DISCRIMINATION LAW: TEXT, CASES AND MATERIALS

Aileen McColgan
King's College London

·HART·
PUBLISHING

OXFORD – PORTLAND

Hart Publishing
Oxford and Portland, Oregon

Published in North America (US and Canada) by
Hart Publishing c/o
International Specialized Book Services
5804 NE Hassalo Street
Portland, Oregon
97213-3644
USA

Distributed in the Netherlands, Belgium and Luxembourg by
Intersentia, Churchillaan 108
B2900 Schoten
Antwerpen
Belgium

Hart Publishing Ltd is a specialist legal publisher based in Oxford, England.
To order further copies of this book or to request a list of other
publications please write to:

Hart Publishing Ltd, Salter's Boatyard,
Folly Bridge, Abingdon Road, Oxford OX1 4LB
Telephone: +44 (0)1865 245533 or Fax: +44 (0)1865 794882
e-mail: mail@hartpub.co.uk
www.hartpub.co.uk

British Library Cataloguing in Publication Data
Data Available
ISBN 1 84113–146–6 (paperback)

Typeset by Hope Services (Abingdon) Ltd
Printed in Great Britain on acid-free paper
by Biddles Ltd, *www.biddles.co.uk*

Contents

To Lucy "it's outrageous" Anderson
for helping to shape my understanding of discrimination
and
to Robbie for paying for the child care!

Acknowledgements

The author and publisher gratefully acknowledge the authors and publishers of extract material which appears in this book, and in particular the following for permission to reprint material from the sources indicated:

AB Academic Publishers for permission to quote from:
International Journal of Discrimination and Law (**C. Bell:** *The Employment Equality Review and Fair Employment in Northern Ireland,* 2 IJDL; **R Townshend Smith:** *Justifying Indirect Discrimination in English and American law* 1 IJDL; **C. McCrudden:** *The Constitutionality of Affirmative Action* 1 IJDL; **Vera Sacks** *What do we think about alternative action now?* 2 IJDL; **M Hedemann-Robinson:** *Indirect Discrimination and the EC; Appearance Rather than Reality* 2 IJDL.

Cavendish Publishing Limited, for permission to quote from:
D. Ashiagbor, in Sheldon (ed), *Feminist Perspectives on Employment Law* Chapter 6

Cambridge University Law Faculty, for permission to quote from:
Peter Wallington *Ladies First – Or How Mr Peake was piqued* 1978 Cambridge Law Journal 37, 39 and **G T Pagone** The Lawyers Hunt for Snarks, Religion and Racism (1984) CLJ 218,

Continuum Publishing for permission to quote from:
Bhikhu Parekh, *"The Case for Positive Discrimination"* in Hepple and Szyszczak Discrimination: The Limits of Law 272; **Nicola Lacey,** *From Individual to Group* in Hepple and Szyszczak (above); **M Coussey,** *The Effectiveness of Strategic Enforcement of the RRA 1976* in Hepple and Szyszczak (above); **B Hepple** *Have 25 years of the Race Relations Act in Britain Been a Failure* in Hepple and Szyszczak (above); **Sacks** *Tackling Discrimination Positively in Britain* in Hepple and Szyszczak (above).

Oak Tree Press for permission to quote from:
M McDonagh *Disability Discrimination in Australia* in G. Quinn, M McDonagh and C Kimber (eds) Disability Discrimination law in the US, Australia and Canada

Oxford University Press for permission to quote from:
S Fredman *Women and the Law* Pp 40–43, 49–51, 61–62, 65–66, 79–80; **J Jowell** *Is Equality a Constitutional Principle* (1994) Current Legal Problems, p1 at 2; **Paul Davies** *The Central Arbitration Committee and Equal Pay* (1980) 33 Current Legal Problems 165, 173–176;

E Collins and E Meehan, in Chambers and McCrudden (eds) *Individual Rights and the Law in Britain* 383–88, 403–405; **C McCrudden,** *Racial Discrimination* in McCrudden and Chambers (eds) *Individual Rights and the Law in Britain* Pp 445–6, 451; **D Pannick** Sex Discrimination law, pp 250–1, pp 255–270, pp 147–50, pp 189–95, p 105, p 96–7; **K. O'Donovan and E Szyszczak** *Redundancy Selection and Sex Discrimination,* (1985) Industrial Law Journal, 252, 253–4; **Keith Ewing** *The Human Rights Act and Labour Law,* (1998) 27 Industrial Law Journal, 275, 281–9; **G. Mead,** *Intentions, Conditions and Pools of Comparison,* (1989) 18 Industrial Law Journal; **C. McCrudden,** *Rethinking Positive Action,* (1986) Industrial Law Journal, 219, 230–2, 233–4; **N. Lacey** *Dismissed by Reason of Pregnancy,* 15 ILJ 43, 44–5; **Ivan Hare** *Pregnancy and Sex Discrimination* (1991) 20 ILJ 124, 128; **Claire Kilpatrick** *"Deciding When Jobs of Equal Value can be Paid Uniequally: an Examination of s 1(3) of the Equal Pay Act 1970"* (1994) 23 ILJ 311 ; **B. Ryan** *Employer Enfordment of the Immigration Rules,* (1997) ILJ 26, 136, 140–1; **Mark Jeffrey** *Not Really Going to Work etc* (1998) 27 Industrial Law Journal 193, 199–201; **Leo Flynn** *Gender Equality Law and Employer Dress Codes* (1995) 24 ILJ 255, 256–60; **Paul Skidmore** *Sex, Gender and Comparators in Employment,* (1997) 26 ILJ 51, 54–6; **C. McCrudden** *The Northern Ireland Fair Employment White Paper,* 17 ILJ 162, 162–3; **S. Poulter** *Muslim Headscarves in Schools: Contrasting approaches in England and France* (1997) Oxford Journal of Legal Studies, 43,44, 65, 66–7.

Palgrave Press for permission to quote from:
Alan Arthurs in J Gregory, R Sales and A Hegewisch (eds), "Women, Work and Inequality etc" (1999) *Independent Experts in Equal Pay* p 168 at 173

Sweet & Maxwell Ltd, for permission to quote from:
L. Lustgarten: *The New Meaning of Discrimination,* Public Law; **St John Robilliard:** *Should Parliament enact a Religious Discrimination Act?*(1978) Public Law, p 379, 386–7; **E. Ellis and J. Miller:** *The Victimisation of Anti-Discrimination Complainants,* Public Law 80–81, 82–4; **D. Pannick:** *Homosexuals, Transexuals and the Law,* (1983) Public Law 279,281; **E. Ellis and G. Appleby:** *Formal Investigations: The CRE and ECOC as Law Enforcement Agencies,* (1984) Public Law 236, 247; **J. Kentridge:** (1994) Public Law 198, 203, 206; **E. Ellis:** *The Definition of Discrimination in European Sex Equality Law,* (1994) 19 European Law Review, 561, 564–6; **S. Fredman:** *A difference with Distinction,,* 110 LQR 106–9; **E. Ellis and G. Appleby:** *Blackening the Prestige Pot: Formal Investigations and the CRE,* (1984) LQR 349, 354; **Benyon and Lowe:** *Mandla and the Meaning of Racial Group,* (1984) 100 LQR 120; **J. M. Thompson:** (1981) LQR 107, 10 ,11–12.

Industrial Relations Services, for permission to quote from:
Equal Opportunities Review

Blackwell Publishers Ltd, for permission to quote the following extracts from the Modern Law Review:

John Gardner 50 Modern Law Review 345, 346, 349–51, 351–2; **John Bowers** *More Bonds for the Fettered Runner* (1980) 43 Modern Law Review 215–219; **Vera Sacks** *Unnatural Justice for Discriminators* 47 Modern Law Review 334–5, 336, 337–8, 339; **Vera Sacks and Maxwell** *The Equal Opportunities Commission – Ten Years on* (1986) 49 MLR, 560, 581–2, 582–5, 566–7; **McEvoy and White** *Security Vetting in Northern Ireland* (1998) 61 MLR 341, 343–5, 353–7; **Brian Doyle** *Enabling Legislation or Dissembling Law?* 60 MLR 64, 74; **C McCrudden** *Codes in a Cold Climate* (1988) 51 MLR, 409, 429; **I McKenna** (1983) MLR; **Dine and B Watts** *Sexual Harassment: moving away from discrimination* 50 (1995) Modern Law Review, 343, 347–52; **E Szyszczak** *Pregnancy Discrimination* (1996) 59 MLR 58, 59–62; **M Wynn** *Pregnancy and Discrimination* (1999) 62 MLR 435, 441–5; **R Mullender** *Racial Harassment, Sexual Discrimination etc* (1998) 61 MLR 236, 240–1.

The ***Web Journal of Current Legal Issues***, (http://webjcli.ncl.ac.uk/) for permission to quote from:
W Mcleod *Autochtonous Language Communities and the RRA* 1998 Web Journal; **Ursula O'Hare** *Positive Action before the European Court of Justice: Case C–450/93 Kalanke v Freie Hansestadt Bremen* Web Journal of Current Legal Issues

Thompsons, for permission to quote from:
http://www.thompsons.law.co.uk/altindex.htm, Head Office, Congress House, Great Russell Street, London WC1B 3LW 0171 637 9761

Commission for Racial Equality, for permission to quote from:
CRE, *Irish in Britain;* **CRE** *Second Review of the RRA*, 1992, para 12 (1992); **CRE** *The RRA Time for a Change* (1983)

Justice for permission to quote from:
Justice *Improving Equality Law: The Options* (1997)

Table of Cases

Table of Legislation

INTERNATIONAL CONVENTIONS

1

Introduction

INTRODUCTION

The last quarter century has seen a burgeoning of anti-discrimination law in the UK and elsewhere. Prior to 1975 there was in operation, in the UK, legislation which prohibited race discrimination (the Race Relations Act 1968[1]). Also on the statute books were the Sex Disqualification (Removal) Act 1919, the Disabled Persons (Employment) Act 1944 and the Equal Pay Act 1970 (EqPA). But there were significant flaws in the Race Relations Act's enforcement mechanisms[2]; the 1919 Act, further discussed below, was of very limited application; the quotas imposed by the 1944 Act were rarely complied with and the EqPA, though on the books, was not implemented until the end of 1975.

At the start of 1975, legislative intervention in the field of discrimination was very limited indeed. By the end of that year the EqPA was in operation and the Sex Discrimination Act 1975 (SDA) in place. The following year saw the passage of the Race Relations Act 1976 (RRA) and, in Northern Ireland, the Fair Employment Act 1976 (FEA, which prohibited discrimination on grounds of religious belief or political opinion).[3] In 1989 the second FEA extended the regulation of religious and political discrimination (again only within Northern Ireland); 1995 saw the enactment of the Disability Discrimination Act 1995 (DDA), 1996 and 1999 its progressive implementation.[4]

The years since the establishment of the (New) Labour Government in May 1997 have seen a flurry of new provisions. While the Government has set its face firm against increasing pressure for root-and-branch reform of the law relating to discrimination (an issue further considered in the concluding chapter), the current administration has presided over the passage and implementation of the Fair Employment and Treatment (Northern Ireland) Order 1998, which extended the reach of the FEAs beyond the area of employment, and the amendment in 1999 of the SDA expressly to

---

[1] Prior to this the Race Relations Act 1965 Act.

[2] For discussion of this see C. McCrudden, "Racial Discrimination", in C. McCrudden and G. Chambers (eds), *Individual Rights and the Law in Britain* (Oxford: OUP, 1995), 415–417.

[3] Northern Ireland also boasted the Sex Discrimination (Northern Ireland) Order 1976, whose provisions precisely mirrored those of the SDA, but was not covered by race relations legislation until the implementation of the Race Relations (Northern Ireland) Order1997.

[4] Implementation will be completed in 2004, see Chapters 4 and 8.

regulate discrimination based on gender-reassignment. Also of significance in the discrimination field are the 1998 Human Rights Act (HRA) and Northern Ireland Act (NIA), and the Race Relations (Amendment) Bill 1999 (RR(A)B), which is passing through Parliament at the time of writing. The first of these, which incorporates many of the provisions of the European Convention on Human Rights into UK law and which will be fully implemented in October 2000, provides (Article 14):

> The enjoyment of the rights and freedoms set forth in this Convention shall be secured without discrimination on any ground such as sex, race, colour, language, religion, political or other opinion, national or social origin, association with a national minority, property, birth or other status.

The Article 14 right to freedom from discrimination is not free-standing, regulating as it does only discrimination in the "enjoyment of the rights and freedoms set forth in th[e] Convention". Further, the HRA is binding in the fullest sense only on public authorities. We shall, however, see below that the implications of the HRA in the discrimination field are significant. This significance will increase if the twelfth Protocol to the Convention, which requires that "the enjoyment of any right set forth by law shall be secured without discrimination" on the grounds set out in Article 14, is adopted and ratified by the UK.

S.75 NIA imposes upon "public authorities" an obligation "in carrying out [their] functions relating to Northern Ireland" to have "due regard to the need to promote equality of opportunity" on grounds of sex, race, religious belief and political opinion, age, marital status or sexual orientation, disability and responsibility for dependants. S.76 of the same Act provides that:

> (1) It shall be unlawful for a public authority carrying out functions relating to Northern Ireland to discriminate, or to aid or incite another person to discriminate, against a person or class of person on the ground of religious belief or political opinion.

S.75 puts into statutory form the Policy Appraisal and Fair Treatment Guidelines in operation (at least in theory) in Northern Ireland since 1994. The PAFT guidelines and s.75 which replaces them will be considered in more detail in Chapter 5. Here it is sufficient to note that s.75 was the first significant legislative example of equality "mainstreaming" in the UK. "Mainstreaming" refers to the policy of incorporating an emphasis on equality into "into all policies and programmes, so that, before decisions are taken, an analysis is made of the effects on" protected groups. Gender mainstreaming was adopted in the "platform for action" by the Fourth UN World Conference on Women in September 1995 (the Beijing conference), strongly backed by the EU delegation to the Conference. Mainstreaming has subsequently been incorporated into European thinking: Article 3 of the Treaty Establishing the European Community, as amended by the Treaty of Amsterdam stating that "In all the activities [of the Community], the Community shall aim to eliminate inequalities, and to promote equality, between men and women".

The 1998 First Annual Report from the European Commission on Equal Opportunities for men and women in the European Union reported that "[t]hroughout 1998, the Commission continues and consolidated its strategy of assessing all general policies and measures for their gender impact", particular attention having been paid to the targeting of structural funds and mainstreaming having been adopted as the "general principle and the primary strategic objective" of the Medium-term Community action programme on equal opportunities for men and women. A gender-dimension was incorporated into educational and research programmes, into development co-operation programmes and into the Commission input on Member States National Plans for Employment. Most recently the race discrimination directive (further considered below) emphasises that its impact on both women and men must be assessed and reported on by Member States (Article 16).

S.76 NIA, which was originally contained in the Northern Ireland Constitution Act 1973, applies only in relation to direct discrimination. This limitation was echoed, in relation to race discrimination, by the RR(A)B as it was originally introduced in the House of Lords in December 1999. Much criticism was voiced, both in the debates on the NIA and in relation to the RR(A)B, of the failure to regulate indirect discrimination, a particular problem in view of the approach taken by the courts to the "services" in respect of which discrimination is prohibited by the various legislative enactments (see, in particular, the discussion of the *Amin v Entry Clearance Officer, Bombay* [1983] 2 AC 818 in Chapter 4). Such was the opposition generated by the Bill's exclusion of indirect discrimination that it was amended at the report stage to regulate this form of discrimination also. The Government also agreed to amend the Bill to impose an obligation on public authorities to promote equality of opportunity on grounds of race.[5]

In addition to UK legislation dealing with discrimination, a great deal of development has taken place on the European Community front. Britain was a member of the EEC (as it then was) 25 years ago, and Articles 39 and 141 (ex Articles 48 and 119 respectively of the Treaty Establishing the European Community TEC) prohibited "discrimination based on nationality between workers of the Member States as regards employment, remuneration and other conditions of work and employment" and required the application by Member States of the principle of equal pay for equal work regardless of sex. The intervening quarter century has seen the implementation of directives on equal treatment as between men and women in employment and social security; the inclusion within the TEC of Article 13, which confers European jurisdiction in the area of discrimination "based on sex, racial or ethnic origin, religion or belief, disability, age or sexual orientation"; and the publication by the European Commission of draft directives prohibiting employment-related discrimination on any of these prohibited grounds, and race discrimination more generally.[6]

[5] Announcement by Home Secretary Jack Straw, 26th January 2000. This duty is further discussed in Chapter 5, below.
[6] Article 141 was also amended to give an explicit basis for equal treatment, as distinct from equal pay, between men and women and to permit positive action—see further Chapter 3.

All of the legislation mentioned above is considered in detail elsewhere in this book. It is referred to here only to give a flavour of the pace of development of the subject. Nor has the development been limited to the passage and implementation of legislation. Judicial understanding of the meaning of existing legislation has also developed over the past twenty-five years. The amendment of the SDA to regulate discrimination on grounds of gender-reassignment, for example, followed the European Court of Justice decision in *P* v *S & Cornwall* (Case C–13/94) [1996] ECR I–2143, [1996] All ER (EC) 397, [1996] IRLR 347 that such discrimination amounted to sex discrimination contrary to the Equal Treatment Directive. And while the same Court balked from applying this analysis, in *Grant* v *South-West Trains* (Case C–249/96) [1998] ECR I–3739 to discrimination based on sexual orientation, the European Court of Human Rights ruled, in *Lustig-Prean & Beckett* v *UK* 29 EHRR 548 and in *Smith & Grady* v *UK* 29 EHRR 493 that sexual orientation discrimination was in breach of the Convention.[7] Less dramatic, but equally important over time, has been the interpretation of Article 141 to require sex equality in "pay" ever more broadly defined.

DISCRIMINATION AND THE COMMON LAW

Developments in the legislative arena, and in the judicial interpretation (both at UK and, more particularly, at European, level) of legislation have been very substantial. These developments have also impacted on administrative law. In *EOC* v *Secretary of State for Employment* [1995] 1 AC 1, [1994] 1 All ER 910, [1994] 2 WLR 176, 92 LGR 360, [1994] ICR 317, [1994] IRLR 176, for example, the House of Lords struck down the extended qualifying periods for unfair dismissal and redundancy protection imposed on (predominantly female) part-time workers on the grounds that they contravened EU sex equality law.[8] The legislation at issue there was delegated but it is clear that the English courts can be obliged to disapply even primary legislation where it contravenes EU law. Where discrimination/equality developments have yet to occur is in the area of common law more generally. Sandra Fredman, immediately below, considers the historical approach of the common law to women. Further below we will address the question of the extent to which this approach has changed.

Sandra Fredman, *Women and the Law* **(Oxford, OUP, 1997) pp.40–3, 49–51, 61–2, 65–6, 79–80**

Liberal principles of individual freedom were not extended to married women until deep into the twentieth century. Instead, the Diceyan ideal of formal equality of all individuals before the law unabashedly excluded married women from the category "individuals". This truth is

[7] The cases concerned dismissals from the armed services in pursuit of the UK's then ban on gays in the military. They are further discussed below.

[8] Even more dramatic was *Factortame (No.2)* [1990] ECR I 2433 in which the ECJ ruled that the domestic courts (there the British House of Lords) were required to provide an effective interlocutory remedy on a plea that domestic legislation contravened directly effective EC law.

epitomised by the common law of coverture which entailed that "the very being or legal existence of the wife is suspended during the marriage or at least incorporated and consolidated into that of the husband under whose wing, protection and cover she performs everything." Coverture gave the husband near-absolute control over the wife's property as well as her person. Married women were perpetual legal minors, divested of the possibility of economic independence. Any property which a married woman had owned as a single woman became her husband's property on marriage: personal property vesting absolutely, real property during the lifetime of the husband. Similarly, he had absolute rights to all property which came into her hands during her marriage, including all her earned income. Moreover, money given to her by him as housekeeping money remained his property at all times. . . .

Control over her person reached into every aspect of legal dealings. A married woman could not sue or be sued unless her husband were a party to the suit; in tort, for example, she retained her liability but her husband had to be joined as a defendant. An important implication was that she could not sue him in tort. She could not make a valid will unless her husband consented to its provisions, and he could withdraw his consent at any time until probate. He decided where the family would live and had ultimate authority over where and how the children were raised. He could "correct" her physically; but he was so much her sovereign that if she killed him she committed treason, not simple murder. Contractual capacity was similarly denied her: a married woman could not enter into a contract except as agent for her husband, and then only with his express authority. This was especially harsh if a wife was evicted or neglected by her husband. . . .

The persistence of married women's legal disabilities was at the heart of their general inferiority. For example, it was frequently argued that it was impossible to grant married women equal voting rights if they remained legal minors. Their inability to own their own property or even retain their own income made it impossible for them to achieve economic independence. At the same time, the economic pressures on single women to marry were intense: marriage was not an institution which could be avoided by most women. . . . Women were held to have impliedly consented not only to their own legal obliteration on marriage, but also to every act of sexual intercourse demanded by their husbands. Indeed, until as recently as 1991, a husband who forced his wife to have intercourse against her will could not be found guilty of rape except in limited circumstances. Married women's legal subordination was also frequently justified by means of the familiar technique of asserting that the family was outside the political arena and therefore authority need not be legitimated by consent. Blackstone went further and confidently asserted that these restrictions actually benefited women. "Even the disabilities which the wife lies under, are for the most part intended for her protection and benefit. So great a favourite is the female sex of the laws of England!" . . .

Until the limited reforms of 1839, a married woman had no rights of custody whatsoever over her children. "The basic premise of both law are equity in custody disputes over legitimate children was one of strict patriarchy—'the sacred right of the father over his own children'." As Blackstone put it: "A mother as such is entitled to no power, but only to reverence and respect." The courts would order a mother to surrender a child to the father even if the child was still being breast-fed. Thus in a nineteenth century case, the court upheld the father's rights to custody over the child even though he had forcibly snatched the baby from its mother's breast and taken it away almost naked in an open carriage in bad weather. The court did not even hold that this fell within the exception for cases where a child required judicial protection: Lord Ellenborough CJ could see no reason to believe that the child had been 'injured for want of nurture or in any other respect" [citing *R v De Manneville* [1804] 5 East 221]. Nor would the courts consider that the father had given up his rights to children just because he was living in adultery. Even after his death, the father's rights remained intact. He had absolute right to name a testamentary guardian to take care of his children after his death, and if he chose to name someone other than the mother, she had no rights whatever over her children. . . . The Custody of Infants Act of 1839 gave a mother the right to petition courts of Chancery for custody of children under seven, and for access to children over seven. It took more than three decades for this to be broadened to allow mothers to petition for custody of children under sixteen. . . . patriarchal assumptions about the father's absolute rights over his children remained so strong in the minds of the judges that the impact of the 1873 Act was largely undermined. In *In re Besant* [1879] 11 Ch 508, for example, the Court of Appeal held that a refusal by the mother to bring up the child in the religion of the father was a good reason for removing the child from her custody. . . .

Judges were first given the power to adjudicate divorce in 1857. However, the new provisions were clearly aimed at continued protection of husbands' rights to assure their own paternity, rather than at spousal equality. Thus the Matrimonial Causes Act 1857 gave statutory authority to the "double standard of adultery": "Simple" adultery would be a matrimonial offence if committed by the wife; but not if committed by the husband. Instead, a wife petitioning for divorce would need to prove that the husband had committed "aggravated" adultery, that is incestuous adultery, bigamy with adultery, adultery with desertion for two years, adultery with cruelty, or rape, sodomy or bestiality. Moreover, the newly created Divorce Court simply reinforced current assumptions. Even though the Act gave the Court a wide discretion to make such provision as it deemed just, regardless of the guilt of the parties, "guilty" wives were almost invariably refused custody and access. "It will probably have a salutary effect on the interest of public morality, that it should be known that a woman, if found guilty of adultery, will forfeit as far as this court is concerned, all rights to the custody of or access to her children." [*Seddon v Seddon & Doyle* (1862) 2 Sw. & Tr 640] This was the case even if the court acknowledged that the husband's conduct towards the wife had precipitated the adultery. This attitude continued well into the twentieth century. . . .

In an important victory, women ratepayers were given the municipal franchise on the same terms as men in 1869, reflecting grudging acceptance of the principle of "no taxation without representation". Once again, however, the judiciary were quick to grasp at semantic niceties to pare down women's rights. The [Municipal Franchise] Act 1869 clearly provided that "words importing the masculine gender . . . shall be held to include females for all purposes connected with . . . the right to vote". Nevertheless, within three years of the passing of the 1869 Act, the Queen's Bench Division held that married women were excluded. "Marriage is at common law a total disqualification, and a married woman, therefore, could not vote, her existence for such a purpose being merged in that of her husband . . . [The 1869 Act] only removes the disqualification by reason of sex, and leaves untouched the disqualification by reason of status" [citing *R v Harrald* [1872] LR VII QB 361] Nor was this the last of judicial incursions. When a new structure of local government was established during the 1880s, women were included among those entitled to vote, using the usual provision that "for all purposes connected . . . with the right to vote at municipal elections words . . . importing the masculine gender include women." This time, the judges turned from the right to vote to the right to be elected. On the face of it, the intention of Parliament seemed clear: the Act provided that those entitled to elect should also be entitled to be elected. Nevertheless, the Court of Appeal held, the right to be elected did not extend to women.

Even the Sex Disqualification (Removal) Act 1919 was easily undermined by tenacious opponents of equality for women. This was clearly evidenced in 1922, when Lady

Rhondda, a hereditary peeress, claimed that the 1919 Act meant that she could no longer be disqualified by her sex from the exercise of the public function of membership of the House of Lords [*Beresford-Hope* v *Lady Sandhurst* [1889] 23 QBD 79]. However, the Committee of Privileges of the House of Lords decided by a majority of twenty-two to four that the Act did not entitle her to sit as a peer. Semantic niceties were pushed to their extreme: it could not be denied that membership of the House of Lords was a public office, and therefore a woman could not be disqualified on grounds of her sex. But, argued Viscount Cave, women had never had the right to sit in the House; and therefore there was no "disqualification" in the strict sense of the Act. "The 1919 Act", he stated, "while it removed all disqualifications, did not purport to confer any right." The Committee also resorted to the familiar artifice of "Parliamentary intention" to reinforce the point. Since Parliament had not expressly given women the right, it must be assumed that the intention was not to confer such a right. It was not sufficient that the Act specifically sued the words "A person shall not be disqualified by sex or marriage from the exercise of any public function." According to the Lord Chancellor, Viscount Birkenhead: "The Legislature . . . cannot be taken to have . . . employed such loose and ambiguous words to carry out so momentous a revolution in the constitution of this House." . . .

Whereas the legislature refused to intervene to correct unequal pay, the judges went so far as to strike down employers' voluntary institution of equal pay, in the public sector at least. In the seminal case of *Roberts* v. *Hopwood*, the House of Lords was asked to consider the case of the Poplar Borough Council, which had decided to pay all its lowest grade of workers, both male and female, the same minimum subsistence pay. "The vanity of appearing as model employers of labour, . . . [and] ardent feminists" was not something the House of Lords would tolerate. The Council's statutory power to pay "such wages as [it] may think fit" had to be exercised reasonably; and, according to the court, equal pay was clearly not within the bounds of reason. The council had exceeded the bounds of its legitimate power by allowing itself, in the words of Lord Atkinson, "to be guided . . . by some eccentric principles of socialistic philanthropy, or by a feminist ambition to secure the equality of the sexes in the matter of wages in the world of labour."

The common law's inadequacies in the context of discrimination were not restricted to the field of sex.

St John A. Robilliard, "Should Parliament Enact a Religious Discrimination Act" (1978) *Pubic Law* 379, p.380

. . .One of the reasons for enacting the Race Relations Acts was that the common law came down heavily on the side of freedom to contract no matter how capriciously such a right was exercised whilst it ignored the feelings of the innocent victim of prejudice. An Irish case which can still be considered declaratory of the common law in the field of religious discrimination is *Schegel* v. *Corcoran* [(1942) IR 19]. A tenant wished to alienate a tenancy to a Jew. The landlord, who had to live in the same building as the tenant, refused to grant her consent to the transfer. Under the lease consent to substitute tenants could not be unreasonably withheld and it was also submitted that as the constitution of the Irish State provided that public authorities must treat citizens of differing religious belief alike there was a constitutional right of freedom from religious discrimination. However the court held that in the circumstances the landlord's sincere religious objection was a reasonable one to hold. Furthermore a restrictive view of the constitution was taken and it was only held to be relevant to the State's conduct but not to the activities of private individuals.

It is clear from the Fredman extract that women's advances over the centuries were the result of legislation, rather than of judicial developments. Even where legislation did attempt to right the balance, judicial interpretation of that legislation undermined its impact as in the case of the Custody of Infants Act 1873, the Municipal Franchise Act 1869 and the SD(R)A 1919.

The 1919 Act, which was passed primarily in order to extend women's franchise,[9] declared that:

> A person shall not be disqualified by sex or marriage from the exercise of any public func-
> tion, or from being appointed to or holding any civil or judicial office or post, or from
> entering or assuming or carrying on any civil profession or vocation, or for admission to
> any incorporated society . . . and a person shall not be exempted by sex or marriage from
> the liability to serve as a juror.[10]

Fredman mentions the approach of the judiciary to the provisions of the 1919 Act in the *Viscountess Rhonnda* case. But that decision was not an isolated example of judicial obstinacy in the face of this enabling statute. In *Price v Rhondda Urban District Council* [1923] 2 Ch 372, a woman teacher who was (as was then common) dismissed because she was married claimed that the dismissal was in breach of the Act. The High Court dismissed her claim, Eve J declaring that he was not "prepared to hold that an Authority commits a breach of that Act if in some of its appointments it indicates that applications from one sex only can be received".

In 1966 Salmon LJ, in *Nagle v Feilden* (1966), accepted that the Act might assist a woman discriminatorily denied a training licence by the Jockey Club. But the court's decision to permit a trial of the claim, which had originally been struck out as showing no cause of action, was made on the ground that, the Jockey Club exercising a monopoly in the control of horseracing, the practice of refusing licences to women trainers was arguably "unlawful and in restraint of trade and contrary to public policy". According to Lord Denning:

> If [Ms Nagle] is to carry on her trade without stooping to subterfuge, she has to have a
> licence. When an association, who have the governance of a trade, take it on themselves to
> license persons to take part in it, then it is at least arguable that they are not at liberty to
> withdraw a man's licence—and thus put him out of business—without hearing him. Nor
> can they refuse a man a licence—and thus prevent him from carrying on his business—in

---

[9] The Representation of the People Act 1918, which first gave women the vote, applied only to those over thirty who were university graduates, householders or the wives of householders. The 1919 Act also enabled women to sit as jurors for the first time, and permitted them to serve as justices of the peace and on a variety of public bodies.

[10] The mode of admission to and terms of service relating to some civil service posts was exempted, as was the reservation of some foreign and colonial service positions—see generally W. Creighton, *Working Women and the Law* (London: Mansell, 1979), pp.67ff.

their uncontrolled discretion . . . When [licensing] authorities exercise a predominant power over the exercise of a trade or profession, the courts may have jurisdiction to see that this power is not abused.

In this case Mrs Nagle alleges that the Stewards of the Jockey Club make a practice of refusing any woman trainer who applies for a licence. She is refused because she is a woman, and for no other reason. The practice is so uniform that it amounts to an unwritten rule. . . It seems to me that this unwritten rule may well be said to be arbitrary and capricious. It is not as if the training of horses could be regarded as an unsuitable occupation for a woman, like that of a jockey or speedway-rider. It is an occupation in which women can and do engage most successfully. It . . . is an occupation which women can do as well as men, and there would seem to be no reason why they should be excluded from it. If this practice—this unwritten rule—is invalid as being contrary to public policy, there is ground for thinking that the court has jurisdiction to say so.

Lord Denning took the view that horse training was not capable of amounting to a "vocation" within the SD(R)A. Salmon LJ thought this point was arguable, but joined Denning and Dankwerts LJJ in basing his decision on the restraint of trade doctrine:

I should be sorry to think that we have grown so supine that today the courts are powerless to protect a man against an unreasonable restraint on his right to work to which he has in no way agreed and which a group with no authority, save that which it has conferred on itself, seeks capriciously to impose on him. I certainly refuse to believe that it is not even arguable that in such circumstances that courts have power to protect the individual citizen. It follows that Mrs Nagle may succeed in this action if she can show that the stewards, whilst recognising her good character and long experience and ability as a trainer, have refused her a licence solely on the ground that she is a woman. It would be as capricious to do so as to refuse a man a licence solely because of the colour of his hair. No doubt there are occupations, such as boxing, which may reasonably be regarded as inherently unsuitable for women; but evidently training racehorses is not one of them . . .

We shall see, in chapter 4, that a different view has subsequently been taken, under the SDA itself, to sex discrimination in the boxing ring. But it should be stressed that the decision in *Nagle* was a very narrow one, turning as it did on the restraint of trade doctrine and the absolute monopoly of the Jockey Club. Nor did the Court of Appeal decide in that case that the Jockey Club had acted in restraint of trade. Concerning as the case did an appeal against the striking out at first instance of Mrs Nagle's claim, the decision was only to the effect that the claim should be heard. In the event, the Jockey Club capitulated to "the gallant millionairess who . . . could afford to battle on level financial terms" with it[11] and the case never came to trial.

The SD(R)A has never successfully been pleaded against employment-related discrimination. In *Hugh-Jones* v *St John's College Cambridge* [1979] ICR 848, EAT upheld a tribunal ruling that the exclusion of women from membership of that college by its statutes did not breach the Act. The applicant, whose application for a research fellowship had been rejected, lost her SDA claim on the ground that those provisions

[11] Edward Grayson in *The Times*, April 8th 1993.

of the College's statutes which governed such fellowships were "charitable instruments" "conferring benefits" and therefore exempted from that Act by s.43. Her SD(R)A claim also failed because the fellowship was not a "civil post" (taken by EAT to mean a post "in the public service"); that exclusion from a particular college did not amount to "disqualification from entering a civil profession or vocation"; and, most restrictively of all (*per* Slynn J):

> this Act is not to be seen as creating a right to a post or admission to a society or profession. It removes a disqualification in general terms, but the question whether in any particular case there is a right to the post or admission to the society or profession remains. Here such right does not exist. The right to refuse to appoint or admit women in particular cases has been upheld in earlier authorities, though it is now subject to the other arguments with which we are concerned [those arising under the SDA]: see *Viscountess Rhondda's Claim* and *Price* v *Rhondda Urban District Council*. We see nothing in the Court of Appeal decision in *Nagle* v *Feilden* . . . which compels us to a different view of the meaning of the Act . . .

A similar lack of enthusiasm for anti-discrimination measures can be seen in the judicial approach to the RRA 1968[12] and to the administrative enforcement of the RRA and the SDA (see further Chapter 5), and in the decisions reached on s.71 RRA, which imposes upon local authorities a duty "to make appropriate arrangements with a view to securing that their various functions are carried out with due regard to the need (a) to eliminate unlawful racial discrimination; and (b) to promote equality of opportunity, and good relations, between persons of different racial groups".[13]

Wheeler v *Leicester City Council* [1985] 2 All ER 1105 involved a challenge by the members of a rugby club to the Council's decision to deny it access to the training facilities it generally used because of its failure to bring pressure to bear upon club members not to tour South Africa in contravention of the Commonwealth Gleneagles Agreement which discouraged sporting links with that country (this being during the apartheid era). The club argued that the tour was not unlawful, nor was it contrary to the rules of the club or of the Rugby Union. The Council relied successfully upon s.71 RRA against an action for judicial review and in the Court of Appeal, drawing attention in particular to the fact that African-Caribbeans and Asians accounted for a quarter of the city's population. But the House of Lords ruled in favour of the club on the grounds (*per* Lord Templeman) that "[t]he club could not be punished because the club had done nothing wrong"; (*per* Lord Roskill) that:

> Persuasion, even powerful persuasion, is always a permissible way of seeking to obtain an objective. But in a field where other views can equally legitimately be held, persuasion,

---

[12] "The dominant approach adopted by the House of Lords to the 1968 Act (that the legislation should be restrictively interpreted because it interfered with common law liberties)": C. McCrudden, fn 2 above, p.447. McCrudden was discussing *Charter* v *Race Relations Board* [1973] AC 868 and *Dockers' Labour Club and Institute Ltd* v *Race Relations Board* [[1976] AC 285, see further Chapter 5.

[13] The duty applies also to housing authorities, Housing Act 1988. It will be strengthened by the adoption of the RR(A)B 1999, further discussed throughout.

however powerful, must not be allowed to cross that line where it moves into the field of legitimate pressure coupled with the threat of sanctions.

And in *R v Lewisham Borough Council ex p Shell* [1988] 1 All ER 938, the High Court declared the Council's boycott of Shell's products because of that company's involvement in South Africa unlawful. Neill LJ ruled that, the Council's wish to promote good race relations being mixed with an intention to put pressure on the company to sever its lawful links with South Africa, it could not rely on s.71 RRA to defend the boycott.

It has been argued that equality is a constitutional principle in English law.

Jeffrey Jowell, "Is Equality a Constitutional Principle?" (1994) *Current Legal Problems* 1, p.4

In elaborating the Rule of Law Dicey said that "With us every official, from the Prime Minister down to a constable or a collector of taxes, is under the same responsibility for every act done without legal justification as any other citizen." Dicey is here espousing a concept of what has been called formal equality, by which he meant that no person is exempt from the enforcement of the law. Rich and poor, revenue official and individual taxpayer are all within the equal reach of the arm of the law.

This kind of equality has been derided but it is important. It is inherent in the very notion of law, and in the integrity of law's application, that like cases be treated alike over time. Its reach however is limited because its primary concern is not with the content of the law but with its *enforcement* and *application* alone. The Rule of Law is satisfied as long as laws are applied or enforced equally, that is, evenhandedly, free of bias and without irrational distinction. The Rule of Law requires formal equality which prohibits laws from being enforced unequally, but it does not require substantive equality. It does not therefore prohibit unequal laws. It constrains, say, racially-biased enforcement of laws, but does not inhibit apartheid-style laws from being enacted.

Turning to the question whether English common law contains a principle prohibiting the unequal treatment of people without justification, a principle which he regards as "deriv[ing] from the nature of democracy itself", Jowell continues:

Jowell, pp.9–14

. . . we find some ancient duties placed upon the likes of inn-keepers, common carriers and some monopoly enterprises such as ports and harbours, to accept all travellers and others who are "in a reasonably fit condition to be received".

Does this specific enunciation of forbidden discrimination imply that other forms of discrimination are permissible? To answer this question we have to turn to our administrative law. Here we find first that the courts imply that decisions of public officials should not be taken in "bad faith". Decisions should not therefore be infected with motives such as malice, fraud, dishonesty or personal animosity. Such motives are impermissible because they bias or distort the decision-maker"'s approach to the applicant. The applicant is therefore in a sense subject to unfair discrimination, in breach of the principle of formal equality.

. . .

Most decisions invoking substantive inequality have been struck down under the ground of judicial review known as "unreasonableness". In cases of this kind, wide discretionary power has normally been conferred on the decision-maker, and the courts—through judicial review—must be careful to allow the decision-maker a sufficiently wide margin of discretion. Courts therefore intervene under the formula set out by Lord Greene in the 1947 case of *Wednesbury* [*Associated Provincial Picture Houses Ltd* v *Wednesbury Corporation* [1948] 1KB 223] only when the decision is "so unreasonable that no reasonable decision-maker would so act". . . .

Underneath the *Wednesbury* camouflage, however, a principle of equality can be discerned.

A century ago the notion of unreasonableness was less obscure. In 1898 in the case of *Kruse* v. *Johnson* [1889 2 QB 291] Lord Russell of Killowen was asked to invalidate a by-law for unreasonableness. "Unreasonable in what sense?" he asked, and then proceeded to provide some relatively specific examples including the following: The by-laws would be unreasonable, he said "if, for instance, they were found to be partial and unequal in their operation as between different classes". . . .

In 1955 in *Prescott* v. *Birmingham Corporation* [1955] Ch 210] the local authority, which had power to "charge such fares as they may think fit" on their public transport services introduced a scheme for free bus travel for the elderly. The decision was declared to be unlawful because it conferred out of rates" "a special benefit on some particular *class* of inhabitants . . . at the expense of the general body of ratepayers". The reasoning in *Prescott* might have benefited from attention to a more sophisticated conception of equality, but its approach was followed in other cases involving differential transport fares schemes, each of which grapples with some notion of equality. In the GLC Fares Fair case, for example [*Bromley LBC* v *GLC* [1983] 1 AC 768], justification was required for the differential costs and benefits of the transport fare cut to the inhabitants of Bromley, other ratepayers in London, and travellers from outside London using London's public transport.

Looking behind recent applications of *Wednesbury* unreasonableness we do see stark examples of the application of the principle of equality. In 1988 a councillor in Port Talbot was allowed to jump the housing queue in order to put her in a better position to fight the local election from her own constituency. The decision was held unlawful because unfair to others on the housing waiting list, adversely discriminated against [*R* v *Port Talbot BC ex p Jones* (1988) 2 All ER 207]. The principle of equality was not mentioned, but surely applied.

It has recently been held that schools may not discriminate in the allocation of school places against children living outside the school's catchment area. In *R.* v. *Hertfordshire County Council ex parte Cheung* [*The Times* 4th April 1986] the Master of the Rolls Lord Donaldson held that the Home Secretary, in considering the remission of a prisoner's sentence, must have regard to the length of time served by the applicant's co-defendants. He said that: "It is a cardinal principle of good public administration that all persons in a similar position should be treated similarly".

Some of these cases provide examples of formal equality, but there are many other cases where, whether explicitly mentioned or not, substantive equality was the standard by which administrative decisions have been tested. Planning conditions that insist that local businesses only have access to new office premises have been upheld on the ground that their primary intent was to fuel the local economy—a legitimate planning consideration. On the other hand, conditions attached to planning permissions requiring local people only to occupy new or converted housing in the area (and thus discriminating against second home owners, or indeed anyone from outside the area) are of more doubtful validity. In *Great Portland Estates* v. *Westminster Council* [(1985) AC 661] the council's local district plan was challenged on the ground that it favoured the retention in the area of certain small industries only. The plan was upheld but the apparent discrimination had indeed to be carefully justified.

The clearest recent articulation of equality as a substantive standard was applied by Mr Justice Simon Brown in the case of *R.* v. *Immigration Appeal Tribunal, ex parte Manshoora Begum* [1986] Imm AR 385], when he struck down part of immigration regulations promulgated by the Home Secretary. The regulation made provision for a dependent parent to be admitted to the United Kingdom in exceptional and compassionate circumstances, but required as one such circumstance that the parent should have a standard of living "substantially below that of his or her own country". Citing Lord Russell's formulation of unreasonableness as, inter alia, involving "partial and unequal" treatment, it was held that these regulations would benefit immigrants from affluent countries and discriminate against those from those from poor countries. The particular provision was however struck down on the explicit ground that it was "manifestly unjust and unreasonable"

Sometimes, in our administrative law, we see the principle of legal certainty, of formal equality, the Rule of Law value, in conflict with the principle of substantive equality I have outlined, involving treatment as equals. The doctrine of the fettering of discretion is a case in point. Public officials are permitted to make rules that make it easier for them to exercise their discretion and which have the benefit of making their policy clear to the public. For example, local authorities devise a points system for the allocation of council housing. But the decision-maker must always be prepared to listen to someone with something new to say. Discretion may not be fettered. The decision-maker must be willing to depart from a rule aimed at all equally (that is, seeking formal equality), by allowing the applicant to show that difference in treatment is justified in the particular case (that is, in order to achieve substantive equality).

There is no doubt that equality is used as a test of official action in our law.

The extent to which equality is a factor of judicial review decisions is returned to below. But Jowell's conception of equality is a rather thin one. As he himself points out of the *Prescott* case, the striking-down of a benefit directed at the aged can hardly be regarded as a blow for equality. Equally, the decision of the House of Lords in the *GLC* case can be seen as a victory of the relatively advantaged over the less so. The same is true of any decision favouring the interests of those who wish to purchase second homes, this type of home ownership tending to drive the price of rural properties beyond the range of local buyers and adversely to affect local retail and other businesses. As to the question whether some small businesses should be favoured over others, the answer is not one likely unduly to attract the attention of those involved in using discrimination law as a mechanism to tackle disadvantage. What remains are the decisions in the *Port Talbot, Hertfordshire* and *Begum* cases. The search for decisions favourable to the interests of the clearly disadvantaged is not a particularly fruitful one.

Further illustration of the limitations of Jowell's conception of equality is to be found in his treatment of the House of Lords decision in *Roberts* v *Hopwood*, discussed by Fredman in the extract above. Their Lordships upheld the imposition on the

Councillors of a surcharge in respect of their "overpayment" (i.e., equal payment) of the women workers on the grounds that the Councillors had breached their duty to administer their funds "with a due and alert regard to the interests" of ratepayers:

> in each and every case the payment of all wages and salaries must be "reasonable" . . . What is a reasonable wage at any time must depend, of course, on the circumstances which then exist in the labour market. . . But it does not appear to me that there is any rational proportion between the rates of wages at which the labour of these women is paid and the rates at which they would be reasonably remunerated for their services [in the absence of an equal minimum wage]. . . what has been given to the women as wages is really to a great extent gifts and gratuities disguised as wages.

In defending the decision of the House of Lords, Jowell states that, while "the case is often produced as an exhibit of a typically blatant example of judicial opposition towards social equality . . .[its] ratio . . . was based upon a more sober consideration of the lack of 'rational proportion' between the rates paid to the women and the going market rate". But the reason for this lack of proportion lay, precisely, in the market undervaluation of women's work relative to that of men. In the face of such widespread and blatant labour market discrimination as then prevailed, any attempt to pay men and women comparably was bound to produce a wage radically different from the going rate.

It is possible that very recent years have witnessed an evolution in the common law's approach to discrimination. In *Matadeen & Anor* v *Pointu & Ors, Minister of Education and Science & Anor* [1999] 1 AC 98, [1998] 3 WLR 18 the Privy Council stated, *per* Lord Hoffman, that:

> treating like cases alike and unlike cases differently is a general axiom of rational behaviour. It is, for example, frequently invoked by the courts in proceedings for judicial review as a ground for holding some administrative act to have been irrational . . .
>
>   But the very banality of the principle must suggest a doubt as to whether merely to state it can provide an answer to the kind of problem which arises in this case. Of course persons should be uniformly treated, unless there is some valid reason to treat them differently. But what counts as a valid reason for treating them differently? And, perhaps more important, who is to decide whether the reason is valid or not? . . .

The plaintiffs argued that, Mauritius being a signatory to the International Covenant on Civil and Political Rights, its constitutional prohibitions on discrimination must be read so as to give effect to Article 26 of the Covenant, which provides that:

> All persons are equal before the law and are entitled without any discrimination to the equal protection of the law. In this respect, the law shall prohibit any discrimination and guarantee to all persons equal and effective protection against discrimination on any ground such as race, colour, sex, language, religion, political or other opinion, national or social origin, property, birth or other status.

Lord Hoffman went on to declare, however, that "the power to quash the Minister's decision as unreasonable, under the principles in *Associated Provincial Picture Houses v Wednesbury*, would have been entirely adequate to secure compliance with the equal treatment provisions of Article 26".

On the assumption that this declaration is to the effect that discrimination contrary to international obligations should, *per se*, be regarded as contravening *Wednesbury*, it marks a significant recent change in administrative law. As recently as 1996, the English Court of Appeal rejected such an argument in *R v Admiralty Board ex p. Lustig-Prean, R v Ministry of Defence ex p. Smith*, extracted below, a judicial review case brought by servicemen and women dismissed in pursuance of the ban (since lifted) on gays in the military.

Mr Justice Simon Brown, in the Divisional Court, had remarked on the lack of evidence put before him to justify the " 'blanket, non-discretionary, specific', 'status based' ban" but had " 'albeit with hesitation and regret' ", decided that the ban was not so irrational as to fail the *Wednesbury* test which requires the court to be satisfied that the administrative action at issue "is beyond the range of responses open to a reasonable decision-maker".[14] The Court of Appeal upheld his decision.

R v *Ministry of Defence, ex parte Smith and other* [1996] QB 517, [1996] 1 All ER 257, [1996] 2 WLR 305, [1996] IRLR 100

Sir Thomas Bingham MR

Mr David Pannick QC (who represented three of the appellants, and whose arguments were adopted by the fourth) submitted that the court should adopt the following approach to the issue of irrationality:

> The court may not interfere with the exercise of an administrative discretion on substantive grounds save where the court is satisfied that the decision is unreasonable in the sense that it is beyond the range of responses open to a reasonable decision-maker. But in judging whether the decision-maker has exceeded this margin of appreciation the human rights context is important. The more substantial the interference with human rights, the more the court will require by way of justification before it is satisfied that the decision is reasonable in the sense outlined above.

> This submission is in my judgment an accurate distillation of the principles laid down by the House of Lords . . .

The Court of Appeal went on to decide that the policy, which was justified by the Ministry of Defence on the grounds of "morale and unit effectiveness, the . . . role of the services as guardian of recruits under the age of 18, and . . . the requirement of communal living in many service situations", was not irrational. Pannick argued that the first reason was rooted in irrational prejudice, the second also in the assumption "that homosexuals were less able to control their sexual impulses than heterosexuals", and

---

[14] Divisional Court citation from M. Bowley QC, The Strasborg Flight is Boarding Now (1996) 1 *International Journal of Discrimination and the Law* 376, 376–7.

that, while "[t]he lack of privacy in service life was . . . a reason for imposing strict rules and discipline [it was] not a reason for banning the membership of any homosexual . . . each of the appellants had worked in the armed forces for a number of years without any concern being expressed or complaints made about inappropriate behaviour".

> Above all, Mr Pannick criticised the blanket nature of the existing rule. He placed great emphasis on the practice of other nations whose rules were framed so as to counter the particular mischiefs to which homosexual orientation or activity might give rise. He pointed out that other personal problems such as addiction to alcohol, or compulsive gambling, or marital infidelity were dealt with by the service authorities on a case by case basis and not on the basis of a rule which permitted no account to be taken of the peculiar features of the case under consideration.

The Master of the Rolls, with whose judgment the others concurred, ruled that "The threshold of irrationality is a high one. It was not crossed in this case". Further:

> The fact that a decision-maker failed to take account of [ECnHR] obligations when exercising an administrative discretion is not of itself a ground for impugning that exercise of discretion.

Quite how irrational was the ban on homosexuals in the armed forces was made clear in the subsequent decisions of the ECtHR in *Smith & Grady* v *UK*,[15] in which that Court ruled that the ban breached Article 8 of the ECnHR. Before being dismissed from the service they were subjected to intense and invasive investigation and questioning by the military on the subject of their sexual inclinations, tastes and relationships and their HIV status. The ECtHR not only ruled against the UK in respect of the nature of the investigations carried out on the plaintiffs, but also in respect of the ban itself:

Smith & Grady v *UK* **29 EHRR 548 (2000)**

> 89. . . . each State is competent to organise its own system of military discipline and enjoys a certain margin of appreciation in this respect . . . it is open to the State to impose restrictions on an individual's right to respect for his private life where there is a real threat to the armed forces' operational effectiveness, as the proper functioning of an army is hardly imaginable without legal rules designed to prevent service personnel from undermining it. However, the national authorities cannot rely on such rules to frustrate the exercise by individual members of the armed forces of their right to respect for their private lives, which right applies to service personnel as it does to others within the jurisdiction of the State. Moreover, assertions as to a risk to operational effectiveness must be "substantiated by specific examples" . . .
>
> 95. The core argument of the Government in support of the policy is that the presence of open or suspected homosexuals in the armed forces would have a substantial and negative effect on morale and, consequently, on the fighting power and operational effectiveness of the armed forces. . .

[15] *Lustig-Prean & Beckett* v *UK* was in similar terms.

99. The Court notes the lack of concrete evidence to substantiate the alleged damage to morale and fighting power that any change in the policy would entail. . . Given the number of homosexuals dismissed between 1991 and 1996 . . . the number of homosexuals who were in the armed forces at the relevant time cannot be said to be insignificant. Even if the absence of such evidence can be explained by the consistent application of the policy, as submitted by the Government, this is insufficient to demonstrate to the Court's satisfaction that operational effectiveness problems of the nature and level alleged can be anticipated in the absence of the policy . .

102. . . . The Government . . . underlined that it is "the knowledge or suspicion of homosexuality" which would cause the morale problems and not conduct, so that a conduct code would not solve the anticipated difficulties. However, in so far as negative attitudes to homosexuality are insufficient, of themselves, to justify the policy . . . they are equally insufficient to justify the rejection of a proposed alternative. .

The Government maintained that homosexuality raised problems of a type and intensity that race and gender did not. However, even if it can be assumed that the integration of homosexuals would give rise to problems not encountered with the integration of women or racial minorities, the Court is not satisfied that the codes and rules which have been found to be effective in the latter case would not equally prove effective in the former. The "robust indifference" . . . of the large number of British armed forces' personnel serving abroad with allied forces to homosexuals serving in those foreign forces, serves to confirm that the perceived problems of integration are not insuperable . . .

104. The Court . . . notes the evidence before the domestic courts to the effect that the European countries operating a blanket legal ban on homosexuals in their armed forces are now in a small minority. It considers that, even if relatively recent, the Court cannot overlook the widespread and consistently developing views and associated legal changes to the domestic laws of Contracting States on this issue . . .

In *Smith & Grady* the ECtHR specifically addressed the contention of the UK Government that the applicants' right to judicial review (the exercise of which had eventually resulted in their application to that Court, was sufficient to constitute an effective remedy in respect of ECnHR violations as required by Art 13 of the Convention ("Everyone whose rights and freedoms as set forth in [the] Convention are violated shall have an effective remedy before a national authority . . .")

In *Vilvarajah and Ors v UK* (1991, Series A no. 215), the ECtHR had accepted that proceedings by way of judicial review could amount to an effective remedy for the purposes of Article 13. There, the ECtHR had found that the test applied by the domestic courts in the judicial review of extradition and expulsion decisions made by the Secretary of State coincided with the ECtHR's approach under the relevant provision of the ECnHR (Article 3). In the *Smith & Grady* case, however, the Court took a different view of the compatibility of judicial review with the requirements of Article 13 read with the relevant Article 8.

135. . . . to require the provision of a domestic remedy allowing the competent national authority both to deal with the substance of the relevant Convention complaint and to grant appropriate relief . . .

136–7. . . . the applicants' right to respect for their private lives . . . was violated . . . As was made clear by the High Court and the Court of Appeal in the judicial review proceedings, since the Convention did not form part of English law, questions as to whether the application of the policy violated the applicants' rights under Article 8 and, in particular, as to whether the policy had been shown by the authorities to respond to a pressing social need or to be proportionate to any legitimate aim served, were not questions to which answers could properly be offered. The sole issue before the domestic courts was whether the policy could be said to be "irrational" [i.e., according to Lord Bingham MR in the instant case, whether] . . . the court was satisfied that the decision was unreasonable in the sense that it was beyond the range of responses open to a reasonable decision-maker. In judging whether the decision-maker had exceeded this margin of appreciation, the human rights context was important, so that the more substantial the interference with human rights, the more the court would require by way of justification before it was satisfied that the decision was reasonable.

It was, however, further emphasised that, notwithstanding any human rights context, the threshold of irrationality which an applicant was required to surmount was a high one. This is, in the view of the Court, confirmed by judgments of the High Court and the Court of Appeal themselves. The Court notes that the main judgments in both courts commented favourably on the applicants' submissions challenging the reasons advanced by the Government in justification of the policy. . . .

Nevertheless, both courts concluded that the policy could not be said to be beyond the range of responses open to a reasonable decision-maker and, accordingly, could not be considered to be "irrational".

138. In such circumstances, the Court considers it clear that, even assuming that the essential complaints of the applicants before this Court were before and considered by the domestic courts, the threshold at which the High Court and the Court of Appeal could find the Ministry of Defence policy irrational was placed so high that it effectively excluded any consideration by the domestic courts of the question of whether the interference with the applicants' rights answered a pressing social need or was proportionate to the national security and public order aims pursued, principles which lie at the heart of the Court's analysis of complaints under Article 8 of the Convention.

It should be noted that the approach taken to the irrationality test by Lord Bingham in *ex p. Smith* was more generous than the norm, accepting as it did that additional justification would be required in respect of decisions which interfered with Convention rights. Unless the approach taken by the House of Lords in *Matadeen* constitutes a considerable advance from that impugned by the ECtHR in *Smith & Grady*, it remains unlikely, to say the least, that the principle of non-discrimination is effectively incorporated within the irrationality limb of judicial review.

It may be that judicial review will develop more fully to take into account the principle of non-discrimination, in particular after the implementation of the Human Rights Act 1998. But it remains true at present to state that the common law has yet to develop any general proscription against discrimination. In *Amin v Entry Clearance*

Officer, Bombay [1983] 2 AC 818, [1983] 2 All ER 864 [1983] 3 WLR 258, the House of Lords considered a challenge under the SDA to discriminatory immigration practices.

Before 1968 holders of British passports were, generally speaking, free to enter and settle in the United Kingdom without restriction. From about 1965 onwards the governments of certain East African states, formerly British colonies, adopted a policy of excluding persons who were not citizens of their state from trading or taking employment there. The consequence was that persons who did not hold local citizenship of the East African state in which they were living were virtually obliged to leave it. Many of them came to the United Kingdom, as they were then entitled to do, but the influx became difficult to absorb. The Commonwealth Immigrants Act 1968 therefore extended immigration control, which had previously applied only to persons not holding British passports, to apply also to citizens of the United Kingdom and Colonies holding British passports unless they had certain prescribed connections with the United Kingdom. Difficulties then arose because many holders of British passports, particularly Asians living in East Africa, found themselves obliged to leave the countries where they had been living and with nowhere else to go because they were not allowed into the United Kingdom. To ease their position, the British Government in 1968 introduced the special voucher scheme, whereby vouchers are issued to heads of households, who are holders of British passports, and who are under pressure to leave their countries of residence. The scheme has no express statutory basis and no rules have been published defining the conditions on which special vouchers will be issued. The reason is that the scheme is intended to be flexible and is operated by the exercise of administrative discretion, according to the needs of particular individuals and to the circumstances prevailing in their country of residence at the time. It is subject to an overall ceiling of 5,000 vouchers per annum. The ceiling applies to the number of heads of families, but the number of persons actually admitted to the United Kingdom as a result of the scheme is much larger than that as dependants, including children up to 25 years old provided they are unmarried and dependent on the voucher holder, are allowed to accompany the head of the family to the United Kingdom if they have entry clearance. . . .

In my opinion the entry clearance officer who dealt with the appellant's application for a special voucher did discriminate against the appellant on the grounds of her sex. He had to do so because the special voucher scheme is in its nature discriminatory against women. . . . The . . . scheme proceeds upon the assumption that in a household which consists of, or includes, a married couple the husband is normally the head of household. Only in exceptional circumstances, where the husband suffers from long term medical disability, is the wife regarded as the head of household.

But not all sex discrimination is unlawful. Part I of the Act merely defines discrimination and it contains no provision for making it unlawful. Discrimination is only unlawful if it occurs in one of the fields in which it is prohibited by Parts II, III or IV or the Act.

Lord Justice Mann made the same point in *Bernstein* v *Immigration Appeal Tribunal & Department of Employment* [1988] Imm AR 449:

I do not wish to be taken as impugning in any way any of the criteria used by the Department of Employment in deciding whether or not to issue a work permit. However, let it be assumed that those criteria do involve a discrimination against women. . . it must ever be remembered that *sex discrimination of itself is not unlawful*. It is unlawful only in circumstances prescribed by the [SDA]. (My emphasis.)

Returning to the *Amin* decision Lord Fraser, with whom Lords Keith and Brightman agreed, took the view that the discrimination at issue did not fall within Part III of the SDA. This aspect of the decision is considered in Chapter 4. Lords Scarman and Brandon dissented on this issue, but agreed with the majority that "Parts II to IV of the [SDA] are exhaustive of the circumstances in which sex discrimination is unlawful".

DISCRIMINATION AND DISADVANTAGE

It is clear from the previous section that there is no common law right to be free from discrimination. There are however, as we saw above, a variety of statutory prohibitions covering, at the present time, discrimination based on sex (including gender reassignment), race, disability and, in Northern Ireland, religious belief and political opinion. These "protected grounds" have not been plucked out of the air, legislation having followed the recognition of disadvantage suffered by women, ethnic minorities, the disabled (and, in Northern Ireland, Catholics/ Nationalists).

The disadvantage suffered by these various groups, and the extent to which it persists, is discussed in the chapters dealing, respectively, with the SDA, RRA, DDA and FETO. What is of interest here to note is that, with the exception only of the DDA, legislation passed in recognition of the disadvantage suffered by particular groups (women, ethnic minorities and, in Northern Ireland, Catholics/ Nationalists) has taken a formal approach to equality, rather than seeking to prohibit discrimination, exclusively or for the most part, on the grounds of membership of the disadvantaged group. In other words, the SDA prohibits discrimination on grounds of sex[16] rather than discrimination against women; the RRA prohibits discrimination on racial grounds rather than discrimination against blacks, Asians, African Caribbeans, etc; and the FETO prohibits discrimination (in Northern Ireland) on the grounds of religious belief or political opinion, rather than discrimination against Catholics/ Nationalists.

The DDA, by contrast, prohibits discrimination only against the disabled.[17] The significance of this is that the DDA approach permits all forms of positive steps to be taken to ameliorate the disadvantage suffered by the disabled, whereas the other legislation allows only such positive steps as are expressly permitted (see Chapter 3) or which do not contravene the general prohibitions on "discrimination", discussed in Chapter 2. While there have not been a great number of claims brought under the RRA or SDA by whites and men challenging attempts to reduce the disadvantage

---

[16] Or being married or undergoing or having undergone gender-reassignment, see further Chapter 6.

[17] Save only where the discrimination takes the form of victimisation, discussed in Chapter 2.

experienced in particular spheres by women and persons of particular ethnic minority background, the symmetrical approach to discrimination adopted under those Acts has stifled efforts which might otherwise have been made to achieve increased substantive equality.[18]

Another area in which the current legislative approach fails to map onto the disadvantage suffered by particular groups concerns multiple discrimination. This is particularly a problem for women of colour who must select either the SDA or the RRA in order to mount a challenge to discriminatory treatment. This is reasonable in a case where, for example, an Asian woman has been less favourably treated than a white woman (in which case the RRA may provide a remedy) or than an Asian man (where the SDA would apply). But difficulties arise in cases where a woman of colour has been less favourably treated than a white man.

Christine Bell has criticised the fragmented nature of anti-discrimination law in the Northern Irish context, prior to the enactment there of the Race Relations (Northern Ireland) Order 1997 which prohibited race discrimination for the first time.

C. Bell, "The Employment Equality Review and Fair Employment in Northern Ireland" (1996) 2 *International Journal of Discrimination and the Law* **53, 58–9**

The anti-discrimination regime in Northern Ireland, as in the rest of the UK, is a piece meal one. Some types of discrimination are outlawed by legislation, for example sex and religious/political discrimination, and some are not, for example race or sexual orientation . . . some legislation has statutory enforcement bodies, and some does not, and the powers and funding of these bodies differ. . .

It can be argued that the nature of discrimination in these different spheres is so different that different approaches are warranted. It seems, however, that often the legislative approach is based more on political contingencies than the need to address different inequalities differently. Moreover, for those experiencing discrimination the compartmentalization of identities which must take place to take a case is problematic—is a woman discriminated against as a Catholic or as a woman, or both? Compartmentalization can hide important conceptual problems from view, and can prevent broad strategies being developed to respond to what is often a multifaceted issue.

A similar point is made by Fredman and Szyszczak in relation to black and Asian women.

S. Fredman E. Szyszczak, "The Interation of Race and Gender", in B. Hepple and E. Szyszczak (eds) *Discrimination: The Limits of Law,* **221–5**

The cumulative effect of race and sex discrimination is not simply additive. Black women experience problems not shared by either white women or black men. Scales-Trent argues:

By creating two separate categories for its major social problems—"the race problem" and "the women's issue"—society has ignored the group which stands at the interstices of these two groups, black women.

[18] Women-only railway carriages would, for example, breach the SDA, but fear of attack prevents many women from travelling after dark.

In the United States a third way forward has been explored in recognizing the dilemma posed by the interaction of race and gender. This is the holistic approach of recognizing black women as a distinct group, worthy of legal protection, with its own legal identity. It is to this question that we now turn. . . .

In the US, black activists and scholars have addressed the issue of how a new legal status for black women could be derived by using the disadvantages of their multiple status. Initially the US courts were not sympathetic to multiple status claims. As in Britain, black women were forced to separate their sex and race discrimination claims. . . .

Some progress was made in the USA in 1980 in *Jeffries* v *Harris County Community Action Association* [615F 2d 1025 (5th Circuit, 1980)] where a court rejected the *Degraffenreid* approach [413F Supp 142 (ED Niss 1976] and substituted the analogy of "sex-plus" concept. In *Jeffries* the court addressed the race and sex discrimination claims separately and then categorized the claim as one of sex discrimination with a secondary category of race discrimination. Although this decision recognizes the possibility of a claim based on both sex and race discrimination, it required the race claim to be subordinated to the sex discrimination issue. The decision has been heavily criticized since it merely repeats the choice that black women must make in bringing legal claims, "thereby perpetuating a fundamental misunderstanding of the nature of the discrimination experienced by black women, most of whom do not consider their race to be secondary to their sex."

Despite criticism, the sex-plus analogy has been allowed by other courts in the United States. However, in order not to splinter Title VII "beyond use and recognition" the subsequent decision of *Judge* v *Marsh* [649F 2d 1025 (5th Circuit 1980)] has limited the use of the sex-plus concept to the combination of only one "plus" with the dominant protected immutable trait (or fundamental right). Thus black women are limited to arguing only that their sex *plus* their race have been the cause of their discriminatory treatment. This prevents the courts from addressing other factors which may be contributory causes, for example, their colour, religion, national origin, marital status. The limitations and the irony of this approach are summarized by Scarborough:

> The more someone deviates from the norm, the more likely s/he is to be the target of discrimination. Ironically, those who need Title VII's protection the most get it the least under *Judge's* limitation.

In addition to these limitations of the "sex-plus" approach, the doctrine has come under attack from black scholars since it refuses to recognize the reality of black women's lives. By combining sex and race discrimination the law is seeing and conceptualizing black women as the *sum* of two parts, sex + race, rather than as whole persons. Attempts have been made to argue beyond the sex-plus approach to establish that black women, because of their unique historical, social and economic experiences, form a separate and special class worthy of particular attention in law. Such a holistic approach is capable of being achieved in the US because the Constitution already recognizes the complexity of the *forms* discrimination can take. Although technical, it also provides a process whereby groups may establish their distinct identities. In Britain this process is limited to the establishment of groups defined by the Race Relations Act 1976. . . .

DISCRIMINATION AND THE HRA

We saw, above, that the grounds upon which discrimination is currently regulated in the UK include sex, gender reassignment, race, disability and (in the case of Northern Ireland alone) religious belief and political opinion. The exact source, nature and extent of the prohibitions vary between protected grounds, and their discussion forms the subject matter of the book.

In addition to these "core" grounds which are specifically regulated by UK legislation (albeit, in the case of religious belief and political opinion, only in Northern Ireland), we saw that Article 14 ECnHR, which is incorporated as part of UK law by the HRA regulates discrimination on grounds of sex, race, colour, language, religion, political or other opinion, national or social origin, association with a national minority, property, birth or other status. Article 14 may provide additional protection in relation to discrimination on a ground recognised as "protected" by UK legislation (such as, for example, race, colour, national origin and association with a national minority, all of which would fall within the RRA), where the particular discrimination complained of falls outside that legislation (where, for example, it consists of indirect discrimination by the police in the exercise of their powers of arrest—see further chapter 4). It may also provide protection where the ground of discrimination falls entirely outwith current UK legislation (as is the case, for example, with discrimination on grounds of opinion[19], social origin, property or birth or, outside Northern Ireland, religious belief[20] or political opinion).

Article 14 does not give rise to "free-standing" rights against discrimination in general, rather, to rights not to be discriminated against in the exercise of the other rights and freedoms guaranteed by the ECnHR. These rights and freedoms include the right to life; the right to freedom from torture and "inhuman or degrading treatment or punishment" and from slavery and forced labour; the right to "liberty and security of person" and to a fair trial; the right to marry and to found a family and the right to respect for "private and family life"; the right to freedom of thought, conscience and religion and to freedom of expression, association and peaceful assembly. A violation of the Convention can be established under Article 14, and another Article where the subject matter of the discriminatory treatment "relate[s] to" or "falls within the scope of"[21] or is "covered by"[22] a right or freedom elsewhere guaranteed by the Convention. In the *Smith & Grady* case the interference was with the applicants" "private and family life". And in a number of cases in which applicants have complained of religious discrimination, they relied either on Article 9's protection of freedom of religion or on

---

[19] Except, in Northern Ireland, political opinion, see further Chapter 9.

[20] Unless it falls within the RRA, see further Chapter 7.

[21] Appl. 5763/72 *X* v *Netherlands* (1973) *Yearbook* XVI 274, p.296; Appl. 5935/72 *X* v *Federal Republic of Germany* (1976) *Yearbook* XIX 276, p.288.

[22] Appl. 6573/74 *X* v *Netherlands* DR 1 (1975) p.87 at 89 cited by P. van Dijk and G. van Hoof, *Theory and Practice of the European Convention on Human Rights* (2nd ed) (The Netherlands: Kluwer, 1990), p.535.

this together with Article 14 in cases where the state dealt differently with persons of different religious beliefs.[23]

The HRA, which incorporates many of the ECnHR rights into domestic law, becomes fully operational throughout the UK in October 2000. All those who believe that their ECnHR rights have been infringed can sue in the UK courts. Only public authorities (broadly defined) are obliged to comply with the HRA and only public authorities can be sued under it. But the courts, in addition to their powers to declare primary legislation incompatible with the Convention rights, to strike down incompatible secondary legislation and to award damages for breaches by public authorities of their Convention obligations, will be obliged to develop the common law and, where possible, to interpret primary legislation, consistently with those rights.

While someone dismissed by a private employer on grounds of sexual orientation would not be able to sue under the HRA, she would be able to argue that the unfair dismissal provisions should be interpreted so as to comply with her Articles 8 and 14 right to be protected from sexual orientation discrimination. If she were to be refused employment on the same ground, she could argue that the provisions of the SDA ought to be interpreted to provide her with protection.[24]

A similar argument could be made by someone dismissed on grounds associated with his religion, though he would be able to challenge his non-employment only if the courts were prepared to interpret the RRA to this end. We saw, above, that the legislation has been interpreted to provide protection from discrimination to Jews and Sikhs, but that the protection provided to anti-Moslem discrimination turns on the degree of association between that religion and the applicant's racial group.

It may be that the HRA would provide the impetus for an across-the-board recognition of Moslems as a racial group under the Act. But however broadly read, the RRA could not provide protection to those refused employment because they are Jehovah's witnesses, Mormons, Catholics or Presbyterians. Equally, whereas religious discrimination can be challenged on the basis of Article 9, read alone or with Article 14, and sexual orientation discrimination under Article 8, alone or in conjunction with Article 14, the grounds for challenge to the other heads of discrimination listed in Article 14 are less clear. Whether sex discrimination, race discrimination[25] or discrimination on grounds of "language . . . political or other opinion . . . social origin . . . property, birth or other status' will contravene the Convention rights as incorporated by the HRA will turn on the nature of the treatment at issue (and, where the discrim-

---

[23] *Ahmad* v *United Kingdom* (1981), 4 EHRR 126, *Karaduman* v *Turkey* (1993), 74 D & R 93, *Casimiro* v *Luxembourg* (No. 44888/98) (27 April 1999).

[24] The requirements of the ECnHR with respect to non-appointment to, as distinct from dismissal from, employment are less clear—see, in particular, the contrasting decisions in *Kosiek* v *Germany* (1986) 9 EHRR 328 and *Glasenapp* v *Germany* (1987) 9 EHRR 25, on the one hand, and *Vogt* v *Germany* (1996) 21 EHRR 205, on the other. The cases are discussed by John Bowers and Jeremy Lewis, "Wistleblowing: Freedom of Expression in the Workplace" [1996] EHRLR 637, pp 638 ff.

[25] As understood in the UK this would include colour, national origin and association with a national minority, see further Chapter 7.

inator is not a public authority, on the availability of another legal claim on which to "piggyback" the HRA claim).

There may be scope under the HRA for extending the boundaries within which discrimination on grounds of sex, race, disability (and, in Northern Ireland, politics and religion) is currently regulated. In particular, the implementation of the 1998 Act is likely to impact on the scope of judicial review and to result in further expansion of the irrationality limb of judicial review. There may also be scope for extending the heads of discrimination regulated by law. But in addition to the limitations discussed in the preceding paragraphs, the scope for discrimination-based claims under the HRA is restricted for the reasons discussed by Keith Ewing in the following extract, and in the text which follows it. Dealing with the area of employment, Ewing warns that:

K. Ewing, "The Human Rights Act and Labour Law" (1998) 27 *Industrial Law Journal* 275, 288–9

. . . it would be a mistake to be over optimistic about the potential of incorporation for there are several reasons for thinking that the progress here too will be measured in inches rather than miles.

The first of these is the very narrow approach to the construction of the Convention adopted by the Strasbourg authorities, at least in relation to its application to employees. In *Ahmad* [(1981) 4 EHRR 126] the Commission held that there had been no violation of the applicant's article 9 right to freedom of religion, partly because the content of the right could "as regards the modality of a particular manifestation, be influenced by the situation of the person claiming that freedom", including any employment contract to which he or she was a party. And in *Stedman v United Kingdom* [(1997) 23 EHRR CD 168], where the applicant was dismissed by her employer "for refusing on religious grounds to accept a contract which meant that she would have to work on Sundays", the Commission concluded that the applicant had been dismissed "for failing to agree to work certain hours rather than for her religious belief as such and was free to resign and did in effect resign from her employment". Although directed to take these decisions into account, controversially the British courts are not bound by the Strasbourg jurisprudence, which they are free to disregard. It would indeed be disappointing if the courts were to take the view that Convention rights could be qualified by contract, and they would be rightly excoriated were they to adopt the formalism of the Commission's reasoning in *Stedman*.

The second reason for caution, however, is that the rights in the Convention are by no means unqualified. Indeed as the Commission reminded us in *Ahmad* "the freedom of religion, as guaranteed by Article 9, is not absolute, but subject to the limitations set out in Article 9(2)". This has important implications for any court or tribunal faced with a complaint that a dismissal breaches a Convention right. The applicant will first have to establish that the right claimed is in fact a Convention right, a not inconsiderable obstacle in view of the fact that much of the jurisprudence is so embryonic, and in view of the fact that the content of the right can be determined by the contract itself. Consideration will then have to be given to the second paragraph in cases relating to articles 8–11 which permit restrictions where "prescribed by law" and "necessary" in "a democratic society" on a number of grounds including in each case "the rights and freedoms of others". Assuming that restrictions imposed by the contract of employment are restrictions "imposed by law" (though *quaere* the position of implied terms where there is a self evident lack of transparency), the rights and freedoms in whose interests restrictions may be imposed presumably will include those of employers: it is a fair bet that commercial and business considerations will not always take second place.

In addition to the reservations expressed by Ewing about ECnHR rights in general, and to his qualms about the application of those rights by the British judiciary, the utility of the HRA as a weapon against discrimination is limited by the concept of discrimination adopted by the Convention organs.

Violations of Article 14 are not generally found unless the discrimination at issue is direct and overt. The ECtHR referred, in the *Belgian Linguistics* case, to the "aims *and effects*" (my emphasis) of legislation.[26] But, according to Harris *et al*, "the burden upon the applicant to establish that it exists is severe".[27] And the Court tends to evaluate indirectly discriminatory treatment according to its aims, failing to take into account its disparate impact. In *Abdulaziz* v *UK* (1968) A6, 1 EHRR 252, for example, in which the ECtHR rejected a complaint that an immigration rule indirectly discriminated against men from the Indian sub-continent, the Court ignored the disparate impact of the rule and simply examined the purpose behind it. And in *Dudgeon* v *UK* (1981) 4 EHRR 149, the Court accepted the imposition of differential ages of consent for homosexual and heterosexual sex by focusing on the protective intent of the (higher) homosexual age limit without considering whether such arguments justified the differential treatment of homosexuals, as distinct from the restriction of intercourse with young persons generally.

The protections afforded by the ECnHR are inferior to those found (albeit in a more limited sphere) under EC law because of the "parasitic" nature of Article 14 and the under-developed nature of indirect discrimination under the Convention. Further, while direct discrimination cannot be justified, in the context of race or sex, under UK and (where relevant) EC law, Article 14 does permit the justification of direct discrimination. This is inevitable given the breadth of grounds covered in Article 14 (an issue returned to in the concluding chapter). But the ECtHR's test for justification is considerably more relaxed than that applied by the ECJ. In the *Belgian Linguistics* Case, the Court ruled that Article 14 is violated by discrimination having "no objective and reasonable justification". Discrimination in pursuit of a "legitimate aim" would be justified unless it was "clearly established that there is no reasonable relationship of proportionality between the means employed and the aim sought to be realized". In subsequent decisions the Court asked only whether the treatment at issue had a justified aim in view or whether the authorities pursued "other and ill-intentioned designs."[28] Finally, by contrast with the equality provisions of EC law,

---

[26] (1968) A 6, 1 EHRR 252.
[27] D. Harris, M. O'Boyle and C. Warbrick, *Law of the European Convention on Human Rights* (London: Butterworths, 1995).
[28] *Belgian Police* and *Swedish Engine Drivers Union* cases, respectively (1975) 1 EHRR 578 (1975) 1 EHRR 617.

Article 14 permits the removal of discrimination by levelling-down, rather than up, of the provisions at issue.[29]

EC LAW AND DISCRIMINATION

Many reservations have been expressed about the potential of the HRA as an anti-discrimination tool. There is no doubt, however, that the incorporation of the ECnHR into UK law will spawn a great deal of litigation in the discrimination field. Nor is the HRA the only source of rapid development in the law relating to discrimination. Mentioned above were the draft directives published by the European Commission in 1999 as part of a package of anti-discrimination proposals including a proposal for a Council decision establishing a five year anti-discrimination programme to run from 2001–2006.[30]

The directive on race discrimination[31] which was adopted by the Council of Ministers in June 2000 and which will come into force within three years extends beyond the employment field (broadly defined[32]) to regulate discrimination in access to voluntary work, training including practical work experience, social protection including social security and healthcare, social advantages (concessionary travel on public transport, access to cultural events, subsidised school meals, etc.), education and access to goods, services and housing. Some of these areas are currently covered by the RRA (see Chapter 7) and the implications of the new directive for the coverage of the RRA are further considered there and in Chapter 4.

The framework directive on establishing equal opportunities in employment would, if it is adopted, have more radical impact on UK law. The framework directive seeks to prohibit discrimination on grounds of "racial or ethnic origin, religion or belief, disability, age or sexual orientation". Its impact would go beyond the gap-plugging potential of the race discrimination directive by creating entirely new heads of actionable discrimination—age and sexual orientation and, outside Northern Ireland, religion and belief.

The draft directive on equal opportunities will not become law unless it receives the unanimous approval of the Council of Ministers, approval which may be very difficult to secure given "one size fits all" approach. Acceptance of the race discrimination directive was driven in part by concerns over the election of a right-wing government in Austria. But no decisions have, as yet, been reached on the framework directive,

---

[29] Britain's response to the decision of the Court in *Abdulaziz*, above (in which Britain's immigration rules were found to violate Article 14 read together with Article 8, in that they provided less favourable treatment to the husbands and fiancés of patrial women than to the wives and fiancées of patrial men), was to withdraw the more favourable treatment from the wives of patrial men.

[30] Com (1999) 567 final.

[31] Com (2000) 328(01).

[32] As is the case under the RRA.

and morally conservative states may object to the inclusion of sexual orientation as a protected ground. Any prohibition of disability discrimination has significant cost implications and legitimate questions may be raised in some cases as to whether age or religion/ belief discrimination ought to be categorised as the same kind of wrong as, for example, discrimination based on race or sex. These issues will be considered further in the concluding chapter, which anticipates developments in discrimination law.

Here it is useful to consider the application of EC law in the UK. Some of the detail of the EC equality legislation (Articles 39 and 141 of the Treaty of Rome, Council Directives 75/117, 76/207, 79/7, 86/378, 92/85, and 97/80 on, respectively, equal pay, equal treatment in employment, the progressive implementation of equal treatment in social security and in occupational social security schemes, pregnant workers and the burden of proof in cases of sex discrimination) is considered throughout the book. Here the focus is on the relevance and application of EC law in the UK.

Article 141 of the Treaty has both horizontal and vertical direct effect in domestic law. This means that plaintiffs can rely on it in the UK courts regardless of any UK provisions to the contrary, and can do so regardless of whether the legal action is taken against the state or another individual. The difficulty which arises in this context, however, concerns the manner in which Article 141 may be relied upon in the domestic courts.

In the normal course of events, individuals rely on Article 141 through the mechanisms of the EqPA. Where these are inadequate fully to implement Article 141, they can be done whatever violence is necessary to give effect to the rights guaranteed by it. In *Worringham* v *Lloyds Bank plc* Case C–69/80 [1981] ECR 767, for example, the applicant challenged the employer's differential contributions to male and female pensions. The ECJ ruled that the contributions were "pay" within Article 141. When the case returned to the Court of Appeal ([1982] IRLR 84), the Court simply ignored that provision of the EqPA which excluded claims in relations to pensions and declared in favour of the applicant.[33] A similar approach was taken by EAT in *Bossa* v *Nordstress & Anor* [1998] ICR 694, [1998] IRLR 284 to Article 39 (see further Chapter 4).

In other cases, for example where the EqPA's restriction to contractual terms precludes an Article 141-based claim in respect of a gratuitous benefit, applicants can bring their claims under the SDA. This was the case in *Garland* v *British Rail* Case C–12/81 [1982] 2 All ER 402, [1982] ECR 359, where the applicant challenged the discriminatory provision of gratuitous travel benefits. Again, the ECJ ruled that the benefits constituted "pay" within Article 141, and the applicant's claim succeeded despite the exclusion from the SDA of (s.6(4)) "provision in relation to death or retirement".

In some cases, claims based on Article 141 fall entirely outside UK legislation concerned with discrimination. The most notable example of this arose in the wake of the

---

[33] The applicants in *Gillespie* v *Eastern Health and Social Services Board* Case C–342/93 [1996] ECR I–0475, [1996] IRLR 214 brought their claims in part under the EqPA, claiming (unsuccessfully) that their contracts should be amended to include more favourable terms relating to maternity pay. See also *Levez* v *Jennings (Harlow Pools) Ltd* Case C–326/96 ([1999] All ER (EC) 1, discussed in Chapters 5 and 10, in which the plaintiff successfully sought the disapplication of the two-year limit on backdating in the EqPA.

House of Lords decision, in *R* v *Secretary of State for Employment ex p. EOC* [1993] 1 All ER 1022, that discrimination against part-timers in terms of access to redundancy payments and unfair dismissal protection breached EC law. (It also appeared from the decision that unfair dismissal compensation might and redundancy payments did qualify as "pay" within Article 141—suggestions later confirmed by the House of Lords in *R* v *Secretary of State for Employment, ex parte Seymour-Smith & Perez (No. 2)* [2000] 1 RLR 263. The post-*EOC* claims (*Biggs* v *Somerset County Council* [1996] IRLR 203 and *Barber* v *Staffordshire County Council* [1996] ICR 379, [1996] IRLR 209, discussed below and in Chapter 5) were made under the unfair dismissal and redundancy provisions (currently found in the Employment Rights Act 1996).

It is clear that, to the extent that the ERA (or its successor legislation) failed to give effect to Article 141, the national courts would be under an obligation to do whatever violence to its provisions was required to implement the rights guaranteed by that Art. The same is true where an Article 141 claim is brought under the SDA or the EqPA itself. But attempts have been made to circumvent national provisions barring actions by applicants who have argued that they should be permitted to rely on "freestanding" Article 141 rights. In *Shields* v *Coomes* [1979] 1 All ER 456, Lord Denning suggested that: "a married woman could bring an action in the High Court to enforce the right to equal pay given to her by article [141]". But the remark was made *obiter* and, while the "freestanding right" approach has found intermittent support both in the Court of Appeal (*Macarthys* v *Smith (No 2)* [1980] IRLR 209 and *Pickstone* v *Freemans* [1987] IRLR 218)[34] and in EAT,[35] it has recently been rejected by the Court of Appeal in *Biggs* v *Somerset* and in *Barber* v *Staffordshire County*. In *Biggs* Neill LJ, for the Court of Appeal, declared that Article 141:

> does not confer a right to compensation for unfair dismissal where there is no sex discrimination . . . Article [141] does not provide a separate claim for compensation for unfair dismissal. Moreover, even if such a separate basis of claim existed, it would not fall within the jurisdiction of an industrial tribunal.[36]

And in *Barber* v *Staffordshire*, which was decided on the same day as *Biggs*, Neill LJ adopted the reasoning of Mummery J for EAT in *Biggs* v *Somerset*:

---

[34] The House of Lords reached their decision on different grounds. See also Lord Denning's speech in *Worringham*.

[35] *Amies* v *Inner London Education Authority* [1977] ICR 308, *Snoxell and Davies* v *Vauxhall Motors Ltd* [1977] IRLR 123, *Albion Shipping Agency* v *Arnold* [1982] ICR 22, [1981] IRLR 525, *Hammersmith & Queen Charlotte's Special Health Authority* v *Cato* [1987] IRLR 483, *Stevens and others* v *Bexley Health Authority* [1989] IRLR 240, *Secretary of State for Scotland & Greater Glasgow Health Board* v *Wright & Another* [1991] IRLR 187, *Diocese of Hallam Trustees* v *Connaughton* [1996] ICR 860, [1996] IRLR 505, *Scullard* v *Knowles & Southern Regional Council for Education & Training* [1996] ICR 399, [1996] IRLR 344.

[36] Auld LJ and Sir Iain Glidewell agreed, the latter adding that "Article [141] does not . . . provide any remedy for breach of th[e] right [not to be discriminated against in redundancy pay or unfair dismissal compensation]. . . The remedy is provided by national law in this country by the [Employment Rights Act]".

(a) The industrial tribunal has no inherent jurisdiction. Its statutory jurisdiction is confined to complaints that may be made to it under specific statutes, such as the [ERA, the SDA, the RRA, the EqPA] . . . and any other relevant statute. We are not able to identify the legal source of any jurisdiction in the tribunal to hear and determine disputes about Community law generally.

(b) In the exercise of its jurisdiction the tribunal may apply Community law. The application of Community law may have the effect of displacing provisions in domestic law statutes which preclude a remedy claimed by the applicant. In the present case the remedy claimed by the applicant is unfair dismissal. That is a right conferred on an employee by the [ERA] and earlier legislation. If a particular applicant finds that the Act contains a barrier which prevents the claim from succeeding but that barrier is incompatible with Community law, it is displaced in consequence of superior and directly effective Community rights.

(c) In applying Community law the tribunal is not assuming or exercising jurisdiction in relation to a "free-standing" Community right separate from rights under domestic law. In our view, some confusion is inherent in or caused by the mesmeric metaphor, "free-standing". "Free-standing" means not supported by a structural framework, not attached or connected to another structure. This is not a correct description of the claim asserted by the applicant. She is not complaining of an infringement of a "free-standing" right in the sense of an independent right of action created by Community law, unsupported by any legal framework or not attached or connected to any other legal structure. Her claim is within the structural framework of the employment protection legislation, subject to the disapplication of the threshold qualifying provisions in accordance with the EOC case . . .

Having adopted the approach taken by EAT in *Biggs*, Neill LJ continued:

Article [141] can be relied upon by an applicant to disapply barriers to a claim which are incompatible with Community law. The statutory conditions which have to be satisfied before compensation can be obtained can therefore be disapplied if they are discriminatory and contrary to Community law . . . But, as I understand the matter, the impact of Community law on claims brought before industrial tribunals is that Community law can be used to remove or circumvent barriers against or restrictions on a claim but that Community law does not create rights of action which have an existence apart from domestic law. We are not of course concerned in this case with a claim for compensation such as that which was considered by the ECJ in *Francovich* v *Italian Republic* [joined cases C–6/90 and C–9/90 [1995] ICR 722; [1991] ECR I–5357, ECJ [1992] IRLR 84 ECJ] . . . But, unless parliament otherwise decided, such a claim would not come within the jurisdiction of an industrial tribunal.

The position with respect to Article 39 of the treaty is a little less clear. The Article provides that:

1. Freedom of movement for workers shall be secured within the Community.
2. Such freedom of movement shall entail the abolition of any discrimination based on nationality between workers of the Member States as regards employment, remuneration and other conditions of work and employment. . .

The extent to which Article 39 is *horizontally* effective is, as yet, unclear. In *Bossa* v *Nordstress & Anor* [1998] ICR 694, [1998] IRLR 284, which is discussed in Chapter 4, EAT relied on the decision of the ECJ in the *Bosman* case (C–415/93) to rule that the provision was so effective. It is unclear whether this is wholly true, the ECJ ruling in that case that the Article applied "not only to the action of public authorities but . . . likewise to rules of any other nature aimed at regulating in a *collective* manner gainful employment and the provision of services" (my emphasis). This suggests that only collective agreements and the like are covered (*Bosman* itself concerned the transfer rules governing footballers). But the Court went on to rule that "Since . . . working conditions in the various Member States are governed sometimes by means of provisions laid down by law or regulations and sometimes by agreements or other acts concluded or adopted by private persons, to limit the prohibition in question to acts of a public authority would risk creating inequality in their application." This would appear to extend to purely individual instances of discrimination.

Article 39 does not merely prohibit *discrimination* connected with nationality but regulates all measures which interfere with the free movement of workers within the Community. The measure impugned in *Bosman* was the rule which required payment between football clubs in connection with the transfer of players after the completion of their contracts. There was no question that this rule discriminated as between players of different EU nationality. It was clear, on the other hand, that it had the potential to interfere with their freedom of movement between the Member States.

Art 39 is limited in that, despite its reference to "workers", it has been interpreted to apply only to those having nationality of one of the Member States.[37] The final point to make about Article 39 is its non-application in "wholly internal" situations. In *R* v *Saunders* Case C–175/78 [1979] ECR 1129, [1979] 2 CMLR 216 a Northern Irish woman claimed that a sentence whereby she was bound over to return from Bristol to Northern Ireland and to remain there for three years restricted her right to free movement under Article 39 (this provision, as was pointed out above, not being restricted to discriminatory restrictions). Her claim was rejected on the grounds that it had no extra-British element such as to bring it within the scope of Article 39. In *Knoors* v *Secretary of State for Economic Affairs* Case C–115/78 [1979] ECR 399, the fact that a Dutch plumber was refused permission to work as a plumber in the Netherlands, his qualifications having been gained in Belgium, did provide such an external element as to bring his claim within Article 39.

By contrast with Article 141 and, it appears, Article 39, directives have only vertical direct effect.[38] This means that, assuming that their terms are sufficiently clear, precise and unconditional to be enforceable at all,[39] directives can be directly enforced only against Member States. This can occur where, as in *Marshall* v *Southampton and South*

---

[37] See discussion in Chapter 2, R. Nielsen and E. Szyszczak, *The social dimension of the European Community*, 3rd ed.) Copenhagen: Handelshøjskolens Forlag, 1997).

[38] *Marshall*, Case C–152/84 [1986] ECR 723, discussed below.

[39] *Van Gend en Loos* Case C–26/62 [1963] ECR 1.

West Hampshire Area Health Authority (Teaching) Case 152/84 [1986] 2 All ER 584, [1986] QB 401, an individual employed by the State (widely defined)[40] relies on the terms of a directive against her employer. Secondly, an individual may sue the State, other than as his or her employer, for failure to implement the terms of Directives in national legislation. (This is the so-called *Frankovich* claim, after the decision of the ECJ in *Francovich*, above). Organisations such as the EOC and, on occasion, individuals may also seek judicial review of UK legislation on the grounds of its failure to conform with EC law.[41]

Directives may not be relied upon directly against private individuals. But, increasingly, they are giving rise to *indirect* vertical and horizontal effect by the interpretative obligation imposed upon national courts by the Treaty of Rome and by section 2(4) of the European Communities Act 1972 (ECA).

The directive in respect of which most relevant litigation has arisen is the equal treatment directive, whose provisions are given effect in Britain through the SDA (which, however, predates the directive). In *Duke* v *GEC Reliance* [1988] IRLR 118 [1988] 1 All ER 626, [1988] AC 618, the House of Lords took a narrow approach to the interpretive obligation, ruling that it did not apply as between the SDA and the directive because the former:

> was not intended to give effect to the Equal Treatment Directive . . . Section 2(4) of the [ECA] does not . . . enable or constrain a British court to distort the meaning of a British statute in order to enforce against an individual a Community Directive which has no direct effect between individuals."

In *Marleasing SA* v *Comercial Internacional de Alomentacion SA* Case C–106/89 [1990] ECR I–4135, the ECJ ruled that national courts were obliged to interpret domestic legislation "*so far as possible*, in the light of the wording and the purpose of [any related] directive in order to achieve the result pursued by the latter" (my emphasis), this obligation not being restricted to legislation passed in order to give effect to the directive.

In *Webb* v *EMO Air Cargo (UK) Ltd (No 2)* [1994] QB 718, [1994] 4 ALL ER 115, [1994] 3 WLR 941, [1994] ICR 770, [1994] IRLR 482, which is discussed in Chapter 6, the House of Lords took a more generous approach to the interpretive obligations imposed by the Equal Treatment Directive than it had previously been prepared to do. Prior to referring the case to the ECJ Lord Keith, for the Court,[42] had taken the view that the SDA was unambiguously unfavourable to the applicant but allowed that, if the ECJ ruled that her treatment breached the terms of the Directive: "it would be necessary for this House to consider whether it is possible to construe the relevant

---

[40] *Foster* v *British Gas* Case 188/89 [1990] ECR I–3313 and (House of Lords) 2 CMLR 217, [1990] IRLR 353.

[41] See *ex p. EOC* v *Secretary of State for Employment* and *R* v *Secretary of State for Employment ex p Seymour-Smith*. Both cases are discussed in Chapter 2.

[42] [1992] 4 All ER 929, [1993] 1 WLR 49, [1993] ICR 175, [1993] IRLR 27.

provisions of the [SDA] in such a way as to accord with such a decision". When the case returned to the House of Lords, their Lordships appeared to have no difficulty in construing the relevant provisions to this effect and made no complaint about interpreting the SDA in a way which they had previously apparently regarded as impossible.

STRUCTURE OF THE BOOK

It is clear from the foregoing that discrimination law is a very complex subject, combining as it does a wealth of UK legislation with EC law and issues relating to the ECnHR. This book attempts to make some sense of the area by ordering the material into general and specific parts and incorporating, where it sheds light on problematic areas, non-European material. The structure is shaped on the framework of the UK legislation—the general part largely utilising concepts taken from the UK Acts (direct and indirect discrimination, victimisation, the types of discrimination prohibited under the various regimes) and the specific part dealing in detail with each of the UK anti-discrimination enactments (the SDA, the RRA, the DDA, the EqPA and. applicable only in Northern Ireland, the FETO). But the European provisions, in particular those stemming from our membership of the European Union, have played a significant role in shaping the UK legislation (in particular, the SDA and the EqPA) and in the development of the jurisprudence thereunder. Their significance will become apparent throughout the book.

Part I of the book—the general part—consists of four chapters (2–5) entitled, respectively, "Discrimination", "Positive Discrimination", "Prohibited Discrimination" and "Eliminating Discrimination". These chapters deal with issues common to most or all of the legislation dealing with discrimination. Part II of the book considers the specific issues which arise under the various legislative regimes dealing. respectively, with (Chapter 6) the SDA, (Chapter 7) the RRA, (Chapter 8) the DDA, (Chapter 9) the FETO and (Chapter 10) the EqPA. Chapter 11 concludes with some remarks as to the likely development of discrimination jurisprudence.

2

"Discrimination"

"Discrimination" is the subject matter of this book, and it is the concept which ties together all the legislation here considered. The concept of "discrimination" is not unique to the legislation generally regarded as central to the study of that subject. In addition to the sex discrimination, race relations, disability discrimination, equal pay and fair employment and treatment legislation considered in this book, the Trade Union and Labour Relations (Consolidation) Act 1992 prohibits employment-related discrimination on grounds of trade union membership and non-membership (ss.137–8, 146, 152–3) and the Employment Rights Act 1996 prohibits discrimination on grounds that someone has exercised any of the rights provided by the Acts (ss.44–47 and 99–104). The Employment Relations Act 1999 also prohibits discrimination on a number of grounds.

Many pieces of legislation prohibit discrimination on various grounds. But what is of particular significance in the case of the legislation here studied is the central importance to them of the discrimination prohibition and its articulation as a prohibition on "discrimination" (rather than, as is the case in the 1992 and 1996 Acts, as a prohibition on "detriment" and "dismissal" on grounds of, *inter alia*, trade union membership, assertion of a statutory right, health and safety reasons). Further, four of the five pieces of legislation here under discussion share the same concept of discrimination as extending to direct and indirect discrimination. Only the Disability Discrimination Act (DDA) excludes a prohibition on indirect discrimination, and this exclusion is balanced to a significant extent by its imposition of a duty to make reasonable accommodation for the disabled. The DDA is unique amongst UK anti-discrimination law also in providing a general justification defence to direct discrimination—this, too, as we shall see in chapter 8, being balanced to some extent by the duty of reasonable adjustment. Here, we consider the three types of discrimination regulated by UK anti-discrimination law legislation—direct and indirect discrimination and victimisation.

DIRECT DISCRIMINATION

The concept of direct discrimination applies across the regimes under discussion though, as was mentioned above, with modifications in the case of the DDA. S.1(1)

Sex Discrimination Act (SDA) provides that:

> A person discriminates against a woman in any circumstances relevant for the purposes of
> any provision of this Act if—
> (a) on the grounds of her sex he treats her less favourably than he treats or would treat a
> man . . .

S.1(1) Race Relations Act (RRA), and Art3(2)(a) Fair Employment and Treatment
(Northern Ireland) Order (FETO) are in similar terms, the prohibited grounds of discrimination consisting, respectively of race, and "religious belief or political opinion".
The DDA's approach is slightly different, s.5(1) prohibiting discrimination for "a reason which relates to the disabled person's disability". The significance of this will
become apparent below. No distinction is drawn by the Equal Pay Act (EqPA)
between "direct" and "indirect" discrimination—indeed, the term "discrimination" is
not even employed by the Act. But, as we shall see in chapter 10, the concepts of direct
and indirect discrimination have a significant role to play for the purposes of that Act.
  Neither the SDA nor the RRA, the DDA nor the FETO, require that the complainant point to an actual person who has been more favourably treated. By contrast
with the EqPA, the other regimes permit a claim on the basis of a hypothetical comparator alone. Whether an actual or a hypothetical comparator is used, s.5(3) SDA
provides that:

> A comparison of the cases of persons of different sex . . . under section 1(1) . . . must be such
> that the relevant circumstances in the one case are the same, or not materially different, in
> the other.

Ss. 3(4) RRA and Art3(3) FETO are in similar terms, the comparisons being,
respectively, between persons of different racial grounds and persons of different religions or political beliefs. The DDA includes no such provision. It also, alone,
expressly permits the justification of direct discrimination,[1] s.5(3) providing in the
employment context that discrimination will not be justified unless "the reason for it
is both material to the circumstances of the particular case and substantial". (Different
tests, discussed in Chapter 4, are applied to discrimination in relation to services,
housing, etc.) But we shall see, below, that ss.5(3)/ 3(4) and Article 3(3) may operate
covertly to permit the justification of direct discrimination under the SDA, RRA and
FETO respectively.

The development of direct discrimination

The definition of direct discrimination appears relatively straightforward. But, particularly in the early application of the SDA, the courts at times appeared reluctant to

---

[1] Other than by particular provisions such as the GOQ defences provided by both RRA and SDA and
discussed in Chapters 6 and 7.

apply it in its full force. The first case to reach the Court of Appeal under that Act was *Peake* v *Automotive Products Ltd*, in which a man challenged his employer's practice of allowing women to leave the factory five minutes before men. Men and women finished work at the same time, but women were permitted to leave first, according to Lord Denning, "in the interests of safety so that the women should not be jostled or hurt in the rush through the gates when the men leave work".

Peake v Automotive Products Ltd [1978] QB 233, [1978] 1 All ER 106, [1977] 3 WLR 853, [1977] ICR 968, 12 ITR 428, [1977] IRLR 365

Lord Denning MR:

Although the [SDA] applies equally to men as to women, I must say it would be very wrong to my mind if this Act were thought to obliterate the differences between men and women or to do away with the chivalry and courtesy which we expect mankind to give womankind. The natural differences of sex must be regarded even in the interpretation of an Act of Parliament. Applied to this case it seems to me that, when a working rule is made differentiating between men and women in the interests of safety, there is no discrimination contrary to s.1(1)(a). Instances were put before us in the course of argument, such as a cruise liner which employs both men and women. Would it be wrong to have a regulation: "Woman and children first"? Or in the case of a factory in case of fire? As soon as such instances are considered, the answer is clear. It is not discrimination for mankind to treat womankind with the courtesy and chivalry which we have been taught to believe is right conduct in our society.

Shaw LJ:

The [SDA] was not, in my judgment, designed to provide a basis for capricious and empty complaints of differentiation between the sexes. Nor was it intended to operate as a statutory abolition of every instinct of chivalry and consideration on the part of men for the opposite sex. The phrase used in all the prohibitions imposed by the [SDA] is "discrimination against" one sex or the other. This, to my mind, involves an element of something which is inherently adverse or hostile to the interests of the persons of the sex which is said to be discriminated against. . .

In the present case the union unreservedly approved the arrangements which were made in the interests of safety and which have existed for 30 years. The union thought them desirable and sensible and not in the least discriminatory, and I entirely agree.

In applying statutory provisions which touch human conduct and relationships in infinite ways, it is vitally important to cling to common sense. Otherwise it may be argued by some troublemaker some day that the provision of separate and different arrangements for hygiene and sanitation constitutes an act of discrimination against the males or the females or both. Some acts of differentiation or discrimination are not adverse to either sex and are not designed so to be. Nor, without surrendering to absurdity, can they be so regarded. The discrimination alleged in this case appears to me to fall within that category. I too would allow the appeal.

The decision in *Peake* was described by Peter Wallington as one "redolent of all the values that the [SDA] had sought to lay to rest . . . a contribution from the Court of

Appeal which must rank as intellectually one of its weakest in recent years". According to Wallington, its logic was that:

P. Wallington "Ladies First—How Mr Peake was piqued" [1978] CLJ 37, 39

A person who refused to employ women as bricklayers because he envisaged that they would be embarrassed by the language used by the male employees, or the landlord who kept women out of his dockland pub because they might be molested by drunken male customers, would not be discriminating. That in itself is bad enough—women are capable of making such judgements for themselves without the need for a judicially-sired wet-nurse—but what must cause greater concern is the formidable burden of proof if some element of subjective hostility on the part of the respondent needs to be proved in every case of discrimination. Proof of discrimination even on an objective standard of conduct is difficult enough: it would be well-nigh impossible if the respondent could put on his best honest expression, disclaim any malevolent intent towards the applicant, and wait for the Tribunal to shelter behind the burden of proof and dismiss the claim.

The difficulty with the approach of the Court of Appeal in *Peake* is that it is just the attitudes of "chivalry" and those regarding the "natural differences of sex" which are in large part responsible for the disadvantages suffered by women which the SDA attempted to eradicate. Recognition, albeit belated, of this prompted the Court of Appeal in *Ministry of Defence* v *Jeremiah* to modify the approach it had adopted in *Peake*.

Ministry of Defence v *Jeremiah* [1980] QB 87, [1979] 3 All ER 833, [1979] 3 WLR 857, [1980] ICR 13, [1979] IRLR 436

Mr Jeremiah complained that that, whereas men who volunteered for overtime were required to work in the "colour-bursting shop" (an unpleasant environment in respect of which work attracted an additional premium), women who worked overtime were not so required.

Lord Denning MR:

A woman's hair is her crowning glory, so it is said. She does not like it disturbed: especially when she has just had a "hair-do". The women at an ordnance factory in Wales are no exception. They do not want to work in a part of the factory . . . which ruins their "hair-do" . . .

Mr Jeremiah has little regard for chivalry or for the women's hair-dos. He is a modern man. He says that there should be equality between the sexes. Either the women should be required to do their stint (in the colour-bursting shop), just like the men. Or the men should not be required to do it any more than the women . . .

it is plain that Ministry of Defence here discriminated against Mr Jeremiah. They required him to work in the dirty shop. They treated him less favourably than they treated a woman; and they did it on the ground of his sex, because he was a man . . .

the Ministry relies on *Peake* v *Automotive Products Ltd* . . . There were two grounds for the decision. Now on reconsideration, I think the only sound ground was that the discrimination was *de minimis* [2]. Counsel for Mr Jeremiah told us that on a petition to the House of Lords, they refused leave to appeal for that very reason. They thought that the decision was correct on the *de minimis* ground.

In these circumstances, the other ground (about chivalry and administrative practice) should no longer be relied on . . .

Direct discrimination may, as in the cases considered above, consist in treating people differently *simply* because of a difference in sex, racial group, etc.[3] But it may also, and will more commonly, consist in treating them differently on the basis of attributes stereotypically associated with persons of either sex or a particular racial group.

T. Modood "Cultural Diversity and Racial Discrimination in Employment Selection" in B. Hepple and E. Szyszczak (eds) *Discrimination: the Limits of Law* (London: Mansell, 1992)

Stereotyping is an intellectually crude, patronizing and unfair method of providing a context in which to judge individuals who are deemed to be of a collective type; in the extreme case individuals are seen completely in terms of a collective type. The greater the ignorance about a group of people by an outsider or observer, the greater the reliance on a stereotype (which may not be completely unfavourable to the group). It follows that to decrease the use of unfavourable stereotypes one has to increase the level of knowledge about the groups and to make sure that the knowledge used is not only of the outsider's generalizing type but includes some understanding of how the group understands itself, of what it believes to be some of its distinctive qualities or virtues. We need to allow favourable as well as unfavourable generalizations to come into play. The more one knows about a group the more one is able to penetrate beyond the group to the individual; it is when the context is easily understood and taken for granted that the individual stands out and so can be noticed in his or her own right. The less familiar one is with the group, the less one is able to perceive the individual for "they all look alike" (not just in terms of physical appearance but also in terms of behaviour). See for instance how easily all assertive Muslims have been branded as "fundamentalists" by the media, and indeed how there *was* no media interest in Muslim concerns until they were seen as a threat. The choice, then, is not between identifying someone as an individual and identifying him or her as a group member; without understanding the group, one lacks the context for identifying the variables out of which individuality is composed. Until one can penetrate into the forest one cannot see one tree as being different from another.

These generalities are relevant to the employment selection process. Consider the cultural variables of an interview for example. What I have in mind are the following types of features: desired length of interview, desired ratio of talk between interviewer and interviewee, length of introductions, eye-contact, posture, body language, deference, willingness to talk about oneself and various areas of one's life, tendency to answer directly or in circumlocutions and elaborate context-setting ways, standards of politeness and informality, willingness to "sell oneself" and inhibitions about boasting, sexual modesty, anxieties built up from previous rejections and fear of discrimination, etc. How we treat

---

[2] Wallington, p.40, points out that the difference amounted to two days *per annum*.
[3] In such a case an employer, if replying honestly, would affirm that the reason for the differential treatment was the difference in sex, race, etc.

and evaluate other people in an interview is dependent on how we relate to them, how comfortable we are with them. The very same qualities that in one individual may be perceived as pushy and aggressive may in another be commended as the raw materials to be developed into leadership skills. The difference in perception may be nothing more than racial—or for that matter, sexual—prejudice. Such prejudice may be unconscious and unexamined because it is shared and reinforced by our own peer group and, when combined with a lack of familiarity with the nuances of a different cultural manner, is bound to produce mutually unsatisfactory interviews and fail in bringing out or identifying the capabilities of ethnic minority candidates. Where we as selectors do not make an effort to guard against unconscious discrimination, we invariably select those individuals who are most like ourselves—for after all not only are they the people it is easiest to get close enough to for their strengths to be spotted, but they are the ones whom we are likely to feel we had a good interview with because they are the individuals that we are likely to enjoy the experience of being with. Conversely, with those that we don't easily hit it off with, we do not make the same effort to seek their positive qualities and therefore undervalue them.

Stereotyping was recognised as a form of direct discrimination in *Skyrail Oceanic Ltd* v *Coleman* a sex discrimination case brought by a travel agent who was dismissed when she married an agent from a competing firm. Both employers had got together and agreed that Ms Coleman should be dismissed on the assumption that her husband would be the primary breadwinner. The Court of Appeal re-instated the tribunal's decision that she had been dismissed on grounds of sex, EAT having overturned that decision in the meantime ([1980] ICR 596, [1980] IRLR 226).

Coleman v Skyrail Oceanic Ltd (trading as Goodmos Tours) [1981] ICR 864, [1981] IRLR 398

Lawton LJ:

The foundation of Mr Lester's submission [for the plaintiff] that there had been unlawful discrimination against Mrs Coleman because of her sex was . . . [the employer's] evidence when he said: "We [decided to dismiss her] on the assumption that the husband was the breadwinner". The respondents made no inquiries about the financial position of the husband. Had they done so they would have discovered that he was earning a modest wage of £46 per week net, which in 1978 would have provided a poor standard of living for himself and his wife if she did not make any contribution to the family income. . . I am satisfied that the dismissal of a woman based upon an assumption that men are more likely than women to be the primary supporters of their spouses and children can amount to discrimination under the [SDA].

The problem which Mr Lester had to overcome in this case was that the respondents had a reason for dismissing Mrs Coleman which had nothing to do with her sex. What mattered to them was the fact that she was on intimate terms with an employee of a rival firm. Mr Lester submitted, however, that what triggered off their decision to dismiss Mrs Coleman was their assumption that her husband would be the breadwinner after their marriage. It was this which led them to treat her less favourably than they would have treated a man in their employment who happened to have a wife working for a rival firm . . .

There was evidence that the respondents and Mr Levinson of the rival firm had discussed the problem arising from the fact that they were employing a married couple. Following this discussion Mrs Coleman had been dismissed because of the assumption which was made. The evidence is not clear who made the assumption. It seems to me likely that the assumption was made by both the respondents and Mr Levinson in the course of their discussion; and even if it was not, it was made by the respondents . . .

[Counsel for the employers] also submitted that the evidence did not establish that the respondents discriminated against Mrs Coleman on the ground of her sex. The assumption which they made had no sexual connotation because a breadwinner can be of either sex. This is so; but, in the circumstances of this case, the assumption was that husbands are breadwinners and wives are not. Such an assumption is, in my judgment, based on sex.

Shaw LJ (dissenting)

The circumstances which give rise to this appeal have been recounted in the judgment which has just been delivered. I need not, therefore, dwell in detail upon the history. I must acknowledge at the outset that it appears to me to be trivial and banal even when topped up with much legalistic froth. However, this court is required to examine the claims erected upon it. The appellant asserts that the respondents discriminated against her on the ground of her sex and that she was unfairly dismissed by them. In the light of the history those claims are, in my view, artificial and pretentious; but the . . . Tribunal thought otherwise and their only concern appears to have been as to how great a sum they could award to this excessively outraged victim of sex discrimination. As the other members of this court are of the mind that on the evidence there is a narrow factual ground for awarding her something, though it be a small sum, I must take a little time to explain why I consider Mrs Coleman's claim to be unmeritorious and an abuse of the idealistic principle sought to be embodied in the [SDA] . . .

Before the appellant was married, the respondents had a legitimate ground for terminating her contract of employment with them. Their only obligation then was to give her due notice and to avoid any implication that she had been guilty of impropriety as an employee. Her relationship with a fiancé in the service of a competing organisation made her continued employment with the respondents a source of risk which they were not called upon to accept. If she had been told this and given due notice that would have been the end not only of her employment with the respondents, but of any possible claim against them. Whatever tears she may have shed because of her dismissal at a time when she was contemplating marriage, no solatium could have been extracted or extorted from her employers. She would have had to be content with such consolation as her fiancé and her family could give her. When she had dried her tears she would have had to look for new employment and to have counted herself lucky to find it, as she has indeed done . . .

After the appellant had made her original claim for unfair dismissal, the respondents were incautious enough to assign a purported reason for her dismissal. Those who advised her pounced upon this as a manifestation of sex discrimination and the Industrial Tribunal embraced the proposition and awarded her a thousand pounds for the injury thus done her. This appears to me to make nonsense of s.1 of the [SDA]. Mrs Coleman gave evidence before the Tribunal. She does not appear to have been asked whether she would have been more content (or would have suffered less) if (i) her husband had been dismissed and she had not, or if (ii) both her husband and she had been dismissed. If either of those events had occurred no cry of "unfair discrimination because I am a woman" would have availed her before the Industrial Tribunal. Had she appeared there in those circumstances not even the most unrestrained sympathy could have evoked support for a claim resting on so unreal a foundation. This *reductio ad absurdum* demonstrates, in my view, that the appellant's claim is founded on a fallacy . . .

Each employer might have adopted the harsh expedient of respectively dismissing the husband and the wife. They might have tossed a coin to decide which of them should dispense with the services of the embarrassing employee. The tears might still have followed, but no execrating noises about sex discrimination . . .

This was so unmeritorious a case on the facts that I deplore the encouragement given to the appellant to pursue what was at best a phantom claim. The promotion of such claims can only have the consequence of bringing the laudable aims of the legislation against sex discrimination into disrepute. The principles which the [SDA] are designed to promote and protect are disserved when it is sought, with all the attendant anxieties and expense to others, to apply those principles to cases as empty as the present . . .

Shaw LJ's blustering dissent notwithstanding, *Coleman* was followed by EAT in *Horsey* v *Dyfed CC*. The plaintiff was a social worker who was refused secondment to a course because her manager, Mr Evans, took the view that, on its completion, she would fail to return to work for them, her husband having accepted a job elsewhere. EAT overturned a tribunal rejection of her claim that she had been discriminated against on the grounds of sex or marital status.

Horsey v *Dyfed CC* [1982] ICR 755, [1982] IRLR 395

Browne-Wilkinson J:

. . . Under both ss.1 and 3 of the Act (and also the corresponding provisions of . . . the [RRA]) unlawful discrimination consists in treating someone less favourably "on the ground of" sex, marital status or race. . . In our view it is now established by authority that those words do not only cover cases where the sole factor influencing the decision of the alleged discriminator is the sex, marital status or race of the complainant. The words "on the ground of" also cover cases where the reason for the discrimination was a generalised assumption that people of a particular sex, marital status or race possess or lack certain characteristics, eg "I like women but I will not employ them because they are unreliable," "I will not lend money to married women because they are not wage earners," or "I will not employ coloured men because they are lazy". Most discrimination flows from generalised assumptions of this kind and not from a simple prejudice dependent solely on the sex or colour of the complainant. The purpose of the legislation is to secure equal opportunity for individuals regardless of their sex, married status or race. This result would not be achieved if it were sufficient to escape liability to show that the reason for the discriminatory treatment was simply an assumption that women or coloured persons possessed or lacked particular characteristics and not that they were just women or coloured persons.[4]

The cases thus far considered suggest (*Jeremiah*'s disapproval of *Peake* being taken into account) that a respondent's motive for treating the claimant less favourably will not preclude a finding of discrimination as long as that discrimination was "*on the*

---

[4] See further *Hurley* v *Mustoe* [1981] IRLR 208, below. More recently see *Griffin* v *Red Star Parcels* 38 EORDCLD p.7, which concerned racial stereotyping.

grounds of" sex or race, etc. The prohibited ground does not have to be the sole ground for the less favourable treatment (*Owen & Brigg* v *James* [1982] ICR 618, [1982] IRLR 502, Court of Appeal) but it must be "the principal or at least an important or significant cause of the less favourable treatment".[5]

The lack of any requirement that the discriminator be motivated by the prohibited ground was confirmed by the House of Lords in *R* v *Birmingham City Council ex p. EOC*.[6] The same decision established that "less favourable treatment" occurred when a plaintiff was deprived of a choice which was valued by her and by others on reasonable grounds. The case was brought by the EOC because, the Council having fewer grammar school places available for girls than for boys, it set the pass mark higher for the former in the "11 plus" examination by which children in the area were selected for secondary education. The House of Lords ruled that, in order to establish that the girls had been discriminated against, it did not have to be shown that grammar school education was better than the alternative. Lord Goff went on to consider, for their Lordships, the meaning of "on the grounds of sex".

R v *Birmingham City Council ex p. EOC* [1989] 1 All ER 769, [1989] AC 1155

There is discrimination under the statute if there is less favourable treatment on the ground of sex, in other words if the relevant girl or girls would have received the same treatment as the boys but for their sex. The intention or motive of the defendant to discriminate, though it may be relevant so far as remedies are concerned . . . is not a necessary condition to liability . . . if [it were] it would be a good defence for an employer to show that he discriminated against women not because he intended to do so but (for example) because of customer preference, or to save money, or even to avoid controversy.[7]

This statement of the law seems clear. But it did not settle the meaning of "on the grounds of" within s.1(1)(a) of the SDA and RRA. Only one year later, the House of Lords considered the matter once again in *James* v *Eastleigh Borough Council*, a case brought by a man who was charged entrance to the local swimming pool on the grounds that, both he and his wife being aged between 60 and 65, she but not he had reached state pensionable age upon which free entrance depended.

---

[5] Reaffirmed in *Swiggs & Ors* v *Nagarajan* [1999] 3 WLR 425 further considered below. By contrast, in the US the Civil Rights Act 1991 reversed the decision of the Supreme Court in *Price Waterhouse* v *Hopkins* (1989) 490 US 228 to the effect that the prohibited reason in a mixed motive case must at least "tip the balance". *James* v *Eastleigh Borough Council* and *Nagarajan* used the "but for" test adopted *restrictively* by a US Court of Appeals in *Lewis* v *University of Pittsburg* 33 US Cases 1091 (1983) (i.e., to require that the discriminatory reason had to tip the balance), see D. Pannick, *Sex Discrimination Law* (Oxford: OUP, 1985), p.87. But the House of Lords, in adopting the "but for" test in these cases, did not do so restrictively but, as we saw above, expansively to deny the need for motivation. It may be that the discriminatory reason may *either* satisfy the "but for" test or, in a case where a discriminatory motive is established (this not being necessary in a "but for" case), be an "important and significant cause".

[6] Prior to this see *R* v *Commission for Racial Equality, ex p Westminster Council* [1985] ICR 827, [1985] IRLR 426 (CA).

[7] Citing *Jenkins* v *Kingsgate (Clothing Productions) Ltd* [1981] 1 WLR 1485 at 1494 *per* Browne-Wilkinson J and *R* v *Secretary of State for Education and Science, ex p Keating* (1985) 84 LGR 469 at 475 *per* Taylor J. See also Lord Denning MR in *Ministry of Defence* v *Jeremiah*.

Jones v Eastleigh Borough Council [1990] 2 AC 751, [1990] 2 All ER 607, [1990] 3 WLR 55, 88 LGR 756, [1990] ICR 544

Lord Bridge of Harwich

. . . the statutory pensionable age, being fixed at 60 for women and 65 for men, is itself a criterion which directly discriminates between men and women in that it treats women more favourably than men "on the ground of their sex" . . . It follows inevitably that any other differential treatment of men and women which adopts the same criterion must equally involve discrimination "on the ground of sex". . . .

The Court of Appeal's attempt to escape from these conclusions lies in construing the phrase "on the ground of her sex" in s.1(1)(a) as referring subjectively to the alleged discriminator's "reason" for doing the act complained of. As already noted, the judgment had earlier identified the council's reason as "to give benefits to those whose resources would be likely to have been reduced by retirement" and "to aid the needy, whether male or female". But to construe the phrase, "on the ground of her sex" as referring to the alleged discriminator's reason in this sense is directly contrary to a long line of authority confirmed by your Lordships' House in [*ex p. EOC* above].

Lord Goff's test, it will be observed, is not subjective, but objective. Adopting it here the question becomes: would the plaintiff, a man of 61, have received the same treatment as his wife *but for* his sex? (My emphasis) An affirmative answer is inescapable.

Lord Goff

. . . As a matter of impression, it seems to me that, without doing any violence to the words used in [s.1(1)(a)], it can properly be said that, by applying to the plaintiff a gender-based criterion, unfavourable to men, which [the Council has] adopted as the basis for a concession of free entry to its swimming pool, they [sic] did on the ground of sex treat him less favourably than it treated women of the same age, and in particular his wife. In other words, I do not read the words "on the ground of sex" as necessarily referring only to the reason why the defendant acted as he did, but as embracing cases in which a gender-based criterion is the basis on which the complainant has been selected for the relevant treatment. Of course, there may be cases where the defendant's reason for his action may bring the case within the subsection, as when the defendant is motivated by an animus against persons of the complainant's sex, or otherwise selects the complainant for the relevant treatment because of his or her sex. But it does not follow that the words "on the ground of sex" refer only to cases where the defendant's reason for his action is the sex of the complainant and, in my opinion, the application by the defendant to the complainant of a gender-based criterion which favours the opposite sex is just as much a case of unfavourable treatment on the ground of sex. . .

. . . as I see it, cases of direct discrimination under s.1(1)(a) can be considered by asking the simple question: would the complainant have received the same treatment from the defendant but for his or her sex? This simple test possesses the double virtue that, on the one hand, it embraces both the case where the treatment derives from the application of a gender-based criterion, and the case where it derives from the selection of the complainant because of his or her sex and on the other hand it avoids, in most cases at least, complicated questions relating to concepts such as intention, motive, reason or purpose, and the danger of confusion arising from the misuse of those elusive terms.

Lord Ackner concurred with Lords Bridge and Goff. Lords Griffiths and Lowry gave dissenting speeches, Lord Griffith on the ground that the Council had not discriminated against Mr James "because" he was a man, Lord Lowry on the ground that Lord Goff's "causative construction not only gets rid of unessential and often irrelevant mental ingredients, such as malice, prejudice, desire and motive, but also dispenses with an essential ingredient, namely the ground on which the discriminator acts . . . the causative test is too wide and is grammatically unsound, because it necessarily disregards the fact that the less favourable treatment is meted out to the victim on the ground of the victim's sex".

Despite the objections of the dissenters, the approach taken by the majority in *James* attracted wide support:

Evelyn Ellis, "The Definition of Discrimination in European Sex Equality Law" (1994) 19
***European Law Review* 561, 564–6**

All sorts of explanations can be advanced for differing success levels in different groups of people. However, before enacting the sex, race, and religious and political anti-discrimination legislation of the mid-1970s, the United Kingdom legislature seems to have been particularly convinced by two specific explanations. The first, and less palatable, notion was that there was active prejudice in operation against these disadvantaged sections of society. The second, and more subtle, was that discrimination had become "institutionalised" in certain sectors, so that traditional and unquestioned practices were having the effect of unnecessarily and unfairly excluding equality of opportunity. . . .

Three vital deductions follow from such an understanding of the origins of anti-discrimination laws. The first is that the anti-discrimination laws were created as devices for the relief of disadvantage; the law created was not intended to be in any sense criminal or punitive in nature. The logic understanding it is the compensation of the victims of the prior system and, by doing so, the deterrence of others in the future from repeating the injustices of the past. Thus, however, this may become disguised as a result of technical legal definition and judicial interpretation, it is at the very heart of the notion of discrimination that it is the *effect* on its victims with which the law is truly concerned, not the precise nature of the conduct of its perpetrators.

The second deduction is that the legislation has to recognise two different situations in which discrimination can occur; this has been reflected by the law's general acceptance of the twin concepts of direct and indirect discrimination, an acceptance made both by domestic systems and by the European Community system. Thirdly, however, it has to be concluded that these concepts are indeed twins, in other words that they are very closely related and have both sprung from identical roots. Their underlying rationale is the same and this means that they must both consist essentially of the same two elements: some sort of adverse impact on their victims and a prohibited classification underlying that impact. Adverse impact and causation, at least in a broad, non-technical sense, must as a matter of basic logic be the constituent elements which underpin all systems of sex discrimination law. The question then becomes whether or not the definition of discrimination provided by a particular system of law, and thereupon applied by the relevant group of judges, adequately recognises this logic. . . . What sometimes leads to confusion in cases of direct discrimination is the fact that the clearest instance of its occurrence is provided where the perpetrator makes plain an intention to disfavour the victim, in other words, the case of intentional direct discrimination. The temptation here is to extrapolate from the malign motive and to conclude that it is this element which renders the conduct offensive. This, however, is to fall into the trap of analysing discrimination as quasi-criminal in nature rather than treating the notion as essentially remedial in character. An intention to disfavour the victim simply helps to prove the case. It is *not* a necessary ingredient of the statutory tort.

Rather more prosaically, perhaps, another commentator pointed out that:

Geoffrey Mead, "The Role of Intention in Direct Discrimination" (1990) 19 *ILJ*, 250, 252

The practical upshot of all this is that direct discrimination has become easier to establish. The adoption in *James* of the "but for" test of direct discrimination, both simplifies the law and clearly brings within the scope of direct discrimination instances of the use of gender-*based* criteria. This, combined with the decision in *West Midlands P.T.E.* v. *Singh* [1988] I.C.R. 614[8] that if there is statistical evidence of an employer's reluctance to employ members of a particular race or sex, this can help an individual of that race or sex to show she was treated less favourably, removes two major obstacles to successful claims. Nevertheless, it is perhaps unfortunate that it has taken some 15 years for this position to be reached.

Ellis' and Mead's approval of the decision in *James* was not echoed by Bob Watt.[9] Describing the "but for" test as "not a test at all", he interpreted Lord Goff's approach as "contain[ing] two questions:

—Was the complainant subjected to unfavourable treatment?
—Was the complainant a member of a group defined by that which the law declares to be a forbidden ground?

If the answers to these two questions are "yes", the "but-for test provides the answer that unlawful discrimination has occurred".[10]

It is true, as Watt points out, that "the "but-for" test does not contain the explicit question, "was the unfavourable treatment meted out to the applicant because of their group membership?" He is, however, mistaken in his supposition that the "but-for" test is satisfied by "yes" answers to the two questions put above.

Everyone—whether white or ethnic minority, male or female and, in Northern Ireland, regardless of religious belief or political opinion—is entitled not to be discriminated against on grounds of race, sex, etc. Everyone, therefore, is a "member of a group defined by that which the law declares to be a forbidden ground" (indeed, is a member of several such groups). If it were the case that such membership, coupled with the fact of less favourable treatment, was itself sufficient to satisfy the "but-for" test, then any detriment suffered by any worker would always amount to unlawful dis-

---

[8] Discussed in chapter 5.

[9] B. Watt, "Goodbye 'but-for', hello 'but-why?' " (1998) 27 *ILJ* 121.

[10] Watt proceeds to argue that the "but-for" test should be replaced with a "but-why" test, this test replacing the second question above with: "Did the subject of the complaint . . . impose that unfavourable treatment because of the complainant's membership of a group defined on the basis of a forbidden ground?" Watt argues that the Courts are, in fact, moving towards this "but-why" test, an argument we shall consider in Chapter 5.

crimination, depending on how that worker chose to define himself or herself and so long as the worker could point to someone of a different sex, racial group or (in Northern Ireland) religion or political opinion who had not or would not have been subjected to that detriment. No causal link would be required between membership of the group and the treatment complained of.[11]

But the "but-for" test does impose a causation requirement. It is not sufficient to point out a coincidence of group membership and less favourable treatment. The worker must, in addition, be able to convince the tribunal that the less favourable treatment would not have occurred "but-for" his or her membership of the relevant group. The worker does not, on this test, have to establish that the less favourable treatment was *motivated* by the group membership—but s/he does have to establish that the two were causally connected. So, for example, a black woman refused promotion will, in order to establish a discrimination claim, have to prove either (under the SDA) that she would have been differently treated if she were a man or, (under the RRA) that she would have been differently treated if she was not black. The concerns expressed by Watt and by Lord Browne-Wilkinson appear to stem from a perception of the anti-discrimination legislation as creating "protected categories" of people (presumably women, ethnic minorities and, in Northern Ireland, Catholics) who have to be treated favourably, regardless of merit, lest they exercise their power to bring automatically successful discrimination suits. We shall see in Chapter 5 that the reality is very different.

Whatever the reservations of the dissenting Law Lords and commentators such as Watt, the "but for" test is now the established criterion for identifying direct discrimination. It applies equally to discrimination based on race, religious belief or political opinion, and disability[12] and was most recently confirmed by the House of Lords (Lord Browne-Wilkinson dissenting) in *Nagarajan* v *London Regional Transport*. The decision dealt with victimisation (discussed below), but it was agreed by their Lordships that the term "by reason that" in the victimisation provisions had to be interpreted consistent with "on the grounds of" in the context of direct discrimination. Lord Browne-Wilkinson argued that the decisions in *ex p. EOC* and in *James* v *Eastleigh* did not establish the "but for" test as the sole, objective, test for direct discrimination. While he accepted that Lord Bridge had, in *James*, expressly preferred what the former termed an "objective approach" to s.1(1)(a) (i.e., one which asked

---

[11] The jump made by the tribunal in *Barclays Bank* v *Kapur (No.2)* from finding less favourable treatment of applicants who were Asian to concluding that they had been directly discriminated against in the absence of an established causal link was overruled by EAT and EAT's judgment upheld by the Court of Appeal [1995] IRLR 87 precisely on this ground.

[12] See, for example, *The Belfast Port Employer's Association* v *The Fair Employment Commission for Northern Ireland* 29th June 1994 unreported (available on LEXIS), in which Northern Ireland's Court of Appeal accepted the application of *James* to the Fair Employment Act, overruling its previous decision in *Armagh District Council* v *FEA* [1989] AC 1155, in which Lord Lowry LCJ had ruled that "although malice (while often present) is not essential [for direct discrimination], deliberate intention to differentiate on the [prohibited] grounds . . . is an indispensable element in the concept of [direct] discrimination". See also *British Sugar* v *Kirker* [1998] IRLR 624 (disability) and *Swiggs* v *Nagarajan* fn5 and *Chief Constable of Greater Manchester Police & Anor* v *Hope* [1999] ICR 338 (race).

"was a substantial cause of less favourable treatment the race or sex of the claimant?"),[13] he suggested that Lord Goff did not fully accept the "but for" test:

Nagarajan [1999] 3 WLR 425 v *London Regional Transport* [1994] 4 All ER 65 [1999] ICR 877, [1999] IRLR 572

Lord Browne-Wilkinson, dissenting

. . . It is to be noted that Lord Goff picks his words carefully. He finds the "but for" test a useful practical approach to determining the discriminator's reason "in the majority of cases." Moreover, it is to be noted that his formulation is purely subjective: the question is whether the claimant would have received the same treatment "from the defendant." The "but for" test is not a rule of law but a rule of convenience depending on the circumstances of the case. I find it difficult in these circumstances to know exactly what was decided by the James case. Although it is binding on your Lordships I do not regard the question under section 1 as finally determined: it may require to be revisited in the future . . . The only yardstick (in the field of direct discrimination) must be the mental state of the alleged discriminator. To dismiss somebody who comes from an ethnic minority is not, per se, unlawful. Only if what lies within the mind of the employer is the race of the employee and it is that factor which provides the reason why the employee is dismissed does one come into the field of race discrimination at all.

There can be no doubt that the mental state of the alleged discriminator is important to whether direct discrimination has occurred. But the categorisation as "objective" of the "but for" test is flawed. The race, sex, etc., of the employee does lie within the mind of the direct discriminator in a *James* v *Eastleigh* situation in that s/he *knowingly* and *intentionally* applies a criterion which itself *directly* discriminates as between men and women/ different racial groups, etc.[14] Thus, contrary to the view taken by Lord Browne-Wilkinson in *Nagarajan* and by Bob Watt in the extract above, it is not the case that the "but for" test requires a finding of discrimination simply on the basis of less favourable treatment accorded to a ethnic minority worker than to another.[15] This was recognised by Lord Nicholls who, with Lord Steyn, delivered the majority speeches:

Nagarajan v *London Regional Transport*

Lord Nicholls

. . . in every case it is necessary to inquire why the complainant received less favourable treatment. This is the crucial question. Was it on grounds of race? Or was it for some other reason, for instance, because the complainant was not so well qualified for the job? Save in obvious cases, answering the crucial question will call for some consideration of the mental processes of the alleged discriminator. Treatment, favourable or unfavourable, is a con-

---

[13] Or, in a victimisation claim, the fact that the applicant had done a protected act.

[14] The knowing and intentional application of indirectly discriminatory criteria is (intentional) indirect discrimination, see *London Underground* v *Edwards* [1995] IRLR 355, *JH Walker Ltd* v *Hussain & Others* [1996] ICR 291, [1996] IRLR 11.

[15] Or, for that matter to a woman than to a man or *vice versa*, or to a white worker than to another.

sequence which follows from a decision . . . The crucial question just mentioned is to be distinguished sharply from a second and different question: if the discriminator treated the complainant less favourably on racial grounds, why did he do so? The latter question is strictly beside the point when deciding whether an act of racial discrimination occurred. For the purposes of direct discrimination under section 1(1)(a), as distinct from indirect discrimination under section 1(1)(b), the reason why the alleged discriminator acted on racial grounds is irrelevant. Racial discrimination is not negatived by the discriminator's motive or intention or reason or purpose (the words are interchangeable in this context) in treating another person less favourably on racial grounds . . . If racial grounds were the reason for the less favourable treatment, direct discrimination under section 1(1)(a) is established . .

The same point was made in *James* . . . The reduction in swimming pool admission charges was geared to a criterion which was itself gender-based. Men and women attained pensionable age at different ages. Lord Bridge . . . described Lord Goff's test in the *Birmingham* case as objective and not subjective. In stating this he was excluding as irrelevant the (subjective) reason why the council discriminated directly between men and women. He is not to be taken as saying that the discriminator's state of mind is irrelevant when answering the crucial, anterior question: why did the complainant receive less favourable treatment?

Circumventing direct discrimination: appropriate comparators

Taken to its logical conclusion, the "but for" approach might have permitted the British courts to find that both pregnancy discrimination and discrimination on the grounds of sexuality amounted, of necessity, to direct discrimination on grounds of sex. A woman dismissed on grounds of pregnancy could claim that, "but for" the fact of her sex, she would not have been so treated. In *Geduldig* v *Aiello* (1974) 417 US 484 the US Supreme Court refused to accept that pregnancy discrimination amounted to sex discrimination, upholding the exclusion of pregnancy from a state unemployment insurance plan on the grounds that:

[t]here is no risk from which men are protected and women are not. Likewise, there is no risk from which women are protected and men are not . . . The program divides potential recipients into two groups—pregnant women and nonpregnant persons. While the first group is exclusively female, the second includes members of both sexes.

By contrast, the Supreme Court of Canada in *Brooks* v *Canada Safeway* [1989] 1 SCR 1219 ruled that "pregnancy cannot be separated from gender". There the Court found that the exclusion of pregnancy from an insurance policy contravened the equality provisions of Canada's Charter of Rights: "[t]he fact . . . that the plan did not discriminate against all women, but only against pregnant women, did not make the impugned distinction any less discriminating".

The UK courts focused on the "relevant circumstances" of the appropriate comparator under ss.5(3) of the SDA, and defined those circumstances so as to defeat direct discrimination claims based on pregnancy (and, as we shall see in chapter 6, sexual orientation).[16] European developments eventually forced the British courts to accept pregnancy discrimination (though not, as yet, sexual orientation discrimination) as direct sex discrimination, a development further discussed in chapter 6. Meanwhile, the decision of the Court of Appeal in *Dhatt* v *McDonalds Hamburgers* [1991] 3 All ER 692, discussed below, illustrates the potential of s.5(3) [s.3(4) RRA] to undermine the prohibition of direct discrimination and, in particular, of the "but for" test.

Prior to the decision in *Dhatt*, the courts had refused to apply the "same relevant circumstances" requirement to this effect. In *Showboat Entertainment Centre Ltd* v *Owens*, EAT upheld a finding of race discrimination against an employer who dismissed the applicant for his refusal to obey an instruction to exclude young blacks from his place of work (an amusement centre). Much of the decision dealt with the applicability of s.1(1)(a) to discrimination against someone other than the applicant, a matter further discussed in Chapter 7. But the final point dealt with by EAT was the employer's argument that, in order to satisfy s.3(4) RRA, the treatment received by the applicant had to be compared with that which would have been meted out to another manager who refused to obey a racist instruction.

Showboat Entertainment Centre Ltd v Owens [1984] 1 All ER 836, [1984] 1 WLR 384, [1984] IRLR 7, [1984] ICR 65

Browne-Wilkinson J (for the Court)

. . . Although one has to compare like with like, in judging whether there has been discrimination you have to compare the treatment actually meted out with the treatment which would have been afforded to a man having all the same characteristics as the complainant except his race or his attitude to race. *Only by excluding matters of race can you discover whether the differential treatment was on racial grounds.* Thus, the correct comparison in this case would be between Mr Owens and another manager who did not refuse to obey the unlawful racialist instructions (my emphasis)

The approach taken in *Showboat* certainly seemed consistent with that subsequently adopted by the House of Lords in *James* v *Eastleigh*, in which Lord Bridge declared that:

Because pensionable age is itself discriminatory it cannot be treated as a relevant circumstance . . . It is only by wrongly treating pensionable age as a relevant circumstance under s 5(3) that it is possible to arrive at the conclusion that the provision of facilities on favourable terms to persons of pensionable age does not involve direct discrimination under s 1(1)(a) . . . On a proper application of s 5(3) the relevant circumstance which was

---

[16] See also the decision of the ECJ in *Grant* (Case C–249/96) [1998] ECR I–3739 [1998] All ER (EC) 193, [1998] 1 FCR 377, [1998] 1 FLR 839, [1998] IRLR 206, [1998] ICR 449 and, on gender reassignment, that of EAT in *Bavin* v *The NHS Trust Pensions Agency & Secretary of State for Health* [1999] ICR 1192, both discussed in Chapter 6.

the same here for the purpose of comparing the treatment of the plaintiff and his wife was that they were both aged 61.[17]

In *Dhatt*, however, the Court of Appeal permitted a race-related circumstance to be considered for the purposes of s.3(4) RRA. The claim was brought by a man of Indian nationality who was dismissed by McDonalds because of his failure to satisfy his employers that he was entitled to work in the UK. His passport was stamped in such a way as to indicate his entitlement to work, but McDonalds did not recognise this stamp as sufficient to comply with their requirement, imposed only in respect of non-EC workers, of evidence of entitlement to work. On the face of it, Mr Dhatt had clearly been discriminated against contrary to s.1(1)(a) ("racial grounds" being defined by s.3(1) RRA as "any of the following grounds, namely colour, race, nationality or ethnic or national origins"). "But for" the fact that he was not an EC national, he would not have been dismissed because of his failure to provide evidence of his entitlement to work. Despite this, the claim was rejected by a tribunal, EAT and the Court of Appeal.

All three Lords Justice of Appeal accepted the relevance of the decisions in *Showboat* and in *James* but distinguished the latter on the basis that, while the Council had freely chosen to condition free entrance on directly discriminatory criteria, here McDonalds had, *per* Neill LJ, a "general responsibility to ensure that those who work in his business comply with the law". Stocker LJ agreed that employers had a "public duty to assist in the enforcement of the immigration laws. They had, in my view, no alternative but to enquire whether or not an applicant was lawfully entitled to accept employment. Such an enquiry for this purpose did not arise in the case of British citizens or those from EEC countries".

The Court of Appeal took the view that this was sufficient to render a job seeker's nationality a "relevant circumstance" under s.3(4). Lord Justice Neill did not attempt to distinguish the dicta in *Showboat*, but Stocker and Staughton LJJ agreed that *Showboat* did not lay down any principle of "universal application".

The Court of Appeal in *Dhatt* purported to rely on the employers' legal obligation to read into s.3(4)'s "relevant circumstances", in a claim of nationality discrimination, the factor of nationality. If it were the case that the failure so to do would prevent employers from meeting their legal obligations, this would perhaps have been inevitable. But s.41 RRA provides that a discriminatory act is not unlawful under the RRA if it is done: "(a) in pursuance of any enactment or Order in Council or (b) in pursuance of any instrument made under any enactment by a Minister of the Crown or (c) in order to comply with any condition or requirement imposed by a Minister of the Crown (whether before or after the passing of this Act) by virtue of any enactment."

---

[17] Although Browne-Wilkinson LJ in the Court of Appeal [1990] QB 61, [1989] 2 All ER 914. [1989] 3 WLR 123, [1989] ICR 423, [1989] IRLR 318 took a different view.

In *Hampson* v *Department of Education and Science* [1991] 1 AC 171, [1990] 2 All ER 513, [1990] 3 WLR 42, [1990] ICR 511, which is considered in Chapters 4 and 7, the House of Lords took a restrictive approach to s.41(b). Their Lordships did not consider s.3(4) RRA. But, if the approach taken by the Court of Appeal in *Dhatt* were correct, s.41 would be otiose and Ms Hampson's claim would certainly have failed. Not being in possession of a UK qualification (or, perhaps, a three-year equivalent as proscribed by the Secretary of State for Education), the applicant's appropriate comparators would have been others similarly failing to comply with the regulations as applied. All such applicants would, it must be presumed, have been given equally short shrift.

We will return to direct discrimination in Chapter 5, in which the issue of proof is considered, and in the Chapters 6–9 which deal specifically with the SDA, RRA, DDA and FETO. Here it is sufficient to conclude from our initial consideration of direct discrimination the importance of the "but for" test; the fact that reliance on stereotypical views of women (men, persons of different racial or national groups, etc) is directly discriminatory; and the potentially problematic role of the requirement (imposed, respectively, by s.5(3), s.3(4) and Article 3(3) of the SDA, RRA and FETO) that the "comparison of the cases of persons of different sex [race, etc] . . . must be such that the relevant circumstances in the one case are the same, or not materially different, in the other".[18]

Harassment as discrimination

The recognition by the British courts of harassment as, at least in some cases, a form of discrimination, began with the decision of the Scottish Court of Sessions in *Strathclyde Regional Council* v *Porcelli* [1986] ICR 564, [1986] IRLR 134. Catharine MacKinnon has defined sexual harassment as "the unwanted imposition of sexual requirements in the context of a relationship of unequal power",[19] and Canada's Labour Code has defined it as:

> any conduct, comment, gesture or contact of a sexual nature
> (a) that is likely to cause offence or humiliation to any employee; or
> (b) that might, on reasonable grounds, be perceived by that employee as placing a condition of a sexual nature on employment or on any opportunity for training or promotion.[20]

The European Commission's Recommendation on the Protection of the Dignity of Men and Women at Work defines sexual harassment in the following terms:

---

[18] For an unproblematic application of s.3(4) RRA see *Wakeman* v *Quick Corporation* [1999] IRLR 434, discussed in Chapter 4.

[19] *Sexual Harassment of Working Women: A Case of Sex Discrimination* (New Haven, Connecticut: Yale University Press, 1979), p. 1.

[20] RSC, 1985, c. L–2, 247.1.

conduct of a sexual nature, or other conduct based on sex affecting the dignity of women and men at work [which] . . . is unwanted, unreasonable and offensive to the recipient; is used . . . as a basis for an [employment] decision; and/or . . . creates an intimidating. hostile or humiliating work environment for the recipient.

More recently, the new race discrimination directive (Directive 2000/43/EC) defines discrimination to include harrassment with the "purpose or effect of violating the dignity of a person" and of creating an "intimidating, hostile, degrading humiliating or offensive environment."

The US Equal Employment Opportunity Commission (EEOC) in 1980 produced guidelines on sexual harassment which defined harassment as a violation of Title VII's prohibition on sex discrimination.[22] And in Canada, the Supreme Court recognised sexual harassment as sex discrimination in *Janzen* v *Platy Enterprises Ltd.* Manitoba's Court of Appeal had ruled that sexual harassment did not amount to discrimination:

Janzen v *Platy Enterprises Ltd* (1986) 43 Man R(2d) 293, 33 DLR (4th) 32 (CA)

Twaddle JA (with whom Hubard JA concurred)

Harassment is as different from discrimination as assault is from random selection. The victim of assault may be chosen at random just as the victim of harassment may be chosen because of categorical distinction, but it is nonsense to say that assault is random selection just as it is nonsense to say that harassment is discrimination. The introduction of a sexual element, be it the nature of the conduct or the gender of the victim, does not alter the basic fact that harassment and assault are acts, whilst discrimination and random selection are methods of choice.

The fact that harassment is sexual in form does not determine the reason why the victim was chosen. Only if the woman was chosen on a categorical basis, without regard to individual characteristics, can the harassment be a manifestation of discrimination . . .

Where the conduct of an employer is directed at some but not all persons of one category, it must not be assumed that membership in the category is the reason for the distinction having been made. The distinction may have been based on another factor . . .[23]

The gender of a woman is unquestionably a factor in most cases of sexual harassment. If she were not a woman, the harassment would not have occurred. That, however, is not decisive . . . We are concerned with the effective cause of the harassment, be it a random selection, the conduct, or a particular characteristic of the victim, a wish on the part of the aggressor to discourage women from seeking or continuing in a position of employment or a contempt for women generally.

Only in the last two instances is the harassment a manifestation of discrimination.

The Supreme Court allowed the plaintiff's appeal.

---

[21] Discussed in chapter 1 and throughout, especially Chapters 4, 5, 6, 7 and 11.

[22] EEOC, Guidelines on Discrimination Because of Sex, 29 CFR 1604.11(a) (1985)).

[23] Citing *Bliss* v *Attorney General of Canada* [1979] 1 SCR 183, in which the Supreme Court ruled that pregnancy discrimination was not sex discrimination. That decision was overturned by the Supreme Court in *Brooks* v *Canada Safeway* [1989] 1 SCR 1219.

Janzen v Platy (1989) 1 SCR 1284 (SC)

Dickson CJ (for the Court):

When sexual harassment occurs in the workplace, it is an abuse of both economic and sexual power.

Sexual harassment is a demeaning practice, one that constitutes a profound affront to the dignity of the employees forced to endure it. By requiring an employee to contend with unwelcome sexual actions or explicit sexual demands, sexual harassment in the workplace attacks the dignity and self-respect of the victim both as an employee and as a human being.

Perpetrators of sexual harassment and victims of the conduct may be either male or female. However, in the present sex stratified labour market, those with the power to harass sexually will predominantly be male and those facing the greatest risk of harassment will tend to be female . . .

Sexual harassment as a phenomenon of the workplace is not new. Nor is it confined to harassment of women by men, though this is by far the most prevalent and significant context. It may be committed by women against men, by homosexuals against members of the same sex. According to a Canadian survey published in 1983[24], women reported far more exposure to all forms of unwanted sexual attention than did men. Forty-nine percent of women (as compared to 33% of men) stated that they had experienced at least one form of this kind of harassment. The frequency of sexual harassment directed against women was also significantly higher. In the case of sexual harassment experienced by women, most (93%) of the harassers were men, while men complained of harassment by women (62%) and men (24%) . . .

There appear to be two principal reasons, closely related, for the decision of the Court of Appeal of Manitoba that the sexual harassment to which the appellants were subjected was not sex discrimination. First, the Court of Appeal drew a link between sexual harassment and sexual attraction. Sexual harassment, in the view of the Court, stemmed from personal characteristics of the victim, rather than from the victim's gender. Second, the appellate court was of the view that the prohibition of sex discrimination in s. 6(1) of the Human Rights Act was designed to eradicate only generic or categorical discrimination. On this reasoning, a claim of sex discrimination could not be made out unless all women were subjected to a form of treatment to which all men were not. If only some female employees were sexually harassed in the workplace, the harasser could not be said to be discriminating on the basis of sex. At most the harasser could only be said to be distinguishing on the basis of some other characteristic.

The two arguments raised by the Manitoba Court of Appeal may in fact be seen as alternate formulations of the following argument. Discrimination implies treating one group differently from other groups, thus all members of the affected group must be subjected to the discriminatory treatment. Sexual harassment, however, involves treating some persons differently from others, usually on the basis of the sexual attractiveness of the victim. The harasser will typically choose one, or several, persons to harass but will not harass all members of one gender. As harassers select their targets on the basis of a personal characteristic, physical attractiveness, rather than on the basis of a group characteristic, gender, sexual harassment does not constitute discrimination on the basis of sex.

[24] Canadian Human Rights Commission, Research and Special Studies Branch, *Unwanted Sexual Attention and Sexual Harassment: Result of a Survey of Canadians* (Ottawa: Minister of Supply and Services Canada (1983)).

This line of reasoning has been considered in both Canada and the United States, and in my view, quite properly rejected . . .

The fallacy in the position advanced by the Court of Appeal is the belief that sex discrimination only exists where gender is the sole ingredient in the discriminatory action and where, therefore, all members of the affected gender are mistreated identically. While the concept of discrimination is rooted in the notion of treating an individual as part of a group rather than on the basis of the individual's personal characteristics, discrimination does not require uniform treatment of all members of a particular group. It is sufficient that ascribing to an individual a group characteristic is one factor in the treatment of that individual. If a finding of discrimination required that every individual in the affected group be treated identically, legislative protection against discrimination would be of little or no value. It is rare that a discriminatory action is so bluntly expressed as to treat all members of the relevant group identically. In nearly every instance of discrimination the discriminatory action is composed of various ingredients with the result that some members of the pertinent group are not adversely affected, at least in a direct sense, by the discriminatory action. To deny a finding of discrimination in the circumstances of this appeal is to deny the existence of discrimination in any situation where discriminatory practices are less than perfectly inclusive. It is to argue, for example, that an employer who will only hire a woman if she has twice the qualifications required of a man is not guilty of sex discrimination if, despite this policy, the employer nevertheless manages to hire some women.[25]

In *Strathclyde* v *Porcelli* the Court of Sessions ruled that sexual harassment could amount to sex discrimination. The case was brought by a woman laboratory technician driven from her job by the sustained verbal and physical harassment, of a sexual nature, to which male colleagues had subjected her. A tribunal rejected her sex discrimination claim on the grounds that the reason for the harassment lay in her aggressors' dislike of her, and that a man who was so disliked by them would have been treated equally badly. On this ground the tribunal found that she had not been treated less favourably than an (equally disliked) man would have been and had not, therefore, been discriminated against contrary to the SDA. EAT allowed an appeal, a decision upheld by the Court of Session.

Strathclyde Regional Council v *Porcelli* [1986] ICR 564, [1986] IRLR 134

Lord Emslie (P):

S1(1)(a) is concerned with "treatment" and not with the motive or objective of the person responsible for it. Although in some cases it will be obvious that there is a sex related purpose in the mind of a person who indulges in unwanted and objectionable sexual overtures to a woman or exposes her to offensive sexual jokes or observations that is not this case. But it does not follow that because the campaign pursued against Mrs Porcelli as a whole had no sex related motive or objective, the treatment of Mrs Porcelli by Coles, which was of the nature of "sexual harassment" is not to be regarded as having been "on the ground of her sex" within the meaning of s.1(1)(a). In my opinion this particular part of the campaign was plainly adopted against Mrs Porcelli because she was a woman. *It was a*

---

[25] Citing *Brooks*, fn 23 above.

particular kind of weapon, based upon the sex of the victim, which . . . would not have been used against an equally disliked man [my emphasis].

The Industrial Tribunal reached their decision by finding that Coles' and Reid's treatment of an equally disliked male colleague would have been just as unpleasant. Where they went wrong, however, was in failing to notice that a material part of the campaign against Mrs Porcelli consisted of "sexual harassment", a particularly degrading and unacceptable form of treatment which it must be taken to have been the intention of Parliament to restrain. From their reasons it is to be understood that they were satisfied that this form of treatment—sexual harassment in any form—would not have figured in a campaign by Coles and Reid directed against a man. In this situation the treatment of Mrs Porcelli fell to be seen as very different in a material respect from that which would have been inflicted on a male colleague, regardless of equality of overall unpleasantness . . .

Lord Grieve

In order to decide whether there ha[s] been a breach of s.1(1)(a) consideration . . . ha[s] to be given . . . to the weapons used against the complainer. If any could be identified as what I called "a sexual sword", and it was clear that the wound it inflicted was more than a mere scratch, the conclusion must be that the sword had been unsheathed and used because the victim was a woman. In such a circumstance there would have been a breach of s.1(1)(a).

In considering the approach taken by the Court of Sessions, the reader ought to remember that treatment, whether it is apparently sexualised or otherwise, will also amount to sex discrimination (less favourable treatment on grounds of sex) in any case where sex is the motive (e.g., where a manager or colleagues do not wish to work with women and so take steps to drive out women workers). The problem with "sexual harassment" is precisely that it will usually be unlawful only where it is recognised as less favourable treatment *on the ground of sex*.[26] Absent any provable sex-based motivation, the solution lies in the Court of Session's recognition of the "sexual sword".

The point made in *Porcelli*, that sexual harassment need not be motivated by sex, should be stressed. Sexual harassment is frequently regarded as "to do with" sex, men accused of such behaviour defending themselves on the basis that that they were not attracted to their alleged victims. But, as Lord Emslie put it in *Porcelli*, such harassment can consist of "a particular kind of weapon, based upon the sex of the victim". Some sexual harassment is particularly problematic in that "hostility" is denied by the harasser who seeks to categorise his conduct as "friendly", with the effect that "detriment" may be difficult to establish (see further Chapter 4). But in many cases there is be little substantive difference between racial and sexual harassment—nor, indeed, between sexual harassment and harassment on the grounds of disability, religious belief or political opinion (these forms of harassment are further discussed below). In all cases the treatment at issue may involve the use of particular weapons related to the particular racial, sexual or other characteristics of the victim.

---

[26] Unless it amounts to a criminal assault, harassment under the Protection from Harrassment Act (see below) or that the failure to protect from harassment amounted to a breach by the employer of implied contractual terms relating to, for example, trust and confidence or health and safety.

It is clear from the decision of the Court of Session in *Porcelli* that harassment on the grounds of sex will not automatically amount to discrimination under the SDA (nor, accordingly, will harassment on the grounds of the relevant characteristic necessarily amount to a breach of the RRA, DDA or, in Northern Ireland, the FETO). While a claim of discrimination will be made out as long as the particular type of "weapon" used would not have been used on a person of the opposite sex/ a different racial group, etc., such a claim will generally be defeated by a credible claim that the same weapon (whether sexual assault or, arguably, race, religion or disability-specific abuse) had or would have been used against a man, or a person lacking the particular characteristic targeted. This point is illustrated by the decision in *Stewart* v *Cleveland Guest (Engineering) Ltd* [1996] ICR 535, [1994] IRLR 440.

The case was brought by a woman who had been exposed to "pin-ups" in the workplace. She had been subject to a number of incidents of sexual harassment, including several indecent assaults, none of which formed the subject matter of her sex discrimination claim. She complained on several occasions to her employer about the pictures but met with no success. Eventually, after Ms Stewart enlisted the help of her union, the pictures were removed but management made known the reason for their removal to protesting employees and Ms Stewart felt unable to return to the workplace. Her sex discrimination claim was rejected by a tribunal on the basis that

> the display of these pictures was not necessarily aimed at women, or a woman, in the way that direct touching or sexually suggestive remarks can be said to be aimed at the individual woman. The display itself was neutral. A man might well find [it] . . . as offensive as the applicant did.[27]

The tribunal distinguished *Porcelli* on the grounds that, while in that case it was accepted that a man would have been treated differently, here "the nature of the treatment by way of display of the pictures would have been the same to men and women". EAT rejected Ms Stewart's appeal.

Stewart v *Cleveland Guest (Engineering) Ltd* [1996] ICR 535, [1994] IRLR 440

Mummery J(P):

. . . It was argued that it was perverse of the Tribunal to conclude that the display of pictures was not aimed at women and was sexually neutral. The display was of women in a sexually explicit fashion in a workplace where most of the workers were men and where there was a prevalent attitude of the men epitomised by remarks and conduct which treated women as sex objects. The display was "gender-specific", operating in a "gender-specific environment" where women, not men, were exposed to the treatment complained of by Miss Stewart.

It was also [argued that it was] perverse of the Tribunal to conclude that a man might well find this sort of display as offensive as Miss Stewart did. A man's objection to such a

---

[27] Ms Stewart also successfully claimed constructive dismissal on the ground that, given the way in which management had handled her complaint, she had had to leave.

display would be based on other grounds (eg moral grounds), not on the ground of his sex. As the pictures depicted women, and not men, a man, even one who objected to the pictures, would not have found the pictures offensive in the same way as Miss Stewart did. The display was not in an environment where men were in the minority, nor in an environment where men, as against women, were subjected to suggestive remarks. The true position was that, in the words of Lord Brand in *Porcelli* . . . this form of treatment was unfavourable to a woman because she was more vulnerable to it than a man was. . . no error of law on the part of the Industrial Tribunal has been demonstrated . . . the decision in every case of this kind must turn on its particular circumstances. It is important to state what this case does not decide. The decision to dismiss this appeal does not mean that it is never an act of sex discrimination for a company to allow its male employees to display pictures of that kind in the workplace. A decision to allow this appeal would not mean that such an employer would in every such case be liable for sex discrimination.[28] The crucial point is to clarify the legal position by stating that whether or not there has been less favourable treatment of a woman on the ground of her sex must depend upon the particular facts of every case.

EAT's decision was unfavourable to Ms Stewart. But it did fall appear to leave open the possibility that discrimination could be established by "treatment" of general application (here in the form of a display) which was nevertheless aimed at women, or the impact of which was not regarded as "neutral" between men and women. In either case, the s.1(1)(a) test would be satisfied because women (or men) would be "less favourably" treated by being subjected (whether deliberately or otherwise) to a particular type or degree of "offense", humiliation, outrage, intimidation, embarrassment, etc. Ms Stewart's claim failed because of the tribunal's conclusion that exposure to the display at issue was objectively "neutral" as between men and women, which conclusion was bizarre given the tribunal's findings that [t]he conditions in the workplace . . . tended to be suggestive of the treatment of women as sex objects, not as people and that [m]anagement had encouraged a general ethos that was male orientated.

The tribunal accepted that Ms Stewart's objections to the pictures were reasonable, but appears to have reached its decision on the basis of evidence that her views were not shared by other women in the workplace.[29] The adoption of an objective test is perhaps understandable: without some such standard, sexual (racial or other) harassment could be found in treatment which no-one other than an exceptionally sensitive (even irrational) plaintiff would have regarded as offensive, intimidating or humiliating, etc. But the application of this test here, as in the context of clothing and appearance rules (discussed in Chapter 6) is problematic. How is the tribunal to assess the views of the "reasonable woman"? In *Stewart*, the tribunal appeared to take account of the views of other women in the workplace. But, especially in light of the finding

---

[28] In *Salmon* v *David & Ors* 38 EORDCLD, p.6 a tribunal found that a woman exposed, *inter alia*, to pornographic material was discriminated against on grounds of sex.

[29] A similar approach was adopted to sex-specific dress codes by the Court of Appeal in *Burrett* v *West Birmingham Health Authority* (unreported, but noted in the (1995) 24 *Industrial Law Journal* 177 and discussed in Chapter 6).

that women in that workplace were regarded "as sex objects, not as people", and of Ms Stewart's experience of repeated sexual assault in that workplace, one could justifiably conclude that the plaintiff's perception of the pin-ups as contributing to "an intimidating, hostile or humiliating working environment" was objectively reasonable in this case, and that her female colleagues had been desensitized by the ' general ethos that was male orientated".

The importance of the subjective was recognised by EAT in its subsequent decisions in *Reed* v *Stedman* [1999] IRLR 98 and in *Driskel* v *Peninsula Business Services*, both duscussed in Chapter 4. *Driskel* is of particular interest because of the appeal tribunal's express recognition of the subjective element in relation not only to the question whether the applicant had suffered a "detriment" within s.6(2)(b) SDA (this aspect of the decision is considered in Chapter 4) but also in determining whether the treatment to which she had been subjected was *less* favourable than that which was or would have been experienced by a man.

In *Driskel*, the question for EAT was whether, in considering a particular incident in respect of which harassment-as-sex-discrimination was alleged, the tribunal should have regard to the subjective perceptions of alleged harasser and victim in determining whether less favourable treatment had been established. There, a tribunal had found that the incident, in which a manager advised a member of staff with whom he was at loggerheads that she should wear a transparent blouse and show plenty of cleavage in a one-to-one promotion interview with him, "was intended as a flippant remark which could not reasonably have been taken seriously, and was not taken seriously by the applicant when the words were spoken". EAT accepted that subjective perceptions were relevant to whether or not discrimination had occurred. On the facts of the present case, however:

Driskel v Peninsula Business Services Ltd [2000] IRLR 151

Holland J (for EAT)

that which was complained of amounted prima facie to discrimination of a high order. [The applicant] was in the unenviable position of having to seek promotion by way of a one-to-one interview with a man for whom she had an antipathy. In such circumstances . . . that which was complained of was objectively *prima facie* discriminatory and it would need some exceptional findings to negate that inference by reference to the respective perceptions of [the complainant and the manager]. As it was, the tribunal was heavily influenced by [her] failure to make an immediate complaint without reminding itself that any instinct to complain must perforce be inhibited by the fact that she wanted the promotion that would come from the approval of [the manager]—and that she did in fact complain on the day following when she perceived that she had no chance of promotion. Further and in any event, given the nature of the remarks, how significant was any failure to complain? Turning to [the manager], the tribunal's finding . . . that the remark was flippant and was not meant to be taken seriously effectively misses the point. It is irrelevant that he never expected her to turn up for the interview in sexually provocative dress—what is relevant is that by this remark (flippant or not) he was undermining her dignity as a woman when, as a heterosexual, he would never similarly have treated a man . . .

Returning to the *Stewart* case, the sex discrimination claim failed because neither the tribunal nor EAT accepted that she had been sexually harassed. In *British Telecommunications plc* v *Williams* [1997] IRLR 668, Morison J expressed the view that, where sexual harassment (or, by implication, other forms of harassment) was proven, it would always amount to discrimination under s.1(1)(a) (of the relevant Act):

> Because the conduct which constitutes sexual harassment is itself gender-specific, there is no necessity to look for a male comparator. Indeed, it would be no defence to a complaint of sexual harassment that a person of the other sex would have been similarly so treated: see *Porcelli* . . .

But in *Smith* v *Gardner Merchant Ltd* [1998] 3 All ER 852 a majority of the Court of Appeal disagreed. Ward LJ remarked that it was precisely on this issue that the Court of Session in *Porcelli* differed from Scottish EAT (which had asked itself merely whether sexual harassment had occurred):

> it is not the case that because the abusive conduct is gender-specific that there is no necessity to look for a male comparator; but it is rather the case that *if it is gender-specific*, if it is sex-based, then, in the nature of the harassment, it is almost certainly bound as a matter of fact to be less favourable treatment as between the sexes (my emphasis).

Ward LJ's approach, was condemned by Michael Rubenstein in his commentary to the IRLR report. Pointing out that it would provide a defence, on a sex discrimination claim, to an employer guilty of sexual harassment who would harass (or had harassed) an employee of the opposite sex as well, Rubenstein declared that the approach:

> would be risible, if it did not threaten to do such damage to sexual harassment law. It is, indeed, difficult to credit that a sexual assault on a woman will amount to sex discrimination only if the perpetrator would not sexually assault a man. This is the conclusion demanded by the Court of Appeal in *Smith* v *Gardner* which, although it claimed to follow *Porcelli*, seems to narrow it in asserting that treatment which is "sex-based" or "gender-specific" (such as, for example, grabbing a woman's breast) is not *per se*, but only "almost certain . . . as a matter of fact" to amount to sex discrimination (because it is unlikely that, for example, a man who committed an indecent assault upon a woman would also indecently assault a man (or do so in the same manner).[30]

By contrast, Dine and Watt criticise what they see as a loosening of the requirement in US and Canadian law for differential treatment in establishing discrimination on grounds of harassment.

[30] Whether, in such a case, the treatment (real or hypothetical) differed between the sexes depends on how narrowly the harassment was defined—i.e., "indecent assault" or by reference to the particular part touched or, indeed, to the sexual significance of the part touched (in which case touching the chest area of a woman would be less favourable treatment than touching the chest area of a man). For a decision on the significance of sex-specific verbal abuse see *Pearce* v *Governing Body of Mayfield Secondary School* (EAT, 7th April 2000) available at www.employmentappeals.gov.uk.

J. Dine and B. Watt "Sexual Harassment: Moving Away from Discrimination" 58 (1995) *Modern Law Review* **343, 347–52**

There are discernible trends within the United States law away from the strict use of discrimination law and the requirement to prove differential treatment. The American courts appear to place less and less emphasis on the disparate treatment element of behaviour and, correspondingly, more emphasis on whether or not a hostile working environment was created as a result of sexually motivated behaviour. This accords with the authors' view that sexual harassment raises issues which primarily involve a misuse of sexuality rather than issues relating to different treatment on grounds of gender.

The roots of this view are present in *Meritor Savings Bank F.S.B.* v *Vinson*, 477 US 57 (1986). Here, Rehnquist J seemed willing to accept that sexual harassment might not amount to discrimination when he said:

> Respondent argues, and the Court of Appeals held, that unwelcome sexual advances that create a hostile or offensive working environment violate Title VII. Without question, when a supervisor sexually harasses a subordinate because of that subordinate's sex, that supervisor "discriminates" on the grounds of sex. Petitioner (i.e. *Meritor*) apparently does not challenge this proposition.

This seems to indicate that the Supreme Court had some reservation about the applicability of the principle of discrimination in the sense of disparate treatment. This reading of Rehnquist J's view has been recognised in some later cases, one of which is discussed below.

In more recent United States cases, the requirements for establishing a harassment case are listed as (i) that the conduct in question was unwelcome; (ii) that the harassment was based on sex; (iii) that the harassment was sufficiently pervasive or severe so as to create an abusive working environment; and (iv) that some basis exists for imputing liability to the employer. In determining whether the harassment created an abusive working environment, the harassment must be sufficient "to interfere with the plaintiff's ability to perform her work or significantly affect her psychological well-being." No mention is made of the disparate treatment issues which are lost in the determination that the behaviour was based on sexuality.

Such an action amounts to a claim that a particular plaintiff was treated badly because of her sexuality rather than a claim that discrimination against a particular sex has taken place. Harassment issues have outgrown the customary concepts of sex discrimination, since the above analysis could be applied to a situation where sexual issues were poisoning a working atmosphere regardless of the sex of the persons working there. Indeed, such an extension was attempted in *Drinkwater* v *Union Carbide*, 3rd Circ, 1990 904 F 2d 853, where the allegation was that an intolerable atmosphere was created by the consensual sexual relationship between the plaintiff's supervisor and a co-worker.

The link between discrimination and hostile environment claims was explained in *Drinkwater* as deriving from the underlying theory of sexual harassment developed by Catharine MacKinnon, in particular the idea that: "The relationship of sexuality to gender is the critical link in the argument that sexual harassment is sex discrimination." For MacKinnon:

> women's sexuality largely defines a women as women in this society, so violations of it are abuses of women as women, whereas the sexual power asymmetry between men and women means that men are not defined by their sexuality so that a man's hostile environment claim would be much harder to plead and prove.

This explanation is incomplete and unconvincing, particularly so in cases like *Drinkwater* where the alleged hostile environment is created by overt sexuality and thus would affect men and women alike. In *Drinkwater*, the Court of Appeals held that there was not enough evidence to establish the claim on the facts proved, but did not rule out the possibility of admitting such a claim in future cases where the evidence before the court was stronger.

In the most recent sexual harassment case to reach the Supreme Court, *Harris* v *Forklift Systems Inc*, (1993) 114 Sup. Ct 36, Ms Harris complained that she had been subjected to a campaign of sexual insults and innuendos. There is no evidence in the opinion of the Court, delivered by O'Connor J, that any of the courts considering Ms Harris' claim ever addressed the question as to whether the harasser treated men and women differently. The three Justices delivering opinions, O'Connor J for the Court, and Scalia and Ginsberg JJ concurring, confirm that behaviour which creates an abusive working environment is actionable under Title VII of the Civil Rights Act of 1964. However, this appears to ignore the focus of the Civil Rights Act, the purpose of which is to outlaw discriminatory treatment. Accordingly, if the Act were correctly applied, proof of disparate treatment would be a *sine qua non* for success of an action. . . .

The difficulty of identifying the social position of women as important in proving the equivalence of harassment and discrimination became apparent in the Canadian Supreme Court in *Janzen et al* v *Platy Enterprises Ltd*. [discussed above] Dickson CJC's judgment follows closely the argument of MacKinnon in defining sexual harassment as a type of sex discrimination and he disapproved of the reasoning of the lower court which refused to make this link. . . .

Dickson CJC accepts the argument made by Aggarwal that "sexual harassment is used in a sexist society to underscore women's difference from, and by implication, inferiority with respect to the dominant male group and to remind women of their inferior ascribed status." This argument is clearly consonant with that of MacKinnon, who views women's susceptibility to sexual harassment as being based upon their subordinate status in society.

The problem with statements of this kind is that they fail to establish the causal link between economic and social subordination, and disadvantage and sexual harassment. The relevant statement asserts the link but does not prove it, yet Dickson CJC seems to take it as true. Whilst the subordinate economic position of women undoubtedly provides situations in which sexual harassment is likely to thrive, it does not provide a complete explanation of the phenomenon and wholesale adherence to the theory may prevent justice being done where no power differential exists or where women occupy the more powerful position.

The central theme of Dickson CJC's judgment is more questionable still. He states:

> in *Brooks* v *Canada Safeway Ltd* I stated that pregnancy-related discrimination is sex discrimination. The argument that pregnancy-related discrimination could not be sex discrimination because not all women become pregnant was dismissed for the reason that pregnancy cannot be separated from gender. All pregnant persons are women. . . . The reasoning in *Brooks* is applicable to the present appeal. Only a woman can become pregnant; only a woman could be subject to sexual harassment by a heterosexual male such as the respondent.

This last sentence is plainly wrong. The respondent could have sexually harassed a man by, for example, asserting that he had a tiny penis and that he would prove more sexually satisfactory to the man's wife. The respondent might go so far as to expose his own penis and invite comparison. He might simulate masturbation and anal intercourse with a male colleague and suggest that such activities were desirable to his victim, or he could feign buggery with his victim in order to embarrass and humiliate him. He might grab his victim's penis and derogate it. All of these activities are sexual harassment of a male by a heterosexual male.

Whilst criticisms may be levelled at other aspects of their judgments, it seems that the quoted portion of the judgments of Huband and Twaddle JJA are fundamentally sound. However, the judgment of Dickson CJC can be challenged on two bases. An acceptance of the theory that the power differential between men and women turns harassment into discrimination is too narrow a view of the problem of harassment. The view that women may only be subjected to harassment by heterosexual men is clearly wrong and also should not be used to turn harassment into discrimination.

The approach taken by Dine and Watt is open to criticism, in particular inasmuch as they equate sexual harassment of a woman by a heterosexual male with that of a man. The behaviour outlined by the authors in the penultimate paragraph of the extract above is deeply unpleasant, and the feigned intercourse ought to be unlawful as discrimination on grounds of (perceived) sexual orientation. But, save in the case where a heterosexual man harasses another man who is, or is seen to be, gay; even harassment which, as in the penis-grabbing example used above, constitutes a physical assault, is absent the element of wrong which is at the core of sexual harassment as sex discrimination. Such harassment is damaging, at least in part, because it carries the real threat of sexual assault. It is true that the grabbing of a man's penis by another man would amount to an indecent assault and would, no doubt, be experienced as painful and perhaps humiliating. Such an assault would not necessarily, however, be experienced as a sexual assault by its victim. Absent from it is the threat which applies in male-female harassment (and, indeed, in much male heterosexual harassment of men perceived as gay) of invasive sexual violence. This being the case, even the reasoning of EAT in the *Stewart* case would permit a finding of sex discrimination in a case in which a man who would have harassed a man in the manner described by Dine and Watt subjected a woman to a sexual assault. The same is true of the *Driskel* case, above, in which EAT recognised that, in the case of "sexual badinage . . . the sex of the alleged discriminator [and discriminatee] . . . potentially adds a material element absent as between two heterosexual men".

In *Sidhu* v *Aerospace Composite Technology Ltd* [1999] IRLR 683, EAT ruled that no comparator was required in a case in which the plaintiff had been subject to race-specific conduct (there harassment). The plaintiff had, together with his abusers, been dismissed after he reacted violently to a racist assault, his employers having decided not to take account of the fact that the original assault on Mr Sidhu was racist. A tribunal found against Mr Sidhu but was overruled because of the employer's decision not to take into account the racial nature of the original attack on Mr Sidhu:

Sidhu v *Aerospace Composite Technology Ltd* [1999] IRLR 683, EAT

Charles J:

. . . In our judgment, a decision to disregard the fact that the cause of an attack, or harassment, or provocation, or anything else, is racial is a "race-specific" decision which has a "race-specific" effect and is thus "race-specific conduct". In our judgment this is so whatever the motive for the decision because its effect is inevitably that the treatment arising from the decision is treatment on racial grounds because it is the racial element of the relevant incident that is being deliberately left out of account. In our judgment, (i) the nature and effect of such a decision in the circumstances of this case is such that amounts in itself to racial discrimination within s 1(1)(a), and (ii) there was no need for Mr Sidhu to show that a white person (or a person from a different racial group) had been, or would have been, treated differently . . .

Whether the approach taken by Ward LJ in *Smith* v *Gardner Merchant* or that of Morison and Charles JJ proves more durable, the requirement for gender-specific conduct (or, in cases brought under the other anti-discrimination legislation, conduct specific to the protected heads) remains. As the decision in *Stewart* demonstrates, the recognition of such conduct by reference to its impact is problematic. This position would be improved were the government to accede to the EOC's suggestion, made in its 1998 proposals (*Equality in the 21st Century: A New Sex Equality Law for Britain* (Manchester: EOC)) that the European Commission's definition of sexual harassment be incorporated into UK law, and such harassment specifically prohibited. The race discrimination directive defines as descrimination harassment "related to racial or ethnic origin" and will require amendment of the RRA. Similar amendment of the SDA, FETO and DDA would be required if the 1999 draft equal treatment directive is adopted.

The express incorporation of the EC definition in the relevant Acts would eliminate the problems of proving that harassment amounts to less favourable treatment "on the grounds of . . . sex [race, etc.]", as is currently required for a finding of unlawful discrimination under the various Acts. It would also avoid some of the problems, discussed in Chapter 4, which are created by the additional requirement that the plaintiff prove "detriment" to succeed in claiming discrimination by way of harassment. Further, it is at least arguable that those who find themselves in the position of the complainant in *Stewart* v *Cleveland Guest*, whether or not they can demonstrate gender [race, etc.]—specific "treatment", may nevertheless be able to show "conduct of a sexual [racial, etc.] nature, or other conduct based on sex [race, etc.] affecting the dignity of women and men at work [which] . . . is unwanted, unreasonable and offensive to the recipient . . . and . . . creates an intimidating, hostile or humiliating work environment for the recipient".

INDIRECT DISCRIMINATION

"Indirect discrimination" is the term which has come to be used for the type of discrimination set out in s.1(1)(b) of both SDA and the RRA and in Article 3(2)(b) FETO. S.1(1) RRA provides as follows:

> A person discriminates against a another in any circumstances relevant for the purposes of any provision of this Act if—
> (b) he applies to that other a requirement or condition which he applies or would apply equally to persons not of the same racial group as that other but—
> (i) which is such that the proportion of persons of the same racial group as that other who can comply with it is considerably smaller than the proportion of persons not of that racial group who can comply with it and
> (ii) which he cannot show to be justifiable irrespective of the colour, race, nationality or ethnic or national origins of the person to whom it is applied and
> (iii) which is to the detriment of that other because he cannot comply with it.

S.1 SDA and Article 3(2)(b) FETO are in similar terms, the prohibited grounds of discrimination consisting, respectively, of sex and religious or political belief. The DDA contains no equivalent to s.1(1)(b) but the government claimed, during the debates on the DDA, that indirect discrimination was included within the s.5 prohibition. S.5(2) defines as discrimination an unjustified failure to comply with the duty of reasonable accommodation imposed by s.6 S.6, in turn, obliges employers ' to take such steps as it is reasonable, in all the circumstances of the case, for [them] to have to take" to prevent "arrangements made by or on [their] behalf" or "any physical feature of premises occupied by" them from placing a(n actual) disabled person "at a substantial disadvantage in comparison with persons who are not disabled". Similar definitions of discrimination are imposed in relation to non-employment related matters covered by the DDA. These, and the duty of reasonable accommodation more generally, are discussed in chapter 9.

Indirect discrimination was intended to reflect that concept of "disparate impact" discrimination recognised in the United States in *Griggs* v *Duke Power Co* (1971) 401 US 424.[31] There, black employees sued under Title VII of the Civil Rights Act 1964 (which, *inter alia*, prohibits race discrimination), claiming that the employer's practice of requiring a high school diploma or success in an IQ test as a condition of employment in particular jobs discriminated against them on grounds of race, a disproportionate number of blacks being rendered ineligible by the practice. The lower courts had found that the employer's previous practice of race discrimination had ended, and that there was no evidence that the requirements had been adopted in order to discriminate on racial grounds. The Supreme Court found in favour of the plaintiffs.

[31] See R. Townshend-Smith, below, 111–113.

Griggs v Duke Power Co (1971) 401 US 424

Chief Justice Burger, for the Court:

The objective of Congress in the enactment of Title VII is plain from the language of the statute. It was to achieve equality of employment opportunities and remove barriers that have operated in the past to favor an identifiable group of white employees over other employees. Under the Act, practices, procedures, or tests neutral on their face, and even neutral in terms of intent, cannot be maintained if they operate to "freeze" the status quo of prior discriminatory employment practices.

The Court of Appeals' opinion, and the partial dissent, agreed that, on the record in the present case, "whites register far better on the Company's alternative requirements" than Negroes . . . This consequence would appear to be directly traceable to race. Basic intelligence must have the means of articulation to manifest itself fairly in a testing process. Because they are Negroes, petitioners have long received inferior education in segregated schools . . . Congress did not intend by Title VII, however, to guarantee a job to every person regardless of qualifications. In short, the Act does not command that any person be hired simply because he was formerly the subject of discrimination, or because he is a member of a minority group. Discriminatory preference for any group, minority or majority, is precisely and only what Congress has proscribed. What is required by Congress is the removal of artificial, arbitrary, and unnecessary barriers to employment when the barriers operate invidiously to discriminate on the basis of racial or other impermissible classification.

Congress has now provided that tests or criteria for employment or promotion may not provide equality of opportunity merely in the sense of the fabled offer of milk to the stork and the fox. On the contrary, Congress has now required that the posture and condition of the job-seeker be taken into account. It has—to resort again to the fable—provided that the vessel in which the milk is proffered be one all seekers can use. The Act proscribes not only overt discrimination but also practices that are fair in form, but discriminatory in operation. The touchstone is business necessity. If an employment practice which operates to exclude Negroes cannot be shown to be related to job performance, the practice is prohibited.

On the record before us, neither the high school completion requirement nor the general intelligence test is shown to bear a demonstrable relationship to successful performance of the jobs for which it was used. Both were adopted, as the Court of Appeals noted, without meaningful study of their relationship to job-performance ability. Rather, a vice president of the Company testified, the requirements were instituted on the Company's judgment that they generally would improve the overall quality of the work force . . . good intent or absence of discriminatory intent does not redeem employment procedures or testing mechanisms that operate as "built-in headwinds" for minority groups and are unrelated to measuring job capability . . .

Previous UK anti-discrimination legislation (the Sex Disqualification (Removal) Act 1919,[32] and the Race Relations Acts of 1965 and 1968,[33] had concerned itself only with direct discrimination, and the Government had not originally intended to include

---

[32] The Act, discussed in Chapter 1, removed formal legal barriers to women's employment and holding of public office.

[33] The 1965 RRA prohibited discrimination in public places, the 1968 Act more generally.

any prohibition on indirect discrimination within the SDA (the first piece of legislation to do so). *Equality for Women* (the White Paper preceding the SDA) suggested that only intentional discrimination should be prohibited: "to understand the meaning of unlawful discrimination, it is essential not to confuse motive with effect".[34] But between the publication of the White Paper and that of the Sex Discrimination Bill, Secretary of State Roy Jenkins visited the United States and was familiarised with the decision in *Griggs*. On his return, Jenkins declared that "the Bill would be too narrow if it were confined to direct and intentional discrimination".[35] *Race Discrimination*, the White Paper preceding the RRA, instanced the failure of previous legislation to include this concept as one of the reasons for its limited success.[36]

Indirect discrimination is intended, to reiterate, to capture "practises that are fair in form, but discriminatory in operation".

R. Townshend-Smith, "Justifying Indirect Discrimination in English and American Law: How Stringent Should the Test Be?" (1995) 1 *International Journal of Discrimination and the Law* 103, 104–5

The standard socio-economic rationale for a law on indirect discrimination (adverse impact) is well-known. Some practices of employers operate to disqualify certain groups at a greater rate than other groups. Some such practices may be the deliberate choice of employers, whereas others may reflect a deep-rooted social difference. One rationale for the law is that individuals have the right to what might be termed a level playing-field or the removal of "built-in headwinds." This individualistic explanation fails to do justice to the notion of group disadvantage. If as a society we are to a greater or lesser extent committed to the economic advancement of those groups, such practices need examination and possibly removal. This explanation is particularly potent as regards *Griggs* itself, where the employer utilised educational requirements as a criterion for filling lower level positions. For various reasons, including the amount of resources the state of North Carolina had chosen to devote to the education of African-Americans in a still segregated school system, white people passed the requirement at a far greater rate than African-Americans. It is a paradigm case, as the differentiation was both very marked and also applicable state-wide or nationwide. The pattern of inequality might well have been equally manifest whichever employer had been defendant.

Group economic inequality is thus the key to indirect discrimination law. It takes as a starting-point a belief that economic power (average earnings?) should in an ideal world be equally distributed between different relevant groups. This redistributive ideal is highly significant as an objective, even though it could be countered that attaining it would be both uneconomic and impossible. Under current English law the only relevant groups are those based on race and gender [this article preceded the implementation of the DDA], though

---

[34] *Equality for Women* (London: Department of Employment, 1974) Cmnd. 5724, para. 33.

[35] 889 H.C. Debs (26 March 1975), col. 513.

[36] London: Department of Employment, 1975, Cmnd. 6234, para 35. See generally I. MacDonald, *Race Relations: the New Law* (London, Butterworths, 1977). C. McCrudden, "Racial Discrimination", in C. McCrudden and G. Chambers (eds), *Individual Rights and the Law in Britain* (Oxford: OUP, 1995), pp.417–8, points out that "Acceptance of the American approach was not wholesale . . . In two respects the American experience was rejected; monitoring of the . . . composition of employer's work-forces was not made compulsory; and proposals to set up a system of effective "contract compliance" were still born". These issues are discussed further in Chapter 5.

in principle indirect discrimination analysis could be applied to almost any group: there is nothing magical about race and gender. The key is the extent to which members of a group regard the economic and social well-being of other members of their group as being significant for them.

The potential operation of the concept of indirect discrimination is further illustrated by the following extract:

Thompson's "Sex Discrimination and Employment"[37]

The following requirements or conditions, with which a considerably smaller proportion of women than men can comply, may be indirectly discriminatory.

AGE BARS can indirectly discriminate against women who have taken time out of employment to bring up children.

EXPERIENCE/LENGTH OF SERVICE REQUIREMENTS can exclude women who have taken time out of employment to bring up children both in respect of the length of time actually employed and in respect of experience gained. It is too often assumed that the experience of managing a family should be discounted—presumably because men so rarely do it.

MOBILITY CONDITIONS can indirectly discriminate against women who, because of family commitments or partners' income are less likely to be able to comply with such conditions than men.

UNSOCIAL HOURS REQUIREMENTS can exclude women because of their family responsibilities. This can be particularly discriminatory—and unjustifiable—where the job requires an availability for call-out which, in practice, is likely to occur very rarely.

QUALIFICATIONS are often used to weed out applicants. Where the qualifications are such that women are less likely to be able to comply with them than men (and women have widely been excluded from training) unless they can be justified as an absolute requirement for a job, their requirement is an indirect discrimination.

HEIGHT/WEIGHT REQUIREMENTS must be justified in terms of the job to be done as men are demonstrably taller and heavier than women.[38]

CONDITIONS RELATING TO FULL-TIME WORK may be discriminatory if it can be shown that the job could be undertaken part-time or on a job-sharing basis. Separate provisions for part-time staff such as a provision that part-time staff be dismissed first in a redundancy situation or the exclusion of part-time staff from certain benefits.

Thompson's *Race Discrimination and Employment*[39]

[Discussing *Hussein* v *Saints Complete House Furnitures* [1979] IRLR 337.]

A Liverpool furniture store refused to consider applicants from Liverpool 8 which had a high rate of unemployment because unemployed friends of staff from that district would loiter outside the premises and discourage custom. Fifty per cent of the population of

---

[37] Available at http://www.thompsons.law.co.uk.

[38] Differential physical requirements would be directly discriminatory—see in the case of physical fitness teating *Allcock* v *Chief Constable, Hampshire Constabulary* 36 EORDCLD, p.1. Employers must, accordingly, adopt a single standard whose disparate impact, if any, will be objectively justifiable by reference to the needs of the undertaking.

[39] Available as at fn 37 above.

Liverpool 8 was black compared with two per cent in Merseyside as a whole. The Tribunal held this to be an unlawful requirement or condition because it was one that applied to one racial group more than another. The condition could not be justified.

Selection tests have been held to constitute a requirement or condition such that the proportion of one racial group who can comply is considerably smaller than the proportion of persons who are not of that racial group. In other words, a selection test may be indirectly discriminatory.

A requirement that an applicant for a manual job should be able to read and write English where there is virtually no reading or writing required is unlikely to be justifiable. An age bar has been held indirectly to discriminate against people who had immigrated to this country as adults and therefore started their careers later than others [citing *Perera* v *Civil Service Commission* [1983] ICR 428, [1983] IRLR 166, below] . . .

Any requirement for particular UK-based examinations will discriminate indirectly on grounds of nationality and, in Northern Ireland, any stipulation that job applicants come from a particular geographical area will, in most cases, disproportionately favour Catholics or Protestants. The same is true in Great Britain in relation to the racial composition of particular areas, and in both jurisdictions residence requirements will discriminate indirectly on nationality grounds. And such is the disparity in unemployment rates between the Northern Irish communities (for decades, the Catholic rate has been about twice that among the Protestant workforce) that recruiting from the unemployed will generally favour Catholics. Recognition of this, coupled with the social justice (and political) imperatives in favour of tackling disadvantage through targeted employment, resulted in the amendment of the fair employment legislation in 1998 specifically to permit targeted recruitment from amongst those not in employment (see further Chapter 3).

By contrast with direct discrimination, it is of the essence of indirect discrimination that some practices which impact unfavourably upon one or other sex, upon different racial or other groups, may nevertheless be lawful. The point is made in the extract below:

Townshend-Smith, p. 106–8

if quotas are to be avoided an employer must be allowed as a matter of both logic and policy to explain a disparity in achievement between different groups. The task of the law is to reconcile the competing interests of the employer in efficiency and profits with those of members of the group seeking economic advancement. The assumption is that the employer must be allowed to hire, promote and pay more to those who are truly better employees, while at the same time artificial and irrational barriers to the economic advancement of protected groups can be challenged. As it will already have been shown that the challenged condition has a disparate impact, it logically follows that the burden of proof is on the employer to show that it is justified. As the rationale for permitting justification is that the employer's economic and other business objectives must be respected, it further follows that the employer's argument is only worthy of respect if it can be shown to a satisfactory level of proof that the employer's policy will indeed have the result claimed for it.

This point is the heart of the requirement for objective justification. But even if success-ful in proving this causal connection, the employer may still fail on the basis of what has come to be known as the principle of proportionality. First, the plaintiff may win if it can be established that there was a means of achieving the same objective which had less of a disparate impact. Secondly, the employer may also lose if the court considers that the ben-efit of being allowed to continue with the practice is outweighed by the discriminatory con-sequences to the protected group. This is problematic for two reasons. First, it is unclear whether regard should be had to the degree of adverse impact only at the defendant enter-prise, or whether regard should be had to the extent the relevant practice is utilised in soci-ety generally. Secondly, the decision on this issue is at bottom an issue of competing social policy values, is a matter for the court and of course depends enormously on judicial sen-sitivity to the social objectives of the legislation. It is at this point that a plaintiff may argue that removal of indirectly discriminatory practices may require some positive reorganisa-tion of workplace practices by the employer rather than merely removing barriers such as tests with an adverse impact on black people. Again, is the focus more on employer respon-sibility or on overall economic inequality? As Kelman puts it: "[a]n obligation to alter prac-tices might be seen as necessary to correct historically imposed burdens, whether or not the employer . . . imposed those burdens, or to allow people to be treated in accordance with the potential that they cannot realise unless the employer restructures the work setting."
. . .

On the one hand, employers must not be permitted to utilise practices with an adverse impact which cannot be proved to achieve business objectives. On the other hand, the stan-dard at which that proof is set must not be so stringent as to be virtually unattainable, for that would logically lead to the use of surreptitious quotas, contrary to legislative policy. It is intellectually dishonest to demand such a stringent standard because one supports quo-tas, in the belief that this is the likeliest way that quotas will in practice be introduced.

The task of the law is to produce a standard of justification which is sensitive to both of these policy objectives. "The theory of disparate impact represents an uneasy compromise between the abstract and ambiguous ideal of economic equality and the means that Congress thought sufficient to achieve it." While it is important to examine what courts have said on the matter, it is contended that too often judicial dicta have been uttered with no awareness of the practical problems of application, or of how employers are supposed to discharge the burden laid upon them.

We saw in *Griggs* that the US Supreme Court adopted "business necessity" as the "touchstone" of justifiability. More recently, in *Wards Cove Packing Co.* v *Atonio*, 490 US 642 (1989), a less liberal Supreme Court set a lower standard .[40] According to Justice White (who carried a bare majority of the Court):

the dispositive issue is whether a challenged practice serves, in a significant way, the legiti-mate employment goals of the employer . . . The touchstone of this inquiry is a reasoned review of the employer's justification for his use of the challenged practice. A mere insub-stantial justification in this regard will not suffice, because such a low standard of review would permit discrimination to be practiced through the use of spurious, seemingly neutral employment practices. At the same time, though, there is no requirement that the chal-

---

[40] *Wards Cove* was reversed on this issue by the Civil Rights Act 1991 which, however, because of Bush's Presedential veto, did not make the test as rigorous as was originally planned.

lenged practice be "essential" or "indispensable" to the employer's business for it to pass muster: this degree of scrutiny would be almost impossible for most employers to meet, and would result in [inter alia, the imposition of racial quotas].

The European Court of Justice, in applying the equality directives and the provisions of the Treaty, has ruled that indirectly discriminatory practices may be lawful where they are shown to "correspond to a real need on the part of the undertaking, [be] appropriate with a view to achieving the objectives pursued and [be] necessary to that end" (*Bilka-Kaufhaus GmbH* v *Weber von Hartz* (Case 170/84), [1986] ECR 1607). This, in subsequent cases, has been taken to exclude the justification of discrimination against part-timers in terms of their perceived lower degree of integration into the workforce (*Rinner-Kühn* v *FWW Spezial-Gebaudereinigung GmbH* (Case 171/88) [1989] ECR 2743); and to demand that the disparately-impacting reward of training, flexibility and seniority be justified in terms of workers' ability to do their particular jobs (*Handels-og Kontorfunktionaererner Forbund I Danmark* v *Dansk Arbejdsgiverforening (acting for Danfoss)* (Case C–109/88) [1989] ECR 3199, *Nimz* v *Freie und Hanse-Stadt Hamburg* (Case C–184/89) [1991] ECR I–297). These cases are further discussed in Chapter 10.

Bilka-Kaufhaus concerned discrimination by employers. In cases where the discrimination is practised by the state against categories of persons (such as part-time workers), "somewhat broader considerations apply",[41] the ECJ having accepted in *Rinner-Kühn* that such discrimination may be justifiable where the disputed practices "meet a necessary aim of [a Member State's] social policy and . . . are suitable and requisite for attaining that aim". On the other hand, the ECJ ruled, in that case, that the claim that part-timers were excluded from sick-pay entitlement because they were less integrated into the workforce and therefore less in need of income during illness was not even potentially capable of justifying the established discrimination.

In *Danfoss* the ECJ ruled that, insofar as they resulted in differential payments for women and men, factors such as training and flexibility must be justified in terms of the workers' ability to do their particular jobs. The court also ruled that differentials in the average payments of men and women attributable to "merit" were evidence of direct sex discrimination, and permitted the inference of discrimination from sex-related pay differentials and a non-transparent pay structure. And in *Nimz* v *Freie* the ECJ withdrew its approval (expressed in *Danfoss*) of seniority-related pay and stated that it, too, would have to be justified in relation to the ability to perform the particular job in question where it impacted disparately on male and female wages. In *Enderby* v *Frenchay* (Case C–127/92) [1993] ECR I–5535, the court ruled that pay disparities could not be justified by reference to different pay structures (in this case collective bargaining arrangements) applicable to the male and female jobs in respect of which a comparison was made. According to the ECJ:

[41] Lord Keith in *EOC* v *Secretary of State for Employment* [1995] 1 AC 1, [1994] 1 All ER 910, [1994] 2 WLR 176, 92 LGR 360, [1994] ICR 317, [1994] IRLR 176 on *Rinner-Kuhn*. See also the recent decisions of the ECJ in *Nolte* and of that Court and of the House of Lords in *ex p. Seymour Smith*, discussed overleaf.

the fact that the respective rates of pay of [female and male jobs of equal value] were arrived at by collective bargaining processes which, although carried out by the same parties, are distinct, and, taken separately, have in themselves no discriminatory effect, is not sufficient objective justification for the difference in pay between those two jobs . . .

The cases discussed above arose in the employment context. In *Nolte* v *Landes-versicherungsanatalt Hannover* C–317/93 [1995] ECR I–4625 (a social security case), the ECJ accepted that Member States had a broad margin of discretion in selecting the means to further particular social policies. There, the Court upheld German rules excluding from the statutory pension scheme employment of fewer than 15 hours per week which attracted less than a threshold wage. The Court noted the German government's arguments :

(1) that the exclusion of persons in minor employment from compulsory insurance corresponded to a structural principle of the German social security scheme;
(2) that there was a social demand for minor employment to which the government considered that it should respond in the context of its social policy by fostering the existence and supply of such employment and that the only means of doing this within the structural framework of the German social security scheme was to exclude minor employment from compulsory insurance; and
(3) that the jobs lost would not be replaced by full- or part-time jobs subject to compulsory insurance. On the contrary, there would be an increase in unlawful employment . . . and a rise in circumventing devices (for instance, false self-employment) in view of the social demand for minor employment.

The ECJ went on to rule that:

in the current state of Community law, social policy is a matter for the Member States . . . Consequently, it is for the Member States to choose the measures capable of achieving the aim of their social and employment policy. In exercising that competence, the Member States have a broad margin of discretion. . . . the social and employment policy aim relied on by the German Government is objectively unrelated to any discrimination on grounds of sex and that, in exercising its competence, the national legislature was reasonably entitled to consider that the legislation in question was necessary in order to achieve that aim.

This judgment was indicative of an apparent retrenchment on the part of an increasingly conservative court contrasting as it did, in particular, with the earlier decision in *Rinner-Kühn* in which the court held that statements to the effect that part-time workers "were not as integrated in, or as dependent on, the undertaking employing them as other workers" and should not, therefore, be afforded access to statutory sick pay, were "only generalizations about certain categories of workers [which did] not enable criteria which are both objective and unrelated to any discrimination on grounds of sex to be identified". But more recently, in *R* v *Secretary of State for Employment ex parte Seymour-Smith and Perez* Case C–167/97 [1999] ECR I–623 [1999] 2 CMLR 273

[1999] 2AC 554 [1999] All ER (EC) 97, [1999] 3 WLR 460, [1999] ICR 447, [1999] IRLR 253, further discussed below), the ECJ ruled that the effect of *Nolte* was not to permit Member States to satisfy the Court as to the justification of indirectly discriminatory practices simply by showing that it was reasonably entitled to consider that the disputed measure would advance a social policy aim. [42]

71 ... It cannot be disputed that the encouragement of recruitment constitutes a legitimate aim of social policy.

72 It must also be ascertained, in the light of all the relevant factors and taking into account the possibility of achieving the social policy aim in question by other means, whether such an aim appears to be unrelated to any discrimination based on sex and whether the disputed rule, as a means to its achievement, is capable of advancing that aim ...

74 It is true that in ...the *Nolte* case the Court observed that, in choosing the measures capable of achieving the aims of their social and employment policy, the Member States have a broad margin of discretion.

75 However, although social policy is essentially a matter for the Member States under Community law as it stands, the fact remains that the broad margin of discretion available to the Member States in that connection cannot have the effect of frustrating the implementation of a fundamental principle of Community law such as that of equal pay for men and women.

76 Mere generalisations concerning the capacity of a specific measure to encourage recruitment are not enough to show that the aim of the disputed rule is unrelated to any discrimination based on sex nor to provide evidence on the basis of which it could reasonably be considered that the means chosen were suitable for achieving that aim.[43]

The question of justification is returned to below. But what should be noted here is that the relatively simple concept of indirect discrimination, as it was recognised by the US Supreme Court in *Griggs*, has been translated in the SDA, RRA and FETO into a complex series of tests.[44]

In *Kidd* v *DRG* [1985] ICR 405, [1985] IRLR 190, Waite J, then President of EAT, stated that "[t]he concept of indirect discrimination was one which clearly needed to be framed from the outset with the maximum flexibility if it was fully to encompass the mischief at which the anti-discrimination laws are directed". But, as it has been interpreted by the UK courts the test for indirect discrimination is far from flexible.

A successful claim of indirect discrimination requires that the plaintiff establish the existence of (a) a requirement or condition with which (b) a considerably smaller

---

[42] Ironically, the House of Lords in *ex p. Seymour Smith* (extracted below) took the opportunity to ease the burden of justification previously imposed by the domestic courts in relation to social policy aims.

[43] See *Kruger* v *Kreiskrankenhaus Ebersberg* Case C-281/97, 9th September 1999 available on the web at www.europa.eu.int/eur-lex/en/index.html. on the different tests applied in respect of state and private action.

[44] Described recently by Lord Lester, the architect of the 1975 and 1976 Acts, as "unnecessarily restrictive", "Making Discrimination Law Effective: Old Barriers and New Frontiers" (1997) 2 *International Journal of Discrimination and the Law* 167, 173.

proportion of his/her sex or racial group can comply, and with which (c) the plaintiff him or herself cannot comply. At this point it falls to the employer to show (d) that the application of the requirement or condition was justifiable. Each of these tests will be considered in more detail.

Requirement or condition

Early decisions applied this provision flexibly, taking a purposive approach to ss.1(1)(b) of the SDA and the RRA. In *Clarke* v *Eley (IMI) Kynoch Ltd* [1982] IRLR 482, for example, EAT (*per* Browne-Wilkinson J) ruled that:

> it is not right to give these words a narrow construction. The purpose of the legislature in introducing the concept of indirect discrimination into the [SDA] and the [RRA] was to seek to eliminate those practices which had a disproportionate impact on women or ethnic minorities and were not justifiable for other reasons. The concept was derived from that developed in the law of the United States which held to be unlawful practices which had a disproportionate impact on black workers as opposed to white workers: see *Griggs* v *Duke Power Company* [above]. If the elimination of such practices is the policy lying behind the Act, although such policy cannot be used to give the words any wider meaning than they naturally bear it is in our view a powerful argument against giving the words a narrower meaning thereby excluding cases which fall within the mischief which the Act was meant to deal with.[45]

In *Watches of Switzerland Ltd* v *Savell* [1983] IRLR 141, too, EAT (Waterhouse J presiding) followed *Clarke* in according to the words "requirement or condition "a liberal interpretation in order to implement the object of the legislation". But in *Perera* v *The Civil Service Commission & The Department of Customs and Excise*, the Court of Appeal took a different approach.

Mr Perera, who had unsuccessfully applied for a number of jobs in the Civil Service, claimed that the imposition of a number of criteria relating to nationality, experience in the United Kingdom, ability to communicate in English and an upper age preference in respect of these positions discriminated against him indirectly on grounds of his colour or national origin. The Court of Appeal agreed with EAT that Mr Perera had failed to show that a "requirement or condition" had been applied to him.

Perera v *The Civil Service Commission & The Department of Customs & Excise* [1983] ICR 428 [IRLR] 166

Stephenson LJ:

. . . The matters which have to be established by an applicant who claims that he has been discriminated against indirectly are, first of all, that there has been a requirement or condition, as Mr Perera put it, a "must"; something which has to be complied with. Here there

---

[45] For favourable comment upon this decision see C. Docksey, "Part-time Workers, Indirect Discrimination and Redundancy" (1983) 46 *Modern Law Review* 504.

was a requirement or condition for candidates for the post of legal assistant in the Civil Service; it was that the candidate should be either a qualified member of the English Bar or a qualified Solicitor of the Supreme Court of this country—an admitted man [sic] or a barrister; and those conditions or requirements—those "musts"—were fulfilled by Mr Perera. But, as he admitted in his argument before the Appeal Tribunal and before this court, there is no other express requirement or condition, and he has to find a requirement or condition in the general combination of factors which he says the Interviewing Board took into account [whether the applicant had experience in the United Kingdom; whether he had a good command of the English language; whether he had British nationality or intended to apply for it, and his age]. He cannot formulate, as in my judgment he has to, what the particular requirement or condition is which he says has been applied to him and to his attempt to obtain a post of legal assistant. That is the hurdle which, as it seems to me, he is unable to get over . . . in my opinion none of [the four] factors could possibly be regarded as a requirement or a condition in the sense that the lack of it, whether of British nationality or even of the ability to communicate well in English, would be an absolute bar. The whole of the evidence indicates that *a brilliant man whose personal qualities made him suitable as a legal assistant might well have been sent forward on a short list* by the Interviewing Board in spite of being, perhaps, below standard on his knowledge of English and his ability to communicate in that language [my emphasis].

The decision in *Perera* is perhaps the most widely criticised discrimination case of recent years. Geoffrey Mead pointed out that its effect was that:

G. Mead, "Intentions, Conditions and Pools of Comparison" (1989) 18 *Industrial Law Journal* 59, 61–2

if an advertisement states that applicants for the job of a cleaner should either have lived in the area for 20 years or have a degree of law, then although the first criterion might have a detrimental effect on certain racial groups, who might be new to the area, the fact that they could get the job if they had a law degree means that they have not been indirectly discriminated against. It is submitted that this result is absurd, and means that there is much room for abuse of the law. Employers who do not wish to employ certain racial groups could simply add another criterion to the one which is indirectly discriminatory, and be immune from challenge. It seems clear that this second criterion may even be indirectly discriminatory itself. Thus, if an employer specifies that applicants must possess either attribute A or attribute B in order to get the job, then both of these criteria might be such that they will have a detrimental effect on a larger proportion of a particular racial group, but as neither of them was decisive, then a claim for discrimination will fail. This holding means that if the employer can establish that a criterion is not a requirement or condition, then he need not even go on to the stage of trying to justify it. Thus, in the hypothetical postulated above, the employer need not go on to try to show that it is objectively necessary in order to be a cleaner that one has lived in the area for 20 years or has a law degree. This is despite the fact that prima facie neither specification is related to the job in question, and the both will almost certainly have a detrimental effect on a larger proportion of certain racial groups.

Section 4(1)(*a*) of the R.R.A. 1976 makes it clear that an employer who expresses a "preference" not to be sent blacks for interviewing for a job, is directly discriminating on grounds of race. It thus seems difficult to argue that Parliament, although outlawing the expression of preferences when expressed directly, should have intended them to be permitted if expressed indirectly.

Mead's arguments are difficult to refute. In addition, the fact that "a brilliant man" might have been chosen despite his failure to comply with the normal criteria for selection does not alter the fact that men (even persons) of Mr Perera's racial group would (assuming that the other criteria for indirect discrimination had been made out) have had to be better than other candidates in order to stand any chance of getting the job. It is inconceivable that this was the intention of the Act's framers, or of the framers of the SDA. Nevertheless, when confronted with the matter once again in *Meer* v *Tower Hamlets* [1988] IRLR 399, the Court of Appeal declared itself bound by its earlier decision.

The applicant in *Meer* was a solicitor of Indian origin who had unsuccessfully applied for a job as head of Tower Hamlets' legal department. The applications had been judged on the basis, *inter alia*, of whether candidates had experience in Tower Hamlets, which factor Mr Meer challenged on the basis that it discriminated indirectly against those of Indian origin. All four candidates with Tower Hamlets experience were longlisted. Mr Meer was not.

Meer v *Tower Hamlets* [1988] IRLR 399

Balcombe LJ:

[Counsel for Mr Meer] sought to distinguish *Perera* on the ground that whether a condition or requirement is a "must" depends on what it is needed for. He submits that Tower Hamlets' experience was not a "must" for getting on the long list, but it was a "must" for having the maximum chance of selection. But applying the analogy, so was the knowledge of English language, for example, in the *Perera* case, although that was not spelt out in so many words. If we were to distinguish *Perera* on this ground, it would be making a distinction of the kind which in my judgment tends to bring the law into disrepute. . . . there are strong arguments . . . that the absolute bar construction of "condition or requirement" may not be consistent with the object of the Act. But *Perera* is binding upon us . . . I accept that there are arguments . . . which suggest that the law as stated by *Perera*, might need reform. But that is not a matter for this court to speculate upon; it may be for Parliament
. . .

Staughton and Dillon LJJ agreed that the appeal must fail, the former expressing a degree of satisfaction with the decision in *Perera*: "s.1(1)(b) of the RRA would have such an extraordinarily wide and capricious effect" otherwise, and the latter not finding it necessary to express a view.[46]

Michael Connolly, "How an ECJ Decision on Equal Pay May Affect British Indirect Discrimation Law" [1996] 1 *Web Journal of Current Legal Issues*

An unscrupulous employer can avoid the law simply by reclassifying his job conditions as "mere preferences". His, or her, job advertisement might read:

---

[46] See also *Clymo* v *Wandsworth London Borough Council* [1989] IRLR 241, discussed below.

Librarians wanted. Candidates must have an excellent command of English. Preference will be given to those who: have a Home Counties accent; are over 6 feet tall; are under 30 years old; are willing to wear trousers to work; wear a beard; and have lived in the area all of their lives.

This advertisement, which effectively would debar almost all except burly white men would not be unlawful under British legislation according to *Perera* and *Meer*. Clearly then the Court of Appeal favours a narrow interpretation of the legislation. This approach can be contrasted with the Australian approach. Australian discrimination legislation carries the same phrase "requirement or condition". However in *Secretary of Department of Foreign Affairs and Trade* v *Styles* (1989) 88 ALR 621 the Federal Court of Australia (New South Wales district) held that an employer's preference" for higher grade journalist amounted to a "requirement or condition" for the purposes of the Sex Discrimination Act 1984. And the High Court of Australia held in *Waters* v *Public Transport Corporation* (1991) 173 CLR 349 that the phrase "requirement or condition" in the Equal Opportunity Act 1984 should be given a wide interpretation. Thus it was held that the removal of conductors from trams imposed a requirement or condition that complainants (certain disabled persons) could fully avail themselves of the tram service only if they could use trams without the assistance of conductors.

In *Brook* v *London Borough of Haringey* [1992] IRLR 478 the Court of Appeal took a similar approach, in a sex discrimination case, to that adopted in *Perera* and in *Meer*.[47] And in *Hall and others* v *Shorts Missile Systems Ltd* [1996] NI 214, Northern Ireland's Court of Appeal purported to apply *Brook* to rule that indirect discrimination could not be established under the Fair Employment Act 1989 (FEA, as it then was) where the discrimination complained of resulted from the application of a [disparately impacting] factor not itself that of religious belief, rather than "by reason of" religious belief. There, the Court overruled a tribunal decision to the effect that the application by a company of a "last-in, first-out" (LIFO) redundancy procedure, in circumstances where recent attempts by it to redress chronic under-representation among its workforce of Catholic employees had the result that such employees had shorter periods of service than their Protestant counterparts, would have been indirectly discriminatory under the FEA. According to MacDermott LJ (with whom the others agreed):

I do not accept that the [LIFO] agreement applied a requirement or condition. In coming to the contrary conclusion the [tribunal] does not appear to have had regard to Brook's case. . . .
The last section of the judgment of Wood J . . . is that which is of relevance in the present case and he is there considering whether or not length of service is a condition or requirement having an indirect discriminatory effect . . .

Lastly, it is argued that the applicants were required to obtain a preset number of points to avoid redundancy and that this in itself was a condition. It seems to us that no-one could have told what the "cut-off" point would be in each particular trade

[47] *Cf Jones* v *University of Manchester* [1992] ICR 52, discussed below.

until after the points had been calculated and there could not, in reality, be said to be any predetermined figure. A person who is rejected because he is not the best candidate on an amalgam of factors has not been subjected to any requirement or condition but he has simply failed to defeat his competitors. It is the position of the individual on the list which is the determining factor, not the amount of points scored. The cut-off is unknown until after the event.

I am attracted by that reasoning and would readily adopt it in the present case. I am satisfied that the [LIFO] agreement . . . did not apply either conditions or requirements and there was no "must" provision in [it]. Those who were not declared redundant were those who were assessed as better than those who were made redundant—it was, and I repeat the tribunal's phrase, a competitive ranking scheme.

It is useful to subject to scrutiny Wood J's assertion, adopted by Northern Ireland's Court of Appeal, that: "A person who is rejected because he is not the best candidate on an amalgam of factors has not been subjected to any requirement or condition but he has simply failed to defeat his competitors". This approach was taken, in *Brook*, to exempt from scrutiny for its sex-related impact the taking-into-account of length of service as one of four redundancy selection criteria. In *Hall* it blocked scrutiny of the impact on the religious make-up of length of service as one of seven such criteria. In each of these cases the factor in dispute (length of service) was no more than indirectly related to the sex or religion of the applicants selected for redundancy. But the declaration by Wood J which is reproduced above would apply equally where a selection of criteria, none of which individually amounted to a "must", included preferences expressly related to sex, race or, in Northern Ireland, religion or political opinion. In *Hall* and in *Brook*, the courts were prepared to take into account, as related to merit, disparately impacting factors the justification for reliance upon which had not been ascertained. Logically, the "best candidate" could be defined also in terms of sex, race, etc., as long as these factors were no more than part of an "amalgam".

It has been argued that the UK approach to indirect discrimination is, at least in the context of sex discrimination, inadequate to implement EU law.[48]

E. Ellis, "The Definition of Discrimination in European Sex Equality Law" (1994) 19 *European Law Review* 561, 573–4

As a matter of United Kingdom law, it is not enough to show simply that the way things are organised within a particular enterprise works to the disadvantage of women; it is essential to be able to point to a particular hoop through which women are required to jump. This of course can be extremely difficult to identify and to prove. European

---

[48] More recently, the Opinion of Advocate General Fennelly in *Petrie and Others* v *Universita Degli Studi di Verona and Camilla Bettoni* Case C–90/96 available at www.europa.eu.int/eur-lex/en/index.html interpreted the ECJ decision in *O'Flynn* (discussed below) to the effect that "migrant workers do not have to explain the pattern of conduct which results in their being disproportionately adversely affected by a national rule. . . Furthermore, as the Court indicated in *O'Flynn*, a national rule can be deemed to have a discriminatory effect if it is liable to have such disproportionate effects, even if they have not been established in practice".

Community law is unencumbered by this technicality. It remains free to find adverse impact proved in whatever way seems appropriate in the circumstances. Admittedly, the Court of Justice has not yet devoted a great deal of attention to this matter; this is because the vast majority of indirect discrimination cases which have been presented to it have involved part-time workers. For this group, a requirement or condition in the United Kingdom sense is imposed, namely, the requirement or condition that they work full-time in order to receive better treatment. The issue of other detrimental situations has not yet often been clearly presented to the Court of Justice. However, it has several times expressed itself in quite broad terms nevertheless, demonstrating its sensitivity to the purposes intended to be achieved by the legislation and its intention not to be deflected from such purposes by legal niceties. For example, in both *Bilka-Kaufhaus* . . . and in *Danfoss*, the Court referred to pay "practices" which were illegal because they were indirectly discriminatory.Indeed, in *Danfoss*, the Court was satisfied simply with statistical evidence which created the suspicion that there was sex discrimination going on, accepting that because of the "non-transparent" nature of the computation of pay in the organisation concerned there was really no way in which the women employees could discover *how* they were being prejudiced. The element of adversity thus being broadly satisfied, the Court was content to go straight to the issue of causation.

More recently, in the *Enderby* case, the Court of Justice held that:

[W]hen a measure distinguishing between employees on the basis of their hours of work has in practice an adverse impact on substantially more members of one or other sex, that measure must be regarded as contrary to the objective pursued by Article 119 EC, unless the employer shows that it is based on objectively justified factors unrelated to any discrimination on grounds of sex.

It is strongly arguable that the Court did not intend this statement to be confined to the equal pay situation, but rather that it meant that, whenever and however a plaintiff establishes a "prima facie" case of sex discrimination. the burden shifts to the employer to prove that discrimination has not occurred. If this is correct, the United Kingdom's restrictive formulation of the circumstances in which indirect discrimination arises is contrary to Community law. Such a view was rejected by the Employment Appeal Tribunal in *Blaidi v. IMI Refiners Ltd* [1994] ICR 307, [1994] IRLR 204] but may yet be accepted by the higher courts.

In *Falkirk Council* v *Whyte*, EAT relied on EU law to uphold a tribunal finding that a woman had been subject to unlawful indirect discrimination where she was denied a managerial post in respect of which management training and supervisory experience were stated to be "desirable".

Falkirk Council v Whyte [1997] IRLR 560

Lord Johnston

It was [the plaintiffs'] essential submission that one should not interpret the words "requirement or condition" on any narrow or restricted basis, having regard to the fact that the legislation was based upon European Directive No 207/76 covering sex discrimination which therefore fell to be treated differently from discrimination on grounds of race. Since the employers here were part of the emanation of the State, this tribunal, and indeed the industrial tribunal, could apply the Directive without reference to the legislation; but, in any event, if the legislation required it to be interpreted on any particular basis it should be consistent with the purpose of the Directive—the so-called "purposive approach" which can be found supported by the House of Lords in *Litster* v *Forth Dry Dock Engineering Co Ltd* [49] [Counsel for the plaintiffs] . . . submitted that *Perera* had been rightly criticised even in the context of race relations (*Meer* v *Tower Hamlets* . . .), which was all the more reason for not applying it to the scope of sex discrimination. The proper approach should be whether or not the factor, to give it a neutral phrase, hindered women as opposed to men in the particular context, here the application for the post in question. . . .

the tribunal were . . . liberally interpreting what is meant by "a requirement or condition" within the meaning of the legislation. We consider this approach was open to the tribunal and, being based upon the evidence, not one with which we feel able to interfere as an appellate tribunal. We would observe in passing that if the case turned upon whether or not the relevant factors to become a requirement or condition had to be an absolute bar to qualification for the post in question, we would not be inclined to follow the race discrimination cases and, in particular, that of *Perera*. We consider that each case has to be determined on its own merits, and the status of the factors in question relevant to the application for the post in question very much depends upon the circumstances of a particular case. Some may be too trivial to be regarded as a condition or requirement; but, equally, if material, and it is shown otherwise that qualifying for the particular factor is more difficult for women than for men in the appropriate workplace, we do not see why that should not be a condition or requirement in terms of the legislation in relation to applications for the post, particularly when the relevant factor or factors turn out to be decisive.

The decision in *Falkirk* has not escaped criticism. Michael Connolly pointed out that, in distinguishing *Meer* as an RRA case, "EAT did not consider a number of cases where the construction in *Perera* was applied to the [SDA]."[50] Nevertheless, Connelly supported the decision on the basis that EAT's interpretation of the SDA consistent with the equal treatment directive was preferable to the same court's earlier refusal, in *Bhudi* v *IMI Refiners*, so to do.[51]

The stumbling block currently presented by the decision in *Perera* is likely to be removed by the implementation in the UK of Council Directive 97/80, on the burden of proof in cases of discrimination based on sex. The Directive, which must be implemented by 22nd July 2001, defines indirect discrimination as existing:[52]

---

[49] [1990] 1 AC 546, [1989] 1 All ER 1134, [1989] 2 WLR 634, [1989] ICR 341, [1989] IRLR 161. [1989] 2 CMLR 194.

[50] "Discrimination Law: Requirements and Preferences" (1998) 27 *ILJ* 133, p. 138.

[51] EAT in *Bhudi*, a private sector case in which, unlike the position in *Whyte*, the Directive had only indirect effect, applied *Duke* v *GEC Reliance* [1988] IRLR 118 [1988] 1 All ER 626, [1988] AC 618 (discussed in Chapter 1) to deny an interpretive obligation where, as there, the court regarded consistent legislation as impossible.

[52] The Directive was passed under the Protocol on Social Policy and so did not originally apply to the UK. The other Member States were to implement the Directive by 1st January 2001 and, the UK having signed up to the Protocol (the terms of which have, accordingly, been enacted as part of the Treaty Establishing the European Community, as amended by the Treaty of Amsterdam), Council Directive 98/52 on the extension of Directive 97/80 on the burden of proof in cases of discrimination based on sex to the UK, applied the burden of proof directive to the UK.

where an apparently neutral provision, criterion or practice disadvantages a substantially higher proportion of the members of one sex unless that provision, criterion or practice is appropriate and necessary and can be justified by objective factors unrelated to sex.

The Directive applies only to sex discrimination, but the government has indicated that it is likely to bow to pressure from the CRE and others to amend the RRA (and, presumably, the FETO also).[53] The formulation adopted by the race discrimination directive is the same "apparently neutral provision, criterion or practice", the directive to be implemented by 19 July 2003. So, too, is that of the 1999 draft equal treatment general framework directive.

The recent decision of the House of Lords in the deeply confusing *Barry* v *Midland Bank plc* case, [1999] 1 WLR 1465, [1999] ICR 859, [1999] 3 All ER 974 [1999] IRLR 581, illustrates a loophole which remains. There, dealing with a claim arising under the EqPA in which a woman challenged, as indirectly discriminatory, the terms of a severance package (she argued that the calculation of redundancy pay disadvantaged those, such as herself, who had transferred from full-time to part-time work), the House of Lords took account of the intention of the scheme (to compensate job loss) in deciding that the applicant had not been disadvantaged. This approach, which is reminiscent of that recently adopted by Canada's Supreme Court in determining the application of the equality provisions of the Charter of Rights[54], would blow holes in the protection of the anti-discrimination provisions if widely adopted in the UK. It is further discussed in Chapter 10.

Considerably smaller proportion . . . can comply

In order that a complaint of indirect discrimination can succeed, the claimant must, at present (see further below), demonstrate that the requirement of condition applied is such that a "considerably smaller proportion" of his or her sex or racial group, etc., than of others, can comply with it. It is vital to stress that the question does not relate to the relative proportions of men and women, persons of different ethnic groups, etc. within the population of those who can comply—one would not expect, absent discrimination, that 50% of those complying with any particular set of job-related requirements would be black, Asian or, in Northern Ireland, Catholic or Protestant. Rather, the question relates to the representation of the relevant racial or other group in the qualifying population *relative to* their representation in the wider population or other relevant "pool" (how this "pool" can be determined is further discussed below). The questions which arise are (1) how to determine the relative proportions of the

---

[53] The Better Regulation Task Force (See http://www.cabinet-office.gov.uk /bru/1999/task_force/anti-discrimination.pdf) supported the extension of the Directive to the DDA and the RRA (the FEA, as it then was, was outside the Task Force's remit). The Government agreed in principle to extension to the RRA.

[54] See *Miron* v *Trudel* [1995] 2 SCR 418 and *Egan* v *Canada* [1995] 2 SCR 513, briefly considered in Chapter 11. See also, more recently, the decision of the ECJ in the *Wiener* case (C–309/97) also discussed in Chapter 10 and available on the web as at footnote 43 above.

claimant's group and of others who can comply with the disputed requirement or condition and (2) what is meant by "a considerably smaller proportion".

In order to establish the relative proportions of the plaintiff's relevant group and of others who can comply, tribunals select an appropriate "pool for comparison", i.e., a description of those who (leaving aside the disputed requirement or condition) are in the same "relevant circumstances" as the applicant (see discussion of ss.5(3), 3(4) and article 3(3) of the SDA, RRA and FETO respectively, above). The proportions of the claimant's group (whether defined in terms of sex, race, or, in Northern Ireland, religion or political belief) and of others who can comply with the requirement or condition is determined by comparing those of the claimant's group and of others who are within this pool and who can[55] comply with the disputed condition.

A number of difficulties are associated with the "pool" approach. In the first place, should the "pool" of those who are regarded as being in the "same relevant circumstances" as the applicant be drawn within the workplace? Should it take into account others in the relevant travel-to-work area? Or should some wider approach be taken? Secondly (and this is related), we saw above that the question of who should be regarded as being within the "same relevant circumstances" as the applicant is not without complications.

Some of the difficulties which can arise in connection with the selection of an appropriate pool can be illustrated by the following example. Assuming that A, a female doctor who previously worked full-time, unsuccessfully applies to transfer to part-time work after maternity leave, in a case in which all the doctors who work for her employer are both female and full-time; her indirect discrimination claim cannot succeed if the pool for comparison is taken as being those currently employed by her employer. Given the exclusively female nature of that pool, a tribunal might decide that, for example, the relevant pool would be all doctors employed by the NHS. But if it were the case that all doctors were required to work full-time, any comparison between the proportion of men and women doctors in practice who could work full time would be meaningless, the pool being restricted from the outset to those who could, in fact, work full-time. This being the case, the pool would have to take into account those who were qualified to work as doctors, whether or not they were in fact working. Even this, however, might be inappropriate—if it were commonly known that doctors were required to work full-time, or that for this or other reasons medicine was a particularly difficult career for women, the pool of those qualified as doctors might itself be already tainted.[56]

The choice of pool made by the tribunal may well be crucial to the success or failure of a discrimination claim. The extent to which this pool may be reviewed on appeal, therefore, is a matter of some importance.

---

[55] or, on occasion, who cannot—see decision in *London Underground* v *Edwards (No. 2)* and the speeches of Lord Nicholls in *ex parte Seymour Smith* and in *Barry* v *Midland Bank*, below (text to footnotes 66 to 69).

[56] This was recognised by Potter LJ in *London Underground Ltd* v *Edwards (No. 2)* [1998] IRLR 36, below.

Kidd v *DRG (UK) Ltd* (EAT) [1985] ICR 405, [1985] IRLR 190

Waite J:

We reject the argument that the choice of section of the population [the pool for comparison] . . . is a question of law . . . The choice of an appropriate section of the population is in our judgment an issue of fact (or perhaps strictly a matter of discretion to be exercised in the course of discharging an exclusively fact-finding function) entrusted by Parliament to the good sense of the tribunals, whose selection will be influenced by the need to fit it as closely as possible to the varying circumstances of each case. Of course in those exceptional cases where it can be shown that good sense has not prevailed, and the tribunal has chosen to make the proportionate comparison within an area of society so irrationally inappropriate as to put it outside the range of selection for any reasonable tribunal, then the tribunal would have fallen into an error of law which could be corrected in the appellate jurisdiction.[57]

EAT will overturn the choice of pool if it is not, as a matter of law, such that the "relevant circumstances" of those (both of and not of the claimant's relevant group) within it are "the same or not materially different". In *University of Manchester* v *Jones* [1992] ICR 52 and in *London Underground* v *Edwards* [1995] ICR 574, [1995] IRLR 355, EAT ruled that tribunals had erred in artificially restricting the category of people included in the pool. The *Jones* case was brought by a 44 year old woman who was turned down for a job limited to graduates aged 27–35. The woman had taken her degree as a mature student and she claimed that the age limit discriminated against women who had obtained their degrees as mature students. The tribunal selected, as the pool for comparison, men and women who had obtained degrees at the age of 25 or over. Of these, the proportion of women aged under 35 was smaller than the proportion of male students under that age. The tribunal's finding in favour of Ms Jones was overturned on appeal and EAT's decision upheld by the Court of Appeal:

Jones v *University of Manchester* [1993] ICR 474, [1993] IRLR 218

Lord Justice Evans:

If . . . the numbers of women and of men, respectively, remaining after the requirement is applied are to be compared as "proportions" of something other than the total number of those who can comply, then the question arises, as proportions of what? One possibility is, as proportions of "all men" and "all women", even of "all humanity" subdivided in this way [58]. The other possibility is . . . "the relevant population", meaning all persons who satisfy the relevant criteria apart from the requirement or condition which is under consideration [59]. The latter approach is supported by . . . *Perera* . . . and by *obiter dicta* in *Price* v *Civil Service Commission and another* (Phillips J) [extracted below]. In my judgment, it is much to be preferred. This means that the proportion of women in the "group" (those who can comply) must not be considerably smaller than the proportion of women in the

---

[57] For criticism of the pool allowed by EAT in *Kidd* see K. O'Donovan and E. Szyszczak, below.
[58] Citing *R* v *Secretary of State for Education ex parte Schaffter* [1987] IRLR 53, *per* Schiemann J.
[59] Citing *Jones* v *Chief Adjudication Officer* [1990] IRLR 533, *per* Mustill LJ.

"relevant population" or "pool". (Section 5(3), which requires comparisons of women with men to be such that the "relevant circumstances" are the same, supports this construction, in my view.)

It follows that the statutory concept, in my judgment, is that of a "pool" or "relevant population", meaning those persons, male and female, who satisfy all the relevant criteria, apart from the requirement in question. It is, in effect, the total number of all those persons, men and women, who answer the description contained in the advertisement, apart from the age requirement. Here, that means all graduates with the relevant experience.

The next question raised by this appeal is whether the number of women and men, respectively who can comply with the requirement, must be compared as proportions of the total numbers of women and men, respectively, in the whole of the relevant population (graduates with the relevant experience), or whether they may be subdivided so as to form some smaller group which then is compared with a corresponding subdivision of the larger "pool" (mature graduates with the relevant experience) . . . I find it difficult to identify the basis on which any subdivision might be done . . . the Industrial Tribunal erred in law in having regard to a "pool" which consisted of mature graduates with relevant experience only.

The decision in *Jones* was applied by EAT in *London Underground* v *Edwards* to overturn a tribunal's choice of pool. The case concerned a sex discrimination claim brought by a single mother who was unable to comply with a newly imposed shift system which rendered alternative childcare impossible. A tribunal compared the proportion of male and female single parent train operators who could comply with the shift systems. EAT ruled that the appropriate comparison was between all male and female train operators. In *Greater Manchester Police Authority* v *Lea* [1990] IRLR 372, by contrast, EAT rejected an appeal against a pool which, it accepted, was imperfect.

Knox J, for EAT (citing the tribunal):

"In view of the very wide range of persons who could have applied for the job in question [the tribunal] considered that to take the economically active population was a proper approach and one they were prepared to accept."

The submission that was made to us in support of the attack on the Industrial Tribunal's conclusion on that first issue—namely was the pool taken the right one—was that although the pool did admittedly include the right people, it was far too wide. It was submitted to us that it was too wide in two directions both in terms of intellectual ability and other capacity. It included those who were not equipped realistically to apply for the post; they would be the people who did not have the necessary mental or other equipment to hold down what obviously did require certain important qualities. At the other end of the scale it was suggested that the pool did include people who would have been—putting it shortly—overqualified, that there were people whose abilities would have been amply sufficient to enable them to carry out these functions but who, because of their position, would not have been interested in applying for such a job.

The reply was not that the pool was statistically perfect but that statistical perfection is not properly to be sought in this field. . . The underlying consideration that this is an issue of fact and judgment and that this is a matter in which it has to be shown that the tribunal has adopted a course which is outside the range of selection for any reasonable tribunal are submissions that we accept as being applicable for this case and indeed generally.

The final issue which arises here concerns how a tribunal might determine the proportions of those of and not of the claimant's sex or race-based group able to comply with the relevant requirement or condition (what is meant by "can comply" is dealt with below). This depends on the pool for comparison chosen by the tribunal but, in general, tribunals will not demand the production of elaborate statistics and will, in appropriate cases, take account of their members' knowledge and experience.[60]

O'Donovan and E. Szyszczak, "Redundancy Selection and Sex Discrimination" 1985, 14 *Industrial Law Journal* 252, 253–4

Prior to *Kidd* motherhood, especially in caring for young children, had been treated by tribunals and official discourse generally as a major factor limiting women's participation in the labour market. This "social fact" was challenged by both the industrial tribunal and by the E.A.T. in *Kidd* v. *D.R.G.* Therein lies a source of uneasiness about the E.A.T. decision. The E.A.T. approved the tribunal's view that "mothers of young children in the modern community are no longer conforming universally to the traditional notion that their place is in the home; and that there are plenty of couples (married or unmarried) today with young children, where the male partner stays at home for the whole or part of the time to release his female partner to undertake full-time work." No evidence was given for this new "social fact" despite the statutory reference to considerably smaller proportions.

The problem with looking at households with children is that this assumes that all adult members of the household are equally incapacitated by the presence of children or others who need care. In other words, this overlooks the sexual division of labour. The correct pool, we suggest, should be those at risk under the first element of the statutory definition of indirect discrimination, that is those at risk from the ostensibly neutral requirement or condition. Having identified those who are at risk, the appropriate comparison is between those who can comply with the requirement and those who are at risk under it. In the particular circumstances of *Kidd* those at risk are part-time workers and those who can comply are full-time workers. The issue of childcare commitments which was raised by the complainant is not strictly relevant. In social terms there are a number of reasons why married women work part-time. In addition to domestic responsibilities, state policies such as the tax and social security thresholds provide incentives for married women to choose part-time rather than full-time employment. In legal terms there must be a direct connection between the requirement or condition and the question of compliance. The requirement in *Kidd* is the ability to work full-time to avoid being "first-out" in the redundancy procedure. Compliance by married women is the issue, not the presence of children in the household. It is enough for a complainant who alleges indirect discrimination to give statistical evidence that the numbers of persons in her class (women under s.1(1)(*b*); married persons under s.3(1)(*b*)) who can comply with the requirement are considerably less than the numbers in the comparative class.

This raises the question why there was no such statistical evidence before the tribunal and E.A.T. It seems that once the error of identifying the pool as households with children (instead of identifying those at risk under the requirement) was made, both tribunals wanted to hear statistical evidence about such households. But the complainant's counsel produced "extracts from the national census figures" which were "too broadly based" and which were held merely to confirm that more full-time jobs are held by men than are held

---

[60] See, for example, *Briggs*, below, *Home Office* v. *Holmes*, *Price* and *Perera*.

by women. The E.A.T. wanted figures on the effect as between the sexes, or as between married and unmarried persons, of responsibility for children as a factor potentially precluding the acceptance of a full-time job. Such figures are available in Social Trends or (now) from Martin and Roberts, *Women and Employment* (H.M.S.O. 1984). It is submitted that the statistical evidence of women's or married persons' lesser ability to comply is enough to show a prima facie case of indirect discrimination. The reasons for that inability rank as supplementary.

In *Briggs* v *North Eastern Education and Library Board* [1990] IRLR 181, Northern Ireland's Court of Appeal accepted that a considerably smaller proportion of women than of men could comply with a requirement to work late. In *Jones* v *University of Manchester*, Evans LJ remarked that the wording of s.1(1)(b) "make[s] some statistical evidence inevitable, but I have wondered throughout this appeal whether Parliament can have envisaged the kind of detail which has been produced in this case".[61] And in *London Underground Ltd* v *Edwards (No. 2)* [1998] IRLR 364, the relevant part of which is extracted below, the Court of Appeal accepted that the tribunal was entitled to take into account "common knowledge" of the preponderance of female over male lone parents as well as the statistical evidence relating to the ability of women in the workplace concerned to comply with the requirement in dispute.

But the *Kidd* approach is not entirely obsolete. As recently as 1999, the tribunal in *Sanderson* v *BAA plc* (40 EORDCLD, p.2) refused to accept, without proof, that a requirement to work an early morning shift discriminated against women.[62] Some evidence of disparate impact will generally be necessary, and the requirement for it can make the tribunal's selection of pools crucial to the applicant's success. In *Pearse* v *City of Bradford Metropolitan Council* [1988] IRLR 379, for example, the applicant's claim failed because, her statistics on disparate impact relating only to the pool upon which she argued the tribunal should rely, the rejection of that pool had the effect that the tribunal found no evidence of disparate impact. Ms Pearse challenged the ring-fencing of applications for a full-time academic job to those already holding a full-time position in the college. The statistics she had prepared showed that, of those academics working in the college, 21.8% of the women and 46.7% of the men were full-time. The tribunal, however, accepted the employer's argument that the correct pool for comparison was restricted to those otherwise qualified for the post although, as EAT subsequently accepted, it was not clear whether the tribunal chose as the appropriate pool all those otherwise qualified, or only those also employed at the college.

The potential pitfall for applicants created by the tribunal's almost unregulated power over the choice of pool makes any insistence by tribunals on statistical evidence deeply problematic. Extremely important here is the decision in *O'Flynn* v *Adjudication Officer* case C–237/94 [1996] ECR I–2617 [1996] All ER (EC) 541, in

---

[61] See also *Perera* and *Kidd*.
[62] *Cf Cowley* v *South African Airways* 41 EORDCLD, pp.2–3 in which a tribunal ruled that using its "knowledge of working practices there will be far less women with young children who would be able to comply with [a requirement for] back-to-back double-shift working than males".

which the ECJ ruled that indirect discrimination could be established where conditions were imposed which, although they applied irrespective of nationality, carried a *risk* that a relevant group of workers would be less able to comply with them.[63] The case was brought by an Irish man who, being resident in the UK, applied for a funeral grant to bury his son in Ireland. The grant was refused, the governing regulations providing that such grants were available only in respect of burials in the UK.[64] The ECJ ruled that the regulations were incompatible with Article 39 (ex Article 48), imposing as they did a disparate burden on migrant workers:

> 20. It follows from all the foregoing case-law that, unless objectively justified and proportionate to its aim, a provision of national law must be regarded as indirectly discriminatory if it is intrinsically liable to affect migrant workers more than national workers and if there is a consequent risk that it will place the former at a particular disadvantage.
> 21. It is not necessary in this respect to find that the provision in question does in practice affect a substantially higher proportion of migrant workers. It is sufficient that it is liable to have such an effect.

The decision in *O'Flynn* requires that a similar approach is taken by the UK courts under the RRA where indirect discrimination is based on nationality and affects an EEA national.

The dicta in *Briggs* v *NEELB*, *Jones*, and *London Underground Ltd* v *Edwards (No. 2)* to the effect that tribunals are entitled to take into account "common knowledge" of disparate impact have already been mentioned. In order to give effect to *O'Flynn*, however, the discretion currently vested in tribunals in this area must be restricted. One way this could be achieved would be the redefinition of indirect discrimination along the lines recently suggested by the CRE. In its 1998 reform proposals, that body suggested that indirect discrimination should be regarded as occurring:

> where an apparently neutral provision, criterion, practice or policy which is applied to persons of all racial groups cannot as easily be satisfied or complied with by persons of a particular racial group *or where there is a risk that the provision, criterion, practice or policy may* operate to the disadvantage of persons of a particular racial group, unless the provision, criterion, practice or policy can be justified by objective factors unrelated to race (my emphasis).[65]

Despite the lapse in time since the decision in *O'Flynn*, the government has not yet acted to give effect to it. It declined to amend the definition of indirect discrimination

---

[63] The case concerned free movement of workers, the protected group being non-nationals.

[64] In *R* v *Secretary of State for Social Services ex parte Nessa Times* 15th November 1994, discussed in Chapter 7, the Divisional Court relied on the House of Lords' decision in *R* v *Entry Clearing Officer, Bombay, ex parte Amin* [1983] 2 AC 818, [1983] 2 All ER 864 (discussed in Chapter 4) to rule that funeral grants were not covered by the RRA.

[65] This proposal was endorsed by the FEC in its 1997 Review of the FEAs and by the Standing Advisory Commission on Human Rights (see further Chapters 5 and 9) in its recommendations for reform—*Employment Equality: Building for the Future* (HMSO, cm 3684, June 1997).

in the FETO on the basis of maintaining consistency between that statute and the RRA and SDA, although the White Paper preceding the FETO stated (para 5.48) that: "[t]he Government will continue to monitor developments, including obligations arising from the European Union Treaty of Amsterdam, and will consider further the potential implications for fair employment legislation in Northern Ireland". The 1999 draft equal treatment general framework directive defines indirect discrimination, consistent with *O'Flynn* and the race discrimination directive and the definition proposed by the CRE. This directive would, if adopted, apply to discrimination on grounds of "religion or belief, disability, age or sexual orientation". The new directive on race discrimination directive (Directive 2000/43/EC) defines indirect discrimination as occuring:

> where an apparently neutral provision, criterion or practice *would put persons of a racial or ethnic group at a particular disadvantage* compared with other persons, unless that provision, criterion or practice is objectively justified by a legitimate aim and the means of achieving that aim are appropriate and necessary [my emphasis].

This formulation, agreed by the Council of Ministers, is not as strong as the one which went to them for approval, which had expressly incorporated the *O'Flynn* risk-based approach. To the extent that the *O'Flynn* test is easier to satisfy, it should continue to be applied in cases falling within Article 39 TEC. The other significant change which took place between the proposed and the finally agreed definition of race discrimination under the new directive was the removal of the proviso that the aim pursued by indirectly discriminatory provisions, criteria, etc., had to be 'unrelated to the racial or ethnic origin of a person or group of persons'. Discrimination will be easier to justify under the terms of the directive, therefore, than under the RRA.

Turning to (2), the question of what amounts to "a considerably smaller proportion" was also considered by the Court of Appeal in the *London Underground* case, which concerned an indirect discrimination claim brought by a woman train driver after her employer imposed shift changes. The woman, a single parent, claimed that a considerably smaller proportion of women (95.2%) than of men (100%) train drivers could comply with the new shifts. An industrial tribunal found in her favour, taking into account "common knowledge that females are more likely to be single parents and caring for a child than males", the disparity in the numbers of male and female train drivers (2,023 men to 21 women) and the fact that only one person (the applicant) could not comply with the employer's condition. London Underground appealed.

London Underground Ltd v Edwards (No. 2) [1998] IRLR 364

Potter LJ:[67]

In my view, there is a dual statutory purpose underlying the provisions of s1(1)(b) and in particular the necessity under subparagraph (i) to show that the proportion of women who

---

[67] Having acknowledged acknowledged the comment of Neill LJ in *R* v *Secretary of State for Employment ex parte Seymour-Smith*, below, that "before a presumption of indirect discrimination on the

can comply with a given requirement or condition is "considerably smaller" than the proportion of men who can comply with it. The first is to prescribe as the threshold for intervention a situation in which there exists a substantial and not merely marginal discriminatory effect (disparate impact) as between men and women, so that it can be clearly demonstrated that a prima facie case of (indirect) discrimination exists, sufficient to require the employer to justify the application of the condition or requirement in question: see subparagraph (ii). The second is to ensure that a tribunal charged with deciding whether or not the requirement is discriminatory may be confident that its disparate impact is inherent in the application of the requirement or condition and is not simply the product of unreliable statistics or fortuitous circumstance. Since the disparate impact question will require to be resolved in an infinite number of different employment situations . . . an area of flexibility (or margin of appreciation), is necessarily applicable to the question of whether a particular percentage is to be regarded as "substantially smaller" in any given case . . . [a]n industrial tribunal does not sit in blinkers. Its members are selected in order to have a degree of knowledge and expertise in the industrial field generally. The high preponderance of single mothers having care of a child is a matter of common knowledge. Even if the "statistic", ie the precise ratio referred to is less well known, it was in any event apparently discussed at the hearing before the industrial tribunal without doubt or reservation on either side. It thus seems clear to me that, when considering as a basis for their decision the reliability of the figures with which they were presented, the industrial tribunal were entitled to take the view that the percentage difference represented a minimum rather than a maximum so far as discriminatory effect was concerned.

Equally, I consider that the industrial tribunal was entitled to have regard to the large discrepancy in numbers between male and female operators making up the pool for its consideration. Not one of the male component of just over 2,000 men was unable to comply with the rostering arrangements. On the other hand, one woman could not comply out of the female component of only 21. It seems to me that the comparatively small size of the female component indicated, again without the need for specific evidence, both that it was either difficult or unattractive for women to work as train operators in any event and that the figure of 95.2% of women unable to comply was likely to be a minimum rather than a maximum figure. Further, if for any reason fortuitous error was present or comprehensive evidence lacking, an unallowed-for increase of no more than one in the women unable to comply would produce an effective figure of some 10% as against the nil figure in respect of men; on the other hand, one male employee unable to comply would scarcely alter the proportional difference at all. . . . In many respects, no doubt, it would be useful to lay down in relation to s1(1)(b) a rule of thumb or to draw a line defining the margin within, or threshold beyond, which, in relation to small percentage differences, the lower percentage should not reasonably be regarded as "considerably smaller" than the higher percentage. However, it does not seem to me appropriate to do so. For the various reasons discussed in this judgment, and because of the wide field and variety of situations in which

ground of sex arises there must be a considerable difference in the number or percentage of one sex in the advantaged or disadvantaged group as against the other sex and not simply a difference which is more than de minimis", of Peter Gibson LJ in *Barry* v *Midland Bank plc* [1998] IRLR 138, that: "the consistent approach of the European Court has been . . . to see whether the measure works to the disadvantage of far more women than men" and of Otton LJ in *R* v *Secretary of State ex parte Unison* [1996] IRLR 438 that a 4% disparity between the proportions of men and women able to comply with a particular requirement "would fall within the *de minimis* exception". He also referred to Greater *Manchester Police Authority* v *Lea*, above, in which EAT upheld a tribunal determination that the difference between 95.3% and 99.4% was "considerable".

the provisions of the section are to be applied, the circumstances and arguments before the adjudicating tribunal are bound to differ as to what in a particular case amounts to a proportion which is "considerably smaller" for the purposes of determining the discriminatory or potentially discriminatory nature of a particular requirement or condition. If a figure were to be selected in the field of employment, it would be likely to vary according to the context, and in particular as between a case where the requirement or condition is applied on a national scale in respect of which reliable supporting statistics are available and those where it is applied in relation to a small firm or an unbalanced workforce where the decision may have to be made on far less certain evidence and to a large degree upon the basis of the industrial tribunal's own experience and assessment as applied to such figures as are available. The difficulties are well illustrated by this case.

Plainly, a percentage difference of no more than 5% or thereabouts is inherently likely to lead an industrial tribunal to the conclusion that the requirements of s 1(1)(b) have not been made out, but I am not prepared to say that such a conclusion must inevitably follow in every case.[68]

R v *Secretary of State for Employment, ex parte Seymour-Smith & Perez* [1996] All ER (EC) 1, [1995] ICR 889, [1995] IRLR 464 involved a challenge to the 1985 increase in the qualifying period for unfair dismissal, in 1985, from one to two years. It was argued that women were substantially more disadvantaged than men by the increase and that, therefore, it breached the *equal* treatment directive. The Court of Appeal accepted (overruling the Divisional Court) that proportions of between 88.4 and 94.6% were "considerably smaller" than 100%. The appeal court felt constrained by the equal treatment directive not to place an exaggerated emphasis on the word "considerably". On appeal, the House of Lords referred to the ECJ, *inter alia*, the question: "[w]hat is the legal test for establishing whether a measure adopted by a Member State has such a degree of disparate effect as between men and women as to amount to indirect discrimination for the purposes of Article [141, ex Article 119] of the EC Treaty unless shown to be based upon objectively justified factors other than sex?" The ECJ ruled:

60 . . . it must be ascertained whether the statistics available indicate that a considerably smaller percentage of women than men is able to satisfy the condition of two years' employment required by the disputed rule. That situation would be evidence of apparent sex discrimination unless the disputed rule were justified by objective factors unrelated to any discrimination based on sex.

61. That could also be the case if the statistical evidence revealed a lesser but persistent and relatively constant disparity over a long period between men and women who satisfy the requirement of two years' employment. It would, however, be for the national court to determine the conclusions to be drawn from such statistics.

62. It is also for the national court to assess whether the statistics concerning the situation of the workforce are valid and can be taken into account. . . . It is, in particular, for the national court to establish whether, given that it was a matter for the national court to

---

[68] In *Kang* v *R F Brookes Ltd* 40 EORDCLD, p.2, a tribunal ruled that a requirement with which 94% of Sikh and 100% of non-Sikh workers could comply was not indirectly discriminatory.

determine whether differences in ability to comply were purely fortuitous or short term phenomena, and whether, in general, they appear to be significant.

63. In this case, it appears from the order for reference that in 1985, the year in which the requirement of two years' employment was introduced, 77.4 per cent men and 68.9 per cent of women fulfilled that condition.

64. Such statistics do not appear, on the face of it, to show that a considerably smaller percentage of women than men is able to fulfil the requirement imposed by the disputed rule.

When the case returned to the House of Lords the decision of the Court of Appeal was overturned. The majority decided on the grounds that a *prima facie* case of discrimination had been made out but that the discrimination was justified. This aspect of the decision is considered below. Lords Slynn and Steyn concurred on the basis that no discrimination had been proven.

R v Secretary of State for Employment, ex parte Seymour-Smith & Perez [2000] IRLR 263

Lord Nicholls (with whom Lords Goff and Jauncey agreed):

In paragraph 61, unlike paragraph 60, the [ECJ] gave no guidance on the extent of statistical disparity required to establish apparent sex discrimination. Nor did the court spell out, in so many words, how these two approaches fit together.

As I see it, the reasoning underlying these paragraphs is that, in the case of indirect discrimination, the obligation to avoid discrimination . . . is to avoid applying unjustifiable requirements having a considerable disparity of impact. In this regard the European Court has adopted an approach similar to that provided in section 1(1)(b) of the [SDA]. A considerable disparity can be more readily established if the statistical evidence covers a long period and the figures show a persistent and relatively constant disparity. In such a case a lesser statistical disparity may suffice to show that the disparity is considerable than if the statistics cover only a short period or if they present an uneven picture.

Having set out the applicable principles, the European Court addressed the facts in the present case. In doing so the court focused exclusively on the 1985 statistics . . . Before your Lordships it was common ground that 1991, not 1985, was the relevant date for the purpose of the issue now being considered. The position at this later date was not considered by the European Court . . . These figures show that over the period of seven years, from 1985 up to and including 1991, the ratio of men and women who qualified was roughly 10:9 . . . This disparity was remarkably constant for the six years from 1985 to 1990, but it began to diminish in 1991. These figures are in borderline country. The question under consideration is one of degree. When the borderline is defined by reference to a criterion as imprecise as "considerably smaller" it is inevitable that in some cases different minds may reach different conclusions. The decisions of the two courts below illustrate this. . . I find myself driven to the conclusion that a persistent and constant disparity of the order just mentioned in respect of the entire male and female labour forces of the country over a period of seven years cannot be brushed aside and dismissed as insignificant or inconsiderable. I agree with the Court of Appeal that, given the context of equality of pay or treatment, the latitude afforded by the word "considerably" should not be exaggerated. I think these figures are adequate to demonstrate that the extension of the qualifying period had a considerably greater adverse impact on women than men . . .

Of significance here also is the recent decision of the House of Lords in *Barry* v *Midland Bank plc* [1999] 1 WLR 1465, [1999] IRLR 581 in which case Lord Nicholls suggested that:

> a comparison must be made between, on the one hand, the respective proportions of men . . . who are not disadvantaged by the [disputed practice] and those who are disadvantaged and, on the other hand, the like proportions regarding women in the workforce . . . These proportions by themselves can be misleading, because they are affected by the comparative sizes of the non-disadvantaged group and the disadvantaged group. The smaller the disadvantaged group in proportionate terms, the narrower will be the differential. Take an employer whose workforce of 1,000 comprises an equal number of men and women. Ten per cent of the staff (100 employees) work part-time, and of these 90 per cent are women. A scheme which disadvantages part-timers will disadvantage 10 men (2 per cent of the male employees) and 90 women (18 per cent of female employees). If the figures were the same save that the total workforce was 10,000 employees, the disadvantaged part-timers would comprise 10 men (0.2 per cent of male employees) and 90 women (1.8 per cent of female employees). A better guide will often be found in expressing the proportions in the disadvantaged group as a ratio of each other. In both my examples the ratio is 9:1. For every man adversely affected there are nine women. Absolute size, in terms of numbers, remains relevant, since a low ratio may be of little significance in a small company but of considerable significance in a large company.

Lord Nicholls returned to this theme in his *Perez* speech:

> In paragraph 59 of its judgment the European Court described the approach which should be adopted to the comparison of statistics:

> > . . . the best approach to the comparison of statistics is to consider, on the one hand, the respective proportions of men in the workforce able to satisfy the requirement of two years' employment under the disputed rule and of those unable to do so, and, on the other, to compare those proportions as regards women in the workforce. It is not sufficient to consider the number of persons affected, since that depends on the number of working people in the Member State as a whole as well as the percentages of men and women employed in that State."

> This statement appears to envisage that two comparisons should be made: a comparison of the proportions of men and women able to satisfy the requirement ("the qualifiers"), and a comparison of the proportions of men and women unable to satisfy the requirement ("the non-qualifiers"). Thereafter in its judgment the court considered only the proportions of men and women who were qualifiers.

> Some of the ramifications involved in looking at the composition of the disadvantaged group, as well as the composition of the advantaged group, were explored by the Divisional Court and the Court of Appeal in the present case. Suffice to say, I do not understand the European Court to have rejected use of the figures relating to the non-qualifiers in a suitable case. Indeed, the European Court has looked at the composition of the disadvantaged group in several cases, although in none of them was there an issue on this point [69] . . .

[69] Citing *Bilka-Kaufhaus*, *Nimz* and *Kowalska* v *Freie und Hansestadt Hamburg* (Case C–33/89) [1990] ECR 1–2591.

Having regard to the conclusion I have expressed above on the issue of disparate impact, it is unnecessary to reach a firm conclusion on this point. I prefer to leave this question open for another occasion.

The implications for this area of law of the decision of the ECJ in *O'Flynn* and of the new race discrimination directive have been considered above.

One of the particular difficulties which may arise in establishing disparate impact concerns multiple discrimination, mentioned in Chapter 1.

S. Fredman and E. Szyszczak, "The Interaction of Race and Gender" p. 20

In *Degraffenreid* v *General Motors Assembly Division* [413F. Supp 142 (ED Miss 1976)], the court foresaw the potential for moving discrimination law beyond the standard of comparability with the white male norm and rejected a joint sex and race discrimination challenge to a "last-in-first-out" lay-off policy. The justifications for the rejection of a *combination* of sex and race claims were well rehearsed. First, it was argued that by allowing the interaction of race and sex claims the courts would create a "super remedy" for black women that "would give them relief beyond what the drafters of the relevant statutes intended". Black women should come to the courts on an equal footing with white women and black men. They should not, and could not, obtain better *locus standi* and remedies by creating an unauthorized class of plaintiff. (At this juncture it is interesting to note that the US courts have not encountered any difficulty in recognizing white men as a distinct class deserving special treatment in reverse discrimination claims.) A second justification was that by allowing the growth of "special group" interests, Title VII would become unmanageable. It would open the door to allow other interest groups to make special pleadings. Finally, the creation of a new group interest would open a "Pandora's box" or lead to the creation of a "many-headed Hydra". It is easy to understand the reasoning of *Degraffenried*. As Crenshaw points out, black women have difficulty making any gains under the present law because they are two steps removed from the legal norm which "is not neutral but is white male." Sex discrimination and race discrimination are relatively easy to tackle because they are politically acceptable targets for legal intervention and reform. Asking law to listen to a plurality of voices upsets the hegemony of law and forces it to "lose a sense of ready solutions and steady certainties.

"Which is to [her] detriment of that other because she cannot comply"

L. Lustgarten, "The New Meaning of Discrimination" (1978) *Public Law* 178, pp. 190–3

s1(1)(b)'s "detriment" requirement presents two practical hindrances to the effectiveness of the Act that are potentially extremely serious.

Virtually every suit under the American civil rights laws is brought as a class action. This procedural device enables a litigant whose claims are typical of numerous other persons to represent their interests in court. If he prevails, remedial action, including substantial compensation, may be granted to all members of the class. Class action procedure was designed and first used in commercial and corporate litigation, but it proved ideal for plaintiffs in discrimination cases, all of whom were suffering identical disabilities. Once the court approves the class action the suit goes forward on behalf of the plaintiff "and all those similarly situated." It is therefore not uncommon for the plaintiff to fail to establish his own case, whilst proving discrimination against the class.[70] The court may then order remedial action against the discriminatory practices, even if the named plaintiff obtains no relief.

The absence of any such procedure in Britain, coupled with the "detriment" clause, may seriously handicap enforcement of the law. Whether even an unmistakably discriminatory practice is held illegal will depend on the more or less fortuitous occurrence that a given individual has the interest, tenacity and courage to assert his rights. He may also require an unusual degree of asceticism. An employer worried about the cost or other problems that may attend changing an entrenched practice might find it politic to make a particularly good settlement offer to the occasional black complainant. What would seem good fortune to the latter would for the employer be far cheaper than compliance with the law. This "resist and withdraw" tactic was quite common in early American employment litigation until the courts made clear that such arrangements would not block their scrutiny of the employer's practices. But under the present statute, once the complainant withdrew his case, the tribunal would lose jurisdiction to correct the illegality of the employment practice, regardless of how severely it affected others.

Conversely if a complainant is clearly unsuitable for the position that is the subject of the claimed discrimination, the "detriment" provision would seem to preclude further inquiry. This restriction, and the demonstrated reluctance of victims of overt discrimination in this country to seek redress, compounded by the fact that for certain kinds of jobs, notably white collar and supervisory posts, there are likely to be relatively few black applicants in the near future, may effectively insulate the discriminatory practices of many firms from correction by the law. It seems wrong that so much of the law's effectiveness should depend on the personal characteristics and qualifications of individuals. . . . it seems likely that in numbers and in importance, private complaints will be the primary means of implementing the Act. It is therefore essential that the "detriment" requirement does not block its central artery. Even if the complainant stays the course, an additional practical problem concerning proof of "detriment" is that he will often be unable to establish the extent of his injury. He may, for example, have been one of 15 applicants; and whilst indirect discrimination caused him not to be hired or even short-listed, some of his competitors were in fact equally qualified or indeed preferable on legitimate grounds. If the "detriment" clause is interpreted to require that the complainant prove that his application would have succeeded in the absence of discrimination, the Act will be eviscerated, for this will often be untrue.

These compelling practical objections apart, the imposition of such a requirement would be based on a fundamental misconception of the purpose of anti-discrimination legislation. It is not intended to ensure that a non-white (or woman) gets the job or promotion he or she wants; it insists only that the applicant be fairly considered. The new understanding of discrimination broadens the category of what will be regarded as "unfair" criteria and practices, but—here the rejection of a pure "fair share" approach is explicit—its focus still centres on the process of decision, not the ultimate result. Thus the minority person suffers injury, and the statute is transgressed, whenever the process of decision is tainted by discrimination, not only when he would obviously have succeeded had he been white. Practicality and principle conjoin to urge that "detriment" be interpreted to mean simply that the process of hiring, promotion or whatever has been in any degree affected by the existence of the challenged requirement or condition.

---

[70] See discussion of *Osamor* (*Coker & Osamor v Lord Chancellor* [1999] IRLR 396 Chapter 4). The tribunal's finding that Osamor was not qualified for the appointment and that she had not, therefore, suffered any detriment, meant that the racially discriminatory nature of the Lord Chancellor's appointment could not be challenged in that case.

The question whether or not the claimant (together with others of his or her sex or race-based group) "can comply" with the requirement or condition imposed by the employer is obviously of crucial importance to whether or not indirect discrimination has been made out. Disputes over ability to comply may occur vis-à-vis the plaintiff him or herself, or in relation to his or her relevant group. Ability of the group to comply appears to be measured by statistical or other evidence of actual compliance, this having been discussed above.

The approach to be taken to the possibility of compliance by the individual claimant was established by EAT in *Price* v *Civil Service Commission*. This case arose under the SDA, and the question of "can comply" related to the group rather than the individual plaintiff (compliance by the latter being clearly impossible on the facts). The approach taken in *Price* was, however, subsequently applied, however, by the House of Lords in *Mandla* v *Dowell Lee* [1983] 2 AC 548, [1983] 1 All ER 1062, [1983] IRLR 209 vis-à-vis the individual plaintiff, as well as his group. See also *Clarke* v *Eley*, above *Mandla*, which arose under the RRA, is considered further below.

The claim in *Price* was brought by a 35 year old woman who challenged a maximum age limit of 28 imposed in relation to a Civil Service post. She argued that the age limit discriminated indirectly against women, many women being engaged in child bearing in their later twenties. Her claim was dismissed by a tribunal on the ground that the words "can comply" had to be interpreted strictly and, given that it was theoretically possible for any woman between 17½ and 28 to apply, the proportion who were able to do so was not considerably smaller than the proportion of men also so able. Ms Price appealed to EAT.

Price v Civil Service Commission [1978] 1 All ER 1228, [1977] 1 WLR 1417, [1978] ICR 212, 12 ITR 483, [1997] IRLR 291

Phillips J:

. . . In one sense it can be said that any female applicant can comply with the condition. She is not obliged to marry, or to have children, or to mind children; she may find somebody to look after them, and as a last resort she may put them into care. In this sense . . . any female applicant can comply with the condition. Such a construction appears to us to be wholly out of sympathy with the spirit and intent of the 1975 Act. Further, it should be repeated that compliance with sub-para (i) is only a preliminary step, which does not lead to a finding that an act is one of discrimination unless the person acting fails to show that it is justifiable. "Can" is . . . a word with many shades of meaning, and we are satisfied that it should not be too narrowly, or too broadly, construed in its context in s 1(1)(b)(i). It should not be said that a person "can" do something merely because it is theoretically possible for him to do so: it is necessary to see whether he can do so in practice. Applying this approach to the circumstances of this case, it is relevant in determining whether women can comply with the condition to take into account the current usual behaviour of women in this respect, as observed in practice, putting on one side behaviour and responses which are unusual or extreme.

Knowledge and experience suggest that a considerable number of women between the mid-twenties and the mid-thirties are engaged in bearing children and in minding children, and that while many find it possible to take up employment many others, while desiring to do so, find it impossible, and that many of the latter as their children get older find that they can follow their wish and seek employment. This knowledge and experience is confirmed by some of the statistical evidence produced . . . This demonstrates clearly that the economic activity of women with at least one A level falls off markedly about the age of 23, reaching a bottom at about the age of 33 when it climbs gradually to a plateau at about 45.

Basing ourselves on this and other evidence, we should have no hesitation in concluding that our own knowledge and experience is confirmed, and that it is safe to say that the condition is one which it is in practice harder for women to comply with than it is for men. We should be inclined to go further and say that there are undoubtedly women of whom it may be properly said in the terms of s1(1)(b)(i) that they "cannot" comply with the condition, because they are women; that is to say because of their involvement with their children.

Phillips LJ stopped short, however, of concluding that a considerably smaller proportion of women than of men could comply with the age limit, remitting this point to a different tribunal for determination.

In *Mandla* v *Lee*, the House of Lords accepted that Sikhs were less able to comply with a "no turban" requirement not to wear a turban than were others—while it was perfectly possible for Sikhs to remove their headwear, any such action was incompatible with their religious convictions and so should not be considered practically possible. This decision went a step further than that in *Price*: whereas, in the earlier case, the plaintiff could not under any circumstances *presently* meet the age requirement imposed (albeit that she could have done so several years previously had she organised her life differently); the plaintiff in *Mandla* could (although not consistent with his religious beliefs) have removed his turban.

In *Home Office* v *Holmes* [1984] IRLR 299, too, EAT upheld a tribunal decision that a woman who was refused permission to return to work part-time after the birth of her child could not have done so consistent with her "parental responsibilities . . . [without suffering] excessive demands on her time and energy". Ms Holmes was a lone parent, and EAT stressed that it was not imposing a blanket entitlement for mothers to work part-time. Nevertheless, EAT did not disapprove of the tribunal's finding that "despite the changes in the role of women in modern society, it is still a fact that the raising of children tends to place a greater burden on them than it does on men". Similar conclusions were reached by the courts in *Greater Glasgow Health Board* v *Carey* [1987] IRLR 484, *Briggs* above, and *Meade Hill* v *British Council* [1995] IRLR 478 (although in the earlier cases EAT and Northern Ireland's Court of Appeal respectively found the conditions imposed to be justifiable).

The correct approach to this issue is relatively clear. Despite this, in *Clymo* v *Wandsworth London Borough Council* [1989] ICR 250, [1989] IRLR 241 EAT refused to overrule a tribunal decision that a woman librarian "could comply" with a requirement that she work full-time despite her view that this course of action was inconsistent with her childcare responsibilities. Citing *Price* in support of the decision, Mr Justice Wood stated:

It is a question of reasonableness. The applicant should not be in a position to demand, nor should she be coerced into a position of complying with a situation wholly alien to her womanhood or motherhood. All the surrounding circumstances will be relevant and must be examined. No doubt society is changing and will continue to change and with it the findings of the judges of fact may alter . . . A reasonable and responsible management decision had been reached and it seems clear in trying to fit society into the framework of the statute and the statute into our society that in every employment ladder from the lowliest to the highest there will come a stage at which a woman who has family responsibilities must make a choice. That situation was one facing this mother.

Clymo stands as a triumph of the technical approach and is as far-removed from the purposive approach taken to the concept by the ECJ in *O'Flynn* and, in the equal pay context, in *Enderby* v *Frenchay*, as it is possible to be.[71] Not only did EAT in that case uphold the tribunal's decision that the applicant could work full-time; the appeal tribunal also agreed with the tribunal that no requirement had been "applied" to Ms Clymo—full-time working was one of the terms of employment which she was initially offered and accepted when she took the job. According to EAT:

for the local authority to tell their current employees that a job continues to be "full time" is not applying anything and that on the facts of the present case "full time" is part of the nature of the job itself [72] . . . in many working structures . . . there will be a grade or position where the job or appointment by its very nature requires full-time attendance. At one end of the scale if a cleaner was required to work full time it would clearly be a requirement or condition. Whereas in the case of a managing director it would be part of the nature of the appointment. In between there will be many gradations but it will be for an employer, acting reasonably, to decide—a managerial decision—what is required for the purposes of running his business or his establishment.[73]

EAT further ruled that there was no "firm evidence" that the proportion of qualified women librarians who can work full-time was considerably smaller than the proportion of qualified male librarians (although "[t]here was evidence . . . that considerably fewer qualified women remained in the library service than fully qualified men. This was attributed to the child minding responsibilities of women"). According to the tribunal "at this level of income, and most particularly in the London

---

[71] See also *Turner* v *Labour Party Superannuation Scheme* [1987] ICR 101 in which the Court of Appeal ruled against a claim ot the effect that the scheme discriminated against an unmarried person on the ground that she might, prior to the date at which benefits became payable, be married.

[72] Preferring *Francis and others* v *British Airways Engineering Overhaul Ltd* [1982] IRLR 10 to *Holmes*.

[73] This approach was disapproved by Northern Ireland's Court of Appeal in *Briggs* v *North Eastern Education and Library Board*, in which Hutton LCJ (for the Court) preferred the approach taken by Waite J in *Holmes*: " 'It appears to us that words like "requirement" and "condition" are plain, clear words of wide import fully capable of including any obligation of service whether for full or for part time, and we see no basis for giving them a restrictive interpretation in the light of the policy underlying the [1975] Act, or in the light of public policy . . .' " In *Ministry for Justice, Equality & Law Reform* v *Hand* DEE 5/98, the Irish Labour Court applied *Clymo* to the effect that "it is for the employer, acting reasonable, to decide what is required for the purpose of running the organisation for which it is responsible" (there a refusal to job share).

area, with child minding facilities readily available, people of these qualifications and this combined income [£24 000 in London in the late 1980s] and with a professional career both behind and ahead of them could certainly conduct their family arrangements on less old-fashioned bases than the less qualified and more lowly paid". EAT declined to interfere with this conclusion.

The approach taken by the courts to indirect discrimination cases has improved, the standards of justification (discussed below) having tightened and the distinction drawn by the tribunal and EAT in *Clymo* between job-related "requirements" and features regarded as part of the "very nature" of the job not having resurfaced since its disapproval by the Northern Ireland Court of Appeal in *Briggs*. But the attitude of the tribunal and EAT towards the question whether the applicant could comply with the full-time work requirement has persisted, with women who rely on family reasons to claim that they are not able to comply with hours-related work requirements being subject to increasingly close scrutiny.

In *Zurich Insurance Co* v *Gulson* [1998] IRLR 118 (EAT), for example, the employers of a woman dismissed for failure to comply with extended working hours on her return from maternity leave sought to cross-examine her at great length about her finances. Their purpose was to establish that, on a net salary of under £1 000 per month, she and her husband could tighten their belts and afford a full-time nanny. The tribunal restricted the employers" questioning and EAT upheld the decision, Kirkwood J pointing out that the applicant's inability to comply did not rest solely on the affordability of a nanny and referring to the wide discretion given to tribunals by the Industrial Tribunals (Constitution and Rules of Procedure) Regulations 1993 to regulate their own proceedings:

> It is of course a discretion that must be exercised judicially. The primary purpose of para 9(1) [of Schedule 1 to the Regulations] is to allow the appropriate enquiries for the clarification of the issues before the tribunal. Beyond that, it is in no sense incumbent upon the tribunal and forms no part of the judicial exercise of the discretion it has, to allow lengthy and detailed cross-examination on matters that do not appear to the tribunal to be of assistance to it, however enthusiastically the advocate endeavours to pursue that line.

The discretion vested in tribunals can operate to the advantage of applicants, as in the *Zurich Insurance* case. But it can result in distinctly questionable decisions being upheld on appeal. In *Stevens* v *Katherine Lady Berkeley's School* (EAT/380/97, 15th January 1998), for example, EAT rejected an appeal against the dismissal of an indirect sex discrimination claim brought by a woman teacher who had been refused permission to return part-time after maternity leave. The tribunal ruled against her solely on the grounds that she had failed to show her inability to comply with the requirement for full-time work. The case was referred back to the tribunal by EAT because Ms Steven's failure to adduce evidence on this point was due to the employer's having conceded the woman's inability to comply. The tribunal again decided that the plaintiff had not shown herself unable to comply, a finding challenged by the plaintiff on the grounds that the test applied by the tribunal was more stringent than that established by EAT in *Price*. In particular, the appellant claimed that the tribunal had erred in finding that she had merely expressed a " 'preference' to work part-time, rather than an 'inability' to do so." Further, her counsel claimed that

> the tribunal . . . have quite deliberately, bearing in mind the first Employment Appeal Tribunal judgment, found that there was no evidence to support the applicant's case that she could not in practice comply with the requirement. He points in particular to [the plaintiff's evidence that] "I decided that I was no longer able to work full-time. As a full-time teacher I spent most evenings and usually an entire day at the weekend in preparation and marking. Such a time-commitment would not be possible now that I had a small child." That, he submits, is some evidence as to the practicalities of her ability to comply with the requirement.

In this case EAT refused "too close an examination of the language of the Industrial Tribunal's reasons" and found that the tribunal "reached a permissible conclusion of fact that she had failed to satisfy them as to her inability to comply with the requirement". EAT's decision in this case is alarmingly reminiscent of that in *Clymo*, which Jeremy Lewis criticised in the following terms:

J. Lewis "Refusing to Allow Job Sharing" (1989) 18 *Industrial Law Journal* 244, 246–7

In *Holmes* very little evidence was needed to satisfy the E.A.T. that the parental responsibilities of a single mother prevented her complying with a requirement of full-time work. In *Clymo*, by contrast, there were adequate child-minding facilities which the complainant could easily afford. Thus, the E.A.T. concluded, Ms. Clymo's failure to comply was due to a mere "personal preference" to bring up her own children. . . . While the E.A.T. set out a workable test of ability to comply, their application of the test was inept. The E.A.T. asserted that ultimately a question of reasonableness was involved. It must be ascertained whether Ms. Clymo could comply "in practice," taking into account "the current usual behaviour of women in this respect" (see *Price* v. *Civil Service Commission*). The need to consider social trends was thus recognised. The dominant social ideology of this country still stresses the importance of bringing up one's own children and, as recognised in *Holmes*, the burden still tends to fall on the mother. Of course many would prefer to take advantage of child care facilities rather than give up employment altogether. However job sharing opens the possibility of combining a continued career with personal care of one's own children. Indeed this was the motivation for Ms. Clymo's claim. In the face of this the E.A.T. not only dismissed the pressure and influence of the dominant social ideology as mere "personal preference," but also dogmatically denied that job sharing allows any new choice:

> A reasonable and responsible management decision has been reached and it seems clear in trying to fit society into the framework of the statute and the statute into our society that in every employment ladder from the lowliest to the highest there will come a stage at which a woman who has family responsibilities must make a choice.

Thus the employer's autonomy is again prioritised. It is mothers who must choose and not employers who must justify the denial of an adequate choice.

Thompson's *Part-time Workers and the Law*[74] suggests that:

> although *Clymo* has not been followed in subsequent cases it is helpful to show evidence of why the particular woman cannot comply [with a requirement to work full-time]. Examples will include the availability of affordable reliable child care, any special needs of the child concerned and any other domestic circumstances, such as the proximity of other relatives of the child to assist in caring.

Justifiability

The final hurdle at which an indirect discrimination claim can fall is that of justification. By contrast with the other elements discussed above, it is for the alleged discriminator to satisfy the tribunal on this matter. The DDA offers some legislative guidance, s.5(3) stating that discrimination in employment "is justified if, but only if, the reason for it is both material to the circumstances of the particular case and substantial". But the DDA is unique in this respect,[75] the SDA, RRA and FETO leaving the issue to the courts to determine.

L. Lustgarten, pp. 193

Once the complainant establishes discrimination, it is open to the employer—who carries the burden of proof—to demonstrate that the practice is "justifiable." In a purely negative sense, this is perhaps the most important single term in the Act, for an interpretation that gave extensive deference to customary employment practices would reduce it to insignificance. It is a critical failing of the statute that it articulates no standards to direct tribunals called upon to make this judgment.

One may begin the task of interpretation by asking why this provision is in the statute. Put another way, why does it not simply proscribe any practice proven to be disadvantageous to minorities? The explanation is grounded in policy: the value of preventing the exclusion of non-whites cannot always be paramount. But in the scheme of what, for Britain, is an innovative and comprehensive enactment, this can be true for only the most compelling reasons, which may be roughly defined as the safe and efficient operation of a business. Thus no anti-discrimination law requires an employer to hire unqualified persons, but effective legislation does insist that the criteria governing qualifications truly measure competence, and do not simply express prejudice, preconception or unthinking custom.

If this analysis is correct, much of the extended Standing Committee debate over whether "justifiable" should have been replaced by "necessary" was misconceived, a point nicely illustrated by the confusion of the Under-Secretary for Employment, who managed to define the former by reference to the latter. He offered two main arguments against the proposed amendment. He defined necessary to mean something like "inescapable"—a somewhat strained interpretation—and thus contended that it was too restrictive. Conversely those who favoured the substitution gave an unduly latitudinarian meaning to "justifiable," taking it to denote any explanation not patently specious. The Minister's second

---

[74] Available as at fn 37 above.

[75] As in others—it will be remembered that the DDA, by contrast with the SDA, RRA, and FETO, permits the justification of direct discrimination—and of a failure to make reasonable accomodation.

point was more cogent. He thought "justifiable" connoted a more objective test than "necessary." Both sides in the debate seemed to share the same ends, whilst having conflicting understandings of each other's formulations, . . . the idea of job-relatedness first articulated in *Griggs* is not to be found in the statute; it is understood as *inherent* in the concept of discrimination itself. Bearing in mind that Britain has received the *Griggs* concept of discrimination whilst setting out in a clearer and more systematic manner the sequence in which the reviewing body must make particular legal judgments, it seems appropriate that the justifiability test should require the employer to prove that the practice in question is job-related. This interpretation gives effect to the explanation of the new concept of discrimination offered in the White Paper, which used the phrase "substantially related to job performance" without acknowledging its origin in *Griggs*. It also accords quite strongly with the sense, if not the precise language, of what both sides in the Standing Committee discussions were attempting in their disparate fashions to convey.

Job-relatedness—"a manifest relationship to the employment in question"—means above all that the requirements of the job itself, not the expressed or assumed preferences of customers or other employees must prove the guidelines. Thus it is no justification of a discriminatory practice to argue that it was agreed with trade union representatives, or that its elimination and the employment of non-whites might cause withdrawal of business, strikes or other labour trouble, or would necessitate expenditure on developing new employment criteria. Of course it is more convenient and cheaper to continue existing practices, or to pander to the prejudice of employees or customers, but acquiescence in the discriminatory status quo is precisely what laws against discrimination are designed to disturb. Though these consequences may well ensue, they are precisely the sort of considerations the statute subordinates to achieving equality of opportunity.

Only requirements inherent in the job may be regarded as justifiable. This seemingly abstract concept is in fact quite realistic, for it forces employers at first instance and then tribunals to make a practical appraisal of job content, cocking a sceptical eye at traditional restrictions and the more recent, albeit limited, vogue for credentials and testing. The result will surely be to eliminate many practices that have excluded able people and have been carried on primarily through habit and neglect. In numerical terms, more whites than non-whites will be the gainers. An effective anti-discrimination law is a powerful force for what is truly "rationalisation" of industry—the clearing away of mythologies surrounding employment practices, and their replacement by prerequisites that demonstrably help select the most competent people. . . .

The justification provision is an integral part of the compromise of principle embodied in the Act. Had an unalloyed "fair share" approach been taken, the mere under-representation of minorities would have been proscribed. The reason for their disadvantage would have been irrelevant. However, the statute also accepts that industrial efficiency (and fair treatment of qualified whites) are values which should not be trampled in the pursuit of racial equality. the tension between the two competing considerations can be satisfactorily resolved by a rigorous and sceptical approach towards efforts at justification. This would require firm evidence that the challenged practice actually enhanced industrial safety or efficiency. This sort of scrutiny would ensure the maximum scope for both industrial efficiency and racial equality, and achieve the greatest possible reconciliation between them where they conflict.

Notwithstanding Lustgarten's early commentary, the test of justification turned out to be rather less than rigorous. His discussion was concerned with the RRA but the

SDA, whose approach to indirect discrimination is identical, has been in place for slightly longer. (Northern Ireland's fair employment regime has only prohibited indirect discrimination since 1989.) But since the mid–1970s, and prior to any rulings being made expressly in the light of EC law and its impact, in particular, on the SDA, the approach of the courts to justifiability under the SDA and RRA appeared to diverge.

In *Steel* v *Union of Post Office Workers and others*, for example, EAT considered, as a case arising under s.1(1)(b) SDA, a complaint concerning the application by the Post Office of what should have been regarded as a directly discriminatory seniority requirement in allotting "walks" (women having, until 1975, been barred from gaining such seniority). On the matter of justification, EAT ruled as follows:

Steel v *Union of Post Office Workers and others* [1978] 2 All ER 504, [1978] 1 WLR 64, [1978] ICR 181, [1977] IRLR 288

Phillips J

There is no doubt that the onus of proof here lies on the employer, and that it is a heavy onus in the sense that before it is discharged the industrial tribunal will need to be satisfied that the case is a genuine one . . . The question is what considerations are relevant and proper to be taken into account when determining whether the requirement or condition was justifiable . . .[76]

. . . It may be helpful if we add a word of detail about what we consider to be the right approach to [the question of justifiability]. First, the onus of proof lies on the party asserting this proposition, in this case the Post Office. Secondly, it is a heavy onus in the sense that at the end of the day the industrial tribunal must be satisfied that the case is a genuine one where it can be said that the requirement or condition is necessary. Thirdly, in deciding whether the employer had discharged the onus the industrial tribunal should take into account all the circumstances, including the discriminatory effect to the requirement or condition if it is permitted to continue. Fourthly, it is necessary to weigh the need for the requirement or condition against that effect. Fifthly, it is right to distinguish between a requirement or condition which is necessary and one which is merely convenient, and for this purpose it is relevant to consider whether the employer can find some other and non-discriminatory method of achieving the object.

. . . a practice which would otherwise be discriminatory (which is the case here) is not to be licensed unless it can be shown to be justifiable, and it cannot be justifiable unless its discriminatory effect is justified by the need, not the convenience, of the business or enterprise
. . .

In *Panesar* v *Nestle Co Ltd* [1980] ICR 144, [1980] IRLR 64, by contrast, the Court of Appeal accepted the employer's argument that a "no beards" rule which excluded Sikhs from employment was justifiable under s.1(1)(b)(ii) of the RRA on grounds of

---

[76] "Furthermore, it is necessary as far as possible to construe the [SDA] and the [EqPA] so as to form a harmonious code", citing EAT's decision in *Snoxell* v *Vauxhall Motors Ltd* [1977] 3 All ER 770, [1978] QB 11, [1977] 3 WLR 189, [1977] ICR 700: "The onus of proof under s 1(3) [of the EqPA] is on the employer and it is a heavy one".

hygiene, despite the fact that the employer did not prohibit the wearing of "moustaches, whiskers and sideburns". According to Lord Denning MR:

> ... The scientific evidence was all in support of the practice which the Nestle company had adopted in their factory at Hayes as a matter of pure hygiene. It had nothing to do with the colour of the individual or his religious beliefs. It applied to all men of all races ... the industrial tribunal held that the rule about the wearing of beards was justifiable. ... It seems to me that that finding was essentially one of fact in the circumstances of the case, against which there is no appeal except on a point of law.

The approach to justification in this case was extraordinarily lax, the tribunal and the Court of Appeal appearing to ask simply whether the alleged discriminator had been improperly motivated. It is hard to see how beards could be considered unhygienic *per se*, while other forms of facial hair were viewed as acceptable even if uncovered.[77]

In *Ojutiku and Oburoni v Manpower Services Commission*, the Court of Appeal once again ruled that the test for justification under the RRA did not, contrary to EAT in *Steel*, require that the employer prove that the requirement was necessary for the good of his business.

Ojutiku and Oburoni v Manpower Services Commission [1982] ICR 661 [1982] IRLR 418

Eveleigh LJ:

> ... I am very hesitant to suggest another expression for that which is used in the statute, for fear that it will be picked up and quoted in other cases and then built upon thereafter, with the result that at the end of the day there is a danger of us all departing far from the meaning of the word in the statute. For myself, it would be enough simply to ask myself: is it justifiable? But if I have to give some explanation of my understanding of that word, I would turn to a dictionary definition which says "to adduce adequate grounds for"; and it seems to me that if a person produces reasons for doing something, which would be acceptable to right-thinking people as sound and tolerable reasons for so doing, then he has justified has conduct.

At issue in *Ojutiku* was a requirement that candidates for student bursaries had managerial experience, a requirement which had a disproportionately exclusionary impact on West African applicants. Notwithstanding the evidence that the applicants' lack of experience was the result of direct discrimination on the part of would-be employers, the Court of Appeal accepted that the requirement was justified:

Eveleigh LJ:

> What the respondents have to justify is their own conduct, not that of other people. If it is justifiable to require a qualification, although it is discriminatory in the indirect sense, in

---

[77] See also *Kang*, fn 68 above, in which a refusal to permit a woman wearing a Sikh bracelet to work on a sensitive part of the food production line was regarded as justifiable on grounds of hygiene, no consideration having apparently been given to the possibility of covering the offending item.

my opinion it could not alter the position if the qualification were made impossible of attainment by the act of another. The latter's discrimination would be in no way the responsibility of the respondents; it would of course be deplorable, but that is another matter. Many people are without the necessary qualifications for certain pursuits—indeed, most of us are without the necessary qualifications for something or another. Some lack them through their own fault; some through misfortune or lack of opportunity, but that is life; and if an employer imposed a similar qualification to that imposed in this case by the Commission, one could not expect him to waive it in the case of a person who lacked the qualification through misfortune, even if that misfortune were to be discrimination against him by another.

Kerr LJ

. . . In *Steel* . . .[EAT] . . . put something of a gloss on the word "justifiable" by suggesting that it was equivalent, or close to having the same meaning as "necessary". But that gloss was rightly shaded, to put it no higher, by another decision of [EAT] in *Singh* v *Rowntree MacKintosh Ltd*, [1979] IRLR 199 . . . in which the approach was in effect that "justifiable" means "reasonably necessary in all the circumstances" . . . I decline to put any gloss on the word "justifiable", which is a perfectly easily understandable ordinary word, except that I would say that it clearly applies a lower standard than the word "necessary" . . .

Problems of consistency began to appear in the wake of the ECJ's decision in *Bilka-Kaufhaus* (Case C–170/84) [1986] ECR 1607 in which that Court, in the context of an Article 141 claim, ruled that disparately impacting pay practices were permissible only where they "correspond to a real need on the part of the undertaking, are appropriate with a view to achieving the objectives pursued and are necessary to that end".

The approach of the ECJ was adopted, in the context of the EqPA, by the House of Lords in *Rainey* v *Greater Glasgow Health Board* [1987] 1 AC 224, further discussed in chapter 10.[78] Neither *Bilka-Kaufhaus* nor *Rainey* were decisions on the meaning of s.1(1)(b)(iii) of the SDA, much less on the RRA or the FEA (as it then was). But it was accepted by the Court of Appeal in *Shields* v *Coomes* [1979] 1 All ER 456 (1978), discussed in Chapter 10) that the SDA and the EqPA should be interpreted "as far as possible . . . so as to form a harmonious code".[79] In *Rainey*, Lord Keith of Kinkel for the House of Lords stated that there was no "material difference in principle" between indirect discrimination under the EqPA and SDA.

The House of Lords decision in *Hampson* v *Department of Education and Science* was considered above. Their Lordships overturned the decision of the Court of Appeal ([1990] 2 All ER 25, [1989] IRLR 69, [1989] ICR 179), which had accepted the Department's s.41 argument. But they expressly refrained from dealing with the issue of justifiability. The Court of Appeal, by contrast, had found against the Department on the justification issue after considering the effect of the decisions in *Bilka-Kaufhaus* and *Rainey*. Balcombe LJ (for the Court) categorised the approaches of Eveleigh and

---

[78] Their Lordships accepted that justification could be established by reference to "administrative efficiency" as well as economic reasons.

[79] Citing Phillips J in *Steel*.

Kerr LJJ in *Ojutiku* as of "little help", neither in his view indicating "what tests should be applied" in reaching the "value judgment" inherent in the words "[j]ustifiable" and "justify".

Balcombe LJ

whatever test is to be applied it is an objective one: it is not sufficient for the employer to establish that he considered his reasons adequate. However I do derive considerable assistance form the judgment of Stephenson LJ [who] referred to:

> . . . the comments, which I regard as sound, . . . given by Phillips J in *Steel v Union of Post Office Workers* . . . What Phillips J there said is valuable as rejecting justification by convenience and requiring the party applying the discriminatory condition to prove it to be justifiable in all the circumstances on balancing its discriminatory effect against the discriminator's need for it. But that need is what is reasonably needed by the party who applies the condition . . .

In my judgment "justifiable" requires an objective balance between the discriminatory effect of the condition and the reasonable needs of the party who applies the condition. This construction is supported by the recent decision of the House of Lords in *Rairey* . . . The House of Lords held, applying the decision of the European Court in *Bilka-Kaufhaus* . . ., that to justify a material difference under s 1(3) of the [EqPA], the employer had to show a real need on the part of the undertaking, objectively justified, although that need was not confined to economic grounds; it might, for instance, include administrative efficiency in a concern not engaged in commerce or business. Clearly it may, as in the present case, be possible to justify by reference to grounds other than economic or administrative efficiency. . . .

Nourse LJ agreed with Balcombe LJ that the best interpretation which could be put on the authorities was that the test: "requires an objective balance to be struck between the discriminatory effect of the requirement or condition and the reasonable needs of the person who applies it. If, and only if, its discriminatory effect can be objectively justified by those needs will the requirement or condition be 'justifiable' within s.1(1)(b)(ii) of the [RRA]."

The approach taken by the Court of Appeal in *Hampson* was not endorsed by the House of Lords in that case. While their Lordships expressly refrained from considering the justification issue, the parties not having argued it before them, Lord Lowry did remark that "what was said in the Court of Appeal [in *Ojutiku* on the issue of justification] seems to me to merit the closest attention". But in *Webb v EMC* [1992] 4 All ER 929, [1993] 1 WLR 49, [1993] ICR 175, the House of Lords approved the approach taken by Balcombe LJ for the Court of Appeal in *Hampson*.

Balcombe LJ's approach did mark a significant improvement over that taken in *Ojutiku*. Many practices which serve disproportionately to exclude women and ethnic minorities from the workforce have been practised by many employers over many years (preference for full-time employees and for those who can work "flexibly" to suit the employer,[80] age and experience stipulations, IQ testing,[81] clothing and appearance

---

[80] This requires childlessness or the presence of a (usually female) support at home.
[81] Such tests are frequently culturally skewed—see *Griggs*, above.

rules[82]) and are therefore, of their very nature, capable of being explained in a manner "acceptable to right-thinking people as sound and tolerable". The same practices, if scrutinised in the light of their impact on those excluded by them, may appear in a different light.[83]

The ECJ in *Bilka-Kaufhaus* framed the test of "objective justification" (by which it required that indirect sex discrimination be justified) in terms of necessity (disparately impacting practices being justifiable only where they "correspond to a real *need* on the part of the undertaking, are appropriate with a view to achieving the objectives pursued and are *necessary* to that end"). The test established by the Court of Appeal in *Hampson* fell short of this, replacing a requirement for business necessity with a demand for balance between the *reasonable* needs of the employer[84] and the discriminatory impact of the requirements or conditions adopted. It is likely, even under the test as it was established in *Bilka-Kaufhaus*, that the selection of the ends necessary to an undertaking would be treated as a matter in respect of which employers should be accorded a significant degree of autonomy. In this sense, the ends *necessary* to the undertaking might be interpreted as those ends which an employer could reasonably regard as necessary. By contrast, where the pursuit of those ends has a disproportionately negative impact on women, ethnic minorities, etc., the means chosen should be subjected to rigorous scrutiny.[85]

Turning to the application, in practice, of the *Hampson* test, there have been a number of cases in which the courts have ruled against employers on this issue. In *London Underground Ltd v Edwards*, for example (the facts of which are set out above), EAT upheld a tribunal decision that the employers had failed to justify a shift system with which women were less able than men to comply (and with which the applicant, as a lone parent, was unable to comply).

London Underground Ltd v Edwards

Mummery J (for EAT)

The tribunal referred to the "Single Parent Link" scheme proposed . . . to assist employees in the position of the applicant and to its disbandment in September 1992 because agreement on it could not be reached with the unions . . .

> From the fact, as we have found, that a scheme for single parents was contemplated, it is clear that the employer regarded such a scheme as feasible. Provisions could have been made, without significant detriment to the savings sought to be made, for single parents like the applicant to be catered for.

---

[82] Which may impact particularly on those bound by religious obligations concerning appearance which are (see Chapters 7), race-related.

[83] This was applied by the Northern Ireland Court of Appeal in *Kennedy* v *Gallagher Ltd* (discussed in the FEC review, para 1.22): "in measuring the reasonable needs of the employer significant weight should be given to the fact that the majority of the workforce suffered no detriment by resaon of the requirement".

[84] In this the decision in *Hampson* echoed that of Browne-Wilkinson J (as he then was) in *Jenkins* v *Kingsgate* (2) [1981] 1 WLR 1485, [1981] ICR 715, [1981] IRLR 388.

[85] Some support for this can be found in the approach taken by the ECJ in relation to social policy of member states and the means used to pursue it, see above.

[Counsel for LUL] submitted that these statements ignored the question whether a scheme of positive discrimination in favour of a small sector of the workforce was feasible, if the workforce as a whole, through its elected representative, opposed it. There was no evidence or reasoning to support the conclusion that provision could, in those circumstances, have been made to cater for single parents. The tribunal failed to address questions as to why the law should require the employer to give single parents preference in rostering over other categories of employees, such as those with sole responsibility for a disabled spouse or partner, or sole responsibility for an infirm parent, or those who have care of children shared with a spouse or partner who is a night security guard, or for those who experience serious strain on a marriage or relationship as a result of working unsocial hours. The tribunal failed to consider whether the [SDA] compelled the employer to require those of its workforce who are not single parents to work more night shifts than average in order to allow a privileged class of single parents to avoid night shifts altogether, and whether, if the tribunal's reasoning is correct, this in turn might give rise to sex discrimination claims by the disadvantaged majority. The adverse effect of the new rostering on the applicant had to be balanced against the reasonable needs involved in introducing the company plan with its attendant saving of £10m a year and doing so without creating anomalies and inequalities between categories of the workforce . . .

We agree with the applicant that it was for the employer to satisfy the tribunal that the requirement was justifiable. That was an issue of fact and degree which cannot be disturbed on appeal if the tribunal directed themselves, as they did, to the correct test, and came to a conclusion for which there was some evidence . . . In our view, the tribunal were entitled to come to the conclusion on that evidence that it was feasible to cater for single parents or those with primary care of children who were able to work social hours, without significant detriment to the objectives of the employer to achieve savings. The tribunal took account of the need of the employer to make savings and found that there was no significant detriment. In our view, there was no error of law in the tribunal's treatment of this issue.

When the case returned to EAT a freshly constituted tribunal having applied the correct pool for comparison, Morison J found that the second tribunal had correctly applied *Hampson* in deciding that the imposition of the disputed shift system was not justified. The tribunal had ruled that:

> We have to consider the needs of the respondents and their objectives to save money and to be more efficient and on the other hand the discriminatory effect it had on the applicant and others who were single parent carers. We find from these facts that the respondents could have easily, without losing the objectives of their plan and reorganisation, have accommodated the applicant who was a long-serving employee. They were aware of her particular difficulties quite early on and after the failure of the single parent link in September 1991, she had set out her misgivings and her difficulties in writing to the management. *They did not address themselves to these issues* [my emphasis] and therefore we find that they have not justified this act of discrimination."

London Underground Ltd v Edwards (No 2) [1997] IRLR 157

Morison J:

There was evidence to justify the conclusion that London Underground could—and, we would add, should—have accommodated Ms Edwards's personal requirements. She had been working for them for nearly ten years. Her family demands were of a temporary nature. There were no complaints about her work, which she appeared to enjoy . . . there was good evidence that London Underground could have made arrangements which would not have been damaging to their business plans but which would have accommodated the reasonable demands of their employees. It may be that London Underground would have wished to implement the single parent link but gave in to pressure from their predominantly male workforce.

We would wish to add three observations. In the first place, employers should recognise the need to take a reasonably flexible attitude to accommodating the particular needs of their employees. In a case such as this, had it been obvious that London Underground could have accommodated Ms Edwards's needs, without any difficulty or expense, there might have been a case for alleging direct discrimination. Changing the roster in a way which they must have appreciated would cause her a detriment might have justifiably led to an inference that they had treated her less well than they would have treated male train operators who had been in a similar position. In other words, the more clear it is that the employers unreasonably failed to show flexibility in their employment practices, the more willing the tribunal should be to make a finding of unlawful discrimination . . .

Second, in many cases, an employer will be able, readily, to justify a roster system, even if people with childcare responsibilities could not sensibly be accommodated within it. But the lesson from this case is that employers should carefully consider the impact which a new roster might have on a section of their workforce.

Third, nothing we have said in this judgment should be construed as favouring positive discrimination. Such discrimination is unlawful, and for what it is worth, none of the members of this court would wish the position to be otherwise.

In *London Underground* the employers failed to take a reasonable step which they had themselves identified (and which, as EAT pointed out, would have involved no "difficulty or expense") in order to reduce the impact of the disputed requirement on the applicant. It would be difficult to argue that such a failure was justified. This is true also in cases where employers simply refuse to engage with an employee's representations in respect of an indirectly discriminatory practice. So, for example, in *Oddbins Limited* v *Robinson* (EAT/188/96, unreported), EAT rejected an appeal against a finding of discrimination in favour of an applicant whose request to job-share her position as branch manager of an off-licence on her return from maternity leave was refused by her employers. She applied for the job-share because of the impossibility of arranging childcare consistent with her contractual obligation, as a full-time manager, "to work such [additional unpaid] hours as may be necessary to carry out your duties to the satisfaction of the company".

Oddbins Limited v *Robinson (EAT/188/96, unreported)*

Buckley J (for EAT):

The real debate before us, as indeed it is recorded as having been understood by the tribunal, was whether the respondents could justify the clause. . . . The respondents had to show that its reasonable needs outweighed the discriminatory effect of the condition . . . the general proposition that flexible hours in a contract, particularly a contract of this type—namely covering the employment of a branch manager of an off-licence—is a clause that may be necessary to give effect to the efficient running of the business, is a proposition that this tribunal would readily accept. What went wrong here from [Oddbin's] point of view . . . was that their evidence was discredited in the eyes of the tribunal . . Some of the evidence . . . was held to be just plain wrong by reference to other objective criteria. Other areas of the evidence was found to be evasive and equivocal . . . individuals looking into the question had done so with closed minds, and had not fairly given consideration to the matter in hand. Finally, that some relevant evidence on cost had simply not been placed before the tribunal . . .

It may well be that had the respondents given fair-minded consideration to alternative means of operation, which was what was in question, in particular job sharing, and had they, to put in bluntly, got their house in order and placed sensible credible evidence before the tribunal, they might well have satisfied them that job sharing was not an acceptable way to run their branches. We cannot comment further on that, but it would not surprise this tribunal if the matter arose again, Oddbins were able to satisfy a different tribunal of that without too much difficulty.

It follows from what we have said that this decision should not be taken as any precedent at all about job sharing in general, none even so far as Oddbins own business is concerned.

It is clear from Buckley J's judgment (and, indeed, from those of Morison J and Mummery J in the *London Underground* decisions) that, however apparently rigorous the test established by the ECJ in *Bilka-Kaufhaus* and which the Court of Appeal in *Hampson* purported to adopt, in practice the burden of justification is relatively easy to satisfy. Tribunals will find themselves overruled where they expressly apply the *Ojutiku* approach and ask only whether the employer's action was "acceptable to right-thinking people as sound and tolerable".[86] But, as the cases extracted below will show, the application in practice of the *Hampson* approach appears to have little to distinguish it from that in *Ojutiku*.

One example of this can be seen in the decision of Northern Ireland's Court of Appeal in *Briggs v North Eastern Education and Library Board*. The case concerned a school's refusal to permit a teacher to switch badminton coaching from after school to lunchtime, or to retain her scale 2 position (awarded in respect of "additional duties" including "assist[ing] with extra-curricular school games") without undertaking that coaching (which a tribunal found as a matter of fact comprised only a small part of these additional duties). Mrs Briggs, having adopted a baby, could not continue to coach games after school and she claimed indirect discrimination under s. 3(1)(b) SDA (discrimination against married persons). A tribunal upheld her complaint but Northern Ireland's Court of Appeal (to which appeals from tribunals go directly in Northern Ireland) overturned the decision.

---

[86] See, for example, *Hellewell v Manchester Metropolitan University* (EAT/835/95, unreported), *Furber v Wirral Borough Council* (EAT/1141/96, unreported) and *Eddy & Others v Cassette & Record Services Ltd* (EAT/790/93, unreported), all available on *Lexis*.

Briggs v North Eastern Educational Library Board [1990] IRLR 181

Hutton LCJ

[citing the decision of the tribunal] "the respondent's evidence was that it was not acceptable for the girls to have badminton practice at lunchtime since that did not allow sufficient time for proper practice sessions to be undertaken . . . that the only effective way of developing badminton within the school was to provide for badminton practice after school. In addition, as noted above, the school had decided that an appropriate way of developing badminton within the school was to provide badminton practice at the local leisure centre where there were more courts than at the school and thus greater opportunities for all the girls to have longer periods of practice at each session . . . the majority of the Tribunal noted that [the employers had not] . . . considered the possibility of re-organising the duties of the applicant's post or providing for some other method which would be acceptable of fulfilling the requirements relating to badminton. This was in spite of evidence that the duties of other scale posts had previously been changed in individual cases". . .

the Tribunal concentrated on how the school authorities negotiated with the respondent without, it appears, paying regard to the most important question, which was whether badminton coaching in the lunch hour would or would not be for the advantage of the girls whom it was intended to benefit. Furthermore, we consider that the points made by the majority of the Tribunal . . . that the coaching duties were a minor part of the contract and that the duties were not clearly defined do not support their conclusion that the attitude of the appellant was unjustifiable . . . Coaching games, even if a minor part of the contract, is a not unimportant function in a school and it was at no time suggested by the respondent that badminton coaching did not constitute part of her duties. Moreover we consider that the term "extra-curricular school games" means that games may be played after school hours. Indeed it is quite clear that at the time the respondent entered into the contract with the school authorities they both did so on the basis that her duties would be to take badminton practice and that both understood that she would continue to take the practice in the afternoon after school hours as she had done in the past.

Accordingly we consider, applying the test stated by the Court of Appeal in *Hampson's* case, that the reasonable needs of the appellant that badminton practice should be conducted in the interest of the school and for the benefit of the girls clearly necessitated that the badminton practice should not be carried out in the lunch break but should be carried out in the afternoon after school, and that the discriminatory effect of the requirement applied to the respondent was clearly objectively justified by those needs.

For all the Court of Appeal's articulated obeisance to *Hampson*, the Lord Chief Justice gave little appearance of attempting to balance the impact of the employer's decision against its reasonable needs. This is particularly the case given that the applicant was protesting, not the school's refusal to let her coach during lunchtime, but her demotion in respect of her inability to continue with coaching on their terms, such coaching forming only a minor part of the additional duties required for the higher post. The same failure to balance in fact can be seen in *Bullock v Alice Ottley School* [1993] ICR 138, in which the English Court of Appeal rejected a sex discrimination claim by a domestic worker against her mandatory retirement at 60 in circumstances in which maintenance workers and gardeners were permitted to work until 65.

The school had originally set retirement ages at 65 for men and 60 for women. When this was rendered unlawful, a retirement age of 60 was set in respect of domestic workers (who were all women) and teachers (all but two of 70 were women) while the retirement age for the (exclusively male) maintenance workers and gardeners was set at 65. A tribunal and the Court of Appeal (overruling EAT) rejected the applicant's direct discrimination claim on the basis that women were not prevented from applying for employment as gardeners or maintenance staff (all refused to draw any conclusions from the remarkable consistency between retirement ages applied in relation to individual employees prior to and after the change of rules required under the SDA). On the issue of indirect discrimination, the Court of Appeal ruled that the disparate impact by sex of the retirement ages did not prevent their being justified.

Bullock v *Alice Ottley School* [1993] ICR 138

Neill LJ

It was argued on behalf of the applicant that the only reasonable conclusion that the industrial tribunal could have reached on the evidence was that she was the victim of indirect discrimination. There was no need for the school to require that the applicant should retire at 60. I am unable to accept this argument. The general retiring age adopted at the school was 60. I do not understand that this general retiring age was the subject of criticism. The later retiring age of 65 was applied for personnel who worked as gardeners or members of the maintenance staff. The question is: was this later retirement age for this group of the staff objectively justified?

Neill LJ referred to the requirement imposed by *Hampson* "that an objective balance should be struck between the discriminatory effect of the condition and the reasonable needs of the party who applied the condition", and cited the decision of the House of Lords in *Rainey*.

As the law stands at present, it seems to me to be clear that in order to justify a later retirement age for a group which in fact though not by design consists wholly or largely of men it is necessary for the employer to show a real and genuine need for this later retirement age. It is further clear, however, that that need is not confined to economic grounds but may include administrative efficiency and possibly other grounds . . .

In the present case the industrial tribunal accepted the bursar's evidence that a later retirement age for the gardeners and the maintenance staff was necessary because of the difficulty of recruiting such staff and the need to retain them as long as possible. As compared with a gardener the applicant was undoubtedly indirectly discriminated against. But this indirect discrimination was justified by the needs of the school . . . the industrial tribunal's acceptance of the bursar's evidence enables this court to reach a clear conclusion on indirect discrimination.

It may well have been the case that the school needed to retain maintenance staff and gardeners (though no evidence of this was apparent except for the bursar's statement). But the Court did not question why, in light of the retirement age permitted these (male) staff, the school nevertheless adopted a "general retiring age" of 60, this retirement age applying almost exclusively to women.

Finally it is useful to consider the decision of the Court of Appeal in *Jones* v *University of Manchester* (the facts of which are set out above). The tribunal had found against the university on the justification issue, ruling that the reasons put forward by the university for imposing a maximum age limit (35) on the particular appointment were inadequate to balance the discriminatory impact of the limit on women. EAT overruled the tribunal on the basis that it had "effectively dismissed the matters relied upon by [the university] once it was demonstrated that they were not essential". The University had put forward two factors in support of the application of an upper age-limit to the particular careers adviser post for which Ms Jones had applied, arguing that (1) it was desirable that careers advisers be "not too far removed in age from the students"; (2) there was a need to achieve a better spread in the ages of advisers in the department whose staff were presently aged 62, 63, 54, 47, 45 and 42. The Court of Appeal upheld EAT's decision:

University of Manchester v Jones [1993] ICR 474, [1993] IRLR 218

Ralph Gibson LJ (with whom the others concurred)

The test for deciding whether application of a requirement is justifiable . . . turns upon balancing the reasonable needs of the University for application of the requirement: it does not require proof of necessity.

I agree that . . . the [tribunal] was at least setting a perilously high standard of proof of reasonable need . . . On this ground alone, however, I am not confident that this Court could properly hold that the conclusion of the [tribunal] on justification could not stand. The [tribunal] had formulated the test correctly and I think that the matters complained of may properly be regarded as matters of expression rather than substance.

The second error on the part of the [tribunal] with reference to justification was, accordingly to the majority in the EAT, that the balancing of the grounds of justification put forward by the University as against the effect of the requirement was carried out subjectively instead of objectively: not objectively in relation to mature women students in general, but subjectively to the particular case of Miss Jones and other women who had suffered under her disadvantages. Further, the discrimination that was found to exist was towards only a very small proportion of the total of eligible women graduates, namely about 3% of the total number of eligible women.

For my part, I cannot find any real assistance in the concept of subjective or objective assessment of the discriminatory effect of the requirement in a case of this nature. The [tribunal] is required to determine the discriminatory effect of the requirement. That seems to me to require the IT to ascertain both the quantitative effect, ie how many men and women will or are likely to suffer in consequence of the discriminatory effect; and, also, what is the qualitative effect of the requirement upon those affected by it, ie how much damage or disappointment may it do or cause and how lasting or final is that damage?

I therefore do not agree that it is improper in the balancing exercise to take into account the particular hardships which have lain in the way of the particular applicant, provided that proper attention is paid to the question of how typical they are of any other men and women adversely affected by the requirement. That, I think, is what the [tribunal] did. . .

Nevertheless, in my judgment, the [tribunal] did misdirect itself in carrying out the balancing exercise. As against the reasonable needs of the University, the [tribunal] must set the discriminatory effect of the application by the University of the requirement to Miss Jones and any others excluded by it. If, contrary to my view, the [tribunal] was entitled to hold as it did that the application of the requirement to Miss Jones was indirectly discriminatory . . . yet in carrying out the balancing exercise it was necessary, in my judgment, for the [tribunal] to keep in mind the process by which their conclusion was made out and, in particular, that the women in that small section of the total number of graduates represents a small proportion of the total of eligible women graduates . . .

For the reasons I have already stated, I consider that the [tribunal] was entitled to assess as it did the effect upon "women like Miss Jones" of the impact of such a requirement when, after finally getting their degrees, they are excluded from suitable employment by an age bar. I share the [tribunal's] view of the nature of such an obstacle upon mature women graduates generally. It is, however, clear that the [tribunal], in carrying out the balancing exercise, was putting into the scale their assessment of the impact of such a requirement upon the "thousands of women enrolled as mature students in English universities who will not obtain their degree until they are aged 30 or more and that many of them will come up against the obstacle of gaining the type of employment for which those qualifications make them suitable if such a requirement or condition as the one applied by the [University] to [Miss Jones] in this case is imposed". Thus, in my judgment, the [tribunal] was placing in the balance the discriminatory effect of this requirement if permitted to be applied by employers. That was not right. This is not a case concerned with the potential effect of age requirements generally or of a university seeking to justify an age limit for general or normal recruitment of a particular class of employee. It was claiming to justify the imposition of an age requirement on this occasion of recruiting a replacement to fill one permanent post, enlarged to two permanent posts in the circumstances described, for a department which has, in addition, to the director and his deputy, seven careers advisers. The discriminatory impact is not to be measured for this purpose with reference to the impact upon the thousands of women mentioned by the [tribunal]. The indirect discrimination as established to the satisfaction of the [tribunal] was upon a small section of the total relevant number and with reference to the selection upon one occasion of two recruits to the careers advisory department of the University. There was thus, in my judgment, misdirection by the [tribunal] in the conduct by them of the balancing exercise in their consideration of the issue of justification . . .

A very significant area of indirect sex discrimination concerns return to work after maternity leave. Many women find it impossible to return to full-time work as a result of childcare difficulties (cost and availability, particularly in relation to the increasing number of jobs which require (employer-defined) "flexible" working). Other women find that the very long hours required by their employers mean that, regardless of how much they can afford to spend on childcare, continuing with "full-time" work is not compatible with adequate parenting of their child(ren). In theory, this is an issue equally applicable to men. In practice, and with occasional exceptions, women absorb the bulk of responsibility for parenting.

The difficulties experienced by new mothers make the operation of indirect discrimination law of particular importance in relation to full-time work requirements.

A number of potential difficulties were canvassed above, in relation to the question whether the woman (and others) "can comply" with the requirement to work full-time. Even in those cases where women do satisfy tribunals as to the other technical requirements imposed by s.1(1)(b), many claims fail on the justification issue. The suggestion made by EAT in *Clymo* was that a requirement of full-time working would, almost automatically, be justifiable in relation to all but the most menial jobs. Whether or not the courts would embrace this as a principle it seems that, as long as employers are seen to have applied their minds, however superficially, to accommodating a request to work part-time (or to job-share, or alter their working hours), refusals will be regarded as justified.

One example of this can be seen in *Eley* v *Huntleigh Diagnostics Ltd*, in which the appeal tribunal considered an indirect discrimination claim by a woman whose request for altered hours (made because of her difficulty in scheduling child-care) was rejected. She worked as a telephonist/receptionist for a manufacturing company, and wished to change her hours from those of the sales department (9.30 am to 5.30 pm Monday to Thursday and 9.00 am to 5.00 pm on Fridays, in each case with an hour for lunch) to those of the manufacturing department (8.30 am to 5.00 pm Monday to Thursday, with a half hour lunch, and 8.30 am to 1.30 pm on Fridays). The refusal of her repeated request for a change in hours (latterly to part-time) resulted in her resignation.

Eley v Huntleigh Diagnostics Ltd, EAT/1441/96 (unreported, 1st Dec. 1997)

Lindsay J (for EAT) [having cited Bilka-Kaufhaus *and* Hampson*]*

The onus as to justifiability is upon the employer. He is required to justify his measure upon an objective balance being struck between the discriminatory effect of the condition he has applied and his reasonable needs, objectively regarded. In the striking of that balance the three-fold test proposed in *Bilka-Kaufhaus* is to be taken as an important guide . . . the Appellant's case here is that the Industrial Tribunal merely paid lip service to that correct test but, in truth, applied some other and more subjective a test. It is first convenient to look at the reasons which the . . . Tribunal itself expressly mentioned . . . the Industrial Tribunal, considering whether Ms Eley's requests had, indeed, been fairly considered by the company, was, in effect, holding that it was, in general, likely that the request had been fairly considered as the company was the kind of employer who, in general, did take care over its employees' needs.

Secondly, the Industrial Tribunal paid particular attention to the nature of Ms Eley's work in relation to the commercial needs of the company. She was more, they held, than "just a receptionist" . . . The company had taken the view that continuity and familiarity with customers made it essential for there to be a full-time receptionist. The company also feared that Ms Eley's request might set a precedent which, if acceded to, would make administration difficult. The . . . Tribunal also had evidence from which they concluded . . . [that]:

> there would have to be taken into consideration the training costs and the appointment of a further employee to cover the applicant who herself on occasions might be unavailable for work, which would give rise to potential further difficulties in cover of

a sufficient quality and standard . . . the employer in considering the requests in the light of the needs of the company decided on good grounds that anything other than a full time employee filling the receptionist position would result in disruption of customer continuity which would be detrimental to the company's business . . . this was a company which was based essentially on telesales where the receptionist provided a vital role in that area and also in the supporting role of clerical assistant. We consequently are of the view that the condition which was discriminatory was nevertheless objectively justifiable.

The Appellant has, on balance, failed to persuade us that that represents a subjective test. The good grounds are found not merely because the company said they were so and believed them to be so, although that cannot be wholly left out of account, but because the Industrial Tribunal had received evidence as to, *inter alia*, the disruption which would result from Ms Eley not working the full hours of the sales department . . . there was in, our view on balance evidence such that the Industrial Tribunal could have concluded that the application of the requirement that Ms Eley should work until 5.00 pm on Fridays and not work part-time did correspond with a real need of the company, namely the need to ensure that in a business very dependent on the telephone there would only be one experienced receptionist (and a well-informed one at that) to field and allocate enquiries so that customers would, throughout the Sales Department hours, deal with only one respondent, however frequently they needed to make contact. That we might have concluded differently upon the same evidence is utterly immaterial. As to the appropriateness of the condition (working the full hours of the Sales Department) as a means of achieving that end, there was evidence from which the Industrial Tribunal could have concluded that it was entirely appropriate in that such condition would, if satisfied achieve the objective sought, would do no more than achieve the objective sought and had, in any event, been made clear to Ms Eley from the moment that the variation in her hours had been considered.

As to whether the term was necessary, which is perhaps the very heart of the appeal, it is to be remembered that, even in our domestic statutes the word "necessary" can, taking colour from its context, mean nothing more exacting than "really needed" . . . *Bilka-Kaufhaus* is not to be approached as if the judgment of the European Court of Justice was a statute. Whether a condition is "necessary" and where precisely the meaning needs to be put for the word "necessary" in the spectrum . . . from "useful" at the one end to "indispensable" at the other, is very much a matter best left to the Industrial Tribunal. It is not to be adjudged by considering whether some other approach, however impractical or inconvenient, could have avoided the application of the particular condition in question and whether, in that sense, the condition could be said to be unnecessary.

Here, looking to see what evidence the Industrial Tribunal received, we see from the Chairman's notes and from the witness statements expressions on subjects such as these:- These days you cannot afford to lose or confuse customers; that the company had looked at Ms Eley's request from all aspects; that it was not suitable for sales or reception not to be available to 5.30 pm; that another member of the sales staff could not be switched as he or she would have been required to be at his or her sales desk; that to employ someone just for Friday afternoons would cause huge problems; that it was essential for the receptionist to have a fundamental knowledge of the organisational structure of the business and a knowledge of the products and the customer base; that it was essential to have continuous cover; that there would be a significant breakdown in communication if the company had two part-time telephonists; that the company placed great importance on continuity and familiarity with customers and it was considered that a full-time receptionist was essential.

In this, as in the other cases discussed above, it is difficult to ascertain any attempt to balance the "needs" of the employer against their discriminatory impact. Nor is it clear why the employers were able to rely on the cost of training a second worker as a justification for refusing to permit the applicant to work part-time, where the result of that refusal was that they would have to train her replacement. Indeed, it is ironic that the applicant here, by having made herself indispensable to her employers, had placed herself in a position where they apparently took the view that they would rather not employ her at all than employ her part-time. The very finding of the tribunal that hers was not a job that could be done part-time turned, it appeared, on her employer's testimony as to quite how marvellous an employee the applicant was.

In *Eley*, as in *Briggs* and *Bullock*, it seems that disparately impacting practices are accepted as justified largely because employers have decided that they are necessary, and this despite the lip-service paid to the balancing requirement. The impact of this is particularly problematic in the context of attempts by women to job-share or to work part-time, given that it is precisely the resistance of many employers to countenance anything other than full-time working in jobs with any degree of responsibility and/or status which accounts for the damage done to women's careers by childbearing.

The gap between the formal adoption of *Hampson* by a tribunal and its application in practice of the *Ojutiku* approach was one of the grounds of appeal in *Nelson* v *Chesterfield Law Centre* (EAT/1359/95, unreported) as it was in *Eley*. There, a solicitor challenged a Law Centre's refusal to permit her to take on a post on a job-share basis. A grant had enabled the law centre to create an additional post. Prior to the creation of that post there were three solicitors, one of whom had a co-ordinating role involving development and administrative work and who did not perform individual case work. On receipt of the grant, the workers' committee of the centre favoured splitting the co-ordinator's role between development and administrative work with the latter being performed by an incoming office manager. They were overruled by the management committee which preferred that the co-ordinator absorb the new duties in respect of which the grant was made, but that her work should then be shared with a new "co-ordinator (development work)". It was for this latter post that the applicant unsuccessfully applied to do on a part-time or job-share basis, being turned down on the ground that the job was full-time.

When challenged, the law centre claimed that the requirement that the new position be performed by a single, full-time worker was justified on the grounds (1) that the "post is sharing tasks and responsibility for tasks with the current co-ordinator and it is envisaged that the two post holders will jointly undertake tasks and allocate tasks between them. The two post holders will have to work very closely together and it was felt that it would be more difficult to achieve this level of co-operation between the posts if the new post was split", and (2) that "the new post will be working within a geographical area not previously served by the Law Centre. A vital part of the development work is to establish links with agencies, groups, politicians and other workers in the area. The success of this work will depend on the new post holder developing links within the area and extending those links to other Law Centre workers. That process already requires a high level of co-ordination and was again a consideration when deciding whether this job could be split."

A tribunal rejected Ms Nelson's indirect discrimination claim. The tribunal did consider the impact of the full-time work requirement as well as the "needs" of the employer. Distinguishing "quantitative" from "qualitative" effects they concluded that the former were "by any standards small"—this turning on the fact that, while "there was nothing in the original advertisement to deter potential part-timers or job-sharers", all 31 applicants with the exception only of Ms Nelson applied to work full-time. As to the "qualitative" effects (i.e., those on the applicant herself):

> she suffered no humiliation in that she was not rejected on her merits and she had qualifications which fitted her for many other part-time jobs. On the other hand she was entitled to think that she was very well suited and qualified to work in a law centre which was confirmed subsequently by the fact that she now has a job at Sheffield Law Centre . . . from the covering letter [in which the applicant stated that her child care responsibilities permitted her to work only on a part-time or job-share basis] . . . the applicant appears to have been deliberately "setting up" the respondents for this present application and to that extent we do not think that she was surprised by her rejection[87]. We conclude that the discriminatory effect was by any standards at the lower end of the scale.

The reasoning of the tribunal can only be described as extraordinary. The decision, on the one hand, read into those 30 applications other than Ms Nelson's a choice to work full-time (this choice being discerned from the failure of the advertisement expressly to require full-time work, coupled with the failure of the other 30 applicants expressly to state an inability to work full-time). On the other hand, the tribunal's conclusion that Ms Nelson was "setting-up" the employers can only have been drawn from the fact that she applied to do, on a part-time or job-share basis, a job which the tribunal regarded as having impliedly been offered exclusively on a full-time basis. Further, the humiliation or lack of humiliation involved in the applicant's rejection was surely a matter for consideration in relation to remedy, rather than in determining whether she had been discriminated against. However hurt or otherwise Ms Nelson may have been, the fact was that the full-time work requirement imposed by the Law Centre denied her the opportunity to be considered for the job for which, in the tribunal's own view, she was "very well suited and qualified".

The tribunal's reasoning in relation to the needs of the employer was scarcely more satisfactory. The tribunal noted that the reorganisation could have occurred in line

---

[87] This comment is difficult to understand . The "covering letter" stated merely that she was not able to work full-time due to child-care responsibilities but would like to be considered for part-time work or job-share.

with the recommendation of the workers' committee, in which case "there would have been an opportunity for part-time or job-share which would have been hard to resist".

> However, the respondents are entitled to make their own management decisions and it is not appropriate for us to impose our ideas as to how their business should be run. . . . We bear in mind that it is always easy for an organisation to raise objections to job-share although in our experience once a decision to adopt job-share has been taken, the previous objections often turn out to be groundless. We think that job-share could have been accepted in the present case and we think it would have probably worked satisfactorily. Nevertheless, that is not the proper basis for our decision and we have to remind ourselves of the tests set out above.
>
> The majority of us accept that the respondents gave consideration to the question of job-share although we are conscious that nobody attempted to persuade them to adopt the idea. However, the majority of us feel that the respondents were justified in their decision to insist on a full-time employee. It seems to that the respondents were entitled to have regard to the fact that the job was to be shared with [the co-ordinator] and that a further division of responsibility would be unsatisfactory . . .

The minority member dissented on the ground that:

> . . . the respondents did not have a properly formulated equal opportunities policy and in particular that they did not follow what he understands to be the local authority's guide-lines on job-share. In his experience local authorities insist that whenever practicable all jobs should be offered for job-share and he feels that a law centre that is publicly funded should adopt that practice themselves as an example to other employers . . .

EAT rejected the applicant's appeal:

Nelson v *Chesterfield Law Centre* (EAT/1359/95 unreported)

Peter Clark J (for EAT):

There was and is no dispute as to the correct legal test to be applied when considering justification. . . the tribunal directed themselves in accordance with the test formulated by Balcombe LJ in *Hampson* . . . [and] the guidance to be found in the judgment of Ralph Gibson LJ in *Jones* v *University of Manchester* [above] . . . Ms Mountfield [for the applicant] accepts that the correct [*Hampson*] test for establishing justification is set out [by the tribunal]. However she submits that the majority did not in fact apply that test. Instead they approached the question in the way that the Court of Appeal did in *Ojutiku* . . . She relies upon the tribunal's observation that in their view job-share could have been accepted in the present case and would probably have worked satisfactorily, and submits that in applying the *Bilka-Kaufhaus* test, as adopted in *Hampson* . . . the tribunal ought to have applied its own view that the full-time requirement was not objectively necessary, instead of considering whether the employer was entitled to conclude that a full-timer was needed. On this analysis, submits Ms Mountfield, the tribunal have applied the incorrect *Ojutiku* . . . test . . . In our judgment there is nothing . . . to suggest that the majority misapplied the true test of justification, or departed from the test which it set itself . . . It was entitled to conclude that the two reasons advanced by the respondent justified the requirement . . .

Some of the difficulties associated with attempting to balance working and family life will be addressed by the implementation in the UK of the directives on part-time work and on parental leave (directives 97/81/EC and 96/34/EC), which are further discussed in Chapter 6.

The application of the justification test was, for a period, at its most rigorous in the UK[88] where the courts have considered disparately impacting conditions imposed by central government, rather than by employers. In *R v Secretary of State for Education, ex p Schaffter* [1987] IRLR 53, for example, the High Court ruled that the practice of restricting additional lone-parent student "hardship grants" to those who had been married impacted disadvantageously upon women, a far greater proportion of them than of men being never-married lone parents. The High Court ruled that this amounted to a breach of the equal treatment directive. In that case, the Secretary of State had failed even to put forward a purported justification. But in *R v Secretary of State for Employment ex p. EOC*, in which the House of Lords struck down, as in breach of Article 141, the application of differential qualifying periods in respect of unfair dismissal protection and redundancy payments to full-time and part-time workers, the justification put forward by the Secretary of State was dismissed by their Lordships.

R v Secretary of State for Employment ex p. EOC [1995] 1 AC 1, [1994] 1 All ER 910, [1994] 2 WLR 176, 92 LGR 360, [1994] ICR 317, [1994] IRLR 176

Lord Keith (for the court):

In the *Bilka-Kaufhaus* case the European Court said ... "It is for the national court, which has sole jurisdiction to make findings of fact, to determine whether and to what extent the grounds put forward by an employer to explain the adoption of a pay practice which applies independently of a worker's sex but in fact affects more women than men may be regarded as objectively justified on economic grounds. If the national court finds that the measures chosen by Bilka correspond to a real need on the part of the undertaking, are appropriate with a view to achieving the objectives pursued and are necessary to that end, the fact that the measures affect a far greater number of women than men is not sufficient to show that they constitute an infringement of Article [141]."

Somewhat broader considerations apply where the discriminatory provisions are to be found in national legislation [citing *Rinner-Kühn*, above] ... The original reason [for the differential qualifying periods] ... appears to have been the view that part-time workers were less committed than full-time workers to the undertaking which employed them. In his letter of 23 April 1990 the Secretary of State stated that their purpose was to ensure that a fair balance was struck between the interests of employers and employees ... It is now claimed that the thresholds have the effect that more part-time employment is available than would be the case if employers were liable for redundancy pay and compensation for unfair dismissal to employees who worked for less than 8 hours a week or between 8 and 16 hours a week for under five years. It is contended that if employers were under that liability they would be inclined to employ less part-time workers and more full-time workers, to the disadvantage of the former.

---

[88] *Cf* the approach taken by the ECJ, discussed elsewhere in the chapter.

The bringing about of an increase in the availability of part-time work is properly to be regarded as a beneficial social policy aim and it cannot be said that it is not a necessary aim. The question is whether the threshold provisions . . . have been shown, by reference to objective factors, to be suitable and requisite for achieving that aim. As regards suitability for achieving the aim in question, it is to be noted that the purpose of the thresholds is said to be to reduce the costs to employers of employing part-time workers. The same result, however, would follow from a situation where the basic rate of pay for part-time workers was less than the basic rate for full-time workers. No distinction in principle can properly be made between direct and indirect labour costs. While in certain circumstances an employer might be justified in paying full-time workers a higher rate than part-time workers in order to secure the more efficient use of his machinery (see *Jenkins* v *Kingsgate (Clothing Production) Ltd* Case C–96/80 [1981] ECR 911, [1981] 1 WLR 972) that would be a special and limited state of affairs. Legislation which permitted a differential of that kind nationwide would present a very different aspect and considering that the great majority of part-time workers are women would surely constitute a gross breach of the principle of equal pay and could not possibly be regarded as a suitable means of achieving an increase in part-time employment. Similar considerations apply to legislation which reduces the indirect cost of employing part-time labour. Then, as to the threshold provisions being requisite to achieve the stated aim, the question is whether on the evidence before the Divisional Court they have been proved actually to result in greater availability of part-time work than would be the case without them. In my opinion that question must be answered in the negative. The evidence for the Secretary of State consisted principally of an affidavit by an official in the Department of Employment which set out the views of the Department but did not contain anything capable of being regarded as factual evidence demonstrating the correctness of these views. . . . no other member state of the European Community, apart from the Republic of Ireland, ha[s] legislation providing for similar thresholds . . . In the Netherlands the proportion of the workforce in part-time employment was in 1988 29.78% and in Denmark 25.75%, neither country having any thresholds similar to those in the 1978 Act. In France legislation was introduced in 1982 providing for part-time workers to have the same rights as full-time, yet between 1983 and 1988 part-time work in that country increased by 36.76%, compared with an increase of 26.71% over the same period in the United Kingdom. While various explanations were suggested on behalf of the Secretary of State for these statistics, there is no means of ascertaining whether these explanations have any validity. The fact is, however, that the proportion of part-time employees in the national workforce is much less than the proportion of full-time employees, their weekly remuneration is necessarily much lower, and the number of them made redundant or unfairly dismissed in any year is not likely to be unduly large. The conclusion must be that no objective justification for the thresholds in the 1978 Act has been established.

A similar approach was taken by the Court of Appeal in *ex parte Seymour-Smith & Perez*, in which that Court considered an argument that the increase in qualifying period for unfair dismissal in 1985 from one year to two constituted unlawful discrimination (under Article 141) against women:

R v Secretary of State for Employment, ex p. Seymour-Smith & Perez [1995] ICR 995 (CA)

Neill LJ:

. . . The question for the court is whether on the evidence the threshold of two years has been proved to result in greater availability of employment than would be the case without it. . . . Before us, as before the Divisional Court, the Secretary of State relied upon a number of studies. They are examined in detail in the judgments below. That examination led the Divisional Court to the conclusion that the Secretary of State had not proved his case. No suggestion has been made in front of us by Mr Richards that the judges below had misunderstood any of the material or that their criticisms of it as proof were ill-founded. Indeed, he accepts that there is no empirical evidence directed towards the specific issue of the effect of moving from a one-year to a two-year threshold. He submits that in so far as there is evidence that unfair dismissal rights do substantially affect employment opportunities then it is reasonable to infer that the increase of the threshold from one year to two years must increase employment opportunities to some degree. His approach is similar to that adopted in argument on behalf of the Secretary of State in the *EOC* case.

However, we have found nothing in the evidence, either factual or opinion, which obliges or enables us to draw the inference that the increase in the threshold period has led to an increase in employment opportunities . . .

We have come to the conclusion that on the evidence before us the Secretary of State has failed to prove that the increase in the threshold has increased employment opportunities. On that evidence the threshold of two years is neither suitable nor requisite for attaining the aim of increased employment. It follows that this discriminatory measure has not been justified.

The House of Lords overturned the decision of the Court of Appeal, three of the five Law Lords basing their decision on the issue of justification. According to Lord Nicholls, who delivered the leading speech:

Ex p. Seymour-Smith & Perez (No. 2) [2000] IRLR 263

the test applied by the Court of Appeal was whether the threshold of two years had been "proved to result" in greater availability of employment than would have been the case without it. The Court of Appeal declined to incorporate into this formulation any margin of appreciation: . . .

The answer given by the European Court to the fifth question referred to the court by this House has now shown that this test was too stringent. The burden placed on the government in this type of case is not as heavy as previously thought. Governments must be able to govern. They adopt general policies, and implement measures to carry out their policies. Governments must be able to take into account a wide range of social, economic and political factors. The European Court has recognised these practical considerations. If their aim is legitimate, governments have a discretion when choosing the method to achieve their aim. National courts, acting with hindsight, are not to impose an impracticable burden on governments which are proceeding in good faith. Generalised assumptions, lacking any factual foundation, are not good enough. But governments are to be afforded a broad measure of discretion. The onus is on the member state to show (1) that the allegedly discriminatory rule reflects a legitimate aim of its social policy, (2) that this aim is unrelated to any discrimination based on sex, and (3) that the member state could reasonably consider that the means chosen were suitable for attaining that aim.

There is no difficulty with the first two requirements. The object of the 1985 Order was to encourage recruitment by employers. This was a legitimate aim of the government's social and economic policy, and this aim was unrelated to any sex discrimination. Whether the third requirement was satisfied in 1985 is more debatable. In March 1985 the Secretary of State, Mr. Tom King, stated with regard to the proposed change in the qualifying period:

> The risks of unjustified involvement with tribunals in unfair dismissal cases and the cost of such involvement are often cited as deterring employers from giving more people jobs. This change which now puts all new employees on the same basis as that already existing for those small firms should help reduce the reluctance of employers to take on more people.

The relevant question is whether the Secretary of State was reasonably entitled to consider that the extension of the qualifying period should help reduce the reluctance of employers to take on more people.

This question raises an issue of fact, to be decided on the basis of the extensive documentary evidence adduced by the parties . . . On balance, I consider the Secretary of State discharged the burden of showing his view was reasonable. It is apparent that obtaining hard evidence, including evidence of employer perceptions, is essentially a difficult task in this field. But this is not a case of a mere generalised assumption, as occurred in *Rinner-Kühn* . . . Here, there was some supporting factual evidence. To condemn the minister for failing to carry out further research or prepare an impact analysis . . . would be unreasonable . . .

The requirements of Community law must be complied with at all relevant times. A measure may satisfy Community law when adopted, because at that stage the minister was reasonably entitled to consider the measure was a suitable means for achieving a legitimate aim. But experience of the working of the measure may tell a different story. In course of time the measure may be found to be unsuited for its intended purpose. The benefits hoped for may not materialise. Then the retention in force of a measure having a disparately adverse impact on women may no longer be objectively justifiable. In such a case a measure, lawful when adopted, may become unlawful.

Accordingly, if the government introduces a measure which proves to have a disparately adverse impact on women, the government is under a duty to take reasonable steps to monitor the working of the measure. The government must review the position periodically. The greater the disparity of impact, the greater the diligence which can reasonably be expected of the government. Depending on the circumstances, the government may become obliged to repeal or replace the unsuccessful measure.

In the present case the 1985 Order had been in operation for six years when the two claimants were dismissed from their jobs. The Divisional Court and the Court of Appeal noted there was no evidence that the extension of the qualifying period in 1985 led to an increase in employment opportunities. Ought the government to have taken steps to repeal the 1985 Order before 1991? In other words, had the Order, lawful at its inception, become unlawful by 1991?

Here again, the matter is debatable. As time passed, the persistently adverse impact on women became apparent. But, as with the broad margin of discretion afforded to governments when adopting measures of this type, so with the duty of governments to monitor the implementation of such measures: the practicalities of government must be borne in mind. The benefits of the 1985 Order could not be expected to materialise overnight, or even in a matter of months. The government was entitled to allow a reasonable period to elapse before deciding whether the Order had achieved its objective and, if not, whether the Order should be replaced with some other measure or simply repealed. Time would then be needed to implement any decision. I do not think the government could reasonably be expected to complete all these steps in six years, failing which it was in breach of Community law. The contrary view would impose an unrealistic burden on the government in the present case. Accordingly I consider the Secretary of State discharged the burden of showing that the 1985 Order was still objectively justified in 1991.

The focus in this section has been on indirect sex discrimination, rather than indirect discrimination on grounds of race, disability or, in Northern Ireland, religion or political opinion. There is an abundance of appellate decisions, post-*Hampson*, dealing with the justifiability of indirect discrimination under the SDA while decisions under the RRA and FEA (now the FETO) are scarce. Some of the early RRA decisions on justifiability are considered above.[89] Another is *Barclays Bank* v *Kapur & Others No.2)* [1992], in which EAT ruled that a pension fund rule which had been applied in order to prevent double recovery in respect of pensionable service accrued by Asians expelled in the "Africanisation" of Tanzania and Kenya was justifiable. (The applicants had been paid off on termination of their employment, and subsequently re-employed in the UK on the basis that their African service did not count. Overruling a tribunal decision in favour of the applicants, Tucker J for EAT declared that it was "clearly justifiable" for the bank to take steps to prevent double recovery, "the only question" being whether the particular course adopted by the bank was justifiable (alternatives being open to it):

> There is sufficient evidence to enable us to make a finding (as we do) that the Appellants considered the alternative courses open to them and [took] the course which appeared to be the more appropriate . . . In reaching this conclusion we have applied the test formulated by Balcombe LJ in *Hampson*.

The Court of Appeal upheld EAT's decision ([1995] IRLR 87) without discussion of the appropriate test for justification. In *Board of Governors of St Matthias Church of England School* v *Crizzle* [1993] ICR 401, [1993] IRLR 472, EAT ruled that the restriction of a headteacher post to applicants who were communicant Christians was justified. Dealing with a race discrimination claim from an Asian woman who was, although a Christian, not a communicant,[90] Wood J accepted that the requirement operated disproportionately to exclude Asians from the post but, overruling the tribunal, declared that it was justified:

Board of Governors of St Matthias Church of England School v *Crizzle* [1993] ICR 401

It seems to us, on the authorities, that the approach of an industrial tribunal should be upon the following lines. (a) Was the objective of the governors [who applied the requirement]a legitimate objective? It is not for the industrial tribunal to redraft or redefine the

---

[89] See, for example, *Panesar* v *Nestle, Ojutiku* v *MSC. Cf* the rigorous approach to justification taken by the House of Lords in the pre-Hampson *Orphanos* v *Queen Mary College* [1985] IRLR 349.

[90] It appears from this case that the applicant's own inability to comply with a disputed requirement does not have to be causally related to his or her membership of the group which is less able to comply than others.

objective. In the present case it was to have a headteacher who could lead the school in spiritual worship and in particular the administering of the sacrament at the weekly mass to those who were confirmed. The headteacher should have full membership of the Church in order to foster the Anglo-Catholic ethos of the school. (b) Were the means used to achieve the objective reasonable in themselves? (c) When balanced, on the principles of proportionality between the discriminatory effect upon the applicant's racial group and the reasonable needs of the governors, were they justified? The same tests would apply to any board of governors who restricted the headteacher to being a Jew, or a Muslim, or a Sikh, or a Buddhist or any other religion . . . in the present case the objectives of the governors related to the spiritual practices at St Matthias and its ethos. They thought it to be in the best interests of the school if it was led by a headteacher who assisted at mass and gave communion. All parents seem to have supported this view, whatever their own religious background.

The tribunal had ruled against the school on the basis that the governors had placed the religious ethos of the school over the need for efficient education by "exclud[ing] the possibility of a balanced choice of the most suitable candidate for headteacher", drawing attention in particular to the ethnic and religious mix of the pupils and "the great difficulty in recruiting teachers generally and of appointing headteachers". The tribunal also found as a fact that "the assistance of the headteacher in administration of the sacrament at school mass was a convenience rather than a need, as this could be done by anyone licensed by the bishop".

Wood J:

The test in *Hampson* . . . as approved in *Webb* . . . "requires an objective balance between the discriminatory effect of the condition and the reasonable needs of the party who applies the condition."

Was the objective sought to be achieved a reasonable one of the governors to take? Was the way in which it was sought to achieve it, namely, by imposing the condition, justifiable in the objective sense set out by Balcombe LJ [in *Hampson*]? . . .

We consider that this industrial tribunal did not apply the correct test in *Hampson*, namely, whether the objective of the governors was a reasonable one for them to seek, and whether the way in which they sought to achieve it was justifiable in the sense set out by Balcombe LJ. In determining the need which they assessed, they misdirected themselves and erred in law. It is in the field of worship that the governors' objective was based and it is in that context that the test of justifiability must be applied. In our view, the objective was legitimate and reasonable, the means used to achieve the objective were reasonable and, when balanced on the principles of proportionality between the discriminatory effect upon the applicant's racial group and the reasonable needs of the governors, the objective was justifiable.

In *R* v *The Secretary of State for Social Services ex parte Nessa* (*The Times* 15th November 1994), the Court of Appeal considered the justifiability of the rules on funeral grants which were subsequently challenged before the ECJ in *O'Flynn* [1996] ECR I–2617. The challenge was there brought, unsuccessfully, by a Bangladeshi woman denied reimbursement of that part of her husband's funeral expenses which was incurred in the UK, on the ground that he was buried in Bangladesh. The Court ruled against her on the basis that funeral grants did not fall within the RRA (see further chapter 4), but went on to declare that, had the grants been so covered, their restriction to burials held within the UK would have been unjustifiable.

R v *The Secretary of State for Social Services ex parte Nessa* (*The Times*, 15th November 1994)

Auld J:

As recently stated by the House of Lords in *Webb* . . . the concept of justification in this context requires the court to consider: "an objective balance between the discriminatory effect of the condition and the reasonable needs of the party who applies the condition."

As to the extent of the discriminatory effect, the Secretary of State relies upon the ready availability in this country of Muslim burial place[s]. As to the reasonable needs for the reg 7(1)(c), the Secretary of State's case is that it would be complicated and expensive to administer a scheme to provide, and verify claims for, payments for funeral expenses incurred in this country where the burial is abroad, and that there are many other calls on the United Kingdom Government's resources.

The availability of Muslim burial places in this country does not seem to me to assist on the question of justification if, despite that availability, the requirement were discriminatory. The complications of apportionment of burial expenses between those incurred in this country and those in the place of burial do not seem to me to be of such weight as to justify discrimination if there were any. The principal candidates for payment would be the matters provided for in reg 7(2)(a) to (c), namely documentation, the cost of a coffin and transport within the United Kingdom. It is hard to see why those costs should not be equally and readily payable whether the burial takes place here or abroad.

Leaving aside issues of pay (which are considered in Chapter 10) it appears that the imposition, in relation to particular employees, of full-time and flexible work requirements and age limits will readily be accepted as justifiable by the courts. Again, significant changes will be wrought in this area by the implementation of the EC directives on part-time work and, to a lesser extent, on parental leave. Both are discussed in Chapter 6. Practices such as psychometric testing, which have been demonstrated in the US to have an adverse impact on ethnic minority applicants, have barely been considered here by the courts. And the discriminatory impact of requiring particular qualifications has yet to be the subject matter of any significant litigation in this jurisdiction. It remains to be seen, if and when these race-related factors come before the courts, whether reliance upon them will be as easy to justify to the satisfaction of those courts as reliance on many sex-related factors is today.

VICTIMISATION

Sections 4(1), 2(1), and 55(2) and Article 3(5) respectively of the SDA, the RRA, the DDA and the FETO define, as "discrimination" for the purposes of the various anti-discrimination regimes, less favourable treatment "by reason that the person victimised has—

(a) brought proceedings against the discriminator or any other person under [the relevant Act[91]]; or

(b) given evidence or information in connection with proceedings brought by any person against the discriminator or any other person under [the relevant Act]; or

(c) otherwise done anything under or by reference to [the relevant Act] in relation to the discriminator or any other person; or

(d) alleged that the discriminator or any other person has committed an act which (whether or not the allegation so states) would amount to a contravention of [the relevant Act],

or by reason that the discriminator knows that the person victimised intends to do any of those things, or suspects that the person victimised has done, or intends to do, any of them.

(2) Subsection (1) does not apply to treatment of a person by reason of any allegation made by him if the allegation was false and not made in good faith.

A straightforward application of the victimisation provisions occurred in *Northern Health and Social Services Board* v *Fair Employment Agency*,[92] in which an applicant sued successfully in respect of a remark made by one member of an appointments panel to another to the effect that he had previously made a complaint under the FEA (as it then was). The Fair Employment Agency ruled that the making of the remark amounted to discrimination by way of victimisation "in the arrangements the employer makes for the purpose of determining who should be offered employment". Northern Ireland's Court of Appeal agreed.

Cases such as *NHSSB* v *Fair Employment Agency* aside, the victimisation provisions have not served adequately to protect discrimination complainants from dismissal and other ill-treatment. One difficulty which arises in relation to any provision concerned with the intentions of an actor (here the alleged discriminator) is that of proof. This issue is discussed more generally in Chapter 5, as is the potential significance of Council Directive 97/80, on the burden of proof in cases of discrimination based on sex, which must be implemented in the UK by 22nd July 2001 and of the new race discrimination directive which must be implemented by December 2002. The dif-

---

[91] The SDA also prohibits victimisation in relation to proceedings brought under the EqPA and the sex discrimination provisions of the Pensions Act 1995.

[92] Unreported 20th September 1994, available on LEXIS. See also *Bameih* v *Crown Prosecution Service* 41 EORDCLD, pp.3–4, a case in which "extra care" was written on the interview notes of the applicant, who had previously complained of discrimination, marks were awarded subjectively, no proper records kept and hers was the only performance not properly marked.

ficulties inherent in proving discrimination are not unique to the victimisation provisions. But additional hurdles are imposed in this matter by the interpretive approach taken by the courts to victimisation.

In *Kirby* v *Manpower Services Commission* [1980] IRLR 229, EAT ruled that the victimisation provisions required that the applicant be less favourably treated than a person who had acted similarly, but other than in connection with the relevant Act. Mr Kirby had been demoted because he breached his duty of confidentiality towards client employers by reporting to the Council for Community Relations racially discriminatory actions taken by them. EAT accepted the employer's argument that, as any employee who had "give[n] away information of this kind or information which [was] received in confidence would [have been] treated on broadly the same basis", the victimisation claim failed.

The first victimisation claim to reach the Court of Appeal was *Aziz* v *Trinity Street Taxis Ltd and Ors* [1989] 1 QB 463, [1988] 2 All ER 860, [1988] 3 WLR 79, [1988] ICR 534, [1988] IRLR 204, in which that court characterised as "absurd" the approach taken by EAT in *Kirby*. The Court ruled that a finding of victimisation did not require the complainant to demonstrate that s/he had been less favourably treated than someone who had not done an act under (a)–(d) above ("a protected act"). Slade LJ, for the Court, declared that:

> [a] complaint made in reliance on s 2 necessarily presupposes that the complainant has done a protected act . . . If the doing of such an act itself constituted part of the relevant circumstances, a complainant would necessarily fail to establish discrimination if the alleged discriminator could show that he treated or would treat all other persons who did the like protected act with equal intolerance. This would be an absurd result.

Slade LJ identified as the "clear legislative purpose of s.2(1) . . . to ensure, so far as possible, that victims of racial discrimination shall not be deterred from" seeking redress. This being the case, it might be assumed that the Court of Appeal would replace the *Kirby* test with one more likely to afford protection. But in *Aziz* the Court of Appeal replaced the approach taken in *Kirby* with one whose effect was precisely the same.

Mr Aziz, a taxi driver, formed the view that he was being unfairly treated by TST, a company of which he was a member and which promoted the interests of taxi drivers in Coventry. He was concerned that some of his fellow members who were sympathetic in private would not be so publicly, and he tape-recorded some conversations with them. He subsequently filed a race discrimination complaint as a result of which the existence of the tape recordings became public and, after Mr Aziz's race discrimination complaint was dismissed by a Tribunal, he was expelled from TST. His victimisation complaint was rejected by tribunal, EAT and the Court of Appeal.

The Court of Appeal accepted that Mr Aziz had been treated "less favourably than . . . [TST] treat[ed] other persons" in that he had been expelled from membership. But the industrial tribunal found that the expulsion had been by reason of Mr Aziz's breach of trust, rather than because of any link between his actions and the RRA. This being the case, Slade LJ declared that the less favourable treatment suffered by Mr Aziz could not be regarded as having been:

> by reason that the appellant had (within the meaning of s 2(1)(c)) "otherwise done anything under or by reference to" the RRA . . . on the true construction of s 2(1), if the necessary causal link is to be established, it must be shown that the very fact that the protected act was done by the complainant "under or by reference to" that legislation, influenced the alleged discriminator in his unfavourable treatment of the complainant.[93]

Despite the criticism directed at *Kirby* by the Court of Appeal in *Aziz*, the practical effect of the decisions is the same. Under *Aziz*, Mr Kirby would have had to establish, not that he was less favourably treated than someone who had made the complaint to the CRE, but than someone who had not made a complaint. So far, so good. But Mr Kirby would then have had to establish that his less favourable treatment was *by reason that* his act was connected with (in that case) the RRA (in another case it could equally have been the SDA, DDA or FETO). This, in turn, would have required him to establish that he had been less favourably treated than a person who had acted similarly, but other than in connection with the RRA. Yet this is precisely the test which was applied to him by EAT, but which was dismissed by the Court of Appeal in *Aziz* as "absurd".[94]

The result of the decision in *Aziz*, as it had been of *Kirby*, was that the victimisation provisions did not provide protection in respect of less favourable treatment which an employer can suggest was motivated, however unreasonably, by the complainant's actions themselves, rather than the relationship between those actions and the SDA, RRA or EqPA.

E. Ellis and C.J. Miller, "The Victimisation of Anti-Discrimination Complainants" 1992, *Public Law* 80, 82–4

The earliest reported judicial decisions on the victimisation sections also had the effect of further narrowing the scope of the behaviour caught by the statutory definition, in particular by restrictive construction of the requirement of less favourable treatment. [citing, in particular, *Kirby*] it can perhaps be regarded as symptomatic of a technical rather than purposive attitude of judges to this area of the law.

The decided cases also show that the element of causation can give rise to difficulties for the complainant. In *Cornelius* v. *University of Swansea*, the Court of Appeal held that the victim has to prove not merely victimisation on account of having participated in *any* legal proceedings, but rather on account of participation in *anti-discrimination* proceedings. The Court of Appeal explained the matter rather more fully in the *Aziz* case, saying:

---

[93] See also the decision of the Court of Appeal in *Cornelius* v *University College of Swansea* [1987] IRLR 141.
[94] Albeit in relation to the question whether the applicant had been "less favourably treated", rather than whether that treatment was "by reason of" his having done a protected act.

[W]e are unable to accept that Parliament would have intended that a claimant, in reliance on category (c) of section 2(1), can establish unlawful discrimination within that section, even though the evidence shows that the fact that the protected act had been done under or by reference to the race relations legislation in no way influenced the alleged discriminator in his treatment of the complainant. In such a case, in our judgment, on the true construction of section 2(1), if the necessary causal link is to be established, it must be shown that the very fact that the protected act was done by the complainant "under or by reference to" that legislation influenced the alleged discriminator in his unfavourable treatment of the complainant.

The Court went on to add that:

[A] person can treat another "less favourably than . . .he treats or would treat other persons" within the meaning of the opening words of section 2(1), even though the relevant treatment itself has no racial element. Paragraphs (a), (b), (c) and (d) of section 2(1) however are all concerned with the motive which caused the alleged discriminator to treat the complainant less favourably than other persons. In our judgment paragraph (c) no less than paragraphs (a), (b) and (d) contemplates a motive which is consciously connected with the race relations legislation.

Once again, this conclusion, even if literally accurate, mocks the spirit of the victimisation prohibition. It is surely the act of revenge for having honestly asserted *any* legal rights which ought to ground the action, not revenge for having asserted *particular* legal rights.

The approach to the victimisation provisions has been altered by the recent decision of the House of Lords in *Nagarajan* v *London Regional Transport.* Their Lordships overruled the Court of Appeal's decision (*Nagarajan* v *London Regional Transport* [1998] IRLR 73) to the effect that a victimisation complainant must prove that the less favourable treatment was *consciously* influenced by the applicant's commission of a protected act. An industrial tribunal had found an interview panel's assessment of the applicant, who had taken action under the RRA against the organisation on previous occasions, inexplicable and so, given the knowledge of the interviewing panel members of the background, had felt bound to draw an inference of victimisation. Both EAT and the Court of Appeal disagreed, Peter Gibson LJ for the latter requiring "conscious motivation" on the part of the alleged discriminator. The decision of the House of Lords is likely to have a significant impact on the way in which the courts deal with victimisation claims.

Nagarajan v London Regional Transport [1999] 4 All ER 65, [1999] 3 WLR 425, [1999] ICR 877, [1999] 1 RLR 572

Lord Nicholls

All human beings have preconceptions, beliefs, attitudes and prejudices on many subjects. It is part of our make-up. Moreover, we do not always recognise our own prejudices. Many people are unable, or unwilling, to admit even to themselves that actions of theirs may be racially motivated. An employer may genuinely believe that the reason why he rejected an applicant had nothing to do with the applicant's race. After careful and thorough investigation of a claim members of an employment tribunal may decide that the proper inference to be drawn from the evidence is that, whether the employer realised it at the time or not, race was the reason why he acted as he did . . . If . . . the discriminator treated the person victimised less favourably by reason of his having done one of the acts listed in section 2(1) . . . the case falls within the section. It does so, even if the discriminator did not consciously realise that, for example, he was prejudiced because the job applicant had previously brought claims against him under the Act. In so far as the dictum in *Aziz* ("a motive which is consciously connected with the race relations legislation") suggests otherwise, it cannot be taken as a correct statement of the law.

This was sufficient to deal with the problem presented by the Court of Appeal in *Nagarajan*. But their Lordships went further. Lord Steyn (with whom Lords Hutton and Hobhouse agreed) stated that:

Section 2(1) in effect provides that, in order for there to be unlawful victimisation, the protected act must constitute the "reason" for the less favourable treatment. The contextual meaning of the words "by reason that" is at stake. The interpretation upheld by the Court of Appeal requires that under section 2(1) a claimant must prove that the alleged discriminator had a motive which is consciously connected with the race relations legislation. On the other hand, the interpretation put forward by the applicant merely requires that a claimant must prove that the principal or at least an important or significant cause of the less favourable treatment is the fact that the alleged discriminator has done a protected act . . . If the Court of Appeal's interpretation is accepted, it would follow that motive becomes an ingredient of civil liability under section 2(1). As evidence motive is always relevant. But to make it the touchstone of civil liability would be unusual. Even in criminal law motive is only an ingredient of the offence in exceptional cases . . . the applicant's interpretation . . . contemplates that the discriminator had knowledge of the protected act and that such knowledge caused or influenced the discriminator to treat the victimised person less favourably than he would treat other persons. In other words, it postulates that the discriminator's knowledge of the protected act had a subjective impact on his mind. But, unlike the first interpretation, it is a broader construction inasmuch as it does not require the tribunal to distinguish between conscious and subconscious motivation . . . Quite sensibly in section 1(1)(a) cases the tribunal simply has to pose the question: Why did the defendant treat the employee less favourably? It does not have to consider whether a defendant was consciously motivated in his unequal treatment of an employee. That is a straightforward way of carrying out its task in a section 1(1)(a) case. Common sense suggests that the tribunal should also perform its functions in a section 2(1) case by asking the equally straightforward question: Did the defendant treat the employee less favourably because of his knowledge of a protected act? Given that it is unnecessary in section 1(1)(a) cases to distinguish between conscious and subconscious motivation, there is no sensible reason for requiring it in section 2(1) cases . . .[95]

The Court of Appeal relied strongly on an observation by Slade LJ in *Aziz* v *Trinity Street Taxis Ltd* [above]. The passage in *Aziz* is . . . to the effect that section 2(1) contem-

[95] Moreover, the threshold requirement laid down by the Court of Appeal in respect of section 2(1) cases would tend to complicate the task of the tribunal and would thus render the protection of the rights guaranteed by s.2(1) less effective: see *Coote* v *Granada Hospitality*, below.

plates "a motive which is consciously connected with the race relations legislation." But as the headnote of *Aziz* makes clear the case was decided on a causative approach. In any event, the case pre-dates the decisions of the House of Lords in the *Birmingham* . . . and *Eastleigh* . . . cases [above]. A contemporary reviewer of *Aziz* argued convincingly that in the light of the decision in the House of Lords in the *Birmingham* case the observation of Slade LJ cannot stand[96]. She said . . . that the *obiter dictum* of Slade LJ "wrongly emphasises the underlying motivation of the alleged discriminator rather than the immediate cause of the unfavourable treatment." I agree.

The significance of Lord Steyn's speech is its indication that the motivation of the discriminator is as irrelevant to a victimisation claim as it is to a claim of direct discrimination. In both cases, the applicant merely needs to show that, *but for* his or her either being of a particular sex or racial group (in a claim of direct discrimination) or performing a protected act (in a claim of victimisation), s/he would not have been subjected to less favourable treatment. What remained unclear, even after the House of Lords decision in *Nagarajan* was the question what constituted the "protected act" *but for* the performance of which the victimised person would not have suffered less favourable treatment. Was it (A) the act of bringing legal proceedings, giving evidence in connection with such proceedings, otherwise doing anything "under or by reference to" legislation or alleging that the discriminator or another has contravened legislation? Or was it (B) bringing legal proceedings *under the relevant anti-discrimination legislation*, giving evidence in connection with proceedings *under the relevant anti-discrimination legislation*, otherwise doing anything "under or by reference to" *the relevant anti-discrimination legislation* or alleging that the discriminator or another has contravened *the relevant anti-discrimination legislation*? Only if the answer was (A) could the victimisation provisions be regarded as even beginning to offer protection to those who would pursue their legal rights.

The Court of Appeal in *Aziz* demanded a connection between the specific legislation in connection with which the victimised person acted and the motivation of the discriminator. It was clear from the decision in *Nagarajan* that this *motivation* does not have to be established. But it was still possible that the causal question was linked directly to the particular anti-discrimination legislation under which the victimised person acted.

At this point it is useful to consider how the "but for" test is applied. In order to establish that the victimised person has been discriminated against "by reason that" s/he did the protected act, the treatment accorded to that person has to be compared with that (which would have been) accorded to someone who did not do the protected act. We know from *Aziz*, overruling *Kirby*, that the comparison has to be between the applicant and someone who did not do the act, as distinct from someone who did the act other than in connection with the relevant anti-discrimination legislation. In other words, if an applicant has been dismissed for bringing action under the RRA, the

---

[96] J. Ross, "Reason, Ground, Intention, Motive and Purpose" (1990) 53 *Modern Law Review* 351.

appropriate comparison is with someone who has not taken legal action (as distinct from someone who has taken action, for example, under the SDA or the Employment Rights Act 1996). This being the case, it must be that the question of causation upon which, according to the House of Lords in *Nagarajan*, victimisation turns is: *but for* the fact that the applicant took or assisted legal action, alleged a breach of the law or otherwise did anything else of a legal nature, would s/he have suffered the less favourable treatment of which s/he complains.

This approach has recently been affirmed by the Court of Appeal in *Chief Constable of the West Yorkshire Police* v *Khan*. The case involved a victimisation claim by a police officer who had sued his employers under the RRA. Prior to the tribunal hearing, his employers responded to a request from a prospective employer for a reference which was to the effect that, given the outstanding tribunal application, "the Chief Constable is unable to comment any further for fear of prejudicing his own case before the Tribunal".

An employment tribunal ruled that Mr Khan had been discriminated against contrary to s.2 RRA. Both EAT and the Court of Appeal upheld this decision, rejecting the employer's contention that the appropriate comparison was with someone who "had started proceedings against the respondent on grounds other than racial discrimination". Lord Woolf MR, for the Court of Appeal, stated his "initial reaction" that "as the legislation is concerned with racial discrimination, victimisation which has nothing to do with race is unlikely to be intended to be unlawful under s.4 . . .". Nevertheless, he ruled that s.4 had to be construed in context so as "to prevent those who have taken steps to resist racial discrimination from being victimised in consequence of doing so". Adopting the "but for" test embraced by the House of Lords in *Nagarajan*, and the approach of Slade LJ in *Aziz* to the selection of the appropriate comparator, the Court of Appeal upheld the decision of the employment tribunal that Mr Khan "was treated less favourably [because] . . . he had done a protected act".

Chief Constable of the West Yorkshire Police v *Khan* **[2000] IRLR 324**

Woolf LJ (for the Court)

The correct approach to the application of s.2 in this context is to identify the appropriate comparator, not by looking at the reason why the reference was not provided, but by considering what was requested. Here what was requested was a reference and it is necessary to compare the manner in which other employees in relation to whom a reference was requested would normally be treated and compare the way they would normally be treated with the way in which the respondent was treated. It is the request for a reference which is the circumstance which is relevant in finding the comparator under s.2 of the Act.

The decisions of the House of Lords in *Nagarajan* and of the Court of Appeal in *Khan* have done much to improve the protection afforded by the victimisation provisions of the RRA (and thus, by implication, of the other anti-discrimination legislation). It remains to be seen, however, whether their application in practice will be such that, if *Kirby* and *Aziz* were to be litigated today, their outcomes would differ. *Khan* was a relatively straightforward case in the sense that the police officer was discriminated against because he was taking legal proeedings. But it could not necessarily be said that Mr Kirby would not have been dismissed *but for* his reporting a suspected breach of the law—had he broken confidence in any other circumstances he would, presumably, also have been dismissed. Mr Aziz, too, would have been expelled from TST regardless of whether he was pursuing legal action—the grievance against him related not to the fact of litigation, rather to his action in tape-recording conversations. On the other hand, the generous approach adopted both by the House of Lords in *Swiggs* and the Court of Appeal in *Khan* might be taken to require that the comparators against whom the treatment of these complainants must be judged would be persons who had not breached confidence or trust respectively, rather than those who had done so for any reason concerned with litigation.

The decision of the House of Lords in *Nagarajan* was influenced in part by the recent ECJ ruling, in *Coote v Granada Hospitality Ltd* (Case C–185/97) [1998] All ER(EC) 865 (further discussed in Chapter 4), that the SDA's victimisation provisions were inadequate to comply with the equal treatment directive. Article 6 of the directive requires Member States "to introduce into their national legal systems such measures as are necessary to enable all persons who consider themselves the victims of discrimination 'to pursue their claims by judicial process' ". The shortcoming highlighted in that case related to the lack of protection from retaliation by an ex-employer after the termination of an employment relationship (there by refusing to supply a reference). But the principle of Article 6 is much wider, and was interpreted by the ECJ in that case to require "that the Member States . . . must ensure that the [sex equality] rights . . . conferred [in accordance with the directive] can be effectively relied upon before the national courts by the persons concerned".[97] The decision in *Nagarajan*, to the extent that it overruled the approach taken by the Court of Appeal in that case, goes some way towards achieving that end.

A remaining flaw in the victimisation provisions became apparent in *Waters v Commissioner of Police of the Metropolis*, in which the Court of Appeal rejected a claim brought by a WPC who suffered detriment as a result of her allegation of rape and buggery by a fellow police officer while they were off-duty. Her counsel argued that the SDA: "has to be construed in such a way as to treat as protected acts any allegations which, objectively considered, are aimed at claiming (ie provide the basis for development of a claim for) protection under the equality legislation". For reasons discussed in Chapter 4, the WPC's complaint relating to the assault did not amount to a claim that she had been discriminated against contrary to the SDA.

---

[97] EAT's decision subsequently interpreted the SDA accordingly but noted that *Adekeye v Post Office (No.2)* [1997] ICR 110, [1997] IRLR 105 (discussed in Chapter 4), to the effect that post-employment victimisation would not constitute victimisation under the RRA, still held under that Act.

Waters v Commissioner of Police of the Metropolis [1997] ICR 1073, [1997] IRLR 589

Waite LJ (for the Court of Appeal):

True it is that the legislation must be construed in a sense favourable to its important public purpose. But there is another principle involved—also essential to that same purpose. Charges of race or sex discrimination are hurtful and damaging and not always easy to refute. In justice, therefore, to those against whom they are brought, it is vital that discrimination (including victimisation) should be defined in language sufficiently precise to enable people to know where they stand before the law. Precision of language is also necessary to prevent the valuable purpose of combating discrimination from becoming frustrated or brought into disrepute through the use of language which encourages unscrupulous or vexatious recourse to the machinery provided by the Discrimination Acts. The interpretation proposed by [counsel for WPC Waters] would involve an imprecision of language leaving employers in a state of uncertainty as to how they should respond to a particular complaint, and would place the machinery of the Acts at serious risk of abuse. It is better, and safer, to give the words of the subsection their clear and literal meaning. The allegation relied on need not state explicitly that an act of discrimination has occurred—that is clear from the words in brackets in s 4(1)(d). All that is required is that the allegation relied on should have asserted facts capable of amounting in law to an act of discrimination by an employer within the terms of s 6(2)(b). The facts alleged by the complainant in this case were incapable in law of amounting to an act of discrimination by the Commissioner because they were not done by him, and they cannot (because the alleged perpetrator was not acting in the course of his employment) be treated as done by him for the purposes of s 4(1).

In his concern for the interests of those engaged in victimisation, Waite LJ perhaps exhibited too little regard for the interests of the victimised. From the point of view of the employer, and contrary to Waite LJ's view, it makes no difference whether any allegation made by an employee would, if proven, disclose a breach of the relevant legislation.

According to WPC Water's testimony, she was subject to appalling behaviour in the wake of her rape complaint. She was aggressively treated; transferred between police stations without consultation or the normal periods of notice; her complaint improperly investigated; any semblance of confidentiality related to it breached (this in part resulting in her being ostracised by her colleagues and superior officers). She was transferred from police to civilian duties; denied appropriate time off; her applications for particular placements refused; her personal diary stolen and the theft never investigated. She was given unfair reports; "harassed and unfairly treated" by her superiors; told "that she should leave the police force before she was forced to go"; given the impression that she, rather than her alleged attacker, was under investigation and told that there would be no disciplinary proceedings against him. She was denied back-up and subjected to pornography by her fellow officers. No attempts were made by senior officers to prevent her harassment (in connection with the rape allegation) by her fellow officers. She was not given notice of court appearances and her complaints about this went unheeded. She was threatened with violence by her Chief Superintendent and "quite unjustifiably and with a view to intimidating and harassing her", was required to undergo "psychological analysis" to see if she was "fit for duty". Her paperwork started to disappear and she was advised to leave the force by a colleague in his capacity as Police Federation representative. She eventually took sick leave.

The Court of Appeal's ruling in this case meant that WPC Water's allegations were never proven. But, in view of their seriousness, it is difficult to comprehend Waite LJ's assertion that "[t]he interpretation proposed by [counsel for WPC Waters] would involve an imprecision of language leaving employers in a state of uncertainty as to how they should respond to a particular complaint, and would place the machinery of the Acts at serious risk of abuse". The facts alleged in *Waters* are certainly at the extreme end of the spectrum. But Waite LJ's approach suggests that, in cases other than those which fall within the victimisation provisions, employers have a right, worthy of legal protection, to respond to complaints by subjecting the complainer to ill-treatment.

E. Ellis and C.J. Miller, pp. 80–1

Recent studies have shed light on the prevalence in practice of the victimisation of anti-discrimination complainants. Graham and Lewis, examining the role of ACAS in the conciliation of sex discrimination and equal pay cases, reported that the complainants they interviewed "often came across as morally outraged at the treatment they had received." It became apparent to them that many "were complaining not only about their particular case, but about a culture of job segregation about which, perhaps, they could do little in legal terms. Their objections often revolved around the fact that they were working for bad employers." Graham and Lewis's study was primarily concerned with complainants who had settled or withdrawn their claims. Leonard subsequently embarked on research designed to discover whether successful complainants also suffered similar problems and this project examined all (116) cases in England, Wales and Scotland in which an individual had succeeded in either a sex discrimination or equal pay claim at an industrial tribunal between January 1, 1980, and December 31, 1984. Leonard's conclusions were bleak: commonly workplace relationships deteriorated as soon as applicants filed their case; for several the situation became untenable and they left their jobs, some before the hearing and some afterwards. A number of applicants were dismissed or made redundant because they had brought a case. None of the applicants who were still in their jobs after tribunal hearings found that their working conditions and prospects had improved. Of the many who left their jobs, about one-third of those who looked for new jobs experienced difficulties which they attributed to having taken their tribunal case. Among those who did *not* encounter difficulties, several did not reveal the matter to prospective employers, or did not use their former employer as a reference. "In short, for many, taking a case wholly disrupted their work situation or created a problem in securing other employment, and, for some, did both."

Research has shown extraordinary rates of attrition in relation to sex discrimination and equal pay applicants, both successful and unsuccessful.[98] It remains to be seen

---

[98] A. Leonard, *Pyrrhic Victories: Winning Sex Discrimination and Equal Pay Cases in the Industrial Tribunals, 1980—1984* (London: HMSO, 1987); J Gregory, *Trial by Ordeal: A Study of People Who Lost Sex Discrimination Cases in the Industrial Tribunals in 1985 & 1986* (London: HMSO, 1989).

whether the decisions in *Nagarajan* and *Khan* have any impact on this. Both the CRE and the EOC have recently called for the revision of the victimisation provisions as, in the context of fair employment legislation, did Northern Ireland's Standing Advisory Commission on Human Rights (SACHR). The EOC's 1998 reform proposals state that "there is very little protection for individuals and no effective penalty that would discourage would-be victimisers' and called for a reverse in the burden of proof and the award of an automatic penalty. The CRE called for a statutory reversal of *Waters* to allow a victimisation finding where "the initial complaint of discrimination is . . . made in good faith but . . . because of the limitations of the Act, is held not to constitute a complaint or proceedings "under the Act". SACHR criticised, *inter alia*, the failure of the provisions to cover victimisation of A on the grounds of B's complaint.[99] It as yet unclear what, if any, amendments the government intends to meet these criticisms although the implementation of the burden of proof and the new race discrimination directives will require the reversal of the burden of proof in victimisation claims as in other discrimination claims under the SDA and RRA respectively.[100] The former directive was already in place (although not, as yet, binding on the UK) when the government amended and consolidated the former FEAs into the FETO 1998 (see further Chapter 9). The opportunity was not, however, taken at that time to amend the Northern Irish provisions to render them consistent with the anticipated amendments to the SDA.

[99] This was not given effect in the FETO.

[100] The race discrimination directive also requires that "associations, organisations or other legal entities may pursue any judicial and/or administrative procedure provided for the enforcement of the obligations under this Directive on behalf of the complainant with his or her approval".

3

Positive Action

INTRODUCTION

This chapter considers the extent to which employers in the UK may take steps positively to improve the employment position of those whose disadvantage the Race Relations Act (RRA), Sex Discrimination Act (SDA), Disability Discrimination Act (DDA) and Fair Employment and Treatment (Northern Ireland) Order (FETC) were passed in order to address.

Steps taken in order to redress disadvantage, whether in the labour market or elsewhere, are generally termed "positive discrimination", "affirmative action", "reverse discrimination" or "employment equity". None of these terms has an uncontroverted meaning, and all are as politically controversial as they are linguistically indeterminate.

Of all the terms mentioned, "affirmative action", originally embraced in the US, has the longest vintage. Bell, Hegarty and Livingstone define "affirmative action" broadly to include "any measures which go beyond the prohibition of discrimination and seek to positively alter the composition of a public or private institution, such as a school or workplace [whether those] . . . measures [are] voluntarily undertaken by the institution [or] . . . are imposed upon it".[1] Christopher McCrudden has distinguished "at least three different types of affirmative action":[2]

C. McCrudden, "The Constitutionality of Affirmative Action in the United States: A Note on *Adarand Constructors Inc* v *Pena*" **(1996) 1** *International Journal of Discrimination and the Law* **369**

- Needs-based programmes, such as federal assistance targeted at particular inner city areas, resulting in some racial or ethnic groups benefiting disproportionately because they are disproportionately in need. These are relatively uncontroversial ideologically, particularly if they are seen as an alternative to other (unacceptable) types of affirmative action. They do, however, cost money and at a time of budget cuts, advocating increased funding of such programmes may therefore be politically unacceptable.

[1] C. Bell, A. Hegarty and S. Livingstone, "The Enduring Controversy: Developments in Affirmative Action in North America" (1996) 1 *International Journal of Discrimination and the Law*, 207.
[2] McCrudden distinguishes five different forms in "Rethinking Positive Action" (1986) 15 *ILJ* 219: "eradicating discrimination" in addition to "facially neutral but purposefully inclusionary policies' which is similar to the first of the categories distinguished above, "outreach programmes", "preferential treatment" and, which will be considered further below, "redefining merit".

- Outreach programmes have traditionally been popular across the political spectrum. These programmes are designed to attract qualified candidates from the previously under-represented group in two ways: first, by bringing employment opportunities to their attention and encouraging them to apply; second, by providing training the better to equip them for competing on equal terms when they do apply.
- Preferential treatment is the affirmative action issue which elicits the most heated debate. There are, however, considerable differences under this broad heading, relating to the type of preference accorded, and the situation in which the preference is accorded: for example, a preference where candidates are equally well qualified, as opposed to a preference where the preferred candidate is less well-qualified. There are also different aspects of the employment relationship in which preferences may be used, with some programmes involving preferences only in hiring, while others extend to promotion and lay-offs.

As McCrudden himself makes clear, his third type of affirmative action can be divided into a number of subcategories. At one extreme are "quotas" which, in their most extreme form, are used as a caricature by opponents of affirmative action. At the other end of the spectrum, arguably, is a "tie-break" model whereby, where candidates are equally qualified, the "disadvantaged" candidate (female, disabled, ethnic minority, etc) will generally be appointed.

The term "affirmative action" is used above simply because, globally, it is the most common. "Employment equity" is largely used in Canada, where federal and provincial levels have seen the imposition of obligations on employers to take steps to integrate their workplaces (usually with respect to women, aboriginal and "visible minority" (ethnic minority) employees and the disabled). The term "reverse discrimination" is more frequently reserved for McCrudden's third type of "affirmative action", i.e., deliberate favouring of the "disadvantaged" candidate at the point of recruitment (promotion or redundancy-related dismissal). Terms such as "reverse" or "positive" discrimination are not used in UK legislation. Nor is "affirmative action" save in the context of the FETO where, as we shall see below, it bears a distinct and narrower meaning than it generally does elsewhere. Nevertheless, the expression "positive discrimination" is more familiar here than "affirmative action", although its meaning is no more settled. It will, for that reason, be employed in this chapter with the same meaning as that assigned by Bell *et al* to "affirmative action".

POSITIVE DISCRIMINATION—THE UK POSITION

"Positive discrimination" is not expressly regulated by the SDA, the RRA, the DDA or the FETO. This does not, however, mean that it is lawful. The "symmetrical" approach to discrimination adopted by the SDA, RRA and FETO (although not by the DDA) has the effect that much of what could be defined as "positive discrimination" amounts to direct discrimination and is, therefore, unlawful. The RRA protects white as well as black and Asian people from discrimination on racial grounds. The SDA protects men as well as women. And the FETO applies equally to Protestants and to Catholics. With a very few exceptions (discussed below) "positive discrimination" which consists of the preferential treatment of persons defined along gender, racial (or, in Northern Ireland, religious or political grounds) will breach the relevant anti-discrimination legislation. The legality of acts which amount to indirect discrimination in favour of disadvantage groups is further considered below.

The Disability Discrimination Act 1995

The DDA does not adopt a symmetrical approach, prohibiting discrimination against those with disabilities (currently or in the past), rather than discrimination on grounds of (dis)ability.[3] Private sector employers are free to discriminate in favour of those with disabilities. But it was pointed out by Brian Doyle in 1996 that s.7 of the Local Government and Housing Act 1989 requires that all local authority workers be appointed on the basis of "merit". The Disabled Persons (Employment) Act 1944, which was repealed by the DDA, imposed (almost universally ignored) quotas for the employment of registered disabled people, these quotas being permitted by s.7(2) of the LGHA. Some local authorities practised "priority interviewing" whereby any registered disabled candidate who satisfied the minimum job requirements was interviewed as a matter of course. Such a course of action would not have been unlawful under s.7 of the 1989 Act.

The repeal of s.7(2) LGHA has had a "chilling" effect on local authorities, according to a survey published in the 1998 *Industrial Relations Journal*. The two local authority employers (of six surveyed) who articulated concern over the repeal expressed regret over the removal of what they had regarded as beneficial "priority interviewing" schemes and one was quoted to the effect that:

> The DDA wants employers to do more and be more aware in order to encourage and allow special initiatives and recruitment schemes . . . What of course it has actually done is that the one sector that has taken on this message and tried to put these schemes in place is now prohibited from doing so.[4]

Paragraph 4.66 of the Code of Practice for the Elimination of Discrimination in the Field of Employment Against Disabled People provides:

> The [DDA] does not prevent posts being advised as open only to disabled candidates. However, the requirement . . . under Section 7 . . . that every appointment to local authorities must be made on merit means that a post cannot be so advertised. Applications from

[3] Save in the case of victimisation.

[4] I. Cunningham and P. James, "The Disability Discrimination Act—an early response of employers" (1988) 29 *Industrial Relations Journal* 304. S. 729 HA does, however, provide that the duty to appoint on "merit" is subject to the duty of reasonable adjustment imposed by ss. 5(2) and 6 DDA (see further Chapter 8) as well as to the SOQ provisions of the SDA and RRA (see Chapters 6 and 7 respectively).

disabled people can nevertheless be encouraged. However, this requirement to appoint "on merit" does not exclude the duty under the [DDA] to make adjustments (see further Chapter 8) so a disabled person's "merit" must be assessed taking into account any such adjustments which would have to be made.[5]

The question of whether "positive discrimination" should be permitted, in what form and in what circumstances, is further addressed below. First it is useful to consider the limited extent to which UK legislation currently permits any such discrimination. That discrimination expressly permitted by UK anti-discrimination legislation will be called "positive action" in order to distinguish it from positive discrimination which is not permitted, or the legality of which is in doubt.

The Sex Discrimination Act 1975 and Race Relations Act 1976

The SDA and RRA (ss.47 and 48, and 37 and 38 respectively) expressly permit "positive action" in limited circumstances by training bodies and employers. Ss.48 SDA provides:

> (1) Nothing . . . shall render unlawful any act done by an employer in relation to particular work in his employment at a particular establishment in Great Britain being an act done in or in connection with—
>   (a) affording his female employees only, or his male employees only access to facilities for training which would help to fit them for that work; or
>   (b) encouraging women only, or men only to take advantage of opportunities for doing that work at that establishment . . .

S.48(2) also permits trade unions and employers' organisations, in limited circumstances, to provide single-sex training for posts within the organisation and to encourage applications for posts from men or women and s.48(3) permits sex-targeted recruitment drives in the same circumstances. S.38 RRA is in similar terms.[6] The circumstances under which such "positive action" is permitted are that (in the SDA context) "at any time within the twelve months immediately preceding the doing of the act there were no persons of the sex in question among those doing that work or the number of persons of that sex doing the work was comparatively small". The RRA (s.38(1)) permits such positive action "where any of the conditions in subsection (2) was satisfied at any time within the twelve months immediately preceding the doing of the act". Those conditions are (s.38(2))

> (a) that there are no persons of the racial group in question among those doing that work at that establishment; or

---

[5] The relationship between s.7 LGA and the DDA was considered by EAT in *London Borough of Hillingdon* v *Morgan* EAT/1493/98 27th May 1999, discussed in Chapter 8 and available at www.employmentappeals.co.uk

[6] S.38(3) and (5) RRA echo s.48 (2) and (3) SDA.

(b) that the proportion of persons of that group among those doing that work at that establishment is small in comparison with the proportion of persons of that group-
  (i) among all those employed by that employer there; or
  (ii) among the population of the area from which that employer normally recruits persons for work in his employment at that establishment.

Ss.47 SDA and 37 RRA permit targeted training by persons other than employers along lines similar to those provided by ss.48 SDA and 38 RRA in cases of under-representation in "particular work" either nationally or in the relevant local area. Crucially, however, ss.47(4) SDA and 37(3) RRA disapply this provision in relation to "any discrimination which is rendered unlawful by" s.6 SDA and s.4 RRA respectively. This has the effect of prohibiting race and sex preferences in the allocation of apprenticeships, which are defined as a form of employment under the SDA and the RRA. Ss.47(4) SDA and 37(3) RRA were inserted by the Sex Discrimination Act 1986, which widened ss.47 SDA and 37 RRA by permitting training by "any person", as distinct from those especially accredited for the purpose. But the narrowing effect of ss.47(4) SDA and 37(3) RRA was significant. Prior to 1986, it was at least arguable that apprenticeships could be awarded under ss.47 SDA and 37 RRA.[7] More recently, the CRE has called for the express inclusion within "training" of legal training contracts in an effort to remedy the racial imbalance in access to the legal profession.[8]

In addition to the sex-specific training and advertising allowed by ss.47 and 48 SDA, s.47(3) of that Act provides that:

> Nothing . . . shall render unlawful any act done by any person in, or in connection with, affording persons access to facilities for training which would help to fit them for employment, where it reasonably appears to that person that those persons are in special need of training by reason of the period for which they have been discharging domestic or family responsibilities to the exclusion of regular full time employment.

While this section is couched in sex-neutral terms, the disproportionately female composition of those taking time out of the workforce in connection with domestic or family responsibilities means that this provision is potentially significant for women in particular.

The employment-related "positive action" provisions of the SDA and the RRA fit McCrudden's second type of affirmative action—"outreach" programmes. It is important to note that these provisions do not in any event permit discrimination in

---

[7] Although the CRE did call in 1985 for express legislative provision to this end. This call went unheeded, the 1986 Act making it clear that apprenticeships were not subject to positive action by the inclusion of ss.37(3) and 47(4).

[8] Further discussed in Chapter 7. S.35 RRA also permits any act done in affording persons of a particular racial group access to facilities or services to meet the special needs of that group in relation to their education, health, welfare or any other ancilliary benefit. This might cover special black sections in the Labour Party (note the lack of equivalent to s.33 SDA, discussed in Chapter 4). As is clear from the decision in *Hughes* v *London Borough of Hackney*, discussed by McCrudden below, s.35 RRA does not apply in relation to employment.

terms of access to jobs (as distinct from encouragement to apply for them). By contrast, the non-employment related provisions of the SDA do allow some affirmative action of McCrudden's third type. Whereas trade unions are generally prohibited from discrimination under the SDA, s.49 allows them to reserve female seats on elected bodies "where in the opinion of the organisation th[is] is in the circumstances needed to secure a reasonable lower limit to the number of members of that sex serving on that body". S.33 SDA provides that political parties may discriminate by making special provision for persons of one sex only in the constitution, organisation or administration of the political party. This section, however, operates only in relation to s.29's prohibition on discrimination in the provision of goods, services, etc. In *Jepson* v *Labour Party* [1996] IRLR 116, an industrial tribunal ruled that single-sex shortlists, being in breach of s.13 SDA (discussed in Chapter 4) were not saved by s.33. None of the other discrimination legislation contains an equivalent to s.33. But the RRA (s.35) permits any act done in affording persons of a particular racial group access to facilities or services to meet the special needs of that group in relation to their education, health, welfare or any other ancillary benefit. This might cover special black sections in the Labour Party but does not cover employment (see further McCrudden, below).

The Fair Employment and Treatment (Northern Ireland) Order 1998

The FETO appears to go far beyond the SDA and RRA in permitting positive discrimination. Article 4 defines "affirmative action" as:

> action designed to secure fair participation [undefined] in employment by members of the Protestant, or members of the Roman Catholic, community in Northern Ireland by means including—
> (a) the adoption of practices encouraging such participation; and
> (b) the modification or abandonment of practices that have or may have the effect of restricting or discouraging such participation.[9]

Article 5 defines "equality of opportunity" under the FETO as "ha[ving] the same opportunity [in terms of employment or occupation] . . . as [an]other person has or would have . . . due allowance being made for any material difference in their suitability". Article 5 goes on to stipulate:

> (3) . . .a person is not to be treated as not having the same opportunity as another person has or would have by reason only of anything lawfully done in pursuance of affirmative action.

[9] Whereas the direct and indirect discrimination and the victimisation provisions of the FETO extend protection beyond Catholic and Protestant to anyone discriminated on grounds of "religious belief or political opinion", those provisions dealing with "fair participation" and "affirmative action" concern themselves only with the "two communities". Such is the overriding significance of the Protestant/ Catholic divide in Northern Ireland that a very old and familiar joke concerns a Jewish person quizzed as to whether s/he is a "Protestant Jew" or a "Catholic Jew".

(5) Any reference in this Order to the promotion of equality of opportunity includes a reference to the promotion of affirmative action and, accordingly, any reference to action for promoting equality of opportunity includes a reference to affirmative action.

Northern Irish employers may engage in "affirmative action" at will and are not constrained by the under-representation requirements imposed by the RRA and SDA. In addition, where mandatory workforce monitoring (see further Chapters 5 and 9) discloses an actual or anticipated lack of "fair participation" on the part of either Catholics or Protestants, employers must (Article 55) "determine the affirmative action (if any) which would be reasonable and appropriate". Such action may include the establishment of goals and timetables to set out the "progress towards fair participation in employment in the concern that can reasonably be expected to be made by members of a particular community". Finally, the Equality Commission is required (Article 56):

> where a review discloses that members of a particular community are not enjoying, or are not likely to continue to enjoy, fair participation in employment in the concern, make such recommendations as it thinks fit as to the affirmative action to be taken and, assuming the action is taken, as to the progress towards fair participation in employment in the concern, by reference to any period or periods, that can reasonably be expected to be made by members of the community.

The failure of the FETO and of its predecessors to define "fair participation" in pursuit of which affirmative action ought to be undertaken was mentioned above. The Fair Employment Commission's Code of Practice suggests that affirmative action "should certainly be considered. For example, if either Protestants or Roman Catholics":[10]

> are applying in fewer numbers than might be expected for either employment training or promotion,
> are being recruited, trained or promoted in numbers proportionately lower than their rate of application,
> hold jobs carrying higher pay, status and authority in numbers proportionately lower than their rate of application or availability,
> are, in larger undertakings, concentrated in certain branches, shifts, sections or departments, enjoy less attractive terms, hours or working conditions than others, are likely to be adversely affected by possible redundancies and agreed or traditional schemes such as "last in first out".

The FETO appears to provide a much more significant role for positive discrimination than exists under either the SDA or the RRA. But Christine Bell pointed out, in 1996, that only three (now four) forms of "affirmative action" are explicitly permitted by the FETO (then the FEA):

[10] Para 3.1 of the FEC guide to affirmative action, available on *http://www.fec-ni.org* (soon to be incorporated within the new Equality Commission's website)

Christine Bell, "The Employment Equality Review in Northern Ireland" (1996) 2
***International Journal of Discrimination and the Law* 53, 60**

* special training to enhance limited or non-existent skills amongst members of the under-represented group . . .
* adoption of alternative redundancy procedures designed to ensure that attempts to recruit members of the under-represented community into the workforce are not dissipated, for example by disapplying last in first out policies in redundancy situations (not to be defined with specific reference to religion or politics)
* targeted advertising to attract applicants from an under-represented group. . . .

There are several problems with affirmative action as defined by the legislation. Firstly, the fact that only three forms of affirmative action enjoy explicit protection from charges of unlawful discrimination, suggests that other forms of affirmative action are not favoured and are vulnerable to charges of discrimination. This can act to inhibit employers from taking other affirmative action measures because of fear of discrimination suits. . . .

Since Bell's article was written the scope of lawful affirmative action under that regime has been widened. Prior to the implementation of the FETO, and despite first impressions, the scope for positive action within the fair employment legislation was, despite the talk of "affirmative action" and "fair participation", much narrower in some respects than that provided by the British Acts. Although the express exception covering redundancy selection was unique to the fair employment legislation,[11] the FEAs did not permit any religion-specific training regardless of the degree of under-representation of one or other community in the workplace, employers being restricted in these circumstances to training which, being based in a particular geographic area or confined to a class of persons defined other than on grounds of religious belief or political opinion, was more accessible to the under-represented group.

The 1998 Order widened the scope of the training provision, Article 76 permitting employers and other training bodies to provide single-religion training:

(1) . . . in relation to employment with the employer at a particular establishment in Northern Ireland, being an act done in or in connection with affording only persons of a particular religious belief access to training which would help to fit them for that employment where the conditions in paragraph (2) are satisfied at any time within the 12 months immediately preceding the doing of that act.

(2) The conditions referred to in paragraph (1) are—
    (a) that it appears to the Commission that—
        (i) there are no persons of the religious belief in question among those engaged in that employment at the establishment; or
        (ii) that the proportion of persons of that belief among those engaged in that employment at that establishment is small in comparison with the proportion of persons of that belief among all those employed by the employer there or among the population of the area from which that employer might reasonably be expected to recruit persons for employment at that establishment . . .

---

[11] See *Brook & Others* v *London Borough of Haringey* [1992] IRLR 478.

The scope for positive action in the provision of training remains considerably narrower under the FETO than under the RRA and SDA in two ways. First, the Equality Commission (which administers all Northern Irish equality legislation) must give prior approval of any such training. Second, that training may not be provided "by an employer, or a person providing training services on behalf of an employer, in relation to any person who is employed by the employer at the time when the act is done". It would, of course, amount to (unlawful) direct discrimination under the FETO for an employer to provide single-religion training for the under-represented community and thereafter to recruit only from that group.

POSITIVE ACTION AND INDIRECT DISCRIMINATION

Another significant amendment to the fair employment legislation was Article 75 FETO which provides:

(1) The application of any requirement or condition to any person applying to fill a vacancy for employment where the requirement or condition is one that the person applying to fill the vacancy has not been in employment for a specified period of time is not . . . by virtue of Article 3(2) unlawful . . .

This provision was inserted into the fair employment legislation to deal with the fact that, because Catholic unemployment rates in Northern Ireland have remained fairly stable at around twice the Protestant level for decades, any attempt to target the unemployed would amount, *prima facie*, to indirect discrimination the lawfulness of which would turn on the issue of justification. In 1986, Christopher McCrudden wrote that:

C. McCrudden, "Rethinking Positive Action" (1986) 15 *ILJ* 219, 230–2

It is arguable that an attempt by an employer to redress underrepresentation by adopting a policy which is neutral but intentionally inclusive is unlawful as a discriminatory arrangement under the S.D.A., the R.R.A. and the F.E.A. An employer decides to give preference to those who are unemployed in order to reduce the imbalance between majority and minority groups in his workforce. This would have the effect of disproportionately including, for example, racial minorities (given the considerably greater rate of black unemployment) without explicitly or intentionally excluding whites who, if they are unemployed, would also be able to benefit. There would, however be a disparate impact on whites. That is both the intention and the problem. The decision may amount, first, to direct discrimination under the three Acts. It would, second, be for the courts to decide whether this policy was indirectly discriminatory and whether it would be "justifiable" under the S.D.A. and R.R.A.

If the approach to justifiability currently adopted by the courts in their interpretation of the S.D.A. and R.R.A. continues (*i.e.* one sympathetic to subjective processes actions taken in furtherance of this second type of positive action would be lawful, given the lack of intrusiveness into employers' practices which that approach seems to imply. In this context, therefore, there is the rather ironic situation that supporters of positive action might well be arguing for an interpretation of indirect discrimination which they would otherwise be anxious to reject. This is of particular relevance should the proposal to substitute some more restrictive idea of justification, such as that proposed by the C.R.E., be accepted. It may be reasonable to distinguish between an interpretation of "justifiability" when the condition or requirement is adverse to the minority group or women, from its interpretation when it is favourable to these groups. However, it may be more realistic to assume that the judiciary would be unlikely to bring these assumptions to bear in this way.

Since 1986, the narrow approach to justification adopted by the ECJ has been applied to the Equal Pay Act (and, by implication, to the SDA and RRA) by the House of Lords in *Rainey*. More specifically, the possibility of justifying indirect discrimination on the part of employers by reference to wider social issues was dismissed by EAT in *Greater Manchester Police Authority* v *Lea*.

The case concerned a police authority's policy of preferring applicants for employment who were not already in receipt of an occupational pension. The reasoning behind the policy was that occupational pension recipients were less in need of an employment-related income than were others. It was, however, demonstrated to the satisfaction of EAT (no issue being raised as to the status of the factor as a "preference" rather than an "absolute must")[12] that the policy impacted disadvantageously on men who were in the (un)fortunate position of being more likely than women (4.7% as against 0.6%) to receive such a pension. Dealing with the matter of justification, EAT ruled (applying *Hampson* v *Department of Education and Science* [1990] 2 All ER 25, [1989] ICR 179, [1989] IRLR 69, discussed in Chapter 2):

Greater Manchester Police Authority v Lea [1990] IRLR 372

Knox J:

It is therefore now clear if it was not before that the test is, as thus stated by Lord Justice Balcombe in particular, of an objective balance being struck between the discriminatory effect of the requirement or condition and the reasonable needs of the person who applies it.

   In our judgment if one applies that test the Police Authority fails to satisfy the requirement because . . . it was held and properly held by the Industrial Tribunal that there was no relevant need of the Police Authority in connection with this condition. It was of course not enough as appears from the judgments in *Hampson* for it to be shown, as no doubt the Police Authority did show, that the condition was imposed in pursuance of an intrinsically entirely laudable and otherwise reasonable policy of helping the unemployed. *There has in our judgment to be a nexus established between the function of the employer in this type of case and the imposition of the condition* otherwise it is impossible to carry out the objective balance that the Court of Appeal has identified as the test of justifiability in relation to the needs of the employer [my emphasis]. There was some discussion before us on the question whether or not different tests might properly be applied to public authority employers as

---

[12] See *Perera* v *Civil Service Commission* [1983] ICR 428, [1983] IRLR 166 discussed in Chapter 2.

compared with private employers. It would not in our judgment be useful or safe to seek any general principles in that field. What is appropriate to a public authority employer will, inevitably, in our view, be conditioned by the status, almost certainly statutory, of the employer in question. Generalisations would be inappropriate in that type of context because the particular framework, usually statutory, would need to be considered in any given case.

It would appear, as a matter of UK law (and leaving aside specific FETO exceptions covering recruitment of the unemployed and redundancy), that an altruistic employer would have to show that a recruitment practice which was designed to favour the disadvantaged (the poor, the disaffected) but which had a disparate impact by race, sex (or, in Northern Ireland, religion or political opinion) "correspond[ed] to a real need on the part of the undertaking, [was] appropriate with a view to achieving the objectives pursued and [was] necessary to that end".[13]

It is perhaps reasonable to make this demand in circumstances where the targeting of one disadvantaged group (for example, the unemployed) serves to exclude disproportionate numbers of another disadvantaged group (women, for example, if definition as unemployed turns on receipt of benefits);[14] or where targeting one disadvantaged (predominantly white) housing estate disproportionately excludes blacks and Asians. But where the group to whose advantage the targeting works is disadvantaged both in the sense (for example) of being unemployed and, further, by reason of race or sex (it being clearly demonstrable that ethnic minorities, women and, in Northern Ireland, Catholics are disadvantaged in the labour market) one has to question whether the severity of the approach adopted in *Lea* is warranted.

Returning to the point made by Christine Bell, and despite the apparently generous scope of Articles 55, 56 and 5 (the latter defining "equality of opportunity" as compatible with "anything lawfully done in pursuance of affirmative action"), the scope afforded for positive discrimination under the FETO is almost as narrow (and in some respects is narrower) than that provided under the SDA and the RRA. The FETO, like the SDA and RRA, permits such action in relation to the under-represented only to the extent that it encourages them to apply for jobs and, if necessary, provides them with training.[15] What it does not do is to permit discrimination in favour of the disadvantaged *at the point of hiring*.[16]

---

[13] That this approach is not required as a matter of European Community law, even where it is applicable, is clear from the discussion of *Marschall* and *Badeck*, below.

[14] *Partnership for Equality* (Northern Ireland Office, March 1998), the White Paper preceding the FETO, initially suggested targeting at the unemployed. This was altered after representations from SACHR and the CAJ (see further Chapters 5 and 9), that women would be disadvantaged by any requirement for unemployment as distinct from non-employment.

[15] Also, in the case of the FETO, with *indirect* discrimination in redundancy selection.

[16] See, for example, *Jones v Chief Constable of Northamptonshire Police* 41 EORDCLD. 2.6).

THE USE OF POSITIVE ACTION IN THE UK

"Affirmative action" along the lines permitted by the FETO, previously the FEAs, has been a significant feature of Northern Irish employment for some years. The FEC's annual report for 1996/7, for example, reports that affirmative action plans had been agreed between the Commission and 110 organisations. Statements welcoming applications from under-represented groups "are now a common feature in newspaper recruitment campaigns'.[17] The FEC "actively promoted community orientated affirmative action programmes, linked to goals and timetables through a programme of formal investigations [see further Chapter 5] and its work with employers on their [workforce] reviews" [see Chapter 9]. The 110 affirmative action programmes agreed in 1996–7 included undertakings regarding the development of school and community links, the inclusion of welcoming statements in advertisements and the adoption of goals and timetables for increased integration.

The positive action provisions of the RRA and the SDA are much less used than those of the FETO and its predecessor legislation. In 1987, the EOC criticised the Training Opportunities Scheme for having made no use of its power to direct training towards women, while a study published in the same year found that only seven of the 441 employers surveyed had made any use of s.48 SDA.[18] Vera Sacks' subsequent study of the application of ss.47 and 48 concluded that:

Vera Sacks, "Tackling Discrimination Positively in Britain", in B. Hepple and E. Szyszczak, *Discrimination: The Limits of Law* **pp. 380–1**

the law in this field is little known, misunderstood, and minimally used. How has this come about?

Two related factors provide important clues. One is the symmetrical approach of the . . . which, as Lacey argues, "does not match the nature of the social problem to which sex discrimination legislation should be addressed . . . The result . . . of this symmetrical principle . . . is to outlaw any form of reverse discrimination or affirmative action". Yet experience over the past fifteen years has underlined the fact that men and women are running different races and that a neutral stance tends to legitimize and confirm inequality. The second fact is the obvious one that such exceptions as are presented by sections 47 to 49 are permissive and not mandatory. Experience elsewhere reveals that little is done as long as employers are not compelled to develop affirmative action measures.

In the course of this research many organizations of both employers and trainers emphasized the resource problem and the lack of commitment by those in charge. Doubtless, resources in the public sector are always subject to competing demands, and diverting resources to women's promotion and training is seen by decision-makers as controversial, expensive and unpopular, and therefore as of low priority. Commitment is essential and that is most likely to come from women, but women thus far constitute only 20 per cent of local

[17] Annual report para 1.5, available on the Commission's website, fn 10 above.
[18] EOC, *Review of the Training Opportunities Scheme* (Manchester: EOC, 1978); EOC, *Equality Between the Sexes in Industry: How Far Have We Come?* (Manchester: EOC, 1978).

councillors, and are in even smaller proportions in the managerial and trade union hierarchy. Thus placing a duty on employers, at least in the public sector, to provide training for women and to achieve a more balanced workforce is essential here as it has been elsewhere. To quote Marano: "All of the systematic studies done on the issue indicate that affirmative action has had a positive effect and has resulted in increased employment opportunities and training programmes for women and minority men." Marano also described how, in turn, this more highly trained part of the workforce continued on the same path but without compulsion. In Australia and Canada recent legislation places employers under a duty to submit a programme whose objective is to achieve tangible changes in the employment profile as it relates to women, and the same should be done in this country.

The RRA's positive action provisions appear to have been used rather more than those of the SDA. Research carried out by Welsh and others in the early 1990's, mainly in the public sector, found that 82% of employers had used advertisements to encourage applications from ethnic minority workers and that 33% had provided targeted training for ethnic minority workers. These "targeted" advertisements, however, rarely consisted of more than statements that "all [were] welcome", or that applicants were "welcome regardless of race". Welsh concluded that the use of the provisions was generally "patchy" and their "overall impact . . . probably limited".[19]

Christopher McCrudden had reported, in 1986, that the positive action provisions of the RRA were being utilised, particularly in the public sector. But the extract below illustrates some of the difficulties into which attempts to increase the diversity of workforces ran:

C. McCrudden, "Rethinking Positive Action", 233–4

Relatively little used until recently, the provisions have given rise to relatively little controversy. However, the increasing scrutiny by some London Boroughs of the composition of their workforces has encouraged a greater use of these provisions. Not surprisingly , it has also produced the first litigation in Britain over the permissible limits of action taken ostensibly under them, and this has demonstrated some uncertainties in their scope [discussing *Hughes* v *LB of Hackney*].

The London Borough of Hackney developed an equal opportunities policy in 1982 which included an element of outreach for racial minorities. This was intended to help in the recruitment and training opportunities of members of ethnic minorities. A number of posts were created as part of this programme. An advertisement appeared for two of these posts (for park apprentices) which not only described the training that would be associated with the posts but continued:

> Black and ethnic minorities are heavily underrepresented in the Parks and Open Spaces Services. Where such conditions exist the RRA (section 38) allows an employer to establish extra training opportunities specifically for those groups. We would therefore warmly welcome applications from black and ethnic minority people for the two apprenticeships.

[19] C.Welsh, J. Knox and M. Brett, *Acting Positively: Positive Action Under the Race Relations Act 1976* (Sheffield: Employment Department, 1994) Research Series No. 36 p.37. The research found that 61% of employers were influenced in their decision to take some form of positive action by the CRE.

The three complainants, all of whom were white, applied for the posts. The application form asked for information on the candidate's ethnic group and the complainants indicated that they were white. They received a letter from he Council's personnel officer which said these posts were "open only to black and ethnic minority people." The three complained to an industrial tribunal which upheld their complaint . . .

The Council argued that the provision of employment of this type in these circumstances was, in accordance with section 38 of the R.R.A., an act done by an employer in connection with encouraging only persons of a particular racial group to take advantage of opportunities for doing particular work at a particular establishment. The proportion of persons of that group amongst those doing that work was small in comparison with the proportion of persons of that group among the population of the area from which the Council normally recruited persons for employment at that establishment. The tribunal rejected this argument, again for two reasons. The words "in connection with" were not wide enough to cover an employer providing job opportunities restricted to racially disadvantaged members of the community. Second, the Council failed to show that the proportion of black and ethnic minority workers doing relevant work at the establishment was small within the meaning of the section. Although 9 per cent of gardeners were black or ethnic minority compared with 37 per cent of the Borough's population, since only 58 per cent of recruits came from within the Borough, there was no reason to restrict the words "the area" to recruits from the Borough of Hackney. Since there was no evidence of where, outside the Borough the remaining recruits came from or what the percentage of black and ethnic minorities were within that population, the Council failed to satisfy the conditions set out in section 38.

THE POLITICS OF POSITIVE DISCRIMINATION

In 1986, McCrudden reported a significant degree of support for the legalisation in the UK of preferential treatment on grounds of race and sex. Such support came, *inter alia*, from the CRE[20] and the Council of Social Democracy of the Social Democratic Party.[21] Since that time, however, the climate has changed. Under "positive action" the CRE's 1998 reform proposals stated only that:

The [RRA] recognises training as an important means of enabling members of racial groups that have been underrepresented in the past to compete on equal terms for jobs and promotion . . . the Act should clearly specify what positive action is permitted, and that it should include: training for the exclusive benefit of members of a part icular racial group; reserved places on non-exclusive courses; training bursaries; on-the-job training and apprenticeship training for up to two years.

[20] In its 1985 proposals for reform of the RRA, discussed in McCrudden, "Rethinking Positive Action", fn 2 above.

[21] Citizens' Rights, Policy Document No. 10, p.21 cited by McCrudden, *ibid*, p.237. McCrudden also cites G. Bindman, "Reforming the RRA II" *New Law Journal* 22nd November 1985, p.1169.

The EOC's 1998 reform proposals included the statement that "[i]n general, the EOC does not support positive discrimination".[22] And even while the government has been adopting "goals and timetables" for increasing sex and race diversity in the public sector (see further below), it has been at pains to emphasise that this does not amount to "positive" or "reverse" discrimination.

The degree of suspicion with which "positive discrimination" is viewed in the UK is far from universal. In *Action Travail des Femmes* v *CNR* [1987] ISCR 1114, Canada's Supreme Court accepted the imposition of quotas as a remedial measure to counter the effects of past discrimination. There the Court upheld an order that at least a quarter of those hired by the railway company for traditionally male, blue-collar jobs be women until women accounted for 13% of workers in that sector (this being the average level of participation of women in such jobs across Canada). The Supreme Court accepted that "systematic discrimination" ("discrimination that results from the simple operation of established procedures of recruitment, hiring and promotion, none of which is necessarily designed to promote discrimination") had occurred and that the programme ordered was "essential to combat [its] effects . . . specific hiring goals . . . are a rational attempt to impose a systemic remedy on a systemic problem".

S.15 of Canada's Charter of Rights now provides that: "Every individual is equal before and under the law and has the right to the equal protection and equal benefit of the law without discrimination and, in particular, without discrimination based on race, national or ethnic origin, colour, religion, sex, age or mental or physical disability". Section S.15(2) states that the prohibition on discrimination does not apply to "any law, program or activity that has as its object the amelioration of conditions of disadvantaged individuals or groups including those that are disadvantaged because of . . . sex".

Some of the objections to positive discrimination are set out by Justice Stewart in his dissenting opinion in *Fullilove* v *Klutznick*, in which the United States Supreme Court upheld the constitutionality of a 10% "minority business enterprise" set-aside in a Federal public works programme.

Fullilove v *Klutznick* 448 US 448 (1980)

Justice Stewart

> Our Constitution is color-blind, and neither knows nor tolerates classes among citizens. . . . The law regards man as man, and takes no account of his surroundings or of his color. . . .

Those words were written by a Member of this Court 84 years ago [citing Harlan J, dissenting, in *Plessy* v *Ferguson*, 163 US 537]. His colleagues disagreed with him, and held that a statute that required the separation of people on the basis of their race was constitutionally valid because it was a "reasonable" exercise of legislative power and had been "enacted in good faith for the promotion [of] the public good" . . .

---

[22] EOC, *Equality in the 21st Century: A new sex equality law for Britain*, available from the EOC'S website at www.eoc.org.uk.

Today, the Court upholds a statute that accords a preference to citizens who are "Negroes, Spanish-speaking, Orientals, Indians, Eskimos, and Aleuts," for much the same reasons. I think today's decision is wrong for the same reason that *Plessy* v *Ferguson* was wrong, and I respectfully dissent. . .

The command of the [US Constitution's] equal protection guarantee is simple but unequivocal: In the words of the Fourteenth Amendment: "No State shall . . . deny to any person . . . the equal protection of the laws." Nothing in this language singles out some "persons" for more "equal" treatment than others. Rather, as the Court made clear in *Shelley* v *Kraemer*, 334 US 1, 22, the benefits afforded by the Equal Protection Clause "are, by its terms, guaranteed to the individual. [They] are personal rights." From the perspective of a person detrimentally affected by a racially discriminatory law, the arbitrariness and unfairness is entirely the same, whatever his skin color and whatever the law's purpose, be it purportedly "for the promotion of the public good" or otherwise . . . The Court's attempt to characterize the law as a proper remedial measure to counteract the effects of past or present racial discrimination is remarkably unconvincing. The Legislative Branch of government is not a court of equity. It has neither the dispassionate objectivity nor the flexibility that are needed to mold a race-conscious remedy around the single objective of eliminating the effects of past or present discrimination . . . since the guarantee of equal protection immunizes from capricious governmental treatment "persons"—not "races"—it can never countenance laws that seek racial balance as a goal in and of itself. . . Second, there are indications that the [minority business set aside] . . . may have been enacted to compensate for the effects of social, educational, and economic "disadvantage." No race, however, has a monopoly on social, educational, or economic disadvantage, and any law that indulges in such a presumption clearly violates the constitutional guarantee of equal protection. Since the . . . provision was in whole or in part designed to effectuate objectives other than the elimination of the effects of racial discrimination, it cannot stand as a remedy that comports with the strictures of equal protection, even if it otherwise could . . .

Laws that operate on the basis of race require definitions of race. Because of the Court's decision today, our statute books will once again have to contain laws that reflect the odious practice of delineating the qualities that make one person a Negro and make another white. Moreover, racial discrimination, even "good faith" racial discrimination, is inevitably a two-edged sword . . . Most importantly, by making race a relevant criterion once again in its own affairs the Government implicitly teaches the public that the apportionment of rewards and penalties can legitimately be made according to race—rather than according to merit or ability—and that people can, and perhaps should, view themselves and others in terms of their racial characteristics. Notions of "racial entitlement" will be fostered, and private discrimination will necessarily be encouraged . . .

Justice Stewart was in the dissent in *Fullilove*. In *Adarand Constructors* v *Pena*, Justice Thomas concurred with a majority decision finding a similar set-aside programme unconstitutional in delivering the following judgment:

Adarand Constructors v *Pena 515 US 2000 [1995]*

I believe that there is a "moral [and] constitutional equivalence," between laws designed to subjugate a race and those that distribute benefits on the basis of race in order to foster some current notion of equality. Government cannot make us equal; it can only recognize, respect, and protect us as equal before the law . . .

As far as the Constitution is concerned, it is irrelevant whether a government's racial classifications are drawn by those who wish to oppress a race or by those who have a sincere desire to help those thought to be disadvantaged. There can be no doubt that the paternalism that appears to lie at the heart of this program is at war with the principle of inherent equality that underlies and infuses our Constitution. (See the Declaration of Independence "We hold these truths to be self-evident, that all men are created equal, that they are endowed by their Creator with certain unalienable Rights, that among these are Life, Liberty, and the pursuit of Happiness") . . .

Purchased at the price of immeasurable human suffering, the equal protection principle reflects our Nation's understanding that [racial] classifications ultimately have a destructive impact on the individual and our society. Unquestionably, "[i]nvidious [racial] discrimination is an engine of oppression,". It is also true that "[r]emedial" racial preferences may reflect "a desire to foster equality in society". But there can be no doubt that racial paternalism and its unintended consequences can be as poisonous and pernicious as any other form of discrimination. So-called "benign" discrimination teaches many that because of chronic and apparently immutable handicaps, minorities cannot compete with them without their patronizing indulgence. Inevitably, such programs engender attitudes of superiority or, alternatively, provoke resentment among those who believe that they have been wronged by the government's use of race. These programs stamp minorities with a badge of inferiority and may cause them to develop dependencies or to adopt an attitude that they are "entitled" to preferences . . .

In my mind, government-sponsored racial discrimination based on benign prejudice is just as noxious as discrimination inspired by malicious prejudice. In each instance, it is racial discrimination, plain and simple.

The views of Justices Stewart and Thomas have, for the moment, gained the upper hand in the US Supreme Court (see further below). But they are not universally shared.

Bhikhu Parekh, "The Case for Positive Discrimination", in B. Hepple and E. Szyszczak *Discrimination: The Limits of Law* 272–5

The opponents of preferential treatment for disadvantaged groups object to it on the grounds that it disregards merit and that it is unjust and violates individual rights. This is so because it introduces irrelevant and arbitrary criteria, excludes deserving candidates, and favours those with no claim to be favoured. It is unjust also because it punishes the present generation for the deeds of its predecessors, unjustly penalizes members of the dominant group, especially those superseded in specific cases, and privileges all disadvantaged groups, particularly those lucky enough to receive preferential treatment in specific cases.

The first argument makes important points. It rightly stresses that admissions and appointments should be based on clearly specified, rationally defensible and impartially applied criteria, that merit should never be disregarded, that the better qualified should not be passed over in favour of the less qualified, that patronage in all its forms must be avoided, and that efficiency is an important value. However, the definition of merit is far more problematic than its advocates realize.

When people talk about merit, whether in educational institutions or in employment, they define and determine its content in the following three rarely articulated stages. First, an organization or an area of life is abstracted from its wider social context, and its purposes are defined without reference to its place and role in the society at large. Second, a job is abstracted from its larger organizational context and treated as a self-contained unit. An organization is broken up into and viewed as an aggregate of so many separate tasks or jobs, each requiring a specific kind of competence. As a result the overall culture, ethos, ambience of the organization in question is left out of consideration and its claims are defined out of existence. Third, the complex requirements of a job are reduced to and defined almost exclusively in terms of relevant intellectual qualities as measured by examination results and, where appropriate, interview. Merit thus comes to be defined almost entirely in terms of the intellectual requirements deemed necessary to undertake an abstractly and insularly defined job.

When the critics of preferential treatment insist on the inviolability of merit, they have broadly this view of it in mind. There is no reason why we should accept this view, or agree that to depart from *this* view of merit is to depart from merit *itself*. We may question each of the three stages by which the dominant view of merit is arrived at. We might argue that no organization exists or flourishes in a vacuum, and that its purposes cannot be defined without reference to its obligations and responsibilities to the wider society. We might argue too that if the reified concept of job were to be deconstructed, we could find that it is not some independent entity with a unitary structure, but a fragment of a process, a cluster of tasks embedded in and deriving meaning from a larger structure. We might therefore conclude that the very concept of "qualifications for a job" or of "job-related qualifications" is misleading and even logically incoherent. Finally, we might argue that a job is not a task but a social relationship in the sense that it is done by an individual in association with other individuals and involves relating to a specific group of men and women whom it is designed to serve, and that it therefore calls for a complex range of skills and abilities of which the intellectual qualities are only a part. As a result of such a critique we might arrive at a very different conception of merit to the one currently dominant, or we might find the very concept of merit problematic, or we might arrive at some other concept of which merit as traditionally defined is an important but only one constituent.

Take admissions to medical schools. The purpose of medical schools is to produce good doctors, and our admission requirements are necessarily determined by our conception of a good doctor. By and large we define him or her as one who is competent at his or her job, and ask for good grades at public examinations as conditions of admission. But we would easily take a different and perhaps more satisfactory view of a good doctor. We could argue that a good doctor should be not only intellectually competent but also possess specific qualities of character and temperament, compassion and a sense of social concern. We could argue too that in a culturally and racially diverse society like ours, he [sic] should be able to relate to and inspire the confidence of people of different backgrounds, and be knowledgeable about their life-styles, stresses and strains, needs and approaches to health and disease. We could also argue that he should be able to appreciate that modern medicine is not the last word in scientific knowledge and that it can benefit from a dialogue with other medical traditions.

We might conclude that a man is more likely to acquire a well-rounded education and to become a better doctor if he had in his medical school students from different cultural, racial and social backgrounds, provided of course that they were reasonably bright and capable of coping with the demands of medical education. They might not have very high grades at public examinations, but they might bring with them invaluable cultural skills, intuitions and experiences necessary for creating an environment conductive to the production of better doctors overall. Judged by the criterion of narrowly defined merit, they do not deserve admission. But judged by the standards of a broadly defined "merit" based on differently defined purposes of medical education, they do. There is no reason why, subject to certain minimum necessary qualifications, we could not trade off one set of qualities against another. We could go a step further and argue that as a highly visible and elite institution, the medical school has an obligation to set a good example to a divided society, to tap new talents and to provide them with role models. The case for admitting competent but a little less "meritorious" black and other candidates then becomes even stronger. . . .

Our remarks about admission to medical schools apply also to other areas of education and to employment.

As for the second argument that preferential treatment is inherently unjust and violates individual rights, it is open to several objections. We have already conceded that the present generation cannot be held responsible for the deeds of its predecessors. Insofar as the case for preferential treatment rests on such a view, it is obviously untenable. However, we have shown that a different kind of case can be made out for the present generation's responsibility for the consequences of past harm, and hence preferential treatment is not without a moral basis. The other points made by its critics are equally unconvincing. Preferential treatment does introduce irrelevant criteria when a person is preferred *solely* because of his or her sex or colour, but not when he or she comes out better on a broader definition of merit or when he or she makes a distinct contribution to the culture and functions of an institution. In such cases merit in the narrow conventional sense of examination results, intelligence tests and so forth is *not* disregarded but balanced against other equally legitimate considerations. And people are not selected simply because of their colour or sex, for they do satisfy the necessary requirements of competence *and* additionally possess qualities declared and shown to be desirable. A more "meritorious" or formally better qualified candidate has then no right to complain against his or her rejection if the criteria of selection are widely known, rationally defended and impartially applied. . . .

The advantages of preferential treatment are several. As both the American and Indian experiences show, it has a great symbolic significance. It reassures the disadvantaged that the dominant groups appreciate their predicament, accept the responsibility to do something about it, and have the political will to act decisively, including reconsidering such traditional bastions of their power as the principle of merit. Preferential treatment is also a powerful means of integrating disadvantaged groups into the mainstream of society and reducing their feeling of existential marginality. True, it benefits only a small number of men and women and its effects are necessarily limited. However, that is enough to persuade the rest that the dominant and otherwise frightening world is not inaccessible to them and that, if they were to exert themselves, the coveted prizes will not be denied to them.

As we saw, disadvantaged groups cannot overcome their handicaps without substantial help, But such help is often blocked by vested interests, or is of the wrong kind, or is subverted by those in charge of implementing it. It is here that preferential treatment becomes important. It ensures that those knowledgeable about the needs of, and committed to promoting the interests of the disadvantaged are involved in making and implementing decisions, offering advice and keeping a critical watch on the policies of the organisations in question. Such people also act as points of contact for their communities.

Preferential treatment also serves the valuable purpose of providing role models. This is a difficult area about which much remains unknown. We do not know how people are inspired and motivated, why and how they pluck up the courage to take their first tentative steps along a road they have never travelled before, and how over time they build up their confidence and cultural resources. But we do know that men and women whose pride and self-confidence have been shattered often draw their courage and strength from the struggles and achievements of those with whom they identify.

Nicola Lacey, "From Individual to Group?" in Hepple and Szyszczak, *Discrimination: The Limits of Law*, 113–16

Group rights may be understood in a variety of different ways, several of which might be worth considering in reforming anti-discrimination law. For the purposes of this discussion, I shall distinguish between just two senses of group rights. The first I shall call "cultural" or "protective" rights. These may be adopted to protect and express respect for the particular and distinctive ways of life of peoples from specific ethnic, racial or religious groups. An example would be the rights of a Sikh to wear the dress appropriate to his or her religious beliefs, or the right of a Muslim worker to observe traditional religious holidays or hours of prayer. . . .

In this essay I want to assess the potential of a second conception of group rights, which I shall call "remedial" rights. These "remedial" rights focus on socio-economic disadvantage and the distribution of basic goods rather than on cultural discrimination and the value of cultural pluralism. These rights would apply to groups which were suffering disadvantage as a result either of present oppression or the present effects of past oppression. The essence of the right would be that positive and effective steps be taken to combat and overcome that disadvantage within a reasonable period of time. This would mean that the holders of such rights would typically be members of minority ethnic and religious groups and women, rather than white men, and that the very instantiation of the rights would therefore express the perceived social problem to which they purport to respond.

The enforcement of these group rights would need to be supported by adequately resourced public agencies which would offer counselling, legal advice and representation, and which would monitor the effectiveness of remedies over a substantial period of time. The assertion of group rights would be met with remedies not only of the traditional legal kind—for example, damages distributed among or with an impact upon assignable individuals who are members of the group—but also a wide range of radically different remedies which would not necessarily be susceptible of such distribution. This feature would be crucial in breaking the conceptual link between loss and remedy which characterizes the individual legal form. Hence contract compliance, quota systems and affirmative action programmes, urban development programmes, educational reforms and money to set up community projects of various kinds would be possible responses to the legal assertion of the violation of a group right.

Should such rights be instantiated as legal rights, or must they rather be conceptualized as political rights? Would courts and tribunals as currently constituted be capable, politically or professionally, of administering legal actions asserting such claims? I would argue that it would be possible to legislate for such group rights in certain areas. For example, this might be done by allowing a group defined in terms of the Race Relations Act and Sex Discrimination Act categories (which it is to be hoped might be extended to include religion and sexual orientation) whose representation in an area of employment fell below its numbers in the general pool by a certain margin, or a group whose share of valuable educational resources was disproportionately low, to bring a claim for appropriate remedial action. As such, the action would have much in common with the procedural notion of a class action, but would have the additional feature of de-individualizing the legal subject and opening the way for more wide-ranging remedies which are not tied to specific legally recognized harms. The essence of the action would be seen not so much as an assertion of the existence of widespread individual acts of discrimination against members of the group, but of an unjust disadvantage suffered by the group, the ultimate source of which would note the subject of technical legal proof. This would overcome some of the main problems of legal proof and enforcement, and would be informed by an ideal of a substantive equality of outcome which goes well beyond the commitment of the present legislation. And although the structure of such actions would inevitably be complex, many of the technical problems which would arise have already been encountered and at least partially resolved in indirect discrimination cases under the existing Sex and Race Discrimination Acts. . . .

. . . the recognition of collective rights would mean the direct and overt legal recognition of the specificity of the objects of racial and sexual discrimination. In other words, group rights would empower groups of people who experience a common socio-economic or educational disadvantage which is structured along racial, ethnic, gender or religious lines to assert themselves and the patterned nature of their disadvantage. Rather than stopping at giving all citizens *the same right* not to be discriminated against, which, as an exclusive strategy, as we have seen, obscures the nature of the real political problem, the collective approach would make those problems visible in the legal and political arena. It would represent a move beyond the obfuscating exclusive reliance on a symmetrical approach, criticized earlier in this essay, and could mean that the legal sphere might become a more symbolically, as well as a more instrumentally, powerful forum in which to assert and voice the disadvantages and injustices suffered by certain oppressed groups in our society. This would help to overcome the problem raised by the symmetrical individual enforcement model's implication that discrimination is something unusual, pathological, abnormal, and would put institutional discrimination centre stage. It would represent a significant step away from the notion of the abstract, gender- and race-neutral individual legal subject who is equal with all other subjects before the law, and towards a legal recognition that sexism and racism mean that all subjects are *not* equal before the law, and that compensatory legal recognition and remedy is called for to combat the unfair disadvantage suffered by some legal subjects. It introduces into the courtroom the historical realities of racism and sexism, which could no longer be marginalized on the legal agenda by being divided up into individual pathological acts of discrimination of no general political significance. Litigation might become a forum in which an oppressed group actually advanced its cause and further developed its sense of solidarity and resistance to its race- or gender-related disadvantage. Arguably, in other words, the notion of collective rights might help to politicize the legal process in a positive way.

Conversely, certain disadvantages and potential dangers are also inherent in the notion of collective rights. First of all, if we were to add a system of group rights to an otherwise unmodified structure of individual enforcement (and indeed to an essentially individualist liberal legal system), might the very starkness of the contrast itself serve further to marginalize racism and sexism as legal issues? Could the legal institutionalization of a specific group paradoxically undermine the struggle against racism and sexism either by calling forth political hostility or by becoming a "specialist" or marginal area of legal practice? The first problem is met by the fact that such a change would not occur without some measure of political will and hence a change in the political climate, but the inhospitableness of the legal system even to the limited models of agency enforcement introduced by current anti-discrimination legislation suggests that we should not merely dismiss the marginalization point as a non-problem.

GOALS AND TIMETABLES

We will return to consider the arguments relating to positive discrimination below, after we address current developments in the UK. We saw, above, that positive discrimination is very strictly regulated under the SDA, RRA and FETO. The recent adoption by Government of widespread "goals and timetables" projects is, therefore, of very considerable interest.

The terms "goals and timetables" is taken from the US, in which from 1968 and 1971 the federal government required government contractors to adopt, first race-based and then also sex-based, "goals and timetables" guidelines in an attempt to assimilate the racial and sexual balance of workforces to those of locally available workforces.[23] Such "affirmative action" has also been practised voluntarily in the US, notably by universities in relation to admissions and by public sector employers. Finally, courts have ordered employers and others to engage in "affirmative action" where they have been found guilty of practising discrimination. The various forms such "affirmative action" may take are discussed below.

In the UK, "goals and timetables" are available to (and sometimes required of) Northern Irish employers under the FETO. The practice was first imposed by the FEA 1989. More recently, in July 1998 the government established a target of 50:50 male: female appointment ratio for men and women in public life[24] and, in the *Modernising Government* White Paper (March 1999),[25] committed itself to "pro rata representation of ethnic minority groups" among the 100,000 public appointments (those serving on NHS Trusts and advisory and executive bodies, school governors, magistrates etc.). In late 1998, fewer than one third of public appointments were held by women, and only 3.6% by members of the ethnic minorities.[26]

Modernising Government also stated the need to "accelerate progress on diversity" in the public sector, expressing concern at the "serious[] underrepresent[ation]" of women, ethnic minority and disabled people "in the more senior parts of the public service". The Government committed itself to targets, for 2004–5, of 35% women in the top 3 000, and 25% women in the top 600 civil service posts;[27] and 3.2% ethnic

---

[23] In the same year the Philadelphia Plan, adopted by President Nixon, required all those bidding for federal contracts to establish numerical goals for integration. As Attorney General, the later Chief Justice Rehnquist assured the President that the plan was in conformity with the Civil Rights Act—see R. McKeever, *Raw Judicial Power?: the Supreme Court and American Society* (2nd ed., Manchester: Manchester University Press, 1995), pp.125–6.

[24] Speech by Joan Ruddock, Minister for Women, to a regional TUC conference on women's work 9th July 1999, press release on *www.dss.gov.uk/hq/press/1998/july98/ 186.htm*. A publication from the Women's Unit (*Delivering for Women: the Progress so Far*, available at *www.cabinet-office.gov.uk*/womens-unit, reports that 1998 appointments were 39% female, up from 32% in 1997).

[25] (CM 4310), the forerunner to the Local Government Act 1999, further discussed in Chapter 5. The White Paper is available at www.official-documents.co.uk

[26] (1998) 81 *Equal Opportunities Review* News (1998), p.8.

[27] 17.8% and 12.7% respectively in 1998.

minority incumbents in the top 3 000 civil service posts, and promised an equivalent target for people with disabilities.[28]

Perhaps most high profile of all these commitments has been Home Secretary Jack Straw's goals for ethnic minority representation in the police, the fire and prison service, set in the aftermath of the McPherson enquiry into the death of Stephen Lawrence and its exposition of "institutional racism" among the police.[29] Subsequently, Chris Patten's report on the RUC, *Policing for Northern Ireland*, set targets of 50% Catholic recruitment over the next 10 years in an attempt to redress the current position, whereby over 40% of the population but only 8% of RUC officers are Catholic. The Patten recommendations were accepted by Government, Secretary of State for Northern Ireland (Peter Mandelson):

> attach[ing] particular importance to [the] recommendations for action to transform the composition of the police service. They are essential to gaining widespread acceptability. I endorse the proposal for 50:50 recruitment of Protestants and Catholics, from a pool of candidates, all of whom—I stress this—will have qualified on merit. We propose that the requirement for that special measure should be kept under review on a triennial basis, with rigorous safeguards to ensure that the rightly challenging targets for recruitment do not diminish the standard required of recruits.[30]

The introduction in the UK of "goals and timetables" has generally been accompanied by protestations that they, unlike "quotas", do not entail positive discrimination which would be unlawful under the RRA and SDA.[31] In setting targets for racial integration of the police service, Home Secretary Jack Straw declared:

> Let me be clear about what I am not doing. I am not setting quotas and saying that you have to take somebody on because of the colour of their skin. I am setting targets that will enable the police service to more fairly represent the community [the police] serve.[32]

The *Modernising Government* White Paper, too, was at pains to emphasise that the targets in respect of women and ethnic minority representation in public appointments were to be "on the basis of merit". This indicates, perhaps, that the targets are to be achieved by the outreach methods currently permitted under the SDA and RRA

[28] A headline in the (1999) 87 *Equal Opportunities Review*, p.4 read "Middle class white men still rule Civil Service", reporting that ethnic minorities comprise 1.6% women 16% and disabled people 1.5% of the senior Civil Service "the current culture is perceived as encouraging those who are different to comply with the "norms" in order to get on . . . being prepared to work long and additional hours was the highest ranked enabler to career progression by two-thirds of [the 1701] respondents. Networking and patronage were also seen as too influential in assisting career development.

[29] Goals in particular forces to be consistent with the relevant population—Press Association Newsfile 28th July 1999, and 85 *Equal Opportunities Review* pp.21ff, Ethnic Minority Targets Set for Police.

[30] HC Debs 19th January 2000 Column 847, available on *http://www.parliament.the-stationery-office.co.uk/pa/cm/cmhansrd.him.*

[31] See, for example, statements of Home Secretary Jack Straw quoted in Press Association Newsfile and *Equal Opportunities Review*, fn 29 above.

[32] Speech to a major police conference in April 1999 reproduced in *Equal Opportunities Review*, fn 29 above.

provisions discussed above.[33] But it would be irrational for an employer or appointing body presented with two "equally" qualified candidates and a recruitment goal favouring one or the other to choose the candidate whose appointment would tend to frustrate that goal. The choice of the candidate whose appointment would further the goal, on the grounds that their appointment would have that effect, would qualify as "tie-break" positive (even "reverse") discrimination.

The insistence that "goals and timetables" do not amount to "positive" or "reverse" discrimination appears to depend on a view of the latter as requiring the appointment of women/ ethnic minority/ other candidates, regardless of merit, until particular numerical quotas are fulfilled. This certainly corresponds to the caricature of "affirmative action" as practised in the US. But, in truth, the distinction between (US) "affirmative action" and (UK) "goals and timetables" is far less clear-cut.

Strict quota-based "affirmative action" was prohibited by the Supreme Court in *Regents of University of California* v *Bakke* 438 US 265 (1978), the first such case to reach that Court. There, a white student successfully challenged the medical school's "set-aside" policy whereby 16 places each year were reserved for disadvantaged ethnic minority students, these places being allocated on the basis of competition within that group alone. Bakke had failed to achieve the grades required in respect of admissions other than in respect of one of these 16 places, but would have qualified academically if he had met the criteria for a "reserved" place. Five of the nine justices of the Supreme Court disapproved of the university's "affirmative action", one (Justice Powell) on the grounds only that particular model adopted (a strict quota-based system based, not upon proof of discrimination by the university itself, but upon the vaguer notion of "societal discrimination) was unacceptable. Justice Powell, together with the four dissenters, accepted that the university was entitled to pursue "a diverse student body". But "the reservation of a specified number of seats in each class for individuals from the preferred ethnic groups" was not the only method for achieving this aim. Given the particular hardship such a quota system placed on those excluded by it, it would be acceptable only if it were the only means by which such an aim could be pursued.

It has been clear since 1978 that, in the US, ethnic diversity cannot be achieved by means of rigid quotas. Court-ordered quotas have been upheld in the wake of judicial rulings that particular employers have themselves been guilty of discrimination. But in these cases (*Sheet Metal Workers* v *EEOC* (1986) 478 US 421, *US* v *Paradise* (1987) 480 US 149) such quotas were imposed only after "egregious" discrimination on the part of the offender who, in both cases, consistently flouted court orders. In both of these cases the "quotas", being flexible, were more in the nature of goals. In neither case was there any question of the unqualified being advanced.

In addition to court-ordered affirmative action programmes, until 1989 at least educational establishments could pursue race-based diversity policies (not including rigid quotas); public and private sector employers could adopt voluntary and temporary

---

[33] One example of this would be the civil service Careers Fair for Ethnic Minorities held in July 1999.

training quotas or other race-conscious methods in hiring and promotion "to eliminate conspicuous racial imbalance in traditionally segregated job categories";[34] and
federal programmes could operate race-based set-asides where severe inequality of
access had been shown. The lawfulness of affirmative action has become more uncertain since that year, a series of restrictive decisions[35] culminating in *Adarana* v *Pena*
(above) in which the Supreme Court applied to race-based programmes the same
"strict scrutiny"[36] as they adopted in other cases of race discrimination. It remains the
case, however, that some affirmative action programmes would withstand such judicial scrutiny.

Returning to "goals and timetables" in the UK, the question was raised whether,
confronted with such targets for the recruitment of women and ethnic minority candidates, employers might not be tempted to favour the woman / ethnic minority candidate at the point of recruitment (such preferential treatment being, at present,
unlawful in the UK). The "tie-break" form of positive discrimination has been mentioned above. Far more radical would be a requirement that an employer should,
regardless of merit, appoint any candidate whose recruitment would further the goals
set. It is this latter option which is sometimes conceived of (albeit wrongly) as the
"quota" method. In reality, no serious proponents of affirmative action would favour
such an approach. But it is possible to support a policy of favouring the appointment
of a candidate who satisfies the minimum qualifications for a job (or academic course),
and whose recruitment would further the goal (a workplace integrated by sex, race or
other characteristic) over a "more" qualified candidate whose appointment would
serve to undermine that goal.

This latter option appears very much more radical than a "tie-break" approach. But
the difference is one of degree rather than kind. No two candidates will ever be precisely similar, and the extent to which candidates may be regarded as "equally qualified" depends on what qualifications are accepted as relevant to the appointment. On
the one hand, it could be argued that to ignore a masters qualification or doctorate is
unfair, regardless of whether or not the qualification is relevant to the job in respect of
which appointment is sought. On the other hand, to the extent that appointment on
the basis of particular qualifications disadvantages a group definable under the SDA,
or the RRA (or, in Northern Ireland, the FETO), reliance on those qualifications will
be lawful only where they impact on the ability of the candidate to perform that particular job.[37] This being the case, the specification of that which will be regarded as

---

[34] *United Steelworkers of America* v *Weber* 443 US 193, *Bushey* v *New York State Civil Service
Commission* 469 US 1117.

[35] *Croson* v *City of Richmond* 488 US 469, *Martin* v *Wilks* 490 US 755, *Metro Broadcasting* v *FCC* (1990)
497 US 547, 490 US 755.

[36] See A.McColgan, *Women under the Law: the False Promise of Human Rights* (Harlow: Addison
Wesley Longman, 1999), Chapters 3 and 3.

[37] See the decisions of the ECJ in *Bilka-Kaufhaus GmbH* v *Weber von Hartz* Case 170/84, [1986] ECR
1607, *Rinner-Kühn* v *FWW Spezial-Gebaudereinigung GmbH* Case 171/88 [1989] ECR 2743, *Handels-og
Kontorfunktionaerernes Forbund I Danmark* v *Dansk Arbejdsgiverforening (acting for Danfoss)* Case 109/88
[1989] ECR 3199, *Nimz* v *Freie und Hanse-Stadt Hamburg* Case C–184/89 [1991] ECR I–297 in Chapter 2.

going to qualification for appointment should, arguably, be as narrow as possible. In addition, when candidates are being compared, the extent of their qualifications should be measured only on the basis of the factors related to the particular job. One result of this would be to multiply the cases in which candidates can be regarded as "equally qualified" (i.e., equally fitting the "equal opportunity-conscious" specifications).

It is possible, despite the protestations of the government, that the increasing commitment within the public sector to equal opportunities measured in numerical terms will result in a form of such discrimination, albeit not one which conforms to the caricature of appointment regardless of "merit". The report of the Patten Commission on policing in Northern Ireland has been the only document, thus far, which has acknowledged the full implications of a "goals and timetables" approach. While accepting that "[m]erit must remain a critical criterion for selection for the police service", stating that "religious or cultural identity, gender or ethnicity should [not] be regarded as a makeweight for merit", and emphasising the importance of "outreach programmes" designed to attract applications from Catholics, the report recommends that all candidates reaching a specified standard of merit "should then enter a pool from which the required number of recruits can be drawn . . . an equal number of Protestants and Catholics should then be drawn from the pool".[38] The Report concludes that this approach would require amendment to the FETO, which amendment it recommends.

POSITIVE DISCRIMINATION AND EC LAW

The amendment of the FETO to permit the adoption of the Patten recommendations relating to Northern Ireland's police force is a matter purely for domestic government.[39] At least at present, no issues of European law arise, though the implementation of the Human Rights Act 1998 (see further Chapters 1 and 11) will no doubt, assuming the Patten recommendations are implemented, lead to challenges under that Act by aggrieved Protestants whose applications to join the police force are rejected. But the position with respect to positive discrimination in favour of women and, to a lesser extent, ethnic minority workers is rather more complex.

The Patten report acknowledges a severe under-representation of women in the RUC (12.6%, of whom a third are part-time reservists). It made no recommendations for radical reform of recruitment practices to address the male/female imbalance,

---

[38] *Report of the Independent Commission on Policing*, paras 15.9–15.10. The report is available at www.belfast.org.uk.

[39] That this will not be a straightforward matter is clear from the response of Ian Paisley, leader of the Democratic Unionist Party to the report: "The Patten Commission is, as we said it would be, the death-knell of the RUC. . . Deliberate discrimination against Protestants is to be legally engaged in. Protestants within the Police will be forced out with no hope of receiving justice. . . Protestant money will finance those who have wrecked our Province and are now to be custodians of the Protestant people"—8th September 1999, available on the DUP website at *http://www.dup.org.uk*.

citing the advice it had "regrettabl[y]" received that such a radical approach was precluded by EU law. This being the case, it is useful to consider the extent to which EU law is or might be compatible with any "positive discrimination" implied in a "goals and timetables" approach.

At present, the only direct relevance of EU law here is to sex discrimination and to that part of race discrimination which falls within Article 39 (formerly Article 48) of the Treaty (see further, Chapter 2). This position will change when the new directive on race discrimination (COM (2000) 328 (01)) is implemented and if the 1999 draft equal treatment general framework directive[40] is adopted. Both the race discrimination directive, and the draft general framework directive (which regulates discrimination on grounds of racial or ethnic origin, religion or belief, disability, age or sexual orientation) permit positive discrimination by Member States. They shall be considered below, as shall the "positive action" amendment to Article 119 (now Article 141) of the founding Treaty, inserted by the Treaty of Amsterdam in the wake of the ECJ decisions discussed below.

Before turning to consider the ECJ decisions on positive action, it is useful to outline the legislation on which they were based. Article 2(1) of Council Directive 76/207 (the equal treatment directive) prohibits discrimination "on grounds of sex either directly or indirectly by reference in particular to marital or family status" "in the conditions, including selection criteria, for access to all jobs or posts" (Article 3), "with regard to access to all types and to all levels, of vocational guidance, vocational training, advanced vocational training and retraining" (Article 4) and "with regard to working conditions, including the conditions governing dismissal" (Article 5). Article 2 provides that the directive is (3)"without prejudice to provisions concerning the protection of women, particularly as regards pregnancy and maternity" and (4) "without prejudice to measures to promote equal opportunity for men and women, in particular by removing existing inequalities which affect women's opportunities" in access to employment, promotion, vocational training and working conditions.

In addition, Recommendation 84/635/EEC on the promotion of positive action for women, passed after the failure of the Council of Ministers and the Commission to pass a directive on positive action, encourages Member States to "adopt a positive action policy designed to eliminate existing inequalities affecting women in working life and to promote a better balance between the sexes in employment . . .". The document recommends, *inter alia*, that Member States take steps to "eliminate or counteract the prejudicial effect on women in employment or seeking employment which arise from existing attitudes"; to encourage the recruitment and promotion of women "in sectors and professions and at levels where they are underrepresented, particularly as regards positions of responsibility"; and to adapt working conditions and adjust the organisation of work and working time. The Recommendation, which is not binding, should be taken into account in the interpretation of Article 2(4).[41]

---

[40] Discussed in Chapter 1 and throughout the book.
[41] *Grimaldi* v *Fonds de Maladies Professionnelles* [1989] ECR 4407.

Even in the absence of the Recommendation on positive action, the equal treatment directive lacks the rigidly symmetrical approach adopted by the SDA, with its requirement for comparison (whether real or hypothetical). The ECJ might have chosen to adopt a relatively generous approach to positive discrimination by interpreting Articles 3, 4 and 5 as imposing obligations on Member States to eliminate the effects of discrimination, as well as its overt manifestations. Article 2(4), in particular, could have been applied to this end.

In *Commission* v *France* Case C–312/86 [1988] ECR 6315, the ECJ ruled that France's retention of a package of rights specific to women employees amounted to a failure adequately to transpose the equal treatment directive. Among the offending provisions were extended maternity leave; shortened working hours; leave to care for sick children; additional annual leave in respect of each child; one day's leave at the beginning of the school year; the time off work on Mother's Day; daily breaks for women working on keyboard equipment or employed as typists or switchboard operators; additional points for pension rights in respect of the second and subsequent children and childcare allowances for mothers.

The decision in *Commission* v *France* turned, in part, on the application of Article 2(3) which concerns rights connected with pregnancy and maternity. The Court ruled that "the protection of women in relation to maternity is designed to protect the special relationship between a woman and her child over the period which follows pregnancy and childbirth, by preventing that relationship from being disturbed by the multiple burdens which would result from the simultaneous pursuit of employment". It did not apply, therefore, to "measures relating to the protection of women in capacities, such as those of older workers or parents, which are not specific to [women]." As far as Article 2(4) was concerned, the Court ruled that the exception it provided:

15 . . . is specifically and exclusively designed to allow measures which, although discriminatory in appearance, are in fact intended to eliminate or reduce actual instances of inequality which may exist in the reality of social life. Nothing in the papers of the case, however, makes it possible to conclude that a generalized preservation of special rights for women in collective agreements may correspond to the situation envisaged in that provision.

The ECJ did not, in *Commission* v *France*, specify which of the special measures retained by France breached the equal treatment directive.[42] Though the package offended, it remained possible that any of the particular measures, whether alone or in various combinations, did not. The scope of Article 2(4) next came before the ECJ in *Kalanke* v *Freie Hansestadt Bremen* Case 450/93 [1995] ECR I–3051 [1996] All ER (EC) 66, [1996] ICR 314, [1995] IRLR 660, in which the Court interpreted that provision narrowly to prohibit direct positive discrimination. Very shortly thereafter, however, *Marschall* v *Land Nordrhein-Westfalen* Case C–409/95 [1997] ECR I–6363 [1998] IRLR 39, [1997] All ER (EC) 865, [1998] 1 CMLR 547 signalled a change of direction.

---

[42] See, however, the recent decision of the ECJ in *Abdoulaye*, case C–218/98, available on the web at www.europa.eu.int/eur-lex/en/index.html.

Kalanke involved a challenge to a German regional regulation whereby, in the case of equally qualified candidates, a woman would be given priority over a man where women were underrepresented in the particular post. Advocate General Tesauro interpreted Article 2(4) of the directive as a derogation from the principle established by Article 2(1), and categorised the priority given to women in the instant case as "only too obvious[ly] . . . discrimination on grounds of sex". He accepted that any action in favour of a disadvantaged group "conflicts with the principle of equality in the formal sense" and declared that positive action was permissible only to the extent that it was within Article 2(4), interpreting that provision narrowly to allow only those actions "designed to promote and achieve equal opportunities", "equal opportunities" being in turn defined to extend only to "putting people in a position to attain equal results and hence restoring conditions of equality as between members of the two sexes as regards starting points", as distinct from aiming at equality as regards results.[43]

The "formal equality" model described by Advocate General Tesauro is similar to that which pertains under the SDA and the RRA.[44] He went on to acknowledge, however, that:

> [t]he principle of substantive equality . . . [defined as] basing itself [on] . . . factors [such as sex] in order to legitimise an unequal right, which is to be used in order to achieve equality as between persons . . . complements the principle of formal equality and authorises . . . such deviations from that principle as are justified by the end which they seek to achieve, that of securing actual equality. The ultimate objective is therefore the same: securing equality as between persons.

Advocate General Tesauro took the view that Article 2(4), together with the other derogations, was based on the principle of substantive equality and authorised "such inequalities [of treatment] as are necessary in order to achieve" equality, and that "the rationale for the preferential treatment given to women [by Article 2(4)] lies in the general situation of disadvantage caused by past discrimination and the existing difficulties connected with playing a dual role".

Thus far, the Advocate-General's reasoning appears to permit formally unequal treatment under Article 2(4). But he went on to declare it "obvious" that "such difficulties will certainly not be resolved by means of quota systems and the like, which are even irrelevant to that end" and stated that Article 2(4) permitted only:

> measures relating to the organisation of work, in particular working hours, and structures for small children and other measures which will enable family and work commitments to be reconciled with each other . . . Positive action must therefore be directed at removing the obstacles preventing women from having equal opportunities by tackling, for example,

---

[43] Advocate General Tesauro also drew the rather surprising conclusion that "[t]he very fact that two candidates of different sex have equivalent qualifications implies in fact by definition that [they] have had and continue to have equal opportunities". This was contradicted by Advocate General Jacobs in *Marschall* who, nevertheless, shared Tesauro's conclusion.

[44] Not the DDA and, as we saw above, the position under the FETO is complex.

educational guidance and vocational training. In contrast, positive action may not be directed towards guaranteeing women equal results from occupying a job, that is to say, at points of arrival, by way of compensation for historical discrimination. In sum, positive action may not be regarded, even less employed, as a means of remedying, through discriminatory measures, a situation of impaired inequality in the past . . .

The ECJ ruled that the granting of automatic preference to women, where candidates were equally qualified and women underrepresented, breached the equal treatment directive. Article 2(4), in the Court's view:

> is specifically and exclusively designed to allow measures which, although discriminatory in appearance, are in fact intended to eliminate or reduce actual instances of inequality which may exist in the reality of social life . . . [citing *Commission* v *France*]. It thus permits national measures relating to access to employment, including promotion, which give a specific advantage to women with a view to improving their ability to compete on the labour market and to pursue a career on an equal footing with men . . .

The Court accepted that "existing legal provisions on equal treatment, which are designed to afford rights to individuals, are inadequate for the elimination of all existing inequalities", but ruled nevertheless that:

> as a derogation from an individual right laid down in the directive, Article 2(4) must be interpreted strictly[45] . . . National rules which guarantee women absolute and unconditional priority for appointment or promotion go beyond promoting equal opportunities and overstep the limits of the exception in Article 2(4) of the directive. Furthermore, in so far as it seeks to achieve equal representation of men and women in all grades and levels within a department, such a system substitutes for equality of opportunity as envisaged in Article 2(4) the result of which is only to be arrived at by providing such equality of opportunity.

The decision in *Kalanke* was greeted with a great deal of disquiet. The European Commission issued a Communication to the European Parliament and the Council on the interpretation of the judgment to the effect that the decision condemned only the granting of an "absolute and unconditional right to appointment or promotion", leaving it open to states to take and to permit to be taken "all other forms of positive action including flexible quotas"[46]. The Commission proposed an amendment to the equal treatment directive to the effect that "Possible measures [permissible under Article 2(4)] shall include the giving of preference, as regards access to employment or promotion, to a member of the under represented sex, provided that such measures do not preclude the assessment of the particular circumstances of an individual case".[47] The proposed amendment was rejected by the Economic and Social Committee on the grounds, *inter alia*, that it did not serve to clarify the existing law.

---

[45] Citing *Johnston* v *Chief Constable of the Royal Ulster Constabulary* Case C–222/84 [1986] ECR 1651, pp.1686–1687, [1986] 3 All ER 135, p.158.
[46] COM (96) 88 final, p.3.
[47] (97/C 30/19) OJ C.30/57 30th January 1997.

Ursula O' Hare, "Positive Action Before the European Court of Justice: Case C–450/93
Kalanke **v** ***Freie Hansestadt Bremen"*** **[1996] 2** *Web Journal of Current Legal Issues*

It may be argued that the interpretation given to the relevant legal provisions [by the ECJ in *Kalanke*] reveals a narrow vision of the principle of equality . . . the Advocate-General's analysis proceeds on the basis that the premise for [the "tie-break"] form of positive action is compensation for past discrimination. Arguments based around the social utility of such measures are also relevant but are not addressed . . . It is now commonly accepted that the achievement of *de facto* equality is a legitimate social objective. That leads to the question what, if anything, is discriminatory, where all else is equal, about utilising objective criteria in order to achieve that de facto equality; sex here being used as a functional means of distinguishing the candidates. (At the point of the exercise of discretion, it can be argued that the exercise of management prerogative may give effect to assumptions about one group which work to their disadvantage and therefore, does not automatically proceed on the basis of the "merit" principle.) Finally, strict quotas are for many, unacceptable because they are deemed to offend the merit principle. Tie-break positive action schemes, on the other hand, do not. However, there is no consideration of this issue by either the Court or the Advocate-General. These arguments should at least be addressed by the Court in the context of Articles 2(1) and 2(4) and the failure to do so renders the position taken here less convincing . . .

If, as the Advocate-General contends, the objective of the directive is ultimately substantive equality, then the insistence that the legislative provisions can only bear an interpretation which permits this objective to be achieved by means of procedural equality may be unduly narrow. Although Article 2(1) is undoubtedly an anti-discrimination measure and Article 2(4) can be read narrowly to give effect to this interpretation, a more expansive interpretation of that provision may also be possible. If Article 2(4) is read in light of the Recommendation [above] then it may be possible to give a broader interpretation to that provision than has been followed here . . .

It may be argued that the fair representation of women in employment, and particularly, the presence of women in senior positions could go some way towards challenging those existing attitudes which bar women's integration in the labour market which, in turn, might encourage the appointment of more women to senior positions. The adherence by the Court and the Advocate-General to a formal vision of equality fails to recognise that the achievement of "material equality" may ultimately require more than merely ensuring access to a "level playing field."

Increasingly, women do have access to the same educational opportunities and training and are entering the labour market well qualified. However, women continue to fail to achieve upper management positions ("the glass ceiling"). A number of reasons may be proffered for this failure which the Court neglects to consider; the employment culture traditionally reflects the male career-model of full-time and continuous employment with which many women are unable to comply; traditional assumptions about the role of women often work to thwart women's advancement and the absence of women from senior posts both confirms a stereotype and becomes a self-fulfilling prophecy in itself. Women remain segregated in the labour market and continue to earn proportionally less than men, notwithstanding the existence of equality laws which should have the effect of levelling the playing field . . . The exclusion of women from senior management fails to harness the full talents of society. Furthermore, without role models in key areas, younger women are in fact disadvantaged as compared with their male counter-parts and it becomes more difficult to break out of a cyclical pattern of disadvantage . . . For these reasons a more expansive interpretation of the principle of equal treatment could go some way to addressing these issues.

Vera Sacks, "What do we think about affirmative action now?" (1996) 2 *International Journal of Discrimination and the Law* 129, 134–7

There are those who believe that, if disadvantaged groups are to be helped to overcome existing obstacles in the competition for desirable goals, then sooner or later, underrepresentation of such groups will cease. To this end measures such as special training and education, relief from domestic responsibilities and the like are seen by them as sufficient and appropriate. These measures do not cause any injustice to others, do not interfere with the merit principle. . . . they are hostile to preference at the selection stage. The reasons centre around the individual injustice to the person who "loses out", arguments about merit (or lack of it), and that the reward is misdirected "for the beneficiaries were not themselves victims of ill treatment, merely the heirs of those who were" (Lustgarten, *Legal Control of Racial Discrimination* (Basingstoke: Macmillan, 1980) at p. 21) . . .

thus discriminatory selection which aims at redistributing desirable goods is too unfair to particular individuals, and thus a denial of justice. In the words of the Advocate-General [in *Kalanke*]: "the imposition of quotas . . . most affects the principle of equality as between individuals . . . in sum, positive action may not be regarded, even less employed, as a means of remedying, through discriminatory measures, a situation of impaired inequality in the past".

Others believe that underrepresentation needs to be addressed directly. The reasons for desiring proportionate representation, whether in the legislature or in other spheres, are centred round ideas about compensation, and justice and has great symbolic significance. . . . In the European Union now the only help is of the kind which reinforces women's role as workers and carers, ignoring the argument advanced by Parekh (and impliedly accepted by the A.G. [in *Kalanke*]) that this makes the visible and invisible walls almost impossible to scale.

This is a very limited view of the difficulties faced by women especially in those areas of employment where they are most underrepresented. Attitudes and past practices are often unthinking and unconscious and the setting of goals is a small attempt to overcome this fact. The challenged legislation set a legally enforceable but very limited goal. Without such goals equality of opportunity remains elusive. . . .the reasoning of the Advocate-General that Art. 2(4) could not have been intended to confer benefits on women simply because they are women, and hence that such measures are unlawful, is by no means self-evident. Viewed in the more global context, where such measures have become quite common as a means of addressing inequality of opportunity, the rejection by the E.C.J. of the experience and growing understanding of the necessary mechanisms needed to remedy discrimination is very sad. . . . The Bremen law which only related to the public sector, was a minimal attempt at redressing imbalances at the higher and more impenetrable management level. . . . The decision in *Kalanke* is to be regretted and will have serious consequences in many member states. It seems that old democracies have something to learn from new democracies.

Within two years, the ECJ had adopted the approach advocated by the Commission in its Communication on the *Kalanke* decision. *Marschall* v *Land Nordrhein-Westfalen* concerned a challenge to a rule which provided that, where there were fewer women than men in a particular career bracket, women were to be given priority for promotion in the event of equal suitability, competence and professional performance "unless reasons specific to an individual [male] candidate tilt the balance in his favour". Advocate General Jacobs argued that the decision in *Kalanke* was correct, and that no distinction could properly be drawn between its facts and those in the present case, although he accepted the argument that legislative reform might well be required. The Court, however, seized upon the "savings clause" to reach a different conclusion. Having reiterated the first paragraph of *Kalanke* reproduced above, the Court went on to acknowledge that:

Marschall v Land Nordrhein-Westfalen Case C–409/95 [1997] ECR I–6363

even where male and female candidates are equally qualified, male candidates tend to be promoted in preference to female candidates particularly because of prejudices and stereotypes concerning the role and capacities of women in working life and the fear, for example, that women will interrupt their careers more frequently, that owing to household and family duties they will be less flexible in their working hours, or that they will be absent from work more frequently because of pregnancy, childbirth and breastfeeding. For these reasons, the mere fact that a male candidate and a female candidate are equally qualified does not mean that they have the same chances.

It is at this point that the *volte-face* on the part of the Court occurs:

It follows that [my emphasis] a national rule in terms of which, subject to the application of the saving clause, female candidates for promotion who are equally as qualified as the male candidates are to be treated preferentially in sectors where they are under-represented may fall within the scope of Article 2(4) if such a rule may counteract the prejudicial effects on female candidates of the attitudes and behaviour described above and thus reduce actual instances of inequality which may exist in the real world.

While this is arguably [just] consistent with the Court's prohibition, in *Kalanke*, of the according of "absolute and unconditional priority" to women, it is irreconcilable with the Court's demand in that case that "as a derogation from an individual right laid down in the directive, Article 2(4) must be interpreted strictly", and its condemnation of the rule in that case for "substitut[ing] for equality of opportunity as envisaged in Article 2(4) the result which is only to be arrived at by providing such equality of opportunity". The only qualification imposed by the Court in *Marschall* to its newly permissive approach to positive discrimination was that:

since Article 2(4) constitutes a derogation from an individual right laid down by the directive, such a national measure specifically favouring female candidates cannot guarantee absolute and unconditional priority for women in the event of a promotion without going beyond the limits of the exception laid down in that provision (see *Kalanke* . . .) Unlike the rules at issue in *Kalanke*, a national rule which, as in the case in point in the main

proceedings, contains a saving clause does not exceed those limits if, in each individual
case, it provides for male candidates who are equally as qualified as the female candidates
a guarantee that the candidatures will be the subject of an objective assessment which will
take account of all criteria specific to the individual candidates and will override the priority accorded to female candidates where one or more of those criteria tilts the balance in
favour of the male candidate . . . It is for the national court to determine whether those conditions are fulfilled on the basis of an examination of the scope of the provision in question
as it has been applied.

The ECJ seized upon the "savings clause" in *Marschall* in order to distinguish the case
from *Kalanke*. But, as Advocate-General Jacobs pointed out in his opinion in
Marschall: "the national rule at issue in *Kalanke* was not in fact absolute and unconditional": the Court noted the national court's point that the rule had to be interpreted
"with the effect that, even if priority for promotion is to be given in principle to
women, exceptions must be made in appropriate cases". Equally, and somewhat
bizarrely, it appears that the savings clause in *Marschall* permitted consideration of
the very factors which, the German legislature had acknowledged in passing the preference rule, operated to women's disadvantage and necessitated the preference rule in
the first place:

> where qualifications are equal, employers tend to promote men rather than women because
> they apply traditional promotion criteria which in practice put women at a disadvantage,
> such as age, seniority and the fact that a male candidate is a head of household and sole
> breadwinner for the household.[48]

"Limited Positive Discrimination Allowed" (1998) 77 *Equal Opportunities Review* **38, 39–40**

From a legal standpoint, there is little to be said for this decision other than its outcome,
though many will think that the outcome is all that really matters. The reasoning, however,
is undistinguished. It is extremely difficult to see how this kind of positive discrimination
can be said to fall within the scope of the derogation from the principle of non-discrimination allowed by article 2(4) for "measures to promote equal opportunity". The ECJ refers
to whether the rule "is designed to promote equality of opportunity", whether it is "in fact
intended to eliminate or reduce actual instances of inequality". The intention of the rule-
maker, however, should have been of little weight: all positive discrimination measures
are intended to reduce inequality, including the measure held unlawful in *Kalanke*. The relevant issue is not intent, but whether the rule properly falls within the description of a
"measure to promote equal opportunity". Many would say that a measure which discriminates at the point of selection against one sex cannot also be a measure to promote equal
opportunity.
   Nor is there much of a basis for a principled distinction between *Marschall* and *Kalanke*.
The North Rhine-Westphalia rules [permitted by the ECJ in *Marschall*] have all the heavy-
handedness found in Bremen [and prohibited by the ECJ in *Kalanke*], other than the vague

[48] Observations of the Länder reported in the ECJ decision. Indeed the flexibility built into the preference system was such that "the administration can always give preference to a male candidate on the basis
of promotion criteria, traditional or otherwise".

savings clause allowing the preference in favour of women to be overridden in individual cases. This is valuable, in that it offers the scope to deal with the most anomalous of cases. But it does not deal with the more fundamental objection to this kind of positive discrimination policy: that it presumes prior sex discrimination by the employer and sets quotas without regard to whether such discrimination really did take place. This may be a reasonable assumption in the higher grades of teaching, the facts of *Marschall*. More generally, however, operation of the rule does not require any prior assessment of how likely it is that women would be equally represented in the grade if there had been no discrimination by the employer. In many jobs, the proportion of women is a function of sex discrimination in education or vocational training, or of occupational choice by women, not of sex discrimination in recruitment by the employer. An employer can appoint 20% of all female applicants and 20% of all male applicants, but if there are 10 times as many men as women applying, there will be far fewer women than men in post. Does that mean that women are "underrepresented" and should be given preferential treatment?

The European Court appears to place great weight on the assertion that "even where male and female candidates are equally qualified, male candidates tend to be promoted in preference to female candidates, particularly because of prejudices and stereotypes concerning the role and capacities of women in working life . . . For these reasons, the mere fact that a male candidate and a female candidate are equally qualified does not mean that they have the same chances." No empirical support for this generalisation is offered, however, and it is improbable that any proof for it exists. To the extent that there is such proof that equally-qualified women are discriminated against by employers, the most obvious remedy is to enforce the sex discrimination law of the country concerned, and it is startling that the Court makes no acknowledgement of this.

The truth is that "equally qualified" in this context is being given a very limited meaning. Paragraph 9 of the Advocate-General's Opinion records the Land's justification for giving "equally-qualified" women preferential treatment: "a man would tend to be appointed over an equally-qualified woman . . . because he is likely to be older and to have had longer service, attributable to fewer career breaks." It is certainly questionable whether most human resource practitioners would regard a female candidate for promotion as "equally qualified" as a man with longer service. Service is normally regarded as part of the qualifications for the job, broadly defined, though its relevance depends on the factual circumstances. If a man is appointed because he has more service—or because he is older—that may pose a legal issue of indirect discrimination, which can be dealt with without reference to positive discrimination (see the recent ECJ decision in *Kording v Senator für Finanzen* [Case C–100/95 [1997] ECR I–5289] [1997] IRLR 710).

Conversely, if professional qualifications are all that are at issue, it is arguable that a woman who has achieved the same standard as a man, despite taking time off for family reasons, should be regarded as "better qualified". Who is the more impressive candidate: the man aged 36 who has just passed his IPD exam, or the woman of the same age who has done it while taking time off to have three children?

Positive discrimination thus can only be regarded as permissible by giving a very broad interpretation to article 2(4); that amounts to a rewriting of the provision. Of course, there may be nothing wrong with that per se. It is what the Court did to the Equal Treatment Directive in respect of transsexuals in *P v S* [Case C–13/94 [1996] ECR I–2143]. . . . the best way of viewing *Marschall* is to recognise that the Court is interpreting the Equal Treatment Directive as a "living" document, taking account of changes in attitude since the Directive was drafted. The Advocate-General advised against this. He said: "Admittedly, the legislation was drafted two decades ago, and social developments since then may mean that a provision whose intention and scope were apposite when adopted is now in need of review. Revision of Community legislation is, however, also a matter for the legislature and not for this Court."

The European Court rejects this conservative approach to statutory construction. In so doing, the Court is reflecting the current political will of the Community. It is widely felt that limited positive discrimination, such as the use of gender as a tie-break, does no major harm. The Court's decision in *Kalanke* was criticised for frustrating the will of national legislatures. Following *Kalanke*, the European Commission issued a Communication setting out its view that the judgment only prohibited positive action taking the form of rigid quotas, which did not leave open any possibility to take account of individual circumstances. This is the approach now endorsed by the European Court in *Marschall*.

However spurious the grounds for distinction adopted by the ECJ in *Marschall*, that Court has moved towards a more substantial model of equality than currently prevails in the UK. The decision in *Marschall* was followed by that in *Badeck*, in which the ECJ approved German provincial legislation which, *inter alia*, required that public administrative departments "women's advancement plans" and take other measures to "work towards equality of women and men in the public service and the elimination of under-representation of women and to eliminate discrimination on grounds of sex and family status".

Part of the legislation at issue was concerned with the elimination of indirect discrimination, requiring that selection decisions were to be made on the basis of the "requirements of the post to be filled or the office to be conferred" and, where relevant, "capabilities and experience which have been acquired by looking after children or persons requiring care in the domestic sector (family work)" had to be taken into account "in so far as they are of importance for the suitability, performance and capability of applicants". Part-time work, leave and delays in completing training as a result of family commitments were to be excluded from consideration as were the applicant's family status and the income of the applicant's partner and, save where they were "of importance for the suitability, performance and capability of applicants", seniority, age and the date of last promotion.

But the advancement plans went beyond this to require equality of outcome to a significant degree. They were to contain binding targets for increasing the proportion of women in sectors in which they were under-represented and more than half of all positions arising during the two year duration of each plan were to be designated for women, save where a GOQ applied or it was "convincingly demonstrated that not enough women with the necessary qualifications are available", in which case a smaller proportion of posts could be designated female.

Promotions of women had, at least, to be in proportion to their relative position in the lower rung of employment and the proportion of women had to be protected in the event of redundancies. Particular measures applied to academic jobs, the appointment of women having to correspond, at least, with the proportion of women graduates, higher graduates or students in the discipline (the latter in the case of academic assistants without degrees).

Quotas were also established for training positions in occupations in which women were under-represented and, in sectors in which women were under-represented, at least as many women as men (or all the women applicants) were to be interviewed as long as they satisfied the minimum conditions for the position.

Finally, if the targets were not fulfilled in respect of each two-year plan, every further appointment or promotion of a man in a sector in which women were under represented was to require the approval of the body which had approved the advancement plan or, in some cases, the provincial government.

The ECJ ruled that measures intended to give priority to women in sectors of the public service where they are under-represented were compatible with the equal treatment directive as long as (a) they did not *automatically and unconditionally* give priority to women when women and men were equally qualified, and (b) the candidatures were the subject of an objective assessment which took account of the specific personal situations of all candidates. While it was for the national courts to decide whether these conditions were satisfied, the Court went on to suggest that none of the provisions at issue breached the equality directive. It ruled that the equal treatment directive "does not preclude a national rule which":

Badeck & Ors v Landesanwalt beim Staatsgerichtshof des Landes Hessen Case C–158/97 [2000] All ER (EC) 289, [2000] IRLR 432

—in sectors of the public service where women are under-represented, gives priority, where male and female candidates have equal qualifications, to female candidates where that proves necessary for ensuring compliance with the objectives of the women's advancement plan, if no reasons of greater legal weight are opposed, provided that that rule guarantees that candidatures are the subject of an objective assessment which takes account of the specific personal situations of all candidates,[49]
—prescribes that the binding targets of the women's advancement plan for temporary posts in the academic service and for academic assistants must provide for a minimum percentage of women which is at least equal to the percentage of women among graduates, holders of higher degrees and students in each discipline,
—in so far as its objective is to eliminate under-representation of women, in trained occupations in which women are under-represented and for which the State does not have a monopoly of training, allocates at least half the training places to women, unless despite appropriate measures for drawing the attention of women to the training places available there are not enough applications from women,
—where male and female candidates have equal qualifications, guarantees that qualified women who satisfy all the conditions required or laid down are called to interview, in sectors in which they are under-represented,

---

[49] While this was a question for the national courts, the ECJ seemed to suggest that, because the targets absolutely required the appointment of a woman over an equally qualified man only where no reasons of greater legal weight are opposed, and could be overridden by virtue of the preference given to the appointment of former public service employees returning after family-related periods of absence or to full-time work after family-related part-time working; to certain categories of service personnel; to the seriously disabled and to the long-term unemployed, sufficient consideration of factors specific to individuals was permitted by the plans.

—relating to the composition of employees' representative bodies and administrative and supervisory bodies, recommends that the legislative provisions adopted for its implementation take into account the objective that at least half the members of those bodies must be women.

It is clear, as a result of the decisions in *Marschall* and in *Badeck*, that there is wide scope for positive discrimination under the sex equality provisions of European law. This has recently been underlined by new Article 141 of the Treaty which, post-Amsterdam, provides:

(4) With a view to ensuring full equality in practice between men and women in working life, the principle of equal treatment shall not prevent any Member State from maintaining or adopting measures providing for specific advantages to make it easier for the under-represented sex to pursue a vocational activity or to prevent or compensate for disadvantages in professional careers.

Both the 1999 draft directive establishing a framework for equal opportunities and the newly adopted race discrimination directive provide, as was mentioned above, permit positive discrimination. The race discrimination directive provides (Article 5) that:

With a view to ensuring full equality, in practice, the principle of equal treatment shall not prevent any Member State from maintaining or adopting specific measures to prevent or compensate for disadvantages linked to racial or ethnic origin.

This formulation differs from that in the draft equal treatment framework directive ("This Directive shall be without prejudice to the right of the Member State to maintain or adopt measures intended to prevent or compensate for disadvantages concerning persons to whom any of the [prohibited grounds of discrimination—racial or ethnic origin, religion or belief, disability, age or sexual orientation] apply"), the stronger amended version having been adopted in the race discrimination directive at the behest of the European Parliament.

There is considerable scope for positive discrimination within EU law. Certainly, the provisions upheld by the ECJ in the *Marschall* case go far beyond anything currently available in the UK. It is now for the Government to determine whether to legislate in order to further the "goals and timetables" established by it in relation to ethnic minority recruitment and retention in the police, prison and fire service, as well as to ethnic minority and female advancement in public appointments and the senior civil service. It is most unlikely, given the government's hostility to intervention in the private sector (see further Chapter 5), that positive action will be required other than in the public sector. But in the absence of legislative amendment to permit at least "tie-break" reverse discrimination, the goals and timetables set in respect of female and ethnic minority advancement have very little chance of being met. Every white man rejected in favour of a woman or ethnic minority candidate will have an incentive to litigate. And the fact that an employer is self-consciously in the business of seeking to appoint more women/ ethnic minority candidates will operate so as to render a judgment in favour of the aggrieved white man more likely.

The difficulties of proving discrimination are discussed in Chapter 5. Here it is useful to consider a recent EAT decision which illustrates the potential difficulties facing those employers seeking deliberately to increase the diversity of their workforces.

ACAS v *Taylor* EAT/788/97, (Transcript) 11 February 1998

The decision concerned an appeal from a tribunal finding that Mr Taylor had been discriminated against by being refused promotion. Applications for promotion had been made by 126 ACAS officers of whom 40% were female (women accounted for 38% of those eligible to apply). Applications were assessed in the first place by their line managers, the grades awarded resulting either in rejection or in the case of "A" grades, in progress to the next stage of the promotion procedure. The highest scoring "B" grade assessed by each line manager also went forward as did, in cases where the line manager" scorings were regarded as low, the second highest ranking "B".

Mr Taylor was ranked fourth of the 4 "Bs" in his region, and was not put forward to the next stage. A tribunal found that he had been discriminated against on the basis that, whereas all eight of the women ranked "B" were put forward, only six of the sixteen men so ranked were put forward. In relation to four of the six recommending officers, two "B" candidates were put forward. In each of these cases, the second "B" was female.

The decision of the tribunal was questionable, the fact being that, whether or not two B candidates had been put forward in relation to the applicant's region, his application would not have been put forward. Further, the fact that women in each case benefited from a judgment that their recommending officers had been parsimonious could well have reflected the common practice whereby women are undervalued by virtue of their being women. But the tribunal took the view that Mr Taylor had been the victim of a policy of positive discrimination. This decision was reached, in part, because ACAS had circulated the following recruitment guidelines to its recommending officers.

> Please remember that more needs to be done to ensure the reality of the claim that ACAS is an equal opportunity employer. For example women make up only 17% of those at SEO level at present and ethnic minorities staff less than 1%. All staff should be considered on their merits as individuals. Where you have any doubts about the fairness of the Annual Reports you should not hesitate to take appropriate action.

Morison J, for EAT

It seems to us that the guidance provisions to which we have referred should be reconsidered by ACAS. The sentence "Please remember that more needs to be done to ensure the reality of the claim that ACAS is an equal opportunity employer" is readily capable of being misconstrued. Furthermore, it begs the question as to what is to be done and by whom. It seems to us that it would have been more appropriate and quite sufficient for the guidance to have reminded the line managers that ACAS was an equal opportunity employer and to draw attention to the fact that women and ethnic minorities staff at SEO level were poorly represented. Such poor representation was itself suggestive of potentially discriminatory practices in the past and the employers were entitled to draw that to the attention of those who had the responsibility for making decisions about promotions in the future. The way the guidance was composed seems to us to be capable of leading the unwary into positive discrimination.

It would be deeply ironic if, absent legislation to extend the scope of lawful positive discrimination, even if only in certain sections of the public sector, the adoption by government of a "goals and timetables" approach to equal opportunities served only to arm disappointed white male applicants with material from which tribunals will readily infer that they have been discriminated against. We saw, above, that EC law leaves considerable scope for an extension of the positive discrimination currently lawful in the UK. Few would argue that positive discrimination should be anything other than a last resort. But twenty five years after the enactment in the UK of fairly comprehensive, symmetrical legislation prohibiting discrimination on grounds of race or sex (in Northern Ireland, religious belief and political opinion), disadvantage on these grounds remains deeply entrenched, as we shall see in chapters 6, 7 and 9.

4

Prohibited discrimination

INTRODUCTION

We saw in Chapter 1 that discrimination on the grounds covered by the Sex Discrimination Act, the Race Relations Act, the Disability Discrimination Act and the Fair Employment and Treatment (Northern Ireland) Order is not regulated except by the relevant legislation—the common law imposes no general prohibition on discrimination. This position will change with the implementation of the Human Rights Act 1998, the judiciary being obliged to develop the law to give effect to the provisions of the European Convention on Human Rights and, in particular, to Article 14's prohibition of discrimination in relation to those provisions "on any ground such as sex, race, colour, language, religion, political or other opinion, national or social origin, association with a national minority, property, birth or other status." At present, however, the position is as discussed in Chapter 1. Some of the possible implications of the HRA are discussed in the concluding chapter.

None of the anti-discrimination legislation here discussed imposes a blanket prohibition on discrimination on the covered grounds (race, sex, disability, etc.). Instead, each enactment details a number of areas—employment; facilities, goods and services; housing, etc.—in respect of which discrimination is regulated. Even in these areas, discrimination is prohibited by the various regimes only in specific instances.

EMPLOYMENT

S.4 RRA, which is extracted below, regulates employment-related discrimination. Its provisions are echoed by s.6 SDA, s.4 DDA and Article 19 FETO, all of which are discussed further below. "Employment" is defined by the RRA, SDA and FETO as "employment under a contract of service or of apprenticeship or a contract personally to *execute any work or labour*", the DDA substituting the words "to do any work" for those italicised.[1] These definitions serve to extend the protection of the anti-discrimination provisions[2] to a wider category of workers than those entitled to claim unfair dismissal,

---

[1] Ss. 78, 82, Article 69 and s.68 respectively.

[2] But not, significantly, the 1992 Trade Union and Labour Relations (Consolidation) Act's prohibition of discrimination on grounds of trade union membership.

redundancy payments, etc., under the Employment Rights Act 1996. The ERA applies only to workers employed under contracts *of service*, as distinct from contracts *for services*, which latter category includes many of the most disadvantaged workers. The anti-discrimination protections also apply, save in the case of the DDA,[3] to barristers (in Scotland, advocates) in relation to pupillage, tenancy and the assignment of work[4].

Ss.11–16 SDA (ss.10–15 RRA and Article 26 FETO) prohibit discrimination in relation to partners (though, save in the case of the SDA, only in partnerships of at least six). Save in the case of the DDA, agency/ contract workers are protected from discrimination by "principals" as if they were employed by the principal,[5] and are also protected from discrimination on the part of the supplying agency.[6] A significant limitation on the protection afforded to contract workers was imposed by EAT in *Lloyd* v *IBM (UK) Ltd* (EAT/642/94, 3rd February 1995), in which the fact that the applicant supplied her services to an employment agency through a company established by her, as is common in the IT sector, excluded her from the protection of the SDA.[7] In *Abbey Life* v *Tansell*, however, the Court of Appeal took a different view in a case brought under the DDA.

Abbey Life Assurance Company Ltd v *Tansell*, Court of Appeal, 6th April 2000

Mummery LJ (for the Court):

The language of section 12 clearly covers the standard case in which, for example, a person makes office work available for doing by individuals employed by a temping agency. The agency enters into a contract with that person to supply individuals to do that work. That person is a principal. The individuals who are supplied are contract workers doing contract work. By section 12 they are protected from discrimination by the principal. . . .

the language of the section is also reasonably capable of applying to the less common case in which an extra contract is inserted, so that there is no direct contract between the person making the work available and the employer of the individual who is supplied to do that work. . . .

This result does not involve any unconstitutional border crossing by the court. It is achieved by a conventional process of judicial construction of legislation. The normal meaning of the language of the section is capable of covering this case, as well as the standard case. An interpretation which applies the section to the less common case, as well as

---

[3] Ss.35A & B SDA (ss.26A & B RRA) and Article 32 FETO. The Disability Rights Task Force's final report, *From Exclusion to Inclusion* (1999, available at http://www.disability.gov.uk/drtf/index2.html), recommended that the DDA be brought into conformity with the other regimes.

[4] Barristers' and advocates' claims must be brought to the County or Sheriff Court rather than to the employment tribunal.

[5] Ss.9 SDA and 7 RRA and Article 20 FETO. For the application of the provisions see the decision of the Court of Appeal in *Harrods Ltd* v *Remick and others* [1998] 1 All ER 52, [1998] ICR 156, [1997] IRLR 583, *BP Chemicals Ltd* v *Gillick & Anor* [1995] IRLR 128 and *Taylor* v *Arthur Andersen & Ors* (1999) 41 EORDCLD 4.

[6] Ss.15 SDA, 14 RRA and Article 22 FETO. See *Cobb & Ors* v *Secretary of State for Employment* [1989] IRLR 464.

[7] A similar decision was reached in *Rice* v *Fon-a-Car* [1980] ICR 133, in which that which was lacking was a contractual obligation on the part of the supplier.

to the standard case, is more consistent with the object of the section and of the 1995 Act than an interpretation which does not do so. In a number of authorities the appellate courts have stressed the importance of giving the wide ranging provisions of the discrimination legislation a generous interpretation [citing, *inter alia, Jones* v *Tower Boot Co Ltd* [1997] ICR 254, [1997] 2 All ER 406, [1997] IRLR 168]. The general purpose of the 1995 Act is to outlaw discrimination on the ground of disability. Employment is one of the fields in which it aims to achieve that goal. In order to achieve that result Parliament decided not to confine liability for discrimination in employment to the employer who discriminates against those employed by him under a traditional contract of service. Under section 12 liability is also imposed on those who, without entering into contracts of service with individual employees, make contracts for individuals employed by others to do work made available for them to do. It would not be consistent with the legislative object to withhold protection from discrimination by a person to whom an employee, who was entitled to protection from his employer, had been supplied to do some work. Hence the provisions for the protection of contract workers in all the discrimination Acts. . . .

it is my view that *Lloyd* v *IBM* was wrongly decided and that *Rice* v *Fon-a-Car* [see footnote 7] is irrelevant.

Both the CRE and the EOC, in their 1998 reform proposals, called for the extension of the Acts to volunteers. In addition, the CRE pointed out that the definition of employee adopted by the RRA [and, accordingly, under the SDA] excludes most office holders (whether judges or members of commissions or authorities, etc.). The CRE points out that "the position of office-holder, by its nature, is normally an influential one" and declares it "particularly important that there should be no racially discriminatory barriers to access to such positions" or, indeed, be any such discrimination during or at the termination of office-holding. The Race Relations (Amendment) Bill, currently before Parliament, extends the provisions of the RRA to cover the appointment of office holders.[8] The government has also indicated the intention to deal with volunteers by means of a Code of Practice.[9] We shall see, below, that significant amendments to the RRA will be required in order to implement the new race discrimination directive.

The boundaries of "employment" under the SDA and other anti-discrimination legislation are illustrated by the decision of the Court of Appeal in *Mirror Group Newspapers Ltd* v *Gunning*. Ms Gunning sought to sue MGN under the SDA when the group refused to permit her to take over her father's area distributorship on his retirement. She, like her father, was an independent newspaper wholesaler who bought papers from newspaper publishers and sold them on to newsagents. A tribunal ruled that the distributorship came within the SDA's definition of "employment", the contract between MGN and Ms Gunning's father requiring that he exercised day-to-day supervision over the distribution tasks, although he was not obliged to carry them out himself. The tribunal further found that MGN had discriminated unlawfully against

[8] See also *Perceval-Price & Ors* v *DED & NI Civil Service* 41 EORDCLD 1, in which a tribunal ruled that tribunal chairs were "workers" within Article 141.

[9] Ian McCartney, Minister of State for the Cabinet Office, in an equality statement 30th November 1999, available on http://www.cabinet-office.gov.uk/1999/news/ 991130_discrimination.htm.

Ms Gunning. EAT, by a majority, refused MGN's appeal ([1985] IRLR 60), but the Court of Appeal allowed it on the basis that the contract at issue was not one "personally to execute any work or labour" under s.82(1).

Ms Gunning's counsel had argued that "any" should be read as applying to the *extent* as well as to the *nature* of the work or labour contracted for, so as to afford the protection of the SDA to any contract a "material" term of which required the personal execution of work or labour by a contracting party. The Court of Appeal, however, preferred an interpretation suggested by Alexander Irvine QC (now Lord Chancellor), for MGN.

Mirror Group Newspapers Ltd v Gunning [1986] 1 All ER 385, [1986] 1 WLR 546, [1986] ICR 145 [1986] IRLR 27

Balcombe LJ:

I cannot accept [Mr Irvine's] primary submission that the phrase "contract personally to execute any work or labour" contemplates only a contract whose sole purpose is that the party contracting to provide services under the contract performs personally the work or labour which forms the subject matter of the contract. As was suggested during the course of argument, this would exclude from the definition a contract with a sculptor, where it was contemplated that some of the menial work might be carried out by persons other than the contracting party, a contract with a one-man builder, who might be expected to sub-contract some of the specialist work, or even a contract with a plumber, who might be expected to have his mate with him on all occasions.

However, I do accept Mr Irvine's alternative submission that the phrase in its context contemplates a contract whose dominant purpose is that the party contracting to provide services under the contract performs personally the work or labour which forms the subject matter of the contract. In the course of oral argument before us, Mr Beloff [for Ms Gunning] conceded that a single obligation to provide personal services in a contract is not of itself sufficient to bring the contract within the phrase; you have to look at the contract as a whole to see the extent to which that obligation colours the contract, which goes a long way towards accepting the "dominant purpose" test. In my judgment, you have to look at the agreement as a whole, and provided that there is some obligation by one contracting party personally to execute any work or labour, you then have to decide whether that is the dominant purpose of the contract, or whether the contract is properly to be regarded in essence as a contract for the personal execution of work or labour, which seems to me to be the same thing in other words.

The *Gunning* case has been applied subsequently to exclude sub-postmasters from the protection of the RRA and DDA (respectively, *Chambers* v *Post Office Counters Ltd* (CA), 21st February 1995, unreported (CA) and *Sheenan* v *Post Office Counters* EAT/417/98, 16th November 1998, unreported). In *Kelly & Loughran* v *Northern Ireland Housing Executive* [1998] ICR 828, [1998] 3 WLR 735, [1998] IRLR 593, on the other hand, a majority of the the House of Lords took a very generous approach to the equivalent provisions of the Fair Employment Act (as it then was) in accepting that a "contract personally to execute any work or labour" could arise between a body and individuals within an organisation to which that body contracted work.

The *Kelly & Loughran* case arose as a result of the refusal by the Housing Executive to appoint the applicants—respectively, one of two partners in a firm of solicitors and a sole practitioner—to a panel which defended public liability claims made against it. The applicants sought the appointment of their firms and named themselves the designated solicitors who would be responsible for the work. The Fair Employment Tribunal ruled that neither applicant was seeking "employment" under the FEA's wide definition, a finding upheld in respect of the first applicant only by Northern Ireland's Court of Appeal, but rejected (by a bare majority) by the House of Lords in respect of both.

Dealing first with the *Loughran* case, Lord Slynn agreed with the Court of Appeal that Mr Loughran, as a sole practitioner, was "In substance . . . seeking to have himself appointed to the panel. He designated himself as the solicitor who would be mainly concerned with the work to be done for the executive." The effect of this designation was that Loughran agreed, if appointed, to "give priority to panel work". This, according to Lord Slynn (with whom Lord Steyn agreed) fell within the *Gunning* test. Their Lordships regarded this test as permitting some delegation in a case, such as this, in which an individual was legally responsible for the work:

> it does not cease to be a contract "personally to execute any work" because his secretary types and posts the executive's defence to any claim or that his assistant solicitor goes along to file such a defence. The dominant purpose is that he will do the essential part of the work.

Lord Griffiths concurred on similar grounds, Lords Lloyd and Clyde dissenting as they did in *Kelly*. Their speeches are discussed below. Turning to the *Kelly* case, Lord Slynn (with Lord Steyn) took the broadest approach, deciding that a contract "personally to execute any work or labour," could be made with a firm as well as with a natural person.[10] This conclusion rested on the Interpretation Act 1978 provision to the effect that " 'unless the contrary intention appears' 'person' includes a body of persons unincorporate". Lord Slynn could discern no contrary intention, the FEA's purpose being "to outlaw discrimination on the grounds of religious or political opinion in the employment sphere" and it being "factually possible to discriminate against the partners of a firm or against the firm itself as it is against a sole practitioner":

> the [FEA] clearly and deliberately adopts a wide definition of employment so as to include a contract to provide services and a firm can contract to provide services. If the definition had included only "workman" or "artificer" or "a contract of service" the position might well be different but with the extended definition of employment I consider that a contract by a firm to provide services is capable of being a contract "personally to execute any work or labour.

---

[10] See *Tinnelly & Sons Ltd and others and McElduff and others* v *United Kingdom* Cases 62/1997/846/1052–1053, available on http://www.dhcour.coe.fr/eng/Judgments .htm, discussed in Chapter 9, where this point was not, however, argued. The approach of the House of Lords in *Loughran* should also apply to the SDA and the RRA.

Lord Griffiths concurred with Lords Slynn and Steyn as to result, but decided the *Kelly* case on the basis that the applicant, as a partner, was a "contracting party":

> A firm of solicitors has no legal existence, independent of the partners of the firm. The contract . . . if it had come into existence, would have been a contract between the executive and both partners of the firm. That being so Bernadette Kelly was seeking to enter into a contract personally to execute work . . .

Lord Griffiths was unable to agree with Lord Slynn's interpretation of the FEA which, in his view was "aimed at giving protection to individuals and not to companies or unincorporated corporations. It would be a wholly unnatural use of language to say a company or corporation had personally agreed to carry out work". Lord Griffith's judgment was sufficient to secure to Ms Kelly, as well as to Mr Loughran, the protection of the FEA despite the dissents of Lords Lloyd and Clyde. The former took the view that, the contracts in both cases being sought by the *firms*, they would not have been made with the persons who would have carried out the personal service:

> Had Mrs Kelly's firm been successful in the application for appointment to the panel, the contract would have been with the firm, but the actual work would have been performed by Mrs Kelly as the designated solicitor. If one assumes for a moment that Mrs Kelly had been an assistant solicitor, and not a partner, it seems clear enough that she could not have complained. The contract would not have been with her. Nor could the firm have complained, since a firm (as distinct from an individual) cannot agree to execute work personally . . .
>
> Parliament cannot have intended that [the FEA] should apply to some partnerships but not others, according to whether the person actually carrying out the work is a partner or not. In many cases a potential employer would not even know (unless he inquired) whether the person carrying out the work was a full partner, a salaried partner, or an employee. Moreover the status of the person carrying out the work might change. Thus if in the present case Mrs Kelly had been an assistant solicitor at the time of the contract she could not have complained, even though she was due to become a partner within a month or a week. The liability of a potential employer for unlawful discrimination should not depend on such chances as these. In her complaint Mrs Kelly describes herself as having applied for the job in question. But, except in the most technical and refined sense this was not the case it was the firm who applied, and not Mrs Kelly, as indeed my noble and learned friend, Lord Slynn, acknowledges . . .
>
> As for Mr Loughran, the Court of Appeal drew a distinction between his case and that of Mrs Kelly on the ground that Mr Loughran was "in substance" seeking to have himself appointed to the panel. The Court of Appeal did not regard this as a desirable distinction, and nor do I. But, whereas the Court of Appeal felt constrained to reach an undesirable conclusion . . . I do not myself feel the same constraint. Parliament cannot have intended the application of [the FEA] to depend on the number of partners in the firm . . .

Lord Clyde took the view that neither applicant fell within the *Gunning* test:

> What [the proposed contract in each case] sought to do was to secure the appointment of a particular solicitors' business enterprise with a view to the giving of instructions in the

future for the conduct of litigation in which the executive would be involved. The executive was also concerned to identify individual practitioners in the solicitors' business. It was not concerned to see that the party with whom it made the contract was the individual who would himself or herself predominantly do the work. As the tribunal described it, it would be fortuitous if the same person was both the contracting party and the person who was principally to do the work. The proposed appointment was not one under which the appointee was personally to execute work, but only one under which the appointee would be able to make arrangements for the personal execution of work by one of the solicitor members of the business. Under the construction which has been given to the critical phrase the offer of appointment which was made in the present case does not seem to me to fall within the scope of the definition . . .

There was no majority in *Kelly & Loughran* to the effect that the FETO (as it now is) or the other discrimination provisions apply to "firms" or "companies", as distinct from individuals. Organisations are, of course, liable for their own acts of discrimination, whether as employers or as providers of goods and services, etc. But, save within the narrow confines of the *Kelly & Loughran* case, they are not protected against discrimination by others. This remains the case even where, as was alleged in that case, the discrimination is at the hands of a public authority.

Lord Griffith, in his concurring speech, drew attention to the "formidable difficulties" of requiring "tribunals . . . to decide on the religious beliefs or political opinions of companies or corporations". But, where there is evidence that a would-be contractor has been discriminated against because of the alleged discriminator's perception of its religious or political composition, the actual composition of the organisation should not be relevant. The same point could be made in respect of other forms of discrimination.

The new directive on race discrimination applies its protections to 'persons' rather than 'individuals', this by virtue of an amendment carried in the European Parliament. There is evidence that ethnic minority who run businesses, in particular, suffer discrimination. The RRA will have to be extended to permit companies as well as natural people. The other issue of relevance here concerns the obligations imposed in Northern Ireland by s. 75 Northern Ireland Act 1998 and to be imposed in Britain by the Race Relations (Amendment) Bill currently before Parliament. The Act and the Bill impose upon public authorities obligations to "have regard to the need to promote equality of opportunity" in carrying out their functions (the Northern Ireland Bill only in Northern Ireland). The Northern Ireland Act covers equality of opportunity on a variety of grounds and is further discussed in Chapter 5. So, too, is the duty to be imposed by the RRA after amendment. The point to make here is that the promotion of equality of opportunities between persons of different racial groups must include an obligation not to discriminate without justification between white and ethnic minority businesses, even if it is not possible to define the businesses themselves as 'persons' of any particular racial group.

PROHIBITED DISCRIMINATION

We have seen that the "employment" in relation to which discrimination is prohibited is, though wide, not sufficiently generous, as yet to encompass all those (like Ms Gunning and Mr Sheenan) who are in an economically subordinate contractual relationship involving, as a matter of fact, the personal execution of work. We will now turn to consider the terms of s.4 RRA and the equivalent provisions of the other anti-discrimination legislation.

> (1) It is unlawful for a person, in relation to employment by him at an establishment in Great Britain, to discriminate against another—
>> (a) in the arrangements he makes for the purpose of determining who should be offered the employment; or
>> (b) in the terms on which he offers that employment; or
>> (c) by refusing or deliberately omitting to offer him that employment.
> (2) It is unlawful for a person, in the case of a person employed by him at an establishment in Great Britain, to discriminate against that employee—
>> (a) in the terms of the employment which he affords him; or
>> (b) in the way he affords him access to opportunities for promotion, transfer or training, or to any other benefits, facilities or services, or by refusing or deliberately omitting to afford him access to them; or
>> (c) by dismissing him, or subjecting him to any other detriment.

S.6 SDA is of precisely the same effect, save that it omits (2)(a), discrimination in contractual terms being governed by the Equal Pay Act 1970 (discussed in chapter 10). S.4 DDA and Article 19 FETO are drafted in similar terms to s.4 of the RRA.

Before we consider the operation of s.4 RRA and the equivalent provisions of the SDA, DDA and FETO, it is useful to draw attention to the geographical qualification to the scope of the anti-discrimination provisions. The RRA, SDA and DDA apply only to employment "at an establishment in Great Britain", the SD(NI)O, RR(NI)O and FETO to "employment in Northern Ireland". S.8 RRA provides that "employment is to be regarded as being at an establishment in Great Britain unless the employee does his work wholly or mainly outside Great Britain" or, in the case of those working on British registered ships or on aircraft or hovercraft registered in the UK and operated by British residents, "unless the employee does his work wholly outside Great Britain".[11]

The geographical limitation of the RRA's employment-related provisions must now be considered in the light of *Bossa* v *Nordstress & Anor* [1998] 1 CR 694, [1998] IRLR 284. The plaintiff, who was an Italian national resident in the UK, applied in the UK for a cabin crew job based in Italy. His application was rejected on the basis

---

[11] See also ss.10 SDA and 68 DDA and *Carver* v *Saudi Arabian Airlines* [1999] IRLR 371. S.9 RRA also exempts from the provisions of the Act seamen recruited abroad.

that "as a foreign company providing a leasing service to Alitalia", the company was not permitted to employ Italian nationals in Italy. His RRA claim was rejected on the grounds that it was excluded by s.8 RRA. On appeal, EAT ruled that the RRA failed to give effect to Article 39 (ex 48) of the Treaty of Rome, which prohibits "discrimination based on nationality between workers of the Member States as regards employment, remuneration and other conditions of work and employment".[12]

Reservations were expressed in Chapter 1 about the extent to which Article 39 has full horizontal effect. Nevertheless, the decision in *Bossa* serves as a reminder that, in the area of race as well as sex discrimination, European law is relevant. This will become all the more true when the new race discrimination directive comes into effect. It, like the equal treatment directive, is not subject to any geographical limitations. Article 3 of the equal treatment directive provides that "there shall be no discrimination whatsoever on grounds of sex in the conditions, including selection criteria, for access to all jobs or posts, whatever the sector or branch of activity, and to all levels of the occupational hierarchy.[13] The race discrimination directive provides (Articles 2 and 3) that "there shall be no direct or indirect discrimination based on racial or ethnic origin" in relation "[w]ithin the limits of the powers conferred upon th[e] Community" to conditions for access to employment, working conditions, social security, social advantages and so on. These directives, having only vertical direct effect, are binding only on public sector employers, and the clear exclusion of employment outside Great Britain is probably not susceptible to interpretation so as to give indirect effect to the directives.[14] Nevertheless, it appears that the exclusion of employment outside Great Britain from the SDA and the RRA is suspect. The same will be true, in the context of the DDA, if the 1999 draft equal treatment general framework directive adopted. The directive would also extend European anti-discrimination provisions to "religion or belief . . . age or sexual orientation".

Returning to s.4 RRA, a number of its provisions are very straightforward. Ss.4(1)(a) and (c) overlap to some extent, most instances of discriminatory refusals to employ arising out of discrimination in the arrangements upon which selection for employment relies. But, whereas an applicant under s.4(1)(c) and the equivalent provisions must actually have applied for and been rejected from the job in question, s.4(1)(a) is apt to cover complaints from those who have been rendered unable to apply.[15] This point was clarified by the recent employment tribunal decision in *Coker & Osamor* v *Lord Chancellor* discussed below.

S.4(1)(a) and its equivalents prohibit discrimination "in the arrangements [made] for the purpose of determining who should be offered . . . employment". Such arrangements

---

[12] In *Walgrave and Koch* (Case C–36/74) [1974] ECR 1405 the ECJ ruled that Art 141 applies even in respect of work done outside the Community, as long as the legal employment relationship was entered into within the Community.

[13] For a tribunal decision on this see *Murray* v *Navy Army & AirForces Institute* reported in 34 EORD-CLD, pp.11–12.

[14] See discussion in Chapter 1.

[15] Although it does require—*London Borough of Croydon* v *Kuttapan* [1999] IRLR 349—that an actual vacancy existed.

might include advertising (including questions of how any advertisements are drafted and where they are placed);[16] the use of recruitment sources such as schools, careers offices, job centres etc. (including the selection of these sources and any instructions issued to them);[17] selection and training of short-listers and interviewers, together with the manner in which short-listing, interviewing, and final selection is conducted.[18]

The CRE's Code of Practice for the Elimination of Racial Discrimination and the Promotion of Equal Opportunity in Employment advises (Part I) that:

> It is unlawful to use recruitment methods which exclude or disproportionately reduce the numbers of applicants of a particular racial group and which cannot be shown to be justifiable. It is therefore recommended that employers should not recruit through the following methods:
>
> Recruitment, solely or in the first instance, through the recommendations of existing employees where the workforce concerned is wholly or predominately white or black and the labour market is multi-racial.
>
> Procedures by which applicants are mainly or wholly supplied through trade unions where this means that only members of particular racial group, or a disproportionately high number of them, come forward.

Coker & Osamor v *Lord Chancellor* arose from the appointment by the Lord Chancellor of a "Special Adviser", a position not governed by the normal rules governing civil service appointments. These advisers, one or two of whom may be appointed by Cabinet ministers, work very closely with their respective ministers, impart political advice and play a role in policy development. The person appointed by the Lord Chancellor was Garry Hart, a longstanding friend and godfather, incidentally, to a child of the Prime Minister with whom the Lord Chancellor himself had longstanding ties. The appointment was made without advertisement of the vacancy.

Jane Coker and Martha Osamor challenged the appointment under s.6(1)(a) of the SDA and 4.(1)(a) RRA respectively, arguing that Lord Irvine had discriminated against them by denying them the opportunity to apply for the position. By restricting the potential candidates for the position to those within his predominantly white, male circle of friends, they argued that he had discriminated against otherwise quali-

---

[16] Though EAT in *Cardiff Women's Aid* v *Hartup* [1994] IRLR 390 ruled that only the CRE, under s.29 RRA, could take action in respect of a discriminatory advertisement. As Michael Rubenstein pointed out in the IRLR commentary to the case, the distinction drawn by EAT in that case between an *act* of discrimination (this being required under s.4(1)(a)) and evidence of an *intention* to discriminate (in respect of which only the CRE can take action), was "unconvincing", and EAT's interpretation of s.4(1)(a) "unduly restrictive".

[17] The CRE's Code of Practice states that "it is recommended that employers should not confine recruitment unjustifiably to those agencies, job centres, careers offices and schools which, because of their particular source of applicants, provide only or mainly applicants of a particular racial group".

[18] See *In re Ballymena Borough Council* Queen's Bench Division (Crown Side)18th June 1993 (unreported, further discussed in Chapter 5), where selection took place by secret ballot by counsellors divided along sectarian lines. The applicant, who was rejected, succeeded in a complaint under the FEA's equivalent of s.4(1)(c) RRA. Had, for some reason, a decision been reached after the ballot to abandon the new position and not appoint, an application could still have been made under s.4(1)(a), see *Brennan* v *J H Dewhurst Ltd* below.

fied women and African/ Caribbean/ Afro-Caribbean people. The tribunal found in favour of Jane Coker while rejecting Martha Osamor's claim. In doing so, it rejected the Lord Chancellor's argument that, the women not having applied for the post of Special Adviser, they could not bring themselves within ss 6(1)(a) SDA and s.4(1)(a) RRA respectively:

Coker and Osamor v Lord Chancellor [1999] IRLR 396

As we have noted, it is common ground that the position to which Mr Hart was appointed was not advertised. Further, it is contended by the respondents that the Lord Chancellor was never aware of the applicants or their interest to become Special Advisers. Mr McManus submitted that, as a matter of law, an application is required for a specific post before there can be a breach of s.6 of the Sex Discrimination Act; it would be wrong in principle to hold that discrimination legislation makes it obligatory to advertise in all cases; and the consequences of finding such an obligation could not be restricted to this case and would mean that "headhunting", a familiar practice in recruitment, was unlawful. . . .

As we have noted, s.6(1)(a) makes it unlawful to discriminate against a woman in the arrangements a person makes for the purpose of determining who should be offered employment. That is clearly intended to apply to facts which are other than a refusal or deliberate omission to offer employment, which are addressed separately in para. (a). It appears to us that the phrase "the arrangements he makes" is very broad in its effect. . . . the legislation is intended to apply to a situation in which the employer by one means or another avoids receiving applications from people. We do not see what difference in principle there could be between the situation referred to by Mr Justice Morison, of telling people not to apply for a job, and the situation which appears to arise in this case, of not letting people know that there is a vacancy.

As to the relevance of Article 3 of the Directive, its provisions also appear to be in broad and absolute terms, relating to access to "all jobs or posts" and not restricted to such jobs or posts as may be the subject of invitations for applications.

As to the statutory purpose and intent, it seems clear to us that, on balance, it would be contrary to the policy of the discrimination legislation to allow an employer to avoid it completely by an absence of recruitment, and its replacement by appointment of friends and relatives. It was submitted by Ms Monaghan that the Act incorporates safeguards against unrestricted classes of individuals being able to bring complaints, ie the floodgates argument. Firstly, there is the provision for a comparison of similar circumstances. A complainant must be able to bring herself or himself within that provision. Secondly, if an employment practice in fact affects a large class of individuals, then there is no good reason why they should be prevented from bringing actions. She submitted that headhunting would not be outlawed if her argument were accepted, provided the headhunting was not discriminatory on the grounds of race or sex.

The tribunal accepts and adopts those submissions by Ms Monaghan. We therefore accept that the applicants were entitled to bring their complaints of discrimination in the absence of specific applications by them for employment. Whether these applications succeed is to be determined by the application of the statutory provisions, and the provisions of the Directive to which we have referred.

The tribunal went on to find that Lord Irvine had applied a requirement or condition that the "Special Adviser" be personally known to him, with which condition a substantially smaller proportion of women and African/ Caribbean/ Afro-Caribbean people than of men/ white people could comply. They also found that the application of the condition was not justifiable, the Lord Chancellor's own articulation of the qualities needed in his Special Adviser not having required it. The decision is awaiting hearing by EAT, the Lord Chancellor having taken the unusual step of retaining two leading QCs for the appeal. It is further discussed below.

It is clear from the *Coker* decision that s.4(1)(a) RRA and its equivalent provisions extend to the decision whether or not jobs will be advertised. The word-of-mouth recruitment method is widely acknowledged as one which perpetuates existing race and/or sex imbalances in the workforce. (In his evidence to the Northern Ireland Select Committee for its 1998–99 Fourth Report, *The Operation of the Fair Employment (Northern Ireland) Act 1989: Ten Years On*, the then-Chair of the FEC attributed much of the success of the fair employment legislation in integrating private sector employment to the formalisation of recruitment methods.)[19]

The traditional paradigm of word-of-mouth recruitment is in manual work, in which recruitment frequently took place via family connections. But, as counsel for the Lord Chancellor pointed out in *Coker*, recruitment via headhunters could be categorised as subject to the same failings. (So, too, could current methods for appointing judges and QCs.)[20] It is important to note, however, that even if *Coker* was generally binding (which, as an employment tribunal decision, it is not), the decision does not prohibit such "informal" recruitment methods. Rather, as the tribunal pointed out, reliance upon informal methods of selection such as those applicable to "Special Advisers" should be accompanied with awareness of "the imbalance of gender or race in the circles in which [an appointer] is minded to find someone for an appointment". It has been noted, above, that the RR(A) Bill 1999 will, if implemented in its present form, apply the provisions of the RRA to the appointment, *inter alia*, of judges. Given the reliance of the current selection method on informal "secret soundings",[21] the impact of the amended legislation in this area will be a matter of significant interest.

In relation specifically to the appointment of such advisers the tribunal "do not say that all such posts should be subject to civil service recruitment standards, only that the particular minister should ensure that his selection is free from discrimination". What this means, in practice, is that the Minister (and others applying informal

---

[19] The Select Committee on Northern Ireland, 1998–1999 session Fourth Report, *The operation of the Fair Employment (Northern Ireland) Act 1989: Ten Years On*, question 160 appended in the minutes of evidence for the 13th January 1999 (available at http://www.parliament.the-stationery-office.co.uk/pa/cm199899/cmselect/cmniaf /95/9502.htm#ev. "That was probably the single greatest stumbling block towards the provision of equality, not deliberate direct discrimination but those sort of practices".

[20] This area is currently outwith the Acts but the RR(A)B will, if adopted in its current form, apply the RRA's prohibitions on discrimination to office holders. It is likely, given the government's apparent commitment to consistency between the regimes (see, for example, Ian McCartney's statement, fn 9 above) that this extension will apply also to the SDA and the DDA.

[21] For further discussion of this see A. McColgan, *Women under the Law* (Harlow: Addison Wesley Longman, 1999), Chapters 1 and 10.

methods of selection) should have regard to the racial and/ or sexual constitution of the pool from which selection is to be made and, where the pool is unbalanced, to rely solely upon it where such reliance would be justified according to the test discussed in chapter 2.[22]

Turning to the more general application of s.4.(1)(a) RRA and its equivalent provisions, much of the case law which has arisen concerns allegedly discriminatory interview. In particular, women frequently complain that they are subjected to questioning as to their family status and, if they have children, their childcare arrangements, from which men are generally exempt. The EOC's Code of Practice for the elimination of discrimination on the grounds of sex and marriage and the promotion of sex equality in employment (para 23) recommends that:

> (c) questions should relate to the requirements of the job. Where it is necessary to assess whether personal circumstances will affect performance of the job (for example, where it involves unsocial hours or extensive travel) this should be discussed objectively without detailed questions based on assumptions about marital status, children and domestic obligations . . . Questions about marriage plans or family intentions should not be asked, as they could be construed as showing bias against women . . .

In *Brennan v J H Dewhurst Ltd*, EAT confirmed that particular questions asked of a candidate could breach s.6(1)(a) SDA. The applicant had applied and been rejected for a job as a butcher's assistant. A tribunal accepted that the shop's manager "both from the questions [he] asked . . . and his manner and demeanour at the interview . . . had no desire or intention to employ a woman as butcher's assistant". In the event, the area manager, who had advertised the position, decided that there was no need to appoint. There was no suggestion that the area manager had himself been guilty of discrimination:

Brennan v J.H. Dewhurst Ltd [1983] IRLR 357, [1984] ICR 52

Browne-Wilkinson J:

S.6(1)(a) deals with discrimination against a woman in the arrangements the employer makes for the purpose of determining who should be offered that employment. There are broadly two ways in which that might be construed. The first, which is the basis upon which the argument originally turned on the hearing of this appeal, is that the discrimination has to be found in the making of the arrangements by the employer; the second is that it is enough that the effect of the arrangements made is discriminatory, whether or not the employer was guilty of any discriminatory conduct in the actual making of the arrangements . . .

It seems to us slightly ambiguous, in relation to subsection (a), whether the phrase "to discriminate against a woman in the arrangements he makes" requires it to be shown that in the making of the arrangements there was discrimination, or whether it is sufficient if the

---

[22] The Sixth Report of the Committee on Standards in Public Life (the Neill Committee), Cm 4557, available at http://www.public-standards.gov.uk/), which dealt with special advisers, did not consider their appointment, dealing rather with considerations of numbers, payment and accountability.

arrangements made operate so as to discriminate against a woman. In our judgment the latter is the right view . . . if the true construction of the section is such that it is not unlawful to operate, in a discriminatory way, arrangements made in a non-discriminatory way, there would be a gap in the Act. The policy of s.6 is to ensure that at all stages in applying for and obtaining employment the woman is on an equal footing with a man in her ability to obtain the job. If s.6(1)(a) does not cover arrangements for the purpose of determining who should be offered employment which are operated in a discriminatory way, to that extent the plain policy of the Act would not be carried out. We accept . . . that it is not our function to insert into an Act of Parliament something which the Act, on its fair reading, does not contain. But when one is faced with a doubt whether the discrimination is to be found in the operation of the arrangements or in the making of the arrangements, we think it is legitimate for us to take into account the manifest policy of the Act as stated in the long title to the Act. Therefore, we think we are entitled and, indeed, bound to hold that the provisions of s.6(1)(a) are satisfied if the arrangements made for the purpose of determining who should be offered that employment operate so as to discriminate against a woman, even though they were not made with the purpose of so discriminating . . .

In *Brennan* EAT agreed with the tribunal that the applicant had been subject to discrimination. Differential questioning does not, however, always result in this conclusion. In *Saunders* v *Richmond upon Thames Borough Council*, EAT considered the s.6(1)(a) claim brought by a woman golf professional who claimed that her interview and also her non-selection for a golf position were discriminatory. The tribunal found that her non-selection was not by reason of her sex, a finding EAT upheld. Here, we deal with the separate issue which arose under s.6(1)(a), the questions asked of her at interview having included the following: "Are there any women golf professionals in clubs?"; "So you'd be blazing the trail, would you"?; "Do you think men respond as well to a woman golf professional as to a man?"; "If all this is true, you are obviously a lady of great experience, but don't you think this type of job is rather unglamourous?"; "Don't you think this is a job with rather long hours?"; "I can see that you could probably cope with the playing and teaching side of the job, but I am rather concerned as to whether you could cope with the management side"; and "If some of the men were causing trouble over the starting times on the tee, do you think you would be able to control this?".

Saunders v Richmond upon Thames Borough Council [1977] IRLR 362

Phillips J

. . . the question whether [interview questions discriminate] must be one of fact in each case. The issue would be whether by asking the question she was, on the ground of her sex, treated less favourably than a man would be treated (section 1(1)(a)). This would involve a consideration of the circumstances in which, and the purposes for which, the question was asked . . .

   Mr Beloff [for the applicant] stressed the fact that since the enactment of the [SDA] it is necessary for everyone, and in particular employers, to reconsider their approach to such matters and to rid themselves of what are now out-of-date ideas and prejudices. . . There is probably not much doubt that such questions as (1) "Are there any women golf professionals in clubs?" or (4) "Do you think men respond as well to a woman golf professional as to a man?" reflect, in part at least, what is now an out-of-date and proscribed attitude of mind. That such questions were asked may be very relevant when it comes to be determined . . . whether there has been discrimination in not appointing a woman . . . But we do not think that it is unlawful to ask such questions, or that Mr Beloff is right when he says that it is now unlawful to ask a woman (or a man) any question which would not be asked of a man (or a woman). Indeed it may be desirable to do so . . . suppose a man to be considered as an applicant for the headship of a single sex girls' boarding school. If appointed it is obvious that in practice he might have problems with the girls which would be different from those which a female head would have. An appointing committee might well think it proper to inquire whether he had insight into this problem, and was prepared, and was the sort of man who would be able, to deal with it. For that reason they might well wish to inquire whether he had given consideration to his ability as a man to deal with pupils all of whom were girls. It would be absurd to regard such a question as in itself and by itself discriminatory. Indeed, so to rule would scarcely assist the cause of those who are active in the promotion of sex equality. If such questions were to be forbidden, they would not be asked; but not to ask them would not change the mental attitudes of those who would have asked them had they been allowed to do so. All that would be achieved would be that those of that cast of mind would continue to act in the same way as they would have acted had they been allowed to ask the question, but it would never be known, by examining the type of questions they do ask, the way in which they approached the problem. Assuming an employer who is in fact biased and prejudiced, this fact is much more likely to be revealed, and redress to be obtained, if he is free to ask what questions he likes, and thereby to show his true colours.

The publication in 1985 of the EOC's Code of Practice might have been expected to have some impact in this area, s.56A(10) SDA providing that its provisions "shall be taken into account" where they appear relevant to the tribunal. But the Code appears to have had little impact on EAT's decision in *Woodhead* v *Chief Constable of West Yorkshire Police*. In *Woodhead*, EAT rejected a s.6(1)(a) SDA claim based on the questioning of a police force applicant about her family circumstances. The plaintiff had been subjected to the following questions: "How old are your children?" "How does your husband manage to work flexible hours?" "Do you have a reliable babysitter?" "Who else looks after your children?" "Is your husband in danger of becoming a house husband?" "How would you feel being without the children for 14 weeks whilst you are at training school?" "Who will care for the children while you and your husband are at work?" "Where does your husband work?" "What job does he do?" "What are your husband's feelings regarding you becoming a police constable?"

Woodhead v *Chief Constable of West Yorkshire Police* EAT/285/89 (unreported 1990)

Ian Kennedy J

It was not disputed that in substance those . . . plainly do involve an enquiry into this lady's personal circumstances in relation to her husband, his work, her children, their care, and to her husband's attitude towards her new career both generally and in terms of the impact that it may have upon his life.

The applicant gave evidence that after she left the interview she spoke with two of her fellow applicants, both men, to ask whether they had been asked questions about the care of their children. She was told that they had not. There was no evidence before the . . . Tribunal as to which those two applicants were: whether they were married or had children. What the nature of the questioning of those two men was we do not know, and the . . . Tribunal did not know. The officers responsible for the interview, each of Superintendent rank, said that broadly speaking they made the same sort of enquiries of both male and female applicants.

Was it necessary that such matters should be investigated, or was this a raw manifestation of prejudice and discrimination? Why was it relevant to ask such things? The first point that has to be had in mind is this: the police service appears to be a purely civilian service, yet its members are subject to a very strict discipline and a discipline moreover which puts the duties of the office before private interest. The police officer is not entitled to go home at the end of a shift, perhaps leaving the enquiry until he returns. Secondly, a person who joins the police does join a body with a esprit of its own in the same way as a person who joins the armed services: he or she has a new series of loyalties which are more intense than the loyalties which normally bind employer and employee. Thirdly, the job involves stresses, difficulties and unpleasantnesses which people may not always have thought out as carefully as they should.

These considerations will in reality make many married women with children think twice before they join. . . It is not to our mind sexist or discriminatory to want to be sure that a woman has thought about these things fully, and that she has the support of her husband. Her service will mean, because of shift patterns, that there will be many times when her husband will have to look after the children in the evening or get them ready for school in the morning. How is he likely to respond to that? Will he do it cheerfully or grudgingly? Thus "Where does he work and what job does he do" are very relevant questions as is "How does your husband manage to work flexible hours?" It must be difficult enough in a household to have one partner working flexible hours; what, we ask ourselves, happens when there are two and one of them has no choice in the matter. In that context to ask "Do you have a reliable babysitter" and "Who else looks after your children?" are questions which have got to be addressed. Those questions do not imply that it is the woman's task to look after the children, they simply raise the simple question of how are your children going to be cared for?

[The tribunal] concluded that there was nothing discriminatory about the questions although they did add the observation that they felt too much time had been spent upon that aspect and not enough on the generality of matters. That is their observation, their finding and therefore that concludes the matter for us. It is however as well to make this point: interview techniques do vary, sometimes some aspect of an interviewee's capacity may be so obviously appropriate that it need attract no more than one or two token questions, whereas the interviewer may prefer to spend a greater length of time upon those questions where there may be real cause for concern. It is a matter for the interviewer.

the . . . Tribunal did not overtly refer to the Code of Conduct. That again is true but the whole tenor of their decision . . . tends to show that they must have had these matters well in mind, and [Ms Woodhead's counsel] says that he made great point of the Code. The Code is to be had in mind but it is not essential that every Tribunal should on every occasion recite as if it were a rubric. An experienced Tribunal will pay regard to something so obvious as that, and there is certainly nothing in their findings to show that they put it aside . . .

If an interview is conducted in such a way that there is a prejudicial manner to it, the very nature of that interview may amount to an arrangement within the import of section 6(1)(a). But that does not mean that every question which may, on reflection, be one which it would be better not to have asked is itself an arrangement, or that each such question offends against the provisions of the Act. In that context, notwithstanding the caution that this was a case decided before the Act had been amended to include a reference to the Code, the words of Mr Justice Phillips in *Saunders* . . . are much in point . . . We would, in exactly the same way, here say that those interviewing must be in a position where they can probe points of concern without it being suggested that they are by that very fact offending against the [SDA]. The . . . Act has been enacted to proscribe discrimination, and not to change reality. It was not enacted to make it more difficult for people to ventilate problems which are inherent in the particular employment, where it would be no kindness to an applicant (whether he be male or female) that he or she should go into the post with any illusions about what he or she is proposing to undertake.

The cases considered above relate to alleged breaches of the SDA. It should be borne in mind that s.4(1)(a) RRA and the equivalent provisions of the DDA and FETO would also be relevant in cases in which interview questions or other selection arrangements appeared to discriminate against a relevant group. *Osamor v Lord Chancellor* provides an example of a s.4(1)(a) RRA claim, albeit one which was unsuccessful because Ms Osamor, who was relying on an indirect discrimination argument, could not establish detriment (see further Chapter 2). (Where s.6(1)(a) SDA or its equivalent was argued in connection with direct, rather than indirect discrimination, prohibited "less favourable treatment" under this head ought to be challengeable whether or not the aggrieved person would otherwise have been a possible appointee). Whereas, in an indirect discrimination claim such as *Osamor*, the applicant must establish detriment, only "less favourable treatment" (which should be satisfied by the application of the discriminatory arrangements) needs to be established in a direct discrimination claim.

Other examples of discriminatory arrangements might be where an Asian woman is interviewed on the basis of stereotypical assumptions about familial expectations (though here she would have to decide—see Chapters 1 and 6—whether to sue under the SDA or the RRA, there being no category of "racially specific woman" apparently known to law); where a wheelchair bound applicant is subjected to the "does she take sugar" treatment; or where (see *in re Ballymena BC* (Northern Ireland HC, 1993, unreported, discussed in Chapter 5) an appointment decision is reached by means of a secret vote in circumstances where sectarian affiliations are present. It should also be noted that, whether or not differential questioning amounts, in any particular case, to a breach of s.4(1)(a) RRA or its equivalent provisions, a challenge under s.4(1)(c) or equivalent to a failure to appoint would frequently be boosted by evidence of such questioning. Nevertheless, as we saw in the *Saunders* case, even the most bizarrely inappropriate questioning will not necessarily result in a successful discrimination claim

S.4(1)(c) RRA and its equivalents (ss.6(2)(b) SDA, 4(2)(d) DDA and Article 19(b)(iii) FETO) require that the aggrieved individual has actually applied for the position and been rejected. The CRE Code of Practice suggests, *inter alia*, that refusal to employ a Sikh by virtue of his inability to comply with uniform requirements might breach s.4(1)(c).[23] Among the cases which have arisen under these sections have been *Martin* v *Marks & Spencers* [1998] ICR 1005, [1998] IRLR 326, discussed in Chapter 5 and below; *Price* v *Civil Service Commission and another* [1977] IRLR 291, *Meer* v *Tower Hamlets* [1988] IRLR 399 and *Falkirk Council* v *Whyte* [1997] IRLR 560 (see Chapter 2). As is the case with claims of discriminatory dismissals, the most significant problems which arise under s.4(1)(c) and its equivalents concern difficulties of proof. The same is true in respect of s.4(2)(b)—discrimination in terms of access (or the refusal of access) to "opportunities for promotion, transfer or training, or . . . any other benefits, facilities or services".

Before we consider s.4(2)(c), it is useful to mention ss.4(1)(b), 4(2)(a) & (b). As we saw, above, s.4(1)(b) and 4(2)(a) prohibit discrimination in the terms on which employment is, respectively, offered and afforded. The SDA contains no equivalent of s.4(2)(b), discrimination in contractual terms afforded to men and women being covered by the EqPA. There are relatively few appellate decisions on these subsections, or on their equivalents. *Barclays Bank plc* v *Kapur and ors* [1991] 2 AC 355, concerned alleged race discrimination in contractual terms. More recently, in *Wakeman* v *Quick Corporation* [1999] IRLR 424, the Court of Appeal considered a s.4(2) claim made by locally-recruited staff of a Japanese firm who compared their conditions to those applied to staff seconded from Japan. The case was dismissed, EAT upholding the tribunal decision on the grounds that the Japanese staff, being seconded, were not in "the same relevant circumstances" as the applicants.[24]

S.6(1)(b) and the EqPA equivalent of s.4(2)(a) RRA may prove to be the subject of increased litigation in future years. The rejection by the ECJ in *Grant* v *South West Trains* C–249/96 [1998] ECR I–0621, of the "sexual orientation discrimination as sex discrimination" argument is discussed in Chapters 1 and 6, as are the subsequent decisions of the ECtHR in *Smith & Grady* v *UK* (2000) 29 EHRR 548 and *Lustig-Prean & Beckett* (2000) EHRR 493. Given that the former decision relied on the incorrect view that sexual orientation discrimination was consistent with the ECnHR, and given also the possibility of an EC directive prohibiting employment-related discrimination on grounds, *inter alia*, of sexual orientation, it is likely that such discrimination will soon be prohibited in the UK.[25] One of the most common areas of litigation is likely to concern terms and conditions of employment. The following article from the *Equal Opportunities Review* discusses discrimination in this context.

---

[23] The legality of such a refusal turns on justification though s.11 Employment Act 1989 exempts Sikhs from hard hat requirements on building sites.

[24] Non-Japanese seconded staff would also have had the better conditions. Indirect discrimination would probably have been made out on the facts, subject to the issue of justification.

[25] At present, though, the commitment is only to a non-statutory (non-binding) Code of Practice, discussed in Chapters 1 and 11.

"Work and Sexual Orientation" (1997) 74 *EOR*, 20, 22–5

A central aspect of equal treatment in the workplace is ensuring that lesbians and gay men are employed on the same terms and conditions as other employees. What this means in practice is that any benefits which are made available to a heterosexual partner should apply equally to a partner of the same sex. . . .

Workplace benefits include leave arrangements, pensions, health insurance, and free or subsidised use of the employer's services, such as travel concessions. . . .

The main types of leave provided by employers are special leave (including bereavement leave and leave for family reasons), and maternity and paternity leave.

Special leave usually covers the death or serious illness of a family member. If the wording of a policy uses the term "spouse" then this will usually be construed as not applying to same-sex partners. . . .

In the case of paternity leave, an organisation may decide to restrict eligibility for leave to the biological father, or to extend it to a "nominated carer". In the latter case, the nominated person could be a same-sex partner. Most pension schemes make provision for two kinds of benefits in the event of a scheme member's death before retirement: lump sum benefits and dependant's benefits. It is usually possible for a member to nominate anyone they choose as the recipient of the lump sum. But with respect to the survivor's benefits, the scheme may specify that the widow's or widower's pension can only be paid to a married partner. This is true of the majority of public and private sector schemes. In some cases the scheme allows the survivor's pension to be paid to an unmarried partner, but specifically excludes a same-sex partner.

A survey by *Pensions World* in June 1996 of the treatment of non-married partners in 24 public and private sector pensions schemes found a wide variation of provision. Some schemes made provision for same-sex partners, including BT, Powergen and Scottish Power, subject to eligibility criteria of financial dependency. But a number of schemes, including the Ford Motor Co, did not include same-sex partners. Many schemes said that ultimately the payment of benefits was at the discretion of the trustees. . . .

The National Association of Pension Funds carries out an annual survey of occupational pension schemes. Its 1996 survey, which covered over 640 employers and around 40% of all occupational scheme members in the UK, confirmed a trend for categories of people other than spousesto be eligible for benefits. Over 60% of private sector schemes can provide pensions to a dependant other than a partner or children, and 31% of public sector schemes can do so. Just over 20% of private sector schemes and nearly 10% of public sector schemes will consider making provision for same-sex relationships, according to the survey.

All pension schemes are subject to Inland Revenue rules which provide that pensions may be paid to widows and widowers as of right, but in other cases can only be made where the beneficiary is "financially dependent" on the member. After discussions with Stonewall, the Inland Revenue revised their previous restrictive definition of financial dependence to include "inter-dependence" . . .

According to Stonewall, "there is now nothing in law to prevent any private occupational scheme making survivor's benefits payable to unmarried partners, including same-sex partners, or to their children." It recommends that if the current rules of a scheme do not allow payments to same-sex partners, an employee should "draw the trustees' attention to the recent Inland Revenue Practice Note and ask them to change the rules."

. . .

The TUC is actively campaigning on the issue of equal treatment in public sector pension schemes. In 1995, with the backing of unions across the public sector, it published a report. *Pensions and prejudice in public sector pension schemes*, highlighting the discrimination against unmarried partners and same-sex partners in six public service schemes, including the Teachers' Superannuation Scheme, the NHS Superannuation Scheme and the Principal Civil Servants' Pension Scheme.

Individual unions are also pressing for change. For example, the Civil Service unions are actively campaigning for changes to their pension scheme to include unmarried and same-sex partners. When Unison—the UK's largest trade union—held its annual national lesbian and gay conference this year, a key motion was on equal rights for pensions. The motion supported a national campaign to end discrimination in public sector pension schemes against unmarried partners, including same-sex partners. Part of the campaign is for the right of each individual public sector worker to nominate a person he/she wishes to receive their pension in the event of their death. The motion was passed at the conference and is now the policy of the union as a whole.

Some organisations provide employees with private health insurance cover. Provision may be restricted to the employee or the employee's family may also be covered.

According to one of the major providers of private health insurance, BUPA, the issue of whether same-sex partners are covered by the scheme is entirely at the discretion of the employer, not BUPA. There is no reason why same-sex partners should not be covered, but it is up to the company to specify who, and how many people, are covered.

Among the benefits that may be provided for employees are free or concessionary travel for staff of public transport companies and discounts on products in retail organisations. Where these benefits exist, they may be extended to employees' partners. In these cases, equal treatment requires that same-sex partners be included.

Many organisations have customarily restricted such privileges to spouses or to spouses and heterosexual non-married partners. But recently some organisations have reviewed their policies and explicitly extended the provisions to same-sex partners.

British Airways extended its travel concessions and issued a new policy in April 1995, which states that unmarried staff have the option to nominate a close relative, travelling companion or a partner of their choice—who can be of the same gender—to enjoy the same travel concessions that are available to married members of the workforce.

It ought to be noted that, if discrimination on grounds of sexual orientation were to be prohibited simply by amending the definition of sex discrimination under the SDA to include discrimination on grounds of sexual orientation, the restriction of benefits to "spouses" would amount only to indirect, and therefore potentially justifiable, discrimination under that Act. By contrast, restriction to differently-sexed partners would amount to (unjustifiable) direct discrimination.

Turning, finally, to s.4(2)(c) RRA and its equivalent provisions, it is clear from *Weathersfield* v *Sargent* [1998] IRLR 14 that "dismissal" extends to cover constructive as well as other forms of dismissal. The SDA, as it was originally enacted, provided wide exceptions in relation to discrimination in retirement provisions. These exceptions have been removed as a result of the ECJ's decision in *Marshall* v *Southampton and South-West Hampshire Area Health Authority* Case C–152/84 [1986] ECR 723 and successive decisions on equality in relation to pensions and redundancy pay (see

Chapter 10) s.6(4) now providing a very limited exception relating to pensions (discussed in that chapter).[26]

The decision of the Court of Appeal in *Adekeye* v *Post Office (No.2)* [1997] ICR 110, [1997] IRLR 105 highlighted a significant gap in the protection afforded by the employment-related provisions of the various anti-discrimination enactments. There the Court ruled that discrimination in a post-dismissal appeal fell outwith the scope of the RRA on the grounds (*per* Peter Gibson LJ) that the "ordinary and natural meaning" of s.4(2)'s "a person employed by him" was restricted to present, rather than past, employees.[27]

In *Coote* v *Granada Hospitality Ltd* Case C–185/97 [1998] ECR I–5199, the ECJ ruled that the equal treatment directive required that those complaining of sex discrimination be protected from victimisation (in the form of a refusal to supply a reference) after the termination of their employment. EAT subsequently ruled in the applicant's favour:

Coote v *Granada Hospitality Ltd (No. 2)* [1999] ICR 942, [1999] IRLR 452, [1999] 3 CMLR 334

Morison J:

The main issue before this Court is whether it is possible to construe the [SDA] so as to enable a claimant to make a victimisation complaint in relation to events that occurred after the employment relationship had terminated.

On behalf of the employers, Mr Preston submitted that to construe the Act so as to accommodate the appellant's claim would require the Court to distort the meaning of the statute or re-write it [see *Duke* v *Reliance Systems Limited* [1988] ICR 339]. Neither was a permissible option. This part of the appeal is, he submitted, effectively determined by the Court of Appeal's decision in *Adekeye* . . .

Ms Rose [for the applicant] submitted that it was possible to construe the Act so as to give effect to the ECJ's ruling. She agreed that the *Adekeye* decision was, technically, not binding on this Court on the issue before us and she submitted that, in any event, the decision of the Court of Appeal does not bear close analysis . . . She noted that the Court expressly refused to take account of the directive when reaching its conclusion, on the grounds that it had no application to racial discrimination. She submitted that "in these circumstances, the decision of the Court of Appeal on that point of construction does not preclude this tribunal from interpreting the SDA consistently with the decision of the ECJ." But even if it did, then she submitted that the EAT was bound to give effect to the ECJ's decision since a court could not be bound to refuse to make a reference by reason of a higher court's decision. Since the lower court could make a reference it must be assumed that when it has received the ECJ's ruling it was competent and required to act upon it . . .

---

[26] Equal state pensionable ages will be phased in between 2010 and 2020.

[27] Citing with approval the decision of EAT in *Nagarajan* v *Agnew* [1994] IRLR 61. The Court, further, characterised as "unrealistic" the argument, accepted by the industrial tribunal, that Ms Adekeye, in appealing against her dismissal, was seeking employment within s.4(1): "On the appeal the appellant is not seeking an offer which can be accepted or refused; the appellant is seeking the reversal of a decision to dismiss".

What . . . is the effect of the Court of Appeal's judgment, which is recognised by both counsel not to be binding in relation to the [SDA]? Both parts of the discrimination legislation were regarded by the Government of the day as being part of a piece. The White Papers preceding them make that clear. In almost all respects the language of the two Acts is identical, as are the concepts within them. It was plainly Parliament's intention that they should be construed in the same way. We are instinctively reluctant to adopt an argument which leads to two different results.

We have, therefore, with counsel's assistance, given careful thought to the reasoning in *Adekeye*.

As we understand it the Court placed reliance on the fact that section 4 [in this case section 6] is drafted in the present tense. But with great respect it seems to us that the present tense would have been quite apt had the section been intended to apply to former employees, since what is made unlawful is a present act of discrimination.

Secondly, the Court was of the view that there was no room for the application of the "access to benefits" to ex-employees, since access would "seem to me likely to occur during employment". During the course of argument, quite apart from the important matter of references, to which the Court made no reference, a number of matters were raised, and the Court itself, in its deliberations has considered others: for example, the continued use of sports facilities to retirees, the payment of bonuses to present and former staff and the provision of concessionary travel facilities. All these matters might be decided or altered after the employment had ceased. If Mrs Garland (*Garland* v *British Rail Engineering Ltd* [1983] 2 AC 751) had been employed by a privatised railway company, so that she could not rely on the direct effect of the directive, is it to be said that she, or her partner, fell outside section 6 because she had ceased to be employed? . . . for many different purposes the contact between employer and former employee may continue after the employment relationship has ceased . . .

We have not been persuaded that it could be said that the Court of Appeal's decision was so mistaken [*per incuriam*] that it need not be followed. We quite see the force of the criticisms made of it. Indeed, we would go further and respectfully say that we disagree with it. But the doctrine of precedent requires us to follow it and had it been applicable to this case we would have done so. However, the Court expressly rejected [the] argument that reference could be made to the [SDA] and to European materials: "I know of no authority that compels so extraordinary a result". Furthermore, the Court noted that [counsel for Ms Adekeye] had been:

> unable to point to any relevant interpretation of [the equal treatment directive] laid down by the ECJ. It seems to me to be open to argument whether the words of the directive "working conditions, including the conditions governing dismissal" are apt to cover an appeal procedure where the dismissal has already occurred.

The ECJ decision in this case determines the argument to which the Lord Justice was referring. On this basis, we do not regard the decision in that case as constraining us from arriving at our conclusion that Ms Rose's construction of section 6 of the [SDA] is correct: both as a matter of language and Parliamentary intention and in the light of the ECJ decision. In any event, we accept her further argument that the supremacy of the ECJ's decisions would be undermined were a lower court to feel obliged to follow a higher court's decision in preference to giving effect to what the European Court of Justice has determined.

As Mr Justice Morison made clear in *Coote*, *Adekeye* remains the law in relation to race discrimination (and, persuasive in relation to discrimination under the DDA and FETO). But it is likely that the Court of Appeal would decline to follow *Adekeye* were it to come before it again.

The implementation of the new race discrimination directive (2000/43/EC) will require that the *Coote* approach be adopted in relation to discrimination on grounds of ethnic or racial origin. The directive supplements the standard provision on effective remedy by providing (Article 7) that it applies "even after the relationship in which the discrimination is alleged to have occurred has ended" and further requires (Article 9) that:

> Member States shall introduce into their national legal systems such measures as are necessary to protect persons from *any* adverse treatment or adverse consequence as a reaction to a complaint or to legal proceedings aimed at enforcing compliance with the principle of equal treatment.

A similar approach has been taken in the 1999 draft equal treatment general framework directive in relation to discrimination on grounds of religion or belief, disability, age or sexual orientation.

Turning to the "any other detriment" provision, this serves as a "catch all" category capable of covering most types of discrimination which might arise during employment and not otherwise covered by s.4 RRA or the equivalent provisions of the SDA, DDA and FETO. The "any other detriment" head of s.4(2)(c) RRA and its equivalents has given rise to a considerable number of appellate decisions. The difficulty associated with it is that, whereas discrimination in respect of the other matters covered by s.4 RRA etc. is actionable *per se*, the applicant who alleges discrimination under the second head of s.4(2)(b) must convince the tribunal not only that less favourable treatment was accorded her, but also that the treatment was sufficiently disadvantageous to be regarded as an actionable "detriment".

The difficulties to which the "detriment" requirement have given rise were indicated as early as 1977 in the Court of Appeal's decision in *Peake* v *Automotive Products Ltd* [1978] QB 233. The decision, which was extracted in Chapter 2, was reached primarily on the ground that the employer's policy of allowing women to leave work five minutes before men was not "discrimination" within the meaning of s.1(1)(a) SDA. This aspect of the decision was disapproved of by the same court in the subsequent decision in *Ministry of Defence* v *Jeremiah* [1980] QB 87. But the alternative basis for the *Peake* ruling, which was upheld in the latter decision, was that the additional five minutes which the men were required to work was, if it amounted to a "detriment" at all, *de minimis* and therefore outside the scope of the Act.

The *de minimis* approach has not subsequently been expressly applied to exclude discrimination complaints from the scope of s.6(2)(b) SDA and its equivalent provisions, having been called into question by the subsequent decision of the Court of

Appeal in *Gill & Coote* v *El Vino Ltd* .[28] But a similar outcome has been achieved by the categorisation of particular forms of discrimination (in the sense of differential or differently-impacting treatment) as "not detrimental" to their challengers. This approach has been particularly evident in the context of alleged harassment and clothing and appearance rules (the former are discussed below, the latter in Chapter 6) but has been applied elsewhere also. In *Staffordshire County Council* v *Black* [1995] IRLR 234, EAT rejected the claim that a factory check on all black workers entering the building, imposed in order to prevent entry by one particular black man, amounted to a "detriment" under the RRA. EAT did not accept that the applicant had been "put under a disadvantage" by the check.[29] And in *Clymo* v *Wandsworth*, EAT ruled that a woman refused permission to return to work on a job-share basis had not been subjected to any detriment:

Wood J (for EAT)

it seems to us that the word "detriment" as used in this subsection . . . must be some unpleasantness or burden or less favourable treatment arising out of or in the course of that employment. It cannot amount to a failure to provide some advantage so long as such an advantage is not offered to others in the same grade of employment, ie to other branch librarians. Thus for instance it would not be a detriment to the applicant if the local authority failed to offer her the perk of a company car or the right to work overtime which it had not offered to others in the same grade.

In the present case job sharing was not an option for branch librarians and thus the applicant was no worse off than other branch librarians. She resigned—left of her own accord—and this does not seem to us to be a "detriment" caused by anyone but herself.

It is clear from s.4 RRA, extracted above, that the RRA (in common with the other anti-discrimination legislation) does not, as yet, expressly prohibit harassment. (This may change with the implementation of the new directive on race discrimination). The recognition of sexual and other harassment as treatment "on the grounds of sex" has been discussed in Chapter 2. What is of concern here is not the question whether sexual, racial, etc. harassment is treatment "on the ground of" sex, race, etc. Rather, the hurdle at which applicants occasionally fail is in the requirement that such treatment amount to a "detriment" within s.4(2)(c) RRA or the equivalent provisions.

Sexual (and by implication, other forms of) harassment was recognised as falling potentially within the scope of the anti-discrimination prohibitions in *Strathclyde*

---

[28] In *Gill & Coote* [1983] 1 QB 425, 206, a goods and services case discussed further below, the Court of Appeal refused to apply the *de minimis* maxim where (in a case where women were refused service in a bar unless seated at a table, men being allowed to stand at the bar). Eveleigh LJ found it: "very difficult to invoke the maxim *de minimis non curat lex* in a situation where that which has been denied to the plaintiff is the very thing that Parliament seeks to provide, namely facilities and services on an equal basis". The *de minimis* approach was also rejected on the facts in *R* v *Secretary of State for Education and Science, ex parte Keating and Others, The Times* 3rd December 1985. Cf, however, the decision in *Schmidt* v *Austicks Bookshops* [1978] ICR 85, discussed in Chapter 6.

[29] One has to wonder to what extent the blanket testing was on the basis that "they all look the same".

Regional Council v *Porcelli* [1986] ICR 564, [1986] IRLR 134, which case was discussed in chapter 2. But it was remarked of the case at that time that:

J. M. Thompson, note on the *Porcelli* case (1985) 101 *Law Quarterly Review* 471, 471–2

discrimination was only unlawful if it fell within section 6(2)(b) of the Act *i.e.* the employer had (vicariously) unlawfully discriminated "by dismissing her, or subjecting her to any other detriment." Lord McDonald refused to accept the contention that "the words 'subjecting her to any other detriment' were so universal that they covered acts of sexual harassment committed against [the complainant] during her employment, without reference to any consequence thereof so far as her employment was concerned";... In other words, sexual harassment at work does not *per se* constitute unlawful sex discrimination within section 6. It is only if, as a result, the woman suffers a detriment related to her employment, *e.g.* dismissal, or action short of dismissal, for resisting unwanted sexual advances, that section 6(2) would be satisfied. On the facts of the case, however, the complainant had suffered such an "employment" detriment as she felt obliged to seek a transfer to another school: the request for the transfer had not been voluntary but had been forced upon her as a result of the sexual harassment.

It is thought that given the structure of the Sex Discrimination Act 1975, Lord McDonald's decision is correct. But at a time of record unemployment, it is a serious limitation of the Sex Discrimination Act 1975 that it is of no assistance to women who are subjected to sexual harassment at work but, for economic reasons, continue at their jobs. It remains to be seen whether either the criminal law or the law of tort will be sufficiently flexible to protect unfortunate women in these circumstances.

In *De Souza* v *The Automobile Association* [1986] ICR 514 [1986] IRLR 103, the Court of Appeal accepted that harassment could be actionable within s.6(2)(b) even where its victim continued in employment, providing that "the putative reasonable employee could justifiably complain about his or her working conditions or environment . . . whether or not these were so bad as to be able to amount to constructive dismissal, or even if the employee was prepared to work on and put up with the harassment".[30] But the Court of Appeal in that case rejected a race discrimination claim by a woman who had overheard herself being referred to by a manager in racially derogatory terms. What was lacking, according to the court, was the necessary link between the employer and the hurt suffered by the appellant, such that the employer could be said to have "*subject[ed] her* to any other detriment" (my emphasis) within s.4(2)(c) of the RRA. Nevertheless, and despite the fact that the racially insulting remark was in this case made by a manager (which may have meant, according to May LJ, that the appellant "was being considered less favourably, whether generally or in an employment context, than others"):

I for my part do not think that she can properly be said to have been "treated" less favourably by whomsoever used the word, unless he intended her to overhear the

---

[30] In *Bracebridge Engineering Ltd* v *Darby* [1990] IRLR 3, EAT accepted that a single incident of sexual harassment could, if it were sufficiently serious, amount to a "detriment" (there the harassment consisted of a serious sexual assault).

conversation in which it was used, or knew or ought reasonably to have anticipated that the person he was talking to would pass the insult on or that the appellant would become aware of it in some other way . . .

More recently, in *Reed & Another* v *Stedman* [1999] IRLR 98, a case in which the treatment complained of consisted of bullying and the use of sexual innuendo, EAT defined sexual harassment as "words or conduct which are unwelcome to the recipient", undermining her dignity at work and creating a "hostile" and "offensive" working environment. Interesting in the decision was EAT's insistence that "It is for recipients to decide for themselves what is acceptable to them and what they regard as offensive". The dicta in *Reed* could equally be applied to a case in which the unwanted treatment consisted of "friendly", if persistent, advances, rather than apparently "hostile" actions though in such a case there might be an obligation on the recipient of the actions to make known her feelings about them if they could reasonably be regarded as inoffensive.

In *Driskel* v *Peninsula Business Services Ltd* [2000] IRLR 151, EAT again emphasised the significance of subjective perceptions. The complainant had, *inter alia*, been advised by her manager to wear a transparent blouse and show lots of cleavage at a promotion interview to be conducted by him. This was the culmination of a series of incidents in which he had made sexual remarks to her. A tribunal dismissed the claim of sex harassment, ruling in respect of the early incidents that the complainant "made no objection at the time to the remarks", that the manager "could not have known that she found them offensive", and that "she suffered no detriment from such remarks being made". As to the final incident, the tribunal ruled that the remark, which "was wholly inappropriate and unacceptable in a modern employment context, and was capable of being regarded as an act of sexual harassment . . . was intended as a flippant remark, which could not reasonably have been taken seriously, and was not taken seriously by the applicant when the words were spoken".

EAT stressed the importance of viewing the final incident of alleged harassment in context, against its background of sexual remarks, and continued (in this case against a background of sexual remarks made by the harasser to the complainant) and continued.

Holland J (for EAT)

The ultimate judgment, sexual discrimination or no, reflects an objective assessment by the tribunal of all the facts. That said, amongst the factors to be considered are the applicant's subjective perception of that which is the subject of complaint and the understanding, motive and intention of the alleged discriminator. Thus, the act complained of may be so obviously detrimental, that is, disadvantageous . . . to the applicant as a woman by intimidating her on undermining her dignity at work, that the lack of any contemporaneous complaint by her is of little or no significance. By contrast she may complain of one or more matters which if taken individually may not objectively signify much, if anything, in terms of detriment. Then a contemporaneous indication of sensitivity on her part becomes obviously material as does the evidence of the alleged discriminator as to his perception. That which in isolation may not amount to discriminatory detriment may become such if persisted in notwithstanding objection, vocal or apparent. . . . By contrast the facts may simply disclose hypersensitivity on the part of the applicant to conduct which was reasonably not perceived by the alleged discriminator as being to her detriment—no finding of discrimination can then follow . . .

A breach by way of harassment of the anti-discrimination legislation requires that a nexus be established between the employer and the detriment suffered by the employee. There are two ways in which this can be done. In the first place, ss.41, 32, 58 and Article 36 of the SDA, RRA and DDA and FETO respectively impose vicarious liability upon employers for "[a]nything done by a person in the course of his employment . . . whether or not it was done with the employer's knowledge or approval". This, in turn, is subject to a "due diligence" defence whereby employers can escape liability by proving that they "took such steps as were reasonably practicable to prevent the employee from doing that act, or from doing in the course of his employment acts of that description". Secondly, the employer might incur direct or personal liability for the detriment, in a case in which s/he was him or herself the harasser, or where s/he subjected the harassed employee to a detriment by failing to deal with past harassment about which the employer had knowledge and other harassment over which s/he had control.

Dealing first with the issue of vicarious liability, the decision of the Court of Appeal in *Irving and Anor* v *The Post Office* [1987] IRLR 289 made it very difficult for harassed employees to pin liability on employers. In that case, the Court applied the common law test of vicarious liability to find the Post Office not liable in respect of racist remarks scrawled upon the post delivered to the home of a black couple. According to the court, an employer was liable under the RRA only for

acts actually authorised by him . . . [and] acts which he has not authorised, provided they are so connected with acts which he has authorised that they may rightly be regarded as modes—although improper modes—of doing them . . . if the unauthorised and wrongful act of the servant is not so connected with the authorised act as to be a mode of doing it, but is an independent act, the master is not responsible: for in such a case the servant is not acting in the course of his employment, but has gone outside of it".[31]

In the instant case, the Post Office authorised employees to write on mail only "for the purpose of ensuring that they were properly dealt with in the course of the post", and "wholly improper" scrawlings unrelated to this purpose were outside the sphere of the employment.

The difficulty with the common law test adopted in the context of the RRA (and, by implication, the SDA, DDA and FEA, as it then was) by the Court of Appeal in

---

[31] Citing the 9th edition of Salmond on Torts, and approved by the Privy Council, in *Canadian Pacific Railway* v *Lockhart* (1942) AC 591, p.599.

Irving was that (1) it tended to restrict employers' vicarious liability for acts of harassment to those employees who were in some type of managerial position vis-à-vis the harassee[32] and (2) the more egregious the conduct of the harasser, the more likely it was to be considered outside the course of his/her employment. In *Tower Boot Co Ltd v Jones* [1995] IRLR 529, for example, EAT applied the *Irving* approach to reject a race discrimination complaint made by a man who had been repeatedly called "chimp", "monkey" and "baboon", had been attacked and burnt with a hot screwdriver, had metal bolts thrown at his head, been whipped and had a notice pinned on his back reading "Chipmonks are go". An industrial tribunal found in his favour, but EAT ruled that the acts complained of could not be described, by any stretch of the imagination, as an improper mode of performing authorised tasks and that the employers were not, accordingly, liable under s.32(1).

The Court of Appeal ([1997] ICR 254, [1997] 2 All ER 406, [1997] IRLR 168) allowed Mr Jones' appeal, pointing out that the Court of Appeal in *Irving* had not taken into account s.32(1) in adopting the common law test of vicarious liability. "Free of authority", the Court in the current instance declined to follow *Irving*. Adopting, instead, a purposive approach, Waite LJ cited the words of Templeman J (as he then was) in *Savjani* v *IRC* [1981] 1 QB 458, (discussed below) "the [RRA] was brought in to remedy a very great evil. It is expressed in very wide terms, and I should be slow to find that the effect of something which is humiliatingly discriminatory in racial matters falls outside the ambit of the Act" and interpreted "course of employment" in s.32 (and, correspondingly, in the other Acts) broadly, in an everyday rather than a legalistic fashion. The alternative, as Waite LJ recognised, was that

> the more heinous the act of discrimination, the less likely it will be that the employer would be liable . . . [This would] cut[] across the whole legislative scheme and underlying policy of s32 (and its counterpart in sex discrimination), which is to deter racial and sexual harassment in the workplace through a widening of the net of responsibility beyond the guilty employees themselves, by making all employers additionally liable for such harassment, and then supplying them with the reasonable steps defence under s32(3) which will exonerate the conscientious employer who has used his best endeavours to prevent such harassment, and will encourage all employers who have not yet undertaken such endeavours to take the steps necessary to make the same defence available in their own workplace.[33]

The difficulties associated with establishing vicarious liability have been eased by the decision of the Court of Appeal in *Tower Boot*, although the decision in *Waters* v *Commissioner of Police of the Metropolis* [1997] ICR 1073, [1997] IRLR 589 (also discussed in Chapter 2) indicates that legal protection from harassment is not absolute.

---

[32] See, for example, *Bracebridge*, fn 30 above, where vicarious liability for a serious indecent assaulted rested upon the fact that the assaulters were at the time "engaged in disciplinary supervision" of the complainant. Even then, according to EAT in *Tower Boot*: "*Bracebridge* seems to stretch the [*Irving*] test to its limit".

[33] *Cf*, in the non-employment field, the retention of the *Irving* approach, *ST* v *North Yorkshire County Council* [1999] IRLR 98.

According to Lord Justice Waite, who was considering the alleged rape and buggery of a WPC by a fellow officer in the bedroom of a police "section house" while both were off-duty:

> He lived elsewhere, and was a visitor to her room in the section house at a time and in circumstances which placed him and her in no different position from that which would have applied if they had been social acquaintances only, with no working connection at all. In those circumstances it is inconceivable, in my view, that any tribunal applying the *Tower Boot* test could find that the alleged assault was committed in the course of [his] employment.

More recently, in *Chief Constable of the Lincolnshire Police* v *Stubbs and Ors* [1999] IRLR 81, EAT accepted that sexual harassment which took place at a social gathering which could be regarded as "an extension of the employment" of those involved could be "within the course of" the harasser's employment as understood post-*Tower Boot*. A similar conclusion was reached by EAT in *Sidhu* v *Aerospace Composite Technology Ltd* [1999] IRLR 683 (also discussed in Chapter 2), in which an employee was subject to racist violence from colleagues during a work-organised family day out.

Even where an act of harassment or other discrimination is found to be within ss. 41, 32, 58 or Article 36 of the SDA, RRA and DDA and FETO respectively, employers can escape liability by proving that they "took such steps as were reasonably practicable to prevent the employee from doing that act, or from doing in the course of his employment acts of that description".[34]

S.41(3) SDA was considered by EAT in *Higgins* v *Home Counties Newspaper Holdings Ltd,* in which a woman complained of sexual harassment by her general manager. The tribunal and EAT accepted that she had been sexually harassed, but ruled that the employers had made out the defence.

Higgins v *Home Counties Newspaper Holdings Ltd* EAT/1048/97

Smith J (for the Court)

The tribunal found that the respondent had conducted a proper investigation of the appellant's complaint according to the procedures. This was so, although Mr Coppen-Gardner [the respondent's manager] had come to a different conclusion about Mr Steed's [the harasser's] conduct than had the tribunal. He had not thought it amounted to sexual harassment whereas the tribunal did. Nonetheless, the respondent had acted properly in taking disciplinary action against Mr Steed for his inappropriate behaviour.

The tribunal considered whether the respondent had made out its defence under s.41(3). A proper response to a complaint was not enough. The respondent had to show that they had taken such steps as were reasonably practicable to prevent the sexual harassment. The tribunal considered the respondent's evidence about their equal opportunities policy and their policy for dealing with sexual harassment. The policy was incorporated in the company handbook and the tribunal found that staff were made aware of it. Sexual harassment

---

[34] S.41(3) SDA, s.32(3) RRA, s.58(5) DDA and Article 36(4) FETO.

was treated as gross misconduct in the disciplinary code. Managers were given awareness training. Both Mr Steed and Mr Coppen-Gardner had attended a course. The tribunal found that the respondent could not have been expected to do more. The nature of Mr Steed's harassment was such that no one knew about it until the appellant complained. When she did complain the respondent took appropriate action. This showed that the respondent took its policies seriously and acted upon them. They were not "paper policies". They found that the respondent had made out its defence under s.41(3) . . . the tribunal was entitled to conclude that the steps taken by the respondent in April and May 1995 were such steps as were reasonably practicable to prevent Mr Steed from sexually harassing the appellant in May 1996. They were entitled to regard the awareness training as adequate. As for the European Commission Recommendations and Code of Practice, we think the tribunal might well have been aware of their contents and had them in mind when deciding this issue. The document was not brought specifically to their attention during this case and they cannot be criticised for not mentioning it. However, we endorse Miss Pollard's suggestion [for the applicant] that this is a document which should inform the thinking of industrial tribunals faced with issues of this kind . . . The decision reveals no error of law on this point and the finding under s.41(3) is not perverse . . .

Almost invariably where employers plead the "due diligence" defence, the issue is one of harassment. *Martin* v *Marks & Spencers* is an unusual case. There the employers disputed liability for alleged discrimination by their own interviewing panel. A tribunal made an inference of racial discrimination from an interviewing panel's "bias", and ruled against the employer's on the s.32(3) issue. Both EAT and the Court of Appeal, however, ruled in favour of the employer on both issues. That part of the decision concerned with the tribunal's finding of discrimination is discussed in chapter 5. Here we consider the s.32(3) RRA point.

Martin v *Marks & Spencers* [1998] ICR 1005, [1998] IRLR 326

Mummery LJ (for the court)

s 32(3) is directed to providing a defence for an employer who has taken, in advance of the alleged discriminatory treatment, all reasonable and practicable steps to prevent discrimination from occurring. . . It is relevant for the purposes of s 32(3) to have regard to what was done by Marks & Spencer in advance of and prior to the interview to determine whether they had taken reasonably practicable steps to prevent discrimination by the employees in the interview, which inevitably led to the decision of Marks & Spencer not to offer employment to Ms Martins . . . there can be no doubt that Marks & Spencer made out the defence on the findings of fact about . . . their equal opportunities policy; their compliance with the Code of Practice issued by the Commission for Racial Equality in relation to selection procedures, criteria and interviewing; and their selection of the interviewing panel to include a person with an interest in recruiting from ethnic minorities.

Ss.42 SDA, 33 RRA, 57 DDA and Article 35 FETO provide that it is unlawful to assist the discriminatory act of another. This enables harassers to be found liable for aiding the discriminatory acts of their employers who are vicariously liable for the acts of the harassers. In *Hallam & Anor* v *Avery & Anor* [1999] ICR 547 [1999] IRLR 81 the

Court of Appeal ruled (*per* Judge LJ) that liability under s.33 RRA required the aider to know "that the party from whom his liability is alleged to derive is treating, or is about to treat, or is contemplating treating someone less favourably on racial grounds, and with that knowledge, or knowing that such treatment would be the likely result of doing so, he provides him with aid". This will rarely cause any difficulties in harassment cases.[35]

More problematic is the decision of the Court of Appeal in *Anyanwu & Anor v South Bank University & Anor* [2000] ICR 221, [2000] IRLR 36, in which that Court, by a majority, ruled that s.33 RRA (and, by implication, the corresponding provisions of the other legislation) was not applicable to those who could properly be described as "prime movers". According to Laws LJ, with whom Butler-Sloss concurred (Pill LJ dissenting), the use of the term "aid" by s.33 RRA "contemplates a state of affairs in which one party, being a free agent in the matter, sets out to do an act or achieve a result, and another party helps him to do it".

Applied to harassment cases, this decision would appear to preclude the possibility of harassers themselves being found liable under the anti-discrimination provisions (liability for aiding the employer's act of discrimination being the only route available under the discrimination legislation to impose liability on the harassers). If the decision in *Anyanwu* stands, it creates a significant flaw in the law relating to harassment.

Direct, as distinct from *vicarious* liability on the part of employers is best illustrated by EAT's decision in *Burton and Rhule v De Vere Hotels*, a case in which no vicarious liability could have been incurred by the employer in circumstances where the harassers were neither employed by it nor acting under its authorisation. *Burton* involved a race discrimination claim brought by two black waitresses after they had been exposed to racist jokes made by Bernard Manning, and associated racial and sexual abuse, at a police function at which they served. A tribunal dismissed the women's race discrimination claims on the grounds that, while the applicants had suffered a "detriment" within the meaning of the RRA, "[i]t was not . . . the respondent which subjected them to it". The tribunal further ruled that the manager's failure to ensure that staff were not offended by the act did not amount to "less favourable treatment on racial grounds" because his failure to address his mind to what the act might contain was not related to the employees' ethnic origins. EAT overruled the tribunal's decision.

Burton and Rhule v De Vere Hotels [1997] ICR 1, [1996] IRLR 596

Smith J

. . . the problem is to decide what an applicant must prove in order to show that the employer "subjected" the employee to the detriment of racial abuse or harassment, where the actual abuser or harasser is a third party and not a servant or agent of the employer for whose actions the employer would be vicariously liable. Put another way, the problem is to

---

[35] Though see *Hallam* for the difficulties created by that requirement on the facts there.

decide the extent of the duty of an employer to protect the employee from racial harassment from third parties. . .

It is not enough that the appellants suffered racial harassment while in the course of their
employment. . . The duty is not to subject the employee to racial harassment. We think that
the statutory test is best understood by consideration of the true meaning of the word "subjecting". We do not think "subjecting" is a word which connotes action or decision . . .
Rather we think it connotes "control" . . . An employer subjects an employee to the detriment of racial harassment if he causes or permits the racial harassment to occur in circumstances in which he can control whether it happens or not.

We do not think it is necessary or appropriate that any particular degree of foresight on
the part of the employer need be established . . . However, we can see that on occasions
what the employer knew or foresaw might be relevant to what control the employer could
exercise. Lack of possible foresight and the unexpected nature of an event might be relevant to the question of whether the event was under the employer's control. But foresight
of the events or the lack of it cannot be determinative of whether the events were under the
employer's control. An employer might foresee that racial harassment is a real possibility
and yet be able to do very little, if anything, to prevent it from happening or protect his
employees from it. For example, the employer of a bus or train conductor may recognise
that the employee will face a real risk of racial harassment at times. Yet the prevention of
such an event will be largely beyond the control of the employer. All he will be able to do
is to make his attitude to such behaviour known to the public and to offer his employees
appropriate support if harassment occurs. On the other hand, if the harassment occurs
even quite unexpectedly, but in circumstances over which the employer has control, a tribunal may well find that he has subjected his employee to it . . .

EAT went on to rule that, in the present case, the hotel manager ought to have
instructed his assistant managers, who were on duty at the event, to remove the waitresses from the hall should the entertainment take an unpleasant turn. His failure to
do so resulted in their subjection by the employer to the racial harassment which they
suffered from Mr Manning and his audience.[36]

Mullender suggests that harassers themselves, even if they fall outside the relevant
Acts, might be held liable at common law:

**Richard Mullender "Racial Harassment, Sexual Harassment, and the Expressive Function of
Law" (1998) 61 *Modern Law Review* 236, 240–1**

Law has an expressive function. Encoded in legal norms are statements or messages.
Examples of such statements or messages abound. Tort law sends out the message that
we bear personal responsibility for our actions. Criminal law identifies some forms of
behaviour as "seriously antisocial". It, moreover, works to impose the "strongest formal
condemnation that society can inflict" on those who engage in such behaviour. What is true

---

[36] See also *Go Kidz Go Ltd* v *Bourdouane* reported in Thompson's Labour and Employment Law Review
Issue 7 (available at http://www.thompsons.law.co.uk/ltext/libindex.htm). In that case, decided a week
before *Burton*, a differently constituted EAT required a degree of foresight, rather than just control, on the
part of the employer. See also *Jagot* v *Benefits Agency* 40 EORDCLD, p.3. Cf *Coyne* v *Home Office*
EAT/244/97, 23rd April 1999, available at www.employmentappeals.gov.uk, in which EAT took a very narrow approach to *Burton*.

of Tort and Criminal Law is also true of the law relating to racial and sexual harassment. The RRA and SDA send out messages to the effect that discrimination on the grounds with which they are respectively concerned is wrongful.

The anti-discriminatory message contained in the RRA is, of course, encoded in the *Burton* decision. Given, moreover, that the Tribunal's decision is a response to "sexualised racism", it echoes the SDA's anti-discriminatory message. Three points lend, however, plausibility to the view that more powerful expression could have been given to the messages contained in the EAT's decision had liability been imposed on the person identified by the Tribunal as primarily responsible for the abuse at stake in the case. First, to engage in racist-cum-sexist abuse is to attack an egalitarian principle that informs both the RRA and the SDA: *viz*, the principle that all persons possess the same moral worth. Secondly, to impose legal liability on the perpetrators of racist and/or sexist abuse is to make an unequivocal statement to the effect that such conduct does not merit a tolerant response. Thirdly, while the liability rule established by the EAT in *Burton* can be expected (other things being equal) to give employers an incentive to provide protection against racist and/or sexist abuse, the message it sends out *vis-à-vis* expressive activity of the sort engaged in by Bernard Manning is not without equivocation. This is because the expression of pernicious prejudice is, *at once*, identified as conduct that calls forth a legal response and yet is *not*, itself, the direct object of a legal sanction.

The Protection from Harassment Act 1997, which was passed in order to deal with stalking, rather than workplace harassment, makes it an offence, punishable by up to six months' imprisonment, (1(1)) "to pursue a course of conduct—(a) which amounts to harassment of another, and (b) which he knows or ought to know amounts to harassment of the other", "harassment" being defined to include causing alarm or distress. In addition to being a criminal offence, such harassment may result in the award of an injunction and/or damages. It is not defined by reference to sex, race or any other factor. S.4 of the Act creates an aggravated offence of "caus[ing] another to fear, on at least two occasions, that violence will be used against him [where the defendant] knows or ought to know that his course of conduct will cause the other so to fear on each of those occasions". This offence is punishable by up to five years' imprisonment.

QUALIFYING BODIES

In the next section we consider the extent to which discrimination in the provision of goods and services etc. is restricted by anti-discrimination legislation. First, however, we will complete our survey of employment-related issues by mentioning a number of restrictions on employment-related discrimination which falls outwith s 4 RRA and the equivalent provisions.

In Chapter 5 we will discuss the formal investigation powers of the various commissions and the restrictions imposed by the anti-discrimination legislation on instructions and pressure to discriminate, discriminatory advertisements, etc. We also saw, above, that barristers, partners, contract and agency workers share, for the most part, employment-related protection from discrimination. In addition, discrimination by trade unions and persons concerned with vocational training is prohibited under the various anti-discrimination provisions.[37] We saw, in chapter 3, that the prohibition on discrimination by trade unions is subject to some "positive action" exceptions. In addition, s.12 SDA provides that the prohibition on sex discrimination by trade unions in relation to the benefits afforded to members "does not apply to provision made in relation to the death or retirement from work of a member".

S.13 SDA provides;

> (1) It is unlawful for an authority or body which can confer an authorisation or qualification which is needed for, or facilitates, engagement in a particular profession or trade to discriminate against a woman—
>   (a) in the terms on which it is prepared to confer on her that authorisation or qualification, or
>   (b) by refusing or deliberately omitting to grant her application for it[38]; or
>   (c) by withdrawing it from her or varying the terms on which she holds it.

S.12 RRA is in similar terms as is Article 25 FETO (which, however, uses the terms "qualification" rather than "authorisation or qualification" and "engagement in employment in any capacity, or in a particular employment or occupation in Northern Ireland" rather than "engagement in a particular profession or trade".[39] The DDA does not, at present, regulate "qualifying body" discrimination.[40]

Ss.13 SDA and 12 RRA have given rise to a substantial amount of litigation. Some such litigation has concerned whether the alleged discriminator was a "qualifying body". In *Malik* v *Post Office Counters Ltd* [1993] ICR 93, EAT ruled that selection for the position of post-master did not fall within s.12. Although the words of the section should not be construed narrowly, the Post Office did not have exclusive authority as to the granting or witholding of the position. In *Tattari* v *PPP Ltd* [1998] ICR 106, [1997] IRLR 586, 38 BMLR 24, the Court of Appeal ruled that the refusal by the health insurance company to add the already qualified doctor to their list of approved plastic surgeons did not fall within s.12 RRA.

---

[37] Article 26 FETO covers partnerships (again of at least 6) while Articles 21–25 prohibit discrimination, respectively, by persons with statutory power to select employees for others, by employment agencies, by vocational organisations, by persons providing training services and by persons with power to confer qualifications. S.13 DDA prohibits discrimination by trade organisations (defined as "organisation[s] of workers . . . employers or any other organisation[s] whose members carry on a particular profession or trade for the purposes of which the organisation exists". For the application of the trade union provisions (there of the SDA), see *Fire Brigades Union* v *Fraser* [1998] IRLR 697 (CS).

[38] But not, according to the Northern Ireland Court of Appeal in *McLoughlin* v *The Queen's University of Belfast* [1995] NI 82, refusal of permission to enrol (the FEA did not apply to education and the FETO applies now only in relation to third level education).

[39] Article 27 now prohibits discrimination by establishments of higher and further education.

[40] The DRTF Final Report recommends: "5.13 Qualifying bodies should be covered in civil rights legislation on employment with careful consideration being given as to what adjustments they might be expected to make (for example, they should not be expected to make adjustments that altered requirements essential to the qualification)."

Beldam LJ (for the Court)

... referring as it does to an authority or body which confers recognition or approval, [s.12 RRA] refers to a body which has the power or authority to confer on a person a professional qualification or approval needed to enable him to practice a profession, exercise a calling or take part in some other activity. It does not refer to a body which is not authorised to or empowered to confer such qualification or permission but which stipulates that for the purpose of its commercial agreements a particular qualification is required . . .[41]

A similar decision was reached by Northern Ireland's Court of Appeal in *Loughran & Kelly* v *Northern Ireland Housing Executive* [1998] IRLR 70, in which that Court ruled that inclusion on the Housing Executive's panel of solicitors did not fall within s.23 FEA (now Article 25 FETO). The case proceeded to the House of Lords as one relating to employment. And in *Arthur* v *Attorney-General & Ors* (unreported, cited by EAT in *Sawyer* v *Ahsan* [1999] IRLR 609, below) EAT ruled that non-selection by the Attorney-General as a lay magistrate did not come within s.12 RRA. According to the appeal tribunal in that case, s.12:

... is directed to circumstances in which A confers on B a qualification which will enable B to render services for C. A and C are the same entity, the section would appear to be inapplicable, otherwise it would apply to every selection panel.

The Council of Legal Education has been recognised as a "qualifying body" under s.12 RRA (*Bohon-Mitchell* v *Common Professional Examination Board and Council of Legal Education* [1978] IRLR 526 (IT)), the issue concerning discrimination against overseas applicants in terms of access to the Common Professional Examination course. In *Jepson & Dyas-Elliott* v *the Labour Party & ors* [1996] IRLR 116 and in *Sawyer* v *Ahsan* the Labour Party was accepted as being a "qualifying body" in relation, respectively, to Labour MPs and Labour Councillors. The first of these cases was brought by way of a challenge to the Labour Party's all-women shortlists, the second was a complaint against the de-selection of an Asian Councillor in favour of a centrally-imposed white man. The decisions are considered further below. So, too, has been the British Judo Association in relation to judo referees and the Financial Intermediaries Managers and Brokers Regulatory Association (FIMBRA) whose members are authorised under the Financial Services Act 1986 to carry out investment business.

Many of the cases brought under ss.12 RRA and 13 SDA relate to proceedings of the General Medical Council which licenses doctors in the UK.[42] In *Rovenska* v *GMC* [1998] ICR 85, [1997] IRLR 367, for example, a Czechoslovakian-qualified doctor challenged, as indirectly discriminatory under the ss.1(1)(b) and 12 RRA, the Council's language-related qualifying criteria for full registration in the UK.[43] A complicating feature of such claims is often s.54(2) RRA/ s.63(2) SDA which provide

---

[41] See also *Balamoody* v *Manchester Health Authority* EAT/1288/97, unreported.
[42] Respectively, *British Judo Association* v *Petty* [1981] ICR 660 and *Zaidi* v *FIMBRA* [1995] ICR 836.
[43] See also *Trivedi* v *General Medical Council* EAT/544/96 (unreported, 1st July 1996).

that s.54(1) and 63(1) RRA and SDA respectively, which allow for the enforcement of the employment-related provisions of the Acts in the employment tribunals, "do not apply to a complaint under section 12(1) [RRA/ s.13(1) SDA] of an act in respect of which an appeal, or proceedings in the nature of an appeal, may be brought under any enactment . . ."[44]

The impact of s.54 was felt in *Khan v General Medical Council* [1993] ICR 627, [1993] IRLR 378 in which the applicant challenged, as indirectly discriminatory, the GMC's requirements for full registration of overseas practitioners after twice being refused such registration. His application, pursuant to s.29 Medical Act 1983, to the Review Board for Overseas Qualified Practitioners for review of the Council's decision had been unsuccessful.

The issue for the Court of Appeal was whether the Review Board procedure was "in the nature of an appeal" under s.54(2) despite the fact that the Board had no power to reverse the decision of the Council, its role being restricted to providing an opinion to the President of the Council.[45] What the case illustrates, however, is that s.54(2) can operate to prevent challenge to alleged discrimination. Further, according to the Court of Appeal in *Khan*, the appeal procedure could not, if it were alleged itself to be discriminatory, found a claim under s.12.

It was argued in the *Khan* case that s.54(2) ought to be given the same construction as s.63(2) of the SDA which would have to be interpreted so as to provide an "effective remedy" under the equal treatment directive. But, according to Hoffman LJ:[46]

> I do not see why it should not be regarded as an effective remedy against sex or race discrimination in the kind of case with which s. 12(1) of the [RRA] deals. That concerns qualifications for professions and trades. Parliament appears to have thought that, although the industrial tribunal is often called a specialist tribunal and has undoubted expertise in matters of sex and racial discrimination, its advantages in providing an effective remedy were outweighed by the even greater specialisation in a particular field or trade or professional qualification of statutory tribunals such as the Review Board, since the Review Board undoubtedly has a duty to give effect to the provisions of s.12 [this having been established by the Divisional Court in *R v Department of Health ex p Gandhi* [1991] ICR 805, [1991] 1 WLR 1053, [1991] 4 All ER 547] . . . This seems to me a perfectly legitimate view for parliament to have taken. Furthermore, s.54(2) makes it clear that decisions of the Review Board would themselves be open to judicial review on the ground that it failed to have proper regard to the provisions of the [RRA]. In my view, it cannot be said that the Medical Act 1983 does not provide the effective remedy required by European law.

[44] Complaints could not be made under the RRA or the EqPA in relation to service in the armed forces until the amendment of those Acts by the Armed Forces Act 1997. The SDA provides (s.85) that "(4) Nothing in this Act shall render unlawful an act done for the purposes of ensuring the combat effectiveness of the naval, military or air forces of the Crown. (5) Nothing in this Act shall render unlawful discrimination in admission to the Army Cadet Force, Air Training Corps, Sea Cadet Corps or Combined Cadet Force, or to any other cadet training corps for the time being administered by the Ministry of Defence." These provisions must be read subject to the decision of the ECJ in *Sirdar v The Army Board, Secretary of State for Defence* Case C–273/97 [1999] All ER (EC) 928, discussed in Chapter 6.

[45] *Cf Zaidi v FIMBRA* note 42 above.

[46] Concurring with Neill LJ with both of whose speeches Waite LJ agreed.

In the *Gandhi* case the Divisional Court had ruled that the Secretary of State, in exercising an appellate function in respect of the Medical Practices Committee of the NHS,[47] was bound to consider the allegation of race discrimination upon which the appeal rested (the Secretary of State had resisted this conclusion). The Secretary of State was not required, however, to make a specific finding in relation to the allegation in dismissing the appeal. Further, the appeal being "nearer the administrative end of the spectrum than the judicial end", the requirements of natural justice were not onerous. In that case Dr Gandhi had not received an oral hearing.

An additional complication in the application of ss.13 SDA/ 12 RRA was threatened in *General Medical Council* v *Goba* [1988] IRLR 425, in which case the GMC argued that any discrimination under s.12 was rendered lawful by s.41 RRA. The complaint in that case, as in *Rovenska*, concerned the Council's qualifying criteria for registration of overseas doctors. The Council sought to rely on s.41(1):

Nothing in Parts II to IV shall render unlawful any act of discrimination done
(a) in pursuance of any enactment or Order in Council or
(b) in pursuance of any instrument made under any enactment by a Minister of the Crown or
(c) in order to comply with any condition or requirement imposed by a Minister of the Crown (whether before or after the passing of this Act) by virtue of any enactment.

The Council argued that s.41(1)(a) provided "an umbrella protection" for any act done in pursuance of its statutory registration duty, the duty having been imposed on it by s.22 of the Medical Act 1983. EAT ruled that s.41(1) provided a defence only in respect of those acts that were "reasonably necessary" in order to comply with any condition or requirement imposed". It is now clear, from the decision of the House of Lords in *Hampson* v *Department of Education and Science* [1991] 1 AC 171 that s.41 covers only those acts done i the necessary performance of an express obligation contained in the instrument (see, further, Chapter 7).

The cases considered above are concerned with the nature of "qualifying bodies" under ss.12 RRA and 13 SDA. In both *Jepson* v *Labour Party* and in *Sawyer* v *Ashan*, the Labour Party argued that it was not a "qualifying body" in relation to Labour Party election candidates, relying on the freedom of candidates to stand for election other than as Labour Party candidates, and on the fact that selection by the Party did not guarantee election. In both cases the argument was rejected.

Also raised by the Labour Party in *Jepson* was the argument that "profession" within s.13 SDA should be restricted to "employment" (that being the subject heading of Part II of the Act within which s.13 appears). This would have served to disqualify membership of Parliament as a "profession", MPs being office-holders and therefore outside the employment-related provisions of the Act. The tribunal rejected this argument as a matter of construction:

[47] Under the National Health Service Act 1977 and the National Health Service (General Medical and Pharmaceutical Services) Regulations 1974.

It soon becomes apparent from the wording of s.13 that more than employment as defined in s.82 [SDA] is intended to be covered by that section. It would have been quite easy for s.13 to have been drafted in such a way as to have restricted its operation just to employment as so defined.

Nor did it matter that Councillors were not paid. In *Sawyer* EAT cited *British Judo Association* v *Petty* (above), EAT in that case having accepted that qualification as an unpaid judo referee was within s.13 SDA. The substantive argument put forward by the Labour Party in *Jepson* was to the effect that, s.33 SDA permitting political parties to discriminate by making special provision for persons of one sex only in the constitution, organisation or administration of the party, all-women shortlists were lawful.

Jepson and Dyas-Elliott v *Labour Party and Ors* [1996] IRLR 116

Mr Goudie says first that s.13 comes within part II of the Act which is headed "Discrimination in the employment field". He submits that that heading is an aid to construing the Act and in particular to construing the limits of that part of the Act. Having regard to the definition of employment in s.82, s.13 cannot, he says, cover a Member of Parliament who is an office-holder and not a person in employment. Moreover, the heading in s.13 itself is qualifying bodies which from the text cannot be said to cover the Labour Party and Constituency Labour Parties.

Secondly, he submits that adopting an individual as a Labour Party prospective parliamentary candidate amounts to a commitment to the provision by the Party and the Constituency Party of facilities and services for the prospective Parliamentary candidate as a member of the public under s.29 in Part III of the Act. Discrimination in the selection of the candidate would, he submits, be unlawful discrimination under s.29 were it not for s.33, which provides an exception from s.29 for any special provision for persons of one sex only in the constitution organisation or administration of the political party (in this case the Labour Party). Consequently, he says, s.33 expressly exempts the Labour Party for its positive discrimination in attempting to redress the current underrepresentation of women in the House of Commons. That being so, it would be inconsistent with the scheme of the Act to have the matter also dealt with in Part II. The two parts are mutually exclusive and even if they are not it would be illogical to make the discrimination unlawful under one part and lawful under another. Mr Goudie submits that further support for this view is by reference to relevant Parliamentary Committee Meetings in 1975, utilising the principle in the House of Lords decision in *Pepper* v *Hart* [[1993] AC 593].

Thirdly, Mr Goudie submits that neither the appointment of a prospective Parliamentary candidate nor election as an MP is engagement in a particular profession or trade. The candidate is not paid. The MP is not an employee. The definition of a profession in s.82 does not refer to the well-known category of office-holder and, he submits, in no way can be described as covering prospective Parliamentary candidates or MPs. When a Constituency Labour Party appoints a prospective Parliamentary candidate that is not, says Mr Goudie, declaring an authorisation of qualification on a candidate. . . .

Finally he refers to European law and the Equal Treatment Directive—Directive 76/207—in that he submits that Article 2(4) covers the positive discrimination of having women-only shortlists notwithstanding the *Kalanke* case [[1995] ECR I–3051].

We are not satisfied that s.29 of the Act applies at all to this situation. . . . s 29 is clearly intended to cover situations where persons or bodies provide goods, facilities and services *to the public*, that is to say what may broadly be described as "trade" or matters similar thereto. It is an ingenious but fallacious argument to bring the matter we are considering into the ambit of s.29 although we can understand why Mr Goudie has endeavoured to do this because he believes it provides a defence for the respondents under s.33. Whatever be the correct interpretation of the ambit of s.33 we are unable to accept tht s.29 should take precedence over s.13.

The matter may perhaps be tested in this way. If a person gained employment as defined in s.82 with the Labour Party it could also be said that consequent upon that employment he would also gain facilities and services from the Labour Party as a member of the public under s.29. There would on account of s.33 then be a possible direct conflict in the Act. We apprehend that in that situation Mr Goudie would be obliged to concede that the rights of the individual as covered by Part II of the Act should prevail. Consequently it follows that once this tribunal is satisfied, as indeed we are, that s.13 applies to this situation any argument under s.29 and s.33 (which relates back *only* to s.29) must fall away.

We do not regard the principle in *Pepper v Hart* as assisting us having regard to there being in our view no real ambiguity to resolve, nor we are bound to say have we gained much assistance from references to the European Court of Human Rights.

We certainly reject there being any justification for this positive discrimination arising from Article 2(4) of the Equal Treatment Directive as submitted by Mr Goudie. That would have to be in the context of the Equal Treatment Directive applying directly in the first place which it clearly does not since the respondents are not emanations of the State (although as we have seen we can refer to the Directive as assisting the construction of the national law).

In any event such a total block on one sex as occurs here cannot have been the intention in that Article, a view which we regard as fully endorsed by the decision of the European Court in the *Kalanke* case.

We conclude therefore that the complaints of both applicants that they have been unlawfully discriminated against on the grounds of their sex are well-founded and the tribunal makes a declaration to that effect.

The final issue in *Sawyer* concerned whether qualification as a Labour MP should be regarded as akin to a professional qualification within s.12 RRA or whether it fell within *Arthur* v *Attorney-General*, above:

Sawyer v Ashan

The EAT's references [in Arthur] to "A", "B" and "C", the continuation of the point first mentioned in Malik and developed through *Tattari* and *Kelly* [& *Loughran*], require us to identify the player who fits each letter.

"A", to both Mr Goudie [for the Labour Party] and Mr Allen [for Mr Ahsan], is the Labour Party and each has Mr Ahsan as "B" but the difference between them appears when, to Mr Goudie, it is the Labour Party which is "C",[48] with the result that "A" and "C" are the same and accordingly, if Arthur is right, as Mr Goudie contends, section 12

---

[48] The argument put by the Labour Party—that an elected Councillor should be regarded as serving the Party, rather than the constituents, is extraordinary.

does not apply. To Mr Allen "C" is the general public or at least that section of it which lives or works in the Sparkhill Ward, with the result that "C" differs from "A" and that the Arthur argument does not put Mr Ahsan outside section 12.

We prefer Mr Allen's argument. To select a candidate as the Labour candidate for Sparkhill or any other Local Government constituency is, in our view, very different to appointing an agent (as in *Malik*), to reaching a commercial agreement of similar effect (*Tattari*) or to appointing a Solicitor or other person to provide professional services for oneself (*Kelly*). In each case the appointor in those cases was selecting for its own purposes, even though those purposes included the appointee, if selected, dealing on its behalf with some sector of the public . . . No doubt in each of those cases the appointee could, in an appropriate case, be removed by the appointor or could in many cases be given mandatory directions as to how to conduct matters on pain of dismissal. By contrast, a Labour candidate, if elected, cannot be removed as Councillor by the Labour Party and, whilst, on pain of losing the whip or party membership, pressure can be put upon him by the party, he is left to make up his own mind. He can retire at will or remain independent of the wishes of the Party, for his elected term. He cannot be directed by the Party in any mandatory way if he chooses to ignore its wishes, its whip and its membership. He would even remain a Councillor if after election he chose to describe himself as an independent or as a Councillor of a rival party. We were told, moreover, that his oath of office (which we were not shown) is not only common to all Councillors of whatever political persuasion, but also (as we would expect) is of a duty to the public rather than to party . . .

EDUCATION

Ss.17 and 22 of the RRA and SDA respectively prohibit discrimination by an educational establishment:[49]

  (a) in the terms on which it offers to admit . . . [pupils] to the establishment, or
  (b) by refusing or deliberately omitting to accept an application for . . . admission to the establishment, or
  (c) . . . [in relation to existing pupils]:
      (i) in the way it affords . . . access to any benefits, facilities or services, or by deliberately omitting to afford . . . access to them, or
      (ii) by excluding [them] . . . from the establishment or subjecting [them] . . . to any other detriment.

Article 27 FETO is in similar terms, although it applies only to further and higher educational establishments, religion-specific schooling being the norm in Northern Ireland. The Fair Employment Acts which preceded the FETO did not regulate discrimination in the education field. The DDA does not prohibit discrimination in education, ss.29–31 being concerned only with rights to information about provision

---

[49] The establishments are listed and orders may be made under s.24(1) SDA to alter these from time to time.

made for the disabled. In December 1999 Secretary of State for Education and Employment David Blunkett announced that the DDA would be amended to cover access to schools, colleges and the curriculum.[50]

Education authorities are liable under ss.17 and 22 RRA and SDA respectively in relation to maintained schools, and are also prohibited by ss.18 and 23 respectively from discriminating in relation to any of their statutory functions.[51] Exceptions are being provided by s.26–28 SDA in relation to single sex establishments, formerly single sex establishments in the process of becoming co-educational, and physical education courses.[52] Discrimination which arises *between* rather than *within* institutions (such as where, for example, pupils at a boys' school are treated more favourably than those at a girls' school)[53] falls under ss.18 and 23 RRA and SDA. Thus, for example, while *Mandla* v *Dowell Lee* [1983] 2 AC 548 was brought under s.17 RRA, *EOC* v *Birmingham City Council* [1989] AC 1155 concerned discrimination under s.23 SDA. Both cases are considered in detail in Chapter 2.

Perhaps the most infamous case of discrimination in the education field came to light as a result of a Formal Investigation by the CRE (see further Chapter 5). In *Medical School Admissions: A CRE Investigation*, the Commission found that the computer programme utilised by St George's Medical School to sift applications included a (deliberate) bias against women and non-whites. Perhaps the most worrying thing about the use of the programme was that it had been designed to replicate the decision-making formerly undertaken by academics.[54]

In *R* v *Cleveland County Council ex p. CRE* (1992) 91 LGR 139[55] the Court of Appeal ruled that the parental choice provisions of the Education Act 1988 overrode those of the RRA to the effect that a local authority which be obliged to accommodate even racially discriminatory parental preferences. The CRE argued that the apparently unqualified nature of the EA should be read in the light of s.18 RRA (above).

DISCRIMINATION IN HOUSING/PREMISES

Ss. 21–24 RRA and 30–31 SDA regulate discrimination in relation to the disposal of premises. The equivalent provisions of the FETO and the DDA are Articles 29–30 of the former and ss.22 and 23 of the latter:

[50] Press release 589/99 15th December 1999, in response to the report of the Disability Rights Task Force published 13th December 1999, see fn 3 above.

[51] Ss. 19 and 25 RRA and SDA respectively impose, in addition, general duties of non-discrimination on public sector education providers. These are concerned with planning and are enforceable only by the Secretary of State for Education. Also s.71 RRA, discussed in Chapter 5, obliges local education authorities to promote good race relations.

[52] This includes teacher training courses.

[53] See, for example, *R* v *Secretary of State for Education and Science, ex p. Keating* [1985] LGR 469.

[54] C. Bourn and J. Whitmore, *Anti-discrimination Law in Britain* (3rd ed., London: Sweet and Maxwell, 1996), para 7.07.

[55] *The Times* 25th August 1992, *The Independent* 6th August 1992, [1993] 1 FCR 597.

FETO, Article 29:

(1) It is unlawful for a person with power to dispose of any premises to discriminate against another—
  (a) in the terms on which he offers him those premises; or
  (b) by refusing his application for those premises; or
  (c) in his treatment of him in relation to any list of persons in need of premises of that description.
(2) Paragraph (1) does not apply to a person who owns an estate in the premises and wholly occupies them unless, for the purpose of disposing of the premises, he—
  (a) uses the services of an estate agent; or
  (b) publishes an advertisement or causes an advertisement to be published.[56]
(3) It is unlawful for a person managing any premises to discriminate against a person occupying those premises—
  (a) in the way he affords him access to any benefits, or by refusing or deliberately omitting to afford him access to them; or
  (b) by evicting him, or subjecting him to any other detriment.
(4) It is unlawful for any person whose licence or consent is required for the disposal of any premises comprised in a tenancy to discriminate against a person by withholding his licence or consent for the disposal of the premises to that person.

Article 29 is subject to an exception in relation to small premises in which an occupier "resides, and intends to continue to reside" and shares accommodation on the premises with others, not household members, who live on the premises.[57] Small premises are defined as those which either (30(4)) do not usually comprise more than three separate households including that of the occupier, this last containing only the occupier and his or her household; or do not include residential accommodation for more than six persons in addition to the occupiers household. The occupier can consist either of the discriminator or of his or her spouse, parent, child, grandparent, grandchild, or brother or sister (whether of full or half blood or by affinity).[58] This exception does not apply in relation to discrimination against existing tenants.

S.24 DDA defines discrimination in this context so as to exclude the failure to make reasonable adjustment which applies elsewhere throughout the DDA. Discrimination (less favourable treatment for a reason which relates to the disabled person's disability) may be justified if the discriminator reasonably believes that it is necessary in order not to endanger the health or safety of any person or that the disabled person or that "the disabled person is incapable of entering into an enforceable agreement, or of giving an informed consent, and for that reason the treatment is reasonable in that case". Discrimination in the terms upon which a disabled tenant is permitted to make use of

---

[56] Evidence from the Chair of the FEC to the Northern Ireland Select Committee Fourth Report, 1998–1999 session (see fn 18 above) suggested (answer to question 148) that discrimination in the sale of land remained a significant problem in rural areas.

[57] Not being access or storage.

[58] Art. 30(6) also excludes from the prohibition on discrimination the disposal, etc., of educational premises.

any benefits or facilities is subject to an additional justification where the discrimina-tor reasonably believes that it is necessary "in order for the disabled person or the occupiers of other premises forming part of the building to make use of the benefit or facility", and a discriminatory refusal to permit a disabled person to make use to any benefits and facilities where the discriminator reasonable believes that it is necessary "in order for the occupiers of other premises forming part of the building to make use of the benefit or facility".

Relatively few cases have been litigated under the premises sections of the anti-discrimination legislation. The CRE has carried out a number of Formal Investigations (see further Chapter 5) into race discrimination by local authorities in the provision of housing. In 1984 it found that the London Borough of Hackney had been guilty of "direct discrimination against black applicants and tenants who had been allocated housing from the waiting list . . . in that whites had received better-quality allocations of housing than blacks".[59]

> Although there were almost as many black applicants on the council waiting list as whites (45 per cent. compared with 49 per cent.), among white applicants 16 per cent. were allo-cated houses, 19 per cent. maisonettes and 65 per cent. flats, whereas 4 per cent. of blacks received houses, 11 per cent. maisonettes and 85 per cent. flats. Whites were more likely to be allocated new property than blacks (25 per cent., compared with 4 per cent.) moreover, a higher proportion of white tenants were awarded ground or first floor accommodation.[60]

Discrimination in the provision of accommodation by Hackney was regarded by the CRE as discrimination in access to services under s.20 RRA (see below); discrimina-tion in relation to waiting lists as discrimination under s.21(1)(c).[61] The Commission's 1978 Annual Report also records that the London Borough of Islington complied with CRE pressure to change a rule whereby dependants were recognised for the pur-pose of its waiting list only if they were resident in the UK.[62] And the Formal Investigation at issue in *Hillingdon London Borough Council* v *Commission for Racial Equality* [1982] AC 779 (see Chapter 5) also concerned housing.[63]

According to the CRE Factsheet *Housing and Homelessness*, 44% of Caribbean households and 42% of Bangladeshi households lived in flats by comparison with 29% of white households, while in 1991 2% of white, 5% of Caribbean, 30% of Pakistani and 47% of Bangladeshi families were living in overcrowded conditions:

> In Greater London, ethnic minority households formed 45% of the statutory homeless households in 1998. Excluding Irish, ethnic minorities were about three times as likely to be homeless as whites . . . In London . . . at 0.78% the homelessness rate was highest for

[59] Bourn and Whitmore, fn 54 above, para 7.48. See also M. Bryan, *Discrimination in the Public Provision of Housing: the Commission for Racial Equality Report on Housing in Hackney*, 1984 *Public Law* 194.

[60] Bryan, *ibid*, p.196.

[61] S.35(3) SDA, s.23(1) RRA.

[62] This was altered to permit consideration of those entitled to live in the UK.

[63] The RRA alone prohibits discrimination by planning authorities, s.19A having been inserted after the *Amin* case in order to deal with pressure to discriminate upon planning authorities.

Caribbeans and Africans, compared with an average of 0.26% . . . In Tower Hamlets, Bangladeshi families made up nearly 60% of all homeless families in 1994, but only 10% of families in the borough . . .[64]

DISCRIMINATION IN THE PROVISION OF GOODS AND SERVICES

Turning to those areas of discrimination entirely unrelated to employment, the most significant provision of the SDA in this area is s.29 which provides:

(1) It is unlawful for any person concerned with the provision (for payment or not) of goods, facilities or services to the public or a section of the public to discriminate against a woman who seeks to obtain or use those goods facilities or services—
    (a) by refusing or deliberately omitting to provide her with any of them, or
    (b) by refusing or deliberately omitting to provide her with goods, facilities or services of the like quality, in the like manner and on the like terms as are normal in his case in relation to male members of the public or (where she belongs to a section of the public) to male members of that section.
(2) The following are examples of the facilities and services mentioned in subsection (1)—
    (a) access to and use of any place which members of the public or a section of the public are permitted to enter;
    (b) accommodation in a hotel, boarding house or other similar establishment;
    (c) facilities by way of banking or insurance or for grants, loans, credit or finance;
    (d) facilities for education;
    (e) facilities for entertainment, recreation or refreshment;
    (f) facilities for transport or travel;
    (g) services of any profession or trade, or any local or other public authority.

S.20 RRA is in exactly the same terms as is article 28 FETO while s.19 DDA provides:

(1) It is unlawful for a provider of services to discriminate against a disabled person-
    (a) in refusing to provide, or deliberately not providing, to the disabled person any service which he provides, or is prepared to provide, to members of the public;
    (b) in failing to comply with any duty imposed on him by section 21 in circumstances in which the effect of that failure is to make it impossible or
    (c) in the standard of service which he provides to the disabled person or the manner in which he provides it to him; or
    (d) in the terms on which he provides a service to the disabled person.
(2) For the purposes of this section and sections 20 and 21-
    (a) the provision of services includes the provision of any goods or facilities;
    (b) a person is "a provider of services" if he is concerned with the provision, in the United Kingdom, of services to the public or to a section of the public; and
    (c) it is irrelevant whether a service is provided on payment or without payment.

---

[64] The fact sheet is available on the CRE website at www.open.gov.uk.

S.19(3) DDA lists the same examples as does s.29(2)SDA, with the addition of "(b) access to and use of means of communication; (c) access to and use of information services" and "(g) facilities provided by employment agencies or under section 2 of the Employment and Training Act 1973". Education is specifically excluded from the protection of the DDA, though schools, colleges and universities are required to provide information for disabled people. The 1999 Code of Practice on Rights of Access states (para 2.18) that the education exception covers services very closely related to education such as "youth services provided by a local education authority" and "social, cultural and recreational activities and facilities for physical education and training designed to promote personal or educational development provided by a voluntary organisation (for example, a local branch of the scouts or guides)". Transport is also expressly excluded, though the Government may set minimum access standards for new taxis, trains and buses and transport infrastructure such as railway and bus stations and airports are covered.

The Disability Discrimination (Services and Premises) Regulations 1996[65] impose special rules relating to insurance for disabled persons and to occupational pension schemes. Less favourable treatment of disabled persons in relation to insurance is permitted by the regulations where the treatment is in connection with insurance business carried out by the discriminator; the treatment is based on information relevant to the assessment of the risk to be insured; the information is from a source upon which it is reasonable to rely and the less favourable treatment is reasonable on the basis of this information and any other relevant factors.[66] The Code of Practice on Rights of Access to Goods, Facilities, Services and Premises suggests that the refusal of life insurance to a person expected, on good medical evidence, to die within six months would not be regarded as unlawful whereas the charging of higher motor insurance to a manic depression sufferer, though based on actuarial tables relating to sufferers during manic episodes, would be unlawful in the face of credible evidence that the applicant's condition had been stable over a period of years and his driving record clean.

The 1996 Regulations (Reg 4) provide that less favourable treatment of a disabled person in relation to benefits provided under an occupational pension scheme in respect of termination of service; retirement, old age or death; or accident injury, sickness or invalidity is justified where "by reason of the disabled person's disability (including any clinical prognosis flowing from the disability) the cost of providing [the] . . . benefit is likely to be substantially greater than it would be for a comparable person without that disability". The same Regulations (Reg 4) deem to be justified any requirement that a disabled person pay the same rate of contributions as others "notwithstanding that [s/he] . . . is not eligible under that scheme, for a reason related to his disability, to receive a benefit or to receive a benefit at the same rate as a comparable person to whom the reason does not apply".

---

[65] SI 1996/1836.
[66] The Disability Discrimination (Description of Insurance Services) Regulations 1999, SI No.2114, available at http://www.legislation.hmso.gov.uk/stat.htm.

The 1996 Regulations have been criticised, not least on the basis that they have encouraged discrimination where none before existed.[67] The Disability Rights Task Force commissioned (small scale) research which found that discrimination in this area was not common, save in respect of access to particular benefits. The DRTF Final Report, *From Exclusion to Inclusion*, recommended that the scope for discrimination in this area be reduced:

> Occupational pension schemes should be required to offer equal access to scheme membership for disabled people when starting their employment. Restricted access to certain benefits should be permitted for disabled people choosing to join a scheme later in their employment or re-joining a scheme, but only if: restricted access to benefits is strictly limited to a specific pre-existing impairment or condition; such restrictions can be justified, eg. based on relevant and reliable information such as up-to-date actuarial or statistical data; and schemes regularly review any restrictions or impose time limits on them.[68]

S.20 defines discrimination for the purposes of the DDA's goods and services provisions in terms both of direct discrimination (less favourable treatment) and failure to comply with a duty of reasonable adjustment, both forms of discrimination being capable of justification under the Act (see further Chapter 8). The implementation of this part of the DDA is not yet complete, the current obligations (imposed in October 1999) for service providers to take reasonable steps to change practices, policies or procedures which make it impossible or unreasonably difficult for disabled people to use a service; to provide auxiliary aids or services to enable disabled people to use the service and to overcome physical barriers by providing the service by a reasonable alternative method being upgraded, in 2004, to obligations to take reasonable steps to remove, alter, or provide reasonable means of avoiding, physical features that make it impossible or unreasonably difficult for disabled people to use the service.

Northern Ireland's fair employment legislation did not apply in relation to goods and services prior to the implementation of the FETO. All the caselaw on goods and services discrimination, therefore, arises under the SDA and RRA. The same is true in respect of the other non-employment provisions of the anti-discrimination enactments.

Ss.33 and 34 SDA, create exceptions from that Act's prohibition on discrimination in goods and services in respect of political parties and voluntary bodies, the former permitting "special provision" and acts done to give effect to such provision, "for persons of one sex only in the constitution, organisation or administration of the political party". In the *Jepson* case, discussed above, the tribunal rejected the argument that s.33 applied to permit discrimination in the selection of parliamentary candidates (see extract).

---

[67] Contribution to the January 2000 seminar hosted by the Independent Review of Discrimination Law from a public sector trade union official.

[68] Fn 3 above, recommendation 5.34. See also DTRF 26/99 working group, *Report on Outstanding Recommendations on Occupational Pensions*, available on http://www. disability.gov.uk/drtf/.

S.34 SDA allows non-statutory, non-profit making bodies to restrict membership wholly or mainly to one sex, and the provision of benefits, facilities or services to members of such bodies. S.35 also allows the provision of single-sex facilities or services in hospitals and "other establishment[s] for persons requiring special care, supervision or attention"; in sex-segregated places "occupied or used for the purposes of an organised religion [where] the facilities or service are restricted to men so as to comply with the doctrines of that religion or avoid offending the religious susceptibilities of a significant number of its followers"; and in circumstances where:

(c) the facilities or services are provided for, or are likely to be used by, two or more persons at the same time, and
    (i) the facilities or services are such, or those persons are such, that male users are likely to suffer serious embarrassment at the presence of a woman, or
    (ii) the facilities or service are such that a user is likely to be in a state of undress and a male user might reasonably object to the presence of a female user.
(2) A person who provides facilities or services restricted to men does not for that reason contravene section 29(1) if the services or facilities are such that physical contact between the user and any other person is likely, and that other person might reasonably object if the user were a woman.

S.46 SDA permits discrimination in admission to communal accommodation and associated benefits, as long as the treatment of each sex is "fair and equitable". This provision, unsurprisingly, has no equivalent in the RRA. S.43 SDA permits charitable instruments to confer benefits (disregarding exceptional or insignificant benefit) entirely on persons of one sex, ss.78 and 79 providing for the alteration of such instruments connected with education. S.10 DDA permits charitable instruments to discriminate by "conferring benefits on one or more categories of person determined by reference to any physical or mental capacity" and charities to pursue their charitable purposes "so far as those purposes are connected with persons so determined".[69] S.34 RRA is to similar effect save that distinctions may not be made by reference to colour. S.44 SDA provides that the Act shall not:

> In relation to any sport, game or other activity of a competitive nature where the physical strength, stamina or physique of the average woman puts her at a disadvantage to the average man, render unlawful any act related to the participation of a person as a competitor in events involving that activity which are confined to competitors of one sex.

This exception does not permit all sex discrimination in sport. In April 1998, Jane Couch won a tribunal case brought against the British Boxing Board of Control over that body's refusal to grant her a boxing licence. The board sought to defend their decision on the grounds that:

---

[69] S.10 also permits positive discrimination by persons providing supported employment in relation to particular groups of disabled persons.

The Times, **April 28th 1998,**

. . . women were more prone to accidents than men because of pre-menstrual tension; they were more susceptible to bruising and therefore to brain damage; and monthly hormonal changes resulted in fluid retention and weight gain, making weight categorisation harder . . . [the] tribunal . . . held that the decision was prompted solely by "gender-based stereo-types and assumptions" . . . Ms Couch was never examined by a board doctor, and that there was no evidence that "boxing poses a higher risk to women than to men or vice versa". In a damning decision, it criticised the board for not obtaining any medical evidence about Ms Couch . . . "No male boxer would have been rejected on medical grounds without having had a medical investigation."

S.39 RRA permits discrimination on grounds of nationality, birthplace or length of residence in the selection of persons to represent areas, places or countries in any sport, or in competition rules regarding eligibility.

A number of the leading cases under the RRA and the SDA have arisen under the non-employment related provisions of the Acts. These include *Mandla* v *Dowell Lee*, *EOC* v *Birmingham* and *James* v *Eastleigh* [1990] 2 AC 751, all of which are discussed in Chapter 2. The issues raised by these cases, however, related to the "general part" of the anti-discrimination legislation—that is, the meaning of direct discrimination, the meaning and justification of indirect discrimination and, in the *Mandla* case (which is also considered in Chapter 7) to the meaning of "racial group", rather than specifically to the non-employment provisions of the Acts which we now consider.

S.29 SDA and 20 RRA prohibit discrimination in the provision of goods, services and facilities. S.29 has been applied by the Court of Appeal in *Gill* v *El Vino Co Ltd* [1983] QB 425 to cover a wine bar's refusal to serve women unless they were seated and, in *Quinn* v *Williams Furniture Ltd* [1981] ICR 328, a shop's refusal to extend credit facilities to a woman unless her husband stood as a guarantor. S.20 RRA has also been applied by that court in *Savjani* v *Inland Revenue Commissioners* [1981] QB 458 to race discrimination by the Inland Revenue in affording tax relief and, as we saw above, by the House of Lords in *James* v *Eastleigh* to discriminatory charges for access to a public swimming pool.

In addition to the qualifications to s.29 mentioned above, s.45 permits sex discrimination in relation to annuities, life assurance policies, accident insurance policies or similar matters concerning the assessment of risk where the discrimination results from reasonable reliance upon actuarial or other statistical material, and is reasonable in the light of the statistical and other factors. The test of reasonableness is not onerous, the County Court accepting in *Pinder* v *Friends Provident*, *The Times*, 16th February 1985 that a practice of charging women 50% more than men for health insurance on the basis of 1953 statistics fell within s.45.[70]

The insurance-related exception was criticised by David Pannick:

---

[70] Bourn and Whitmore, fn 54 above, para 7.41.

David Pannick, Sex Discrimination Law (Oxford, OUP, 1985), 189–95

Sex discrimination is a common feature of insurance policies. Because of a belief that women are more prone to illness than men, women tend to be charged higher premiums than men in order to receive the same benefits in permanent health insurance and in many other forms of cover. Because women tend to live longer than men, they often pay lower premiums than men for life assurance and receive lower annuity rates.

It is strongly arguable that, as a matter of principle, the 1975 Act should not exempt insurance policies. The criterion of sex is an unreliable, unnecessary, and unfair one to use in the assessment of risk in insurance policies. In any event, it is doubtful whether many of the insurance policies which currently discriminate on the ground of sex would satisfy the criteria of section 45.

The practice of charging women more for equal benefits, or giving women lesser benefits for the same premium, is justified by insurance companies on the basis that statistics show that women, as a group, are more frequently ill than men, as a group, and that women tend to live longer than men. Sex discrimination in insurance cannot be defended unless this statistical basis is a reliable one. The problem for insurance companies is that "[i]nsurance rates are calculated from mortality tables based on persons already dead, and charged to persons who will live far into the future. Thus there is no reason to expect sex differences among current insureds to match those reflected in the tables." Insurance companies use old, sometimes antiquated, statistics which are based on the behaviour of previous generations of men and women whose occupational and social experiences were vitally different from those of the current generation of insured persons. Because sex differences in the statistics are largely due to behavioural rather than genetic factors, the relevance of the statistics will critically depend on whether women (and men) have similar occupational and social patterns today. Changes in such patterns since the time to which the statistics relate will obviously have an impact on sickness and death rates for men and women. Often, the statistics will tell us little or nothing about sickness and mortality rates today because of important changes in society since the period to which the statistics relate. Furthermore, the sickness statistics may merely reflect occupational segregation between men and women: since women tend to do less responsible work, they are likely to take more time off work.

Even if the statistical information relied on by an insurance company shows that there are differences between the sickness and mortality rates which can be predicted for men and women working today, it may be unnecessary for insurers to discriminate between men and women in this way. Other factors, such as a person's age, class, occupation, family medical history, and whether the person smokes, may be far better predictors of illness and death than sex. In *Los Angeles Department of Water and Power* v. *Manhart* [435 US 702], the US Supreme Court held that it was unlawful sex discrimination contrary to Title VII of the Civil Rights Act 1964 for an employer to require female employees to make larger contributions than male employees to a pension fund in order to receive the same benefit. The employers argued that their practice was valid because women tend to live longer than men and so the average woman will tend to receive more out of the fund than the average man. One reason for the decision of the Court to reject this argument was that "[s]eparate mortality tables are easily interpreted as reflecting innate differences between the sexes; but a significant part of the longevity differential may be explained by the social fact that men are heavier smokers than women". Often, insurance companies give no weight, or inadequate weight, to these other statistically valid factors; they merely charge one premium (or allow one payment) for women and a different premium (or payment) for men. Such policies take insufficient note of the fact that "[w]hile actuarial tables may be relatively accurate in predicting the average longevity of men and women respectively, quite a substantial deviation occurs within either sex", for many non-sex based reasons.

A third reason for questioning sex discrimination in insurance is that it is unfair to individual men and women. Assume that sex-based differentials in health insurance or pension plans are statistically valid: that they are based on valid material and ignore no other relevant classifications, so that an insurance company can accurately predict significantly different risks for relevant men and for relevant women. In such circumstances, it may well be that the scheme treats men (as a group) equally with women (as a group), allocating roughly equal amounts of benefits to, and taking approximately equal contributions from, each sex when there are equal numbers of men and women who participate in the scheme. All women who belong to the scheme will be charged a higher premium for health insurance or for a pension than all men because of an assumption that, by reason of their sex, they will tend to become ill more frequently than, and to die later than, comparable men. This is irrespective of the characteristics of an individual woman, who may in fact be a good health risk or may die much sooner than a man of her age doing a similar job. The question is whether it is fair to impose this detriment on any woman because she is a woman, irrespective of her own individual attributes.

It is a general principle of anti-discrimination law that people should not be treated by reference to a stereotyped assumption based on their race or sex. They are entitled to treatment by reference to their individual characteristics irrespective of their race or sex. Two arguments are used to defend the use of stereotyped assumptions in the context of insurance. First, that here the assumption is a true one: women do live longer than men. Secondly, that insurance is concerned with the assessment of risk and so it is here permissible to treat people by reference to the risk associated with persons of their sex.

In *Manhart*, the US Supreme Court recognized that the case before it did not "involve a fictional difference between men and women. It involves a generalisation that the parties accept as unquestionably true: women, as a class, do live longer than men." But, said the Court, it is improper to act on a stereotyped assumption unless it is true of all women so treated. It may well be true that women tend to be less able than men to lift heavy weights. Still it would be unlawful sex discrimination for an employer to reject a woman for a job involving the lifting of such weights simply because she is a woman: she is entitled to be considered on her individual ability to do the job, not to be rejected because of an assumption true of most women. The concept of direct discrimination under the 1975 Act is concerned with the individual. Like Title VII of the US Civil Rights Act, it "precludes treatment of individuals as simply components of a . . . sexual . . . class . . . Even a true generalisation about the class is an insufficient reason for disqualifying an individual to whom the generalisation does not apply." Those women who do not live as long as the average man will pay higher contributions to the pension fund while working, yet they will receive no compensating advantage when they retire. The fact that the erroneous assumption made about them was true of some other women—that those others would live longer than the average man—does not alter the fact that they have been classified according to their sex and that this has resulted in them suffering a disadvantage compared with similar men. Such treatment is particularly unfair because it penalizes a person for a factor outside her control and offers her no opportunity to decrease the relevant risk. Conversely, there will be many men who live longer than the average woman. They will pay lower pension premiums during their working lives, yet will receive considerable benefits during their prolonged retirement. They will receive these benefits, by comparison with comparable women, not because of their individual characteristics, but simply because of their sex. Since anti-discrimination law is primarily designed to entitle individuals to be treated by reference to their individual characteristics, it is as discriminatory to treat people by reference to a stereotyped assumption true of most women (or men) as it is to treat them according to an assumption true of few women (or men).

Nor is it a convincing defence of sex-based insurance policies that insurance is fundamentally concerned with the assessment of risk for people defined by reference to class characteristics. As the US Supreme Court emphasized in *Manhart*, "[i]t is true that insurance is concerned with events that are individually unpredictable, but that is characteristic of many employment decisions". When deciding whether to appoint, promote or dismiss a worker, employers need to weigh risks and to assess future potential. But employers are prohibited from doing this by reference to stereotyped assumptions. No doubt it is more expensive for employers to undertake an individual assessment of whether a woman applicant is capable of lifting the heavy weights, which is part of the job, rather than merely refusing the application of all women because most women could not lift such weights. Why should different principles apply to insurance practices? Indeed,

> when insurance risks are grouped, the better risks always subsidise the poorer risks. Healthy persons subsidise medical benefits for the less healthy; unmarried workers subsidise the pensions of married workers; persons who eat, drink or smoke to excess may subsidise pension benefits for persons whose habits are more temperate. Treating different classes of risk as though they were the same for purposes of group insurance is a common practice that has never been considered inherently unfair. To insure the flabby and the fit as though they were equivalent riks may be more common than treating men and women alike; but nothing more than habit makes one "subsidy" seem less fair than the other.

One further factor suggests that insurance companies are capable of avoiding discriminatory policies even when those policies could be justified statistically. The US Supreme Court noted in *Manhart* that "[a]ctuarial studies could unquestionably identify differences in life expectancy based on race or national origin, as well as sex". Insurers did, at one time, use race-segregated insurance tables. Yet the Race Relations Act 1976 does not allow insurance companies to treat persons of different races in a disparate manner by reference to actuarial data on which it is reasonable to rely. As the US Supreme Court said in *Arizona Governing Committee* v. *Norris* [463 US 1073 (1983)] (applying the *Manhart* principle of equality between the sexes so as to find it unlawful sex discrimination for an employer to pay out lower monthly annuity payments to women than to men who had made equal contributions prior to retirement), it is impossible to see any difference of principle between race classifications and sex classifications in this context.

The objective of securing equal treatment for men and women, irrespective of sex, requires the avoidance of different insurance terms for each sex. A woman may be charged a higher premium than a man because of her individual characteristics, but not because she is a woman and he is a man. In insurance, as elsewhere, "[p]ractices that classify [persons] in terms of . . . sex tend to preserve traditional assumptions about groups rather than thoughtful scrutiny of individuals". To impose higher premiums on persons, or to give them lower benefits, because of their sex and because of assumptions based on sexual stereotypes is to use unreliable, unnecessary, and unfair criteria.

Section 45 of the 1975 Act, by including references to whether it is "reasonable" to rely on the actuarial data in all the relevant circumstances, no doubt offers courts the opportunity to limit the amount of sex discrimination which may lawfully be practised by insurance companies. But even the references to reasonableness cannot excuse section 45 and its approval of some such sex discrimination. The existence of section 45 owes much to the lobbying powers of the insurance industry in 1975. It is time for section 45 to be repealed.

Despite these and other criticisms, s.45 remains intact and has been given implied approval by the decision of the ECJ in *Neath* v *Hugh Steeper Ltd* Case C–152/91[1993] ECR I- 6935, in which that court permitted some pension-related actuarial discrimination. The application of s.29 SDA and the equivalent provisions to social security and social services is discussed further below.

S.29 and its equivalent provisions apply only where the goods, facilities or services are provided "to the public or a section of the public", a proviso intended to preclude the application of the Acts from "genuinely private social clubs, [and] other personal and private relationships".[71] This qualification, which has come under increasing attack in the context of the SDA, was interpreted widely by the courts to exempt from the provision of the RRA 1968 discrimination in access to a Conservative club and by a working men's club to a member of an associated club.[72] S.25 RRA 1975 prohibits discrimination by incorporated and unincorporated bodies having at least 25 members[73], but the SDA has no equivalent provision. Accordingly, sex discrimination in relations to goods, services or facilities is unlawful only where the facilities, etc., are provided to "the public or a section of the public", which qualification will not be satisfied where, for example, membership of a club depends on "genuine selection on personal grounds".[74] The Private Member's Sex Discrimination (Amendment) Bill currently before Parliament would amend the SDA in similar terms to the RRA, save in respect of clubs which are entirely single-sex (i.e., would require that where clubs do admit women, they do so on equal terms). It is, however, unlikely to become law.

Perhaps the most significant issue relating to the non-employment provisions of the RRA and the SDA has concerned their application to the public sector. In *Kassam* v *Immigration Appeal Tribunal* the Court of Appeal ruled that s.29 SDA did not apply to the Secretary of State for the Home Department in the exercise of his immigration function.

---

[71] White Paper, *Equality for Women* Cmnd 5724 (1974), para 66.
[72] Respectively *Charter* v *Race Relations Board* [1973] AC 868 and *Dockers' Labour Club and Institute Ltd* v *Race Relations Board* [1976] AC 285.
[73] S.25 RRA—as long as the discrimination falls outside s.12 (trade unions) and s.20.
[74] *Charter, Dockers and Applin* v *Race Relations Board* [1975] AC 259, though the application of the test was disputed in the last of these cases. Bourn and Whitmore, fn 54 above, para 7.23, point out the contrast with *Applin*, in which their Lordships applied the RRA to foster-parents. The case is discussed by Colin Munro "A Matter of Public Concern" (1975) 38 *Modern Law Review* 93. The outcome in *Applin* was ousted by s.23(2) RRA, which provides that "s.20(1) does not apply to anything done by a person as a participant in arrangements under which he (for reward or not) takes into his own home, and treats as if they were members of his family, children, elderly persons, or persons requiring a special degree of care and attention". As the recent decision in *Conwell* v *London Borough of Newham* [1999] 3 FCR 625, [2000] ICR 42, illustrates, this exception does not apply to local authorities or private agencies in their fostering role.

Kassam v Immigration Appeal Tribunal [1980] 2 All ER 330 [1980] 1 WLR 1037, [1979–1980] Imm AR 132

Stephenson LJ

Counsel for the appeal tribunal . . . submits that the Secretary of State does not provide facilities and the immigrant does not obtain or use them when he or she obtains leave from him or his immigration officers. Section 29 is concerned with what he called marketplace activities. The Secretary of State is exercising statutory powers to control immigration and any facilities he may be said in the course of their exercise to provide or to be concerned in providing are not within the aim or purview of the section.

I am of the opinion that the Secretary of State is not a person concerned with the provisions of facilities to a section of the public. Subsections (1) and (2) of s 29 repeat *mutatis mutandis* s 2(1) and (2) of the [RRA] 1968 (now repealed and reenacted in s 20(1) and (2) of the 1976 Act) and so are not free from judicial interpretation. But read in their natural and ordinary meaning they are not aimed at and do not hit the Secretary of State concerned with giving leave to enter or remain in the exercise of his powers under the 1971 Act. The kind of facilities with which the sections of the [RRAs] are concerned is of the same order as goods and services, and though it may not always be easy to say whether a particular person (or body of persons) is a person concerned with the provision of any of those three things to the public or a section of the public and although a minister of the Crown or a government department might be such a person (for instance, in former days the Postmaster General, as Sir David Cairns suggested in argument), I am clearly of the opinion that the Secretary of State in acting under the Immigration Act and rules is not such a person, and he cannot be held to have unlawfully discriminated against the appellant . . . He is operating in a field outside the fields in which Parliament has forbidden sex discrimination.

In *Savjani v Inland Revenue Commissioners* the Court of Appeal applied s.29 RRA to the activities of the Inland Revenue. According to Lord Denning MR:

the Revenue are entrusted with the care and management of taxes. They provide a service to the public in collecting tax. They also provide a service to a section of the public in so far as they give relief from tax or make repayments of tax or, I would add, give advice about tax. Those are all most valuable services which the Revenue authorities provide to the public as a whole and to sections of the public. It seems to me that the provisions for granting relief, giving advice, and the advice which is given, are the provision of services.

Lord Denning distinguished *Kassam* on the ground that, while in that case the Court of Appeal: "held that, in dealing with people coming in under the immigration rules, the immigration authorities were not providing 'services' within the meaning of the [SDA, t]his case is very different. The Revenue are providing "services" in regard to relief from tax or repayment of tax. Those services come within the provisions of the Act. If there is discrimination in the carrying out of those services, it is unlawful."

Templeman LJ:

the board and the inspector are performing duties, those duties laid on them by [statute] . . . but, in my judgment, it does not necessarily follow that the board and the inspector are not voluntarily or in order to carry out their duty also performing services for the taxpayer. The duty is to collect the right amount of revenue; but, in my judgment, there is a service to the taxpayer provided by the board and the inspector by the provision, dissemination and implementation of regulations which will enable the taxpayer to know that he is entitled to a deduction or a repayment, which will entitle him to know how he is to satisfy the inspector or the board if he is so entitled, and which will enable him to obtain the actual deduction or repayment which Parliament said he is to have. For present purposes, in my judgment, the inspector and the board provide the inestimable services of enabling a taxpayer to obtain that relief which Parliament intended he should be able to obtain as a matter of right subject only to proof . . .

Counsel for the commissioners submitted that the [RRA] does not apply to the Inland Revenue at all, but he naturally and wisely recoiled from the suggestion that the inspector of taxes might decline to interview a taxpayer if the taxpayer were coloured. He made forcibly the submission that, when the board decides for sensible reasons that a higher standard of proof is required from taxpayers who come from the Indian subcontinent, the board are not providing a service to that taxpayer; they are carrying out their duty to the Crown. As I have already indicated, it does not seem to me that the two concepts are mutually exclusive. The board and the inspectors perform their duty and carry out a service and, in my judgment, it is a service within the meaning of s 20 [RRA].

Counsel for the commissioners relied on *Kassam*, where this court had to consider the very different case of the powers of the Secretary of State under the Immigration Act 1971. In relation to those powers, wide discretions are conferred on the Secretary of State. Ackner LJ said in that case . . .

> In my judgment, when the Secretary of State is exercising his discretion in relation to powers granted to him by the Immigration Act 1971, he is not providing a "facility" within the meaning of [the similar, almost identical, SDA].

In the present case, as I have indicated, subject to the question of proof, the taxpayer is absolutely entitled to the relief which he prays; and the Inland Revenue performs the service of enabling him to get the relief to which he is absolutely entitled. Accordingly, I do not think the *Kassam* case stands in the way of our reaching the conclusion which I have mentioned . . .[75]

John Gardner "Section 20 of the Race Relations Act: Facilities and Services" (1987) 50 Modern Law Review 345, 346

Savjani makes it clear that a person who has a primary statutory function which does *not* amount to the provision of a "facility or service" to the complainant may nevertheless have some other function which *does*. There is nothing inconsistent in saying that H.M. Inspector has, apart from the (detrimental) function of collecting taxes, a further (advantageous) function which falls within section 20, since section 20 is "not particularly concerned with the nature of the body which discriminates . . . it is concerned with what the body does in the course of which it discriminates."

---

[75] Dunn LJ, albeit reluctantly, agreed with Lord Denning and Templeman LJ. Similarly, in *Alexander* v *Home Office (Prison Dept)* which went to the Court of Appeal on damages (see Chapter 5 the Court of Appeal decision is at [1988] 2 All ER 118), the County Court ruled that the allocation of work to prisoners was within s.20 and in *Farah* below the Court of Appeal accepted that police services, as distinct from police powers, came within s.20.

This could be applied with equal force to the case of a Prison Officer, who it could be claimed, is predominantly concerned with ensuring the detention of a prisoner, but might still "provide facilities" to prisoners, for example by allocating work or privileges to them [see *Alexander* v *Home Office*].

A related point which arises from *Savjani* is this: there is no conceptual reason why, in the course of subjecting someone to a detriment, a person cannot provide that other with a "facility" for lightening the burden of the detriment. The point was made by Templeman L.J. in *Savjani*: H.M. Inspector might "voluntarily, or in order to carry out [his] duty, also perform . . . services for the taxpayer." The example which *Savjani* itself suggests is that of advice on income tax liabilities; another would be the optional "facility" of Television Licence Stamps offered by the Home Office, which renders less onerous the obligation of paying for a television licence.

These observations reveal that there is no necessary relationship between a person's primary function under statute and his subjection or non-subjection to section 20. Nor is there any necessary relationship between public conceptions of his role and his subjection or non-subjection to section 20. A government officer may conceive of himself as primarily an agent of control. The general public (even those who are successful in extracting some favourable decision from him) may also view him as an agent of control. Nevertheless, he may provide "facilities" to the public for the purpose of section 20 if, for example, he accepts applications for some advantage or concession; he also provides "services" by advertising the facility, advising on it, and considering applications.

Shortly after the decision of the Court of Appeal in *Savjani*, the House of Lords considered a challenge under the SDA to discriminatory immigration practices in *Amin* v *Entry Clearance Officer, Bombay*. The facts of the case are set out in Chapter 1. Their Lordships took the narrow view of the "goods and services" provisions, restricting the application of s.29 RRA to those activities of the Crown which resembled those carried out by private actors.[76]

Amin v *Entry Clearance Officer, Bombay* [1983] 2 AC 818, [1983] 2 All ER 864 [1983] 3 WLR 258

Lord Fraser, with whom Lords Keith and Brightman agreed

It was said that the granting of special vouchers for entry into the United Kingdom was provision of facilities or services to a section of the public, and that the wide general words of subsection (1) of section 29 were not cut down by the examples given in subsection (2) which are only "examples" and are not an exhaustive list of the circumstances in which the section applies. Reliance was also placed on paragraph (*g*) of section 29(2) which expressly refers to services of a public authority and which has been held to apply to the Inland Revenue . . .

My Lords, I accept that the examples in section 29(2) are not exhaustive, but they are, in my opinion, useful pointers to aid in the construction of subsection (1). Section 29 as a

---

[76] See also *Home Office* v *Commission for Racial Equality* [1982] QB 385 [1981] 1 All ER 1042, [1981] 2 WLR 703. The decision in *CRE* v *Riley*, CRE *Annual Report 1982*, p.18, in which a County Court judge had ruled that the granting of planning permission fell outwith s.20 RRA, resulted in the insertion of s.19A RRA which reverses that decision in the planning sphere.

whole seems to me to apply to the direct provision of facilities or services, and not to the mere grant of permission to use facilities. That is in accordance with the words of subsection (1), and it is reinforced by some of the examples in subsection (2). Example (*a*) is "access to *and use of* any place" and the words that I have emphasised indicate that the paragraph contemplates actual provision of facilities which the person will use. Example (*d*) refers, in my view, to the actual provision of schools and other facilities for education, but not to the mere grant of an entry certificate or a special voucher to enable a student to enter the United Kingdom in order to study here. Example (*g*) seems to me to be contemplating things such as medical services, or library facilities, which can be directly provided by local or other public authorities. So in *Savjani*, Templeman L.J. took the view that the Inland Revenue performed two separate functions—first a duty of collecting revenue and secondly a service of providing taxpayers with information. He said, at p. 467:

> As [counsel] on behalf of the revenue submitted, the board and the inspector are performing duties—those duties laid upon them by the Act which I have mentioned—but, in my judgment, it does not necessarily follow that the board and the inspector are not voluntarily, or in order to carry out their duty, also performing services for the taxpayer. The duty is to collect the right amount of revenue; but, in my judgment, there is a service to the taxpayer provided by the board and the inspector by the provision, dissemination and implementation of regulations which will enable the taxpayer to know that he is entitled to a deduction or a repayment, which will [enable] him to know how he is to satisfy the inspector or the board if he is so entitled, and which will enable him to obtain the actual deduction or repayment which Parliament said he is to have.

In so far as that passage states the ground of the Court of Appeal's decision in that case I agree with it. . . . In the present case the entry clearance officer in Bombay was in my opinion not providing a service for would-be immigrants; rather he was performing his duty of controlling them.

Counsel for the appellant sought to draw support for his contention from section 85(1) of the [SDA] which provides:

> This Act applies—(*a*) to an act done by or for purposes of a Minister of the Crown or government department, or (*b*) to an act done on behalf of the Crown by a statutory body, or a person holding a statutory office, as it applies to an act done by a private person.

That section puts an act done on behalf of the Crown on a par with an act done by a private person, and it does not in terms restrict the comparison to an act *of the same kind* done by a private person. But in my opinion it applies only to acts done on behalf of the Crown which are of a kind similar to acts that might be done by a private person. It does not mean that the Act is to apply to any act of any kind done on behalf of the Crown by a person holding statutory office. There must be acts (which include deliberate omissions—see section 82(1)), done in the course of formulating or carrying out government policy, which are quite different in kind from any act that would ever be done by a private person, and to which the Act does not apply [citing Woolf J. in *Home Office* v. *Commission for Racial Equality* [1982] Q.B. 385] Part V of the SDA makes exceptions for certain acts including acts done for the purpose of national security (section 52) and for acts which are "necessary" in order to comply with certain statutory requirements: section 51. These exceptions will no doubt be effective to protect acts which are of a kind that would otherwise be unlawful under the Act. But they do not in my view obviate the necessity for construing section

29 as applying only to acts which are at least similar to acts that could be done by private persons.

Lords Scarman and Brandon dissented from the conclusion of the majority:

Lord Scarman

Entry into the United Kingdom for study, a visit, or settlement is certainly a facility which many value and seek to obtain. And it is one which the Secretary of State has it in his power under the Immigration Act to provide: section 3(2) of that Act. The special voucher scheme which he has introduced does provide to some this very valuable facility, namely the opportunity to settle in this country. It is a facility offered within Great Britain, albeit to persons outside: the exception in section 36 of the SDA does not apply.

Upon the literal meaning of the language of section 29(1), I would, therefore, construe the subsection as covering the facility provided by the Secretary of State.

It is, however, said that the kind of facilities within the meaning of the subsection are essentially "market-place activities" or activities akin to the provision of goods and services, but not to the grant of leave to enter under the Immigration Act. Reliance is placed upon section 29(2) as an indication that this was the legislative intention of the section and upon the decision of the Court of Appeal which interpreted the section in this way in *Kassam's* case.

In *Kassam's* case, Stephenson L.J. found the submission, which is now made to the House in this case, namely that in giving leave to immigrants to enter the country and to remain here the Secretary of State provides a facility to a section of the public, so plausible that he was tempted to accede to it . . . I agree with him. But I have yielded to the temptation, if that is a fair description of selecting a sensible interpretation of a statutory provision. He, however, did not. He appears to have accepted the submission that section 29 was concerned with "market-place activities." If he did not restrict the section to the full extent of that submission, he certainly took the view, which was also expressed by Ackner L.J. and concurred in by Sir David Cairns, that the section applies only to facilities which are akin to the provision of goods and services. Ackner L.J. . . . held that "facilities" because of its juxtaposition to goods and services must not be given a wholly unrestricted meaning but must be so confined.

I reject this reasoning. I derive no assistance from subsection (2) in construing subsection (1) of section 29. I can find no trace of this House accepting any such assistance when in . . . *Applin* . . . this House had to consider the directly comparable provision in section 2(1) and (2) of the Race Relations Act 1968. Section 29(2) does no more than give examples of facilities and services. It is certainly not intended to be exhaustive. If some of its examples are "market-place activities" or facilities akin to the provision of goods and services, others are not: I refer, in particular, to examples (*a*), (*d*), and (*g*). And, if the subsection cannot, as I think it cannot, be relied on as a guide to the construction of subsection (1), one is left only with Ackner L.J.'s point as to the juxtaposition of goods, facilities and services in subsection (1).

This is too slight an indication to stand up to the undoubted intention of Parliament that the Act is to bind the Crown. Section 85(1) provides:

This Act applies—(*a*) to an act done by or for purposes of a Minister of the Crown or government department, or (*b*) to an act done on behalf of the Crown by a statutory body, or a person holding a statutory office, as it applies to an act done by a private person.

An attempt was made in reliance upon the concluding three words of the subsection to argue that in its application to the Crown the Act is limited to the sort of acts which could be done by a private person, e.g. "marketplace activities" or the provision of facilities akin to the provision of goods and services. I do not so read the subsection. It means, in my judgment, no more and no less than that the Act applies to the public acts of Ministers, government departments and other statutory bodies on behalf of the Crown as it applies to acts of private persons. It would be inconceivable that the generality of subsection (1)(*a*) and (*b*) could be restricted by words which in drawing a distinction between two classes of act are intended to show that the distinction is immaterial. I cannot accept that so short a tail can wag so large a dog.

Section 52 also is consistent with the view that the Act has a wide cover in respect of acts of the Crown. It is designed to ensure that nothing in Parts II to IV of the Act (which include section 29) shall render unlawful an act done for the purpose of safeguarding national security.

Accordingly I think that on this point *Kassam* was wrongly decided. In my view, the granting of leave to enter the country by provision of a special voucher or otherwise is the provision of a facility to a section of the public. Indeed, I have no doubt that some see it as a very valuable facility. It is certainly much sought after. Section 29(1) is wide enough, therefore, to cover the special voucher scheme which, in my judgment, is properly described as offering a facility to some members of the public, i.e. United Kingdom passport holders, who seek access to this country for the purpose of settlement but have no lawful means of entering other than by leave.

In the course of argument, your Lordships' attention was drawn to the Court of Appeal's decision in *Savjani* in which it was held that by putting the plaintiff because of his ethnic origin to a higher standard of proof of his entitlement to a tax relief than is normally required of a claimant the revenue had unlawfully discriminated against him in the provision of services to the public within the meaning of section 20(1)(*b*) [RRA]. The decision was, I am satisfied, correct and is certainly consistent with the approach which I would hold that the courts should adopt to section 29(1) [SDA]. But it was a different case on its facts from this case in that the revenue did provide, however informally, an advisory service to taxpayers seeking guidance on their problems.

The majority decision in *Amin* has been widely criticised:

D. Pannick *Sex Discrimination Law* (OUP)

Lord Fraser said that section 29 applies "to the direct provision of facilities or services and not to the mere grant of permission to use facilities". That is rather a fine distinction on the facts of the case. The voucher is itself a facility: if it is not, then any shop or restaurant can escape the effect of section 29 (and the similar provision in the Race Relations Act 1976) by admitting people only if they have a voucher and by refusing to distribute such vouchers to women (or blacks). In any event, section 50(1) of the 1975 Act (to which none of their Lordships referred) states that indirect access to benefits is covered by section 29.

Secondly, the majority opinion of Lord Fraser contended that section 29 only applies to acts by the Government which "are at least similar to acts that could be done by private persons". But, as Lord Scarman pointed out in his dissenting opinion, the examples of facilities and services given in section 29(2)—in particular the services of any local or public authority—are hardly confined to "market-place activities". Section 29(1) applies to provision "for payment or not". Moreover, the special exemption from liability under section 29 for sex discrimination relating to political parties and religious bodies shows that section 29 covers more than market-place activities. The majority opinion placed reliance on section 85(1) of the 1975 Act. This states that the Act covers State action "as it applies to an act done by a private person". However, it would not seem that this takes the matter any further. Lord Fraser acknowledged that it "does not in terms restrict the comparison to an act *of the same kind* done by a private person". The crucial issue is the nature of the benefits provided, not their source, public or private. All that section 85(1) does, as Lord Scarman argued, is to ensure that "the Act applies to the public acts of Ministers, Government departments and other statutory bodies on behalf of the Crown as it applies to acts of private persons".

The House of Lords has in *Amin*, without any justification from the language or purpose of the 1975 Act, denied much of the statute's application to State action even though that action discriminates against women, even though the action concerns the provision of facilities to the public and even though the 1975 Act contains an express exception for acts done under statutory authority (suggesting that State action is covered by section 29). The decision of the House of Lords in *Amin* is particularly unfortunate when so much sex discrimination in immigration, social security, and tax law directly results from Government conduct. The decision in *Amin* adopted a similar approach to the earlier Court of Appeal decision in *Kassam*.

John Gardner criticised the decision in the following terms:

Gardner (1987) 50 *Modern Law Review* **349–351**

In order to reach this conclusion, Lord Fraser examined some of the examples in section 29(2), which he considered to be "useful pointers to aid in the construction of subsection (1)." He thought that some of the examples excluded mere passive permissions. "Access to and use of any place" seemed to him to suggest not a simple permission to enter a place, but the active provision of something there; "the services of any profession or trade, or any local or other public authority" seemed to him to cover "things such as medical services, or library facilities, which can be directly provided . . ."

There is nothing in subsection (2) to suggest that it is designed to place any restrictions on the meaning of "facilities or services" in subsection (1), which, as we have seen, prima facie bears its ordinary meaning. If this is wrong, however, it does not seem likely that the restriction is the one which Lord Fraser suggested. There is no implication in any of the examples that "facility" to which they refer need to be a "directly provided" (active) facility. Indeed, the action of an Entry Clearance Officer is *precisely* that of facilitating "access to and use of" a place.

Moreover, an "active facility" cannot be anything other than a "service," so that Lord Fraser's view entails that the word "facility" in subsection (1) is redundant . . .

Lord Fraser also approved the distinction drawn by Templeman L.J. in *Savjani*, between "services" and "duties."

. . . the more plausible basis for *Savjani* is the distinction between benefits and detriments. In some respects the Entry Clearance Officer in *Amin* does seem to belong to the same category as a tax collector: for it was a decision *not* to grant a special voucher that was challenged, a decision which appears detrimental. To this degree the distinction between "controlling" immigrants and "providing a service for" them does have some attraction.

It is probably true to say that a *decision not to grant* a special voucher is not a "facility or service" within the ordinary meaning of those words. On the other hand, this does not mean that an Entry Clearance Officer does not, or did not in *Amin*, "provide . . . facilities or services" to would-be immigrants. Both the 1975 Act and the 1976 Act are concerned with "what [someone] does, in the course of which [he] discriminates." What the Entry Clearance Officer in Bombay did, in the course of which he discriminated against Mrs. Amin, was to *consider her application* for a special voucher. The activity of considering applications is not detrimental, but is a "facility or service" within the ordinary meanings of those words. The Officer (whether acting out of duty to Parliament or otherwise) provides a "facility" by entertaining applications for leave to settle, and a "service" by considering the merits of such applications, Lord Fraser's second reason is thus misconceived.
. . .

Quite apart from the absence of any express limitation on Crown liability, example (g) of subsection (2) makes Lord Fraser's restriction appear extremely implausible: "the services of . . . any . . . public authority" clearly aims at encompassing more than just those "services" which could also be provided by individuals.

However, even if it were plausible to claim that the 1975 Act and the 1976 Act only bind the Crown in respect of actions which are "similar" to those of private persons, we need to provide a criterion of similarity. In some respects the process of considering an application for leave to settle is very similar to the process of considering whether to grant a gratuitous licence to another to reside on one's land. In other respects the process of considering whether to grant leave *does* seem peculiar to governments. Unless the criterion of similarity is spelled out, we cannot tell whether Lord Fraser is right to treat the grant of a clearance voucher as being a peculiarly governmental power. It is really only peculiarly governmental in the obvious sense in which all statutory powers of the Crown are peculiarly governmental. So even if it were cogent as a general principle, Lord Fraser's third argument would not apply comfortably to the case of a refused special voucher. . . .

As long as the House of Lords' decision in *Amin* represents the law, the words "facilities or services" in section 20 of the 1976 Act do not bear their ordinary meanings.

More recently, in *Farah v Commissioner of Police of the Metropolis* the Court of Appeal considered the application of s.20 RRA to the police.

Farah v Commissioner of the Police of the Metropolis [1998] QB 65, [1997] 1 All ER 289, [1997] 2 WLR 824

Hutchinson LJ (with whom Gibson and Otton LJJ agreed)

The case pleaded by the plaintiff, who is a citizen of Somalia and a refugee and who was aged 17 at the time, is that on that date she and her 10-year-old cousin were attacked near their home by some white teenagers, who set a dog on her and injured her. By a 999 call she summoned police assistance, but the police officers who came in response, instead of helping her and seeking to detain her attackers, arrested her without cause, detained her for a time, and charged her with affray, common assault and causing unnecessary suffering to a dog. She was released on bail the same day. On 12 January 1995 she appeared to answer the charges and, no evidence being offered, was acquitted . . . the plaintiff [alleged] . . . that the conduct of the attending police officers amounted to unlawful racial discrimination . . . She puts her claim on the basis that she was a person seeking to obtain the use of services from a person concerned with the provision of services to the public within the terms of s 20 of the [RRA], and that the officers deliberately omitted to provide her with the services she sought or with services of a like quality or in like manner or on the like terms to those normally provided by the officers to other members of the public. She particularises, in support of this assertion, the acts or omissions of which she says the officers were guilty as follows: (a) officers in the employment of the defendant failed to react, alternatively chose to ignore her call for assistance by way of an emergency telephone call to the police emergency service before the attendance of the said officers; (b) the said officers at the scene of her detention and involved with the interview of the plaintiff failed to investigate her account of events both at the scene of her apprehension and thereafter; (c) the defendant and the officers in his employment failed to afford the protection accorded victims of crime in like manner to the plaintiff as to white members of the public. Then . . . the plaintiff says that the officers brought the criminal proceedings against her on racial grounds and so treated her less favourably than they would treat other persons. All of this was sought to be struck out as disclosing no cause of action . . .

As a matter of construction, Mr Seabrook [for the Police Commissioner] submits s 20 does not apply to police officers performing the duties of their office—they are not providing services. The acts alleged against them all entail the exercise of discretion and judgment. What they were engaged on, from the moment the 999 call was received, was the exercise of their powers of investigation, detection and the bringing of offenders to justice . . . it is arguable that the limited service for which the plaintiff looked to the police comes within Lord Fraser's test . . . prima facie, s 20 is wide enough to apply to at least some of the acts undertaken by police officers in the performance of the duties of their office. The crucial words— to be interpreted of course in the light of the examples given, but not on the basis that the examples are definitive of the circumstances to which the section can apply—are "any person concerned with the provision (for payment or not) of . . . services to the public".

I accept Mr Nicol's contention [for the plaintiff] that these words are entirely apt to cover those parts of a police officer's duties involving assistance to or protection of members of the public. Mr Nicol emphasised that it is in regard to that aspect of the officers duties that the claim in the present case is advanced—it is not suggested that pursuing and arresting or charging alleged criminals is the provision of a service. What is said is that the service sought by the plaintiff was that of protection and that she did not, because of her race, obtain the protection that others would have been afforded. It seems to me that that is no less the provision of a service than is the giving of directions or other information to a member of the public who seeks them.

Turning to the examples in sub-s (2) I find nothing expressly or impliedly to exclude police officers; and in my view they can properly be regarded as falling within para (g)— "the services of any profession or trade, or any local or other public authority".

Furthermore, I find in *Savjani*'s case support for the conclusion that the police, in some aspects of their activities, fall within the [RRA]. The passage in Templeman LJ's judgment approved in *Amin*'s case shows that there is no reason why a person performing a public duty may not also be providing a service, and strongly supports the plaintiff's arguments . . .

Taking the view I do on construction, I do not consider that there is any basis for entertaining Mr Seabrook's policy arguments. I would observe, however, that (as the judgment of Templeman LJ [in *Savjani*] recognises) there are in any event powerful arguments on each side of the public policy issue and I do not find the spectre of claims of racial discrimination against the police, with the inconvenience and expense that that may involve, to be more disturbing than the prospect that a member of the public who, seeking assistance in dire need, has been the subject of racial discrimination, should be without remedy.

Otton LJ (having agreed with Hutchinson LJ)

Like Templeman LJ in *Savjani* . . . I should be slow to find that the effect of something which is humiliatingly discriminatory in racial matters falls outside the ambit of the [RRA]. I accept that the police officers perform duties in order to prevent and detect crime and to bring offenders to justice. They are also vested with powers to enable them to perform those duties. While performing duties and exercising powers they also provide services in providing protection to the victims of crimes of violence.

Thus applying Templeman LJ's reasoning with regard to the position of the police, the two concepts are not mutually exclusive. In *Kassam* . . . the entry clearance officer in Bombay was not providing a facility to intending immigrants when he performed the act complained of; he was solely performing his duty of controlling them. Ackner LJ in *Kassam* . . . considered that the—

> word "facilities" . . . is flanked on one side by the word "goods" and on the other by the word "services". This suggests to my mind that the word "facilities" is not to be given a wholly unrestricted meaning but must be limited or confined to facilities that are akin to goods or services.

In my view the provision of services of protection are akin to the provision of facilities (if not goods). Given the dual role of a policeman I can see no reason why he is not performing those services within s 20.

I am unable to accept the submissions of Mr Robert Seabrook QC that public policy requires that Pt III of the [RRA] should not apply to the police at all, not even when they are providing a service. He (like counsel in Savjani's case) naturally and wisely shied away from the suggestion that a policeman might with impunity decline to investigate a complaint or to protect a person from violence on account of his or her colour. If an ambulance person and police officer attended at a scene of a road accident and they deliberately withheld medical services on the ground of a victim's race it would be illogical for the former to be guilty of an act of discrimination and for the latter to be immune from suit, criminal or civil.

In my judgment, if it was the intention of the Parliament to provide such immunity it would have expressly said so. In such a sensitive area as relations between the ethnic minorities and the police it would be to my mind surprising that Parliament would have countenanced such an exclusion from the ambit of the [RRA] or allowed immunity to be inferred by the courts as a matter of construction. Moreover, Pt VI of the [RRA] contains specific exceptions to its provisions, reflecting in some instances public policy (see s 42). It is significantly silent on an exception for the police, and more so for individual police officers. To my mind the examples of facilities and services in s 20(2) (and in particular at (g)) are wide enough to accommodate (and so not exclude) the services of protection for individuals . . .

These acts (or services) which the plaintiff sought from the police were, to my mind, acts which might have been done by a private person. The second category envisaged by Lord Fraser covers those acts which a private person would never do, and would normally only ever be performed by the police, eg gaining forcible entry into a suspected drugs warehouse.

Here the officers would be carrying out government policy to which the [RRA] would not apply. Moreover, they would be performing duties in order to prevent and detect crime and exercising their powers to enable them to perform those duties . . .

The s.20 aspect of the *Farah* decision was favourable to the plaintiff in the instant case,[77] but fell far short of declaring that the provisions of the RRA applied to all aspects of policing. Further, the Court of Appeal also ruled in *Farah* that the Commissioner was not vicariously liable for the discriminatory actions of police officers. This ruling was particularly controversial given its coincidence in time with the public unrest which followed the bungled investigation into the Stephen Lawrence case.[78] The CRE's 1998 *Annual Report* began with the words:

In years to come 1998 will be seen as a watershed for race relations in Britain. No one will ever forget that it was the year of the MacPherson Inquiry into the racist murder of the black teenager, Stephen Lawrence.[79]

The report, which concluded that: "institutional racism . . . exists both in the Metropolitan Police Service and in other Police Services and other institutions countrywide",[80] recommended that:

the full force of the Race Relations legislation should apply to all police officers, and that Chief Officers of Police should be made vicariously liable for the acts and omissions of their officers relevant to that legislation.

Amongst the responses of the Home Secretary, Jack Straw, to the MacPherson report was the establishment of goals and timetables whereby each police force is expected to increase ethnic minority representation within its ranks.[81] This issue was discussed in chapter 3. But for all of the concern expressed by the Government, the CRE's funding was cut by some 10% in 1998.[82] Its commitment to the eradication of "institutional racism" was questioned by Professor Paul Gilroy in the first ICA annual lecture in a critique which was to prove remarkably prescient:

A fully independent system for managing complaints against the police is as far away as ever . . . The idea that "institutional" racism could have significant implications for the way

[77] See also *Conwell* v *Newham*, note 74 above, in which EAT (*per* Charles J) ruled that the provision of care to children by a local authority came within s.20—this with the result that a worker victimised for protesting the authority's refusal, on racial grounds, to let a black child holiday with a white family fell within the RRA.

[78] In *SPV* v *AM & Anor*, 27th August 1999 unreported, the Court of Appeal refused to apply this reasoning in a case where a police officer was sued under s.42 SDA for harassment of a fellow officer.

[79] P.3, available from the CRE's homepage fn 64 above.

[80] *Report of an Inquiry by Sir William MacPherson of Cluny*, February 1999 Cm 4262-I. para 6.39 (available at http://www.official-documents.co.uk).

[81] The *Press Association Newsfile* 28th July 1999 reports that targets have been set also for the fire service and for Home Office civil service staff.

[82] This, according to then Chairman Sir Herman Ousley in his foreword to the 1998 *Annual Report* (available from the CRE website, as at fn 64 above), was the fourth successive annual cut.

political processes were conducted or understood did not appear to have dawned on any-body. Here, the populist legacy of Conservative rule was the main intimidating factor. Paul Boateng . . . was first dispatched to defend Commissioner Condon against the unjoined-up demand that he resign, and then to warn the nation's black muggers and marginals that they would not be able to "use the Macpherson Report as a cloak for their criminal activities".

Boateng continued: "Stop and search is there to be used as part of the Police's armoury." In this lost world of politics without conflict, division or even debate, the spin doctors are always right. You can have business as usual in the street-level operations of police power but you can also "use" stop and search "in a way that attracts the support of the whole community, black and white". The compromised imperatives of sensible, joined-up politics dictate that no one is to be estranged, offended or perturbed, that everyone can board this privatised bus to post-political utopia. You can please all of the people all of the time.

Power is there to be administered, and Middle England will never be inner London. Politics, joined-up or otherwise, eventually yields meekly to the different rules of statecraft. In the key constituencies where control of government will be lost or retained, the British love of playing fair does not currently include recognising the possibility that blacks can belong. Far better then to manage the problem of diversity and inclusivity, theatrically and aesthetically, by, for example, putting up Trevor Phillips to be a celebrity mayor, or by gild-ing the withering boughs of the House of Lords with the delicate blooms represented by a few carefully selected ethnic peerages. Minority business people will supply the incontro-vertible proof that this country is, after all, modern! . . . To quote Keith Vaz MP: "Bill Clinton showed an acute appreciation of the fact that in the modern world, good race rela-tions and good business practice are synonymous." It's hard to see how this deluded pro-fundity might have helped Stephen Lawrence, but then he seems to have passed outside the present. To all intents and purposes, that wrong resolved into a financial transaction that provides an uncomfortable alternative to more substantive forms of judicial restitution.

"Institutional racism" was defined by the McPherson report, as:

> The collective failure of an organisation to provide an appropriate and professional service to people because of their colour, culture, or ethnic origin. It can be seen or detected in processes, attitudes and behaviour which amount to discrimination through unwitting prejudice, ignorance, thoughtlessness and racist stereotyping which disadvantage minority ethnic people.[83]
>
> It persists because of the failure of the organisation openly and adequately to recognise and address its existence and causes by policy, example and leadership. Without recogni-tion and action to eliminate such racism it can prevail as part of the ethos or culture of the organisation. It is a corrosive disease.

Almost twenty years before, Lord Scarman's inquiry into the Brixton riot contained the following passage:

---

[83] Fn 80 above, para 6.34. The report was at pains to point out that (para 6.26): "We repeat that we do not pretend to produce a definition which will carry all argument before it" The definition was criticised *inter alia* by the alternative Lawrence report commissioned by UNISON and co-authored by Lee Jasper, on the ground that: "its emphasis on unwitting and collective failure, allows institutional racism to become almost accidental"—*The Independent*, 18th July 1999.

If by [institutionally racist] it is meant that [Britain] is a society which knowing y, as a matter of policy, discriminates against black people, I reject that allegation. If, however, the suggestion being made is that practices may be adopted by public bodies as well as private individuals which are unwittingly discriminatory against black people, then this is an allegation which deserves serious consideration, and where proved, swift remedy.[54]

Publication of the MacPherson report led to a lemming-like rush on the part of all manner of institutions to declare themselves guilty of "institutional racism", apparently on the basis that this form of racism was rather less reprehensible than the raw version. In July 1999, the National Officer of the Fire Brigades Union "acknowledged that the service suffered from the institutional racism that affected many public bodies, and had its share of 'bigoted, racist staff' ".[85] In August, the firemaster of Lothian and Borders "admitted . . . that his force was guilty of institutionalised racism under the definition set out in the MacPherson report" and reported that only two of 1000 firefighters were of ethnic minority background[86]. "Institutional racism" has also been acknowledged within the NHS[87] and, as a problem for her union, by the General Secretary of the Royal College of Nursing.[88] And in June, Scotland's Lord Advocate accepted that there was "institutional racism" within the Scottish criminal justice system.[89]

It is easy to be cynical about the rush to confess. But the focus on racism which has followed the MacPherson report has served to highlight the extent of the problem. In July, a letter to the *Glasgow Herald* pointed out that: "[d]espite consistent lobbying, the body politic has successfully manufactured an all-white Scottish Parliament. This defines [sic] structured and institutionalised racism and maybe cultural racism too . . . How was it possible to structure in (white) women to the Scottish Parliament and not parallel that action for black people?".[90] In the same month, an Asian woman barrister won her claim of "institutional racism" against the CPS—she had been denied promotion for 12 years.[91] In March 1999, Ofsted had accused "virtually all schools" of the same failing.[92] Defining as "institutional racism", the "collective failure of an organisation to provide an appropriate and professional service to people because of their colour, culture or ethnic origin . . . It could be detected in processes, attitudes and

[84] Cited by Baronness Howells, HL Debs 14th Dec 1999, col. 149, available at http://www.publications.parliament.uk/pa/ld/ldhansrd.htm.
[85] Press Association *Newsfile*, 28th July 1999.
[86] *Guardian*, 10th August 1999.
[87] Director of Nursing Nottingham Healthcare Trust, Nottingham *Evening Post*, 10th July 1999.
[88] *Guardian*, 12th March 1999.
[89] *Daily Record*, 16th June 1999. The newspaper reports that the same Lord Hardie had castigated as "uninformed and ill-advised" a trial judge's anger that only one of three men arrested in respect of the racist murder of Surjit Chhokar ("Scotland's Stephen Lawrence") faced trial—he was convicted only of assault.
[90] July 28th, letter from Andrew Johnson, Director, Equality and Discrimination Centre, University of Strathclyde.
[91] *Daily Mail*, 10th June 1999.
[92] *Daily Telegraph*, 11th March 1999.

behaviour that amounted to discrimination through 'unwitting prejudice' that disadvantaged ethnic minority people", the chief inspector of secondary schools, Jim Rose, stated that "the poor performance of black pupils, the fact that they often achieved more than their teachers expected and the disproportionate number who were excluded from school" made it "difficult . . . to imagine a school not being guilty of 'institutional racism' ".[93]

The government's response to the apparently newly discovered problem of "institutional racism" came in the form of the RR(A) Bill 1999, which plugs the vicarious liability gap in the RRA (though not in the SDA), and initially proposed only a partial reversal of *Amin*. Clause 1 introduces a new s.19B RRA which would provide that:

> 19B. (1) It is unlawful for a [public authority, the definition of which is set out in Schedule 1 of the 1999 Act to include, *inter alia*, the police, prosecuting authorities and immigration service] to discriminate, in carrying out any of its functions, against another person.

The proposed new s.19(2), in its original form, provided that "For the purposes of this section and section 19C, section 1 has effect with the omission of subsection (1)(b)"— in other words, that only direct discrimination is prohibited in this context. Cl.19C provides that s.19B "does not make it unlawful for a relevant person to discriminate against another person on grounds of nationality or ethnic or national origin [as distinct from colour or race] in carrying out immigration and nationality functions".

The Act's failure to apply the prohibition on indirect discrimination to public authorities was greeted with a tidal wave of condemnation during its second reading in the Lords (where the Act was introduced). Criticism was focused, in particular, on the fact that the "institutional racism" identified by the MacPherson report was, for the most part, indirect. (Equally odd is the exclusion from the RR(A)B of decisions not to prosecute, given that this was at the heart of the Stephen Lawrence scandal.) Lord Bassam, for the Government, explained the exclusion of indirect discrimination from the proposed new provisions of the RRA:

> The Government did not take this decision lightly . . . To outlaw indirect discrimination in all the functions to be newly covered by the Act would have uncertain and potentially far-reaching effects on the Government's ability to make policy. Any policy or practice that had a differential impact on different racial groups because of a requirement or condition could be challenged in the courts. That could potentially include any age-based policy because of the different demographic profiles of different racial groups, and also any regional policy because of the different regional spread of different racial groups. Not least, challenges could be mounted to those policies that are helping individuals from ethnic minority communities the most.
>
>   The Government are working to ensure that discriminatory policy-making and practice must stop. But we believe that the most effective way of ensuring this is to retain the flexibility necessary to pursue policies which can benefit ethnic minorities and others without

---

[93] Quotes from the *Daily Telegraph* article.

the risk of frequent and counter-productive challenges in the courts while obliging public authorities to tackle unjustifiable discriminatory practices through the promotion of race equality. That means, for example, consulting those affected by policy proposals and monitoring the differential impact of policy on different groups so that unexpected, unjustifiable outcomes can be remedied. As announced in the Government's equality Statement, we are pursuing this administratively and are committed to placing a statutory duty on public authorities to promote equality as soon as parliamentary time permits.[94]

The RR(A)B was introduced in the House of Lords. Lord Lester's remarks, below, are fairly representative of the general reaction among Labour and Liberal peers.[95]

Instead of having a greater responsibility because of the public nature of its vital functions, under the Bill much of the public service is to be less legally responsible. It is to be immunised from the statutory duty to justify indirectly discriminatory practices to individuals affected, the courts and the CRE . . . under the Bill it will not be unlawful for Ministers, their officials, the police and immigration services, Her Majesty's Customs and Excise, the Inland Revenue, the Benefits Agency and other public authorities to operate practices and procedures which have a disproportionate adverse impact on ethnic minorities and which cannot be justified.

The victims of indirect discrimination by the public sector will remain unprotected. For example, British Muslims, who cannot obtain a remedy for religious discrimination, will not be protected against indirect racial discrimination by public authorities in providing services stemming from hostility to Islam.

The CRE will be unable to use its strategic law enforcement powers to tackle indirectly discriminatory practices and procedures in key public sector functions, because, unless such discrimination is direct, it will be outside the scope of the Bill. That is a particularly serious defect . . .

Because of the immunity to be given to indirect discrimination by public authorities, there will also be much legal uncertainty and unnecessary litigation about opaque distinctions between what is direct and what is indirect discrimination by public authorities, about what discrimination (direct or indirect) by public authorities is already forbidden by Section 20 [RRA].

Both the [RRA] and the [SDA] already apply the concept of indirect as well as direct discrimination, not only to the employment field but also to public authorities and private bodies, in education and housing and in the provision of goods, facilities and services to the public or a section of the public. We are not aware of any complaint that has ever been made that the operation of the concept of indirect discrimination in any of these areas is unworkable or unfair. I should be grateful if the Minister would tell the House whether he and his department have any evidence that it has operated in a harmful way.

Section 20 outlaws direct or indirect discrimination in the provision of certain services by public authorities. If a service falls within Section 20, it must be provided without direct

[94] Fn 84 above, cols. 129–130.

[95] Lord Cope for the Conservatives appeared critical also though Lord Astor reserved the right to comment later, torn as the Tories were on policing. Lord Lester made similar criticisms in relation to s.76 Northern Ireland Act 1998, see HL Debs 7th December 1998, col. 770 (available as at fn 34 above). Lord Cope stated that he wanted "the *Amin* gap . . . filled". The defence used during the FETO debates by Lord Dubs for the Government was (col. 769) that "[t]o make any changes now to fair employment legislation would lead to it being out of step with that on sex and race discrimination".

or indirect discrimination. If it falls outside Section 20 but within the proposed new Section 19B, it must be provided without direct discrimination but it will not be unlawful if it is indirectly and unfairly discriminatory in its impact on ethnic minorities . . .

It is entirely fortuitous whether a function of a public body falls within or outside Section 20. It is quite ridiculous—I understate my indignation—for the concept of unlawful discrimination to depend upon making such an artificial distinction based upon an uncertain legal test in circumstances where the factual issues about purpose and effect will often be tangled together.

It is difficult to imagine how vulnerable people—the alleged victims of institutional racism by the police, prison, immigration or social services—could reasonably be expected to untangle the legal and factual knots. Disentangling those knots will simply add to the legal costs of employing counsel like myself.

By clothing themselves and their departments with the immunity from liability for indirect racial discrimination, Ministers are judges in their own cause. They seek to be immune, not for reasons of principle but for administrative convenience. The problems suggested by the Minister about policy-making are, with respect, fanciful and unreal. There is no reason whatever why regional policies and policies related to a person's age cannot be objectively justified. If, under the Bill, decisions about national security need to be justified, why on earth should other less serious policy decisions not also need to be justified? . . .

Lord Lester also challenged the government's assumption that the RR(A)B complied with the Human Rights Act 1998, and expressed his concern over the very limited prohibition against discrimination in the field of immigration:

[If] the concept of discrimination contained in the European Convention on Human Rights covers indirect as well as direct discrimination . . . as I believe is indicated in case law, how can the Minister possibly make a statement that the legislation complies with the convention if it will authorise breaches of Article 14 of the convention, read with Article 5 in relation to police powers and Article 6 in relation to access to justice? . . .

Unlike discrimination on grounds of nationality or place of residence, discrimination based on ethnic or national origins is as much racial discrimination as is discrimination based on colour or race, as the definition of racial discrimination in Article 1 of the United Nations Convention on the Elimination of All Forms of Discrimination 1966 makes crystal clear. Such discrimination involves treating one individual less favourably than another for what is not chosen by them but for what is innate in them at birth—their genetic inheritance—whether as ethnic Jews, Roma gypsies or Hong Kong Indians. It is as invidious and unfair as is discrimination based on the colour of a person's skin. . .

The sweepingly broad exception in Section 19C is incompatible with the very principle of non-discrimination which the legislation is intended to secure. If the Home Office wishes to make special arrangements aimed at providing protection to particular groups seeking shelter in the United Kingdom, such as the Bosnians and Kosovars who were granted exceptional leave to remain during the recent crisis in the Balkans, it is difficult to understand how that would require an exception. The reason for affording favourable treatment to some of those groups is surely not their ethnic or national origins but their well-founded fear of persecution, the urgency of their humanitarian needs and the need to comply with the UK's obligations under the refugee convention. The policy is not based upon or caused by their ethnicity. It does not involve discriminating against anyone on the grounds of their ethnic or national origins . . . Even if it were appropriate, for the avoidance of doubt, to include an exception to cover situations of that kind, the exception to the fundamental right to equal treatment without discrimination would need to be prescribed in legislation in a way carefully tailored to what is necessary to give effect to the Government's legitimate aims, with adequate judicial safeguards against the abuse of this extraordinary power, to ensure that the doing of a discriminatory act is justified by its purpose, as with national security.

The functions covered by Section 19C include decisions to deport, exclusion directions, leave to enter or remain, the grant of asylum, exceptional leave to remain, and even naturalisation as a British citizen. Section 44 of the British Nationality Act 1981 provides that any discretion vested by that Act in the Secretary of State, a governor or lieutenant governor, must be exercised, "without regard to the race, colour or religion of any person who may be affected by its exercise".

Yet Section 19C would allow the discretion to be exercised on the basis of ethnic or national origins which are part of the international legal definition of what constitutes "racial discrimination".

As it stands, Section 19C authorises breaches by a future populist illiberal Home Secretary, or by a prejudiced administration, of the various international human rights conventions by which the UK is bound: notably, Articles 2, 5 and 6 of the Convention on the Elimination of Racial Discrimination and Articles 2 and 26 of the International Covenant on Civil and Political Rights. . .

In 1975 the previous Labour government's White Paper, *Racial Discrimination*, observed that legislation was the essential pre-condition for an effective policy to combat discrimination and promote equality of opportunity and treatment. I quote that White Paper:

> Where unfair discrimination is involved, the necessity of a legal remedy is universally accepted. To fail to provide a remedy against an injustice strikes at the rule of law. To abandon a whole group of people in society without legal redress against unfair discrimination is to leave them with no option but to find their own redress. It is no longer necessary to recite the immense damage, material as well as moral, which ensues when a minority loses faith in the capacity of social institutions to be impartial and fair.[96]

Faced with the barrage of condemnation, Lord Bassam could only reiterate his opening remarks that "to prohibit indirect discrimination in relation to the functions that will be caught by the new provisions of the Act would have uncertain and potentially far-reaching effects" and to claim, contrary to the conclusions of the MacPherson report, that "the widely acknowledged element of discrimination in the stop and search figures is due to the cumulative effects of direct discrimination, whether witting or unwitting, rather than indirect discrimination".

This latter contrasts rather sharply with remarks made by Jim Wallace, Scotland's deputy first minister, in a mere six months before. Asserting that "institutional racism" was also a problem in Scotland, he suggested that the term referred to "unwitting" racism "such as by asking for a Muslim's Christian name; or enforc[ing] procedures that unintentionally discriminate against people from a different language or culture, such as by failing to provide an interpreter for non-English speakers in

[96] Fn 84 above, col.141.

court or at the police station". Both of these practices would amount to indirect, rather than direct, discrimination.

> I think the problem with the definition is that to describe this as "institutional racism" is to imply a malevolence that isn't there, when it is more about ignorance and lack of sensitivity . . . Possibly it is used to describe people who would be appalled at the idea that they were racist, who if taken one to one would condemn racism out of hand . . . What is being implied is things you might not be conscious of unless you actively have to think: "How are my actions being interpreted here, am I approaching this in a way which, with no offence intended, could lead to offence being taken?"[97]

Lord Bessam also made the somewhat surprising assertion that prohibiting indirect discrimination "does not fit well with law enforcement where there is no requirement or condition with which an individual must comply".[98] It should be recalled that, not only is this definition of indirect discrimination a peculiarly narrow one, but it will have to be amended in the SDA from July 2001 and, in the RRA either then or as required by the new race discrimination directive, by December 2002.[99] The definitions of indirect discrimination utilised by the directives are considered in Chapter 2.

The government's preferred option for dealing with indirect discrimination by public authorities (save that which falls within s.20 RRA and equivalent provisions) lay in the imposition of an obligation on such authorities to promote equality.[100] This has already occurred in Northern Ireland (see Chapters 5, and 9). But the weight of pressure caused a rethink between the second reading and the report stage in the House of Lords, the Bill being amended to prohibit indirect discrimination also and to impose an obligation on public authorities to promote equality of opportunity on grounds of race on lines similar to those of s.75 Northern Ireland Act.[101] The result of this is to fill the gap left by the *Amin* decision in the RRA. Until the SDA is amended consistent with the RR(A)B, the difficulties associated with *Amin* will remain.

SOCIAL SECURITY

One very significant gap in the protection afforded by the RRA and SDA relates to social security. This area is not expressly excluded from the provisions of the Acts but

---

[97] *Scotsman*, 7th July 1999.
[98] Fn 84 above, col.177.
[99] Noted also by SACHR in the Northern Ireland context: "SACHR particularly regrets that inadequacies in the existing definition are given as reasons for not" including a prohibition against indirect discrimination by public authorities—see memorandum of evidence to the Northern Ireland Select Committee 3rd Feb 1999, appended to the Fourth Report of that Committee, 1998–1999 session, fn 19 above.
[100] See Lord Bassam's speech, text to fn 94 above.
[101] Announcement by Jack Straw, 26th January 2000 (Home Office press release 012/2000, available on http://195.44.11.137/coi/coipress.nsf). David Blunkett committed to a like provision in relation to sex, according to press release 331/99, 14th July 1999, in response to EOC proposals for change to the SDA and EqPA (also available on the same website).

the combination of the decision in *Amin* and the exclusion from the provisions of the RRA and from the non-employment-related provisions of the SDA of acts done under statutory authority (ss.41 and 51) serves to exclude from the reach of ss.20 RRA and 29 SDA most social security related decisions.[102] This is not to say that malign discrimination on the part of a social security adjudicator could not amount to a breach of the RRA. Such discrimination would most probably not be cloaked with statutory authority (see discussion of *Hampson* v *Department of Education and Science* [1991] 1 AC 171 above and in Chapter 7) and it might well fall within *Savjani*, rather than *Amin*. But much discrimination has been protected from challenge by s.41 RRA (which will survive the RR(A)B), s.51 SDA and by the decision in *Amin*.

The position under the SDA has always been complicated as a result of EC law, in particular, Council Directive 79/7 on the progressive implementation of equal treatment in social security schemes relating to sickness, invalidity, old age, accident and unemployment, which provides:

4(1). The principle of equal treatment means that there shall be no discrimination whatsoever on ground of sex either directly, or indirectly by reference in particular to marital or family status, in particular as concerns:
—the scope of the schemes and the conditions of access thereto,
—the obligation to contribute and the calculation of contributions,
—the calculation of benefits including increases due in respect of a spouse and for dependants and the conditions governing the duration and retention of entitlement to benefits.
4(2). The principle of equal treatment shall be without prejudice to the provisions relating to the protection of women on the grounds of maternity.
7(1). This Directive shall be without prejudice to the right of Member States to exclude from its scope:
(a) the determination of personable age for the purposes of granting old-age and retirement pensions and the possible consequences thereof for other benefits;
(b) advantages in respect of old-age pension schemes granted to persons who have brought up children; the acquisition of benefit entitlements following periods of interruption of employment due to the bringing up of children;
(c) the granting of old-age or invalidity benefit entitlements by accidents at work and occupational disease benefits for a dependent wife;
(d) the consequences of the exercise, before the adoption of this Directive, of a right of option not to acquire rights or incur obligations under a statutory scheme.

E. Collins and E. Meehan "Women's Rights in Employment" in C. McCrudden and G. Chambers (eds.) *Individual Rights and the Law in Britain* (Oxford, Clarendon, 1994) 383–8

The social security system was not affected by the introduction of the equal pay and sex discrimination legislation in 1975, although changes were introduced in both the Social Security Act and the Social Security Pensions Act of 1975 to provide for equal treatment in some areas, such as the right to unemployment benefit and sickness pay for married

---

[102] See, for example, *ex p Nessa*, *The Times* 15th November 1994, discussed in Chapters 2 and 7.

women on the same basis as men. The same legislation, however, also introduced new discriminatory elements into the system, such as invalid care allowance and the non-contributory invalidity pension, for which married and cohabiting women were ineligible. A "housewives' version" of the non-contributory invalidity pension was introduced in 1977, giving these women an entitlement to the pension if they could prove that they were incapable of carrying out normal household duties, a test which did not apply to the general invalidity pension.

In general terms, however, the main changes which have been introduced since the 1970s have been as a result of Community directives applying the principle of equal treatment to both statutory and occupational social security schemes. The former, adopted in 1979, aimed to ensure the application of the principle of equal treatment to statutory social security schemes, and member states were obliged to implement any necessary changes by 23 December 1984. The Directive is designed primarily to cover the main employment-related risks, such as sickness, invalidity, old age, accidents at work, and unemployment, and it applies to the "working population" which is defined to cover those in work and seeking work, as well as those whose employment is interrupted by accident, sickness, or involuntary unemployment.

A series of changes was implemented from the end of 1983 to bring the United Kingdom into compliance with the provisions of the Directive. This included changes to the discriminatory rules relating to adult and child dependency additions, for which a variety of approaches was adopted, involving both levelling up (extending benefit to previously excluded groups) and levelling down (taking benefits away from previously included groups). The rules regarding eligibility for supplementary benefit were amended at this time, to allow married and cohabiting women to claim for the first time—but only if they could establish themselves as the "breadwinner" rather than a "dependant", a concept which has remained problematic for women under social security rules. Changes were also made to family income supplement and the non-contributory invalidity pension and its housewives' equivalent were repealed. Invalid care allowance was not repealed at this time, however, and it was not until the judgment of the European Court in the *Drake* case, which challenged the allowance, was pending that the Government took steps to provide the entitlement on the same basis as men and single women to married and cohabiting women.

Despite these changes, there has been a significant amount of litigation about the scope of European obligations since the Directive came into force. For example, the European Court ruled in *Johnson* v. *Chief Adjudication Officer* [Case C–31/90 [1991] ECR I–3723], a case concerning eligibility for severe disablement allowance, the successor to non-contributory invalidity pension, that the personal scope of Article 2 of Directive 79/7 does not apply to a person who had interrupted her occupational activity for child-caring purposes and who is prevented from returning to work because of illness *unless* the person was seeking employment and her search was interrupted by the onset of one of the risks set out in Article 3 of the Directive, the reason for previously leaving employment being irrelevant. It also held that the Directive could be relied on to set aside national legislation which makes entitlement to a benefit subject to rules for eligibility to a preceding benefit which contained discriminatory conditions. In the absence of appropriate measures implementing Article 4 of the Directive, women placed at a disadvantage by the maintenance of discriminatory conditions are entitled to be treated in the same manner as men.

Questions concerning the requirement on a man to pay national insurance contributions for five years longer than women in order to be entitled to the same basic pension and the requirement that, should a man continue to work between the ages of 60 and 65, he still has to pay national insurance contributions when women over 60 years of age do not, whether they are working or not, were also considered by the European Court in a case in the name of the Equal Opportunities Commission. The Court ruled in 1992, that the United Kingdom is not in breach of Directive 79/7 by imposing this requirement. Cases concerning eligibility for supplementary benefit and income support were also decided by the European Court in 1992. It held that Directive 79/7 does not apply to such benefits.

National courts themselves of course have to apply the provisions of the Directive and, in respect of social security, a 1990 judgment of the Court of Appeal augurs well. In *Thomas* v. *Adjudication Officer and Secretary of State for Social Security* [Case C–328/91 [1993] CMLR 880], it held that the female claimants, who were over 60 years of age, were entitled to rely on the 1979 Directive to claim severe disablement allowance or invalid care allowance, despite the fact that these benefits were restricted to those under the state retirement age. The Court held that the Secretary of State had failed to prove that the restriction properly fell within the scope of the exclusion in the Directive relating to the determination of pensionable age for the purposes of old-age and retirement pensions and the possible consequences thereof for other benefits. The House of Lords referred questions arising from this case to the European Court in November 1991.

The other social security Directive, concerning occupational schemes, was due to come into effect on 1 January 1993, though some aspects will not be effective until 1999. Its aim is to extend the principle of equal treatment to schemes not covered by the 1979 Directive whose purpose is to provide workers with benefits intended to supplement or replace benefits provided by statutory schemes, whether membership of such schemes is optional or compulsory. The Directive allows member states to defer the compulsory application of a number of its provisions. These include the determination of pensionable age for the purposes of granting old-age or retirement pensions until a directive requires such application or until the date on which such equality is achieved in statutory schemes, and the application of the Directive to survivors' benefits until a directive requires such application. The Directive also provides that different actuarial calculation factors may be taken into account until 1999. The decision in the *Barber* case, [Case C–262/88 [1990] ECR I–1889] led to uncertainty over the precise scope of these wide exceptions and the scope for further Community legislation is unclear, despite being in the pipeline for some time. In national terms, however, the Government has sought to implement the Directive with the Social Security Act 1989.

The personal taxation system was also excluded from the scope of the 1975 Act and yet the system in place at the time and until recently contained blatantly discriminatory features, which undermined the spirit of the legislation and impeded advances made with regard to pay and employment opportunities of women, particularly married women, in respect of economic independence. Among the features of the tax system subject to the most vociferous criticism was the lack of privacy for married women in respect of their financial affairs, the husband being responsible for declaring his wife's income. A wife's earned income was automatically aggregated with that of her husband unless she elected to be taxed separately and, in the case of her investment income, it had to be aggregated. The Married Man's Allowance, payable to the husband except on very rare occasions when he was not working and after lengthy negotiations with the Inland Revenue, was also considered an anachronism.

The European Commission, while respecting the competence of the member states over the question of personal taxation, has taken an interest in this issue and in 1984 presented a Memorandum to the Council on Taxation and Equal Treatment for Women and Men. This recommended that there should be a system of totally independent taxation for all and that at least the option of separate taxation should be available to couples. Whether this led to the changes announced by Government in 1988 or not, the changes were broadly welcomed as long overdue but regarded as not extensive enough. These changes made provision for women to manage their own financial affairs from 1990. Specifically, married women, like all others, will have their own personal allowance and the capacity to make separate returns to the Inland Revenue in respect of their earned and unearned income. The Married Man's Allowance has been replaced with a Married Couples Allowance, although this remains payable to the husband and the wife does not have the same entitlement except in limited circumstances. While this falls short of a completely independent taxation system and it remains to be seen how it operates in practice, the changes are at least partially positive.

More recently, the ECJ decided in joined cases C–377/96—C–384/96, *De Vrient* v *Rijksdienst voor Pensionenen* [1998] ECR I–2105 that the derogation permitted by Article 7 applied only in respect of matters "necessarily and objectively related to the difference in pensionable age". If a Member State abolished discriminatory retirement ages, it could not retain differential methods of calculating pensions by reference to the earlier, discriminatory pensionable ages. And in *Taylor* v *Secretary of State for Social Security* Case C–382/98[103], the ECJ ruled that the directive was breached by the UK's restriction of winter fuel payment to those of pensionable age—i.e., to women of 60, men of 65. Ruling that the benefit was "directly and effectively linked to . . . the risk of old age" (this on the grounds that it was payable even to elderly people "without financial or material difficulties"), the ECJ rejected the argument put forward by the UK that the aim of the payment was to protect against a lack of financial means. On this ground, and on the ground that "if the benefit is designed to provide protection against the risk of old age . . . it does not follow that the [qualifying age for receipt] . . . must necessarily coincide with the statutory age of retirement", the ECJ ruled that differential access to the benefit breached the directive and was not saved by the derogation permitted by Article 7.

It was noted, above, that the RRA has limited impact on social security matters, legal challenges being restricted, on the one hand, by the exemption provided by s.41 RRA, on the other by the decisions in *Amin* and other s.20 cases. The RR(A)B will have some impact on the area, providing as it does for the reversal of *Amin*. It will not, however, impact on the scope of s.41 RRA. Although s.19B of the RRA, as it will be amended, will make it "unlawful for a body or other person specified in Schedule A1 or of a description falling within that Schedule A1 to discriminate, in carrying out any of its functions, against another person", that Schedule applies to Ministers of the Crown and government departments (only) "*other than* (para 1, my emphasis) in relation to any function of or relating to–

---

[103] Available at http://europa.eu.int/eur-lex/en/index.html.

(a) making, confirming or approving Orders in Council and other instruments of a kind mentioned in section 41(1); or

(b) making or approving arrangements, or imposing requirements or conditions, of any kind mentioned in section 41.

After amendment of the RRA, social security matters will be amenable to review under that Act only insofar as they fall outside the protected sphere imposed by s.41 and accepted by the House of Lords in *Hampson* (discussed above). However, the race discrimination directive, which must be implemented in the UK by July 2003, provides for the elimination of discrimination on grounds of racial or ethnic origin in relation, *inter alia*, to "social protection", "social security" and "social advantages". Given, in particular, its application to indirect as well as direct discrimination, it may be that the implementation of the directive will result, in the medium term, in changes to social security rules where, for example, they can be shown to be inherently disadvantageous to particular racial groups.

Before we leave the area of social security it is useful to mention the significance of the Human Rights Act 1998. In *Cornwell* v *United Kingdom* (Application no. 36578/97)[104], the European Commission of Human Rights ruled that the UK's discrimination as between "widows" and "widowers" in the provision of benefits (widow's allowance and widow's payment) gave rise to an actionable claim under Articles 8 and 14 of the ECnHR taken with Article 1 of Protocol No. 1 which provides that:

> Every natural and legal person is entitled to the peaceful enjoyment of his possessions. No one shall be deprived of his possessions except in the public interest and subject to the conditions provided for by law and by the general principles of international law.

The Commission referred the case to the ECJ for determination, but a settlement was reached between the applicant and the UK government before any decision was forthcoming. The Welfare Reform and Pensions Act 1999 amends the discriminatory provisions at issue, but the case indicates another avenue of challenge available in the case both of race and of sex discrimination in social security matters

---

[104] Available at http://www.echr.coe.int/eng/Judgments.htm.

5

Enforcement

INDIVIDUAL ENFORCEMENT

The approach to discrimination adopted by the SDA, RRA and DDA is, for the most part, a highly individualistic one. While consideration of "group" characteristics (such as women's childcare responsibilities, or the religious affiliations of particular racial groups) can be taken into consideration in an indirect discrimination claim; most intervention in discrimination consists in legal cases brought by individuals, whose outcomes apply only to those individuals. Trade unions and the EOC and CRE support "test cases" whose outcome will, in practical terms, reach beyond the individual. And "sample cases" can be selected where many litigants are involved in similar claims.[1] But the focus of the law is on the individual, and legal success turns on the demonstration of detriment suffered by the individual as a result of discrimination.

In order to win discrimination cases, individuals have to bring their claims to employment tribunals (or, in non-employment cases, the county court).[2] No legal aid is available to them. Those who regard themselves as the victims of discrimination can apply to the relevant commission for financial and other assistance (the commissions are further discussed below). Doyle contrasted the position of DDA claimants (at the time denied a Commission) with that of claimants under the RRA and the SDA, who could apply to the CRE and the EOC, respectively, for financial and other assistance. But the demand for such assistance far outweighs the available resources. In 1998, for example, the CRE received 1657 formal applications for assistance (and a further 10 000 telephone calls from potential applicants). Advice and assistance was offered by the Commission to 972 applicants, but only 163 received full legal representation.[3] In the same year, the EOC granted legal assistance to 47 of the 187 applicants who formally applied.[4] The various Commissions have petitioned for the extension of legal aid to discrimination cases.[5]

[1] See for example *Ashmore v British Coal* [1990] IRLR 283, in which the Court of Appeal stayed as abusive cases brought after the dismissal of 12 sample cases of 1500.

[2] These include claims of discrimination by advocates/ barristers under the SDA, RRA and FETO.

[3] CRE *Annual Report* pp.23–4. A further 101 received limited advice and 92 were referred on to other organisations such as trade unions (53) and racial equality councils (15).

[4] *Annual Report* 1998. Advice was provided in a further 18 cases.

[5] See for example the FEC, *Review of the Fair Employment Acts* (1997, available from the FEC website at *http://www.fec-ni.org/*, and the CRE's 1998 proposals, *Reform of the Race Relations Act 1976*, available from the CRE.

The funding which has been made available to the commissions has fallen over time.[6] The Better Regulation Task Force suggested that the various commissions might do better "to target their own investigative and enforcement activity on novel or test cases, and on flagrant or persistent offenders". The Task Force expressed the "hope" that "the current reforms of legal aid . . . will pave the way for an extension of legal aid to discrimination cases". But given the overarching concern of government to reduce the cost of legal aid, it cannot be considered probable that legal aid would, even if available in theory, be granted in any but the rarest cases.

Some change may be forced in this area by the implementation of the new race discrimination directive which provides (Art 7) that "Member States shall ensure that associations, organisations or other legal entities may pursue, on behalf of the complainant with his or her approval, any judicial and/or administrative procedure provided for the enforcement of obligations under the directive". This provision might be read so as to require practical steps such as adequate funding of the CRE.

Turning to the legal position, the burden of proof in discrimination, as in other employment cases, is on the applicant. We saw, above, that the concept of indirect discrimination is a complicated one, and that its proof frequently turns on statistical evidence. Direct discrimination, by contrast, is conceptually straightforward. But its proof gives rise to enormous problems. Success in a direct discrimination claim requires that the claimant persuades a tribunal, not only that s/he has been less favourably treated than his/her comparator (real or hypothetical), but also that the discrimination (less favourable treatment) was "on the grounds of" race, sex, religious belief or political opinion.[7] The protected factor need not be established as the sole cause of the less favourable treatment, but must be proven to have been "the principal or at least an important or significant cause of the less favourable treatment".[8]

The UK courts have frequently acknowledged the difficulties of proving direct discrimination—in particular, the fact that direct evidence of such discrimination will only rarely be available. It is one thing to demonstrate that a complainant has been treated less favourably than someone of a different sex, racial group, etc; and to demonstrate that s/he has suffered a detriment thereby. But only in the rarest cases will a discriminator admit that the less favourable treatment was "by reason of" the com-

---

[6] This, according to then Chairman Sir Herman Ousley in his foreword to the 1998 Annual Report (available from the CRE website at http://www.cre.gov.uk/), was the fourth successive annual cut.

[7] Cf disability, discussed in Chapter 8.

[8] *Owen & Brigg* v *James* [1982] ICR 618, [1982] IRLR 502, *Seide* v *Gillette*, reaffirmed in *Swiggs* v *Nagarajan* [1999] 3 WLR 425, discussed in Chapter 2. By contrast, in the US, the Civil Rights Act 1991 reversed the decision of the Supreme Court in *Price Waterhouse* v *Hopkins* 490 US 228 (1989) to the effect that the prohibited reason in a mixed motive case must at least "tip the balance". The 1991 Act provides that discrimination, where present, does not have to tip the balance (though relief is limited in a case where it does not). Having said this, *James* v *Eastleigh* and *Nagarajan* (discussed in Chapter 2), which used the "but for" test adopted *restrictively* by a US Court of Appeals in *Lewis* v *University of Pittsburg* 33 US Cases 1091 (1983) did not do so restrictively as in the US cases (see D. Pannick, *Sex Discrimination and the Law* (Oxford: OUP, 1985), p.87) but expansively to deny the need for motivation. It is likely that direct discrimination will be satisfied where the prohibited reason is *either* the "but for" cause of *or* the motivating factor for the less favourable treatment.

plainant's sex, race, etc—in other words, that s/he would not have been so treated "but for" the protected reason. It falls to the tribunal, therefore, to *infer* unlawful discrimination (i.e., to conclude that the reason for the less favourable treatment was a prohibited one). Such inference may also be necessary in a case which turns on a hypothetical, rather than actual, comparator, in order to establish less favourable treatment. Particularly in relation to the former situation, significant difficulties have arisen in determining when inferences of discrimination may appropriately be drawn.

The leading authority is the decision of the Court of Appeal in *King* v *The Great Britain-China Centre*, most recently reaffirmed by the House of Lords in *Glasgow City Council* v *Zafar*. The *King* case was brought by a Chinese woman who claimed that she had been subject to race discrimination in a job application. Her claim succeeded at tribunal, a majority finding that the employers "had failed to demonstrate that the applicant had not been treated unfavourably [in not being shortlisted], or that such unfavourable treatment was not because of her race". EAT allowed the employers' appeal, ruling that the tribunal had incorrectly placed the burden of proof on them. The Court of Appeal, however, reinstated the tribunal's decision, Neill LJ for the Court summarising the existing authorities as follows:

King v *The Great Britain-China Centre* [1992] ICR 516, [1991] IRLR 513

(1) It is for the applicant who complains of racial discrimination to make out his or her case. Thus if the applicant does not prove the case on the balance of probabilities he or she will fail.

(2) It is important to bear in mind that it is unusual to find direct evidence of racial discrimination. Few employers will be prepared to admit such discrimination even to themselves. In some cases the discrimination will not be ill-intentioned but merely based on an assumption "he or she would not have fitted in".

(3) The outcome of the case will therefore usually depend on what inferences it is proper to draw from the primary facts found by the Tribunal. These inferences can include, in appropriate cases, any inferences that it is just and equitable to draw in accordance with s 65(2)(b) of the 1976 Act from an evasive or equivocal reply to a questionnaire [discussed below].

(4) Though there will be some cases where, for example, the non-selection of the applicant for a post or for promotion is clearly not on racial grounds, a finding of discrimination and a finding of a difference in race will often point to the possibility of racial discrimination. In such circumstances the Tribunal will look to the employer for an explanation. If no explanation is then put forward or if the Tribunal considers the explanation to be inadequate or unsatisfactory it will be legitimate for the Tribunal to infer that the discrimination was on racial grounds. This is not a matter of law but, as May LJ put it in [*North West Thames Regional Health Authority* v *Noone* [1988] IRLR 195], "almost common sense".

(5) It is unnecessary and unhelpful to introduce the concept of a shifting evidential burden of proof. At the conclusion of all the evidence the Tribunal should make findings as to the primary facts and draw such inferences as they consider proper from those facts. They should then reach a conclusion on the balance of probabilities, bearing in mind both the

difficulties which face a person who complains of unlawful discrimination and the fact that it is for the complainant to prove his or her case . . .

Miss King is an ethnic Chinese. So were four other of the 30 candidates. Eight candidates were called for interview. None of these eight candidates was an ethnic Chinese. The majority of the Tribunal were satisfied that Miss King's paper qualifications fulfilled the requirements set out in the advertisement and in the job specification, and that she had been treated less favourably than the candidates called for interview . . . The majority were also impressed by the fact that no ethnic Chinese had ever been employed by the centre.

In these circumstances the Tribunal were clearly entitled to look to the centre for an explanation of the fact that Miss King was not even called for an interview. The majority, however, found the explanation unsatisfactory and were also dissatisfied with the reply to the questionnaire. They therefore concluded that Miss King had made out her case . . . reading the relevant parts of the [tribunal's] reasons as a whole the majority's decision was not flawed by an error of law. They clearly had in mind that it was for Miss King to make out her case . . . They were entitled to look to the centre for an explanation of the fact that Miss King was not selected for interview. They were not satisfied with the explanation and they were entitled to say no. It was therefore legitimate for them to draw an inference that the discrimination was on racial grounds. This process of reasoning did not involve a reversal of the burden of proof but merely a proper balancing of the factors which could be placed in the scales for and against a finding of unlawful discrimination.

The question whether an applicant has proven his or her claim of discrimination is one of fact and, as such, cannot be appealed unless the tribunal has applied the wrong legal test or otherwise reached a perverse decision. In *King*, as we saw above, the Court of Appeal took the view that the tribunal had been entitled to draw an inference of discrimination. Similarly, in *The Belfast Port Employer's Association* v *FEC*, Northern Ireland's Court of Appeal ruled that the FET had been entitled to infer discrimination, in the absence of a satisfactory explanation from the employer, where "there were 167 applicants for 15 posts, 29 from Roman Catholics. No Roman Catholics were short-listed, although it was established that the complainants were experienced dockers and at least as well qualified for consideration as a number of those included in the short list."[9] And in *In re Ballymena Borough Council*,[10] Northern Ireland's High Court, *per* Carswell J, accepted that a tribunal had been entitled to infer discrimination where a Catholic's application for employment was rejected after a secret ballot. Having drawn attention to a number of procedural irregularities, and failures on the part of the appointers to follow the FEC's Code of Practice, Carswell J continued:

One of the major factors was that set out by the Tribunal . . . [for its decision was t]hat very little evidence was forthcoming from those councillors who voted for the successful candidate in preference to the applicant . . . As the Tribunal also observed, the assessment forms, to which it might have turned in default of direct personal evidence, were not all completed, returned or marked consistently. In these circumstances there appears to me to be force in the Tribunal's remarks . . . [that]:

[9] Court of Appeal (Civil Division) 29th June 1994 unreported, *per* Carswell LJ, approving the Fair Employment Tribunal's application of *King*.
[10] Queen's Bench Division (Crown Side) 18th June 1993, unreported.

We do not know precisely who voted for whom. If we are asked not to draw an inference of unlawful discrimination from our finding of less favourable treatment, the method of appointment by secret ballot as adopted by the respondent, and the failure to record assessments of the candidates, obviously makes the task of the Tribunal extremely difficult if not impossible. The use of a secret ballot does not reconcile with the recommendation in the Fair Employment Code of Practice that recruitment should be systematic and objective so that it can be tested if a complaint is made. If there is anonymity in appointments, as well as absence of records of assessment, it makes the respondent's explanation for selection of candidates much more difficult to defend.

The higher courts will overturn decisions where tribunals have failed to follow the approach set out in *King*. In particular, a tribunal which considers itself bound to infer unlawful discrimination from a finding of less favourable treatment, coupled with an unsatisfactory explanation from an employer, will err as a matter of law.

Neill LJ stated in *King* that "a finding of discrimination [in the sense of less favourable treatment] and a finding of a difference in race [or sex] will often point to the possibility of racial discrimination . . . If no explanation is then put forward or if the Tribunal considers the explanation to be inadequate or unsatisfactory *it will be legitimate* for the Tribunal to infer that the discrimination was on racial grounds" (my emphasis). In *Khanna* v *Ministry of Defence* [1981] IRLR 331, [1981] ICR 653 *Chattopadhyay* v *Headmaster of Holloway School* [1981] IRLR 487, [1982] ICR 132, *Baker* v *Cornwall County Council* [1990] IRLR 194 and *West Midlands Passenger Transport Executive* v *Singh* [1987] IRLR 351 the courts suggested that inferences of discrimination *ought* to be drawn in cases in which apparent discrimination was not adequately explained. The issue was resolved in *Glasgow City Council* v *Zafar*, in which the House of Lords ruled that a tribunal had erred in regarding itself as *bound* to infer unlawful discrimination from the employer's unsatisfactory explanation of the disputed treatment.

Glasgow City Council v Zafar [1998] 2 All ER 953, [1997] 1 WLR 1659, [1998] ICR 120, [1998] IRLR 36

Lord Browne-Wilkinson (for the Court)

Claims brought under the [RRA] and the [SDA] present special problems of proof for complainants since those who discriminate on the grounds of race or gender do not in general advertise their prejudices: indeed they may not even be aware of them . . . The best guidance is that given by Neill LJ in *King* [citing principles 1–5 extracted above] . . .

In my judgment that is the guidance which should in future be applied in these cases. In particular, certain remarks of mine in the Employment Appeal Tribunal in *Khanna* v *Ministry of Defence* and *Chattopadhyay* v *Headmaster of Holloway School* to the effect that such inference "should" be drawn put the matter too high, are inconsistent with later Court of Appeal authority and should not be followed.[11]

---

[11] See also *Leicester University Students' Union* v *Mahomed* [1995] IRLR 292.

The House of Lords in *Zafar* also ruled that the tribunal had erred in inferring *less favourable* (i.e., *prima facie* discriminatory) treatment from *bad* treatment.

Lord Browne-Wikinson

The [RRA] requires it to be shown that the complainant has been treated by the person against whom the discrimination is alleged less favourably than that person treats or would have treated another. In deciding that issue, the conduct of a hypothetical reasonable employer is irrelevant. The alleged discriminator may or may not be a reasonable employer. If he is not a reasonable employer he might well have treated another employee in just the same unsatisfactory way as he treated the complainant in which case he would not have treated the complainant "less favourably" for the purposes of the [RRA]. The fact that, for the purposes of the law of unfair dismissal, an employer has acted unreasonably casts no light whatsoever on the question whether he has treated the employee "less favourably" for the purposes of the [RRA]. . . .

   The industrial tribunal, having wrongly drawn the inference of less favourable treatment, then held that, in the absence of any satisfactory non-racial explanation for such treatment, it was bound by authority to draw the inference that such less favourable treatment was on the grounds of the applicant's race . . .

A commentary in the *Equal Opportunities Review* warned that, although the Lord Browne-Wilkinson's approach was:

   logically indisputable . . . Whether the employer was reasonable is not relevant to whether the employee was treated less favourably . . . there is a danger that Lord Browne-Wilkinson's dictum will be taken out of context and misapplied . . . like the statement in *Qureshi* v *London Borough of Newham* [1991] IRL R 264 . . . that incompetence by an employer does not equate to discrimination, as indicating that it is for the applicant to prove that the unexplained treatment was on racial grounds rather than because the employer was simply unreasonable or incompetent.[12]

More recently, in *Martins* v *Marks & Spencer* [1998] IRLR 326 the Court of Appeal ruled that a tribunal had been "perverse" in inferring race discrimination from their finding that an interview panel had been "biased" against an applicant.[13] Michael Rubenstein's commentary to the IRLR report of the case remarked on "a disturbing trend in higher court decisions on allegations of race discrimination" (this trend including the decision of the House of Lords in *Zafar*):

   Why should the tribunal's finding of bias be displaced by the speculative, rather implausible thesis that the interviewer would also have acted in a biased way towards someone from

---

[12] 77 *Equal Opportunities Review* 44, pp.45–6.

[13] Somewhat bizarrely, the Court also ruled that, even had the panel discriminated against the applicant, the employer would not have been liable because, under s.32(3), it had taken "such steps as were reasonably practicable to prevent" discrimination by the interviewers—i.e., "the employers" equal opportunity policy; their compliance with the Code of Practice issued by the [CRE] in relation to selection procedures, criteria and interviewing and their selection of the interviewing panel to include . . . a person with an interest in recruiting from ethnic minorities". This aspect of the decision was touched upon in Chapter 4.

a different racial group? And how is the applicant to prove that there was no bias in someone else's interview while the tribunal at the same time avoids investigating the process in such detail as to render itself liable to being accused of "usurping the functions of the interviewers"?

Bob Watt, on the other hand (whose disapproval of *James* was noted in Chapter 2), regarded the decision as no more than confirmation by the House of Lords of the importance of the alleged discriminator's *reason* for treating the complainant less favourably:

> even when [a complainant] are [sic] a member of a group ostensibly protected by the anti-discrimination legislation, it is not necessarily the case that their unfavourable treatment was premised upon their group membership. . . .The central point which is to be found in Lord Browne-Wilkinson's speech in *Zafar* [14] . . is that what really counts in turning a neutral decision into a discriminatory decision is the effective reason for which the putative discriminator acted. This is to be addressed at the level of "what did the actor wish to bring about" (i.e. intention) rather than at the level of motive.[15]

Watt's favourable view of *Zafar* (and, indeed, of the decision in *Martins*) is not widely shared. Rubenstein's comments have been noted above. And the CRE's 1998 proposals for reform of the RRA, suggested that, despite *Zafar*'s approval of *King*, the House of Lord's decision had rendered "courts and tribunals . . . less willing to . . . draw an inference of racial discrimination".

The CRE suggested that such an inference might be permitted on the basis of unreasonable treatment, where that treatment was contrary to employment legislation and codes of practice and where there was no evidence that an employer had taken steps to prevent discrimination of the type alleged:

> employers . . . must not be allowed to hide behind poor or unreasonable practices or decisions to avoid inferences of discrimination being drawn. Implicitly this was the policy which Parliament sought to establish in the [RRA], since they made employers responsible for the discriminatory acts of their employees unless, under section 32(3), an employer could prove that he or she had taken such steps as were reasonably practicable to prevent such acts. Where . . . the employer not only took no positive steps to avoid race discrimination but permitted poor employment practice, which may well either include or conceal race discrimination, then courts or tribunals should not be prohibited from drawing an inference of discrimination where there is evidence of unreasonable treatment of a person from a racial group which constitutes a minority within the whole, or a relevant section, of that employer's workforce.

---

[14] He also included Lord Lowry's speech in *James* which (dissenting) would have upheld the decision of Browne-Wilkinson VC (as he them was) in the Court of Appeal, and Advocate-General Tesauro's subsequent opinion in *P v S & Cornwall County Council* Case C–13/94 [1996] ECR I–2143.

[15] B Watt "Goodbye 'but-for', hello 'but-why?' " (1998) 27 *ILJ* 121, pp.124–6.

The CRE also called for primary legislation to bring the RRA into line with the Council Directive 97/80 on the burden of proof in cases of discrimination based on sex. The burden of proof directive requires (Article 4(1)) that:

> Member States shall take such measures as are necessary, in accordance with their national judicial systems, to ensure that, when persons who consider themselves wronged because the principle of equal treatment has not been applied to them establish, before a court or other competent authority, facts from which it may be presumed that there has been direct or indirect discrimination, *it shall be for the respondent to prove that there has been no breach of the principle of equal treatment* (my emphasis).

It has been suggested that this replicates existing practice, albeit that tribunals in the UK are only permitted, rather than required, to draw inferences of discrimination from unsatisfactory or absent explanations of less favourable treatment. But the appear increasingly reluctant to draw inferences of discrimination. In 1992, Geoffrey Bindman wrote that the test established in *Noone* was:

> Far from satisfactory. It still means that a respondent will be able to avoid a finding of racial [or other prohibited] discrimination by producing *plausible* explanation other than race [etc.] for an act of discrimination (i.e. less favourable treatment. . .) without being under a positive obligation to prove that the alternative explanation was the *true* one . . . it is all too easy to find a plausible subjective ground, especially in recruitment or promotion cases, for choosing one candidate rather than another.[16]

The terms of the directive, which bind Member States only in relation to sex discrimination, are to be implemented in the UK by 22nd July 2001.[17] The UK government will give them effect, although it has indicated that the provisions are (subject to "careful assess[ment of] the relative benefits and burdens (including the costs)) likely to be applied to the RRA as well as to the SDA". Of immense significance here is the new race discrimination directive which establishes the burden of proof in those cases to which it applies (see further Chapter 4 and 7) in precisely the same terms as the burden of proof directive. If the 1999 draft directive on equal treatment is adopted, similar provisions will apply in relation to the discrimination regulated thereby (see Chapters 1 and 11).

Some of the difficulties associated with proving discrimination have been mentioned. The questionnaire procedure established under ss.74, 65, 56 and article 44 of the SDA, RRA, DDA and FETO, respectively, can assist a tribunal to draw inferences of discrimination. A prospective complainant may send to the employer a document which lists a number of questions. The form of the questionnaire is prescribed by statutory instrument under the relevant legislation, the race questionnaire, for example, being set out in the Race Relations (Questions and Replies) Order 1977 (SI 1977 No 842), Schedule 1, as follows:

[16] "Proof and Evidence of Discrimination", in B. Hepple and E. Szyszczak, *Discrimination: the Limits of Law*, (London: Mansell, 1992), pp.57–8.
[17] Council Directive 98/52 on the extension of Directive 97/80 on the burden of proof in cases of discrimination based on sex to the UK, Article 2.

To (name of person to be questioned) of (address)

1. (1) I (name of questioner) of (address) consider that you may have discriminated against me contrary to the [RRA].
   (2) (Give date, approximate time and a factual description of the treatment received and of the circumstances leading up to the treatment.)
   (3) I consider that this treatment may have been unlawful (because (complete if you wish to give reasons, otherwise delete)).
2. Do you agree that the statement in paragraph 1(2) above is an accurate description of what happened? If not, in what respect do you disagree or what is your version of what happened?
3. Do you accept that your treatment of me was unlawful discrimination by you against me? If not—
   (a) why not,
   (b) for what reason did I receive the treatment accorded to me, and
   (c) how far did considerations of colour, race, nationality (including citizenship) or ethnic or national origins affect your treatment of me?
4. (Any other questions you wish to ask.)
5. My address for any reply you may wish to give to the questions raised above is (that set out in paragraph 1(1) above) (the following address).
   (signature of questioner) (date).

   N.B.—By virtue of section 65 of the Act this questionnaire and any reply are (subject to the provisions of the section) admissible in proceedings under the Act and a court or tribunal may draw any such inference as is just and equitable from a failure without reasonable excuse to reply within a reasonable period, or from an evasive or equivocal reply, including an inference that the person questioned has discriminated unlawfully.

The same statutory instrument prescribes the form of response (Schedule 2):

To (name of questioner) of (address).

1. I (name of person questioned) of (address) hereby acknowledge receipt of the questionnaire signed by you and dated .... which was served on me on (date).
2. [I agree that the statement in paragraph 1 (2) of the questionnaire is an accurate description of what happened.] [I disagree with the statement in paragraph 1 (2) of the questionnaire in that ....]
3. I accept/dispute that my treatment of you was unlawful discrimination by me against you. [My reasons for so disputing are .... The reason why you received the treatment accorded to you and the answers to the other questions in paragraph 3 of the questionnaire are ....]
4. (Replies to questions in paragraph 4 of the questionnaire.)
[5. I have deleted (in whole or in part) the paragraph(s) numbered .... above, since I am unable/unwilling to reply to the relevant questions in the correspondingly numbered paragraph(s) of the questionnaire for the following reasons ....]

(signature of person questioned) .... (date)

Similar forms are set down by the Sex Discrimination (Questions and Replies) Order 1975 (SI 1975 No 2048[18]), the Disability Discrimination (Questions and Replies) Order 1996 (SI 1996 No 2793) and the 1989 Fair Employment (Questions and Replies) Regulations.[19] As is noted on the face of the questionnaire itself, a deliberate failure "without reasonable excuse" on the part of the employer to reply to the questionnaire within a reasonable time in full or in part, or an "evasive or equivocal" reply, will permit the tribunal to draw an inference of discrimination as in *King*, above. This provision was objected to in the strongest terms by some Conservative politicians on the ground that it compelled "self-incrimination", and "smack[ed] of the Star Chamber".[20] But its impact has been less than dramatic. Employers can refuse to answer questions on the grounds of irrelevance, or because to do so would impose an onerous and undue burden, and an explanation by the employer of any refusal to answer will prevent any adverse inferences being drawn by a tribunal. Evasiveness or a refusal to respond on the part of an employer can assist an applicant in persuading the tribunal to draw inferences of discrimination,[21] but will not of itself suffice for such an inference.[22] The CRE's 1998 proposals suggested that tribunals ought to be obliged to draw unfavourable inferences from failure of refusal to reply. The government's response to this is as yet unclear.

Perhaps the most powerful evidence from which discrimination may be inferred is statistical evidence relating to an employer's past or current practice in relation to the employment of women, particular racial groups, etc. In *Jalota v Imperial Metal Industries*, EAT had rejected statistical evidence as "irrelevant" to the question whether an applicant had been discriminated against. Mr Jalota, who had been denied a transfer by his employers, sought discovery of the number of ethnic minority workers employed by his employer, broken down according to a number of categories. He also sought information about the education, qualifications, age, length of service, race, colour and the ethnic origin of the successful candidates for the various vacancies for which he applied since beginning employment with the respondents. His request was refused and the refusal upheld by EAT.

Jalota v Imperial Metal Industries [1979] IRLR 313

Talbot J

The ground on which he required that information was (when he made his submission to us) that it would establish a company policy not to employ coloured [sic] persons. On

---

[18] Northern Ireland has its own equivalents.

[19] There are equivalent provisions under the NI Orders.

[20] Leon Brittan MP, 893 HC Debs (18th June 1975), col. 1602. See also Ian Percival MP at col. 1598.

[21] In *Clarke* v *Kay & Co Ltd* 41 EORDCLD 7 inferences were drawn from unsatisfactory replies but the case was strong in any event.

[22] See also *Gamble & Anor* v *Nadal & Anor* EAT/350/98 unreported 16th October 1998 (available at http://www.employmentappeals.gov.uk/), in which EAT overturned a decision in favour of an applicant who alleged race discrimination in spite both of refusal to answer the questionnaire and evidence of racism on the part of the manager. The CRE briefing on the Government's response to the 1998 reform proposals, available on the CRE website, see fn 8 above, suggests that that response is favourable on this issue.

inquiry from him he told us that, although amongst the payroll employees there are a number of coloured persons employed, there are only one or two on the staff and the job he was applying for was a staff job . . .

As to whether or not the respondents were racially discriminating against this appellant on his application of January 1978 this seems to raise issues that could no way, in our view, make it relevant that the respondents should be required to produce particulars of the number of coloured employees that they have . . .

But there is another matter that has to be considered: these employers, the respondents, do not categorise, amongst their many thousands of employees, the colour of the employee. To ask them to comply with this request would be to require them to produce a category from their large number of employees of coloured persons . . . how do you define colour? What is the precise definition that would have to be applied? But much worse than that, what could be more undesirable, and . . . more divisive than requiring the respondents to go around their thousands of employees; to check on the colour; to try to make a decision as to that? We think this request is wholly unreasonable, irrelevant, and should not be answered . . .

[dealing with the request relating to the vacancies he previously applied for] The basis of that request can only be . . . that Mr Jalota is seeking to show that in the case of each, or some, of the previous applications he was discriminated against by reason of his colour and race. He is not permitted, by virtue of [time limits] to make a complaint to a Tribunal in respect of these applications and refusals. What he is seeking to do is to try to show that the particulars of applicants who were accepted would indicate that his refusal must have been based upon race or colour; that he was discriminated against and therefore make it more likely that the complaint he is now bringing, by way of his originating application, is a correct one.

EAT concluded that, the statistics sought going only to "credit" (i.e., whether the employer had discriminated in the past) rather than to whether Mr Jalota himself had been the victim of discrimination, discovery was unavailable in respect of them. The decision in *Jalota* was condemned at the time.

John Bowers, "More Bonds for the Fettered Runner" (1980) 43 *Modern Law Review* 215–19

A complainant on the grounds of race or sex discrimination is like a fettered runner, shackled by bonds at the starting line. The onus of proof rests on the applicant in all discrimination cases, and it is a most difficult burden to discharge. outside the most blatant forms of discrimination, inferences have to be drawn as to an employer's actions and motives. What can be gleaned from discovery of documents is thus a vital issue, recently considered by the House of Lords in *Science Research Council* v. *Nassé* [1979] ICR 921].

In consolidated appeals, Mrs. Nassé and Mr. Vyas sought discovery of confidential assessment reports from their employers to assist in their sex and race discrimination actions. The House of Lords rejected the employers' contentions that confidentiality alone is a ground of privilege from disclosure. The general test to be applied by the court or tribunal is whether discovery of each document is necessary for disposing fairly of the proceedings. The relevance of the document is an important ingredient in this decision, but not sufficient in itself. This makes the case of *Jalota* v. *Imperial Metal Industries (Kynoch) Limited* all the more significant. In this case the door was closed on the creative use of statistics in employment discrimination cases, in marked contrast to the position in the United States. . . .

The decision in *Jalota* is against logic and principle, which suggest that the racial make up of the employers' work force is indeed relevant. In direct discrimination actions tribunals have sown themselves willing to draw inferences from the fact that minorities are employed in a particular workplace. This has been used to rebut discrimination. To hold the converse has proved anathema. For instance, in *Balkaran* v. *City of London Corporation* [COIT 694/31], an Industrial Tribunal was invited to infer that the absence of coloured people in supervisory jobs showed an anti-colour policy. It refused to do so. In *Downer* v. *Liebig Meat* [COIT 820/54], the chairman poured scorn on the very idea: "One can no more read from the statistics that there has been discrimination than one can infer from the fact that of the High Court judiciary only two are females, while 10 per cent of the Bar are of that sex, that there is a policy of sex discrimination in the office of the Lord Chancellor."

It is suggested that, by a skilful use of statistics, inferences can indeed be drawn as to the occurrence of discrimination. This is supported by American experience. "Statistics speak loudly, and the courts listen" is there an oft repeated dictum. They are accepted as of great significance in both class and individual actions brought under Title VII of the Civil Rights Act 1964, which is in terms very similar to Britain's race and sex discrimination legislation. The demonstration of a large disparity between the number of females or members of minority groups in a work force, and the local or national population establishes a prima facie case, while in some cases, statistics have been held "dispositive" of the whole case. The rationale is important; as enunciated in *Hazelwood School District* v. *U.S.P* [534 JF (2d) 805], it runs "absent explanation, it is ordinarily to be expected that non-discriminatory hiring practices will in time result in a workplace more or less representative of the racial and ethnic population in the community from which the employees are hired." . . .

Talbot J.'s second reason against ordering discovery in the instant case would deny any of this development, and is more fundamental than the first. The claim to be shown a racial profile of the work force was "wholly unreasonable, irrelevant, and should not be answered." He instead commends the respondents for not categorising the colour of their employees and asks "What could be more undesirable and more divisive" than keeping such records?

The judgment comes at time when many previously sceptical employers, government departments and civil liberties lobbies are taking the view that ethnic statistics are an essential element in monitoring the Race Relations and Sex Discrimination Acts, and that they should be applauded as providing a springboard for new voluntary initiatives. . . .

Civil liberties and immigrant associations have long been particularly concerned about the use of statistics in an unexplained way by those opposed to integration. Controversy has surrounded, in particular, the ethnic question in the census. The Runnymede Trust, and the National Council for Civil Liberties now advocate the keeping of figures in the employment area, with adequate safeguards. Moreover, the last government "considered that a vital part of our equal opportunities policy is a regular system of monitoring." It proposed, on the lines of the American experience, that the Department of Employment should be given power to request from government contractors details of employment practices, including statistical information.

It would be outrageous to analogise Britain's race problems with those of the United States, but in the use of statistics, both as evidence in court cases, and as a basis for monitoring employment practices, the Americans appear to have more of the answers.

Talbot J's judgment in *Jalota*, if it is followed, will not permit the questions to be formulated.

As Bowers pointed out, the horror with which Talbot J viewed the collection of race statistics by employers sat uncomfortably with the emphasis placed by the CRE on the importance of their collection. The CRE's Race Relations Code of Practice, for the elimination of racial discrimination and the promotion of equality of opportunity in employment, published in 1980, recommends that:

employers should regularly monitor the effects of selection decisions and personnel practices and procedures in order to assess whether equal opportunity is being achieved. The information needed for effective monitoring . . . will best be provided by records showing the ethnic origins of existing employees and job applicants. . . . the need for detailed information and the methods of collecting it will vary according to the circumstances of individual establishments . . . in small firms or in firms in areas with little or no racial minority settlement it will often be adequate to assess the distribution of employees from personal knowledge and visual identification.

It is open to employers to adopt the method of monitoring which is best suited to their needs and circumstances. but whichever method is adopted, they should be able to show hat it is effective . . . Analyses should be carried out of:

The ethnic composition of the workforce of each plant, department, section, shift and job category, and changes in distribution over periods of time.
Selection decisions for recruitment, promotion, transfer and training, according to the racial group of candidates, and reasons for these decisions.
Except in cases where there are large numbers of applicants and the burden on resources would be excessive, reasons for selection and rejection should be recorded at each sage of the selection process, e.g. initial shortlisting and final decisions. Simple categories of reason for rejection should be adequate for the early sifting stages.

. . . in order to identify areas which may need particular attention, a number of key questions should be asked.

Is there evidence that individuals from any particular racial group:
Do not apply for employment or promotion, or that fewer apply than might be expected?
Are not recruited or promoted at all, or are appointed in a significantly lower proportion than their rate of application?
Are underrepresented in training or in jobs carrying higher pay, status or authority?
Are concentrated in certain shifts, sections or departments?

The Code of Practice is not binding. But, as with the other statutory codes, failure to observe its recommendations:

may result in breaches of the law where the act or omission falls within any of the specific prohibitions of the Act. Moreover, its provisions are admissible in evidence in any proceedings under the [RRA] before an industrial tribunal and if any provision appears to the tribunal to be relevant to a question arising in the proceedings it must be taken into account in determining that question. If employers take the steps that are set out in the Code to prevent their employees from doing acts of unlawful discrimination they may avoid liability for such acts in any legal proceedings brought against them.

It was not until 1987 that EAT accepted the relevance of statistical evidence in *West Midlands Passenger Transport Executive* v *Singh*, a decision upheld by the Court of Appeal.

The *Singh* case involved a race discrimination claimant who applied for discovery of the ethnic origins of all applicants for senior inspector posts with the employer over a particular period, which post he had unsuccessfully applied for.[23] This information was collected by the employer in pursuit of its equal opportunities policy. The Transport Executive resisted the application and appealed against an industrial tribunal order which was subsequently upheld by EAT. EAT ruled that the statistics sought were logically probative as evidence from which an inference might be drawn that the employers had adopted a racially discriminatory policy. The Court of Appeal also rejected the employer's appeal, overruling *Jalota*.

West Midlands Passenger Transport Executive v Singh ([1988] 2 All ER 873, [1988] 1 WLR 730, [1988] ICR 614, [1988] IRLR 186)

Balcombe LJ (for the Court):

The issue is whether evidence that a particular employer has or has not appointed any or many coloured [sic] applicants in the past is material to the question whether he has discriminated on racial grounds against a particular complainant; and whether discovery devoted to ascertaining the percentage of successful coloured applicants with successful white applicants should be ordered . . .

[Balcombe LJ remarked on the special difficulties of proving discrimination, and the need for inferences to be drawn from primary facts] . . . Statistical evidence may establish a discernible pattern in the treatment of a particular group: if that pattern demonstrates a regular failure of members of the group to obtain promotion to particular jobs and to under-representation in such jobs, it may give rise to an inference of discrimination against the group. That is the reason why the Race Relations Code of Practice . . . recommends ethnic monitoring of the workforce and of applications for promotion and recruitment, a

---

[23] Rule 4(1)(b)(ii) of the Industrial Tribunals Rules of Procedure 1985 (contained in Schedule 1 to the Industrial Tribunals (Rules of Procedure) Regulations 1985 (SI 1985 No 16)) provides that discovery is available in the industrial tribunals as in the county courts, this in turn being governed by Order 14, Rule 8(1) of the County Court Rules 1981 which provides that "On hearing of an application [for discovery or disclosure of particular documents] the court . . . shall in any case refuse to make an order if and so far it is of opinion that discovery [or] disclosure . . . as the case may be, is not necessary either for disposing fairly of the action or matter or for saving costs." Rule 8(1) of the Industrial Tribunals Rules of Procedure 1985 further gives Industrial Tribunals the power to conduct hearings as it thinks fit and provides that Tribunals "shall not be bound by an enactment or rule of law relating to the admissibility of evidence in proceedings before the courts of law." See also *Martins* v *Marks & Spencer*, below, in which the Court of Appeal found that a tribunal had been perverse in concluding from its finding of "obvious bias" in an interview that race discrimination had occurred.

practice adopted by the appellants in their own organisation. Statistics obtained through monitoring are not conclusive in themselves, but if they show racial or ethnic imbalance or disparities, then they may indicate areas of racial discrimination . . .

If a practice is being operated against a group then, in the absence of a satisfactory explanation in a particular case, it is reasonable to infer that the complainant, as a member of the group, has himself been treated less favourably on grounds of race. Indeed, evidence of discriminatory treatment against the group in relation to promotion may be more persuasive of discrimination in the particular case than previous treatment of the applicant, which may be indicative of personal factors peculiar to the applicant and not necessarily racially motivated . . . [24]

The suitability of candidates can rarely be measured objectively; often subjective judgments will be made. If there is evidence of a high percentage rate of failure to achieve promotion at particular levels by members of a particular racial group, this may indicate that the real reason for refusal is a conscious or unconscious racial attitude which involves stereotyped assumptions about members of that group . . .

[referring to *Jalota*] if and insofar as the case purported to lay down any general principles as to the probative effect of statistical evidence in racial discrimination cases, then it is inconsistent with the principles we have endeavoured to state above and should no longer be followed. In particular, the passage in the judgment . . . that it is unreasonable to expect employers to maintain records of the colour or ethnic origins of their employees, is inconsistent with the provisions as to monitoring contained in the Race Relations Code of Practice . . .

The Employment Appeal Tribunal in *Jalota* ended their judgment in the instant case with the following words:

> "Proceedings before an Industrial Tribunal are intended to be informal and the full panoply of inquiry open to litigants for instance in the commercial court was never intended to be part of the Industrial Tribunal structure". Industrial Tribunal chairmen are fully aware of this. However, the fact that it is of an informal nature does not mean that a litigant should be deprived of a proper weapon in the armoury provided by Parliament in seeking to establish facts known to the other side but unknown to him in order to advance his case.
>
> Industrial Tribunal chairmen have enormous experience in the hearing of these applications and on the few occasions when the matter comes before us it appears generally that they have approached the applications with common sense and we have rarely interfered. This leads us to the conclusion that the result of today's hearing will not lead to any undue increase in the length of interlocutory proceedings or in the length of trials or add an unreasonable additional burden to the parties."

We agree. We dismiss this appeal.

Balcombe LJ pointed out that an order for discovery did not follow automatically upon a finding of relevance, the question being whether such an order was necessary

---

[24] "If evidence of a non-discriminatory attitude on the part of an employer is accepted as having probative force, as being likely to have governed his behaviour in the particular case [as was the case in *Owen and Briggs*, fn 8 above], then evidence of a discriminatory attitude on his part may also have probative effect . . ."

for the fair disposal of the proceedings[25] and, in particular, whether the party seeking the request was "fishing" or the request "oppressive" in the sense that: "(1) It may require the provision of material not readily to hand, which can only be made available with difficulty and at great expense [or] . . . (2) It . . . may . . . require the party ordered to make discovery to embark on a course which will add unreasonably to the length and cost of the hearing". It was for the tribunal to decide, as it had done here, whether the discovery order ought to be granted.

The limits of the *Singh* decision became apparent in *Carrington* v *Helix Lighting Ltd* which involved an employer who, unlike the West Midlands Transport Executive, did not conform to the CRE's Code of Practice in respect of ethnic monitoring. Ms Carrington, who had applied for a light assembly job, was interviewed for only a couple of minutes and was rejected without notification, advertisements for the jobs in question continuing to appear in the local press. She sought discovery of statistical material relating to the ethnic composition of the respondents' workforce, an application refused by the tribunal on the grounds that, the documents sought not already being in existence, discovery of them could not be ordered. EAT rejected her appeal, Wood J stating that legislative provision had been made, in respect of the difficulties of proving discrimination, by the questionnaire procedure and by the power given to tribunals to draw adverse inferences in relation thereto.

Carrington v *Helix Lighting Ltd* [1990] ICR 125, [1990] IRLR 6

Wood J MC (P) (for EAT):

. . . There are always two sides to an issue, and whilst the elimination of discrimination—unfairness—whether of race or sex is the object of the legislation, it is important to remember that it is the function of the Industrial Tribunal, just like any other judicial body, to maintain the balance—doing that which is fair, just and reasonable between the parties.

Whilst the Tribunal in each case will adopt its own approach to the problems facing it, it seems to us that an order for discovery of documents may be a useful first step before considering any second or subsequent questionnaire, and that in any event it may be possible for the parties to agree to draft a schedule of facts. However, in our judgment, it is not within the power of a Tribunal to order such a schedule—at least where there is no documentation upon which the schedule is to be based and where the production of the schedule is in the nature of creating evidence.

The CRE['s] . . . Code of Practice encourages the keeping of records in order to monitor possible elements of unfairness . . . failure to comply with the provisions and spirit of the Code of Practice can be taken into account by a Tribunal and when it considers the whole of the case an adverse inference may be drawn.

Finally, the learned chairman in the present case decided that to make an order would be oppressive. This is essentially a matter within his discretion. In the present case there were only some 155 employees, but he may very well have had in mind the fact that the only relevant employees were those in employment on 26 May 1988; that there was a considerable turnover in the workforce, and that he had been assured there was no documentation which was relevant to the issue. It would therefore have meant an investigation throughout

---

[25] Citing *Science Research Council* v *Nassé* above.

the workforce, and in considering oppression he might have taken into account the possibility of exacerbating relationships in the factory.

The potential usefulness of ethnic monitoring (and, by implication, the monitoring of other employee characteristics such as sex, etc) is clear from the decisions in *Singh* and in *Carrington*, above.[26] The CRE's guidance on ethnic monitoring was reproduced above. But relatively few employers comply with the Code and, despite the tribunals' power to draw unfavourable inferences from such failure, this does not appear to happen in practice.

Both the EOC and the CRE called, in their 1998 reform proposals, for the imposition of "positive obligations" on employers to conduct sex and race monitoring and to pass such information to the relevant statutory bodies.[27] The Better Regulation Task Force's report made clear its opposition to statutory monitoring along the lines supported by both CRE and EOC. The Task Force concluded that "imposing additional statutory burdens on business would be counter-productive at this stage" and preferred to encourage "larger businesses to promote proportionate equality policies actively to their small suppliers and customers . . . to adopt equality and monitoring policies and promote compliance throughout their supply chains". The issue of obligatory monitoring and the deliberations of the Better Regulation Task Force are further discussed below.[28]

TIME LIMITS

A further significant difficulty which discrimination complainants frequently encounter relates to the time limits imposed by legislation. Ss.76 and 68 of the SDA and RRA respectively provide that:

(1) An [employment] tribunal shall not consider a complaint . . . unless it is presented to the tribunal before the end of the period of three months beginning when the act complained of was done . . . [29]
(5) [(6)[30]] A court or tribunal may nevertheless consider any such complaint . . . which is out of time if, in all the circumstances of the case, it considers that it is just and equitable to do so.[31]

[26] Though, as Bindman's article goes on to consider, no such inference was actually drawn in *Singh*.

[27] The CRE proposes this, in relation to private sector employers, only in relation to those having at least 250 employees (the EOC to all save private households).

[28] The Government has, however, issued monitoring guidelines for the public sector. These are available from the Cabinet Office at http://www.cabinet-office.gov.uk/ civilservice/1999/documents/equal_opportunities_monitoring_guidance_V2.pdf.

[29] Both the CRE and the EOC called in 1998, to no avail, for this to be extended to six months.

[30] RRA.

[31] In non-employment cases a questionnaire is available and the time limit is generally six months although this is subject to extension in some education cases involving notification requirements to the Secretary of State for Education.

The time-limits imposed by the EqPA are considered below. Schedule 3, para 3 of the DDA is in similar terms to ss.76 and 68 SDA and RRA, while Article 46(1) FETO establishes, as a time-limit: "whichever is the earlier of (a) the end of the period of three months beginning with the day on which the complainant first had knowledge, or might reasonably be expected first to have had had knowledge, of the act complained of, or (b) the end of the period of six months beginning with the day on which the act was done". Article 46(5) FETO is in similar terms to s.76(5) SDA above. Subsections 68(7) and 76(6) of the RRA and SDA go on to provide that:

For the purposes of this section
(a) when the inclusion of any term in a contract renders the making of the contract an unlawful act, that act shall be treated as extending throughout the duration of the contract; and
(b) any act extending over a period shall be treated as done at the end of that period; and
(c) a deliberate omission shall be treated as done when the person in question decided upon it; and in the absence of evidence establishing the contrary a person shall be taken for the purposes of this section to decide upon an omission when he does an act inconsistent with doing the omitted act or, if he has done no such inconsistent act, when the period expires within which he might reasonably have been expected to do the omitted act if it was to be done.

Again schedule 3 DDA is in similar terms as is Article 46(6) FETO.[32] Leaving aside, for the moment, the significance of ss.76(5)/ 68(6), it is clear from subsection 76(6)/68(7)(a) that, where the discrimination relates to a contractual term, the three month time limit applies only from the end date of the claimant's employment or, where this is sooner, from the removal of the offending term.[33] Of rather more controversial import is subsection (b), by virtue of which a doctrine of "continuing discrimination" has been developed which has permitted workers, on occasion, to sidestep the three month limitation period.

The courts have been at pains (in *Sougrin* v *Haringey Health Authority* [1992] IRLR 416 (CA), for example, in *Owusu* v *London Fire & Civil Defence Authority* [1995] IRLR 574 and in the FEA case of *Kearney* v *Northern Ireland Civil Service Commission*)[34] to distinguish "continuing acts" from "continuing consequences". Whereas any act of discrimination will have consequences which persist over time (a discriminatory dismissal or refusal to employ may result in a period of unemployment, a discriminatory refusal to promote may give rise to continuing financial losses), a "continuing act" refers to "some policy, rule or practice, in accordance with which decisions are taken

---

[32] Prior to its amendment in 1989, the FEA contained similar provisions (though the normal time-limit was then two months). These provisions were repealed by the FEA 1989.

[33] Attempts by the employer in *Barclays Bank plc* v *Kapur and Ors* to argue that the (allegedly discriminatory) refusal of the bank to credit, for pension purposes, the East African service of Asian employees who moved to Britain in the 1970s as a result of the "Africanisation" policies in that region, was a "deliberate omission" within s.68(7)(c) were dismissed by the House of Lords ([1991] 2 AC 355, [1991] 1 All ER 646, [1991] 2 WLR 401, [1991] ICR 208, [1991] IRLR 136).

[34] Court of Appeal, 16th February 1996, unreported.

from time to time" (*per* Mummery J in *Owusu*). In that case, a fire safety caseworker complained of a persistent failure on the part of his employers to promote, regrade, or shortlist him for promotion. The effect of EAT's acceptance that the "continuing act" complained of was the practice of discriminatorily excluding the applicant from regrading was that a race discrimination complaint which specified a number of failures on the part of the employer to regrade the applicant was within the three month time limit, despite the fact that more than three months had elapsed since the last act alleged.

A similar approach was taken by the Court of Appeal in *Cast v Croydon College* [1998] IRLR 319, [1998] ICR 500, which concerned a woman denied permission to transfer from full-time to part-time work after her return from maternity leave. The employer's written policy was one of "receptiveness to proposals for jobsharing at all levels", but Ms Cast was informed that it was essential for the holder of her post (information centre manager) to work full-time in order properly to coordinate the work of the centre's part-time employees. The applicant resigned a month after her return to work and made her sex discrimination claim two months later. The claim was rejected by an industrial tribunal and EAT on the grounds that the act of discrimination (if it was such an act) took place prior to the applicant's return from maternity leave (the date of her first request). The complaint, accordingly, was long out-of-time. Further, both the tribunal and EAT denied that the employer's refusal (despite repeated requests on Ms Cast's part) amounted to a policy. According to EAT (per Judge Hargrove):

> [t]he mere repetition of a request . . . cannot convert a single managerial decision into a policy, practice or rule. In the *Owusu* case, it does not hold that a series of refusals must amount to a practice. In our view, the tribunal was forced to the view that this was a single act and being a finding of fact after considering correctly the question of law, it cannot be impeached.

The Court of Appeal allowed Ms Cast's appeal.

Auld LJ (for the Court):

The fact that a specific act out of time may have continuing consequences within time does not make it an act extending over a period . . .[35]

As to an act extending over a period, the authorities make clear—at least in the case of discrimination in the field of employment under s 6 of the 1975 Act and s 4 of the 1976 Act[36] . . . that it is the existence of a policy or regime, not a specific act of an employer

---

[35] Citing *Amies v Inner London Education Authority* [1977] ICR 308 EAT—failure to appoint to a position; and *Sougrin v Haringey Health Authority* [1992] IRLR 416 CA—refusal to upgrade an employee. For a decision on this issue under the FEA (as it then was) see *Kearney v Northern Irish Civil Service Commission* [1996] NI 415.

[36] *Cf* Brooke LJ in *Rovenska v General Medical Council* [1997] IRLR 367 on s.12 of the RRA, which deals with professional qualifications. Auld LJ in *Cast* appeared to doubt this which was, in any event, *obiter*, no discriminatory policy being required where the complaint follows within three months of the last act alleged.

triggering its application to the complainant, that matters. A moment's consideration of the concluding words of s 76(6)(b) "any act extending over a period shall be treated as done at the end of that period" (my emphasis)—shows that that must be so. If the "act extending over a period" required a specific act by an employer to give it effect there would be no need or room to "treat . . . it as done at the end of the period" . . .

There may be a policy or regime for this purpose even though it is not of a formal nature or expressed in writing; and it may be confined to a particular post or role[37] . . .

The passage from . . . Judge Hargrove's judgment [above] confuses the question whether the repetition of requests, and it would seem corresponding refusals, can convert a single decision into a policy with the question whether there was a single decision or several decisions. His conclusions that the industrial tribunal had been "forced to the view that this was a single act" and, implicitly, that it had so found are not, in my judgment, justified on the material before the tribunal or evident from the way it expressed its findings . . .

To acknowledge that there may be successive acts of discrimination in this way does not negate the time bar provided by s 76, provided that decision-makers make clear in responding to further requests whether they have reconsidered the matter. If they have, time begins to run again; if they have not, and merely refer the complainant to their previous decision, no new period of limitation arises. However, where the successive acts are such as to indicate and/or are pursuant to a policy or regime, different considerations arise . . .

Tribunals remain free to disapply time limits if they regard it as just and equitable so to do (SDA, s.76(5); RRA, s.68(6); DDA, schedule 3, para 3(2)) FETO Article 46(5)). This discretion is much wider than that afforded under the Employment Rights Act 1996, s.111(2) of which provides that a tribunal "shall not consider" a claim made out-of-time unless made "within such further period as the tribunal considers reasonable in a case where it is satisfied that it was not reasonably practicable" for the complaint to be presented in time. Nor will EAT readily overturn the exercise of such discretion. In *Director of Public Prosecutions and another* v *Marshall*, a tribunal exercised its powers under s.76(5) SDA to allow an out-of-time sex discrimination claim brought in the wake of *P* v *S & Cornwall* (Case C–13/94) [1996] ECR I–2143, [1996] All ER (EC) 397, [1996] IRLR 347 (see Chapters 3 and 6).[38] The claim was brought by a transsexual whose job offer was withdrawn when he announced that he would take up his position as a woman, and was filed within three months of the decision in *P* v *S* below. The respondents claimed that the interests of legal certainty were against such an extension of the time limit.

---

[37] Citing *Owusu* and Lord Griffiths in *Barclays Bank* v *Kapur* who, in turn, cited with approval a passage from the judgment of Bristow J in *Amies*: "So, if the employers operated a rule that the position of head of department was open to men only, for as long as the rule was in operation there would be a continuing discrimination and anyone considering herself to have been discriminated against because of the rule would have three months from the time when the rule was abrogated within which to bring the complaint."

[38] See also *British Coal Corporation* v *Keeble and others* [1997] IRLR 336. In *Aniagwu* v *London Borough of Hackney, Thompson's European and Employment Law Review* 34, available at *http://www.thompsons.law.co.uk/ltext/ libindex.htm*, EAT ruled that a tribunal ought to have allowed an extension of time where one day over was due in part to the respondent's delay in processing the appeal.

Director of Public Prosecutions and another v *Marshall* [1998] ICR 518 [1998] IRLR 494

Morison J:

... The proposition that to allow the applicant to present her complaint offends against the principle of legal certainty begs the question: what is the nature and extent of the principle? There are, as it seems to us, a number of general factors which suggest that every mature legal system should adopt limitation provisions, of which legal certainty is but one. The state has an interest in avoiding trials of actions which are so stale that justice cannot be seen to have been done. If all the evidence is so stale that it is inherently unreliable, then the parties' rights cannot be judicially determined Further, the citizens of the state have an interest in not being troubled by proceedings brought long after the event people are entitled to arrange their affairs on the basis that what happened in the past is, after a defined period, over and done with. But, equally, citizens are to be allowed a reasonable opportunity to bring their legitimate grievances to the court . . . legal certainty does not require that a person's perception of his rights to bring a valid complaint cannot be taken into account in every case . . . Some discretionary provisions will permit the court to take that factor into account; some will not. It is a question of construction of the words used which determines the answer.

In this legislation, the [SDA], the court's power to extend time is on the basis of what is just and equitable. These words could not be wider or more general. The question is whether it would be just or equitable to deny a person the right to bring proceedings when they were reasonably unaware of the fact that they had the right to bring them until shortly before the complaint was filed. That unawareness might stem from a failure by the lawyers to appreciate that such a claim lay, or because the law "changed" or was differently perceived after a particular decision of another court. The answer is that in some cases it will be fair to extend time and in others it will not. The industrial tribunal must balance all the factors which are relevant, including, importantly and perhaps crucially, whether it is now possible to have a fair trial of the issues raised by the complaint. Reasonable awareness of the right to sue is but one factor . . .

It is arguably the case that EAT was obliged under the terms of the equal treatment directive to exercise its discretion in favour of Ms Marshall. The ECJ has accepted that Member States may impose time limits in respect of claims based on Community law provided (*Rewe-Zentralfinanz eG* v *Landwirtschaftskammer fur das Saarland* (Case C–33/76) [1976] ECR 1989) that they are no less favourable for such actions than for similar rights of a domestic nature, and that they do not render the exercise of rights conferred by Community law impossible in practice. The difficulty which arises relates to claims in respect of which the relevant national time limit has expired before a Member State has properly implemented the EC legislation. In *Emmott* v *Minister for Social Welfare and Attorney General*, Case C–208/90 [1991] IRLR 387 the ECJ ruled that, while time limits were acceptable within the provisos established by *Rewe*, the obligation on Member States to implement EC law must be taken to provide that, until a directive had been properly transposed, Member States could not rely on delay against an individual seeking to exercise rights granted by that directive.

The approach taken by the ECJ in *Emmott* would appear to indicate that no time limits could be applied in respect of European-related claims until after the relevant

EC law has been properly implemented by Member States. Thus, where inadequacies of transposition become apparent in future years, the three month time limit would not begin to run until after further amendments. But the result of this application of *Emmott* would be such as to do away, in practice, with the principle, discussed in Chapter 1, that directives, as distinct from a number of Treaty provisions and other EC legislation, do not have horizontal direct effect.

If *Emmott* were to be applied in all its logic by the ECJ, private actors (in this case, employers) would be rendered liable, perhaps long after the event, for breaches of EC law of which they were unaware and could not have been aware at the time of the breach. The rationale behind *Marshall* and *Francovich and others* v *Italian Republic*, joined cases C–6/90 and C–9/90 [1995] ICR 722; [1991] ECR I–5357, ECJ [1992] IRLR 84 ECJ (see Chapter 1) has been, in part, to encourage compliance with EC law by Member States otherwise tardy in the transposition of directives. But no such logic applies in relation to private sector actors such as employers who would be caught by any wide application of the *Emmott* principle.

It was perhaps the recognition of this dilemma which caused the about-turn taken by the ECJ in the *Steenhorst-Neerings* v *Bestuur van de Bedrijfsvereniging voor Detailhandel, Ambachten en Huisvrouwen* (Case C–338/91 [1993] ECR I–4575 and *Johnson* v *Chief Adjudication Officer (No 2)* (Case C–410/92 [1994] ECR I–5483) cases. Both concerned Council Directive 79/7 and, in particular, national rules which limited the back-dating of benefits to one year prior to any claim made. In both cases, the plaintiffs sought the non-application of the limit on the grounds that the social security legislation in question had not previously provided for equal treatment as required by the directive. Both applicants argued that their claims should be back-dated to the end of 1984, the date when the Netherlands and the UK should properly have transposed the directive so as to provide for equality in respect of the benefits at issue. But, while Advocate General Damon took the view, in *Steenhorst-Neerings*, that *Emmott* mandated a decision favourable to the applicant in the instant case, the Court distinguished the earlier case on the grounds that, while it related to time-limits, *Steenhorst-Neerings* concerned back-dating. Time limits, according to the ECJ, served to ensure that the legality of administrative decisions could not be challenged indefinitely. Limitations on backdating of benefit claims, on the other hand, served the interests of sound administration and financial balance. The Court did not, however, explain why the latter, but not the former, trumped the principle of equality.[39]

In *Denkavit Internationaal BV* v *Kamer van Hopophandel en Fabrieken voor Middengelderland*, Case C–2/94 [1996] ECR I–2827 [1996] 3 CMLR 504, Advocate-General Jacobs suggested that *Emmott* was properly understood, in the light of the intervening decisions:

> as establishing the principle that a Member State may not rely on a limitation period where a Member State is in default both in falling to implement a directive and in obstructing the

---

[39] In *Johnson* the ECJ relied on *Steenhorst*.

exercise of a judicial remedy in reliance upon it, or perhaps where the delay in exercising remedy and hence the failure to meet the time limit—is in some other way due to the conduct of the national authority. In *Emmott*, the delay had been caused by the state itself, the administrative authorities refusing to adjudicate the applicant's social security claim until litigation in a relevant case had been concluded.[40] A further factor in *Emmott* was that the applicant was in the particularly unprotected position of an individual dependent on social welfare.

Seen in those terms, the *Emmott* judgment may be regarded as an application of the well-established principle that the exercise of Community rights must not be rendered "excessively difficult" . . . That view is consistent with the Court's remark in *Johnson* that the time bar in *Emmott* "had the result of depriving the applicant of any opportunity whatever to rely on her right to equal treatment under the Directive," whereas the application of the rules in *Steenhorst-Neerings* and *Johnson* did not "make it impossible to exercise rights based on the Directive." . . .

The *Emmott* judgment may nevertheless be seen as a new application of that principle in so far as it demonstrates that a national court may be obliged to set aside a limitation period which is in principle unobjectionable where the special circumstances of the particular case so demand. It seems to me, in the interests of legal certainty the obligation to set aside time limits should be confined to wholly exceptional circumstances such as those in *Emmott*.

Particular problems have arisen concerning the time limits applicable in respect of claims related to Article 141 (ex Article 119) of the Treaty Establishing the European Community. In *Biggs* v *Somerset County Council* and in *Barber* v *Staffordshire County Council* [1996] ICR 379, [1996] IRLR 209 (both cases are further discussed below), the applicants sought to argue that the time-limit in respect of claims based on Article 141 could not begin to run until the provision had been implemented in UK law. Both cases arose in the wake of the House of Lords decision in *EOC* v *Secretary of State for Employment* and were brought by women who, having been dismissed from part-time employment with less than the five years' service then required for redundancy pay/unfair dismissal claims, sought to make their claims years after dismissal. Their claims were rejected and their appeals dismissed by both EAT and the Court of Appeal. In Chapter 1 we considered whether Article 141 gave rise to "free-standing" rights enforceable in the tribunal system (the Court of Appeal in *Biggs* and *Barber* declared that it does not). Here we consider the issued raised in relation to time limits only.

Neill LJ considered a number of ECJ cases including those in *Amministrazione Delle Finanze Dello Stato* v *San Giorgio* Case C–811/79 [1980] ECR 2545 [1983] ECR 3595, *Johnson* v *Chief Adjudication Officer*, *Francovich* and *Rewe*. From *Rewe* he cited the following extract before going on to consider the case before him:

Biggs v Somerset County Council [1996] IRLR 203

In the absence of Community rules on this subject, it is for the domestic legal system of each Member State to designate courts having jurisdiction and to determine the procedural

---

[40] *McDermott* v *Minister for Social Welfare* Case C–286/85 [1987] ECR 1453.

conditions governing actions at law intended to ensure the protection of the rights which citizens have from the direct effect of Community law, it being understood that such conditions cannot be less favourable than those relating to similar actions of a domestic nature . . . The position would be different only if the conditions and time limits made it impossible in practice to exercise the rights which the national courts are obliged to protect.

Neill LJ

It was . . . argued on behalf of Mrs Biggs that the statutory time limit should be disapplied because its application would run counter to the principle that it must not be impossible or extremely difficult to present a claim . . .

   In reliance on the decision in *Emmott* . . . it was argued on . . . that the council could not rely on any time limit until UK law had been brought into conformity with Community law. It is necessary to consider this argument first in relation to Article [141]. It is clear from the decision of the ECJ in *Francovich* . . . that even where a Directive is capable of having direct effect, an individual cannot rely on its terms while the Directive is unimplemented. Until implemented it has no force of law in the relevant jurisdiction, though the fact that it has not been implemented may give rights to compensation. . . . But a provision in the Treaty itself which has direct effect stands on a different basis. Thus the validity of Article [141] in UK law does not depend on any implementation by the UK Parliament; it is part of UK law. It follows therefore in my view that the principle set out in *Emmott, supra*, has no application to a claim involving Article [141]. Indeed, it is to be noted that in paragraph 17 of the judgment in *Emmott* attention was drawn to the "particular nature of Directives".[41]

Biggs and *Barber* v *Staffordshire* fell at the time-limits imposed by the ERA, the claims relating to unfair dismissal and redundancy (albeit interpreted in light of Article 141's equality guarantee). In *Preston* v *Wolverhampton NHS Trust*, the time limit at issue was that imposed by s.2(4) EqPA.

s.2 EqPA

(1) No claim in respect of the operation of an equality clause relating to a woman's employment shall be referred to an industrial tribunal . . . if she has not been employed in the employment within the six months preceding the date of the reference.

This provision appears more generous than the position under the SDA, RRA, DDA or the FETO, discussed above. Having said this, the anti-discrimination legislation does not treat time as running from the point at which a discriminatory contractual term is imposed, the act of imposing a discriminatory term being treated as "extending throughout the duration of the contract".[42] In addition, while the SDA and RRA permit the time limit to be extended where such extension is "just and equi-

---

[41] Nor did the Court of Appeal accept that Ms Biggs could rely on the non-conformity of UK law at the time of her dismissal to bring an *Emmott* claim under the Equal Pay Directive: "The Equal Pay Directive was adopted in order to implement the principle in Article 141. In these circumstances it does not seem to me that the Equal Pay Directive conferred any new or separate right".

[42] See above.

table" (and the ERA where an earlier claim was not "reasonably practicable"), the six month period imposed by the EqPA is absolute.

In *Preston and others* v *Wolverhampton Healthcare NHS Trust and others; Fletcher and others* v *Midland Bank plc* ECJ considered the compatibility of s 2(4) with Community law. The applicants had been denied access to occupational pension schemes by virtue of their part-time status. The ECJ had ruled, in *Vroege* v *NCIV Institut voor Volkshuisvesting BV* Case C–57/93 [1995] All ER (EC) 193, [1995] ICR 635, [1994] ECR I–4541, ECJ, [1994] IRLR 651,[43] that Article 141 entitled women and men to equal access to membership of pension schemes (as well as to payments thereunder). *Barber* v *Guardian Royal Exchange* imposed a time constraint on equal pay claims relating to pension *payments* (the ECJ permitting claims in relation to pension payments in respect of service prior to the date of judgment only where the claims were filed before the date of the *Barber* v *Guardian Royal Exchange* judgment). But, according to the Court in *Vroege*, that time limit did not apply to claims relating to the denial of *membership* on grounds of sex.

Preston was among the tens of thousands of women who launched equal pay claims in the wake of the *Vroege* decision. A number of cases were selected in order that preliminary issues such as time limits could be resolved. These claims, of which Preston's was one, were rejected by a tribunal, EAT and the Court of Appeal. One of the stumbling blocks concerned the six month timelimit imposed by the EqPA. Many of the women had left employment years before commencing their actions. Others had been employed on a succession of fixed term contracts. Of this group, even those who had filed their claims while they were still working were met with the ruling that the six month period flowed from the end of each successive contract of employment, with the result that their claims in relation to earlier periods of employment were out of time.

All arguments advanced to the effect that the EqPA's six month limit conflicted with EC law were rejected. In response to the argument that the limit made it impossible in practice for applicants to press their Article 141 claims, the courts followed the approach taken by the Court of Appeal in *Biggs* and said that, Article 141 being directly enforceable by individuals in the national courts, the applicants could have challenged their exclusion from the pension schemes at the time. Nor did the courts accept that the time limits imposed by the EqPA were less favourable than those which applied elsewhere (such as the RRA, whose three month time limit could be extended). In the first place, the courts ruled that the EqPA's limits applied whether cases were based solely on national law or whether they emanated from Article 141. On this basis, there was no discrimination against European law claims.[44] Secondly,

---

[43] See also *Dietz* v *Stichting Thuiszorg Rotterdam* ECR I–5223 [1996] IRLR 692 Case C–435/93 [1996] and *Fisscher* v *Voorhuis Hengelo* Case C–128/93 [1994] ECR I–4583, [1994] ICR 635, [1994] IRLR 662, though (in the case of a contributory pension) the right to retroactive membership depended on the employee making the appropriate contributions. The *Barber* time limits do not apply in relation to joining pension schemes, as distinct from payments received thereunder.

[44] This aspect of the decision will be questioned below.

even if it was appropriate to look beyond the EqPA, the *Rewe* decision did not oblige the courts:

> to cast around the whole of domestic law in order to discover some other legislation . . . which is concerned with some other sort of equality in order to see whether the limitation periods in that Statute are in certain circumstances more generous than those in the [EqPA]. Our domestic law as no doubt the domestic law of other Member States, has innumerable different time limits in relation to innumerable different situations. Some of those time limits incorporate a certain degree of flexibility, (I accept that in the employment field no other claim has a completely rigid time limit which cannot be disapplied by the court) others do not. It is not, and could not be, suggested that this in itself is contrary to Community law. What is objectionable is discrimination in the treatment of similar claims as between claims based on domestic law and claims based on Community law. That does not exist in the present cases.[45]

Preston was appealed to the House of Lords which referred to the ECJ the question whether the six month time limit imposed by the EqPA rendered it "impossible" or "excessively difficult" for applicants to exercise their Article 141 rights, and whether the different time limits which applied to equal pay and other claims (including contractual claims) breached European law. Their Lordships referred similar questions dealing with the two year limit on compensation, which issue is considered in Chapter 10. They agreed, however, with the lower courts that, in the case of successive fixed term contracts, the six month period ran from the end of each contract rather than the end of the final period of employment.

Preston and others v *Wolverhampton Healthcare NHS Trust and others; Fletcher and others* v *Midland Bank plc* (ECJ, available at http://europa.eu.int/eur-lex/en/index.html)

33. As regards the compatibility of a time requirement, such as that contained in section 2(4) of the [EqPA], with the Community-law principle of effectiveness, it is settled case-law, and has been since *Rewe* . . . that the setting of reasonable limitation periods for bringing proceedings satisfies that requirement in principle, inasmuch as it constitutes an application of the fundamental principle of legal certainty . . .

34. Contrary to the contention of the claimants in the main proceedings, the imposition of a limitation period of six months, as laid down in section 2(4) of the EPA, even if, by definition, expiry of that period entails total or partial dismissal of their actions, cannot be regarded as constituting an obstacle to obtaining the payment of sums to which, albeit not yet payable, the claimants are entitled under Article 119 [now Art. 141] of the Treaty. Such a limitation period does not render impossible or excessively difficult the exercise of rights conferred by the Community legal order and is not therefore liable to strike at the very essence of those rights.

35. The answer to the first part of the first question must therefore be that Community law does not preclude a national procedural rule which requires that a claim for membership of an occupational pension scheme (from which the right to pension benefits flows)

---

[45] Nor did the court accept that the treatment of Article 141 claims was less favourable than that accorded under the RRA.

must, if it is not to be time-barred, be brought within six months of the end of the employment to which the claim relates, provided, however, that that limitation period is not less favourable for actions . . .

This part of the ECJ's judgement dealt only with the first limb of *Rewe* – the demand that domestic procedural limitations on the exercise of EC rights must not be such as to render them impossible in practice or excessively difficult to pursue. The ECJ went on to deal with the question whether the six month time limit imposed by the EqPA was less favourable than that which applied to the exercise of similar rights under domestic law. The Court of Appeal had taken the view that the appropriate comparison was between those equal pay claims which did and those which did not rely on Community law, both being governed by the EqPA's limitation. By contrast, the applicants argued that the appropriate comparison was with the time-limits established by the SDA and RRA (which, as we saw above, although, shorter, are not absolute) or that applied to claims for breach of contract (six years). The House of Lords referred to the ECJ a question on the appropriate comparison.

Between the date of reference and that of the ECJ's decision, the latter had handed down judgment in *Levez* v *Jennings (Harlow Pools) Ltd* Case C–326/96 [1999] All ER (EC)1, [1999] 36 in which, dealing with s.2(5) EqPA (discussed in Chapter 10), that court ruled that the comparison required by *Rewe* could not be made between Article 141 claims, on the one hand, and EqPA claims, on the other: "the [EqPA] is the domestic legislation which gives effect to the Community principle of non-discrimination on grounds of sex in relation to pay, pursuant to Article [141] of the Treaty and the [Equal Pay] Directive. Accordingly . . . the fact that the same procedural rules [there s.2(5) EqPA] apply to two comparable claims, one relying on a right conferred by Community law, the other on a right acquired under domestic law, is not enough to ensure compliance with the principle of equivalence, as the United Kingdom Government maintains, since one and the same form of action is involved".

In *Preston*, the ECJ reached a similar conclusion. Although it was for the domestic courts to determine the question of discrimination as between Community and domestic claims:

52. . . . the [EqPA] constitutes the legislation by means of which the United Kingdom discharges its obligations under Article [141] of the Treaty and, subsequently, under the [Equal Pay] Directive. The Act cannot therefore provide an appropriate ground of comparison against which to measure compliance with the principle of equivalence . . .

57. in order to determine whether a right of action available under domestic law is a domestic action similar to proceedings to give effect to rights conferred by Article [141] of the Treaty, the national court must consider whether the actions concerned are similar as regards their purpose, cause of action and essential characteristics.

63. . . . in order to decide whether procedural rules are equivalent, the national court must verify objectively, in the abstract, whether the rules at issue are similar taking into account the role played by those rules in the procedure as a whole, as well as the operation of that procedure and any special features of those rules.

Finally, the ECJ dealt with the question of how the six month time limit should apply in the case of successive fixed term contracts:

67. . . . the Court has held that the setting of reasonable limitation periods is compatible with Community law inasmuch as the fundamental principle of legal certainty is thereby applied. Such limitation periods cannot therefore be regarded as capable of rendering virtually impossible or excessively difficult the exercise of rights conferred by Community law.

68. Whilst it is true that legal certainty also requires that it be possible to fix precisely the starting point of a limitation period, the fact nevertheless remains that, in the case of successive short-term contracts of the kind referred to in the third question, setting the starting point of the limitation period at the end of each contract renders the exercise of the right conferred by Article [141] of the Treaty excessively difficult.

69. Where, however, there is a stable relationship resulting from a succession of short-term contracts concluded at regular intervals in respect of the same employment to which the same pension scheme applies, it is possible to fix a precise starting point for the limitation period.

70. There is no reason why that starting point should not be fixed as the date on which the sequence of such contracts has been interrupted through the absence of one or more of the features that characterise a stable employment relationship of that kind, either because the periodicity of such contracts has been broken or because the new contract does not relate to the same employment as that to which the same pension scheme applies . . .

72. . . . Community law precludes a procedural rule which has the effect of requiring a claim for membership of an occupational pension scheme (from which the right to pension benefits flows) to be brought within six months of the end of each contract of employment to which the claim relates where there has been a stable employment relationship resulting from a succession of short-term contracts concluded at regular intervals in respect of the same employment to which the same pension scheme applies.

INDIVIDUAL REMEDIES

There are very significant differences in this area between the SDA and the RRA, on the one hand, and the FETO and, to a lesser extent, the DDA, on the other (the remedies under the EqPA are considered in chapter 10). The approach taken by the SDA and RRA will be considered here, those of the DDA and FETO (to the extent that they differ from the RRA and SDA), below. Sections 65, and 56 and Article 39 respectively of the SDA, the RRA and the FETO provide that remedies may consist of:

(a) an order declaring the rights of the complainant and the respondent in relation to the act to which the complaint relates;
(b) an order requiring the respondent to pay to the complainant compensation . . .
(c) a recommendation that the respondent take within a specified period action appearing to the tribunal to be practicable for the purpose of obviating or reducing the

adverse effect on the complainant of any act of discrimination to which the complaint relates.[46]

S.8 DDA is in similar terms, save that "practicable" in (c) is substituted by the words "reasonable, in all the circumstances of the case". Declarations and recommendations are almost never made under the SDA or RRA.[47] In 1998 the CRE criticised the individualistic focus of s.56(c) RRA and proposed that it be widened to allow tribunals to make recommendations "regarding the future conduct of the respondent to prevent further acts of discrimination", including recommendations "regarding any of the respondent's practices or procedures which have been at issue and future treatment of the applicant by the respondent . . . whether or not she or he remains in employment".[48] In the same year the EOC criticised the narrow range of remedies available and called for powers to be given to tribunals to order "reinstatement, re-engagement, appointment, or promotion as appropriate" as well as "action needed to end the discrimination [against] the person bringing the complaint *and anyone else who might be affected* (my emphasis)".

Article 39(1)(d) FETO, by contrast with the corresponding provisions of the SDA, RRA and DDA, permits the Equality Commission to recommend:

> that the respondent take within a specified period action appearing to the Tribunal to be practicable for the purpose of obviating or reducing the adverse effect on a person *other than the complainant* of any unlawful discrimination to which the complaint relates.[49]

This power to make recommendations was amended to this effect only in 1998, the previous legislation having been in similar terms to the SDA and RRA. Even before this amendment, the use of recommendations under the fair employment legislation has been vastly more common than under the other provisions. It is important to note here that, whereas pre-tribunal hearing conciliation is attempted, in RRA and SDA cases, by ACAS; conciliation in fair employment cases falls within the remit of the Equality Commission (previously the FEC) in Northern Ireland. Further, when cases do come to court, they are heard by the specialist Fair Employment Tribunal rather than, as is the case in relation to the SDA, RRA (and DDA), the generalist employment tribunals.

Settlements account, in Northern Ireland, for many more fair employment cases than do tribunal determinations in favour of applicants. The same is true under the SDA, RRA and DDA in Great Britain.[50] But, whereas information about the

[46] In *Prestcold v Irvine* [1981] ICR 777 the Court of Appeal ruled that recommendations were confined to non-monetary matters—they could not include a recommendation as to wages.

[47] G. Chambers and G. Horton, *Promoting Sex Equality: The Role of Industrial Tribunals* (London: Policy Studies Institute, 1990).

[48] Fn 5 above.

[49] This provision was included in the 1998 Order after pressure from the FEC.

[50] According to Tribunal Statistics 1993–95 69 *Equal Opportunities Review*, p.26, in 1993–4 around 30% and in 1994–5 around 25% of all sex and race discrimination and equal pay cases were conciliated by ACAS. 9% and 7% of cases were successful at tribunal, 17% and 13% were dismissed and 44% and 53% respectively were withdrawn.

settlements reached under the auspices of ACAS and otherwise is hard to access, the FEC in Northern Ireland published details of settlements reached under the fair employment legislation. Such settlements almost invariably included apologies and undertakings on the part of the employer. Undertakings commonly made included agreements to liaise with the FEC to ensure an "adequate and effective" equal opportunities policy, to create "a harmonious working environment", or to take "pro-active action on sectarian harassment", together with a review of equal opportunities policies.[51]

By far the most common remedy under the SDA and RRA (though still only awarded in a minority of successful cases—see below) is compensation which, until 1993 and 1994 respectively, was capped (most recently at £11 000). The SDA cap was removed in the wake of the decision in *Marshall v Southampton and South-West Hampshire Area Health Authority (No 2)* (Case 271/91) [1993] IRLR 445, in which the ECJ ruled that it contravened the equal treatment directive, and a Private Member's Bill amended the RRA similarly.[52] The FEA's £30 000 cap was removed in 1994 while compensation payable under the DDA, passed after the removal of the other caps in respect of the other forms of discrimination, was never subject to a statutory maximum.

The SDA, RRA and FETO (but not the DDA) contain prohibitions on indirect discrimination. Respondents could avoid the award of compensation (ss.66(3) SDA, 57(3) RRA and 26(2) FEA) by proving "that the requirement or condition in question was not applied with the intention of treating the claimant unfavourably on the ground of" sex, race, married status, religious belief or political opinion. Quite what was meant by "intentional" as distinct from "unintentional" discrimination was not clear until 1995, when EAT reached its decision in *London Underground v Edwards* [1995] IRLR 355. EAT ruled that an intention to apply the disputed requirement or condition, coupled with the knowledge of its impact on the claimant as a member of the group upon which it impacted disadvantageously, sufficed.[53]

The *London Underground* case was brought under the SDA, but a similar decision was reached under the RRA the following year in *JH Walker Ltd v Hussain & Others* [1996] ICR 291, [1996] IRLR 11. There, EAT upheld an award of damages made to a number of Moslems who were disciplined for taking time off during Eid contrary to their employer's recently adopted rule that non-statutory holidays could not be taken during the summer months. According to Mummery J, for the Court:

> as a matter of ordinary English, "intention" in this context signifies the state of mind of a person who, at the time when he does the relevant act (ie the application of the requirement or condition resulting in indirect discrimination),

---

[51] These from four settlements reported 11th March 1997, press report on FEC's website at *www.fec-ni.org*.

[52] Sex Discrimination and Equal Pay (Remedies) Regulations 1993 SI 1993/2798; Race Relations (Remedies) Act 1994.

[53] *Cf* B. Hepple, "Have Twenty-five Years of the Race Relation Acts in Britain Been a Failure?", in B. Hepple and E. Szyszczak, *Discrimination: The Limits of Law* (London: Mansell, 1992), 19, at 22.

(a) wants to bring about the state of affairs which constitutes the prohibited result of unfavourable treatment on racial grounds; and

(b) knows that that prohibited result will follow from his acts . . .

Depending on the circumstances, a tribunal may infer that a person wants to produce certain consequences from the fact that he acted knowing what those consequences would be . . .[54]

In the period between *London Underground* and *Walker*, the SDA was amended to permit compensation for employment-related unintentional indirect discrimination where the tribunal regarded such compensation as "just and equitable'. This action was prompted, it seems, by the government's fear that it would be subject to legal action under *Frankovich* (above),[55] in the wake of a number of tribunal decisions that the SDA did not comply with the equal treatment directive and the decision of EAT in *Macmillan* v *Edinburgh Voluntary Organisations Council* (unreported, EAT/1995/536) that the SDA's "unambiguous" provisions could not be interpreted so as to permit an award in respect of unintentional discrimination). When the FEAs 1976 and 1989 were amended and consolidated into the FETO 1998, a similar change was made. No such amendment has yet been made in respect of the RRA, although the government has indicated its willingness to do so.

The heads of compensation payable under the RRA and SDA were set out by the Court of Appeal in *Alexander* v *Home Office* [1988] 2 All ER 118, [1988] 1 WLR 968, [1988] ICR 685, [1988] IRLR 190.

May LJ:

. . . damages for this relatively new tort of unlawful racial discrimination are at large, that is to say that they are not limited to the pecuniary loss that can be specifically proved . . . compensatory damages may and in some instances should include an element of aggravated damages where, for example, the defendant may have behaved in a high-handed, malicious, insulting or oppressive manner in committing the act of discrimination . . .[56] The material passage from Lord Diplock's speech in *Cassell & Co Ltd* v *Broome* [[1972] 1 All ER 801 at 836, 869] is in these terms:

The three heads under which damages are recoverable for those torts for which damages are "at large" are classified under the following heads. (1) Compensation for the harm caused to the plaintiff by the wrongful physical act of the defendant in respect of which the action is brought. In addition to any pecuniary loss specifically proved the assessment of this compensation may itself involve putting a money value upon physical hurt, as in assault on curtailment of liberty, as in false imprisonment or malicious prosecution on injury to reputation, as in defamation, false imprisonment and malicious prosecution on inconvenience or disturbance of the even tenor of life, as in

---

[54] *Cf Orphanos* v *Queen Mary College* [1985] IRLR 349. See also *Hussain* v *Streamline Taxis* 10th November 1997 36 EORDCLD, pp.12–13.

[55] S.65(1B)(b), as inserted by the Sex Discrimination and Equal Pay (Miscellaneous Amendments) Regulations 1996 SI 1996 No 438.

[56] Citing *Rookes* v *Barnard* [1964] AC 1129, p.1221 *per* Lord Devlin, *Cassell & Co Ltd* v *Broome* [1972] AC 1027, p.1085, 1124 *per* Lord Reid and Lord Diplock.

many torts, including intimidation. (2) Additional compensation for the injured feel-ings of the plaintiff where his sense of injury resulting from the wrongful physical act is justifiably heightened by the manner in which or motive for which the defendant did it. This Lord Devlin calls "aggravated damages". (3) Punishment of the defendant for his anti-social behaviour to the plaintiff. This Lord Devlin calls "exemplary damages".

Although damages for racial discrimination will in many cases be analogous to those for defamation, they are not necessarily the same. In the latter the principal injury to be com-pensated is that to the plaintiff's reputation I doubt whether this will play a large part in the former. On the other hand, if the plaintiff knows of the racial discrimination and that he has thereby been held up to "hatred, ridicule or contempt", then the injury to his feel-ings will be an important element in the damages . . . in the substantial majority of dis-crimination cases the unlawful conduct will cause personal hurt in the sense of injury to feelings . . . I do not think that this must "inevitably" follow. A proper inference to draw in a case such as this may be that the discrimination will cause a plaintiff "hurt" of a particu-lar kind. But, unless the court can and feels it right to draw that inference, then the mere fact that a defendant is guilty of racial discrimination is not in my opinion in itself a factor affecting damages . . .

The ruling of the Court of Appeal that exemplary damages were available in race (and, by implication, sex) discrimination cases was followed by the Court of Appeal in *City of Bradford Metropolitan Council* v *Arora* [1991] 2 QB 507, [1991] 3 All ER 545, [1991] 2 WLR 1377, [1991] ICR 226, [1991] IRLR 165. But the Court of Appeal in *Gibbons* v *South West Water Services Ltd* [1993] 2 WLR 507 held that *Arora* was not binding, and ruled that exemplary damages were available in respect of torts, whether statutory or common law, which existed prior to the decision of the House of Lords in *Rookes* v *Barnard* [1964] AC 1129. On this view, such damages were not available in respect of sex or race discrim-ination.[57] Nor, according to Northern Ireland's Court of Appeal in *McConnell* v *Police Authority for Northern Ireland*,[58] were they available under the FEA.[59]

The FEC called, in 1998, for exemplary damages to be awardable under the FEA (as it then was)[60] and for the FET to have the power to order continuing financial pay-ments until a stipulated event such as a promotion occurred. Neither request was acceded to by government, this despite much criticism of the *Gibbons* decision. Amongst this criticism was that of the Law Commission in *Aggravated, Exemplary and Restitutionary Damages* (Consultation Paper No. 132):

To assert that the role of the law of civil wrongs is only to provide compensation, or less restrictively does not at least include punitive aims [this being the basis for the decision in *Gibbons*], is to assume what is at issue and fails to address the question of policy involved.

[57] See *Deane* v *Ealing London Borough Council and Anor* [1993] ICR 329, [1993] IRLR 209, EAT.
[58] (1997) CARF 2410.
[59] See also *O'Cara* v *Limivady District Council* NICA 6th April 1995, unreported. SACHR's proposal (SACHR—Employment Equality: Building for the Future (HMSO, cm 3684, June 1997)) that exemplary damages be specifically permitted under the FEA (as it then was) was not acted upon by the government.
[60] Fn 7 above, para 1.87. The FEC also recommended, para 1.93, that interim orders should be available in FE cases to maintain the *status quo*.

Both the FEC and the CRE have also called, unsuccessfully, for continuing damages to be made available in discrimination cases in order that pressure could be brought to bear upon employers to take remedial action promptly.

The levels of compensation typically awarded in sex and race discrimination cases have been far from high.[61] Whereas, in the US, discrimination awards can run to millions of dollars, in the period between the removal of the statutory caps on compensation (22nd November 1993 and 3rd March 1994 in sex and race cases respectively) and the end of 1995, over 20% of both sex and race discrimination awards[62] were for less than £1,000 and just over and just under 75% of sex and race discrimination awards were for less than £5,000. Only 10% of race discrimination awards, and 8% of sex discrimination awards, were in excess of £10,000.[63]

While the courts have, in the past, appeared eager not to earn public disapproval by making excessively large awards, they have appeared less fearful of breeding contempt for the law by making very small ones. Perhaps of even more concern is the fact that the majority of successful sex and race discrimination claims do not result in the award of any compensation: in 1995/6, for example, only 30% and 35% respectively of successful race and sex discrimination claims led to the award of compensation. And in the same time frame, only 19% and 38% respectively of those race and sex discrimination claims heard by tribunals resulted in findings in favour of the applicant. In all, only 6% of the minority of race discrimination complainants who had their cases heard (13% of sex discrimination complainants), received any award at all.

A significant proportion of discrimination compensation generally consists of an award for injury to feelings (this being the largest factor, frequently, in sexual harassment claims). Compensation in respect of personal injury also features in some harassment awards such as that in *Stubbs* v *Chief Constable of Lincolnshire Police & Walker* (ET, 41 *EORDCLD* 8) in which a tribunal awarded £41,500 in respect of injury to feelings and personal injury to a woman who suffered symptoms akin to Post Traumatic Stress Disorder and was forced to retire on medical grounds after 14 months of severe harassment by her line manager.[64]

Prior to EAT's decision in *Armitage, Marsden & HM Prison Service* v *Johnson* [1997] IRLR 162, and even after the abolition of the compensation limits in 1993–94, tribunals continued to apply the decision of the Court of Appeal in *North West Thames Regional Health Authority* v *Noone* that, taking into account the then overall

[61] The significant exceptions to this rule have involved servicewomen dismissed for pregnancy—see Lord Lester, HL Debs, 16th February 1995, col. 855 and, more generally, A. Arnull, "EC Law and the Dismissal of Pregnant Servicewomen" (1995) 24 *ILJ* 215.

[62] The former figure excludes Ministry of Defence cases which (*ibid*) skewed the figures for that year.

[63] There is evidence, at least where sex discrimination is concerned, that "employers who have been required to pay only very small amounts of compensation not only fail to engage in follow-up action, but also regard the tribunal process with disrespect, if not outright disdain"—see fn 47 above, p.177.

[64] See also *Sheriff* v *Klyne Tugs (Lowestoft) Ltd* [1999] IRLR 481 and *A* v *B* 40 EORDCLD 1, in which £23,000 was awarded for injury to feelings including symptoms akin to PTSD, in respect of which the judicial studies board currently recommends between £10,000 and £20,000. "The injury extended beyond the more usual humiliation and embarrassment to severe emotional distress". The respondents in *Stubbs* appealed unsuccessfully (see Chapter 4) but did not dispute the quantum of damages.

limit of £7,500 compensation in discrimination cases and the amount of damages typically awarded under this heading, £3,000 should be regarded as the upper limit for injury to feelings compensation. The level of such awards did not significantly change in the years immediately after the removal of the caps for sex and race discrimination compensation (increasing only from £1,825 to £2,823 and £1, 239 to £1,398 respectively, with the median award in sex cases falling from £1,750 to £1,000 in the year immediately after the removal of the cap. In November 1995 EAT ruled, in *Orlando* v *Didcot Power Station Sports and Social Club* [1996] IRLR 262, that *Noone* continued to apply in respect of injury to feelings awards; "We are not persuaded that that the Court of Appeal was so linking the amount of an award for injury to feelings to the then limit on compensation that it can be legitimately argued that without the limit the award would thereby have been higher".

In *Armitage*, however, EAT upheld an award of £21,000 for injury to feelings (and a further £7,500 aggravated damages) to a black prison officer who sued in respect of racial harassment.[65] The award was the highest made by any industrial tribunal at the time, although much larger overall awards (by far the largest proportions of which were in respect of pecuniary loss) have been made since. Many of the largest awards have been made to servicewomen dismissed when they became pregnant in pursuance of a policy expressly pursued by the armed services. (The size of the awards merely reflect the real cost to women of pregnancy-related dismissals, not least in terms of lost pensions, but was seized upon by the right as indicative of "political correctness gone mad".)

In 1997 an award of £65 377 including a sum of £25,000 in respect of injury to feelings, personal injury and loss of congenial employment was made to a former Wren who was discharged for depressive illness developed as a result of sexual harassment (the harassment included sexual assault, being forced to mimic oral sex and to make her clothes transparent by jumping into water).[66] Perhaps most spectacularly, in *D'Souza* v *London Borough of Lambeth* [1997] IRLR 677 (a race discrimination case) EAT increased from £8,925 to £358,289 an award in respect of the "worst case of discrimination it ever had to encounter"[67]. The award was reduced on appeal ([1999] IRLR 241), but on the grounds only that the EAT had not had the power to award an uncapped sum. Compensation had been awarded prior to the removal of the cap by the Race Relations (Remedies) Act 1994, but had been increased by EAT after the employer's subsequent refusal to comply with a reinstatement order made in respect of the applicant's unfair discriminatory dismissal. According to the Court of Appeal,

---

[65]   *Cf* the decision of Northern Ireland's Court of Appeal in *McConnell* v *Police Authority for Northern Ireland* [1997] NI 244, in which it overturned an award of £2500 aggravated damages (which had been made by the FET in addition to £10 000 injury to feelings) on the ground that (*per* Carswell LJ citing Winfield and Jolowicz on Tort, 14th ed, p 637): " 'Aggravated damages may be regarded as truly compensatory, despite the difficulty in quantifying that for which they are awarded . . . it is now clear that, except in the rare cases where exemplary damages are still allowed, any award must be strictly justifiable as compensation for the injury sustained.' "

[66]   19th March 1997 case no. 55542/95 reported in 75 *Equal Opportunities Review*, pp.2–3.

[67]   81 *Equal Opportunities Review* 19, Compensation Awards 1997.

the 1994 act applied only in respect of compensation awarded after the date of the Act's implementation.

An award of over £234,000 was made under the SDA against the London Borough of Southwark in respect of the discriminatory down-grading and dismissal of a senior council employee. £15,500 of the award was for injury to feelings, the rest for past and future loss of earnings including over £45,000 for loss of pension rights.[68] At that point it was the highest ever in a sex discrimination case. The London Borough of Hackney was ordered to pay £113,964 (including £25,000 in respect of injury to feelings) in *Chan* v *Hackney* and this award was upheld by EAT[69] while, in 1998, after a finding of race discrimination against it, the same respondent council received the dubious honour of reaching the largest settlement ever to be made public—£380,000, which included £40,000 paid in respect of injury to feelings.[70] Even this was dwarfed by the reported £5 to £10 million settlement (the details of which remain confidential) between Goldman Sachs and a black bond dealer in respect of his race discrimination claim.[71] More recently, an employment tribunal awarded £131,000 including £20,000 in respect of injury to feelings to an Asian machinist who was "severely traumatised" as a result of racial abuse[72] and another awarded £70,000 including £12,500 in respect of injury to feelings to a transsexual refused a job as an airline pilot.[73]

The perspective taken by EAT in *Armitage* and subsequently on the injuries inflicted by discrimination and, in particular, by racial (and, by implication, sexual) harassment, is new. Previous decisions showed a tendency to play down the emotional impact of discrimination, even of harassment. In *Orlando*, for example, EAT suggested that:

> an admission, or a finding in the complainant's favour, together with an appropriate award [there £750 for injury to feelings, £637 compensatory and £753 basic award for a woman dismissed for pregnancy after 14 years' part-time employment], may put an end to any continuing or further sense of hurt and outrage.[74]

The average award for injury to feelings in sexual and racial harassment cases respectively in 1995–6 was £2,501 and £2,127. In *Armitage*, by contrast, the Appeal Tribunal both accepted that the level of compensation for injury to feelings should be fixed with regard to damages in personal injury claims, and stated with equanimity that:

---

[68] *McLoughlin* v *London Borough of Southwark* 36 EORDCLD, p.12.

[69] *Ibid*, p.19.

[70] *Yeboah* v *Hackney* reported 82 *Equal Opportunities Review*, p.2. The *Guardian* 28th January 2000, reported that a settlement had been reached in *Coote* v *Granada* (see Chapter 4) of £200,000.

[71] 77 *Equal Opportunities Review*, p.2, reporting a settlement reached in December 1997 "if press reports are to be believed".

[72] *Mustafa* v *Ancon Clark Ltd & McNally* 40 EORDCLD, p.6.

[73] *Sheffield* v *Air Foyle Charter Airlines Ltd* 40 EORDCLD, p.7.

[74] See also *Wileman* v *Minilec Engineering Ltd* [1988] ICR 318, [1988] IRLR 144, EAT upheld an award of £50 nominal damages made to a woman who had been sexually harassed for four years by a director of the company for which she worked.

[t]he most severe cases [of post-traumatic stress disorder], resulting in an inability to work, attract awards in the region of £25,000–£35,000. Moderately severe cases where some recovery has occurred or is anticipated attract damages between £10,000 and £20,000. Cases described as "moderate" attract awards in the region of £3,000–£7,500.

Despite EAT's apparent change of heart and cases such as those mentioned above, the average awards for injury to feelings remain low. In 1997, average injury to feelings awards actually fell 5% in sexual cases to £2,441 (the median remained at £1,500 from 1996), although both average and median awards in respect of racial harassment increased (11% to £4,632 and 25% to £2,500 respectively).[75] This may come as a relief to the (disproportionately ethnic minority) residents of those local authorities which appear particularly prone to discrimination (the cost of such discrimination falling on those residents). But the low level of awards is a matter for concern given the findings of Chambers and Horton that, at least in relation to sex, losing discrimination cases had little impact on employers.[76]

The employment provisions of the DDA have not been in force for a sufficient length of time to make comparisons very meaningful. Nevertheless, in its first full year of operation the average compensation award was £3,743, the median £2,000, and awards ranged between £700 and £12,659. Given that all cases in which compensation was awarded involved dismissal, these sums do not appear large. Almost half of the total was awarded in respect of injury to feelings, these awards averaging £1,822 with a median of £1,000. Again, these were considerably lower than the sums awarded in respect of sex and race discrimination.

The unique approach taken to recommendations under the FETO (previously the FEAs), was discussed above, as was the prevalence of FEC-conciliated settlements in which the level of compensation agreed is considerably higher than that generally awarded by employment tribunals. Sums in excess of £25,000 are relatively common even in cases consisting of sectarian harassment alone (the bulk of such awards consisting of compensation for injury to feelings).[77] In the two years to the end of March 1998, for example, 123 complainants settled for an average of almost £10,000 each. Only 20 settlements were for less than £5,000 while 25 settlements were for £15,000 or more (10 in excess of £25,000).

"COLLECTIVE" ENFORCEMENT

The individualistic mechanisms put in place by the SDA, the RRA and the DDA do account for the bulk of activity associated with the Acts. But they do not stand entirely

[75] Fn 67 above.
[76] Chambers and Horton, fn 48 above, p.166 ff.
[77] Four of the five settlements reported on 11th March 1997, the other was for £22 500 (press release available on website, fn 51 above)

alone. The EqPA, as it was originally enacted, provided (s.3) that discriminatory collective agreements or pay structures could be referred to the Central Arbitration Committee (CAC) which had the power to amend the offending terms.[78] This provision was to prove very significant, early commentators on the Act attributing much of the initial hike in women's relative wages to s.3. Zabalza and Tzannatos, for example, who studied the impact of the EqPA on the employment and wages of women, found:

> evidence that collective agreements started to move towards equalisation quite early in the decade, that these increases in relative rates resulted in corresponding and contemporaneous increases in relative earnings, and that the effect on average earnings was not confined to the covered sector but also spilled over to non-covered employees.[79]

And one Australian study attributed the success of the UK legislation, relative to that in the US, precisely to this factor:

> in terms of institutional mechanisms a comparatively centralised wage-fixing system is a more efficient vehicle for implementing equal pay initiatives . . . across the board . . . initiatives such as those seen in Great Britain . . . are the most effective in reducing sex-based differentials.[80]

S.3 was capable of providing the benefits of "equal pay" even to women in exclusively female workplaces, in cases where those workplaces were covered by multi-employer collective agreements. And even where women were not covered by collective agreements, "female rates" within workplaces had to be raised to the level of the lowest "male rate" regardless, again, of the content of the jobs performed by the men and women respectively. But the powers of the Committee were narrowly defined—in particular, they could revise only those provisions which explicitly applied "to men only or to women only". And the CAC's liberal approach to these powers—it was prepared to amend agreements and pay structures in which, in the committee's view, insufficient steps had been taken fully to eradicate the effects of past discrimination[81]—was blocked by the Divisional Court in *R* v *CAC ex p. Hy-Mac Ltd* [1979] IRLR 461, in which it ruled that the Committee had exceeded its jurisdiction in interfering with a collective agreement which did not contain overtly discriminatory "male" and "female" payscales.

---

[78] The provisions of the EqPA extend beyond pay to cover all contractual terms.

[79] A. Zabalza and Z. Tzannatos, *Women and Equal Pay: The Effects of Legislation on Female Employment and Wages* (Cambridge: Cambridge University Press, 1985), p.9. See also Z. Tzannatos and A. Zabalza, 'The Anatomy of the Rise of British Female Relative Wages in the 1970's: Evidence from the New Earnings Survey" (1984) 22(2) *British Journal of Industrial Relations* 177, J. Rubery, "Structured Labour Markets, Worker Organisation and Low Pay" in A. Amsden (ed.), *The Economics of Women and Work* (Harmondsworth: Penguin, 1980), p.120.

[80] K. MacDermott, *Pay Equity: A Survey of 7 OECD Countries* (Canberra: Australian Government Publishing Service, 1987), Women's Bureau, Information Paper No.5, p.77.

[81] *See for example Prestcold & APECCS* (1978) CAC 78/830, reported in EOC *Annual Report* 1978, p.50.

The *Hy-Mac* decision rendered s.3 obsolete. Whereas, between 1976 and 1979 the CAC had ruled on about fifty equal pay cases, between 1981 and 1986 not one case was decided. The SDA 1986 stripped the CAC of its powers under the EqPA, s.3 EqPA being replaced by s.6 SDA 1986, which provided that discriminatory terms in collective agreements and pay structures, were void.[82] But s.6 contained no enforcement mechanism—in particular, no means by which women could demand that their terms be improved to match those enjoyed by men.

The Trade Union Reform and Employment Rights Act 1993 gave individuals the right of complaint to a tribunal in respect of discriminatory terms of collective agreements and "rules of undertakings".[83] Although pursued as an individual remedy, s.6 SDA 1986 (where the right of complaint is found) should be regarded as a collective measure in the sense that, once successfully challenged, the offending provision is struck down in its application across the board. By contrast, ss.77 SDA and 72 RRA, which provide for declarations that unlawfully discriminatory contractual terms are unenforceable, permit such declarations *only* vis-à-vis the complainant herself, where s/he is a party to the disputed contract.[84]

In *Meade-Hill* v *British Council* [1996] 1 All ER 79, [1995] ICR 847, [1995] IRLR 478, it was accepted that s.77 applied to indirectly, as well as directly, discriminatory terms.[85] The same would apply in respect of s.6 SDA 1986 but, by contrast with the position under s.3 EqPA, s.6 does not permit the extension of benefits to those to whom they are at present (discriminatorily) denied.[86] This would not pose a problem in a case where, as in *Meade-Hill*, the disputed term consisted of a wide contractual mobility clause with which women were less likely than men to be able to comply. A successful application under s.6 SDA 1986 would result in the striking-out of the term from the collective agreement or rules of the employer's undertaking as the case may be. But s.6 would not permit, for example, the extension of collectively agreed benefits from full-time to part-time workers where it was established that the non-entitlement of the latter to them amounted to indirect sex discrimination. The aggrieved part-timers would be required to present individual claims under the EqPA or SDA.

---

[82] This despite the suggestion by the AG in *Commission* v *United Kingdom* (Case C–165/82) [1984] CMLR 44 [1984] IRLR 29 at 3453–5 that the CAC was the most appropriate body to deal with collective cases—B. Fitzpatrick "The Sex Discrimination Act 1986", (1987) 50 *Modern Law Review* 934, 945. Fitzpatrick also points out that, s.77 permitting only parties to collective agreements or contractual terms to challenge them, someone covered by discriminatory collectively agreed term had no power to challenge them. Ss.77 SDA and 72 RRA provided for declarations that unlawful terms be unenforceable against the complainant.

[83] The relevant provisions are now to be found in s.77 SDA 1975 and s.6 SDA 1986 (dealing, respectively, with contracts and collective agreements), as amended by the Trade Union Reform and Employment Rights Act 1993.

[84] This is more akin therefore to s.6 SDA/ 2.RRA.

[85] *Cf* doubts expressed by Fitzpatrick, fn 82 above, pp.943–4.

[86] It is arguable that, in this respect, British law falls short of the requirements of Article 141. In *Kowalska* v. *Freie und Hansestadt Hamburg* (Case C–33/89) [1990] ECR I–2591 the European Court of Justice ruled that, in the absence of any national legislation providing for the equalisation of collectively agreed terms as between men and women, the disadvantaged sex would be entitled to be granted the benefits enjoyed by the advantaged sex.

Powers of the EOC, CRE, DRC and EC

The power of individuals to challenge discrimination, other than exclusively as it impacts on them, is very limited.[87] But collective methods of enforcement are available, in addition, to the various enforcement agencies. Each of the categories of anti-discrimination legislation in Great Britain comes with an enforcement body. In the case of legislation dealing with sex discrimination (that is, the SDA and the EqPA), the relevant commission is the EOC which came into existence in December 1975. The RRA's enforcement body is the CRE (effective as of June 1977). Both the CRE and the EOC have an advisory as well as an enforcement function. They are also entitled to issue Codes of Practice which, where relevant, should be taken into consideration by employment tribunals. We have come across some of the provisions of these Codes in Chapters 2 and 4.

The DDA, which was passed in 1995, did not create a commission on the lines of the EOC and the CRE. Rather, and until August 1999, it established a National Disability Council whose role was purely advisory, and whose remit did not extend to the provision of employment advice until mid-1998.[88] Nor did the Council have the power to issue Codes of Practice, this falling to the Secretary of State for Education and Employment. The Disability Rights Commission Act 1999 provides for a Disability Rights Commission (DRC) modelled along the lines of the EOC and the CRE, but with a number of differences discussed below.

The Fair Employment Agency (FEA) was established in Northern Ireland by the FEA 1976. Its powers were wider than those of the EOC and the CRE, extending to conciliation (carried out in Great Britain by ACAS in the case of sex and race discrimination) and to the policing of the monitoring obligations imposed by the fair employment legislation. The FEA also acted as the tribunal dealing with fair employment cases. Northern Ireland also had its own Equal Opportunities Commission while the implementation of the RRA and the creation of the Northern Irish CRE had to wait until 1997,[89] by which stage the FEA had been replaced by the Fair Employment Commission (FEC) which retained the FEA's conciliation role but did not function as a tribunal. Sex and race discrimination claims went to industrial (now employment) tribunals, as in Great Britain, although appeal was directly to the Northern Ireland Court of Appeal, there being no Northern Ireland EAT. In the case of fair employment complaints, however, a special Fair Employment Tribunal was established by the FEA 1989. Appeals from this tribunal, too, went direct to the Court of Appeal. The DDA applied to Northern Ireland as well as to Great Britain, Northern Ireland having its own Disability Council.

---

[87] The inclusion of a detriment requirement in indirect discrimination is discussed in Chapter 2. In cases of direct discrimination the applicant him or herself must have been less favourably treated.

[88] 79 *Equal Opportunities Review*, p. 10, citing a parliamentary answer by Alan Howarth 6th March 1998. The Commission was established on 6th August 1999, the Council to co-exist until April 2000.

[89] Race Relations (Northern Ireland) Order 1997.

The FET has been retained under the FETO 1998, but the FEC has been absorbed from October 1999 into an *uber* "Equality Commission" (EC) with responsibility not only over the FETO, but also over race, sex and disability discrimination legislation in Northern Ireland.[90] The rights and obligations of the EC vary with the legislation at issue.

It appears that the reason for the amalgamation of the various Commissions, in the face of very considerable opposition,[91] lay in large part in the imposition by s.75 NIA on public authorities of the duty to promote equality on grounds, *inter alia*, of sex, race and religion. S.75 was a significant element in the peace process, and the creation of a single Equality Commission (together with the Northern Ireland Human Rights Commission—unique in the UK—and the Commission on Policing), was promised in the pivotal Good Friday Agreement of 1998. The creation of the EC appears to have been particularly important in the view of nationalist political parties, and the EOC for Northern Ireland and the Northern Irish CRE expressed fears that the EC would concentrate on sectarian discrimination at the cost of sex and race. Similar fears were expressed by the Northern Ireland Disability Council. But it may turn out to be the case that amalgamation of the equality bodies has very beneficial impact in the area of sex, race and disability discrimination. The Fourth Report of the Select Committee on Northern Ireland (1998–1999 session) suggested that:

80. . . . it [i]s unlikely, in the longer term, that the single Equality Commission will operate successfully if the plethora of different requirements currently imposed [by the various anti-discrimination regimes] continues. Some degree of harmonisation of the equality requirements therefore seems necessary, and this was supported by a wide range of bodies giving evidence to us (CBI Northern Ireland, [Institute of Directors], Committee for the Administration of Justice). We agree with the IoD that "proposing a single Commission but without proposing a thorough look at the legislation" means that the "job is not complete."

81. **This would raise the difficult question of the level of harmonisation. We have not examined the regulatory frameworks in the equal opportunities, racial equality and disability areas of policy in Northern Ireland, so we have no information on what changes might be appropriate if a common framework is introduced. On the basis of the evidence adduced in the course of this inquiry, however, we would be most reluctant to see any diminution in standards in the area of fair employment legislation. It would also sit very oddly with the enhancements introduced only recently by the [FETO].**

---

[90] Until 1999, the fair employment legislation applied only in relation to employment. The non employment-related provisions of the FETO will be enforced by the ordinary courts. The DDA applies in Northern Ireland while the SDA's provisions are contained, identically, in the Sex Discrimination (Northern Ireland) Order 1976 and the and the RRA's in the 1997 Order, *ibid.*

[91] While the FEC chairman was happy with amalgamation, the EOCNI chairwoman expressed the fear that equality issues other than FE would be downgraded and Christopher McCrudden, a member of SACHR and one of the foremost commentators on NI and other discrimination law, warned that the new commission was "'likely to be riven with infighting", if experience in other countries is anything to go by" (cited in 79 *Equal Opportunities Review*, p.2).

The EOC, the CRE, the DRC and, in Northern Ireland, the EC have powers to act on their own behalf, as well as in support of individuals. Their action can take the form of litigation or the pursuit of "Formal Investigations". The commissions' powers of Formal Investigation (FI) are considered first, their various powers to litigate below. The CRE and EOC will be considered first, the other bodies being of much more recent vintage and, in the case of the EC in particular, being subject to special rules, considered below. What is said in respect of the CRE and EOC, however, applied equally to their sibling organisations in Northern Ireland during the period (however brief) of their existence. It applies today to the EC in its role vis-à-vis the Sex Discrimination (Northern Ireland) Order 1976 and the Race Relations (Northern Ireland) Order 1997.

Formal Investigations

The investigative powers of the EOC and the CRE are set out in ss.57–70 SDA, ss.48–64 RRA. These powers were intended to play a very significant role in the enforcement of the early anti-discrimination legislation.[92] Vera Sacks and Judith Maxwell pointed out, in 1984, that the power granted to the Commissions to carry out Formal Investigations (FIs):

"Unnatural Justice for Discriminators" (1984) 47 *Modern Law Review* **334, 334–5**

was identified in two Government White Papers which preceded the Sex Discrimination Act 1975 and the Race Relations Act 1976 as strategic in identifying and eliminating discriminatory practices: "The Commission's *main tasks* will be . . . to identify and deal with discriminatory practices by industries, firms or institutions" and this could be "on its own initiative" and "whether or not there had been individual complaints about the organisation investigated." Extensive investigatory powers were conferred on the Commission for this purpose for it was recognised that the individual would usually lack the resources to finance and compile proof, and that what was needed was an independent body acting in the public interest who could undertake a thorough appraisal of practices, policies and procedures which, although apparently neutral, might have a discriminatory impact. . . . established business practices often excluded minorities, albeit unintentionally, and it was therefore essential that recruitment, selection and promotion policies be scrutinised as a whole within the context of the entire organisational structure.

The investigative powers of the CRE are set out in ss.48–50 RRA, ss.57–59 of the SDA being in similar terms:

48 (1) Without prejudice to their general power to do anything requisite for the performance of their duties under section 43(1) the Commission may if they think fit, and shall

[92] *Race Discrimination* (London: Department of Employment, 1975), Cmnd. 6234, the White Paper which preceded the RRA, envisaged that the CRE's investigative powers would account for much of the legislative enforcement of the new Act.

if required by the Secretary of State, conduct a formal investigation for any purpose connected with the carrying out of those duties.

49 (2) Terms of reference for the investigation shall be drawn up by the Commission or, if the Commission were required by the Secretary of State to conduct the investigation, by the Secretary of State after consulting the Commission.

(3) It shall be the duty of the Commission to give general notice of the holding of the investigation unless the terms of reference confine it to activities of persons named in them, but in such a case the Commission shall in the prescribed manner give those persons notice of the holding of the investigation.

(4) Where the terms of reference of the investigation confine it to activities of persons named in them and the Commission in the course of it propose to investigate any act made unlawful by this Act which they believe that a person so named may have done, the Commission shall-

(a) inform that person of their belief and of their proposal to investigate the act in question; and

(b) offer him an opportunity of making oral or written representations with regard to it (or both oral and written representations if he thinks fit) . . .

50 (1) For the purposes of a formal investigation the Commission. . .

(a) may require any person to furnish such written information as may be described in the notice, and may specify the time at which, and the manner and form in which, the information is to be furnished;

(b) may require any person to attend at such time and place as is specified in the notice and give oral information about, and produce all documents in his possession or control relating to, any matter specified in the notice.

(2) Except as provided by section 60, a notice shall be served under subsection (1) only where. . .

(b) the terms of reference of the investigation state that the Commission believe that a person named in them may have done or may be doing . . .

(i) unlawful discriminatory acts;[93] . . .

and confine the investigation to those acts.

Sacks and Maxwell point out, of s.49(4),[94] that it was (pp. 336):

added at the latest possible stage when the Race Relations Act was going through Parliament—the third reading in the House of Lords. Proposed by Lord Hailsham in committee as a protection for respondents during the *course of the investigation*, in addition to their right to be heard at the conclusion of the investigation, it was resisted by the Government on the grounds that the C.R.E. should be free to investigate "with a minimum of procedural requirements." But the Government eventually gave way and apparently by mistake the section was added to other amendments as subsection (4) instead of appearing as a new and separate clause 50.

The cost of the Government's mistake will become apparent below, allowing as it did the Commissions' FI powers to be "emasculated by a judiciary which, being

---

[93] (ii) and (iii) expressly list discriminatory practices, discriminatory advertisements and instructions and pressure to discriminate.

[94] The RRA also applied this provision to the SDA (s.58(3A)).

apparently uncommitted to the objectives of the law, have emphasised the narrow letter of the statute and upheld the rights of discriminators in preference to those of the potential victims".[95]

The EOC appeared reluctant from the start to utilise its powers and has conducted only a handful of FIs.[96] Of the EOC's investigations, the first dealt with the allocation of grammar school places by Tameside Education Authority ("a somewhat idiosyncratic first use by the EOC of its enforcement powers since the factual issue was so specialised and unlikely to recur");[97] the second into discrimination in employment by Electrolux, this on the suggestion of Phillips J, (then President of EAT), who was faced with 600 individual claims relating to the company. An investigation into the credit practices of Debenhams stores was threatened in 1978 and resulted in a co-operative exercise which produced recommendations of general application in the retail credit industry. Two of the four FIs begun in 1979 dealt with employment-related discrimination at individual educational establishments; one was into discrimination vis-à-vis its members by the SOGAT trade union; and the other into discrimination in employment practices by Leeds Permanent Building Society. In 1980 the Commission investigated redundancy provisions applied in one British Steel Corporation works. The Provincial Building Society headed off a mortgage FI in the same year with a successful allegation of bias to the Divisional Court and by 1984 the FI agreed in 1983 into the provision of craft, design and technology courses in FE colleges had not yet begun.[98] At that date, two of the FIs begun in 1979 were still ongoing.

The CRE made full use of its FI powers in the early years, launching no less than 17 such investigations in its first eighteen months of operation (June 1977–January 1979), and a total of 63 to the end of 1999.[99] The CRE displayed considerably more relish for its investigative powers than did the EOC though, as Ellis and Applebey pointed out, it did have the benefit of years of experience on the part of the Race Relations Board (whose, albeit considerably expanded, remit it inherited).[100] Having said this, the pace of FI slowed considerably after 1984 in the wake of the *Hillingdon* and *Prestige* cases (discussed below) half of the FIs being completed in the 7.5 years to the end of 1984, the other 50% taking an additional 15 years. The early approach of the CRE to FIs is discussed by Mary Coussey:

---

[95] Sacks and Maxwell, p.334.

[96] Only four of the 13 FIs to 1991 led to the issue of NDNs (see below). CRE investigations tended to relate to broader areas than those conducted by the EOC—typical of the former were investigations into Cardiff employers, the hotel industry and chartered accountancy training: investigations into Dan Air's failure to recruit male cabin staff and into allegations of discrimination in promotion at a number of individual schools were more typical of those carried out by the EOC. See C. McCrudden, D. Smith and C. Brown, *Racial Justice at Work* (London: Policy Studies Institute, 1991), chapter 3 for details of the CRE's record.

[97] E. Ellis and G. Applebey, "Formal Investigations: the CRE and the EOC as Law Enforcement Agencies" (1984) *Public Law* 236, p. 256.

[98] Ellis and Applebey, fn 97 above, p.255–259.

[99] McCrudden *et al*, fn 96 above, p.452.

[100] Fn 97 above. The Board was established under the RRA 1965.

**M. Coussey, "The Effectiveness of Strategic Enforcement of the Race Relations Act 1976",
in B. Hepple and E. Szyszczak (eds),** *Discrimination: The Limits of Law*

The strategic investigations carried out by the CRE before the *Prestige* decision in 1984 were
chosen with reference to the broad labour market position. It was decided to carry out a
rolling programme of general enquiries into the extent of inequality in a number of representative industries located in areas of significant ethnic minority population. In this way, it
would be possible to build up a range of models, demonstrating in practical terms how discrimination operates. Over a dozen such enquiries were started. By selecting large companies in industrial sectors in which ethnic minorities were concentrated, it was anticipated that
the findings of the investigations would be relevant to other employers in the same industry.

These enquiries combined a strategic and inspectorial approach. However, their aims
were not fulfilled because many of the early strategic investigations had to be abandoned
after the *Prestige* decision. But the experience gained was the basis for many of the recommendations in the Code of Practice, as these enquiries identified most of the potentially discriminatory practices and other barriers caused by disadvantage in the labour market.

For example, there were five reports published of general investigations, started before
the *Prestige* decision, into named organizations. The enquiries covered a wide range of personnel decision-making and practices at different job levels. Many potentially discriminatory practices were identified. These included informal word-of-mouth recruitment, which
effectively excluded ethnic minority applicants from access to jobs, and the application of
geographical preferences, which in some circumstances disproportionately excluded ethnic
minorities (e.g. applicants should not live in Liverpool 8). Discriminatory selection criteria
were also found, such as informal oral or written English tests which had little relation to
the standards needed for the work, and which screened out a large majority of Asian candidates. Subjective criteria, acceptability criteria and stereotypical judgments were widespread. The use of sponsorship as a qualification for a hackney cab licence was found to be
a discriminatory practice. One enquiry was restarted as a "belief" investigation, and
focused more narrowly on promotion procedures, identifying the interview as a discriminatory practice because it rejected ethnic minority candidates for lack of communication
skills. This was found to be unjustifiable because the interview did not test the more direct
work-related communication require for the job.

Other early investigations published before 1984 (and therefore unaffected by *Prestige*)
uncovered a similar array of discriminatory practices. These included direct discrimination
and pressure to discriminate by shop stewards, and indirect discrimination by Massey
Ferguson in the use of unsolicited letters for recruitment. The latter practice favoured
applicants with links with the workforce. As the workforce was overwhelmingly white, the
letters of application also came mainly from white people. Inside knowledge also meant
that applicants wrote to apply for a specific vacancy as it arose. Ethnic minority applicants
had no such networks at the plant, and tended to call at the factory gates. When this
occurred, they may have been advised to "write in", but few did so. Many had no confidence that their letters would be successful. The company argued that this recruitment
practice was not a "requirement" (which is one of the criteria in the statutory definition of
indirect discrimination [see further Chapter 2]) because applicants who applied in other
ways were sometimes considered. Had this early case come to the courts, it would have
been an interesting test of the meaning of "requirement or condition" in Section 1(1)(b) of
the Race Relations Act, demonstrating as it does the ease with which employers can point
to one or two exceptions to challenge the existence of a practice or "requirement".

This investigation also showed the powerful effect of a poor company image: the chill factor. It was known among the ethnic minority communities in Coventry, the site of the plant, that it was a "waste of time" applying to Massey Ferguson for a job if you were black or Asian, because "no one like me" was employed there. The "chill factor" is still an important deterrent to ethnic minority candidates, as several recent surveys by employers have shown. See, for example, the recent survey "Ethnic Minority Recruitment to the Armed Services", published by the Ministry of Defence in January 1990. According to this research, one-third of Asians and half of Afro-Caribbeans in the survey expected to find racial discrimination when applying to the armed services.

None of the companies involved in these pre-1984 investigations had taken steps to implement equal opportunities policies. The discriminatory practices could flourish unchecked, as there were no records of the ethnic origin of applicants or employees. Ironically; in the absence of such data, it was difficult for the commission to find sufficient evidence of discriminatory practices. The alternative was to rely on employers' records of reasons for rejection or their accounts of selection practices. Not surprisingly, the evidence gleaned from this was often too weak to justify the use of the enforcement powers.

One significant problem faced by the EOC and the CRE—in particular by the latter, given its more aggressive investigative stance, came from the courts. The disapproval with which much of the judiciary regarded the investigative powers of the Commissions was evident from the start. Lord Hailsham, who, in his legislative capacity, was responsible for the insertion of s.49(4), likened the CRE's powers to those of the Star Chamber in the House of Lords debate on the Bill.[101] In *Science Research Council* v *Nassé* [1979] QB 144 (CA), Lord Denning declared that the Commission's investigative powers enabled it to "interrogate employers . . . up to the hilt and compel disclosure of documents on a massive scale . . . You might think that we were back in the days of the inquisition".

Sacks and Maxwell, p. 338

Lord Oliver in *Mandla* v. *Dowell Lee* [1983] 2 AC 548 has accused the C.R.E. of using the Race Relations Act as an "engine of oppression," Lord Denning has likened an investigation to a criminal charge, while Lord Diplock voiced an implied criticism against the C.R.E. for wasting public money—when the waste was in fact occasioned by the courts' interpretation of their powers. . . . The courts have found in favour of respondents and their multiplicity of challenges to the C.R.E. on procedural grounds.

The bulk of judicial disapproval was reserved for the CRE, probably because, as we saw above, it was less backward about utilising its powers than was the EOC. In *Hillingdon London Borough Council* v *Commission for Racial Equality* [1982] AC 779, [1982] 3 WLR 159, [1982] IRLR 424, 80 LGR 737, the House of Lords took its first substantial step towards curbing what it evidently saw as the excessive powers of the Commission.

[101] 373 HL Debs 20th July 1976, col. 745.

The case concerned a challenge brought by the council to the CRE's decision to launch an FI into possible race discrimination by it in the provision of housing. The CRE believed that the council might be discriminating in providing housing for homeless immigrants. This belief was based, in part, on the contrasting approach of the council to an Asian and a white family who had, respectively, immigrated from Kenya and from Rhodesia (now Zimbabwe). The council took the view that the former were intentionally but the latter were unintentionally homeless, and a council member dumped the Asian family at the Foreign Office, by way of protest that responsibility for housing immigrants who arrived at Heathrow airport fell on the Council, rather than on national government.

The House of Lords interpreted ss.49 (4) and 50 (2)(b) RRA to require that, before it began a named investigation, the CRE must have formed a belief that the persons being investigated might be or have been engaged in unlawful discrimination *of the type* (narrowly defined) which was to be investigated. Unless the instances relied upon by the CRE caused them to form a belief that the Council was engaged in a wider policy of discrimination (which, on the CRE's own evidence, was not the case), they were entitled only to investigate the possibility of discrimination in the provision of housing to homeless immigrants.[102] Further, the House of Lords agreed with the Court of Appeal's (*obiter*) view that s.49(4) required the CRE to carry out a preliminary inquiry prior to any FI during which the subject of the planned FI would have an opportunity to argue against the launch of such an investigation.

The decision of the House of Lords in *Hillingdon* was followed by that in *ex p. Prestige*, in which their Lordships rejected the argument put forward by the CRE that it could carry out "named investigations" without suspicion of unlawful action by the person named, and that in such cases s.49(4) did not apply. The terms of reference of the *Prestige* FI had been "to inquire into the employment of persons of different racial groups by the Prestige Group . . . with particular reference to the promotion of equality of opportunity between such persons as regards [*inter alia*] recruitment [and] access to promotion". The company challenged the FI after the CRE, having uncovered unlawful action by it in the course of the FI, had issued a non-discrimination notice. According to Lord Diplock, who delivered the sole speech in *Prestige* (as he had in *Hillingdon*):

R v CRE ex parte Prestige Group PLC [1984] ICR 472

The requirements of section 49(3) as to the notice to be given of the holding of a general investigation is to be contrasted with the limited notice to be given of a named-person investigation [s.49(4)]. Of the holding of an investigation of the latter type, notice of the holding of it (which obviously must include a statement of its terms of reference) need be, and in practice is, given only to the persons named in it whose "activities" are the subject

---

[102] This, as Ellis and Applebey point out (p.244), appears at odds with the wording of s.49(4). Although the test was drawn quite widely by the HL: (p.246) "the prudent course for the Commission to take will . . . be the minimalist one, resulting in narrow terms of reference and putting a serious practical brake upon the Commission's enforcement powers".

of the formal investigation. The fact that Parliament has thought fit to limit in this manner the notice to be given of a formal investigation of a particular kind, (viz. a named-person investigation) that the CRE is minded to conduct, provides in my view a strong indication of a Parliamentary intention that the nature of such an investigation should not be purely exploratory, as in the case of a general investigation, but should be accusatory in the sense that it is directed to determining whether or not there is justification for pre-existing suspicions of the CRE that the persons to whose activities the named-person investigation is confined had in the course of those activities committed acts made unlawful by the [RRA]. The most likely source of such suspicions before any formal investigation starts is complaints received by the CRE from members of racial groups who claim to have been victims of unlawful discriminatory acts committed by the named persons. In the absence of any belief by the CRE that the named persons may have committed unlawful acts why should those persons alone be picked upon to have their activities investigated to the exclusion of the activities of other employers engaged in the same industries as the persons named? And why, except on the assumption not only that the CRE already had suspicions but also that such suspicions were derived from the most likely source, should Parliament have treated it as unnecessary that the holding of the investigation should be brought to the notice of members of those groups of persons which are likely to include victims or potential victims of unlawful acts committed by the named persons in the course of their activities that are to be investigated?

Lord Diplock's interpretation of Parliamentary intention is in striking contrast to the extract from the White Paper cited by Sacks and Maxwell above and fails to take account of the role of such FIs as outlined by Coussey, also above. The decision in *Prestige*, of course, predated *Pepper* v *Hart* [1993] AC 593, [1993] 1 All ER 42, [1992] 3 WLR 1032, [1993] ICR 291, [1993] IRLR 33, in which their Lordships relaxed the strict rule by which Parliamentary materials could not be referred to in attempting to determine the Parliamentary intent behind legislation.[103] Its impact was to render all but unuseable the Commissions' powers to carry out FIs. Further

G. Appleby and E. Ellis, "Formal Investigations: the CRE and the EOC as Law Enforcement Agencies" (1984) *Public Law* 236, 247

It was far from a foregone conclusion that the legislation would have to be interpreted this way. Section 49(4) refers to the situation where the investigation is into named persons *and* the Commission in the course of it propose to investigate those persons' suspected unlawful discrimination. This wording would appear to suggest that a named-person investigation need not be directed to uncovering discrimination, and the C.R.E. argued in *Prestige* that it was empowered to conduct a general investigation into a named person. In such a case, it would have no coercive powers. Lord Diplock, however, repeated his earlier remarks and held that it is a "condition precedent to the exercise by the C.R.E. of its power

---

[103] In *Pepper*, the House of Lords by a majority of 6:1 (Lord Mackay LC dissenting) ruled that such reference could be made where (a) the legislation was "ambiguous or obscure, or led to an absurdity"; (b) the material relied on consisted of one or more statements by a Minister or other promoter of the Bill together if necessary with such other parliamentary material as was necessary to understand such statements and their effects; and (c) the statements relied on were clear.

to conduct named-person investigations that the C.R.E. should in fact have already formed a suspicion that the persons named may have committed some unlawful act of discrimination . . .

Nor is the judicial approach taken in *Hillingdon* and in *Prestige* on all fours with that adopted in respect of other investigative bodies. Whereas, in *Hillingdon*, Lord Diplock declared that the "first rule of natural justice—*audi alteram partem* is expressly required to be observed at this stage":

Sacks and Maxwell, 339

. . . the courts' treatment of other investigative bodies exercising similar powers suggest that the issue is not as definite as Lord Diplock would have us believe. It appears from the authority of earlier cases not concerning the C.R.E. that, in preliminary proceedings to establish the necessity of undertaking further investigations, there is no right to be heard at this stage. In *Wiseman* v. *Borneman* [1971] AC 297 for example, the House of Lords held that there was nothing inherently unfair in refusing the taxpayer an oral hearing before a tribunal that was concerned only to establish whether there was a prima facie case for an investigation by the Commissioners of Inland Revenue. The Law Lords made it quite clear that at this preliminary stage the requirements of natural justice were minimal. Lord Reid said, "It is, I think, not entirely irrelevant to have in mind that it is very unusual for there to be a judicial determination of the question whether there is a prima facie case. Every public officer who has to decide whether to prosecute or raise proceedings ought first to decide whether there is a prima facie case, but no one supposes that justice requires that he should first seek the comments of the accused or the defendant on the material before him. *So there is nothing inherently unjust in reaching such a decision in the absence of the other party*. This passage was cited with approval in both *Re Pergamon Press Ltd.* [1970] 3 WLR 729, where Lord Denning applied it to inspectors investigating a company's affairs, and *Pearlberg* v. *Varty* [1972] IWLR 524, where Lord Pearson said that "If there were too much elaboration of procedural safeguards, nothing could be done simply and quickly and cheaply. Administrative or executive efficiency and economy should not be too readily sacrificed.' It is clear from these and other cases, that the courts have not invoked *audi alteram partem* at preliminary stages and have not previously thought it necessary to invoke the *audi alteram partem* rule for preliminary hearings designed to establish a prima facie case for proceeding with an investigation.

Indeed the courts have warned against allowing natural justice to be oppressive in its requirements. In a slightly different context of a tribunal exercising licensing functions, Sir Robert Megarry V. C. warned that "the concepts of natural justice and the duty to be fair must not be allowed to discredit themselves by making unreasonable requirements and imposing undue burdens." But this is exactly the situation in which the C.R.E. have now found themselves.

Ellis and Applebey point out some of the difficulties raised by the *Prestige* decision:

E. Ellis and G. Appleby "Blackening the *Prestige* Pot? Formal Investigations and the CRE" (1984) 100 *Law Quarterly Review* 349, 354

For example, what is the Commission to do when minded to begin an investigation into a field of activity exclusively occupied by one individual who, even if not actually named in the terms of reference, is identifiable? An instance would be provided by a Government department (such as in the case of the current C.R.E. investigation into the administration of the immigration service by the Home Office) or a nationalised industry. Perhaps even more intractable is the difficulty that, if a "non-belief" investigation cannot take place into the activities of one named person, neither presumably can such an investigation be concerned with the activities of *any* finite number of named persons. Assuming that the courts would not be satisfied by the mere subterfuge of not naming those involved where is the line to be drawn between an investigation into a number of individuals and a general investigation? Such an argument eventually leads to the conclusion that there may never be able to be a valid general investigation, but this obviously flies in the face of the legislative provisions already cited.

... *Prestige* ... enhances the importance of section 49(4), which in turn gives more scope for respondents seeking judicial review. The House of Commons Home Affairs Committee recommended in 1981 that the subsection be repealed, and the C.R.E. itself has echoed this ... Whilst not for a moment suggesting that individuals should be denied the right to challenge a statutory body's exercise of its powers, the effectiveness of the C.R.E.'s role as a law enforcement agency has certainly been undermined by respondents seizing every opportunity open to them of delaying investigations by seeking judicial review. It is therefore unfortunate if an effect of this judgment has been to provide them with yet more such opportunities.

The latter fear proved well-founded. Subsequent to the *Hillingdon* and *Prestige* decisions, attempts by the CRE to instigate formal investigations became mired in "lengthy and rarely productive challenges before a formal investigation is begun".[104] It took 13 years for the commission to be in a position to launch its formal investigation into the army in 1994, and the number of formal investigations instigated by the CRE has been drastically reduced. The requirements in respect of FIs were listed by Vera Sacks, in an article dealing with the EOC:

V. Sacks, "The Equal Opportunities Commission—Ten Years On" (1986) 49 *Modern Law Review* 560, 581–2

... those who are to be investigated must be informed by way of terms of reference served upon them of the situation which the E.O.C. intend to investigate. Before the investigation begins that party has the right to make representations to the Commission, both oral and in writing if desired, in the hope that the Commission will not proceed with the investigation. If the E.O.C. should revise its terms of reference (as a result usually of representations) then the respondent may make representations again. The Act then provides that, at the conclusion of the investigation, if the Commission is "minded" to serve a non-discrimination

---

[104] CRE, *Annual Report 1988*.

notice on them, the other party has the right to make further representations. A right of appeal against the non-discrimination notice is also available. Such is the procedure laid down by the Act in outline.

However, further requirements have been added by judicial exegesis. The terms of reference must specify the grounds for the suspicion that unlawful acts have been committed, and the Commission may not go beyond them in their investigations unless they revise the terms of reference or the respondent agrees. On appeal all the facts on which the notice was based can be reopened by the appellant in front of a court or tribunal, and are subject to cross-examination—usually years after the events have occurred. at all stages of the investigation the Commission must act in accordance with the principles of natural justice, and here the *Hillingdon* case indicates that the respondent has rights of reply other than those laid down in the Act. Finally it seems that there may be other matters, as yet unexplored, which may be capable of being reviewed—for example, whether an investigation can continue when the factual situation has changed, *i.e.* whether it can refer only to past practices.

The additional rights of reply to which Sacks refers consist, presumably, of the right to reply to a specific charge levelled by the Commission prior to any FI. The significance of this in narrowing the terms of reference of any investigation, and of precluding any departure from those terms as an FI uncovers wider discrimination, is enormous, and would not have arisen had the right to be heard been incorporated in the course of the FI itself, rather than at the preliminary stage. It is the preliminary nature of the right to be heard, too, which underlies the doubts expressed by Sacks in relation to changed circumstances.

Sacks attributes the low number of FIs conducted by the EOC in part both to the technicality of the legal provisions, and to their judicial interpretation. Discussing a number of the investigations begun by the EOC:

Sacks, 582–5

The delay consequent upon stringent legalism can be illustrated by the Ebbw Vale inquiry. The E.O.C. was threatened with judicial review because it appointed a new Commissioner after the warrant of the existing two had expired. Ebbw Vale College argued that the appointment of the new Commissioner part-way through the investigation was unfair (although the existing Commissioners had been re-appointed as additional Commissioners under section 57). This threat was withdrawn after a long delay but by then, in the words of the C.R.E., "It does not matter whether the respondent succeeds; the damage caused by repeated delays is enormous, and all this without touching on the fundamental question whether discrimination has occurred and what should be done about it." The impact has also been devastating on morale, and needed resources are spent obtaining legal opinions to avoid further challenges. Although it would be improper to deny protection to those under investigation, the current situation is neither what was intended by Parliament nor in the interests of victims of discrimination.

Apart from cost and delay the main legal difficulty which now confronts the E.O.C. is that they cannot go on "fishing expeditions" but must confine their investigations to the narrow factual issue which was reported to them. For example both in the Leeds and Barclays investigations the Commission would have liked to extend their investigations into other matters, but since new terms of reference would have had to have been drawn up and new representations made, were understandably deterred. Another current example of this situation is whether statistical evidence showing an imbalance between the sexes in the workforce would provide sufficient suspicion to justify an investigation. The White Paper which preceded the Sex Discrimination Act did not envisage these difficulties; the Commission was to investigate discriminatory practices "on its own initiative" and "whether or not there had been individual complaints about the organisation investigated." Given the fact of widespread inequalities the piecemeal approach to its eradication dictated by case law presents a gloomy prognosis. The way ahead lies in repeal of section 58(3A) and its equivalent in the Race Relations Act and this is currently under consideration by the Government.

The other problem is the extent to which natural justice should be available during the investigative stage. The C.R.E. have said that the courts have added "protection appropriate to law enforcement powers to protection appropriate to a report making process." This writer agrees, especially when the cases in different areas of the law where investigative powers are being used are compared. An investigation is an administrative fact-finding process and although the Commission must act fairly, their fear of judicial review has led them to give respondents extensive rights of reply. Their own guidelines on the conduct of formal investigations specify that the Commission must act fairly, "having regard only to relevant considerations, and complying with the rules of natural justice, so that the Commission is manifestly free from bias and does not condemn anyone unheard or without affording a proper opportunity of answering the case against him." This leads to the Commission seeking respondents' comments each time they have made some finding; and these may be made orally or in writing and with counsel if desired. Since this is in addition to the statutory hearings referred to above it is not surprising that the Ebbw Vale affair took five years and Leeds seven, and only one new investigation has been started since 1982. All the aforegoing problems have led the C.R.E. to ask the Government for far reaching changes which would enable them to obtain a court order without recourse to a full formal investigation when a discriminatory practice is uncovered.

(iii) *Problems arising from the attitudes and behaviour of those under investigation*

The legal challenges outlined above are the result of strong hostility by those under investigation. As time has progressed, investigatees have developed more and different avoidance tactics. Recently an important institution responded to the E.O.C.'s initial inquiries by swamping them with information, then made long oral and written submissions represented by senior counsel, while conducting their own internal investigation. Having established in this way that the complaints were justified, they indulged in a "pincer" movement: on the one hand they agreed to co-operate with the Commission on new recruitment practices while on the other their legal advisers insisted on further clarification of the Commission's findings and threatening judicial review. Either the Commission continued the investigation or settled. It chose the latter course, although wisely only agreed to suspend the investigation pending monitoring. The adversarial stance adopted by the institution and its delaying tactics, especially given the fact that they knew its practices to be wrong, typify many other cases. The Leeds Permanent investigation timetable illustrates all that has been described here and is worth considering:

1977 Complaint received from a woman applicant that much stress was placed on mobility in her interview for management trainee. E.O.C. request application forms so that analysis can be made of other factors which might account for the total lack of female management trainees although a quarter of the applicants are female.

1978   Commission decides to investigate—Leeds seek clarification of complaints; formal terms of reference sent to society after Counsel's opinion sought.

1979   Written and oral representations received; as a result terms of reference revised, further correspondence on these, further representations promised but none received. Application forms analysed and counsel's opinion sought on whether formal investigation could be undertaken.

1980   Questionnaire drafted and sent to applicants whose forms have been analysed. This done i n order to obtain information about interviews. Society consider trying to stop use of questionnaire but do not. Further discussions with Society on current practices and Counsel's advice sought on these relative to whether formal investigation could proceed.

1981   Report on findings drafted and redrafted.

1982   Preliminary report sent to Society (June) who request further representations which are not received until December. Counsel's advice sought.

1983   Final report sent to Society who reject it—more representations made as a result of which Part 3 (containing the Society's representations and the Commission's findings) is redrafted. Further correspondence—E.O.C. agrees to confine its findings to 1978 because practices have changed.

1984   Counsel's opinion sought on redrafting report; Part 3 re-written and sent to Society.

1985   Society's comments received and report considered by Commissioners.

1985   (June) Report published.

The CRE has long campaigned for a reversal of the *Prestige* decision. Even prior to the House of Lords' decision in that case, the Commission's first review (published in 1983), highlighted difficulties it had experienced in carrying out FIs.

The Race Relations Act 1976—Time for a Change? (1983) para. 5[105]

. . . the rate at which legal challenges are mounted to head off an investigation or its results is very high. . . . if enforcement is to be effective the scope for legal challenges must be reduced both by the introduction of greater flexibility and by a shortening of the whole investigative process. The following are some suggestions relating to this:

> There have been legal challenges over investigations on such highly *technical procedural matters* as whether terms of reference are too wide; whether the Commission can investigate named persons without a belief that they are acting unlawfully; whether it is reasonable to embark on an investigation; whether natural justice applies as well as the statutory requirements to hear representations; whether the right to make representations under s.49(4) of the Act applies during the course of an investigation if the Commission forms a belief as to unlawful acts; whether it is reasonable to change from a strategic investigation to one based on a belief that unlawful acts have occurred; whether in drawing conclusions after representations pursuant to s.58(5) of the Act the Commission has acted reasonably.
>
>   None of these matters actually touch on the fundamental question whether discrimination has occurred and what should be done about it. . . . The *Amari* case deal-

---

[105] Available from the CRE website at www.open.gov.uk.

ing with appeals against non-discrimination notices [discussed below] permits the whole factual basis of the non-discrimination notice to be re-opened in an appeal.

Yet, all this has happened in a system which was itself designed to give the person investigated every opportunity to make representation. The result is that they have those opportunities and the right of re-hearing on appeal and plentiful opportunities for requesting a judicial review. In a sense it does not matter whether the respondent succeeds; the damage caused by repeated delays is enormous. In some ways, the possibility of delay on procedural grounds must be reduced.

It may be that the judges will never be able to accept the fact that Parliament has entrusted the CRE with sweeping investigative powers to work towards the eradication of a great social evil being carried out covertly. It may also be that those investigated see the CRE as too partisan for them to be able to accept the conclusions of the CRE administratively reached even after proper hearings. This combination of factors suggests powerfully that a new approach is called for.

The CRE must have wide investigative *powers for any purpose connected with their functions* and should on notifying the terms of reference be able to require the production of information. The only alternative would be a system where legal proceedings subject to wide discovery powers are commenced very early in the day with little or no preliminaries. Yet at the same time the CRE should have power to accept, from persons investigated , binding undertakings to change their practices. (It would have to be established that a judicial review is not possible if the CRE declines to accept such an undertaking—because otherwise this again would hold up work.) there may be many instances where persons will be willing to make changes in practices and procedures to avoid discrimination occurring in future and, if binding undertakings include sanctions against breach, the CRE's public duty may be satisfied by accepting them.

The present system of investigations is designed to have formal investigations directed at large general problems. This makes investigations slow and proceedings complex and, as we have noted, with many opportunities for challenges in the courts as well as the possibility of appeal at the end. A substantial improvement could be effected if the Commission could apply in the course of an investigation to a court or tribunal for a finding that an individual act or practice is discriminatory and for appropriate remedies. (Once again, it would have to be established that the decision to take the matter to court or tribunal was not itself subject to judicial review.)

Commenting upon the Divisional Court's decision in *Prestige*, which the House of Lords was later to uphold, the CRE protested that the restriction of named investigations to cases where unlawful behaviour was suspected would be "a severe, and in our view wrong, constraint on the discretion of the Commission", pointing out in particular that FIs could be used "to highlight and illustrate a particularly desirable practice". The CRE called for the removal of s.49(4), the need for a preliminary hearing at which the person being investigated had a right to be heard being identified by the Commission as a "major delaying factor" in FIs.[106]

---

[106] A view shared by the Employment Select Committee discussed by L. Lustgarten, "The New Meaning of Discrimination" (1978) *Public Law* 178.

CRE (1983) para. 49

. . . the hope of the respondent is raised and as as result representations are frequently made at very great length and by very senior Counsel, at considerable expense and by respondents with high expectations. The expectation is frequently dashed and the expense is unnecessary; the standard of proof at this stage of an investigation has been defined by the House of Lords in the Hillingdon case and is a very low one. It is no more than "to raise in the minds of reasonable men, possessed of the experience of covert racial discrimination that has been acquired by the Commission, a suspicion that there may have been acts by the person named of racial discrimination of the kind which it is proposed to investigate." A mere suspicion is remarkably difficult to dispel and a respondent would, in our view, suffer no disadvantage if we endorsed the recommendations of the Select Committee and **recommended that s.49(4) be repealed**.

The 1983 review by the CRE, and the various reforms it suggested, was ignored by a hostile Conservative Government.[107] The CRE's second review, published nine years later, reiterated the call for statutory reversal of *Prestige* (this call had also been made by the EOC in its 1988 reform proposals), citing in support the view of the White Paper on Racial Discrimination that the CRE's predecessor, the Race Relations Board "has been hampered by its dependence on receiving significant complaints in pursuing the crucial strategic role of identifying and dealing with discriminatory practices and encouraging positive action to secure equal opportunity". According to the CRE:

Second Review of the Race Relations Act, 1992, para. 12

Paragraph 111 of the White Paper preceding the RRA said that under the new legislation the successor body would be able to conduct formal investigations on its own initiative into a specific organisation for any purpose connected with the carrying out of its functions. The new body would also be able to compel the production of information/attendance of witnesses, without the sanction of the Secretary of State where the investigation was confined to unlawful conduct which it believed was occurring. . . .

Until Section 49(4) was added to the legislation there was no doubt that the Government understood that the power of the new Commission to investigate the affairs of an individual or particular organisation was not limited to a situation where there was some initial evidence of unlawful activity.

When the Government accepted the House of Lords amendment which became Section 49(4) the effect was stated as being "to give a person against whom a complaint is made a right to information" (House of Commons Debates 918 c.603). Nothing was said which indicated any belief on the part of Government that it had now accepted a restriction on the Commission's powers to conduct investigations.

A strategic approach to formal investigations is needed. Named person investigations, with or without a suspicion of unlawful acts, should form part of this strategy. Direct discrimination is generally covert. Indirect discrimination is often not recognised as unlawful by those operating the practices involved. Indeed they may not even be applied to any par-

---

[107] Post-consultation the document was sent as the *Review of the Race Relations Act 1976: Proposals for Change* (1985).

ticular member of an ethnic minority, as Section 28 of the Act acknowledges. For example, word of mouth recruiting may be indirectly discriminatory precisely because no one outside the organisation knows the jobs exist. In these circumstances information as to discrimination is unlikely to be brought to the Commission's attention.

The Commission, therefore, needs to be able to look at selected major employers to enable it to identify what practices may be disadvantaging ethnic minorities. In this respect the Commission should be thought of as an inspectorate, bringing technical expertise to bear on identifying the causes of major social problems. We recommend that against this background the intended power taken away by *Prestige* be restored.

As the Policy Studies Institute researchers concluded in their Home Office sponsored research:

> The decision in the *Prestige* case seems to have frustrated the intentions of the legislators. A particularly unfortunate consequence is that formal investigations of specified organisations are bound to be confrontational., since there must be prior belief of unlawful discrimination . . . Investigations of specified organisations which do not allege unlawful discrimination should be available to the Commission in future, as they are by the Fair Employment Commission.

Once again, the 1992 reform proposals were ignored by the Conservative Government and the CRE's 1998 proposals called, yet again, for the statutory reversal of *Prestige*:

> It should be unambiguously stated in the Act that the Commission may conduct a formal investigation—either wide-ranging or confined to a particular organisation or individual—on its own initiative for any purpose connected with the carrying out of its functions. Specifically, the Commission should not be required to obtain and produce evidence of unlawful racial discrimination before embarking on an investigation of a named person . . . The Commission would still be expected to have sufficient information about the respondent to formulate relevant terms of reference for the investigation, and terms of reference which exceeded the Commission's powers could be challenged by judicial review. Where a respondent considers that the terms of reference are ill- or misconceived, the respondent would be able to make representations as at present

The DDA, as newly amended by the DRCA 1999, establishes the DRC's investigative powers in terms which, while they are not precisely the same as ss.49(4) and 58(3A) of the RRA and SDA respectively, fall far short of explicitly excluding *Prestige* even in the disability context. The government has indicated its intention to amend the powers of the CRE and the EOC consistent with those of the DRC[108], a move which the CRE welcomed as a "first step" towards permitting the strategic use of FIs.[109]

S.2 DRCA requires that the DRC draw up terms of reference prior to any FI and give notice, in the case of a named person investigation, to the named person(s) or, in the case of a general investigation, that it "publish a notice . . . in such manner as

---

[108] Ian McCartney, Minister of State for the Cabinet Office, in an equality statement 30th November 1999, available on *http://www.cabinet-office.gov.uk/1999/news/991130_discrimination.htm*.

[109] According to the CRE's briefing on the government's response to the 1998 proposals, fn 22 above.

appears to the Commission appropriate to bring it to the attention of persons likely to be affected by it". S.3 goes on expressly to deal with the investigation of unlawful acts, and provides:

(1) This paragraph applies where the Commission proposes to investigate in the course of a formal investigation (whether or not the investigation has already begun) whether-
   (a) a person has committed or is committing any unlawful act . . .[110]

(2) The Commission may not investigate any such matter u   nless the terms of reference of the investigation confine it to the activities of one or more named persons (and the person concerned is one of those persons).

(3) The Commission may not investigate whether a person has committed or is committing any unlawful act unless—
   (a) it has reason to believe that the person concerned may have committed or may be committing the act in question,[111] or . . .

(4) The Commission shall serve a notice on the person concerned offering him the opportunity to make written and oral representations about the matters being investigated.

(5) If the Commission is investigating whether the person concerned has committed or is committing any unlawful act [[112]] the Commission shall include in the notice required by sub-paragraph (4) a statement informing that person that the Commission has reason to believe that he may have committed or may be committing any unlawful act.

(6) The Commission shall not make any findings in relation to any matter mentioned in sub-paragraph (1) without giving the person concerned or his representative a reasonable opportunity to make written and oral representations . . .

4.(1) For the purposes of a formal investigation the Commission may serve a notice on any person requiring him-
   (a) to give such written information as may be described in the notice; or
   (b) to attend and give oral information about any matter specified in the notice, and to produce all documents in his possession or control relating to any such matter.

   (2) A notice under this paragraph may only be served on the written authority of the Secretary of State unless the terms of reference confine the investigation to the activities of one or more named persons and the person being served is one of those persons.

S.3(1) appears, *contra* the approach taken to the RRA (and, by implication, the SDA) by the House of Lords in *Prestige*, to countenance a named-person FI which is not directed at investigating whether a person has committed an unlawful act, s.3(2) then providing that if, in the course of such an investigation or otherwise, the Commission decides to investigate whether a person is committing an unlawful act, it

---

[110] "or (b) any requirement imposed by a non-discrimination notice served on a person (including a requirement to take action specified in an action plan [discussed below]) has been or is being complied with; (c) any undertaking given by a person in an agreement made with the Commission under section 5 [discussed below] is being or has been complied with.

[111] "or (b) that matter is to be investigated in the course of a formal investigation into his compliance with any requirement or undertaking mentioned in sub-paragraph (1)(b) or (c)."

[112] Otherwise than in the course of a formal investigation into his compliance with any requirement or undertaking mentioned in sub-paragraph (1)(b) or (c)).

must (other than in a follow-up investigation, see further below) not do so without (a) having reason to believe that the unlawful act may have been/ be being committed *and* (b) having complied with the requisite procedures. Crucially, the requirement in s.49(4), as it was interpreted by the courts, that the right to be heard was exercised at a *preliminary* hearing (at which stage, therefore, the terms of reference had to be set in stone), appears not to apply to the DRC—this because of s.3(1)'s express provision that a named person FI can become an *accusatory* named person FI during the course of the investigation.

It appears that the intention of s.3 is to disapply the *Prestige* decision in the context of the DDA. But its contemplation of non-accusatory named person FIs is not much more explicit than was s.49(4) itself, which, by using the conjunctive: "*[w]here* the terms of reference of the investigation confine it to activities of persons named in them *and* the Commission in the course of it propose to investigate any act made unlawful by this Act which they believe that a person so named may have done" (my emphasis); quite clearly contemplated a named person investigation other than one based on a belief in unlawful action. It is possible, therefore, that s.3 will not be sufficient to prevent the judiciary from encasing the DRC in the same straitjacket as it applied to the CRE and, by implication, the EOC.

The Better Regulation Task Force, while tentatively supporting a broadening of the sources of evidence upon which a Formal Investigation could be launched, declared "[u]ntargeted blanket investigation . . . undesirable and counter-productive".[113] It stressed, instead, the importance of "joined up" working between the Commissions and their Government Department sponsors, adverting in particular to the possibility of joint Codes of Practice and investigative work. Removing the statutory barriers which hinder co-operation between the Commissions is, no doubt, important—the law currently prevents the sharing of information even as between the CRE and the CRE for Northern Ireland. But without substantial increases in the investigatory powers of the Commissions, this mode of enforcement will never be the radical tool envisaged by the drafters of the SDA and RRA.

Turning, finally, to the investigative powers of the EC in Northern Ireland, the same rules apply to it in relation to race, sex and disability investigations as apply to the EOC, the CRE and the DRC. In the case of the FETO, however, its powers are considerably wider. Not only does the FETO impose monitoring obligations on employers, which obligations are policed by the EC (see further above); but Article 11 permits the Commission to conduct investigations into, *inter alia*:

(a) "the composition, by reference to religious beliefs" of
  (i) employees of or applicants to any particular employer or class of employers; [and]
  (ii) "persons who have applied for or obtained the services of any employment agency" . . . and
(a) into practices—

---

[113] *Report on Anti-discrimination law*, p.9, available from the Task Force's website at *http://www. cabinet-office.gov.uk/bru/ index/task.htm*

(i) affecting the recruitment, admission to membership or access to benefits of persons belonging to any class referred to in sub-paragraph (a) or the terms of employment or membership or provision of benefits applicable to such persons;

(ii) involving any detriment to such persons . . . including practices discontinued before the time of the investigation so far as relevant for explaining the composition of the class of persons in question at that time".

It is clear that there is no requirement for any suspicion of unlawful action prior to the launch of an investigation by the commission.

The EC's powers of investigation under the FETO cannot be considered in isolation from its obligations in relation to workforce monitoring. A monitoring requirement was imposed by the FEA 1989, in respect of the religious composition of workforces, after the widely acknowledged failure of the voluntary system established under the FEA 1976. The legislative provisions are considered in Chapter 9. It is impossible to judge conclusively how effective the monitoring and review obligations imposed by the FETO are in eradicating discrimination. But what is noticeable is the decline in workplace segregation in Northern Ireland and the degree of consensus which exists as to the decline in religious discrimination. As the Select Committee Report on the FEA 1989 (as it then was) noted:

38 . . . the general view from all the witnesses we heard [was] that unlawful employment discrimination on the grounds of religious belief and political opinion appears to have declined. . . Significant improvement appears to have occurred with lessening segregation of predominantly Roman Catholic firms, and predominantly Protestant firms. . . FEC statistics show that the overall Roman Catholic share of employment has risen by 4.3 percentage points over the period 1990 to1998. . . The employment shifts described above are welcome, but the question arises as to how far they are the result of fair employment legislation. [The Chairman of the FEC] commented that

It is very difficult to give an answer to that and very difficult to disentangle the situation. All I would say is that, during the previous period when the legislation was much weaker . . . there was not as great a change over the previous 15 or 20 years. So I believe that a considerable part of the changes has been as a result of the legislation but I would by no means argue . . . that the changes have been exclusively because of that.

Others shared that basic viewpoint, arguing that the legislation "has created an environment within which the values that legislation encapsulate have been accepted by employers . . ."[114] CBI Northern Ireland considers that the changes in employment "are largely attributable [to the legislation], because [it] would suspect a lot of the changes are due to improved . . . recruitment selection procedures."

The Committee went on to endorse the fair employment legislation's regulatory regime:

[114] Evidence from SACHR to the Select Committee on Northern Ireland, appended to the Fourth Report of that Committee, 1998–1999 session, *The Operation of the Fair Employment (Northern Ireland) Act 1989: Ten Years On.*

66. It has been argued that it might be preferable to reduce the regulatory functions of the FEC, and concentrate resources on resolving individual complaints, making them a more effective mechanism of deterrence.[115] However, it appears to us that such an approach does not recognise the different functions of the individual complaint and the FEC regulatory systems. The former is restricted to dealing with allegations of discrimination, while the latter has a much broader role in encouraging (and ultimately enforcing) fair participation, affirmative action, and equality of opportunity, which (as we have seen above) goes considerably beyond simply eradicating unlawful discrimination. We agree with SACHR, when it said that "you do not necessarily arrive at [fairness and equality] simply by abandoning or abolishing or getting rid of discrimination . . ."

While we welcome the extent to which individual complaints have been used by the [FEC] as the basis for strategic work with employers, we agree with the Commission that if this was the "sole method of dealing strategically with employers then it would be a failure." We recommend that the existing regulatory functions of the Commission be retained in their entirety.

The final point to make in respect of the EC's powers under the FETO is that the Commission has no power to conduct investigations into discrimination on grounds or religious belief or political opinion other than in the employment-related field, broadly defined.

Preventing further discrimination

The EOC and CRE may, during the course of and after the completion of FIs, issue recommendations including recommendations to the Secretary of State for changes to the law. They are obliged, at the close of FIs, to issue reports on them[116] and, if in the course of an FI the relevant Commission is satisfied that the person under investigation is committing or has committed an unlawful act, may issue a non-discrimination notice.[117] NDNs have been issued, *inter alia*, by the CRE into Hackney's housing practices (see Chapter 4) and, more recently, the threat of an NDN in respect of the same borough's employment practices (some of the recent awards against the council having been mentioned above) resulted in an agreed programme for eliminating racism.[118] The programme, details of which have been sent to the 10,500 council employees, includes an apology from the Councillors for the "institutionalised racism" within the organisation.

The contents of such NDNs are prescribed by legislation, s.58 RRA (s.67 SDA) providing that the NDN may require its recipient:

(2) (a) not to commit any such acts; and

---

[115] SACHR dissenting member, fn 59 above, p. 97.

[116] Ss.60 SDA, 51 RRA.

[117] Unlawful discrimination in this context includes pressure, instructions to discriminate, disc advert and disc practices. Appears, from Diplock in *Hillingdon* and *Prestige*, that such notices only after named investigations.

[118] MofD also improved significantly under threat to NDN from CRE—lifted 25th March 1998

(b) where compliance with paragraph (a) involves changes in any of his practices or other arrangements—

    (i) to inform the Commission that he has effected those changes and what those changes are; and

    (ii) to take such steps as may be reasonably required by the notice for the purpose of affording that information to other persons concerned.

(3) A non-discrimination notice may also require the person on whom it is served to furnish the Commission with such other information as may be reasonably required by the notice in order to verify that the notice has been complied with.[119]

Ss.58(5) RRA and 67(5) SDA provides that the relevant Commission will not issue an NDN until it has given the proposed recipient notice of its intention and the grounds for it, has given them an opportunity to make representations and has taken such representations into account. Ss.59 RRA and 68 SDA provide a right of appeal against an NDN, the appeal going to an employment tribunal in employment-related cases, to the county or (in Scotland) sheriff court in other cases. Ss.59(2) RRA and 68(2) SDA provide that:

(2) Where the tribunal or court considers a requirement in respect of which an appeal is brought . . . to be unreasonable because it is based on an incorrect finding of fact or for any other reason, the tribunal or court shall quash the requirement.

This provision was interpreted by the Court of Appeal in *R v CRE ex parte Amari Plastics* [1982] 2 All ER 499, to require a reopening of all the findings of fact, rather than simply the NDN requirements themselves. This approach, defended by Browne-Wilkinson J on the basis that "a requirement "to stop beating your wife" is unreasonable if you have never beaten your wife",[120] had the effect that:

Sacks & Maxwell, 337–8

. . . despite two hearings having already taken place, another hearing is available, this time before the court to examine all the findings of fact. This is so despite the fact that "the Commission have carried out a searching inquisitorial inquiry to satisfy themselves of the truth of the facts on which the notice is based, and have given at least two and probably three opportunities to the person to put his case, whether orally or in writing, either by himself, through solicitors, counsel or any other person of his choice," only to find that the "Act requires that their findings of fact are liable to be re-opened and reversed on appeal." None of the judges felt that section 59(2) could be read any other way, and advised the Commission to seek legislative reform to extricate themselves from the "spider's web spun by Parliament from which there is little hope of their escaping." The effect of the case is to permit the whole factual basis of the non-discrimination notice to be re-opened on appeal.

---

[119] (4) . . . the time at which any information is to be furnished in compliance with the notice shall not be later than five years after the notice has become final.

[120] [1982] 1 QB 265, at 272 (EAT). This approach suggests a degree of judicial arrogance as to the fact-finding capabilities of administrative enforcement bodies such as, in this case, the CRE.

. . .the cost of these proceedings will disable the C.R.E. from doing other and more valuable work and respondents are aware of them.

The other significant difficulty with NDNs relates to their scope. The CRE's 1983 consultative document, *Time for a Change?*, stated that:

> The most serious gap in the non-discrimination notice provisions is the absence of any power to postulate what changes, in the Commission's view, are necessary to avoid a repetition of the discriminatory act. On this the CRE has power to make recommendations only (see s.51, p.30). This has proved, in practice, a very serious constraint and **we recommend that the CRE is given power to state in a non-discrimination notice what changes in the respondents practice are the minimum necessary**. We feel confirmed in this proposal by the very extensive powers of appeal the respondent has against a s.58 notice, which would ensure the avoidance of any unnecessary hardship, which the Notice might inadvertently cause.
>
> Doubts have been raised whether a notice resultant in an unlawful discriminatory act or practice at one particular site of an organisation can give rise to a notice affecting the whole of the organisation or merely its operation at the location investigated. We have always taken the view that as the s.58 notice affects a person (whether human or corporate) it affects the whole of his activity in the particular field covered. However, because it has seriously been questioned, clarification is needed and **we recommend an added provision to make it clear that a non-discrimination notice resultant in an unlawful act or practice makes unlawful the act or practice concerned wherever the respondent may perform it**.

By contrast, the DRCA, which establishes the DRC and sets out its powers, including the powers of FI, not only requires (s.4) that an NDN gives details of the unlawful act which the DRC has found the recipient to be committing or have committed, and ((1)(b)) "requires him not to commit any further unlawful acts of the same kind (and, if the finding is that he is committing an unlawful act, to cease doing so)". In addition, s.4 provides that:

(2) The notice may include recommendations to the person concerned as to action which the Commission considers he could reasonably be expected to take with a view to complying with the requirement mentioned in subsection (1)(b).
(3) The notice may require the person concerned—
    (a) to propose an adequate action plan (subject to and in accordance with Part III of Schedule 3) with a view to securing compliance with the requirement mentioned in subsection (1)(b); and
    (b) once an action plan proposed by him has become final, to take any action which—
        (i) is specified in the plan; and
        (ii) he has not already taken, at the time or times specified in the plan.
(4) For the purposes of subsection (3)—
    (a) an action plan is a document drawn up by the person concerned specifying action (including action he has already taken) intended to change anything in his practices, policies, procedures or other arrangements which—
        (i) caused or contributed to the commission of the unlawful act concerned, or

    (ii) is liable to cause or contribute to a failure to comply with the requirement mentioned in subsection (1)(b); and

(b) an action plan is adequate if the action specified in it would be sufficient to ensure, within a reasonable time, that he is not prevented from complying with that requirement by anything in his practices, policies, procedures or other arrangements; and the action specified in an action plan may include ceasing an activity or taking continuing action over a period.

Schedule 3, part 3, provides that the action plan must be served on the DRC within the time specified in the NDN.[121] If the DRC is not satisfied with the action plan it may request revision of the plan, and make "recommendations as to action which the Commission considers might be included in an adequate action plan" (para 16(2)). If the second plan is inadequate, or if it is not served, the DRC may seek a court order declaring that the plan is inadequate, requiring a revised plan and (para 17(3)(c)) "containing such directions (if any) as the court considers appropriate as to the action which should be specified in the adequate action plan required by the order".

The DRC has a further power, sought by the CRE since 1983, i.e., the power to enter into "voluntary undertakings", binding agreements with suspected discriminators whereby, in exchange for the Commission's undertaking either not to begin[122] or to continue an FI, or (at the completion of an FI) not to issue a non-discrimination notice, the suspected discriminator undertakes (s.5(2)(b) DRCA):

(i) not to commit any further unlawful acts of the same kind (and, where appropriate, to cease committing the act in question); and

(ii) to take such action (which may include ceasing an activity or taking continuing action over any period) as may be specified in the agreement.

Subsection 5(5) goes on to provide that:

The action specified in an undertaking under subsection (2)(b)(ii) must be action intended to change anything in the practices, policies, procedures or other arrangements of the person concerned which—

(a) caused or contributed to the commission of the unlawful act in question; or

(b) is liable to cause or contribute to a failure to comply with his undertaking under subsection (2)(b)(i).

---

[121] Failure to do so may result in the issue of an injunction ordering compliance.

[122] This provision was, presumably, inserted after Roger Berry's complaint (22nd April 1999 col 1087–8) that agreements couldn't be made early enough "According to the CRE, the key time for a written agreement is following the preliminary written inquiry before the start of the formal investigation. It is then that organisations suspected of being discriminatory start getting a little nervous and want to avoid bad publicity". Berry also called (as the CRE and EOC had) for NDNs to "specify the nature of the changes required and the time frame for their implementation" and complained over the DRC's lack of power to take action over discriminatory practices, persistent discrimination and instructions to discriminate. The power to enter voluntary legally binding written undertakings.

"Agreements in lieu of enforcement action" may be varied or revoked by agreement of the parties. Enforcement by the DRC is by way of application to the county or sheriff court.[123] The EC in Northern Ireland has similar powers in respect of the FETO, Article 13 providing that the EC may accept written undertakings "in such terms as appear satisfactory to the Commission for the purpose of ensuring that the person giving it takes such action for promoting equality of opportunity as is, in all the circumstances, reasonable and appropriate". The undertakings may be given in response to notice by the Commission that the latter "in exercising its functions under this Order . . . has formed the opinion that he ought to take action for promoting equality of opportunity" or "from any [FETO-related tribunal] decision . . . or from any evidence given in such proceedings' is of the opinion that such action ought to be taken". Enforcement is by way of notice served by the Commission[124] or by order of the FET on application from the Commission.[125]

The FEC's review of the FEAs suggested that the power to enter into Voluntary Undertakings was unduly narrow:

[t]he Commission would prefer to work with employers rather than to enter into an investigatory procedure . . . the Commission has a statutory function to fulfil and it cannot embark on courses of action which would not ultimately be enforceable. Voluntary Undertakings provide the opportunity for meeting the objectives of a co-operative approach combined with enforcement if necessary. The current requirement that "In exercising its functions under this Order the Commission has formed the opinion that he ought to take action for promoting equality of opportunity" means that Voluntary Undertakings may only be obtained in those circumstances where the Commission has specific power "to form an opinion" . . . Although a bona fide employer may wish to co-operate with the Commission and be able to refer to a public statement of commitment to working with the Commission he/she may not be in a position to conclude a voluntary undertaking.[126]

The FETO does not address the point raised by the FEC. Nor does the DRCA which (s.5(1)) limits voluntary undertakings to situations in which the DRC has reason to believe that discrimination has occurred.

Returning to the formally-issued NDNs, the various Commissions are given the power to follow up the issue of such notices. Ss.60 and 69 of the SDA and RRA respectively permit such investigations absent any belief in unlawful discrimination within five years of the issue of a NDN. S.59(2) DRCA is in similar terms.[127]

---

[123] Introducing the Bill's second reading in the House of Commons (HC 22nd April 1999, Col. 1064). Andrew Smith (Minister for Employment, Welfare to Work and Equal Opportunities), stated that the Lord Chancellor was considering the question of representative actions.
[124] Appealable to the FET.
[125] The EC, at the time of writing, has no powers in respect of the DDA, but changes are anticipated.
[126] FEC *Review*, fn 5 above, paras 3.19 & 3.20.
[127] See further fns 110–112, above.

The Commissions as Litigants

The various Commissions are given exclusive power to litigate in respect of a number of provisions of the RRA and SDA. These consist of "discriminatory practices", such a practice being defined as "the application of a requirement or condition which results in . . . [unlawful indirect sex or race discrimination] . . . *or which would be likely to result in such an act of discrimination*" if those to whom it applied were not all of one sex or if they included people of any particular racial group (my emphasis).[128]

The discriminatory practices provision (SDA s.37, RRA s.28) was aimed at "unintended discrimination [which is] . . . so deeply entrenched or so overwhelmingly effective that it is practically invisible and, therefore, may not give rise to any single individual complaint".[129] Its enforcement is by way of an NDN which, as noted above, can be issued only after an FI with all the difficulties attendant thereon.[130]

Neither the DDA nor the FETO contain any provision relating to discriminatory practices. The DRCA 1999 does contain, as do the SDA, RRA and the FETO, a provision prohibiting "persistent discrimination" (SDA ss.71 and 72, RRA ss.62 and 63). These, again, are enforceable only by the commissions which are permitted to apply to the county (in Scotland, the sheriff) court for an injunction restraining a respondent from engaging in discriminatory practices or otherwise contravening the relevant Act where "it appears to the commission that unless restrained [the respondent] is likely to engage in discriminatory practices or otherwise contravene the relevant Act."[131] Such an application can only be made within five years of a tribunal finding of unlawful discrimination against the respondent, or the service by the same commission of an NDN upon that respondent. Where the action for persistent discrimination follows the issue of an NDN, the Commission must first apply to the tribunal for a declaration that the respondent was guilty of unlawful discrimination. In the period 1977–1992, the EOC's *Annual Reports* record only two cases relating to persistent discrimination by employers. One such case was *CRE* v *Precision Manufacturing Services Ltd* COIT 4106/91, discussed in Chapter 7.

The powers to enforce the provisions relating to persistent discrimination and, where available, discriminatory practices, vest solely in the relevant commissions. In addition, the EOC and the CRE have sole power (ss.38–40 SDA, ss.29–31 RRA), to take action against discriminatory advertisements, instructions to discriminate and pressure to discriminate. Such action may consist of a complaint to an industrial tribunal which may decide that the alleged contravention of the relevant Act occurred. Alternatively, and where "it appears to the Commission . . . that unless restrained [a

---

[128] SDA, ss. 38. 39, 40, 42 & 37(10) and RRA, ss. 29, 30. 31 33 & 28 respectively.

[129] John Fraser, Under-Secretary of State for Employment 906 H.C. Debs (4th March 1976) col. 1430. See cols. 1431–3 and 1434–5 for opposition.

[130] Discriminatory practices can subsequently be challenged as "persistent discrimination" in the manner discussed below.

[131] S.71 SDA, s.62 RRA, s.6 DRCA, art 41 FETO.

person] is likely" to continue to breach the relevant section, the Commission may apply for an injunction from a designated county court.[132]

Again, the utilisation of these powers has not been significant. Between 1977 and 1992 the EOC's took action in two cases each against employers who persistently instructed job centres to discriminate and who placed discriminatory advertisements, and a handful of cases in which employers capitulated to EOC demands in the face of action relating to instructions to discriminate.[133] More recently, a smattering of cases relating to discriminatory advertisements and inducement and/or pressure to discriminate have passed through the tribunals. The EOC's inaction in relation to discriminatory advertisements was criticised by Vera Sacks in 1986:

"The Equal Opportunities Commission—Ten Years On" (1986) 49 *Modern Law Review* 560, 566–7

. . . it appears that in 1984 there were more inquiries relating to advertising than any other topic (2,186 compared to 1,625 on employment), but all the Annual report has to say on this is that there

> has been an increase in the number of complaints to the Commission about apparently unlawful advertisements. The vast majority of such complaints are resolved without recourse to the tribunals or courts; and there has been no deterioration in the generally high level of compliance by publishers with the requirements of section 38 of the Act. The Commission's Advertising Unit has continued to devote any time possible, after dealing with complaints and enquiries, to developing a strategy of prevention by speaking to seminars of publishers and advertisers.

No details of the kind of discriminatory advertising, the places where it occurs, nor any other information is contained in these paragraphs. The only clue to trouble is contained in two sentences:

> Discussions took place with the Employment Services Division of the Manpower Services Commission following a Survey of Job Centres' advertising practice. This had indicated that the indirect discrimination provisions of the Sex Discrimination Act needed clarification in respect of recruitment advertising . . .

At the end of that paragraph on what is clearly a serious source of discrimination all that is known is that discriminatory advertisements are appearing at Job Centres and that the E.O.C. has "surveyed" these practices and "discussed" them with the M.S.C. Considering that this is an area in which *only* the E.O.C. can litigate (individuals must refer complaints to them) the public is entitled to know in more detail about discriminatory advertising and the results which the Commission has achieved "without recourse to the tribunals or courts." The conclusion is that despite 10 years' experience of the Act, there is a growing tide of discriminatory advertisements about which something is being done *informally*. Yet the E.O.C. has only once litigated in respect of an advertisement. Further use of law

---

[132] ss.72 and 63 SDA and RRA.
[133] *Annual Report* 1988, 1986 and 1988 respectively. In 1985, action relating to instructions to discriminate was taken against Barclays, in 1988 against Clarks and in 1986 a further three were threatened and agreement reached.

enforcement powers, perhaps by a formal investigation into job Centres, suggests itself most forcibly.

What has been described here in regard to advertising is true of other activities of the Commission. The Commission is possibly doing itself a grave injustice by the use of anodyne phraseology and lack of hard information. It points out, and this is a comment made repeatedly in regard to other spheres of its work, that it can do more by keeping the identity of offenders anonymous and by persuasion and education. But the lack of real information to the reader seems pointless and unjustifiable. The Annual Report is a clear indication that the Commission has failed to evaluate its work.

As with FIs, the CRE appear to have been rather more active—the Annual Reports 1990–1994, for example, each refer to a number of proceedings started, as well as to agreements reached, in respect of discriminatory advertisements and instructions or pressure to discriminate.[134]

The FETO contains a provision (Article 34) dealing with discriminatory advertisements along the same lines as the SDA and RRA, and prohibits "aid[ing] or incit[ing] . . . direct[ing], procur[ing] or induc[ing] discrimination" (Article 35), rather than instructions or pressure to discriminate. The DDA, controversially, contains no prohibition of discriminatory advertisements, or of instructions or pressure to discriminate.[135] The EC in Northern Ireland is empowered to take action against advertisements which discriminate on grounds of sex, race, religious belief or political opinion though not, similarly to the DRC in Great Britain, disability.[136]

In addition to those powers specifically vested in the various commissions by the relevant legislation, the commissions may make judicial review applications according to the ordinary rules on standing. *EOC* v *Birmingham City Council* [1989] 1 All ER 769, [1989] AC 1155, which was discussed in Chapter 2, was one such case. There the EOC challenged the council's discriminatory provision of grammar school places. In 1990, the EOC's application for judicial review of the Queen's Regulations for the Army and the Royal Air Force, which provided for the dismissal of women who became pregnant, resulted in the abandonment of the policy. As Lord Lester has pointed out, the "good grace" with which the Defence Secretary surrendered to the judicial review application was not matched by the Ministry of Defence's response to the flood of compensation claims which followed: "no doubt because of the very large sums at stake".[137]

In the *Birmingham* case the EOC's standing was not challenged. In *EOC and another* v *Secretary of State for Employment*, on the other hand, the government (as respon-

---

[134] Ironically, the CRE became the first and only body required to submit its advertisements, pre-publication, to the Advertising Standards Authority after allegations of racism were made in connection with a CRE campaign designed to raise awareness of racism.

[135] The Disability Rights Task Force Final Report, *From Exclusion to Inclusion* available from the task force website see fn 113 above, recommends that the DDA be brought into line in this regard with the other legislation (recommendation 5.42).

[136] In Great Britain the CRE, EOC, DRC for the RRA, SDA and DDA respectively in Northern Ireland the EC for all these and for the FETO besides.

[137] "Discrimination: What Can Lawyers Learn From History?" 1994 *Public Law* 224 at 233.

dent) argued that the EOC had no right to challenge its imposition of differential qualifying periods (two and five years respectively) for employment protection on full-time
and part-time workers. The House of Lords rejected the government's argument and
issued a declaration that the discriminatory periods were contrary to Article 141 (see
further Chapter 10).

EOC and another v Secretary of State for Employment **[1995] 1 AC 1, [1994] 1 All ER 910,
[1994] 2 WLR 176, 92 LGR 360, [1994] ICR 317, [1994] IRLR 176**

Lord Keith (Lord Jauncey dissenting on this issue):

RSC Ord 53, r 3(7) provides that the court shall not grant leave to apply for judicial review
"unless it considers that the applicant has a sufficient interest in the matter to which the
application relates". . . Has the EOC a sufficient interest in that matter? Under s 53(1) of
the [SDA] the duties of the EOC include: "(a) to work towards the elimination of discrimination; (b) to promote equality of opportunity between men and women generally . . ." If
the admittedly discriminatory [qualifying periods] . . . are not objectively justified, then
steps taken by the EOC towards securing that these provisions are changed may very reasonably be regarded as taken in the course of working towards the elimination of discrimination. The present proceedings are clearly such a step. In a number of cases the EOC has
been the initiating party to proceedings designed to secure the elimination of discrimination. The prime example is *EOC v Birmingham* . . . in which it was not suggested at any
stage that the EOC lacked *locus standi.*[138] In my opinion it would be a very retrograde step
now to hold that the EOC has no *locus standi* to agitate in judicial review proceedings questions related to sex discrimination which are of public importance and affect a large section
of the population. The determination of this issue turns essentially upon a consideration of
the statutory duties and public law role of the EOC as regards which no helpful guidance
is to be gathered from decided cases. I would hold that the EOC has sufficient interest to
bring these proceedings and hence the necessary *locus standi.*[139]

The potential impact of proceedings such as those in the *EOC* case is difficult to
overestimate. Whereas an individual challenge to the qualifying periods would have to
be brought by an applicant against her employer under the relevant legislation and
would result, if successful, only in the non-application of the period to her alone,
action by the EOC resulted in the removal at the national level of the discriminatory
provisions.

---

[138] His Lordship also relied on *R v Secretary of State for Defence, ex p Equal Opportunities Commission*
(20 December 1991, unreported) in which it was common ground that the EOC had *locus standi.* Another
instance is *R v Secretary of State for Social Security, ex p Equal Opportunities Commission* Case C–9/91
[1992] 3 All ER 577, which went to the European Court.

[139] Lord Jauncey dissented on the basis that: "the fact that the commission may properly initiate judicial
review proceedings in pursuance of their duties against local authorities or other ministers is not, in my view,
conclusive of its ability so to do in relation to the Secretary of State. . . .

If Parliament had intended that the commission should be empowered to challenge decisions of the
Secretary of State and impose its will upon him it is quite remarkable that Pt VI of the Act which sets out
in some detail the powers and duties of the commission, both at large and in relation to the Secretary of
State, should have remained totally silent upon this particular matter.

ALTERNATIVE METHODS OF ENFORCEMENT

The calls from the EOC and CRE in respect of mandatory workplace monitoring have been mentioned. The Better Regulation Task Force acknowledged the benefits of monitoring, but took the view that it should not be made obligatory. This, too, has been the approach of the Government. Government's response to the EOC's call for mandatory pay auditing in workplaces has also fallen upon deaf ears, although the Government has recently promised some improvements to the equal pay legislation.

One of the most significant methods by which anti-discrimination legislation and guidelines are enforced in the United States consists of contract compliance, i.e., the practice of conditioning access to government contracts, grants, etc., on compliance with particular criteria. In the United States, for example, an Executive Order was issued by President Roosevelt in 1914 to prohibit discrimination by defence contractors.[140] The US federal government has used contract compliance since 1968 in order to require government contractors, more generally, to adopt "affirmative action" (first race-based, then also sex-based) in an attempt to assimilate the racial and sexual balance of workforces to those of locally available workforces.[141]

Executive Order 11246 binds federal contractors and subcontractors whose US-based government contracts are worth in excess of $10,000. Such contractors are required to monitor and report on the racial and sexual composition of their workforces. Those whose federal contracts are worth in excess of $50,000 and who employ at least 50 staff must, in addition, produce written affirmative action plans. It is estimated that the contract compliance programme covers over 20 per cent of the civilian workforce.[142]

In Canada, federally regulated employers and contractors bidding for goods and services contracts with the federal government are required to provide "employment equity", defined as "an action-oriented approach that identifies under-representation or concentration of, and employment barriers to, certain groups of people, and provides a number of practical and creative remedies.[143] The Employment Equity Act 1995 and accompanying regulations require employers, in consultation with their workforces to:

- conduct a workforce survey to ascertain the proportion and position of women, aboriginal, disabled and "visible minority" workers;

---

[140] FEC Review, fn 5 above, para 3.55.

[141] In the same year the Philadelphia Plan, adopted by President Nixon, required all those bidding for federal contracts to establish numerical goals for integration. As Attorney General, the later Chief Justice Rehnquist assured the President that the plan was in conformity with the Civil Rights Act—see R. McKeever, 'Raw Judicial Power?: the Supreme Court and American Society' (2nd ed., Manchester. Manchester University Press, 1995) *ibid*, pp.125–6.

[142] Paras 99–100 Fourth Report of the Select Committee on N. Ireland, 1998–1999, fn 114 above.

[143] Human Resources Development Canada, Introduction to Employment Equity available at http://info.load-otea.hrdc-drhc.

- undertake a "workforce analysis" to determine the degree of under-representation, if any, of the groups within the workforce;
- undertake an "employment systems review" to determine what, if any, barriers "prohibit the full participation of designated group members within the employer's workforce";
- develop and implement an "employment equity plan" which "must include . . .
  —positive policies and practices to accelerate the integration of designated group members in employers" workforces;
  —elimination of employment barriers pinpointed during the employment systems review;
  —a timetable for implementation;
  —short term numerical goals;
  —and longer term goals";
- monitor the implementation of the plan, reviewing and revising it as necessary.

The Canadian rules apply to contractors with at least 100 employees wishing to bid for contracts worth at least $200 000. Failure to comply with the rules can result in ineligibility to bid for further contracts.

In the UK itself, contract compliance in the form of the Fair Wages Resolutions was practised between 1891 and 1983. The Fair Wages Resolutions of 1891, 1909 and 1946, which were passed by the House of Commons, required government contractors to provide their employees with terms and conditions that were no less favourable than those generally established by collective bargaining in the relevant trade. The 1946 Resolutions also required government contractors to permit workers the freedom to join trade unions.[144] Many local authorities also imposed fair wages clauses on private sector companies with which they contracted.[145]

None of the Fair Wages Resolutions was concerned with discrimination on grounds of sex, race, etc. Indeed, the generally held view of the 1898 Resolution was that it "says nothing as to the standard rate of wages for women", and that it was not "the intention of the resolution to enforce the payment to women of the rate 'current' for men employed on the same class of work".[146] Nevertheless, and despite their many imperfections, the Resolutions do provide precedent within the UK for the practice of contract compliance by central government.

Those concerned with the efficacy of the various anti-discrimination statutes (and, in the case of Northern Ireland, the FETO) have long called for contract compliance to be utilised as an enforcement method. The CRE's 1992 reform proposals included the statement (para 9) that:

---

[144] The 1946 Resolution was, in addition to being administered by the executive in the allocation and content of government contracts, incorporated into a number of statutes (see further A. McColgan) *Just Wages for Women* (Oxford: OUP, 1997 Chapter 9) although, as in the case of the Resolution itself, the obligations were not directly enforceable by the employees concerned. See also *Simpson v. Kodak Ltd* [1948] 2 K. B. 184.

[145] See generally B. Bercusson, *Fair Wages Resolutions* (London: Mansell, 1978).

[146] *Ibid.*, pp.36–7.

Without any new legislation, a Government could bring its economic power in Britain to bear on the whole question of equal opportunities. Indeed, by not doing so it may be criticised on the moral ground that that power is inevitably being used in many instances to support firms which are not providing equal opportunities, as well as on the practical ground that it is throwing away a chance to influence change for the better.

We believe the economic power of government, both national and local, should be used in support of equal opportunity.

The CRE's call for the adoption of contract compliance was reiterated by that body and by the EOC, in their 1998 reform proposals. And in 1997, the *Justice* report, *Improving Equality Law: the Options*, contained the following recommendation.

The Labour Party has traditionally supported contract compliance, for example, in respect of fair wages. In 1975 the White Paper on racial discrimination proposed a clause in government contracts to ensure that contractors were not practising racial discrimination, but no attempt was subsequently made to monitor compliance with such clauses in government contracts.

Experience in the United States and Northern Ireland, and in Great Britain before the rescission in 1980 of the Fair Wages Resolution, shows that contract compliance of this kind can be a powerful weapon. However, the Local Government act 1988, Section 17, has outlawed contract compliance by public authorities. There is a limited exception in the case of racial discrimination which applies only to local authorities and allows certain approved questions to be asked on workforce matters before a firm's name is put on a list of tenderers. It is unclear how far Section 18(2)(b) of the Act allows a binding undertaking (e.g. to conduct ethnic monitoring) to be included in any contract awarded by a local authority and, if so, what sanctions may be applied. The exception does not apply to discrimination on any grounds other than race. Contract conditions to further social objectives within a Member State are compatible with the EC Treaty provided that they do not discriminate between EC contractors and are mentioned in the notice advertising the contract in the EC official journal. Although a contractor's policy in regard to equal opportunities is probably not a permissible basis in EC law for selection as a contractor, once awarded the contract, the contractor must comply with the contract condition which seeks to enforce a lawful objective, such as compliance with anti-discrimination legislation. The Local Government Act needs to be amended so as to prevent this in relation to all forms of unlawful discrimination. It would be a powerful weapon against discrimination.

Much contract compliance is actually prohibited in the UK. Prior to the implementation of the LGA 1988, many local authorities had adopted policies of contract compliance. Christopher McCrudden wrote of that period:

"Codes in a Cold Climate" (1988) 51 *Modern Law Review* 409, 429

Local authorities have basically the same powers to contract as others, including the power to seek to have firms with which they contract accept conditions on how the contract is to be carried out. In all cases, however, these powers are subject to public law requirements, including the duties to act reasonably, not ultra vires, and in compliance with the fiduciary duty to the ratepayers. The Greater London Council (G.L.C.) in drawing up its contract compliance policy in 1983, sought counsel's opinion on how best to satisfy these public law duties. As a result of that advice, the G.L.C. relied on section 71 of the Race Relations Act, which imposes on councils a duty to seek to eliminate racial discrimination and promote equality of opportunity, as a primary legal support for its contract compliance policy. Though there was no specific legal obligation for other areas of discrimination, it was considered justifiable on moral grounds for public bodies to seek positively to promote the laws against sex discrimination in equivalent ways. Furthermore, it decided that the detail of any compliance sought "should relate as closely as possible to officially recognised standards . . . using the Codes of Practice of the C.R.E. and the E.O.C." Indeed, one of the architects of the policy has written that, "[b]ecause of the clear legal advice the G.L.C. received, the operational core of the policy turned on the Codes of Practice." An equivalent policy was also adopted by the Inner London Education Authority. Most importantly, ethnic monitoring and the submission of statistics became standard elements in contract compliance policy.

Although it was open for those subject to local authority contract compliance policies to challenge them by way of judicial review, the Government eventually acceded to requests from the C.B.I. and the construction and civil engineering employers to introduce legislation restricting local authority powers to impose contract compliance policies on those with whom they contracted.

S.17 of the Local Government Act 1988 prohibited local and other public authorities from taking into account, in their contracting functions: "non-commercial matters", these matters being defined to include:

(5) (a) "the terms and conditions of employment by contractors of their workers or the composition of, the arrangements for the promotion, transfer or training of or the other opportunities afforded to, their workforces".

The only exception to this prohibition was provided by s.18, which permitted only that local authorities:

(2) "ask . . . approved questions seeking information or undertakings relating to workforce matters and consider . . . the responses to them" and/or "include[e] in a draft contract or draft tender for a contract terms or provisions relating to workforce matters and consider . . . the responses to them . . . if, as the case may be, consideration of the information, the giving of the undertaking or the inclusion of the term is reasonably necessary to secure compliance with [RRA s 71]".

S.71 imposes upon local authorities an obligation to "to make appropriate arrangements with a view to securing that their various functions are carried out with due regard to the need:

(a) to eliminate unlawful racial discrimination; and
(b) to promote equality of opportunity and good relations, between persons of different racial groups."[147]

[147] See *R v LewishamBC ex p Shell* [1988] 1 All ER 938 for judicial; interpretation of this section.

According to the CRE's second (1992) report on the RRA (41–2):

> ... we were disappointed by Government action in relation to the local government legislation of 1988. If it had not been for the existence of Section 71 of the Race Relations Act 1976, the probability is that Government would have banned local authorities altogether from considering equal opportunities in their contracting processes. . . . The Sex Discrimination Act contains no similar provision and Government did ban local authorities from considering equal opportunities between men and women in their contracting processes.
>
> Because of Section 71 the Government felt it had to permit some local government action in the area of race, but restricted it. By use of the Approved Questions under the legislation, Government has stopped local authorities obtaining ethnic monitoring data from those they might wish to contract for the supply of goods and services. Yet, in *West Midlands Passenger Transport Executive v Singh* (CA) [1988] IRLR 186 and in the Commission's *Code of Practice in Employment*, the value of that data in determining whether equal opportunities is being provided is recognised.

The impending changes to s.71 RRA and the corresponding provisions are considered below. A wholly fresh approach is now required by Government. In Northern Ireland, the provisions equivalent to s.17 LGA are subject to an limited exceptions permitting public authorities to ascertain whether a contractor is a "qualified person" within the FETO. The prohibition on contract compliance is particularly problematic given the widespread contracting-out of services previously provided by the public sector. Compulsory competitive tendering was introduced in 1980 and has had a devastating on the terms and conditions of former public sector jobs.

L. Dickens, "Gender, race and employment equality in Britain: inadequate strategies and the role of industrial relations actors" (1997) 28 *Industrial Relations Journal* 282

There has been a disproportionate adverse effect on women and ethnic minorities (in particular black women) who tend to be over-represented in those sectors and jobs which have been effected. Some predominantly male areas, such as refuse collection have been affected, although the stronger union and bargaining position of male workers helped reduce some of the adverse consequences of CCT for them. The major impact has been on women who have lost jobs, had hours reduced and work intensified, experienced pay reductions and loss of benefits . . . The government policy shift in the public sector towards subcontracting could have been harnessed for equality through a strategy of contract compliance . . . [which] had been used to some effect by local authorities in the past. Instead a contrary path was taken with contract compliance being curtailed by [the LGA 1988] . . . Nor was there any equality-proofing of the CCT process. Rather than disseminating good practice out from the public sector (which traditionally provides the model of a "good employer"), increased commercialism within a deregulated framework has weakened the good practice itself.[148]

---

[148] Citing T Colling, Renewal or Rigor Mortis? Union Responses to Contracting-Out in Local Government (1995) 26 *Industrial Relations Journal* 134; A Coyle, Going Private: The implications of Privitisation for Women's Work (1985) 21 *Feminist Review*; K Escott and D Whitfield, The Gender Impact of CCT in Local Government, EOC Research Discussion Series no 12, Manchester, EOC; and Public Services Privitisation Research Unit, Privitisation—disaster for Equality London, PSPRU, 1992. See

Dickens states that "some protection of existing terms and conditions was provided by the need for the UK to conform to European requirements relating to transfers of undertakings". But, as she points out, this protection was "belated", the Transfer of Undertakings Regulations 1981 only being amended in 1993 clearly to apply to public sector contracting-out (and even now their application in relation to re-tendering is unclear). In any event, their imperfect protection applies only to existing workers, rather than to jobs, so they have little long-term impact on terms and conditions in contracted-out sectors.

As the CRE pointed out in the extract above, no exceptions are made to s.17 LGA in respect of sex discrimination. The same is true of disability discrimination. The FETO does embrace a form, albeit an extremely limited form, of contract compliance, Article 64 providing that public authorities "shall not enter into [relevant] contract[s] with" an unqualified person, and "shall take all such steps as are reasonable to secure that no work is executed or goods or services supplied for the purposes of [a relevant] contract by any unqualified person".[149] An "unqualified person" is one declared as such by the Equality Commission (Article 62) on the grounds either of failure to register with the Commission (a prerequisite to the monitoring obligations discussed in Chapter 7) or to submit a monitoring return, or of failure to comply with an order issued by the EC. Only one employer has ever been declared "unqualified" and this declaration was subsequently withdraw.[150]

The Standing Advisory Commission on Human Rights proposed, in 1997, that the then-FEA be amended to require that prospective contractors provide information on their "policies, procedures and practices in relation to fair employment and equal opportunities", and that contracts could specify terms which contractors would be obliged to meet. But *Partnership for Equality*, the White Paper which preceded the FETO made clear the government's general disapproval of the CC mechanism (paras 5.25–7)

[C]ontract compliance . . . runs counter to the spirit of market liberalisation in public procurement which has been promoted by the European Union and the UK Government. The Government's policy has been that value for money is central to public sector procurement policy . . . The [fair employment legislation] includes a form of contract compliance [which]

also Report on Formal Investigation into Competitive Tendering in Health and Education Services in Northern Ireland available from the EOC for Northern Ireland (now the Sex Equality Directorate of the Equality Commission).

[149] Such a contract is either (art.64(2)): "a contract made by the public authority accepting an offer to execute any work or supply any goods or services where the offer is made . . . (b) in response to an invitation by the public authority to submit offers" or (art.64(3)) "a contract falling within a class or description for the time being specified in an order made by the Department, where work is to be executed or goods or services supplied by any unqualified person".

[150] Article 64(6) provides that "(6) Nothing in this Article affects the validity of any contract" Prior to the implementation of the FETO, the FEA permitted contracts with unqualified persons if the alternative was either disproportionately expensive or not in the public interest. These qualifications were repealed but Art.64(7) provides that "(7) This Article does not apply to the execution of any work, or the provision of any goods or services, by any person which is certified in writing by the Secretary of State to be necessary or desirable for the purpose of safeguarding national security or protecting public safety or public order".

. . . stand[s] as a significant modification of general government policy on contract compliance and an acknowledgement that the particular circumstances of fair employment in
Northern Ireland might warrant sanctions of a different magnitude from those applying to
other types of discrimination . . . the Government does not propose to extend contract
compliance to achieve fair employment objectives.

The public procurement directives (Council Directives 93/37, 93/36, 92/50 and
93/38) guarantee equal treatment on grounds of nationality in the contracting process
in relation, respectively, to works, supplies, services and utilities. They apply to contracts which exceed specified financial threshholds and require that the tendering
process be transparent and that the selection of candidates in the award of tenders be
based on objective criteria.[151]

The directives permit the tendering authorities to advise prospective contractors as
to the national employment regulations and in the view of the FEC appear to permit
authorities "to request tenderers to provide a guarantee that their future compliance
with national anti-discrimination requirements had been included in their tender price
. . . The fundamental principle applied is that the method adopted by the contracting
authorities in satisfying themselves of future conformity must not directly or indirectly
discriminate against contractors from other member states ."[152]

In *Gebroeders Beentjes BV* v *State (Netherlands)* Case C–31/87 [1990] 1 CMLR 287,
the ECJ distinguished between contractual conditions imposed on contractors, on the
one hand, and selection criteria for contractors on the other. As far as the latter were
concerned, the public procurement directives would be breached if they had a discriminatory impact on grounds of nationality. It had already been established, in
Commission v *Italy* Case C–360/89 [1992] ECR 3401, that the only criteria upon which
tendering authorities could assess the suitability of prospective contractors were those
set out in the directives themselves. The suitability criteria imposed by the public procurement directives provide little scope for enforcing anti-discrimination provisions,
the only potentially relevant criteria included in the works directive for example, being
a legal finding of professional misconduct or a finding of "grave professional misconduct proved by any means which the contracting authority can justify". *Commission* v
Italy dealt with the suitability, rather than the award criteria. As far as the latter were
concerned, the directives require that the contract be awarded to the lowest-priced or
economically most advantageous tender. The *Beentjes* case concerned a contract
awarded to a bidder who was able to employ long-term unemployed, the authority
regarding this as one of the selection criteria. The ECJ took the view that, the public
procurement directives not being intended exhaustively to regulate procurement, such
factors could be taken into account as long as they did not operate in a discriminatory
manner.

[151] Transposed into UK law, respectively, by The Public Works Contracts Regulations 1991 (S.I.
1991/2678), The Public Supply Contracts Regulations 1995 (S.I. 1995/2010); The Public Service Contracts
Regulations 1993 (S.I. 1993/3228), and The Utility Supply and Works Contracts Regulations 1992 (S.I.
1992/3279).
[152] FEC *Review*, fn 5 above, para 3.64.

The EC position on contract compliance was summarised by the FEC in the following terms.

Review of the Fair Employment Act (1997)

3.72 It is clear therefore that there are circumstances in which equality criteria and conditions may be incorporated into the contracting process both at the suitability and the award stages:

1. Requiring the contractor to agree that he/she will comply with national requirements concerning non-discrimination.
2. Enabling the authority to satisfying him/herself that the contractor has not been convicted of a breach of anti-discrimination laws.
3. In some limited circumstances, in the context of the award criteria.

3.73 It is under this third heading that contracting authorities may be required to undertake more far reaching positive action measures to promote the participation and interests of minority groups in the work place. In order to be acceptable such contract conditions must not be discriminatory between contractors in different member states. For example if the positive action condition were such that a contractor was required to carry out affirmative action in his undertaking the key question is whether that affirmative action is of a type which is lawful in one member state but unlawful in another. The tenderer in the country where it is lawful would have a clear advantage in being able to satisfy the positive action criteria . . . . As there is no common policy across the Member States with regard to positive action this would prove difficult. Thus requiring affirmative action without first carefully considering whether contractors in all Member States are legally able to engage in it runs the risk of breaching the Procurement Directives. For example the question arises as to whether it is lawful in other member states to adopt affirmative action measures in a redundancy situation such as those protected by the FETO. One suggested way to resolve this might be to exclude non-national contractors from having to satisfy any affirmative action requirement or at least those which are unlawful in their member state. (Executive Order 11246 in the United States provides that contracts and subcontractors are exempt from the requirement of an equal opportunity clause with regard to works performed outside the United States by employees who are not recruited within the United States). However there are strong arguments that this would amount to reverse discrimination against the domestic contractor.

The Commission took the view that the public procurement directives were consistent, even at the suitability stage, with questions as to the compliance with the provisions of the FETO of "registered employers" (see further Chapter 9), and recommended that contracting authorities be required

to carry out an assessment of each contractor to consider whether there is proof of grave professional misconduct . . . arising from unlawful religious and/or political discrimination . . . If the contracting authority concludes . . . that the contractor has been convicted of any offence concerning professional misconduct . . . or that the contractor has otherwise been guilty of grave professional misconduct and the authority considers it reasonable to do so, then the contractor should be excluded from participation in the contract.[153]

[153] *Ibid.*, para 3.96.

The FEC further expressed the view that they permitted the specification of equal opportunity requirements in tender documents produced by contracting authorities, though "in assessing contracting responses [public authorities should] not discriminate between contractors from different member states". Finally, the FEC proposed that, consistent with the requirements of the various public procurement directives, contracting authorities could include a range of equality conditions in contracts including:

3.97 a) The contractor shall adopt a policy to comply with statutory obligations under the Fair Employment Acts.

b) The contractor shall take all reasonable steps to ensure that all its staff or agents employed in the performance of the contract will comply with the policy. These steps shall include the issue of written instructions to staff, the appointment of a senior manager with responsibility for equal opportunities, and the provision of information to staff on availability of support from staff and from the Commission.

c) The contractor shall take all reasonable steps to observe the Fair Employment Code of Practice.

d) In the event of any finding of unlawful religious or political discrimination being made against the contractor during the period of the contract by any court or Fair Employment Tribunal the contractor shall inform the contracting authority and take such steps as the contracting authority directs and seek the advice of the Commission in order to prevent repetition of the unlawful discrimination.

e) The contractor shall monitor the religious composition of applicants and of its workforce under the contact, it shall review the composition of those employed under the contract and the employment practices for the purposes of determining whether there is more which could be done to promote fair participation in employment in the contractors workforce.

f) If the contractor determines that there is more which could be done to promote fair participation in employment in the contractor's workforce then he/she shall take reasonable and appropriate affirmative action which will include setting goals and timetables.

g) In the event that a contractor during the period of the contract is found to have committed a summary offence under the Fair Employment Acts the contractor shall inform the contracting authority and take such steps as the contracting authority directs and seek advice from the Commission to prevent further offences.

h) In the event that a contractor during the period of the contract is served with notices, directions, orders or recommendations or provides a written undertaking under the Fair Employment Acts, the contractor shall inform the contracting authority, take such steps as the contracting authority directs and seek the advice of the Commission i order to comply with its statutory obligations under the Fair Employment Acts.

i) The contractor shall provide such information as contracting authority may reasonably request for the purpose of assessing contractor compliance with the equal opportunities terms of the contract.

3.98 *As the contracting authority has no direct relationship with sub-contractors, the Commission recommends that a clause in the contract should make the contractor responsible for ensuring that sub-contractors comply with the equality conditions in the contract.*

3.99 *The Commission is of the opinion that the contract compliance provisions should oper-*
ate on contracts above a specified financial threshold and suggests a threshold of
£100,000.[154]

The CRE's and EOC's lobbying on contract compliance was mentioned above. The
Better Regulation Task Force supported "the use of public sector finance to encourage equality policies among suppliers and contractors" and,[155] in contrast to its generally non-interventionist tone, stated that:

> Public sector purchasers should be ensuring that their suppliers and contractors conform
> to the requirements in equality legislation, particularly with regard to employment provi-
> sions. If it transpires that such proportionate measures would contravene Government or
> EC procurement policies, *we would recommend the government seriously reconsiders and*
> *revisit these policies, to develop a broader range of criteria in the contracting process* (my
> emphasis).

The government's response was to the effect that, while government procurement is
to be based on value for money:

> . . . Value for money is the optimum combination of whole life cost and quality, not simply
> initial price . . . Departments can reject suppliers on grounds of impropriety—for example
> if they have . . . committed an act of gross misconduct in the course of their business, includ-
> ing in the employment and equal opportunities areas . . . The principles on which our EU
> procurement obligations are based are very much in line with our own value for money pol-
> icy. The UK has, however, been pushing for some time for the detailed rules, reflecting
> those principles, to be simplified, clarified and brought up to date. The Commission . . . is,
> together with Member States . . . looking at the extent to which social factors can be taken
> into account in the procurement process under the existing regime, consistent with
> Community law. While it is inconsistent with the Government's policy on value for money
> to use procurement to pursue other aims, we are taking careful note of the Task Force's
> recommendation, its potential, and its relevance to the work we are doing in Brussels.[156]

This Government's response to SACHR's proposals was criticised by the Northern
Ireland Affairs Select Committee's Fourth Report (*The Operation of The Fair*
Employment (Northern Ireland) Act 1989—Ten Years On). Having cited the passage
from the White Paper reproduced above, the report went on to state that:

---

[154] The FEC *Review* fn 5, above, points out, further, that EC law permits the grant of state aid, even in
cases where this distorts the competitive position of firms, where *inter alia*, the aid is to promote the economic development of areas where the standard of living is abnormally low or where there is serious under-
employment or the execution of an important project of common European interest. The FEC points out
the obvious relevance of these criteria to fair employment in Northern Ireland. They could also be applied
to cover sex discrimination and, since the adoption of Article 13 of the Treaty Establishing the European
Community, discrimination on the other listed grounds.
[155] Available from the DTI website at *www.opengov.uk.*
[156] *Partnership* for *Equality* 1998 (Northern Ireland Office, 1998) available at www.ccruni.gov.uk/
equality/equality.html.

97. We . . . received evidence which indicated that, provided adequate advice was given by Government to ensure that the criteria did not discriminate against tenderers in other EU Member States,[157] European Community law was a less significant barrier to the use of public procurement than Ministers indicated in evidence. Our view on this was strengthened by the fact that, in a recent Communication on public procurement, the European Commission "encourages the Member States to use their procurement powers to pursue" a range of social objectives, including equality, "providing the limits laid down by Community law are respected."[158] The Secretary of State, subsequent to her oral evidence, has commented that no practical guidance has yet been given by the Commission as to the circumstances in which compliance with conditions of social character could lawfully be included in a contract. The Secretary of State considered that the ambiguity of the Commission's present guidance raised the possibility of legal challenge by an unsuccessful tenderer, should contract compliance be applied.

98. Another objection raised by Ministers was that the use of public procurement for social policy objectives was likely to run counter to the principle of value for money. We take the view that this need not be the case: it can be argued that a definition of best value which excluded the beneficial results of the achievement of the social policy objective at issue would not be supportable, a point which, in evidence, [the Northern Ireland Minister] appeared not to dissent from. . . .

99. We were impressed with the use of contract compliance in the United States. **We recommend that the Government look again at the potential contribution of contract compliance to achieving fair employment objectives, taking account of the full extent to which this may be compatible with EU law and drawing fully on the experience of the United States Federal Government. The Government has acknowledged, in the White Paper, the principle that contract compliance has a part to play in the particular circumstances of fair employment in Northern Ireland. This is, as the Government says, a significant modification of general Government policy on contract compliance. We believe that the present limited provisions can, and should, be developed into a more effective mechanism for helping to deliver fair employment policy objectives . . .**

103. **Government and public bodies award public contracts on behalf of the communities that they serve. It is not therefore, in our view, unreasonable that these communities might expect that public contracts should, all other things being equal, go to contractors who further such a basic policy aim as fair employment. We do not consider the award of public contracts as simply an economic activity by the Administration, in which the Administration can consider itself as equivalent to a private sector organisation.**

104. **We find it difficult to see how public purchasing activity can in principle be regarded as a separate area of state activity in which equality criteria are ignored that are considered self-evident in other areas of state activity, such as public sector employment.** This consideration is strengthened if a company tendering for a contract is able to tender at a lower price for that contract because it does not engage in good employment practices which other ten-

---

[157] Fn 113, above, reply to question 145 (Sir Robert Cooper): "The restriction is in terms that lots of companies, for example, would wish to recruit on a localised basis, but European contract legislation makes that more difficult. I am not an expert on the European situation, but I am told that it will soon be possible for companies perhaps to avoid the difficulties there, but there are pitfalls in that because of the European regulations about contracts being open to people from right across the European Union. Employers cannot differentiate, and that causes some problems".

[158] Commission Communication, Public Procurement in the European Union, COM (98) 143 (March 1998), desposited in Parliament as European Community Document No. 6927/98.

derers do and is thus able to cut costs. Public bodies might reasonably be expected to take account of, and discount, any unfair competitive advantage acquired as a result. Unfortunately, the existing limited linkage between Government contracts and fair employment in Northern Ireland does not encompass this approach.

105. A new dimension to the debate about contract compliance has been added by the existence of the equality duty under the Northern Ireland Act 1998. As a CAJ witness commented: "It would seem only fair and reasonable that public authorities should be free to examine how contractors are fulfilling their legal obligations under the existing legislation before deciding whether or not they may be breaching their statutory duty. They have to consider these matters in terms of fulfilling their statutory duty."[159] **We recommend that Government Departments and public bodies review the position they have taken with regard to public procurement in the context of the preparation of their equality schemes under section 75 of the Northern Ireland Act 1998.**

Linda Dickens suggested, in the article extracted above, that the election of the (New) Labour Government in May 1997 "heralds the end of CCT". In the event, CCT has been replaced, as from April 2000, by "best value", which requires public bodies to engage in a rolling programme of review to ensure the achievement of "best value", whether in-house or contracted-out, in all their services.[160]

Just as was the case with CCT, contracts must exclude "non-commercial matters".[161] *Implementing Best Value—A Consultation Document on Draft Guidance* (1999, Department of the Environment, Transport and the Regions), stated that the Government "recognises that it is important that employees have confidence in the fairness of the competitive process. It intends to amend [s.17 LGA] in such a way as to enable local authorities to take into account appropriate workforce matters in the selection of tenderers and the award of contracts, consistent with its EC obligations and the achievement of value for money."[162]

The RR(A)B will, if carried in its present form, amend s.71 RRA to provide that:

71. (1) [Public authorities, widely defined by Schedule 1A . . . shall make arrangements to secure that its functions are carried out with due regard to the need—
    (a) to eliminate unlawful racial discrimination
    (b) to promote equality of opportunity and good relations between persons of different racial groups.
(2) The Secretary of State may [after consultation with the CRE] by order impose, on such persons falling within Schedule 1A as he considers appropriate, such duties as he considers appropriate for the purpose of ensuring the better performance by those persons of their duties under subsection (1) . . .

---

[159] SACHR evidence to the Select Committee on N. Ireland, appended to the fourth report, 1998–1999, fn 114 above.

[160] Local Government Act 1999.

[161] Para 19 of the White Paper, available from the DETR website at www.detr.gov.uk.

[162] See also clarification of the TUPE application, *Staff Transfers in the Public Sector: Statement of Practice: A Consultation Document* July 1999, Cabinet Office available at www.cabinet-office.gov.uk.

As was noted above, s.17 LGA 1988 currently precludes local authorities and some other public bodies from taking into account "non-commercial matters" in the award of contracts. S. 18 LGA, in its current form, provides that:

(1) Except to the extent permitted by subsection (2) below, section 71 of the Race Relations Act 1976 (local authorities to have regard to need to eliminate unlawful racial discrimination and promote equality of opportunity, and good relations, between persons of different racial groups) shall not require or authorise a local authority to exercise any function regulated by section 17 above by reference to a non-commercial matter.

S. 19 of the Local Government Act 1999, which establishes the new "best value" regime, provides that:

(1) The Secretary of State may by order provide, in relation to best value authorities, for a specified matter to cease to be a non-commercial matter for the purposes of [s.17 LGA 1988] . . .

The Act does not apply to Scotland. Explanatory notes accompanying the legislation state that s.19 "might be used to enable best value authorities to have regard to certain work force matters in the contractual process" and that "Where a matter ceases, by virtue of an order under section 19, to be a non-commercial one, then in the future exercise of the function concerned, best value authorities will be required to have regard to any guidance issued by the Secretary of State." The provision came into force in late 1999.

"MAINSTREAMING" EQUALITY

The concept of "mainstreaming" was mentioned in Chapter 1, as was s.75 of the Northern Ireland Act 1998 which stands, at present, as the Government's most significant commitment to that policy.

S.75 NIA imposes upon "public authorities" an obligation "in carrying out [their] functions relating to Northern Ireland" to have "due regard to the need to promote equality of opportunity—

(a) between persons of different religious belief, political opinion, racial group, age, marital status or sexual orientation;
(b) between men and women generally;
(c) between persons with a disability and
(d) between persons with dependants and persons without".

S.75(2) provides that, without prejudice to the obligations imposed by s.75(1), public authorities shall also have regard to the desirability of promoting good relations between persons of different religious belief, political opinion or racial group.

S.75 sits somewhat uncomfortably with the Government's articulated hostility towards contract compliance, and its continued pursuit of competition in the public sector. It has its roots in the Policy Appraisal and Fair Treatment (PAFT) guidelines, first issued in Northern Ireland in December 1993, which in turn drew upon the British guidelines launched in the 1980s by the Ministerial Group on Women's Issues, which encouraged Whitehall Departments to develop basic guidance with a view to producing tailored guidelines on "equality proofing". According to the Central Community Relations Unit's First Annual Report on PAFT (1995):

> 2.1 The aim of the PAFT initiative is to ensure that, in practice, issues of equality and equity condition policy-making and action in all spheres and at all levels of Government activity, whether in regulatory and administrative functions or in the delivery of services to the public. The guidelines identify a number of areas where there is potential for discrimination or unequal treatment to occur and outline steps which those responsible for the development of policy and the delivery of services should take to ensure that, in drawing up new policies or reviewing existing policies, they do not unjustifiably or unnecessarily discriminate against specified sections of the community.

The groups to which public authorities were instructed to have regard were "people of different gender, age, ethnic group, religious belief or political opinion; married and unmarried people; disabled and non-disabled people; people with or without dependants; and people of differing sexual orientation".

The operation of the PAFT guidelines in Northern Ireland was heavily criticised, Christine Bell pointing out that the guidelines were not made public and, in many cases, did not even reach public authorities responsible for their implementation. Further:

"Employment Equality Review" (1996) 2 *International Journal of Discrimination and the Law*, **69–74**

> ... there are differences both in how the implementation of PAFT is managed by the different departments, and in what departments consider a "PAFT analysis" involves. The inconsistencies in these areas demonstrate a lack of coherence to the implementation of PAFT which severely limits its proposed effect.
>
> When it comes to application of PAFT analysis, again inconsistencies in approaches are evident. In fact the CCRU report abounds with the phrase "no PAFT implications" yet the detail of how this conclusion was arrived at is not given ... for example, notes that three out of four of the policies reviewed were found to have no PAFT implications, although little detail is given as to why not. ... The DHSS Care in the Community Project which "aims to integrate and include people with a mental illness within the community", was dismissed in the report with the comment: "[n]o PAFT issues were identified." Given that the groups for PAFT analysis include both those with dependants and those with disabilities, this report indicates a conceptual flaw. While it is theoretically possible that the policy does not impact differentially on those with as compared to those without dependants (although this seems unlikely) or is objectively justified for some other reasons, this is a different matter to thee being "no PAFT issues".

Implementation by Non Departmental Public Bodies (NDPBs)

While the implementation of PAFT guidelines at departmental level seems patchy, at the level of NDPBs it has been worse if not non-existent. This was well illustrated in a judicial review taken by UNISON against Down Lisburn Trust for refusing to suspend its decision to market test services. UNISON had argued that the decision not to suspend testing discriminated against women involved in service provision. One of the reasons given in support of suspension was the need to consider the PAFT implications of the decision. In the course of the case it was revealed that it was 6 July 1995 (that is about 18 months after their introduction) before Health Trusts received PAFT documentation.

The court found that the decision makers had not been made aware of PAFT at the time of their decision, and were therefore not at fault for not applying it. However, the court rejected the Trust's submissions that "PAFT Guidelines were not a blueprint but more in the nature of a series of strategic objectives", rejecting the Trust's implicit argument "that PAFT provided no more than a lofty aspiration at which bodies such as Trusts should aim and that failure to achieve that aspiration would be a matter of little or no consequence." While the case illustrates at best a casual approach to PAFT, the decision by the Court leaves the door open for further enforcement in the future.

Contracting Out Services

The PAFT guidelines call for consideration to be given to any discriminatory effect which attaches to a particular service delivery or policy, so that alternative approaches can be assessed. Specific reference is made to the application of these principles to contracted-out services in the cover letter sent with the guidelines within departments are urged "to use their best endeavours, consistent with legal and contractual obligations, to secure compliance with PAFT by those performing contracted-out services on their behalf." However, according to the CCRU report, departments merely seek to encourage providers of contracted-out services to be "consistent with the spirit of PAFT."

Education services provides an example of the limitations of PAFT application in this area. In the case of education, article 20 of the Education and Library Boards (Northern Ireland) Order requires Boards to conduct contracting-out activities without reference to non-commercial matters. Despite the conflicts with PAFT, and the DENI clarification to Boards that the Order takes precedence, no explicit reference is made to this tension in the Department's CCRU Report entry. This not only reflects on the quality of the CCRU Report, but given that contracting out of services is a governmental trend at present, it illustrates an important limitation of PAFT. If in practice PAFT is rendered inapplicable to this area then its usefulness is seriously diminished. Further, if legislation automatically takes precedence over PAFT, and PAFT does not require at least consideration of its amendment, then the whole operation and function of PAFT is in question.

Training in the implementation of the guidelines within government departments appeared, in 1995, to have been sketchy at best with no additional resources having been allocated to this end. Nor were resources made available for monitoring.

The CCRU's second Annual Report on PAFT referred to the UNISON case, noting that:

2.13 The PAFT guidelines require Departments to use their best endeavours, consistent with legal and contractual obligations, to secure compliance with PAFT by those performing contracted-out services on their behalf. The primary purpose of this reference was to seek the delivery of contracted-out services to the public on the same basis of fairness and non-discrimination which would be expected from a public body. The controversy over market testing drew attention to the . . . issue of the implications for the workforce in parts of the public sector where polices such as market testing, contracting-out and privatisation are applied. Where PAFT considerations are found to be relevant, it is, however, still entirely legitimate for a Department to conclude, on the basis of an assessment of the full range of factors at play, that greater benefit would be secured from implementation of the initiative. Furthermore, legislation predating PAFT, such as the Education and Libraries Order (NI) 1993, which introduced compulsory competitive tendering for certain functions of the Education and Library Boards, may limit the scope for the application of PAFT, since clearly statutory obligations take precedence over administrative guidance.

The report referred to the findings of an FI conducted by the EOCNI on the impact of competitive tendering in the health and education services, the EOCNI having recommended that the gender implications of CCT in that sector were so severe that the policy should be suspended:

2.15 . . .The Government decided not to suspend the policy, pending a full examination of the evidence contained in the EOC's report. Of the report's 35 recommendations, 6 relate to the application of the PAFT guidelines. The case studies on which the report is based related to the period before the introduction of the PAFT guidance and several of the recommendations would be expected to be part of current procedures. The [EOCNI's] final report was published in 1996 and is currently under consideration."

2.16 The controversy over market testing and competitive tendering points to the potential for tensions between the philosophy of PAFT and aspects of other Government policies. Many forms of discrimination are illegal under Northern Ireland statute and clearly cannot be breached by the Government. Other forms of differential treatment are legally permissible and PAFT requires Departments to consider carefully the potential for rectifying them. This may sometimes involve assessing the competing claims of different policies and this may ultimately be a matter for Ministerial judgement as to public interest. PAFT seeks to ensure that issues of equality and equity are given full weight in these considerations, but it cannot be assumed that PAFT considerations will always predominate.

The third and final report on PAFT noted that:

2.10 . . . The Secretary of State subsequently replied to the EOC on 21 January 1997 stating that the Government was unable to accept certain of the report's recommendations, including those relating to the suspension of competitive tendering in the health and education services . . . the Secretary of State noted the need to establish an appropriate balance, consistent with statutory obligations, between achieving maximum safeguards in relation to equality issues, delivering services to the public as efficiently as practicable, setting the highest quality standards, and attaining best value for money.

In 1999 Christopher McCrudden remarked that the PAFT initiative "proved largely unsuccessful".[163] Criticism by McCrudden and others was not aimed at the substance of the guidelines, rather at their non-binding nature and the failures of implementation within the authorities charged with their application.[164] One of the main criticisms made in respect of s.75, as it was originally proposed, concerned the lack of a robust "internal mechanism" for their enforcement. Initially the Northern Ireland Bill was, according to SACHR's response, "silent on the crucial issue of an internal mechanism to ensure that equality considerations are mainstreamed at the heart of government". It criticised the "collapsing" of the equality bodies in order to create an "external mechanism" and proposed the creation of a Department of Equality headed by the Deputy First Minister of Northern Ireland's Assembly. The Northern Ireland Act did give the Deputy First Minister responsibility for equality but resisted the call for Department of Equality. Amendments were also made to the Bill. Schedule 9 of the NIA requires the relevant bodies to draw up equality schemes:

4 (1) A scheme shall show how the public authority proposes to fulfil the duties imposed by section 75 . . .
  (2) A scheme shall state, in particular, the authority's arrangements-
    (a) for assessing its compliance with the duties under section 75 and for consulting on matters to which a duty under that section is likely to be relevant (including details of the persons to be consulted);
    (b) for assessing and consulting on the likely impact of policies adopted or proposed to be adopted by the authority on the promotion of equality of opportunity;
    (c) for monitoring any adverse impact of policies adopted by the authority on the promotion of equality of opportunity;
    (d) for publishing the results of such assessments as are mentioned in paragraph (b) and such monitoring as is mentioned in paragraph (c);
    (e) for training staff;
    (f) for ensuring, and assessing, public access to information and to services provided by the authority.
  (3) A scheme shall-
    (a) specify a timetable for measures proposed in the scheme; and
    (b) (c) include details of how it will be published . . .
5 Before submitting a scheme a public authority shall consult, in accordance with any directions given by the Commission-

---

[163] *Equality News* available from the DGV website at http://europa.eu.int. See also the EOC's report in mainstreaming in local authorities available from its website
[164] Similar criticisms were made by Bell and others of the "TSN" (Targeting Social Need) initiative whereby resources were to be skewed towards areas of greatest need. This policy, according to SACHR, "was a nice idea waiting in the wings" (evidence to the NIA Select Committee, 3rd February appended to the fourth report, 1998–99, of that Committee, see fn 114, above). The Government has re-committed to the policy, but doubts were expressed to that Committee (notably by the CAJ and SACHR) as to how effective this would be in practice.

(a) representatives of persons likely to be affected by the scheme; and

(b) such other persons as may be specified in the directions.[165]

Guidelines for compliance with the statutory duty are being drawn up by the EC which will have the power either to approve a scheme or to refer it to the Secretary of State who, if s/he does not approve it, may request the public authority to revise it or may impose a new scheme.[166] Public authorities must review their schemes at least once every five years. Failure to comply with their schemes will result, after the opportunity to remedy such breach has been provided by the EC and not taken, in referral to the Secretary of State.[167] The EC must produce an annual report on the operation of s.75.

S.75 has been echoed in Great Britain by the RR(A)B 1999, which will impose upon public authorities a statutory obligation to promote equality of opportunity on racial grounds.[168] The government reaffirmed, in agreeing to amend the Bill to that end, its commitment to "plac[e] the promotion of equality by public bodies on a statutory footing"[169]. At present, positive duties in respect of promoting equality on grounds of disability, sex, etc are non-statutory except in Northern Ireland.[170]

The RRA, as amended, will be an improvement on its current form. But the Bill contains no equivalent of Schedule 9 NIA, which is regarded as of the utmost significance to the success of "mainstreaming". The shortcomings of the non-statutory PAFT guidelines were noted above, and Schedule 9's "equality scheme" provisions are designed to ensure tht "mainstreaming" becomes a reality, as distinct from an empty promise. By contrast, the RRA, in its amended form (as currently proposed) provides only (new s. 71):

- that the authorities covered "shall make arrangements to secure that its functions are carried out with due regard to the need—(a) to eliminate unlawful racial discrimination; and (b) to promote equality of opportunity and good relations between persons of different racial groups";
- that the Secretary of State "*may* [my emphasis] by order impose . . . as he considers appropriate, such duties as he considers appropriate for the puspose of ensuring the better performance by those persons of [these] duties"; and
- that the CRE "may [my emphasis] issue codes of practice containing such practical guidance as the Commission think fit in relation to the performance by persons of [such] duties"

---

[165] The provisions appear to be modelled on C McCrudden's *Benchmarks for Change; Mainstreaming Fairness in the Government of Northern Ireland* (Belfast: CAJ, 1998).

[166] The Assembly has to be involved by the EC and, if the Secretary of State does not approve the original scheme, by him/her.

[167] A different scheme is in place for government departments—see generally schedule 9 NIA 1998.

[168] Controversy rages as to the definition of public authority which is narrower in NIA and in the RR(A)B than in HRA.

[169] HLDebs 27th, Col 1673 available at www.publications.parliament.uk/pa/ld/hansard.htm.27 Jan 2000.

[170] PAFT guidelines available from the Cabinet Office website at www.cabinet-office.gov/uk.

The success of the amended RRA, and of the similar amendments promised to the SDA, will depend in large part on the exercise by the Secretary of State and the relevant Commissions of these discretionary powers.

Another uncertainty which remains concerns the balance which will be struck between the imperatives of equality and others such as "value-for-money", efficiency and job-creation. In *R* v *Secretary of State for Employment ex p. Seymour-Smith & Perez* [2000] IRLR 263, the House of Lords accorded to government a great deal of discretion in pursuing its goals (there encouraging employment of part-timers by reducing burdens on business) at the cost of the legal protection of predominantly female vulnerable workers. That decision was reached in the application of Article 141 whose supremacy is unquestioned. It was clear, in the Northern Irish context, that the non-statutory PAFT guidelines gave way in the face of government commitment to CCT. The balance which will be struck, in the employment field, between the obligation to promote equality and the imperatives of "best value", however that will be ultimately defined, will have very significant repercussions for the pursuit of employment equality.

6

The Sex Discrimination Act 1975

INTRODUCTION

In 1998, women accounted for 44% of those in employment. Two-thirds of women returned to work within 11 months of giving birth (this figure stood at 45% in 1988) and 72% of women (84% men) of working age were economically active. Women have made enormous strides in the working sphere over the last quarter century. The "gender pay gap" (further discussed in chapter 10) has decreased from around 30% to 20% (Full-time women earning an average 80% of full-time male hourly wages). And women have increased significantly their share of management, administration and professional jobs. Girls have been out-performing boys at school for a number of years, boys equalling their performance at GCSE/CSE level only in mathematics and at A Level only in French and History.[1] In Higher Education institutions women outnumber men in every subject area except physical, mathematical and computer sciences and engineering and technology and architecture, building and planning, the overall numbers of women (453,000 full-time and 50,000 part time) outstripping men (426,000 full-time and 37,000 part-time) to a significant extent.[2] Nor is women's numerical strength confined to traditionally female areas of study; women outnumber men in medicine, veterinary science, law, agriculture and related science and business and administrative studies as well as in subjects allied to medicine, biological science, social, political and economic studies; education and other traditionally female areas.

For all of this, women remain significantly disadvantaged. Despite huge increases in the number of women MPs following the 1997 General Election, women account for only 18% of those in the House of Commons, 24% of British MEPs. In 1998, the 45% of working women who worked part-time earned around 60% of men's average hourly rate (experienced a "gender pay gap of around 40%). This gap had barely changed over the preceding twenty-five years. And in the adult population taken as a whole, women's incomes were only 53% of men's at the turn of the millennium. In all but 18% of households, men earn at least 5% more than women. 77% of men belong to occupational pension schemes. For full-time women workers the figure is 67% and

---

[1] EOC, Facts about women and men in Britain, 1999, available on the EOC website at http://www.eoc.org.uk/. The EOC analysed results for 11 popular GSCE and 10 popular A level subjects.
[2] *Ibid.*

for part-time women workers only 33%.[3] Women, particularly those who work part-time, are very badly hit by the lower earnings cut-off for National Insurance, this serving to exclude many from entitlement to benefits including pensions and maternity pay.[4]

Sexual harassment, which is endemic, serves to exclude women from male-dominated working environments and to underline their frequently subordinate position at work (whether that subordination is job-related or the product of physical and sexual intimidation). 54% of working women have experienced such harassment (15% of men).[5] Women are segregated into the lower-paying service sector and, in significant numbers, in only three of the nine major occupational groups.[6] Women also remain concentrated at the lower rungs of occupational hierarchies. In 1996, for example, when women accounted for 50% of medical students and/or house officers, they comprised one in three senior house officers and one in five consultants.[7] A similar pattern prevails in the legal profession, which women have been entering in large numbers for decades, in higher education and in business, women comprising only 5% of directors of *The Times* top 200 companies in 1997.[8]

Nor are relatively advantaged women the only ones to suffer by comparison with men. At the other end of the scale women comprise the large majority of those who benefitted from the implementation of the National Minimum Wage. Women's workplace disadvantage is, at least in part, the result of discrimination.

Evelyn Collins and Elizabeth Meehan, "Women's Rights in Employment", in C. McCrudden and G. Chambers (eds), *Individual Rights and the Law in Britain* (Oxford: Clarendon, 1994) 403, 405

One test of the effectiveness of the Sex Discrimination Act might be a reduction in occupational and industrial segregation but on the basis of official statistics there has been little change since te mid-1970s. We have shown that the development of the right to equal treatment under the Sex Discrimination Act since 1975 has not always been straightforward. The indirect discrimination provisions particularly should have enabled the courts and tribunals to take a purposive approach to tackling the structural discrimination which is embedded deeply in the labour market. Instead, they have focused on technicalities and procedures and there is evidence of "a judicial reluctance to widen the ambit of the debate over equality".

The industrial tribunal system has also been found to be a disappointment as a mechanism for dealing with individual complaints and ensuring the more widespread adoption of non-discriminatory employment practices. Leonard concluded, for example, from her

---

[3] *Ibid.* In 73% of households, women earned at least 10% more than men. There was a gap in the number of men and women with occupational pensions across all major occupational groups.

[4] Though entitlement to Maternity Allowance (see further below) has recently been extended to all those earning at least £30 per week. The EOC's *Lower Earnings Limit in Practice*, available from the website (fn 1 above) explores the gender implications of the threshold.

[5] Industrial Society Survey 1993 discussed in the TUC Women's Conference Report, *No Excuse—No Harassment at Work* (1999), available from the TUC's website at http://www.tuc.org.uk. The TUC's own survey showed 27% women reporting personal experience of sexual harassment.

[6] *Labour Market Trends* 1998, reported in 85 *Equal Opportunities Review*, p.35.

[7] 78 *Equal Opportunities Review*, p.4.

[8] 77 *Equal Opportunities Review*, p.5.

analysis of successful claimants in the period 1980–4, that compensation awarded to individual applicants was inadequate; that often claimants were out of pocket themselves, despite winning their cases; that there were often real difficulties in collecting the compensation; and that the costs for complainants in terms of emotional stress and damaged future employment prospects were extremely high. Also, the fact of winning a case seemed to have little impact on the conditions of co-workers, in that it led to little change in the organization. Gregory, in her analysis of unsuccessful applicants in the 1985–6 period painted a similar, dismal picture. Gregory and Leonard both recorded problems with lack of specialized knowledge of discrimination law in the tribunal system, often due to problems such as the allocation of cases widely across membership and the absence of compulsory formal training. Chambers and Horton looked at the impact of tribunal decisions on employers and their conclusions are also an indictment of a mechanism which had the potential to effect change in the workplace. It is clear that changes are necessary not only to the legislation but also to the systems of advice, assistance and representation; to the tribunal procedure itself; and to the remedies and sanctions which can be applied, to ensure that they impact on employers both as a deterrent and as an incentive to introduce changes.

Comparison between the UK and other countries regarding the scope of rights available and the effectiveness of any equal treatment laws is difficult without a full discussion of the different legal systems, the different laws, and the different social and economic contexts within which the countries operate. Formally, all Community countries have, for example, fulfilled their obligation to implement the equality directives in their jurisdiction, but as directives leave it open to member states to decide the means to do this, the approaches have been different and it is difficult to say which is "better" or "worse". While a significant number of references to the European Court have come from the United Kingdom, for example, it cannot be said that it is the worst in the Community. The references are as likely to be as a result of the fact there are larger independent equality Commissions here then elsewhere, which have strategically used Community law as a means of forcing change nationally. On some counts, however, particularly in respect of child-care provision and parental leave, it is clear that the United Kingdom ranks among the lowest (with Ireland) in the Community.

The *Equal Opportunities Review* reported, in 1999, that even in firms which are "actively involved in the management of diversity . . . 86% of top management . . . [a]re white males."

For many women, the point at which work-related disadvantage bites hardest is after childbirth. Many jobs at the top of the economic hierarchy are structured on the assumption not only that the holder has no caring obligations, but also that he does not even have to look after himself. Women face an almost impossible task in attempting to reconcile such jobs with motherhood no matter how comprehensive and high quality their childcare arrangements. Further down the scale, relatively few jobs pay sufficient to buy good quality childcare so women are dependent on informal arrangements which require a significant degree of flexibility on their part. Many women "choose" part-time work as the solution to the balancing act, only to find themselves denied promotion, downgraded or having to accept work for which they are over-qualified.[9]

[9] See further A. McColgan. *Just Wages for Women* (Oxford: OUP, 1997), Chapters 2 and 6.

The problems faced by black and other ethnic minority women are particularly acute. Women from all ethnic minority groups account for just under 5% of all women in formal employment, but these figures exclude substantial proportions of women employed in the informal economy. Of those ethnic minority women whose employment is recorded Indians form the largest single group (164,000 or 1.5% of all women workers), followed by Black Caribbeans (118,000 or 1%), women of mixed and other origins (92,000), Chinese and other Asian (70,000), Black African (47,000) and Pakistani and Bangladeshi (45,000).[10] Some of the issues are touched upon by Fredman and Szyszczak in Chapter 1, and by Nicola Lacey in Chapter 3. Here, Diamond Ashiagbor further comments on the inadequacies of the existing legislative approach.

D. Ashiagbor, "The Intersection between Gender and 'Race' in the Labour Market", in S. Sheldon (ed.) *Feminist Perspectives on Employment Law* **(London, Cavendish, 1998)**

Notwithstanding 20 years of sex discrimination and equal pay legislation, gender inequalities persist in the workplace, and women in the UK continue to earn, on average, less than three-quarters of men's wages. Empirical studies of women's involvement in the labour market have identified a number of factors to explain this continued disadvantage, in particular, the importance of gender segregation, namely, the overcrowding of women into sectors of the labour market to which lower value or status is attributed. Such analyses of women's employment patterns have been useful in redressing the previously male centred theories of labour market participation. However, in view of the heterogeneity of the category of women workers, the accuracy of those analyses of paid work and gender which treat women as if they were a unitary category is also open to question. This heterogeneity has implications for the effectiveness of measures, including legislative measures, aimed at tackling women's labour market disadvantage, since it is arguable that, within the larger body of "women's work", there exist ethnic niches wherein black and Asian women are, effectively, segregated. If it is the case that black and Asian women are either segregated into particular sectors of the labour market, or even excluded altogether from participation in the formal economy, then a recognition of the cumulative effect of the dynamics of race and sex would seem necessary to anti-discrimination legislation to be truly effective. Strategies of legal intervention which are based on remedying the disadvantage encountered by white women will, arguably, be inadequate to address the disadvantage of women who face different obstacles due to the interaction of race and gender.

The following section will examine the implications of assuming that the experience of white women within the labour market speaks for all women and addresses the diversity of experience of women of different ethnic minorities through an analysis of the ethnic variations in women's labour market positioning and the segregation of the labour market along lines of gender and race.

In a report to the European Commission's Equal Opportunities Unit on changing work patterns and the impact of gender divisions, Jill Rubery and her colleagues identified how women's employment patterns in Britain differ from many other countries in Europe and North America. They identified three distinct typologies: the continuous pattern, where women remain in paid employment (exemplified by Denmark, France and the US); the

---

[10] EOC, fn 1 above, p.9, citing the Labour Force Survey, Spring 1998.

interrupted pattern, found in Britain, The Netherlands and Germany; and the curtailed pattern, found in Ireland and Southern Europe. These differences may be attributed to factors such as differences in public policy regimes—for example, child care provision and employment legislation. However, research since the 1991 census has shown that the "British" pattern of women's employment is, in fact, a white pattern and cannot be generalised to other ethnic groups within Britain.

In particular, in 1995, the economic activity rate of white women within the UK labour market was 72.9%, that of black women (that is, Black African and Black Caribbean) 69%, that of women of Indian origin 61%, and that of Pakistani/Bangladeshi women 22%. However, any analysis of the ethnic variation in women's employment patterns is problematic: first, although the Labour Force Survey has included a question on ethnic origin for some time, it was only with the incorporation of a question on ethnic origin in the 1991 UK Population Census that occupational distribution by gender and ethnic group could be properly analysed. Secondly, the figures must be treated with caution, as ethnic minorities constitute very small groups within the workforce and are, thus, subject to a relatively high number of sampling errors. Thirdly, the Labour Force Survey has been shown to under-record the number of black and female headed households in the population and is most likely to miss the poorer black and Asian households, thereby under-recording homeworking and family employment.

Within the UK, feminist analyses of the position of women in the labour market have, traditionally, placed great emphasis on gender divisions within the family and women's responsibility for domestic work as having necessary implications for women's labour market participation and positioning. For example, the tendency of married women or women with child care responsibilities to work part time is adduced in support of the conventional view that processes prior to entry into the labour market determine women's segregation into lower paying sectors. The fact that the majority of part time workers in the UK are women with family responsibilities has ramifications for the proper role of anti-discrimination law: both domestic courts and the European Court of Justice have recognised that unequal treatment of part time workers may amount to indirect sex discrimination, since any exclusion of part time workers is likely to have a disproportionate impact on women (compared to the impact on men). Furthermore, there has been much empirical research to show that, in spite of equal pay legislation, occupation by occupation, part time workers earn less per hour than full time workers. Whilst the differential between men and women's hourly pay can be explained in part by differences in skill distribution, a persistent percentage of the differential remains attributable to women receiving unequal pay for jobs of similar skill levels.

However, it is questionable whether sex discrimination alone can provide a satisfactory explanation for the labour market disadvantage experienced by black and Asian women. The prominence given to part time work and domestic responsibilities as determinants of the sexual division of labour and of differential rewards between men and women's paid work can be seen as ethnocentric. Whilst this analysis has proved useful to highlight inequalities as between white women and white men and has achieved legally significant gains for part time workers, it also serves to hide the particular experience of black and Asian women within the labour market, since part time working is not, in fact, a major factor in keeping black and Asian women's pay and prospects so far below those of white men. Whilst some 46% of white women employees worked part time in 1993, only 33% of non-white women did so. For black women (namely, Black Caribbean, Black African and Black Other), the figures are starker, with less than 22% of black women working part time.

Whilst responsibility for child care and home management *does* have a major influence on the participation of women in the labour market, this influence varies significantly between ethnic groups. White women who work full time tend to the free of immediate child care responsibilities, while those with such responsibilities tend to work part time. however, this does not appear to apply to Black Caribbean women, who have a high rate of single parenthood relative to other groups but, also, have high rates of participation in the labour market and high rates of full time employment. It would, thus, appear that factors other than domestic responsibilities (for example, economic necessity) determine black women's participation in the labour market. As the Greater London Council noted in 1986, black women are "much more likely [than white women] to have to bring in a second wage and to work full time, partly because black men are also trapped in low status, low paid jobs". Further, Clare Holdsworth and Angela Dale, in their study of ethnic differences in women's employment published in the journal *Work, Employment and Society*, reach the interesting conclusion that, historically, part time jobs were constructed for white women. They point to evidence from the Commission for Racial Equality which suggests that employers have continued to make part time jobs preferentially available to white women, so that full time employment may, sometimes, be the result of discrimination rather than choice.

Another factor explaining the full time and high economic activity rates of black, especially Black Caribbean, women is the nature of the relationship between paid work outside the home and work, whether paid or unpaid, within the home. Patricia Hill Collins has criticised traditional social science research into African-American women's experiences of family and work for using the normative yardstick developed from experiences of middle-class American and European nuclear families. One criticism is that the contrast between a public economy and a private, non-economic domestic sphere creates a distinction between the paid labour of the public sphere and the unpaid labour of the domestic sphere, which does not, in reality, hold true for African-American women's experience of the labour market, since "African-American families exhibit . . . fluid public/private boundaries because racial oppression has impoverished disproportionate numbers of Black families".

Although household arrangements and family structures in the UK also differ enormously across race and culture, the type of intervention into the labour market envisaged by sex discrimination law—in particular, by the concept of indirect discrimination—seems predicated on a unitary view of the position of women in the family and their reasons for seeking paid work outside the home.

What, then, of the incidence of homeworking? The seemingly low economic activity rates of Asian women—in particular, Asian Muslim women—may, in part, be accounted for by the fact that they are more likely than white or black women to be involved in work, such as homeworking and family employment, which is less amenable to official statistical collation. For example, research conducted in the West Midlands clothing industry concluded that, for every factory worker in this industrial sector (that is, for every worker in the formal economy), there were at least two unregistered homeworkers; a pilot study published in 1989 found that the Muslim women interviewed were employed largely as homeworkers or as unpaid workers in family businesses and, in a few cases, in paid work outside the home.

For these 'atypical' workers, therefore, their concentration in the ethnic economy or exclusion from the formal economy must be examined before an appropriate legal response can be forthcoming. Many homeworkers are classed as being self-employed rather than employees, providing a partial explanation for the higher than average incidence of self-employment amongst Asian women (see below). Although self-employment is often seen as an indicator of entrepreneurship, clearly this is an inaccurate description of the position of many homeworkers or those working in the clothing industry. The attribution of the status "self-employed" to such workers, by an employer who is unwilling to accept the fiscal and legal consequences of treating homeworkers as employees, can result in these "atypical" workers being denied the protection of employment legislation in a manner similar to the traditional exclusion of part time workers from the reach of employment protection legislation. However, the extent to which present formulations of indirect discrimination law can be manipulated to provide redress for *all* "atypical" workers, is limited. Reliance on sex discrimination law alone is insufficient to protect the interests of this particular group in the labour market, Asian homeworkers and "self-employed" workers.

The disadvantage suffered by women in the workplace and, in particular, the pay inequalities resulting therefrom, impact profoundly upon women's lives. While some women earn sufficient to maintain themselves and their children, many more do not. Women's economic dependency traps many in abusive relationships, and poverty in old age is a predominantly female state. Women have, since the implementation of the SDA, been entitled not to be discriminated against in terms of their access to mortgages, etc. But the level of women's earnings, relative to those of men, results in precisely that effect. And while women continue to be relatively disadvantaged at work, they continue to shoulder the bulk of childcare responsibility which, in turn, serves to perpetuate their workplace disadvantage.

Much of the discrimination from which women suffer ("domestic" violence, sexual assault, the dual burden of paid and unpaid work) is untouched by the provisions of the SDA. We saw in Chapter 1 that the common law cares little for discrimination and in Chapter 4 that much discrimination by public authorities (whether it consists of the downgrading of "domestic" violence by the police, the sexist assumptions about rape victims which permeate the legal system, or the operation of the immigration system) is outside the scope of the SDA.

The SDA has been discussed at some length in the preceding chapters. In Chapters 2, 3 and 5 we considered those aspects of the Act that it shares with some or all of the other legislation under discussion—the definitions of discrimination it employs, problems of proof and procedural issues such as time limits. In Chapter 4 we discussed the sphere within which anti-discrimination legislation operates, i.e., those aspects of employment, housing, the provision of services, etc., in respect of which discrimination is prohibited by this and other legislation. In this chapter we turn to those issues which are unique to the SDA itself. The main focus of the chapter will be on pregnancy and its coverage by the SDA, dress codes and the extent to which discrimination on grounds of sex includes discrimination on grounds associated with sexual orientation. The legality of dress codes arises also in relation the RRA but the issues differ between the Acts and will be considered both here and in chapter 7. Here we will also consider the GOQ (genuine occupational qualification) defence as it relates to the SDA.

COVERAGE OF THE SDA AND EXCEPTIONS THERETO

The SDA is frequently regarded as an Act which prohibits discrimination against women. Its terms, however, apply equally to men. Further, the SDA prohibits discrimination against married persons as well as discrimination on grounds of sex, although this prohibition applies only in relation to employment. As of 1999, the Act also applies expressly to discrimination against transsexuals, although this prohibition extends only to direct discrimination in the employment sphere and is otherwise more qualified than is the case with discrimination on grounds of sex or married status.[11] S.2A, which extends the protections of the SDA to transsexuals, is extracted immediately below but the issue is dealt with more generally in a subsequent section of the Chapter.

> S.2(1) Section 1 and the provisions . . . relating to sex discrimination against women, are to be read as applying equally to the treatment of men, and for that purpose shall have effect with such modifications as are requisite.
> (2) In the application of subsection (1) no account shall be taken of special treatment afforded to women in connection with pregnancy or childbirth.
> S.2A(1) A person ("A") discriminates against another person ("B") . . . if he treats B less favourably than he treats or would treat other persons, and does so on the ground that B intends to undergo, is undergoing or has undergone gender reassignment.

S.3(1) defines direct and indirect discrimination against married persons in similar terms to s.1 (sex discrimination) and provides that "a provision . . . framed with reference to discrimination against women shall be treated as applying equally to the treatment of men . . ."

A number of the exceptions to the SDA (sports, charities and insurance) have been considered in Chapter 4. We saw there that the Act does not apply in relation to employment outside Great Britain, and in Chapter 3 we considered the scope of positive action permissible under the SDA. In addition, there are limited exceptions to the prohibition on employment-related discrimination for police and prison officers (discrimination in relation to height requirements, uniform, equipment allowances, pregnancy and childbirth and pensions being permitted in the former case, discrimination in relation to height requirements alone in the latter),[12] and positions as religious ministers may be limited to persons of one sex.[13]

Ss.51 and 51A permit discrimination necessary to comply with statutory provisions, (only) where those provisions are concerned with protecting women in connection with pregnancy or maternity or to circumstances affecting only women.[14] S.51 as orig-

---

[11] The SDA does not prohibit discrimination against single people. The tribunal in *Murray v Navy Army Air Force Institute* 1997, case 3100459/96 36 EORDCLD rejected the argument that the Equal Treatment Directive prohibited discrimination on grounds of family status.

[12] Ss.17 and 18 SDA.

[13] S.19 SDA.

[14] Or women and others also covered.

inally enacted, contained a wider statutory exception along the lines of RRA s.41 (discussed in Chapter 7) the effect of which was to preserve "protective" legislation. The CBI had lobbied for the removal of such legislation, the TUC and feminists for its extension to cover men as well as women.[15] The European Commission issued a reasoned opinion in 1987 to the effect that s.51 was too broad to comply with the equal treatment directive, and the provision, which had been modified to some extent by the SDA 1986, was narrowed considerably by the Employment Act 1989.

Article 3(2) of the equal treatment directive permits derogations from the principle of equality in relations to provisions for the protection of women, in particular in relation to pregnancy and maternity. The provision was discussed in Chapter 3 in relation to positive discrimination. In *Johnston* v *RUC*, which concerned a challenge to a ban on women (but not men) police officers carrying guns, the ECJ ruled that:

> Article 3(2)(c), must be interpreted strictly. It is clear from the express reference to pregnancy and maternity that the directive is intended to protect a woman's biological condition and the special relationship which exists between a woman and her child . . . the differences in treatment between men and women that article 2 (3) of directive no 76/207 allows out of a concern to protect women do not include risks and dangers, such as those to which any armed police officer is exposed when performing his duties in a given situation, that do not specifically affect women as such.

In *Johnston* the ECJ accepted that Article 2(2) of the equal treatment directive, which provides that "This Directive shall be without prejudice to the right of Member States to exclude from its field of application those occupational activities and, where appropriate, the training leading thereto, for which, by reason of their nature or the context in which they are carried out, the sex of the worker constitutes a determining factor", could justify a derogation from the principle of equality in that particular case:

Johnston v Chief Constable of the Royal Ulster Constabulary, Case C–222/84 [1986] ECR 1651

> The policy towards women in the RUC full-time reserve was adopted by the Chief Constable because he considered that if women were armed they might become a more frequent target for assassination and their fire-arms could fall into the hands of their assailants, that the public would not welcome the carrying of fire-arms by women, which would conflict too much with the ideal of an unarmed police force, and that armed policewomen would be less effective in police work in the social field with families and children in which the services of policewomen are particularly appreciated. The reasons which the chief constable thus gave for his policy were related to the special conditions in which the police must work in the situation existing in Northern Ireland, having regard to the requirements of the protection of public safety in a context of serious internal disturbances.

[15] E. Collins and E. Meehan in C. McCrudden and G. Chambers (eds), *Individual Rights and the Law in Britain* (Oxford: OUP, 1995), pp.370 and 394–7. *Cf International Union, United Auto Workers* v *Johnson Controls Inc* [1991] 55 FEP Cases 365 in which the US Supreme Court ruled that restrictions based on women's reproductive capacity violated the principle of equal treatment.

As regards the question whether such reasons may be covered by Article 2 (2) of the directive, it should first be observed that that provision, being a derogation from an individual right laid down in the directive, must be interpreted strictly. However, it must be recognized that the context in which the occupational activity of members of an armed police force are carried out is determined by the environment in which that activity is carried out. In this regard, the possibility cannot be excluded that in a situation characterized by serious internal disturbances the carrying of fire-arms by policewomen might create additional risks of their being assassinated and might therefore be contrary to the requirements of public safety.

In such circumstances, the context of certain policing activities may be such that the sex of police officers constitutes a determining factor for carrying them out. If that is so, a Member State may therefore restrict such tasks, and the training leading thereto, to men . . . it is for the national court to say whether the reasons on which the Chief Constable based his decision are in fact well founded and justify the specific measure taken in Mrs Johnston's case. It is also for the national court to ensure that the principle of proportionality is observed . . .

The scope of Article 2(2) was considered more recently by the ECJ in *Sirdar* v *The Army Board, Secretary of State for Defence*, a claim brought by a woman denied a position in the marines. Women are prohibited from serving in the marines by virtue of that organisation's principle of "interoperability"—that is, the rule that all marines must be capable of operating in a commando unit. Women are prohibited from active combat service[16] with the effect that Ms Sirdar, who had applied for transfer as a chef to the marines in order to avoid redundancy, was ineligible for the position. Her claim could not be brought under the SDA, s.85(4) of which provides that "[n]othing in this Act shall render unlawful an act done for the purpose of ensuring the combat effectiveness of the naval, military or air forces".

The UK government sought to argue that "decisions concerning the organisation and administration of the armed forces, particularly those taken for the purpose of ensuring combat effectiveness in preparation for war, fall outside the scope of EC law". The ECJ rejected this argument, ruling instead that the case turned on Article 2(2) of the equal treatment directive.

Sirdar v The Army Board, Secretary of State for Defence Case C–273/97 [1999] All ER (EC) 928 [2000] IRLR 47

it must be noted . . . that, as a derogation from an individual right laid down in the Directive, [Article 2(2)] must be interpreted strictly . . .

The Court has thus recognised, for example, that sex may be a determining factor for posts such as those of prison warders and head prison warders (Case 318/86 *Commission* v *France* [1988] ECR 3559), or for certain activities such as policing activities where there are serious internal disturbances (*Johnston*).

A Member State may restrict such activities and the relevant professional training to men or to women, as appropriate. In such a case, as is clear from Article 9(2) of the

---

[16] This rule is currently under review.

Directive, Member States have a duty to assess periodically the activities concerned in order to decide whether, in the light of social developments, the derogation from the general scheme of the Directive may still be maintained . . .

In determining the scope of any derogation from an individual right such as the equal treatment of men and women, the principle of proportionality. . . must also be observed, as the Court pointed out in paragraph 38 of *Johnston*. That principle requires that derogations remain within the limits of what is appropriate and necessary in order to achieve the aim in view and requires the principle of equal treatment to be reconciled as far as possible with the requirements of public security which determine the context in which the activities in question are to be performed.

However, depending on the circumstances, national authorities have a certain degree of discretion when adopting measures which they consider to be necessary in order to guarantee public security in a Member State. . .

The question is therefore whether, in the circumstances of the present case, the measures taken by the national authorities, in the exercise of the discretion which they are recognised to enjoy, do in fact have the purpose of guaranteeing public security and whether they are appropriate and necessary to achieve that aim.

In addition to the exceptions discussed above, the SDA (s.7(2)) recognises a number of situations in which sex is a "genuine occupational qualification" (GOQ) for a job. These apply where:

(a) the essential nature of the job calls for a man for reasons of physiology (excluding physical strength or stamina) or, in dramatic performances or other entertainment, for reasons of authenticity, so that the essential nature of the job would be materially different if carried out by a woman; or

(b) the job needs to be held by a man to preserve decency or privacy because-
   (i) it is likely to involve physical contact with men in circumstances where they might reasonably object to its being carried out by a woman, or
   (ii) the holder of the job is likely to do his work in circumstances where men might reasonably object to the presence of a woman because they are in a state of undress or are using sanitary facilities; or

(ba) the job is likely to involve the holder of the job doing his work, or living, in a private home and needs to be held by a man because objection might reasonably be taken to allowing to a woman—
   (i) the degree of physical or social contact with a person living in the home, or
   (ii) the knowledge of intimate details of such a person's life, which is likely, because of the nature or circumstances of the job or of the home, to be allowed to, or available to, the holder of the job; or

(c) the nature or location of the establishment makes it impracticable for the holder of the job to live elsewhere than in premises provided by the employer, and—
   (i) the only such premises which are available for persons holding that kind of job are lived in, or normally lived in, by men and are not equipped with separate sleeping accommodation for women and sanitary facilities which could be used by women in privacy from men, and
   (ii) it is not reasonable to expect the employer either to equip those premises with such accommodation and facilities or to provide other premises for women; or

(d) the nature of the establishment, or of the part of it within which the work is done, requires the job to be held by a man because—

  (i) it is, or is part of, a hospital, prison or other establishment for persons requiring special care, supervision or attention, and

  (ii) those persons are all men (disregarding any woman whose presence is exceptional), and

  (iii) it is reasonable, having regard to the essential character of the establishment or that part, that the job should not be held by a woman; or

(e) the holder of the job provides individuals with personal services promoting their welfare or education, or similar personal services, and those services can most effectively be provided by a man, or

(g) the job needs to be held by a man because it is likely to involve the performance of duties outside the United Kingdom in a country whose laws or customs are such that the duties could not, or could not effectively, be performed by a woman, or

(h) the job is one of two to be held by a married couple.

The absence of any GOQ permitting the operation of, for example, women-only taxi services is of note, given the widespread perception on the part of women that the use of minicabs renders them vulnerable to sexual assault.

D. Pannick, *Sex Discrimination Law* (Oxford, OUP, 1985) 271

The late Sir Ronald Bell MP vigorously opposed the 1975 Bill in Parliament. However, he welcomed the clause which became section 7. He described it as "a good, old clause about the authentic male characteristics. It is the lavatory clause—and all that. Nothing would help the Bill to make sense, but if we did not have Clause 7 the Bill would be such manifest nonsense that it would have been laughed out on Second Reading." Section 7 indeed more often furthers the objectives of those who opposed the 1975 Act than the objectives of those who supported the legislation.

Pannick's criticisms of s.7 will be considered further below. In *Sisley* v *Brittania Security Systems Ltd* [1983] ICR 628 EAT accepted, as falling within s.7(2)(b) a job in which the state of undress was incidental to, rather than required by, the job. The case was brought by a man refused a job in a security control room because the women working shifts there were in the habit of removing their uniforms so as to avoid creasing them when they took rests during long shifts. A tribunal found that the rest periods were necessary and accepted that the state of undress was reasonably incidental thereto. Both the tribunal and EAT ruled in favour of the employer. The decision was doubted by Pannick.

D. Pannick, *Sex Discrimination Law* 250

Section 7(3) suggests that sex is a GOQ only where the job "duties" so require. Section 7(2)(b)(ii) refers to the "needs" of the job. The reference to "sanitary facilities" in section 7(2)(b)(ii) does not, as the EAT suggested, show that the subsection extends further than job duties. When men might reasonably object to the presence of a woman because the men are using sanitary facilities, it is the job *duties* of the lavatory attendant which made sex a

GOQ for the job. The attendant *needs*, by reason of the essence of the job, to be present where the sanitary facilities are being used.

Section 7(2) and the EEC Directive 76/207 demand a compelling justification before sex discrimination is validated in employment. *Sisley* does not appear to present such a justification since there was no need for women employees to take off their clothes; in any event, there was no reason why they should not change into leisure clothes in the lavatory area and rest on the bed in those clothes rather than in their underwear. If there is a clash between the desire of female employees not to crumple their uniforms and the desire of Mr Sisley to be considered for a job vacancy irrespective of his sex, the former must give way to the latter. The policy of the 1975 Act and the EEC Directive admits of no other solution.

Section 17(2)(d) of the Irish Employment Equality Act 1977 provided that sex was an occupational qualification "where either the nature of or the duties attached to a post justify on grounds of privacy or decency the employment of persons of a particular sex". After receiving an indication from the European Commission that this body considered section 17(2)(d) to be inconsistent with EEC Directive 76/207/EEC, the Irish Government repealed section 17(2)(d) by the European Communities (Employment Equality) Regulations 1982. This action, expressly carried out "for the purpose of giving effect to Council Directive 76/207/EEC", strongly suggests that section 7(2)(b) of the 1975 Act should be given a narrow construction whenever possible so as to ensure consistency with the Directive. Section 7(2)(b), like the other parts of section 7(2) of the 1975 Act, should be held to make sex a GOQ for a job only where there is "justification for so doing under the EEC Directive.

Among the cases which have arisen under s.7 are *Etam v Rowan* [1989] IRLR 150 in which EAT accepted that a job in a women's clothing shop could come within s.7(2)(b) where it involved assisting in a changing area. In that case the GOQ defence was defeated under s.7(4), see below. And in *Buckinghamshire County Council v Ahmed*, EAT allowed an appeal against a finding of unlawful discrimination in respect of a man who had not been given work as a Punjabi interpreter. His name had been entered on a list of Punjabi and other interpreters, most of the Punjabi interpreters being women, but only female interpreters had actually been used by the Council. EAT ruled that the tribunal had erred in rejecting as a GOQ the Council's evidence that:

Buckinghamshire County Council v Admed EAT/124/98, 18th June 1998 (unreported)

Hull J (for the Court)

in a number of the ethnic communities with which they dealt and in particular the Punjabi Muslim community, there was great delicacy in dealing with women who were concerned in various social or medical or other problems. It was said that if an interpreter were to go into one of the homes, or to see women collectively at perhaps a "well woman" session, or women's health session or something of that sort, it would be regarded generally in the community and by the woman concerned as inappropriate that the interpreter should be a man. It was said that although if (say) a white social worker went to a house that might be in order, if a person who was a Punjabi went there it were better, it said, that it should be a woman than a man, out of feelings of delicacy and tact.

It was not said, of course, that it was essential that it should be a woman interpreter but what was said was that the services could be provided more effectively: it would be easier for a Punjabi Muslim woman, on many occasions, to explain in such matters as the case perhaps where her children had been involved in matters which had attracted the attention of the Police, or where she herself had medico-social problems or something like that. It would be easier for her to speak to a woman and would not attract the sort of comment that might happen if a male Punjabi-speaker, particularly a Punjabi himself, were to go to the house.[17]

It should be noted that s.7(3) provides that discrimination in access to employment is permitted "where only some of the duties of the job fall within paragraphs (a)–(g),[18] as well as where all of them do" and s.7(4) generally precludes the operation of the GOQ defence[19] in relation to vacancies "when the employer already has male [female] employees:

(a) who are capable of carrying out the duties falling within [the relevant] paragraph; and
(b) whom it would be reasonable to employ on those duties; and
(c) whose numbers are sufficient to meet the employer's likely requirements in respect of those duties without undue inconvenience.[20]

In *Timex Corporation* v *Hodgson* [1982] ICR 63, the first GOQ case to reach EAT, that tribunal failed to take account of s.7(4) in finding in favour of an employer who had selected a woman rather than a man for a supervisory position on the basis that, there being no other women supervisors at the factory, it was necessary to have one woman supervisor to deal with the personal problems of women staff, to keep the women's toilets stocked and to take urine samples from women staff working with toxic substances when the woman whose job this was was unavailable. A tribunal rejected the employer's argument that the duties at issue brought the job within s.7(2)(b), ruling that other non-supervisory staff were available for this purpose. Neither the tribunal nor EAT referred to s.7(4), the latter ruling that the tribunal "cannot tell the employers how to manage their business and that they need not have included the additional duties in the . . . job".

David Pannick was critical of the generous scope of the GOQs established by the SDA.

D. Pannick, *Sex Discrimination Law*, 255–70

Part of the difficulty with section 7 is that it attempts to deal with three separate types of cases, those of physical, functional, and social differences between the sexes. The physical differences concern cases where, by reason of his or her sex, a person is simply unable to

---

[17] The case was remitted to a different tribunal for rehearing, the original tribunal having placed undue evidence on the opinion of its Sikh member.

[18] S.7(2)(h) relating to jobs to be held by married couples.

[19] Excepting the defences relating to private homes and married couples.

[20] In *Lasertop Ltd* v *Webster* [1997] ICR 828, [1997] IRLR 498, EAT ruled that s.7(4) had no application in a case in which such employees had not yet been recruited—the job refusal occurred at pre-opening recruitment for a health club and was based on the argument that a man could not show potential clients around the changing facilities.

perform the job. The functional differences concern cases where Parliament has recognized that, by reason of her sex, a person is less able effectively to perform the job. Such cases are hard to reconcile with the fundamental premiss of the 1975 Act that one should consider persons as individuals irrespective of the qualities commonly possessed by or associated with their sex. Section 7(2)(d) and section 7(2)(e) also seem inconsistent with the principle that sex is not a GOQ merely because of customer preference. The social differences between men and women recognized by section 7 include those concerned with privacy and decency. Clearly it is a matter of social policy to what extent privacy and decency should limit the employment opportunities of one sex. Different societies adopt different values relating to the sharing of sleeping accommodation by men and women at work or relating to states of undress at work. . . .

Once one moves away from the obvious examples of cases where the essential nature of the job calls for a person of a particular sex for reasons of "physiology", difficult questions are raised of what is "the essential nature" of a job and when is its performance "materially different" because carried out by a man (or a woman)? Suppose a company which manufactures motor cars wishes to advertise its product by hiring attractive models to be photographed in a state of undress lying on the bonnet. Although it wants to employ women, and not men, for reasons of physiology, it is unclear whether the essential nature of the job would be materially different if performed by a male model. Even if the company is correct in assuming that it will sell more cars by employing *female* models, this is insufficient to make sex a GOQ for the job. There is a thin, but important, line between sex as a GOQ where the essential nature of the job requires a woman, and the case where the job can more effectively be performed by a woman because of customer reaction. A publican cannot refuse to employ men behind the bar because he believes (rightly or wrongly) that a barmaid attracts more custom. The essential nature of the job, that is serving alcohol, would note materially different if performed by a man. The reference in section 7(2)(a) to "the essential nature of the job" and to whether it would be "materially different" if carried out by a man requires the court to look objectively at the job in its context. If a men's club employs topless waitresses, sex may be a GOQ even though in other circumstances the essential nature of the job (serving customers) is not materially different when performed by a man. The court is required to look at the essence of the job and to reject an employer's attempt to add sex appeal to the job definition unless that is part of the essential nature of the job. . . .

The vague criterion of reasonableness in section 7(2)(c)(ii) gives courts and tribunals the unenviable task of deciding how to balance a person's right not to be discriminated against on the ground of their sex and an employer's plea that it should not have to incur a financial burden in employing that person.

In deciding what is "reasonable" under section 7(2)(c)(ii) it is unfortunately not relevant that, as Baroness Seear emphasized in Parliament, in other European countries "it is far more common for men and women to share certain premises and conveniences" (for example, train couchettes). The question under section 7(2)(c)(ii) is whether it is reasonable to expect the employer to provide separate sleeping accommodation and private sanitary facilities for each sex, not whether it is reasonable to refuse to employ women because there are no such facilities provided. Section 7(2)(c) adopts a very conservative approach to this question, allowing employers to refuse jobs to women even if women are prepared to share facilities with men, and even if those men are prepared to share the facilities with the women. It is not a precondition for the applicability of section 7(2)(c), as it is for the applicability of section 7(2)(b), that relevant men (or women) "might reasonably object" to the employment of members of the other sex. Section 7(2)(c) needs amendment to include such a precondition. . . .

The difficulty with section 7(2)(d) is to understand why it is necessary. Why should sex be a GOQ in jobs done in special establishments where the privacy and decency GOQ in section 7(2)(b) does not apply, when the communal accommodation GOQ of section 7(2)(c) does not apply, and where the personal services GOQ of section 7(2)(e) does not apply? If any of these other bases for a GOQ supply the rationale for section 7(2)(d), then section 7(2)(d) is otiose. If these other factors are not relevant, what is the rationale for section 7(2)(d)? No rationale different from those presented in section 7(2)(b) and section 7(2)(e) was suggested by the Government during the Parliamentary debates on the Bill. The argument that prisoners, or patients, or persons in other institutions need to be dealt with by a person of their own sex (even though this is neither to preserve decency or privacy nor because persons of that sex can most effectively provide personal services) badly smells of the offensive sex stereotyping that the 1975 Act aims to eradicate. . . .

Two objections were raised to section 7(2)(g) during Parliamentary debates. Neither of them received a satisfactory answer. First, which countries have laws or customs which prevent the performance (or effective performance) of which jobs by women (or men)? It is difficult to assess the propriety of an exception to the general anti-discrimination principle unless one knows precisely what one is validating.

The second objection to the existence of section 7(2)(g) was that we should not "enshrine in our legislation a concession to the prejudices of other countries . . .". It was emphasized by those unhappy about section 7(2)(g) that the 1975 Act would be a model for amended legislation prohibiting race discrimination: surely we would not allow employers to discriminate against blacks or Jews in filling jobs whose partial duties were performed in Great Britain, on the ground that some duties were to be performed in a less enlightened country where such individuals would, by reason of that country's laws or customs, be unable to perform the duties adequately or at all. Indeed, the Race Relations Act 1976 does not make membership of a particular racial group a GOQ in circumstances similar to those defined in section 7(2)(g). In *American Jewish Congress* v. *Carter*, Aramco, an oil company with interests in Saudi Arabia, were accused of acting contrary to the New York State Law against discrimination by refusing to employ Jews for work which might involve travel to Saudi Arabia. They discriminated in this way because the King of Saudi Arabia not only prohibited the employment of Jews there but also "strenuously objects to the employment of Jews in any part of Aramco's operation". The judge in the Supreme Court of New York rejected the claim that being a non-Jew was a BFOQ for the job. He declared that:

> This court does not pretend to assert that Saudi Arabia may not do as it pleases with regard to whom it will employ within the borders of Saudi Arabia . . . What this court does say is that Aramco cannot defy the declared public policy of New York State and violate its statute within New York State, No matter what the King of Saudi Arabia says. New York State is not a province of Saudi Arabia, nor is the constitution and statute of New York State to be cast aside to protect the oil profits of Aramco.

He said that if Aramco cannot employ Jews because of the orders of the King, "the answer of New York State is simply—Go elsewhere to serve your Arab master—but not in New York State".

The rationale of section 7(2)(h) is difficult to comprehend. If by section 7(2)(h) Parliament merely wished to allow employers to continue to require a married couple to perform the two jobs, then the subsection is otiose. A single person applying for one of the jobs, or an unmarried couple applying for the jobs, would have no legal complaint. There would be no sex discrimination, and section 3 prohibits discrimination on the ground of marital status only when it is against married persons. Presumably, therefore Parliament intended to allow an employer, taking on a married couple for two jobs, to specify which job should be done by which spouse. Why is it unlawful for an employer to require that, in its offices, its caretaker must be male or to require that its cleaner must be female, but lawful for the employer to require a married couple to act as caretaker and cleaner and to specify that the husband must be the caretaker and the wife must be the cleaner? One hopes that courts and tribunals would interpret section 7(2)(h) to prevent employers abusing this exemption by requiring a married couple as a pretext for sex discrimination.

PREGNANCY

It is clear from Chapter 2 that one of the major applications of the SDA has related to women as mothers. Whereas complaints of direct discrimination are concerned with the conscious application of less favourable treatment to women *as women*, many indirect discrimination claims have challenged practices which disadvantage women who have taken time out of the labour market [*Price* v *Civil Service Commission* [1977] IRLR 291, *Jones* v *University of Manchester* [1992] ICR 52, *Falkirk Council* v *Whyte* [1997] IRLR 560), or those whose childcare commitments preclude full-time or other particular patterns of work (*Clymo* v *Wandsworth* [1989] ICR 250, *Cast* v *Croydon* [1998] IRLR 319, [1998] ICR 500, *London Underground* v *Edwards* [1995] ICR 574, [1995] IRLR 355).

Motherhood poses very significant challenges to women in the labour market. Many jobs, certainly most high status jobs, are shaped around workers who are not responsible for the physical care of others. But even more fundamental, in terms of the hurdles to labour market equality, is the discrimination frequently associated with pregnancy itself. Complaints of pregnancy-related discrimination account for a very significant part of the EOC's postbag, and recent research has shown that:

> [p]regnant women workers are still seen as "invalids" who are not physically or emotionally capable of fulfilling the demands of their employment. Two other traditional attitudes to emerge were that pregnant women who were already mothers should be at home, and that pregnant workers were placing themselves, their child, fellow workers and clients in "danger" and selfishly using employers" and taxpayers" resources.[21]

More than one in thirty working women have babies each year. Traditionally, many women left the paid labour market in order to have children. Increasingly, however, women expect to remain in employment during pregnancy and to return to work

---

[21] 81 *Equal Opportunities Review* pp.10–11, citing H. Gross, *Pregnancy and Employment: the perceptions and beliefs of fellow workers*, Department of Human Sciences, Loughborough University, LE11 3TU.

within a relatively short period of the birth. We saw, above, that the proportion of women returning to work within a year of birth has increased very substantially even within the last ten years. Yet many employers persist in seeing pregnancy and motherhood as incompatible with a commitment to paid work. Many women who return to work do so on a part-time basis (almost 50% of all working women working part-time). The problems associated with this practice are considered further below. Here we deal exclusively with the issues of pregnancy and maternity.

The Employment Rights Act 1996 provides some protection against pregnancy-related discrimination.

> S.99(1) An employee who is dismissed shall be regarded . . . as unfairly dismissed if-
>
> (a) the reason (or, if more than one, the principle reason) for the dismissal is that she is pregnant or any other reason connected with her pregnancy,
>
> (b) her maternity leave period is ended by dismissal and the reason (or, if there is more than one, the principle reason) for the dismissal is that she has given birth to a child or any other reason connected with her having given birth to a child,
>
> (c) her contract of employment is terminated after the end of her maternity leave period and the reason (or, if more than one, the principle reason) for the dismissal is that she took, or availed herself of the benefits of, maternity leave . . .

Special provision is made (s.77) for redundancy arising during the course of maternity leave, the employer being obliged to offer the woman any suitable alternative employment which is available and failure so to do being regarded as automatically unfair dismissal within s.99. No qualifying period of employment applies in respect of s.99.

In addition to the right not to be dismissed, all women are entitled under ss.71–85 to maternity leave of eighteen weeks (this right was introduced only in 1996 and between then and April 2000 was for a period of only 14 weeks).[22] Women who have been continuously employed for at least one year have additional rights to absence for a period of up to six months after the birth (this may be extended by a further four weeks in the event of illness). Failure on the part of an employer to permit a woman to return is generally regarded as a dismissal (s.96) which dismissal shall, if it falls within s.99 above, be automatically unfair.

Some provision is made for maternity pay, though this is not generous (being restricted, at best, to 90% of salary for six weeks and around £59.55 a week (from April 1999) for a further twelve).[23] Women earning less than the National Insurance threshold (currently £64 per week) during a particular eight week period of their pregnancy are not entitled to any maternity pay. The *Equal Opportunities Review* pointed out in 1998 that 25,000 women were affected by this rule. Such women are entitled to a maternity payment from the Social Fund (frozen at £100 for ten years to 1999, now £200).

---

[22] Two weeks leave after the birth is compulsory on pain of criminal sanctions for the employer.

[23] Those who have been employed for less than about nine months at the time of the birth are entitled only to Maternity Allowance at the lower rate—this right has recently been extended beyond those earning in excess of the NI threshold to all those earning at least £30 per week.

Had the protection afforded by the ERA and its successors against pregnancy-related discrimination been comprehensive, no issue might have arisen as to the inclusion or otherwise of pregnancy discrimination within the SDA's prohibition on "sex" discrimination. But the provisions discussed above are of relatively recent vintage. Prior to 1996, dismissal on grounds of pregnancy was only prohibited in the case of women having at least two years qualifying service (five in the case of those working for under 16 hours a week).[24] The ERA protections apply only to "employees",[25] rather than to the broader category protected under the SDA and other discrimination-related legislation. Further the right to return was, in respect of babies expected prior to 30th April 2000, subject to fulfilment of technical requirements of mind-numbing complexity. The notice requirements have been simplified by the Maternity and Parental Leave, etc., Regulations 1999.[26] Finally, whereas the compensation which may be awarded under the SDA has, since 1993, been uncapped, the unfair dismissal compensation under the ERA is subject to a maximum limit which currently stands at £50,000 but which, until this year, was a mere £12,000. (By contrast, women who relied on the SDA to challenge their pregnancy-related dismissals from the armed forces (which, until 1990, operated a blanket policy of dismissing pregnant women), proved losses, and secured awards, of up to around £300,000.)

Such were the shortcomings of legislation expressly dealing with pregnancy that women began to argue that pregnancy-related discrimination fell within the prohibitions of the SDA. Whether "pregnancy" equates with "sex" in this context has been one of the long-running debates associated with the legislation. That there should have been some disagreement as to whether or not pregnancy discrimination could be regarded as direct sex discrimination is not surprising. Most employers who discriminate against pregnant women do not do so because they disapprove of pregnancy as such, rather because of its actual or anticipated impact of attendance, flexibility, etc., and the ensuing requirement for maternity leave. Challenging pregnancy-related discrimination as sex discrimination has been problematic because of the formal approach to equality adopted by the SDA.

**Sandra Fredman, "A Difference with Distinction: Pregnancy and Parenthood Reassessed"
110 *LQR* 106, 106–9**

In many areas, such as that of the suffrage, equality has been a useful tool. It has, moreover, had an important influence on anti-discrimination law. In this context, the policy that gender alone should not be a sufficient ground for differentiation translates into the equal

---

[24] Those working for less than eight hours a week never qualified.

[25] S.230 defines "employee" as "an individual who has entered into . . . a contract of employment", this in turn being defined as "a contract of service or apprenticeship".

[26] The Regulations are discussed in more detail by the author at (2000) 29 *ILJ* 125, "Family Friendly Frolics". One significant improvement resulting from the Employment Relations Act 1999 under which the Regulations were passed, is that the contract of employment is declared to subsist throughout maternity leave. For the previous position and the implications therof see *Kelly* v *Liverpool Maritime Terminals* [1988] IRLR 310 (CA), *Crees* v *Royal London* [1998] ICR 848 (CA) and *Haifperny* v *IGE* [1999] ICR 834 (CA).

treatment principle, namely, that those who, apart from their gender, are alike, should be treated alike. However, in the pregnancy context, the equal treatment principle presents some intractable problems Five central limitations will be dealt with here. First, the equal treatment principle requires an answer to the question "Equal to whom?" The answer supplied by anti-discrimination law is, generally, "equal to a man." For example, under the Sex Discrimination Act 1975, it is unlawful for an employer to treat a woman less favourably on grounds of her sex or marital status than a man would have been treated. In the pregnancy context, this central reliance on a male norm leads straight into the awkward question of who the relevant male comparator should be. Secondly, the reach of the equal treatment principle is necessarily restricted to those who are held to be similarly situated. It requires no explanation for the type of treatment meted out to those who are not equal in the relevant ways. Thus, no justification is required for detrimental treatment of women in cases in which there is no similarly situated male. In the pregnancy context, if no relevant comparator can be found, detrimental treatment is in effect legitimated. The third limitation of the equality principle is that it requires only consistency of treatment between men and women, not minimum standards. In the pregnancy context, this means that a women's rights are entirely dependent on the extent to which comparable rights are afforded to comparable men. For example, if it is accepted that a pregnant woman is similarly situated to an ill man, then she is entitled only to the rights he has. If he has no protection against dismissal or sick leave, then she has correspondingly no protection against dismissal on grounds of her pregnancy or rights to maternity leave. Fourthly, the equal treatment principle leads to an inadequate consideration of the question of who should bear the social cost of pregnancy and child-bearing. Because the principle translates into an obligation placed on the individual employer, the courts are prompted to require justification for placing the cost of pregnancy on that employer. But this ignores the fact that sparing an "innocent" employer leaves the whole cost with the woman and prevents any consideration of the potential cost-spreading role of the State. Finally, the equal treatment principle tends to operate symmetrically, striking down inequalities between men and women regardless of whether the differential treatment favours women or men. One implication is that, in the absence of specific legislative exceptions, maternity leave policies might be challenged on the grounds that they constitute a benefit which is not available to men.

Traditional assumptions that pregnancy and maternity belonged to the home, or the "private sphere," are increasingly challenged by the great increase in women working in the market-place, or "public sphere." Indeed, the pregnant worker forces the law to confront the breakdown in traditional divisions between public and private.

In facing this challenge, however, legislatures and courts have become ensnared in another of the dichotomies which bedevil analysis of women's rights: that between equality and difference. Most anti-discrimination legislation follows a well-trodden path: those who are equal deserve equal treatment, and, conversely, those who differ may be treated differently. Unpacking this apparently straightforward formula reveals unsuspected complexity. For example, the principle itself gives no guidance as to which of the myriad differences and similarities between individuals are relevant for the purpose at hand. As Finley argues, "the outcome of the analysis which asks whether someone is different or the same . . . depends entirely on the characteristic or factor selected for emphasis. This selection is a highly political, value-laden choice." Yet too often no attempt is made to articulate or justify the underlying values. This approach generates particular difficulties when applied to pregnancy: clearly a woman is different from a man when she is pregnant, but how significant is this difference, and what legal consequences should follow from it?

If it were the case that women were discriminated against by virtue simply of the fact that they were pregnant, the SDA could quite readily be construed so as to offer protection. This was recognised by David Pannick in 1985, in a commentary on the decision in *Turley* v *Allders Department Stores Ltd*, which is discussed below.

D. Pannick, *Sex Discrimination Law*, 147–50

Because only women can become pregnant, the complainant who is dismissed because she is pregnant can argue that she would not have been less favourably treated but for her sex. It requires a very narrow construction of the statute to exclude less favourable treatment on the ground of a characteristic unique to one sex. It is quite true that not all women are (or become) pregnant. But it is important to note that direct discrimination exists not merely where the defendant applies a criterion that less favourably treats all women.[27] It also exists where special, less favourable, treatment is accorded to a class consisting only of women, albeit not all women. Suppose an employer announces that it will employ any man with stated qualifications but only a woman who has those qualifications and who is over six feet tall. Albeit not all women are excluded, the employer has directly discriminated against women because it has imposed a criterion which less favourably treats a class composed entirely of women. That such treatment must constitute direct discrimination is emphasized by the fact that it would not give rise to a claim of indirect discrimination: the employer has not applied a condition or requirement equally to members of both sexes. There can be no doubt that Parliament intended to proscribe such conduct.

Less favourable treatment by reference to a criterion which affects only women, albeit not all women, has been considered by the US Federal courts in applying Title VII of the Civil Rights Act 1964. Section 703(a) of Title VII makes it unlawful for an employer "to fail or refuse to hire or to discharge any individual or otherwise to discriminate against any individual with respect to his compensation, terms, conditions or privileges of employment, because of such individual's . . . sex . . .". The US courts have held that "sex-plus" criteria, those less favourably treating only women, but not all women, violate Title VII. In *Sprogis* v. *United Air Lines*, [444 F 2d 1194 (1971)] (the US Court of Appeals found that the defendants had breached Title VII by requiring female flight attendants to be unmarried. The court held that:

> The scope of [the statute] is not confined to explicit discrimination based "solely" on sex. In forbidding employers to discriminate against individuals because of their sex, Congress intended to strike at the entire spectrum of disparate treatment of men and women resulting from sex stereotypes. . . . The effect of the statute is not to be diluted because discrimination adversely affects only a portion of the protected class. Discrimination is not to be tolerated under the guise of physical properties possessed by one sex . . .

In *Hurley* v. *Mustoe* [1981] ICR 490, the EAT had no doubt that an employer who refused to employ women with young children was directly discriminating on the ground of sex contrary to the 1975 Act.

It is true that in *Hurley* the less favourable treatment was expressly pointed at *women* who had stated attributes. The employer who dismisses an employee because she is

---

[27] *Cf* the approach taken by Manitoba's Court of Appeal in *Janzen* v *Platy Enterprises Ltd* and overturned by Canada's Supreme Court ([1989] ISCR 1284). The decisions are discussed in Chapter 2.

pregnant does not expressly direct his policy at women. But the distinction is meaningless in this context. Whether the less favourable treatment is "on the ground of her sex" must depend on whether it can, in practice, affect only women, and not on how the employer labels the disadvantaged class. Because only women can become pregnant, the employer who dismisses a woman for reasons connected with pregnancy has treated her on the ground of a characteristic unique to her sex. It has applied special treatment to a class consisting only of women, albeit that class does not consist of all women. The less favourable treatment (if any) is therefore "on the ground of her sex".

Pannick is clearly of the view that treatment by reason of pregnancy is treatment by reason of sex. But a breach of the SDA requires *discrimination*, that is, *less* favourable treatment, by reason of sex. In *Turley* v *Allders* (EAT's first engagement with pregnancy-as-sex discrimination), this was to prove the applicant's undoing. She claimed that she had been discriminated against when she was dismissed by reason, she claimed, of her pregnancy. A tribunal rejected her claim having decided, as a preliminary issue, that pregnancy-related dismissal was not prohibited by the SDA. Her appeal failed.

Turley v *Allders Department Stores Ltd* [1980] IRLR 4

Bristow J (for the majority)

Section 1 (1) [SDA] provides: "A person discriminates against a woman in any circumstances relevant for the purposes of any provision of this Act if—(a) on the ground of her sex he treats her less favourably than he treats or would treat a man, or (b) he applies to her a requirement or condition which he applies or would apply equally to a man but—(i) which is such that the proportion of women who can comply with it is considerably smaller than the proportion of men who can comply with it, and (ii) which he cannot show to be justifiable irrespective of the sex of the person to whom it is applied, and (iii) which is to her detriment because she cannot comply with it."

Section 1 (2) underlines the intention which underlies subsection (1). You are to look at men and women, and see that they are not treated unequally simply because they are men and women. You have to compare like with like. So, in the case of the pregnant woman there is an added difficulty in the application of subsection (1). Suppose that to dismiss her for pregnancy is to dismiss her on the ground of her sex. In order to see if she has been treated less favourably than a man the sense of the section is that you must compare like with like, and you cannot. When she is pregnant a woman is no longer just a woman. She is a woman, as the Authorised Version of the Bible accurately puts it, with child, and there is no masculine equivalent.

So, in our judgment, to dismiss a woman because she is pregnant is not within the definition of discrimination against women in section 1 of the [SDA] . . .

Like Pannick, EAT here accepted that pregnancy-based treatment was "by reason of" sex. But the majority ruled that the applicant had not been *less favourably* treated than a man, this on the ground that no comparison was possible between a pregnant woman and a man. This approach was criticised by Pannick who advocated an approach similar to that taken by the dissenting member in *Turley*.

Pannick states (p. 160) that the conceptual problem with pregnancy is "in its essence an irreconcileable theoretical conflict between those who believe that the gender equality principle can only be applied where men and women are treated differently with respect to a shared characteristic (which pregnancy is not) and those who believe that discrimination on the basis of physical characteristics inextricably linked to one sex must be sex discrimination". Proponents of the first approach would include the majority members of EAT in *Turley* and the Supreme Court of the US in *Geduldig* v *Aiello* (1974) 417 US 484 (in which that Court ruled that pregnancy discrimination did not amount to sex discrimination for constitutional purposes). Advocates of the latter approach include Fredman (extracted above), Lacey and Szyszczak (extracted below).

Pannick goes on to state that "Neither of the suggested approaches is . . . correct. A third, preferable solution is that classification by reference to a characteristic unique to one sex . . . is treatment on the ground of sex. Whether it is less favourable treatment . . . is . . . dependent on how the other sex is treated in 'not materially different' circumstances". It was this "third way" which found favour with EAT in the subsequent case of *Hayes* v *Malleable Working Men's Club*. The applicants were dismissed after they informed their employers that they were pregnant, neither having sufficient qualifying service for a claim under the EP(C)A 1978 (which statute then governed unfair dismissal). Their claims were dismissed in line with *Turley*, but their appeals to EAT were successful and their cases were remitted for rehearing.

Hayes v Malleable Working Men's Club and Institute, Maughan v Northern East London Magistrates' Court Committee [1985] ICR 703, [1985] IRLR 367

Waite J (P)

It must in practice be extemely rate these days for anyone to be dismissed simply because they were going to have a baby, and for no other reason—though in sterner times than ours that might possibly have been thought to provide moral justification for the dismissal of an unmarried employee. It will usually be the consequences of pregnancy, rather than the condition itself, which provides the grounds from dismissal; the general effect, that is to say, upon the employee's performance at work of the need to take time off for her confinement and for periods of rest before and afterwards. Those consequences will vary greatly in importance and significance from case to case and from one instance to another. . .

Turley . . .has no basis of fact apart from the three facts there assumed, namely that the employee is pregnant, that she is dismissed, and that the former provided the grounds for the latter. It enshrines no principle of law of general application. and is too bare of any factual content to be applied by analogy to the circumstances of any other case. . . We think, therefore, that the proper assessment to be made of *Turley's* case is that it is a decision limited to the narrow hypothetical circumstances with which the Appeal Tribunal was there invited to deal. Since circumstances so narrow as those are unlikely to be paralleled in practice in any particular instance where a dismissal associated with the pregnancy of an employee falls to be judged in the light of sex discrimination, it should not be treated as an authority applicable to other cases but should be treated as confined to its own restricted (and assumed) facts. Industrial Tribunals may therefore in our judgment direct themselves for the future upon the basis that there is no principle of law preventing the application of the [SDA] to cases where a woman claims to have been the victim of direct or indirect discrimination on grounds associated or connected with the fact that she is pregnant. If we are wrong in so distinguishing Turley's case and it is an authority of principle, then with respect (and with sympathy for the views of the majority in the predicament presented to them by the need to determine a hypothetical question) we would feel bound to decline to follow it; and to prefer the views of [the dissenter]—for which powerful support is provided, in our judgment, by the crucial requirement in s 5(3) of the Act that for all purposes of comparison (whether direct or indirect discrimination is involved) the two cases must be the same "or not materially different".[28] Like [her], we have not found any difficulty in visualising cases—for example, that of a sick male employee and a pregnant woman employee, where the circumstances, although they could never in strictness be called the same, could nevertheless be properly regarded as lacking any material difference.

Hayes left some scope for women to argue that pregnancy-related discriminations breached the SDA, but its protection was far from comprehensive. To return to the argument made by Sandra Fredman, above, it afforded the protection of the SDA only to women who behaved like men—like those men to whom their employers would have afforded equivalent periods of sick leave to the maternity leave they required. The shortcomings of the *Hayes* approach were further illustrated by the decision in *Berrisford* v *Woodard Schools (Midland Division)* [1991] ICR 564, [1991] IRLR 247, in which EAT rejected an appeal by a woman dismissed because her pregnancy, coupled as it was with a refusal to marry, manifested her participation in extra-marital sex. The extract from Nicola Lacey, below, considers more generally the shortcomings of *Hayes*.

N. Lacey, "Dismissal by Reason of Pregnancy" (1986) 15 *ILJ*, 43, 44–5

It would be a mistake to hail *Hayes* as an unambiguous victory in the battle for genuine equality of opportunity for women. two main factors militate towards the conclusion that if it stands the test of time as a victory at all that victory may well turn out to have been at best, partial; at worst, Pyrrhic. . . . the admission of pregnancy as in principle a source of unlawful less favourable treatment admits the litigant to the perilous minefield of proof endemic to all direct race and sex discrimination cases. In the case of pregnancy, however, these problems may be especially acute. Pregnancy is frequently, and often unjustifiably associated in popular consciousness with factors such as tiredness and loss of concentration as well as with the clear necessity of some period of absence from work. Thus an employer such as the Malleable Working Men's Club, which claimed that Ms. Hayes' dismissal was based not on pregnancy but on past performance at work, may well be able to take advantage of such unreflective attitudes on the part of the adjudicator, with the consequence that the plaintiff will have enormous difficulty in dislodging the argument. Of course, on the reasoning in *Hayes*, even if the employer's initial argument is accepted, so long as the poor performance is thought to be related to the pregnancy, it would then be necessary for the tribunal to ask how a man performing similarly poorly on the basis of illness or perhaps anxiety would have been treated.

---

[28] See discussion of s.5(3) SDA in Chapter 2.

This leads us on to the second, and much more deep-seated problem with the *Hayes* approach. Whichever way the Tribunal decides, an important dimension of the case may well become suppressed. If the Tribunal decides that a sick man would have been equally harshly treated, by the very hypothesis of the comparison, no question can be raised about whether it was appropriate to treat a pregnant woman in the same way. Since the logic of the section lies in formally equal treatment in roughly similar cases, no possible argument can be raised about the special nature of pregnancy which might merit special treatment, as acknowledged in our statutory laws on maternity leave. The limitations of the approach may best be illustrated by taking the different example of hiring, to which the *Hayes* principle would apply. It would probably be held that ill health or inability to start work for several months would be a likely and legitimate reason for a decision not to hire—thus the foothold for a claim of sex discrimination in a decision not to hire a pregnant woman disappears. In such crucial spheres, therefore, the S.D.A. would still be powerless to make any progress towards the goal of ensuring that no quality intrinsically related to femaleness should act as a barrier to equality of opportunity: what the example shows is the dubious propriety of assuming that a pregnant woman and a sick man, or a man seeking compassionate leave for other reasons, are likely to be in a similar situation for the purposes of making even a reasonable range of employment decisions about them or comparisons of them.

This doubt persists if, alternatively, the Tribunal holds that a sick man would not have been dismissed in such circumstances, and thus makes a finding of sex discrimination on ground of pregnancy. The plaintiff wins her case, but at the cost of artificially comparing herself with an ill or otherwise abnormally situated man. This serves to reinforce a gravely damaging stereotyped view of women as having special weaknesses which render them comparable only with men in non-standard circumstances; the equation of pregnancy with ill health or other misfortune grossly misrepresents the nature of that condition and wilfully undervalues the importance still attached in our society to the bearing of children.

One is left with the uncomfortable suspicion that except in cases where pregnancy is being used as a pretext for general sex discrimination, the form of the S.D.A. renders it an unreliable legal tool for ensuring the fair treatment of pregnant women. In a sense, the majority in *Turley* was right: the logic of section 1(1) of the S.D.A. is irresistible—or at least can only be escaped by the making of illegitimate and ultimately damaging comparisons. In the absence of legislative formulation of a specific provision outlawing pregnancy discrimination in the sense of any *unfavourable* rather than *less favourable* treatment on grounds of pregnancy, would the E.A.T. in *Hayes* not have done better to make use of the "golden rule" of statutory interpretation so as to avoid the absurd consequences of a literal reading of the S.D.A. by acknowledging that no real male comparator can exist, thus rejecting any attempted comparison and simply seeking to identify unfavourable treatment on the sex-related grounds of pregnancy?

A different approach to that adopted by EAT in either *Turley* or in *Webb* was taken by the European Court of Justice in *Dekker v Stichting Vormingscentrum Voor Jonge Volwassen Plus* Case 177/88 [1990] ECR I-3941.

E. Ellis, "The Definition of Discrimination in European Sex Equality Law" (1994) 19 *European Law Review* 561, 567–8

Dekker concerned a refusal to employ a pregnant woman who would otherwise have been appointed to a job of training instructor in a youth centre. The employers explained that, as Ms Dekker was already pregnant when she applied for the job, the employer's insurers would not reimburse the sickness benefits paid to Ms Dekker during her maternity leave. It would therefore be impossible for the employers to employ a replacement during Ms Dekker's absence, which would mean in the end that they would lose some of their training places. The first question which the Court of Justice had to answer was whether or not this situation amounted to direct sex discrimination. They held that this depended on whether the most important reason for the refusal to recruit Ms Dekker was a reason which applied without distinction to employees of both sexes or whether it applied exclusively to one sex. Since employment can only be refused because of pregnancy to a woman, such a refusal, the Court held, *must* be direct discrimination on the ground of sex. And a refusal to employ because of the financial consequences of pregnancy must be deemed to be based principally on the fact of the pregnancy. In other words, the Court was saying that, *but for* Ms Dekker's sex, she would have been appointed, so that her adverse treatment must be grounded on her sex; there was no need to prove any subjective consideration of Ms Dekker's sex on the part of the employers. The Court of Justice's conclusion here thus seems to be substantially the same in theory as that of the House of Lords in the *James* case.

However, the Court of Justice added a further point in *Dekker*, which indicates its fundamental grasp of what the law in this area is seeking to achieve. It had been urged to hold that the employers could escape liability if they could establish a "legal justification" for their action. This it refused to do, saying that the only defences to unlawful sex discrimination were those contained in Article 2 of the Equal Treatment Directive. It is highly significant that the Court did not allow itself to be muddled by the introduction of a notion of justification into *direct* discrimination (as distinct from *indirect* discrimination where, as will be explained below, it plays a vital role in relation to causation). In effect it took a very clear-sighted view of direct discrimination, accepting that Ms Dekker would win her case if she could show simply that she had suffered detrimental treatment and that that treatment was grounded on her sex; if the employers could not rely on one of the listed defences, that was the end of the matter for them. Once causation had been established, the discrimination could only be excused for one of the specific reasons articulated by the directive. Looking at this from a different angle, the Court is focusing here on the *effect* of the impugned treatment, rather than being diverted by subjective inquiries into *why* the employers behaved as they did. The important thing which the Court keeps uppermost in its mind is the *remedial* function of the anti-discrimination law, and it is not thrown off course by arguments about culpability which would be appropriate in a criminal law context.

Evelyn Ellis' approval of the *Dekker* decision was not universally shared.

Ivan Hare, "Pregnancy and Sex Discrimination" (1991) 20 *ILJ*, 124, 128

The flaw in . . . is that the fact of the pregnancy is not the true reason for the detrimental treatment. This can be further illustrated by reference to the facts of the *Dekker* case itself, from which it plainly emerges that the true rationale for the company's refusal to employ Mrs Dekker was not the fact that she was pregnant but rather that the employers would not be able to recoup the maternity benefits paid to her from the relevant fund. This reason would apply equally to a male employee who would require a period of absence within six months of commencing work because of a condition which was foreseeable at the time of his recruitment. If one looks at the true reason for the detrimental treatment such a refusal would only be discriminatory if the employer would have treated a similarly situated male worker differently.

The flaw in Hare's argument is, of course, that it permits continued discrimination against women who, by contrast with men, require a period of leave if they are to combine work and motherhood.

At about the same time that the ECJ decided *Dekker*, the pregnancy-as-sex argument came before EAT once again in *Webb v EMO Air Cargo (UK) Ltd* [1990] ICR 442. There, EAT rejected an appeal from a woman who, having been employed, on an indefinite contract, to cover for another employee who was to take maternity leave, was dismissed when she subsequently discovered and announced that she was pregnant her baby due at the same time as that of the employee she was hired to cover for.

Webb v EMO Air Cargo (UK) Ltd [1990] ICR 442, [1990] IRLR 124

Wood J:

The facts in this case could not be simpler, but the issue raised will be thought by those involved in the field of discrimination law to be of fundamental importance. Different divisions of this Court have taken different views [*Turley* and *Hayes*] and for this reason we have sat as a five-member Court . . .

Mr John Melville-Williams [for the applicant] contends that . . . although a comparison should be made between a woman applicant and a notional man, it is only possible to reach a result which accords with the intention of the [SDA] if in considering the phrase "relevant circumstances" in s 5(3) of the Act you proceed, in the first place, to ignore the factor of sex and having then found those circumstances to be the same, but the result of the treatment to be different solely by reason of the physiological function of a woman in her pregnancy, which is unique and which is incapable of comparison with a male condition, then it must follow that the act of dismissal because of pregnancy must be direct discrimination . . . he submits that it would be contrary to the purpose of the Act if the phrase "relevant circumstances" in s 5(3) included circumstances which arose in the case of a woman exclusively from a characteristic unique to her sex; that there is no binding authority in support of the proposition that such characteristics are part of the comparative equation and it is wholly artificial so to treat them; it follows that the relevant circumstances are circumstances other than circumstances arising from the applicant's sex and that therefore the search for a man whose condition is equivalent to the condition of a pregnant woman is unnecessary and distorts the provisions of the Act. It seems to us that this latter part of his argument comes very close to the *Turley* view.

The second main plank in his argument relates to s 2 [SDA] . . . He submits that the purpose of s 2(2) is to obviate the possibility of a man bringing proceedings alleging discrimination because special consideration has been given to a woman in connection with pregnancy or childbirth, and that therefore that such treatment of women is "on the ground of sex". No such exclusion applies in reverse and therefore to treat a woman differently than a man because she is pregnant must fall within s 1(1)(a) . . .

It can be seen that the argument put forward for Ms Webb differed in some respects from the approach of the ECJ in *Dekker*. Whereas the ECJ was interpreting the equal treatment directive which has no rigid requirement for a comparison between men and women, the *Webb* case arose under the SDA which requires (s.5(3)) that the treatment complained of was less favourable than that which was or would have been afforded to a man in the same relevant circumstances. A straightforward application of *Dekker* would have ignored this requirement. By eliminating the sex-specific fact of pregnancy from the "relevant circumstances", the approach argued for by Melville-Williams would amount in practice to treating pregnancy discrimination as sex discrimination (this because the treatment accorded to the pregnant woman would be compared to that of a man who did not need a period of leave). At the same time, the Melville-Williams approach has the advantage of fitting the SDA's framework better than one which simply eschews the requirement for comparison.

EAT, however, preferred the arguments put forward by David Pannick for the respondents. Somewhat bizarrely, the appeal tribunal relied on the fact that counsel for the plaintiff in *Hayes* v *Malleable*, discussed above, (Anthony Lester QC) had not argued that pregnancy discrimination automatically amounted to sex discrimination as support for the fact that it should *not* be so regarded, rather than as indicating that the point had not properly been considered by EAT in the earlier case. Pannick (an extract from whose book appears above), persuaded the tribunal that the position of the applicant—that no man can become pregnant and that, therefore, pregnancy discrimination *is* sex discrimination—was equivalent to the discredited *Turley* approach—that no man can become pregnant and that, therefore, pregnancy discrimination can never be sex discrimination. EAT accepted that the appropriate comparator under s.5(3) was a man who was or would be absent from work.

EAT also relied, in reaching its decision, on the approach taken by the Court of Appeal in *James* v *Eastleigh Borough Council* [1990] 2 AC 751, [1990] 2 All ER 607, [1990] 3 WLR 55, 88 LGR 756, [1990] ICR 544, in which that Court ruled that regard had to be had to the subjective intention of the employer in a case of direct discrimination (applied here—was she discriminated against (a) because of her pregnancy *or* (b) because of her sex?). We saw, in Chapter 2, that the House of Lords in that case took a different view, ruling that direct discrimination was established where, *but for* the sex of the applicant, she would not have been less favourably treated.

It was pointed out that the latter decision, applied to pregnancy, should require discrimination on this ground to be treated as discrimination on grounds of sex. (The reasoning for this was to the effect that *but for* the fact that this woman was a woman she could not have been pregnant and, therefore, would not have been so treated.) The decision of the House of Lords in *James* was one of the planks upon which Ms Webb's appeal from EAT rested. So, too, was the decision of the ECJ in *Dekker* (above), in which that Court decided that a refusal to employ on grounds of pregnancy amounted, without more, to discrimination on grounds of sex contrary to the equal treatment directive.

The Court of Appeal rejected Ms Webb's appeal. Lord Justice Glidewell, with whom Balcombe and Bedlam LJJ concurred, accepted that the test for direct discrimination was the "but for" test embraced by the House of Lords in *James*. But their Lordships insisted that the appropriate comparison under s.5(3) was between a pregnant woman and (*per* Glidewell LJ):

> a male employee in the nearest comparable situation. To postulate a pregnant man is an absurdity, but I see no difficulty in comparing a pregnant woman with a man who has a medical condition which will require him to be absent for the same period of time and at the same time as does the woman's pregnancy . . .

Nor did the Court of Appeal accept that European law (in particular, the decision of the ECJ in *Dekker*) required a different conclusion. The Court took the view both that *Dekker* fell short of categorising all pregnancy-related dismissal as sexually discriminatory and also that, even if *Dekker* was to be interpreted otherwise, the requirements of the equal treatment directive could not be given effect in English law without illegitimate distortion of the SDA. Ms Webb appealed to the House of Lords which referred to the ECJ the question whether her dismissal breached the equal treatment directive.

In deciding to refer the issue to the ECJ, Lord Keith for their Lordships expressed the view that the requirement for time off work must, in *Webb*, be a "relevant circumstance" under s 5(3) SDA. Less favourable treatment on grounds of pregnancy or childbirth itself would generally amount to sex discrimination, "[c]hild-bearing and the capacity for child-bearing [being] characteristics of the female sex" and discrimination on the grounds of gender-specific characteristics amounting to sex discrimination under the "but for" test adopted by the House of Lords in *James v Eastleigh*. But the "but for" test:

Webb v EMO Air Cargo (UK) Ltd ([1992] 4 All ER 929, [1993] 1 WLR 49, [1993] ICR 175, [1993] IRLR 27) (HL)

Lord Keith of Kinkel (with whom their Lordships agreed):

> is not capable of application to the circumstances of this case . . . It is true that but for her sex [the applicant] would not have been pregnant, and but for her pregnancy she would not have been unavailable then. If the "but for" test applies to that situation, it must equally apply where the reason for the woman's being unavailable at the critical time is that she is then due to have an operation of a peculiarly gynaecological nature, such as a hysterectomy. But a man may required to undergo an operation for some condition which is peculiar to males, such as an abnormal prostate. Is the "but for his sex" test to be applied so as to produce a finding of unlawful discrimination where he is not engaged because the impending operation will make him unavailable when his services are particularly required? Both in the *Birmingham City Council* and in James's case [see Chapter 2] members of one sex were treated unfavourably by comparison with actual members of the other sex. The problem of postulating relevant circumstances for the purpose of making a comparison with the treatment accorded to hypothetical members of the opposite sex did not arise. The circumstances in the case of a woman due to have a hysterectomy are different from the circumstances in the case of a man due to have a

prostate operation.[29] The question is whether they are materially different, and the answer must be that they are not, because both sets of circumstances have the result that the person concerned is not going to be available at the critical time. Then it has to be considered whether there is something special about pregnancy which ought to lead to the conclusion that the case of a woman due to be unavailable for that reason is materially different from the case of a man due to be unavailable because of an expected prostate operation. In logic, there would not appear to be any valid reason for that conclusion [save, perhaps, the fact that it was crucial to the pursuit of labour market equality]. It is true that pregnancy may be said to be a normal condition, not an abnormal pathological condition such as to require a hysterectomy, but the consequences of both are the same, namely unavailability of the person when particularly needed. The argument for the appellant is that when comparison is made between a pregnant woman, who is going to be unavailable on account of her confinement at the critical time, and a man, then because a man could not be unavailable for the same reason dismissal of or failure to engage the pregnant woman constitutes discrimination. But the correct comparison is not with any man but with an hypothetical man who would also be unavailable at the critical time. The relevant circumstance for purposes of the comparison required by s 5(3) to be made is expected unavailability at the material time. The precise reason for the unavailability is not a relevant circumstance, and in particular it is not relevant that the reason is a condition which is capable of affecting only women or, for that matter, only men.[30]

Lord Keith found it necessary to refer the case to the ECJ for a preliminary ruling on the position under the equal treatment directive. The ECJ (Case C–32/93 [1994] 4 All ER 115, [1994] QB 718) ruled that the dismissal, by reason of pregnancy, of a woman from indefinite employment breached the equal treatment directive. Again, the ECJ ruled that discrimination on the grounds of a characteristic unique to one sex is necessarily direct sex discrimination, there being no need for a comparator. The House of Lords interpreted the SDA accordingly.

Webb v EMO Air Cargo (UK) Ltd (No 2) [1994] QB 718, [1994] 4 ALL ER 115, [1994] 3 WLR 941, [1994] ICR 770, [1994] IRLR 482) (HL)

Lord Keith of Kinkel (with whom their Lordships agreed):

. . . The reasoning in my speech in the earlier proceedings was to the effect that the relevant circumstance which existed in the present case and which should be taken to be present in the case of the hypothetical man was unavailability for work at the time when the worker was particularly required, and that the reason for the unavailability was not a relevant cir-

---

[29] This reasoning was applied by a tribunal in *Carpenter* v *Business Link London (The City, Hackney & Islington) Ltd* 40 EORDCLD, p.4, to rule that dismissal for a menopause-related reason was not automatically unfair, less favourable treatment than a comparator being required.

[30] Lord Keith took the view that s. 2(2) SDA, which provides that more favourable treatment of a pregnant woman would not amount to unlawful discrimination against men, provided support for his approach, "since that provision appears to envisage that there may be relevant circumstances affecting a man which are not materially different from those attributable to the state of pregnancy in a woman". This he took to contradict any argument that, comparison between a pregnant woman and a man being impossible, pregnancy discrimination was, *per se*, sex discrimination. (S.2(2) is, however, perfectly consistent with the Melville-Williams approach set out above.)

cumstance . . . So it was not relevant that the reason for the woman's unavailability was pregnancy, a condition which could not be present in a man.

The ruling of the European Court proceeds on an interpretation of the broad principles dealt with in articles 2(1) and 5(1) of Directive 76/207. Sections 1(1)(a) and 5(3) of the [SDA] set out a more precise test of unlawful discrimination, and the problem is how to fit the terms of that test into the ruling. It seems to me that the only way of doing so is to hold that, in a case where a woman is engaged for an indefinite period, the fact that the reason why she will be temporarily unavailable for work at a time when to her knowledge her services will be particularly required is pregnancy is a circumstance relevant to her case, being a circumstance which could not be present in the case of the hypothetical man. It does not necessarily follow that pregnancy would be a relevant circumstance in the situation where the woman is denied employment for a fixed period in the future during the whole of which her pregnancy would make her unavailable for work, nor in the situation where after engagement for such a period the discovery of her pregnancy leads to cancellation of the engagement.[31]

In *Webb* the House of Lords took a more generous approach to the interpretive obligations imposed by the equal treatment directive than it had previously been prepared to do. We saw, in Chapter 1, that the House of Lords decision in *Duke* v *GEC Reliance* [1988] IRLR 118 [1988] 1 All ER 626, [1988] AC 618, upon which the Court of Appeal in *Webb* relied, was to the effect that the SDA should not be "distorted" to give effect to the directive.[32] In *Webb* the House of Lords appeared to find it impossible to construe the SDA in the applicant's favour. Yet in *Webb (No.2)* their Lordships did precisely that, and without apparent difficulty.

It is now clear, as a matter of English as well as European law, that discrimination on grounds of pregnancy will generally amount to sex discrimination (whether the discrimination is subjectively motivated by the pregnancy itself, or the woman's anticipated absence or, presumably, any other reason).[33] The word "generally" is necessary because of the approach taken to temporary contracts by the House of Lords in *Webb (No 2)*.

Erica Szyszczak, "Pregnancy Discrimination" (1996) 59 *Modern Law Review*, 58, 590–2

Lord Keith puts forward the argument that both the Court and the Advocate General considered it to be a relevant circumstance that Ms Webb had been engaged upon an indefinite

[31] More recently, in *Jones* v *William Monk Ltd* 38 EORDCLD, p.6, a tribunal found that a woman dismissed for abortion-related absence was discriminated against on grounds of sex without need for a comparator.
[32] Compare the willingness of the House of Lords in this case to revise its previous construction of the Act with its earlier decision in *Duke* v *GEC Reliance Ltd* [1988] 1 AC 618, [1988] 1 All ER 626, [1988] ICR 339, [1988] IRLR 118, [1985] 1 CMLR 719, *per* Lord Templeman: "Section 2(4) of the European Communities Act 1972 does not in my opinion enable or constrain a British court to distort the meaning of a British statute in order to enforce against an individual a Community directive which has no direct effect between individuals. Section 2(4) applies and only applies where Community provisions are directly applicable. . . ."
[33] For further confirmation of this see *Mahlburg* (Case C–207/98), delivered by the ECJ on 3rd February 2000 and available from the EC website at www.europa.eu.int/eur-lex/en/index.html. There the court ruled that a refusal to employ a pregnant woman who was prevented by the criminal law from working in the job for the duration of the pregnancy breached the directive.

contract. The Law Lords were anxious to avoid a situation which was described as being "unfair to employers and as tending to bring the law on sex discrimination into disrepute," by allowing the ruling to apply to temporary or fixed term employees. This is achieved by the caveat (which has the status of an *obiter dictum*) that:

> It does not necessarily follow that pregnancy would be a relevant circumstance in the situation where the woman is denied employment for a fixed period in e future during the whole of which her pregnancy would make her unavailable for work, nor in the situation where after engagement for such a period the discovery of her pregnancy leads to cancellation of the engagement. . . .

But by allowing this exception in equal treatment law, the House of Lords is making inroads into the general principle of prohibition against dismissal of pregnant workers contained in Article 10 of Council Directive 92/85/EEC and also paragraph 26 of the ruling in *Webb*:

> contrary to the submission of the United Kingdom, dismissal of a pregnant woman recruited for an indefinite period cannot be justified on grounds relating to her inability to fulfil a fundamental condition of her employment contract. The availability of an employee is necessarily, for the employer, a precondition for the proper performance of the employment contract. However, the protection afforded by Community law to a woman during pregnancy and after childbirth cannot be dependent on whether her presence at work during maternity is essential to the proper functioning of the undertaking in which she is employed. Any contrary interpretation would render ineffective the provisions of the Directive.

If the Sex Discrimination Act 1975 is applied in the way suggested by the House of Lords, the unavailability of a worker on a fixed term contract because of reasons connected with pregnancy will result in a finding that direct discrimination has not occurred. This is different from the approach taken by the Court of Justice. In *Webb* and *Habermann* Case C–241/92 [1994] ECR I–1657, the Court hints that where a woman was not engaged upon an open-ended contract and thus the amount of time she would be unavailable for work because of her pregnancy would be greater than the time she would normally be at work, then an employer may be able to *justify* the dismissal. Is the Court edging its way towards the idea of justifying acts of direct discrimination? The EC Commission clearly favours this approach, but to date the Court has not ruled definitively on the matter.

The problem highlighted by Szyszczak is significant to the very important question of whether direct discrimination can be justified and may be of importance to women employed (as is increasingly common) on a succession of fixed term contracts. There are, in addition, several other substantial flaws in the protection afforded to women in connection with pregnancy and childbirth. In *Handels-og Kontorfunktionaerer-nes Forbund i Danmark (acting for Hertz) v Dansk Arbejdsgiverforening (acting for Aldi Marked K/S)* (Case C–179/88) [1992] ICR 332, [1991] IRLR 31, which was handed down on the same day as *Dekker*, the ECJ decided that the equal treatment directive did not prohibit dismissal for absence due to pregnancy-related illness which manifested itself outside the national period of maternity leave. A similar approach was taken in *Larrson* (Case C–400/975) [1997] ECR 2757. But in *Brown v Rentokil Ltd*

(Case C–394/96) [1998] IRLR 445 the ECJ took more generous approach, ruling that the directive prohibited discrimination on grounds of pregnancy (or pregnancy-related illness):

> throughout the period of pregnancy . . . dismissal of a female worker during pregnancy for absences due to incapacity for work resulting from her pregnancy is linked to the occurrence of risks inherent in pregnancy and must therefore be regarded as essentially based on the fact of pregnancy. Such a dismissal can affect only women and therefore constitutes direct discrimination on grounds of sex.

Brown was subsequently applied by EAT in *Abbey National* v *Formosa* [1999] IRLR, 222 to find that the dismissal of a woman prevented the opportunity to defend herself at a disciplinary hearing because she was on maternity leave amounted to sex discrimination under the SDA.[34] But *Brown* leaves unregulated discrimination on grounds of pregnancy-related sickness absence which takes place after the period of maternity leave (which may, in the UK, extend as little as seven weeks after childbirth). Also unaffected by EC law is the employer's right to trigger maternity leave where a woman requires sick leave (however unrelated to pregnancy) in the six weeks before the due date[35] and, perhaps most fundamentally, the matter of maternity pay.

The extension of maternity leave in the UK from women with at least two years' qualifying employment to all women came about as a result of Council Directive 92/85/EC (the pregnant workers directive). The directive prohibits pregnancy-related dismissals and provides for payment at no less than the rate of statutory sick pay.[36] The directive has proven beneficial to some women in the UK, if only by extending existing protections to women without the qualifying periods previously required. But the directive's provisions relating to payment have, it seems, operated against the interests of women.

In *Gillespie and Others* v *Northern Health and Social Services Board & Ors* Case C–342/93 [1996] ECR I–0475, [1996] IRLR 214, the applicants argued that Article 141 [ex 119] entitled them to full pay during maternity leave. If discrimination against women during the period of maternity leave is discrimination on grounds of sex, the argument went, then non-payment of wages during this period was contrary to Article 141. The ECJ accepted that maternity pay was "pay" within Article 141. But:

> [t]he principle of equal pay laid down in Article [141] . . . and set out in detail in Council Directive 75/117/EEC [the equal pay directive] . . . neither requires that women should continue to receive full pay during maternity leave, nor lays down specific criteria for

---

[34] See also *Healy* v *William B Morrison* EAT/172/99 30th June 1999, in which EAT ruled that an absence-related selection for redundancy during the period of maternity leave breached the SDA without need for comparison with the treatment of a sick man. The case is available at www.employmentappeals.gov.uk.

[35] This was accepted by the ECJ in *Boyle* v *EOC*, below.

[36] Save (see Art 11(4) of the pregnant workers directive, applied by EAT in *Banks* v *Tesco & Secretary of State for Employment* [1999] ICR 1141), where the applicant has not satisfied the statutory qualifying criteria.

determining the amount of benefit payable to them during that period, provided that the amount is not set so low as to jeopardise the purpose of maternity leave.

When that case returned to the Northern Ireland Court of Appeal (*Gillespie and Others* v *Northern Health and Social Services Board & Ors (No 2)* [1997] IRLR 410), it was considered together with *Todd* v *Eastern Health and Social Services Board & Anor*, in which a pregnant woman challenged, as discriminatory, the setting of maternity pay at 90% of salary for six weeks followed by 50% for 12 weeks, where contractual sick pay was set at five months' full pay followed by five months' half pay. Dealing with the questions (1) whether statutory maternity pay was "set so low as to jeopardise the purpose of maternity leave", and (2) whether a tribunal was entitled to rule in favour of Ms Todd on the grounds that maternity pay was less favourable than sick pay, the Court ruled that maternity pay was adequate so long as it was at least equivalent to statutory sick pay (this being the approach adopted by the pregnant workers' directive). In relation to Ms Todd's claim, the Court of Appeal rejected the argument that contractual maternity pay had to be set at the same level as contractual sick pay:

> the only requirement imposed by the ECJ [in *Gillespie*] was that . . . the amount of maternity pay must not be so low as to undermine the purpose of maternity leave . . . Article 11(3) [of the pregnant workers directive] deems [maternity pay] to be adequate if it is at least equivalent to the amount of statutory sickness benefit. It need hardly be said that this is by no means the same thing as saying that maternity pay must always be fixed at the same level as sickness pay in order to be adequate. It follows necessarily from what we have already held in this judgment that it does not have to be payable at the same level as contractual sickness benefit.[37]

Any doubt as to the correctness, of this decision as a matter of EC law, was laid to rest by the decision of the ECJ in *Boyle & Ors* v *Equal Opportunities Commission* (Case C–411/96 [1998] All ER (EC) 879, in which that Court took a precisely similar approach. In that case the ECJ rejected, *inter alia*, a challenge brought by EOC employees to the practice whereby, if they failed to return to work after maternity leave, they were required to repay any contractual maternity pay which they had received in excess of the statutory requirement.

---

[37] An additional question posed by the *Gillespie* case related to whether the calculation of maternity pay had to take into account a backdated pay increase awarded during the period of maternity leave. The ECJ ruled that it did. See also *Alabaster* v *Woolwich* EAT/558/99 9th April 2000, available as at fn 34 above. In *Abdoulaye & Ors* v *Regie Nationale de Usines Renault SA* Case C–218/98, 16th September 1999, available as at fn 33 above, the ECJ permitted payment of a maternity bonus on top of full pay during maternity leave in recognition of the occupational disadvantages inherent in maternity leave "a woman an maternity leave may not be proposed for promotion . . . her period of service will be reduced . . [she] may not claim performance-related salary increases. . . may not take part in training [and] . . . the adaptation of a female worker returning from maternity leave becomes complicated."

M. Wynn, "Pregnancy Discrimination: Equality, Protection or Reconciliation?" (1999) 62
Modern Law Review **435, 441–5**

Despite the injunction in Article 2 of Directive 92/85/EC that the protection of the health and safety of such workers should not jeopardise equal treatment, the Court of Justice has firmly rejected the possibility of any equality comparison between women on maternity leave and other workers on the basis that such women are in a special position, but are not actually at work; thus the usual obligations deriving from the contract of employment do not arise. Furthermore, the delineation of women on maternity leave as dependant mothers as opposed to productive workers has allowed the Court to by-pass notions of equality and locate the problem in the realm of social protection where economic justifications are more likely to gain recognition. Protected status has thus resulted in a regime which has penal consequences for women in that entitlement to adequate income and immunity from dismissal during maternity leave without the need for inappropriate male comparisons has been substituted for substantive equality. . . .

The logic of *Gillespie* was reiterated in *Boyle* v *Equal Opportunities Commission*, where the Court of Justice again rejected a comparative approach . . .

The result of *Boyle* and *Gillespie* is that women on maternity leave are left without effective recourse where employers exploit the modicum of protection provided by Directive 92/85/EC. Financial detriments will continue to be incurred by women who choose to combine work and childbearing and employers will not be penalised for minimising their costs as long as the threshold of adequacy of income is not undermined. These cases indicate that the limits of maternity protection are determined by the European Court's perception of national autonomy in matters of social welfare. The result of balancing competing interests on the social plane is that the cost of applying the principle of equal treatment militates against the vindication of individual rights. As Advocate General Iglesias noted in *Gillespie*, to give full protection to pregnant mothers "would threaten to upset the balance of the entire social welfare system".

By contrast with these decisions on maternity rights, recent cases concerning pregnant workers indicate that a more favourable regime applies to the pregnant woman *qua* worker. In *Thibault* Case C–136/95 [1998] ECR I–2011, the Court of Justice stated that pregnancy and maternity require substantive, not merely formal rights. Here it was the woman's capacity as a worker which the Court emphasised as the factor which triggered the operation of discrimination law, as pregnancy itself could not act as the cause for any adverse treatment in working conditions. Thus the deprival of the right to an annual performance assessment as a result of absence on maternity leave was regarded as unfavourable treatment. Notably, *Gillespie* was referred to in order to support the conclusion that the taking of maternity leave should not deprive a woman of any benefits from pay rises due to her as a worker.

The bifurcation in the Court's jurisprudence on pregnancy and maternity rights has received more specific confirmation in *Hoj Pedersen* Case C–66/96 [1998] ECR I–7327. The applicants were deprived of full pay when they became unfit for work because of pregnancy-related illness before the beginning of their maternity leave. According to Danish national legislation, pregnancy-related incapacity for work entitled the worker to half pay, whereas incapacity for other illness resulted in full benefits. The Court of Justice held that it was contrary to Article 119 [now 141] of the Treaty of Rome and Directive 75/117/EEC to withhold full pay from a pregnant woman who became unfit for work before the commencement of maternity leave by reason of a pathological condition connected with pregnancy.

The importance of this case lies in the explicit comparison made between pregnancy and maternity rights. Advocate General Colomer had made clear in *Boyle* that there is no basis for comparison between a woman on maternity leave and a man on sick leave because the man's contractual obligations are only suspended for so long as he undergoes treatment for a sickness, whereas maternity leave is a special "block" period granted to protect specific pregnancy and maternity needs ie to protect the biological condition of pregnancy and the relationship between mother and child. This distinction was developed in *Pedersen* where the Advocate General rejected the view that unfitness for work caused by pregnancy before maternity leave began amounted to "pre-maternity" leave. He stated that maternity leave differs from pregnancy-related sickness absence in a number of respects: first, maternity leave has a finite duration; secondly, entitlement is not linked to illness; thirdly, a woman is released from all employment obligations including work. This reasoning focuses on differences in employment rights: whereas pregnant workers must prove unfitness for work in order to be released from employment obligations, workers on maternity leave acquire rights independently of any such obligations. The dichotomy between maternity leave as social protection and pregnancy unfitness as worker incapacity allows the "sick-mate comparison" to operate only in cases of pregnancy. Gender specific rights attaching to maternity leave are diluted because they are welfare rights; pregnancy rights as equal rights emphasise the point of similarity with men and are thus conditioned by factors shaping the rights of male workers.

Pedersen also highlights the inherent instability of the chronological approach to pregnancy adopted in *Hertz* and *Brown*. The Court in *Pedersen* distinguished pathological complaints from routine pregnancy-related inconveniences. As only serious conditions result in incapacity for work, these conditions gain protection whereas routine complaints do not. This distinction, a logical result of basing protection on the concept of capacity for work, could both limit and expand pregnancy rights in the future. It will filter out minor complaints in the pregnancy period but it could also open up the possibility of allowing more serious claims in the post-maternity period. The Court used causation arguments to justify the non-protection of routine conditions by suggesting that adverse treatment resulted from a woman's choice not to work, thereby discounting the special nature of pregnancy as a female condition. The corollary of the Court's emphasis on incapacity in *Pedersen* however, is that the chronological approach to pregnancy risks in *Brown* becomes less tenable. Post-confinement complications of the *Hertz* type are also pathological complaints and should be specifically protected.

There is an implied acceptance in the judgments in *Gillespie*, *Hertz* and *Brown* of economic justifications for inferior treatment of pregnant women. In *Pedersen*, the European Court was faced with an explicit argument based on loss distribution in relation to the costs of pregnancy and firmly rejected this on the premise that discrimination cannot be justified on such grounds. The employers had argued that the discriminatory treatment was justified on the grounds that Danish legislation reflected a sharing of risks and costs of pregnancy between the pregnant worker, the employer and society as a whole. The Court stated that the aim of loss-sharing was not an objective factor within the meaning of previous case law:

> The discrimination cannot be justified by the aim of sharing the risks and economic costs connected with pregnancy . . . That goal cannot be regarded as an objective factor unrelated to any discrimination based on sex . . .

The interests of the employer, in contrast with the interests of the State, require more specific economic justification than broad loss-sharing goals.

COMBINING WORK AND FAMILY LIFE

The inflexibility of the maternity leave provisions introduces us to the wider subject of flexible working. "Flexibility", together with "prudence" and "joined-up government" is one of the mantras of the current government. The emphasis on labour market flexibility is one of those which it shares with its predecessors. And "flexibility" is deeply fashionable in the European Union, the current push towards maximising employment being associated with moves to dismantle "unnecessary" and "inflexible" labour market regulation.

The flexibility which is the rallying call of those on the economic right is concerned with the needs of employers and the perceived needs of the wider economy. By contrast, the flexibility with which we are concerned here is the flexibility which permits workers to combine work and family life. Whether this means a phased return to work after maternity leave (part-time, term-time, job-share or flexi-time work) even just the ability to take time off without retaliation in the event of family illness, a degree of flexibility is crucial unless motherhood (or, less commonly, fatherhood) is to be home-based.[38] Some employers have made significant steps towards accommodating the needs of working parents. Many more have not. As the law currently stands, the obligation on employers to permit a degree of flexibility rests, in large part, on the SDA. The Part-time Workers Regulations, considered below, deal with conditions for part-time rather than to part-time work.

Women who wish to work other than the employer's preferred hours must rely on the indirect discrimination provisions of the SDA. The concept of indirect discrimination turning on the statistical relationship between the complainant's needs and her sex, the indirect discrimination route to flexible working is closed to men. Men may, however, claim direct discrimination if refused access to flexible working in circumstances where women are or would be permitted such access.

The difficulties associated with indirect discrimination claims were discussed in Chapters 2 and 5, many of the cases considered therein dealing precisely with the issue of flexible working. Most of those cases concerned employees' needs for flexibility—*Clymo* v *Wandsworth*, for example, *Cast* v *Croydon College*, *Zurich Insurance Co* v *Gulson*, *Stevens* v *Katherine Lady Berkeley's School*, *Oddbins Limited* v *Robinson*, *Briggs* v *North Eastern Education and Library Board*, *Eley* v *Huntleigh Diagnostics Ltd.*[39] One—*London Underground* v *Edwards*—concerned the employee's inability to

---

[38] According to the EOR's analysis of the Labour Force Survey Spring 1998 (*Women and Men in Britain*, available from the EOC's website, see fn 1 above), p.9, 23.7% of women and 15.6% of men employees have some form of "flexible" working arrangement (this not including part-time work *per se*). 11.7% women and 8% men have flexible working hours, 3.3% of each annualised hours, 7.2 and 1.3% respectively term-time hours, 1.5% and 0.1% job shares, 0.1 and 0.3% a nine day fortnight, 1.3% and 2.4% a four and a half day week, and 0.8 and 0.6% zero hours contracts.

[39] Respectively, [1998] IRLR 319, [1998] ICR 500; [1998] IRLR 118; EAT/380/97, unreported; EAT/188/98, unreported; [1990] IRLR 18; EAT/1441/96, unreported. All are available on Lexis.

comply with the employer's need for "flexibility".[40] We considered the difficulties associated with establishing that the employer's refusal of request for flexible working amounted to a "requirement or condition" (*Clymo*), the problems associated with pools (*Edwards, Kidd v DRG*) and with establishing an inability to comply (*Clymo, Gulson, Stevens*) and, finally, the ease with which employers can justify indirect discrimination (*Kidd, Clymo, Robinson, Briggs, Eley*).[41]

The difficulties associated with changing working conditions after maternity leave, and, for women seeking to change jobs or to return to work after time out of the labour market, of finding flexible jobs of equivalent status to previously-held full-time jobs, means that the inability to perform an "inflexible"[42] full-time job forces some women into jobs in respect of which they are over-qualified, others into jobs which are under-rewarded relative to the demands made by them.[43]

The undervaluation of women's work is further considered in chapter 10. Here it is mentioned simply to underline the point that, if women (and men) are truly to be enabled to combine family and working life, rather than conforming to the existing pattern whereby women sacrifice the latter for the former, men the former for the latter, significant changes must be made in terms of increasing levels of (employee-orientated) flexibility in currently full-time jobs, as well as in improving the terms and conditions associated with part-time jobs (this is addressed in Chapter 10). It would be foolish to pretend that radical change in this direction is imminent. Discrimination against part-timers has been recognised as usually unlawful for at least 15 years[44] and women do successfully take action against employers who refuse access to part-time work, job-sharing or other flexible work after maternity leave.[45] But most discrimination against part-time workers takes place unchallenged, as does most employer intransigence in the face of attempts to engage in flexible work. Nevertheless, the forthcoming implementation in the UK of Council Directives 96/34/EC and 92/85/EEC (the directive on part-time work and the parental leave directive) may have

[40] [1985] ICR 405, [1985] IRLR 190.

[41] In *British Telecommunications plc v Roberts* [1996] IRLR 601 EAT rejected the argument that *Webb* protected a flexible return to work.

[42] Flexibility being assessed from the worker's perspective.

[43] Though see Diamond Ashiaghor, extracted above, on the ethno-specific characteristics of female part-time work.

[44] Since *Bilka-Kaufhaus GmbH v Weber von Hartz* (Case 170/84), [1986] ECR 1607, arguably since *Jenkins v Kingsgate (Clothing Production) Ltd* (Case 96/80) [1981] ECR 911, [1981] 1 WLR 972. K. O'Donovan and E. Szyszczak note, in a commentary to *Kidd v DRG* [1985] IRLR 190 [1985] ICR 405 ((1985) 14 *Industrial Law Journal* 252, 252) that "[d]espite the close correlation between female participation and part-time work, industrial tribunals and EAT have been reluctant to conclude that the concept of sex discrimination may be generally applied to the differential treatment of full-time and part-time workers."

[45] 84 *Equal Opportunities Review*, p.3, for example, reports a £22 500 settlement between Royal & Sun Alliance and a woman manager refused permission to job-share on the basis that such an arrangement was not possible in her managerial position, and a £45 000 settlement between the Solicitors Indemnity Fund and a solicitor refused permission to work on a part-time or job share basis in order that she could care for three under-fives. See also the decisions in *Home Office v Holmes* [1984] ICR 678 [1984] IRLR 229 (*cf* more recently, *British Telecommunications v Roberts*, fn 41 above). See also *Greater Glasgow Health Board v Carey* [1987] IRLR 484.

some impact in this area, if only because the implementing Regulations will grant concrete rights in relation to working time and discrimination on the basis thereof rather than, as is currently the case, vague rights to freedom from sex discrimination, those rights having to be directed, in relation to flexible work, through the prism of indirect sex discrimination.

The directive on part-time work marked the culmination of almost twenty years efforts to regulate "atypical" work at the European level. It was the first directive to be adopted under the Social Chapter, the UK having vetoed attempts to pass the directive under the Article 137 of the Treaty Establishing the European Community. The social partners concluded an agreement on part-time work in accordance with the procedure established by the Social Chapter, the agreement being adopted as Directive 96/34/EC.

The part-time workers directive has been implemented in UK law by the Part-time Workers (Prevention of Less Favourable Treatment) Regulations 2000 (SI 2000 No 1551) which came into force on 1st July of that year.[46] They provide Reg 5) that "A part-time worker has the right not to be treated less favourably by his employer than the employer treats a comparable full-time worker" where the less favourable treatment is "on the ground that the worker is a part-time worker" and "is not justified on objective grounds". A "comparable worker" is (Reg 2(4)) one who is "engaged in the same or in broadly similar work [to that done by the part-time worker] having regard, where relevant, to whether they have a similar level of qualification, skills and experience". The comparator must be employed by the same employer as the claimant and must work at the same establishment unless there is no comparator at that establishment. Finally, the comparator must be employed under the same type of contract as the claimant, Reg 1 distinguishing between contracts applicable to indefinitely retained employees, indefinitely retained workers, fixed term employees, fixed term workers, apprentices and "any other description of worker that it is reasonable for the employer to treat differently from other workers on the ground that workers of that description have a different type of contract".

Claims can be brought under the Regulations without such a narrowly defined comparator only where claimants have transferred within their employment from full-time to part-time work or have returned after an absence of less than one year "to the same job or to a job on the same level", whether on the same or a different type of contract. In either of these cases, the claimants may choose instead (Regs 3 and 4) to compare their treatment with that of a notional full-time worker employed on the terms and conditions s/he enjoyed prior to the transfer or the period of absence or, in the latter case, to the treatment of a notional full-time worker employed on the terms and conditions which would have applied to the worker had s/he continued to be employed full-time during her period of absence.

The Regulations provide that the *pro-rata* principle shall be applied unless inappropriate, and also that part-timers need not be paid over-time rates until they have

---

[46] The Regulations are discussed in more detail by the author at (2000) 29 *ILJ* (forthcoming)

worked the normal full-time hours.[47] They are accompanied by "guidance notes" and a "programme of information" which advise on compliance and best practice.

The government's regulatory impact assessment estimated that the Part-time Workers Regulations would "directly" benefit only 7% of the six million part-time workers in the UK, most of the rest being excluded from protection by the absence of a comparator. This aspect of the Regulations has been severely criticised.[48] The protection afforded by the Regulations is further reduced by their failure to prohibit dismissals in connection with a refusal to transfer between part-time and full-time work. Compensation in respect of injury to feelings is generally precluded by the Regulations which, further, apply the EqPA's two-year limit to compensation in respect of discriminatory access to or treatment by pension scheme (this latter is discussed in Chapter 10).

The 2000 Regulations will provide additional protections to some part-time workers (including male part-timers who, unless treated less favourably than female workers, could not previously challenge discrimination against them as part-time workers). But the failure of the Regulations to regulate the most significant source of the disadvantage experienced by part-time workers – their very denial of access to the same jobs in the same workplaces as full-time workers – their very denial of access to the same jobs in the same workplaces as full-time workers – means that, for the most part, they will continue to have to rely on the SDA, which Act has proved its inadequacies in this respect over the past twenty-five years.

The Part-time Workers Regulations are not the only legislative changes in recent years which have implications for those attempting to combine work and family life. The Parental Leave and Maternity etc. Regulations 1999 (SI 1999 No 3312) which were passed in order to implement the parental leave directive in the UK in the wake of its acceptance of the "Social Protocol" of the Maastricht Treaty (now incorporated within the Treaty Establishing the European Community), came into force in December 1999.[49] Prior to their implementation, workers in the UK had no entitlement to parental or family leave. By contrast, workers in every other EU Member State with the exceptions only of Belgium, Ireland and Luxembourg were entitled to parental leave even prior to the adoption of the parental leave directive (the details which follow were correct in 1996).[50] The period of leave varied between three years in Spain (unpaid), France and Germany (paid at around £380 and £267 monthly respectively); and three months (unpaid) in Greece. Six months leave was available in both Italy and Netherlands (the former at 30% of salary and the latter unpaid) and two years in Austria and Portugal (the former paid at between £344 and £510 monthly, the latter unpaid). Sweden afforded its workers 18 months leave (12 months of which were

---

[47] This approach was accepted by the ECJ in *Stadt Lengerich* v *Angelika Helmig*, (joined cases C–399/92, C–409/92, C–425/92, C–34/93, C–50/93 and C–78/93) [1994] ECR I–5727, but is problematic in failing to mark the inconvenience associated with working in excess of a worker's own normal hours.

[48] See fn 46, above.

[49] The Regulations should be read with the ERA 1999, Sch 4 part 1.

[50] The latter only for two years.

paid at 75%,[51] three months at a flat rate of around £165 monthly); Denmark between 23 and 62 weeks with some remuneration and Finland six months on two-thirds of salary plus child-care leave until the child's third birthday at between £282 and £507 monthly. In addition, all other Member States with the exception of Denmark, Ireland and Italy afforded workers a period of family leave, generally paid and varying in length between one and four days in France to 60 days per year in Sweden.

The 1999 Regulations provide an entitlement to three months' (unpaid) parental leave to be taken by everyone having responsibility for a child during the first five years' of the child's life.[52] This is in addition to maternity leave and the new right accorded under the (s.57A) ERA to: a reasonable amount of time off . . . in order to take action which is necessary—

(a) to provide assistance on an occasion when a dependant falls ill, gives birth or is injured or assaulted,

(b) to make arrangements for the provision of care for a dependant who is ill or injured,

(c) in consequence of the death of a dependant,

(d) because of the unexpected disruption or termination of arrangements for the care of a dependant, or

(e) to deal with an incident which involves a child of the employee and which occurs unexpectedly in a period during which an educational establishment which the child attends is responsible for him.

S.57A(2) provides that the employee must inform the employer as to the reason for absence "as soon as reasonably practicable", and, save where no notice could practically be given, of the likely period of absence.

S.57A is not subject to any qualifying period of employment. The new parental leave rights, by contrast, apply only in respect of employees with at least one year's qualifying service, and do not apply in respect of children born before 15th December 1999.[53] The Regulations provide for the continuation of specified contractual terms (entitlement to notice, redundancy pay and disciplinary procedures; obligations in respect of notice, confidentiality and loyalty).

In respect of parental leave taken in blocks of less than 4 weeks, and of a period of additional maternity leave of similar length,[54] employees are entitled to return to their job, in other cases to that job "or, if it is not reasonable practicable for the employer to permit her to return to that job, to another job which is both suitable for her and appropriate for her to do in the circumstances".[55] The terms and conditions to which

---

[51] Reduced from 90% in 1994 and 80% in 1995—figures from the *Equal Opportunities Review*, fn 48 above.

[52] In respect of children in receipt of Disability Living Allowance, 18 years and five years after adoption or until 18 if sooner or where employer has postponed leave.

[53] Unless adopted after that point.

[54] Additional maternity leave being in addition to the now-basic eighteen weeks.

[55] The directive provides for alternative job where return to original is not "possible" rather than "reasonably practicable". There is no entitlement to return where redundancy provisions apply. In the case of a woman taking parental leave of less than four weeks directly after additional maternity leave, original job unless not reasonably practicable applies both to end date of maternity leave and of parental leave

employees return must be no less favourable than had no leave been taken, and continuous employment unbroken by (but not accumulated) during the leave period. Protection against detriment is accorded to those exercising their rights under the Regulations and a dismissal in connection with the exercise of such rights is automatically unfair for the purposes of the ERA.

The primary method by which the regulations are intended to be implemented is through the mechanism of a "workforce agreement", the statutory detail below being by way of a default arrangement. Workforce agreements can be reached between the employer and recognised unions or, where no such union exists, between the employer and elected representatives of the workforce.

In the absence of such an agreement, the Regulations establish detailed conditions to which the right to parental leave is subject. No more than four weeks' leave may be taken in any year in respect of a single child Employees who wish to avail of their right to take parental leave must provide evidence of the child's birth or adoption and of parental responsibility for the child, together with notice of their intention to take leave. The notice must be given at least 21 days in advance except where the timing of leave turns on the date of birth or adoption, and must specify the start and end date of the leave requested.[56] Employers may postpone the taking of any such leave, except where it is connected with birth or adoption, where s/he "considers that the operation of his [sic] business would be unduly disrupted if the employee took leave during the period identified in his [sic] notice", and where the employer agrees to permit the employee the same period of leave within six months of the requested period. The employer must give the employee written notice of postponement with the reasons for it and the alternative period of leave permitted within seven days of the employee's original request.

The Parental and Maternity Leave, etc. Regulations have been criticised for permitting employers to postpone parental leave, as well as for their adoption of a five-year rather than eight-year cut-off point; their application only to "employees"[57] and in respect of children born after the 19th December 1999;[58] the lack of a clear right to return to the same job for those taking additional maternity leave and lengthy blocks of parental leave and the fact that the parental leave is to be unpaid;[59] and the minimum one-week period of leave permitted under the default arrangements. In addition, the TUC argued that employers should be permitted to postpone leave only for objectively justified reasons and after consultation with workers or their representatives.

---

[56] In these cases specification of EWC and duration of leave or expected week of placement and period of leave. In the latter case 21 days notice or as soon as practicable.

[57] The directive refers to those in "an employment relationship" which is probably wider.

[58] The TUC's challenge to this aspect of the Regulations has resulted in a reference by the High Court to the ECJ (June 2000), the TUC having lodged an appeal against the Court's refusal to suspend the disputed provision pending the outcome of that reference. The TUC has also challenged the restriction to "employees" of the Part-Time Workers Regulations.

[59] See for example the TUC's and EOC's submissions to the Social Security Select Committee, appended to the Ninth Report of the Committee, 1998–1999 Session, *Social Security Implications of Parental Leave* HC 543 ISBN 0 10 556431 1, available at http://www.official-documents.co.uk/.

In those EU Member States in which parental leave is already available (see above), its popularity, according to the *Equal Opportunities Review* (above, pp.23–24):

is more often than not dependent upon whether leave is paid or not. The number of parents taking parental leave in countries where no benefit is available, such as Greece, Portugal, Spain and the Netherlands, is believed to be correspondingly low, even though there are no precise figures available . . . In Germany, where flat-rate payments are available, the vast majority of mothers take parental leave, although men account for only 1% of all leave-takers . . . In Denmark, where an additional entitlement to leave was introduced in 1992, take-up . . . was initially low, due mainly to the fall in income that this would cause . . .

Take-up rates of parental leave are highest in countries paying earnings-related benefit, such as Finland, Norway and Sweden. In Finland, virtually all mothers take parental leave, although fathers account for only 2% of takers . . . Sweden is unusual in that, in addition to nearly all mothers taking leave, a high percentage of fathers—around 50%—also take up their option to parental leave. This may be due to the fact that leave arrangements are very flexible, with parents being able to take short or long periods of full- or part-time leave. In addition, the law stipulates that at least one month of earnings-related leave must be taken by either parent.

The government's own figures projected that only 2% men and 35% women with children will take advantage of the right to parental leave over the five year period, the low take-up rate being in large part due to the lack of payment available.[60] Having lost the argument for paid leave, the TUC lobbied for parental leave to be available "in principle, flexibly, in months, weeks or shorter periods or on a reduced hours basis, subject to objective justification by employers[61] in small chunks" in order to encourage uptake, questioning the government's categorisation of parental leave as a major contribution to its "family friendly" employment strategy on its own projected take-up rates. The availability of such flexible leave is seen as particularly important in encouraging its uptake by men.

TUC, Submissions to the House of Commons Social Security Committee, June 1999

In order to promote gender equality . . . there are wider arguments for not instituting a parental leave system where it is only women who take up unpaid leave. In particular, women taking unpaid parental leave will become almost entirely economically dependent on men which research shows may result in less family income being spent on children. In the long term, periods of unpaid leave for women are likely to result in lesser pension and other social security entitlements and more disparity in lifetime earnings with men. This can lead to poverty for women in old age, particularly following relationship breakdown. In addition, as acknowledged by the objectives behind the Parental Leave Directive, take-up by men of parental leave should encourage greater gender equality, by facilitating more

[60] TUCs submissions to the Committee, *ibid*, and available also on the TUC's website at *http://www.tuc.org.uk*. The possibility of paid parental leave is now under review by the government, and some benefits are available to low-income workers during parental leave.

[61] TUC's response to the DTI consultation on parental leave, available on the TUC's website, *ibid*.

sharing of childcare and other family responsibilities between women and men. The most recent British Social Attitudes Survey shows that in 80% of households, women still do most of the domestic tasks apart from small repairs around the home.

It remains to be seen whether the implementation of the parental leave directive in the UK serves to further or to hinder women's progress towards equality at work.

DISCRIMINATION ON GROUNDS OF GENDER-REASSIGNMENT

The SDA prohibits discrimination between men and women and, since its amendment in May 1999, discrimination on the basis of "gender-reassignment".[62] This amendment was made as a result of the ECJ's decision in *P* v *S & Cornwall* (Case C–13/94) [1996] ECR I–2143, [1996] All ER (EC) 397, [1996] IRLR 347, that discrimination on the grounds of gender reassignment amounted to sex discrimination contrary to the equal treatment directive. The case is considered further below.

The effect of the decision in *P* v *S* was that those employed by the state, broadly defined, were at once entitled to protection from discrimination on grounds of gender reassignment. And in *Chessington World of Adventures Ltd* v *Reed* [1998] ICR 97, [1997] IRLR 556, EAT found itself able to interpret the SDA so as to provide the same protection to private sector employees. The Sex Discrimination (Gender Reassignment) Regulations 1999[63] incorporate this approach expressly into the SDA by inserting into that Act the new s.2A which was reproduced at the start of this chapter. The section, which prohibits only direct discrimination, applies to discrimination in employment and training (further discussed in Chapter 4), and to discrimination in relation to barristers and (in Scotland) Advocates. It remains the case, under English law, that persons who have undergone gender reassignment are regarded, for the purposes of marriage, imprisonment, etc., as retaining the biological sex of their birth. However, in April 1999 the Home Secretary announced the creation of a working group on transsexuals whose terms of reference are' [t]o consider, with particular reference to birth certificates, the need for appropriate legal measures to address the problems experienced by transsexuals . . .".[64]

S.2A(2) SDA provides that subsection (1) applies in relation to absence related to gender-reassignment but subsection (3) states that discrimination will be made out, in relation to absence, only if "he is treated less favourably than he would be if (a) the absence was due to sickness or injury" or (b) "to some other cause and, having regard to the circumstances of the case, it is reasonable for him to be treated no less favourably". This is clearly intended to avoid the application of an approach analo-

---

[62] Sex Discrimination (Gender Reassignment) Regulations: an EOR Guide 85 *Equal Opportunities Review* p.36, estimates that around 5000 people in the UK are affected by gender-reassignment.
[63] SI 1999 No 1102.
[64] Reported in the *Equal Opportunities Review*, fn 62 above, p.41.

gous to that which has finally prevailed in relation to pregnancy-related absence (see *Webb (No. 2)* above) in the context of gender reassignment. S.2(2) of the Regulations amends s.5(3) SDA to the effect that:

> A comparison of the cases of persons of different sex . . . under section 1(1) or 3(1) or a comparison of persons required for the purposes of s.2A must be such that the relevant circumstances in the one case are the same, or not materially different, in the other.

Protection against discrimination on grounds of gender-reassignment starts at the point when a person indicates an intention to undergo gender reassignment, the original proposal to make protection contingent on the person formally having sought medical intervention being dropped after the consultation stage. S.2(3) provides that pay-related discrimination against transsexuals shall be dealt with under the SDA rather than the EqPA and s.2(4) incorporates a new s.7A SDA which provides that discrimination is not unlawful under s.6(1) or (2) of the SDA if:

(a) in relation to the employment in question—
    (i) being a man is a genuine occupational qualification for the job, or
    (ii) being a woman is a genuine occupational qualification for the job, and
(b) the employer can show that the treatment is reasonable in view of the circumstances described in the relevant paragraph of section 7(2) and any other relevant circumstances.

Unlike the existing GOQs, those applying in relation to gender reassignment cover dismissal as well as failure to recruit (this being necessary to cover gender reassignments which take place after recruitment). The Regulations' failure to specify the point at which gender is regarded as having changed may, as the EOR commentary pointed out, create difficulties in the application of these GOQs.[65] In addition to the application of the existing GOQs to persons undergoing gender-reassignment, s.7B provides "supplementary [GOQs] relating to gender reassignment" where:

(2) (a) the job involves the holder of the job being liable to be called upon to perform intimate physical searches pursuant to statutory powers;
    (b) the job is likely to involve the holder of the job doing his work, or living, in a private home and needs to be held otherwise than by a person who is undergoing or has undergone gender reassignment, because objection might reasonable be taken to allowing such a person—
        (i) the degree of physical or social contact with a person living in the home, or
        (ii) the knowledge of intimate details of such a person's life, which is likely, because of the nature or circumstances of the job or of the home, to be allowed to, or available to, the holder of the job;
    (c) the nature or location of the establishment makes it impracticable for the holder of the job to live elsewhere than in premises provided by the employer, and—

---

[65] *Ibid*, p.39.

      (i) the only such premises which are available for persons holding that kind of job are such that reasonable objection could be taken, for the purpose of preserving decency or privacy, to the holder of the job sharing accommodation and facilities with either sex whilst undergoing gender reassignment, and

      (ii) it is not reasonable to expect the employer either to equip those premises with suitable accommodation or to make alternative arrangements; or

  (d) the holder of the job provides vulnerable individuals with personal services promoting their welfare, or similar personal services, and in the reasonable view of the employer those services cannot be effectively provided by a person whilst that person is undergoing gender reassignment.[66]

The GOQs established by paras (c) and (d) do not apply to those whose gender-reassignment is complete (though in many cases the point of completion is unclear; further surgical refinements often being undertaken over a long period. S.7B, unlike ss.7 and 7A, applies whether or not there are other employees capable of carrying out the duties in question.

In order to determine whether the new s.2A SDA brings the UK into compliance with EU law it is necessary to consider the decision of the ECJ in *P* v *S*. Prior to the decision of the Court, Advocate-General Tesauro, while expressly accepting that the 1976 directive was not intended to prohibit discrimination on the basis of transexualism (the condition barely having been recognised at the time), urged that the ECJ interpret the directive "as the expression of a more general principle, on the basis of which sex should be irrelevant to the treatment everyone receives . . . [to include] all situations in which sex appears as a discriminatory factor".[67] The ECJ responded to the Advocate-General's plea, ruling that:

> The principle of equal treatment "for men and women" to which the Directive refers in its title, preamble and provisions means, as Articles 2(1) and 3(1) in particular indicate, that there should be "no discrimination whatsoever on grounds of sex" . . . the Directive is simply the expression, in the relevant field, of the principle of equality, which is one of the fundamental principles of Community law. Moreover, as the Court has repeatedly held, the right not to be discriminated against on grounds of sex is one of the fundamental human rights whose observance the Court has a duty to ensure . . .
>
> Accordingly, the scope of the Directive cannot be confined simply to discrimination based on the fact that a person is one or other sex. In view of its purpose and the nature of the rights which it seeks to safeguard, the scope of the Directive is also such as to apply to discrimination arising, as in this case, from the gender reassignment of the person concerned.
>
> Such discrimination is based, essentially, if not exclusively, on the sex of the person concerned. Where a person is dismissed on the ground that he or she intends to undergo, or has undergone, gender reassignment, he or she is treated unfavourably by comparison with

---

[66] Reg 5 amends s.19 of the SDA to permit discrimination on the basis of gender reassignment in employment for the purposes of organised religion and Reg 7 amends the EOC's responsibilities to include those who "intend to undergo, are undergoing or have undergone gender reassignment".

[67] Calling in support the fact that the European Parliament expressed itself to the same effect in a Resolution on discrimination against transsexuals of 9 October 1989.

persons of the sex to which he or she was deemed to belong before undergoing gender reassignment.

To tolerate such discrimination would be tantamount, as regards such a person, to a failure to respect the dignity and freedom to which he or she is entitled, and which the Court has a duty to safeguard.

Whether or not s.2A is sufficient to implement *P* v *S* in domestic law will depend on the acceptability of (a) exclusion of the *Dekker/Webb* approach to time-off in connection with gender-reassignment, (b) the applicable GOQs and (c) the non-application of the concept of indirect discrimination in this context. A commentary in the *Equal Opportunities Review* stated, of (a), that:

> Once it is accepted that discrimination based on a person's change of sex is equivalent to discrimination based on a person's belonging to a particular sex, treatment by the employer which would not take place but for the fact that the person was undergoing a gender reassignment must be regarded as treatment on grounds of sex, and thus unlawful.[58]

Turning to (b), the supplementary GOQs provided in the Regulations are considerably narrower than those originally suggested (the government having originally countenanced, *inter alia*, an exclusion from the principle of non-discrimination in respect of all work with children). The remaining difficulty is s.7B(2)(a) which will operate as an effective bar to transsexuals in the police force, a situation regarded as unacceptable by an employment tribunal in the (pre-Regulations) *A* v *Chief Constable of the West Yorkshire Police*,[69] a challenge to a refusal to recruit a male-to-female transsexual into the police on the grounds that she would have to conduct intimate searches. The tribunal took the view that, the police being under no obligation to disclose the applicant's status to those undergoing body searches, this should not be allowed to operate as a bar to such employment. The alternative approach:

> would preclude transsexuals from ever becoming police constables and might have a similar effect in those other occupations and in the training leading thereto where close personal interraction is a prerequisite of the job . . . the risks to the respondent in permitting the applicant as a transsexual to carry out the full range of duties including the searching of women are so small that to give effect to them by denying the applicant access to the office of constable would be wholly disproportionate to the denial of the applicant's fundamental right to equal treatment.

Finally, with regard to (c), the equal treatment directive, on which the decision in *P* v *S* was based, expressly prohibits indirect as well as direct discrimination (this was

---

[68] Transsexual legislation proposed, 78 *Equal Opportunities Review* 30, p.30, considering the consultation document. *Cf Equal Opportunities Review*, fn 62 above, p.37: "the government has pragmatically—and arguably sensibly—adopted special rules in the case of absence due to a transsexual undergoing gender reassignment", though this is contradicted on the next page, the special rules being categorised as a "dilution of the principle of nondiscrimination".

[69] 18th March 1999, case 1802020/98, discussed in *Equal Opportunities Review*, fn 62 above, p.39.

recognised also by the Government in its Consultation Paper, *Legislation Regarding Discrimination on Grounds of Transsexualism in Employment*, but the recognition not translated into any proposed protection), and the decision of the ECJ in *P* v *S* defines gender-reassignment as "sex" for the purposes of the directive. It would appear, accordingly, that the express provisions of the SDA, as amended, may fall short of what is required to secure compliance. Scope remains, however, for purposive interpretation of the Act to achieve compliance with the demands of the directive.

The decision in *Chessington*, in which EAT interpreted the SDA's "sex" to cover gender-reassignment, was mentioned above. More recently, the *Independent* (4th May 2000) reported a settlement reached in a legal challenge, backed by the EOC, to the banning from a pub of a customer who had undergone gender-reassignment. Given the amendment of the SDA only inasmuch as it relates to employment, the challenge must have been brought under s.20 of the Act interpreted in the light of *P* v *S* and *Chessington*. No settlement is authoritative, of course. But it is at least arguable that the SDA ought to be interpreted so as to regulate indirect as well as direct discrimination on grounds of gender reassignment. The express provisions concerning leave and GOQs may not be capable of interpretation and so may have to be applied, in advance of litigation before the ECJ, save in the case of those employed by the state.

Whatever the interpretations adopted of the SDA by the domestic courts in relation to the issues, a significant gap remains in the protection of workers who have undergone gender reassignment. The issue was highlighted by EAT's decision in *Bavin* v *The NHS Trust Pensions Agency*. The claim was brought by a woman living with a man who had undergone gender reassignment, and consisted of a challenge to the NHS pension rules which restricted survivors' pension to "widows" and "widowers". Ms Bavin was legally disabled from marrying her partner who remained, in the eyes of the law, a woman. Her claim was rejected by EAT.

Bavin v The NHS Trust Pensions Agency & Secretary of State for Health [1999] ICR 1192.

Morison J (for EAT):

the Scheme discriminates between members who are married and members who are not. The words "widow" and "widower" mean and can only mean the surviving spouse. Thus, unmarried partners can never obtain derived benefits, whatever the reason for the fact that they are not married. richard, as with other unmarried partners of members, is not entitled to derived benefits because he is unmarried and not because he is a transsexual. It is being unmarried which disqualifies him. He is not being discriminated against because he is a transsexual but because he is unmarried (whether because he is a transsexual or because he is gay or because he objects to marriage or because he or Kathleen is already married). If it is not unlawful to deprive transsexuals of the right to get married, it seems to us an odd result if he has a valid claim against the Scheme based on his inability to get married . . .

The casd of *P* v *S* does not carry the argument . . . In that case, P was treated less favourably than he would have been had he not indicated a desire to undergo gender reassignment. In other words, he was treated worse than he would have been had he not given that indication. Thus he was treated less favourably than an "ordinary" male or a transsexual who did not intend, or announce an intention, to undergo the surgery. The case did not establish that transsexuals were entitled to equal rights with those of the sex to which they were seeking re-assignment.

DISCRIMINATION ON GROUNDS OF SEXUAL ORIENTATION

"Equality for Lesbians and Gay Men in the Workplace" (1997) 74 *Equal Opportunities Review* **20, 20–1**

In 1992, the Labour Research Department (LRD) carried out a questionnaire survey ["Out at work: lesbian and gay workers' rights" LRD 1992] distributed by several unions to their branch members (EOR 45). Of the 362 respondents, 61% were lesbians, gay men or bisexual. A key finding was that nearly a quarter of respondents had personally experienced, or knew cases of, harassment or victimisation of lesbian and gay workers. Although 90% said that there was an equal opportunities policy at their workplace, only 62% of this group said that the policy covered sexuality. The proportion who were "out" at work about their sexuality was higher among union post-holders (80%), than among lesbian, gay or bisexual respondents as a whole (60%).

A survey of nearly 2,000 lesbians, gay men and bisexuals at work—the largest survey of its type to be carried out in Britain—was conducted by Stonewall in 1993 (EOR 52). The questionnaire was distributed via mailing lists of gay businesses, publications, and social groups. The report [A. Palmer "Less Equal than Others. A Survey of Lesbians and Gay Men at Work", (London: Stonewall, 1993)] found that one in six respondents (15%) had at least one experience of discrimination; a further 21% suspected that they had, and 8% had been dismissed because of their sexuality. But the findings indicated that "discrimination by employers is only part of the problem. Harassment is a much bigger problem, and discrimination avoidance, including the closet, is the biggest problem of all." In the area of recruitment, 5% said they knew that they had been discriminated against and 17% suspected that they had been. A similar proportion (5%) said they knew they had been denied promotion because of discrimination and 19% suspected they had been.

Almost half the respondents (48%) considered that they had been harassed because of their sexuality. A high proportion concealed their sexual orientation at work to avoid discrimination or harassment. Only 11% said they had never concealed their sexuality at work, compared with over half (56%) who had concealed it in some jobs, and 33% in all jobs.

As in the LRD survey, the majority (79%) said that their employer had an equal opportunities policy. But just over a quarter of private sector employees said that the policy covered sexual orientation, compared with nearly two-thirds of public sector employees, and around nine out of 10 voluntary sector employees.

The most recent study, published by Social and Community Research in 1995 [D. Snape, K. Thompson and M. Chitwynd, "Discrimination against gay men and lesbians", SCPR 1995], found that discrimination was "widespread" against gay men and lesbians (EOR 62). The findings are based on the first representative sample of lesbians and gay men, drawn randomly from the National Survey of Sexual Attitudes and Lifestyles. Of the respondents, 116 defined themselves as homosexual, or as having been homosexual in the past, and 619 people as heterosexual. In the sphere of employment, 21% of those who defined themselves as homosexual had been harassed at work; 8% had been refused promotion because of their sexuality, 6% had tried to get a job and failed, and 4% had been dismissed.

To avoid discrimination many respondents said that they concealed their sexuality. Over half said that none of their work colleagues knew about their sexuality, and one one-fifth said that all their colleagues knew. The report suggests that those who concealed their sexuality were less likely to experience some form of discrimination, but pointed out that "the strain and indignity of keeping such an integral part of their lives a secret is one of the most insidious forms of discrimination that homosexual people experience."

The ECJ's ruling, in *P* v *S*, that "the scope of the Directive cannot be confined simply to discrimination based on the fact that a person is one or other sex" suggests that the provisions of the equal treatment directive might extend also to prohibit discrimination on grounds of sexual orientation. As early as 1983, David Pannick suggested that the SDA ought to be interpreted to this effect:

D. Pannick, "Homosexuals, Transsexuals and the Law" (1983) *Public Law*, 279, 281–284

Adverse treatment of an individual by reason of his or her sexual preferences may constitute sex discrimination notwithstanding that sex discrimination can only be established by comparing the treatment of the complainant with the treatment of a person of the opposite sex. . . .

The simplest case is where the employer refuses to employ male homosexuals but is willing to employ lesbians. A male homosexual who is refused employment by reason of his sexual preferences can establish direct discrimination contrary to the 1975 Act: he has been less favourably treated by reason of his sex than a woman whose "relevant circumstances . . . are the same, or not materially different," the comparison required by section 5(3). The Employment Appeal Tribunal has emphasised that "in deciding whether the circumstances of the two cases are the same, or not materially different, one must put out of the picture any circumstances which necessarily follow from the fact that one is comparing the case of a man and of a woman." . . .

A claim of direct sex discrimination can also be formulated if the defendant adversely treats homosexuals of each sex because of their sexual preferences. The less favourable treatment of the complainant on the ground of his or her sex compared with a person of the other sex might, again, be established. Suppose the employer dismisses a male homosexual from employment because he has a rule that he will employ neither men or women who have sexual preferences for persons of their own sex. The complainant can argue that this is sex discrimination because if two employees—one male, and one female—are romantically or sexually attached to the same actual or hypothetical male non-employee, the employer treats the male employee less favourably on the ground of his sex than he treats the female employee. . . . The California Supreme Court, in deciding a case under the state Fair Employment Practices Act (which prohibits discrimination on the ground of "sex") rejected a similar analysis. While recognising that "as a semantic argument, the contention may have some appeal," the court concluded that the legislation did not contemplate discrimination against homosexuals [*Gay Law Students Association* v *Pacific Telephone & Telegraph Co* 19 FEP Cases 1419 (1979)]. In *DeSantis* v. *Pacific Telephone and Telegraph Co. Inc.* [608 F2d 327 (1979)], the U.S. Court of Appeals considered the argument that discrimination against homosexuals breached Title VII because "if a male employee prefers males as sexual partners, he will be treated differently from a female who prefers male partners . . . [T]he employer thus uses different employment criteria for men and women." The court firmly rejected the "appellants' efforts to 'bootstrap' Title VII protection for homosexuals . . . [W]e note that whether dealing with men or women the employer is using the same criterion: it will not hire or promote a person who prefers sexual partners of the same sex. Thus this policy does not involve different decisional criteria for the sexes."

The judgment of the U.S. Court of Appeals in *DeSantis* emphasises that one's conclusion on the validity of this claim of sex discrimination depends on the classification of the problem and the precise comparison one adopts with regard to the treatment of a man and a woman. Should one conclude that if a male employee is adversely treated for his sexual relationship with a third party X (a male) when a female employee is not so treated for her sexual relationship with the same X, such a disparity in treatment is by reason of the sex of the employee? Or should one conclude that the comparison is false as one of the employees is a homosexual and the other is not. This difficult issue will be determined by an english court or tribunal pursuant to section 5(3) of the 1975 Act. In making the comparison between the treatment of the male employee and the female employee, are we dealing with cases which are "such that the relevant circumstances in the one case are the same, or not materially different, in the other"? The problem is that the 1975 Act provides no criteria of "relevance." The Employment Appeal Tribunal held in *Grieg* v. *Community Industry* [[1979] ICR 356] that section 5(3) is "principally although not exclusively talking about . . . the personal qualifications of the person involved as compared with some other person." It is arguable that, on this criterion, the private sexual preferences of the complainant are not "relevant circumstances" unless the employer can establish that the sexual preferences of his staff are material to their ability to perform the job. This argument is strengthened by the fact that section 5(3) applies an objective test and does not provide for the comparison to be made by reference to those circumstances that the employer deems relevant.

Pannick's argument was made pre-*James* v *Eastleigh*, at a point where it was thought that sex had to be "the activating cause", rather than simply "a *causa sine qua non*" of the less favourable treatment. Nevertheless:

The homosexual who suffers a detriment by reason of his sexual orientation can, by comparing his treatment with the more favourable treatment of the person of the sex opposite to his, show that he has been less favourably treated on the ground of his sex. . . . In the case of sexual preferences, the sex of the complainant (and the sexual stereotypes which the employer associates with that sex) is very much in the foreground as the activating cause of the less favourable treatment of which complaint is made. The employer who has said that a sexual relationship with Mr. X is conduct permissible in a female employee but conduct impermissible in a male employee has clearly differentiated in treatment of male and female employees. The differentiation is on the ground of sex: women may have relationships with Mr. X and retain their jobs; if men have such relationships they will be sacked. The employer may well believe that he has good reason for differentiating between men and women in this respect. But, subject to the express exceptions contained in the 1975 Act, it is no defence for the employer to say that "what was done was done with good motives or was done, even objectively, in the best interests of the person concerned or in the best interests of the business with which the case is concerned." That the employer has an ulterior motive for differentiating in his treatment of men and women cannot abrogate the conclusion that such differentiation is on the ground of sex.

Pannick's approach did not, initially, find favour with the courts. *R v Ministry of Defence, ex parte Smith and Ors* [1996] QB 517, [1996] 1 All ER 257, [1996] 2 WLR 305, [1996] IRLR 100 concerned a discrimination claim brought by a number of ex-servicemen and women who were dismissed on grounds of their homosexuality. The applicants claimed, *inter alia*, that the policy excluding homosexuals from the armed forces breached the equal treatment directive, the provisions of which were directly enforceable by them in respect of their employment by the State. Their claims failed, both High Court and Court of Appeal being so confident of the non-application of the directive to discrimination on the grounds of sexuality as to refuse to refer the case to the ECJ (both decisions were reached prior to *P v S*). According to Simon Brown LJ (in the High Court), the directive:

> says everything about gender discrimination, but to my mind nothing about orientation discrimination . . . I have no doubt that the ordinary and natural meaning of "sex" in this context is gender. Of course the word is apt to encompass human characteristics as well as people's anatomical qualities . . . Orientation . . . is another thing.

Lord Bingham MR, in the Court of Appeal, found "nothing whatever in the EEC Treaty or in the equal treatment directive which suggests that the draftsmen of those instruments were addressing their minds in any way whatever to problems of discrimination on grounds of sexual orientation", a conclusion agreed with by Thorpe LJ on the grounds that:

> any common-sense construction of the Directive in the year of its issue leads in my judgment to the inevitable conclusion that it was solely directed to gender discrimination and not to discrimination against sexual orientation . . . [Noting, as the Master of the Rolls had done, more recent concern on the part of the Commission with discrimination on the grounds of sexual orientation, Thorpe LJ continued] if the European Union is to proscribe discrimination on the grounds of sexual orientation that must be achieved by a specific Directive and not by an extended construction of the 1976 Directive.

In *R v Secretary of State for Defence, ex parte Perkins*, Lightman J relied on the decision in *P v S* in deciding to refer to the ECJ the question whether discrimination on grounds of sexual orientation breached the equal treatment directive. The case, like *ex parte Smith*, concerned the discharge of a homosexual serviceman.

R v Secretary of State for Defence, ex parte Perkins [1997] IRLR 297

Lightman J:

. . . the reasoning and the grounds of the decision [in *P v S*] . . . were. . . that a transsexual has a right to his or her own sexual identity, ie the choice of his or her own sex; that . . . he or she has a right to live, both before (and without) and after any such gender reassignment, as a member of the opposite sex, and this includes a right to a sexual life as such . . .

[The] case shows that protection will be afforded against discrimination in case of persons described as having a personality characterised "with a dual personality, one physical, the other psychological, together with such profound conviction of belonging to the other sex that the transsexual is prompted to ask for the corresponding bodily correction to be made" or as: "those who, whilst belonging physically to one sex, feel convinced that they belong to the other" [internal citations omitted].

The distinguishing feature is: "a state of mind relating to sex". "Homosexual orientation" is likewise a state of mind relating to sex. Further, in many cases the distinction between the two states of mind (most particularly between transsexuals before any gender reassignment and persons of homosexual orientation) may not be easy to draw at the least, there is likely to be (or at least may be) a substantial degree of overlap. It is perhaps difficult to see how the Directive can be directed to outlaw discrimination based on the one state of mind, but not the other, or at least there must be a prospect that like protection will be afforded to both . . .

After the decision in the *Cornwall* case, it is scarcely possible to limit the applicaton of the Directive to gender discrimination, as was held in the *Smith* case, and there must be a real prospect that the European Court will take the further courageous step to extend protection to those of homosexual orientation, if a courageous step is necessary to do so. I doubt, however, whether any courage is necessary, for all that may be required is working out and applying in a constructive manner the implications of the Advocate-General's Opinion and the judgment in the *Cornwall* case. . . .

Lightman J made his reference to the ECJ after that of an employment tribunal in *Grant v South-West Trains Ltd*, an equal pay claim brought by a woman whose lesbian partner was denied the travel concessions afforded to workers' other-sex partners. The *Perkins* referral was withdrawn after the decision of the ECJ in *Grant*.

It was clear from the decision of the ECJ in *Garland v British Rail* Case C–12/81 [1982] ECR 359 (see Chapter 10) that the travel concessions amounted to "pay" within Article 141. The question for the court was whether discrimination on grounds of sexual orientation fell within the principle enunciated by that court in *P v S*. In *Grant*, Advocate General Elmer recognised the significance of the decision in *P v S*, citing the ECJ's ruling in it that:

P v S & Cornwall County Council

the right not to be discriminated against on grounds of sex is one of the fundamental human rights whose observance the court has a duty to ensure . . . Accordingly, the scope of the directive cannot be confined simply to discrimination based on the fact that a person is of one or other sex. In view of its purpose and the nature of the rights which it seeks to safeguard, the scope of the directive is also such as to apply to discrimination arising, as in this case, from the gender reassignment of the person concerned. . . Such discrimination is based, essentially if not exclusively, on the sex of the person concerned.

In *Grant*, Advocate-General Elmer interpreted the decision in *P v S* as:

a decisive step away from an interpretation of the principle of equal treatment based on the traditional comparison between a female and a male employee. The Court of Justice thus held that it did not matter that there was no reason to think that a woman who wished to undergo gender reassignment would have been treated more favourably than a man who wished to do so . . . The essential point was that the discrimination was based exclusively, or essentially, on gender.

The Advocate General pressed the Court to apply the logic of *P* v *S* to the facts before it in *Grant*, a position opposed by the European Commission whose approach the Court chose to adopt:

Grant v *South-West Trains Ltd*, Case C–249/96, [1998] ECR I–3739, [1998] All ER (EC) 193, [1998] ICR 449, [1998] IRLR 206

The refusal to allow Ms Grant the concessions is based on the fact that . . . she does not live with a "spouse" or a person of the opposite sex with whom she has had a "meaningful" relationship for at least two years.

That condition, the effect of which is that the worker must live in a stable relationship with a person of the opposite sex in order to benefit from the travel concessions, is . . . applied regardless of the sex of the worker concerned. Thus, travel concessions are refused to a male worker if he is living with a person of the same sex, just as they are to a female worker if she is living with a person of the same sex.

Since the condition imposed by the undertaking's regulations applies in the same way to female and male workers, it cannot be regarded as constituting discrimination directly based on sex.

The ECJ's decision did not seek to explain the apparent inconsistency between it and that in *P* v *S*, stating baldly that its reasoning in the earlier case ". . . is limited to the case of a worker's gender reassignment and does not therefore apply to differences of treatment based on a person's sexual orientation".[70] The Advocate-General's reasoning re-emerged in the recent EAT decision in *Bavin* v *The NHS Trust Pensions Agency* the facts of which were outlined above

Its effect was there, as we saw above, to deny to a non-married partner (there someone who had undergone gender-reassignment) the benefits open to employee's spouses, there despite the protection afforded, post *P* v *S*, to discrimination on grounds of gender-reassignment itself.

Bavin v *The NHS Trust Pensions*

Morison J (for EAT):

[Having cited *P* v *S* and *Grant*] . . . It was not clear to us whether the claim in this case would have been any different had Richard not undergone gender re-assignment operative procedures. It is likely to be the case that there are many transsexuals who, for a variety of

---

[70] *Cf* the decision of the Canadian Human Rights Tribunal in *Attorney General of Canada* v *Moore* 98 CLLC 230–033, in which the denial of same-sex benefits was held to be discriminatory. Judicial review of that decision was refused by the federal court.

reasons, do not undergo surgery but lead lives in the gender in which they feel more comfortable. If a distinction were to be drawn between those who had, and those who had not, undergone surgery, some transsexuals who have declined surgery for sound reasons would then feel discriminated against and obliged to undergo it. If such a distinction were not made then there would be some homosexual relationships which would be barely distinguishable from relationships involving transsexuals. Whilst this Court might well take the view that all relationships should be treated equally under the law, others might take a different view. Attracted as we were to the invitation to adopt a truly functionalistic approach to the problem at hand, we recognise that this Court would lose all its respect if we ignored the law and tried to do justice according to our own views as to how the underlying complex problems should be resolved.

It was argued, for the applicant, that lthe restriction of the survivors' benefit to "spouses" was indirectly discriminatory. This argument failed because there was no evidence that more women than men had their partners denied the benefits of the survivors' pension. Here it was crucial that Ms Bavin, being the partner of a transsexual rather than a transsexual herself, was obliged, as the employee, to argue her case on grounds of sex-as-gender, rather than sex-as-transsexuality discrimination. Had Ms Bavin herself undergone gender-reassignment and, as a result, had the benefits of the survivors' pension denied to her (originally same-sex) partner, she could have argued that a higher proportion of those who had undergone gender-reassignment than of others were disadvantaged by the spousal rule. It was noted, above, that the express provisions of the SDA to not prohibit indirect discrimination in these circumstances. But it is certainly arguable that the SDA, interpreted in the light of the equal treatment directive and the decision in the *P v S*, does. This is an argument which is not currently open to gay men and lesbians, the ECJ in *Grant* having refused to read the equal treatment directive's prohibition on sex discrimination to cover discrimination on grounds of sexual orientation.

Returning to the decision in *Grant* the ECJ is not bound by precedent in the same manner as the British courts, and might well reach a different decision in future on sexual orientation discrimination. Given that Court's reliance on its understanding of the law under the ECnHR, the decisions of the ECtHR in *Smith & Grady* and in *Lustig-Prean & Beckett*, below, might well provoke a speedy reversal. In any event, as the Court pointed out in *Grant*, the Treaty of Amsterdam "provides for the insertion in the EC Treaty of an article 6a now 13 which . . . will allow the Council under certain conditions. . . to take appropriate action to eliminate . . . discrimination based on sexual orientation". We have already come across Art 13 and the draft general framework directive on equal treatment which, if implemented, would require the prohibition by Member States of employment-related discrimination, subject to the possibility of relevant GOQs, on grounds, *inter alia*, of sexual orientation.

Whether or not the draft directive becomes law, it is very likely that legislative change is imminent in the UK. The government has responded fairly negatively to the recent reform proposals made by the CRE and the EOC, and has resisted even some of the suggestions put forward by the Better Regulation Task Force (see, especially, Chapter 11). That Task Force was half-hearted in its recommendations on sexual orientation discrimination, suggesting that the legal position in this area should be "clarified", perhaps by means of a Code of Practice. It appears that the Task Force favoured reform, a view which would seem to be in line with that of the Government more generally, but were prevented from suggesting legislative reform by an ideological disapproval of increased "regulation", on the one hand, and an apparent misunderstanding of the status of such Codes. It is difficult to see what a Code of Practice could achieve in this area. If discrimination on grounds of sexual orientation is not *per se* unlawful, official disapproval of it, whether expressed in a Code of Practice or elsewhere, will not make it so. A Code can certainly encourage best practice, and instruct employers who wish to act in a non-discriminatory manner about how to avoid discrimination. It could even be taken into account by tribunals considering whether a sexual-orientation-related dismissal was unfair under the ERA.[71] But a Code cannot prohibit such discrimination in relation to recruitment, promotion, etc. The Government has, nevertheless, decided to proceed in this matter by way of a Code of Practice, and in February 2000 requested that the EOC draw up such a Code.[72] The Code, which is to be drawn up in association with Stonewall, will discourage discrimination in relation to benefits paid to partners (with the exception of pensions) as well as in access to jobs, promotion and in relation to dismissal. The Code will be voluntary but Ministers are said to be considering legislation in the event that it is not effective.

It appears that more substantial change might be forced upon the government even in advance of any EU requirements. We saw in Chapter 1 that the ECtHR has ruled, in *Smith & Grady* and in *Lustig-Prean & Beckett* v *UK* that the UK's ban on gays in the military breached Article 8 of the European Convention on Human Rights. The applicants in this case appealed to the European Court after their application for judicial review of the prohibition on gays in the UK armed services was rejected (see *ex p Smith*, above). Before being dismissed from the service they were subjected to intense and invasive investigation and questioning by the military on the subject of their sexual inclinations, tastes and relationships and their HIV status. The ECtHR not only ruled against the UK in respect of the nature of the investigations carried out on the plaintiffs, but also in respect of the ban itself:

Smith & Grady v UK 29 EHRR 493 (2000)

71 . . . the investigations by the military police into the applicants' homosexuality, which
    included detailed interviews with each of them and with third parties on matters relating to their sexual orientation and practices, together with the preparation of a final

---

[71] See the notorious *Saunders* v *Scottish National Camps Association Ltd* [1980] IRLR 174.

[72] *Daily Telegraph* 18th February 2000. C. McCrudden, "Codes in a Cold Climate: Administrative Rule-Making by the CRE" (1988) 51 *Modern Law Review* 409, remarks on the attitude of the then (Labour) Government to codes of practice in 1975, the power to issue having been granted to the EOC only by the RRA after government opposition blocked it initially.

report for the armed forces' authorities on the investigations, constituted a direct inter-ference with the applicants' right to respect for their private lives. *Their consequent administrative discharge on the sole ground of their sexual orientation also constituted an interference with that right* (my emphasis)

The judgment in *Lustig-Prean & Beckett* was in similar terms.

As of October 2000, the Human Rights Act 1998 will be fully implemented through-out the UK, with the effect that the decisions in these cases will have implications for domestic law. What is perhaps most noteworthy about the decisions is that the ECtHR did not restrict its ruling to the facts, i.e., by regarding the intrusive investiga-tions into the applicants as fundamental to the breach of Article 8 in this case. Rather, the Court struck out at the gay ban itself. This being the case, it seems fair to say that discrimination on the basis of sexual orientation may now be regarded as contrary to the ECnHR.

The *Smith* and *Lustig-Prean* decisions will not apply in their entirety to private sec-tor workers. But the Courts are bound to interpret national legislation in light of the ECnHR provisions, including Article 8. The likely impact of this is at least that some-one dismissed on grounds of sexual orientation will be more likely to win an unfair dis-missal case subsequent to the implementation of the HRA than s/he would have been before. The Act will not, however, function so as to give the Convention rights direct horizontal effect. It is unlikely, as a result, that someone refused employment on grounds of sexual orientation could utilise the HRA, save perhaps to remake the argu-ment (comprehensively dismissed by the Court of Appeal in *ex p Smith*) that the SDA should be interpreted to include sexual orientation.[73] The decision of the ECJ in *Grant* gives no support to this argument in the context of the equal treatment directive. But it would certainly not preclude any more generous interpretation of the SDA.

In view of all of the above, and also of the commitment of the present Government to equalising the age of consent for homosexual sex and abolishing section 28 of the Local Government Act 1988, which prohibits the "promotion" of homosexuality by local authorities;[74] legislative amendment to include sexual orientation discrimination within the work-related provisions of the SDA, must be regarded as imminent. And regardless of such change, the decision of the Court of Appeal in *Smith* v *Gardner Merchant* illustrates that, even today, some sexual-orientation related discrimination (that corresponding to David Pannick's first category, above) breaches the SDA.

The applicant alleged a breach of the SDA after he was dismissed following a dis-pute with a colleague. He alleged that the colleague had subjected him to harassment on grounds of his homosexuality—in particular, that she had constantly asked per-sonal questions regarding his sexuality and had made offensive remarks, implying that

---

[73] See discussion in Chapter 1, however, of the possible limitations on the decisions suggested by the deci-sions in *Kosiek* and in *Glasenapp*. The protection of Article 8 may be confined to dismissal rather than non-appointment.

[74] Currently (June 2000) the subject of huge political rows, a House of Lords vote against the govern-ment and cabinet splits about the prospect of educational guidelines underpinning traditional marriage.

he probably had all sorts of diseases. A tribunal dismissed his SDA claim on the ground that sexual orientation discrimination was not within their jurisdiction, a decision upheld by EAT. On appeal to the Court of Appeal, however, his claim was remitted to a tribunal for rehearing.

Smith v Gardner Merchant [1998] IRLR 510

Ward LJ with whom the others concurred

To identify whether or not there has been direct sex discrimination it is necessary to compare the treatment meted out to the employee and the treatment which was or would have been meted out to a member of the opposite sex and to ask whether the employee has received less favourable treatment. There are three points to notice . . .

In conducting that comparative exercise one applies s 5(3), which—is directed to ensuring that like is compared with like. The relevant circumstances in the one case are to be the same as, or not materially different from, those in the other. Of course there is the fundamental difference that the one case concerns a man and the other case concerns a woman . . . [the "relevant circumstances"] cannot include the motive of the defendants . . . because motive is not a valid justification for discrimination. Indeed any other conclusion would be wholly inconsistent with the ruling of the House of Lords in *James* v *Eastleigh* . . .

The industrial tribunal and the Appeal Tribunal were, therefore, correct to conclude that there is a difference between discrimination on the ground of sex and discrimination on the ground of sexual orientation and that a person's sexual orientation is not an aspect of his or her sex . . .

The error lies in the conclusion, which was virtually a conclusion of *cadit quaestio*, when, as I now see it, the right question had not been addressed. The right question framed in terms of s 1(1)(a) is whether the applicant, a man, had been less favourably treated than his employers treated or would have treated a woman. By focusing on the applicants homosexuality, the drift of the argument pushes one almost ineluctably—as I myself was carried along—to ask the wrong question: was he discriminated against because he was a man (sex) or because he was a homosexual (sexual orientation)? In concentrating on that, one falls into the error that one does not make the comparison which the statute requires namely between his position as a man, and the comparative position of a woman. The fault in the argument is that it precludes consideration of a vital question, namely whether or not discrimination against him based upon his homosexuality may not also be discrimination against him as a man. I am grateful to Ms Cox for withstanding a fairly hostile judicial barrage and for opening my eyes to errors made by the tribunal.

It is upon that further reflection that I have come to the conclusion that the task imposed on the tribunal by s 1(1)(a) read with s 5(3) is to ascertain: (a) what, as a matter of fact, was the treatment received by the employee; (b) was he treated less favourably than the woman with whom he falls to be compared; and (c) would he have been so treated but for his sex?
. . .

To compare like with like, a male homosexual must be compared with a female homosexual.

CLOTHING AND APPEARANCE RULES

It is very common indeed for employers (and, indeed, schools), to impose regulations concerning clothing and appearance. In the employment field these rules are generally regarded as falling within the sphere of managerial discretion. A number of challenges have, however, been mounted against the operation of clothing and appearance rules. Such challenges have been made under the SDA, generally in cases where differential rules are imposed on men and women. They have also been made, as we shall see in Chapter 7, under the RRA. These latter claims tend to be quite different from those considered here, the alleged discrimination consisting in the disparate impact of the rules on persons of different race-related religious groups.

If a very straightforward approach is taken, it might be thought that any application of different rules to men and to women should be regarded, in the absence of express provision to the contrary, as breaching s.1(1)(a) SDA. Thus, for example, employers should not be permitted to require that women wear skirts or, indeed, that men wear trousers (unless the same requirement exactly is applied to both sexes). This type of interpretation was rejected by the Court of Appeal in the recent *Smith* v *Safeway plc* decision ([1996] ICR 868, [1996] IRLR 456). In this case, which is further discussed below, Phillips LJ declared that:

> a code which made identical provisions for men and women, but which resulted in one or other having an unconventional appearance, would have an unfavourable impact on that sex being compelled to appear in an unconventional mode. Can there be any doubt that a code which required all employees to have 18-inch hair, earrings and lipstick would treat men unfavourably by requiring them to adopt an appearance at odds with conventional standards?

This statement is difficult to dispute. But what it overlooks is that any code which applied those standards of appearance to women forces them to conform with a particular model of "appropriate" femininity. It is damaging to women in a different and less obvious way than it is damaging to men. But it is damaging nonetheless. And, whereas Phillips LJ used his argument to support the imposition of what were regarded by the court as "sex appropriate" sex-specific appearance codes, it is equally consistent with a different approach.

If dress codes were to be permitted only where they applied, in identical form, to men and women, the imposition of any code which, in practice, presented more difficulties to either men or women would be indirectly discriminatory. This being the case, it could be upheld only to the extent that it was justifiable. It is difficult to picture any circumstances, outside the performing arts, where it would be justifiable for an employer to require that men wore long hair, earrings and lipstick. But it is also difficult to see many circumstances in which an employer could justify the application of such a rule to women. And the beauty of adopting the approach set out above is that, once the code has been declared to discriminate indirectly against men, its use in respect of women would also have to stop. What employers would still be permitted to do would be to require that employees conform to particular standards of hygiene, neatness and smartness.

The weakness which might be identified with the alternative approach set out above is that it would not, for example, allow an employer to permit women to wear skirts or trousers, while prohibiting men from wearing skirts. Few employers would, perhaps, object to men wearing kilts (which are, after all, the favoured apparel of conventional royal males). But "appalling vistas" might be conjured up regarding miniskirted lumberjacks and stiletto-clad postmen.

Assuming that cross-dressing is regarded as a matter over which employers are entitled to have control (an argument which might become more difficult to sustain in view of the Gender Reassignment Regulations, particularly given the early, premedical intervention—point at which protection begins), one could argue that employers be permitted to require that employees adopt "conventional" dress codes. This would permit women to wear trousers (garb which has been widely regarded as acceptable for sixty years), while permitting control over more eccentric forms of dress. This approach is not conceptually very far removed from that which has found favour in the British courts. The difference of degree involved, however, has proven very significant in allowing employers to enforce such "sex appropriate" dress codes as they see fit.

The judicial approach which prevails to this day was established by EAT in *Schmidt v Austicks Bookshops*. The applicant complained that she was prohibited from wearing trousers to work and, in addition, required to wear overalls while serving customers. Men, by contrast, were subject to the sole restriction that they were not permitted to wear t-shirts at work. Her claim failed before the tribunal and EAT. Phillips J, for the Court, disregarded the matter of the overalls (which, presumably, gave female staff a subordinate appearance by comparison with men) as too trivial to amount to a "detriment" (see further Chapter 4) before going on to establish the general approach to clothing rules:

Schmdt v *Austicks Bookshops* [1978] ICR 85, [1977] IRLR 360

Phillips J, for the tribunal

. . . although there was less scope for positive rules [i.e., "no skirts"] in the case of the men, in that the choice of wearing apparel was more limited, there were restrictions in their case, too. For example, they were not allowed to wear [tee] shirts; and it is quite certain, on a reasonable examination of the evidence, that they would not have been allowed to wear, had they sought to do so, any out-of-the-way clothing. And so they were subjected to restrictions, too, albeit different ones—because, as we have already said, the restrictions to which the women were subjected were not appropriate to the men. Experience shows that under the [SDA] a lot depends on how one phrases or formulates the matter of which complaint is made. Here it has been formulated in the terms of skirts and overalls. As has been pointed out, in another case it might be in terms of ear-rings for men, long hair, all sorts of possibilities. But it seems to us that the realistic and better way of formulating it is to say that there were in force rules restricting wearing apparel and governing appearance which applied to men and also applied to women, although obviously, women and men being different, the rules in the two cases were not the same. We should be prepared to accept . . . an alternative contention . . . "that in any event, in so far as a comparison is possible, the employers treated both female and male staff alike in that both sexes were restricted in the choice of clothing for wear whilst at work and were both informed that a certain garment should not be worn during working hours."

It seems to us, if there are to be other cases on these lines, that an approach of that sort is a better approach and more likely to lead to a sensible result, than an approach which examines the situation point by point and garment by garment . .

The *Schmidt* approach operates, within the structure of the SDA, by accepting that a "sex appropriate dress code" can be a "relevant circumstance" within s.5(3), and by finding discrimination only if the terms of the code, as they apply to one sex, are significantly less favourable than those which apply to the other. The approach entails (1) accepting that a "sex appropriate dress code" can be a "relevant circumstance" within s.5(3) of the SDA, and (2) finding discrimination only if the terms of the code, as govern employees of the claimant's sex, are significantly less favourable than those which govern employees of the opposite sex.

Such less favourable treatment has, on occasion, been found by tribunals. In January 2000, for example, Judy Owen's success in an SDA claim against the Professional Golfers' Association, which had required her to wear trousers at work, was widely publicised. Such decisions are, however, rare. In *Schmidt*, as we saw above, a dress code forbidding women from wearing trousers and requiring them to wear overalls was regarded as not significantly less favourable than that forbidding men from wearing tee-shirts. In *Burrett v West Birmingham Health Authority* (unreported, but noted in the *Industrial Law Journal* (1995) 24, p.177), a uniform which required, in respect of female nurses, that a linen cap be worn was not regarded as imposing upon them significantly less favourable treatment than in the case of men, who had no obligation in respect of headgear. Finally, in *Smith v Safeway plc* [1996] ICR 868 [1996] IRLR 456, the Court of Appeal ruled that the prohibition, in the case of male employees, of long hair (female employees were permitted to wear their hair long and tied back) was not discriminatory. In doing so, the Court overruled EAT which had ([1995] IRLR 132) distinguished the code, bearing as it did on the employee's appearance outside employment, from those upheld in *Schmidt* and in *Burrett*.

Schmidt permits employers to reinforce, through dress codes, the very stereotypes of "male" (serious, responsible, mature) and "female" (decorative handmaidens) which disadvantage women at work. Because they are in line with stereotyped notions of what is appropriate to men and women respectively, these dress codes are not seen "objectively" to "demean" women even where they serve to mark them out as "second class". The other difficulty with *Schmidt*, upheld as it has been by the Court of Appeal in *Smith*, is that its approach to discrimination has more in common with that of the Court of Appeal in *Peake* [[1978] QB 233] (subsequently disapproved of in this regard in *Farthing* ([1980] QB 87]) than it does with the decision of the House of Lords in *James* v *Eastleigh* [1990] 2 AC 751] in which their Lordships refused to accept, as a "relevant circumstance" within s.5(3), the attainment of retirement age on the grounds that this was, itself, gender-based (see further Chapter 2).

It is true that the Court of Appeal in *Dhatt* v *McDonald Hamburgers* [[1991] 3 All ER 692] accepted a nationality-related factor as a "relevant circumstance" under s.5(3), but neither this decision nor those in *Schmidt* and *Smith* can properly be viewed as consistent with *James*.

The approach of the British courts to appearance codes has been widely criticised.

Leo Flynn, "Gender Equality Law and Employer's Dress Codes" (1995) 25 *ILJ* 255, 256–60

It is important to clarify the distinction between "sex" and "gender". *Sex* means those irreducible, biological differentiations between those members of the human species who have XX and those who have XY chromosomes which include more or less marked dimorphisms of genital formation, hair growth, fat distribution, hormonal function, and reproductive capacity. *Gender*, the assumptions, expectations habits and usages which identify a particular individual to themselves and to others as being a man or a woman, is socially constructed. The precise form and content of those elements constituting social gender vary greatly over time and from one place to another; historical and anthropological studies show that the signals indicating that a given individual is "really" a man or a woman are contingent and historically situated. In short, gender is a system of categories constructed on the site of the body but lacks any essential, given link with the (sexed) body.

There is an expectation that gender and sex should coincide so that gender, which is socially constructed, acquires an air of inevitability while sex is perceived as being inextricably linked with a range of behaviour which is taken as appropriate even though it lacks any intrinsic connection with biological sex. A demand for coincidence between superficially "feminine" (or "masculine") dress and the sexed reality of the body has been applied and enforced in our society, save in a few socially sanctioned situations, throughout the modern period. Thus dress difference (which is gendered) is assumed to . . .

As a result of its dual function, identifying both what the subject is and what she should be, dress has a significance beyond the conventional; aspects of personal appearance which are regarded as feminine, such as long hair, earrings and make-up, not only indicate that, in general, one is looking at a woman but also serve to identify a deviation from social norms if one knows that the person one is observing is male. This equation of the habitual with the normal means that any move by some members of one sex to take up the elements of dress associated with the other sex are initially treated as a major transgression. That spectre of cross-dressing may, in turn, provoke a panicked defence of masculinity (or femininity) which sometimes spills over into the courts. . . .

Although *Schmidt* stands as the leading English case on this matter, it can be criticized at two key points. The reasoning of the EAT rests on a questionable assumption, namely, that it is not open to men to wear certain items of apparel which are available to women. This premise removes the possibility of strict comparability between the sexes in matters of dress and necessitates the use of a modified, equivalence analysis of the situation. Neither of these elements in the EAT's reasoning—the impossibility of a skirt-wearing male, and the necessity of an identical comparator—stands up to scrutiny. To say that something is not usual or normal is not to say that it is not possible. The starting point produced by the

EAT in *Schmidt* was ill-founded and is not convincing. The boundaries of acceptable male and female dress can, and have, shifted significantly over the centuries and have altered with dramatic speed in the past few decades. Efforts to fix this process through an ascription of natural limits to "female" and "male" apparel cannot be reconciled with the basic philosophy of anti-discrimination legislation. It is true that if one did accept the argument that this requirement, not to wear trousers and to wear skirts or dresses, could never be applicable to men, then a similarly situated male comparator would be absent. However, in the wake of European Court of Justice cases, such as *Dekker* and *Webb*, dealing with pregnancy, a genuinely sex-unique characteristic, this gap need not be fatal to a successful direct discrimination claim. Nonetheless, rather than indulge this fantasy of the impossibility of a man in a dress, one must return to the basic point that *Schmidt* forces an inappropriate inevitability onto the gender of apparel.

Paul Skidmore wrote of the *Smith* v *Safeway* case:

Paul Skidmore, "Sex, Gender and Comparators in Employment Discrimination Law" (1997) 26 *ILJ* 51, 54–6

Phillips LJ considered the proposition put to the Court by counsel for Nicholas Smith "that conditions of employment which place restrictions on men which do not apply to women, or vice versa, are unlawful". This proposition is in accordance with existing case-law: *R v Birmingham CC ex p EOC* [[1989] 1 All ER 769] and *James v Eastleigh BC* which interpreted s 1(1)(a) SDA strictly, holding that the motive of the discriminator is irrelevant. Safeway did not however argue that there was discrimination, albeit with a benign motive, for example, to protect its business reputation and so as not to frighten or offend customers. It argued in line with the decision in *Schmidt* that Smith had not suffered less favourable treatment and that different treatment of men and women could be non-discriminatory. Phillips LJ accepted this by placing an unacceptable gloss on "less favourable treatment" (as had been done in *Schmidt*). He chose firstly to look at the dress code as a whole, rather than item by item, and assumed secondly that any overall package which reinforces conventional gender stereotypes (or as he put it "a conventional standard of appearance") does not give rise to less favourable treatment. He refused to accept the reasoning of the industrial tribunal in *Rewcastle v Safeway* (a case with very similar facts). There the tribunal held that the rationale of the SDA, that is to say challenging traditional assumptions about the sexes, extended to assumptions about dress and appearance.

This gloss on "less favourable treatment" cannot be justified. A restriction on hair length which applies to men and not to women is less favourable treatment of men. In the light of *James*, this should be the full extent of the analysis. All the surrounding factors are totally irrelevant. Thus Peter Gibson LJ's discussion of the employer's motives or rationale should have had no place in this judgment. He also suggests that it is a matter of fact and degree whether the employee has been subjected to less favourable treatment. This seems to be allowing the tribunal too great a degree of discretion—the comparison he makes with *Boychuk v Symons* [[1977] IRLR 395] is inappropriate—the unfair dismissal legislation gives the tribunal considerable discretion, which is not present under s 1(1)(a) SDA. For a man to lose his job for having long hair when a woman with hair of the same length would not have done so, should on any interpretation constitute less favourable treatment. . . .

The misunderstanding of the judges, clearly evident in *Nicholas Smith*, is that they think that those challenging conventional gender roles and assumptions want so to disrupt conventionality that it itself becomes unconventional, with compulsory cross-dressing as a rule. For many workers and campaigners, the aim is to have sufficient freedom in law for all workers to have autonomy and control over their gendered appearance and relationships, without this infringing the autonomy to others. Using sex discrimination legislation to the full is one way of attempting this. . . . the prospects for gays and lesbians at least to achieve this autonomy through the traditional political processes of the EC/EU remain remarkably slim, thus litigation is likely to remain high on the agenda.

7

The Race Relations Act

INTRODUCTION

The recent recognition in the UK of the widespread nature of "institutionalised racism" was considered in Chapter 4, together with the steps under way, in the form of recruitment targets and the Race Relations (Amendment) Bill 1999 to begin to tackle this type of racism. Institutionalised racism in the police and Crown Prosecution services and the courts is currently the focus of particular scrutiny. But it would be foolish to regard the racism uncovered by the McPherson Inquiry as unique to the criminal justice area.

In early 1998, the results of an independent inquiry by barrister Lincoln Crawford into the employment practices in the London Borough of Hackney was published. This was not the first time that the Council had come under scrutiny—in 1984, the CRE found that it had been responsible for discrimination in the allocation of housing, white applicants being granted substantially more favourable accommodation than their black fellow rate-payers. In Chapter 5 a number of recent race claims against Hackney were discussed in the context of remedies.

The Crawford report found some of the "worst manifestations of race discrimination" in Hackney's employment practices. The Council had succeeded in transforming itself from an almost exclusively white employer in the mid 1980s (itself quite a remarkable feat for a predominantly non-white borough)[1] but, the report found, had failed to give ethnic minority staff support and career development.

"[M]ediocre performance from white staff was ignored, but managers came down 'like a tonne of bricks' on the heads of visible minority staff for similar performance '. More disciplinary actions were taken against ethnic minority staff for misconduct than against white staff whose conduct "appeared to be excused . . . many ethnic minority staff remained in the posts into which they were recruited, and were never promoted; very few were given the opportunity to perform higher level duties or to 'act-up' to more senior positions; and more of them than of white staff were displaced through the process of restructuring. The result was that the confidence of many ethnic minority staff was regularly undermined, and 'psychological damage may have been done to many visible minority staff though their experience of working for the council' ".[2]

[1] See C. McCrudden, "Rethinking Positive Action" (1986) 15 *Industrial Law Journal* 219, extracted in Chapter 3.
[2] 77 *Equal Opportunities Review*, p.7.

Hackney may provide a particularly egregious example of race discrimination at work. But it is far from an isolated one. In Spring 1997 the Office of Public Management reported that racism was a "pervasive, long-running and deeply entrenched problem" within the armed services (in which ethnic minorities, comprising 5% of the population, account for 1.4% of personnel).[3] A survey by the European Commission, published in December 1997, found that a third of adults in the UK admitted to being "very" (8%) or "quite" (24%) racist. Two-thirds of those interviewed in the UK thought that "minority groups are being discriminated against in the job market".[4] Even among firms which include an equal opportunities statement in the annual report, 42% responded less favourably to an apparently Asian job applicant than to one who was apparently white and similarly qualified. The study, which was carried out by the Employment Policy Institute among the *Times* Top 100 companies, found that 10 of the 24 companies which had stressed their equal treatment of ethnic minority candidates responded less favourably to the Asian than to the white application. The findings of this 1998 study were consistent with those of the CRE in 1996.[5]

A recent study of 56,000 job applications found that white graduates were almost twice as likely as ethnic minority graduates to be recruited. The study, presented to the British Psychological Society's Annual Conference in 1998 by researchers from the University of East London, found that ethnic minority candidates were disproportionately likely to be weeded out at the initial sifting stage and at the final stage, generally an "assessment centre" exercise. Racism within the police service has been a matter of significant public comment over recent years. In April 1999, in a speech announcing the imposition of targets on police forces for the recruitment of ethnic minority officers, Home Secretary Jack Straw reported that, of 111 applicants accepted onto the police fast-track promotion scheme, only three had been from ethnic minorities. No ethnic minority candidates had been selected for fast-tracking over the preceding three years.[6]

Christopher McCrudden, "Racial Discrimination" in C. McCrudden and G. Chambers (eds.), *Individual Rights and the Law in Britain* (Oxford: Clarendon, 1994) 451

Despite the legislation . . . and despite relatively favourable interpretation by the higher courts, research has shown that there is a widespread view, as gleaned from opinion polls, that there remain high levels of racial discrimination in contemporary Britain. This view seems to be more the case amongst black people than amongst Asian and white people. There is also empirical research which tends to show that these perceptions are accurate. Racial discrimination and inequality of opportunity between racial groups continue at substantial levels, for example, in employment and housing. Racial minority groups differ sub-

---

[3] 77 *Equal Opportunities Review*, p.7.

[4] 78 *Equal Opportunities Review*, pp.6–7. This compares to 55% in Belgium, 48% in France and 42% in Austria.

[5] 81 *Equal Opportunities Review*, p.11.

[6] Speech to a major police conference reported 85 *Equal Opportunities Review*, p.21. Ethnic minority workers are also significantly disadvantaged in terms of pay—see 73 *Equal Opportunities Review*, p. 000 Minimum Wage Benefits Women and Ethnic Minorities.

stantially from the white population in economic conditions generally, in housing conditions, in being unemployed, and in employment opportunities. In 1992, for example, the total of black people unemployed was more than twice the national average. Some 25 per cent of black adults were jobless. These are, however, substantial differences between the ethnic minority groups in economic conditions, with Indian, African-Asian and Chinese groups being closer to the white population than the Afri-Carribean, Pakistani, and Bangladeshi ethnic groups.

Policy Studies Institute research of the legal enforcement of the 1976 Act in employment, covering the period up to 1989, and published in 1991, argued that the 1976 Acts was not working as intended. An important aim of the 1976 Act was, as we have seen, to tackle institutional discrimination: the whole range of policies and practices that are unfair to racial minorities in effect, even though that may not have been the intention. The PSI research concluded, however, that the new concept of "indirect discrimination", introduced as part of the attempt to tackle institutional discrimination, had been of limited use.

We have considered, in Chapters 2 and 3, those aspects of the RRA—direct and indirect discrimination, victimisation, etc.—which it shares with the other anti-discrimination legislation. In Chapters 1 and 6 we touched on the "multiple disadvantage" suffered by black and other ethnic minority women and in Chapter 4 we considered the scope of operation of the RRA and other anti-discrimination legislation—those aspects of employment, policing, housing, immigration, etc., to which the RRA applies. In Chapter 5 we dealt with issues of enforcement. Here we turn our attention to those legal issues which are unique to the RRA. These include the meaning of "racial group" and the genuine occupational qualification (GOQ) defence. Before we consider the RRA itself, however, it is useful briefly to deal with the relevance in this area of EC law.

RACE DISCRIMINATION AND EUROPEAN LAW

For many years now, it has been impossible adequately to understand sex discrimination law without taking into account the relevant provisions of European law. The same will soon be true in respect of race discrimination. Article 39 (formerly Article 48) of the Treaty Establishing the European Community provides:

1 Freedom of movement for workers shall be secured within the Community.
2 Such freedom of movement shall entail the abolition of any discrimination based on nationality between workers of Member States as regards employment, remuneration and other conditions of work and employment.

Christopher McCrudden, "Racial Discrimination" in McCrudden and Chambers (eds.), 445–6

There have, however, been limited developments since the mid-1980s which may lead to the EC taking a more active role. The European Parliament has taken some interest in the question of racism and xenophobia, beginning in 1984, after an increase in the number of elected representatives of extreme right-wing groups in the European Parliament. A committee of inquiry was established to study the rise of fascism and racism in Europe and to submit a report to the Parliament. The report was submitted in December 1985. Following this, a joint declaration against racism and xenophobia was signed in June 1986 by the Presidents of the European Parliament and the Council, the representatives of the member states, and the Commission.

The European Commission was pressed to go further but considered that it had no legal competence under the Treaty to do so. The Parliament disagreed. In 1988 the Commission proposed a limited formal resolution on racism and xenophobia, together with an action programme. However the resolution finally passed by the Council in 1990 was so changed from even the limited draft resolution proposed by the Commission that the Commissioner responsible disassociated herself from the final product. The resolution called upon member states to adopt "such measures as they consider appropriate" to counter racism and xenophobia. A further European Parliament committee of inquiry reported in July 1990, with further recommendations for action.

More specifically related to employment, the preamble to the Social Charter, agreed to by all member states except the United Kingdom in December 1989, provides that "in order to ensure equal treatment, it is important to combat every form of discrimination, including discrimination on grounds of sex, *colour*, *race*, opinions and beliefs, and . . . in a spirit of solidarity, it is important to combat social exclusion [*emphasis added*]". The general introduction to the Action Programme accompanying the Social Charter stressed the need for member states to eradicate discrimination on the grounds of race, colour, or religion, "particularly in the workplace and in access to employment", but no plans were announced for carrying these declarations into legislation. However in 1991 the Directorate-General for Employment, Industrial Relations, and Social Affairs commissioned a study seeking a "comparative assessment of the legal instruments implemented in the various Member States to combat all forms of discrimination, racism and xenophobia and incitement to hatred and racial violence". The report of this study recommended that each state "review existing legislation for gaps in coverage and consider the adoption of comprehensive anti-racism and anti-discrimination legislation". Achieving a limited degree of consensus on the content of any future legislation by the Community may be facilitated by the adherence of all but one EC member state (Ireland) to the Convention on the Elimination of All Forms of Racial Discrimination, though, according to a comparative analysis by Forbes and Mead of measures to combat racial discrimination in the member states of the Community, few of the other EC states have anything approaching the conceptual sophistication and detailed enforcement apparatus of the British legislation. In December 1991, the European Council asked Ministers of the Member States *and the Commission* "to increase their efforts to combat discrimination and xenophobia, and to strengthen the legal protection for third country nationals in the territories of the Member States".

The absence of EC legislation did not mean that EC law was irrelevant to issues of racial equality. On the one hand, the possibility of read-across into the RRA from the SDA of interpretations required by EC legislation was potentially beneficial. But the disadvantages of the EU dimension are discussed in the extracts below.

E. Szyszczak, "Race Discrimination: The Limits of Market Equality" in Hepple and Szyszczak *Discrimination: The Limits of Law* pp. 126–9

It is felt that many black and ethnic minorities, particularly when they are only "guest workers" in the European economy, will be adversely affected by the consequences of the Internal Market. Wong vividly describes the future Europe as a ". . . landscape for increasing problems of social polarisation and exacerbation of racial tensions and uprisings". The fears of black and ethnic minority communities may be separated into three recognized issues for the purposes of analysis, although obviously the three areas overlap and interrelate to form a web of what could be classified as institutionalized discrimination.

The first fear is the invisibility of black and ethnic minority rights in the Social Charter and in Community law generally. . . . A second fear is that indirect discrimination may occur as a result of the operation of the Internal Market. Freedom of movement is an illusory right to a non-Community national. Equally, discrimination at the national level may lead to black and ethnic minorities having difficulty in obtaining the transportable Euro-skills.

Examples of the kind of indirect discrimination which may occur are given by the Commission for Racial Equality. In analyzing the implications of Council Directive 89/48/EEC on a "general system for recognition of higher education diplomas awarded on completion of professional education and training of at least three years' duration", several issues of indirect discrimination emerge. The Directive requires member states to recognize Community professional qualifications subject to the completion of one of the adaption procedures provided where the qualifications are lower than those of the host state. Article 1 of the Directive states that a diploma must show:

> . . . that the education and training attested . . . were received mainly in the Community, or the holder thereof has three years' professional experience certified by the Member State which recognises a third country diploma . . .

There is nothing in the Directive to allow a challenge by an individual alleging that a decision by a competent authority is racially discriminatory. . . .

Another example of the indirect discrimination consequences of the Internal Market is in the area of public procurement. Community law has already been used by the Conservative government as an excuse not to introduce local labour contracts as a way of alleviating local unemployment after the Broadwater Farm and Handsworth disturbances. Anxieties are now expressed about the decision in *Gebroeders Beentjes BV v State (Netherlands)*, [Case C–31/87] [1990] CMLR 387 discussed in Chapter 5]. . . . A third fear of the consequences of the Internal Market is that by promoting a common European identity, even further alienation of black and ethnic minority groups will occur, fuelled by the lack of legal protection in national and Community law, the indirect discrimination consequences of the Internal Market and the growth of rightwing fascist groups in Europe. Even Mrs Thatcher, not the greatest supporter of the Internal Market, alluded to this in her famous speech at Bruges in 1988:

> From our perspective today, surely what strikes us most is our common experience. For instance the story of how Europeans colonised and (yes, without apology) civilised much of the world, is an extraordinary tale of talent, skill and courage.

The fostering of a common European identity may prevent the acceptance of different "non-European" forms of religion, languages, cultural ideas and education. Sivanandan has warned: "We are moving from an ethnocentric racism to a Eurocentric racism, from the different racisms of the different member states to a common, market racism."

Issues have already arisen in Europe over multi-racial schooling and the wearing of traditional clothes at school and at work. These are indicative of some of the features of alienation already experienced. With cutbacks in public expenditure it is felt that even fewer resources will be available to finance projects relating to the education of black and ethnic minorities and that more attention will be paid to the teaching of European languages, history, policies and culture.

Article 39 has been supplemented, since the Treaty of Amsterdam, by Article 13 which provides:

Without prejudice to the other provisions of the Treaty and within the limits of the powers conferred by it upon the Community, the Council, acting unanimously on a proposal from the Commission and after consulting the European Parliament, may take appropriate action to combat discrimination based on sex, racial or ethnic origin, religion, belief, disability, age or sexual orientations.

The limitations of Article 39 were discussed in Chapter 2. The provision generated scant litigation in the UK context, its protections being considerably weaker for most purposes than those provided by the RRA. But the decision of the ECJ in *O'Flynn* v *Adjudication Officer* Case C–237/94, [1996] ECR I–2617 [1996] All ER (EC) 541 was of significant interest in the context of indirect discrimination. There (in a case which fell outwith the provisions of the RRA), the ECJ ruled that indirect discrimination was established where conditions were imposed which, although they applied irrespective of nationality, carried a *risk* that non-national workers would be less able to comply with them. This, as was pointed out in Chapter 2, is a considerably easier test to satisfy than that which currently prevails under the RRA or, indeed, any other domestic anti-discrimination legislation.

Part of the significance of the *O'Flynn* decision, and of Article 39 in general, lies in its potential to challenge discrimination which, arising in the social security field, falls outside the provisions of the RRA. (See further Chapter 4.) But the case serves, more generally, as a reminder that EC law can provide a source of protection in some race-related cases as it can in the area of sex discrimination. This was underlined by EAT's subsequent decision in *Bossa* v *Nordstress & Anor* [1998] ICR 694, [1998] IRLR 284, which was discussed in Chapter 4.

The new directive on race discrimination (directive 2000/43/EC), which was adopted under the new Article 13 TEC, has been mentioned throughout the book. Here it is useful to recap the changes which it will require to be made to the RRA.

Article 2 requires a less formulaic approach to indirect discrimination than at present (see Chapter 2), such discrimination being taken to occur (subject to the possibility of justification) "where an apparently neutral provision, criterion or practice would put persons of a racial or ethnic group at a particular disadvantage compared with other persons. Article 2 also provides that harassment 'related to racial or ethnic origin . . . *shall be deemed* to be discrimination' (my emphasis), this precluding the application of a rigid comparator requirement as is currently the case (see Chapter 2).

Article 3 provides that its protections apply to *persons* rather than individuals, this being designed to bring companies (as legal persons) within the scope of the directive as victims as well as perpetrators of discrimination (this has been discussed in Chapter 4). It also sets out the scope of the discrimination prohibition will, as we saw in Chapter 4, require the extension of the RRA into social security.

Article 7(2) requires that "associations, organisations or other legal entities may engage, either on behalf or in support of the complainant with his or her approval, in any judicial and/or administrative procedure provided for the enforcement of obligations under this Directive". The significance of this has been considered in Chapter 5.

Article 8 requires a reversal of the burden of proof on the establishment of 'facts from which it may be presumed that there has been direct or indirect discrimination' (this provision, although it does not apply to criminal proceedings, resulted in howls of outrage from the right-wing British press). Its significance has also been considered in Chapter 5 while that of Article 9 'Member States shall introduce into their national legal systems such measures as are necessary to protect persons from any adverse treatment or adverse consequence as a reaction to a complaint or to *legal* proceedings aimed at enforcing compliance with the principle of equal treatment'.

It should be noted that the Directive applies only in respect of discrimination on grounds of racial or ethnic origin, Article 3(2) providing, *inter alia*, that it 'does not cover difference of treatment based on nationality'. But it is highly unlikely that any consequent amendments to the RRA will be restricted to discrimination on these grounds alone.

COVERAGE OF THE RRA

The first very significant issue which arises under the RRA concerns the people to whom it applies. In one sense the RRA, adopting a formal approach, applies to all people.[7] But the concern of the Act is with discrimination *on racial grounds* (s.1(1)(a)) and, in the context of indirect discrimination, treatment which disadvantages particular *racial groups*. S.3(1) of the RRA defines these terms as follows:

> In this Act, unless the context otherwise requires—
> "racial grounds" means any of the following grounds, namely colour, race, nationality or ethnic or national origins;
> "racial group" means a group of persons defined by reference to colour, race, nationality or ethnic or national origins, and references to a person's racial group refer to any racial group into which he falls.
> (2) The fact that a racial group comprises two or more distinct racial groups does not prevent it from constituting a particular racial group for the purposes of this Act."

---

[7] After the implementation of the new directive, whether legal or natural.

In Northern Ireland, but not in Great Britain, members of the "Irish Traveller Community" are expressly included as a racial group under the Race Relations (Northern Ireland) Order 1997, which implemented the provisions of the RRA in Northern Ireland for the first time.

Showboat Entertainment Centre Ltd v *Owens* [1984] 1 All ER 836, [1984] 1 WLR 384, [1984] IRLR 7, [1984] ICR 65

Mr Owens, who was white, was dismissed because he refused to carry out a racially discriminatory instruction from his employers to exclude young blacks from his place of work. A tribunal finding that he had been unlawfully discriminated against under the RRA was appealed, unsuccessfully, to EAT.

Browne-Wilkinson J

In our judgment, the words of s.1(1)(a) are capable of two possible meanings, the one reflecting the broad approach of Mr Hytner and the other the narrower approach of Mr Harvey.

Certainly the main thrust of the legislation is to give protection to those discriminated against on the grounds of their own racial characteristics. But the words "on racial grounds" are perfectly capable in their ordinary sense of covering any reason for an action based on race, whether it be the race of the person affected by the action or of others . . .

We can therefore see nothing in the wording of the Act which makes it clear that the words "on racial grounds" cover only the race of the complainant. As we have said, it seems to us that on the words of the Act alone it is open to give the words either a narrow or a broad construction . . .

We find it impossible to believe that Parliament intended that a person dismissed for refusing to obey an unlawful discriminatory instruction should be without a remedy. It places an employee in an impossible position if he has to choose between being a party to an illegality and losing his job. It seems to us that Parliament must have intended such an employee to be protected so far as possible from the consequences of doing his lawful duty by refusing to obey such an instruction . . .

We therefore conclude that s.1(1)(a) covers all cases of discrimination on racial grounds whether the racial characteristics in question are those of the person treated less favourably or of some other person. The only question in each case is whether the unfavourable treatment afforded to the claimant was caused by racial considerations . . .

We . . . gain considerable support from certain remarks made in the Court of Appeal in *Race Relations Board* v *Applin* (1973) 1 QB 815 . . . Counsel had put to the Court of Appeal the example of two white women who were refused entrance to a public house if accompanied by coloured [sic] men. After quoting s.1 of the [RRA 1968], Lord Denning said . . .

That definition of discrimination is wide enough to cover the case of the two women. They are treated less favourably than other women on the ground of colour.

The *Applin* case went to the House of Lords: see (1975) AC 259. Only Lord Simon in the House of Lords dealt with this particular point. He said this:

Moreover, I respectfully agree with the learned Master of the Rolls . . . It is inadmissible to read s.1(1) as if it read "on the ground of his colour". Not only would this involve reading into the subsection a word which is not there; it would also mean that some conduct which is plainly within the "mischief" would escape—for example, discriminating against a white woman on the ground that she had married a coloured man . . .

Although there are substantial differences between the 1968 Act and the 1976 Act which normally render it dangerous to treat authorities on the earlier Act as helpful on the later Act, in this instance the definition of discrimination in the two Acts is very similar. . . although we are not bound by the dicta, they are in our view persuasive authority for holding that "A" can discriminate against "B" on the ground of "C's" colour. Once this point is reached, there seems to be no stopping point short of holding that any discriminatory treatment caused by racial considerations is capable of falling within s.1 of the 1976 Act . . .

the correct comparison in this case would be between Mr Owens and another manager who did not refuse to obey the unlawful racialist instructions . . .

EAT's decision in *Showboat* was approved of by the Court of Appeal in *Weathersfield (trading as Van & Truck Rentals)* v *Sargent* [1999] IRLR 94 in which it upheld a tribunal finding that Mrs Sargent, who resigned after being instructed to discriminate against "coloured or Asians", had been subject to constructive discrimination on racial grounds. In that case, counsel for the employers argued that the RRA should be interpreted consistently with the SDA which prohibits discrimination (s.1(1)(a)) "on grounds of her sex". The Court of Appeal, however, took the view that a "broad approach" should be taken to "racial grounds" to the same effect as the decision in *Showboat*.[8]

Before we turn to consider the meaning of "racial grounds" it is useful to note that the RRA, by contrast with the other anti-discrimination legislation, expressly defines segregation as discrimination. S.1(2) of the Act provides that "for the purposes of this Act, segregating a person from other persons on racial grounds is treating him less favourably than they are treated".

Only one appellate decision has been reached on this provision—that of EAT in *FTATU* v *Modgill*. The case was brought by a number of African Asians who were employed by PEL in the paint shop. They complained, *inter alia*, that the employers had discriminated against them by segregating them contrary to s.1(2). EAT overturned a tribunal decision in their favour.

FTATU v *Modgill*; *PEL Ltd* v *Modgill* [1980] IRLR 142

Slynn J:

There is no doubt that if an employer does keep apart one person from others on the grounds of his race, that amounts to discrimination on the part of the employer. If it can be shown that it is the policy of the company to keep a man of one colour apart from others, and that it does in fact happen, then a Tribunal clearly is entitled to find that there has been discrimination contrary to the provisions of the Act . . .

[8] If the SDA was in similar terms, it would preclude the application of that Act of the reasoning in *Grant* v *South-West Trains* Case C–249/96 [1998] ECR I–3739, discussed in Chapter 6, and would prohibit much discrimination related to sexual orientation.

Had it here been clear that there was this policy of the company, and had the facts been that through the personnel department only Asians had been sent to this particular section of the factory, it seems to us that there would have been evidence upon which the Tribunal could have reached the conclusion which it did in fact reach. But that is not the way that the Tribunal, at the end of the day, put it. They had evidence which they appear to have accepted, in the body of their decision, that when vacancies arose in the paint shop they were filled by persons introduced by those who were already working there or those who were leaving . . . Indeed, the evidence was that, in a significant number of cases, people had applied for employment even before the company know that there was either a vacancy or was about to be a vacancy because one of the Asian workers was to leave . . . for a period of something like two years, the personnel department of the company had not had to select or interview persons for employment in this particular area. Those who worked there had produced candidates for appointment to [the manager] and he had found men who were able and willing to take on the job. It seems to us that the Tribunal accepted that there arose a situation, really by the acts of those working in the paint shop itself, that all the workers were in fact Asian . . .

The Tribunal, as we read their decision, really decided the case on the basis that there had been what they called "indirect" or "secondary" discrimination because the company had not had a more positive employment policy which would have removed any element of factual segregation, or suspicion of it, arising in the paint shop. This appears to suggest that it was the opinion of the Industrial Tribunal, not so much that the company had by its own acts segregated these men in this particular area away from others, but that it had not prevented the men themselves from coming together in this way. What appears to be suggested is that the company ought to have taken steps to ensure that for some of these jobs, white or non-Asian or coloured men were put in, and that Asians were not allowed to take on these jobs on the grounds of their colour, in order to prevent this segregation in fact arising . . . We do not consider that the failure of the company to intervene and to insist on white or non-Asian workers going into the shop, contrary to the wishes of the men to introduce their friends, itself constituted the act of segregating persons on racial grounds within the meaning of s.1(2) of the Act. A refusal to appoint other applicants because of their colour, or because they were Asians, might in itself indeed have amounted to discrimination within the meaning of the Act.

J.M. Thompson (1981) 97, *Law Quarterly Review* 10, 11–12

While it is perhaps understandable that the EAT was reluctant to compel an employer to ensure that his workforce was racially balanced, nevertheless the decision is open to criticism. Throughout his judgment, Slynn J. emphasised that there would have been discrimination if an intention to segregate on the part of the company could have been established. But why should intention be relevant? The Act simply states that "segregating a person" is treating him less favourably: Slynn J's construction in effect adds the restrictive gloss "*intentionally or deliberately* segregating a person." In the parallel field of equal pay, the Court of Appeal has held that an employer has no defence to a claim merely because he had no intention to discriminate. Thus in *Clay Cross (Quarry Services) Ltd.* v. *Fletcher* [1978] I.C.R. 1, 5 Lord Denning M.R. maintained that "The issue does not depend on the employer's state of mind. It does not depend on his reasons for paying the man more. The employer may not intend to discriminate against a woman by paying her less; but, if the result of his actions is that she is discriminated against, then his conduct is unlawful whether he intended it or not."

The EAT's decision in *Modgill* would seem to ignore this important principle. Instead, it is submitted that the EAT should have adopted the approach of an industrial tribunal in *Hussein* v. *Saints Complete House Furnishers* [1979] I.R.L.R. 337, where an employer was held guilty of indirect racial discrimination as a result of his policy of not employing youths from the "City Centre" of Liverpool. Since a large proportion of the population living there was coloured, the effect of this policy was to treat coloured youths less favourably than their white counterparts who lived in the suburbs and the tribunal held that it was irrelevant that the employer had not intended to discriminate on the grounds of race. Similarly, it is thought that the issue of intention to discriminate is out of place when considering whether there was segregation for the purpose of section 1(2). There can be few better examples than *Modgill* of a hard case making bad law.

RACIAL GROUNDS, RACIAL GROUP

Turning to the meaning of "racial grounds" and "racial group", "ethnic origins" has proven the most problematic subcategory and has given rise to substantial case law. The leading decision is that of the House of Lords in *Mandla and Anor* v *Dowell Lee and Anor* [1983] 2 AC 548, [1983] 1 All ER 1062, [1983] 2 WLR 620, [1983] ICR 385, [1983] IRLR 209, in which case their Lordships considered whether Sikhs were properly considered a racial group. Prior to this decision EAT had accepted, in *Seide* v *Gillette* [1980] IRLR 427, that Jews were properly regarded as a racial group, with the result that anti-Jewish discrimination was caught by the provisions of the RRA.

I. McKenna (1983) 46 *Modern Law Review* 759, 759–60

In a number of cases it appeared to have been taken for granted that Sikhs were a racial group for the purposes of the Race Relations Act 1976. In *Singh* v. *Rowntree Mackintosh Ltd.* [1979] ICR 504 and *Panesar* v. *Nestlé Co. Ltd.* [1980] ICR 144 the Scottish and the English E.A.T.s respectively appeared to accept this implicitly. The issue was more explicitly dealt with in *C.R.E.* v. *Genture Restaurants Ltd.* [unreported] where the County Court judge held that Sikhs were a "group of persons defined by reference to . . . ethnic origins" within the meaning of section 3(1). Thereafter, judicial doubt began to creep in. When the *Genture* case went to the Court of Appeal on a different point, two members expressed reservations *obiter*.

This scepticism was taken a step further by Judge Gosling in *Mandla* v. *Lee* when he ruled that Sikhs were not a racial group. In confirming this, the Court of Appeal had to find that Sikhs did not constitute a group capable of classification by reference to "colour, race, nationality or ethnic or national origins." The appellants contended that Sikhs were a group defined by reference to "ethnic origins" relying, in part, on a definition of "ethnic" in the 1972 Supplement to the *Oxford English Dictionary*: ". . . pertaining to or having common racial, cultural, religious or linguistic characteristics especially designating a racial or other group within a larger system. . . ." The Sikhs, the appellant contended, are a classic example of an "ethnic" group because of their distinctive cultural traditions.

Lord Denning preferred the definition of "ethnic" in the 1934 edition of the *Concise Oxford Dictionary*: "pertaining to race." Thus, "ethnic origins" meant "racial origins." Both Lord Denning and Kerr L.J. indicated clearly that they considered the term "race" (embracing the notion "ethnic") as used in the Act to refer, as Kerr L.J. put it, to "characteristics or attributes which are, by their nature, unalterable."

There are difficulties with this. First, if the term "race" as used in section 3(1) does indeed refer to immutable characteristics, it is difficult to explain why Parliament should have included both the terms "race" and "ethnic" origins (meaning "racial origins" according to the Court of Appeal). The Court's literal interpretation thus made one of the statutory terms redundant.

A second difficulty is the attempt to distinguish Sikhs and Jews. Lord Denning considered Jews definable by "ethnic origins" not by virtue of any cultural or religious bonds but by the common "racial" characteristic of being descended, however remotely, from a common ancestor. In contrast, Sikhs were not definable by "race" but by religion and culture.
. . .

So spurious was this distinction that the Jewish Employment Action group urged action by the House of Lords or Parliament to ensure that the protection of Jews under the Act had not been jeopardised.

As McKenna points put, the early assumption that Sikhs were protected by the RRA was not, perhaps, surprising, given that this was the very firm intention of its drafters.

I. McKenna 760–1

In the Standing Committee debates on the Race Relations Bill, the Opposition spokesman sought to introduce "religion" for the express purpose of protecting Sikhs. The amendment was withdrawn on the Government's express assurance that they would be protected. Mr. Brynmor John stated "I hope to be able to show . . . that the Bill is a considerable advance in protecting the religions of people in its concept of indirect discrimination. . . . Where any requirements laid down by an employer are notionally equal but, in fact, discriminatory against *the Sikhs* because of their religion, they would be caught, where it is unjustifiable, by indirect discrimination." Withdrawing his support for the amendment, Mr. Frederick Willey said "I accept . . . that the minorities on whose behalf we are expressing disquiet will have all the protection within the present definition that they would probably obtain even from an extended definition."

In the House of Lords a similar amendment was again withdrawn upon identical Government assurances. The Lords also debated an amendment to *delete* the term "ethnic origins" from the list of prohibited grounds of discrimination. The Government spokesman argued that the term "ethnic origin" was essential to ensure the protection for a group such as, *inter alia*, the Sikhs which was not definable by race, colour, nationality or national origin. He contended that the term "ethnic origin" "gets away from the idea of physical characteristics which inform the words 'colour' and 'race' and introduces the idea of groups defined by references to cultural characteristics geographic location, social organisation and so on." In withdrawing his proposed amendment, Lord O'Hagan accepted that the word "ethnic" was part of the whole formula of protection against discrimination and not merely a redundant term that meant the same as "race."

Debates in both Chambers leave no doubt that it was explicit Government, Opposition and back-bench opinion that the enacted statute both should and did protect Sikhs on grounds of their ethnic origin. How was it possible for the unanimous Court of Appeal to thwart the clear intention of Parliament? The judicial convention not to take official notice of parliamentary statements produced, in *Mandla* v. *Lee*, a perverse result. There is a clear case for admitting this evidence at least where it is as unequivocal as in *Mandla* v. *Lee*. On occasion judges clearly do consult informally legislative materials but evidently the Court of Appeal did not here.

As McKenna accepts, convention at the time prevented judges from looking officially at statements made in Parliament in interpreting the meaning of legislation. This position was altered by the decision of the House of Lords in *Pepper* v *Hart and others* [1993] 1 All ER 42, [1993] IRLR 33, a decision which shall be mentioned further below and which was intended to meet precisely the flaw pointed out by McKenna at the time:

> Although [the convention] is eminently sensible where a statute is dated or when either subtle issues of policy are involved or parliamentary debates are equivocal, the *Mandla* case [pre House of Lords] illustrates the shortcomings of disregarding entirely statements which point unequivocally to a particular interpretation.

The *Mandla* case was brought on behalf of a schoolboy who was refused access to a private school on the grounds that he, consistent with the requirements of his Sikh religion, wore a turban. The school's argument was that the turban would draw attention to the boy's origins and "accentuate religious and social distinctions in the school which, being a multiracial school based on the Christian faith, the headmaster desired to minimise".[9]

The House of Lords decided unanimously, and contrary to the County Court and the Court of Appeal, that Sikhs comprised a "racial group" within s.3(1). The effect of this was that the application of a "no turban" rule amounted, subject to its justifiability, to indirect discrimination against the boy.

Mandla and Anor v *Dowell Lee and Anor* ([1982] 3 All ER 1108, [1983] QB 1)

Lord Fraser

It is suggested that Sikhs are a group defined by reference to colour, race, nationality or national origins. In none of these respects are they distinguishable from many other groups, especially those living, like most Sikhs, in the Punjab. The argument turns entirely on whether they are a group defined by "ethnic origins". It is therefore necessary to ascertain the sense in which the words "ethnic" is used in the 1976 Act . . . an ethnic group in the sense of the 1976 Act . . . must . . . regard itself, and be regarded by others, as a distinct community by virtue of certain characteristics. Some of these characteristics

---

[9] IRLR headnote [1983] IRLR 209. By denying the manifestation of difference, the school just assimilated all racial groups to the presumably white "norm".

are essential others are not essential but one or more of them will commonly be found and will help to distinguish the group from the surrounding community. The conditions which appear to me to be essential are these: (1) a long shared history, of which the group is conscious as distinguishing it from other groups, and the memory of which it keeps alive (2) a cultural tradition of its own, including family and social customs and manners, often but not necessarily associated with religious observance. In addition to those two essential characteristics the following characteristics are, in my opinion, relevant: (3) either a common geographical origin, or descent from a small number of common ancestors (4) a common language, not necessarily peculiar to the group (5) a common literature peculiar to the group (6) a common religion different from that of neighbouring groups or from the general community surrounding it (7) being a minority or being an oppressed or a dominant group within a larger community, for example a conquered people (say, the inhabitants of England shortly after the Norman conquest) and their conquerors might both be ethnic groups.

A group defined by reference to enough of these characteristics would be capable of including converts, for example, persons who marry into the group, and of excluding apostates. Provided a person who joins the group feels himself or herself to be a member of it, and is accepted by other members, then he is, for the purpose of the 1976 Act, a member. That appears to be consistent with the words at the end of sub-s (1) of s 3: "references to a person's racial group refer to any racial group into which he falls." In my opinion, it is possible for a person to fall into a particular racial group either by birth or by adherence, and it makes no difference, so far as the 1976 Act is concerned, by which route he finds his way into the group . . .

Sikhs . . . were originally a religious community founded about the end of the fifteenth century in the Punjab by Guru Nanak, who was born in 1469. But the community is no longer purely religious in character. Their present position is summarised sufficiently for present purposes in the opinion of the county court judge in the following passage:

> The evidence in my judgment shows that Sikhs are a distinctive and self-conscious community. They have a history going back to the fifteenth century. They have a written language which a small proportion of Sikhs can read but which can be read by a much higher proportion of Sikhs than of Hindus. They were at one time politically supreme in the Punjab.

The result is, in my opinion, that Sikhs are a group defined by a reference to ethnic origins for the purpose of the 1976 Act, although they are not biologically distinguishable from the other peoples living in the Punjab.

Lord Templeman pointed out that the RRA did not prohibit discrimination on grounds of religion and ruled that, for the purposes of the Act:

a group of persons defined by reference to ethnic origins must possess some of the characteristics of a race, namely group descent, a group of geographical origin and a group history. The evidence shows that the Sikhs satisfy these tests. They are more than a religious sect, they are almost a race and almost a nation. As a race, the Sikhs share a common colour, and a common physique based on common ancestors from that part of the Punjab which is centred on Amritsar. They fail to qualify as a separate race because in racial origin prior to the inception of Sikhism they cannot be distinguished from other inhabitants of the Punjab. As a nation the Sikhs defeated the Moghuls, and established a kingdom in the Punjab which they lost as a result of the first and second Sikh wars they fail to qualify as a separate nation or as a separate nationality because their kingdom never achieved a sufficient degree of recognition or permanence. The Sikhs qualify as a group defined by ethnic origins because they constitute a separate and distinct community derived from the racial characteristics I have mentioned. They also justify the conditions enumerated by my noble and learned friend Lord Fraser. The Sikh community has accepted converts who do not comply with those conditions. Some persons who have the same ethnic origins as the Sikhs have ceased to be members of the Sikh community. But the Sikhs remain a group of persons forming a community recognisable by ethnic origins within the meaning of the 1976 Act.

The approach taken by the House of Lords in *Mandla* has not gone uncriticised:

G.T. Pagone, "The Lawyer's Hunt for Snarks, Religion and Races" [1984] *Cambridge Law Journal* **218, 218–222**

To the social scientist . . . the lawyer's attempt at definition must seem like the famous hunt for Snarks described by Lewis Carroll and the object of the hunt as dangerous as the Boojum, for if you ever catch sight of a Boojum you "will softly and suddenly vanish away." So too with "race," "ethnicity" and "religion," since the closer the definition approaches the concept the less it appears as a definition at all . . .

Lord Fraser . . . considered the competing senses in which "ethnic" is used and attempted to strike a balance between (a) the need of lower courts and public officials for guidance and certainty in the administration of the law and (b) an awareness that a rigid legal definition of such concepts would be inappropriate . . . in deciding that Sikhs were an "ethnic" group and hence a "racial group" for the purposes of the Act, the House of Lords has adopted a definition which seeks to contain the elusiveness of the concept under discussion by allowing for future changes and variation in the nature of the concept . . .

It could be argued that there is no compelling reason why the House of Lords . . . needed to provide any definition at all. The court[] could, for example, have taken the view that what is a "race" is a question of fact to be determined by the trier of fact. . .

In the final analysis, however, [the] court[] provide[d a] solution[] which g[a]ve recognition to the impossibility of fixed and certain meanings. Ultimately, whether any group of people can be called an "ethnic group" or "race" . . . requires a judgment for which no amount of legal training can assist. The lawyer is neither equipped nor entitled to give fixed legal definitions for such important social phenomena and at best the law can do little more than point to the general direction of what seems an elusive concept. It is thus not surprising that in the end the approach[] of . . . the House of Lords should be to list what appear to be some relevant factors and leave additions, weightings and orderings of importance in each case as, and when, it arises.

Pagone takes issue with the very attempt to define "ethnic group". Benyon and Lore, whose article is extracted below, comment on the disparities between Lord Fraser's judgment and that of Lord Templeman who, while setting out a substantially different test, appeared also to agree with Lord Fraser. (The three remaining Law Lords expressed their agreement with both speeches.)

H. Benyon and N. Love, "*Mandla* and the Meaning of 'Racial Group' " (1984) 100 *Law Quarterly Review* 120, pp. 121–3

A very cursory reading of *Mandla* might suggest that Lord Fraser gave the leading speech, which Lord Templeman merely repeated in an abbreviated form. But closer inspection reveals important discrepancies between the two speeches. They both regard a sense of history (a "long shared history" (Lord Fraser) or a "group history" (Lord Templeman)) as an essential characteristic of a group of persons defined by reference to ethnic origins. But there the similarity ends. The second of Lord Fraser's two essential characteristics (*i.e.* a "cultural tradition," etc.,) and the last four of his five relevant characteristics (*i.e.* "language," "literature," "religion" and "oppressed or dominant group") do not feature in Lord Templeman's definition at all; whilst Lord Templeman's two other essential characteristics (*i.e.* "group descent" and "group of geographical origin") only appear in Lord Fraser's speech in the alternative, as the first of his five non-essential but relevant characteristics. This creates a difficulty in identifying the *ratio* of the case, in view of the fact that the remaining Law Lords concurred in *both* speeches. Is the true *ratio* to be found in Lord Fraser's speech, in Lord Templeman's, or perhaps in both?

No doubt, one should strive as hard as possible to avoid finding any inconsistency between the two formulations, so that one true *ratio* emerges. Is this possible here? It scarcely seems so. Granted, towards the end of his speech Lord Templeman remarked that "they [the Sikhs] also justify the conditions enumerated by [Lord Fraser]," and this might conceivably be taken as indicating his concurrence in anything in Lord Fraser's speech that went beyond his own. The difficulty arises in establishing Lord Fraser's agreement with those parts of Lord Templeman's speech which different from his. Can such a consensus be found if conditions which Lord Templeman states "must" exist ("group descent" and "geographical origin") Lord Fraser merely regards as "relevant"? Surely not. There is surely a crucial difference between "must" and "may," of between a necessary condition and a contingent characteristic, even if, as will shortly be shown, other aspects of Lord Fraser's speech suggest that in other respects he attached little importance to the distinction he was here at pains to draw. So, at the very least, even if (a dubious point) Lord Fraser and Lord Templeman concurred in requiring a "cultural tradition" as well as a "group history" (lengthy or otherwise), they did not concur as to whether or not "group descent" and "geographical origin" were essential (Lord Templeman) or merely relevant (Lord Fraser). It is true that sentences and phrases in judgements should not *normally* be treated as if they were provisions in an Act of Parliament, because it is not *normally*—at common law—the function of judges to frame definitions so much as to enunciate principles. But when judges are interpreting an Act of Parliament—are, in other words, performing their function as constitutionally-appointed semasiologists—then the case is rather different. Some conceptual and verbal precision can be expected. . . . Lord Fraser's interpretation of "racial group" might well embrace gipsies as nomads and itinerants, even though Lord Templeman's clearly would not, since nomads and itinerant as such would fall foul of Lord Templeman's second requirement of "geographical origin." In fact, Lord Fraser's definition would seem to embrace many groups quite outside the intended scope of the Race Relations Act, such as the British Royal Family, or the working class. Do they not each possess, in their different ways, "long shared histories" and "cultural traditions, including family and social customs and manners . . ."? One response to this might be that although both the Royal Family and the working class possess Lord Fraser's characteristics, they are not "defined by reference to" them. They are instead probably "defined by reference to" consanguinity or affinity with a reigning monarch, and occupation, respectively. A perfectly sensible response, indeed, but not one open to anyone supporting Lord Fraser's interpretation of the Act, since he himself, as will be shown, did not use "defined by reference to" in this limiting sense. So, another possible response might be that, however distinctive the family and social customs of the Royal Family and the working classes, they do not amount to a "cultural tradition," but only to a "sub-cultural" tradition. But if so, the infinite regress towards which that tends is another argument against Lord Fraser's interpretation. The law should try, if it can, to offer clearer criteria for recognising what practices might be unlawfully discriminatory, and on that ground Lord Templeman's formulation is possibly preferable to Lord Fraser's—irrespective of any greater narrowness it may possess.

In *Dawkins* v *Department of the Environment Sub nom Crown Suppliers PSA* [1993] ICR 517, [1993] IRLR 284, the Court of Appeal ruled that Rastafarians did not comprise a racial group for the purposes of the RRA. The applicant, whose job application had been rejected because he refused to cut his hair, claimed that he had been discriminated against on grounds of race. His claim had been accepted by a tribunal but rejected by EAT on the ground that, Rastafarians having existed as a group for only 60 years, they did not have a "long shared history" which, in the EAT's view, was required in order that Rastafarians might be regarded as an "ethnic" group. (Unless Rastafarians could be regarded as such a group they could not qualify as a "racial group" within s.3(1)—Rastafarians, who comprise only a small subsection of black people and African Caribbeans, a subsection of those of Jamaican or African origin—cannot be identified by reference to colour, race, nationality or national origins.)

Before the Court of Appeal, counsel for Mr Dawkins argued that the tribunal's acceptance of 60 years as a "long" shared history was a question of fact which was not amenable to review. He also drew attention to the conflicts between Lord Fraser's and Lord Templeman's speeches in order to argue that, the decision in *Mandla* having obscured rather than clarified the meaning of s.3(1), the Court should rely on the intervening decision in *Pepper* v *Hart* and look to the Parliamentary debates in determining the question whether Rastafarians should be regarded as an ethnic group. These, he claimed, supported the understanding of ethnicity in the following terms:

> A group is identifiable in terms of its ethnic origins if it is a segment of the population distinguished from others by a sufficient combination of shared customs, beliefs, traditions and characteristics derived from a common or presumed common past, even if not drawn from what in biological terms is a common racial stock. It is that combination which gives them an historically determined social identity in their own eyes and in the eyes of those outside the group. They have a distinct social identity based not simply on group cohesion and solidarity but also on their belief as to their historical antecedents.[10]

---

[10] Richardson J in *King-Ansell* v *Police* [1979] 2 NZLR 531, approved of by Lord Fraser in *Mandla*.

Dawkins v Department of the Environment sub nom Crown Suppliers PSA [1993] ICR 517, [1993] IRLR 284

Lord Justice Neill rejected the argument that there was sufficient ambiguity between the speeches of Lord Templeman and Lord Fraser to justify recourse to Parliamentary material, declaring that counsel for Mr Dawkins:

falls into the error of equating the language used in speeches or judgments with that of a statute. In giving reasons for a decision a judge seeks to explain the basis on which he has reached his conclusion. The speech or judgment has to be read as a whole. It is very often possible to find one passage in a judgment which, because different language is used, gives a slightly different impression or has a slightly different nuance when compared with another passage. For my part, however, I cannot detect any real difference in substance between what Lord Fraser said and what Lord Templeman said. Both of them stressed that the words "ethnic origins" had to be construed in the light of the fact that they occurred as part of a definition of "a racial group". Lord Fraser . . . said that the word "ethnic" still retained a racial flavour. Lord Templeman . . . agreed that in the context ethnic origins had a good deal in common with the concept of race.

I am satisfied therefore that in these circumstances this was not a case where it would have been appropriate for the court to be referred to statements in Hansard. . .

I am unable to accept that the Industrial Tribunal's decision by a majority that Rastafarians had a sufficiently long shared history to satisfy Lord Fraser's first condition was merely a finding of fact with which an appellate court cannot interfere. The finding that the group originated in 1930 was indeed a finding of fact, but a decision as to the length of a shared history, which is necessary for the purpose of satisfying a statutory test, is a very different matter. In any event it is important to remember that the relevant words in the statute are "ethnic origins" . . .

It is clear that Rastafarians have certain identifiable characteristics. They have a strong cultural tradition which includes a distinctive form of music known as reggae music. They adopt a distinctive form of hairstyle by wearing dreadlocks. They have other shared characteristics of which both the . . . Tribunal and [EAT] were satisfied. But the crucial question is whether they have established some separate identity by reference to their ethnic origins. In speaking about Rastafarians in this context I am referring to the core group, because I am satisfied that a core group can exist even though not all the adherents of the group could, if considered separately, satisfy any of the relevant tests.

It is at this stage that one has to take account of both the racial flavour of the word "ethnic" and Lord Fraser's requirement of a long shared history. Lord Meston submitted that if one compared Rastafarians with the rest of the Jamaican community in England, or indeed with the rest of the Afro-Caribbean community in this country, there was nothing to set them aside as a separate ethnic group. They are a separate group but not a separate group defined by reference to their ethnic origins. I see no answer to this submission . . .

In my judgment it is not enough for Rastafarians now to look back to a past when their ancestors, in common with other peoples in the Caribbean, were taken there from Africa. They were not a separate group then. The shared history of Rastafarians goes back only 60 years or so. One can understand and admire the deep affection which Rastafarians feel for Africa and their longing for it as their real home. But, as Mr Riza recognises, the court is concerned with the language of the statute. In the light of the guidance given by the House of Lords in *Mandla*, I am unable to say that they are a separate racial group.

Wilson McLeod, "Autochthonous language communities and the Race Relations Act" (1998) *Web Journal of Current Legal Issues* Issue 1

Lord Fraser's . . . initial observation that "the word "ethnic" still retains a racial flavour" . . . received undue emphasis in *Dawkins* . . .

The "racial flavour" required for "ethnic group" status is not . . . coterminous with the broader term "race". The inquiry appears to be somewhat more specific. Lord Fraser amplified his reference to "racial flavour" by noting that "the word "ethnic". . . is used nowadays in an extended sense to include other characteristics which may be commonly thought of as being associated with common racial origin". . . Lord Fraser cited with approval the decision of the New Zealand Court of Appeal in *King-Anseil* v *Police* . . . "a group is identifiable in terms of its ethnic origins if it is a segment of the population distinguished from others by a sufficient combination of shared customs, beliefs, traditions and characteristics derived from a common or presumed common past even if not drawn from what in biological terms is a common racial stock" . . . This nuanced approach to the concept of "racial flavour" means that traits based on a relatively recent shared tradition can be sufficient even in the absence of a common racial stock; Lord Fraser concluded in *Mandla* that Sikhs constitute an ethnic group for RRA purposes "although they are not biologically distinguishable from the other peoples living in the Punjab" . . . It should be noted, however, that Lord Templeman's speech in *Mandla* appeared to emphasise the racial dimension to a rather greater degree, arguing that "a group of persons defined by reference to ethnic origins must possess some of the characteristics of a race, namely group descent, a group of geographical origin and a group history" . . .

We saw, from *Dawkins*, that "gipsies" (but not "travellers") were accepted as a "racial group" by the Court of Appeal in *Commission for Racial Equality* v *Dutton*. The case concerned a "no travellers" sign displayed in a pub, "traveller" being defined by the landlord as a "person who travels around in a caravan and parks on illegal sites and gives him 'hassle.' "

Commission for Racial Equality v *Dutton* [1989] QB 783, [1989] 1 All ER 306 [1989] IRLR 8

Nicholls LJ:

The [CRE's] case was that in these notices "travellers" is synonymous with gipsies . . .

the judge rejected the view that the words are synonymous. I agree with him But before proceeding further it is necessary for me to comment on the word "gipsy." One of the difficulties in the present case, in my view, is that the word "gipsy" has itself more than one meaning. The classic "dictionary" meaning can be found as the primary meaning given in the Oxford English Dictionary (1933):

> A member of a wandering race (by themselves called Romany), of Hindu origin, which first appeared in England about the beginning of the 16th century and was then believed to have come from Egypt.

Hence the word "gipsy," also spelled as "gypsy." It is a corruption of the word Egyptian. . . Alongside this meaning, the word "gipsy" also has a more colloquial, looser meaning.

This is expressed in the Longman Dictionary of Contemporary English (1987) . . . "a person who habitually wanders or who has the habits of someone who does not stay for long in one place." In short, a nomad.

I can anticipate here by noting that if the word "gipsy" is used in this second, colloquial sense it is not definitive of a racial group within the Act. To discriminate against such a group would not be on racial grounds, namely, on the ground of ethnic origins. As the judge observed, there are many people who travel around the country in caravans, vans converted buses, trailers, lorries and motor vehicles, leading a peripatetic or nomadic way of life. They include didicois, mumpers, peace people, new age travellers, hippies, tinkers, hawkers, self-styled "anarchists," and others, as well as (Romany) gipsies. They may all be loosely referred to as "gipsies," but as a group they do not have the characteristics requisite of a racial group within the Act . . .

In this judgment, save where I indicate otherwise, I shall henceforth use the word "gipsy" in the narrower sense, of the first of the two means mentioned above . . .

In my view, [in the circumstances] . . . "No travellers" will be understood by those to whom it is directed, namely, potential customers, as meaning persons who are currently leading a nomadic way of life, living in tents or caravans or other vehicles. Thus the notices embrace gipsies who are living in that way. But the class of persons excluded from the Cat and Mutton is not confined to gipsies. The prohibited class includes all those of a nomadic way of life mentioned above. As the judge said, they all come under the umbrella expression "travellers," as this accurately describes their way of life.

It is estimated that nowadays between one-half and two-thirds of gipsies in this country have wholly or largely abandoned a nomadic way of life, in favour of living in houses. I do not think that the notices could reasonably be understood as applying to them, that is, to gipsies who are currently living in houses. Gipsies may prefer to be described as "travellers" as they believe this is a less derogatory expression. But, in the context of a notice displayed in the windows of a public house near a common on which nomads encamp from time to time, I do not think "No travellers" can reasonably be understood as other than "No nomads." It would not embrace house-dwellers, of any race or origin.

For this reason I cannot accept that the defendant's notices indicate, or might reasonably be understood as indicating, an intention by him to do an act of discrimination within section 1(1)(a). Excluded from the Cat and Mutton are all "travellers," whether or not they are gipsies. All "travellers," all nomads, are treated equally, whatever their race. They are not being discriminated against on racial grounds . . .

Nicholls LJ went on to consider whether "gypsies" were a "racial group" for the purposes of deciding whether the notice amounted to unlawful indirect discrimination against them.

On the evidence it is clear that such gipsies are a minority, with a long-shared history and a common geographical origin. They are a people who originated in northern India. They migrated thence to Europe through Persia in medieval times. They have certain, albeit limited, customs of their own, regarding cooking and the manner of washing. They have a distinctive, traditional style of dressing, with heavy jewellery worn by the women, although this dress is not worn all the time. They also furnish their caravans in a distinctive manner. They have a language or dialect, known as "pogadi chib," spoken by English gipsies (Romany chals) and Welsh gipsies (Kale) which consists of up to one-fifth of Romany words in pace of English words. They do not have a common religion, nor a peculiar, common literature of their own, but they have a repertoire of folktales and music passed on from one generation to the next. No doubt, after all the centuries which have passed since the first gipsies left the Punjab, gipsies are no longer derived from what, in biological terms, is a common racial stock, but that of itself does not prevent them from being a racial group as widely defined in the Act.

I come now to the part of the case which has caused me most difficulty. Gipsies prefer to be called "travellers" as they think that term is less derogatory. This might suggest a wish to lose their separate, distinctive identity so far as the general public is concerned. Half or more of them now live in houses, like most other people. Have gipsies now lost their separate, group identify, so that they are no longer a community recognisable by ethnic origins within the meaning of the Act? The judge held that they had. This is a finding of fact.

Nevertheless, with respect of the judge, I do not think that there was before him any evidence justifying his conclusion that gipsies have been absorbed into a larger group, if by that he meant that substantially all gipsies have been so absorbed. The fact that some have been so absorbed and are indistinguishable from any ordinary member of the public, is not sufficient in itself to establish loss of what Richardson J, in *King-Ansell* v *Police* . . . referred to as "an historically determined social identity in [the group's] own eyes and in the eyes of those outside the group." There was some evidence to the contrary from Mr Mercer, on whose testimony the judge expressed no adverse comment. He gave evidence that "we know who are members of our community" and that "we know we are different." In my view the evidence was sufficient to establish that, despite their long presence in England, gipsies have not merged wholly in the population, as have the Saxons and the Danes, and altogether lost their separate identity. They, or many of them, have retained a separateness, a self-awareness, of still being gipsies.

Nicholls LJ went on to decide that the "no travellers" rule amounted to indirect discrimination against gypsies, subject to the question of justification which he referred back to the county court for decision. Taylor and Stocker LJJ concurred, though the latter expressed reservations about the qualification as an "ethnic group" of gypsies given what he saw as the degree of their absorption into the wider population. We saw, above, that the "Irish Traveller Community" is expressly recognised as a racial group by the Race Relations (Northern Ireland) Order 1997.

Two of the very significant gaps in the coverage of the RRA, as interpreted by the House of Lords in *Mandla*, have become apparent in recent years. The first concerns discrimination, whether direct or indirect, against Moslems. This has increasingly been seen as a significant social problem, not least in the wake of the Salman Rushdie affair. The second, which will become an increasingly important issue in light of the devolution of power to Scotland, Wales and Northern Ireland, concerns discrimination in relation to "autochthonous" languages—that is, indigenous minority languages such as Scots Gaelic and Welsh.[11]

Discrimination against Moslems will sometimes, and sometimes not, amount to discrimination on racial grounds.

[11] The issue under the FETO would be religion/ political opinion and Irish language.

Sebastian Poulter, "Muslim Headscarves in School: Contrasting Approaches in England and France" (1997) 17 *Oxford Journal of Legal Studies* **43, 64**

So far,—in four cases decided by industrial tribunals and the Employment Appeal Tribunal, it has been held that Muslims are not an ethnic group but a religious one. As the South London Industrial Tribunal explained in *Nyazi* v *Rymans Ltd*:–

> Muslims include people of many nations and colours, who speak many languages and whose only common denominator is religion and religious culture.

More importantly, perhaps, Muslims worldwide do not possess a "shared history" and many perceive themselves not as members of an ethnic group but as part of an essentially religious community or *"ummah"*. To some extent, this definitional hurdle can be circumvented through a plaintiff's reliance on membership of a group which does fall clearly within the terms of the Act. A Muslim pupil whose parents came to Britain from Pakistan could plead, for example, that any discrimination against her was based on her Pakistani nationality, her Pakistani "national origin" (if she was a British citizen) or her Asian "race". On the other hand, the daughter of one of the growing number of white or black (Afro-Caribbean) British converts to Islam could not take advantage of this approach.

Nyazi v *Rymans Ltd* concerned a complaint from a Moslem woman who had been denied leave to celebrate Eid. There was some dispute as to the facts and as to whether the applicant was an observant Moslem (this being relevant to whether she could comply with a requirement to work through the festival). The issue of more general interest related to the status of Moslems as an ethnic group. The tribunal had ruled that:

Nyazi v *Rymans Ltd* EAT/6/88 (unreported)

we are unable to conclude that Muslims . . . come within the meaning of "ethnic group". All we can say is that Muslims profess a common religion in a belief in the Oneness of God and the prophethood of Muhammed. No doubt there is a profound cultural and historical background and there are traditions of dress, family life and social behaviour. There is a common literature in the sense that the Holy Quaran is a sacred book. Even so, many of the other relevant characteristics would seem to be missing.

The Muslim faith is widespread, covering many nations, indeed many colours and languages, and it seems to us that the common denominator is religion and a religious culture. In other words we believe Muslims are a group defined mainly by reference to religion and that being so we must find that we have no jurisdiction under the Act.

EAT rejected the applicant's appeal, ruling that the tribunal had not "erred either in the exercise of its discretion, or in the conclusion it reached on the facts which were before it". In *CRE* v *Precision Manufacturing Services Ltd* COIT 4106/91 (26th July 1991), on the other hand, a tribunal found that discrimination against Moslems amounted, on the facts, to race discrimination. The case concerned an instruction issued by an employer to a job centre to the effect that he would not employ Moslems (or, indeed, men). In determining whether discrimination against Moslems breached the RRA the tribunal distinguished between "coloured" and "non-coloured" people and cited evidence to the effect that 6000 of the 250,000 residents of the local area

(Rotherham Metropolitan Borough Council) were ethnic minority. Of these, 100% of the 5300 Pakistanis were Moslems as were 100% of the 200 Yemeni Arabs. 50% of the 100 Ugandan Asians, 30% of the 100 Bangladeshis, 10% of the 200 Indians and a negligible proportion of the 100 others—i.e., 93% of the local ethnic minority population was Moslem.

Another case in which an RRA claim succeeded was *Walker* v *Hussain* in which a tribunal accepted that discrimination against Moslems amounted to discrimination against Asians and thence to race discrimination.[12] There, Asians were less able to comply with a requirement to work through the summer than were non-Asians in the workplace. Eid fell during the summer months and observant Moslems could not work during that period. Their race discrimination claim succeeded because, most Asians in the workplace being Moslem and the tribunal adopting a workplace pool for comparison, the applicants could demonstrate that Asians were significantly less likely than non-Asian employees to be in a position to comply.

The reasoning adopted by the tribunal in *Walker* would not have applied in a workplace in which the majority of Asian workers were not Moslem, and, if a tribunal were to select the pool from the general population, rather than the workplace. Asians may not be significantly more likely than non-Asians to be devout Moslems so as to be unable to comply, for example, with a requirement to work through Eid. In any event, it is arguable whether "Asians" even amount to a "racial group" within the RRA.

The approach taken by the tribunal in *Precision Manufacturing* was to distinguish between "coloured" and "non-coloured" members of the local population, which appears consistent with the RRA's prohibition of discrimination on grounds of "colour" and the Act's provision (s.3(2)) that "[t]he fact that a racial group comprises two or more distinct racial groups [there Pakistanis, Yemeni Arabs, Ugandan Asians, Bangladeshis, Indians and "others"] does not prevent it from constituting a particular racial group for the purposes of this Act").[13] But the demonstration of discrimination against Moslems as discrimination on grounds of colour turned in that case on the specifics of the local, largely Pakistani, non-White population.

"Asians" cannot be categorised according to colour, nationality or national origins". It is possible that Asians might be categorised as a "race", but it may be the case that South and East Asians would have to be distinguished. Again, even if "Asians", "South Asians" or "East Asians" are accepted as a racial group, it remains a question of fact whether, in any particular case, anti- Moslem discrimination amounts to race discrimination within the RRA. The test is less likely to be satisfied, as is apparent from Sebastian Poulter's article (extracted below) where the discrimination against

---

[12] This aspect of the decision was not appealed to EAT whose decision in the case is at *J H Walker Ltd* v *Hussain & Others* [1996] ICR 291, [1996] IRLR 11.

[13] Lustgarten points out ("The New Meaning of Discrimination" (1978) *Public Law* 178) that the provision was included in order to permit training to be targeted at more than one racial group. In *Orphanos* v *Queen Mary College* [1985] 2 WLR 703 the House of Lords accepted that racial groups could be defined in negative terms "non-British", "non EC". Ian Leigh ((1986) 49 *MLR* 235, at 236–7) questions the correctness of this approach.

Moslems takes the indirect form (it again being a question of fact whether, in any particular case, a considerably smaller proportion of the relevant racial group than of others can comply with the requirement or condition at issue.

Where direct discrimination against Moslems is at issue, the question whether indirect race discrimination has occurred depends upon whether a substantially smaller proportion of the applicant's racial group[14] than of others can comply with a requirement not to be Moslem. But where the discrimination against Moslems takes the indirect form (as in the discussion of *hijab* wearing, below), the RRA will be breached only where the relationship between religion and race is so close that the proportion of the relevant *racial* group able to comply with the disputed requirement or condition is considerably smaller than the proportion of other *racial* groups able so to do.

The question here addressed by Poulter is whether a "considerably smaller proportion" of (say) Pakistani girls than of non-Pakistanis or non-Asians could comply with a "no scarf" requirement:

S. Poulter, (1997) *OJLS*, 65

. . . In practice, the general impression is that very few Muslim girls in England, of whatever nationality or national origin, wear the *hijab* as part of their normal clothing out of school. Certainly, the figure seems unlikely to be anywhere near twenty percent of any national group, save possibly in the case of those pupils from states in the Arabian Gulf, of whom there are extremely few. The crucial point is that, in statistical terms, the wearing of Muslim headscarves by girls in this country appears to be just as rare a phenomenon as it is in France, where it has been estimated at below two percent. There is a stark contrast here with the wearing of *shalwars*, the loose-fitting trousers worn by large numbers of Asian women and girls in this country in pursuance of religious norms or cultural traditions. With *shalwars*, the proportionality test could easily be satisfied and therefore a school rule which prescribed the wearing of skirts certainly could constitute indirect indiscrimination.

Even if a *prima facie* case of indirect discrimination is established, discrimination against Moslems can be justified under the RRA. Whereas this is true only in respect of indirect discrimination against Jews and Sikhs (in the form, for example, of a requirement to work on Saturday, for men to be clean shaven or women to have short hair); both direct and indirect discrimination against Moslems may be justified.

S. Poulter, (1997) *OJLS*, 66–7

Even if a Muslim pupil, necessarily relying on her national origins overseas, did manage to satisfy the court on the proportionality test, her school would still not be acting unlawfully if it could establish the statutory defence that its general headwear regulation was "justifiable irrespective of the colour, race, nationality or ethnic or national origins" of the pupil concerned. In recent years this defence of justifiability has been considerably tightened and a test of objective necessity has been developed. A balance now has to be struck between the discriminatory effect of the rule and the reasonable needs of the school. The school

[14] Whether at the level of the workplace or more generally, the choice of pool being one for the tribunal.

would have to demonstrate that the rule corresponded to a real need, rather than mere convenience, and that there was no viable alternative solution available to meet that need. Such necessity might be established in cases where a *hijab* could put the health or safety of a pupil at risk, for instance in some scientific experiments or activities involving vigorous physical exercise . . .

If the foregoing analysis leads to the inexorable conclusion that Muslims, as such, have no legal right to wear headscarves at school and that there is only a remote prospect of even a pupil of Pakistani or Bangladeshi origin succeeding in a claim under the 1976 Act, the irony of the situation should at least be noted at this stage. Any triumph in court would be derived from reliance upon national origins, whereas the whole reason for wearing the headscarf would be totally unconnected with such origins and be derived in fact from religious beliefs. It would indeed be a hollow victory for Islam in those circumstances. By contrast, the turban is invariably portrayed by Sikhs as a communal religious symbol and the decision in *Mandla* v *Dowell Lee* is thus perceived as upholding their religious freedom rather than protecting them from racial discrimination.

Turning to the question of autochthonous languages, this issue relates to the wider question whether, for example, discrimination between English and Scots people, or between Irish and Welsh, offends the RRA.

According to the CRE Factsheet, *The Irish in Britain*:

> The Irish are Britain's largest ethnic minority group . . . Since the Commission was established in 1977, Irish people have been coming to it with complaints of unlawful discrimination. Academic research and official statistics have revealed inequalities in Irish people's experience of the labour and housing markets, the health service and the benefits system. Many Irish people in Britain have also objected to being made the butt of humour and remarks which they find offensive . . . There has been a failure, both at an official level and in general discussions of race relations, to recognise the difficulties that many Irish people experience in Britain . . . "Irish people are constantly reminded that they are not entitled to an equal place in British society. On the other hand they are not seen as sufficiently distinct for this racism to be acknowledged and to be afforded some measure of protection". [5]

There is no doubt that anti-Irish discrimination comes within the RRA, such discrimination having successfully been challenged on a number of occasions. Among the cases cited by the Commission were *O'Driscoll* v *Post Office* (1990) in which an Irish applicant was questioned as to whether he had a drink problem: *Nicholl* v *London Staff Bureau* (1991) in which an woman was refused a job interview because she was Irish and therefore unreliable; and *Bryans* v *Northumberland College* (1995) in which an Irish man was victimised for complaining about his abuse in front of colleagues and visiting professionals.

"Discrimination against the Irish is discrimination on grounds of nationality or national origin". More problematic, however, is the Scots/ Welsh/ English/ Northern Irish distinction. Neither colour nor, presumably, race would be implicated. As far as

---

[15] Citing *Discrimination and the Irish Community in Britain* (ISBN 1 85442 200 6), a national research project commissioned by the CRE in 1994.

nationality is concerned, it could be argued that all are British. The questions which remain concern whether these groups could be distinguished either in terms of their national or their ethnic origins.

In *Ealing London Borough Council* v *Race Relations Board*, a case which arose under the RRA 1965, the House of Lords considered the meaning of "national origins".

Ealing London Borough Council v Race Relations Board [1972] AC 342

Lord Simon of Glaisdale:

[The] words ["national origins"] are part of a passage of vague terminology in which the words seem to be used in a popular sense. "Origin", in its ordinary sense, signifies a source, someone or something from which someone or something else has descended. "Nation" and "national", in their popular, in contrast to their legal, sense, are also vague terms. They do not necessarily imply statehood. For example, there were many submerged nations in the former Hapsburg Empire. Scotland is not a nation in the eye of international law, but Scotsmen constitute a nation by reason of those most powerful elements in the creation of national spirit—tradition, folk memory, a sentiment of community. The Scots are a nation because of Bannockburn and Flodden, Culloden and the pipes of Lucknow, because of Jenny Geddes and Flora MacDonald, because of frugal living and respect for learning, because of Robert Burns and Walter Scott. So, too, the English are a nation—because Norman, Angevin and Tudor monarchs forged them together, because their land is mostly sea-girt, because of the common law and of gifts for poetry and parliamentary government,[!] because (despite the Wars of the Roses and Old Trafford and Headingley) Yorkshireman and Lancastrian feel more in common than in difference and are even prepared at a pinch to extend their sense of community to southern folk. By the Act of Union English and Scots lost their separate nationalities, but they retained their separate nationhoods, and their descendants have thereby retained their national origins. So, again, the Welsh are a nation—in the popular, though not in the legal, sense—by reason of Offa's Dyke, by recollection of battles long ago and pride in the present valour of their regiments, because of musical gifts and religious dissent, because of fortitude in the face of economic adversity, because of the satisfaction of all Wales that Lloyd George became an architect of the welfare state and prime minister of victory. To discriminate against Englishmen, Scots and Welsh, as such, would, in my opinion, be to discriminate against them on the ground of their national origins . . .

In *Boyce* v *British Airways plc*, EAT ruled that the Scots and the English could not be distinguished on the grounds of ethnic origins. The applicants appealed to EAT against a tribunal finding that anti-Scots discrimination fell outwith the RRA. The appeal was rejected. On the question whether the Scots were a group identified by reference to their ethnic origins, EAT ruled:

Boyce v British Airways plc (31st July 1997, EAT 385/97)

Lord Johnston (for EAT)

In determining the guidance afford by the House of Lords in *Mandla*, we consider it essential to have regard (1) to all that was said in that case, and not simply to those parts of Lord

Fraser's speech dealing with the tests to be applied, in determining whether a given group was an ethnic group and (2) the facts of that case. . .

As we understand the matter, the House of Lords insisted (as did the Court of Appeal) that the word "ethnic" had a strong racial flavour, and it is against that background that the factors, specified by Lord Fraser, fall to be considered.

Turning to the facts of *Mandla*, it is clear that there was a strong racial flavour. . . .

Turning to the facts of this case, we can find no racial flavour, and, indeed, none was ever suggested, and, in these circumstances, in the total absence of any racial flavour or element, we are satisfied that the applicants cannot claim that they have been discriminated against on the grounds of their ethnic origins. . . .

We would add that, even if we were not satisfied that the racial flavour, insisted upon by the House of Lords, were absent in this case, we would have some doubt about the wisdom of our proceeding to consider the factors mentioned by Lord Fraser . . . We were urged, for example, to find that the Scots have a cultural tradition of their own, including family and social customs and manners often, but not necessarily, associated with religious observance. We were urged to hold that the Scots had a cultural tradition of their own, and reference was made to the works of Scott, Burns and (!) McGonigle. In our view, it would not be appropriate for us to attempt to determine whether or not Scott and Burns were peculiarly Scottish writers, and thus evidence of, or constitutive of a Scottish cultural tradition, as opposed to being merely part of—say—a wider European movement.

We do not see how we could even begin to address the third factor mentioned by Lord Fraser. Lord Fraser said that either a common geographical origin or descent from a small number of common ancestors was a relevant factor. Given the waves of immigration to Scotland, and emigration from it to England, we do not see how we could answer that question unaided. As already noted, we have some doubt as to whether or not we could determine whether or not "Scottish literature" is peculiar to Scotland or part of a wider cultural movement. Always assuming that we were prepared to hold that Scotland did have a religion, it would be again difficult for us to determine whether the Church of Scotland was a peculiarly Scottish institution, or part of a wider European religious movement . . .

It will be noted that the decision in *Boyce* was restricted, expressly, to the question whether Scots could be regarded as a racial group by virtue of their *ethnic* origins. In *Northern Joint Police Board v Power* [1997] IRLR 610, EAT considered whether a Scots/ English distinction could be drawn, for the purposes of the RRA, on grounds of *national* origin.

Mr Power claimed that the failure of the respondents to shortlist him was because he was English rather than Scots. A tribunal accepted that discrimination between English and Scots was on "racial grounds", "racial" being defined by reference to "national origins". The tribunal based its decision on the reasoning of the House of Lords in *Ealing*, above.

It seemed to the tribunal sufficient in applying the ratio of the decision in *Ealing* to ask itself the question whether England and Scotland are nations in the popular or non-legal sense and to try to answer the question objectively.

In the unanimous opinion of the tribunal, they are separate nations in that sense. That they are is attributable principally to the fact that prior to the Act of Union the two countries were separate nations in the legal sense, that is to say, they were each formerly sovereign states in their own right. The two countries have since the Act of Union continued to be separated geographically.

They have retained their separate names. There was preserved to Scotland under the Act of Union its legal system, its church and its education system. In the words of Lord Simon [above], "By the Act of Union, English and Scots lost their separate nationalities, but they retained their separate nationhoods." Each country has thus retained a separate status and identity notwithstanding having been absorbed into what is the United Kingdom. Although the circumstances are wholly different, England and Scotland as part of the United Kingdom are in this context "nations" in the same way that Poland was a "nation" as part of the Russian Empire before it became a sovereign state. There are many manifestations of the separate status of the two countries in present-day life. It is not something which is merely historical. It is continuing. There is no difficulty in saying now . . . that the Scots and the English are each a group of people who can be described as a "nation".

EAT rejected the employer's appeal. Having expressed the view that the speech of Lord Simon in *Ealing*, extracted above, was "not particularly helpful, other than to point to the nature of the elements which may enter the equation determining whether or not, in a particular context of England and Scotland, there are national attributes", Lord Johnston continued:

Nationality, we consider, has a juridical basis pointing to citizenship, which, in turn, points to the existence of a recognised state at the material time. Within the context of England, Scotland, Northern Ireland and Wales the proper approach to nationality is to categorise all of them as falling under the umbrella of British, and to regard the population as citizens of the United Kingdom. Against that background, what context, therefore, should be given to the phrase "national origins"? It seems to us, so far as there needs to be an exhaustive definition, what has to be ascertained are identifiable elements, both historically and geographically, which at least at some point in time reveals the existence of a nation. Whatever may be difficult fringe questions to this issue, what cannot be in doubt is that both England and Scotland were once separate nations. That, in our opinion, is effectively sufficient to dispose of the matter, since thereafter we agree with the proposition that it is for each individual to show that his origins are embedded in such a nation, and how he chooses to do so requires scrutiny by the tribunal hearing the application. In our opinion, whatever factors are put forward to satisfy the relevant criteria will be self-evidently relevant or irrelevant as the case may be. There is, therefore, no need for the tests such as enunciated by Lord Fraser in *Mandla*, with regard to the question of groups based on ethnic origins in relation to the issue of national origins, since the former by definition need not have, although it might have, a defined historical and geographical base. It is perfectly possible that the two defined groups may overlap, but that does not affect the issue which is required to be approached in each context from a different direction. The existence of a nation, whether in the present or past, is determined by factors quite separate from an individual's origins, and those factors are easily established in any given case by reference to history and geography. That the same cannot be said in relation to groups based on ethnic origins creates the need for Lord Fraser's test.

We are also entirely satisfied that it is legitimate, assuming there is any doubt in the matter as to whether Parliament intended to include the constituents within the United

Kingdom as part of the "races" to be considered within the legislation, to examine the surrounding materials in order to determine the intention, and indeed the mischief being addressed. On doing so, it is manifest that Parliament's intention was to include the constituent races, so-called, within the United Kingdom under the umbrella of the legislation. The matter is, therefore, put beyond doubt.

The legal status of language requirements designed to encourage, for example, the continued and expanded use of Welsh or Scots Gallic is problematic. This is likely to become an issue of increasing importance in the wake of devolution. It could be argued that any requirement that an employee be conversant with Welsh or Scots Gallic would amount to race-based discrimination. On the reasoning in *Power*, such a requirement might, depending on its justifiability, amount to unlawful indirect discrimination on grounds of national origin against, for example, English Irish and Scots (in Wales), Welsh Irish and English (in Scotland).[16] It might also, subject to questions of justification, amount to indirect discrimination under Article 39 of the Treaty of Rome.[17] A non-Welsh-speaking Welsh person who wishes to challenge the application of a Welsh language requirement, or a non-Gallic-speaking Scot who wishes to challenge the application of a Gallic language requirement, can rely neither on any claim of discrimination on grounds of national origins nor, generally, on Art 39.[18] In *Gwynedd County Council* v *Jones and another*, however, two non-Welsh-speaking Welsh complainants sought to argue that they had been discriminated against on grounds of their ethnic origin by the application of a Welsh language requirement. A tribunal accepted their claims, ruling that the Welsh could be divided into two ethnic groups—English-speaking-Welsh and Welsh-speaking-Welsh. EAT allowed the employers' appeal.

Gwynedd County Council v *Jones and another* [1986] ICR 833

Sir Ralph Kilner Brown

. . . it was wrong in law to use the language factor alone and in isolation as creating a racial group. Even if . . . this approach is said to be a question of fact, the decision is wholly unreasonable . . . We cannot believe that, for example, a Mrs Jones from Holyhead who speaks Welsh as well as English is to be regarded as belonging to a different racial group from her dear friend, a Mrs Thomas from Colwyn Bay who speaks only English. This concept seems to us to be as artificial as the proposition that 5,000 or so spectators at Cardiff Arms Park who are fluent in Welsh are a different racial group from the 45,000 or so whose command

---

[16] Justification would have to relate to operational needs of the business—see *Greater Manchester Police Authority* v *Lea* [1990] IRLR 372, discussed in Chapter 2.

[17] Justification is not difficult in this area—In *Groener* v *Minister for Education* Case 397/87 [1989] 2 ECR 3967 the ECJ permitted the imposition of an Irish language requirement in a teaching job in which it was not required in practice, although there it was because the language had constitutionally guaranteed official status. For discussion of this see McLeod cited above.

[18] As we saw in Chapter 2 Art 39 does not apply in "wholly internal" situations and could protect nationals from discrimination within their Member State only to the extent that, as in *Knorrs* Case C–115/78 [1979] ECR 399, some external element was present.

of the Welsh tongue is limited to the rendering of the Welsh national anthem, or "Sospan fach". An Englishman who dared to suggest this would be in danger of his life!

Wilson McLeod, "Autochthonous language communities and the Race Relations Act" (1998)
Web Journal of Current Legal Issues **Issue 1**

How are Gaelic speakers in Scotland and Welsh speakers in Wales to be classified within the framework of the [RRA], and how are their rights—if any—to be measured against those of other protected groups?

These questions have scarcely been considered at all by industrial tribunals or by the courts, and the little treatment they have received has been problematic and unsatisfactory . . . The analysis in *Jones* was superficial, indeed cryptic, and a range of important sociological and legal questions were ignored. These questions have become all the more critical in light of changing policies and increasing attention at the UK and European levels to the rights and needs of autochthonous linguistic groups. If carefully and sensitively construed, the RRA may serve as a mechanism to reinforce these policies and solidify the position of the autochthonous languages . . .

the critical question with respect to the Gaels and to Welsh speakers must be whether they properly constitute an "ethnic group"—"a group of persons defined by reference to . . . ethnic origins"—since it would seem clear that none of the other enumerated categories applies . . .

Although Lord Fraser's speech in *Mandla* emphasised the need to construe the word "ethnic" "relatively widely, in a broad, cultural/historic sense," his initial observation that "the word "ethnic" still retains a racial flavour" . . . has received undue emphasis in subsequent decisions. . . [citing *Dawkins* and *Boyce*] . . .

In concluding that English-monoglot Welsh people did not constitute a protected racial group, the EAT [in *Jones*] adopted a view of the Welsh as an undifferentiated unit and thus implicitly determined that Welsh speakers were also not a protected group. Noting the criteria identified in *Mandla*, *Jones* opined that language, standing alone, is not an essential factor in the determination, and that the analytic emphasis should be on the combination of factors. . .

Although its decision may ultimately have been correct in light of the overall position of the Welsh language in Wales and the nature of the Welsh-speaking community, the EAT in *Jones* clearly failed to consider the question with any serious analysis. Language cannot properly be considered something that stands alone; in particular, it very often tends to create among its speakers "a cultural tradition of [their] own" (*Mandla* . . .), and it is certainly arguable that such a distinct tradition can be discerned among Welsh speakers. It is unfortunate that the status of the Welsh language community was determined in this essentially negative context; a much more vigorous and culturally sensitive case could have been mounted within the *Mandla* framework if the question affirmatively presented had been the status of the Welsh-speaking minority community, rather than the English-monoglot majority.

The analysis in *Jones* was also distorted to some extent by the unhelpful terminology of the RRA, with its reliance on the term "racial group" as the unit of analytic currency. Although *Mandla* took the proper analytic approach and spoke of "ethnic groups"—the pertinent subset of the "racial group" under the statute—the EAT's reasoning in *Jones* seems to have been confused by the "racial group" terminology. The EAT's evident difficulty in seeing Welsh-speakers and English-monoglots as separate "racial groups" in the ordinary lay sense led it to explain its decision with peculiar images [Mrs Jones and Mrs Thomas] . . .

Although the principal factor differentiating the Gaels from other Scots is the use of the Gaelic language itself, it can well be argued that the language is actually the medium of a distinct and separate culture, manifested in a variety of ways including deep-rooted traditions of poetry, song and music, and unique forms of religious worship. To some extent at least, this distinctiveness extends to material existence as well, the present-day crofting communities remaining substantially different in their way of life from the highly urbanised Scottish mainstream. The claim of Gaelic speakers to recognition as an ethnic group is also strengthened by the fact that a very high proportion of Gaelic speakers, relative to the UK's other autochthonous language communities, are native speakers born and brought up in Gaelic-speaking communities in the Hebrides and West Highlands. It would be safe to say that at least 90% of Gaelic speakers come from such backgrounds, whereas the Welsh language community contains significant proportions of learners and non-traditional speakers. In the case of Gaelic, then, there is a very significant link between the ability to speak the language and a distinct culture and way of life, and the language is the badge of a community that has long been outside the societal mainstream.

Significantly from a legal standpoint, this "combination of shared customs, beliefs, traditions and characteristics" is largely "derived from a common . . . past", distinct from the social institutions and practices of Lowland Britain . . . Although Gaelic was once the language of almost all Scotland, language shift and cultural divergence began as early as 1100, and already by 1380 the Gaels were identified as an entirely distinct and separate group. Marginalised by geography and outsiders" hostility, the Gaels have without question emerged from a common history and experience not shared by others . . .

GENUINE OCCUPATIONAL QUALIFICATIONS AND OTHER EXCEPTIONS

S.8 RRA provides that the Act does not apply in respect of workers employed wholly or mainly outside Great Britain (this must now be read in the light of the *Bossa* case, discussed below). Seafarers recruited abroad are likewise denied the protection of the Act (s.9), as are non-resident workers who are subject to discrimination in relation to employment designed to provide skills which the worker "appears to the employer to intend to exercise wholly outside Great Britain" (s.6). The RRA does not apply in relation to employment in private households (save in respect of victimisation)[19], s.10 exempts from the Act discrimination in respect of partners in firms with less than six partners, and some exceptions are provided in respect of charities and sports (discussed in Chapter 4) and of positive action (discussed in Chapter 3).

The most significant exceptions provided to the RRA's prohibition of discrimination are found in ss.41 and 42, in s.75, and in the "genuine occupational qualifications" set out in s.5 and discussed below. S.75 RRA provides that:

[19] This exception was removed from the SDA as a result of *Commission v UK* Case C–165.82 [1983] ECR 3431.

(5) Nothing in this Act shall—

   (a) invalidate any rules (whether made before or after the passing of this Act) restricting employment in the service of the Crown or by any public body prescribed for the purposes of this subsection by regulations made by the Minister for the Civil Service to persons of particular birth, nationality, descent or residence.

This provision appears to be consistent with Article 39 of the Treaty Establishing the European Community whose prohibition of discrimination on grounds of nationality does not apply to employment "in the public service" (para 4). The Government has, nevertheless, agreed that civil service rules ought to be changed in order to allow non-EEA and non-Commonwealth citizens, who are currently ineligible for positions in that service, to be eligible and to minimise the number of posts reserved for UK nationals.[20]

> S 42. Nothing in [the RRA] shall render unlawful an act done for the purpose of safeguarding national security.

Prior to the implementation of the Race Relations (Amendment) Bill 1999 s.69 (2) RRA provides that a Ministerial certificate to the effect that "(a) any arrangements or conditions specified in the certificate were made, approved or imposed by a Minister of the Crown and were in operation at a time or throughout a period so specified; or (b) . . . an act specified in the certificate was done for the purpose of safeguarding national security, is to be regarded as conclusive evidence of the matters certified. The 1999 Bill, if passed in its present form, will append to s.42 the words "if the doing of the act was justified by that purpose" and will establish procedures for judicial decisions on justification. S.69(2) will be repealed and a new s.67A inserted:

   (1) Rules may make provision for enabling a court in which relevant proceedings have been brought, where it considers it expedient in the interests of national security-

      (a) to exclude from all or part of the proceedings-

         (i) the claimant;

         (ii) the claimant's representatives; or

         (iii) the assessors (if any) appointed by virtue of section 67(4);

      (b) to permit a claimant or representative who has been excluded to make a statement to the court before the commencement of the proceedings, or the part of the proceedings, from which he is excluded;

      (c) to take steps to keep secret all or part of the reasons for its decision in the proceedings.

   (2) The Attorney General or, in Scotland, the Advocate General for Scotland, may appoint a person to represent the interests of a claimant in, or in any part of, any proceedings from which the claimant and his representatives are excluded by virtue of subsection (1).

---

[20] Government Response to the CRE's *Reform of the Race Relations Act 1976* (1998), Home Office press release 219/99 14th July 1999 available at http://195.44.11.137/coi/ coipress.nsf.

(4) A person appointed under subsection (2) shall not be responsible to the person whose interests he is appointed to represent.

This amendment is necessary in order to give effect to the decision of the ECtHR in *Tinnelly & Sons Ltd and others and McElduff and others* v *United Kingdom*, discussed in Chapter 9, is modelled on the amended version of the FETO and is subject to the same criticisms made thereof. S.42 is of immensely wide reach, but, while the equivalent provision of the fair employment legislation (discussed in Chapter 9), has been relied on frequently in the courts, s.42 has been little used. Only one appellate decision has considered it, the question there being whether it could be relied upon by the Commonwealth of Australia in the British Courts. In *Yendall* v *Commonwealth of Australia* EAT 515/83 (unreported) 11th October 1984, the applicant's claim was dismissed on other grounds.

S 41(1) Nothing in [the RRA] shall render unlawful any act of discrimination done—
    (a) in pursuance of any enactment or order in Council; or
    (b) in pursuance of any instrument made under any enactment by a Minister of the Crown; or
    (c) in order to comply with any condition or requirement imposed by a Minister of the Crown (whether before or after the passing of this Act) by virtue of any enactment.
References in this subsection to an enactment, Order in Council or instrument include an enactment, Order in Council or instrument passed or made after the passing of this Act.
  (2) Nothing in [the RRA] shall render unlawful any act whereby a person discriminates against another on the basis of that other's nationality or place of ordinary residence or the length of time for which he has been present or resident in or outside the United Kingdom or an area within the United Kingdom, if that act is done—
    (a) in pursuance of any arrangements made (whether before or after the passing of this Act) by or with the approval of, or for the time being approved by, a Minister of the Crown or
    (b) in order to comply with any condition imposed (whether before or after the passing of this Act) by a Minister of the Crown.

In *Hampson* v *Department of Education and Science*, the House of Lords took a narrow approach to s.41 RRA. The appellant was a Hong Kong Chinese who was excluded from UK teaching positions by the Secretary of State's requirement that, in order to qualify for such posts, overseas-trained teachers had to have undertaken a teaching course over three consecutive years. The applicant's third year of training was completed eight years after the initial two-year course normal in Hong Kong. She had taught during the intervening years.

The Secretary of State's regulations were made under s. 27 of the Education Act 1980, which provided that:

The Secretary of State may by regulations make provision . . . for requiring teachers at schools . . . to possess such qualification as may be determined by or under the regulations . . .

Ms Hampson's indirect discrimination claim was rejected by an industrial tribunal on the grounds, *inter alia*, that s.41(1) applied. EAT ([1988] IRLR 87) upheld this conclusion and, in the alternative, ruled that any discrimination was justifiable in accordance with the approach taken by the Court of Appeal in *Ojutiku* v *Manpower Services Commission* [1982] IRLR 418. The Court of Appeal ([1990] 2 All ER 25, [1989] IRLR 69, [1989] ICR 179) swept away the *Ojutiku* test (this aspect of the decision is discussed in chapter 2), but upheld the tribunal and EAT on s.41. The House of Lords allowed Ms Hampson's appeal.

Hampson v Department of Education and Science [1991] 1 AC 171, [1990] 2 All ER 513, [1990] 3 WLR 43, [1990] ICR 511

Lord Lowry (who delivered the sole speech)

Balcombe LJ [who dissented in the Court of Appeal] framed the question clearly when, having summarised the respondent's point on s 41, he said . . .

> This argument, which succeeded below, is controvertible if the words "in pursuance of any instrument" are apt in their context to include, not only acts done in necessary performance of an express obligation contained in the instrument (the narrow construction) but also acts done in exercise of a power or discretion conferred by the instrument (the wide construction). Both constructions are possible . . . I accept that the wide construction is the more natural meaning of the words used. I turn, therefore, to consider whether there is anything in the context which leads to an indication that the narrow construction is here correct.

> My Lords, I shall have occasion to refer again to Balcombe LJ's judgment, with which on the s 41 point I completely agree . . .

> s 41 . . . introduces over a wide field . . . as exceptions to the [RRA's] general purpose of outlawing discrimination, five cases in which an act of discrimination shall not be unlawful and in each such case the relevant enactment, Order in Council, instrument, condition, requirement or arrangement may be either pre- or post-Act. In view of the wide sweep of these provisions, the exceptions ought therefore, I suggest, to be narrowly rather than widely construed where the language is susceptible of more than one meaning . . .

> It is . . . the consideration of the wider context that demonstrates the need to adopt the narrow construction of the words "in pursuance of", since the wide construction is seen to be irreconcilable with the purpose and meaning of the [RRA] . . .

> There is a sound argument, based on public policy, for drawing the line in this way. I refer to the need and the opportunity for parliamentary scrutiny . . . To adopt the Balcombe principle, if I may so describe it, will mean that racial discrimination is outlawed (or at least needs to be justified under s 1(1)(b)(ii)) unless it has been sanctioned by Parliament, whereas, if the respondent's argument were correct, a wide and undefined area of discrimination would exist, immune from challenge save, in very exceptional circumstances, through the medium of judicial review . . .

> To sum up, the majority in the Court of Appeal rejected the wide construction but did not

come down in favour of the narrow construction or, indeed, of any specific alternative interpretation of the words "in pursuance of". They appear, however, to have held that the Secretary of State acted, as no doubt he did, in pursuance of the 1982 regulations when he discharged the duty of considering and the further duty of deciding the appellant's application therefore, they held, his allegedly discriminatory act was protected by s 41(1)(b). It is this reasoning, my Lords, that did not commend itself to Balcombe LJ and that I find myself unable to accept. In my view it disregards, and has to disregard, the fact that, in order to decide the application one way or the other, the Secretary of State had first to set up and apply a non-statutory criterion, the setting up and application of which involved the exercise of his administrative discretion and led to the discriminatory act complained of.

What I would venture to describe as the fallacy of that approach can be recognised when one reflects that almost every discretionary decision, such as that which is involved in the appointment, promotion and dismissal of individuals in, say, local government, the police, the national health service and the public sector of the teaching profession, is taken against a statutory background which imposes a duty on someone, just as the 1982 regulations imposed a duty on the Secretary of State. It seems to me that to apply the reasoning of the majority here to the decisions I have mentioned would give them the protection of s 4 and thereby achieve results which no member of the Court of Appeal would be likely to have thought acceptable.

It is clear from the *Hampson* extract that the scope of s.41 is quite narrow. Having said this, in combination with the decision in *Amin* v *Entry Clearance Officer, Bombay* [1983] 2 AC 818, [1983] 2 All ER 864 [1983] 3 WLR 258, discussed in Chapter 4, it has, at least prior to the enactment of the RR(A) B 1999, served to exclude the entire area of social security from the provisions of the RRA. This exclusion is illustrated by the decision in *R* v *The Secretary of State for Social Services ex parte Nessa, The Times* 15th November 1994, in which the applicant unsuccessfully challenged, as contrary to the RRA, the refusal of a funeral grant in respect of the burial of her husband in Bangladesh.

The facts were similar to those in *O'Flynn* v *Adjudication Officer*, discussed in Chapter 2, save that the discrimination at issue did not fall within the prohibition on discrimination on grounds of nationality against citizens of EU Member States imposed by Article 39 of the Treaty Establishing the European Union.

R v *The Secretary of State for Social Services ex parte Nessa*, The Times, 15th November 1994

Auld J:

The [Social Security Administration Act, ss.167(1) and 138(1)] provided for the establishment of the "social fund" to enable payments to be made in prescribed circumstances for, *inter alia*, funeral expenses. The prescribed circumstances for a "funeral payment" are set out in the Social Fund Maternity and Funeral Expenses (General) Regulations 1987, Regulations . . . The amount of the payment, by Regulation 7(2), is that which is sufficient to meet, *inter alia*, the cost of necessary documentation, of an ordinary coffin and of transport of the coffin. One of the prescribed circumstances for payment, and the only one in issue here, is that . . . "the funeral takes place in the United Kingdom".

The applicant . . . arranged for [her husband's] body to be returned to Bangladesh for burial. She applied for a funeral payment to cover such of the funeral costs as were incurred in the United Kingdom. An adjudication officer, who under the Regulations determines such applications, refused her application because of the condition in reg 7(1)(c) that such payment can only be made where the funeral takes place in the United Kingdom.

Mr Drabble, on behalf of the applicant, maintained that reg 7(1)(c), in its prohibition of payment of any funeral expenses incurred in this country where the ultimate disposal of the body takes place abroad, discriminates against residents in this country of overseas origin. He submitted that, therefore, it is unlawful because it is contrary to s 20 of the [RRA]. Mr Drabble attacks the legality of the Regulation rather than the adjudication officer's act of refusal in compliance with it. He is bound to approach the matter in that way because of s 41 of the 1976 Act . . .

The decision of an adjudication officer refusing to make a funeral payment in accordance with reg 7(1)(c) is clearly protected by s 41(1)(a), since, if it was an act of discrimination, it was done "in pursuance of" the Regulation. See *Hampson* . . .

Mr Pannick challenged that approach by reference to s 75(1) of the [RRA] and the decision of the House of Lords in . . . *ex p Amin*. The ratio of the majority decision in *ex p Amin*, as Lord Fraser's words make plain . . . is that acts of a governmental nature, as distinct from those of a kind that may be done by a private person, are not the subject of control under the [RRA] . . .

Accordingly, in my judgment, the subject matter of the applicant's complaint, the making of reg 7(1)(c) of the 1987 Regulations, is not within the scope of s 20 of the 1976 Act, and the fact that the Secretary of State is also responsible for the making of the payments under the Regulations does not bring it within that scope . . .

The implementation of the RR(A)B will apply the prohibition on race discrimination to public authorities, thus reversing the effect of *Amin*. But the provisions of the RRA, even after amendment, will not apply (schedule 1 para 1(1)) to:

A Minister of the Crown or government department . . . in relation to any function of or relating to—
(a) making, confirming or approving Orders in Council and other instruments of a kind mentioned in section 41(1); or
(b) making or approving arrangements, or imposing requirements or conditions, of any kind mentioned in section 41.

The significance of this is discussed in Chapter 5 as is the potential impact of the new race discrimination directive.

Before we turn to the GOQ defence, s.8 of the Asylum and Immigration Act 1996 should be mentioned. It provides that it is an offence to employ someone "subject to immigration control" where ((1)(a)) that person has not been granted leave to enter or remain in the UK; ((1)(b)) that person's leave is either "no longer valid and subsisting" or is "subject to a condition precluding the taking up of employment". S.8(2) provides a defence to an employer who either retained "a document which appeared . . . to relate" to the worker (or a copy thereof), that document being one of several listed in the Immigration (Restrictions on Employment) Order 1996,[21] unless the employer knew that the employment was in breach of immigration law. A fine of up to £5000 may be imposed on offenders

S.8 has been widely criticised, not least because it is at once under- and over-inclusive:

Bernard Ryan, "Employer Enforcement of Immigration Law after S.8 of the Asylum and Immigration Act 1996" (1997) 26 *ILJ* **136, 140–1**

On the one hand, notwithstanding the comprehensiveness of the 1996 Order, some individuals may still find it difficult to prove their right to take up employment. It seems likely that most employers will give priority to the possession of a national insurance number as evidence of a right to work. National insurance numbers are issued automatically at sixteen to British residents in respect of whom child benefit has been claimed. But many individuals do not have a national insurance number when they first look for employment This category includes nationals of other states, British nationals who have lived abroad, British residents who reached sixteen before national insurance numbers were issued automatically, and others for whom child benefit has not been claimed. Until they acquire a national insurance number, the practical result of section 8 may be to make it harder for these individuals to find employment.

The possibility of forgery and personation will also pose problems for some job applicants. Employers may have genuine doubts as to validity of documents presented to them, especially those with which they are unfamiliar. They may also doubt that a document relates to the particular individual where, as with a birth certificate or document bearing a national insurance number, it does not contain a photograph. In such cases, employers may choose to reject the applicant or to request further information. As we have seen, they will be encouraged to do so by the exclusion of the statutory defence where the employer "knew" the employment was invalid. For this reason too, it seems likely that employer checks of immigration status will make it harder for some workers to prove their right to take up employment than others.

On the other hand, the comprehensiveness of the 1996 Order means that many individuals *without* a right to work will be able to produce one of the listed documents. In some circumstances, they may possess the document legitimately. For example, they may have a national insurance number even though they have no right to work, where they have worked on a work permit for a particular employer or have previously lived and worked in the United Kingdom. It was partly for this reason that, in the consultation paper which preceded the introduction of the employer offence, the Government admitted that national insurance numbers were "limited as an indicator of entitlement to work" (Home Office, *Prevention of Illegal Working: Consultation Document*, para 31—henceforth "*Consultation Document*"). Similarly, individuals may have a British birth certificate without British citizenship: since the coming into force of the section 1 of the British Nationality Act 1981 on 1 January 1983, children born in the United Kingdom acquire British citizenship only if they have a parent who is a British citizen or settled in the United Kingdom.

Alternatively, reliance upon one of the permitted documents may be entirely fraudulent. In particular, the absence of a photograph on birth certificates or on documents bearing national insurance numbers makes personation a substantial possibility. The possibility of

---

[21] SI 1996 No. 3225.

personation is itself enhanced by the existence of many unused national insurance numbers. (A Social Security Select Committee report in November 1995 found that there were up to 20 million more numbers in existence (over 65 million on one estimate) than the United Kingdom population over 16 (roughly 45 million): see *The Work of the Department of Social Security and its Agencies*, (1994–95) HC Papers 382, pp. ix–x.) Remarkably however the Home Office guidance to employers states that "you do not need to worry about whether National Insurance numbers are genuine or belong to the person if you have seen an appropriate document" (*Guidance*, p. 15). It may be thought surprising that a system which is supposed to discourage illegal working should leave open so many possibilities for it to occur.

Perhaps of more concern here is the potential for increased discrimination. The CRE argued that the section imposed on employers an immigration control function

which should rightly and properly be carried out by the [state, whose staff] are trained specifically to carry out this function and are publicly accountable for the performance of this duty. Individual employers . . . will not be accountable for their performance of their public control function . . . many employers are likely to avoid both the administrative burden of making checks and the risk of prosecution by simply not offering employment to any person whose immigration status might in their view be uncertain. This may include, for example, people with names which are not of UK origin; people of visible ethnic minority origin; and people with accents which identify them as being not of UK origin[22]

Ryan, (1997) 26 *ILJ*, 141–3

If Section 8 does make it harder for some workers to take up employment, then it is likely to have its greatest impact upon workers from abroad and from ethnic minorities. There is already substantial evidence of discrimination in the British labour market, with official surveys finding that workers from ethnic minorities have a significantly higher rate of unemployment than other workers at every level of qualifications. (See F. Sly, "Ethnic Groups and the Labour Market," *Employment Gazette*, May 1994, 147.) Against this background, it is not unreasonable to suspect that employer checks following section 8 will lead to greater discrimination. To quote from the Commission for Racial Equality's response to the *Consultation Document* which preceded the introduction of section 8, "an inevitable result will be the creation of additional barriers to the employment of people from ethnic minorities." . . .

Litigation on the application of equal treatment law to employer checks of immigration status is to be anticipated. It will raise difficult questions as to the definition of unlawful discrimination in this area. These are examined here by looking first at the implications for employer checks of the Race Relations Act 1976, which prohibits discrimination . . .

The coming into force of section 8 adds to the uncertainty as to the authority of *Dhatt*. If the Court of Appeal was correct to conclude [in *Dhatt*, Chapter 2] that it was not inherently discriminatory to treat EEC and non-EEC nationals differently, then its reasoning is strengthened by the distinction drawn in section 8 between "persons subject to immigration control," in relation to whom the offence may be committed, and others. Alternatively, if *Dhatt* was wrongly decided, and the result turns on section 41, then a court

---

[22] Reported in 66 *Equal Opportunities Review*, p.8 News.

might conclude that at least some discrimination against non-EEA job applicants has been made "necessary" by section 8. . . .

If *some* distinctions between job applicants are to be allowed, the question remains—which ones? The most straightforward case would be where an employer asked all applicants their nationality, and then required proof of a right to work only from those who did not declare an EEA nationality. That kind of distinction was permitted in *Dhatt*. It might also be defensible under section 41, in that there would be a broad correspondence between the offence in section 8 and the distinction drawn. But what if an employer questioned the nationality and immigration status of only the applicants about whom there were doubts? Or what if, having asked all applicants their nationality, the employer required proof of EEA nationality of only some applicants? In those circumstances, an employer would probably be distinguishing between applicants on the basis of their ethnic background, or accent, or possible nationality. That would be a prima facie case of discrimination—but one which might nevertheless be allowed under the *Dhatt* principle or the section 41 exception.

A second situation to examine under the Race Relations Act is where an employer declines to hire a worker because of doubts as to their immigration status. This was considered by the Scottish EAT in *Grampian Health Board v Cole* (unreported decision of 21 October 1985, summarised in *Industrial Relations Legal Information Bulletin* 382, August 1989, p. 9). That case concerned a South African national who was denied employment out of a mistaken belief that she would require a work permit. The industrial tribunal had held this to be direct discrimination under the Race Relations Act, and the result was accepted by the EAT.

The main issue is whether there are any limits to the principle. What if an employer refused to hire someone because of the difficulty of establishing that they had a right to work? Or what if, having investigated the applicant's status, the employer genuinely reached the wrong conclusion? Each of these outcomes would undermine an individual's right to work. Nevertheless, a court might decide that it was too much to require employers to have a full investigation, or to require them to reach the right answer in every case. This conclusion is supported in particular by the defence set out in section 8(2), which gives statutory recognition to the undesirability of imposing a strict requirement upon employers. Here too, it is possible that the impact of section 8 will be to weaken a claim of discrimination under the Race Relations Act.

The Better Regulation Task Force recommended the repeal of s.8 on the basis that it:

Has caused particular concerns in placing a blanket duty on all employers to identify job applicants who may be illegal immigrants. The problem of illegal working appears largely confined to racketeers operating in a few specific sectors but a lack of targeting has created the potential for well-intentioned employers across all employment sectors to discriminate against ethnic minority applicants.[23]

Somewhat surprisingly the Government, which had opposed s.8 in opposition, rejected the Task Force's recommendation:

---

[23] Better Regulation Task Force Report on anti-discrimination legislation, p.10, available on the BRTF website at http://www.cabinet-office.gov.uk/regulation/ ndex/task.htm.

Illegal working is a growing problem . . . Illegal employment leads not only to abuse of vulnerable employees who will not have the full protection of the law but also serves to deny job opportunities to those who are lawfully entitled to work here. . . controls on employers are needed . . . in order to deal with the problem comprehensively.

Experience suggests that Section 8 can be a valuable tool if targeted against unscrupulous or exploitative employers. Having looked very carefully at the way in which it is operating in practice, the Government has decided to retain Section 8 to test its effectiveness in dealing with those who are engaging in systematic abuse. The proposals . . . for a Statutory Code of Practice will increase safeguards against discrimination.

Turning, finally, to the RRA's GOQ defences; s.5 provides that the RRA's prohibitions on discrimination in relation to appointments, promotion, transfer or training do not apply where (s.5(1)(a)) "being of a particular racial group is a genuine occupational qualification for the job". S.5(2) goes on provide that a GOQ defence may apply only where:

(a) the job involves participation in a dramatic performance or other entertainment in a capacity for which a person of that racial group is required for reasons of authenticity; or

(b) the job involves participation as an artist's or photographic model in the production of a work of art, visual image or sequence of visual images for which a person of that racial group is required for reasons of authenticity; or

(c) the job involves working in a place where food or drink is (for payment or not) provided to and consumed by members of the public or a section of the public in a particular setting for which, in that job, a person of that racial group is required for reasons of authenticity; or

(d) the holder of the job provides persons of that racial group with personal services promoting their welfare, and those services can most effectively be provided by a person of that racial group.

SS. 5(3) and 5(4) are in similar terms to ss. 7(3) and 7(4) SDA, discussed in Chapter 6.

S.5(2)(a)–(c) have not really been litigated, though they are regarded as overly wide by the CRE which proposed in 1998 that they be replaced by a GOQ "where the employer can demonstrate that the racial group of the job-holder is an essential defining feature":

Return of the Race Relations Act 1976: Proposals for Change, Submitted by CRE to Jack Straw MP, Home Secretary, 30th April 1998

The current criterion of "authenticity" is too wide. It enables the unjustifiable underrepresentation of ethnic minorities in theatre, opera, cinema, television drama etc to continue indefinitely. The new formulation would enable actors to be selected on racial grounds where the race or colour of the character to be portrayed is central to the portrayal, for example to select a black actor to appear in a drama about Nelson Mandela, but would not enable only white actors to be recruited for a production of Hamlet. The Commission also advises that the criterion of racial "authenticity" should not be relevant to future employment patterns in the catering industry in Britain. The new formulation would also enable people to be selected on racial grounds where the purpose of the job is to test for racial discrimination, and for the tests to have validity it is essential to employ people from particular racial groups.

Subsection (d) provides that a genuine occupational qualification (GOQ) will apply where "the holder of the job provides persons of that racial group with personal services promoting their welfare, and those services can most effectively be provided by a person of that racial group". The interpretation of this section by the courts is discussed below.

Turning to the operation of s.5(2)(d), the leading case is *Lambeth London Borough Council v CRE* [1990] ICR 768, in which the CRE challenged advertisements placed by the Council which stipulated African-Caribbean or Asian applicants for jobs in the Council's housing department.[24] The advertisements were placed in line with the Council's policy of making the housing benefits system "more sensitive to the needs and experiences of black people" who, with Asians, comprised over 50% of Council tenants. In pursuit of this aim the Council had reserved two positions in the housing benefits section for black workers. A tribunal ruled that, the jobs being of a managerial or administrative nature involving limited contact with the public. they did not involve "personal services" and the Council, accordingly, had failed to make out the s.5(2)(d) defence. The tribunal further ruled that the racial groups of the post holder and the recipient of his services were not sufficiently identified so as to establish that the holder and the recipient were of the same racial group. Both EAT ([1989] ICR 641) and the Court of Appeal rejected the Council's appeal. Having rejected the idea that s.5(2) permitted positive discrimination, Balcombe LJ continued:

Lambeth London Borough Council v CRE [1990] ICR 768

The services provided by the local authority's housing benefits department undoubtedly promote the welfare of the recipients to those benefits, but the rest of the phrase is qualified by the word "personal." "Personal" is defined by the Oxford English Dictionary as "Of, pertaining to, concerning or affecting the individual or self (as opposed. variously, to other persons, the general community, etc . . .); individual; private; one's own."

The use of the word "personal" indicates that the identity of the giver and the recipient of the services is important. I agree with the appeal tribunal when they say that the Act appears to contemplate direct contact between the giver and the recipient—mainly face-to-face or where there could be susceptibility in personal, physical contact. Where language or a knowledge and understanding of cultural and religious background are of importance,

---

[24] S.63(2)(a) RRA gives the CRE the power to bring claims in respect of discriminatory advertisements, themselves prohibited under s 29 of the Act "[I]t is unlawful to publish or to cause to be published an advertisement which indicates, or might reasonably be understood as indicating, an intention by a person to do an act of discrimination, whether the doing of that act by him would be unlawful or, by virtue of Part II ["Discrimination in the Employment Field"] or III ["Discrimination in Other Fields"], unlawful". To this, there is an exception under subsection (2) if, inter alia, the intended act would be lawful by virtue of section 5 (which establishes the GOQs).

then those services may be most effectively provided by a person of a particular racial group . . .

the decision in any particular case whether the holder of a particular job provides persons of a particular group with personal services promoting their welfare is a question of mixed law and fact, and . . . unless the industrial tribunal have come to a decision which is wrong in law, neither the appeal tribunal nor this court can interfere. The industrial tribunal held that the holders of the jobs advertised, being managerial positions, did not provide personal services promoting the welfare of persons of a particular racial group. I can find no error of law in that decision. On this ground alone I would dismiss this appeal. . . .

If a person is providing persons of a racial group defined by colour (eg black people) with personal services promoting their welfare (eg a health visitor), it will be open to an industrial tribunal on the particular facts of the case to find that those services can be most effectively provided by a person of that colour, from whatever ethnic group she (or he) comes, and even though some of her (or his) clients may belong to other ethnic groups.[25]

The approach laid down by the Court of Appeal in *Lambeth* is narrow, but the approach to GOQs is wide in two respects, both of which are illustrated by *Tottenham Green Under Fives Centre* v *Marshall* [1989] IRLR 147, a decision approved by the Court of Appeal in the *Lambeth* case. The case involved a challenge brought by a white man to a GOQ put forward by a nursery which had advertised for an "Afro-Caribbean worker". The nursery had a policy of maintaining an ethnic balance both for children and for staff, but had four white, one Greek-Cypriot and one African-Caribbean worker. In addition to specifying racial group, the advertisement placed by the nursery stipulated that the applicant would need "a personal awareness of Afro-Caribbean culture" and "an understanding of the importance of anti-racist and anti-sexist child care". An industrial tribunal took the view, contrary to the nursery's contention, that the "personal services" exception would relate only to reading and talking where necessary in dialect and not, in addition, to maintaining the cultural background link for children of African-Caribbean background; dealing with the parents and discussing those matters with them and generally looking after their skin and health, including plaiting their hair. This decision rested on the finding that workers of other ethnic origins would be able to perform the same functions. EAT allowed the nursery's appeal on the grounds, *inter alia*, that s.5(2)(d) required only that the services at issue (*per* Wood J):

can most effectively be provided by a person of that racial group" [rather than that they] "can only be provided" [by that group]. The Act assumes that the personal services could be provided by others, but can they be "most effectively provided?" Would they be less effective if provided by others? Welfare of a child will include the broad understanding and handling of the child, and in the present circumstances an understanding of the background of the culture and the ways of the family. This issue is a matter of fact for the Tribunal, and in so deciding the Tribunal will need to carry out a delicate balancing exer-

---

[25] Mann LJ concurred on the basis that the question was one of fact for the tribunal, and Mustill LJ agreed with both judgments.

cise bearing in mind the need to guard against discrimination, and the desirability of promoting racial integration. However, it seems to us that if a Tribunal accepts that the conscious decision of a responsible employer to commit an act of discrimination and to rely upon s 5(2)(d) is founded upon a genuinely held and reasonably based opinion that a genuine occupational requirement will best promote the welfare of the recipient, then considerable weight should be given to that decision when reaching a conclusion whether or not the defence succeeds.

The tribunal reached a second decision unfavourable to the nursery, which again resulted in a successful appeal to EAT (*Tottenham Green Under Fives' Centre* v *Marshall (No 2)* [1991] ICR 320, [1991] IRLR 162). The issue this time related to s.5(3), the tribunal having rejected the s.5 defence on the grounds that the reading requirement was "the least emphasised of the four" and was "in the nature of a desirable extra and no more".

Knox J [26]

The issue before us . . . is: whether it is open to an Industrial Tribunal to disregard a duty in coming to the conclusion that it does not figure for the purposes of deciding whether s 5(2)(d) applies. One can set on one side two particular categories which it was common ground between the parties did not apply in this case . . . The first of those two categories is what lawyers call matters which are *de mirimis* . . . The other category which would clearly very properly be disregarded in any case, is one where the duty in question is included as a sham or a smokescreen to avoid the requirement that there should be no racial discrimination or indeed for any other purposes. It is common ground that this is not relevant in this particular case . . .

What remains is a relatively unimportant but not trivial duty and we have reached the conclusion that it is not the correct view of the meaning of this paragraph that the Industrial Tribunal can make an evaluation of the importance of the duty in question and disregard it although it is satisfied that it is something that is not so trivial that it can properly be disregarded altogether. It seems to us that subsection (3) indicates clearly that one of the duties of the job

if it falls within any of the relevant paragraphs, in our case paragraph (d) of the preceding subsection, will operate to make the exception available. That is what one can discern that Parliament intended to provide.

---

[26] Citing in support *Timex Corporation* v *Hodgson* [1981] IRLR 530.

8

The Disability Discrimination Act

DISABILITY AND DISADVANTAGE

According to the Department of Education and Employment (DfEE) Disability Briefing (November 1999):

- Disabled people account for nearly a fifth of the working-age population in Great Britain, but for only about one eighth of all in employment. There are over 6.5 million people with a current long-term disability or health problem which has a substantial adverse impact on their day-to-day activities or limits the work they can do.
- The level of disability increases with age: only 11% of those aged 20–29 years have a current long-term disability or health problem compared with 31% of those aged 50–59 years . . .
- Disabled people are over six times as likely as non-disabled people to be out of work and claiming benefits. There are over 2.6 million disabled people out of work and on benefits: over a million of them want to work . . .
- Disabled people are more than twice as likely as non-disabled people to have no qualifications.
- Disabled people are only half as likely as non-disabled people to be in employment. There are currently around 3.1 million disabled people in employment; they make up 12% of all people in employment. When employed, they are more likely to work part-time or be self-employed.[1]
- Around three quarters of those with mental illness and two thirds of those with learning difficulties are out of work and on state benefits.
- ILO unemployment rates for long-term disabled people are nearly twice as high as those for non-disabled people, 10.1% compared with 5.7%. Their likelihood to be long-term unemployed is also higher: 38% of unemployed disabled people have been unemployed for a year or more compared with 24% of non-disabled unemployed.

Of the long-term disabled analysed by the DfEE, 19 % (the largest group) had back or neck trouble, 14% chest or breathing difficulties, 11% each problems with legs and feet or heart and blood pressure, 8% mental illness, 6% problems with hands or arms, 5% problems with stomach, liver, kidney or digestion, 5% diabetes and 2% each learning difficulties, epilepsy, skin or allergy, sight and hearing problems. It is one of the

[1] Employment rates vary greatly between types of disability. Some types of disability are associated with relatively high employment rates (such as diabetes, skin conditions and hearing problems) while other groups (such as those with mental illness and learning disabilities) have much lower employment rates.

disability community's messages that the picture of the disabled person as wheelchair bound is inaccurate.

TUC, *Civil Rights or a Discriminating Law?* (1996)

Sixty-nine per cent of adult disabled people are unemployed . . . Employers are six times more likely to turn down a disabled person for interview than a non-disabled applicant with the same qualifications.

Most public transport is inaccessible:

—Only one in eight long-distance National Express coaches is accessible.

—Only 130 British Rail stations are fully accessible.

—Wheelchair users wishing to use the London Underground are advised to give 24 hours' notice of their intention to travel, to go with a non-disabled companion and to avoid the rush hour.

—There are 4–5 million people with mobility impairments but only 80,000 accessible houses.

—Public information is rarely given in ways that are accessible to people with sensory impairments and to people with learning difficulties.

Public meetings and TV are rarely accessible to Deaf people.

Because of lack of information, based on figures for October 1992, the proportion of Deaf people who have died of AIDS-related illnesses is one in 3,200, compared to one in 68,000 of the total population.

Shops, pubs, restaurants, theatres, cinemas, sports stadia, town halls, law courts and churches are inaccessible to many disabled people.

If disabled people cost more than £500 a week to support, they are forced into institutions.

At the last general election, 88 per cent of polling stations were inaccessible to disabled people . . .

Some of the problems faced by the disabled (in particular, unequal access to employment) bear some similarities to the difficulties encountered by women and ethnic minority groups. But the attempt to provide equality for the disabled is immensely more complicated, in legal terms, than is the case with gender, race or, in Northern Ireland, religion and political opinion. This complexity arises both in the concept of "equality" and in the nature of its absence.

The debates about sex and race equality have, to a very significant extent, been shaped by a notion of formal equality which, concerned as it is with treating like alike, has resulted in a failure fully to grapple with the accommodation of difference. This has been seen particularly in the pregnancy-as-sex discrimination saga (Chapter 6) and, more generally, in the integration of work with (at present predominantly female) family responsibilities. Both the SDA and the RRA prohibit unjustified "indirect discrimination", which concept has the potential to promote substantive equality by requiring the removal of rules, etc., which serve to disadvantage particular genders or racial groups, by reason of characteristics common to that gender or group. But indirect discrimination has been dogged by the rigidity of its legislative expression (see

Chapter 2) and by the reluctance of the courts to challenge (through the concept of justification) the white maleness of the stereotypical worker. Thus, for example, indirectly discriminatory policies and practices have not been capable of challenge under the RRA (or, arguably, the SDA[2]) unless they amounted to "complete bars", and managers retain a wide measure of discretion to organise their affairs as they see fit, despite thereby subjecting non-white, non-male workers (and would-be workers) to disadvantage.[3]

The difficulty, in the context of race and sex discrimination, is that ethnic minority men and (in decreasing degree) white and ethnic minority women appear, in many respects, to be similar to white men. Such differences as there are tend (save in the case of pregnancy) to be social or cultural, rather than physical. This has the effect that these differences (whether they involve responsibility for childcare, elder-care or religious observance) are regarded, to a degree, as being questions of choice. Thus, for example, in *Clymo v Wandsworth London Borough Council* [1989] ICR 250 [1989] IRLR 241 and in *Stevens v Katherine Lady Berkeley's School* EAT/330/97 (unreported, 15th January 1998), (both discussed in Chapter 2), women's decisions that they were unable to combine new motherhood with full-time work were regarded as matters of their free choice. Even where (as is more common) this view is not expressly taken, the justification of indirect discrimination can be a relatively easy matter (see, for example, *Greater Glasgow Health Board v Carey*, *Briggs v North Eastern Education and Library Board*, *Eley v Huntleigh Diagnostics Ltd*, *Nelson v Chesterfield Law Centre*, *Panesar v Nestle Co Ltd* and *Kang v R F Brookes Ltd* all discussed in Chapter 2).[4]

In the case of disability, adherence to a formal equality approach is untenable. Part of the difficulties faced by the disabled is the result of stereotyping by the able-bodied (the "does he take sugar?" approach frequently cited by wheelchair users). In this context the prohibition of direct discrimination against real or perceived disability will, properly enforced, be effective in promoting equality. But much of the difficulty faced by disabled people relates to their denial of access to a world shaped for the able-bodied (a point taken up below in the context of the medical model/ social model debate). Without the imposition of a duty to accommodate the needs of disabled people, any formal guarantee of equality would be a cynical exercise.[5]

The DDA does away with the concept of indirect discrimination, but adopts a wider definition of (direct) discrimination than that in the RRA or the SDA. The DDA

[2] Subject to the requirements of EC law, see *Perera v (1) The Civil Service Commission (2) The Department of Customs and Excise* [1983] IRLR 166, [1983] ICR 428 and *Falkirk Council v Whyte* [1997] IRLR 560, discussed in Chapter 2. For the impending changes to the RRA in this respect see Chapters 2 and 7.

[3] See, for example, *Panesar v Nestle Co Ltd* [1980] ICR 144, [1980] IRLR 64, *Eley v Huntleigh Diagnostics Ltd*, EAT/1441/96 (unreported, 1st December 1997), discussed in Chapter 2.

[4] Respectively, [1987] 1 AC 224; [1990] IRLR 181; EAT/1441/96, unreported; EAT/1359/95, unreported; [1980] ICR 144; (1999) 40 EORDCLD, p. 2.

[5] This is not to say that formal equality is not also important. The mentally ill, in particular, face enormous stigma discrimination. 71 *Equal Opportunities Review*, 7 cites a MIND survey which found that almost 40% had been harassed and one third dismissed or forced to resign. 40% had been denied jobs because of their history and over half concealed their history of mental illness.

defines discrimination as less favourable and unjustified treatment *"for a reason which relates to the disabled person's disability"*, as distinct from less favourable treatment "on the grounds of . . . sex"/ "on racial grounds". The Act also imposes (save in the context of housing) a duty of reasonable adjustment, defining discrimination to include the unjustified failure to comply with such a duty.

The second very significant issue about disability is the sheer scope of the inequality experienced by the disability community. Race discrimination permeates the workplace, the police, the criminal justice system, housing, immigration and education (this list does not purport to be comprehensive). Sex discrimination is felt also in the workplace, in social security arrangements and (in its indirect form) in the crippling impact of motherhood on women's lifetime earnings. But, whereas some people with disabilities (such as, for example, heart disease in middle age) lead relatively affluent lives, many others are denied access not only to work but also to education, housing, transport, healthcare and every other aspect of normal life.

The Disability Rights Task Force, which was established in 1997 to "to look at the full range of issues that affect disabled people's lives and to advise the Government on what further action it should take to promote comprehensive and enforceable civil rights for disabled people", drew attention to the weight of discrimination against some members of the disability community. Among the case studies included by the Task Force in its final report, *From Exclusion to Inclusion*, were the following:

> A company director with spinal muscular atrophy . . . was admitted to hospital with a chest infection. To her horror she found a doctor had placed a "Do Not Resuscitate" notice on her medical notes because it was considered that her quality of life did not warrant such intervention.[6]

> An adult man and woman who lived in a residential care home were prevented by staff from becoming engaged to marry and denied the privacy to form a close and loving relationship. The staff refused to take them to a jeweller's shop to buy a ring and used various methods to keep the couple apart. After three years, the couple persuaded some friends outside of the home to help them leave for a day; they married in a registry office in 1997. They are now in a supported living flat, employing personal assistants.

The Task Force also cited Department of Health statistics showing that "[p]eople with schizophrenia have standardised mortality ratios two and a half times the national average". "One reason for this is that they often receive late, or inadequate, physical investigations. The complaints of psychiatric service users are all too readily put down to their anxiety, or delusions, or other psychiatric symptoms". People with disabilities frequently find themselves under significant pressure not to reproduce and, in the event of having children, some have to work hard to counter the presumption that their parenting skills will be inadequate.

---

[6] Available at http://www.disability.gov.uk/.

SCOPE OF THE DDA

It is clear from the above both that disability affects a considerable number of people in the UK and that its impact on employment and other areas of life is significant. Yet the passage of legislation in this area required a prolonged battle.

In 1982 Peter Large's Committee of Inquiry into Restrictions Against Disabled People (CORAD), "stressed and documented the urgent need to make unjustified discrimination unlawful by means of a commission with powers and duties to conciliate and, where necessary, to take enforcement action".[7] The then Conservative government took the view that "education and persuasion" were preferable to legislation, a view that persisted through thirteen successive attempts to introduce backbench disability rights legislation in the House of Commons.

Alf Morris MP (now Lord Morris) introduced the Civil Rights (Disabled Persons) Bill in November 1991, this Bill being blocked then and in three successive years when it was introduced by Roger Berry and Harry Barnes MP. In 1994–5 the Bill achieved an almost unopposed second reading, at which stage the government was "shamed into introducing their own Bill".[8] The much more radical Civil Rights Bill was talked out.

Given the background to the DDA it was not surprising that the DDA was not as ambitious a piece of legislation as had been the SDA and the RRA in their time. The Act, characterised by Brian Doyle as "at best, half measures and reluctant reform was". He pointed out that, " within a few months of [its] Royal Assent, [the] same government was voicing its opposition to the extension of disability rights across the European Union where the DDA ... has been viewed with great interest".[9] The Treaty of Amsterdam, agreed after the election in the UK of the (New) Labour Government, gave the EU competence in the area of disability discrimination for the first time (see Chapter 1) and the Commission's draft directive on establishing a general framework for equal treatment in employment and occupation includes disability as a head of prohibited discrimination.

The DDA was passed in 1995. Its employment-related provisions came into effect in December 1996 but its implementation in the non-employment field will not be complete until 2004. The prohibition on direct discrimination in relation to goods and services was brought into effect in December 1996 but the duty to make reasonable adjustments in this area (see below) did not begin to bite until October 1999 and will not operate fully for a further five years.

---

[7] Lord Morris of Manchester (who, in 1979, had as Minister for the Disabled set up the inquiry) speaking in the House of Lords Second Reading of the Disability Rights Commission Bill, 17th December 1998, col 1475, available at http://www.publications. parliament.uk/pa/ld/ldhansrd.htm.

[8] *Ibid*

[9] B. Doyle, Enabling Legislation or Dissembling Law? The Disability Discrimination Act 1995 (1997) *Modern Law Review* 64, pp. 64–5 and 78.

   Unlike the SDA, RRA and FETO, the DDA prohibits only direct, rather than indirect, discrimination,[10] although this has been balanced by the duties of reasonable adjustment it imposes. Again by contrast with the position under the other legislation, direct discrimination may be justified under the DDA. The Act applies only to those employers having at least 15 employees (prior to the end of 1998, this figure was 20). Finally, whereas the EOC and CRE respectively were established by the SDA and the RRA respectively, the DDA provided only for the establishment of a National Disability Council which, unlike the EOC and CRE, had an advisory capacity only. Even this was limited, until mid-1998, to the non-employment area.

   The failure of the DDA to establish a commission has been put right by the Disability Rights Commission Act 1999, which establishes the DRC from early 2000. We saw in Chapter 5 that, although similar to those of the CRE and the EOC, the DRC's powers have been altered slightly from those of the older commissions in order to avoid a number of shortcomings. In Northern Ireland, the Disability Council was subsumed within the new Equality Commission (discussed in Chapters 5 & 9) in August 1999.

   The scope of the DDA is similar to that of the SDA and the RRA, and was discussed in Chapter 4. The only distinctions to note here are its non-application to barristers, advocates, firefighters and the military, and to employment in the police force or prison service.

   The exclusion of small employers from the scope of the DDA has been severely criticised (nine out of ten employers are exempt from the provisions of the DDA, and 25% of employees are denied its protection[11]). The legislation itself permits the Minister to reduce the threshold to a minimum of two employees and it was widely expected that the review announced in December 1997 by Alan Howarth MP, then the responsible Minister, would result in a very substantial reduction.[12] The Labour Party, in opposition, had resisted the imposition of thresholds for application of the Act. But Howarth was replaced as Minister for Employment and Equal Opportunities by Margaret Hodge in 1998 and it was she who announced the 15 employee threshold, defending it on the basis that:

> There is not a body of evidence out there . . . which demonstrates to employers that there will not be a hefty cost to them of employing disabled people [[13]] . . . I have asked officials here to assemble that evidence, so that we can start to challenge the suspicion and fear that does exist among employers.[14]

---

   [10] The Berry Bill also prohibited indirect discrimination. The then-Government took the view that the variety of disability made adverse impact too difficult to assess.

   [11] Prior to the change, 95% of employers were exempt from the provisions of the Act.

   [12] *Times* 9th September 1998, *Guardian* 4th November 1998.

   [13] According to the *Times*, *ibid*, "the Government's own figures' put the cost of lowering the threshold to two employees at £6.88 per employee.

   [14] *Guardian* 4th November 1998. On the government's figures the reduction to 15 covered an additional 60,000 disabled employees. Had the limit been reduced to 10, 5 or 2 (the other options consulted upon by *The Employment Provisions and Small Employers—a Review* (DfEE), an additional 130,000, 280,000 and

This approach has been criticised by disability rights activists.[15] Lord Ashley (formerly Jack Ashley MP, a long-time campaigner for the disabled) described the lowering of the threshold as "a minuscule improvement" and criticised Hodge for pandering to the fears of employers:

> When Hodge made the very limited change, she was at pains to reassure the firms that they had nothing to fear since the act required them only to make "reasonable adjustments" which, she said, "are generally low" . . .
> It was because these facts were generally known among the disability lobby that campaigners fully expected the number of exempted companies to be reduced almost to zero . . .
> The Employers' Forum on Disability pointedly said: "(We) can see no logical reason why small firms should be exempt from any aspect of the act." The decision was particularly ironic because she stood political logic on its head. She claimed she preferred to overcome the prejudices of small firms through education and persuasion. This is precisely the argument used by the Tories when they were trying to stop the legislation.
> Labour, the All-Party Disablement Group and disability organisations all argued then that legislation needs to be accompanied by education and persuasion, but that legislation is essential. We now have the legislation but Hodge maintains the exemption of most employers and goes back to education and persuasion!
> Regrettably, this decision has sent a damaging signal to 92.5 per cent of British companies—no matter how blatantly you discriminate in the workplace, it will be perfectly legal. Is it really too much to hope that those who work in small firms will have the same protection against discrimination as those in large ones? . . .
> What is required is an act of political will to give the protection of the law to all disabled workers, irrespective of the size of their firms.[16]

More recently, the Better Regulation and Disability Rights Task Forces[17] have recommended the removal of the small employer exemption which, according to the latter, serves to deny the protection of the DDA to almost a third of a million disabled employees.[18]

380,000 disabled employees would have been protected—78 *Equal Opportunities Review*, p. 3 (in addition to the 1.3 million currently protected).

[15] *The Times*, fn 12 above, reported complaints that the review was "piffling and pathetic", and "derisory".

[16] *Guardian* 14th October 1998.

[17] The latter task force was established by the Government "to advise Government on improving the quality of government regulation". For the Task Forces' reports see, respectively, fn 6 above and http://www.cabinet-office.gov.uk/regulation/index.htm.

[18] Fn 6 above, Chapter 5, para 21. The Government has also been criticised for its opposition to Lord Ashley's Private Member's Bill seeking to safeguard community care services for the disabled, for its failure to carry through its support in opposition for an ex-services unit and for its failures to tackle discrimination against the disabled in connection with building society sell-offs and housing renovated or built by money released from the same of council houses—*Guardian* 23rd July 1997.

"DISABILITY"

S.1(1) DDA provides that "[s]ubject to the provisions of Schedule 1, a person has a disability for the purposes of this Act if he has a physical or mental impairment which has a substantial and long-term adverse effect on his ability to carry out normal day-to-day activities."[19] Section 2 states that the Act applies equally to "a person who *has had* a disability (my emphasis), but not to someone who will have one in the future. It is, in every case, for the complainant to establish that s/he has or had a disability.

The model of disability adopted by the DDA is a medical, rather than a social, one. The "social" model of disability recognises "the close connection between the limitation experienced by individuals with disabilities, the design and structure of their environments and the attitude of the general population".[20] The "medical model", by contrast, locates the problem of disability in the disabled person, regarding disability as an individual impairment.

The medical approach to disability rights has long been criticised by the disability community. Anne Begg MP expressed a common view in the House of Commons Second Reading debate on the Disability Rights Commission Act:

> It's not my disability that stops me playing an equal part in society, it's the fact that some people put steps in buildings that I can't get into. I have no limitations in what I can do in a fully accessible building . . . It is society that has built the physical barriers and it is people in society who have the attitudes that cause the problem—not the disability.

That this approach to disability is not shared by the present government, any more than it was by its successors, was made clear by Margaret Hodge in an article for the Newcastle *Journal*. The newspaper had published criticism by a disability activist of the a government disability awareness campaign:

> disability is not about victims, tragedy or understanding the person—feeling sorry for someone does not make public transport become magically accessible overnight. Being patronising towards people does not remove physical barriers to allow access to facilities, services or leisure activities . . . Understanding how difficult it must be and then moving away to get on with life does not ensure that housing providers design and build with access in mind or grant access to mainstream education. . . .

What is increasingly apparent is the gulf between the disability movement's definition of disability . . . the social model, and that of the policy makers [the medical model]. The social model identifies social barriers and the infrastructure of society as the cause of disability; preventing participation on equal terms and denying equality

---

[19] S.1(2) "In this Act "disabled person" means a person who has a disability".

[20] See United Nations Standard Rules on the Equalization of Opportunities for Persons with Disabilities, para 5, cited by B. Doyle, Disabled Workers" Rights, the Disability Discrimination Act and the UN Standard Rules (1996) 25 *ILJ* 1, 11.

of opportunity. The medical model refers solely to a physical condition or impairment.[21]

Margaret Hodge's response was to "wonder how men and women in the North-East understand the accusation that disability is their problem. That the shopper in the MetroCentre is somehow responsible for oppressing disabled people".

Even as a medical model of disability, the approach taken by the DDA is very narrow, excluding protection on grounds of *perceived*, rather than *actual* disability,[22] and adopting a functional approach which requires actual, substantial, impairment in relation to normal, day-to-day activities. This latter aspect of the DDA echoes the approach taken by the Americans with Disabilities Act 1990, upon which the DDA is modelled in many respects. The ADA prohibits discrimination against those who are "disabled" in the sense that they have: (a) a physical or mental impairment that substantially limits one or more of the[ir] major life activities . . . or (b) a record of having such an impairment; or (c) [that they are] . . . regarded as having such an impairment".

As we shall see below, the ADA's requirement for substantial limitation of major life activities renders its protection less comprehensive than that provided by Australia's Disability Discrimination Act 1992, whose definition is satisfied by:

(a) total or partial loss of the person's bodily or mental functions; or
(b) total or partial loss of a part of the body; or
(c) the presence in the body of organisms causing . . .; or
(d) . . . capable of causing disease or illness; or
(e) the malfunction, malformation or disfigurement of a part of the person's body; or
(f) a disorder or malfunction that results in the person learning differently from a person without the disorder or malfunction; or
(g) a disorder, illness or disease that affects a person's thought processes, perception of reality, emotions or judgement or that results in disturbed behaviour.

The Australian definition of "disability" requires no limitation of activities (as in the case of the ADA) or "effect on" the disabled person"s "ability to carry out . . . activities" (as is required by the DDA 1995) over and above the medical conditions listed.

M. McDonagh, "Disability Discrimination in Australia", in G. Quinn, M. McDonagh and C. Kimber (eds.), *Disability Discrimination Law in the US, Australia & Canada* (Oak Tree Press, Dublin, 1993) p. 128

The definition of disability in the [Australian] DDA follows closely the recommendations of the HREOC's (Human Rights & Equal Opportunities Commissions) Draft Position

[21] D. Wood "Initially, New Labour seemed willing to dismantle much of what they inherited from the Tories, and was keen to promote the concept of active citizenship and equality of opportunity. One example of this was indicated in their manifesto, heralded by the promise of "comprehensive and enforceable civil rights" for disabled people"—*The Journal* (Newcastle, UK) 21st June 1999.
[22] This omission was quite deliberate, the government of the day resisting every attempt to amend the Bill to include perceived disabilities—79 *Equal Opportunities Review*, Interpreting the DDA—Part 1, p.17.

Paper. It is interesting to note therefore that the HREOC in that document expressly rejected the definition of disability set out in the . . . (ADA).

The HREOC argued that the requirement that a person's impairment substantially limits major life activities is a source of unnecessary legal difficulties or complexities. In particular, it saw such a definition as posing difficulties for people whose condition has disabling effects only intermittently rather than continuously or whose condition is controlled by medication and/or other treatments (for example many people with epilepsy, some forms of mental illness or asthma). In addition there are those people whose disability relates to physical disfigurement, rather than loss of any functional capacity and who are not limited in any major life activities but who are nonetheless discriminated against because of prejudice. Finally, there are people who have overcome any loss of capacity (through their own efforts, with or without any assistance and the use of aids or appliances), for example, many hearing impaired people who would deny that they are limited in their ability to lead a full and active life, other than by prejudice and discrimination. As the HREOC argues "the need for protection against discrimination does not disappear as a person becomes more able to participate in the community". Apart from the legal difficulties raised by such definitions, it is also questionable whether a person in seeking the assistance of anti-discrimination law in asserting their ability and entitlement to participate equally may paradoxically find it necessary to argue that their ability to participate fully is in fact limited by their impairment in order to qualify for the protection of the law.

Even the ADA definition of "disability" is wider than that adopted by the DDA 1995, extending as it does to *perceived* rather than actual disability (this is further discussed below) and accepting as "inherently substantially limiting" HIV infection.[23] In the UK, by contrast, someone sacked because s/he is (or is thought to be) HIV positive, in circumstances where, as is usual, s/he is perfectly capable of living a normal life, is outside the protection of the Act. So, too, is someone dismissed because their employer (wrongly) regards their heart condition as disabling according to the definition adopted by the DDA. Employees are not protected either in the UK or in the US where a relatively minor medical condition has some real or perceived impact on their ability to do their particular job; or where their employer's pre-employment screening has disclosed a genetic predisposition to cancer or some other condition. Such screening, which was already used by 6% of US employers in 1997, is likely to become ever more common.

The *Independent on Sunday* 16th November 1997

Weeding out employees who are shown to have a predisposition to an illness associated with particular industrial conditions, such as asthma, eczema or cancer, could have a significant impact on insurance, compensation and re-recruitment costs, while testing potential employees for predispositions to conditions such as heart disease, cancer, arthritis or mental illness could reduce sickness absence costs, identify potential poor performers, prevent the drain of early retirements on pension funds, and reduce premiums on corporate health insurances. Some go as far as suggesting that employers might even find it useful to

---

[23] Guidance issued by the US Equal Employment Opportunity Commission, available at www.eeoc.gov.

know whether a potential recruit has a high risk of having a child with a serious genetic illness which could detract their attention, time and energy from work.

And even if the company you work for, or want to work for, isn't keen on genetic spying, insurance companies, who see genetics as another way to load the risk dice, are likely to start applying pressure, increasing premiums or refusing compensation claims to employers they see as neglecting to minimise health risks . . . employees have no legal right to refuse to take a genetic test, nor to claim discrimination or unfair dismissal as a result of refusing. And since taking a genetic test for any reason is now insurance-form declarable . . . the genetic test you have been forced to undergo in order to get a job could jeopardise your ability to secure life insurance, pension or a mortgage.[24]

In the UK, the Human Genetics Advisory Commission 1999 Report, *The Implications of Genetic Testing for Employment* reported that "with one exception [the Ministry of Defence[25]] employers in the UK are not currently using genetic test results" and that "[i]t will take major developments both in our understanding of common diseases and in genetic testing itself before genetic testing becomes a serious issue for employment practice".[26] The Report contrasted the position in the UK and Europe with the greater prevalence of testing in the US where:

In a competitive climate, employers will naturally be concerned to manage the cost of employment efficiently. They will wish to minimise absenteeism and are likely to be concerned about the cost of taking on an employee with an existing health problem (subject to the terms of the DDA), especially if it is a chronic disease leading to repeated periods of absence or incapacity . . . In view of the rapid pace of developments in human genetics and the possible development of cheaper multi-tests, it might become attractive for employers to make use of genetic test results to predict future health and illness in a cost effective way . . .

The current level of understanding of the implications of most genetic test results for future ill health is quite limited. Since many employees stay in a given job for relatively short times, it would not be reasonable to use this limited ability to predict future health for employment purposes. We note in particular the possibility that unfair discrimination (possibly leading to stigmatisation) might arise if employers use genetic test results for employee selection. We therefore conclude that it would not be acceptable for genetic test results to be used to exclude people from employment or advancement on the grounds that they have a predisposition to future ill health.

We note, however, that there are exceptional circumstances in which the use of genetic tests might be justified [screening for increased occupational risks "where there is strong evidence of a clear connection between the working environment and the development of

---

[24] 16th November 1997.
[25] The MOD tests for sickle cell disease and trait among applicants for air crew positions. According to the report "MoD reports that this is a common approach in military aviation medicine, which is designed to protect the individual and others from the potentially catastrophic effects of a sickling crisis provoked by low oxygen pressures in flight. Individuals with sickle cell trait, although generally asymptomatic, can develop symptoms of sickling if exposed to very low oxygen pressures. The real risk of sickle cell trait at altitude remains uncertain and the MoD is currently re-examining its policy on sickle cell trait screening for military aircrew training".
[26] Para 1, summary. Available from the HGAC site at http://www.dti.gov.uk/hgac/.

'a serious health' condition for which genetic testing can be conducted", the condition being one "for which the dangers cannot be eliminated or significantly reduced by reasonable measures taken by the employer to modify or respond to the environmental risks".[27]

HGAC went on to recommend that "if and when genetic testing in employment becomes a real possibility", individuals should not be required "to take a genetic test for employment purposes", or "to disclose the results of a previous genetic test unless there is clear evidence that the information it provides is needed to assess either current ability to perform a job safely or susceptibility to harm from doing a certain job". The Advisory Commission further recommended that "employers should offer a genetic test (where available) if it is known that a specific working environment or practice, while meeting health and safety requirements, might pose specific risks to individuals with particular genetic variations"; "[f]or certain jobs where issues of public safety arise . . . employer[s] should be able to refuse to employ . . . person[s] who refuse[ ] to take a relevant genetic test; and that "any genetic test used for employment purposes must be subject to assured levels of accuracy and reliability, reflecting best practice".

The Disability Rights Task Force's final report, *From Exclusion to Inclusion* (1999), recommended that the definition of "disability" be extended "to cover both people with HIV from diagnosis and cancer from when it has significant consequences on people's lives", and that the guidance on matters to be taken into account in determining questions relating to the definition of disability (below) should be improved and clarified.[28] It stated its concern that "rapid advances in this field should not leave the Government taking reactive, rather than proactive, action to protect people's civil rights" and suggested that "the DRC and the Equality Commission for Northern Ireland should work closely with the Government Department or Agency taking forward monitoring of this issue", but recommended that "[a]t this time, genetic predispositions to impairments should not be considered a disability under the DDA".[29] The Task Force suggested, however, that:

> [d]isability or disability-related questions before a job is offered should only be permitted in limited circumstances, such as where it is necessary to establish the need for a reasonable adjustment to the interview or selection process or thereafter to do the job and for certain monitoring purposes.[30]

The pressure for genetic testing of employees and others, when it does come, is likely to emanate from the insurance industry. The Association of British Insurers currently

---

[27] Citing *Genetic Screening—Ethical Issues*, Nuffield Council on Bioethics,1993.

[28] Though it did, in addition to the extensions mentioned above, recommend consultat[ion] on aspects of the DDA definition of disability with a view to ensuring an appropriate and comprehensive coverage of mental health conditions; consideration of extension to include " those with severe conditions which are not long-term, as can sometimes be the case with some heart attacks, strokes or depression" and the adoption of a presumption that blind/ partially sighted people fulfilled the definition of disabled.

[29] Fn 6 above, recommendation 3.10.

[30] Fn 6 above, recommendation 12.

bans its members from them requesting genetic tests from applicants for life assurance. But the Code is subject to annual revision and the Association is, according to a report in *Scotland on Sunday*, 4th June 2000, under pressure from members to change this rule. In addition, the Code requires disclosure of tests which have already been carried out if the insurer requests it, save in respect of mortgage-linked life assurance of no more than £100,000. The Alzheimer's Association has accused the insurance industry of breaching its terms (*Daily Telegraph*, 22nd April 2000) by requesting the disclosure of all medical tests in such cases.

Liberal Democrat health spokesman Nick Harvey has warned of a new "underclass" of people unable to get health or life insurance, mortgages, loans or jobs and thereby financially excluded from society'.[31] His Genetic Testing (Consent and Confidentiality) Bill, which was introduced in the Commons on 25th May 2000, is unlikely to become law and the Government has thus far failed to take action in line with the banning recommendation of the Human Genetics Advisory Commission. It has, however, established a Commission under Baroness Helena Kennedy QC to advise on the ethical and social implications of genetic testing. In April 2000, the German government declared its intention to ban compulsory genetic testing on staff and customers after insurers suggested that such testing could reduce insurance premiums. The US Government acted similarly in relation to Federal employees in February 2000.

Returning to consider that which is regulated by the DDA, s. 1 of the Act defines disability in terms of "physical or mental impairment which has a substantial and long-term adverse effect on [the person's] ability to carry out normal day-to-day activities."[32] Except in the case of severe disfigurement this requires (schedule 1) the impairment of "mobility; manual dexterity; physical co-ordination; continence; ability to lift, carry or otherwise move everyday objects; speech, hearing or eyesight; memory or ability to concentrate, learn or understand; or perception of the risk of physical danger".[33] The Secretary of State has issued guidance about the matters to be taken into account in determining whether an impairment has a substantial adverse effect on a person's ability to carry out normal day-to-day activities; and whether such an impairment has a long-term effect".[34] As is the case with statutory Codes of Practice issued by the discrimination commissions and other bodies, the provisions of the guidance must be taken into account, where they appear relevant, by any tribunal or court "which is determining . . . whether a person's impairment has a substantial and long-term adverse effect on his or her ability to carry out normal day-to-day activities" under s.1.

[31] Writing in the *Western Morning News* 30th May 2000.
[32] According to EAT in *Vicary* v *British Telecommunications plc* 41 EORDCLD, p.11, it is for the tribunal (rather than any medical witness) to decide what is a "normal day-to-day activity" and a substantial effect".
[33] Save that (Schedule 1, para 3,) a severe disfigurement is to be treated as having a substantial adverse effect on the person's ability to carry out normal day-to-day activities.
[34] *Guidance on matters to be taken into account in determining questions relating to the definition of disability*, Statutory Instrument No 1996/1996.

The guidance excludes from "impairment" within s.1 "addiction to or dependency on alcohol, nicotine, or any other [non-prescribed] substance",[35] although the results of such addiction (cirrhosis, emphysema, lung cancer, psychosis) are covered by the DDA. In excluding addictions the DDA takes a comparatively narrow approach to disability. In the US, although the ADA excludes current illegal drug users and "current" alcoholics, its provisions do protect non-using addicts.[36] In Canada, by contrast, human rights legislation recognises addiction as a disability.

The DDA also excludes from its definition of "impairment" hayfever ("except where it aggravates the effect of another condition"); exhibitionism; voyeurism; a tendency to steal, to set fires, or to abuse others either physically or sexually. The guidance also provides that "disfigurements which consist of a tattoo (which has not been removed), non-medical body piercing, or something attached through such piercing, are to be treated as not having a substantial adverse effect on the person's ability to carry out normal day-to-day activities". "Mental impairment" includes "a wide range of impairments relating to mental functioning, including what are often known as learning disabilities". Mental illnesses are, however, excluded by the Act (schedule 1) save where they are "clinically well-recognised".[37]

Whether any particular impairment should be considered "substantial" ("more than "minor" or "trivial") requires consideration of: the time taken by the person "to carry out a normal day-to-day activity"; the way in which such an activity is carried out; the "cumulative effects" where more than a single day-to-day activity is affected; the extent to which the person has or ought to have developed "coping strategies"; and the effects of the environment on the impairment. The Guidance provides examples of what may and might not be regarded as a significant adverse effect on normal day-to-day activities. These examples, which are described as "indicators and not tests", suggest "what it would, and what it would not, be reasonable to regard as substantial adverse effects". Among the former category are:

- "difficulty in going up or down steps, stairs or gradients";
- "inability to use one or more forms of public transport";
- "inability to handle a knife and fork at the same time";
- "ability to pour liquid into another vessel only with unusual slowness or concentration";
- "even infrequent loss of control of the bowels";
- "loss of control of the bladder while asleep at least once a month";
- "inability to carry a moderately loaded tray steadily";
- "inability to ask specific questions to clarify instructions";
- "taking significantly longer than average to say things";

[35] "Liver disease" resulting from alcoholism would amount to an impairment however, according to para 10 which provides that "It is not necessary to consider how an impairment was caused, even if the cause is a consequence of a condition which is excluded".

[36] ADA s.104(c)(4).

[37] Para 13. Para 14 goes on to provide that "A clinically well-recognised illness is a mental illness which is recognised by a respected body of medical opinion. It is very likely that this would include those specifically mentioned in publications such as the World Health Organisation's International Classification of Diseases."

- "inability to hear and understand another person speaking clearly over the voice telephone";
- "inability to see to pass the eyesight test for a standard driving test";
- "total inability to distinguish colours";
- "intermittent loss of consciousness and associated confused behaviour";
- "persistent inability to remember the names of familiar people such as family or friends";
- "inability to adapt after a reasonable period to minor change in work routine";
- "inability to operate safely properly-maintained equipment";
- "inability to nourish oneself (assuming nourishment is available)";
- "inability to tell by touch that an object is very hot or cold".

Regarded by the Guidance as not capable, *considered alone*, of amounting to a "substantial adverse effect" are:

- "difficulty walking unaided a distance of about 1.5 kilometres or a mile without discomfort or having to stop";
- "inability to undertake activities requiring delicate hand movements, such as threading a small needle";
- "inability to reach typing speeds standardised for secretarial work";
- "mere clumsiness";
- "infrequent minor leakage from the bladder".
- "inability to carry heavy luggage without assistance";
- "inability to articulate fluently due to a minor stutter, lisp or speech impediment";
- "inability to speak in front of an audience";
- "having a strong regional or foreign accent;
- "inability to hold a conversation in a very noisy place";
- "inability to read very small or indistinct print without the aid of a magnifying glass";
- "inability to distinguish between red and green";
- "occasionally forgetting the name of a familiar person, such as a colleague";
- "inability to fill in a long, detailed, technical document without assistance";
- "minor problems with writing or spelling";
- "fear of significant heights";
- "underestimating the risk associated with dangerous hobbies, such as mountain climbing".

In the case of people with progressive conditions such as cancer, multiple sclerosis, muscular dystrophy and HIV, a substantial adverse effect under s.1 will be established "from the moment any impairment resulting from that condition first has some effect on ability to carry out normal day-to-day activities. The effect need not be continuous and need not be substantial. For this rule to operate medical diagnosis of the condition is not by itself enough".[38]

The failure of the DDA to protect those who are discriminated against on the basis of asymptomatic HIV or other asymptomatic conditions, or on the basis that they are incorrectly perceived to be disabled, has been noted above, as has its failure to extend

---

[38] Schedule 1, para 8.

protection to those discriminated against on the basis of impairments not classified as "disabilities" by the Act. Some illustrations of this latter can be seen the employment tribunal decisions in *Cook* v *Kitchen Range Foods*, *Thorpe* v *The Royal Hospitals NHS Trust* and *Alexander* v *Driving Standards Agency*.[39]

These cases involved allegations that employees had been discriminated against on the basis, respectively, of a back injury, having sight only in one eye, and having an epileptic fit. In the *Cook* and *Alexander* cases, the applicants were dismissed as a direct result of their medical conditions (in the former case this was itself the result of a work-place accident). Yet in all three cases, tribunals ruled that the applicants' medical conditions did not have a "substantial . . . adverse effect on his or her ability to carry out normal day-to-day activities" as required by s.1. Mr Cook was able to carry normal weights and to stand for periods of up to two hours, with the effect that his back injury could not be said to have affected his "normal day-to-day activities". Although Ms Alexander had had two epileptic fits, these had both occurred at night and the chances of daytime recurrence were "extremely small". She could not, accordingly, be regarded as suffering from a recurring illness. Further, the effects of each fit having lasted less than 24 hours, her condition could not be regarded as "long-term". Finally, and in a decision which must have been particularly baffling for the unsuccessful applicant, Ms Thorpe could not be regarded as disabled because "she lives a full life, largely unaffected by her disability due to the good sight in her left eye and *due undoubtedly to her determination not to let her partial-sightedness prevent a normal life*" (my emphasis). The *Thorpe* decision was questionable in the extreme, and resulted in a call from the Disability Rights Task Force for the automatic definition as disabled of the blind and partially excited.

Decisions such as those in *Cook*, *Thorpe* and *Alexander* result, in part, from the very narrow approach to disability taken by the DDA. The Act's combination of medical rather than social approach and requirements of *actual* (rather than perceived), *substantial* and *long-term* adverse impact on *normal* day-to-day activities can be contrasted with the definition of disability adopted by Australia's DDA 1992, above and, to a lesser extent, by the ADA. The Australian DDA's protection would extend to the plaintiffs in *Cook*, *Thorpe* and *Alexander*. So, too, would Ireland's Employment Equality Act 1998, which defines "disability" as:

a. the total or partial absence of a person's bodily or mental functions, including the absence of a part of a person's body, or
b. the presence in the body of organisms causing, or likely to cause, chronic disease or illness, or
c. the malfunction, malformation or disfigurement of a part of a person's body, or
d. a condition or malfunction which results in a person learning differently from a person without the condition or malfunction, or

---

[39] Reported, respectively, at 36 EORDCLD, p.4, 36, EORDCLD, p.4 and 37 EORDCLD pp.11–12.

e. a condition, disease or illness which affects a person's thought processes, perception of reality, emotions or judgement or which results in disturbed behaviour.[40]

The absence in the EEA of any requirement for functional impairment should have the effect that *Cook*, *Alexander* and *Thorpe* would qualify as disabled under (c), (e) and (c) respectively. And while the ADA's definition is, like the DDA's, functional (in requiring substantial limitation of activities), we saw, above, that it includes *perceived*, rather than actual, impairment (so, too, does the EEA). According to the EEOC regulations:

There are three different ways in which an individual may satisfy the definition of "being regarded as having a disability":
(1) The individual may have an impairment which is not substantially limiting but is perceived by the employer or other covered entity as constituting a substantially limiting impairment . . . For example, suppose an employee has controlled high blood pressure that is not substantially limiting. If an employer reassigns the individual to less strenuous work because of unsubstantiated fears that the individual will suffer a heart attack if he or she continues to perform strenuous work, the employer would be regarding the individual as disabled.
(2) the individual may have an impairment which is only substantially limiting because of the attitudes of others toward the impairment; or
(3) the individual may have no impairment at all but is regarded by the employer or other covered entity as having a substantially limiting impairment.

Under this approach it is likely that Ms Alexander would be categorised as disabled, it probably being the case that her dismissal was motivated by the employer's over-reaction to her medical condition. The position with respect to Mr Cook and Ms Thorpe, by contrast, would turn on whether their functional impairments were sufficient to render them disabled under the ADA.[41] According to the US Equal Employment Opportunity Commission (EEOC) regulations:

An impairment rises to the level of disability if the impairment substantially limits one or more of the individual's major life activities [these "include caring for oneself, performing manual tasks, walking, seeing, hearing, speaking, breathing, learning, and working . . . sitting, standing, lifting, reaching] . . . an impairment is substantially limiting if it significantly restricts the duration, manner or condition under which an individual can perform a particular major life activity as compared to the average person in the general population's ability to perform that same major life activity . . . several factors . . . should be considered in making the determination of whether an impairment is substantially limiting. These factors are (1) the nature and severity of the impairment, (2) the duration or expected

[40] Again, by contrast with the DDA, the Irish prohibitions on discrimination extend beyond discrimination on grounds which exists at present to that which "previously existed but no longer exists; *or may exist in the future*; or is imputed to the person concerned (my emphasis)".
[41] Unless they were discriminated against on the basis that they were perceived to be more impaired than they actually were.

duration of the impairment, and (3) the permanent or long term impact, or the expected permanent or long term impact of, or resulting from, the impairment . . .

On the one hand, this approach appears not to differ substantially from that taken by the DDA. On the other hand, the regulations specifically provide that:

> If an individual is not substantially limited with respect to any other major life activity, the individual's ability to perform the major life activity of working should be considered . . . [s]pecific factors that may be used in making the determination of whether the limitation in working is "substantial" . . . are:
> (1) the geographical area to which the individual has reasonable access;
> (2) the job from which the individual has been disqualified because of an impairment, and the number and types of jobs utilizing similar training, knowledge, skills or abilities, within that geographical area, from which the individual is also disqualified because of the impairment (class of jobs); and/or
> (3) the job from which the individual has been disqualified because of an impairment, and the number and types of other jobs not utilizing similar training, knowledge, skills or abilities, within that geographical area, from which the individual is also disqualified because of the impairment (broad range of jobs in various classes) . . .
> an individual does not have to be totally unable to work in order to be considered substantially limited in the major life activity of working. An individual is substantially limited in working if the individual is significantly restricted in the ability to perform a class of jobs or a broad range of jobs in various classes, when compared with the ability of the average person with comparable qualifications to perform those same jobs. For example, an individual who has a back condition that prevents the individual from performing any heavy labor job would be substantially limited in the major life activity of working because the individual's impairment eliminates his or her ability to perform a class of jobs. This would be so even if the individual were able to perform jobs in another class, e.g., the class of semi-skilled jobs. Similarly, suppose an individual has an allergy to a substance found in most high rise office buildings, but seldom found elsewhere, that makes breathing extremely difficult. Since this individual would be substantially limited in the ability to perform the broad range of jobs in various classes that are conducted in high rise office buildings within the geographical area to which he or she has reasonable access, he or she would be substantially limited in working. . . .

According to this approach Mr Cook would, it appears, be regarded as "substantially limited in the major life activity of working" because of his inability to carry out heavy manual work.

In order to qualify as "disabled" under the DDA, the "substantial. . . adverse effect" of the applicant's impairment "on his or her ability to carry out normal day-to-day activities" has to be "long-term" (s.1), a "long-term" effect being defined as one which has lasted or is likely to last for at least 12 months from onset, or which is likely to last for the remainder of the disabled person's life.[42] "It is not necessary for the effect to be the same throughout the relevant period",[43] and an impairment will be regarded as continuing if it is likely to recur.

[42] Schedule 1, para 2.
[43] Para B2.

Save in relation to the correction of sight defects by glasses or contact lenses, no account should be taken by a tribunal or court, in assessing the question of disability, of the effects of treatment upon it. "This applies even if the measures result in the effects being completely under control or not at all apparent" (para A12).[44] Thus (para A13):

> if a person with a hearing impairment wears a hearing aid the question whether his or her impairment has a substantial adverse effect is to be decided by reference to what the hearing level would be without the hearing aid. And in the case of someone with diabetes, whether or not the effect is substantial should be decided by reference to what the condition would be if he or she was not taking medication.

Given the clarity of the law in this area, it is perhaps surprising that early analysis of DDA cases showed "the failure of some tribunals to address these provisions where they may have been highly relevant".

"Interpreting the Disability Discrimination Act—Part 1: the Meaning of Disability" 79 *Equal Opportunities Review* pp. 16–17

In *Powell v Manchester City Council*, the applicant was employed as an administrative assistant. She stated that she was disabled on her application form and in her pre-medical assessment disclosed that she had had asthma since childhood. She took medication daily.

The council medical officer found the asthma to be "well controlled" and classified her as fit. A Manchester tribunal . . . held that she was not a "disabled person" able to bring a DDA complaint after she was dismissed. "Clearly, asthma can be such a disability in particular circumstances," it said. "But was it here? Was it an impairment that had a substantial adverse effect such as to affect her ability to carry out normal day-to-day activities? She had confirmed in her pre-medical assessment that she had never had breathing problems and, indeed, she had never been away absent for breathing-related problems. Her colleagues had seen no evidence of any alleged breathing difficulty or her using her medication. There was no substantive evidence that her condition, such as it was, affected her ability to carry out her job."

Bulimia nervosa was the impairment at issue in *Toogood v Glan Clwyd Hospital Trust*. The applicant, a registered nurse who had been employed at Newcastle General Hospital, was appointed to a post at Stanley Hospital in North Wales, subject to satisfactory completion of a medical exam. She had a history of bulimia for which she received ongoing psychiatric and medical treatment, including medication, while she was employed. She had attempted suicide on several occasions. When this emerged, the employer's occupational health consultant recommended that her appointment should not be confirmed on grounds that she was unfit because of her disability.

The employer accepted that recommendation. It relied on the Clothier Report, which recommended that "no candidate for nursing in whom there is evidence of major

---

[44] Similarly under the ADA "The determination of whether an individual is substantially limited in a major life activity must be made on a case by case basis, without regard to mitigating measures such as medicines, or assistive or prosthetic devices. . ." According to EAT in *Kapadia v London Borough of Lambeth* 41 EORDCLD 41, p.11, counselling amounted to medical treatment in a case in which there was evidence that, without it, a depressed person might have had a mental breakdown requiring in-patient treatment—the tribunal had decided that the depression did not have a substantial effect on the applicant's normal day-to-day activities.

personality disorders should be employed in the profession." It was admitted that bulimia nervosa and depression were mental impairments. However, the tribunal, by a majority decision, decided that the applicant was not disabled within the meaning of the DDA on grounds that her impairment did not have a substantial adverse effect on her ability to carry out normal day-to-day activities. The applicant relied on the effect of her condition on her ability to concentrate and/or the perception of the risk of physical danger.

The majority of an Abergele tribunal . . . focused on the fact that Miss Toogood had managed to hold down her job with Newcastle General Hospital over a lengthy period, notwithstanding her alleged lack of ability to concentrate and her alleged inability to perceive a risk of physical danger. "The members consider that the mental impairments from which the applicant suffered were long term but did not have a substantial adverse effect on her ability to carry out her normal day-to-day activities." The chairman dissented, but neither he, nor the lay members, despite the applicant's long history of treatment for anxiety-based symptoms, addressed themselves to the provisions requiring that the effects of medical treatment must be discounted.

The correct approach was taken by a Manchester tribunal . . . in *Calvert v Jewelglen Limited t/a Parkview Nursing Home*. This case involved an applicant with epilepsy. He used to suffer seriously from it, but for 18 years was free of any attack or fit and managed that by virtue of prescribed medication. The tribunal noted the part of the Guidance which says that "it would be reasonable to regard as having a substantial adverse effect, intermittent loss of consciousness and associated confused behaviour." It concluded that Mr Calvert fell within the definition of disability since he "acknowledges that but for the medication which he receives he would suffer symptoms of epilepsy and those could involve fits and blackouts."

Similarly, in *Cox v The Post Office*, a Birmingham tribunal . . . found that a postman with bronchial asthma had a physical impairment and "disregarding the effect of any treatment which the applicant receives for his impairment, the applicant's condition doe shave a substantial adverse effect on his ability to carry out normal day-to-day activities . . . Activities affected include the ability to lift, carry or otherwise move everyday objects."

In *Kapadia* v *London Borough of Lambeth* [2000] IRLR 14, the Employment Appeal Tribunal considered the proper application of s. 1 in this context. The claim was brought by a man who was retired on medical grounds because of absences associated with depression. His claim was dismissed by a tribunal (the chairman dissenting) on the grounds that, while he was suffering from a well-recognised mental illness, its effect on his day-to-day activities was no more than trivial.

Peter Clark J:

. . . It is common ground that in evidence the medical men called on behalf of the appellant were of the opinion that without the counselling sessions [which the applicant was undertaking] there would have been a very strong likelihood of total mental breakdown and the need for psychiatric treatment including in-patient treatment. Mr Basu [for the council] does not seriously argue that if that state of affairs existed then the appellant's impairment would not have had a substantial effect on his day-to-day activities. We repeat, no medical evidence was called by the respondent to contest those expressions of opinion . . .

In the absence of any medical evidence to the contrary, we are quite satisfied that counselling sessions with a consultant clinical psychologist constitute treatment within the meaning of . . . In so holding we reject Mr Basu's further contention that the counselling sessions with Mr Revell did not constitute treatment because they were directed to reduction of the appellant's symptoms, not to the correction of the mental impairment. It seems to be suggested that a series of counselling sessions which prevents the patient from needing drug treatment for his condition does not amount to treatment. We simply cannot accept that assertion . . .

It follows, in our judgment, that the majority fell into error in . . . wholly disregarding the deduced effects of that impairment, despite submissions on the point made by Mr Neaman below.

EAT replaced the finding of the tribunal with its own decision that Mr Kapadia was disabled within the meaning of the Act. The tribunal had taken the view that there was "no evidence" that the applicant was significantly impaired, this in the face of evidence to the contrary by his two medical witnesses in the absence of any contrary evidence by the employer. It was argued by counsel for the employer that the "[t]he majority were entitled to apply their own judgment as to the effect on the appellant by seeing how he behaved in the witness box" and by taking into account the fact that he had been able to hold down a demanding job with the council. EAT accepted that it was open to tribunals to reject even undisputed medical evidence. But it was not open to them to ignore it as had happened here. Such evidence is likely to be particularly important in a case, such as this, where the medical treatment of the applicant's condition is such that there may be no evidence from friends, family or colleagues as to its effect.

Kapadia concerned the effect of treatment on the characterisation of the applicant as "disabled". Turning to the types of conditions covered by the term "disability", the DfEE's Report, *Monitoring the Disability Discrimination Act (DDA) 1995*, reveals that the most common disabilities amongst those who instituted claims under the DDA in its first year of operation were back or neck problems, depression, bad nerves or anxiety, and arm or hand problems.[45] But a more accurate impression of the scope of "physical or mental impairment" can be gleaned from the appellate decisions, which have involved plaintiffs suffering from conditions ranging from repetitive strain injury and ME ("yuppy flu")[46] through partial sightedness, back injuries and epilepsy[47] to MS and cerebral palsy.[48] In all of these cases the conditions have been accepted, *in relation to the specific complainants*, as having a substantial and long-term adverse effect on his [or her] ability to carry out normal day-to-day activities".

[45] *Monitoring the Disability Discrimination Act (DDA) 1995* (DfEE Research Series RR 19), May 1999.
[46] Respectively *Grigg* v *HM Land Registry* and *O'Neill*. In *London Borough of Hillingdon* v *Morgan* discussed below, EAT upheld a tribunal decision based on ME.
[47] *British Sugar, Clark* v *Novacold, Butterfield* and *Rideout*. Epilepsy was also at issue in *Holmes* v *Whittingham & Porter* (1802799/97), reported in Thompson's *Labour and European Law Review* Issue 17, available at http://www.thompsons. law.co.uk/ltext/libindex.htm.
[48] *Buxton* v *Equinox Design Ltd* [1999] ICR 269, [1999] IRLR 158, *Kenny*. Diabetes was also accepted as disabling in *Greenwood* v *United Tiles Ltd* (1101067/97/C), Thompson's *Labour and European Law Review* Issue 17, *ibid.*

20% disability after a car accident was accepted as being within s.1 in *Morse* v *Wiltshire County Council* [1998] ICR 1023, [1998] IRLR 352, 44 BMLR 58, discussed below, while a tribunal in *Howden* v *Capital Copiers (Edinburgh) Ltd*[49] accepted that a complainant who suffered from abdominal pains without specific medical diagnosis was, on the facts, disabled within the meaning of the Act. In *Walton* v *LI Group Ltd* a tribunal accepted that a person with learning difficulties was within s.1 after hearing the evidence of his parents and on the grounds that he received Disability Living Allowance.[50] In *Rowley* v *Walkers Nonesuch Ltd*, *Hopkins* v *ERF Manchester Ltd*, *Ishiguro* v *Financial Times Ltd*, on the other hand, tribunals found against complainants who suffered, respectively, from back injuries, rheumatoid arthritis and stress.[51] In the first two cases the tribunals ruled that insufficient medical evidence had been produced as to whether the condition was "substantial and long-term". In *Ishiguro* the tribunal took the view that "Stress may be the cause of or related to ill-health. If that ill-health is sufficiently handicapping it may be either a physical or mental impairment, but it is the medical condition itself which must amount to the impairment not the stress". And in *Foster* v *Hampshire Fire and Rescue Service*[52] EAT upheld a tribunal decision that the complainant's asthma and migraine did not have "a substantial and long-term adverse effect on his [or her] ability to carry out normal day-to-day activities".

The general approach to determining whether an applicant is disabled within the meaning of the DDA was set out by EAT in *Goodwin* v *Patent Office* [1999] ICR 302, [1999] IRLR 4. There, EAT stressed the importance of the Guidance and the Code of Practice for the Elimination of Discrimination in the Field of Employment against Disabled Persons or Persons who have had a Disability (1996), to which tribunals should have reference in determining whether a complainant satisfied s.1. Morison J accepted that: "in many cases the question whether a person is disabled within the meaning of the Act can admit of only one answer. In these cases it would be wrong to search the Guide and use what it says as some kind of extra hurdle over which the applicant must jump". But here the tribunal had erred in failing to make reference to the Guidance in reaching what he characterised as a "surprising" decision "that a person admittedly diagnosed as suffering from paranoid schizophrenia and who had been dismissed partly because of what one might call bizarre behaviour, consistent with that diagnosis, fell outside the definition in s 1 of the Act".

The tribunal had decided that the applicant's normal day-to-day activities were not substantially adversely affected by his condition, which resulted in paranoia, "thought broadcasting", when he imagined that other people could access his thoughts, and auditory hallucinations which, in turn, affected his ability to concentrate on his work and to watch television. According to the majority, the applicant "must have been able

[49] Case 400005/97, Thompson's *Labour and European Law Review*, issue 17, fn 47 above.

[50] Case 1600562/97, Thompson's *Labour and European Law Review*, issue 17, fn 47 above.

[51] 40 EORDCLD 10–11. Thompson's *Labour and European Law Review*, issue 17, fn 48 above, states that the second decision is wrong, the condition "undoubtedly" being a progressive one.

[52] 43 *Butterworths Medical Law Reports* 186.

to remember, to organise his thoughts and plan a course of action and execute it, in order to carry out his day-to-day activities of looking after himself at home, getting to and from work and carrying out his work." EAT ruled that the tribunal had erred in concluding "from the finding that the applicant was able to cope at home . . . that, therefore, he fell outwith the provisions of the Act. Rather than remit to a tribunal the question whether or not the applicant fell within s.1, EAT concluded that he did: "It seems to us that in this case the question whether the applicant was, at the relevant time, disabled within the meaning of the Act admitted only one conclusion: he was".

Morison J, for the Court, interpreted the Guidance as establishing four "conditions" which had to be satisfied before a complainant could be regarded as "disabled":

(1) The impairment condition

The applicant must have either a physical or mental impairment. Mental impairment includes an impairment which results from or consists of a mental illness provided that the mental illness is "a clinically well-recognised illness" . . .

If there is doubt as to whether the impairment condition is fulfilled in an alleged mental illness case, it would be advisable to ascertain whether the illness described or referred to in the medical evidence is mentioned in the WHO's International Classification of Diseases. That Classification would very likely determine the issue one way or the other

. . .

(2) The adverse effect condition

In many ways, this may be the most difficult of the four conditions to judge . . The fact that a person can carry out such activities does not mean that his ability to carry them out has not been impaired . . . Furthermore, disabled persons are likely, habitually, to ' play down" the effect that their disabilities have on their daily lives. If asked whether they are able to cope at home, the answer may well be "yes", even though, on analysis, many of the ordinary day-to-day tasks were done with great difficulty due to the person's impaired ability to carry them out . . ."

(3) The substantial condition

"Substantial" might mean "very large" or it might mean "more than minor or trivial". Reference to the Guide shows that the word has been used in the latter sense . . . The tribunal will wish to examine how the applicant's abilities had actually been affected at the material time, whilst on medication, and then to address their minds to the difficult question as to the effects which they think there would have been but for the medication: the deduced effects. The question is then whether the actual and deduced effects on the applicant's abilities to carry out normal day-to-day activities is clearly more than trivial.

In many cases, the tribunal will be able to reach a conclusion on these matters without reference to the statutory Guidance (which is there to illuminate what is not reasonably clear . . . Although Parliament has linked the effect of medication to the "substantial condition", as we have already said, splitting the statutory words into conditions should not divert attention from the definition as a whole. and in determining whether the adverse effect condition is fulfilled the tribunal will take into account deduced effects.

(4) The long-term condition

Paragraph 2 of Schedule 1 applies, as does paragraph B of the Guidance, where reference to it is necessary. The provisions appear to be straightforward and we have nothing useful to say about them.

Goodwin was subsequently applied by a differently constituted EAT in *Vicary* v *BT*, in which that tribunal considered the significance of medical evidence as well as the proper approach to the guidance. A tribunal had ruled that a woman who suffered from an upper limb disorder to the extent that she had a long-term inability to "prepare vegetables, cut meat or roast potatoes, carry saucepans full of water, manually open jars, tins or packets, carry baskets of washing, read without resting the book on the arm of a chair, do heavy shopping, do any DIY tasks, file her nails, tong her hair, and shake quilts, groom animals, polish furniture, knit, sew cut with scissors, hold a briefcase, suitcase or handbag with handheld handles, or carry a chair", was not "disabled" for the purposes of the DDA.

In reaching this conclusion the tribunal had reasoned that the applicant was "able to use both her hands and, in our view, a loss of strength cannot be equated to a loss of function". The tribunal went on to emphasise that she could handle a knife and fork simultaneously and press the buttons on a keyboard "albeit more slowly than she was able to formerly"; that she could modify her behaviour to cope with an inability to lift or carry anything of substantial weight; and that her inability to cut up food was "an isolated example [which did not] make the impairment substantial". Further, the tribunal did:

> not regard the doing of DIY tasks, filing nails, tonging hair, ironing, shaking quilts, grooming animals, polishing furniture, knitting and sewing and cutting with scissors as normal day-to-day activities as set out in the guidance, since it cannot be said that these activities are carried out by most people on a daily or frequent and fairly regular basis.

In reaching its conclusion the tribunal relied heavily upon the evidence given by the employer's medical officer who did not regard the applicant's impairment as "substantial". EAT allowed the appeal.

Vicary v British Telecommunications [1999] IRLR 680

Morison J (for EAT)

On behalf of the Appellant, Mr Brown submitted that the whole approach of the Employment Tribunal was flawed . . . [EAT] has given guidance as to the approach to the question whether a claimant suffers from a disability in the case of Goodwin . . . Under that guidance, the Tribunal should have been concentrating more on the things that the Applicant could not do as opposed to the things that she could do, and should have had proper regard to the context in which the guidance is given . . .

It seems to us with great respect to the Employment Tribunal that their decision can be described as perverse . . .

the Employment Tribunal has not considered the interpretation of the word "substantial". It seems to us clear that they must have approached the case on the basis that "substantial" means more than what the word means in this context [i.e., according to the guidance: "more than minor or trivial"] . . .

Paragraph 1 of part 1 [of the guidance states] . . . "In the vast majority of cases there is unlikely to be any doubt whether or not a person has or has had a disability, but this guidance should prove helpful in cases where it is not clear."

The guidance, therefore, will only be of assistance in what might be described as marginal cases. We agree with Mr Brown that in this case there was in fact no need for the Employment Tribunal to refer to the guidance once they had properly understood the meaning of the word "substantial". Having concluded that the ability of the Applicant to do the activities specified in paragraph 7(3) of the decision was impaired, the Tribunal inevitably should have concluded that the Applicant was a person suffering from a disability within the meaning of the Act. Instead, the Employment Tribunal appears to have used the guidance in a somewhat literal fashion so as to arrive at the surprising conclusion that the Applicant was not substantially impaired in her ability to carry out normal day-to-day activities . . .

the Employment Tribunal assert that a loss of strength cannot be equated to a loss of function. We do not understand what is being said. A loss of strength may well have a substantial adverse effect on the Applicant's manual dexterity. They then refer to the things that she was able to do which in our view is not the right focus of attention . . an ability to prepare vegetables, cut up meat and carry a meal on a tray would all be regarded as examples of normal day-to-day activities. An inability to carry out those functions would, in our view, obviously be regarded as a substantial impairment of an ability to carry out normal day-to-day activities.

Furthermore, the Tribunal's conclusion in that paragraph that DIY tasks, filing nails, tonging hair, ironing, shaking quilts, grooming animals, polishing furniture, knitting and sewing and cutting with scissors were not normal day-to-day activities "as set out in the guidance" misunderstands the nature of the guidance given. Paragraph C9 of the guidance makes it plain that the lists of examples which follow "are not exhaustive; they are only meant to be illustrative." It seems to us obvious that making beds, doing housework (polishing furniture), sewing and cutting with scissors would be regarded as normal day-to-day activities as would minor DIY tasks, filing nails, curling hair and ironing . . .

The fact that a person is able to mitigate the effects of their disability does not mean that they are not disabled within the meaning of the Act . . .

The Employment Tribunal has misdirected themselves as to the relevance of the medical evidence which they received from the Respondent's Occupational Health Advisor . . . It is not for a doctor to express an opinion as to what is a normal day-to-day activity. That is a matter for them to consider using their basic common sense. Equally, it was not for the expert to tell the Tribunal whether the impairments which had been found proved were or were not substantial. Again that was a matter for the Employment Tribunal to arrive at its own assessment. What of course a medical expert was entitled to do was to put forward her own observations of the Applicant carrying out day-to-day activities and to comment on the ease or otherwise with which she was performing those functions. She obviously also was entitled to give any prognosis that might be relevant and to give an opinion as to the position about the effect of medication.

In summary, therefore, in our judgement the Tribunal has erred in law in the following respects:

1. it has arrived at a conclusion which is perverse.
2. it has misdirected itself in law as to the way the guidance is to be used.
3. it has misdirected itself in law as to the meaning of the word "substantial", and
4. it has misdirected itself in law in the way it dealth with the expert evidence . . .

in the light of their findings of fact in paragraph 7(3) the only conclusion open to an Employment Tribunal was to conclude that the Applicant suffered from a disability within the meaning of the Act. We accordingly allow the appeal and substitute that finding in its place.

DEFINITIONS OF DISCRIMINATION

In this part of the chapter we consider only "discrimination" as it is defined in the DDA. The more general approach to discrimination in the anti-discrimination legislation is considered in Chapter 2, while Chapter 4 considers those areas in which discrimination is regulated under the DDA and other legislation.

The DDA's approach to discrimination differs significantly from the RRA, SDA and FETO in a number of respects. In the first place, the Act contains no prohibition of indirect discrimination, discrimination being defined as less favourable treatment "for a reason which relates to the disabled person's disability".[53] Secondly, such discrimination is not unlawful if the employer shows that the less favourable treatment is "justifiable".[54] "Justifiability" differs according to the context in which the alleged discrimination occurs and is discussed in the penultimate section of this chapter.

As was mentioned above, the DDA contains no equivalent to SDA s. 5(3), RRA s.3(4), and FETO Article 3(3), which require that comparison for the purposes of determining whether discrimination has occurred should be between persons (real or hypothetical) in the same "relevant circumstances". The significance of this omission became apparent in the Court of Appeal's decision in *Clark* v *TDG Ltd (t/a Novacold)* [1999] IRLR 318.[55] An employment tribunal had rejected a claim that a man dismissed for disability-related absence from work had been discriminated against contrary to s.5 DDA. According to the tribunal, and to EAT, the treatment meted out to Mr Clark had to be compared with that which a non-disabled employee who was absent for a similar period of time had or would have received (this, the reader will recognise, is the approach taken, pre-*Webb* v *EMO Air Cargo (UK) Ltd (No 2)* [1995] 4 All ER 577, [1995] ICR 1021, [1995] IRLR 645, by the UK courts to pregnancy dismissal). The tribunal took the view that such an employee would also have been dismissed.

The Court of Appeal disagreed. Having pointed out that the differences between the RRA and SDA, on the one hand, and the DDA, on the other, were such that the interpretation of the latter "is not facilitated by familiarity" with the former, Mummery LJ (for the Court) relied both on statements made by the Minister for Social Security and Disabled People during the second reading of the Bill[56] and upon the Code of Practice on Rights of Access to lay down the following principles:

---

[53] Ss.5(1)(a), 14(1)(a), 20(1)(a) and s.24(1)(a). S.5 deals with discrimination in employment, s.14 with discrimination by "trade organisations", s.20 with discrimination in relation to goods and services, etc, s.24 with discrimination in relation to premises.

[54] Ss.5(1)(b), 14(1)(b), 20(1)(b) and 24(1)(b).

[55] A similar decision was reached by EAT in *British Sugar* v *Kirker* [1998] IRLR 624.

[56] The Bill is drafted in such a way that indirect as well as direct discrimination can be dealt with . . . A situation where dogs are not admitted to a cafe, with the effect that blind people would he unable to enter it, would be a prima facie case of indirect discrimination against blind people and would be unlawful" HC Debs vol 253, 24th January 1995, col.150.

(1) Less favourable treatment of a disabled person is only discriminatory under s 5(1) if it is unjustified.

(2) Treatment is less favourable if the reason for it does not or would not apply to others.

(3) In deciding whether that reason does not or would not apply to others, it is not appropriate to make a comparison of the cases in the same way as in the [SDA] and the [RRA]. It is simply a case of identifying others to whom the reason for the treatment does not or would not apply. The test of less favourable treatment is based on the reason for the treatment of the disabled person and not on the fact of his disability. It does not turn on a like-for-like comparison of the treatment of the disabled person and of others in similar circumstances . . .

Mummery LJ's reference to the Code of Practice on Rights of Access is significant. Tribunals are also, where relevant, bound to take into account the provisions of the Disability Discrimination Code of Practice, which came into force in December 1996. This Code provides "general advice to help employers avoid discrimination" (encouraging flexibility, avoidance of stereotyped assumptions and, where appropriate, the seeking of advice). It also gives large numbers of examples of less favourable treatment, potential justifications for such treatment, reasonable adjustments, etc.

The DDA does not expressly cover indirect discrimination. But it was recognised by the Court of Appeal in *Clark* v *Novacold* that the definition of discrimination adopted—in particular, the omission of any section equivalent to s.5(3) SDA—was such as to include that which would be characterised as indirect discrimination under the RRA or SDA. The Court drew attention to the comments made by the Minister responsible for the Act and the examples of unlawful discrimination given in the Code of Practice:

On the second reading of the Bill for this Act the Minister for Social Security and Disabled People stated: "The Bill is drafted in such a way that indirect as well as direct discrimination can be dealt with . . . A situation where dogs are not admitted to a cafe, with the effect that blind people would be unable to enter it, would be a prima facie case of indirect discrimination against blind people and would be unlawful"[57] . . .

The same point can be made on the example given in the Code of Practice on Rights of Access issued by the Secretary of State at para 2.12: "A waiter asks a disabled customer to leave the restaurant because she has difficulty eating as a result of her disability. He serves other customers who have no difficulty eating. The waiter has therefore treated her less favourably than other customers. The treatment was for a reason related to her disability— her difficulty when eating. And the reason for her less favourable treatment did not apply to other customers. If the waiter could not justify the less favourable treatment, he would have discriminated unlawfully."

Both of these cases would be characterised as indirect discrimination under the RRA/SDA/FETO scheme:—the café and restaurant customers were subject to conditions (respectively, being without a dog and eating without difficulty) with which they,

[57] HC Debs vol 253, 24th January 1995, col.150.

as disabled persons, were less able to comply with than non-disabled persons would be. Further, the approach taken by the DDA avoids the technical difficulties (of establishing the existence of a "requirement" or "condition" for example, and selecting the appropriate pools for comparison) associated with the definitions of indirect discrimination adopted by these Acts. Certainly, the Under-Secretary of State for Employment, in Standing Committee, stated that the DDA: "firmly cover[s]—and [is] intended to cover—the use of standards, administrative methods, work practices or procedures that adversely affect a disabled person".[58]

In *O'Neill* v *Symm & Co Ltd* [1998] ICR 481, EAT ruled that an employer could not discriminate "by reason of" disability under s.5(1) unless s/he knew or ought reasonably to have known of the complainant's disability. The claim was made by a woman suffering from ME. On the facts as the tribunal found them, she had not informed her employers of the diagnosis, although she did inform them that she had suffered (and recovered) from viral pneumonia a number of months before her appointment. She was dismissed for absence (15.5 days in her first three months) having, contrary to her contractual obligations, failed to provide sick notes.

A tribunal accepted that Ms O'Neill came within s.1 of the Act, but ruled that the employer's ignorance of her condition, coupled with the fact that her dismissal was because of her uncertified absences, meant that she was not discriminated against because she had a disability. On the face of it, this was inconsistent with the decision of the Court of Appeal in *Clark*. EAT (prior to the Court of Appeal decision in *Clark*) upheld the tribunal's ruling, Kirkwood J for the court rejecting the appellant's argument that s.5(1) was satisfied on proof: "(a) that the employee is a disabled person; (b) [of] less favourable treatment; [and] (c) for a reason that relates to the disabled person's disability".

In *Heinz Co Ltd* v *Kendrick*, however, EAT took a different approach. The case concerned a man who had been dismissed after a period of a year's absence but before he received a confirmed diagnosis to the effect that he was suffering from ME. Having pointed out that the tribunal's decision pre-dated reports of the Court of Appeal, the appeal tribunal rejected the argument that the reason for the less favourable treatment had to be judged, subjectively, from the employer's point of view.

Heinz Co Ltd v *Kendrick* [2000] IRLR 144

Lindsay J (for EAT)

Amongst the points made by *Clark* v *Novacold* in the Court of Appeal is that a textual comparison between the disability discrimination legislation and that relating to sex or race discrimination is not helpful and may even be midleading . . .

O'Neill . . . appears to conclude that there cannot be some less favourable treatment of a person by an employer within Section 5(1)(a) of the 1995 Act being properly held to be for a reason that relates to that person's disability unless the employer has knowledge of the disability "or at least the material features of it as set out in Schedule I of the Act" . . .

---

[58] HC Standing Committee E, col. 142, cited by Doyle, fn 9 above, p.6.

We would hesitate before adopting that view. Firstly, its adoption, if Mr Linden's argument on behalf of Heinz in this case is a guide, would, we fear, lead in many cases to hair-splitting medical evidence. We were addressed on whether CFS was a physical or mental condition or some combination of the two, was it psychosomatic, was it clinically well-recognised, was it long-term? One can readily imagine cases in which, if detailed knowledge were to be relevant as *O'Neill* was argued to require, there would need to be medical evidence as to the labels which could be attached to this or that symptom or aggregation of symptoms as a person's condition deteriorated or improved. We cannot think such an approach was within the legislature's broad intendment.

Secondly, the conclusion arrived at in *O'Neill* was based partly on a comparison between the legislative provisions relating to disability discrimination and those relating to other forms of discrimination, a comparison which, as *Clark* v *Novacold* has since held, can be misleading.[59] . . .

one can imagine, for example, a postman or messenger who, at his engagement and for a while afterwards, successfully conceals the fact that he has an artificial leg and can walk only for short distances at a time. He may later be dismissed for a conduct or capability ground, namely that he had proved to be unacceptably slow in making his rounds, but still without his disability being spotted. His slowness could have been taken by the employer to have been by reason of idleness or absenteeism. If, however, the employee were then able to show that his slowness was by reason of his having an artificial leg then, as it seems to us, he would, in such a case, have been treated less favourably "than others to whom that reason does not apply" (namely, as *Clark* v *Novacold* requires, less favourably than other employees who did their rounds at an acceptable pace).

Moreover he would have been so treated for a reason—unacceptable slowness—which related to his disability. That, it seems to us, would be the case whether or not the employer ever knew before the dismissal that the reason for the slowness was that the employee was disabled. The employee would, as it seems to us, have been discriminated against within the Act even if the employer had assumed that the slowness was attributable only to laziness or absenteeism. As another example, one might imagine a secretary dismissed because he or she, despite repeated training, persisted in typing hopelessly misspelt letters, yet without the employer or, perhaps, even the employee knowing that the reason for the errors was not ignorance or carelessness but dyslexia . . .

there is no language in section 5(1) that requires that the relationship between the disability and the treatment should be adjudged subjectively, through the eyes of the employer, so that the applicable test should be the objective one of whether the relationship exists, not whether the employer knew of it. Indeed, unless the test is objective there will be difficulties with credible and honest yet ignorant or obtuse employers who fail to recognise or acknowledge the obvious . . .

The phrase, "which relates to" in the expression, in Section 5(1)(a), of "for a reason which relates to the disabled person's disability" widens the description of the reasons which may be relevant beyond what the case would have been had the Act said "by reason of . . . the disability". As we see it, the expression may include a reason deriving from how the disability manifests itself even where there is no knowledge of the disability as such. This, we think, opens no floodgates but it does require employers to pause to consider whether the reason

---

[59] EAT further suggested that the decision of EAT in *Del Monte Foods* v. *Mundon* [1980] IRLR 224 to the effect that a woman can be dismissed "in connection with" pregnancy only where an employer knows that she is pregnant was incorrect.

for some dismissal that they have in mind might relate to disability and, if it might, to reflect on the Act and the Code before dismissing. There is, in our judgment, no need to imply into the statute a requirement not expressly present, namely that the employer should know of the disability as such or as to whether its material features fell within or without Schedule 1 of the 1995 Act. It may be that *O'Neill* does not, in any case, go that far. This is not to say, though, that such knowledge or its absence may not be highly material to justifiability under Section 5(1)(b) or Section 5(2)(b) or as to the steps to be considered or taken under Section 6—see also Section 6(6)(b).

DUTY TO MAKE ADJUSTMENTS

The next major difference between the RRA, SDA and FETO, on the one hand, and the DDA, on the other, is in the "duty . . . to make adjustments". In the employment context, this duty is set out in s.6(1) DDA. Ss.5(2) and 6 DDA provide:

> 5(2) . . . an employer . . . discriminates against a disabled person if—
>   (a) he fails to comply with a s.6 duty imposed on him in relation to the disabled person; and
>   (b) he cannot show that his failure to comply with that duty is justified.
> 6(1) Where:
>   (a) any arrangements made by or on behalf of an employer, or
>   (b) any physical feature of premises occupied by an employer,
>   place the disabled person concerned at a substantial disadvantage in comparison with persons who are not disabled, it is the duty of the employer to take such steps as are reasonable, in all the circumstances of the case, for him to have to take in order to prevent the arrangements or feature having that effect.[60]
> (2) Subsection (1)(a) applies only in relation to—
>   (a) arrangements for determining to whom employment should be offered;
>   (b) any term, condition or arrangements on which employment, promotion, a transfer, training or any other benefit is offered or afforded.[61]

The duty to make adjustments arises, in the employment field,[62] only when a disabled person is placed at a "substantial disadvantage" as a job applicant or employee by selection arrangements, working conditions or a physical feature of the workplace. Adjustments by trade organisations are required only when the disabled person is placed at a substantial disadvantage in terms of access to membership or the terms of membership or benefits associated therewith. And, while s.21 imposes upon service providers a "duty to take such steps as it is reasonable, in all the circumstances of the

---

[60] S.15 provides a duty of reasonable adjustment by trade organisations in similar terms.

[61] In relation to discrimination by trade organisations (s.15(2)), to "arrangements for determining who should become or remain a member . . . [and] any term, condition or arrangements on which membership or any benefit is offered or afforded".

[62] Including discrimination by trade organisations (15(2)).

case" to change any "practice, policy or procedure which makes it impossible or unreasonably difficult for disabled persons to make use of a service which he provides", the obligation is enforceable only by a disabled person who is discriminated against.

The Disability Discrimination (Employment) Regulations 1996 define physical features of the workplace as those arising from the design or construction of buildings; access and exits to buildings; fixtures, fittings, furnishings, equipment or materials and any other physical element or quality of land or buildings. S.16 DDA provides that, where an employer (or trade organisation) is under an obligation to make reasonable adjustments to premises and "but for this section . . . would not be entitled to make a particular alteration to the premises", s.16 implies a contractual term to the effect that the lessor shall, on application from the lessee, not "withhold his consent unreasonably".[63]

In the non-employment arena, s.22's prohibition on discrimination in relation to the disposal (whether by sale or lease) or management of premises does not include a duty of adjustment. S.19 DDA, which defines discrimination in relation to the provision of goods and services, etc., does include such a duty, prohibiting discrimination by service providers:

(a) in refusing to provide, or deliberately not providing, to the disabled person any service which he provides, or is prepared to provide, to members of the public;

(b) in failing to comply with any duty imposed on him by section 21 in circumstances in which the effect of that failure is to make it impossible or unreasonably difficult for the disabled person to make use of any such service;

(c) in the standard of service which he provides to the disabled person or the manner in which he provides it to him; or

(d) in the terms on which he provides a service to the disabled person.

S.21 provides:

(1) Where a provider of services has a practice, policy or procedure which makes it impossible or unreasonably difficult for disabled persons to make use of a service which he provides, or is prepared to provide, to other members of the public, it is his duty to take such steps as it is reasonable, in all the circumstances of the case, for him to have to take in order to change that practice, policy or procedure so that it no longer has that effect.

(2) Where a physical feature (for example, one arising from the design or construction of a building or the approach or access to premises) makes it impossible or unreasonably difficult for disabled persons to make use of such a service, it is the duty of the provider of that service to take such steps as it is reasonable, in all the circumstances of the case, for him to have to take in order to—

(a) remove the feature;

(b) alter it so that it no longer has that effect;

---

[63] Save where the lease expressly otherwise provides.

(c) provide a reasonable means of avoiding the feature; or

(d) provide a reasonable alternative method of making the service in question available to disabled persons. . . .

(4) Where an auxiliary aid or service (for example, the provision of information on audio tape or of a sign language interpreter) would-

    (a) enable disabled persons to make use of a service which a provider of services provides, or is prepared to provide, to members of the public, or

    (b) facilitate the use by disabled persons of such a service,

it is the duty of the provider of that service to take such steps as it is reasonable, in all the circumstances of the case, for him to have to take in order to provide that auxiliary aid or service.

(6) Nothing in this section requires a provider of services to take any steps which would fundamentally alter the nature of the service in question or the nature of his trade, profession or business.

(7) Nothing in this section requires a provider of services to take any steps which would cause him to incur expenditure exceeding the prescribed maximum . . .

S.20(1) came into effect in December 1996, s.21(1) in October 1999. S.21(2) will not come into effect until 2004.

According to Brian Doyle:

"Enabling legislation or dissembling law? The Disability Discrimination Act 1995" (60) *Modern Law Review* **64, 74**

The duty to make reasonable adjustments will assume . . . great[] importance as a means to prevent (or to require the adjustment of) unjustifiable practices, rules, policies, requirements or conditions which have a harsh or adverse impact upon access by disabled persons and to compensate for the absence of an explicit prohibition on indirect disability discrimination. The concept of a reasonable accommodation or adjustment is at the heart of disability discrimination statutes in other jurisdictions. It is an example of legally mandated positive action rather than a requirement of reverse or positive discrimination. A failure without justification to comply with a duty to make reasonable adjustments will amount to an act of discrimination.

The issue of justification is further considered below. The rights accorded to disabled people under s.5(2) (and 19(2)) are additional to those under s.5(1) (19(1)). The rights accorded by ss.5(2) and 19(2) are, in one sense, radical, neither the RRA nor the SDA imposing, *in express terms*, any duty of adjustment. It is true that the concept of indirect discrimination can, on occasion, impose an obligation to adjust (by, for example, permitting mothers to work part-time). But under the DDA, by contrast with the position under the other Acts, the expectation is that the employer or service provider will adjust. Under the RRA, the SDA and the FETO, a complaint about a failure to adjust currently requires that the claimant prove (a) the application of a requirement or condition (b) that the applicant's "group" is less able than others to comply with that requirement or condition (c) that the applicant is unable to comply and (d) that this inability to comply amounts to a detriment.[64] We saw, in Chapter 2, that the technicalities of indirect discrimination prove an insuperable barrier to many. The wide definition of direct discrimination as less favourable treatment "for *a reason which relates to* the disabled person's disability", rather than "by reason of" that disability, coupled with the duty of adjustment, appears to cover the ground otherwise covered by indirect discrimination.

The case-law which exists on the issue of reasonable adjustments has arisen under the employment-related ss.5(2) and 6 of the Act. The proper approach to s.5(2) was set out by EAT in *Morse* v *Wiltshire County Council*, in which EAT allowed an appeal by a partially disabled man who was made redundant from his job as a road worker. His employers had decided that only those workers who could drive could retain their jobs, a requirement which, because of his disability, excluded Mr Morse. An industrial tribunal found that his dismissal, though related to his disability, was justified by the employers' "showing that no reasonable adjustment to the working conditions or job description would have avoided the dismissal, and that the reason for the treatment was material to the circumstances of the case and substantial within the meaning of s 5 of the Act:

Morse v *Wiltshire County Council* [1998] ICR 1023, [1998] IRLR 352, 44 BMLR 58

Bell J (for EAT)

if a driving licence is essential, and that discriminates against persons with a disability which makes them unable to hold a licence, then that is unfortunate, but it is hard to see how it can be avoided . . . As to adjustments, it is hard to see what they could be. Nothing was suggested on the applicant's behalf, and anything we could speculate upon would inevitably involve the respondent in considerable expense, in having to have a team effectively "carry" the applicant, which was precisely a situation which the respondent could not afford.

EAT overturned the tribunal's decision because of its failure to apply the appropriate test to the determination of the s.5(2)issue:

In our judgment, ss.5(2) and (4), and 6(1), (2), (3) and (4) of the Act require the industrial tribunal to go through a number of sequential steps when dealing with an allegation of s.5(2) discrimination.

Firstly, the tribunal must decide whether the provisions of s.6(1) and s.6(2) impose a s.6(1) duty on the employer in the circumstances of the particular case.

If such a duty is imposed, the tribunal must next decide whether the employer has taken such steps as it is reasonable, in all the circumstances of the case, for him to have to take in order to prevent the s. 6(1)(a) arrangements or s.6(1)(b) feature having the effect of placing the disabled person concerned at a substantial disadvantage in comparison with persons who are not disabled.

This in turn involves the tribunal enquiring whether the employer could reasonably have taken any steps including any of the steps set out in paragraphs (a) to (1) of s.6(3). The

---

[64] See Chapter 2 for discussion of impending changes to this definition

purpose of s.6(3) is to focus the mind of the employer on possible steps which it might take in compliance with its s.6(1)duty, and to focus the mind of the tribunal when considering whether an employer has failed to comply with a s.6 duty.

At the same time, the tribunal must have regard to the factors set out in s.6(4) paragraphs (a) to (e).

If, but only if, the tribunal (having followed these steps) finds that the employer has failed to comply with a s.6 duty in respect of the disabled applicant, does the tribunal finally have to decide whether the employer has shown that its failure to comply with its s.6 duty is justified, which means deciding whether it has shown that the reason for the failure to comply is both material to the circumstances of the particular case and substantial (see s.5(2) and (4)).

In taking these steps, the tribunal must, in our view, apply . . . an objective test, asking for instance whether the employer has taken such steps as were reasonable, whether any of the steps in s.6(3) were reasonably available in the light of the actual situation so far as the factors in s.6(4) were concerned; and asking whether the employer's failure to comply with its s.6 duty was in fact objectively justified, and whether the reason for failure to comply was in fact material to the circumstances of the particular case and in fact substantial.

No doubt, in carrying out these exercises, the tribunal will pay considerable attention to what factors the employer has considered or failed to consider, but it must scrutinise the explanation for selection for redundancy, for instance, put forward by the employer, and it must reach its own decision on what, if any, steps were reasonable and what was objectively justified, and material and substantial.

We reject, therefore, [the] argument . . . that it is sufficient if the tribunal judges that a reasonable employer could have acted as the respondent did or, more specifically, that the respondent must advance an explanation for its conduct but that, once it has done so, the tribunal can only consider whether that explanation is reasonably capable of being material and substantial.[65]

It is clear from the decision in *Morse* that, in applying s.5(2), the tribunal must ask (1) whether there is a duty on an employer to make any adjustment, (2) whether the employer has taken such steps as are reasonable to make such an adjustment and (3) whether any failure on the part of an employer to take such steps was justified. These questions shall be considered in turn.

A DUTY TO ADJUST?

S.6 DDA does not, on its face, apply to disability-related dismissals, s.6(2) providing that the duty applies only in relation to "(a) arrangements for determining to whom employment should be offered, [and] (b) any term, condition or arrangement on which employment, promotion, a transfer, training or any other benefit is offered or

---

[65] In *Heinz* v *Kendrick*, which is extracted above, EAT also stressed, *per* Lindsay J, the importance of considering ss 5(2) and 6 before reaching the conclusion that less favourable treatment was justifiable (though not if the treatment was found to be *unjustifiable* under s 5(1)).

afforded". But in *Morse,* above, EAT applied s.6 to a dismissal situaticn, ruling (*per* Mr Justice Bell) that "the valuable and specific protection" afforded by s.6 "would be lost to many vulnerable employees at the time of their greatest need if it did not apply to the question of dismissal and especially, perhaps, to dismissal by reason of redundancy". On this basis EAT interpreted s.6(2)(b) purposively to cover "arrangements in relation to whether employment continues or is terminated". In *Clark* v *Novacold,* too, EAT ruled, *per* then President Morison J:

Clark v Novocold [1998] ICR 1044 [1998] IRLR 420

We reject the submission that s 6 has no application to a case where an employee is complaining of dismissal. "I was dismissed because you failed to make necessary adjustments which would have enabled me to stay in useful employment" seems to us a perfectly legitimate complaint. Employers will be forced to think carefully before dismissing a person who has become disabled whilst in their employment. Paragraph 6.21 of the Disability Discrimination Code of Practice provides, *inter alia*, as follows:

> Dismissal—including compulsory early retirement—of a disabled person for a reason relating to the disability would need to be justified and the reason for it would have to be one which could not be removed by any reasonable adjustment.

If Mr Oldham's submission [for the employers] was correct, the Code of Practice is inappropriate since dismissal was not covered by the adjustment provisions in s 6 . . .

The decision in *Morse* was doubted by a differently constituted appeal tribunal in *Baynton* v *Saurus General Engineers Ltd* [1991] IRLR 604. The question whether s.6 applied to dismissal was subsequently considered by the Court of Appeal.

Clark v Novacold (CA) [1999] IRLR 318

Mummery LJ (for the Court):

It is contended that the wide language of s 6(2) and 6(3) is capable of applying to a "dismissal situation" as was held by the appeal tribunal in *Morse* . . .
It is important to note, however, that the complaint in that case under s 5(2) and s 6 was about arrangements of the employer relating to the criteria for selection for redundancy and the pre-dismissal failure of the employer to make reasonable adjustments to them under s 6.
The position in this case is that the only act complained of by Mr Clark . . . was dismissal. His complaint was that the dismissal was discriminatory, because it was less favourable treatment within s 5(1)(a) and it was not justified under s 5(1)(b) because reasonable consideration had not been given to alternative jobs within the company which he could do even with his injury . . . the act of dismissing Mr Clark was not in itself a breach of the s 6 duties. I should add, however, that there is a possible source of confusion in . . the reference to "dismissal situations" not being included in s 6(2). There may well be cases (but this is not one of them) where a person who has been dismissed complains of both s 5(1) discrimination by unjustified dismissal and also of s 5(2) discrimination by pre-dismissal breaches of s 6 duties while he was still in employment. There is no reason why an employee should not be able to pursue both claims: they are separate acts of discrimination and the

fact that the employee has been dismissed does not deprive him of the right to complain of a wrong committed against him while he was still employed, in the employer failing to comply with the duty to make reasonable adjustments to arrangements and to premises. I would add that, in an appropriate case, there is no reason why the compensation recoverable for a s 5(2) case should not include compensation for the loss of a job which flows from the failure to make the reasonable adjustments, though I would normally expect such compensation to be awarded on a successful claim for s 5(1) discrimination rather than under s 5(1).[66]

An example of pre-dismissal adjustments was given in *Kerrigan* v *Rover Group Ltd* (EORDCLD 40, p.11) in which an employment tribunal ruled in favour of a chronic asthmatic who had taken early retirement in order to avoid dismissal. The employers exempted serious progressive illnesses such as cancer from an "attendance improvement scheme" under which high levels of sickness absence such as the applicant's could result in dismissal. Asthma was not included in the scheme. The tribunal ruled that the employers could have made a reasonable adjustment during the time of his employment by including (or at least considering the inclusion of) asthma within the exemptions to the AIS scheme.

In *Kenny* v *Hampshire Constabulary*, EAT ruled that the duty of reasonable adjustment did not extend to the provision of personal assistance to enable a cerebral palsy sufferer to use the toilet.

Kenny v *Hampshire Constabulary* [1999] ICR 27 [1999] IRLR 76

It was contended on behalf of the applicant that the reference to "arrangements" in section 6 of this Act must cover matters of provision and omission and specifically included the provision of any care and equipment needed whilst at work. This would include the provision of personal carers if they were required by an employee to overcome a disadvantage at work . . .

[This] submission amounts to a contention that every arrangement which could be made to facilitate the disabled person's employment falls within the definition in section 6(2). Yet, as it seems to us, a line must be drawn somewhere otherwise the statute would have been drafted differently. Subsection (2), as the word "only" foreshadows, is not intended to cover everything an employer could do. For example, the provision of transport for getting to and from the employers" premises is outwith the section . . . not every failure to make an arrangement which deprives an employee of a chance to be employed is unlawful.

It is to section 6(2) that one must turn for a definition of what is covered. It seems to us that in the context of the language used, namely, "any term, condition or arrangements on which employment, promotion, a transfer, training or any other benefit is offered or afforded," Parliament had in mind what might be called "job-related" matters. In other

---

[66] In *Timex Corporation* v *Hodgson* [1981] IRLR 530, discussed in Chapter 6, EAT applied the GOQ defence (which, save in the case of ss 7A and B SDA, applies only to appointment, rather than to dismissal) in a redundancy case, taking the view that the defence could be applied to selection in respect of remaining jobs.

words, Parliament is directing employers to make adjustments to the way the job is structured and organised so as to accommodate those who cannot fit into existing arrangements
. . .

A broad construction seems inconsistent with the word "only" in section 6(2); the opposite point of view does not automatically lead to the employer succeeding because, as here, there will be discrimination under section 5(1) which the employer will be required to justify. As a matter of first impression it seems to us that, had Parliament intended to impose on employers the duty to cater for an employee's personal needs in the toilet, it would have said so, and the Code of Practice would have laid out the criteria to be applied. In fact, the Code of Practice is not consistent with such a duty . . .

Access to a toilet during working hours is a necessary ancillary to a person's work to bring the Act into play. Therefore, a failure to make physical arrangements for a disabled person to use the toilet would fall within section 6(1)(b); equally a failure to make physical arrangements to accommodate the carer would fall within that section; but it is going too far, in our judgment, to suggest that employers are under a statutory duty themselves to provide carers to attend to their employees' personal needs . . .

The decision in *Kenny* does appear to be consistent with the Code of Practice, upon which EAT relied. But perhaps unduly restrictive of the protection offered by the DDA was EAT's decision in *Ridout* v *TC Group* [1998] IRLR 628, in which it considered the application of s.6(6):

Nothing in this section imposes any duty on an employer in relation to a disabled person if the employer does not know, and could not reasonably be expected to know . . . (b) in any case, that that person has a disability and is likely to be affected in the way mentioned in subsection (1).

It should be noted that the decision of EAT in *Heinz* concerned discrimination under s.5(1) of the Act, rather than in connection with the s.5(2) and s.6 duty to adjust. Only the latter includes an express provision dealing with the employer's knowledge of the disability

S. 6(6) was applied by a tribunal in *Foord* v *JA Johnstone & Sons* to find no duty of adjustment by an employer in relation to an employee's fallen arches, in a case in which the employer did not know of the condition and, according to the tribunal, "could not reasonably be expected to know of it", given the absence of any medical certificate, signs of disability or complaint by the applicant.[67] This seems reasonable. But in *Ridout*, EAT rejected an appeal from a complainant who, having brought her (medically controlled) photosensitive epilepsy to the attention of her prospective employers and remarked, on being shown into an interview room with "bright fluorescent lighting without diffusers or baffles", that she might be disadvantaged by the lighting, was nevertheless interviewed in the room. The basis of her claim (under s.5(2)) was that her prospective employers failed to make reasonable adjustments to their interview arrangements to prevent them from substantially disadvantaging her.

[67] Reported in "Interpreting the DDA: Part 2", 80 *Equal Opportunities Review*, p.18.

The complainant was wearing sunglasses around her neck at the time, and the tribunal accepted the employers' contention that they took her remark as an explanation of the glasses (which she did not wear during the interview). EAT took the view that the employers were not, having been told that the applicant's epilepsy was medically controlled, under any duty to make further inquiry. Nor could they be criticised for not taking Ms Ridout's remark when she entered the room as a suggestion that the room was unsuitable: "it would have been possible for the applicant to be much more forthcoming about what she regarded as being required." The tribunal did not accept that, once the applicant had mentioned that she had epilepsy, the onus passed to the employers to do everything which was necessary to be done:

> The Act is phrased in such a way that the respondent must react in the appropriate way to that which it knows and to that which it could reasonably be expected to know. There is an onus on the employers to make "reasonable inquiry based upon information given to it" but there is no "absolute onus to make every inquiry possible".

EAT upheld the tribunal's decision, ruling that s.6(6):

> requires a tribunal to measure the extent of the duty, if any, against the actual or assumed knowledge of the employer both as to the disability and its likelihood of causing the individual a substantial disadvantage in comparison with persons who are not disabled. Tribunals should be careful not to impose upon disabled people a duty to give a long detailed explanation as to the effects of their disability merely to cause the employer to make adjustments which it probably should have made in the first place. On the other hand, it is equally undesirable that an employer should be required to ask a number of questions as to whether a person with a disability feels disadvantaged merely to protect themselves from liability.

Here EAT accepted that, given the very rare form of epilepsy suffered by the applicant, "the tribunal was entitled to conclude that no reasonable employer could be expected to know, without being told in terms by the applicant, that the arrangements which were made for the interview might disadvantage her . . . Whether the employers should have taken any other steps as a result of what was said at the interview was a matter of fact and evidence for the tribunal".

Once again, Thompson's *Labour and European Law Review* commented that:

> As with other recently reported disability decisions, [the decision in *Ridout*] flags up the difficulty that disabled people face, in having to decide whether to alert employers to a disability so running the risk of potential discrimination, or saying nothing and then losing the protection of the legislation.[68]

It would not, perhaps, have been requiring a great deal from employers to place the onus on them to enquire as to the suitability of the interview arrangements in a situa-

[68] Issue 30, available as at fn 48 above.

tion in which the applicant had (1) notified them of her disability, albeit in general terms and (2) given some indication that the arrangements made by them were such as to place her at a disadvantage. But the *Equal Opportunities Review* suggests that:

"Interpreting the Disability Discrimination Act—Part 2" (1998) 80 *EOR* 14, 14–15

Although the outcome of some of the decisions relying upon s.6(6) may appear somewhat harsh, it must be borne in mind that the alternative to emphasising the employee's responsibility to request an adjustment is to intensify the employer's duty to inquire Where the disabled employee is already doing the job adequately, it is arguable that the law should not encourage an employer to be too proactive, since the line between inquiry and intrusion may be a thin one. In *Davies v Toys R Us*, the applicant was missing part of his arm and wore an artificial limb. Part of his duties involved climbing a ladder and handling goods. After his dismissal, an issue arose as to whether an adjustment to his duties should have been made in this respect. A Leicester industrial tribunal . . . said that: ' Even if the applicant was placed at a substantial disadvantage . . . he covered that up. He was asked on a number of occasions if he had problems and said he did not. On the facts of this case we do not consider that the respondent should have gone beyond the applicant's assertion that he did not have a problem. It would be contrary to the general intention of the Disability Discrimination Act if employers were to determine that a disabled person, who apparently can do the work and maintains when asked that he is capable of doing the work, should be denied that work on a contrary assumption made by the employer".

The decision in *Ridout* was one of fact for the tribunal. Perhaps of more significance than the outcome of the particular decision was the emphasis placed by EAT on the Code of Practice:

we do criticise the industrial tribunal for not making specific reference to the Code of Practice. It seems to us that as the case law develops in relation to the Disability Discrimination Act, industrial tribunals will build up a knowledge of how the Act should be applied in practice. At this period of development it is particularly important, in my judgment, that industrial tribunals should always refer to the relevant provisions of the Code of Practice as they are required to do under s 53. The code will help them in resolving questions at issue since the code sets out the standards to be expected, in relatively straightforward language.

In the instant case, however, EAT found "nothing in the code . . . which is of particular assistance to the appellant".

REASONABLE STEPS TAKEN?

S.6(3) provides a list of examples of the type of action an employer might have to take under s.6(1):

(a) making adjustments to premises;
(b) allocating some of the disabled person's duties to another person;
(c) transferring him to fill an existing vacancy;
(d) altering his working hours;
(e) assigning him to a different place of work;
(f) allowing him to be absent during working hours for rehabilitation, assessment or treatment;
(g) giving him, or arranging for him to be given, training;
(h) acquiring or modifying equipment;
(i) modifying instructions or reference manuals;
(j) modifying procedures for testing or assessment; ·
(k) providing a reader or interpreter;
(l) providing supervision.

The Code of Practice provides concrete examples of the types of steps which might be required under each of these headings (suggesting, for example, that "making adjustments to premises" might include: "widening a doorway, providing a ramp or moving furniture for a wheelchair user; relocating light switches, door handles or shelves for someone who has difficulty in reaching; providing appropriate contrast in décor to help the safe mobility of a visually impaired person".

S.6(4) provides that "[i]n determining whether it is reasonable for an employer to have to take a particular step in order to comply with subsection (1), regard shall be had, in particular", to factors such as (a) "the extent to which taking the step would prevent the effect in question" (b) the practicability and (c) costs of and disruption associated with taking the step as well as (d) the employer's resources and (e) any financial or other assistance available. These following extract illustrates the practical operation of these provisions:

"Interpreting the Disability Discrimination Act—Part 2" pp. 20–1

[In] *Ridley v Severn NHS Trust*, a Bristol industrial tribunal held that more consideration should have been given to finding alternative work for a health visitor with a leg injury before dismissing her. The tribunal noted that s.6(3)(c) refers to the stop of "transferring him to fill an existing vacancy" and the Code of Practice says that the employee "might have to be considered for any suitable alternative posts which are available (such a case might also involve reasonable retraining)." In this case, at the time of dismissal, there were 90 vacancies in the organisation, but the employers admitted that no further steps were taken by them to find the applicant suitable alternative posts, other than sending her lists of existing vacancies.

In *Forder v Southern Water Services Ltd*, a process technician/mechanical fitter with emphysema as dismissed after refusing to transfer to a job involving climbing ladders. . . . a Southampton industrial tribunal held that the employer was under a duty to make adjustments, in particular by allocating some of the duties to another person within s.6(3)(b) of the DDA or by assigning him to a different place of work within s.6(3)(e). "There was no evidence before the tribunal that the respondent had considered making any adjustments," and the tribunal was satisfied that in view of the size and resources of the employer, it was reasonable for them to have taken steps to comply with their duties under s.6 and to have considered an alternative position for the applicant.

On the other hand, in *Matty v Tesco Stores Ltd*, a diabetic was turned down for a job as a fitter at the company's distribution centre because it involved working alone on an irregular shift rota, climbing ladders up to 40 feet, and having to spend several hours a week working in an environment of –25°C. A Leicester industrial tribunal found that the failure to make an adjustment was justified. "As far as the premises are concerned, no adjustment was reasonably practicable. The racking could not be lowered to a height at which it would be safe to allow the applicant to work and the freezer could not be run at a higher temperature . . . The nature of the fitter's job was that, in an emergency, he might have to spend long periods carrying out work in and on the freezer. As a diabetic, the risk of his sustaining injury from such work was increased and the risk could not be reduced by supplying or modifying equipment. There was no way in which the nature of the job could be changed. For reasons of cost, it was not possible to have two fitters on duty all the time, thereby allowing the applicant to work in ambient temperatures and on the ground. Altering his hours would not help."

Financial costs are expressly made a consideration for whether an adjustment is reasonable by s.6(4). In *Smith v Carpets International UK plc*, an epileptic was not allowed to carry on working as a warehouse operative after having seizures. A Leeds industrial tribunal said that the employer "had carried out reasonable investigations as to what adjustments could possibly be made to accommodate" Mr Smith. However, taking "into account the questions of practicability and financial cost", the tribunal took the view that it was "not reasonable to expect the respondent to do what would have amounted . . . to a total change in the way in which the respondent carried out its work. The respondent could not reasonably be expected to have made arrangements which removed fork-lift trucks from the warehouse, for example. They did, however, offer the applicant a different place of work . . . The steps were ones which the tribunal found to come within s.6(3)(a)."

In *Hillingdon v Morgan* and in *Kent v Mingo*, EAT has considered the obligation on employers to provide alternative work for disabled staff otherwise threatened with job loss. In *Morgan* the appeal tribunal, *per* Morison J, upheld an employment tribunal's finding that the employer had failed in its s.6 duty by failing to consider, at least in the short term, whether an applicant who suffered from ME could have been provided with work at home; and by applying to her the normal rules governing redeployment of those who were on long-term sick leave or whose jobs were to be made redundant.

London Borough of Hillingdon v Morgan EAT/1493/98

Morison J (for EAT)

It seems to us clear that the Employment Tribunal's decision can be summarised in this way:

First, with a graded return to work there was reason to believe that she could, after one or two months, have been able to fulfil the duties of many of the jobs which fell for consideration under the [employer's] redeployment scheme, and for which she was well qualified.

Secondly, as a large employer the authority had the capacity to make adjustments, as they had with other staff, to enable her to have a graded return to work, for example, a short period of working at home doing work which she was qualified to do for short periods of time.

Thirdly, the Personnel Department were less than active in seeking to ensure her graded return to work, adopting a supine rather than a positive attitude to finding her a position in other departments.

It seems to us, in a nutshell, that what has happened here is that the employers have treated the Applicant as they would have treated any other person who fell for redeployment within their redeployment scheme. To that extent they have failed in their duty. It was, since the coming into force of the Disability Discrimination Act, their duty to deal with people who became disabled at work in accordance with the statutory requirements as amplified by the Code of Practice. If they had approached the matter in that way, they would not have simply regarded this as another redeployment case where they had to see if there was a job available and, if not, to offer one which was below the level at which she had been working. The Act requires more, as its terms make clear. They are required to see if they can make reasonable adjustments so as to enable a person who is disabled to be retained in their employment. In this case the disablement was by November, regarded as being something which could be overcome with care and attention paid by the employers to her redeployment needs. For example, she could have been provided with secretarial or administrative work to do for short periods of time at home and the judgment of the Employment Tribunal on the facts, as they found them to be, was that if that attitude had been taken towards her, she would, in fact, have been able to return to full-time employment within about two months of her starting to do that temporary work.

Accordingly, it seems to us that the employers have never really addressed the questions at issue in this case, and the Tribunal was quite entitled to . . . [the] view that the Council had failed to comply with the particular statutory obligations which are imposed on an employer when dealing with a disabled person. She was not simply to be treated as a potential redeployee. She needed specific measures being considered and taken in her case.

The employers in *Morgan* had argued that they were bound to appoint only on "merit" by s.7 of the Local Government and Housing Act 1989. Morison J pointed out that s.7, which was considered in Chapter 3, is subject to an exception to accommodate employer's obligations under ss.5(2) and 6 DDA.

The question of re-deployment was considered again in *Kent* v *Mingo*, in which EAT (again under Morison J) ruled that s.6(2) required a measure of positive discrimination in favour of an applicant rendered unfit, by a back injury, for his former position.

Kent County Council v Mingo EAT/1097/98

Morison J (for EAT)

The applicant was classified as a Category B re-deployee and he was told that there was no flexibility about his classification . . . The procedures were designed to match internal job vacancies within the Council with existing re-deployees. Category A re-deployees were those at risk, or under notice of, redundancy. Category B staff consisted of, *inter alia*, "staff to be deployed on incapability/ill-health." The order of treatment was such that Category A staff were the best placed to obtain re-deployment:

"When applying for a post which is graded no higher than the grade of their redundant post they [Category A staff] must be interviewed unless the manager has very good reasons as to why they were unsuitable . . . They have priority consideration for suitable alternative employment and must be seen before, and without regard to the abilities of, other non-category A applicants . . .

"Although Category B staff are given the same access to the Central Clearing House, they are not entitled to preferential treatment in relation to other internal applicants (although their particular circumstances should be taken into account when assessing their application)."

A new Clearing House procedure was introduced in or about November 1996. Under the new procedure Category A staff were defined as before, but a new category was introduced to cover staff with a disability. They were defined as the following:

staff who are covered by the Disability Discrimination Act and where a reasonable adjustment cannot be made to their present post to accommodate their disability."

Staff to be re-deployed on incapacity/ill-health grounds, other than those covered by the Disability Discrimination Act, were defined as Category B staff. The order of treatment of staff still appeared to place Category A staff on a different level to others, as the descriptive paragraph read:

"If no suitable candidates have been found from the above categories then before looking at the other categories these staff must be considered providing they are applying for a post at a level no higher than the post in which they have been employed." . . .

the Tribunal were entitled to consider that the re-deployment procedures of the Council did not adequately reflect the statutory duty on employers under the Act. The Council's policy was to give preferential treatment to redundant or potentially redundant employees. That meant that those with disabilities were relatively handicapped in the system of re-deployment.

The structure of the Act is such as to require employers to take reasonable steps to accommodate disabled staff, or those who become disabled in the course of employment, as set out in section 6 of the Act and in the light of the statutory guidance and Code of Practice.

Whilst we have no doubt that the Council endeavoured to act in accordance with its own procedures, we agree . . . that they did not give effect to the employer's obligations under the Act.

Had the Council's policy permitted the applicant to be treated as a Category A re-deployee, on the facts found by the Tribunal, he would have been re-deployed and not dismissed. On that basis the Tribunal were quite entitled to conclude that the Council had been guilty of unlawful discrimination.

JUSTIFICATION

Discrimination, whether by way of less favourable treatment or a failure to make reasonable adjustments, occurs only where the employer fails to show that the differential treatment or the failure was "justified". S.5(3) provides that, for the purposes of s.5(1): "treatment is justified if, but only if, the reason for it is both *material* to the circumstances of the case and *substantial*" (my emphasis) and 5(5) provides:

> If, in a case falling within subsection (1), the employer is under a Section 6 duty in relation to the disabled person but fails without justification to comply with that duty, his treatment of that person cannot be justified under subsection (3) unless it would have been justified even if he had complied with the Section 6 duty.

The justification of non-employment related discrimination is dealt with somewhat differently under the DDA, s.20(3) states that discrimination in the provision of goods, services, etc is justified only where the service provider reasonably believes that (s.20(4)):

> (a) . . . the treatment is necessary in order not to endanger the health or safety of any person (which may include that of the disabled person);
> (b) . . . the disabled person is incapable of entering into an enforceable agreement, or of giving an informed consent, and for that reason the treatment is reasonable in that case; [or]
> (c) in a case falling within section 19(1)(a), the treatment is necessary because the provider of services would otherwise be unable to provide the service to members of the public;
> (d) in a case falling within section 19(1)(c) or (d), the treatment is necessary in order for the provider of services to be able to provide the service to the disabled person or to other members of the public;
> (e) in a case falling within section 19(1)(d), the difference in the terms on which the service is provided to the disabled person and those on which it is provided to other members of the public reflects the greater cost to the provider of services in providing the service to the disabled person.
> (5) Any increase in the cost of providing a service to a disabled person which results from compliance by a provider of services with a section 21 duty shall be disregarded for the purposes of subsection (4)(e).

Similarly, s.22's regulation of discrimination in relation to premises provides that less favourable treatment in this context is justified only where the alleged discriminator reasonably believes that the treatment is necessary on grounds of health and safety, that the disabled person is unable to enter into a legally enforceable agreement or to give informed consent; where (in a case in which the differential treatment relates to the terms on which premises are offered) it "is necessary in order for the disabled person or the occupiers of other premises forming part of the building to make use of the benefit or facility; or (in a case in which the less favourable treatment consists of a refusal to dispose of the premises) where it "is necessary in order for the occupiers of other premises forming part of the building to make use of the benefit or facility". Reported cases on justification, in common with that on reasonable adjustments, have arisen in relation to employment rather than the other areas covered by the DDA.[69]

Prior to the development of case law on the justification defence, Brian Doyle remarked that "[h]ow [it] . . . works in practice will be the making or breaking" of the DDA. This is particularly the case in view of the generous approach adopted to "less favourable treatment" by the Court of Appeal in *Clark*. The easier it is to prove less favourable treatment (i.e., the fewer hurdles are erected in terms of the appropriate comparator—*Clark*, and the need for knowledge of disability on the part of the employer, etc),[70] the greater the significance of the justification defence.

Early employment cases on the justification defence were not particularly encouraging, a tribunal in *O'Dea* v *Bonart Ltd* finding that a threat to withhold (discretionary) sick pay from a disabled man was "a proper exercise of the [employer's] discretion having regard to the amount of sick pay the applicant had received over the years".[71] In *Clark* v *Novacold* (the first case to reach EAT), the appeal tribunal once again emphasised the importance of the Code of Practice in this matter. So, too, did the Court of Appeal.

The Code of Practice addresses the issue of justification by asserting that less favourable treatment will be justified only if the reason for it . . . relate[s] to the individual circumstances in question and [is] not just . . . trivial or minor."[72] It goes on to suggest that "[a] general assumption that blind people cannot use computers would not in itself be a material reason—it is not related to the particular circumstances"; that the fact that clerical worker with a learning disability "cannot sort papers quite as quickly as some of his colleagues [where t]here is very little difference in productivity . . . is very unlikely to be a substantial reason" for his dismissal; that the muttering of a mentally ill worker, where other workers make similar levels of noise of a mentally ill person who mutters to himself at a level accepted in relation to other employees "is unlikely to be a substantial reason" for his transfer. The Code also points out that:

> less favourable treatment cannot be justified where the employer is under a duty to make a reasonable adjustment but fails (without justification) to do so, unless the treatment would have been justified even after that adjustment . . . [if] an employee who uses a wheelchair is not promoted, solely because the work station for the higher post is inaccessible to wheelchairs—though it could readily be made so by rearrangement of the furniture . . . [t]he refusal of promotion would . . . not be justified.

By contrast, the rejection of someone with "psoriasis (a skin condition) . . for a job involving modelling cosmetics on a part of the body which in his case is severely

---

[69] Though in *Rose* v *Bouchet*, reported at 85 *Equal Opportunities Review*, p.1, Edinburgh Sheriff Court ruled that the opinion could be factually inaccurate or based on a stereotype, so long as the judge finds the opinion was not unreasonable.

[70] See *Heinz* v *Kendrick*, above.

[71] Case 1700168/97, Thompson's *Labour and European Law Review*, issue 17, fn 47 above.

[72] Code of Practice for the Elimination of Discrimination in the Field of Employment against Disabled Persons or Persons who have had a Disability (1996), para 4.6.

disfigured by the condition . . . would be lawful if his appearance would be incompatible with the purpose of the work. This is a substantial reason which is clearly related—material—to the individual circumstance."[73] Equally, the rejection of a blind applicant for a job "which requires a significant amount of driving" is likely to be justified "[I]f it is not reasonable for the employer to adjust the job so that the driving duties are given to someone else".[74]

The question of justification will be one of fact, subject to the tribunal taking into account the relevant provisions of the Code of Practice. Certainly, the standard suggested by the Code of Practice is not onerous—it comes nowhere near the "business necessity" test adopted by the US Supreme Court in *Griggs*,[75] or to the "objective justification" test established in the sex discrimination sphere by the ECJ in *Bilka-Kaufhaus* (see Chapter 2).[76] In *Clark* the Court of Appeal rejected the tribunal's finding that the discrimination was not justified because, although the tribunal had adverted to the Code of Practice, it had not taken into account that document's provision that:

> It would be justifiable to terminate the employment of an employee whose disability makes it impossible for him any longer to perform the main functions of his job, if an adjustment such as a move to a vacant post elsewhere in the business is not practicable or otherwise not reasonable for the employer to make.

The tribunal had ruled that the dismissal of Mr Clark would, had it been discriminatory, have been unjustified because "there could have been no prejudice to [Novacold] in continuing the applicant's employment if his employment . . . It would have had no organisational nor economic consequences at all in terms of wages or other matters . . . if they had continued the applicant's employment and not continued to pay him sick pay, it would have been of no economic loss to them for them to continue that employment under those circumstances." The issue of justification was remitted for reconsideration in light of the Code's provisions.

Further guidance on the justification test was provided by EAT in *Baynton* v *Saurus*, in which a tribunal had ruled in favour of the employer on the basis that the employee was unable to do his job and (in a redundancy situation) no suitable alternative work was available.

---

[73] Ibid, fn. 72 above.

[74] Fn 72 above, para 4.7. In *O'Neill* v *Symm* the Court of Appeal ruled that the dismissal, for absence, of an employee whose disability was not known to the employer would certainly be justified under s.5(1).

[75] In relation to Title VII Civil Rights Act 1964, which prohibits discrimination on grounds of race and sex, but not disability.

[76] Canada's human rights statutes require accommodation to the point of undue hardship. A similar test was struck down by Ireland's Supreme Court in *re Article 26 and in the Matter of the Employment Equality Bill 1996*, Supreme Court Case no.118/97, 15 May 1997.

Baynton v *Saurus* [1999] IRLR 604

Peter Clark J:

Here, although not specifically mentioned, it is clear that the tribunal had in mind the guidance contained in paragraph 6.21 of the Code; the tribunal found that the respondent had justified the dismissal of an employee whose disability made it impossible for him to perform the main functions of his job . . .

Just as the Employment Tribunal and EAT in *Novacold* fell into error in adopting the comparator approach to the question of less favourable treatment in s. 5(1)(a) of the Act, by importing a concept from the differently worded provisions of the sex and race discrimination legislation, so we must be careful to observe the difference in wording between the concept of justification under the [DDA] and the race and sex discrimination Acts.

Under the [DDA] the defence of justification is available to a claim of direct disability discrimination under s. 5(1)(a). It is not available as a defence to claims of direct sex and race discrimination. . . .

It is now accepted that the word "justifiable" in s. 1 of the sex and race discrimination Acts requires an objective balance between the discriminatory effect of the condition and the reasonable needs of the party who applies the condition. [citing Balcombe LJ *Hampson* v *Department of Education and Science* [1989] ICR 179].

We accept that the statutory test laid down in s. 5(3) of the [DDA] is unique. The reason for the discriminatory treatment must be material to the circumstances of the case and substantial. "Material to the circumstances of the case" must, in our judgment, include the circumstances of both the employer and employee.

In *Novacold* the Employment Tribunal fell into error, so the Court of Appeal held, in focusing, too narrowly, on their finding that the employer could continue the applicant's employment without economic consequences. They did not take into account all the relevant circumstances.

In the present case we have concluded that the Employment Tribunal's approach precisely mirrored the Employment Tribunal's error in *Novacold*. Whereas in that case the tribunal concentrated only on one aspect of the facts which favoured the employee, here, the tribunal has focussed only on those facts which favour the employer.

In reaching a conclusion on the issue of justification this tribunal was bound to consider, before finding that the appellant was dismissed because he could not do his job, whether the respondent had, at the date of dismissal . . . found out from the appellant what the real effects of the disability might be. Code, paragraph 3.2. There was no apparent consideration by the tribunal of the effect of the failure by the respondent to warn the appellant that he was at risk of dismissal, or to find out the up-to-date medical position before dismissing him. Had those steps been taken the respondent would have discovered that the appellant was due to see his consultant on 4th February 1998. Bearing in mind that the appellant was not then in receipt of sick pay, how does the tribunal balance the desirability of awaiting the outcome of that consultation with the present need to save an employee from redundancy in the sister company? There is no indication in the tribunal's reasons that they have carried out this consideration of all the circumstances of the case in judging whether the respondent has justified the discriminatory treatment, that is the dismissal.

In these circumstances, like the Court of Appeal in *Novacold*, we find that this Employment Tribunal has fallen into error.

In *Heinz* v *Kendrick*, EAT upheld the tribunal's decision that the applicant's dismissal was unjustified where the employer had not considered whether the applicant, who was on long-term sick leave, could be found alternative employment, and had not followed fully its own procedures for medical dismissals. But Lindsay J stressed the low threshold of justification, in particular, expressing the view that the balancing exercise required by EAT in *Baynton* was a narrow one.

Heinz v *Kendrick* [2000] IRLR 141

Lindsay J (for EAT)

During the hearing [in *Clark* v *Novacold*, Morison J] flirted with the idea that Section 5(3) provided only a necessary rather than a sufficient condition for justification, meaning that a Tribunal could not hold there to be justification unless the reason for the treatment was "both material to the circumstances of the particular case and substantial" but that even if the reason satisfied that test there was not necessarily justification . . . it might be thought such a very low threshold for justification was itself indicative of Section 5(3) providing, surely, only a necessary condition rather than a sufficient one. Were the condition to be merely necessary Tribunals would have been able, as many would applaud, to adopt a broad approach to justification based on their views, as "the Industrial jury", of the substantial merits of the case rather as is required of them under s. 98(4). However, we must recognise that Section 5(3) provides that the treatment "is justified" if the condition is met, not that it "can" or "may" be. It thus seems, in the category we are dealing with, that the condition stipulated in Section 5(3) is both necessary and sufficient. As the Code has to be taken into account . . . then whatever one might think about the lowness of such a threshold, (lower, it might be thought, than the word "substantial" would usually indicate), if the reason for the treatment relates to the individual circumstances in question and is not just trivial or minor then justification has to be held to exist in the category of case which we are dealing with, namely that in which no Section 6 duty falls upon the employer. This is not a conclusion we reach with enthusiasm but as the language of the domestic statute is clear (and no reference has been made to Community law) the remedy for the lowness of the threshold, if any is required, lies in the hands of the legislature not of the Courts . . .

In *Baynton* . . . the EAT preferred a submission that in applying a test of justification under Section 5(3) a Tribunal had to carry out a balancing exercise between the interests of the disabled employee and the interests of the employer. We have already noted that the "circumstances of the particular case" referred to in Section 5(3) can include the employer's circumstances. Whilst we would not preclude some balancing exercise, the comparatively limited reuirements of Section 5(3) are to be borne in mind. It does not require a wider survey of what is reasonable having regard to specific features such as is found in Section 6(1) and Section 6(4). Under Section 5(3) all that is material is whether the reason for the treatment is "both material to the circumstances of the particular case and substantial" which, under the Code, as we have cited, means that the reason has to relate to the individual circumstances in question and not just be trivial or minor.[77]

---

[77] Though in *Post Office* v *Jones* [2000] IRLR 388, EAT accepted that the application, without consideration of the individual circumstances of the case, of the employer's driving ban on insulin-dependent diabetics was not justified within the DDA.

While behaviour which is "unreasonable" within s.98(4) ERA will not be justified under s.5, the converse is not necessarily true. Thus, for example, in *Ridley* v *Severn NHS Trust*, a tribunal ruled that an employer breached the DDA in dismissing a health visitor who was unable, as a result of injury, to work in her previous role.[78] The Trust put her on a redeployment list but did not actively seek to place her in an alternative post, and rejected "for somewhat vague reasons" her application for a receptionist's post. A tribunal found that she had been fairly dismissed for the purposes of the ERA, but that the rejection of her application for the receptionist's job breached the DDA—the reasons given by the Trust were not substantial enough and any shortcomings on her part could have been remedied by training or some other adjustment. And in *Heinz* v *Kendrick*, EAT ruled that the tribunal had erred in treating a dismissal in breach of the DDA as *necessarily* unfair, though in *Kent* v *Mingo* on the facts, EAT found that the dismissal in breach of the DDA was also unfair.

The fact that the DDA permitted the justification even of direct discrimination was criticised at the time of the Act's implementation. Certainly, tribunal decisions have, at times, been less than rigorous in assessing the justifiability of disability-related discrimination. On the other hand, some type of justification defence is inevitable—without it, someone discriminated against on the ground that she lacked the academic qualifications to be a doctor (this lack being connected with a learning difficulty) or because he was unable (by virtue of being wheelchair bound) to meet the physical criteria for a job as a member of a lifeboat crew, would succeed in a DDA claim.

The American ADA is frequently put forward as a model for disability discrimination legislation and, in many respects, has been the model for the DDA. But while the ADA does not expressly permit the justification of discrimination (save, in the case of a failure to make reasonable adjustment, in the case of "undue hardship"[79] to the employer); its restriction of protection against disability-based discrimination to "qualified persons" has much the same effect.

A person is not "qualified" for the job unless (a) she "satisfies the prerequisites for the position, such as possessing the appropriate educational background, employment experience, skills, licenses, etc"; and (b) she "can perform the essential functions of the position . . . with or without reasonable accommodation". According to the EEOC:

"Reasonable accommodations" include: (1) accommodations that are required to ensure equal opportunity in the application process; (2) accommodations that enable the employer's employees with disabilities to perform the essential functions of the position held or desired; and (3) accommodations that enable the employer's employees with disabilities to enjoy equal benefits and privileges of employment as are enjoyed by employees without disabilities . . . This determination of whether or not a particular function is essential will generally include one or more of the following factors . . . [(a)] whether the position

---

[78] Thompson's *Labour and European Law Review*, issue 19, available as at fn 48 above.
[79] According to the EEOC regulations, " 'Undue hardship' refers to any accommodation that would be unduly costly, extensive, substantial, or disruptive, or that would fundamentally alter the nature or operation of the business."

exists [solely] to perform a particular function . . . [(b)] the number of other employees available to perform that job function or among whom the performance of that job function can be distributed . . . [(c)] the degree of expertise or skill required to perform the function. In certain professions and highly skilled positions the employee is hired for his or her expertise or ability to perform the particular function. In such a situation, the performance of that specialized task would be an essential function . . .

The time spent performing the particular function may also be an indicator of whether that function is essential . . . The consequences of failing to require the employee to perform the function may be another indicator of whether a particular function is essential. For example, although a firefighter may not regularly have to carry an unconscious adult out of a burning building, the consequence of failing to require the firefighter to be able to perform this function would be serious . . .

An employer may require, as a qualification standard, that an individual not pose a direct threat to the health or safety of himself/herself or others. Like any other qualification standard, such a standard must apply to all applicants or employees and not just to individuals with disabilities. If, however, an individual poses a direct threat as a result of a disability, the employer must determine whether a reasonable accommodation would either eliminate the risk or reduce it to an acceptable level. If no accommodation exists that would either eliminate or reduce the risk, the employer may refuse to hire an applicant or may discharge an employee who poses a direct threat.

The employer should identify the specific risk posed by the individual. For individuals with mental or emotional disabilities, the employer must identify the specific behavior on the part of the individual that would pose the direct threat. For individuals with physical disabilities, the employer must identify the aspect of the disability that would pose the direct threat. The employer should then consider . . .

(1) the duration of the risk;

(2) the nature and severity of the potential harm;

(3) the likelihood that the potential harm will occur; and

(4) the imminence of the potential harm.

Such consideration must rely on objective, factual evidence—not on subjective perceptions, irrational fears, patronizing attitudes, or stereotypes—about the nature or effect of a particular disability, or of disability generally . . . Relevant evidence may include input from the individual with a disability, the experience of the individual with a disability in previous similar positions, and opinions of medical doctors, rehabilitation counselors, or physical therapists who have expertise in the disability involved and/or direct knowledge of the individual with the disability.

One significant evidential factor taken into account in assessing the essential features of a job is any written job description which predates the disabled person's application for the job:

employers [are not required] to develop or maintain job descriptions [but] written job descriptions prepared before advertising or interviewing applicants for the job, as well as the employer's judgment as to what functions are essential are among the relevant evidence to be considered in determining whether a particular function is essential.

The DRTF considered the "essential function" approach to justification:

We found no evidence that the justification test was not sufficiently objective or sufficiently demanding to balance the interests of disabled employees and employers. Tribunals are considering: the reason for the treatment; whether it was substantial and material; and whether, on the evidence, it was sufficient.

We rejected using an approach similar to that in the [ADA] of Genuine Occupational Requirements (GORs)—the essential requirements of a particular post—to provide employers with a defence for less favourable treatment. Given the wide scope of work activities and employee benefits, it was felt impracticable to require employers to specify GORs for every post in their organisation, for every training and development opportunity and for every benefit offered. Such an approach would limit employers' ability to be flexible in assigning duties and generate unacceptable bureaucratic burdens.[80]

REMEDIES

Much of the relevant material here is considered in Chapter 5. But one issue of particular importance under the DDA is that of medical evidence. The significance of such evidence became apparent in *Buxton* v *Equinox Design* [1999] IRLR 158, [1999] ICR 269, in which EAT remitted for rehearing a tribunal decision to limit the award made to an MS sufferer in respect of loss of earnings (he had been dismissed in connection with his disability) to one year.[81] Morison J, for EAT, suggested that:

What one might describe as the relatively brief and informal hearing on remedy appropriate in unfair dismissal cases may not be appropriate where the compensation is uncapped. In the former category of case, the judgment and experience of the lay members may be especially important in relation to the state of the job market in the locality, and the potentiality for the applicant obtaining new employment, and thus, the tribunal may not be assisted by much, if any, evidence. But where the case involves unlimited compensation, it will often be the case that the remedies hearing should involve the parties in careful pre-preparation under the management of the tribunal . . .

in discrimination cases, the remedy hearing will require careful judicial management. In disability cases, a medical expert might be required if the parties have been unable to agree the evidence . . .

In *McLauchlan* v *Stolt Comex Seaway Ltd* 41 EORDCLD 1, a Scottish tribunal awarded almost £78 000, including £33 000 in respect of future loss, to a man dismissed after a diagnosis of terminal cancer. The award in respect of future loss was based on the medical evidence of his oncologist that his life expectancy was eight months.

---

[80] Fn 5 above, executive summary paras 9–11.
[81] £7,627.50 compensation, including £500 injury to feelings, was awarded.

DISABILITY DISCRIMINATION AND THE DRAFT
EQUAL TREATMENT DIRECTIVE

The 1999 draft directive on equal treatment has been mentioned throughout the book. Here it is useful to outline its possible implications for the DDA. Article 2 provides that indirect discrimination on the enumerated grounds may be justified where the "provision, criterion or practice" at issue "is objectively justified by a legitimate aim and the means of achieving it are appropriate and necessary". The prohibition on direct discrimination does not provide any general justification defence, but Article 4 permits "genuine occupational qualifications . . . where, by reason of the nature of the particular occupational activities concerned or of the context in which they are carried out, such a characteristic constitutes a genuine occupational qualification".

The first point to be made concerns the coverage by the draft directive of indirect discrimination. True it is, as we saw above, that much of that which would constitute indirect discrimination under the RRA, SDA and FETO is caught within the DDA's (qualified) prohibition on "less favourable treatment . . . for a reason which relates to the disabled person's disability", read with the duty of reasonable adjustment. But to the extent that these are insufficient to catch all practices which would come within the broad and generous definition of indirect discrimination adopted by the draft directive, legislative change would be required if the measure were to be adopted. The approach to "justification" taken under the DDA is considerably more generous than that which prevails under Article 141, which appears to form the model for the test of justification adopted by the draft directive. And the draft directive permits justification of direct discrimination only where a "genuine occupational qualification", an approach which is certainly narrower than the position under the DDA. Finally, although the draft directive does not at present define "disability", it will be interesting to see if this approach changes prior to the adoption of it or any other European legislation regulating disability discrimination. The many inadequacies of the DDA in this respect have been considered above.

9

The Fair Employment and Treatment (Northern Ireland) Order 1998

Northern Ireland is unique in the UK in having legislation (currently the Fair Employment and Treatment (Northern Ireland) Order 1998—FETO) which prohibits discrimination on the grounds of religion or political opinion.[1] This latter extends beyond religion-related political opinion to encompass, *inter alia*, "left" and "right" (*McKay* v *Northern Ireland Public Service Alliance* [1994] NI 103) although it excludes opinions "which consist of [or include] approval or acceptance of the use of violence for political ends connected with the affairs of Northern Ireland, including the use of violence for the purpose of putting the public or any section of the public in fear".[2]

The FETO, and the Fair Employment Acts of 1976 and 1989 which it amends and consolidates, have their roots in Northern Ireland's troubled sectarian history. From its creation, the Northern Irish "state" prohibited religious discrimination, the Government of Ireland Act 1920 providing that Northern Ireland's Parliament must not "give a preference, privilege or advantage, or impose any disability or disadvantage, on account of religious belief".[3] From the outset, however, such discrimination was and remained endemic both in the private sector (Protestants and Catholics living largely separate lives) and in Government, broadly defined.

Much of the difficulty arises from the intertwined nature of religion and Northern Irish political affiliation. Very broadly speaking, Northern Irish Catholics tend to favour the creation of a single Ireland, while their Protestant compatriots prefer the continued position of Northern Ireland as part of the UK. The close relationship between religion and political affiliation (and between religion and *perceived* political affiliation) has resulted in the construction of Catholics as disloyal to the state. This,

---

[1] Article 2(3) provides that "references to a person's religious belief or political opinion include references to—(a) his supposed religious belief or political opinion; and (b) the absence or supposed absence of any, or any particular, religious belief or political opinion".

[2] Article 2(4).

[3] The Constitution Act 1973, which abolished the Stormont Parliament and created an Assembly with lesser powers, also prohibited (direct) discrimination by that body and by public authorities. The Assembly was short-lived, however, and direct rule was re-imposed in 1974. S.2 has been replaced by s.76 Northern Ireland Act 1998, discussed below.

predictably, has had repercussions in terms of their employment in the public sector and, in particular, in the security forces.[4]

K. McEvoy & C. White, "Security Vetting in Northern Ireland: Loyalty, Redress and Citizenship" (1998) 61 *Modern Law Review* **341, 343–5**

Since its inception, the Northern Ireland state has placed a great deal of emphasis on ensuring the loyalty of its employees. After the partition of Ireland and the creation of a devolved parliament in the six North Eastern counties, the new government viewed itself as under threat from the Nationalist government in the South and the potentially seditious minority of Catholic/Nationalists in the North who made up approximately one third of the population of Northern Ireland.

. . . Unsurprisingly, it was viewed as crucial by members of the new government that the loyalty of civil servants could be relied upon. In 1923 the Promissory Oaths Act was introduced which required civil servants and teachers (Catholic educational establishments were viewed as particularly worthy of suspicion in the Stormont era) to swear an Oath of Allegiance to "His Majesty King George the Fifth, his heirs and successors according to Law and to his Government of Northern Ireland." Section 1(3) required all government departments to keep a record of people who had taken the Oath and section 1(5) empowered the Minister of Finance to apply the oath to full or part time duties in all departments or authorities as he thought fit.

While a similar Oath had been required in Great Britain during the first World War, it had expired, as far as the Civil Service was concerned, by the time of the introduction of this Act in Northern Ireland. However as the then Prime Minister of Northern Ireland, Sir James Craig, explained, it was felt necessary: ". . . to leave no loophole for people to crawl into departments . . . those who were not favourable to British Rule, for instance, to use their positions in the Civil Service, to undermine the loyalty of those departments towards the Crown and the Government." . . . the fear of disloyalty and mistrust of the Catholic minority, confirmed in the minds of the majority by the periodic outburst of Republican violence, became deeply embedded in the political and social fabric of the state. Catholic/Nationalist disloyalty was viewed as axiomatic, synonymous with those who were against the British connection and wanted to withdraw from the Union, whereas Protestant Unionists were by definition loyal.

These high levels of distrust were demonstrated in security terms in the enactment of Emergency legislation—namely the 1922 Special Powers Act—with extraordinarily wide powers and the maintenance of a paramilitary police force (the RUC) backed up by auxiliary units (the "B" Specials), both of which were specifically designed to deal with the potential threat from seditious Catholics. On a political level, the guaranteed inbuilt Unionist majority ensured that the Unionist Party, dominated by "a laager mentality", remained in power uninterrupted for fifty years without any great incentive to attract Catholic votes. . . . There are a number of references to the question of the loyalty of Civil Servants recorded in the Northern Ireland Hansard during [the Cold War] period.

---

[4] Angela Hegarty, "Examining Equality: The Fair Employment Act (NI) 1989 and Its Review". [1995] 2 *Web Journal of Current Legal Issues* (available at http://webjcli.ncl.ac.uk/admin/wjclidex.html) points out that two other recent prime-ministers (Captain Terence O'Neill and Lord Brookeborough respectively) "stood by while his wife advertised for a Protestant domestic help . . . and . . . publicly declared that [Roman Catholics] . . . ought not to be employed as they are not to be trusted and in any event are enemies of the state".

However the concerns expressed by the Unionist government remain consistent throughout with no noticeable shift of emphasis in the Cold War era. The exchange below between Minister of Finance Maginess and a member of the Nationalist opposition, at the beginning of the Cold War era, is worth reproducing.

Mr Maginess

It is not a question of one religion or another; it is a question of loyalty or disloyalty and that is just the way it should be . . . it is degrading, to my mind, to bring religion into politics, just as it is degrading to bring politics into religion.

Mr Diamond

Then to get employment in the Civil Service you must be a Unionist?

Mr Maginess

If the honourable member complains that not sufficient of his supporters are employed by the Government, then the person most to blame for it is the honourable Member himself who has taught these people disloyalty . . . We have heard proverbs about nursing vipers in the bosom and that sort of thing. If the honourable member would say to his own followers—Look here, Northern Ireland is established under law, and whether you like it or not, act as a citizen of Northern Ireland, and so long as it is in existence do your best for it—then you would see a great change in this country.

McEvoy and White go on to report that in 1969, by which stage Catholics accounted for one third of the population, they occupied 6%, 7% and 14% respectively of technical and professional civil service posts, higher administrative civil service positions and government nominated public body appointments.[5] In the same year political violence broke out leading to the imposition, in 1972, of direct rule (Northern Ireland having been governed, since its inception, from Belfast). It was a British Government which passed the Fair Employment (Northern Ireland) Act 1976, this Act being amended and supplemented by the Fair Employment (Northern Ireland) Act 1989 and, in the context of the 1990s "peace process", being replaced by the FETO.

The FETO differs most significantly from the SDA, RRA and DDA in terms of the monitoring and review obligations it places upon employers (save private sector employers of 10 of fewer). These obligations were first imposed by the FEA 1989, the 1976 FEA having merely encouraged monitoring (the same encouragement is provided, in the context of the SDA and the RRA, by the relevant Codes of Practice).

During the 1980's, evidence that the 1976 legislation had been largely ineffective, coupled with pressure from US investors, led to the demand for reform.

---

[5] K. Mc Evoy and C. White, "Security Vetting in Northern Ireland: Loyalty, Redress and Citizenship" (1998) 61 *Modern Law Review*, p.346.

C. McCrudden, "The Northern Ireland Fair Employment White Paper: a Critical Assessment" (1988) 17 *ILJ* **162, 162–3**

The most authoritative recent study of the effectiveness of this legislation in reducing the extent of inequality of opportunity in Northern Ireland between the two sections of the community was published in 1987 by the Policy Studies Institute. The single most dramatic illustration of the continuing dimensions of the inequality is to be found in comparing the Catholic and Protestant unemployment rates. According to the P.S.I. study, Catholic male unemployment remains at a staggering 35 per cent, two-and-a-half times that of Protestant male unemployment. This has continued despite 10 years of legislation, and despite there being over 100,000 job changes a year. Religion remains a major determinant of this differential unemployment rate.

This P.S.I. study also found that the legislation passed in the mid-1970s had little effect on employers' practices. The vast majority of employers interviewed for the P.S.I. study believed that the Act had made little, if any, impact on their practices and procedures. Job discrimination was still thought to be justifiable in certain circumstances by a considerable number of employers. Informal recruitment and appointment procedures contributed to continuing levels of segregation. Investigations by the F.E.A. . . . did not appear to have made an impact beyond the individual organisation investigated. Very few establishments were formally monitoring the religious composition of the workforce. Indeed, very few establishments were carrying out any type of equal opportunity measure.

There were a number of reasons for the ineffectiveness of the legislation. There was an almost complete lack of interest in the issue of both Labour and Conservative Governments between the mid-1970s and the mid-1980s, despite the limited effect that the legislation was having. The F.E.A. adopted a restrained approach to enforcement; negotiation rather than litigation was the dominant approach even when it delivered relatively little. Employers' organisations, soon after the legislation came into effect, adopted a belligerent approach to the Agency and to the issue. The main constitutional party representing Catholics (the Social Democratic and Labour Party), and the trade unions, seldom adverted to the issue.

Since the mid-1980s, however, inequality of opportunity between Catholics and Protestants in Northern Ireland has again become a key political issue, largely due to pressure from *outside* the Province. A campaign in the United States was begun to bring pressure to bear on American corporations, state legislatures and municipal governments with investments in Northern Ireland to adopt a set of anti-discrimination principles (inspired by the Sullivan Principles) called the "MacBride Principles." The MacBride campaign, despite well-orchestrated opposition from the British and American Governments, has proved popular with state legislators. By July 1988 eight States had already enacted legislation requiring American companies in which they invest to ensure fair employment practices in their Northern Ireland subsidiaries, and many more were considering similar moves.

This American campaign began to fill, however partially and inadequately, the political vacuum caused by the failure of Northern Ireland's political institutions to address the issue adequately.

The Standing Advisory Commission on Human Rights (SACHR), whose task it was to "advis[e] the Secretary of State on the adequacy and effectiveness of the law for the time being in force in preventing discrimination on the ground of religious belief or political opinion and in providing redress for persons aggrieved by discrimination on either ground"[6] announced in 1985 that it intended to review the effectiveness of the 1979 Act. The review was welcomed by Douglas Hurd MP, at the time Secretary of State for Northern Ireland, and in the same year the government itself published statistics which showed:

> marked differences between the characteristics of the Protestant and Catholic sections of the community in Northern Ireland. The statistics illustrated differences in such areas as employment, educational background and housing. They underlined the fact that, in spite of the institutional safeguards in place and the action taken over recent years, substantial differences between Catholics and Protestants continued to exist, notably in terms of employment and unemployment . . .[7]

The Policy Studies Institute conducted more detailed research, the results of which are mentioned by Christopher McCrudden in the extract above, and SACHR made a number of recommendations for amendments to the FEA 1976.[8] As McCrudden goes on to note, the White Paper (and the ensuing 1989 Act) did not wholly embrace the SACHR proposals. But it did introduce the compulsory monitoring mentioned above, and this obligation is now to be found in articles 52–54 FETO, discussed below.

The Government announced during the passage of the 1989 FEA that a comprehensive review of the legislation would be carried out after five years. In the event, this was conducted by the SACHR (which was replaced, in 1999, by the Northern Ireland Human Rights Commission).[9] The Government had initially entrusted the process of review to the Central Community Relations Unit of the Northern Ireland Office, but concerns over this body's lack of independence resulted in responsibility for the review being transferred to SACHR which reported in 1997.[10] Subsequent amendment of the fair employment legislation by the FETO took place in haste, as part of the legislative package associated with the Good Friday peace agreement and ensuing moves towards devolution in Northern Ireland.[11]

The decision of the Government to legislate in 1998 by way of an Order in Council (resulting in very curtailed parliamentary scrutiny) was criticised by the Northern

---

[6] S.20 Northern Ireland Constitution Act 1923.

[7] SACHR, *Religious and Political Discrimination and Equality of Opportunity in Northern Ireland—Report on Fair Employment*, available on http://cain.ulst.ac.uk /hmso/sachr87.htm.

[8] SACHR was abolished by the NIA which created the EC and the Human Rights Commission.

[9] The review was initially to have been conducted by the non-independent Central Community Relations Unit.

[10] See C. Bell, "The Employment Equality Review and Fair Employment in Northern Ireland" (1996) 2 *International Journal of Discrimination and Law* 53, p.53.

[11] Lord Blease, speaking in the House of Lords debates on FETO (HL Debs 7th Dec 1998, col 763, available at http://www.publications.parliament. uk/pa/ld/ldhansrd.htm.), stated that it was "one of the main pillars upon which the real function and work of the Northern Ireland Assembly will be built '. Also evidence given by the CAJ to the Select Committee (and appended to that Committee's Fourth Report of the 1998–99 session, *The Operation of the Fair Employment (Northern Ireland) Act 1989: Ten Years On*, available at available at http://www.parliament.the-stationery-office.co.uk/pa/ cm199899.cmselect/cmniaf/cmniaf.htm) was to the effect that fair employment legislation was central to the peace process—see, for example, answer to question 453.

Ireland Select Committee, whose Fourth Report (*The Operation of The Fair Employment (Northern Ireland) Act 1989—Ten Years On*) stated:

> 26. . . . the [FETO] . . . contained substantial changes from the earlier legislation. In contrast to the previous occasions, the House had no opportunity to seek to amend the proposals. Originally, indeed, the Government proposed taking the Order in the Standing Committee before [the Minister for Northern Ireland] gave evidence to us.
>
> 27. Our concern was, if anything, intensified by the way in which the draft Order in Council was presented to Parliament. . . In other circumstances in which an Order in Council approach to legislating for Northern Ireland had been adopted, the Government frequently published a proposal for the draft Order in Council before the draft itself was published, in order to enable interested parties to comment on the proposal before it was finalised. The 1998 Order was not first published as a proposal and so even that possibility of influencing the draft was substantially reduced. . .
>
> **28. While we appreciate that the Government wanted to make "rapid progress" with the legislation in order to ensure that the terms of its obligations under the [Good Friday] Agreement were fulfilled, we do not consider that the procedures used in this case provided for adequate Parliamentary scrutiny of important new legislation in a sensitive policy area where, hitherto, primary legislation has been the norm. We regret that Government felt it should proceed by way of an Order in this case.**

The Government did not in 1998 accept all of SACHR's submissions. In particular, it rejected the imposition of a statutory obligation on employers to consult employees and recognised trade unions as part of the tri-annual review (discussed below), and the extension of legal aid to the Fair Employment Tribunal (FET, the specialist tribunal established to deal with fair employment cases). It also declined to amend the definition of "victimisation" to include victimisation of A by virtue of FETO-related action by B; to extend contract compliance and to permit the award of exemplary damages by the FET.[12] But it did take into account SACHR's finding that "disadvantage"—in particular, long-term unemployment—was the main obstacle to fair employment.

In 1997, Catholic men were 2.9 times more likely to be unemployed than Protestant men, Catholic women 1.4 times more likely to be unemployed than their Protestant counterparts. Catholics comprised 40% of those employed in Northern Ireland, 41% of the economically active but 62% of the unemployed. The "unemployment differential" (the unequal impact of unemployment between Catholics and Protestants) had actually increased for Catholic men from 2.0 to 2.9 in the seven years to 1997 (for all Catholics, from 1.9 to 2.4 in the same period)—this despite a substantial reduction in unemployment rates (from 9% to 5% for Protestants, 17% to 12% for Catholics[13]).

---

[12] White Paper *Partnership for Equality* 1998 (Northern Ireland Office, 1998) available at www.ccruni. gov.uk/equality/equality.htm., responding to SACHR, Employment Equality: Building for the Future (HMSO, Cmnd 3684, June 1997). 77 *Equal Opportunities Review*, pp.8–9 quoted SACHR Chair Michael Lavery QC to the effect that "it did not augur well for the future of Northern Ireland if the Government could not accept . . . SACHR's "modest proposals' ".

[13] 7–5% for Protestant and 10% to 7% for Catholic women, 11–6% for Protestant and 22%—16% for Catholic men. Statistics taken from the Committee for the Administration of Justice, *News* July 1999.

According to Adam Ingram MP, Minister of State for Northern Ireland, in his evidence to the Select Committee on Northern Ireland Affairs in its review of the fair employment legislation (December 1998): "there remains a gap between the Catholic share of employment and the Catholic share of the economically active population . . . There is also evidence of continuing imbalances at the top of large organisations, not least the civil service".[14]

The reasons behind the differential unemployment rates of Catholics and Protestants in Northern Ireland are a matter of some controversy.[15] Nevertheless the chart below, which was published by the FEC in 1995, shows that the differential is not explained by relative levels of education. In the chart below, level 1 indicates degree level or higher; level 2 BTEC (higher) or equivalent; level 3 "A" level or equivalent; level 4 BTEC (national) or equivalent; level 5 "O" level or equivalent; level 6 CSE (other than grade 1) and level 7 no formal qualifications.[16]

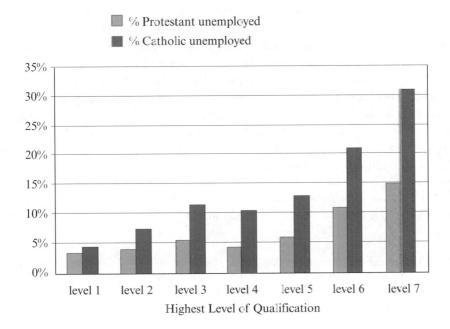

The Committee for the Administration of Justice (CAJ[17]) declared in 1997 that:

the single most important contribution that government can make to ensuring equality of opportunity is to show by its words and actions that it considers inequality in Northern

[14] Fn 11 above.

[15] While SACHR was satisfied, in its review, that some discrimination was involved, one of its members (Ulster Unionist Dermott Nesbitt) disagreed and published a dissenting note on the matter.

[16] FEC, *The Key Facts*, (March 1995), available from the FEC website http://www.fec-ni.org/.

[17] Winner of the Council of Europe's Human Rights Prize 1998, described by Mary Robinson, UN High Commissioner for Human Rights, as "a beacon of light in Northern Ireland's long, hard night . . one of

Irish society to be totally unacceptable. It must accordingly be prepared to put energy and resources into ensuring change . . . in particular . . . a culture of equality [must] be signalled by establishing specific equality goals along with the introduction of appropriate measures and funding to ensure that these goals can be met within a clearly defined time frame. The setting of goals and timetables is particularly important in those public services where representation from across the community is lacking . . . specific and public goals and timetables should be set in the achievement of lesser differentials in unemployment figures (as recommended by SACHR in its 1987 report). Specific (financial) incentives should be made available both to encourage employers to recruit from the long term unemployed and to enable the [latter] to compete on a realistic basis for employment opportunities.[18]

The issue of public service goals and timetables was considered in Chapter 5, in the discussion of s.75 of the Northern Ireland Act. Government spokespersons went out of their way to emphasise the government's commitment to reducing the unemployment differential.[19] But for all of the importance expressly placed on this matter by the government, the time-frame set for the elimination of the differential was 13 years and the task was established as one for the new "Equality Commission" (of which more below), rather than government itself. SACHR criticised the pace of proposed change as well as the delegation by the government of responsibility for the establishment of goals and timetables.[20] The report of the Select Committee on Northern Ireland Affairs was also critical of the time frame imposed by the government, and recommended that the first review of the FETO, which was to take place no later than 2005, should "consider any deviations between the benchmarks established and the available data. This would provide a suitable opportunity for appropriate policy initiatives on the unemployment differential".

In addition to the issues already touched upon, the FETO and the Northern Ireland Act 1998 have made substantial changes to the law as it relates to discrimination on grounds of religious belief or political opinion. The most significant of these have been:

- the replacement of the notorious s.42 FEA (discussed below), by which the issue of an unchallengeable "national security" certificate by the Secretary of State could block action under the FEA, by article 80 FETO and s.91 Northern Ireland Act 1998, which provide a review mechanism for such certificates;[21]
- the merger of all four Northern Irish equality bodies (the Fair Employment Commission, the EOC for Northern Ireland, the CRE for Northern Ireland—itself established only in

the few groups which works across the range of human rights, civil, political, economic and social" at an address to "Equality and Human Rights: Their Role in Peace Building", a conference held in Belfast on 2 December 1998.

[18] Submission to SACHR's Employment Equality Review (February 1996).

[19] See for example the evidence of the Minister of State to the Select Committee, 9th December 1998, appended to the report, fn 11 above.

[20] SACHR response to the White Paper, discussed in SACHR's submissions to the Northern Ireland Affairs Committee, appended to the Report of that Committee, fn 11 above.

[21] The Race Relations (Amendment) Bill 1999 does the same in the race relations context where, by contrast with the position under the FEAs, it has not been frequently used.

August 1997—and the Northern Ireland Disability Council) into a super "Equality Commission";[22]

- the imposition upon all public authorities of a statutory duty to promote equality of opportunity. This duty, at present unique in the UK[23] is to be implemented by equality schemes enforced by the new Commission and extends beyond religion/ political opinion, race, sex and disability to age, marital status, sexual orientation and the presence or absence of dependants;[24]
- the consolidation of the previously unwieldy FEAs 1976 and 1989 into a single piece of legislation—the FETO;
- the extension of the fair employment legislation to cover the provision of goods, facilities, services and premises as well as employment (hence the change of name from Fair Employment Act(s) to Fair Employment *and Treatment* Order (my emphasis).

These changes are further discussed, where relevant, below. In addition to the very major changes introduced by the FETO and the Northern Ireland Act 1998, a substantial number of "housekeeping" amendments were made to the fair employment legislation which had the effect of bringing it more into line with the race and sex discrimination provisions. Many of these changes had been called for by the EEC. Amongst them are Articles 26 and 32 which, respectively, prohibit discrimination by partnerships of at least six partners and by and in respect of barristers; Articles 41and 34, which empower the EC to take action against "persistent discrimination" and in respect of discriminatory advertisements;[25] Article 7(d) which imposes upon the EC an obligation to review the FETO; Article 39 which permits the award of compensation in cases of employment-related unintentional indirect discrimination;[26] Article 46(6) which recognises contractual discrimination as continuing for the purposes of time-limits. By contrast, Article 39(1)(d) creates a new distinction between the fair employment regime and those imposed by the other Acts by permitting the FET, on making a finding of unlawful discrimination, to make "a recommendation that the

---

[22] Northern Ireland Act 1998. This was done despite strong opposition with 29 respondents to the White Paper *Partnership for Equality* supporting merger and only 29 in favour. The FEC was in favour but there is a fear, voiced *inter alia* by SACHR, the EOC and CRE for Northern Ireland and the NI Disability Council, that the other forms of discrimination will lose out to fair employment (see also Lords debate 5th Oct 1998, cols 183ff and debates on the NI Bill 26th Oct HL, available as at fn 11 above). The creation of an Equality Commission for Northern Ireland, as one of three new commissions including a Commission on Policing and a Human Rights Commission, was seen as an important step in the peace process and formed part of the Belfast Agreement of Easter 1999.

[23] Though s.71 LGA imposes upon local authorities an obligation to "to make appropriate arrangements with a view to securing that their various functions are carried out with due regard to the need (a) to eliminate unlawful racial discrimination; and (b) to promote equality of opportunity and good relations, between persons of different racial groups,—see further Chapter 5. For the changes made in this respect by the Race Relations (Amendment) Bill 1999, see Chapter 4.

[24] Northern Ireland Act 1998, s.75. Though the Government set out, for the first time in 1998, targets for the achievement of equal/ pro-rata representation of women and ethnic minorities in public appointments (and proper consideration for the disabled—see *Quangos: Opening up Public Appointments* available on http://www.open.gov.uk. The plans published by each department under this scheme are not legally binding

[25] S.33 FEA forbade discriminatory advertisements but the FEC had no power to apply to the FET for a ruling.

[26] Leaving the RRA the only regime not permitting this—see Chapter 7.

respondent take within a specified period action appearing to the Tribunal to be practicable for the purpose of obviating or reducing the adverse effect on a person *other than* the complainant of any unlawful discrimination to which the complaint relates". This power is in addition to those of declarations, compensation and recommendations (Article 39(1)(c)) "that the respondent take . . . action . . . for the purpose of obviating or reducing the adverse effect *on the complainant* of any unlawful discrimination . . .".

In many respects the FETO resembles the SDA or RRA with the addition of what might be termed "collective" measures such as workforce monitoring, contract compliance and a form of affirmative action, discussed below. By contrast with the other discrimination legislation, the employment provisions of the FETO[27] are enforced by a specialist tribunal (the Fair Employment Tribunal/ FET). SACHR's proposals that non-employment aspects of the legislation went to the FET were rejected by the government in 1998.

EXCEPTIONS TO THE PROHIBITION ON DISCRIMINATION

The FETO does not apply in relation to school teachers (segregated schooling is the norm in Northern Ireland) or clergymen, or to employment "for the purposes of a private household" (Article 70).[28] Nor do its provisions prohibiting discrimination on grounds of religious belief or political opinion apply, respectively, "to or in relation to any employment where the essential nature of the job requires it to be done by a person holding, or not holding" a particular religious belief (Article 70(3)) or political opinion (Article 70(4)). The school teacher exemption was challenged, *inter alia*, by the Committee for the Administration of Justice and by the NAS/UWT but retained in the FETO, subject to the provision (Article 71(2)) that the EC "shall keep under review the exception . . . with a view to considering whether, in the opinion of the Commission, it is appropriate that any steps should be taken to further equality of opportunity in the employment of teachers in schools".

The affirmative action provisions of the FETO have been considered in Chapter 3. In addition to Article 78, which exempts from the provisions of the FETO "anything done in order to comply with a requirement" of primary legislation predating the Act, or of "an instrument made or approved" under such legislation,[29] Article 79 provides that:

No act done by any person shall be treated . . . as unlawfully discriminating if—
(a) the act is done for the purpose of safeguarding national security or protecting public safety or public order; *and*
(b) *the doing of the act is justified by that purpose* (my emphasis).

[27] See Chapter 4.
[28] Both the CAJ and the NAS/UWT opposed the continuation of this exemption by the 1998 legislation—see evidence to the Select Committee on Northern Ireland Affairs.
[29] Or legislation re-enacting (with or without modification) such primary legislation.

Under s.42(2) FEA, which predated Article 80 FETO, the issue of a certificate by the Secretary of State to the effect that an act challenged under the FEA was "an act done for the purpose of safeguarding national security or of protecting public safety or public order" (there being no equivalent to Article 79(b)), was conclusive evidence that the act was done for the stated purpose. Article 80, however, provides that a certificate may be challenged before a special tribunal set up for that purpose under the Northern Ireland Act 1998. The tribunal may uphold such a certificate only if satisfied that the disputed act fulfilled the requirements of Article 79. (The national security exception in the Northern Irish race relations legislation has been altered in the same manner, the Sex Discrimination (Northern Ireland) Order 1976 and the SDA having been amended in the wake of the ECJ decision in *Johnson* v *Chief Constable of the RUC* (Case C–224/84) [1986] ECR 651, in which that Court ruled that the unavailability of judicial review to challenge a similar exemption in the SD Order breached the obligation regarding justiciability in the Equal Treatment Directive.[30]

The new system for the scrutiny of national security certificates was established in the wake of *Tinnelly & Sons Ltd and others and McElduff and others* v *United Kingdom*,[31] in which (in July 1998) the European Court of Human Rights ruled that s.42 FEA breached Article 6(1) of the European Convention on Human Rights, in denying applicants in respect of whom certificates were served access to the courts.[32]

The *Tinnelly* case was brought by a building firm which had tendered unsuccessfully for demolition work with the Northern Ireland Electricity Service (NIE), despite having entered the lowest bid. The firm had initially been led to believe that its tender had been successful, but was subsequently informed that the work had been awarded to another firm with more experience. Tinnelly had then been told by the successful bidder that his (Tinnelly's) bid was rejected because "the unions would not let [his firm] on to the site . . . because they believed them to be terrorists or sympathetic to terrorists". Such an attitude on the part of the NIE workers could only have resulted from the fact that Tinnelly was Catholic.

Tinnelly complained to the FEA whose investigation of the complaint the NIE attempted (unsuccessfully) to prohibit by judicial review. Two months later, a s.42 certificate was issued by the Secretary of State with the effect that Tinnelly's challenge had to fail. A s.42 certificate was also issued in respect of a complaint to the FET by the McElduffs, who were denied the security clearance necessary to undertake work for the Department of the Environment.

The FEA (as it then was) sought judicial review of the *Tinnelly* certificate, arguing it "was procured and issued in bad faith, was irrational, unfair and unreasonable and

[30] The amendment of the RRA is discussed in Chapter 7.

[31] Cases 62/1997/846/1052–1053, available on http://www.dhcour.coe.fr/eng/ Judgments.htm

[32] This followed a similar judgement made some twelve years before by the ECJ in *Johnson* v *Chief Constable of the RUC* (Case 224/84) [1986] ECR 651, in which that Court ruled that the unavailability of judicial review to challenge a similar exemption in the Sex Discrimination (NI) Order (identical in terms to the SDA) breached European law.

made for an improper collateral purpose, namely to prevent the FEA from investigating a complaint of unlawful discrimination". The application was refused.

Mr Justice McCollum[33] castigated the NIE for the "deep hostility" it had displayed to the objectives and activities of the FEA. Nevertheless, he was not satisfied that the decision had not been reached on the basis of security reports by the RUC, at least some of which "appear[ed] not to give security clearance" to workers employed by Tinnelly. And if it was appropriate for NIE to seek a s.42 certificate, the issue of the certificate could not be challenged as long as proper procedures were followed by the Secretary of State. McCollum J took the view that he was unable to go behind the s.42 certificate in order to ascertain whether, as a matter of fact, there were grounds to consider Tinnelly a risk to national security.

The ECHR ruled that the s.42 certificates issued in the Tinnelly and McElduff cases were "a disproportionate restriction on the applicants' right of access to a court or tribunal".[34] According to the Court:

> The conclusive nature of the section 42 Certificates had the effect of preventing a judicial determination on the merits of the applicants' complaints that they were victims of unlawful discrimination. The court would observe that such a complaint can properly be submitted for an independent judicial determination even if national security considerations are present and constitute a highly material aspect of the case. The right guaranteed to an applicant under Article 6 §1 of the Convention to submit a dispute to a court or Tribunal in order to have a determination on questions of both fact and law cannot be displaced by the "ipse dixit" of the executive . . .
>
>   The introduction of a procedure, regardless of the framework which would allow an adjudicator or tribunal fully satisfying the . . . requirements of independence and impartiality to examine in complete cognisance of all relevant evidence documentary or other, merits of the submissions of both sides, may indeed serve to enhance public confidence . . . Mr Justice McCollum was unable under the present arrangements to dispel his own doubts about certain disturbing features of the Tinnelly case since he, like Tinnelly and the Fair Employment Agency, was precluded from having cognisance of all relevant material in the possession of [NIE] . . .
>
>   This situation cannot be said to be conducive to public confidence in the administration of justice.

Under the FEA regime, the issue of s.42 certificates was commonplace. Many jobs in Northern Ireland's public sector require that applicants be security-vetted by the RUC, as do jobs in British Telecom (Northern Ireland), the NIE, and some BBC

---

[33] *In Re the Fair Employment Agency for Northern Ireland*, Queen's Bench Division MCCD 0590.T, unreported, 12th November 1991.

[34] It awarded the Tinnellys and the McElduffs £10 000 and £15 000 respectively in compensation. The McElduffs, who had no criminal convictions save for minor motoring offences, and who had never been involved in any criminal or terrorist activity, claimed that they were discriminated against by the DOE on the grounds of their perceived nationalist views, although they are not members of any political party and are not engaged in any form of political activity. They had in the past been mistaken by members of the security forces for different persons of the same name, and they suspected that this was a case of mistaken identity.

jobs.[35] Where the outcome of such vetting was negative and an FEA complaint ensued, s.42 certificates were frequently issued to protect respondents' appointment procedures from scrutiny.

On the one hand, terrorist allegiances are clearly undesirable amongst employees in security-sensitive jobs. But the operation of s.42 was not even-handed. McEvoy and White point out that, of the 39 certificates issued between 1976 and 1993, 33 (85%) were in respect of Catholic applicants (Catholics comprise around 40% of the population).[36] The FEC's *Review of Fair Employment Acts* (1998) stated the "strongly held belief" of that body that "security checks may have an adverse impact of the employment of Roman Catholics in particular".[37] Further, there is evidence that s.42 certificates have been issued in order to disguise errors on the part of employers.[38] Vetting arrangements changed in 1993 to bring them more into line with those which operate in Great Britain. But McEvoy and White argue that:

"Security Vetting in Northern Ireland" (1998) 61 MLR 341, 353–7

. . . the ideology and practice which continue to inform the process of information-gathering remains a major flaw in the security vetting system in Northern Ireland. . . . vetting is intended to uncover anyone who is or has been involved in, or associated with:

> . . . terrorism, espionage, sabotage, actions intended to overthrow or undermine Parliamentary democracy by political, industrial or violent means, or who is or has been a member of any organisation advocating such activities, associated with any such organisation, or any of its member sin such a way as to raise reasonable doubts about his or her reliability; or is susceptible to pressure or improper influence . . .

Information gathering for the purpose of security vetting in Developed Vetting cases and in Extended Security Check cases, where interviews are not normally conducted, are carried out by investigation officers working within the "Security Branch" of the Department of Finance and Personnel. These officers are normally former policy officers with investigative experience who liaise with the RUC in carrying out the necessary checks. As Sir Patrick Wall has opined with regard to the similar process within the Ministry of Defence, ". . . a great deal depends upon the vetting officer." Linn has argued with regard to the equivalent investigative officer in Great Britain that there are inherent dangers in having such a body staffed exclusively by former male police officers in their mid 50s, in so far as it is unlikely that such a group would reflect the plurality of political views and experiences of those being investigated. We would argue that in the context of the RUC, with over 90 per cent of the officers both male and Protestant, and substantial evidence of a difficult relationship between the police and sections of the Catholic community, those concerns are considerably enhanced.

In a community such as Northern Ireland, a more complete understanding of the realities of community life amongst those who gather information for security vetting purpose

---

[35] The Civil Service, the RUC and Police Authority for Northern Ireland, the Prison Service and construction workers on sensitive projects as well as BT, NIE and some BBC posts. For another example of the impact of security vetting see *Kearney v Northern Irish Civil Service Commission* [1996] NI 415.

[36] Fn 5 above, p.352.

[37] Para 1.114, available from the FEC website, fn 16 above.

[38] Fn 5 above, p.352.

sic crucial. Poor quality intelligence, and a failure to understand the complexities of the minority community, have previously been attributed as significant factors in some of the most noteworthy failures in security policy in Northern Ireland. However, any analysis criticising the quality of intelligence provided by the RUC must go beyond superficial notions of sectarianism amongst former or serving police officers. While there is considerable literature to suggest that such attitudes do exist amongst some officers, it is more fruitful to locate our analysis in the ideological and practical mechanics of information gathering in the Northern Ireland context.

It has been suggested repeatedly that family and extended family networks are closer, more important and more extensive in Northern Ireland. Northern Ireland's predominantly rural heritage, small geographical size, large families, high unemployment and relative poverty have all been referred to as factors to be included in analysing this phenomenon. With the largest rate of imprisonment in Europe per capita, it has been estimated that Northern Ireland has the largest proportionate number of families which have been directly affected by imprisonment of a family member.

McEvoy and White explore the notions of "loyalty" which served to exclude Catholics from many jobs long before the introduction of formal or "overt" vetting, and conclude that:

In this context a new form of "loyalty" may have emerged with regard to security vetting. The old system, of in effect excluding Catholics unless they could demonstrate sufficient "loyalty" to Crown and government, has been replaced by one whereby none will be excluded other than those with "an association with terrorism". Whilst such a formulation may have a superficial attractiveness, it is arguable that it may disproportionately disadvantage those from working class Catholic backgrounds. It may for example lead to an implicit reversal of the onus of proof, whereby people from certain postal districts have to demonstrate their "bona fides" because of where they live, or their family or community backgrounds rather than any specific incident for which they are responsible. These are the areas where Sinn Fein are politically strongest. As noted above, these are also the areas in which police/community relationships are most strained. And these are also often the areas with the highest levels of unemployment where access to employment in the public sector (in its broadest sense) is crucial for the economic and social regeneration of the jurisdiction. . . . the current system of security vetting is flawed because of a number of historical features. It is a system which grew from an exclusionary notion of loyalty in the public sector as synonymous with Unionism. It was refined during a period of violent political conflict where the avenues of redress which should protect the citizen from discriminatory practices were demonstrated to be wholly inadequate. Finally . . . the practical mechanisms for the gathering and assessment of information for security vetting purposes continue to have the potential to operate in a discriminatory fashion against the Catholic community. While Northern Ireland will undoubtedly continue to require some system of security vetting, it is one which will require a range of legal, practical and ideological changes in the administration of the system.

The extent to which the availability of review in respect of national security certificates will make a significant difference to their use (in particular, their unequal use as between Catholics and Protestants), remains to be seen. The provisions made for exclusion of the applicant from national security hearings in FETO cases mirror those, discussed in Chapter 7, proposed by the RR(A)B. The Northern Ireland Affairs Select Committee's report on the fair employment legislation took the view that the changes introduced in this regard might be inadequate to comply with the ECHR protections:

109. The [national security] Tribunal is appointed by the Lord Chancellor: the chairman must be a current or former judge of the High Court or the Court of Appeal in England or Northern Ireland. The legislation authorises Rules which will enable proceedings before the Tribunal to take place without a party being given full particulars of the reasons for the issue of the certificate, and enable the Tribunal to hold proceedings in the absence of any person, including a party and any legal representative appointed by a party. Further provisions permit the Attorney General for Northern Ireland to appoint a Member of the Bar of Northern Ireland to represent the interests of a party to proceedings before the tribunal in any proceedings from which he and any legal representative of his are excluded, but the Order further provides that the person so appointed "shall not be responsible to the party whose interests he represents."

110. These provisions might be thought to represent a reasonable compromise between the need to ensure that the certificates are properly reviewed by an independent body and the need to ensure that information is not disclosed contrary to the public interest . . . On the other hand, these provisions might be thought to enable the Government to have the best of both worlds, enabling the appearance of independent adjudication to take place, but so interfering with the usual adversarial process as to render the process unacceptable. SACHR expressed the view to us that "individuals who are affected by these certificates may not be happy at the end of the day that they have been fully and independently and properly represented by the tribunal. . . . And we feel that these provisions, while enabling some sort of independent scrutiny, do not go far enough, certainly with regard to winning the confidence of the person who is affected by them that he has been properly dealt with."

111. If these provisions are ever used, it is possible that the issue of their compatibility with the European Convention on Human Rights will come before the European Court of Human Rights or, indeed, our own courts once the Human Rights Act 1998 is fully in force. SACHR considered "there must be some reservations" about whether the provisions comply. We hope that the new Northern Ireland Human Rights Commission will consider this issue in due course, and also the desirability of an alternative approach. . .

112. In the interim, another issue has arisen which needs to be resolved. The Northern Ireland Bar Council, which represents the practising Bar, has taken the preliminary view that counsel appointed to represent a person in these proceedings, while not being responsible to that party, may be at risk of being in breach of Bar ethics requirements. Since the legislation requires such counsel to be a member of the Northern Ireland Bar, and thus subject to Northern Ireland Bar Council ethics rules, this is a serious issue.

In 1996 the CAJ had called for the immediate repeal of s.42, and in its submissions to the Select Committee on Northern Ireland Affairs in 1999 it favoured an approach such as that adopted in the sex discrimination context. There, the equivalent of s.42 had been declared in breach of the Equal Treatment Directive by the ECJ in *Johnston* v *RUC*.[39] According to that Court:

[39] Case C–222/84 [1986] ECR 1651.

A provision which . . . requires a certificate . . . to be treated as conclusive evidence that the conditions for derogating from the principle of equal treatment are fulfilled allows the competent authority to deprive an individual of the possibility of asserting by judicial process the rights conferred by the directive. Such a provision is therefore contrary to the principle of effective judicial control . . .

As a result of the *Johnston* decision the UK Government simply disapplied the relevant provisions of the sex discrimination legislation insofar as they applied to employment cases. The Fair Employment Commission's *Review of the Fair Employment Acts* (1997) criticised the ensuing inconsistency between the FEA (as it then was) and the race relations legislation, on the one hand, and the sex discrimination legislation on the other. That position remains.

INVESTIGATIONS OF PRACTICES, MONITORING AND REVIEW OBLIGATIONS

We saw in Chapter 5 that the investigative powers of the EC in relation to the FETO are broader than those of the other commissions (or, indeed, of the EC in relation to sex and race). We noted also there, however, that the FETO provides no investigative powers in relation to discrimination outside the area of employment (broadly defined).

Turning to those collective dimensions of the FETO which are unique to that legislation, the Order, by contrast with the SDA, RRA and DDA, imposes statutory obligations on employers (albeit only those having more than ten employees) to monitor their workforces and applicants by religion (as distinct from political opinion), and to submit records to the Equality Commission.[40] In addition, all public sector employers and those in the private sector having at least 250 employees must monitor the religion of their promotees and of those ceasing to be employed. The FETO introduced the obligation to monitor promotees and those ceasing to be employed, and extended the obligation to monitor applicants to private sector employers of between 11 and 250 staff. It also extended the monitoring obligation to cover part-time workers (although these workers, defined as those working less than 16 hours per week, are not counted for the purposes of establishing the size of the workforce).

Failure to supply the EC with monitoring returns is a criminal offence.[41] The Fair Employment (Monitoring) Regulations (Northern Ireland) 1999 provide the method by which the religious affiliation of employees, applicants, etc., may be determined

---

[40] In respect of information relating to the workforce, applicants, etc., prior to January 2001, the obligation in respect of applicants applies only to public sector employers and those in the private sector having more than 250 employees. Regulations provide for methods of determining religion, primarily on the basis of schools attended.

[41] Art. 27(5) though employer who has a reasonable excuse for missing a deadline and who returns as soon as practically possible shall have a defence—FEC has recommended abolition of the defence.

and require that monitoring returns classify employees not only by religion but also by sex and, within this, by part-time/ full-time status[42] and occupational group.[43] The Regulations provide that (save for specified uses) information gathered for monitoring purposes is to be treated as confidential.

Article 55 FETO requires that employers "review the composition of those employed . . . and the employment practices of the concern for the purposes of determining whether members of each community [Protestant and Catholic] are enjoying, and are likely to continue to enjoy, fair participation in employment in the concern". "Fair participation" which, in the words of the FEC in 1997, was "arguably the most novel departure" of the FEA 1989, is not defined.[44] These reviews must take place at least once every three years and must include review of practices relating to recruitment, training and promotion. Where it appears to an employer, as a result of such a review, that "members of a particular community are not enjoying, or are not likely to continue to enjoy" "fair participation", Article 55 FETO provides that the employer "shall . . . determine the affirmative action (if any) which would be reasonable and appropriate".

The issue of affirmative action was considered in Chapter 3. Tri-annual reviews are not subject to an automatic obligation of return to the EC (SACHR's 1997 proposal that such an obligation should be imposed having been rejected by the Government). Also rejected by the Government was SACHR's proposal that employers should be obliged to consult with recognised trade union or employee representatives during the review process and the FEC's proposal that reviews should consider "the extent to which a harmonious working environment is being provided by staff".[45]

CONTRACT COMPLIANCE

The contract compliance provisions of the FETO are limited, the government having refused to accept SACHR's 1997 proposal for their extension. Article 62 empowers the EC to declare "unqualified" employers who either fail to register (a prerequisite to the monitoring obligations of all but private sector employers of no more than 10 employees) or to submit a monitoring return, or who fail to comply with an order issued by the EC after an investigation such as that described above. Article 64 provides that public authorities "shall not enter into [a relevant] contract with" an

---

[42] The FETO, for the first time, included part-time workers amongst those who must be monitored by race.

[43] i.e., "managers and administrators, professional occupations, associate professional and technical occupations, clerical and secretarial occupations, craft and related occupations, personal and protective service occupations, sales occupations, plant and machine operatives and other occupations".

[44] The government did not act on the FEC's 1997 proposal (*Review*, fn 37 above) that the legislation ought to "clarify that fair participation will not be present where there is an under-representation of one community defined as "fewer members of that community than might be expected"." (para 3.34).

[45] *Review*, fn 37 above, para 3.29.

unqualified person, and "shall take all such steps as are reasonable to secure that no work is executed or goods or services supplied for the purposes of [a relevant] contract by any unqualified person".[46] But Article 64(6) provides that "(6) Nothing in this Article affects the validity of any contract".[47]

Writing in 1996, Christine Bell remarked that:

"The Employment Equality Review and Fair Employment in Northern Ireland" (1996) 2 *International Journal of Discrimination and Law*, **53**

Since the legislation was introduced in 1989 the disqualification provisions have only been applied on one occasion and then only for a short period. This occurred after an employer failed to register. However, the employer registered quickly thereafter and the disqualification was lifted. As no non-compliance findings have been made by the FET no opportunity has arisen to utilize that route of disqualification. The fact that recourse has only been made to the disqualification provisions on one occasion does not mean that these provisions have had no impact. Contract compliance does much of its work as a deterrent and the threat of disqualification may have been one factor which led so many companies to register and send in monitoring returns.

There are several ways in which this regime could be strengthened. Under the present system the contract compliance requirements operate as a penalty mechanism where grants and contracts are removed after evidence of discriminatory practice. They could operate as an incentive scheme whereby to be eligible for a grant or contract one must demonstrate compliance with equality goals or good practice. Incentive operated schemes as utilized in the U.S. and by some local authorities in England (prior to the Local Government Act 1988), have proved a successful tool for increasing the proportion of an under-represented group in the workforce.

Even if the present scheme is not amended SACHR's Employment Equality Review should examine to what extent equality considerations are taken into account by public entities . . . which exercise significant powers to make grants or award contracts. Have pressures towards greater "value for money" and cost reduction in the public sector led to the marginalization of equality concerns when grants or contracts are awarded? Further, the penalty scheme model could be extended. The possibility of disqualification could be added to enforce the present remedy available in an individual complaint, whereby the FET can order the employer to take action to reduce the affect of discrimination on the complainant, within a specified period. An employer who fails to do this could be disqualified. This would make the deterrent of disqualification for maintenance of discriminatory practices a more visible one than it is under the present provisions.

---

[46] Such a contract is either (Article 64(2): "a contract made by the public authority accepting an offer to execute any work or supply any goods or services where the offer is made . . . (b) in response to an invitation by the public authority to submit offers" or (Article 64(3)) "a contract falling within a class or description for the time being specified in an order made by the Department, where work is to be executed or goods or services supplied by any unqualified person". The Local Government (Miscellaneous Provisions) (Northern Ireland) Order 1992, which prohibits local authorities from taking into account "non-commercial matters" in awarding contracts, has an exemption in relation to employers in default.

[47] Prior to the FETO, the FEA permitted contracts with unqualified persons if the alternative was either disproportionately expensive or not in the public interest. These qualifications were repealed but Article 64(7) provides that "(7) This Article does not apply to the execution of any work, or the provision of any goods or services, by any person which is certified in writing by the Secretary of State to be necessary or desirable for the purpose of safeguarding national security or protecting public safety or public order"

SACHR made proposals in 1997 for the extensive amendment of the FEA's contract compliance provisions,[48] suggesting that prospective contractors should be required to provide information on their "policies, procedures and practices in relation to fair employment and equal opportunities", and that contracts could specify terms which contractors would be obliged to meet. These proposals received short shrift in the White Paper which preceded the FETO. The White Paper, together with the response of the Select Committee on Northern Ireland (4th Report, 1998–1999 session) thereto and the wider issue of collective methods of enforcement, is considered in Chapter 5.

AFFIRMATIVE ACTION

Affirmative action under the FETO was discussed in Chapter 3. Here it is useful to note once again that affirmative action obligations may be imposed by the Commission where an Article 55 review demonstrates an absence of fair participation (discussed in Chapter 3) or may be pursued by employers, whether voluntarily (after an employment review or otherwise).

The review obligation imposed by Article 55 FETO, and the role of affirmative action in this area, was mentioned above. Article 55(3) provides that affirmative action may include goals and timetables by which progress towards "fair participation" may be measured and Article 56(5) requires the Commission "where a review discloses that members of a particular community are not enjoying fair participation [to] make such recommendations as it thinks fit as to the affirmative action to be taken and . . . the progress . . . that can reasonably be expected" (again by way of goals and timetables). As was mentioned above, employers are under no general obligation to submit reviews to the Commission but (Article 56(4)) the Commission may require information from employers regarding such reviews (in particular, whether an employer has determined that fair participation is not occurring and, if such a determination has been made and a programme of affirmative action decided upon, any goals and timetables set). Where the EC has recommended affirmative action, it is empowered to require follow-up information (not more than once every six months) as to the progress being made. And where the Commission is of the view that an employer's monitoring or review processes are not adequate, it may seek written undertakings from the employer as to changes to those processes and may, in the absence or breach of such undertaking, issue mandatory directions to the employer (Article 58). These may, in the final analysis, be enforced by the FET.

Where "action appearing to the Commission to be affirmative action" is agreed by undertaking, directed by the Commission or ordered by the FET, the EC may issue a

---

[48] Its first report in 1987 had also proposed extensive contract compliance provisions.

"goals and timetables" notice specifying the expected progress towards "fair employment" and may require follow-up information (Article 60). These powers are in addition to the EC's powers to carry out the "investigations into practices" discussed above. Discrimination uncovered by such an investigation can be remedied either by way of undertaking or direction from the Commission, such direction being enforceable as above.

Christopher McCrudden pointed out that the definition of affirmative action established by s.58 FEA (and largely retained by the FETO) differs also from that originally proposed in the 1988 White Paper—"special measures to promote a more representative distribution of employment in the workforce". Whereas the White Paper's definition suggested that a wide variety of measures would be acceptable, the FEA 1989 permitted only a small number of departures from the formal equality approach. The same is true of the FETO, although it does go one step further than the previous legislation by permitting direct discrimination in training, albeit in very limited circumstances. According to Angela Hegarty, another critic of the legislation:

A. Hegarty, "Examining Equality: The Fair Employment Act (NI) 1989 and its Review" [1995] 2 *Web Journal of Current Legal Issues*

It is clear that it has been the "formal equality" which has prevailed in Northern Ireland in the past and it is equally clear that formal equality has largely failed to redress the imbalance in employment between Protestants and Catholics. . .

Employment discrimination has been a running sore in Northern Ireland since the foundation of the state. The imbalance between the two major communities remains a source of domestic and international dissatisfaction, which the enactment of the 1989 legislation failed to stem. The UK government's attitude to the implementation of truly effective equality laws and practice can most kindly be described as ambivalent. Throughout the evolution of equality policy improvements have only been wrung from the government after much effort from activists and campaigners. The government seems reluctant, at best, to match its words about the absolute necessity for true equality of opportunity with action which guarantees those policies in practice . . . It is unfortunate that the government seems to regard change as a concession to be made only after much lobbying and international pressure. As an attitude it hardly helps promote equality . . . The UK government cannot continue to beg the question of its commitment to equality of opportunity in Northern Ireland.[49]

---

[49] Fn 4 above.

10

Equal Pay

THE BACKGROUND

One of the clearest indications that women experience discrimination at work lies in the level of their wages relative to those earned by men. In 1999, full-time women workers earned 81% of the male hourly rate, 74% of the male weekly rate for 91% of the hours. If manual and non-manual workers are considered separately the picture deteriorates—manual and non manual women working full time earned, respectively, 74% and 69% of the comparable male hourly rate. And part-time women workers do less well again. In 1999, part-time women workers earned 60% and part-time women manual and non-manual women workers 67% and 53% respectively of the equivalent full-time male rate. Male part-time workers fare little better, but are far less numerous.[1] Rates of pay for full-time women workers have improved over the last few decades. In 1970, for example, manual and non-manual women workers earned 61% and 52% of the equivalent male rate, all women 63%. In 1980 these figures had improved to 71%, 61% and 72% respectively, and in 1990 to 72%, 64% and 77%. But part-time women workers' wages have remained relatively static since 1976 when they stood at 59%, up from 52% in 1972. The precise figure fluctuates between 56% and 60% (the rates for manual and non-manual workers, respectively, between 62% and 65% and between 48% and 53%). The 1% rise between 1998 and 1999 is due, most probably, to the implementation of the National Minimum Wage Act which holds out some promise of improvement for the lowest paid workers.

Equal pay legislation has been in place in the UK since 1975, in which year the Equal Pay Act 1970 (EqPA) was implemented. Despite this, very significant disparities remain between men's and women's pay. Women are paid less than men whether their wages are measured hourly or weekly. They are paid less than men both at the top of the hierarchy and at the bottom. In 1998, taking only those women who worked full-time, women doctors and financial managers earned 80% and 64% respectively of their male colleagues' hourly rate, women barstaff and petrol pump forecourt attendants 88% and 91% . Women who do "women's jobs" are paid less than men who do "men's jobs"—in 1998, full-time female nurses, for example, earned 85% of male engineering technicians' hourly rate. Women who do "women's jobs" are paid less than

---

[1] Part-time male workers consist, in the main, of students and workers approaching retirement.

men who do "women's jobs"—full-time women financial clerks and nurses earned only 85% and 96% of their male colleagues' rates. And women who do "men's jobs" are paid less than men who do "men's jobs"—full-time women police officers and women machine tool operatives earned 91%[2] and 69% of the male rate. However the information is categorised, however large or small the occupational categories examined, women earn less than men.[3] Women and, in particular, ethnic minority women and those who work part-time, have been the main beneficiaries of the National Minimum Wage.

Orthodox economists sometimes attempt to explain the gender-wage gap in terms of what they call "compensating differentials". Stephen Rhoads, for example, claims that:

> Part of the wage differential between men and women may be explained by the former's relatively greater interest in obtaining high pay or in taking a leadership role, which generally commands a higher salary . . . men put more emphasis on wages and leadership opportunities . . . women . . . are more apt to stress nonmonetary benefits, such as good physical conditions, convenient hours, or rewarding interpersonal aspects of the job—relations with co-workers and supervisors, the opportunity to help others, and the like.[4]

Mathys and Pincus have waxed lyrical about the "job security and safety" apparently associated with "female" jobs; the "pleasant, sanitised working conditions in many office settings", the "friendships and sociability, opportunities for "social interaction" and "scheduling flexibility" which, we are asked to believe, characterise women's jobs.[5]

The spurious nature of these theories should be apparent to the most untutored eye. Low-paid jobs are frequently associated, not with pleasant working conditions, but with repetitive, stressful, dirty and dangerous work.[6] If, as Rhodes claims, predominantly female jobs are associated with "better supervisors and better relations with co-workers", this may be precisely *because* they are predominantly female, women generally being regarded as more co-operative than men. But it is as absurd to claim that this justifies paying women less as it would be to select "opportunities to play football after work" as a "compensating differential" and to reduce male wages accordingly. There is no evidence, *contra* Rhodes, that women have "easier time off

---

[2] These figures apply only in respect of sergeants and below.

[3] All figures are taken from the NES 1998.

[4] S. Rhoads, *Incomparable Worth: Pay Equity Meets the Market* (New York: Cambridge University Press, 1993), p.14. See also M. Killingsworth, "The Economics of Comparable Worth: Analytical, Empirical, and Policy Questions", in H. Hartmann (ed.), *Comparable Worth: New Directions for Research* (Washington DC: Academy Press, 1985).

[5] N. Mathys and L. Pincus, "Is Pay Equity Equitable? A Perspective That Looks Beyond Pay" (1993) 44 *Labor Law Journal* 351, pp.352–3.

[6] The lowest paid jobs include—F. Wilkinson, *Why Britain Needs a Minimum Wage* (London: Institute for Public Policy Research, 1992), table 1—nursing auxiliaries and assistants, shop assistants, security guards and patrolmen, bar staff, hospital ward orderlies, road sweepers, sewing machinists, footwear workers and repetitive assemblers. See further the discussion in A. McColgan, *Just Wages for Women* (Oxford: OUP, 1997), Chapter 6.

for personal reasons", and women are less likely than men to enjoy a host of work-related benefits such as pensions, sick-pay, company cars, transport subsidies, discounted goods, finance and/or loans, life assurance, private health care recreation facilities, and paid time off for domestic reasons.[7] It seems that men, rather than women, benefit from compensations other than those found in their pay packets.

"Compensating differentials" theory appears to owe more to sexist assumptions about the nature of men's and women's jobs than it does to fact. In *American Nurses Association v State of Illinois* 783 F 2d 716, Judge Richard Posner characterised nursing in terms of "flexible hours" and opportunities for "nurturing".[8] The first is simply inaccurate, at least in the UK where most nursing jobs require shift work. And it begs the question to treat "nurturing" as a reward, rather than a skill or demand associated with the job. Why are men rewarded for "leadership", while "nurturing" is regarded as a reward in itself? Why is dirt seen as an unattractive aspect of waste collection, while the contact with human waste which is a feature of nursing is overlooked in what is generally regarded as a "clean" job? And why is policing seen as a dangerous job while nursing and social work, both of which can require unaccompanied workers to enter sometimes hostile environments equipped with little more than their interpersonal skills, are regarded as "nice jobs for a woman"? (The TUC recently reported that one in three nurses had been attacked by a member of the public (this is four times the national average), and 455 had been threatened with physical violence. Twice as many nurses as other women workers (86%) had to lift heavy loads, 70% had to work in awkward or tiring positions and 25% nurses were exposed to breathing fumes, dusts and harmful substances.)[9]

Nor do "compensating differentials" theories explain why women are paid less than men when they perform the same jobs, why movements of women into previously male jobs are accompanied with falls in the status and rewards of those jobs, why women moving into male jobs (such as management and medicine) are frequently steered into particular specialities (personnel, paediatrics, geriatrics), and those areas of work paid less than those in which men predominate (financial and general management, surgery). Advocates of "compensating differentials" theory serve precisely to illustrate the point frequently made by feminists—that women are underpaid because the demands and difficulties associated with their jobs appear invisible to (male) observers.

---

[7] J. Rubery, S. Horrell, and B. Burchell found that pensions were available in 73% of male full-time and 68% of female full-time jobs; sick-pay in 66% and 58% respectively; a company car in 30% and 10%; transport subsidies in 31% and 24%; discounted goods in 47% and 40%; finance/loans in 21% and 20%, life assurance in 39% and 19%; private health care in 31% and 22%; recreation facilities in 40% and 36% and paid time off for domestic reasons in 64% and 48% respectively—"Part-time Work and Gender Inequality in the Labour Market", in A. Scott (ed.), *Gender Segregation and Social Change: Men and Women in Changing Labour Markets* (Oxford: OUP, 1994), table 6.7.

[8] Cited by Mathys and Pincus, fn 5 above., p.356. See also C. Hakim, *Key Issues in Women's Work: Female Heterogeneity and the Polarisation of Women's Employment* (London, New Jersey, Atlantic Highlands: Athlone, 1996), p.66–71 on part-time working.

[9] TUC, *Running Risks at Work*, reporting the results of the Government's self-reported work-related illness survey (available on the TUC website at http://www.tuc.org.uk).

The other common argument put forward by orthodox economists in order to explain the gender pay gap is put in terms of "human capital"—the skills, training and education, etc, in which workers invest. It is often argued that women have lower human capital then men—that they are less well educated, trained, motivated, and/or skilled than men. Solomon Polachek, for example, argued that women invested less in training and that they avoided those (technologically advanced) areas of work in which skills would quickly diminish during career breaks and in which discontinuity of employment was penalised most.[10] Gary Becker, too, claimed (in the 1960s) that "women spend less time in the labour force than men, and therefore have less incentive to invest in market skills", and that the skills which women do choose to acquire are less related to employment than are men's: "[a] woman wants her investment to be useful both as a housewife and as a participant in the labour force".[11] More recently, Becker has argued that women, in particular married women, make less effort at work than do men:

> [m]arried women with primary responsibility for childcare or other housework allocate less energy to each hour of work than married men who spend equal time in the labor force. . . . Since married women earn less per hour than married men when they spend less energy on each hour of work, the household responsibilities of married women reduce their hourly earnings . . . even when both participate the same number of hours and have the same market capital . . . household responsibilities also induce occupational segregation because married women seek occupations and jobs that are less effort intensive.[12]

The arguments of the "human capital" theorists have been countered by research (much of it conducted in Britain) which has shown that women are paid less not *because* they were concentrated in jobs requiring less skill, but *despite* their working in jobs very similar to those performed by men in different organisations;[13] and that women's jobs are frequently ungraded:

> firms would often recognise differences in skill between the women workers . . . but nevertheless pay all of them at the same rate, justifying the practice on the basis that any differentiation would cause resentment amongst the other women workers. The fact of women's

[10] S. Polachek, "Sex Differences in College Majors" (1978) 31 *Industrial Labor Relations Review* 498; "Occupational Self-selection: a Human Capital Approach to Sex Differences in Occupational Structure" (1981) 63 *Review of Economic Statistics* 60. See also H. Zellner, "The Determinants of Occupational Segregation", in C. Lloyd (ed.), *Sex Discrimination and the Division of Labour* (New York: Columbia University Press, 1975) p.125; J. Mincer and S. Polachek, "Women's Earnings Re-examined", (1978) 13 *Journal of Human Resources* 118 and "Family Investments in Human Capital: Earnings of Women" (1974) 82(2) *Journal of Political Economy* S. 80–1.

[11] G. Becker, "Investment in Human Capital: A Theoretical Analysis" (1962) 70(5)(II) *Journal of Political Economy* 9, p.38-.39. See also Hakim, fn 8 above. At p.133 Hakim suggests that the concentration of women in liberal arts at third level education is motivated by suitability for homemaking. Hakim also claims, p.170, that female occupations are low-skill occupations.

[12] p.S52. For a very recent articulation of this approach see Hakim, fn 8 above, p.69.

[13] S. Horrell, J. Ruberry and B. Burchell, "Unequal Jobs or Unequal Pay?" (1990) 20 *Industrial Relations Journal* 176. Job skills were compared using index allocating points for responsibility, degree of supervision, autonomy, training & education.

pay being less than men's cannot therefore simply be explained on the grounds that women's work is less skilled, for even within women's work there is little or no differentiation of reward by skill . . . the *predominant influence* on the shape and structure of the pay and employment system was the *sex of the workers* (my emphasis).[14]. . .

The differences in education between men and women are narrow and closing fast, well-educated women also being more likely than their counterparts to remain in the workforce after having children. And a recent Workplace Industrial Relations Survey found that:

establishment performance is not significantly affected by the level of female concentration. We therefore find no support for the hypothesis that higher female concentration is an indicator of lower human capital.[15]

Jan Waldfogel found that

only a small proportion of the gender gap . . . is due to differences in characteristics between young men and women . . . if women had the same characteristics they do now but received the same returns as men in the labour market, the gender gap at age 23 would fall 84% (from 19% to 3%) and at age 33 would fall 70% (from 30% to 7%). This means that the much greater part (84% at age 23 and 70% at age 33) of the gender gap is due to differential *treatment* (my emphasis).[16]

Other recent estimates of the relationship between "human capital" and the gender-wage gap in Britain suggest that:

---

[14] C. Craig, J. Rubery, R. Tarling and F. Wilkinson, *Labour Market Structure, Industrial Organisation and Low Pay* (Cambridge: CUP, 1982), p.84.

[15] N. Millward and S. Woodland, *Gender Segregation and Male/Female Wage Differences*, (London: LSE, 1995), p.21. As interesting as their findings on the human capital issue were Millward and Woodland's comments on their fellow economists. Noting that analysts of the Workplace Industrial Relations Survey (WIRS) data tended not to remark on the wage premium associated with working in a predominantly male workplaces, "save to cast female concentration in the role of a proxy measure of low labour quality", they declared the contrast between this assumption and the recognition that the negative wage impact of concentrations of ethnic minority workers could be attributed to discrimination "difficult to understand" (pp.8–9). Certainly, the economists who attributed lower female wages to lower human capital accumulation appeared to do so simply on the basis that "one would expect that a higher quality workforce would result in a higher gross weekly pay of the "typical" employee", and that women's wages were lower (p.8, citing D. Blanchflower, "Union Relative Wage Effects: a Cross-section Analysis using Establishment Data" (1984) 22(3) *British Journal of Industrial Relations* 311).

[16] *Women Working For Less: A Longitudinal Analysis of the Family Gap* (London: LSE, 1993), p.47. P. Sloane, "The Gender Wage Differential", in Scott (ed), fn 7 above, p.191 found that discrimination accounted for approximately one third of the wage gap between single men and women, one quarter of that between married men and women. It should be noted, however, that Sloane included as factors distinct other than "sex" (the latter being the measure of discrimination) some, such as marriage and experience, which might be considered themselves to be discriminatory.

[t]he primary reason for women's lower pay is smaller remuneration for human capital attributes in their jobs: if women's human capital was remunerated at the same rate as men's, their hourly pay would be substantially—of the order of one fifth—higher.[17]

Waldfogel's research has been supported very recently by the Government Women's Unit which reported in 1999 that:

having children is possibly the most significant factor affecting women's income and earnings opportunities. For many working women, having children means a drop in personal income, a loss of momentum on the career ladder and often leaving employment for several years.

There has been a dramatic increase in recent years in the number of women who work during pregnancy and are back in work within nine to eleven months of the birth of their child. But most commonly, women who return to work after having children do so on a part-time basis. Working mothers still bear the primary responsibility for care of their children . . .

A working life fragmented by caring responsibilities and low earnings, together with the lack of pensions provision, combine to make women more likely to be reliant on means-tested benefits in old age. They are more likely to be frail or ill, and to need professional care.

Joshi and Davies estimated, in 1992, that a typical woman who had two children, relatively short periods of maternity leave followed by a few years' part-time work before returning to full-time work, would lose 57.4% of her lifetime earnings after the age of 25.[18] Finally, figures published by the Cabinet Office in February 2000 calculated that their sex cost women an average £250 000 over a lifetime in lost earnings. The study reported that unqualified women forfeited almost £200 000 over a lifetime, women with GCSE qualifications almost £250 000 and women with degrees and professional careers almost £150 000 "simply by being female".[19] This cost to women of motherhood (is additional to the figures mentioned above), is the greatest loss of income in relation to this factor being experienced by women on low incomes who tend to have children earlier and take more time "out" than women with higher qualifications.

There is a great deal of evidence that women are paid less because they are women, that women's jobs are undervalued because they are done by women and that workers are frequently advanced and rewarded for stereotypically male attributes which, accordingly, managers are inclined to overlook even when they are possessed by women workers.[20] And even when women's jobs have been assessed as being of equal

[17] J. Ermisch and R. Wright, "Differential Returns to Human Capital in Full-time and Part-time Employment", in N. Folbre, B. Bergmann, B. Agarwal and M. Floro (eds.), *Issues in Contemporary Economics: Volume 4, Women's Work in the World Economy* (New York: New York University Press, 1992), p.208.

[18] H. Joshi and H. Davies, *Childcare and Mothers' Lifetime Earnings: Some European Contrasts* (London: Centre for Economic Policy Research, 1992) Discussion Paper 600, table 4.

[19] K. Rake, *Women's Incomes over the lifetime*, report for the Women's Unit, February 2000.

[20] S. Bevan and M. Thompson, *Merit Pay Performance Appraisal and Attitudes to Women's Work* (Brighton: University of Sussex, 1992), Institute of Manpower Studies Report No. 234.

value to those of their male colleagues, women still find themselves paid less. Local authority workers have for years had their jobs evaluated and basic wages pinned to these evaluations. It is still the case that men, but not women, workers receive considerable supplements by way of bonuses which are payable only in respect of "male" jobs. In 1999, the *Equal Opportunities Review* reported that "bonus payments represent 15% of average male earnings [for local authority workers] compared with just over 1% of female earnings":

> ... There is a growing acceptance that most of the schemes in operation are indefensible in terms of equal pay, but the total cost of equalisation could run into many millions of pounds. In the West Midlands alone, employers have put the annual cost of equalising bonus payments . . . at over £20 million . . . At the beginning of 1997, 1,500 schools meals workers employed by the former Cleveland County Council settled their equal pay claim based on bonuses for £4 million . . .[21]

The issue of discriminatory bonuses is one, we shall see below, which should in theory be easy to challenge under the EqPA. That such bonus payments persist more than a decade after criticism was first directed at them should indicate that the current state of equal pay legislation leaves much to be desired, at least in terms of its practical application. We turn now to consider the UK and EC legislation which permits challenge to pay discrimination, followed by a brief analysis of the extent to which this legislation is appropriate to challenge that discrimination.

INTRODUCTION TO THE EQUAL PAY ACT

The EqPA, deals only with male/female wage disparities, rather than with pay differences which arise between disabled and other workers, or between workers of different racial groups or, in Northern Ireland, workers of different religious beliefs or political opinion. Like the RRA, the SDA and the FETO, the EqPA adopts a symmetrical approach. It does not specifically address women's underpayment, any more than the other Acts specifically address discrimination against women. Blacks and Asians or, in Northern Ireland, Catholics. Rather, the EqPA prohibits some (and only some) sex-related pay differences. Men, like women, can claim under the Act.

The similarities between the EqPA, on the one hand, and the SDA, RRA and FETO, on the other, do not extend far beyond their shared symmetry of approach. The other legislation prohibits "discrimination", direct or indirect, in a number of situations. It places the burden of proof on the applicant and permits such proof to rest on a hypothetical comparator: "I would not have been treated thus were I not a woman" (/ a man/ black/ Asian/ white/ Catholic/ Protestant/ nationalist/ unionist, etc).

---

[21] 84 *Equal Opportunities Review*, p.4.

The EqPA, on the other hand, does not actually use the term "discrimination", much less distinguish its direct and indirect varieties. Instead, it sets out three situations in which there is a *de facto* right to the same contractual terms (including pay) as another.[22] The applicant must prove that she (or he) falls within one of these three situations—i.e., that she does the same work, work which has been rated by the employer as equivalent (in value) or work which a tribunal has determined to be of equal value, to that done by someone of the opposite sex in the "same employment" as her. (The concept of "same employment" is discussed below.) Where the applicant does this, she is entitled to have an "equality clause" inserted into her contract which gives her the same contractual term(s) as that (those) enjoyed by her comparator and sought by her.

The EqPA does not permit a hypothetical comparator. On the other hand, the Act must be read to permit comparison with a woman's predecessor, according to the Court of Appeal in *Macarthys Ltd* v *Smith (No.2)* [1981] 1 All ER 111, [1980] ICR 672. The Court's decision followed that of the ECJ that such comparators must be permitted to be made under Article 141 of the Treaty Establishing the European Community (as it then was). Accordingly, the Court of Appeal ruled that the EqPA must be read, however inelegantly, to give effect to this. More recently, in *Diocese of Hallam Trustees* v *Connaughton* [1996] ICR 860, [1996] IRLR 505, EAT ruled that Article 141 required the possibility of comparison with a successor in employment.

The equal pay applicant does not have to prove that she has been discriminated against, simply that she has been less favourably treated in some contractual term than a suitable comparator.[23] In these circumstances, one might say that a presumption of discrimination arises. The employer can displace that presumption, and escape the imposition of an equality clause, by proving that the difference in pay (or other contractual term) is due to a "material factor" which is "not the difference of sex". This is called the "GMF" (genuine material factor) or s.1(3) defence (being laid down by s.1(3) of the EqPA). It, together with the various types of equal pay claim, are considered further below. Here it is sufficient to note that, once the applicant has proven that she is paid less than an appropriate comparator, the burden of proof is on the employer to *disprove* discrimination. In order that a "material factor" is "not the difference of sex", it must not discriminate directly between men and women and, if it is indirectly discriminatory (in the sense that reliance upon it disfavours women as a matter of fact), reliance upon it must be justified.

Another significant difference between the EqPA, on the one hand, and the SDA and the RRA, on the other, characterised the early years of the EqPA but was removed from the legislation by the SDA 1986. This difference was to be found in s.3 of the EqPA, as it was originally drafted which established a collective mechanism for the pursuit of equal pay. . s.3, which is also discussed in Chapter 5, provided that

[22] As we shall see below, the applicant can pick and choose the terms.
[23] i.e., like work, work rated as equivalent or work of equal value.

(1) Where a collective agreement . . . contains any provision applying specifically to men or women only, the agreement may be referred . . . to the Central Arbitration Committee . . . to declare what amendments need to be made to the agreement . . . so as to remove that discrimination between men and women.

The reference could be made by trade union or employer or, where the discriminatory term was contained in a pay structure, by the employer or the Secretary of State.

S.3 had the potential radically to improve women's pay. It did not depend on women being able to show that they were employed in the same or similar jobs to those done by men. It had the potential to extend the benefits of collective bargaining to unorganised women (where, for example, the then-common "female rate" in a workplace had to be raised to the closest (possibly unionised) "male rate". S.3 could benefit women who worked in entirely female workplaces, as long as those workplaces were party to multi-workplace collective agreements containing "male" and "female" rates (the latter were invariably lower than the former). Its only real weakness lay in the narrowness of its approach to discrimination. As is evident from the above, s.3 only applied where there was discrimination on the face of the agreement or pay structure—i.e., where the offending instrument referred "specifically to men or women only".

The CAC initially took a broad view of its powers under s.3, reviewing and ordering amendments to pay structures and collective agreements in which, in their view, employers (and/or unions) had taken insufficient steps to eradicate in practice the effects of past discrimination.[24] The breadth of the CAC's approach is apparent in the following extract.

Paul Davies, "The Central Arbitration Committee and Equal Pay" (1980) 33 *Current Legal Problems* 165, 173–6

In its 1977 Report the Committee says:

Discrimination does not always appear on the face of the agreement. For example, an agreement may have been re-negotiated or altered with Grade 1 and Grade 2 replacing the previous male clerks and female clerks with no other change. Such a change cannot be said to have ended the matter. The Committee has to ensure that discrimination has been truly removed and replaced with unisex grades bearing appropriate rates.

In some ways, however, this passage underestimates the reach of the Committee's approach, for it suggests that only alterations of a fairly cynical kind deliberately aimed to avoid the application of section 3 will be caught. There have certainly been references to the Committee which have something of this air about them. Thus, in Award No. 328 (1977) the employer before 1973 had separate wage rates for "General Staff-Male" and "General Staff-Female," the rate for adult females being only about 70 per cent of that for adult males. The women (some 360) were engaged in packing and the men (some 59) on

---

[24] See for example *Prestcold & APECCS* (1978) CAC 78/830, reported in EOC *Annual Report* 1978, p.50. See further Chapter 5.

warehouse duties. In 1973 the employer changed the designations attached to the rates to "Warehouse Staff" and "Packing Staff" respectively, but the wage differential was maintained and only some six males were recruited as packers and no females for warehouse duties. The employer's argument was that the collective agreement contained no provisions applying specifically to men only or to women only so that the Committee had no power to make a declaration (although the employer also argued that the difference in wage rates reflected the difference in job content between packers and warehouse workers). The Committee found that it did have jurisdiction:

> The Committee has also sought to interpret the Act in accordance with its aims which are set out succinctly in the preamble as "An Act to prevent discrimination as regards terms and conditions of employment, between men and women." The Committee accordingly tries to establish whether in reality an agreement contains provisions which discriminate by reference to sex. If a pay structure has been established which overtly discriminates between male and female employees and that pay structure has persisted unchanged in essentials from year to year, then the mere removal of identifying labels and the formal, but not in practice significant, admission of either sex to any grade does not, in the Committee's view, alter the reality of discrimination which it becomes the Committee's duty to remove.

However, the Committee has found itself to have jurisdiction where the employer has not merely removed discriminatory labels attached to wage rates, but has also taken steps to raise the rates attached to jobs done by women. The union's argument here typically is that the employer has not gone far enough, as it is often put, "to eradicate properly the historical concept of a women's rate of pay." This is a development of the utmost significance given . . . high proportion of women workers engaged on "women only" work. The notion of a "woman's rate of pay" is that the rate for a particular kind of job has been fixed at such a low level that women necessarily are the only workers attracted to that type of job. It is necessary, in order for the employer to keep the work as "women's work," for him neither to fix an explicit "female" rate in the collective agreement nor to exclude males from the job in contravention of the Sex Discrimination Act 1975, because of the level of the remuneration set will achieve that end. The essence of the complaint on behalf of the women workers is that their work is undervalued in comparison with that done by men. This is not to say that such discrimination by employers is usually prejudiced. As Henry Phelps Brown has said, in describing the various forms of discrimination by status:

> Secondly, the employer will be led to discount the value of the services of disfavoured persons if his assessment of that value is not firmly based on the actual results of their work, but is guided and biased by their status. He may simply see it in the nature of things that lower status should be matched by lower pay, or he may assume that the lower pay that already prevails is the reliable outcome of general experience of what the work is worth.

In short, the employer may claim that he is paying the rate of the job, but his assessment of what the work is worth to him may be unconsciously biased by the status of the people who are performing the work.

In implementing this approach to discrimination the Committee has to distinguish between cases where the low rate of pay attached to a type of work predominantly performed by women is an accurate reflection of what the work is worth to the employer and cases where the rate reflects status discrimination, *i.e.* it is a "woman's rate of pay." Four factors seem to have predominated in the Committee's Awards, which are encapsulated in the following questions. Is there a preponderance of men at the top and of women at the bottom of an apparently facially neutral (or unisex) grading structure? Is there a history of the work being performed predominantly by women? Is the rate of pay such that it is likely to attract males? Are there very uneven differentials among the rates attached to the various grades in the pay structure? A positive answer to the first, second and fourth questions and a negative one to the third are regarded by the Committee as strong evidence of discrimination still being present in a pay structure which has historically contained separate provisions relating to men and to women, even if these specific references have subsequently been deleted and even if some further steps towards the implementation of equal pay have been taken.

Thus in Award No. 43 (1976) the employer had a 10 grade pay structure, grades 1A to 6 of which had originally been described as male grades and grades 7 to 7B as female. Before the reference of the structure to the Committee the employer had already eliminated the specific references to males and females, had promoted five women to grade 5 and seven to grade 6, and reduced slightly the differential between grades 7 and 6. The Committee concluded that the agreement was discriminatory because "(a) the rate for grade 7, which is theoretically a unisex rate, is at a level which is unlikely to attract and retain male wage earners (b) the differential between grade 7 and grade 6 is about three times as wide as the differential between any other two consecutive grades in the pay structure."

Of the factors used by the Committee to identify continuing discrimination the first is perhaps the least happy. In its Annual Report 1977 the Committee says that "very uneven distribution may indicate that real discrimination has not been eliminated." In so far as this statement points to the absence of women in the higher paid grades a recent Award of the Committee seems to recognise that this may reflect more a shortage of qualified women applicants (which may itself, of course, reflect what Phelps Brown has termed "discrimination before the market") or an employer's discriminatory hiring or promotion policies rather than an inequality in terms and conditions of employment, at which the 1970 Act is directed. In so far as the statement is directed at the absence of men from the lowest paid grades then that factor is, of course, crucial but adequately catered for in the second and third factors listed above. In any case, this factor by itself does not lead the Committee to find discrimination and, as far as can be judged from the published Awards, the Committee has been sensitive in applying the criteria to the various situations before it. Nevertheless, nearly all claims that apparently neutral structures are discriminatory have to the end of 1979 been successful.

The efforts of the Committee were thwarted by the Divisional Court which ruled, in *R v CAC ex p. Hy-Mac Ltd* [1979] IRLR 461, that the CAC had acted improperly in purporting to amend a collective agreement which was not overtly discriminatory. Five years (and one single s.3 decision later), the SDA 1986 stripped the CAC of its powers in respect of equal pay. S.6 of the same Act provided that discriminatory terms in collective agreements and pay structures, were void. But no enforcement mechanism was provided until 1993, when the Trade Union and Labour Relations (Consolidation) Act (TULR(C)A) established a right of complaint to a tribunal. The tribunal cannot, however order the extension of any beneficial term to those discriminatorily denied it (as could the CAC under s.3 EqPA). Rather, it is restricted to declaring the offending provision void. S.6 SDA 1986 was considered in Chapter 5.

ARTICLE 141

Before we turn to the detail of the equal pay regime, it is useful to mention, by way of introduction, the relevant EC provisions. The EqPA, passed some five and a half years prior to its implementation in 1975, predated the UK's accession to the EEC (as it then was). The right to equal pay which it established (i.e., the right to equal pay for like work or for work which had been rated as equivalent by the employer) was thought by the government of the time to be more generous than that required by Article 119 (now 141) TEC.

Article 119 stipulated merely that: "Each Member State shall during the first stage ensure and subsequently maintain the application of the principle that men and women should receive equal pay for equal work. . . ." This was understood by many to require only that men and women were paid equally in respect of the *same* work. The UK acceded to the EEC in 1973, and with this accepted the supremacy of Community (now EC) law. In 1975, Council Directive 75/117 (the Equal Pay Directive) defined the "principle of equal pay" to require the elimination of sex-related pay differentials in respect of "the same work or . . . *work to which equal value is attributed* (Article 1, my emphasis). Article 2 required Member States to

> introduce into their national legal systems such measures as are necessary to enable all employees who consider themselves wronged by failure to apply the principle of equal pay to pursue their claims by judicial process after possible recourse to other competent authorities.

Council Directive 117/75 proved to be a Trojan horse. Having agreed to it on the understanding that it was already adequately implemented by the EqPA, the UK found itself pursued by the Commission on the grounds that it was not. The Commission eventually took enforcement action against the UK on the grounds that, the evaluation of dissimilar jobs being entirely at the discretion of the employer, the latter had not implemented "equal pay for work of equal value" as required by Article 141 and Council Directive 117/75. In *Commission* v *United Kingdom* (C–61/81), [1982] ECR 2601, the ECJ ruled that: "where there is disagreement as to the application of the concept of "work to which equal value is attributed" . . . the worker must be entitled to claim before an appropriate authority that his work has the same value as other work". The Equal Pay (Amendment) Regulations 1983, presented to the Commons by a drunk and derisive Alan Clark (then Under-Secretary of State for Employment),[25] amended the EqPA to provide for an equal value claim.

In *Defrenne* v *Sabena (No 2)* Case 43/75 [1976] ECR 455, the ECJ accepted that Article 141 was directly effective.[26] Since that date (8th April 1976), individuals within the various Member States can rely on Article 141 to claim equal pay in their national

[25] SI 1983/1794.
[26] The effect of the decision was "backstopped" at the date of the judgment, 8th April 1976.

courts. We saw in Chapter 1 that the effect of EU law in relation to sex discrimination (not including pay) is felt:

- where infringement action by the Commission results in legislative change;
- where workers employed by the state (broadly defined by the ECJ in *Foster v British Gas* Case C–188/89 [1990] ECR I–3313) rely on directives against their employer, in which cases:
  —those workers directly reap the benefit of EC law, and
  —rulings against the state in respect of state employees result in legislative change for all;
- where, subsequent to *Francovich* Cases C–6 and 9/90 [1991] ECR I–5357, individuals sue the state for damages in respect of losses resulting from failure adequately to implement directives;
- where courts are obliged to give *indirect effect* to directives by interpreting national legislation, where possible, to accord with EC law. (See, for example, the discussion on *Webb* v *EMO* in Chapter 1).

In the case of Article 141, the added dimension of *horizontal* direct effect means that individuals can rely upon it in the national courts regardless of any provisions of national law and of the identity of the respondent.[27] In 1979, Lord Denning explained the direct effect of Article 141 in the following terms:

Shields v E Coomes (Holdings) Ltd [1979] 1 All ER 456, [1978] 1 WLR 1408. [1978] ICR 1159.

If you were to read article [141] with the eyes of an English lawyer, you would think that that article, and the directives following on it, imposed on the member states an obligation to pass legislation so as to ensure equal pay for equal work, but that it had no direct application of its own force in England. You would think that the English courts could wait and do nothing until they saw an Act on the statute book to give effect to "the principle of equal pay", or "the principle of equal value", or "the principle of equal treatment". But, if you should think that, you would be wrong.

Long before the United Kingdom joined the European Community, the European Court had laid down two principles of great importance to all member states and their citizens. When we joined the Community, our Parliament enacted that we should abide by those principles laid down by the European Court: see s.3(1) of the European Communities Act 1972. These two principles are the twin pillars on which Community law rests. They uphold the standing of Community law as an independent legal order. It is a law which is common to all member states and must be applied in all of them. The first is the principle of "direct applicability". It arises whenever the EEC Treaty imposes an obligation on member states to pass legislation on this subject or that. For instance, article [141] says: "Each member state shall ensure . . . that men and women shall receive equal pay for equal work." It is obvious that, if any member state failed to pass legislation to implement that article, it might become a dead letter within that state. In order to overcome any such evasion of the treaty, the European Court has declared that many of the articles of the treaty are "directly applicable" in any member state. This means that any citizen in a member state can bring

---

[27] For the significance of this see Chapter 1.

proceedings in his own national courts to enforce the rights and obligations contained in this or that article of the treaty . . .

The second is the principle of "the supremacy of Community law". It arises whenever there is a conflict or inconsistency between the law contained in an article of the EEC Treaty and the law contained in the internal law of one of the member states, whether passed before or after joining the Community. It says that in any such event the law of the European Community shall prevail over that of the internal law of the member state.[28] . . . Suppose that the Parliament of the United Kingdom were to pass a statute inconsistent with article [141] : as, for instance, if the [EqPA] gave the right to equal pay only to unmarried women . . . I should have thought that a married woman could bring an action in the High Court to enforce the right to equal pay given to her by article [141].

Lord Denning's affirmation of the supremacy and direct effect of Article 141 is uncontroversial. What is more problematic is his last remark concerning the enforcement of the rights granted under the provision. This point is considered in Chapter 1.

Here it is useful to set out the text of Article 141 as amended and renumbered by the Treaty of Amsterdam (1997, effective 1999). Whereas, prior to that date, Article 141 relied on Article 1 of the Equal Pay Directive to affirm the application of its equal pay principle to work of equal *value*, the new Article 141 reads as follows:

> Each Member State shall ensure that the principle of equal pay for male and female workers for equal work or work of equal value is applied.
>
> For the purposes of this Article, "pay" means the ordinary basic or minimum wage or salary and any other consideration, whether in cash or in kind, which the worker receives, directly or indirectly, in respect of his employment from his employer.
>
> Equal pay without discrimination based on sex means:
> (a) that pay for the same work at piece rates shall be calculated on the basis of the same unit of measurement;
> (b) that pay for work at time rates shall be the same for the same job. . . .

The significance of the amended text is largely symbolic. In the early years, ECJ decisions suggested that applicants could rely on the provision only in cases where discrimination was identifiable "*solely* with the aid of criteria of equal work and equal pay referred to by . . . [Article 141], without national or Community measures being required to define them with greater precision in order to permit of their application" (*Jenkins, Worringham, McCarthys v Smith*[29]). This appeared to place equal *value* claims outwith the scope of the provision.[30] Whatever the original position, the ECJ has for some time permitted claims based on equal value to be brought on the strength

---

[28] Citing *Costa v Ente Nazionale per l''Energia Elettrica (ENEL)* [1964] ECR 585, and *Amministrazione delle Finanze dello Stato v Simmenthal SpA* [1978] ECR 629.

[29] Respectively, Case C–96/80 [1981] ECR 911, Case 69/80 [1981] ECR 767 and Case C–129/79 [1979] ECR 1275.

[30] In *Macarthy's* the ECJ used the first part of the quote. The full quote is taken from *Worringham* although for reasons associated with *Van Gend en Loos's* requirement Case 26/62 [1963] ECR 1 that directly effective provisions need no further implementation (in the form presumably of establishing a procedure) rather than the lack of reference to equal value

of Article 141, albeit that the method for establishing equivalence is one for national law.[31] It would appear that this remains unchanged under the amended Article 141.

Turning to the domestic provisions the EqPA, as amended by the Equal Value Regulations 1983, sets out three types of equal pay claim together with one defence (albeit in two slightly different forms) thereto. First we will consider the meaning of "pay" both within the EqPA itself and, more broadly, in terms of the guarantees afforded by Article 141. Having established that in respect of which "discrimination" is prohibited by the EqPA, we will go on to look at the three types of claim provided by the Act. We will then consider the possible scope of equal pay claims—that is, the extent to which applicants are free to go beyond their own workplace in search of a suitable "comparator". Finally, the employer's defence will be discussed.

'PAY', THE EqPA AND ARTICLE 141

"What is pay?" is not a question which arises under the EqPA. Rather than legislation about "pay" as such, the EqPA operates (as was mentioned above) by way of an "equality clause" which accords to the successful applicant the contractual term(s) enjoyed by her comparator and in respect of which she seeks equal treatment S.1(2) EqPA provides that:

> An equality clause is a provision which relates to terms (whether concerned with pay or not) of a contract under which a woman is employed (the "woman's contract"), and has the effect that [(s.2(a) (b) and (c))] . . .
> (i) if (apart from the equality clause) any term of the woman's contract is or becomes less favourable to the woman than a term of a similar kind in the contract under which that man is employed, that term of the woman's contract shall be treated as so modified as not to be less favourable, and
> (ii) if (apart from the equality clause) at any time the woman's contract does not include a term corresponding to a term benefiting that man included in the contract under which he is employed, the woman's contract shall be treated as including such a term.

The majority of claims brought under the EqPA concern pay. But it is clear from s.1(2) that the Act's scope is wider than this.

The significance of Article 141 has been discussed above. It is clear that Article 141 may be relied upon in the UK courts, generally by way of having the EqPA (or, in the case of non-contractual "pay", the SDA) interpreted (however contrary to their express terms) so as to give effect to the European provision. The question of what is "pay" is not significant to the EqPA itself. But its scope within Article 141 is crucial to the wider picture: to the extent that work-related discrimination falls outwith the scope of the SDA and the EqPA, it can be challenged most effectively where it falls within Article 141. The strength of the provision lies, as we saw above, in its application

---

[31] *Danfoss* Case C–109/88 [1989] ECR 3199, *Enderby* v *Frenchay* Case C–127/92 [1993] ECR I–5535.

horizontally—between individuals—as well as *vertically*—between the individual and the state (this is not true of the equal treatment which regulates employments related discrimination other than in relation to pay). In addition, the equality provisions which relate to "pay" are considerably stronger that those which deal with "social security" in respect of which Member States have traditionally been given more discretion.

We saw, above, that Article 141 categorises as "pay" all benefits, contractual or otherwise, "receive[d], directly or indirectly, in respect of . . . employment from [the] employer". Early decisions on the scope of "pay" tended to be restrictively decided. In *Defrenne* v *State of Belgium (No 1)* Case C–80/70 [1971] ECR 445 the ECJ ruled that Article 141 did not extend to retirement pensions. Ms Defrenne had been dismissed from Belgium's Sabena airline at 40, in line with their discriminatory retirement ages. The pension scheme which she challenged was established according to a Royal Decree which imposed special rules on the aviation sector. According to the Court:

> A retirement pension established within the framework of a social security scheme laid down by legislation does not constitute consideration which the worker receives indirectly in respect of his employment . . . within . . . Article [141]

In *Worringham* v *Lloyds Bank plc* Case C–69/80, which was mentioned above, the ECJ accepted that contributions made by an employer to a pension scheme were "pay" within Article 141 where they were included in employees' gross pay. But in *Burton* v *British Railway Board* Case C–19/81 [1982] IRLR 116 the court ruled that membership of a pension scheme was a matter of treatment, rather than pay, and so fell outside the scope of Article 141. And in *Newstead* v *Department of Transport & Her Majesty's Treasury* Case C–192/85 [1987] ECR 4753, [1988] IRLR 66, deductions made (compulsorily) by an employer in respect of a pension scheme were excluded from Article 141's definition of "pay". The ECJ relied in part on the ground that, the pension scheme in question replacing, in part, the state scheme, it was a matter of "social security" rather than of pay.

Even prior to *Newstead*, the 1986 decision in *Bilka-Kaufhaus GmbH* v *Weber von Hartz* Case C–170/84 [1986] ECR 1607 had already signalled the beginning of a more expansive approach to the scope of "pay". *Bilka-Kaufhaus* was concerned with a contractual pension scheme which supplemented the basic German pension. The scheme was financed solely by employer contributions which were not included within the employees' gross pay.[32] The applicant challenged her exclusion, as a part-time worker, from the scheme (discrimination against part-time workers amounting, in this case, to discrimination against women). The ECJ accepted that the claim fell within Article 141.

Subsequent to the decision in *Bilka-Kaufhaus* the ECJ has extended the scope of "pay" well into what was originally regarded as the area of social security. In *Bilka,*

---

[32] See also *Liefting* v *Directie van het Academish Zienkenthuis* Case C–23/83 [1984] ECR 3224.

the pension scheme in question served exclusively to *supplement* the state pension (so resulting solely from the employment relationship). In *Barber* v *Guardian Royal Exchange Assurance Group* Case C–262/88 [1990] ECR 1889, [1990] IRLR 240[33] the ECJ extended the reasoning in *Bilka* to cover a non-contributory "contracted-out" pension scheme (i.e., one which replaced, in part, the state pension). This decision was regarded as sufficiently momentous that the court agreed to block retrospective reliance upon it—only those workers who had already instituted claims at the date of the decision (17th May 1990) could challenge pension payments based on service prior to that date.[34] The decision also ruled that statutory, as well as contractual, redundancy payments fell within Article 141.

A number of pension cases subsequent to *Barber* were concerned with the nature of the temporal limitation imposed by that decision. Among these were *Ten Oever* v *Stichting Bedrijspensioenfonds voor het Glazenwassers-en Schoonmaakbedrijf* Case C–109/91 [1993] ECR I–4879, [1993] IRLR 601, in which the ECJ confirmed that Article 141 extended to survivors' pensions.[35] In *Bestuur van het Algemeen Burgerlijk Pensioenfonds* v *Beune* Case C–7/93 [1993] ECR I–0131, [1995] IRLR 103,[36] Article 141 was interpreted to include civil service pensions paid by the state as employer. And in *Vroege* v *NCIV Instituut voor Volkshuisvesting BV* Case 57/93 [1994] ECR I–4541, [1994] IRLR 651 and *Fisscher* v *Voorhuis Hengelo* Case 128/93 [1994] ECR I–4583, [1994] ICR 635, [1994] IRLR 662,[37] the ECJ categorised as "pay" access to membership of a pension scheme, as distinct from payments thereunder. What was perhaps most significant about these decisions (which reflected the earlier *Bilka* case) was that they were not subject to the temporal limitation imposed in *Barber*. Nor, according to the ECJ in *Magorrian & Cunningham* v *Eastern Health and Social Services Board* Case 246/96 [1999] ECR I–7153, [1998] IRLR 86, was access to a scheme conferring additional benefits on employees who qualified for it.[38]

In addition to all of the above, the ECJ has accepted as "pay" within Article 141: gratuitous (and, *ipso facto*, contractual) travel concessions—*Garland* v *British Rail*

---

[33] See also (on time-limits imposed by *Barber*) *Moroni* v *Firma Collo GmbH* Case C–110/91 [1993] ECR I–6591, [1994] IRLR 130, *Neath* v *Hugh Steeper* Case C–173/91 [1993] ECR I–6935, [1994] IRLR 91.

[34] The exact meaning of the temporal restriction was established over a succession of cases discussed immediately below. The Maastricht Treaty was subject to the "Barber protocol" which restricted the impact of the decision to pension payments relating to service after the date.

[35] Though temporal limitation precluded the exact claim. Also *Smith* v *Avdel* Case C–408/92 [1994] ECR I–4435 and *Van den Akker* v *Stichting Shell* Case C–28/93 [1994] ECR I–4527 permitted the upwards equalisation of retirement ages in pursuit of "equality".

[36] Accordingly, the decision of EAT in *Griffin* v *London Pension Authority* [1993] IRLR 248 was clearly wrong.

[37] See also *Dietz* v *Stichting Thuiszorg Rotterdam* Case C–435/93 [1996] ECR I–5223, [1996] IRLR 692 though (in the case of a contributory pension) the right to retroactive membership depended on the employee making the appropriate contributions. The *Barber* time limits do not apply in relation to joining pension schemes, as distinct from payments received thereunder.

[38] Had this been construed as relating to the amount of pension the time limit applied in *Barber* would have precluded the claim. See also *Neath* v *Hugh Steeper*, fn 33 above, in which that court permitted some pension-related actuarial discrimination and *Birds Eye Walls Ltd* v *Roberts* Case C–132/92 [1993] ECR I–5579 allowed discrimination in bridging pensions, a position preserved by Directive 96/97.

Case 12/81 [1982] ECR 359 (*Grant* v *South West Trains* Case C–249/96 [1998] ECR I–3739, [1998] IRLR 206); paid leave and over-time pay paid in respect of attendance at trade union training etc—*Arbeiterwohlfahrt der Stadt Berlin eV* v *Bötel* Case C–360/90 [1982] ECR I–3589, [1992] IRLR 423;[39] and rules governing the accrual of seniority, where seniority is directly related to pay—*Hill & Stapleton* v *Revenue Commissioners* Case C–243/95 [1998] ECR I–3739, [1998] IRLR 466.

Also arguably in the nature of "social security", though embraced by the ECJ as "pay", have been sick pay (*Rinner-Kühn* v *FWW Spezial-Gebaudereiningung GmbH & Co KG* Case C–171/88 [1989] ECR 2743); unemployment payments made by an employee's last employer on a periodic basis (*European Commission* v *Kingdom of Belgium* Case C–173/91 [1993] ECR I–0673, [1993] IRLR 404); unfair dismissal compensation (*R* v *Secretary of State for Employment ex p. Seymour-Smith & Perez* Case C–167/97)[40] and maternity pay (*Gillespie* v *Northern Health and Social Security Board* Case C–342/93 [1996] ECR I–0475, [1996] IRLR 214, *Boyle* v *EOC* Case C–411/96 [1998] ECR I–6401, [1998] IRLR 717).[41] As far as the latter is concerned, however, the ECJ ruled that (*Gillespie*):

> 16 . . . discrimination involves the application of different rules to comparable situations or the application of the same rule to different situations. . . women taking maternity leave provided for by national legislation . . . are in a special position which requires them to be afforded special protection, but which is not comparable either with that of a man or with that of a woman actually at work . . . neither Article [141] . . . not Article 1 of Directive 117/75 [the Equal Treatment Directive] require[s] that women should continue to receive full pay during maternity leave".

Pay during maternity leave, and the issue of pregnancy more generally, was considered in Chapter 6.

CLAIMING "EQUAL PAY"

In Chapter 1 we considered the various mechanisms through which Article 141 rights can be relied upon. Here we confine our attention to EqPA claims. The Act establishes

---

[39] See also *Kuratorium Für Dialyse und Nierentransplantation eV* v *Lewark* Case 457/93 [1996] ECR I–0243, [1996] IRLR 637 and see *Manor Bakeries* v *Nazir* [1996] IRLR 604 for a conflicting decision by EAT to absence at a trade union conference.

[40] [1999] 2 CMLR 273 Prior to the ECJ decision there were a substantial number of decisions to the same effect from British courts—*Nash* v *Mash* [1998] IRLR 168 (tribunal), *Mediguard Services Ltd* v *Thame* [1994] IRLR 504, *R* v *Secretary of State for Employment ex p EOC* (DC) [1991] IRLR 493 but the House of Lords in the *EOC* did not regard this issue as clear ((1993) 1 All ER 1022), nor did the Court of Appeal in *ex p Seymour Smith* ([1995] ILR 889). Excluded from the ambit of pay under Article 141 are differential transfer payments arising from the application to the pension contributions of actuarial tables which discriminated on grounds of sex—*Neath* v *Hugh Steeper*, fn 33 above, and rules which govern promotion, even where promotion directly determines pay—*Gerster* v *Freistaat Bayern* Case C–1/95 [1997] ECR I–5253, [1997] IRLR 699.

[41] The ECJ takes the view that no discrimination occurs as absence on maternity leave is not comparable to other situations. See also the *Pedersen* case, Case C–66/96 [1998] ECR I–7327.

three types of claim. S.1 provides for the inclusion of an equality clause into a woman's contract in respect of "any term of [her] . . . contract [which] is or becomes less favourable to [her] than a term of a similar kind in the contract under which [her comparator] is employed", that comparator being employed on (s.1(2)(a)) "like work", (s.1(2)(b)) "work rated as equivalent or (s.1(2)(c)) "work . . . of equal value" to hers. The comparator must be "in the same employment" as the woman (this is further discussed below) and the effect of the "equality clause" is to modify the offending contractual term so "as not to be less favourable". S.1(4) goes on to define as "like work":

work . . . of the same or a broadly similar nature . . . the differences (if any) . . . not [being] of practical importance in relation to terms and condition of employment; and accordingly in comparing her work with theirs regard shall be had to the frequency or otherwise with which any such differences occur in practice as well as to the nature and extent of the differences.

S.1(5) defines as "work rated as equivalent" work which has:

been given an equal value, in terms of the demand made on a worker under various headings (for instance effort, skill, decision), on a study undertaken with a view to evaluating in those terms the jobs to be done by all or any of the employees in an undertaking or group of undertakings, or would have been given an equal value but for the evaluation being made on a system setting different values for men and women on the same demand under any heading.

As was noted above, employers cannot be obliged to carry out job evaluation schemes such as would found equal pay claims under s.1(1)(b) (such schemes are discussed further below).

S.1(2)(c) states that an "equal value" claim may be made by a woman

employed on work which, not being work in relation to which paragraph (a) or (b) above applies, is, in terms of the demands made on her (for instance under such headings as effort, skill and decision), of equal value to that of a man in the same employment.

We consider the various types of equal pay claim in some detail below. First it is useful to deal with an issue which arses by virtue of the particular "equalising" mechanism employed by the EqPA—i.e., the insertion of an "equality clause" to modify "any term of the woman's contract [which] is or becomes less favourable to [her] than a term of a similar kind in the contract under which [her comparator] is employed".

On the face of it, this approach would appear to allow "leap-frogging", i.e., attempting to "cherry pick" any particularly favourable terms of a comparator's contract which may, in theory or practice, be balanced by terms which are more favourable to the applicant than her comparator's equivalent are to him. It was argued by the employers in *Hayward* v *Cammell Laird Shipbuilders Ltd*, that the EqPA did not permit such an approach.

Hayward was brought by a canteen worker who named, as her comparators, a painter, a joiner and an insulation engineer. By way of defence her employers claimed that, although her basic and overtime rates of pay were lower than those of her comparators, her sickness benefits and meal breaks were better than theirs with the effect that, taken as a whole, her contractual terms were no less favourable to her than theirs were to them. A tribunal, EAT and the Court of Appeal all agreed that the applicant would not have been entitled to relief if, as the respondent employer argued, her contract, taken as a whole, was no less favourable than those of her comparators.[42] The House of Lords allowed her appeal, unanimously deciding that s.1(2) of the EqPA meant what it said.

Hayward v Cammell Laird Shipbuilders Ltd ([1988] 1 AC 894, [1988] 2 All ER 257, [1988] 2 WLR 1134, [1988] ICR 464, [1988] IRLR 257, [1988] 2 CMLR 528)

Lord Goff with whom Lords Griffiths, Bridge and Brandon agreed, Lord Mackay delivering a concurring judgment

. . . If I look at the words used [in s.1(2)(c)(ii), this being an equal value claim], and give them their natural and ordinary meaning, they mean quite simply that one looks at the man's contract and at the woman's contract, and if one finds in the man's contract a term benefiting him which is not included in the woman's contract, then that term is treated as included in hers. On this simple and literal approach, the words "benefiting that man" mean precisely what they say, that the term must be one which is beneficial to him, as opposed to being burdensome. So if, for example, the man's contract contains a term that he is to be provided with the use of a car, and the woman's contract does not include such a term, then her contract is to be treated as including such a term.

The respondents, and the lower courts, had made much of the "absurd and unreal consequences" which would follow a literal interpretation of s.1(2), the former using an example of a woman with a salary of £7,500 and a car worth £3,500 p.a. who sought to compare her wages with those of a man paid £11,000 but without a company car. Lord Mackay accepted that "one can envisage difficult examples" but "in the ordinary case such as the present . . . it would be wrong to depart from the natural meaning of the words Parliament has used because of the difficulty in their application to particular examples especially when those examples do not arise in actual cases". (Neither Lord Mackay nor Lord Goff found it necessary to refer to the European legislation in view of their conclusion on the clarity of the UK provisions. Nevertheless, both took the view that it supported their approach.)

Dealing with the concern of the lower courts as to the potential of their interpretation to lead to "mutual enhancement or leap-frogging, as terms of the woman's contract and the man's contract are both, so to speak, upgraded to bring them into line with each other", Lord Goff expressed the opinion that s.1(3) might provide a defence in relation to "compensating" terms such as those upon which the employer in the present case sought to rely. Lord Mackay was not convinced of this, suggesting "at the very least" that s.1(3) required the establishment of a causal link between the woman's unfavourable term and that which claimed to balance it.

---

[42] [1987] 2 All ER 344, [1988] QB 12 (CA) and [1987] 1 All ER 503 (EAT).

This question has never really been resolved, but Lord Goff's provisional view was supported by Lord Bridge in *Leverton* v *Clwyd County Council* [1989] 1 AC 706, [1989] 1 All ER 78, [1989] 2 WLR 47, [1989] ICR 33, [1989] IRLR 28, [1989] 1 CMLR 574. The decision is considered in more detail below. On the question, however, whether a woman's unfavourable pay could be balanced against her shorter hours, Lord Bridge concluded, perhaps not surprisingly, that:

> Where a woman's and a man's regular annual working hours, unaffected by any significant additional hours of work, can be translated into a notional hourly rate which yields no significant difference, it is surely a legitimate, if not a necessary, inference that the difference in their annual salaries is both due to and justified by the difference in the hours they work in the course of a year and has nothing to do with the difference in sex.

The decision of the House of Lords in *Hayward* denied employers *carte blanche* to decide on their workers' behalf the manner in which they should be paid, to the extent that the manner discriminated between men and women. But if the "equality clause" approach to equal pay operated in this matter to women's benefit (by permitting leap-frogging, at least in theory, and subject to the s.1(3) defence), it operated against women's interests in several other respects. We have already mentioned that the EqPA, unlike the other anti-discrimination legislation, requires an actual comparator, it being insufficient for a woman to claim that, had she been a man, she would have been paid more. Added to this has been a degree of confusion, on the part of EAT in particular, as to what is meant by a "contractual term".

In *Benveniste* v *University of Southampton* (unreported, the Court of Appeal decision is at [1989] ICR 617, [1989] IRLR 122), EAT rejected an appeal by a woman academic who was paid less than men doing the same jobs in the same university. A tribunal reached the extraordinary decision that there was no term in Dr Benveniste's contract which was less favourable than the terms enjoyed by her male colleagues. Despite the fact that she was paid less the tribunal stated, and EAT agreed, that the relevant contractual term simply incorporated the pay *scale*, where the applicant was placed on that scale then being a matter purely for the discretion of the employers!

The Court of Appeal overruled EAT: "there was indeed a term in the appellant's contract, namely the term as to her salary, which was less favourable to her than the terms of a similar kind in the contracts of the comparators who were paid more than she was". But technical difficulties with the EqPA arose again in *Barry* v *Midland Bank plc*. The case was brought by a woman who claimed that the bank's contractual redundancy scheme breached the EqPA by discriminating against her. The applicant had switched from full-time to part-time employment a few years before she was made redundant. Her complaint was made on the grounds that, her redundancy payment being calculated on the basis of her final salary, she was not fully compensated in terms of her previous full-time work. The case will be considered again below, when we come to discuss the GMF defence. What is of significance here is EAT's response to her claim that the redundancy terms discriminated against her as a part-time worker.

Barry v *Midland Bank plc* [1997] ICR 192

Mummery J (for EAT)

The critical question is . . . whether the relevant terms of the applicant's contract of employment were less favourable than the terms of a similar kind in the contract of a male comparator. The answer is "No," for the following reasons.

(1) The scheme as a whole does not treat a woman such as the applicant less favourably than a man in her situation. If the applicant had (a) remained a full-time worker throughout the period of her employment, or (b) been a part-time worker throughout her employment, she would have had no complaint under the [EqPA] or under any other statute, treaty article or directive. Her terms of employment and her treatment as an employee would have been exactly the same as in the case of a male comparator employed by the bank working full-time or part-time . . .

(3) As with the statutory redundancy scheme, the rules of the bank's scheme are not formulated so as to treat either (a) women less favourably than men, or (b) part-time workers less favourably than full-time workers. The same rules apply to both men and women, to both full-time and part-time workers. In all cases the calculation of the entitlement to the severance payment is on the basis of pay at the date of redundancy. . .

(5) The force of the applicant's case is that the scheme has the appearance of being arbitrary and unfair in its effect on a group of bank employees which include her, ie, those full-time employees who, before opting for redundancy, have become part-time. That group includes men as well as women. Men in that group are the comparators in like circumstances. Women in that group receive the same treatment as men in that group.

(6) The essence of the applicant's complaint is not that she has been treated less favourably than a male comparator in that group of full-time workers who have switched to part-time employment before opting for redundancy (she has not been so treated). It is that the bank ought to have constructed the scheme, but failed to do so, to include rules which would ensure that payments for voluntary severance mirrored more precisely the nature of past service rendered by employees before redundancy, for example, where past service of a part-time worker included full-time employment. The bank should have ensured that those in her position—both men and women—should have received a more generous payment. One way of securing that would be a proportional arrangement reflecting the past service both full-time and part-time.

(7) In other words, the applicant would like to have a different scheme, with different provisions in it for men and women in her position. Such a scheme might have been fairer than the present scheme when compared with the treatment under this scheme of those who worked full-time throughout or those who worked part-time throughout and those who, before redundancy, changed from part-time to full-time status. Such a provision might well have benefited more women than men, though no statistics are available in the tribunal decision as to the number and proportions in the group switching from full-time to part-time employment. But none of these matters mean that the bank has treated the applicant less favourably in the matter of pay than a male comparator was or would be treated. The essential point is that the rules of the scheme are not in themselves discriminatory and the rules have not been applied to the applicant in a discriminatory way. The terms of the contract between men and women in the relevant group are the same and the women's contract does not require any modification made to it in order to make it not less favourable than the contract of a man. There is, therefore, no breach of any equality clause . . .

EAT's decision was upheld on appeal both by the Court of Appeal and by the House of Lords (though in each case on different grounds). What is noteworthy, however, is that, 22 years after the implementation of the EqPA and 16 years after it was accepted by EAT in *Jenkins v Kingsgate* (see below) that the EqPA did prohibit indirect discrimination in pay, EAT in *Barry* interpreted the EqPA in such a way that it was rendered incapable of dealing with indirect discrimination.[43] This is not to suggest that this approach is generally adopted by that or any other court. But it is testament to the complexities of the Act that this confusion can persist so long after its implementation.

"Like work"

Turning to consider the various equal pay claims in more detail, s.1(2)(a)'s "like work" claim was regarded by the framers of the EqPA as quite a broad and generous provision. Barbara Castle, then Secretary of State for Employment and Production, stressed that the differences between "broadly similar" jobs would have to be "of practical importance" in order to avert a successful claim under this head and suggested that, of about 8.5 million women employees, three million more were engaged on "like work" to that done by men. The government took the view that the combined effect of the "like work" and "work rated as equivalent" provisions as originally set out in the EqPA provided the same result as ILO Convention No. 100, which required "remuneration established without discrimination based on sex". It was on the strength of the EqPA that the UK, in 1971, ratified the Convention.

The Government's view of the breadth of s.1(2)(a) turned out to have been optimistic indeed. The courts adopted an extraordinarily narrow approach to the "like work" provision from the start. In *Amey v Tidmars & Sons*, for example, a tribunal ruled that the jobs done by a curtain cutter and a blind cutter were not "broadly similar". The former involved marking and cutting material with a scissors or shears, the latter the use of a knife and was, in the tribunal's view, "a heavier and generally bigger operation".[44] In *Brodie & anor v Startrite Engineering*, the fact that a male drill operator selected as well as fitted a drill part, and that he could perform minor repairs on his machine, was permitted to block a claim by female drill operators who earned only 70% of his wages.[45]

---

[43] This form of discrimination may be challenged under the EqPA only where the contractual terms of the applicant and her comparator are taken to include their application in the particular case (i.e., here the comparator's entitlement to have his service fully reflected in his redundancy package set against the applicant's partial recompense). This having been done, the question becomes whether the difference is justified under S1(3) EqPA, discussed below.

[44] J. Coussins, *The Equality Report* (London: NCCL Rights for Women Unit, 1976), p.28.

[45] The employers may have shared the view, expressed by one of the respondents to a Department of Employment Study undertaken in the late 70's/ early 80's (M. Snell, P. Glucklich and M. Povall, *Equal Pay and Opportunities: A Study of the Implementation and Effects of the Equal Pay and Sex Discrimination Act in 26 Organisations* (London: DE, 1981), Research Paper No. 2, p.58) that: "[w]omen are not machine sophisticated . . . it would not be worth training them'. For the early approach of the tribunals to "like

In *Eaton Ltd* v *Nuttall*, EAT overturned a tribunal decision in favour of a woman production scheduler who, being responsible for ordering 2,400 units per week of a value up to £2.50, received 85% of the salary of a male production scheduler who was responsible for ordering 1,200 units per week of a value ranging between £5 and £1,000. The employers argued that the woman's work involved a lower degree of responsibility than that of the man, an argument rejected by a tribunal on the grounds that both performed the same function with the same degree of competence. According to Phillips J:

Eaton Ltd v Nuttall [1977] 3 All ER 1131, [1977] 1 WLR 549, [1977] ICR 272, [1977] ITR 197, [1977] IRLR 71

Several decisions of the appeal tribunal have said that in applying s 1(4) of the Act [like work] the most important point to consider is what the woman does and what the man does, but we do not think that it is right to disregard the circumstances in which they do it . . . Thus in *Waddington* v *Leicester Council for Voluntary Service*, when considering s 1(4), we said that it was wrong to ignore the responsibility for supervision taken by the woman and not by the man albeit that in the circumstances of that case it was difficult to pin-point particular acts done in performance of the duty to supervise. In earlier cases we have tried to discourage industrial tribunals from applying s 1(4) too narrowly, and this we strongly endorse; and we should expect them to act in that way when considering such matters as responsibility. Nonetheless this is a job aspect highly regarded by all groups of employers and employees alike, and we would think it not only unacceptable, but also wrong, to ignore it as a factor properly to be taken into account . . . For example, suppose two book-keepers working side by side doing, so far as actions were concerned, almost identical work, where on an examination of the importance of the work done it could be seen that one was a senior bookkeeper and another a junior bookkeeper. Such distinctions between two employees are often easy to spot in practice but difficult to distinguish only in the terms of what each of them does. That is the sort of case where we think that the existence of the factor of responsibility might be crucial.

EAT's decision might appear reasonable. But its effect was to preclude consideration of the fact that the only other female production scheduler in employment, who was paid the same rate as the applicant, had replaced a man who had been paid on the same (higher) rate as that paid to the only male production scheduler whose rate of pay was known. It is also worth noting that the decision in *Waddington*, to which Mr Justice Phillips referred, was to the effect that, a woman being paid *less* than a man in respect of a job which was determined to be *more* responsible than his, she could not claim equal pay under s.1(4). She was a Community leader on whose initiative an adventure playground was established, the playleader (a man) being subordinate to her but paid £3426 per annum to her £3009. (Ms Waddington was paid on the Local Authorities Social Worker scale, her comparator on the Youth Leaders and Community Wardens scale.)

work" see A. Leonard, *Judging Inequality* (London: Cobden Press, 1987) and A. McColgan, *Just Wages for Women* (Oxford: OUP, 1997), Chapter 3.

Waddington v *Leicester Council for Voluntary Service* [1977] 2 All ER 633, [1977] 1 WLR 544

Phillips J

Though the daily work done by each of them was much the same . . . there is no doubt that Mrs Waddington was in a superior position, and was, amongst other things, responsible for Mr Southgate . . . The industrial tribunal found that Mrs Waddington did not satisfy the test prescribed by s.1(4) . . . The differences which they found to exist between the respective work of Mrs Waddington and Mr Southgate concerned: (i) The broader aspect of her work as against his, (ii) The added responsibility which she had, and (iii) Her overall control. They found that Mrs Waddington and Mr Southgate "were never doing the same or broadly similar work". . . .

It seems to us that the real question . . . was whether the admitted differences, between what she did and what he did, were differences of practical importance in relation to terms and conditions of employment. . . . S.1(4) is primarily concerned with what the woman and the man do. Thus the Appeal Tribunal in some of the previous appeals under the [EqpA] have said that in applying s.1(4) regard should be had primarily to what the woman and the man do, and not to what the contract of employment requires them to do, except to the extent that it is done in practice . . . [But a]n obligation to supervise, to take responsibility or to control, if it is discharged, is something which in our judgement falls within the words "the things she does and the things they do". It is true that it is often difficult to pin point and to identify the manifestation of responsibility in particular acts, but they are nonetheless real for that, and properly to be taken into account in applying s.1(4).

EAT remitted the case for reconsideration on the basis that the tribunal had failed to distinguish between that which Ms Waddington's contract required by way of supervision, and that which she actually did. If the tribunal decided that she did, in practice, less than her contract suggested, she might have succeeded in establishing like work. That an equal pay claim might require a lower paid woman to minimise the requirements of her job in order to claim pay parity with a male subordinate can only be described as surreal.[46]

In *Capper Pass Ltd* v *Lawton* [1977] 2 All ER 11, [1977] QB 852 [1976] IRLR 366, EAT adopted a broad approach to s.1(3), ruling that no account should be taken, in determining the question of "like work", of "trivial differences or differences not likely in the real world to be reflected in the terms and conditions of employment". In *Shields* v *Coomes* (also extracted above), the Court of Appeal approved of this approach. The applicant, who worked in a betting shop, was paid less than her male colleague who, in addition to those duties he shared with her, was required to work longer hours, to open the shop, and to carry cash to and from it. The employers, who usually staffed their shop with women, had a policy of employing one man in each of their shops which they considered to be in "rough" areas. The employers took the view that these men, who were all paid at the higher rate, functioned "as a cover or precaution against illegal entry".

---

[46] The decision in *Waddington* predated the equal value claim.

A tribunal took the view that the man's security and cash-carrying duties constituted a difference "of practical importance in relation to terms and conditions of employment" so as to defeat a s.1(4) claim. EAT disagreed, a ruling upheld by the Court of Appeal.

Shields v Coomes

Lord Denning MR

When a woman claims equal pay with a man in the same employment, she has first to show that she is employed on "like work" with him . . . her work and that of the men must be "of the same or a broadly similar nature". Instances of the "same nature" are men and women bank cashiers at the same counter; or men and women serving meals in the same restaurant. Instances of a "broadly similar nature" are men and women shop assistants in different sections of the same department store; or a woman cook who prepares lunches for the directors and the men chefs who cook breakfast, lunch and teas for the employees in the canteen: see *Capper Pass Ltd* v *Lawton*. . . .

Second, there must be an enquiry in to (i) the "differences . . . between the things [that the woman] does and the things [that the men do]", and (ii) a comparison of them so as to see "the nature and extent of the differences" and "the frequency or otherwise with which such differences occur in practice" and (iii) a decision as to whether these differences are or are not "of practical importance in regard to terms and conditions of employment".

This involves a comparison of the two jobs, the woman's job and the man's job, and making an evaluation of each job as a job irrespective of the sex of the worker and of any special personal skill or merit that he or she may have. This evaluation should be made in terms of the "rate for the job", usually a payment of so much per hour. The rate should represent the value of each job in terms of the demand made on a worker under such headings as effort, skill, responsibility and decision. If the value of the man's job is worth more than the value of the woman's job, it is legitimate that the man should receive a higher "rate for the job" than the woman. For instance, a man who is dealing with production schedules may deal with far more important items than the woman, entailing far more serious consequences from a wrong decision. So his job should be rated higher than hers: see *Eaton Ltd* v *Nuttall* [above]. But, if the value of the woman's job is equal to the man's job, each should receive the same rate for the job. This principle of "equal value" is so important that you should ignore differences between the two jobs which are "not of practical importance". The employer should not be able to avoid the principle by introducing comparatively small differences in "job content" between men and women; nor by giving the work a different "job description" . . .

Nor should the employer be able to avoid the principle of "equal value" by having the work (at the same job) done by night or for longer hours. The only legitimate way of dealing with night work or for longer hours is by paying a night shift premium or overtime rate assessed at a reasonable figure . . .

In this case the woman and the man were employed on work of a broadly similar nature. They were both counterhands. There were several differences between the things she did and the things which he did. For instance, he started at opening time and worked longer hours; but this did not, by itself, warrant a difference in the "rate for the job". He carried cash from shop to shop or to head office. But this difference was, by itself, "not of practical importance". The one difference of any significance between them was that the man filled a protective role. He was a watchdog ready to bark and scare off intruders. This difference, when taken with the others, amounted to differences which the majority of the industrial tribunal found were "real and existing and of practical importance". Accepting this finding, I do not think these differences could or did affect the "rate for the job". Both the woman and the man worked alongside one another hour after hour, doing precisely the same work. She should, therefore, receive the same hourly rate as he. It is rather like the difference between a barman and a barmaid. They do the same work as one another in serving drinks. Each has his or her own way of dealing with awkward customers. Each is subject to the same risk of abuse or unpleasantness. But, whichever way each adopts in dealing with awkward customers, the job of each, as a job, is of equivalent rating. Each should, therefore, receive the same "rate for the job". It comes within s 1(4) as "like work".

It would be otherwise if the difference was based on any special personal qualification that he had; as, for instance, if he was a fierce and formidable figure, trained to tackle intruders, then there might be a variation such as to warrant a "wage differential" under s 1(3). But no such special personal qualification is suggested. The only difference between the two jobs is on the ground of sex. He may have been a small nervous man, who could not say boo to a goose. She may have been as fierce and formidable as a battle-axe. Such differences, whatever they were, did not have any relation to the terms and conditions of employment. They did not affect the "rate for the job".

I confess, however, that I have felt great difficulty in overcoming the finding of the industrial tribunal that the differences, especially the protective role of the man, were "real and existing and of practical importance". I thought for some time that this protective role should be rewarded by some additional bonus or premium. But my difficulties on this score have been resolved by giving supremacy to Community law. Under that law it is imperative that "pay for work at time rates shall be the same for the same job"; and that "all discrimination on the ground of sex shall be eliminated with regard to all aspects and conditions of remuneration". The differences found by the majority of the industrial tribunal are all based on sex. They are because he is a man. He only gets the higher hourly rate because he is a man. In order to eliminate all discrimination, there should be an equality clause written into the woman's contract . . .

With the advent of the equal value pay claim in 1984, the significance of the "like work" claim and, in particular, of the narrow approach generally taken to it, was reduced. The type of claim which Lord Denning had, in *Shields* v *Coomes*, thought should be accommodated within a stretched s.1(2)(a) in order to give effect to Article 141's "equal pay for work of equal value" could, after that date, be dealt with instead under s.1(2)(c). And, whereas in *Waddington*, "added value" in the woman's job served to block a s.1(2)(a) claim, it is not conceivable today that an equal value claim would be denied on the ground that the woman's work was more valuable than that done by the man.[47] Equal value claims are further considered below.

Work rated as equivalent

S.1(2)(b) allowed comparisons between the wages of women and those of men, working in the same employment, whose jobs had been rated as equivalent by a job

[47] *Murphy* v *Bord Telecom Eireann* Case C–157/86 [1988] ECR 0673, [1988] IRLR 673

evaluation scheme (JES). Had such schemes been designed to "capture" the undervaluation of women's work, and had employees and/or trade unions been able to force job evaluation on employers. S.1(2)(b) might have been a significant tool in the battle against unequal pay. But job evaluation schemes are, for the most part, designed to justify existing wage hierarchies, rather than to subvert them. And the EqPA's five-year phase-in period gave employers ample time, if their schemes had indicated the underpayment of female jobs, to change the schemes or to change the content of male and female jobs therein so as to render them "unequal". Further, the question whether or not to conduct a JES was one for the employer alone.

The EqPA did allow for challenge to blatantly discriminatory job evaluation schemes, s.1(5) providing that:

> A woman is to be regarded as employed on work rated as equivalent with that of any men if . . . her job and their job . . . would have been given an equal value but for the evaluation being made on a system setting different values for men and women on the same demand under any heading;

The significance of this was that, at a time when no other equal value pay claim was available, a woman could take advantage of a clearly discriminatory JES which had *not* rated her job as equivalent to one done by a man in order to, nevertheless, claim equal pay with him. S.1(5) would, for example, have allowed a successful equal pay claim where, for example, a JES, on its face, would have awarded a score of 20, in respect of responsibility, to a woman doing the same job as a man who would have been rated 30 or 40 under that heading. But it did not permit challenge to a system which undervalued (or failed entirely to take account of) the types of skill primarily associated with female jobs.

In order to qualify as a JES for the purposes of s.1(2)(b), the scheme had to satisfy s.1(5)'s requirement that it evaluate jobs "in terms of the demand made on a worker under various headings (for instance effort, skill, decision)". In *Eaton Ltd* v *Nuttall*, EAT declared that, in order to found a claim under the scheme must be:

> thorough in analysis and capable of impartial application. It should be possible by applying the study to arrive at the position of a particular employee at a particular point in a particular salary grade without taking other matters into account except those unconnected with the nature of the work. It will be in order to take into account such matters as merit or seniority etc, but any matters concerning the work (e g responsibility) one would expect to find taken care of in the evaluation study. One which does not satisfy that test, and requires the management to make a subjective judgment concerning the nature of the work before the employee can be fitted into the appropriate place in the appropriate salary grade, would seem to us not to be a valid study for the purpose of s 1(5).[48]

This approach was established in relation to the s.1(2)(b) claim—that is, in respect of cases in which women sought to rely on job evaluation schemes in order to found

---

[48] P.74, *per* Phillips J. This approach was approved by the Court of Appeal in *Bromley* v *Quick*, below.

equal pay claims. We shall see, below, that EAT was prepared to be much less demanding where, in the context of s s.1(2)(c) (equal pay for work of equal value claim) an employer sought to rely on a JES in order to *defeat* a claim.[49]

Most of the case law under s.1(2)(b) deals, not with whether job evaluation systems were discriminatory or not, rather with whether such schemes had been adopted with the effect that the contractual terms of the woman and/or her comparator were "determined by the rating of the work" as required under s.1(2)(b).[50]

O'Brien v *Sim-Chem Ltd* [1980] IRLR 373 concerned a job evaluation scheme carried out in order to eliminate sex discrimination but, as a result of government incomes policy (which restricted pay increases), never implemented. The Court of Appeal dismissed claims based on the scheme on the basis that, the pay of the work force never actually having been determined by the scheme, the contractual terms of the women and their comparators were not "determined by the rating of the work". The House of Lords allowed the applicants' appeal, ruling that comparison between the contractual terms of the women and their comparators became possible once the scheme had concluded that their jobs were of equal value. And in *Arnold* v *Beecham Group Ltd* [1982] IRLR 307, [1982] ICR 744, EAT applied a similar approach to a job evaluation scheme whose implementation (post agreement between management and unions) had been stalled, not by government policy, but by employee resistance.[51]

In *Springboard Sunderland Trust* v *Robson* [1992] ICR 554, [1992] IRLR 261 a question arose as to whether the applicant's job and that of her comparator had, as a matter of fact, been rated as equivalent under the scheme in question. The applicant's job had been awarded 410 points and that of her comparator 429 points on a scheme which placed jobs rated between 360 and 409 points on grade 3, and those rated 410 to 449 points on grade 4. The employers did not pay the applicant a grade 4 salary and, in response to her s.1(2)(b) claim, argued that s.1(2)(b) assisted only those applicants whose jobs had been awarded precisely equal point scores on a job evaluation scheme, rather than those whose point scores placed them within the same grade as that of their comparators. Both the tribunal and EAT ruled in the applicant's favour.[52]

---

[49] *Bromley* v *Quick* discussed below

[50] As noted above, s.1(2)(b) entitles a woman to have an "equality clause" inserted where she is "employed on work rated as equivalent with that of a man in the same employment (i) (apart from the equality clause) any term of the woman's contract determined by the rating of the work or becomes less favourable to the woman than a term of a similar kind in the contract under which that man is employed . . . and (ii) if (apart from the equality clause) at any time the woman's contract does not include a term corresponding to a term benefiting that man included in the contract under which he is employed and determined by the rating of the work.

[51] See also *England* v *Bromley Council* (1978) ICR 1. *Ratcliffe* v *North Yorkshire*, below, arose under s.1(2)(b), but the legal issue concerned the GMF

[52] In *Dibro Ltd* v *Hore and others* [1990] ICR 370, [1990] IRLR 129, EAT ruled that an industrial tribunal had erred in refusing to accept, as a defence to an equal value claim, the results of a job evaluation scheme carried out after the applicants' equal value claims had been made. See however *Avon County Council* v *Foxall and Others; Same* v *Webb and Others* [1989] ICR 407, [1989] IRLR 435 (EAT)—a tribunal did not err in refusing to stay equal value cases pending the outcome of an employer's subsequently implemented JES.

Work of equal value

We saw, above, that the gender-pay gap is associated with occupational sex segregation. If a woman has to prove that she is doing the same job as a man in order to be entitled to receive the same pay, that part of the gender-pay gap which results from this type of segregation goes unchallenged. Under the EqPA as it was first enacted, this aspect of the pay gap could be challenged only through the collective mechanism (discussed above), or in cases in which "female" jobs had been acknowledged by the employer to be equivalent in value to higher paid "male" jobs. The establishment in 1984 of the "equal pay for work of equal value claim" opened the possibility of real challenge to this part of the pay gap.

David Pannick, *Sex Discrimination Law,* **(OUP, 1985) p. 102**

Equal pay for work of equal value is an essential element of anti-discrimination law in a society in which occupational segregation of men and women persists. The anthropologist Margaret Mead explained that all societies tend to undervalue work done by women:

> Men may cook or weave or dress dolls or hunt humming-birds, but if such activities are appropriate occupations of men, then the whole society, men and women alike, votes them as important. When the same occupations are performed by women, they are regarded as less important.

However vital the introduction of a right to "equal pay for work of equal value", the implementation of the principle has a long way to go. In 1984, full-time women workers earned 73% of men's hourly rate, manual and non-manual women 70% and 62% respectively. The headline rate remained at 73% until 1987, jumped to 75% in 1988 and increased by one point a year until 1992, between which time and 1994 it remained at 79%. It increased to 80% in 1995 and to 81% in 1999. The increase in rates for manual and non-manual women, considered individually, has been less; for the former 4 points and for the latter 7 points in the period since 1984. This, in turn, suggests that part of the reduction in the pay gap is explained by a decrease of women in (lower paid) manual jobs the disproportionate concentration of men in which serves to keep the gender-pay gap lower than it would otherwise be.

Some of the criticisms which have been made of the equal pay for work of equal value claim will be considered below. Before this, however, we will consider the claim itself. One preliminary point which should be made concerns the category of applicants permitted to make such claims. We saw, above, that s.1(2)(c) provides the equal pay for work of equal value claim for applicants:

> employed on work which, not being [like] work [or work rated as equivalent] . . . is, in terms of the demands made on her (for instance under such headings as effort, skill and decision), of equal value to that of a man in the same employment.

This could be read either as *restricting* the category of applicants entitled to claim under s.1(3)(c) to those who have no other comparator, i.e., those women employed on work which is not "like" that on which any man is employed, and which has not been rated as equivalent to that done by any man. Alternatively, it could be read merely as a statement that, where a woman is unable to claim that a particular man is either engaged in like work or in work rated as equivalent, she may nevertheless claim that he is engaged in work of equal value.

In *Pickstone and others* v *Freemans plc*, a tribunal and EAT preferred the former, restrictive reading, and rejected an equal value pay claim brought by women warehouse operatives on the ground that, there being in employment a (sole) male warehouse operative, he was their only appropriate comparator. The women wished to compare themselves against a male warehouse checker who was paid more than them.

The Court of Appeal overruled the lower courts. It took the view that s.1(2)(c) was unambiguously unfavourable to the applicants, but permitted a claim to be made directly under Article 141.[53] The House of Lords upheld the Court of Appeal, reaching its decision on a different basis.

Pickstone and Others v *Freemans plc* [1988] 1 AC 66, [1988] 2 All ER 803, [1989] 3 WLR 265, [1988] ICR 697, [1988] IRLR 357, [1988]

Lord Keith of Kinkel:

The [restrictive reading preferred by the lower courts] would leave a large gap in the equal pay provision, enabling an employer to evade it by employing one token man on the same work as a group of potential women claimants who were deliberately paid less than a group of men employed on work of equal value with that of the women. This would mean that the United Kingdom had failed yet again fully to implement its obligations under art [141] of the Treaty and the equal pay directive, and had not given full effect to the decision of the European Court in *EC Commission* v *UK* Case 61/81 [1982] ECR 2601. It is plain that Parliament cannot possibly have intended such a failure . . .[54]

There was no suggestion that the exclusionary words in para (c) were intended to apply in any other situation than where the man selected by a woman complainant for comparison was one in relation to whose work para (a) or para (b) applied. It may be that, in order to confine the words in question to that situation, some necessary implication falls to be made into their literal meaning. The precise terms of that implication do not seem to me to

---

[53] [1987] IRLR 218. The Court of Appeal refused to follow the decision of EAT in which it had adopted the Court of Appeal's decision in *O'Brien* v *Sim-Chem* to the effect that, since work rated as equivalent came within Article 141 only by virtue of the Equal Pay Directive, Article 141 was not directly effective in relation to this category.

[54] Lord Keith's particular reasons for taking into account parliamentary statements: "The draft regulations of 1983 were presented to Parliament as giving full effect to the decision in question. The draft regulations were not subject to the parliamentary process of consideration and amendment in committee, as a Bill would have been. In these circumstances and in the context of s 2 of the European Communities Act 1972 I consider it to be entirely legitimate for the purpose of ascertaining the intention of Parliament to take into account the terms in which the draft was presented by the responsible minister and which formed the basis of its acceptance."

matter. It is sufficient to say that the words must be construed purposively in order to give effect to the manifest broad intention of the maker of the regulations and of Parliament.
. . .

Lord Templeman.

. . . The words in para (c) on which the employers rely were not intended to create a new form of permitted discrimination. Paragraph (c) enables a claim to equal pay as against a specified man to be made without injustice to an employer. When a woman claims equal pay for work of equal value, she specifies the man with whom she demands parity. If the work of the woman is work in relation to which para (a) or (b) applies in relation to that man, then the woman cannot proceed under para (c) and cannot obtain a report from an ACAS expert. In my opinion there must be implied in para (c) after the word "applies" the words "as between the woman and the man with whom she claims equality". This construction is consistent with Community law. The employers' construction is inconsistent with Community law and creates a permitted form of discrimination without rhyme or reason . . .

In cases of like work and work rated as equivalent, the task of deciding whether the applicant has established her case (subject to the employer's defence) is a fairly straightforward one. In equal *value* claims, on the other hand, a tribunal has to consider the relative value of the woman's job and that of her male comparator in terms of (s.1(3)) "the demands made on her (*for instance* under such headings as effort, skill and decision)" (my emphasis). In the absence of any assistance, this would amount to a demand that the tribunal compose and apply a job evaluation scheme to the applicant's job and that (those) of her comparator(s). Worse still, the EqPA does not actually stipulate those headings under which value ought to be assessed, simply suggesting "for instance" headings such as "skill, effort and decision".

The EqPA did not, however, leave tribunals to determine the issue of value alone. Rather, having made provision for the dismissal of "hopeless" cases the EqPA, as amended by the Equal Value Regulations 1983, provided for the appointment of "independent experts" to advise tribunals on the issue of value. These experts, appointed by the tribunal at a preliminary hearing,[55] would go to the relevant workplace and draw up a report and a recommendation on the relative value of the applicant's job and that (those) of her comparator(s). Until 1996, tribunals were not entitled to determine the issue of value in favour of the equal pay applicant until they had received the report of the independent expert. The tribunal did not have to agree with the recommendation of the expert (although in general tribunals did).

The Sex Discrimination and Equal Pay (Miscellaneous Amendments) Regulations 1996 amended the EqPA to permit tribunals to determine the question of value without the report of an independent expert.[56] The amendment followed the decision of a

---

[55] From an ACAS list.
[56] SI 1996 No. 438, Reg 3. The tribunal must also dismiss where there are no reasonable grounds for a finding of equal value.

tribunal in *Cato* v *West Midlands Regional Health Authority* (Case 182/83 88 (IT)) which, the independent expert having failed to reach a finding on value, decided that Council Directive 75/117 (the Equal Pay Directive) permitted it to determine the issue of value itself. The tribunal devised its own job evaluation procedure, took evidence from the applicant and her comparator and decided against the applicant.[57]

The normal procedure for equal value claims is that a preliminary hearing is held at which the tribunal appoints an independent expert or dismisses the equal pay claim. Claims must be dismissed if, in the opinion of the tribunal, (s.2A(1)(b)) "there are no reasonable grounds for determining that the work is of equal value". S.2A(2) provides that:

> Without prejudice to the generality of . . . subsection (1) above, there shall be taken, for the purposes of [that subsection], to be no reasonable grounds for determining that the work of a woman is of equal value . . . if—
> (a) that work and the work of the man in question have been given different values on a study such as is mentioned in section 1(5) above; and
> (b) there are no reasonable grounds for determining that the evaluation contained in the study was . . . made on a system which discriminates on grounds of sex.

According to the framers of the provision, s.2A(1)(b) was intended to catch the "hopeless cases". Whatever the original intention, s.2A(1)(b), taken together with s.2A(2), has operated so as to prevent arguable cases from advancing. In *Davies* v *McCartneys* [1989] ICR 705, [1989] IRLR 439, EAT approved of a tribunal decision to dismiss, as "hopeless", a secretary's claim for equal pay with a "market clerk".[58]

Wood J:

> The assessment which the tribunal made of the applicant's job is summarised . . . where they say: "We do not believe that her duties are exceptional for a secretary, nor do we believe that she has developed any unusual skills. There was talk of knowledge of property etc. We do not think that this extended beyond what most secretaries would pick up in such an environment." [By contrast, while the work done by the comparator was] largely clerical work . . . it was . . . vital work on behalf of the firm. It represented a major responsibility. If the work was done incorrectly, it could result in a substantial loss to the business.

The "just a secretary" approach sits rather uneasily with that taken by Baronness Seear who, taking part in the Lords debate on the 1983 equal value amending regulations, commented that the equal value claim

> will be an affront to common sense because they will be quite contrary to what in the past has been normal practice. . . . The *whole point* is that it will reverse the pecking order at

---

[57] Equal Value Update 76 *Equal Opportunities Review*, p.18.
[58] The tribunal had dismissed on the basis that the employer had established a GMF. EAT upheld the decision, in addition, on the grounds that the claim was hopeless.

any rate in certain cases, and will not at first sight seem reasonable to many people (my emphasis).[59]

The proper application of s.2A(1)(b), in the wake of the Sex Discrimination and Equal Pay (Miscellaneous Amendments) Regulations 1996, was considered by EAT in *Wood* v *William Ball*. The applicants cleaner/packers claimed equal pay with picker/packer comparators. A tribunal dismissed the claims at a preliminary hearing, ruling that there were 'no reasonable grounds for determining that the work of the Applicants is of equal value to that of their comparators". According to the tribunal "[t]he work was clearly and obviously of different value and no expert's report is or would be required to elucidate that fact". On appeal, EAT ruled that the tribunal had erred.

Wood v *William Ball* [2000] ICR 277, [1999] IRLR 773

Morrison J(P) (for EAT)

Under the pre-1996 Statutory Provisions, an Industrial Tribunal had no power to decide an equal value claim itself except in the very limited situation where it took the view that it was hopeless—that is, that there was no reasonable grounds of success—in which case, it could dismiss it. But since July 1996, an amendment to the law [new s.2A(1)(a) EqPA] enables the Tribunal to have the option of determining the question—that is, the equal value question itself as an alternative to sending the matter on for the preparation of an independent expert's report . . .

It is clear and was accepted by both parties on this Appeal that under the post-1996 regime the fact that a Tribunal has concluded that there was no reasonable prospect of the Applicants showing that their work was of equal value with the comparators, did not thereby, put an end to the case, but permitted the parties themselves to adduce expert evidence in support of their claim which they could adduce at a further Hearing.[60]

Accordingly, under the new regime it is contemplated that there is or may be a two-stage process. The first part is to decide whether an expert's report is to be obtained by the Tribunal itself or by the parties themselves. If it is to be by the parties themselves, then the Tribunal will have to determine the case on the basis of the evidence presented to it. That two-stage process is contemplated by the purpose and intention of the change in the statutory regime. It was plainly Parliament's intention that rather than the parties litigating this issue at the Government's expense—that is, at the expense of the Tribunal itself arranging an expert to determine the issues—the parties themselves should be free to do so. It was unlikely that the parties would themselves have gone to the expense of investing in an expert's report before making an application to the Tribunal that it should obtain a report itself and therefore, it must have been Parliament's intention that the mere fact that an Applicant failed to persuade a Tribunal to order an independent report, would not mean that the Tribunal might not in due course reach a completely different conclusion based on expert evidence which the parties then produced . . .

---

[59] 445 HL Debs (5 December 1983) cols. 901–2.
[60] Distinguishing *Sheffield Metropolitan District Council* v *Sibury & Anor* [1989] ICR 208.

In this case, it appears that the Tribunal have moved from Stage I, which is to ask whether they should commission a report, in which case, the proceedings would have to be adjourned for that purpose, to Stage II, namely to determine the matter themselves without giving the parties an opportunity to adduce expert evidence if they wish to do so themselves . . .

The statute is very badly drafted and we are not in the slightest bit surprised that a procedural mishap has occurred as it has in this case.

S.2A(2) EqPA provides, as we saw above, that an equal value case should be dismissed if the jobs of the woman and that (those) of her comparator(s) "have been given different values on a study such as is mentioned in section 1(5) above", there being "no reasonable grounds for determining that the evaluation contained in the study was . . . made on a system which discriminates on grounds of sex" i.e. "where a difference, or coincidence, between values set by that system on different demands under the same or different headings is not justifiable irrespective of the sex of the person on whom those demands are made").[61]

There have been very few appellate decisions on s.2A(2). It was criticised in 1985 on the grounds that the low burden of proof imposed upon the applicant who wishes to challenge an existing job evaluation scheme is "from a personnel and industrial relations standpoint . . . patently absurd" and that the provision would permit challenge to job evaluation schemes which did not discriminate on grounds of sex.[62] But in the few appellate cases in which s.2A(2) has featured, the courts have allowed job evaluation schemes of very dubious merit to block equal value claims.

Neil and ors v *Ford Motor Co Ltd* involved an equal claim by Ford sewing machinists. The saga was a long-running one. A job evaluation scheme had been carried out by the company in 1966 and the machinists, unhappy with the results, had struck for equal pay in 1967. A Court of Inquiry was set up and concluded (the Scamp report) that machinists' grading was in accordance with the job evaluation results, but that the machinists' "job profile", on the basis of which they were slotted into the system, ought to be examined. This was done, and some changes made. But these were insufficient to alter the grading of the machinists' jobs. Grievances about the grading were brought, unsuccessfully, in 1970, 1974, 1981, 1982 and 1983 and an equal value pay claim launched

The machinists' claims were rejected on the grounds that their jobs had been rated as less valuable than those of their comparators by the 1966 JES. The JES, which predated the EqPA by four years, the implementation of the Act by nine years, had used a system whereby:

1. benchmark jobs were given one of four ratings (low, moderate, high and exceptional) for each of 28 factors;
2. the benchmark jobs were (quite separately) placed in a hierarchy by means of "paired comparisons" ("each [evaluation committee] member considered each

[61] EqPA, s.2A(2), "without prejudice to the generality" of s.2A(1) and s.2A(3).
[62] M. Rubenstein, "Discriminatory Job Evaluation and the Law" (1985–86) 7 *Comparative Labour Law* 172, p.178.

benchmark job in relation to each of the other . . . benchmark jobs and recorded his opinion as to which of the two was of greater overall worth to the company. From the five sets of such comparisons a rank order of the . . . benchmark jobs was extracted);

3. a "multiple regression analysis" was performed to see what weightings should be attached to each of the 28 factors *in order to achieve the best match between the hierarchies created by steps 1 and 2.*

4. At this stage all the non-benchmark jobs were evaluated on the basis of the 28 factors, these evaluations checked, and the factors weighed in line with step 3 to find the "correct place in the ranking" for each of the jobs

One of the difficulties with the methodology employed by Ford was that step 3 served simply to rebuild into the evaluation process the traditional "common sense" views about the relative worth of jobs. The applicants argued, to no avail, that the JES had been operated in a discriminatory manner, assumptions about the relative value of male and female jobs affecting the grading results. There was evidence that the company and the unions shared discriminatory assumptions about the value of women's work (indeed Ford had, at that time and for a number of years thereafter, operated "male" and "female" pay scales, women being paid 85% of the comparable male rate). No advice was given to the evaluators about avoiding bias. There were various disparities in the marking of male and female jobs. The applicants further argued that the sewing machinists' job had become much more difficult, complex and demanding since 1966, a development ignored by the company in its repeated refusals to regrade the job. In dismissing the equal pay claim the tribunal (by a majority) ruled that:

Neil and Ors v Ford Motor Co Ltd [1984] IRLR 339

. . . s 2A(2) and (3) require us to ask ourselves in the present case is whether there is any good reason to suppose that any one or more of the demands, or characteristics on which values have been set by the system, ought in fairness to have been given a value more favourable to the applicant and would have been given such a value, if the majority of those from whose assessments the values were derived had not consciously or subconsciously been influenced by consideration of the sex of those on whom the demands would chiefly be made. There would be a sufficient reason for such a supposition, if we found that a traditionally female attribute or skill was undervalued or any traditionally male attribute was overvalued. There is, however, no specifically male attribute among the 28 characteristics valued by the system under consideration . . .

There is . . . no presumption that a job evaluation study is one that discriminates on grounds of sex, and in the absence of a presumption it is difficult to accept that the burden of proof can lie on the respondents to a claim. Nor can the majority of us accept the proposition that the applicants have only to put forward a reasonable argument which is not foredoomed to failure . . . We appreciate that a Tribunal should not be reluctant to draw inferences, where there are reasonable grounds for drawing them, but . . . we should not lightly set in train a new evaluation unless we are tolerably certain that there are reasonable grounds for believing the previous job evaluation study to have been distorted by discrimination . . .

Some values set by a system may be so patently, or even outrageously, excessive in one direction or the other, that one can say confidently that they are wrong and one can infer sex discrimination if they are less favourable to one sex. Other values may look wrong to one person and right to another; here it would not be right to infer sex discrimination, in the absence of other more positive evidence, from a belief that attitudes to sex discrimination were less enlightened in the 1960s.

The tribunal's approach meant that a job evaluation scheme, however flawed, could easily block equal value claims. One tribunal member disagreed on the basis that:

This case is set against an historical background of conscious and continuous discrimination against women at work for a period of at least a century. This discrimination, somewhat diminished, continues today with women's earnings in general being well below those of men and women's work considered to be of less importance.

I therefore find it impossible to accept that in this case, in the prevailing atmosphere, and in regard to this Job Evaluation Scheme at Fords in operation for the past 17 years that "the Job Evaluation Scheme did not and cannot discriminate on grounds of sex" . . .

The evidence of Mr Passingham convenor of shop stewards at the Dagenham River Plant for more than 30 years as to the attitude of the workers at the inception of the scheme was that the men thought women worked for "pin money" and the women themselves "did not expect equal pay".

It is clear that what they did expect was to have their skills recognised, which, but only to some extent, the scheme did and does.

Prior to the scheme the four grades were "skilled, semi-skilled, unskilled, women". No recognition of women's skills at all. It is also clear that the women sewing machinists hoped that the scheme would fully reflect their status as being skilled or at least semi-skilled thus placing them in the upper half of the structure. It did not do so. The summary of paired comparisons (benchmarks) . . . shows that out of 29 jobs which attained at least two "exceptional" levels, from 56 jobs listed they were ranked 39th, again well in the lower half of the structure. These "exceptional" attainments were in "manual dexterity" and "hand, eye co-ordination" (in reality "hand, eye and foot co-ordination") both very skilled. Thus, the full recognition of their skills was denied. This could be because an element of sex bias did creep in when rating the work done in the only section on the shopfloor employing a substantial number of women on work done almost exclusively by women, and/or because the limitation of the scheme to four levels prevented them from achieving higher points for the work in which they were rated "exceptional" thereby having the full value of their skills and their whole position eroded by lower marks in other characteristics.

In a scheme which to all intents and purposes sought to rate the job and not the person doing it, it is surprising that no special educational measures were taken to guard against sex discrimination. Out of 900 women employees of whom 340 were sewing machinists not one was considered good enough or intelligent enough to be trained as an assessor or member of Review Committees or to take part in the administration of the scheme.

None of the sewing machinists was subjected to observation studies during the period when the scheme was being worked out, nor since, and it is still, according to Mr Sparling's evidence, company policy to have no observation studies even on jobs in dispute because to do it for one would necessitate doing it for all. Instead they relied on the compared value of the original benchmarks and on trade union advocacy. In view of the long standing complaint of the women sewing machinists against their grading, I consider that the continued opposition to observation studies of the work in dispute plus direct consultation and negotiation with the operatives who were studied and their shop representatives is a defect in the scheme which can only infer an element of sex discrimination in their case.

No particular allowance has been made for the value to the company of the experience which the sewing machinists have to bring to their job and it is important to note that no other employees are subjected to the kind of trade test which they have to undergo to secure employment. It is also a fact that the attempt to train certain men to do sewing machining in a re-deployment exercise has failed after a lengthy trial period. It is difficult to divide the structure of the scheme from the way it is operated and the results shown and it is therefore necessary to look at details of the claim of the sewing machinists for a grading at least the same as the Eastman Cutters. Making allowances for the exaggerations of some witnesses in pursuing their arguments I nevertheless find that the applicants have shown reasonable grounds for claiming that in the comparisons of their work with that of [their comparators], the difference, or coincidence between values set by the system on different demands under the same or different headings are not justifiable [the minority member went on to detail what he saw as the discriminatory ratings of various factors] . . .

Neil v *Ford* was only a tribunal case, but nevertheless instructive as to the far from radical approach which prevailed on the equal pay issue.[63] The job evaluation scheme which was permitted to block equal pay claims in that case appeared, from an equality perspective, to be deeply flawed. In *Bromley* v *Quick*, too, EAT allowed a job evaluation scheme of highly dubious merit to block an equal value claim.

EAT's decision in *Eaton* v *Nutall* was mentioned above. In it, that tribunal ruled that an equal pay claim could not succeed under s.1(2)(b) unless the job evaluation scheme on the basis of which it was made was "analytical" in the sense of being "thorough in analysis and capable of impartial application". On the one hand, this restriction might be thought unnecessary—if an employer accepts that a man's job and a woman's job are of equivalent value, s/he should perhaps be estopped from deciding to pay the man more unless a s.1(3) defence operates. But, EAT having decided in *Eaton* to restrict job evaluation schemes under s.1(2)(b) and s.1(5) to those which were "analytical", it would seem obvious that the same restriction should apply to s.2A(2) which refers, after all, to "a study such as is mentioned in section 1(5) above".

In *Bromley*, however, EAT characterised as a "gloss upon the words" of s.1(5) the suggestion that only an analytical scheme could block an equal value claim. The job evaluation scheme at issue in the case had ranked "benchmark" jobs by comparing them on the basis of a number of factors. These jobs were then re-ranked on a "felt fair" basis before the remaining jobs (the demands made by which had never been scrutinised in accordance with the chosen factors) were slotted into the established hierarchy. The applicant's job, together with those of her comparators, had been

---

[63] See also *Waddington*, above, and the GMF cases discussed below.

among these unscrutinised jobs, their places in the hierarchy had been determined without benefit even of full job descriptions.

The Court of Appeal [1988] ICR 623, [1988] IRLR 249 overturned EAT's decision, citing the decision of the European Court in *Rummler* v *Dato Druck GmbH* Case C–237/85 [1986] ECR 2101 [1987] IRLR 32 in support of its conclusion that, while the evaluation of jobs entailed a degree of subjective judgment:

Bromley and Ors v *H & J Quick Ltd* [1987] ICR 47, [1987] IRLR 456

. . . the consideration of any job, and of the qualities required to perform that job, under a job evaluation study must be objective [to the extent that this was possible. S.1(5) required, therefore]. . . a study undertaken with a view to evaluating jobs in terms of the demand made on a worker under various headings (for instance effort, skill, decision) To apply that to s 2A(2)(a) it is necessary, in my judgment, that both the work of the woman who had made application to the Industrial Tribunal and the work of the man who is her chosen comparator should have been valued in such terms of demand made on the worker under various headings. . . the word "analytical" . . . is not a gloss, but indicates conveniently the general nature of what is required by the section, viz that the jobs of each worker covered by the study must have been valued in terms of the demand made on the worker under various headings. The original application of s 1(5) to women within subheading (b) in s 1(2) of the Act (women employed on work rated equivalent to that of a man) necessarily required that the woman's work and the man's should each have been valued in terms of the demand made on the worker under appropriate headings; the wording of s 2A(2)(a), read with that of s 1(5), necessarily shows that the same applies to the present appellants who claim to be within subheading (c), and their male comparators. . . .

It is to be noted that the procedure which the respondent company has invoked under s 2A is a procedure which if successfully invoked would put, as the Industrial Tribunal held it did, a summary end to the appellants' applications without the otherwise mandatory reference of the questions raised by those applications to an independent expert under s 2A(1)(b). S 2A(2)(b) puts the onus on the employer to show that there are no reasonable grounds for determining that the evaluation contained in a job evaluation study such as is mentioned in s 1(5) was made on a system which discriminates on grounds of sex. If in the view of the Industrial Tribunal there are reasonable grounds for so determining, the Industrial Tribunal cannot summarily dismiss an application, but must refer the relevant question to an independent expert for report . . .

In *Dibro Ltd* v *Hore and others* [1990] ICR 370, [1990] IRLR 129. EAT ruled that an industrial tribunal had erred in refusing to accept, as a defence to an equal value claim, the results of a job evaluation scheme carried out after the applicants' equal value claims had been made. This decision is of particular concern given the inherently subjective nature of job evaluation and the ease with which its results can, accordingly, be manipulated. Further, as is pointed out in the extract below, even analytical job evaluation schemes may incorporate factors whose impact is to hold female wages down by comparison with those men. The commentator is contrasting the obligation on independent experts (assessing equal value) with the more common approach to job evaluation.

Alan Arthurs, "Independent Experts in Equal Pay", in J. Gregory, R. Sales and A. Hegewisch (eds) *Women, Work, and Inequality: the Challenges of Equal Pay in a Deregulated Labour Market* (Basingstoke: MacMillan, New York: St. Martins Press, 1999) p. 168, at 173

The legislation provides that the work of the applicant and comparator be compared "in terms of the demands made . . . for instance, under such headings as effort, skill and decision" (Equal Pay Act, as amended, section 1(2)(c)). This rules out two other possible ways of assessing relative values, namely comparing market values (what is actually paid in the market) and comparing the marginal productivity of the two jobs. Implicit in the legislation is that job evaluation-type techniques should be used and the headings suggested imply that an analytical approach is needed.

However, assessing equal value is different in important respects from conventional job evaluation. First, the Act does not use the term "job evaluation" to describe the duties of independent experts and it has been suggested that this may be in order to allow the assessment of equal value to be conducted in a less formal and more limited manner than is the case with a fullscale job evaluation study. To some extent some of the early experts' reports reflected this view, but informality is impossible to maintain when reports are subject to detailed scrutiny and cross-examination. Second, job evaluation is normally designed to accord where possible with the labour market. Equal value assessments must ignore the market. Third, in job evaluation an employer may make allowances for traditional differentials which may enshrine past discrimination. Equal value assessments must take no account of existing pay relationships.

Finally, there is the question of acceptability. This is an important test of a job evaluation scheme, since its introduction is normally in order to replace relative pay rates which have lost credibility with employees and managers. To be successful a new structure must gain the acceptance, or at least the acquiescence, of the great majority of employees to whom it applies. The scheme will have to take account of the bargaining strength of the employees involved, otherwise it will be challenged and its credibility damaged. It is when a pay structure acceptable to all parties has not been agreed and conciliation has failed that an equal value case may be instituted.

The independent expert must find the jobs to be equal or not equal; it is not his or her task to seek a compromise. Without the constraints imposed by the need to take account of the market or traditional differentials the expert may find an assessment method acceptable to the parties, but the overriding considerations are the rights of the parties and freedom from sex bias.

Of even more concern is the suggestion made by Sue Hastings, below.

S. Hastings Negative (Pay) Equity—an Analysis of Some (Side-)Effects of the Equal Pay Act, in J. Gregory, R. Sales and A. Hegewisch (eds) *Women, Work and Inequality*, p. 153

The assumption underlying the "job evaluation study" defence is that jobs which have been analysed and evaluated under an acceptable job evaluation system have already been subject to an "equal value" assessment, because they have been compared under headings such as "effort, skill and decision". This assumption ignores the reality that most job evaluation schemes in the UK have been designed, not to implement equal pay for work of equal value, but to reproduce the previous status quo and thus unequal pay. However, this appears still not to be clearly understood by industrial tribunals, which have seen job evaluation as good industrial relations practice. The result is that no applicant to date has mounted a successful challenge to an existing job evaluation scheme (some have evaded the barrier by showing that their jobs were not analysed or evaluated under the relevant scheme, but this is a different matter). The unsurprising consequence of this is that job evaluation schemes have become very popular with employers concerned at the prospects of equal value claims by individuals or groups of women. Moreover, employers have assumed that the legal defence operates only if potential applicant and comparator jobs are covered by the same JES. This has led to organizations attempting to implement single schemes for all their employees (sometimes excluding the most senior managers). Two major developments have resulted from this. First, there is the introduction of new job evaluation schemes into areas which had previously had different bases for their grading structures, particularly public sector organizations and those with a high proportion of female employees: for example, the civil service, higher education, most of the privatized electricity and water companies, and retail and wholesale distribution. Secondly, we see the replacement of distinct job evaluation systems related to collective bargaining structures by single schemes, often "cascading" downwards a scheme already in use for senior jobs in the organization, for example in the banking and finance sectors and in large manufacturing companies such as ICI. In many of these cases the introduction of job evaluation was associated with changes to relevant labour market and/or collective bargaining arrangements. Between them the above examples cover some millions of employees, so their impact is significant.

Ironically, in the early 1980s, before the implementation of the Equal Value (Amendment) Regulations, David Grayson of the Department of Employment Work Research Unit wrote a paper suggesting that job evaluation was not compatible with the trends then being observed towards greater flexibility of both jobs and individuals. Grayson thought that job evaluation would gradually wither away to be replaced by more flexibly based grading systems. Others shared his views. Yet the spread of job evaluation has not only continued since, but has increased.

The evidence suggests that the spread of single job evaluation systems would have been less extensive, had it not been for this feature of the equal pay legislation. Some managers admit this in private conversation. Some also admit that they follow fashions in labour management techniques, and that job evaluation is currently fashionable. There are few who resist the trend and argue that, as long as they construct new grading and pay structures on principles of equality, they do not need to use job evaluation techniques. The problem is that most of these "fashionable" job evaluation schemes are introduced not to move towards equal pay for work of equal value, but to provide a legal defence against equal value claims. This can be observed in the way such job evaluation schemes are selected and implemented. Rarely are these exercises commenced on the premise suggested in the checklist on job evaluation produced by the Equal Opportunities Commission: that there should be no preconceived views on the resulting rank order. Nor is the first question on the checklist often either posed or answered:

> Do the terms of reference [for the job evaluation exercise] recognise that avoiding sex bias will mean challenging existing relativities? (EOC, n.d.)

Other indicators of a scheme whose objective is a legal defence rather than a step towards equal pay for work of equal value include:

- the absence of training in the concepts and principles of equal value for all those

actively involved in the exercise (a one-hour session with job analysts advising them not to refer to jobholders as "he" or "she" does not constitute such training);
- failure to include union, or employee, representatives, and women (with adequate training) in the choice of scheme;
- selection of a "tried-and-tested" "off-the-shelf" scheme, albeit one designed for the sector, rather than ensuring that the scheme is appropriate to the jobs in question;
- unwillingness to take into account the experience in the relatively small number of JE exercises undertaken on equal value principles, in the UK or elsewhere;
- a single job evaluation exercise to cover widely varying jobs without consideration of the implications.

The irony is that, even where the scheme is not genuinely implemented on equal value principles, the outcomes may still include the upgrading of some particularly undervalued female-dominated jobs relative to male-dominated jobs, simply as a result of applying a rational system and a consistent set of principles. A number of mechanisms have been devised to avoid the implications and costs of this. Green circling, or phased introduction of consequential pay increases, is one.

Another mechanism is the development of what are generally called "broad-banded salary structures", which are consistent with trends towards organizational delayering and flatter hierarchies. They also have the advantage, from the employers' perspective, of at least delaying the payment of equal pay, and possibly of preventing it altogether by introducing barriers to progression within the salary range.

Such broad-banded salary structures following job evaluation exercises have been introduced into a significant number of organizations, including public sector organizations. These include the National Rivers Authority (before it became the Environment Agency) and the British Broadcasting Corporation. Some privatized firms, for example British Telecom and some of the utility companies, have also followed this path.

In a traditional incremental structure, those assimilated towards the bottom of a grade salary range move by annual instalments to the top, where they receive the same money as those assimilated towards the top. Normally this would be seen as acceptable by employees and their union representatives, even though it does not give equal pay in money terms immediately. Where the salary range is wide, this is potentially expensive for the organization in the medium term. So many employers operating broad-banded salary structures adopt alternative progression mechanisms, based on performance or competence or acquisition of qualifications, which mean that progression is no longer automatic. Such systems also have the advantage, from the employer's point of view, of allowing for changes to the criteria for progression over time.

From the employees' point of view, such systems result in the perpetuation of unequal pay. In some systems, for example where progression beyond the mid-point requires exceptional performance, equal pay may never be achieved by those with satisfactory or average performance assessments. So the system is used to thwart the attainment of equal pay, even where the jobs have been accepted as being of equal value through that job evaluation scheme.

We have considered preliminary hearings at which the tribunal (or, on appeal, EAT) has decided that the case was "hopeless" either (as in *Davies* v *McCartneys*) because the applicant was "just a secretary", her comparator having a "responsible job"; or because the applicant's job had been rated as other than equal to that of her comparator by a job evaluation scheme (*Neil* v *Ford, Bromley* v *Quick*—though, as we saw, the latter was reversed on appeal to the Court of Appeal). The tribunal can also dismiss a case at this point where the employer successfully advances a s.1(3) defence at this stage.

Until 1994, the employer could argue s.1(3) both at the preliminary hearing and, if s/he did not succeed at this stage and the jobs were subsequently found to be of equal value, at that point. The Industrial Tribunals Complementary Rules of Procedure 1993 now limit the defence to a single usage except "in exceptional circumstances".[64] But employers can still choose to argue s.1(3) at the preliminary stage, this having the effect in cases such as *Enderby* v *Frenchay Health Authority* Case C–127/92 [1993] ECR I–5535, of delaying the assessment of value for years. The s.1(3) defence is further discussed below.

It is clear from the foregoing that the equal value claim is not an easy one to bring. Nor is the possibility of dismissal at the preliminary stage the only difficulty which applicants confront. In common with those who would seek equal pay for like work and for work rated as equivalent, those wishing to claim equal pay for work of equal value must first discover what comparable men earn. This may not pose insuperable problems in a unionised workplace. But in many non-unionised workplaces, employees are not in a position to find out what others earn. And with the increasing move towards individualised, "merit" based pay systems this problem is unlikely to improve.

The information deficit is to some extent a problem common to all would-be equal pay applicants. But equal value claims are subject to additional problems of information about the relative value of jobs. Even if there were established criteria for assessing value, and applicants were able accurately to evaluate their own jobs, they would have enormous problems in determining the value of potential comparators' jobs. But there are no such criteria. Even if prospective applicants were in possession of all possible information relating to their own jobs and those of their comparators, there is simply no way of knowing how the relative value of those jobs will be assessed.

Anne-Marie Plummer's 1991 study of independent experts' reports found "remarkably little consistency" in the approach taken to the assessment of value,[65] the reports studied (40% of those commissioned by that year) showing great variety in the choice of factors analysed, methods of scoring, weighting of factors and interpretation of equal value. The question whether or not an applicant's job was regarded as of equal value to that of her comparator turned, to a large extent, on the method of evaluation. Yet there was no consensus between "experts" on the methodology.

An applicant may be able to decide, with a fair degree of certainty, that her job is the same as that done by a man. She may also be able to make an informed decision

---

[64] This was one of the few concessions granted by the Government to the EOC in response to the latter's proposals for amendments to the Act.

[65] A. Plummer, *Equal Value Judgements: Objective Assessment or Lottery?* Industrial Research Unit, School of Business Studies, University of Warwick.

that her job and that of a man have been rated as equivalent by her employer. But she simply cannot know whether or not her job will be regarded as "equal" to that done by a male comparator. This being the case, the only reasonable chances of success in equal pay for work of equal value cases lie with women who select as their comparators men who are paid more for jobs which are apparently much less demanding, and with women whose pay claims are organised (as in the *Enderby, Ratcliffe, British Coal* cases, all discussed below) by well-informed and well financed unions committed to improving the wages of their women members.

A prudent applicant would, if only one comparator were permitted, use one whose job seemed self-evidently less valuable than hers, in order to maximise the chances of a favourable decision on this issue. But such a comparator would probably be less well paid than one whose job was closer in "value" to that performed by the applicant. It might be thought that the applicant should name a range of comparators. But this tactic was not approved of by the House of Lords in *Leverton.* According to Lord Bridge, with whom the other Lords agreed:

> I think that industrial tribunals should, so far as possible, be alert to prevent abuse of the equal value claims procedure by applicants who cast their net over too wide a spread of comparators. To take an extreme case, an applicant who claimed equality with A who earns LX and also with B who earns L2X could hardly complain if an industrial tribunal concluded that her claim of equality with A itself demonstrated that there were no reasonable grounds for her claim of equality with B . . .

The complexities and uncertainties of the equal value claim have been the subject of much criticism since its introduction in 1984. Some of this criticism is extracted above. Below is one explanation of some of the inadequacies of the EqPA as amended.

D. Pannick, *Sex Discrimination Law*, p. 105

The inadequacies of the 1983 Regulations which amended the Equal Pay Act 1970 were at least partly due to the unsatisfactory manner in which those amendments were made. The Government provided only 90 minutes for debate in each of the Houses of Parliament, using the procedure of a statutory instrument under s. 2(2) of the European Communities Act 1972 which did not enable critics to table substantiate amendments of their own. The draft Regulations were introduced in the House of Commons on 20 July 1983 by Mr Alan Clark, Under-Secretary of State for Employment. He left no doubt about his lack of commitment to the policy of strengthening the Equal Pay Act. He told the House of Commons that "a certain separation between expressed and implied beliefs is endemic among those who hold office". He warned the House that there were in the draft Regulations "certain legalistic passages which I might have to deal with at 78 rpm instead of 33". He did so. The Opposition spokesman, Mr Barry Jones, justifiably complained that the Minister had "made a frivolous speech on an important subject"; his speech was "damaging and even demeaning to his Department". The quality of the speech of the Under-Secretary of State was indicated by the fact that it was warmly applauded by Mr Tony Marlow, a Conservative back-bencher, whose own contribution to the debate was a criticism of the very idea of entitling women to equal pay for work of equal value. Mr Marlow was worried that "[a]ny trouble-maker . . . is going to pretend that her work is of equal value. It is an open invitation to any feminist, any harridan, or any rattle-headed female with a chip on her bra-strap to take action against her employer."

SCOPE OF THE EQUAL PAY COMPARISON

That part of the gender-pay gap which results from occupational sex segregation (the tendency of men and women to do different types of job) is, at least in theory, challengeable through the equal value pay claim. We have seen some of the problems associated with that claim—complexity, delay, etc. But it is possible to imagine that, properly revised, the equal pay for work of equal value claim could prove effective in tackling this aspect of the gender-pay gap.

Part of the gender-pay gap is associated with women's industrial and workplace segregation—that is, their concentration in predominantly female workplaces. The EqPA requires that the "comparator", whether alleged to be engaged in "like work", "work rated as equivalent" or "work of equal value" to that done by the equal pay applicant, must be "in the same employment" as her.

There is no question of women being able to compare their pay with that of men employed in unrelated workplaces, by unrelated employers. But we shall see that the EqPA does permit comparisons to be made beyond the narrow workplace. S.1(6) includes, within "the same employment", employment by the same:

> or any associated employer at the same establishment or at establishments in Great Britain which include that one and at which common terms and conditions of employment are observed either generally or for employees of the relevant classes.

The significance of this section was first explored in *Leverton* v *Clwyd County Council* which culminated with the House of Lord's decision extracted below. Ms Leverton was a nursery nurse. Her comparators occupied a variety of posts the terms of which were, like hers, determined by a collective agreement covering local authority administrative, professional, technical and clerical staff. All were employed by Clwyd County Council, but they worked in a variety of establishments. In response to her claim her employers argued that she was not in the "same employment" as her comparators. This argument failed at tribunal but won favour with the Court of Appeal which ruled, somewhat bizarrely ([1989] 1 AC 706, [1988] IRLR 239), that s.1(6) assisted only those applicants who were employed on the *same* terms and conditions as their comparators. (Such women would, of course, have little need of an equal pay claim.) The House of Lords allowed her appeal.

Leverton v Clwyd County Council [1989] 1 AC 706, [1989] 1 All ER 78, [1989] 2 WLR 47, [1989] ICR 33, [1989] IRLR 28, [1989] 1 CMLR 57

Lord Bridge of Harwich

. . . The concept of common terms and conditions of employment observed generally at different establishments necessarily contemplates terms and conditions applicable to a wide range of employees whose individual terms will vary greatly *inter se*. On the construction of the subsection adopted by the majority below the phrase "observed either generally or for employees of the relevant classes" is given no content. Terms and conditions of employment governed by the same collective agreement seem to me to represent the paradigm, though not necessarily the only example, of the common terms and conditions of employment contemplated by the subsection.

But if, contrary to my view, there is any such ambiguity in the language of s 1(6) as to permit the question whether a woman and men employed by the same employer in different establishments are in the same employment to depend on a direct comparison establishing a "broad similarity" between the woman's terms and conditions of employment and those of her claimed comparators, I should reject a construction of the subsection in this sense on the ground that it frustrates rather than serves the manifest purpose of the legislation. That purpose is to enable a woman to eliminate discriminatory differences between the terms of her contract and those of any male fellow employee doing like work, work rates as equivalent or work of equal value, whether he works in the same establishment as her or in another establishment where terms and conditions of employment common to both establishments are observed. With all respect to the majority view which prevailed below, it cannot, in my opinion, possibly have been the intention of Parliament to require a woman claiming equality with a man in another establishment to prove an undefined substratum of similarity between the particular terms of her contract and his as the basis of her entitlement to eliminate any discriminatory differences between those terms.

The decision of the House of Lords in *Leverton* was to the effect that, in order to make a cross-establishment comparison, an applicant had to establish that "common" terms prevailed between the establishments taken as a whole, rather than between her and her male comparators. Such comparisons are permitted, presumably, on the ground that, had the comparator worked in the applicant's workplace, he would have been employed on the same terms as he was employed on in the other workplace. But in *British Coal Corp v Smith and others*, [1994] ICR 810 [1993] IRLR 308 the Court of Appeal chose once again to adopt a narrow approach to s.1(6) requiring, in order to bring a case within the House of Lord's decision in *Leverton*, that the woman and her comparator(s) were employed in establishments in which the prevailing terms and conditions were, not merely "broadly similar" or "essentially similar" but were (exactly) "the same".

In the *British Coal* case, female clerical and canteen workers compared themselves with men doing a number of jobs including surface minework. Clerical workers shared the same terms nationwide but, while surface mineworkers were covered by a national agreement, this was subject at local level to variations regarding concessionary fuel and incentive bonuses. Canteen workers' terms and conditions were governed by national agreements which entitled them to identical incentive bonuses to those received, in each particular workplace, by surface workers. They were not entitled to concessionary coal.

Both the tribunal and EAT accepted that the men and women were in the "same employment", applying a "broad comparison" under s.1(6) as they regarded themselves bound to do by the decision in *Leverton*. The Court of Appeal disagreed but was overturned by the House of Lords.

British Coal Corp v Smith & Ors [1996] 3 All ER 97, [1996] ICR 515, [1996] IRLR 404

Lord Slynn of Hadley

. . . Your Lordships have been referred to a number of dictionary definitions of "common" but I do not think that they help. The real question is what the legislation was seeking to achieve. Was it seeking to exclude a woman's claim unless, subject to *de minimis* exceptions, there was complete identity of terms and conditions for the comparator at his establishment and those which applied or would apply to a similar male worker at her establishment? Or was the legislation seeking to establish that the terms and conditions of the relevant class were sufficiently similar for a fair comparison to be made, subject always to the employers' right to establish a "material difference" defence under s.1(3) of the EqPA?

If it was the former then the woman would fail at the first hurdle if there was any difference (other than a *de minimis* one) between the terms and conditions of the men at the various establishments since she could not then show that the men were in the same employment as she was. The issue as to whether the differences were material so as to justify different treatment would then never arise.

I do not consider that this can have been intended. The purpose of requiring common terms and conditions was to avoid it being said simply "a gardener does work of equal value to mine and my comparator at another establishment is a gardener". It was necessary for the applicant to go further and to show that gardeners at other establishments and at her establishment were or would be employed on broadly similar terms. It was necessary, but it was also sufficient. Whether any differences between the woman and the man selected as the comparator were justified would depend on the next stage of the examination under s 1(3). I do not consider that the s 1(3) inquiry, where the onus is on the employer, was intended to be excluded unless the terms and conditions of the men at the relevant establishments were common in the sense of identical. This seems to me to be far too restrictive a test . . .

In the present case the industrial tribunal . . . clearly adopted a broad commonsense approach which seems to me to have been in accordance with the speech of Lord Bridge of Harwich [in *Leverton*]. On this basis they concluded that surface mineworkers were governed by a nationally negotiated agreement which sets basic and overtime rates of pay, sick pay, holidays and other similar matters . . .

The capacity of s.1(6) to extend comparison beyond the narrow confines of the applicant's workplace is significant given the relationship (considered above) between workplace sex segregation and unequal pay. The provision does not merely permit comparators to be sought from different establishments of the same employer. It also, to a limited extent, permits cross-employer comparisons though only (and narrowly) where the comparator is employed by an "associate employer", this in turn being restricted to cases where "one [employer] is a company of which the other (directly or indirectly) has control or if both are companies of which a third person (directly or indirectly) has control".

The narrow scope of the equal pay claim under the EqPA has been the subject of adverse comment. One particular area where problems arise is in the contracting-out context. The term "contracting-out" refers to the "hiving-off" of discrete functions from the central employer to contractors. In the public sector, as we saw in Chapter 5, this has been driven until very recently by "compulsory competitive tendering" (CCT), local authorities being required to put cleaning, waste disposal, catering and other functions out to tender at regular intervals, and being allowed to retain these functions only where they were won, in competition, by separately administered Direct Services Organisations (DSOs). These DSOs had to be financially separate from the local authority and run as commercial enterprises.

CCT brought huge deterioration in the terms and conditions of the workers, in particular the women workers, affected by it. Part of that deterioration resulted from the failure of the Transfer of Undertakings Regulations 1981 adequately to give effect to the Acquired Rights Directive—the Regulations originally excluded "non commercial" undertakings, such as most public authority functions, from their protection. The consequence of this was that most contractors competing for public functions did so on the basis of radically reduced labour costs. In many cases low paid workers were brought into the authority from outside. In others, workers were made redundant and re-employed by the private contractors at reduced wages. The reduced working conditions were felt particularly by women workers whose wages had been protected by collective bargaining in the public sector, and had been pegged considerably higher (often as a result of job evaluation) than the rates prevalent in the private sector.

Even where workers managed to retain their jobs, they did so frequently because DSOs, in preparing "in house" bids, slashed labour costs in order to compete with the market. One example of this resulted in *Ratcliffe and others* v *North Yorkshire County Council*, the House of Lords decision in which ([1995] 3 All ER 597) is discussed at some length below. For our current purposes the point of interest is that, whereas the "dinner ladies" DSO had to reduce labour costs by 25% in order to compete with outside tenders, the DSOs employing their comparators did not. According to the tribunal:

> It was clear to [the DSO manager] that he had to have regard to the market forces and, in particular, that because of low pay in the catering industry in general, and particularly in those areas where women were exclusively employed, he could not afford to continue to engage staff on [National Joint Council] terms, conditions and pay . . .
>
> [the DSO manager] . . . perceived that it was necessary to [reduce those terms from the NJC terms] in order to be able to compete in the open market, that is to say due to his perception of market forces in a market which is virtually exclusively female doing work which is convenient to that female workforce and which, but for the particular hours and times of work, that workforce would not be able to do . . . It was clear to [him] that it was a workforce that would, by and large, continue to do the work, even at a reduced rate of pay, when the alternative was no work or ceasing to have the advantages of remaining a county council employee and becoming an employee of a commercial catering organisation doing the same work for less favourable terms in any event.

It is clear that both the DSO and the employees were over the proverbial "barrel" due to the fact that competitors only employed women and, because of that, employed them on less favourable terms than the council did previously under the NJC agreement . . .

In *Ratcliffe*, as we shall see below, the women eventually won their equal pay claim. (Prior to the CCT exercise, their jobs had been rated as equivalent in value to those done by their comparators.) The issue of the employer's defence, with which that case was primarily concerned, is discussed below. But their claim succeeded only because they were, in fact, employed by the DSO which, like their comparators' DSO, was still part of the local authority. By contrast, women whose terms and conditions suffered when their jobs were contracted out (as many were), would be able to use, as comparators, only those men employed by the same contractor. This would remain the case even (see *Lawrence* v *Regent Office Care* [1999] ICR 654, below) where they continued to do precisely the same job in the same workplace as their former colleagues, with whose jobs theirs had (prior to contracting-out) been rated as equivalent.

The TUPE Regulations were amended in 1995 to give effect to the fact that "non-commercial" undertakings are included within the Acquired Rights Directive, to which the regulations were supposed to give effect. Even where workers are transferred on the same terms and conditions, however, there is nothing to prevent those terms and conditions from falling behind those which apply in respect of former comparators' jobs which have remained in the public sector. Nor have DSOs been able to ignore this potential for private-sector cost cutting in determining their own pay and conditions.

CCT, as such, is now at an end. But local authorities and other public bodies remain obliged to achieve "best value" in all their services (see further Chapter 5). The formal requirement to tender at particular intervals has been replaced with a rolling obligation to assess whether services could be better performed other than by the authority itself. It is probable that women workers will continue to shoulder the burden of cost-cutting.

It is clear that the EqPA does not permit cross-employer comparisons save between "associated employers" this concept being very narrowly defined. But it is not clear that Article 141 adopts so narrow an approach. In *Defrenne* (No 2) [1976] ECR 455, the ECJ ruled that Article 141 requires equal pay "for equal work which is carried out in the same establishment or service, whether private or public."

In *Scullard* v *Knowles*, EAT accepted that the approach required under Article 141 was wider than that set out under the EqPA.[66] There, a unit manager employed by a Regional Advisory Council sought to name, as her comparators, male unit managers employed by other such bodies, all of which were independent and of the Secretary of State for Employment, but funded by the Department of Employment.

---

[66] See also *Hasley* v *Fair Employment Agency* [1989] IRLR 106 (NICA).

Scullard v Knowles & Southern Regional Council for Education & Training [1996] ICR 399, [1996] IRLR 344

Mummery J. (P)

. . . s 1(6) . . . excludes, for example, employees of different employers who, though not companies, are all under the direct or indirect control of a third party and have common terms and conditions of employment. The crucial point is that the class of comparators defined in s.1(6) is more restricted than that available on the application of Article [141], as interpreted by the European Court of Justice. Article [141] is not, for example, confined to employment in undertakings which have a particular legal form, such as a limited company . . .

In *Defrenne* no distinction is drawn between work carried out in the same establishment or service of limited companies and of other employers, whether incorporated or not . . .

The crucial question for the purposes of Article [141] is, therefore, whether Mrs Scullard and the male unit managers of the other councils were employed "in the same establishment or service". The tribunal did not ask or answer that question. To the extent that that is a wider class of comparators than is contained in s 1(6) of the [EqPA], s 1(6), which is confined to "associated employers", is displaced and must yield to the paramount force of Article [141] . . .

Scullard went some way towards addressing the shortcomings of s.1(6). But the gaping hole in the protection offered by the EqPA was exposed by EAT in *Lawrence* v *Regent Office Care*. The case was brought by "dinner ladies" who had, like the applicants in *Ratcliffe*, been employed by North Yorkshire County Council. During the course of the *Ratcliffe* litigation the County Council lost some tenders for school meal provision to the private sector. The women in the *Lawrence* case were amongst those whose jobs were transferred into the private sector. Some were transferred on the understanding that TUPE applied, others on the assumption that it did not. Nevertheless (and this is testament to the ineffective nature of TUPE), all women ended up working on less favourable terms and conditions than had applied during their employment by the Council. They sought to rely on Article 141 to compare themselves with men still employed by the Council whose jobs had, pre-contracting out, been rated as equivalent to those of the applicants. Their claims were dismissed both by the tribunal and by EAT.

Lawrence & Ors v Regent Office Care Ltd & Ors [1999] ICR 654, [1999] IRLR 148

Morison J (for EAT)

. . . are the rights conferred by Article [141] wide enough to permit an employee of company A to make a comparison with the work done by an employee of company B, and claim unlawful discrimination? The appellants say that either the answer to that question is "yes" or alternatively we should refer it to the European Court of Justice for them to give guidance . . .

[For the respondents] Mr Elias makes the valid point that an employer not only has to prove that the factors which he alleges have caused the disparity were genuine but also "causally relevant" to the disparity in pay complained of. It would be difficult, if not impossible, for an employer to run a justification defence if he was not the employer of the comparator because he would not know precisely what the factors were that gave rise to the pay of that person. Furthermore, it would be difficult to understand how the applicant's employer could say that any factor was causally connected to the disparity when their pay was most likely determined quite independently of one another, and in ignorance of the differential . . .

There are two general principles of note from the authorities:

(1) The purpose of Article [141], like s 1 of the Equal Pay Act, is not to achieve fair wages but to eliminate discrimination on grounds of sex.
(2) Whilst it is the policy of Article [141] eventually to eliminate all such discrimination across industries (for example, catering and cleaning have traditionally been regarded as "women's work" and probably thereby been poorly paid), a radical assault across industries will require further agreement between Member States, and detailed implementation in domestic laws (see paragraph 19 of the judgment in *Defrenne*). The precise ambit of the Article, as it stands and without further agreement or direction, is not precisely defined. Case law of the Court will assist on a case-by-case basis. Technical limitations, such as the dates when the comparator and applicant were employed, will not be allowed to defeat the application of the Article. But there must be a line to be drawn somewhere, as the ECJ recognised in the *Defrenne* case, as we read it.

The ECJ [in *Defrenne*] distinguished between "individual undertakings" on the one hand and "entire branches of industry" and even of the economic system as a whole" on the other. We agree with Mr Elias that a feature of this distinction is that in the one case there is a single employer and in the other a multiplicity of employers, but that may not be the only distinction. Sometimes the identity of the employer is different from the entity which controls the work and fixes the pay, for example, where a person's services are "assigned" to subsidiary companies within a group, but where the parent is formally the employer. In such a case the subsidiaries would clearly be associated and fall within s 1(6). But what if the employers were different, such as the Northern Ireland EOC and FEA [referring to the facts in *Hasley*, fn 66]? Not in every case where Article [141] applies will the same entity be employer of both applicant and comparator, nor will they necessarily be associated employers within the meaning of the section. But it does not follow that the Article applies whenever the employers are unconnected other than by the nature of the industry to which they belong. There must be something other than common identity or direct association which provides the boundary line.

. . . the ECJ ha[s] not confined the principle of Article [141] to "work carried out in the same establishment or service" as the words "even more" and "at least" in paragraphs 22 and 24 of the judgment in *Defrenne* make clear. It seems to us that, absent any further agreement between Member States or a Directive, we cannot say more precisely where the boundary line lies save that the applicant and comparator must be "in a loose and non-technical sense in the same establishment or service". By "loose and non-technical sense", we mean to embrace within the definition such cases as *Hasley* and *Scullard* and any other similar cases.

It follows, therefore, that we reject Mr Langstaff's argument [for the applicants] that Article [141] is to be given a much wider range of application. Such a construction would be likely to create a substantial economic effect of the sort which, no doubt, the Court had in mind in the *Defrenne* case and which would need "legislation".

Further, without such legislation, a wide interpretation would deny the respondent any effective opportunity for a defence of justification. Again, no doubt, the ECJ had in mind the need for progressive implementation of any industry-wide application, with proper safeguards built in to accommodate some kind of a justification defence.

It seems to us that Mr Langstaff's submission that the line would be drawn naturally on the basis of what an applicant could prove was unrealistic. He cannot escape from the fact that there is nothing about this case which would distinguish it from any other case where an applicant claimed equal pay with a comparator employed by another company, not necessarily even engaged in the same industry.

It appears that Article 141 requires the possibility of comparison beyond the narrow confines of s.1(6) EqPA. What is unclear is whether it also requires that women (or, indeed, men) can challenge pay discrimination other than in the narrow circumstances provided for by s.1(2). In the first place, there is no provision for increasing women's wages where they are shown to be *disproportionately* underpaid by comparison with, for example, a man whose job is 120% as valuable but whose wages are 150% higher. Secondly (and the resolution of this would in large part also solve the first problem), the EqPA does not permit an equal pay claim based on a hypothetical comparator.

D. Pannick, *Sex Discrimination Law*, p. 96

Can a woman claim equal pay to that of a hypothetical male worker by showing that, if she were a man, she would be paid more by her employer? In *Macarthys* the ECJ suggested that a comparison with "a hypothetical male worker" could not be made as it would be "indirect and disguised discrimination, the identification of which" would require "comparative studies of entire branches of industry". Therefore, the direct application of Article [141] is "confined to parallels which may be drawn on the basis of concrete appraisals of the work actually performed by employees of different sex within the same establishment or service". The ECJ here seems to have confused two different concepts. It is understandable that Article [141] should not entitle a woman to compare her pay with that of a man in a different industry. But the practical difficulties there involved are not raised where the woman is able to prove that her employer would pay her more if she were male. The reference to the hypothetical male worker is merely one means of proving that she has been less favourably treated on the ground of her sex.

The notion of the hypothetical male comparison is central to the concept of discrimination in the Sex Discrimination Act 1975. Direct discrimination is there defined as treating the complainant, on the ground of her sex, less favourably than one treats, *or would treat*, a man. The absence of this express concept in the Equal Pay Act is one indication of its lack of sophistication. Since the 1970 and 1975 Acts form an interlocking code and since the mischief aimed at by the 1970 Act cannot be removed unless the statute prohibits an obvious form of sex discrimination, it may well be that the 1970 Act can be interpreted as covering this case. US courts have had similar difficulties as to whether the US Equal Pay Act 1963 entitles a woman to a remedy if she can prove that a hypothetical male employee would receive higher pay. In *County of Washington, Oregon* v. *Gunther* [425 US 161 (1981)], the majority of the US Supreme Court held that Title VII of the US Civil Rights Act 1964 allows a claim for sex-based wage discrimination by reference to the pay of a hypothetical male worker. The majority opinion of Brennan J. explained that any other view of the scope of Title VII would render lawful discriminatory wage policies which could not be brought under the Equal Pay Act. He said that if Title VII gave no remedy, there would be no redress where "an employer hired a woman for a unique position in the company and then admitted that her salary would have been higher had she been male . . .". The dissenting opinion of Rehnquist J. (joined by Burger CJ, Powell and Stewart JJ) argued that there was no need for such a remedy under Title VII since the Equal Pay Act already covered the situation: "However unlikely such an admission might be in the bullpen of litigation, an employer's statement that 'if my female employees performing a particular job were males, I would pay them more simply because they are males' would be" sufficient to establish a claim under the US Equal Pay Act since "[o]vert discrimination does not go unremedied" by that Act.

Paul Davies, "The Central Arbitration Committee and Equal Pay"

. . . section 1.8 EqPA does not deal with the question of appropriate differentials between jobs that are admittedly not equal. No matter how broadly job evaluation becomes available, section 1 will be able to meet only claims for parity of pay for jobs of the same value and will note able to meet claims that differences in the value of the jobs should be accurately reflected in the differentials between the pay rates for those jobs—unless, of course, section 1 is much more radically restructured than the European Commission is apparently suggesting. And yet it may be that a legally enforceable claim to "fair differentials" is much more important to women workers than the more limited claim to equal pay for equal work. A study by the Office of Manpower Economics in 1972 found that over the previous 20 years there had been a rapid growth in women's employment (the number of women employed had increased by 20 per cent, while the number of men increased by less than one half of a per cent) but that "despite their vastly increased numbers, women have continued to work in a range of jobs which have largely been their traditional preserve." Moreover, "even when they work alongside men the tend to perform work which is commonly classified as being of a less skilled nature." About two and a half million women cut of a total female working population of nearly nine million were employed in occupations where men were less than 10 per cent of the workforce. "These were virtually 'women only' jobs where the question of like work would be unlikely to arise to any great extent." This is no doubt particularly true when, as is the case, comparisons are seldom permitted to go outside the establishment. Within the establishment the real grievance of the women workers may well be, not that there are other men engaged on equal work who are paid more, but there are men whose work is admittedly of higher value but whose pay is disproportionately higher. Even the Sex Discrimination Act 1975 does not address itself directly to this problem. It would require an employer to provide non-discriminatory access to the higher paid jobs but not necessarily to alter the differentials between jobs, although, if the result of the Act were to be the presence of substantial numbers of women in the higher paid jobs, this might in the long run undermine the social attitudes that supported the unjustified differentials.

THE EMPLOYER'S DEFENCE

S.1(3) EPA provides that:

> An equality clause shall not operate in relation to a variation between the woman's con-
> tract and the man's contract if the employer proves that the variation is genuinely due to a
> material factor which is not the difference of sex and that factor–
> (a) in the case of an equality clause falling within subsection (2)(a) or (b) above, must be a
>   material difference between the woman's case and the man's; and
> (b) in the case of an equality clause falling within subsection (2)(c) above, may be such a
>   material difference.

Early decisions: the "Category" approach

S.1(3)(b) was added by the Equal Pay (Amendment) Regulations 1983, which introduced the equal pay for work of equal value claim. The section was meant to by-pass
the decision of the Court of Appeal in *Clay Cross (Quarry Services) Ltd* v *Fletcher*
that only "personal" factors could be considered under s.1(3). The employer had put
forward, as a GMF defence, "market forces", i.e., the argument that he had had to
match the comparator's previous salary in order to attract him to the job. This had
been accepted by EAT on the assumption, as Lord Denning put it, that "the issue
depended on the employer's state of mind, on the reason why he paid the man more
than the woman. If the reason had nothing to do with sex, they could pay him
more". Lord Denning went on to proscribe what he saw as the appropriate limits of
s.1(3):

> **Clay Cross (Quarry Services) Ltd v Fletcher [1979] 1 All ER 474, [1978] 1 WLR 1429, [1979]
> ICR 47**
>
> The issue does not depend on the employer's state of mind. It does not depend on his
> reasons for paying the man more. The employer may not intend to discriminate against the
> woman by paying her less; but, if the result of his actions is that she is discriminated against,
> then his conduct is unlawful, whether he intended it or not . . .
>   The issue depends on whether there is a material difference (other than sex) between her
> case and his. Take heed to those words, "between her case and his". They show that the tri-
> bunal is to have regard to her and to him, to the personal equation of the woman as com-
> pared to that of the man, irrespective of any extrinsic forces which led to the variation in
> pay. As I said in *Shields* v *Coomes* [above] . . . the subsection applies when "the personal
> equation of the man is such that he deserves to be paid at a higher rate than the woman".
> Thus the personal equation of the man may warrant a wage differential if he has much
> longer length of service; or has superior skill or qualifications; or gives bigger output or
> productivity; or has been placed, owing to down-grading, in a protected pay category,
> vividly described as "red circled"; or to other circumstances personal to him in doing his
> job.

But the tribunal is not to have regard to any extrinsic forces which have led to the man being paid more. An employer cannot avoid his obligations under the [EqPA] by saying: "I paid him more because he asked for more", or "I paid her less because she was willing to come for less". If any such excuse were permitted, the Act would be a dead letter. These are the very reasons why there was unequal pay before the statute. They were the very circumstances in which the statute was intended to operate.

Nor can the employer avoid his obligations by giving the reasons why he submitted to the extrinsic forces. As for instance by saying: "He asked for that sum because it was what he was getting in his previous job", or "He was the only applicant for the job, so I had no option". In such cases the employer may beat his breast, and say: "I did not pay him more because he was a man. I paid it because he was the only suitable person who applied for the job. Man or woman made no difference to me." Those are reasons personal to the employer. If any such reasons were permitted as an excuse, the door would be wide open. Every employer who wished to avoid the statute would walk straight through it . . .[67]

In *Rainey* v *Greater Glasgow Health Board* (further discussed below), the House of Lords disapproved of the approach taken by both Lord Denning and Lord Lawton (concurring) in *Clay Cross*, Lord Keith for the Court declaring that the decision was:

unduly restrictive of the proper interpretation of section 1(3). The difference must be "material," which I would construe as meaning "significant and relevant," and it must be between "her case and his." Consideration of a person's case must necessarily involve consideration of all the circumstances of that case. These may well go beyond what is not very happily described as "the personal equation," ie the personal qualities by way of skill, experience or training which the individual brings to the job. Some circumstances may on examination prove to be not significant or not relevant, but others may do so, though not relating to the personal qualities of the employee. In particular, where there is no question of intentional sex discrimination whether direct or indirect (and there is none here) a difference which is connected with economic factors affecting the efficient carrying on of the employer's business or other activity may well be relevant.

The decision in *Rainey* will be considered further below. But the difference of approach between the Court of Appeal in *Clay Cross* and the House of Lords in *Rainey* does indicate some of the difficulties to which s.1(3) gave rise. On its face, the section allows any pay difference which is due (1) to a "material factor/ difference" which is (2) "not the difference of sex". Whether a factor is "material", and whether it is or is not "the difference" of sex should, presumably, be judged on the facts of the particular case (this is further explained below). But what appears frequently to happen in practice is that employers (and, indeed, the courts) grasp particular categories of reasons to explain pay differences on the assumption that the categories themselves, rather than their application in any particular case, constitute "GMFs" (or in the

---

[67] Citing in support, *inter alia*, Phillips J in *National Coal Board* v *Sherwin* [1978] ICR 700, p.710 "The general principle [is] that it is no justification for a refusal to pay the same wages to women doing the same work as a man to say that the man could not have been recruited for less". Lawton and Browne LJJ concurred on similar grounds.

Clay Cross decision, do not). This approach was perhaps understandable in *Clay Cross*, which predated EAT's decision in *Jenkins* v *Kingsgate* (see below). But it has proven a blight on the application of s.1(3), engendering whole lines of cases in which "market forces" (post *Rainey*), "separate collective bargaining structures", "administrative reasons", and so on, have been accepted *per se*, as justifying pay disparities.

At the outset (and prior to anyone in the UK considering the concept of indirect discrimination), the GMF defence was intended to permit differentials based on "length of service, merit, output and so on . . . provided that the payments are available to any person who qualifies regardless of sex".[68] It did not appear, at this stage, that regard would be had to the actual impact by sex of any such factors, as distinct from the question whether both men and women could qualify for them. But, as we shall see below, the ECJ gradually developed an understanding of indirect discrimination and applied it, in the equal pay context, to permit only such differentials as were either unrelated to sex, in the sense that they did not impact disparately between men and women or which, although they did have such an (unintended) impact, were nevertheless justifiable in line with the test discussed below. Even this, as we shall see below, did not always prove sufficient to displace the "category" approach.

Tribunals' initial unwillingness to scrutinise the factors put forward by employers under s.1(3) to ascertain whether they were in fact discrimination-free can be seen in a number of "red circle" cases, among them the first equal pay case ever to reach a tribunal. In *Bedwell & ors* v *Hellerman Deutsch Ltd*, a tribunal accepted the employer's defence that the difference between the man's rate and the woman's was due to the protection of the man's pre-EqPA rate of pay. Prior to 1975 men had all been paid as "staff" while women received an inferior hourly rate. As from the Act's implementation date, all jobs were placed on "unisex" hourly rates in accordance with a job evaluation scheme, but all men continued to receive their previously (higher) hourly rate. According to the tribunal: "s.1(3) of the Act is included *for this very purpose*, ie, to enable employers to overcome immediate practical difficulties in complying with the Act" (my emphasis).[69] It need hardly be pointed out that such an approach directly contradicts the intention of the Act's framers as expressed by Barbara Castle, above.

In *Snoxell* v *Vauxhall Motors Ltd* [1978] QB 11 EAT disapproved of the approach taken by the *Bedwell* tribunal and set out a more rigorous approach to s.1(3). The case was brought by female machine inspectors who named, as their comparators, male machine inspectors whose salaries had been "red-circled" when their exclusively male grade had been assimilated into a new unisex pay structure. It seems from the headnote to the EAT decision that the tribunal had dismissed the case without analysis: "the variation was genuinely due to . . . red-circling and . . . the requirements of s.1(3) were *therefore* satisfied" (my emphasis).

Phillips J, for EAT, opined of the *Bedwell* decision that "it cannot be right to justify the variation in pay by another variation between the man's and the woman's contract

[68] Barbara Castle, 795 HC Debs, 9th February 1970, col. 920.
[69] [1976] IRLR 98, p.99.

[the fact that the man used to have staff status] which itself requires to be justified as being genuinely due to a material difference (other than the difference of sex)".[70] Rejecting the employer's argument that the difference in pay between female machine parts inspectors and male inspectors resulted from the "red-circling" of the latter after their previously exclusively male grade had been assimilated into the unisex, pay structure, Phillips J pointed out that women had not been eligible for the grade in respect of which the men's wages were red-circled and continued:

Snoxell & Anor v Vauxhall Motors, Charles Early & Marriott (Whitney) Ltd v Smith & Anor [1978] QB 11, [1977] 3 All ER 770, [1977] ICR 700, [1977] IRLR 123

Phillips J (for EAT):

The onus of proof under s 1(3) is on the employer and it is a heavy one. Intention, and motive, are irrelevant; and we would say that an employer can never establish in the terms of s 1(3) that the variation between the woman's contract and the man's contract is genuinely due to a material difference (other than the difference of sex) between her case and his when it can be seen that past sex discrimination has contributed to the variation. To allow such an answer would, we think, be contrary to the spirit and intent of the [EqPA], construed and interpreted in the manner we have already explained. It is true that the original discrimination occurred before 29th December 1975, and accordingly was not then unlawful; nonetheless it cannot have been the intention of the [EqPA] to permit the perpetuation of the effects of earlier discrimination.[71]

In *Snoxell*, Phillips J had sought out (direct) discrimination which was disguised behind the "red-circling" GMF. But is was a long time before this rigour was extended to "GMF" defences which were tainted by discrimination of the *indirect* variety. One byproduct of this can be seen in the popularity of the "grading" and "separate pay structure" GMFs. Indeed, such was the popularity of these defences that they continued to be relied upon even after EAT accepted, in *Jenkins* v *Kingsgate* (1981), that indirectly discriminatory factors could not be relied on under s.1(3) unless such reliance was "justified". The issue of justification, and the *Jenkins* case itself, are considered below.

The "grading" GMF made its first appearance in *National Vulcan* v *Wade* in which Ormrod LJ expressed the somewhat optimistic hope that:

---

[70] [1977] IRLR 123, p.128. Having said this, even the Court of Appeal, in *Farthing* v *Ministry of Defence* [1980] IRLR 402 accepted, as a material factor "not the difference of sex" the fact that the employers had, in the process of eliminating directly discriminatory pay scales, first moved the women from grade 4 to grade 6 of the women's pay scale (which entitled them to roughly equal pay with men on grade 4 of the male pay scale) then, in response to the women's complaints at being moved down to the unisex grade 4 (where they continued to receive the same wages as they had on grade 6 of the women's pay scale), transferred them up to grade 6 on the unisex scale "on a personal basis". The men employed on grade 4 made an equal pay claim but Lord Denning, in the Court of Appeal, ruled that both the tribunal and EAT had erred in finding that the variation was due to sex: it came about, rather: "because of the system which had been adopted to eliminate the difference in pay between men and women". Waller and Dunn L.JJ. agreed.

[71] Citing, in support, the US decision in *Corning Glassworks* v *Brennan* (1974) 417 US 188.

National Vulcan Engineering Insurance Group Ltd v Wade [1979] QB 132, [1978] 3 All ER
121, [1978] 3 WLR 214 [1978] ICR 800, [1978] IRLR 225

Ormrod LJ:

the object of [the EqPA] . . . was in simple terms to bring into force what was loosely
described as the policy of equal pay for equal work. It is an Act which has to be applied by
hundreds and thousands of ordinary people who are not lawyers, and it should therefore
be kept as simple and as free from legalistic complications as is possible. . . . the crucial
thing is to keep the issue which the tribunal has to decide, as a matter of fact, to as simple
a matter of fact as it can be and not to complicate their task by an ever-increasing number
of technical legal decisions which must be completely bewildering to those who have to
administer this sort of legislation on the ground.[72]

This view is unchallengeable as a statement of the ideal—no-one would wish to
complicate any further than is necessary the application of equal pay. But, in practice,
the determination to keep things simple serves to prevent proper scrutiny of pay-
related factors which serve to disadvantage women. In *National Vulcan* itself, the difference in wages between the applicant and her comparator was due to their different
performance ratings. An industrial tribunal and EAT had taken the view that, in
pleading grading differences, the employers had failed to discharge the burden placed
upon them by s.1(3). The Court of Appeal ruled that the lower courts had imposed an
unduly heavy burden of proof upon the employer. While Ms Wade was one of the two
lowest-graded employees in the department (the other being a man), two of the other
three women in the department shared the highest rating (with five men) and another
women was placed second highest (with five men, the other three of the 14 men in the
department being placed in intermediate grades). It was true that Ms Wade's comparator, who occupied one of the intermediate positions, "had been assessed by the
management as 'a young man going places'" (Ms Wade's own assessment stating that
she had "a fair knowledge of the procedures and works quite well when concentrating,
but unfortunately is easily distracted") and that, according to EAT, "the assignment
of a particular individual, and therefore his remuneration, depends on the personal
assessment of the individual. . . which was of necessity a subjective judgment". But the
distribution between grades of men and women within Ms Wade's department did
suggest a lack of inherent bias within the system.

The Court of Appeal's decision in *National Vulcan* was unsurprising on the facts, as
was Lord Denning's conclusion that "a grading system according to ability, skill and
experience is an integral part of good business management; and, as long as it is fairly
and genuinely applied irrespective of sex, there is nothing wrong with it at all." But the

---

[72] 808–809*e*. See also the judgment of Lawton LJ in *Clay Cross* in which he stated: ". . . Parliament
intended that industrial tribunals should provide a quick and cheap remedy for what it had decided were
injustices in the employment sphere. The procedure was to be such that both employers and employees
could present their cases without having to go to lawyers for help. . . If . . . there are uncertainties in the
statutes, when construing them the courts should, I think, lean in favour of a simplicity in meaning which
will safeguard informality in procedure". Unusually, this cry for simplicity was made in a judgment
favourable to the applicant.

result of the decision was that "grading", and then "pay structures" more generally were accepted by EAT as a complete defence to equal pay claims. This approach continued even after it was clear that Article 141 prohibited indirect, as well as direct, pay discrimination and that, accordingly, indirectly discriminatory factors could be relied on under s.1(3) only where they were "justified".

Sue Hastings suggests that the widespread acceptance of the "separate collective agreements" "GMF" had an impact on labour market practices.

S. Hastings, in J. Gregory, R. Sales and A. Hegewisch (eds) *Women, Work, and Inequality*

... there is some evidence that this line of defence may have deterred some employers from pursuing proposals for harmonization of terms and conditions of employment between different groups. This is certainly apparent in the National Health Service, where most health trusts have held back from trying to develop their own pay structures.

There have been other reasons for the lack of action by trusts, including opposing pressures from trade unions and lack of resources to lubricate change, but evidence from health service personnel conferences suggests that trust managers do see "equal value" as a problem; and regard maintenance of the Whitley arrangements for centralized pay bargaining as "protection", not to be discarded lightly.

The health service is a good example of the maintenance of separate collective bargaining arrangements operating against a movement towards equal pay for work of equal value.

Hastings refers to a graph which shows, *inter alia*, that, in 1994, the Ancillary Staffs Council scheme ran from £4,000 to £7,000, the Estates Officer Scale from about £6,500 to £37,000, speech therapists' rates from £11,000 to £30,000, hospital pharmacists from £12,000 to £35,000, cliincal psychologists from £9,000 to £47,000 and occupational therapists from £11,000 to £27,000:

The top half of the Ancillary Staffs Council (ASC) structure covers jobs such as cooks, kitchen superintendents, domestic and dining-room supervisors, whose roles include responsibility for all or part of a support service and supervision of staff. On any system of assessment, such roles must be of at least equal value to many of the jobs in the lower grades of the Estates Officer structure, which cover maintenance workers and their supervisors.

The [f]igure also illustrates the basis of the speech therapists' claims for equal pay with hospital pharmacists and clinical psychologists, but suggests that similar claims could have been pursued by others from the professions allied to medicine, for instance, radiographers, physiotherapists or occupational therapists, or by some in the senior clinical nursing grades.

So, the "separate collective bargaining arrangements" defence argued by the respondents in *Enderby* in 1987 [and further considered below] has arguably delayed serious consideration of "equal value" issues in the sector. It also appears to have deterred women in the NHS from taking equal pay cases or unions from supporting them. As the health service employs up to one million people, mainly women, the impact in this sector is significant.

The "separate collective bargaining" defence has also arguably delayed until recently any reconsideration of pay structures in higher education, to the potential disadvantage in pay equity terms of many women employees. Again, those in the manual structure are especially disadvantaged in pay terms compared with comparable clerical and related administrative jobs on the one hand, and technical jobs on the other. And, on the basis of the overall demands of the jobs they do, women whose jobs are graded towards the top of the clerical and administrative structure are also likely to be disadvantaged relative to those in the academic and academic-related structures.

The CGMF and indirect discrimination

In *Jenkins* v *Kingsgate* (Case C–96/80) [1981] 1 WLR 972 [1981] IRLR 228, the ECJ was asked to consider whether Article 141 was breached by lower payments to (predominantly female) part-time workers than to (predominantly male) workers. That court ruled that the purpose of Article 141 was: "to ensure the application of the principle of equal pay for men and women . . . The differences in pay prohibited by that provision are therefore exclusively those based on the difference of the sex of the workers".

This, on the face of it, suggested that only direct discrimination was prohibited under Article 141. But the ECJ had gone on to muddy the waters by ruling that:

> the fact that work paid at time rates is remunerated at an hourly rate which varies according to the number of hours worked per week does not offend against the principle of equal pay laid down in Article [141] of the Treaty *in so far as the difference in pay between part-time work and full-time work is attributable to factors which are objectively justified and are in no way related to any discrimination based on sex*" (my emphasis). . . By contrast, if it is established that a considerably smaller percentage of women than of men perform the minimum number of weekly working hours required in order to be able to claim the full-time hourly rate of pay, the inequality in pay will be contrary to Article [141] of the Treaty where, regard being had to the difficulties encountered by women in arranging to work that minimum number of hours per week, the pay policy of the undertaking in question cannot be explained by factors other than discrimination based on sex.

The effect of the ECJ's decision was to leave unclear the question whether indirect pay discrimination was or was not prohibited under Article 141. On the case's return to EAT (*Jenkins* v *Kingsgate (No. 2)* [1981] IRLR 388), however, that court ruled that, whatever the position under European law, s.1(3) EqPA permitted reliance upon indirectly discriminatory factors (here the fact that the woman was engaged in part-time and her comparator in full-time work) only where that reliance was justified.[73] According to Browne-Wilkinson J:

> If the industrial tribunal finds that the employer intended to discriminate against women by paying part-time workers less, the employer cannot succeed under section 1(3). Even if

[73] [1981] 1 WLR 1485.

the employer had no such intention, for section 1(3) to apply the employer must show that the difference in pay between full-time and part-time workers is reasonably necessary in order to obtain some result (other than cheap female labour) which the employer desires for economic or other reasons.

The ECJ had, in *Jenkins*, taken a cautious approach to Article 141. But within a few years it had developed a much more radical line. Most significant for our purposes was the decision in *Bilka-Kaufhaus GmbH* v *Weber von Hartz* Case C–170/84 [1986] ECR 1607, [1986] IRLR 317, which made it clear that Article 141 permitted indirect pay discrimination only where it was "justified". The same decision marked the beginning, in the equal opportunities context, of a line of authority on the meaning of "justifiable"—there the court ruled that disparately impacting pay practices were permissible under Article 141 only where they "correspond to a real need on the part of the undertaking, are appropriate with a view to achieving the objectives pursued and are necessary to that end".

Subsequently, the decisions of the ECJ in *Rinner-Kühn*, *Danfoss*, and *Nimz* set ever more challenging tests for the justification of indirect discrimination in pay. *Rinner-Kühn* concerned a part-time worker's challenge to her employer's refusal to pay her sick-pay, national law requiring (and providing for the reimbursement to the employer of) such payment only for those working more than 10 hours a week. Having decided that sick pay was "pay" within Article 141 (see above) and that its denial to part-timers amounted, *prima facie*, to indirect discrimination against women, the ECJ continued:

Rinner-Kühn v *FWW Spezial-Gebaudereinigung GmbH* (Case C–171/88) [1989] ECR 2743

In the course of the procedure, the German Government stated [by way of justification] . . . that workers whose period of work amounted to less than 10 hours a week or 45 hours a month were not as integrated in, or as dependent on, the undertaking employing them as other workers.

It should, however, be stated that those considertions, in so far as they are only generalizations about certain categories of workers, do not enable criteria which are both objective and unrelated to any discrimination on grounds of sex to be identified. However, if the Member State can show that the means chosen meet a necessary aim of its social policy and that they are suitable and requisite for attaining that aim, the mere fact that the provision affects a much greater number of female workers than male workers cannot be regarded as constituting an infringement of Article [141].

Danfoss concerned a challenge, *inter alia*, to a practice whereby individual pay was set according to factors including adaptability, training and seniority, reliance on these factors serving to disadvantage women by comparison with men.

Handels-og Kontorfunktionaerernes Forbund I Danmark v *Dansk Arbejdsgiverforening (acting for Danfoss)* (Case C–109/88) [1989] ECR 3199

22 . . . The employer may . . . justify the remuneration of [adaptability to variable hours and

varying places of work] by showing it is of importance for the performance of specific tasks entrusted to the employee.

23 In the second place, as regards the criterion of training, it is not excluded that it may work to the disadvantage of women in so far as they have had less opportunity than men for training or have taken less advantage of such opportunity. Nevertheless . . . the employer may justify remuneration of special training by showing that it is of importance for the performance of specific tasks entrusted to the employee.

In *Danfoss* the ECJ was prepared to accept that the reward of seniority, even where it operated so as to disadvantage women: "length of service goes hand in hand with experience and since experience generally enables the employee to perform his duties better, the employer is free to reward it without having to establish the importance it has in the performance of specific tasks entrusted to the employee". This approach was rapidly revised in *Nimz* v *Freie*, in which the challenge related precisely to the reward of service where this served to disadvantage part-time workers and, accordingly, women:

Nimz v Freie und Hanse-Stadt Hamburg (Case C–184/89) [1991] ECR I–297

13 . . . The City of Hamburg claimed during the procedure that full-time employees or those who work for three-quarters of normal working time acquire more quickly than others the abilities and skills relating to their particular job. The German Government also relied on their more extensive experience.

14 It should, however, be stated that such considerations, in so far as they are no more than generalizations about certain categories of workers, do not make it possible to identify criteria which are both objective and unrelated to any discrimination on grounds of sex [citing *Rinner-Kühn*]. Although experience goes hand in hand with length of service, and experience enables the worker in principle to improve performance of the tasks allotted to him, the objectivity of such a criterion depends on all the circumstances in a particular case, and in particular on the relationship between the nature of the work performed and the experience gained from the performance of that work upon completion of a certain number of working hours . . .

The decisions reached in these and other Article 141 cases require a rigorous approach to the application of the GMF defence. In particular it is clear that, in determining the jutsifiability of indirect pay discrimination, the domestic courts must scrutinise the factors relied upon for any disparate impact associated with sex, and must accept only such factors as are demonstrably related to the requirements of the jobs under consideration.

The decision in *Bilka* was embraced by the House of Lords in *Rainey* v *Greater Glasgow Health Board*, in which their Lordships incorporated the ruling of the ECJ in that case into s.1(3) EqPA. The background to the case was a decision taken by the Board to establish an NHS prosthetics service, prosthetic services always previously having been "bought in" from the private sector. The Board decided that, in order to recruit from the private sector, it would have to offer "indirect applicants" (i.e., those recruited from the private sector) the opportunity to retain their private sector terms and conditions indefinitely. This policy was retained for one year, after which both direct and "indirect" applicants (those recruited other than from private sector employment) were employed on the normal NHS rates. Every one of the 20 indirect recruits was male. Directly recruited prosthetists included one man who subsequently left. No attempts were made to phase out the disparities between direct and indirect applicants and, at the time of the hearing, the applicant was paid £7,295 p.a., her comparator (whose qualifications and experience were broadly similar), £10,085.

We saw above that the House of Lords overruled the approach taken by the Court of Appeal in *Clay Cross* and accepted that the GMF defence could extend beyond factors personal to the applicant and her comparator. Lord Keith interpreted the decision in *Bilka* as permitting objectively justified economic grounds and "objectively justified grounds which are other than economic, such as administrative efficiency in a concern not engaged in commerce or business". In the instant case he took the view that:

Rainey v *Greater Glasgow Health Board* [1987] 1 AC 224, [1987] 1 All ER 65, [1986] 3 WLR 1017, [1987] ICR 129, [1987] IRLR 26, [1987] 2 CMLR 11

the difference between the case of the appellant and that of [her comparator] is that the former is a person who entered the National Health Service . . . directly while the latter is a person who entered it from employment with a private contractor. The fact that one is a woman and the other a man is an accident. . . the new prosthetic service could never have been established within a reasonable time if [the comparator] and others like him had not been offered a scale of remuneration no less favourable than that which they were then enjoying. . .

[I]t was argued for the appellant that it did not constitute a good and objectively justified reason for paying the appellant and other direct entrants a lower scale of remuneration. . . from the administrative point of view it would have been highly anomalous and inconvenient if prosthetists alone, over the whole tract of future time for which the prosthetic service would endure, were to have been subject to a different salary scale and different negotiating machinery . . . there were sound objectively justified administrative reasons, in my view, for placing prosthetists in general, men and women alike, on the Whitley Council scale and subjecting them to its negotiating machinery . . . It was not a question of the appellant being paid less than the norm but of Mr Crumlin being paid more. He was paid more because of the necessity to attract him and other privately employed prosthetists into forming the nucleus of the new service . . .

Counsel for the appellant put forward an argument based on section 1(1)(b) of the Sex Discrimination Act 1975 (with which the [EqPA] to be read as one: *Shields* v *E Coomes* . . .) This provision has the effect of prohibiting indirect discrimination between women and men. In my opinion it does not, for present purposes, add anything to section 1(3) of the [EqPA] since, upon the view which I have taken as to the proper construction of the latter, a difference which demonstrated unjustified indirect discrimination would not discharge the onus placed on the employer. Further, there would not appear to be any material distinction in principle between the need to demonstrate objectively justified grounds of difference for purposes of section 1(3) and the need to justify a requirement or condition under section 1(1)(b)(ii) of the Act of 1975. It is therefore unnecessary to consider the argument further.

The return of the "category" approach?

The decision of the House of Lords in *Rainey* was, on the one hand, to be welcomed because of its incorporation of the ECJ's decision in *Bilka*, and therefore of a rigorous approach to the justification of indirect discrimination, into UK law. But in applying the test to the facts before it, the House of Lords fell into the very same trap as had the tribunals in *Bedwell* and in *Snoxell* (above). Rather than taking into account the *impact*, on men and women, of the factor relied on by the employer in determining whether it was (indirectly) discriminatory, their Lordships just looked at the abstracted factor—here the need to attract indirect applicants while making some effort to control labour costs—and decided that it fitted into the "category" of "administrative efficiency", which category their lordships took to be within *Bilka*. The House of Lords characterised as "accident" the composition by sex of the groups of indirect and direct applicants. But this may not have been the case. And given the disparate impact by sex of the factor, the retention of the enhanced rates payable to private sector prosthetists, coupled with the payment of lower rates to directly recruited staff, at least raised a requirement of objective justification which would, in turn, have had to be made out *taking into account its discriminatory impact*. The failure of the House of Lords in *Rainey* to consider the disparate impact by sex of the "market forces" defence had the effect of permitting the employer to say: "I paid him more because he asked for more", or "I paid her less because she was willing to come for less".[74] These, as Lord Denning pointed out, "are the very reasons why there was unequal pay before the statute . . . the very circumstances in which the statute was intended to operate.[75]

The impact of *Rainey* was to be felt for a long time, its interpretation by the lower courts sometimes having the effect that *Bilka* served to *widen*, rather than to control, the scope of the GMF. In *Reed* v *Boozer and another*, for example, EAT regarded itself as fortified by the House of Lords' decision in *Rainey* in allowing an appeal from an employer. The tribunal had rejected the employer's attempt to block an equal pay claim, prior to the assessment of value, on the grounds that the applicants (women dispatch clerks) were graded on the employer's "staff" pay structure and received a weekly wage, but their comparator (a male dispatch clerk) was paid according to the employer's pay scheme for hourly workers. According to the tribunal:

> Despite [the employer's] hint that shock waves would be sent through the system if the two women applicants were allowed to compare themselves with [the man], it seems to the tribunal that the principal difficulty for [the employers] is that the principles of equal pay, now that they are with us, do not take kindly to the somewhat artificial differences between

---

[74] *Per* Lord Denning in *Clay Cross*, above.
[75] Equally, according to Lawton LJ: "an exception based on such a vague conception as economic factors or market pressures . . . would strike at the object of the article. In the labour market women have always been in a worse position than men. Under both Article 141 and the EqPA 1970 that was no longer to be so".

staff and hourly paid workers which are the product of historical development. It is accepted by the [employers] that there is no internal machinery to allow a staff employee to compare herself with an hourly paid worker, or for that matter vice versa. If the tribunal were to allow this defence at this stage, it would mean that these particular women would not be able to break through the artificial barrier which, so far as the internal machinery is concerned, denies them the opportunity of pursuing claims to equal pay with a selected male employee. If there was a single structure they would, of course, be able to do so.

The approach taken by the tribunal was patently correct. The employers had certainly not shown that the difference in pay was "not the difference of sex". They had, rather, merely given an historical account of how that difference had developed. The applicants were represented by the Association of Clerical Workers, the comparators by the Transport and General Workers' Union. No explanation was given as to why the two groups, whose work was very similar indeed, were represented by different unions. Further, the very title of the applicants' union suggested that it was a predominantly female organisation whose industrial strength would, by reason of that, be considerably less than that of the T&G. But EAT took a different view:

Reed Packaging Ltd v *Boozer and another* [1988] ICR 391, [1988] IRLR 333

There is no suggestion that either of the pay structures contains any element of discrimination based upon sex, whether direct or indirect. Two questions therefore remain. Is the variation due to a material factor, namely, the separate pay structures? And is the operation of these structures genuine? . . .

No one suggests that the variation here was due to a difference of sex. No one has suggested that these pay structures are not genuinely operated. Therefore, can the separate pay structures constitute a material factor? We can see no reason why not—a single grading scheme is clearly capable of being such a factor (see [*National Vulcan*[76]]) . . We are also reinforced in our view by the recent case of *Rainey* . . . [in which the House of Lords held] that . . . section 1(3) might apply where a difference in pay was reasonably necessary in order to obtain some result, other than cheap female labour, that the employer desired to achieve for economic reasons or for other reasons such as administrative efficiency in a concern not engaged in commerce or business . . .

The present case, in our judgment, shows an objectively justified administrative reason and therefore a material factor which was genuine or sound. We have therefore reached the conclusion that the only decision which the industrial tribunal could have reached was that the employers had made out this defence under section 1(3) and that the claim should have been dismissed . . .

In *Davies* v *McCartneys*, too, EAT accepted that the employer had made out the s.1(3) defence on the basis, *inter alia*, that the applicant's comparator (a market clerk) spent 30 per cent of his time in "unpleasant" conditions in live stock markets; that he carried out a more demanding and responsible role than the applicant and that market clerks had always been paid at a higher rate than secretaries.

---

[76] Also *obiter* passage in *Waddington*. Both decisions pre-dated the application of indirect discrimination in the equal pay context.

Davies v McCartneys [1989] ICR 705, [1989] IRLR 439

Wood J:

When considering whether there should be any limitation upon the factors relevant to a consideration of a section 1(3) defence it is important to remember that the [EqPA] and its amendments were intended to give effect to Article [141] of the EEC Treaty and to Council Directive (75/117/EEC) . . .

By Community law the defence which is open to the employer is that such discrimination as existed was objectively justified. There is no limitation to those factors and reasons upon which that defence may be based and we see no reason why the factor should be limited in the defence under section 1(3). The essential is that it should be based on a material factor which is genuine and the variation is genuinely due to that material factor which is not a difference of sex. The argument could also be supported by the difference between the wording in section 1(3)(a) and section 1(3)(b). In (a) there is a reference to "difference between the woman's case and the man's"—this indicates a direct comparison in the demands, and in paragraph (b) the words used are "may be" such a material difference and therefore indicates that it goes outside the immediate comparison between the woman's case and the man's case which is the distinction or the difference in comparison in demands . . .

It is quite apparent [referring to the employer's assertion, regarding the comparator, that "we would not get anyone . . . It is an historical fact that when someone leaves who has been with you for several years, when you try to replace him you find that you have not been paying him enough and that you have to pay his successor more. If that answers the question that is the best I can say."] . . . that upon historic and economic grounds a differential is made between the pay of Mr Jones and that of the applicant and that these grounds might properly be said to be market forces. This would be justified under *Rainey* . . .

As in *Rainey* and in *Reed* v *Boozer*, the category of "GMF" (here "market forces") was plucked from its context and examined, in the abstract, to determine whether it was (again, without reference to context) an acceptable category. In *Reed* v *Boozer*, EAT made the bald assertion that "separate pay structures, at least where they were not internally discriminatory, were "an objectively justified administrative reason and therefore a material factor which was genuine or sound". In *Davies*, the same court stated simply that "market forces . . . would be justified under *Rainey*". But whatever its decision on the facts, the House of Lords did not rule in that case that "market forces" constituted a "GMF". What *Rainey* did establish, rather, was that (*per Bilka*), indirectly discriminatory pay factors are consistent with s.1(3) EqPA only if they "correspond to a real need on the part of the undertaking, are appropriate with a view to achieving the objectives pursued and are necessary to that end". That is a question of fact in the particular case, and is not satisfied simply by the characterisation of a reason put forward by the employer as "economic" "administrative" etc.:

Post-*Bilka* developments (specifically, the decisions in *Rinner-Kühn*, *Danfoss*, and *Nimz* v *Freie*) were mentioned above. Given the direct effect of Article 141 (discussed in Chapter 1), these developments have been incorporated, as a matter of European law, into s.1(3)'s GMF defence. The clash between the approach of the domestic courts in cases such as *Reed* v *Boozer* and *Davies* v *McCartneys* came to a head in

Enderby v *Frenchay*, in which the "category" of GMF relied upon by the employer concerned collective bargaining—the pay of the applicant and that of her comparators had been established by separate collective bargaining arrangements. EAT accepted that the determination of pay by such separate arrangements amounted to a GMF, further requiring that, in order to challenge such a GMF, the applicant would have to show direct or indirect discrimination in its operation (this aspect of the decision is further considered below). The ECJ, however, took a different view.

The GMF and indirect discrimination (2)

Enderby v *Frenchay Health Authority* Case C-127/92 [1993] ECR I-5535

The fact that the rates of pay at issue are decided by collective bargaining processes conducted separately for each of the two professional groups concerned, without any discriminatory effect within each group, does not preclude a finding of *prima facie* discrimination *where the results of those processes show that two groups with the same employer and the same trade union are treated differently*. If the employer could rely on the absence of discrimination within each of the collective bargaining processes taken separately as sufficient justification for the difference in pay, he could . . . easily circumvent the principle of equal pay by using separate bargaining processes. [my emphasis] Accordingly . . . the fact that the respective rates of pay of two jobs of equal value, one carried out almost exclusively by women and the other predominantly by men, were arrived at by collective bargaining processes which, although carried out by the same parties, are distinct, and, taken separately, have in themselves no discriminatory effect, is not sufficient objective justification for the difference in pay between those two jobs . . .

The decision of the ECJ in *Enderby* places beyond argument the unacceptability of the "category" approach to the GMF defence. It is not sufficient for an employer, faced with an equal pay claim, to explain the difference in pay by reference to some factor such as "market forces", "different pay structures or collective agreements", "red-circling", etc. He or she must go further and establish to the satisfaction of the tribunal *either* that, as the House of Lords accepted (albeit controversially) in the *Rainey* decision, that the factor is neutral as regards sex *or*, to the extent that it serves to disadvantage either sex (as distinct merely from the applicant(s)[77]), that reliance upon it is nevertheless justified consistent with European law.

Before we go on to consider the application, post-*Enderby*, of the GMF defence, it is useful to note the criticisms that have been made of that decision and, more generally, of the ECJ's approach to the justification of indirect discrimination in pay.

---

[77] The inherent tendency of a pay-determining factor to disadvantage women might be established, as in *Enderby*, by evidence of the outcome of collective bargaining by sex or, as in *Rinner-Kühn*, by the disproportionately female nature of the part-time workers adversely affected. If, on the other hand, pay is determined according to a factor by which the female applicant is disadvantaged, but women in general are not, no justification ought to be required. See, further, the discussions of *Loughran* and *Enderby* below.

J. Kentridge, "Direct and Indirect Discrimination after *Enderby*" **[1994]** *Public Law* **198, 204–206**

[Commenting on the *Enderby* decision] a pay disparity is not objectively justified solely by the fact that it derives from separate and independently non-discriminatory bargaining processes. There is no difference of substance between terms and conditions incorporated into a contract of employment by virtue of a collective agreement and contractual provisions which are the product of individual agreement. Collective bargaining is simply the process by which certain terms and conditions come to be incorporated in the employee's contract of employment. The process by which an agreement is reached cannot in itself justify the terms of that agreement. That the process is fair may go a long way to securing an outcome which is substantively fair—but it does not necessarily do so. What is relevant in this context is that it transpires that women workers are contracting on less advantageous terms than their male comparators, not simply the process of agreement which led to that result.

The ECJ's approach to the labour market defence accords with its general attitude to commercial factors—a shortage of candidates for a job is amongst the objective economic grounds which can justify a pay practice which is indirectly discriminatory—but only to the extent that it meets a real need of the business, and is appropriate in relation to its object as well as necessary to that end. . . .

what is interesting here is that the court is prepared to accept that market factors may justify pay differentials between men and women whereas it will not countenance disparities which result from collective bargaining, even though the bargaining process itself is not discriminatory. Some might argue that this jeopardises the independence and vitality of collective bargaining and that equality claims should yield to the requirements of vigorous collective bargaining.

It is important to remember, though, that collective bargaining is not simply an end in itself. It should embody and facilitate democracy at work. It is a means to the end of industrial democracy and thence to participative social democracy. The principle of equality is rooted in a conception of fairness. The same conception of fairness grounds a commitment to democratic participation—which in turn requires the equality of all participants. Where collective bargaining arrangements perpetuate gender inequality, they are not fully democratic. But equality has a value beyond its process value. In other words, it is important in itself and not simply as a component of democracy. Equality policies and collective bargaining may be complementary at some points, competitive at others; even, at times, antagonistic. Where there is a conflict between them, the claims of equality should be decisive.

Nevertheless, the Court's view that equality trumps collective bargaining is inconsistent with the approach it takes to the market forces defence. This double standard leads to a curious hiatus in the Court's reasoning. It apparently fails to consider the implications of the fact that market forces are themselves part of a matrix of factors which determine the relative strengths of the parties to collective bargaining. In other words, collectively bargained rates may reflect market forces at one remove, since, to a variable extent, bargaining strength will relate to market scarcity. Alternatively, the Court may be saying that collectively-agreed rates will be justified to the extent that the differential between the male-dominated and the female-dominated jobs can be attributed to market forces, provided that the component which relates to market forces can be isolated. It states:

If . . . the national court has been able to determine precisely what proportion of the increase in pay is attributable to market forces, it must necessarily accept that the pay differential is objectively justified to the extent of that proportion.

It is not clear from this statement whether the court is treating market forces as a factor distinct and independent from collective bargaining, or whether it takes into account the relationship between the two. In either case, it seems to give less weight to the claims of collective bargaining than to those of the market.

Yet choices made through the medium of the market may reflect a set of preferences which are themselves conditioned by gender prejudice and inequality. For example, passengers on an airline may prefer the cabin to be staffed by tall, blonde women. Does this justify the airline in refusing to employ men as cabin crew, or women who do not match the type? Applying the *Bilka* test of what is necessary and appropriate to the objectives of the enterprise, discrimination against all applicants other than tall, blonde women is not justified, even though it may reflect customer preferences. As the Court said in *Diaz v. Pan American World Airways, Inc.* [442 F2d 385 (1971)]:

> it would be totally anomalous if we were to allow the preferences and prejudices of the customers to determine whether the sex discrimination was valid. Indeed, it was, to a large extent, these very prejudices [that Title VII of the Civil Rights Act] was meant to overcome. Thus, we feel that customer preference may be taken into account only when it is based on the company's inability to perform the primary function or service it offers . . . discrimination based on sex is valid only when the *essence* of the business operation would be undermined by not hiring members of one sex exclusively.

Conceivably, an airline which does not discriminate in appointing cabin crew may lose custom to another which provides service with an attractive feminine smile. But if the law allows no airline to discriminate in this way, the customer no longer has that choice. The law has intervened to structure market choices differently from what they would have been if they had simply reflected consumer preferences. In fact, the market is constantly being adjusted in ways which are unremarkable and unremarked—trade in certain types of goods or services is banned or restricted, exchanges of goods and services are taxed differentially, anti-competitive behaviour is prohibited and so on—the very parameters of so-called free-market bargaining are defined by law.

The "market," if such there be, is simply another notional social space, as is the generic "workplace." If the dictates of the market are privileged over the demand of social policies promoting equality, those policies are handicapped at the outset.

Martin Hedemann-Robinson, "Indirect Discrimination and the EC: Appearance Rather than Reality?" (1996) 2 *International Journal of Discrimination and the Law* 85, 93–111

Although in *Bilka* the ECJ appeared to lay down model binding principles regarding the test of objective justification, it is highly questionable whether in practice the ECJ has subsequently abided by them. For instance, it is clear that in numerous cases the ECJ has not adhered to the principle, frequently reiterated by itself, that national courts and not the ECJ should apply EC Law to the facts of each case. Instead, it has often come to a definitive judgment. For instance, in *Rinner-Kühn* it dismissed the German Government's defence to excluding part-time workers from its statutory sick pay scheme as being mere "generalised considerations" without objective foundation. . . . In other cases the ECJ, whilst overtly stating that the final decision must rest with the national court requesting a preliminary ruling under Article 177 EC, has made leading comments on the facts, effectively restricting the national court's options. An example is *Jenkins* where the ECJ indicated that if it could be shown that the defendant employer was endeavouring to encourage full-time employment on economic grounds, regard being had to the employer's intentions and the history of the case, then this would provide the requisite objective justification for the practice of paying part-time workers lower wages than full-timers. The clear distinction made in *Bilka* regarding the respective roles of the courts at national and EC level is not reflected in the majority of cases. Even though it can be argued this is not a particularly novel or unique occurrence in EC Law generally, in that the ECJ has long since overridden any strict interpretation of its jurisdictional boundaries under Article 177 EC, this does not change the fact that the adverse effect of this is inconsistency and therefore unpredictability. It is not clear when and to what extent the ECJ will comment on individual case facts. Yet ultimately such intervention may well determine the outcome of the case. The solution to this problem must be for the ECJ to clarify the limits of its powers of interpreting EC Law and apply them comprehensively. Whilst national courts have the responsibility of ensuring that they glean all the necessary information regarding the proper interpretation of EC Law from the ECJ in accordance with Art. 177(1) EC, it must be recognized that, so long as the ECJ refrains from providing clear guidelines as to the extent of its jurisdiction in the context of preliminary rulings, national courts will inevitably vary in the nature of their questions to it. Some courts may expect the ECJ to deliver a comprehensive judgment on the facts whilst others may limit the range of enquiry to questions on the abstract interpretation of Community Law.

A second problem area following on from that outlined above in respect of disproportionate impact is the imbalanced attitude that the ECJ has shown towards defences of private employers and Member States. There is some evidence to show that the ECJ is more lenient on the private than public sector as regards the objective justification test, particularly when the defendant is relying on financial constraints or budgetary considerations as a reason for the discrepancy in treatment between male and female workers. Whilst it is clear from *De Weerd* [Case C–343/92 [1994] ECR I–571] that Member States are not entitled to rely solely on the criterion of budgetary discipline as the basis for a successful defence, the picture is less clear cut for private defendants. The ECJ, for instance, has been prepared to accept that economic considerations in themselves may constitute a "genuine need" of the enterprise. This raises serious questions as to whether the objective justification model provides adequate and consistent protection against indirect sex discrimination or whether it merely facilitates the ECJ and national courts to set limits to the principle of gender equality in accordance with the constraints and demands of free market ideology. Significantly, the UK courts have interpreted the ECJ's jurisprudence as meaning that the objective justification stage requires in essence a balancing of the respective competing interests of the parties rather than an obligation on the defendant to show that his actions comply with the stricter principle of proportionality. [See, for example, the discussion of *Hampson* v *Department of Education and Science* [1990 2 All ER 25 in Chapter 2] . . .

Furthermore, and more importantly, a comparison between different sectors of EC Law [i.e., sex discrimination and free movement of persons] reveals the distinct lack of coherence of analysis on the part of the ECJ in resolving indirectly discriminatory situations. It is important to recognize and appreciate the significance of the absence of a common body of principles on indirect discrimination applicable to all EC equality provisions. The significance lies in the fact it is the sector of EC law upon which private individuals rely rather than the merits of the case which will probably be the most important factor in determining whether or not they will be able to mount a successful indirect discrimination claim. Quite clearly, it cannot be argued that the ECJ would arrive to the same conclusion irrespective of the methodology it has selected in the case law. The procedural variations between the various sectors have been more than enough to distort the outcome. The ECJ has developed a diversity of rules on indirect discrimination, their variation dependent upon the particular substantive context in issue. This sits most uncomfortably with the traditional view of indirect discrimination as an abstract concept capable of being applied generically irrespective of the particular facts and therefore raises the suspicion of the ECJ engaging in overtly political judgment. Certainly, the ECJ appears to impose, for instance, for the most part far stricter procedural hurdles for complainants of indirect discrimination based on gender as opposed to nationality. This may be accounted by the fact that the ECJ is more sensitive to any potential limitation of cross-border free movement, the cornerstone principle of the Single Market. However, there is no justification for such a differentiation, not least given the fact that the ECJ has also held that gender equality is a general fundamental principle in EC Law. In addition, it is surely the case that freedom of movement and equality are two separate and independent personal rights, whereby the former should not affect the analysis of the latter. Moreover, there is some evidence in the case law showing that the ECJ is applying the rules of indirect discrimination prohibitions more flexibly in favour of private as opposed to public law defendants. This may well be accounted for by an overriding sensitivity on the part of the ECJ towards the perception that private enterprise is the single most important foundation upon which the Single Market rests and depends.

A solution to this untenable state of affairs must lie in the ECJ adopting a consistent framework for all indirect discrimination cases which meets the need to establish a sufficient level of predictability as well as at the same time accommodating a substantive awareness of inequality. There is no doubt that the principle of equality has its limits as a rule of law in that it is dependent upon society's definitions and acceptance of who and what count as equals. This paper does not dispute the fact that the indirect discrimination prohibitions are tailored to ensuring that equality of access to markets is ultimately constrained according to the economic limits which may be imposed on the free market system. Within that context, however, the law must provide private individuals with clear guidance as to the relevant legal criteria which determine the extent of the right to equal treatment. In the *Bilka* case the ECJ demonstrated that it is possible to establish a workable framework which accommodates the advantages of abstract principles (legal certainty) with the need to assess the respective position of the parties realistically (substantive equality). Therefore, the basic two stage model of disproportionate impact followed by objective justification should be maintained with the caveat that realistic and workable burdens of proof are imposed on the respective parties.

Determining the issue of disproportionate impact on the basis of "risk" [as in *O'Flynn* v *Adjudication Officer* Case C–273/94 [1996] ECR I–2617, discussed in Chapter 2], as has been adopted in some free movement and sex discrimination cases, has the advantage in that it takes into account the fact that it is often difficult and costly for individual plaintiffs to locate precise and contemporaneous statistical data. The indirect tax discrimination cases illustrate the high level of unpredictability that ensues if judicial discretion is inserted in the definition of disproportionate impact. Adopting the more stringent test of absolute necessity with regard to objective justification would also take into account the greater bargaining power and social responsibility of employers and Member States as defendants vis-a-vis private individuals. This would ensure that the burden of substantiating objective justification remains high with the effect of encouraging potential defendants to take active steps to ensure that any distorted effects of their actions cannot be made more equitable by other measures. However, consideration of the criterion "legitimate needs" of the defendant in the objective justification equation, as is the case in the sex discrimination cases, should be discontinued, as it means that employers and Member States are less likely to be deterred from defending their policies through litigation and more likely to run the risk of not making their policies socially responsible.

However, it remains to be seen whether the ECJ will be in favour of harmonization. For the sake of certainty, if nothing else, it is hoped that it will. Otherwise, if the ECJ continues to abstain from setting down and abiding by some clear and comprehensive normative foundations and guidelines, litigation undertaken by private individuals to enforce indirect discrimination law in the EC will remain to a large extent an unduly costly lottery for them.

It was mentioned, above, that the *Enderby* case raised the question of the relationship, at the level of theory, between discrimination, on the one hand, and the s.1(3) defence on the other. It is clear from the discussion above that the two are related in the sense that that a factor which is "not the difference of sex" within s.1(3) must be one which is neither directly discriminatory nor, in the absence of adequate justification, indirectly discriminatory. But in *Enderby* v *Frenchay Health Authority* [1991] IRLR 44, EAT ruled that a mere difference in pay, in a case where a woman and her comparator were employed on like work, work rated as equivalent or work of equal value, was not sufficient to found an allegation of unintentional indirect discrimination without the identification of a barrier, requirement or condition causing disparate impact.

The Court of Appeal (*per* Neill LJ), saw "force in the argument that . . . discrimination by employers means or involves the application of some test or standard by employers whereby one individual is differentiated from another [and that therefore] before one considers whether there may be some justification for alleged unintentional indirect discrimination one has first to examine whether the employer applies any test or standard or erects any barrier based on sex at all" adopting the approach of the SDA discussed in Chapter 2. Nevertheless, it referred to the ECJ the question whether the employer's reliance on the separate negotiating structures which governed the pay, respectively, of the applicant her comparators, was objectively justifiable within Article 141. The employers (and the UK government) argued that objective justification could only be required in cases which fitted within the SDA's definition of indirect discrimination—where the applicant could point to criteria which a considerably smaller proportion of women than men could comply with and which had discriminatory effects because of the sex of the worker concerned.[78] But the ECJ took a different view:

Enderby v *Frenchay Health Authority* Case C–127/92

It is normally for the person alleging facts in support of a claim to adduce proof of such facts. Thus, in principle, the burden of proving the existence of sex discrimination as to pay

---

[78] This, as the Court of Appeal in *Enderby* pointed out, appears contrary to the dicta of Lord Bridge in *Leverton*: "the appellant, if she could establish that she was employed on work of equal value to that of "a man in the same employment", would prima facie be entitled under s 1(2)(c) to have the terms of her contract treated as modified as provided by the section to bring them into line with the terms of his contract.

lies with the worker who, believing himself to be the victim of such discrimination, brings legal proceedings against his employer with a view to removing the discrimination.

However, it is clear from the case law of the Court that the onus may shift when that is necessary to avoid depriving workers who appear to be the victims of discrimination of any effective means of enforcing the principle of equal pay. Accordingly, when a measure distinguishing between employees on the basis of their hours of work has in practice an adverse impact on substantially more members of one or other sex, that measure must be regarded as contrary to the objective pursued by Article 141 of the Treaty. unless the employer shows that it is based on objectively justified factors unrelated to any discrimination on grounds of sex [citing *Bilka-Kaufhaus . . . Kowalska* v *Freie und Hansestadt Hamburg* (Case C–33/89) [1990] ECR I–2591 [1990] IRLR 447 and *Nimz* v *Freie* (discussed below)]. Similarly, where an undertaking applies a system of pay which is wholly lacking in transparency, it is for the employer to prove that his practice in the matter of wages is not discriminatory, if a female worker establishes, in relation to a relatively large number of employees, that the average pay for women is less than that for men [citing *Danfoss*[79] (discussed above)] . . .

[I]f the pay of speech therapists is significantly lower than that of pharmacists and if the former are almost exclusively women while the latter are predominantly men, there is a *prima facie* case of sex discrimination, at least where the two jobs in question are of equal value and the statistics describing that situation are valid.

It is for the national court to assess whether it may take into account those statistics, that is to say, whether they cover enough individuals, whether they illustrate purely fortuitous or short-term phenomena. and whether, in general, they appear to be significant . . .[80]

Enderby fell to be considered once again by the Northern Ireland Court of Appeal in *British Road Services Ltd* v *Loughran and others*, the issue concerning whether the decision could be relied upon by women whose job was only 75%, rather than almost exclusively, female. The employers put forward, in support of their argument that the ECJ's decision did not apply, its reference, in paragraphs 4 and 6 of the extract above, to jobs "almost exclusively carried out by women". This argument convinced neither the tribunal nor the majority of the Court of Appeal.

British Road Services Ltd v *Loughran and others* [1997] IRLR 92

MacDermott LJ (for the majority):

. . . the mischief at which the legislation is aimed is women being paid less than men for performing work of equal value. Where the women are members of an exclusively female group it is fair to assume that there is discrimination—an assumption could not easily be made if that group were a mixed group. It seems to me that the more women there are in the group the easier it would be to draw an assumption in their favour—conversely, if there were more men in the group it is unlikely that such an assumption could be fairly drawn—indeed it probably could not be drawn at least without convincing evidence. I would also

---

[79] The ECJ also ruled in *Danfoss* that. where a pay system lacked transparency and resulted in lower wages for women than for men, the burden passed to the employer to disprove discrimination.

[80] For a recent problematic decision in one of the *Enderby* cases see *Evesham* v *North Hertfordshire Health Authority & Secretary of State for Health* [1999] IRLR 155.

add that the composition of a group may lead to a presumption one way or the other and in the light of relevant evidence that presumption will be revealed as sound or unsound and a final determination will be reached having regard to all the evidence . . .

Paragraph [2 of the *Enderby* extract immediately above] makes it clear that the existence of two non-discriminatory wage agreements do not "preclude a finding of prima facie discrimination": that reservation being necessary to prevent circumvention of the equal pay principle. In turn, paragraph [3] seems to be saying that where the claimant group is almost exclusively female and the other predominantly male such agreements are not *ipso facto* sufficient objective justification for the difference in pay between the two groups . . . paragraph [3] . . . recognises that a s.1(3) Stage 1 defence will not arise on the mere production of a non-discriminatory wage agreement where the applicant group is almost exclusively female. It does not say that where an applicant group contains fewer women than would exist in an "almost exclusively" situation that the working agreements viewed in the light of all the relevant circumstances may not show objective justification because the more men there are in an applicant group the greater is the chance of the wage differential not being sex-related.

It follows from this that if you get a group such as the present which is predominantly female the tribunal should at Stage 1 examine the facts to ascertain why a wage differential exists and whether or not it is due to sex discrimination.[81]

The Northern Ireland Court of Appeal demanded, in *British Road Services*, that the employer establish that the factor relied upon under s.1(3) was non-discriminatory. That court, on that occasion, broke ranks with the "category" approach which has so often been applied to s.1(3) and took into account the impact of the factor on male and female wages respectively. This is the only correct approach, given that the obligation is on the employer to prove, under s.1(3), that the disputed pay difference "is genuinely due to a material factor which is not the difference of sex". In order to be "not the difference of sex", the factor which gives rise to the pay difference must be one which discriminates either directly or (without justification) indirectly between women and men.

The decision in *British Road Services* was echoed by that of the House of Lords in *Ratcliffe and others* v *North Yorkshire County Council*. The facts of the case have been mentioned above. The applicants initially won their claim, a tribunal ruling that the "market forces" relied upon by the Council in this case could not be said to be "not the difference of sex". EAT allowed the employer's appeal, and the Court of Appeal ([1994] IRLR 342) rejected the women's appeal on the ground that they, *the applicants*, had failed to prove that the "market forces" relied on in this instance were indirectly discriminatory. The House of Lords allowed the women's appeal.

---

[81] The decision of the majority is consistent with the approach of the ECJ in *R* v *Secretary of State for Employment ex p Seymour-Smith*, in which that court took a flexible view to relative proportions of men and women affected by a practice in order that discriminatory impact be established.

Ratcliffe and others v *North Yorkshire County Council* [1995] 3 All ER 597, [1995] ICR 833, [1995] IRLR 441

Lord Slynn of Hadley:

. . . the three appellants . . . like some 1,300 other women, worked in different schools in the council's area serving school dinners, work which was done almost exclusively by women, who found that the hours of work fitted in well with their family responsibilities and who in the area where they lived might have found it difficult to obtain other work compatible with those responsibilities . . .

There has been much argument in this case as to the relationship between s.1 of the [EqPA] and s.1 of the [SDA]. The latter distinguishes between . . . "direct" . . . [and] "indirect" discrimination. It is submitted that this distinction must be introduced equally into the [EqPA]. For my part I do not accept that this is so . . . In my opinion the [EqPA] must be interpreted . . . without bringing in the distinction between so-called "direct" and "indirect" discrimination. The relevant question under the [EqPA] is whether equal treatment has been accorded for men and women employed on like work or for men and women employed on work rated as equivalent . . . In the present case . . . the women were found to be engaged on work rated as equivalent to work done by men. That is sufficient for the women to be entitled to a declaration by the industrial tribunal in their favour unless s 1(3) of the [EqPA], as set out previously, is satisfied.

This was the question for the industrial tribunal to consider. By a majority they were satisfied that the employers had failed to show that the variation between the appellants' contracts and those of their male comparators was due to a material factor which was not the difference of sex.

In my opinion it is impossible to say that they were not entitled on the evidence to come to that conclusion. It is obvious that the employers reduced the appellants' wages in order to obtain the area contracts and that to obtain the area contracts they had to compete with CCG who, the tribunal found, employed only women and "because of that, employed them on less favourable terms than the Council did previously under the NJC agreement". . . . The fact, if it be a fact, that CCG discriminated against women in respect of pay and that the DSO had to pay no more than CCG in order to be competitive does not, however, conclude the issue. The basic question is whether the DSO paid women less than men for work rated as equivalent. The reason they did so is certainly that they had to compete with CCG. The fact, however, is that they did pay women less than men engaged on work rated as equivalent. The industrial tribunal found and was entitled to find that the employers had not shown that this was genuinely due to a material difference other than the difference of sex.

The women could not have found other suitable work and were obliged to take the wages offered if they were to continue with this work. The fact that two men were employed on the same work at the same rate of pay does not detract from the conclusion that there was discrimination between the women involved and their male comparators. It means no more than that the two men were underpaid compared with other men doing jobs rated as equivalent . . .

The fact that they paid women less than their male comparators because they were women constitutes direct discrimination and *ex hypothesi* cannot be shown to be justified on grounds "irrespective of the sex of the person" concerned . . .

Lord Slynn's refusal, in this case, to distinguish between direct and indirect discrimination in the s.1(3) context, did not survive the subsequent decision of the House in *Strathclyde* v *Wallace*, considered below. It is very unlikely, in any event, that his intention was to preclude justification of an indirectly discriminatory GMF (if this was the case, employers could never pay more for seniority, overtime, flexibility, experience, or any other factor which tends to favour men). It is almost certainly the case that Lord Slynn was seeking simply to rule out the possibility that another court could, as the Court of Appeal did in this case, impose the burden of proving pay discrimination under s.1(3) upon the applicant. In *Strathclyde* v *Wallace*, Lord Browne-Wilkinson hastened to label that part of the earlier decision *obiter* and to state that:

Strathclyde Regional Council and others v Wallace and others [1998] 1 All ER 394, [1998] 1 WLR 259, [1998] ICR 205, [1998] IRLR 146

Whilst there is no need to apply to the [EqPA] the hard and fast statutory distinction between the two types of discrimination drawn in the [SDA], this House did not intend, and had no power, to sweep away all the law on equal pay under article [141] laid down by the European Court of Justice, including the concept of justifying, on *Bilka* grounds, practices which have a discriminatory effect on pay and conditions of service.[82]

Lord Browne-Wilkinson went on to suggest, in *Strathclyde*, that:

article [141] . . . does not draw the same firm legal demarcation between [direct and indirect discrimination] as does the [SDA] . . . [t]he correct position under s.1(3) of the [EqPA] is that even where the variation is genuinely due to a factor which involves the difference of sex, the employer can still establish a valid defence under sub-s (3) if he can justify such differentiation on the grounds of sex, *whether the differentiation is direct or indirect* (my emphasis).

Not only is this entirely at odds with the wording of s.1(3) which requires that the factor relied upon by the employer be "not the difference of sex", but it is also inconsistent with the approach taken to discrimination by the ECJ. The European Commission, in its submissions to the ECJ, has argued on a number of occasions for the recognition of a defence of justification to direct discrimination.[83] So, too, has Advocate-General Van Gerven.[84] But the ECJ has consistently refused to accept that direct discrimination can be justified—relying, occasionally, on sleight of hand to

---

[82] "The law on Article [141], whilst recognising that in many cases there is a *de facto* distinction between direct and indirect discrimination, does not draw the same firm legal demarcation between the two as does the [SDA] which permits justification of indirect discrimination but not of direct discrimination. The correct position under s.1(3) of the [EqPA] is that even where the variation is genuinely due to a factor which involves the difference of sex, the employer can still establish a valid defence under sub-s (3) if he can justify such differentiation on the grounds of sex, whether the differentiation is direct or indirect. I am not aware as yet of any case in which the European Court of Justice has held that a directly discriminatory practice can be justified in the *Bilka* sense. However, such a position cannot be ruled out since, in the United States, experience has shown that the hard and fast demarcation between direct and indirect discrimination is difficult to maintain".

[83] In *Birds Eye Walls*, fn 41 above, and in *Webb* v *EMO* Case C–32/93 [1994] 4 All ER 115, [1994] QB 718 [1994] IRLR 482.

[84] In *Birds Eye Walls*, *ibid* and in *Neath* v *Hugh Steeper*, fn 33 above.

avoid what would otherwise be regarded as an unacceptable outcome.[85] In *Grant* v *SouthWest Trains* (see above), Advocate General Elmer declared that:

> in its assessment of whether discrimination based on sex might be justified, the court has traditionally drawn a distinction between direct and indirect discrimination [citing *Dekker* v *Stichting Vormingscentrum voor Jong Volwassenen* (Case C–177/88 [1990] ECR I–3941), *Nimz* and *Enderby*] . . . Only where discrimination is indirect does the court appear to accept the possibility that it might be justified by reference to objective circumstances. . . In the present case, gender discrimination [is direct] . . .

The ECJ declined to follow the opinion of Advocate General Elmer, but did so on the grounds that no discrimination on the grounds of sex had occurred, rather than because any such discrimination was justified.[86]

A number of issues remain to be considered before we turn to the matter of remedies. The first concerns the question whether, in defending an equal pay claim, the employer has to establish that all of the disputed pay difference is explained by the factor put forward as a GMF. The second concerns whether the characterisation as "material" of factors put forward by the employer, as distinct from the requirement that these factors be "not the difference of sex". Finally, we consider the recent decision of the ECJ in the *Wiener* case.

Explaining part of the pay gap

In *National Coal Board* v *Sherwin* [1978] IRLR 122, EAT decided that the GMF put forward by the employer—the fact that the comparator worked on nightshift, explained just over half the pay difference between his pay and that of the applicants. This being the case, the tribunal "without falling into the error of setting itself up as a wage-fixing body may adjust the woman's remuneration . . . so that it is at the same rate as the man's, discounting for the fact that he works at inconvenient hours and she does not". In *Thomas* v *National Coal Board* [1987] IRLR 451, in a case involving different (similarly situated) applicants and the same comparator, a differently constituted EAT ruled that the employers had established that "a variation in . . . pay is genuinely due to a material factor other than the difference of sex". In this second case, as Claire Kilpatrick (extracted below) points out the failure of the factor to explain (all of) *the* difference, rather than *a* difference was "conspicuously ignored".

As Kilpatrick goes on to point out, in *Enderby* EAT accepted, as a GMF, a factor which explained only 10% of the pay differential at issue "where market forces are genuinely material, it is the whole of the difference which is justified", the alternative being

---

[85] In *Birds Eye Walls, ibid* the ECJ ruled that there had been no discrimination between men and women who did and did not respectively receive a bridging pension between 60 and 65, in *Neath, ibid*, that transfer payments did not amount to "pay" within Article 141.

[86] See also *Gillespie*, above, and *Pedersen*, fn 41 above In the latter, the Danish Government argued that justification should be permitted.

to "involve the Tribunal in a wage-fixing role [which] would be an unreal approach". There the Court of Appeal specifically referred to the ECJ the question whether this satisfied Article 141, the response of that Court being to the effect that "if . . . the national court has been able to determine precisely what proportion of the [difference] is due to [there,] market forces [and, it must be presumed, free of sex discrimination], it must necessarily accept that the pay differential is objectively justified to the extent of that proportion. When national authorities have to apply Community law, they must apply the principle of proportionality". If, on the other hand, it is not possible to determine precisely the extent to which the factor relied upon explains the pay differential "it is for the national court to assess whether the role of the [factor] in determining the rate of pay was sufficiently significant to provide objective justification for part or all of the difference".

This, as Kilpatrick puts it 'is weak normative language". In particular, it appears to ignore the ruling of the ECJ in *Danfoss* that:

Handels-og Kontorfunktionaerernes Forbund I Danmark v *Dansk Arbejdsgiverforening (acting for Danfoss)* (Case 109/88)

13 . . . where a system of individual pay supplements which is completely lacking in transparency is at issue, female employees . . . would be deprived of any effective means of enforcing the principle of equal pay before the national courts if the effect of adducing such evidence was not to impose upon the employer the burden of proving that his practice in the matter of wages is not in fact discriminatory.

14 . . . under Article 6 of the Equal Pay Directive Member States must, in accordance with their national circumstances and legal systems, take the measures necessary to ensure that the principle of equal pay is applied and that effective means are available to ensure that it is observed. The concern for effectiveness which thus underlies the directive means that it must be interpreted as implying adjustments to national rules on the burden of proof in special cases where such adjustments are necessary for the effective implementation of the principle of equality.

15 To show that his practice in the matter of wages does not systematically work to the disadvantage of female employees the employer will . . . be forced to make his system of pay transparent.

16 . . . The Equal Pay Directive must be interpreted as meaning that where an undertaking applies a system of pay which is totally lacking in transparency, it is for the employer to prove that his practice in the matter of wages is not discriminatory, if a female worker establishes, in relation to a relatively large number of employees, that the average pay for women is less than that for men.

It could be argued that, *contra* the general practice commented upon by Kilpatrick (citing *Enderby, Calder & Cizakowsky* v *Rowntree Mackintosh Confectionery Ltd* [1992] IRLR 165 and *Byrne* v *Financial Times Ltd* [1991] IRLR 417, *Enderby* and *Danfoss*, read together, ought to require that employers explain at least the bulk of any pay difference by reference to the factors relied upon.

"Material factors" and the GMF defence

Claire Kilpatrick, "Deciding When Jobs of Equal Value can be Paid Unequally: an Examination of s1(3) of the Equal Pay Act 1970" (1994) 23 *ILJ* 311

The interpretative division which has emerged in section 1(3) can be expressed as follows:

Interpretation 1: involves reading the section as follows, "*the* variation [in contractual terms] is [(i)] genuinely due to a *material* factor [(ii)] other than the difference of sex". This interpretation involves asking two different questions which are to be considered in the chronological order in which they are presented in the section. It will be demonstrated that, using this interpretation, a legal photograph is produced which tends to focus less on the employer than on the possibility of structural pay discrimination. This interpretation subjects the employers' reasons to a strict level of scrutiny and sees discrimination as an objective notion in that it views the nub of anti-discrimination legislation as being the fact of one sex being treated less favourably than the other.

Interpretation 2: can be presented as follows, "the variation [in contractual terms] is genuinely due to a material factor *other than the difference of sex*". Under this interpretation, the two questions posed in the first interpretation are elided. This places the stress on a difference other than sex being present and concurrently diminishes the importance of the requirement that the variation in pay is genuinely due to a material factor. Reasoning under Interpretation 2 stresses either the absence of a sexually based factor, the presence of another factor, or both these reasons presented simultaneously. This interpretation is linked to the idea that discrimination is a subjective notion, that is, that it is a particular form of conduct which is being stigmatized. Cases following this interpretation frequently focus on the behaviour or comportment of the "descriminator" and consequently produce a legal photograph which concentrates on the employer running the enterprise rather than on the fact of women being paid less than men for work of equal value. This interpretation is a misinterpretation of section 1(3) in that in practice it ignores the requirement for the factor to be "material". All of the cases raising a section 1(3) defence can be grouped under one of these two interpretations. . . .

Two cases, decided a decade apart, involving the same comparator highlight the different each of the interpretations can make. In both, women canteen assistants working on dayshifts compared themselves with Mr Tilstone who was employed as a canteen assistant on permanent nightshift, having been taken on at a special rate agreed in 1966 but which was subsequently abolished in 1975. The employers argued (i) the fact that he worked at night and (ii) a "red-circling" argument.

The EAT in *Sherwin* clearly utilizes Interpretation 1; "much was said in the course of argument about whether there was an element of sex discrimination involved, and whether the variation was accounted for by a difference of sex. *This, though not unimportant, does not seem to be the starting point.* One starts with the fact that there is a variation between the contracts of Mrs Sherwin and Mrs Spruce and Mr Tilstone's, and the first question is, has the employer shown that that variation is genuinely due to a material difference between their cases and his? *It is necessary to consider that question first* before going on to consider whether that material difference is a difference other than a difference of sex". Using this approach, the court accepted nightwork was a genuine material factor (but refused to accept that it accounted for all of the variation) and categorically rejected the "red-circling" argument stating that this was not a "red-circle case" and even if it was,

". . . the expression 'red-circle' is no more than useful shorthand and should not be used as a substitute for an analysis of precisely what is the material difference" alleged by the employer".

Following this case, the claims were settled with the two women involved and Mr Tilstone's pay continued to be protected, leaving him available to be a comparator a second time in *Thomas v NCB*, with implications for a much larger group of female employees. This time the EAT, employing Interpretation 2, stated the apposite question to be, "has the employer succeeded in establishing that a variation in terms relating to pay is genuinely due to a *material difference other than the difference of sex*". Following from this, the tribunal accepted the finding of the IT that (i) the remuneration was no greater than reasonably reflected the fact that he worked at night alone, and (ii) that if the employer had attempted to remove his personally protected pay rate, the union would have resisted and there might well have been an industrial dispute. The contrast between the approaches taken under the two interpretations is stark. While *Sherwin*, by demanding that the factor be "material", goes beyond the conveniently labelled "red-circle" argument, the approach of the EAT in *Thomas* reflects a marked reluctance to scrutinize the employer's reasons and upset established practice. . .

The mistake cases pose a general problem for equal value law as the factual situation where the pay differential is a genuine mistake and where the comparator does not represent a balanced or predominantly male class does not catch the type of situations which the equal value concept addresses, namely, the structural under-valuation of female-dominated jobs. However, as the Interpretation 1 case in this category argues, this is a matter to be resolved outside the confines of section 1(3) and, for our purposes, these cases highlight the difference between the two interpretations. While a mistake may not be "the difference of sex" (the primary emphasis of Interpretation 2) it may still not be "material" (the primary emphasis of Interpretation 1).

In the first case [*McPherson* v *Rathgael*], Ms McPherson, an outdoor pursuits instructor, brought an equal pay complaint because she was employed on like work with her comparator, Mr Millar, but received £1,500 less pay each year. This was due to the fact that, at the beginning of Mr Millar's employment, he was paid on a teachers' scale because of a mistaken belief that he had teaching qualifications which were recognized in N. Ireland. When this mistake was discovered the employers continued to pay him on the teachers' scale. The CA refused to accept that this reason established a section 1(3) defence. While sympathetic to the argument that the comparator was anomalous and to the finding of the IT that, "the decision to continue paying Mr Millar on the higher scale was a genuine decision, made in good faith without regard to sex", the course stated that the section requires the factor to be "material" and a gross but understandable error does not satisfy this requirement.

In the second case, *Yorkshire Blood Transfusion Service v Plaskitt* [[1994] ICR 74], the employers submitted under section 1(3) that the pay difference was due to their own mistake in placing the comparator on the wrong grade under the Whitley Council Rules. The EAT, overturning the IT's finding, stressed the subjective nature of the section, "As a matter purely of construction, the word 'genuinely', which appears before the words 'material factor' suggests that the question is a subjective one". Having determined this, they accepted the mistake as a material factor as "there was no evidence of intention to discriminate or actual discrimination . . . the plain fact is that the difference occurred because of a mistake and not because of anything which was "tainted with gender-based discrimination".

In *Tyldesley* v *TML Plastics*, EAT ruled that "a difference in pay explained by a factor not itself a factor of sex, or tainted by sex discrimination, should, in principle, constitute a valid defence" to an equal pay claim. There, the employer had appointed the applicant's comparator at a higher wage on the mistaken view that he was in possession of a particular qualification. A tribunal had ruled in the applicant's favour on the basis, *inter alia*, that "the employer had not established a good and objectively justified ground" for the pay differential. EAT allowed the employer's appeal, ruling that (*per* Mummery J) the tribunal had "erred in law in requiring the employer to satisfy a test of objective justification, apparently in addition to the matter specified expressly in s.1(3)".

It is true that s.1(3) requires the objective justification, in line with *Bilka* and subsequent decisions of the ECJ, only in cases where the factor relied upon by the employer was tainted by sex. It is also true that the tribunal had run together the "material factor" issue with that concerning the justification of indirect discrimination in appearing to require "objective justification" of the factor put forward by the employer as the GMF, absent any finding that it was tainted by sex. But it is entirely possible that the tribunal had done no more than to express, albeit imperfectly, a finding that the factor relied upon by the employer was not "material" and that, therefore, the s.1(3) defence failed even prior to the consideration of discrimination. But EAT entirely failed to advert to the need for a "material factor" in ruling in favour of the employers.

Tyldesley v *TML Plastics Ltd* [1996] ICR 356 [1996] IRLR 395

Mummery J (for EAT)

The [EqPA, Art 141] . . . and the Equal Pay Directive . . . have as their purpose the elimination of sex discrimination, not that of achieving "fair wages." Their detailed provisions are to be construed in the light of that purpose.

A difference in pay explained by a factor not itself a factor of sex, or tainted by sex discrimination, should, in principle, constitute a valid defence . . .

In the absence of evidence or a suggestion that the factor relied on to explain the differential was itself tainted by gender, because indirectly discriminatory or because it adversely impacted on women as a group in the sense indicated in *Enderby*, no requirement of objective justification arises [citing *Calder* v *Rowntree* and *Yorkshire Blood Transfusion Service* v *Plaskitt*] Thus, even if a differential is explained by careless mistake, which could not possibly be objectively justified, that would amount to a defence . . . provided that the tribunal is satisfied that the mistkae was either the sole reason for it or of sufficient influence to be significant or relevant. If a genuine mistake suffices, so must a genuine perception, whether reasonable or not, about the need to engage an individual with particular experience, commitment and skills[87].

Tyldesley was approved by the House of Lords in *Strathclyde* v *Wallace* in which their Lordships posed for themselves the question whether any and all factors relied upon by the employer under s.1(3) had to be "objectively justified".

---

[87] *Cf McPherson* v *Rathgael*, discussed by Kilpatrick, above and overruled by the House of Lords in *Strathclyde* v *Wallace*.

The equal pay claim was brought by a number of women teachers who named, as their comparators, male principal teachers with whom they were doing the same work while "acting up" without pay or appointment. A tribunal found that none of the factors relied upon by the employer were related to sex (most of the "acting up" teachers were male) but ruled in favour of the applicants on the ground that the employer's reliance upon these (albeit non-discriminatory) factors was not objectively justified. EAT overturned the decision of the tribunal, and was upheld in turn by the Court of Sessions and the House of Lords.

Strathclyde Regional Council and Others v *Wallace*

Lord Browne-Wilkinson

. . . Of the 134 unpromoted teachers who claimed to be carrying out the duties of principal teachers, 81 were men and 53 women. The selection by the appellants in this case of male principal teachers as comparators was purely the result of a tactical selection by these appellants: there are male and female principal teachers employed by the respondents without discrimination. Therefore the objective sought by the appellants is to achieve equal pay for like work regardless of sex, not to eliminate any inequalities due to sex discrimination. There is no such discrimination in the present case. To my mind it would be very surprising if a differential pay structure which had no disparate effect or impact as between the sexes should prove to be unlawful under the [EqPA] . . .

To establish a sub-s (3) defence, the employer has to prove that the disparity in pay is due to a factor "which is not the difference of sex", ie is not sexually discriminatory. The question then arises "what is sexually discriminatory"? Both the [SDA] and Article [141] of the EEC Treaty recognise [direct and indirect discrimination]. . . Under the SDA, direct sexual discrimination is always unlawful. But, both under the SDA and under Article [141], indirect discrimination is not unlawful if it is "justified" [citing *Bilka-Kaufhaus*]. Indirect discrimination can be "justified" if it is shown that the measures adopted by the employers which cause the adverse impact on women "correspond to a real need on the part of the [employers], are appropriate with a view to achieving the objectives pursued and are necessary to that end" [citing *Rainey*].

The cases establish that the [EqPA] has to be construed so far as possible to work harmoniously both with the [SDA] and Article [141]. All three sources of law are part of a code dealing with unlawful sex discrimination: see *Shields* v *Coomes* . . . and *Garland* v *British Rail Engineering Ltd.* . . . It follows that the words "not the difference of sex" where they appear in s 1(3) of the [EqPA] must be construed so as to accord with the SDA and Article [141], ie an employer will not be able to demonstrate that a factor is "not the difference of sex" if the factor relied upon is sexually discriminatory whether directly or indirectly. Further, a sexually discriminatory practice will not be fatal to a sub-s (3) defence if the employer can "justify" it applying the test in the *Bilka-Kaufhaus* case. . .

There is no question of the employer having to "justify" (in the Bilka sense) all disparities of pay. Provided that there is no element of sexual discrimination, the employer establishes a sub-s (3) defence by identifying the factors which he alleges have caused the disparity, proving that those factors are genuine and proving further that they were causally relevant to the disparity in pay complained of. . . [88]

---

[88] Approving decision of EAT in *Tyldesley* v *TML Plastics Ltd* and overruling that of the NICA in *McPherson* v *Rathgael*.

It appeared, on the facts in *Wallace*, that s.1(3)'s requirement that the pay difference at issue result from "a material factor" was met. But the failure of the House of Lords to advert to that fact, in stressing that only discriminatory factors require to be justified, is unfortunate. Further, their Lordships once again failed adequately to address the question whether the pay-related factor put forward in *Wallace* was in fact untainted by sex.

Lord Browne-Wilkinson did, it is true, state that most of the "acting up" teachers were male. But he did not divulge whether an even greater proportion of principal teachers were men. If this was the case (as is likely), the denial of the disputed payments to "acting up" teachers would have constituted *prima facie* pay discrimination. And if this had been established, the employers should have been required to justify the practice whereby women performing the duties of a principal teacher were considerably less likely than men performing those duties to be accredited and rewarded as a principal teacher.[89] It may have been demonstrable that this situation was unavoidable in the absence of an (unlawful) decision on the part of employers to restrict the proportion of women "acting up". But, had their Lordships taken account of the sex composition of principal teachers, the justifiability of the employer's pay practices would, at least, have been open to scrutiny.

Turning, finally, to the decision of the ECJ in *Angestelltenbetriebsrat der Wiener Gebietskrankenkasse* v *Wiener Gebietskrankenkasse* Case C–309/97 (available at http://europa.eu.int/eur-lex/en/index.html), the case concerned a claim made by women psychotherapists working in the Austrian health service who chose, as their comparators, male psychotherapists employed in the same organisation. The women were graduate psychologists, the men doctors. Their pay was determined in accordance with different scales applicable, respectively, to administrative staff, health staff and dental technicians, and to doctors and dentists. The respondents relied on the different training and qualifications of the two groups of psychotherapists which comprised, respectively, eighteen women and six men (graduate psychologists), and two women and eight men (doctors).

It was clear on the facts that the differential payment of the two groups of psychotherapists served to disadvantage women only 10% of whom (as compared with almost 60% of the men) qualified for the higher rate of pay. The employers, however, argued that the differential impact by sex of its pay practices was, "a pure coincidence". The national court ruled that "the differential rates of pay for doctors and psychologists working as psychotherapists had been agreed upon by the parties to the collective agreements and are justified by the fact that the obligations incumbent on the two groups of professionals are not the same: only doctors employed as specialists are required also to perform other medical tasks in an emergency". This ruling was made despite the acceptance by that court of the fact that "the same tasks [we]re per-

---

[89] If, for example, there were 200 men and 50 women principal teachers, as well as 81 men and 51 women "acting up", only 50/101 women performing as principal teachers would be rewarded as such, by comparison with 200/281 men (49.5% and 71.2% respectively).

formed over a considerable length of time (several salary periods)" by the two groups concerned.

Taking into account the jurisprudence of the ECJ on equal pay, it might have been expected that the Court would have remarked upon the *prima facie* case of discrimination inherent in the differential payment of broadly similar work[90] and progressed to consider the question of objective justification. Instead, it ruled as follows:

15. the Court has consistently held that discrimination involves the application of different rules to comparable situations or the application of the same rule to different situations [citing *Gillespie*, discussed above and in Chapter 6]

16. . . . in *Enderby* the Court did not rule on whether the functions performed by members of the different professions in question were of equal value . . .

17. In order to determine whether the work being done by different persons is the same, it is necessary to ascertain whether, taking account of a number of factors such as the nature of the work, the training requirements and the working conditions, those persons can be considered to be in a comparable situation . . .

18. Thus, where seemingly identical tasks are performed by different groups of persons who do not have the same training or professional qualifications for the practice of their profession, it is necessary to ascertain whether, taking into account the nature of the tasks that may be assigned to each group respectively, the training requirements for performance of those tasks and the working conditions under which they are performed, the different groups in fact do the same work within the meaning of Article 119 of the Treaty.

19. . . . professional training is not merely one of the factors that may be an objective justification for giving different pay for doing the same work [citing *Danfoss*] . . . it is also one of the possible criteria for determining whether or not the same work is being performed.

20. . . . although psychologists and doctors employed as psychotherapists by the Health Fund perform seemingly identical activities, in treating their patients they draw upon knowledge and skills acquired in very different disciplines, the expertise of psychologists being grounded in the study of psychology, that of doctors in the study of medicine. Furthermore, the national court emphasises that, even though doctors and psychologists both in fact perform work of psychotherapy, the former are qualified also to perform other tasks in a field which is not open to the latter, who may only perform psychotherapy.

21. In those circumstances, two groups of persons who have received different professional training and who, because of the different scope of the qualifications resulting from that training, on the basis of which they were recruited, are called on to perform different tasks or duties, cannot be regarded as being in a comparable situation.

22. That finding is not contradicted by the fact that a single tariff is charged for psychotherapeutic treatment, an arrangement which may be the result of social policy.

The result of the decision in *Wiener* was to preclude scrutiny of pay practices which demonstrably served to disadvantage women by dint of denying that comparison was

---

[90] In particular, the *Enderby* case which concerned men and women doing work which was accepted, for the purposes of the reference, as being of equal value.

possible. This was the same approach taken by the Court in *Gillespie*, above, to the issue of maternity pay. And in *Barry* v *Midland Bank plc* case, [1999] 1 WLR 1465, [1999] ICR 859, [1999] 3 All ER 974 [1999] IRLR 581, which was considered in Chapter 2, a similar approach was taken by the House of Lords in an SDA claim. This particular development in the law relating to discrimination should be regarded with alarm. If it is taken to its logical conclusion, its effect would be to deny the protection of anti-discrimination legislation to all except those who are able to conform to the prevailing (generally white, male) model whose pre-eminence it is surely the function of such law to challenge.[91] It is to be hoped that the decision in *Wiener* is indicative only of a temporary lapse in the jurisprudence of the ECJ and, in particular, would not be applied in a case in which equal value had been established as between the male and female jobs at issue.

REMEDIES

The mechanism employed by the EqPA—i.e., the insertion into the successful applicant's contract of an "equality clause"—has been discussed above. The remedy to which applicants become entitled consists both of this, with its impact on subsequent wages, etc. and, where relevant, of damages in respect of the under-payment of past services. These damages are limited by s.2(5), which provides that:

> A woman shall not be entitled, in proceedings brought in respect of a failure to comply with an equality clause . . . to be awarded any payment by way of arrears of remuneration or damages in respect of a time earlier than two years before the date on which the proceedings were instituted".

We saw in Chapter 5 that procedural limitations are acceptable under EU law only where (*Rewe-Zentralfinanz eG* v *Landwirtschaftskammer für das Saarland* Case C–33/76 [1976] ECR (1989) they neither render the Community right impossible or excessively difficult to secure, nor are less favourable than the rules regulating actions in respect of similar rights of a domestic nature.

In *Levez* v *Jennings (Harlow Pools) Ltd*, *Hicking* v *Basford Group Ltd (No.2)* [1999] IRLR 764, [1999] 3 CMLR 715, [2000] ICR 58, EAT ruled that s.2(5) was unenforceable. The decisions followed that of the ECJ in *Levez* v *Jennings* Case C– 326/96 [1999] All ER (EC) 1, in which that Court had ruled that s.2(5) could not be applied in a case in which the delay in bringing proceedings flowed from the employer's deceit, any such application rendering impossible or excessively difficult the exercise of the applicant's rights under Article 141. Similarly, in *Magorrian and Cunningham* v *Eastern Health and Social Services Board and Department of Health and Social Services* Case C–246/96 [1997] ECR I–7153 [1998] All ER (EC) 38, the two-year rule was found in breach of

[91] Litigation arising under the DDA will perhaps be protected by that legislation's express imposition of a duty of reasonable adjustment.

Article 141 on the facts of the particular case (there concerning access to pension rights).[92]

Neither the decision of the ECJ in *Levez* nor that in *Magorrian* excluded the possibility that s.2(5) might, in the general run of cases, be compatible with Community law or that, in any event, the imposition of such a rule coupled with a degree of flexibility in particular cases would be so compatible. In *Levez*, the ECJ went so far as to state that: "a national rule under which entitlement to arrears of remuneration is restricted to the two years preceding the date on which the proceedings were instituted is not in itself open to criticism". But in *Levez* the ECJ accepted EAT's invitation to consider the second limb of *Rewe*—the principle of equivalence as between procedural rules governing domestic and Community causes of action.

Having stated the principle that it was for "the national court—which alone has direct knowledge of the procedural rules governing actions in the field of employment law" to determine this question having considered "both the purpose and the essential characteristics of allegedly similar domestic actions" and taking into account "the role played by that provision in the procedure as a whole, as well as the operation and any special features of that procedure before the different national courts" the judgment in *Levez* went on to dismiss the UK Government's argument that, the EqPA having predated the accession of the UK to the EC and the application in domestic law of Article 141, the appropriate comparison was between the (identical) restrictions imposed by the EqPA on claims arising under domestic and EC law.

> 48. Following the accession of the United Kingdom to the Communities, the Act constitutes the legislation by means of which the United Kingdom discharges its obligations under Article [141] of the Treaty and, subsequently, under the [Equal Pay] Directive. The Act cannot therefore provide an appropriate ground of comparison against which to measure compliance with the principle of equivalence.
>
> 49. It is . . . suggested that claims to those based on the Act may include those linked to breach of a contract of employment, to discrimination in terms of pay on grounds of race, to unlawful deductions from wages or to sex discrimination in matters other than pay.

When *Levez* returned for decision by EAT, it was heard together with a case in which no allegation of deceit on the part of the employer was made. Morison J, for EAT, refused to distinguish between the two cases: "Either section 2(5) is in conflict with European principles or it is not . . . there will be many cases where an employee does not know the true facts about the salaries of the alleged comparators. . . It seems to us inherently improbable that the decision of the ECJ is contingent upon fraud being found . . .". EAT accepted the arguments put forward on behalf of the applicants that the appropriate comparison was between the EqPA's limitation and that— six years—which was imposed by the Limitation Act 1980 in respect of other contract-based claims.

---

[92] See also the more recent decision of that Court in *Preston and others* v *Wolverhampton Healthcare NHS Trust and others*; *Fletcher and others* v *Midland Bank plc* Case C–78/98 (available at http://europa.eu. int/eur-lex/en/index.html) other aspects of which are discussed in Chapter 5.

11

Discrimination Law: Likely Developments

Chapters 1–10 considered the current legal regulation of discrimination in the UK. Many of the weaknesses in the present law have been highlighted throughout the text, and attention has been drawn to impending legal developments (among these the amendment of the domestic definition of indirect discrimination to reflect that set out in the burden of proof directive; the new race discrimination directive; and changes to the investigatory powers of the CRE and EOC to match those of the newly established DRC). Here we consider more fundamental questions about the possible form and substance of future legislation concerning discrimination.

SCOPE OF DISCRIMINATION PROHIBITIONS

The 1999 draft equal treatment general framework directive has been mentioned throughout the text. If it is adopted (and if, in this context, is a big question, as we saw in Chapter 1), the UK will be obliged to implement legislative prohibitions against discrimination based on age and sexual orientation and to extend the legislative prohibition on discrimination based on religion beyond Northern Ireland to Great Britain.[1]

The incorporation by the Human Rights Act 1998 of the European Convention prohibition on discrimination will impose domestically justiciable obligations on the state in respect of sexual orientation and religious discrimination as well as discrimination based on language, political or other opinion, social origin, property, birth or other status" (Article 14). The ECnHR prohibitions on discrimination are currently restricted, as we saw in Chapter 1, to discrimination in the exercise of the rights guaranteed by that Convention. But the acceptance by the ECtHR of matters pertaining to sexual orientation as connected with Article 8's "private and family life", together with the protection accorded by Article 9 to religion, bring discrimination in these areas firmly within the ECnHR frame (although as we saw in Chapter 1, the application of the ECnHR's provisions to the employment field remains uncertain). And the impending adoption by the Council of Europe of the twelfth Protocol to the

---

[1] Assuming here that the prohibition by the FETO of discrimination on grounds of "religious belief" is sufficient to protect from discrimination on grounds of "belief" within the ECnHR.

Convention, which requires that "the enjoyment of any right set forth by law shall be secured without discrimination" on the grounds set out in Article 14, will create a free-standing right to freedom from discrimination on these grounds.

We saw, in Chapter 1, that the approach taken under the ECnHR to "discrimination" is, at times, impoverished, particularly in those cases where, as in *Ahmad* v *UK*, exercise of a Convention freedom (there religion) requires accommodation from others. In addition, the obligations imposed by the HRA are fully binding only on the state. But it is at least possible that the British courts, accustomed as they increasingly are to applying the indirect discrimination provisions of the RRA, SDA and (in Northern Ireland) the FETO, and the duty of reasonable adjustment imposed by the DDA, will adopt a similar approach to discrimination under the HRA.[2] And the imposition by the HRA of duties on the domestic courts to give effect, where possible, to the ECnHR provisions in interpreting domestic legislation and developing the common law, will provide significant scope for progress.

In light of these developments, significant legislative change must be considered likely. The current government has not resisted the expansion of prohibited grounds of discrimination, voluntarily incorporating into domestic law the provisions of the ECnHR and expressing enthusiasm for the 1999 draft directive agreeing the adoption in June 2000 of the new race discrimination directive[3] agreeing on equal treatment in employment in June 1999, the UK also ratified ILO Convention 111 (Discrimination (Employment and Occupation) Convention, 1958) which (Article 3(b)) imposes on the government an obligation "to enact such legislation and to promote such educational programmes as may be calculated to secure the acceptance of" the prohibition of discrimination in employment on grounds (Article 1) of:

> race, colour, sex, religion, political opinion, national extraction or social origin, which has the effect of nullifying or impairing equality of opportunity or treatment in employment or occupation [and] such other distinction, exclusion or preference which has the effect of nullifying or impairing equality of opportunity in employment or occupation as may be determined by the Member State concerned after consultation with representative employers and workers' organisations, where such exist, and with other appropriate bodies.

Ratifying the Convention, Employment and Equal Opportunities Minister Andrew Smith declared that "we see no place for any unjustified discrimination in today's workplace. . . This government's aim is to make equality a reality so that, in the way in which it treats every one of its people, Britain is a beacon to the world".[4]

---

[2] Only individuals, rather than governments, can petition the ECtHR. It is unclear whether this will encourage UK courts to err on the side of applicants, to avoid appeal to the ECtHR or (perhaps more likely) on the side of the government on the basis that a *de facto* right of appeal remains open to applicants.

[3] In his response to the Commission proposals, Secretary of State for Education and Employment David Blunkett stated that he was "confident that we can help develop anti-discrimination practices across Europe. The extension of such measures will ensure fair treatment for British nationals working or studying in other Member States", Press Release, Department for Education and Employment, available at http://195.44.11.137/coi/coipress.nsf.

[4] Press Release 252/99, Department for Education and Employment, *ibid.*

What is noteworthy is the tension between the government's apparent enthusiasm for anti-discrimination provisions, and its reluctance to legislate in these matters. The increasing pressure for the inclusion of sexual orientation as a prohibited ground for discrimination has been adverted to throughout the text. Not only has the ECtHR indicated, in the *Smith & Grady* and the *Lustig-Prean & Beckett* cases (respectively 29 EHRR 493 and 548 (2000)), that employment-related discrimination on these grounds[5] contravenes the convention, but the ECJ may well adopt a similar approach in a suitable case (one which concerns dismissal or non-recruitment on grounds of sexual orientation, rather than the more complex partner-benefit situation which arose in *Grant* v *South-West Trains*).[6]

Whether or not the ECJ does interpret "sex" to include "sexual orientation", and whether or not the 1999 draft equal treatment general framework directive is adopted in its present form, EC legislation must be regarded as likely in the near future. Ireland was always regarded (accurately) as extremely conservative on "moral" issues. It retained a complete criminal prohibition on homosexual sexual activity until obliged by the ECtHR to modify it. Of all EU Member States, Ireland has the most restrictive abortion legislation (a complete Constitutional prohibition).[7] Divorce was constitutionally prohibited in Ireland until 1996. And for all this, in 1998 Ireland's Employment Equality Act prohibited discrimination on grounds of sexual orientation as well as on grounds of gender, age, race, marital status, family status, religious belief, disability or membership of the traveller community.

Almost bizarrely, in view of past and likely developments, the UK Government has set its face against the inclusion of sexual orientation within the SDA (which has, as we saw in Chapter 6, already been amended to regulate discrimination on grounds of gender reassignment). Attempts were made also to amend the Employment Relations Bill 1998 (later the ERA 1999) to permit the Secretary of State to prohibit sexual orientation discrimination in the workplace, the House of Lords Sexual Orientation Discrimination Bill having failed to pass the Commons in 1997. The Government response was to accept that "a gap exists in the protection that we offer some individuals", to "deplore discrimination on the basis of sexual orientation" and declare its revulsion with "the treatment that some gay men and lesbians continue to suffer",[8] but to declare that the Bill was "not the appropriate vehicle to deal with that important, wide-ranging new topic as it would . . . clearly require extensive consultation". The

---

[5] Previous decisions all concerned criminal prohibitions, and in *Dudgeon* (1981) A 45, 4 EHRR 149, even differential ages of consent were regarded as acceptable, a stance altered in *Sutherland v United Kingdom* (Commission's Report of 1 July 1997), App 25186/94 CO 22. For possible implications of *Smith* and *Lustig-Prean* see Chapters 1 and 6.

[6] The decision in *Grant* (Case C–249/96 [1998] ECR I–3739) did not confine itself to the facts, the ECJ stating that discrimination on grounds of sexual orientation simply was not sex discrimination, but, as we saw in Chapter 6, this was based on an incorrect understanding (it transpired) of the ECtHR's position and could easily be confined to its facts.

[7] Subject, at that time, only to the mother's life.

[8] At this time, 23rd March 1999, the ban on gays in the military was still in place and the Government was defending it at the ECtHR.

Government found it "too early to be clear whether a legislative measure would be the appropriate way to proceed" and rejected the proposed amendment while insisting that "our differences are only over the means and not the objectives".

The sexual orientation amendment was moved at Report stage in the Lords,[9] Lord Razall noting the Labour Party's manifesto commitment "to seek to end unjustifiable discrimination wherever it exists" and the Government's commitment, in response to an unsuccessful bill on the issue in 1997, to give serious consideration to the issue:

> A year later, we are still waiting for the Government to bring forward proposals to deal with this important issue. We are . . . only two years or so away from the next General Election. We have been waiting since Labour's election for this important matter to be dealt with and the Government have stated consistently that they will address it. However, my colleagues and I are beginning to suspect that the Government are adopting what I call the St Augustine position: "I have every intention of becoming pure, but not yet. In any event, it is not my departmental responsibility".[10]

The Government maintained its position, Lord Sainsbury stating that:

> we are very sympathetic to the problems faced by people who have been, and will be, discriminated against on grounds of sexual orientation . . . As the issue needs to be handled with great sensitivity, it is incumbent upon us to ensure that, whatever action is taken, the results will not be counter-productive for gay men and lesbians.

The Government has elected to proceed on this matter by means of a non-binding Code of Practice, although it has pledged to reconsider the matter if the Code proves ineffective. The reluctance to legislate on sexual orientation discrimination (and the government's one-time suggestion, noted in Chapter 6, that transsexuals ought perhaps lawfully to be prevented from working with children) may result from the popular opposition to the repeal of "clause 28" (in June 2000 the repeal is pending a third House of Lords vote, though the Scottish Parliament has secured repeal there) and the equalisation of homosexual and heterosexual ages of consent. It may alternatively, or additionally, be due to its more general emphasis on avoiding "unnecessary" regulation.

In 1996, the then opposition Labour spokesman on employment, Ian McCartney MP, stated that "an incoming Labour government will introduce comprehensive legislation to make age discrimination in employment illegal".[11] But in 1998 the Labour Government resisted an attempt to amend the Employment Relations Bill 1998 to permit the Secretary of State to prohibit work-place discrimination on this ground. According to Michael Wills MP, Minister for Small Businesses, Firms and Industry:[12]

---

[9] Also in the Commons 30th March 1999, defeated.

[10] HL Debs 15th July 1999, col. 563, available at http://www.publications.parliament.uk /pa/ld/ldhansrd.htm.

[11] HC Debs 9th February 1996; col. 618, available at http://www.publications. parliament.uk/pa/cm/cmhansrd.htm.

[12] Standing Committee E, new clause 7 and 8 proposed by Mr Chidgey MP who argued that workplace discrimination on these grounds was "just as prevalent and pernicious as any other form of discrimination"

The Government believes that unfair age discrimination in employment is bad for the individual, bad for business and bad for the country . . . The use of legislation has not proved to be the best way forward in such a complex area . . . effective legislation covering age discrimination raise[s] some very complex issues, not least where the retirement age itself is discriminatory. That is why the Government are taking a measured approach, taking forward a range of initiatives that will help older people and bring about cultural change, and using the lessons learned from those initiatives to inform future plans.[13]

The Government published a non-statutory Code of Practice in 1999, having committed itself to monitoring the effectiveness of the Code and carrying out a full evaluation of its effectiveness by February 2001.[14] *Age Diversity in Employment*,[15] by contrast with the Codes issued by the CRE and EOC on discrimination in employment, the Guidance and the Codes of Practice on disability issued by the Department for Education and Employment, is indicative only of good practice. It provides numerous examples of how employers who wish not to discriminate may avoid doing so, and of why age-related discrimination is not in the interests of employers, but can provide no substitute for legally binding rules.

The final ground of discrimination in respect of which regulation is being considered on the domestic level is that of religious belief. We saw throughout the book and, in particular, in Chapter 9, that discrimination based on religious belief and political opinion has been unlawful in Northern Ireland since 1976. Elsewhere in the UK religious belief is unprotected except in cases where it is sufficiently connected with race to fall within the provisions of the RRA (as in the case of Sikhs and Jews—see further Chapter 7). Further, religious discrimination is entrenched within English law to the extent that blasphemy (an almost entirely unused, but symbolically significant, offence)[16] protects only those of Christian sensibilities and (an issue of recent if not, apparently, immediate practical concern) the heir to the throne may not marry a Catholic and accede.[17] In addition, state schools are generally required to adopt a broadly Christian ethos, state funding having been extended to non-Christian schools (two each Jewish and Moslem, one each Seventh Day Adventist and Sikh by December 1999) only since the election of the (New) Labour Government in May

---

(23rd March 1999, Committee on the Employment Relations Bill available at www.publications.parliament.uk/pa/cm199899/cmstand/e/cmemp.htm). The MP cited a recent Institute of Management survey which found 69% of support amongst its managers for the restriction of age limits in job advertisements, 65% support for comprehensive legislation

[13] Similarly with the age and sexual orientation amendments proposed in the Commons (HC Debs 30th Mar 1999, col. 930 ff available as at fn 11 above).

[14] Somewhat oddly, the Labour Party's national policy forum report 1999 promised ' tough action on age, gender and race discrimination".

[15] Available on the DfEE's website at http://www.dfee.gov.uk/agediversity/index.htm.

[16] There was one prosecution (Mary Whitehouse of *Gay News*) in almost 80 years.

[17] *Daily Telegraph* 17th December 1999 reports friction between Scottish and Westminster Parliaments, the ban being part of the Act of Settlement. Prime Minister Blair rebuffed a unanimous demand from the Scottish Parliament to repeal the Act.

1997.[18] (Anglican bishops are soon to be joined in the reformed House of Lords by senior religious figures of different faiths.)

In 1995, Tariq Modood argued for an understanding of "cultural racism" which he defined in terms of "the willingness of white working-class youth to incorporate young black men and women into their culture, and even emulate them, while hardening their attitudes against groups seen to be assertively different and not trying to fit in, such as Asians and Moslems.[19] The CRE was attacked by Moslem newspaper editors in the same year for adopting a secular stance and, in the view of the editors, failing to give due recognition to the fact that more than half of the country's ethnic minority population were Moslem. According to the *Guardian* (20th September 1995):

> Pointing to the increasingly anti-Muslim nature of racial incidents, the two editors claim . . . that only racial categories such as "Asian" or "Black" are recognised by the Commission and say that "pretending that Muslims don't exist in Britain is an exercise in community disaster".

The CRE pointed out in its defence, the restriction of its statutory remit to race rather than religion and its support in its second review of the RRA for the extension of the criminal law to prohibit incitement to racial hatred. In 1996 the Commission decided to take action on religious discrimination whether or not such discrimination fell within the strict terms of its remit,[20] and in 1997 the CRE began to call for legislation against religious discrimination. In the same year the Policy Studies Institute report *Ethnic Disadvantage in Britain: The Fourth National Survey of Ethnic Minorities* reported that 80% of Asians did not regard themselves as black, seeing themselves rather in terms of their Hindu, Moslem or Sikh religious affiliations,[21] and the Runnymede Trust reported that "Islamophobia" was in danger of becoming "part of the fabric of everyday life . . . It's getting more explicit. It's getting more extreme. It's getting more dangerous".[22] The Trust reported that many Moslems "live in poor housing, they have poor education. There's very high level[s] of unemployment. Over 50 per cent of British Moslems in inner cities are unemployed".[23]

In June 1997, the media reported that the newly elected (New) Labour Government intended to incorporate religion within the protections of the RRA in Autumn 1997.[24] Plans to extend the coverage of blasphemy beyond the protection of Anglicans were

---

[18] *Guardian* 1st December 1999. In practice (*Guardian* 9th April 1996), a fudge was adopted with students (sometimes a majority) exercising the right to opt out of Christian religious education and have alternative religious lessons in their own faith.

[19] Fulbright Colloquium on race and racism in Britain and America, discussed in the *Sunday Times* 26th March 1995.

[20] *Guardian* 3rd October 1996.

[21] According to the *Guardian,* 12th June 1997, there are one million Moslems in Britain.

[22] The Policy Studies Institute also found increasingly prevalent discrimination against Moslems. The Runnymede Trust report is discussed in Agence France *Presse* 22nd October 1997.

[23] *Ibid*, citing Gordon Conway of the Trust.

[24] June 12th 1997, *Guardian*, July 30th 1997 *Daily Telegraph*.

also floated, though Home Secretary Jack Straw acknowledged that it was a "very, very difficult area".[25]

In October of the same year the Home Secretary was reported as having rejected calls for a change in the law. [26] According to the Home Secretary: "Race legislation is not the answer to the particular problem of the Moslem community and religious discrimination legislation may not be the answer either".[27] In October 1999, Lord Ahmed introduced a debate on religious discrimination in the House of Lords, calling attention to increasing incidents of anti-Islamic discrimination:[28]

> According to the *Asian Times* this week, another mosque was burned down in Portsmouth by an arson attack last week. A few weeks ago I met a young Asian barrister in Bradford who is unable to get a pupilage or training contract because of his beard. There are scores of people who have difficulty in obtaining permission from their employers to celebrate religious festivals like Eid and Diwali. There are dozens of women who have been discriminated against because of the dress they wear.[29]

Lord Bassam, for the Government, responded to the effect that the Government was committed to a multi-cultural, multi-faith society and that "in order to achieve that vision, the Government are determined to tackle and eliminate discrimination and intolerance." He pointed to the impending implementation of the HRA as:

> a major new initiative and [one which] will help us create a new culture of rights and responsibilities in the UK . . . Those include rights relating directly to religion. In particular of course there is Article 9: the right to freedom of thought, conscience and religion. But other ECHR rights also touch on religion—for example, Article 10; as does Article 8, the right to respect for private and family life.
>
> The ECHR is about balance. Yes, there are rights, but as Strasbourg says, there are limits to those rights. And sometimes the state has to interfere with them. It is a matter of balancing the rights of the individual with the needs of society as a whole. The Human Rights Act is about balance: balancing one right with another and balancing rights with responsibilities.
>
> Nowhere is that balance more important than with religious matters. It is essential that we have an effective dialogue on religious discrimination. And I know that the Human Rights Act will be a great help in developing that dialogue. . .
>
> On the question of racially aggravated offences which were introduced in the Crime and Disorder Act 1998, . . . [its] provisions . . . protect everyone from racist crime. During the passage of the Bill, a number of noble Lords raised the issue of whether those offences would cover an attack made on a Muslim . . . We believe in practice that most cases, which may appear to have a religious element, will also have a racial element. We do not believe

---

[25] The *Scotsman* 30th July 1997, Jack Straw to the Select Committee on Home Affairs.

[26] 22nd October 1997 Press Association *Newsfile*, on Jack Straw's response to the Runnymede Trust. According to the Home Office there were no immediate plans, though future legislation had not been ruled out.

[27] Agence France *Presse* 22nd October 1997.

[28] HC Debs 28th October 1999, col. 454 ff, available as at fn 12 above.

[29] *Ibid*, col. 456.

that when the perpetrators of those offences attack Muslims they do so because of hostility towards the tenets of Islam. They do so because of racist hostility towards the victim and towards the ethnic minority groups that are associated with the Muslim faith in this country. The test of what amounts to "racially aggravated" for the purposes of these offences requires that racial hostility is "wholly or partly" a motivating factor . . .

the [RRA] . . . makes unlawful direct or indirect discrimination against a group of persons in Great Britain defined by reference to colour, race, nationality (including citizenship) or ethnic or national origins. Th[e] decision [in *Mandla*] has led to the anomaly where certain faith groups receive legal protection from discrimination which is denied to other faith groups. However, in practice, the difference might not be so great. The existing evidence, of which there is very little, suggests that in the vast majority of cases discrimination suffered by followers of minority faiths is based on their ethnicity rather than their beliefs. And where discrimination is based on ethnicity there is protection under the 1976 Act; as in the case of an Asian Muslim woman who is discriminated against as a result of wearing the hijab . . .[30]

Is that discrimination motivated by the hijab as a symbol of Muslim identity? We in this House recognise that the hijab is exactly that; a proud declaration of a Muslim woman's identity and faith. I suggest that the mind that harbours ignorant and racist views sees the hijab only as a symbol of ethnicity and the motivation of racism.

The Government are alive to the concerns of the minority faith communities on this issue. We do not have a closed mind. The Prime Minister, in addressing the Muslim Council of Britain in May this year (the first Prime Minister ever to do so), said: We are listening to those in the Muslim community who want to make sure that they get the right protection under the law. I suggest that we would all subscribe to that . . .

[as to] whether the Government would extend to the rest of Britain the [FETO, the Order] . . . is a piece of legislation crafted in response to the particular circumstances that applied at that time in Northern Ireland. I need not remind this House of the terrible history of sectarian hostility and violence that the people of Northern Ireland have suffered and which provided a very real context for this legislation.

One manifestation of that hostility was clear and indisputable cases of discrimination on the grounds of religious belief. In short, whether an individual was Catholic or Protestant influenced his or her ability to secure employment. As yet, no comparable evidence relating to the position of religious minorities in Britain has been put to the Government. There is no quick fix to be administered here. This is a complex and sensitive area and it would be wrong of the Government to legislate without first having a clear understanding of the nature and scale of the mischief that needs to be addressed.[31]

Lord Bassam referred to research being carried out by the University of Derby into "the scale and nature of religious discrimination in England and Wales". The Government's final decision on legislation may turn on its report. In January 2000 the House of Lords agreed in principle to a Home Office bill providing for the inclusion, for the first time, of a question on religious belief in the 2001 census.[32] Some concerns were expressed about requiring people to identify their religious beliefs—the Bill being

[30] See Chapter 7—Lord Bessam's understanding of the law is incorrect.
[31] Fn 19 above, cols. 474–477.
[32] The census will include a question as to whether the respondent has no religion or is Christian, Moslem, Sikh, Buddist, Hindu, Jewish or other.

amended in the Lords to provide that no penalty will attach to refusal or failure to answer that particular question.[33] One Labour peer suggested that Hitler would have found such information useful in his time. But Lord Weatherill, introducing the Bill, stated that it was supported by the CRE and by many "faith organisations" and explained that the information collected was to be used to combat race discrimination and social exclusion, particularly in relation to sub-groups from the Asian sub-continent:[34] "It would help provide baseline figures against which the Government can monitor possible racial disadvantage and social exclusion within particular minority groups" and remarked that the Bill was supported by the CRE and by many "faith organisations".

Among the opposition raised to legislating in respect of religious discrimination were criticisms relating to difficulties of definition. In 1978, Robilliard argued that

S. Robilliard, "Should Parliament Enact a Religious Discrimination Act" (1978) *Public Law*, 379

It . . . there will always be a problem of definition but it is to be hoped that a modern statute would use wide language such as "thought, conscience and religion" in order to fit in with the breadth of religions and quasi religions which could not have been within the contemplation of mid-Victorian legislators. In *R. v. Registrar-General, Ex p. Segerdal* [1970] 3 WLR 479] the "Church of Scientology" was unsuccessful in its attempt to get a Chapel registered as a place of religious worship under the Act. While Scientologists profess a number of philosophical and cosmological beliefs they do not seem to hold any distinct theological doctrines. Nevertheless the activities that went on at their chapel bore some resemblance to the sort of service that can be seen in many Protestant Chapels. The Court of Appeal upheld the Registrar-General's findings that Scientology was not a religion. While Win L.J. was rather cautious, as he foresaw the pitfalls of attempting to define religion in a court of law, Lord Denning M.R. was prepared to rush in where modern theologians fear to tread and declared: "Religious worship means reverence or veneration of God or of a Supreme being," and while he would acknowledge historic exceptions to this definition, such as the Buddhists, he would not acknowledge the Scientologists as a modern one. With the ever increasing multiplication of religions in this country there is a great deal to be said for excusing the courts, especially the Chancery Division, of this task. Religious belief is a delicate plan that cannot bear too much forensic analysis. To a sincere religious believer: "other men's religions are always gross frauds" and in a dissenting judgment Jackson J. once sounded this caution [*US v Ballard* 322 US 78 (1944)]:

When does less than full belief in a professed credo become actionable fraud if one is soliciting gifts or legacies? such inquiries may discomfort orthodox as well as

---

[33] Lord McIntosh for the Government said this would be confusing but suggested no-one would be pursued over failure to answer a single question "if you have a conscientious objection you won"t answer the question and I think that is likely to be the end of the matter". The amended version of the Bill, post House of Lords, provides "no person shall be liable to a penalty . . . for refusing or neglecting to state any particulars in respect of religion". The Act extends to England and Wales only, Northern Ireland already having such a question and The *Herald*, 13th January 2000 reporting a row about failure to include religious question in Scottish census (this being a devolved matter). One of Scotland's leading Moslems, Councillor Bashir Mann, was amongst those voicing criticism of the absence.

[34] Possibly targeted at Moslems in particular.

unconventional religious teachers, for even the most regular of them are sometimes accused of taking their orthodoxy with a grain of sand.

Robilliard's arguments were echoed more recently in the House of Lords debate.

Lord Warner, HL Debs 28th October 1999, cols 462–3

I have always been a strong supporter of using legislation to prevent discrimination on the basis of race, gender and disability . . . But we should exercise considerable caution before extending legislative protection of the kind that exists in the areas of race, gender and disability to the area of religious belief. We would not be able easily to produce legislation that protects only Muslims. It would need to be extended to a range of religious beliefs.

We should bear in mind that we live in a largely secular society. Research published in the 1999 edition of Social Trends shows that UK Church membership, as measured by active adult members, is approximately 8 million out of an adult population of approximately 45 million. With great respect to those who have strong religious beliefs and support faith-based systems, we must take account of other people's views and their ability to challenge all belief systems in a free secular society. There would be many who would see legislation providing protection on the basis of belief systems as a move towards a context of inhibiting people's rights to criticise and to free expression.

I accept fully the need for racial and religious tolerance. The [ECnHR], now enshrined in the [HRA], provides full protection for individuals to pursue and practice their personal religious beliefs. That is as it should be. But I doubt that we should go further for two practical reasons.

First, my noble friend mentioned the issue of cults. It will be extremely difficult to produce a legislative definition of "religious discrimination" that does not protect cults inappropriately. We know from the work of the Information Network on New Religious Movements that there are approximately 2,000 religious cults in Europe. Many are small; some are innocuous; some are less so. There exists a considerable history of cults preying on vulnerable people, breaking up families and obtaining large sums of money from gullible and vulnerable people.

Some cults pose as religions. For example, I recall that some years ago the Court of Appeal ruled against the recognition of the Scientologists" so-called "chapels" and "ministers". The German Government have taken a very strong line in regard to Scientologists. If we produced legislation in the area of religious discrimination we would see more of this kind of approach, and that would inhibit any government of the day from taking action against inappropriate cults.

The other difficulty which applies to legislation in respect of religious discrimination is pointed out by Andrew Grayling:

A. Grayling, *The Guardian*, December 1st, 1999

Discrimination against any individual on any ground of race, creed, or sexual orientation is wrong, and any individual must be allowed to believe, or to do in private, whatever he or she likes, providing it does no harm to others. (This view is far more liberal than most religious practitioners would like; the consideration they seek for themselves they tend not to extend to sexual orientation.)

But these vitally important principles apply only to individuals, not to groups. It would be impossible to carry an argument to the effect that, say, paid-up members of the Conservative party, considered as an identifiable group, have rights by virtue of their group membership: for example, to be protected from sarcastic remarks or scorn, or the taking of their leader's name in vain.

To think in terms of groups is precisely the fault of the racist or snob: he discriminates against another because of the group he thinks the other belongs to, thereby failing to accord him his rights as an individual. Group thinking is the problem, not the solution, in matters of human rights.

Suppose a group forms around the belief that there are UFOs which will one day save mankind. Are they to get extra protections as a result, and perhaps state funding for a school in which children can be raised in unshakeable beliefs about UFOs?

There is nowhere to draw a line between "responsible" religions and unfounded super-stitions. For that reason, what people privately choose to believe cannot be a ground for them to get extra consideration when they band together.

It is certainly an anomaly that Christianity is protected in Britain by laws, for example against blasphemy, whereas other faiths are not. The remedy is not to extend such laws to other religions, but to abandon them altogether, and to disestablish the Church.

On a plain interpretation of what each religion orthodoxly believes, Christianity and Islam mutually blaspheme each other, the former because it does not accept the Prophet, and the latter because it denies the Holy Ghost. If both faiths were legally protected against blas-phemy, it would be open to litigious enthusiasts in either cause to make money for the lawyers.

Problems will also arise, for example, over female circumcision and the rights of women generally. Most minority faiths seeking protection for their ways of life in contemporary Britain have attitudes and practices regarding women which are in conflict with the main-stream, and the differences are deep and important.

Sebastian Poulter makes a similar point in connection specifically with the *hijab* issue (discussed in Chapter 7).

S. Poulter, "Muslim Headscarves in Schools: Contrasting Approaches in England and France" (1997) 17 *Oxford Journal of Legal Studies*, 43

7. The Salience of Sexual Equality

Viewed from an assimilationist perspective, the principle of sexual equality is breached by allowing the *hijab* at school because the sentiment underlying this particular manifestation of Islamic cultural norms arguably runs counter to secular beliefs about the role of women in a modern European society. Republican principles of universality require state schools in France to promote a common set of values, not a variety of different ones. The issue is one of critical importance, for it involves a struggle for the hearts and minds of the younger generation of Muslims and it will be through education that traditionalist leaders will con-centrate their efforts to transmit their own system of morality and counteract secular influ-ences. Hence, an assimilationist would argue, public schooling needs to offer female pupils a means of escape from male domination rather than mirror the pattern of life at home.

Cultural pluralists would tend to view the judgments of the Conseil d'État in a much more positive fashion, as a beacon of light radiating tolerance of religious diversity and affirming the right of minorities to achieve genuinely equal treatment in the public domain.

On this basis, the problem lies rather within the provisions of English law for its failure to accord Muslim pupils the legal right to wear the *hijab*, irrespective of their racial or national origins. Wholehearted endorsement of a pluralist stance towards allowing the *hijab* in school is, however, continent upon achieving a satisfactory resolution of the question whether its acceptance would entail a violation of human rights standards regarding sexual equality. The European Convention insists that the rights contained within it, such as education, must be secured without any discrimination on the ground of sex and the European Court of Human Rights has emphasized that the advancement of the equality of the sexes is today a major goal of the Member States of the Council of Europe. Although there is no agreed method of ranking human rights in order of their importance, it is certainly arguable that the right to sexual equality, being unqualified, should take precedence over the heavily qualified right to religious freedom. However, a law which guaranteed girls the right to wear the *hijab* would hardly seem to constitute sexual discrimination within the terms of the European Convention. Rather than being denied a right, they would be enjoying its exercise. Indeed, to exclude them from school for wearing headscarves would violate the Convention's guarantee of their right to an education free from any religious discrimination.

On the other hand, the UN Convention on the Elimination of All Forms of Discrimination against Women, to which the United Kingdom is a contracting party, imposes much wider responsibilities upon states. Article 5 provides:-

> State Parties shall take all appropriate measures . . . to modify the social and cultural patterns of conduct of men and women, with a view to achieving the elimination of prejudices and customary and all other practices which are based on the idea of the inferiority or superiority of either of the sexes or on stereotyped roles for men and women.

Whether the wearing of Muslim dress falls within the patterns of conduct and customary practices condemned in this article is, of course, extremely controversial. For some, the *hijab* is closely linked with the notion that women should be inconspicuous,preferably confined to domestic roles within their homes, and that their lives should be led almost entirely separately from those of men. From this perspective, women and girls are chiefly guardians of the honour of their families and their dress and appearance should be designed so as not to offer any attraction to strange men. On the other hand, many Muslim women view the modest clothing prescribed by Islam, including the *hijab*, not as a badge of oppression but as a liberating and empowering device, granting them a private and protected space of dignity and responsibility, shielding them both from the lustful gaze of men and from sexual harassment, as well as relieving them from the constant pressure to follow the dictates of Western fashion. It is also a means whereby they can express their religious identity as members of a worldwide community. In France, it is clear that many young women who wear the *hijab* are demanding the right to identify themselves publicly as both French citizens and Muslims and to be respected as such by others. These are modern, well-educated individuals, who are carving out for themselves a distinctive place in the wider society on the basis of autonomous decisions, a specific set of moral values and a search for personal dignity in an unconducive environment. They are searching for a synthesis of cultural norms. In terms of article 5, it is unclear whether the basis of customary practices should be assessed objectively or subjectively. If those who freely choose to wear the *hijab* reject the connotations of inferiority or stereotyping mentioned in this article, it seems doubtful whether the State can legitimately take steps to eliminate the practice in violation of the right to religious freedom.

Naturally, concern may arise in relation to teenage pupils as to whether a genuinely free choice has been exercised in particular cases. Some girls may feel a strong need to conform with parental and family expectations, while others may face pressures from peer groups at school and in the local neighbourhood, or from religious organizations and societies. While some forms of pressure are clearly acceptable, bullying and intimidation are not yet it may be hard to know where to draw the line. It would surely, however, be idle to pretend that parents do not have at least some rights in this sphere and the First Protocol to the European Convention on Human Rights specifically requires state parties to "respect the rights of parents to ensure . . . education . . . in conformity with their own religious and philosophical convictions". Respect for children's religious freedom coupled with the parental right of direction are enjoined by the UN Convention on the Rights of the Child, which also provides, more ambivalently, as follows:-

> States Parties agree that the education of the child shall be directed to . . . the development of respect for the child's parents, his or her own cultural identity, language and values, for the national values of the county in which the child is living, the country from which he or she may originate, and for civilizations different from his or her own.

> The potential conflicts inherent in this provision are mirrored by the further requirement that education also be directed towards both the spirit of tolerance and the equality of the sexes. However, it is vital to appreciate that the mere attendance of veiled girls at schools will, in almost every instance, have a strong tendency to imbue in them the values of sexual equality and independent thought, so that by the time they reach adulthood they will be in a position to make an informed decision as to whether or not to continue to wear the *hijab*.

Robilliard points to further difficulties which may arise in the non-employment context if religious discrimination is prohibited. These comments were directed, in 1978, to the possibility of incorporation of the ECnHR into UK law. The decisions of the European Commission in *Ahmad* v *United Kingdom* (1981), 4 EHRR 126 and *Karaduman* v *Turkey* (1993), 74 D & R 93, in which that body dismissed as "manifestly unfounded" Article 9 complaints based, respectively, on a refusal to grant time-off work for religious worship and a ban on headscarves being worn for official photographs (themselves a prerequisite of graduation) in a Turkish university suggest that Robilliard's fears were unfounded (see, in particular, Ewing's extract in Chapter 1). But the prohibition of religious discrimination at a specifically British level might present challenges such as those he discusses.

Robilliard, 386–7

A problem peculiar to religious freedom is: can it be said that the law discriminates against the sincere polygamist when it punishes a man for taking more than one wife? Since such a law is Christian based should it apply to the non Christian at all or should it apply in a modified form? If an effective right to religious freedom is enacted a court may well, at some future date, have to balance such a right with the injunctions of the criminal law.

The older American view, expressed in the Mormon polygamy case [*Reynolds* v *US* 198 US 145 (1878)] sums up what is still the English attitude on the correct approach of the court when a conflict between the law and religious freedom appears: "Can a man excuse his practices . . . because of his religious belief? To permit this would be to make the professed doctrines of religious belief superior to the law of the land, and in effect permit every citizen to become a law unto himself." This dictum is underlined in the English case law by the problems of the Peculiar People. This sect believed that the best way to treat the sick was by prayer and not by calling in doctors in most circumstances. In *R. v. Downes* [(1875) IQBD 25] a member of this sect had not called in the physician to treat a child, who subsequently died from inflamed lungs, and was convicted on the ground that he had wilfully neglected to provide medical aid for it. The court held that religious belief went to motive and not to intention and could thus be discounted as a defence. *R. v. Senior* [(1899) IQB 283)] was a similar case. The father was also a member of that sect and again would not call in a doctor to save the life of his sick child. It was said that the correct direction on the word neglect was: "medical aid and medicine were such essential things for the child that reasonably careful parents in general would have provided them. . . ." Thus when a crime is one that requires an intention to commit the criminal act a sincere religious motive will afford no defence and when a crime can be committed negligently the measuring standard will ignore unusual religious belief in asking the question "has the defendant acted as a reasonable man?" Despite this attitude the criminal law has made some allowance for a victim's religious belief on the principle that a wrongdoer must take his victim as he finds him. In 1975 [*R v Blaue* [1975] 1 WLR 1411] the Court of Appeal held that the refusal of a Jehovah's Witness to have a blood transfusion after she had been seriously wounded did not break the train of causation. Unlike the earlier attitude in *Senior*, Lawton L.J. did acknowledge the difficulty of attempting to judge anyone's religious based actions from an objective viewpoint.

If a positive right to religious freedom is enacted then an English court might be in a similar position to that of a Californian court some years ago. A small band of native Indians, known as the Native American Church, followed a cult that had existed from before the time that the white man had set foot on the continent. The central part of their worship involved the use of the illegal drug peyole. It was up to the court to blandly decide between their right to religious freedom and the dictates of the criminal law.

If such an overriding right is allowed there will be uncertainty in the criminal law and there may well be fanciful claims of the type that worried Lord Denning in *Ahmad* [v *ILEA* [1978] QB 36]. The alternative is particular amendment to the law when such change appears necessary. If this second view is preferable this is perhaps another reason why the enactment of the European Convention or a bill of rights shall be approached with caution.

The final argument which might be made against the extension of the existing discrimination prohibitions to include, perhaps *inter alia*, sexual orientation, age and religion, is a practical one.

B. Hepple, "Have 25 Years of the Race Relations Act in Britain Been a Failure?" in B. Hepple and E. Szyszczak (eds), *Discrimination: The Limits of Law* (London: Mansell, 1992)

Why have the Race Relations Acts of 1965, 1968 and 1976 failed to change the patterns of racial disadvantage in Britain? The question is often posed but it is based on a false assumption that law is simply an independent instrument of state power, a technical device that is capable of doing as much for ethnic relations as the microchip has done for communications. This kind of "magic belief" is, as Otto Kahn-Freund said in the context of industrial relations, "a superstition of political importance, but a superstition none the less". The separation of law from social life as a whole leads to the expectation that law can, in some way, "act upon" society, and this has been followed by inevitable disillusionment as successive statutes, each more elaborate than its predecessor, have failed to achieve the stated aims of the reformers. We have been slow in Britain to absorb Derrick Bell's insight that "the common thread in all civil rights strategies is eventual failure". The first reason is that the "cycle of disadvantage" in which second and alter generations of ethnic minorities are trapped cannot itself be brought within the scope of the law. Law, as Ehrlich and others have pointed out, demands specificity. Legal concepts have to be relatively clear and they can be enforced only against identified persons. Put another way, the legal process can operate only by individualizing conflict between specific parties. We may say that government policies are a "cause" of high unemployment among black and brown minorities, or that the police are to "blame" for not curbing racial harassment. This kind of attribution of responsibility, which involves tracing consequences, effects or results, may lead us to pass moral judgements, but it is not sufficiently precise for the attribution of legally relevant causation. . . .

Secondly, the law is directed at only one element in the many causes of disadvantage, namely "discrimination".

The law alone cannot eradicate discrimination. But as Hepple goes on to accept, it can have important symbolic functions, and can "give support to those who wish to resist the pressure to discriminate and to educate those who are prejudiced". The extract from Coussey, below, expands on this theme.

M. Coussey, "The Effectiveness of Strategic Enforcement of the Race Relations Act 1976" in *Discrimination: The Limits of Law*

Experience in the United States suggests that employers begin to take voluntary action when they see it as to their advantage to do so. In order to create this perception six conditions are necessary. First, the standard must be established by law. Where standards are not so established, employers will change or waive them for economic or professional reasons. If the standards are set by employers, self-interest will influence their development and use. Although employers should participate in the development of standards, these need to be given authority by government promulgation.

The second condition for self-regulation is that there must be a vigorous enforcement programme, one in which there is significant risk of serious consequences to employers who flout the standards; for example, settlements improving the rights of workers, and extensive use of regulatory agency rule-making to support the enforcement programme. In Great Britain, there are some 285,000 private-sector employers (or 23,000 parent companies) alone. For the CRE's inspectorial role to have a sufficient impact, staffing would have to be at least at the level of the factory inspectorate (500 to 600 staff compared with the Commission's 30 staff in the Employment Division) or, alternatively, industrial tribunal complaints would have to be multiplied twenty- or thirty-fold, with a twenty-fold increase in awards or settlements and provision for class actions.

The third condition is that the results achieved must be objectively measurable. In the United States, disparate impact was defined by the Supreme Court in 1971. No such definition has been attempted in British courts, and the Commission has not defined "underrepresentation" in its reports or in the Code of Practice. Nor has Parliament defined "fair participation" in the Fair Employment Act 1989 in Northern Ireland [or, indeed, in the FETO which replaced it].

The fourth condition is that the law should provide for liability to individuals, so that even where an organization is carrying out equal opportunity programmes which may protect them from state regulatory action, an individual is free to litigate. This condition does apply in this country; insured individual complainants are free to bring action without the support of the Commission.

The fifth condition is that employers should be better off after voluntary compliance. There must be a regulatory inspection, or other periodic reporting requirement, of voluntary affirmative action plans. No such system exists in this country, although there is the basis for it in Northern Ireland, in that the Fair Employment Commission can call for an employer's affirmative action plan if fair participation is not being provided, and require remedial measures.

The final condition is that there must be sufficient and organized public concern. Given that there has never been an effective independent civil rights movement in Great Britain, arguably no such condition exists here.

Enforcement in Britain meets only one of these tests, that of private access to litigation. Courts and tribunals have not set standards, in the sense of defining the specific steps needed to produce equality, nor have they yet objectively defined disproportionate effect or participation levels, although the Commission has begun to do so in recent reports and recommendations.

Enforcement cannot be defined as vigorous and there is little economic pressure. Set against the estimated tens of thousands of acts of direct discrimination in employment, the few hundred cases each year cannot be seen as extensive. There is no satisfactory system for inspection or reporting, and the resources of the Commission do not allow it to attempt any such functions.

The extension of the current prohibitions on discrimination to cover sexual orientation, age and religion must be regarded as almost inevitable in the medium, even if not in the short, term. Recognition of this leads to questions about the form that extended anti-discrimination legislation might take. The 1999 draft equal treatment general framework directive provides that Member States must prohibit discrimination (direct and indirect, including harassment) on the listed grounds "sex, racial or ethnic origin [these already being covered by Community legislation], religion or belief, disability, age or sexual orientation"; in relation to employment broadly defined. If and when such legislation is enacted in the UK, ought it to take the form of amendments to the current SDA (in respect of sexual orientation) and the RRA (in respect of religion) together with a new legislative enactment on age discrimination? Or is there an argument for following the approaches adopted in Ireland, South Africa or Canada?

The Irish Employment Equality Act regulates discrimination on grounds of gender, age, race, marital status, family status, sexual orientation, religious belief, disability or membership of the traveller community. And South Africa's Employment Equity Act regulates discrimination on no less than twenty grounds—race, gender, sex, pregnancy, marital status, family responsibility, ethnic or social origin, colour, sexual orientation, age, disability, religion, conscience, belief, political opinion, culture, language and birth. Canada's Charter of Rights (a constitutional document which prohibits discrimination by the state and extends far beyond the employment field) provides (s.15(1)) that:

Every individual is equal before and under the law and has the right to the equal protection and equal benefit of the law without discrimination and, *in particular*, without discrimination based on race, national or ethnic origin, colour, religion, sex, age or mental or physical disability (my emphasis).

Canada's Supreme Court has ruled that s.15 protection extends beyond the enumerated grounds to "analogous grounds", these grounds having been taken to include sexual orientation in *Egan* v *Canada* [1995] 2 SCR 513 and in *Vriend* v *Alberta* (1998) [1998] 1 SCR 493.

In the House of Lords debates on the FETO, Lord Lester (architect of the SDA and RRA) called for "a single code of legislation tackling discrimination generally: a single equal rights code with harmonised powers of enforcement". The current position in Britain is clearly unsatisfactory. There exist a variety of different regimes and associated enforcement bodies—the SDA, EqPA and EOC deal with sex discrimination; the RRA and the CRE operate in the race discrimination field and the DDA and DRC are responsible for regulating disability discrimination. Only in Northern Ireland does a single Commission deal with all forms of prohibited discrimination (there also with discrimination on religious and political grounds). The laws dealing with these various heads of discrimination (and, in Northern Ireland, with discrimination based on religious beliefs or political opinion) are not consistent, irrational and arbitrary differences co-existing with those associated with the nature of the particular discrimination regulated and those resulting from European Community intervention[35] and political exigencies.[36] At present, the various Commissions are legally prohibited from sharing information and are thus restricted in the extent to which they can co-operate in fighting unlawful discrimination (though the government has made a commitment to remove this handicap). Further, while the EOC and the DRC report to the Department for Education and Employment, the CRE is answerable to the Home Office.

The Government has agreed to rationalise the powers of the various Commissions and the various discrimination regimes. In the long term it is possible that the British Commissions may follow the Northern Irish route of amalgamation, this step being particularly likely if the Government goes ahead with its commitment to "mainstream" equality on grounds of sex and disability in Britain as it has already taken steps in the RR(A)B 1999 to "mainstream" race equality by imposing a positive duty on public authorities. It was the "mainstreaming" provision of the Northern Ireland Act 1998 (see further Chapters 5 and 9) which resulted in the creation there of a single equality Commission.

On the one hand the amalgamation of existing and future anti-discrimination provisions into a single statute would improve clarity and consistency over the various regimes. But Lord Lester's preference for a single anti-discrimination code is not universally shared, attention having been called in particular to the problem of watering

---

[35] Particularly prevalent in relation to sex discrimination.
[36] Resulting in more radical legislation in Northern Ireland.

down existing legislative protections by adding a "shopping list" of additional prohibited grounds with a "one size fits all" approach.[37] The potential for such dilution is
illustrated by considering a hypothetical single statutory prohibition on discrimination based on sex, race or disability.

Race discrimination is rarely justifiable in principle, except perhaps (and these
examples are controversial) where someone of a particular racial group could more
effectively provide welfare services to persons of that group (sexual assault counselling
to first generation Asian women perhaps, or mentoring services for disaffected African
Caribbean boys), or where a person of a particular racial group is required for purposes of authenticity in a dramatic performance.[38] Sex discrimination is also very
rarely justifiable in principle. Again, exceptions may arise—in the counselling and
mentoring examples used above, the services might better be provided by, respectively,
a woman and a man. In addition, discrimination by way of "separate but equal" treatment would generally be regarded as acceptable in connection with toilet and other
sanitary facilities, and many of those campaigning against sexual violence would support "women-only" train carriages and taxi firms. Some would also argue in favour of
"affirmative action"/ "positive" or "reverse discrimination" (these terms are further
discussed in Chapter 3) as a means of restorative justice.

In general terms, and subject to the possible exceptions outlined above, sex and race
discrimination (defined in terms of treating people less favourably because of their sex
or race) are rarely justifiable, because sex or race does not usually affect a person's
ability to perform a particular job.[39] But disability raises different issues.
Discrimination on grounds of disability will in many circumstances be justified
because (in the employment field) the disability will determine the person's ability to
do the job in question. A partially sighted person is, for example, fundamentally
unsuited to a driving job, and a person who suffers from a severe learning disability is
unlikely to be qualified for a place at medical school. The regulation of discrimination
on grounds of disability must, therefore, focus on (1) eliminating *unjustifiable* discrimination—i.e., the operation of prejudicial stereotypes about the abilities of persons with (particular) disabilities and (2) requiring reasonable adjustments which will
give disabled people access to jobs, services etc. which they are capable of performing/
enjoying, etc., once these adjustments have been made.

Just as the range of permissible discrimination connected with disability is wider than
that which ought to be accepted in the context of race or sex, the same is true in respect
of discrimination on grounds of religion and age. The danger of the "scatter-gun"
approach to prohibiting discrimination on a list of grounds (in Canada, on enumerated

---

[37] Evelyn Ellis, commenting on the framework draft directive at the Independent Review of Anti-
Discrimination Law seminar, Cambridge 14th January 2000. See discussion of the current GOQs in
Chapter 6 and 7.
[38] See discussion of the current GOQs in Chapter 6 and 7.
[39] Where sex or race are indirectly connected to the ability to perform the job (where, for example, a
woman's childcare responsibilities render her unable to do it full-time), discrimination on the full-time/ part-
time distinction will be unlawful only where it is unjustified (see further Chapter 2).

and unenumerated grounds and in the US on unspecified grounds) is that the justification defence which is necessary in relation to, for example, discrimination on grounds of disability or age, might be read across into discrimination on grounds of sex, race, etc.

The 1999 draft equal treatment general framework directive contains a broadly drawn genuine occupational qualification defence and allows specific exceptions to the prohibition on age-related and religious discrimination. Article 4(1) permits discrimination "where, by reason of the nature or context in which particular occupational activities are carried out, such a characteristic constitutes a genuine occupational qualification". Article 4(2) allows Member States to "provide that, in the case of public or private organisations which pursue directly and essentially the aim of ideological guidance in the field of religion or belief with respect to education, information and the expression of opinions, and for the particular occupational activities within those organisations which are directly and essentially related to that aim, a difference of treatment based on a relevant characteristic related to religion or belief shall not constitute discrimination where, by reason of the nature of these activities, the characteristic constitutes a genuine occupational qualification". Article 5 provides that

the following differences of treatment, in particular, shall not constitute direct discrimination if they are objectively and reasonably justified by a legitimate aim and are appropriate to the achievement of that aim:
(a) the prohibition on access to employment or the provision of special working conditions to ensure the protection of young people and older workers;
(b) the fixing of a minimum age as a condition of eligibility for retirement or invalidity benefits;
(c) the fixing of different ages for employees or groups or categories of employees for entitlement to retirement or invalidity benefits on grounds of physical or mental occupational requirements;
(d) the fixing of a maximum age for recruitment which is based on the training requirements of the post in question or the need for a reasonable period of employment before retirement;
(e) the establishment of requirements concerning the length of professional experience;
(f) the establishment of age limits which are appropriate and necessary for the pursuit of legitimate labour market objectives.

The inclusion of specific exemptions regarding age and religion-based discrimination suggests, perhaps, that the "genuine occupational qualification" defence in Article 4(1) of the draft directive ought to be interpreted narrowly. This approach has been taken by the ECJ to the equivalent provision of the equal treatment directive.[40] Ireland's Employment Equality Act also appears to have avoided the "watering down" pitfall. The Act prohibits direct and indirect discrimination on the enumerated grounds subject to a small number of exceptions (covering, for example, special

---

[40] See discussions of *Johnston Chief Constable of the RUC* (Case 224/84) [1986] ECR 651 and *Sirdar v The Army Board, Secretary of State for Defence* Case C–273/97 000, in Chapter 6.

treatment of women connected with pregnancy or maternity,[41] limited sex discrimination in the police and prison services in the interests of decency and privacy,[42] "genuine occupational qualifications" and religious discrimination by religious bodies).[43] The Act further specifies that it does not require the recruitment, retention or promotion "of anyone not available or willing to do, or fully capable of doing, the particular job, providing that in the case of a person with a disability, "fully capable of doing the job may include doing it with the assistance of special treatment or facilities".

The duty of reasonable accommodation imposed by the Irish Employment Equality Act is weak, the original Act having been struck down by the Irish Supreme Court on the ground that a stronger such duty rendered the legislation incompatible with employers' property rights. But the point here is that both the Employment Equality Act and, it appears, the 1999 equal treatment general framework draft directive avoid the watering-down pitfalls of the "one size fits all" approach by providing specific rules in relation to the various heads of discrimination which supplement or provide exceptions from the Act's prohibitions on direct and indirect discrimination. On the other hand, the draft directive gives no indication as to the appropriate course of action where, for example, the interests of religious freedom and sexual equality conflict.

The other, even more problematic approach can be seen in the Canadian Charter of Rights which, as we saw above, prohibits discrimination on a variety of grounds (not all of then enumerated). In Canada, the definition of "discrimination" is left for judicial determination. A similar mechanism applies in the US, the Equal Protection Clause of the 14th Amendment, which guarantees to all "the equal protection of the laws", having been interpreted by the Supreme Court to provide varying degrees of protection from race, sex and other forms of discrimination.

The broad approach is flexible and permits, as in Canada, the development of a sophisticated approach to discrimination on the part of the judiciary. In *Law Society of British Columbia* v *Andrews* [1989] 1 SCR 143, the Supreme Court defined discrimination as:

> a distinction, whether intentional or not . . . which has the effect of imposing burdens, obligations, or disadvantages on [an]. . . individual or group not imposed on others, or which withholds or limits access to opportunities, benefits, and advantages available to other[s] . . . every difference in treatment between individuals under the law will not necessarily result in inequality and . . . identical treatment may frequently produce serious inequality.

In a subsequent decision the Court stated that:

> a law [will not] necessarily be bad because it makes distinctions. . .it is only by examining the larger context that a court can determine whether differential treatment results in

---

[41] Including adoption.
[42] As well as, more controversially, situations of violence and the maintenance of an "appropriate" gender balance.
[43] Relatively widely drawn.

inequality or whether, contrariwise, it would be identical treatment which would in the particular context result in inequality or foster disadvantage. A finding that there is discrimination will . . . in most but perhaps not all cases, necessarily entail a search for disadvantage that exists apart from and independent of the particular legal distinction being challenged.[44]

This approach had the effect that the Supreme Court could regard as not "discrimination" within s.15 a practice whereby, although female prisoners were not subject to close surveillance or "frisk" searches carried out by male prison guards, male prisoners were subject to surveillance and search by women guards. In *Conway* v *Canada (Attorney General)* [1993] 2 SCR 872 the Court ruled that:

> the historical trend of violence perpetrated by men against women is not matched by a comparable trend pursuant to which men are the victims and women the aggressors. . . . the effect of cross-gender searching is different and more threatening for women than for men. The different treatment to which the appellant objects thus *may not be discrimination at all* (my emphasis).

The Court's emphasis on substantive equality also resulted, in *Eldridge* v *British Columbia* [1997] 3 SCR 624, in its demand that government make its free health care services accessible to deaf people by providing them with free translation facilities:

> To argue that governments should be entitled to provide benefits to the general population without ensuring that disadvantaged members of society have the resources to take full advantage of those benefits bespeaks a thin and impoverished vision of s.15(1).

Thus far, the survey of s.15 suggests that a broad approach to the prohibition of discrimination might serve the interests of the disadvantaged. Certainly, it appears that this course might be more successful that the Employment Equality Act/draft directive approach when it comes to balancing competing claims for equality. But the problem with the Canadian Charter model of equality provision is that it renders the protection from discrimination a matter of judicial discretion. And while Canada's Supreme Court started very well, in subsequent judgments its approach to discrimination wavered significantly. In *Miron* v *Trudel* [1995] 2 SCR 418 and in *Egan* v *Canada* [1995] 2 SCR 513, four (of nine) judges on the court ruled that distinctions drawn on grounds protected under s.15 (or analogous thereto) did not constitute "discrimination" where the grounds were "relevant" to the object of the legislation. This approach required of the discriminator no more than a rational decision to distinguish between groups on the basis of protected grounds.

The Canadian approach to discrimination is perhaps unlikely, both current legislation and the 1999 draft directives prohibiting specific instances of "discrimination", "discrimination" itself being closely defined. But Canada's experience of s.15 does

---

[44] *R* v *Turpin* [1989] 1 SCR 1296.

point to the dangers of replacing detailed regulation of discrimination with broad and general provisions.

Much attention is being paid, in current debates about reform of discrimination law, to issues of enforcement. We saw in Chapter 5 that increasing calls are being heard for monitoring obligations to be imposed on employers with regard to sex and race as they are, at present, in relation to religious belief in Northern Ireland. In Canada's federal jurisdiction and in a number of provinces, the general prohibitions imposed by the Charter of Rights are supplemented in the employment field by legislation requiring monitoring and affirmative action in respect of women, disabled, aboriginal and "visible minority" current, departing and prospective employees. In the UK there is a broad consensus (not including either business interests or, at present, the Government) that real improvements will not be seen in respect of sex and race-related disadvantage until employers are placed under positive obligations to promote equality on these grounds.

The Government has yet to be convinced, but recent moves in the public sector coupled with encouraging noises about the gender-pay gap suggest that some movement might occur in the medium term. If the expanding scope of anti-discrimination provisions (in terms of the prohibited grounds of discrimination) is not to herald defeat in the struggle towards more collective methods of enforcement, consideration will have to be given to divorcing general anti-discrimination statutes from enforcement of specific grounds of prohibited discrimination by collective means such as mandatory workforce monitoring and the enforcement of such monitoring, as well as of equality good practice more generally, by means of contract compliance.

Index

Sex discrimination:
  burden of proof, 80–1, 126–7, 260
  chivalry/courtesy, 37–8
  compensation, 285–8
  coverage/exceptions, 346–55 , 620
  direct, *see* Direct discrimination
  EC law, 79–81
  goods and services, 220, 222–9, 231–5
  GOQ, *see* Genuine occupational qualification
  harassment, *see* Sexual harassment
  House of Lords, 7
  housing, 223
  immigration, 18–20, 230–6
  insurance, 224–8
  Jockey Club, 8–9
  legal profession, 340
  licensed premises, 224
  management, 340, 341
  marriage, *see* Married women
  medical practitioners, 340
  occupational pensions, 277, 339–40
  pensionable age, 43–5, 49, 50–1, 196, 250
  pregnancy, *see* Pregnancy
  restraint of trade, 8–9
  retirement age, 44–5, 49, 50–1, 196, 250
  schools, provision, 52, 217–18, 295, 318
  segregation, *see* Gender segregation
  shift-work, 84, 86, 88–9, 106–8
  sport, 223–4
  statutory test, 36
  transsexuals, *see* Gender-reassignment
  travel concessions, 28
  universities, 9–10, 83–4, 112–13
Sexual harassment:
  armed forces, 286
  bullying, 201
  Canada, 52, 53–5, 62–3
  common law, 203, 208–9
  compensation, 2, 86–8
  definition, 52–3, 201–2
  detriment, 200–1
  direct discrimination, 52–64
  Equal Opportunities Commission (EOC), 64
  European Commission, 52–3, 64
  hostility, 202
  innuendo, 202
  less favourable treatment, 55–60
  objective test, 58–9, 202–3
  personal injuries, 286–8
  "pin-ups", 57–9
  police women, 204–5
  subordination, 340
  United States, 53, 61–2
  vicarious liability, 201–6
  "weapon", 56, 57
Sexual orientation:
  age of consent, 26
  armed forces, 15–17, 390–1, 394–5

Better Regulation Task Force, 394
Canada, 621
codes of practice, 394, 608
comparators, 388–9, 396
direct discrimination, 49, 387, 396
draft framework directive, 393
EC law, 227, 28, 194, 393, 607
equal opportunities, 387, 388
Equal Opportunities Commission (EOC), 393
equal treatment, 195–6, 390
European Convention on Human Rights (1950), 4, 24, 194, 394–5, 605
harassment, 387–8, 396
health insurance, 196
intrusive investigations, 394–5
Ireland, 607
Labour Government, 607–8
less favourable treatment, 388–9, 396
occupational pensions, 195–6
travel concessions, 196, 392
unfair dismissal, 24, 396
United States, 388–9
Sheldon, S., 342
Shift-work, sex discrimination, 84, 85, 88–9, 106–8
Sick pay:
  disabled persons, 491
  EC law, 536
  maternity leave, 372, 374
  part-time workers, 71, 72
Sikhs:
  clothing and appearance rules, 95, 102–3, 194, 415, 426
  ethnic origins, 415–17
  indirect discrimination, 96, 102–3, 414, 415
  racial groups, 413–433
  schools, 415–16
  uniform requirements, 194
Single parents:
  black women, 344
  choice of pool, 84
  common knowledge, 86, 88, 89
  see also Child care commitments
Skidmore, Paul, 401–2
Smith, Andrew, 606
Social Democratic Party, 150
Social security:
  child benefit, 439
  diability living allowance, 467
  EC law, 72–3, 243–7, 536
  funeral grants, 86–7, 124–50, 437–8
  housing benefit, 443–4
  invalidity pension, 248
  prohibited discrimination, 246–51
  race discrimination, 605
    Race discrimination directive, 27, 185, 251, 409
  redundancy, *see* Redundancy payments
  severe disablement allowance, 248, 249